CONTEMPORARY

COMPLETE PRE-GED

Coordinating Editor
Patricia Mulcrone, Ed.D
Professor/Chair
Adult Educational Development
William Rainey Harper College
Palatine, Illinois

CB

CONTEMPORARY BOOKS

a division of NTC/Contemporary Publishing Group
Lincolnwood, Illinois USA

Library of Congress Cataloging-in-Publication Data

Contemporary's Complete Pre-GED / coordinating editor,
Patricia Mulcrone, William Rainey.
p. cm.
Includes index.
ISBN 0-8092-0930-6
1. General educational development tests—Study guides.
I. Mulcrone, Patricia. II. Rainey, William. III. Contemporary Books, Inc.
LB3060.33.G45C665 1996
373.12'62—dc20 —dc20 96-43778
[373.12'62] CIP

Contributing Writers
Writing Skills: Joan Maruskin-Mott
Social Studies: Kenneth Tamarkin
Science: Nancy F. Knapp
Reading/Literature and the Arts: Patricia Ann Benner
Mathematics: Robert Mitchell

Science Consultant
Robert P. Mitchell

The Coordinating Editor gratefully acknowledges the assistance of Janice S. Phillips, Assistant Professor of Adult Educational Development at William Rainey Harper College, in preparing material for Section 5: Mathematics.

ISBN: 0-8092-0930-6

Published by Contemporary Books,
a division of NTC/Contemporary Publishing Group, Inc.,
4255 West Touhy Avenue,
Lincolnwood (Chicago), Illinois 60712-1975 U.S.A.

Manufactured in the United States of America.

0 1 2 3 4 5 6 7 8 9 VH 13 12 11 10 9 8 7

Contents

SECTION 4: READING/LITERATURE AND THE ARTS

SECTION 5: MATHEMATICS

CHAPTER 5: DIVISION SKILLS

CHAPTER 6: SPECIAL TOPICS IN MATH

CHAPTER 7: DECIMAL SKILLS

Acknowledgments

Cartoon on page 13 by Peter Oakley, *Modern Wonder Cartoons, America OnLine.* Copyright 1994 by Peter Oakley. Reprinted by permission.

Advertisement on page 39 copyright 1987, The Quaker Oats Company. Reprinted by permission.

Poem on page 43: "A Time to Talk" by Robert Frost. Copyright 1916 by Holt, Rinehart and Winston. Copyright 1944 by Robert Frost. Reprinted from *The Poetry of Robert Frost,* edited by Edward Connery Lathem, by permission of Henry Holt and Company, Inc.

Excerpt on page 208 from *A People's History of the United States* by Howard Zinn. Copyright 1980 by Howard Zinn. Reprinted by permission of HarperCollins Publishers.

Excerpt on page 216 (top) from *The Black Americans: A History in Their Own Words,* edited by Milton Meltzer. Copyright 1964, 1965, 1967, 1984 by Milton Meltzer. Reprinted by permission of HarperCollins Publishers.

Excerpt on page 216 (bottom) from *Let Them Speak for Themselves, Women in the American West,* 1849–1900, edited by Christine Fischer. Copyright 1977 by Archon Books.

Excerpts on pages 237 and 239 from *A People's History of the United States* by Howard Zinn. Copyright 1980 by Howard Zinn. Reprinted by permission of HarperCollins Publishers.

Graph on page 249 copyright © 1986 by The New York Times Company. Reprinted by permission.

Graph on page 260 reprinted courtesy of *The Boston Globe.* Copyright 1986 *The Boston Globe.*

Cartoon on page 232 by Michael Keefe, dePIXion Features, Inc. Copyright 1995 by Michael Keefe. Reprinted by permission.

Cartoon on page 234 by Oliphant. Copyright 1967, Universal Press Syndicate. Reprinted by permission. All rights reserved.

Cartoon on page 236 by Dick Locher. Reprinted by permission of Tribune Media Services.

Excerpt on page 240 from *The American Reader* by Paul Angle. Copyright 1958.

Maps on pages 304, 306, 313, and 332 from *American History Atlas* by Martin Gilbert. Reprinted by permission of Routledge.

Cartoon on page 327 by Tony Auth. Copyright 1985, Philadelphia Inquirer. Reprinted by permission of Universal Press Syndicate. All rights reserved.

Cartoon on page 337 by Don Wright. Copyright 1985 by Don Wright, The Miami News.

Cartoon on page 340 by Mike Peters. Copyright 1986 by Dayton Daily News. Reprinted by permission of Tribune Media Services.

Cartoon on page 342 by Bruce Beattie. Copyright 1983 by Daytona Beach Morning Journal. Reprinted by permission of Copley News Service.

Excerpt on page 557 from *Lake Wobegon Days* by Garrison Keillor. Copyright © 1985 by Garrison Keillor. Reprinted by permission of Viking Penguin Inc., a division of Penguin Books USA Inc.

Cartoon on page 574 from: "The Far Side" by Gary Larson. Copyright 1986 Universal Press Syndicate. Reprinted with permission. All rights reserved.

Cartoon on page 584 from: "Cathy" by Cathy Guisewite. Copyright 1986 Universal Press Syndicate. Reprinted with permission. All rights reserved.

Excerpt on page 620 from "Neighbour Rosicky" from *Obscure Destinies* by Willa Cather. Copyright 1933 by Alfred A. Knopf, Inc. Reprinted by permission.

Excerpt on page 626 from *Dragonwings* by Laurence Yep. Copyright © 1975 by Laurence Yep. Reprinted by permission of HarperCollins Publishers.

Poem on page 636: "Fog" from *Chicago Poems* by Carl Sandburg, copyright 1916 by Holt, Rinehart and Winston, Inc. and renewed 1944 by Carl Sandburg. Reprinted by permission of Harcourt Brace & Company.

Poem on page 637: ".05" by Ishmael Reed from *Chattanooga*. Copyright © 1973 by Ishmael Reed. Reprinted by permission of the author.

Poem on page 639: "On Children" from *The Prophet* by Kahlil Gibran. Copyright 1923 by Kahlil Gibran and renewed 1951 by Administrators C.T.A. of Kahlil Gibran Estate and Mary G. Gibran. Reprinted by permission of Alfred A. Knopf, Inc.

Poem on page 640: "Mother to Son" by Langston Hughes. Copyright 1926 by Alfred A. Knopf, Inc. and renewed 1954 by Langston Hughes. Reprinted from *Selected Poems of Langston Hughes* by permission of the publisher.

Excerpts on page 643 from the novel and the play *Of Mice and Men* by John Steinbeck. Copyright 1937, renewed © 1965 by John Steinbeck. Used by permission of Viking Penguin, a division of Penguin Books USA Inc.

Excerpt on page 645 from *The Prisoner of Second Avenue* by Neil Simon. Copyright 1972 by Neil Simon. Reprinted by permission of Random House, Inc.

Excerpt on page 646 from *The Hot L Baltimore* by Lanford Wilson. Copyright © 1973 by Lanford Wilson. Reprinted by permission of Hill and Wang, a division of Farrar, Straus and Giroux, Inc.

Excerpt on pages 647–648 from *Verdict* by Agatha Christie. © 1958 by Agatha Christie LTD. Reprinted by permission of Samuel French, Inc.

Excerpt on pages 649–650 from *The Glass Menagerie* by Tennessee Williams. Copyright 1945 by Tennessee Williams and Edwina D. Williams and renewed 1973 by Tennessee Williams. Reprinted by permission of Random House, Inc.

Cartoon on page 657 by Steve Benson. Reprinted by permission: Tribune Media Services.

Advertisement on page 664 copyright 1986 Loehmann's Inc. All rights reserved. Reprinted by permission.

Advertisement on page 666 copyright 1985 Sears Roebuck & Co. All rights reserved. Reprinted by permission.

Cartoon on page 950 by Michael Keefe, dePIXion Features, Inc. Copyright 1995 by Michael Keefe. Reprinted by permission.

Poem on page 980: "Friendship" by Dinah Maria Mulock Craik from *The Best Loved Poems of the American People,* edited by Hazel Felleman. Copyright 1936, Doubleday & Co., Inc.

The editor has made every effort to trace the ownership of all copyrighted material, and necessary permissions have been secured in most cases. Should there prove to be any question regarding the use of any material, regret is here expressed for such error. Upon notification of any such oversight, proper acknowledgment will be made in future editions.

To The Instructor

Contemporary's *Complete PRE-GED* program is designed to help students develop a firm basis in all the GED skills: writing and language, social studies, science, reading/literature and the arts, and mathematics. Some special features to note are the Pre-Tests and Post-Tests, the chapter reviews, and the answer keys.

- **Pre-Tests and Post-Tests.** These tests are in multiple-choice format, similar to that found on many tests. Questions are drawn from the entire range of skills and content in each section. Evaluation charts correlated to the chapters help you identify strong and weak areas for each student.
- **Chapter Reviews.** These tests, also in multiple-choice format, are brief reviews of the skills taught in the chapter. Evaluation charts help you see which parts of a chapter a student might need to review before moving on.
- **Answer Keys.** An answer key is located at the end of each section. Students should be encouraged to check their answers as soon as they complete an exercise to ensure that they have mastered the material.

Some exercises ask students to write short answers in their own words. They should make every effort to complete these written exercises since writing has been shown to be one of the most effective demonstrations of learning and comprehension.

Finally, encourage your students to read and help them find appropriate materials. The short passages in this book are no substitute for the real reading opportunities available to your students. By becoming more comfortable with reading, they will prepare themselves not only for content area materials but for lifelong learning.

Section 1: Language and Writing Skills
In Section 1, both the process of writing and the conventions of English are covered. In particular, there are three features to note:

- The "Journal Writing" feature provides students with a variety of ideas for writing in their journals. Its main purpose is to help students start to feel comfortable as writers. In this section *only*, grammar and spelling are not emphasized.
- "Putting Your Skills to Work," a highly structured writing activity, appears following language skills exercises. The writing focuses on the grammar point that was just taught. This feature helps students to understand grammar in the context of their own writing.
- "Your Turn to Write" gives students a choice of topics and some suggestions about how to approach the topic. This is followed by a checklist of a few of the major grammar and usage points in the chapter. The checklist guides students in editing their own writing.

As you can see, each of these writing activities serves a slightly different function. It may be useful to alert students to the differences among the three activities.

Other features of the section concentrate exclusively on grammar and usage. Each "Language Skills" section covers a different point in conventions of English. A chapter review follows each "Language Skills" section. "Punctuating Perfectly" highlights punctuation issues related to grammar issues in the text.

Research has shown that teaching the process of writing in conjunction with grammar and usage is a highly effective way of helping students to become better writers. Contemporary's *Comprehensive Pre-GED Program* incorporates this combined approach, and we hope that you and your students will benefit from it.

Section 2: Social Studies

The Social Studies section is designed to help students develop the critical reading and thinking skills they need to successfully work with social studies materials. Students working in this book receive a thorough grounding in the organization and comprehension of written material and illustrations. Then they are introduced to the higher-order thinking skills—application, analysis, synthesis, and evaluation.

This section emphasizes the step-by-step acquisition of skills rather than discrete knowledge. Materials from the five major social studies areas—history, economics, political science, behavioral science, and geography—are represented throughout the text.

Section 3: Science

This section is designed to help students develop the critical reading and thinking skills they need to read and apply scientific information.

Each chapter is divided into two parts: reading skill and science topic. While students may already have mastered some of the reading skills, we recommend that they work through *all* of the science topics in order to assure a solid grounding in key science concepts.

Also, encourage your students to learn more about science and help them find appropriate materials. You may want to discuss science issues in class. Try to help students feel comfortable with science and help them overcome any perceptions of it as a foreign and inaccessible subject. Your students will be much better prepared not only to tackle science topics but also to deal with science in their everyday lives.

Section 4: Reading/Literature and the Arts

The Reading/Literature and the Arts section is designed to help students develop the critical reading and thinking skills that they need to handle a wide range of reading materials. Students working in this section receive a thorough grounding in the organization and comprehension of short reading passages as well as in basic vocabulary skills. They are also introduced to such critical reading skills as making inferences, predicting outcomes, and identifying persuasive techniques.

The section emphasizes the step-by-step acquisition of skills. Attention is given to comprehension, vocabulary, and study skills—which complement each other and build skills gradually. Special thinking-skill questions enable students to practice more challenging inferential and predicting skills. Generally, if a thinking skill is included, it is the last question in an exercise.

Visual aids such as charts, outlines, cartoons, and advertisements reinforce students' comprehension skills. These will enable the more visually oriented student to *see* how written material, from political advertising to poetry, is structured.

As students work through and finish this text, encourage them to read. Help them find materials that are appropriate, engaging, and thought-provoking. The short passages in this section provide a thorough introduction to reading, but they are no substitute for the real reading opportunities available to your students. By becoming more comfortable with reading, students will prepare themselves for lifelong learning.

Section 5: Mathematics

This section instructs students in a range of skills from whole number arithmetic through fractions, decimals, and percents. Students learn to add, subtract, multiply, and divide, and to apply these arithmetic skills in a variety of word problems. Because of the importance of word problems, the section carefully develops word-problem skills to complement a student's progress. Special topics in multi-step problems, measurement, estimation, interest, data analysis, and probability are also included.

The section has several special features:

- "Skill Builders" are used where appropriate to help students make the transition from explanations to actual problem solving. "Skill Builders" are rows of specially-designed, partially-worked problems that the student completes before beginning practice exercises.
- Instruction in problem-solving skills is integrated throughout the text. Lessons in which these skills are emphasized are highlighted. Even when students can master computational skills, they often have difficulty in solving word problems. Carefully sequenced reasoning activities help students to build their problem-solving abilities.
- Two special chapters, called "Special Topics in Math" and "More Special Topics in Math," are included as chapters 6 and 10. In these chapters, students are introduced to special applications of computation and problem-solving skills.
- Practice tests are included in the comprehensive text. A Pre-Test previews the section, and a Post-Test concludes the student's study. Computation reviews are placed at the end of each chapter to enable students to reinforce computation skills before moving on to each new topic.
- A complete answer key is provided. In addition, solutions are worked out for all word problems so that students can see a step-by-step process to solve the problem correctly. This ensures maximum teaching flexibility for instructors and the possibility of immediate feedback for students.

Equally important as quality learning materials is the attitude that students bring to the study of mathematics. Through good books help, it is the instructor who can do the most to help adult students learn the study habits that can make math an enjoyable and successful experience. One technique that is particularly helpful is to encourage students to leave each day's study of math with a positive feeling. A good way for students to do this is to develop the habit of reviewing mastered problems as the last step before putting a math book away. By reworking a few known problems successfully, a student both reinforces concepts learned that day and reminds himself or herself of the progress being made.

To The Student

Congratulations! As you start work in Contemporary's *Complete Pre-GED* program, you are on your way to preparing for a GED course of study.

Before you begin work in any of the five sections in this book, take the Pre-Tests one at a time. Each Pre-Test will help you decide which chapters you need to concentrate on as you work through the book. When you are finished with the book, the Post-Tests will help you evaluate the work you have done.

As you read through each section, do not try to memorize every fact. Instead, try to get a good understanding of the main ideas in each section. Pay special attention to the words that are printed in ***boldface type*** or in *italic type*. These are words that you will need to know when you are reading or talking about writing, social studies, science, literature, or mathematics.

Work through the exercises in each section. You'll find answers to all the exercises at the back of the section. Be sure to check your work at the end of each exercise before you move on. And when an exercise asks you to write, answer fully in your own words.

Language and Writing Skills

You're bound to become a better writer. You'll get plenty of practice in writing, and you'll gain a good understanding of basic grammar and usage. You'll learn about the writing process.

Although you may find many of the exercises in this section to be useful, remember that the best way to learn skills is to practice them. That is, the best way to learn writing is to write. Take advantage of writing opportunities in your everyday life. Every time you write a letter, leave a note for a family member, or even make a grocery list, you are practicing your writing skills.

Social Studies

In this section, you'll learn how to study reading passages as well as illustrations such as charts, graphs, maps, and cartoons.

In addition, read beyond the pages of this book. Read newspapers, magazines, road maps, and anything else you find useful or interesting. Reading will help you prepare not only for social studies materials but also for your future as a citizen of the world.

Science

In this section, you'll learn how to study reading passages as well as illustrations such as diagrams, charts, and graphs. You'll also study many of the basic ideas that are important in science. Most of the chapters are divided into two parts. The first part of the chapter covers a reading skill, while the second part covers a science topic.

Also, try to learn more about science issues in your daily life. Read science articles in newspapers and magazines. Look for science programs on your local radio and television stations. Science awareness will help you not only in school but also in your everyday life.

Reading/Literature and the Arts

In this section, you'll be learning how to interpret reading passages as well as charts, cartoons, and advertisements. Notice that each chapter contains parts on comprehension, vocabulary, and study skills.

Finally, read beyond the pages of this section. Read short stories, poetry, newspapers, magazines, and anything else you can get your hands on. Reading will help you prepare not only for entering a GED preparation program but also for the rest of your life.

Mathematics

First, Section 5: Mathematics is designed to provide you with the skills of whole number arithmetic. You will learn to add, subtract, multiply, and divide whole numbers. You will also learn to use these computation skills in a variety of word problems.

Because word problems are important on math tests, this book pays special attention to the development of problem-solving skills. Your word-problem skills will increase as your computation skills increase.

Section 5 is divided into ten chapters:

- Chapter 1 provides an introduction to the reading and writing of whole numbers.
- Chapters 2 through 5 introduce the computation skills of addition, subtraction, multiplication, and division. While learning these skills, you will apply them in a variety of word problems.
- Chapter 6 is called "Special Topics in Math." Here you'll study topics including multi-step word problems, measurement, averages, and squares, cubes, and square roots. Because these topics are important in everyday life, they are included on many math tests.
- Chapters 7 through 9 focus on decimals, common fractions, and percents. You'll learn to use these in both computation and word-problem-solving ways.
- Chapter 10 is "More Special Topics in Math." Here you'll study estimation, simple interest, data analysis, and probability.

On many pages, a row of "Skill Builders" comes before the problems. These Skill Builders are problems that have been started for you. Look at the work that has been done, then complete each problem.

To get the most out of your work, do each problem carefully. Check your answers to make sure you are working accurately. A complete answer key is included. Answers are given to all problems. In addition, the solutions to all word problems are worked out for you.

PRE-TESTS

PRE-TEST 1: LANGUAGE AND WRITING SKILLS

This Pre-Test is a chance for you to test your present writing skills. The Pre-Test will show you the kinds of things you will be studying in this text and will help you identify the areas you should work on most.

Follow the directions before each section of the Pre-Test and answer as many of the questions as possible. If you're not certain about an answer, use the answer that first comes to mind. For this test, you don't have to worry about your score. It is only important that you answer to the best of your ability.

Once you have completed the Pre-Test, check your answers on pages 8–9. Take time to compare all answers. Sometimes just seeing the right answer to a question will help you remember a writing skills rule you haven't used in a long time.

PART I

TOPIC 1: COMPLETE SENTENCES AND SUBJECTS

This topic area will help you find out if you can recognize a complete sentence. It will also tell you if you can find the subject of a sentence.

Directions: Each of the following pairs of sentences contains one complete sentence and one fragment. Circle the letter of the complete sentence in each pair. Then underline the subject of the complete sentence. The first one has been done as an example.

1. **a.** At Dinah's house after the movie.
   (b.) The party starts after the movie.

2. **a.** The role of computers in the plant.
   b. The computers do much of the work.

3. **a.** Roger is going to the office now.
   b. Going to the office this morning.

4. **a.** Will Carla go out with her parents tonight?
   b. Going out tonight?

TOPIC 2: NOUNS

This topic area tests your understanding of several types of nouns: common and proper nouns, singular and plural nouns, and possessive nouns.

Directions: Circle the correct noun form in each of the following sentences.

1. In the spring, the *(school, School)* will have driver education classes.

2. The *(women, womens)* are on their way home.

3. The *(bus's, bus')* tires were flat.

4. The *(boys, boy's)* caught five fish last summer.

5. Tomorrow *(aunt, Aunt)* Judy will pick you up at 3:00.

6. All the *(doctors', doctors's)* offices have gray carpeting.

TOPIC 3: PRONOUNS

This topic area will help you find out whether you can use pronouns correctly.

Directions: Part of each of the following sentences is underlined. In the blank at the end of the sentence, write the pronoun you could use to replace the underlined part. The first one has been done as an example.

1. Bruno will buy <u>pizza</u>. ___*it*___

2. <u>Patty</u> will bring the tapes. ____________

3. <u>The stereo's</u> speakers are fantastic. ____________

4. <u>Steve and I</u> will entertain. ____________

5. <u>Ethel's</u> best jokes will be told. ____________

6. Those jokes will keep <u>the guests</u> laughing. ____________

TOPIC 4: VERBS

The following topic area will help you find out how much you know about verb tenses, common irregular verbs, and subject-verb agreement.

Directions: Underline the correct form of the verb to complete each of the following sentences.

1. The winner *(will receive, will receives)* $50,000.

2. Yesterday the man *(laughs, laughed)* at the television show.

3. They *(write, writes)* letters to their friends.

4. Mike or Diane *(is, are)* in charge of the meeting.

5. Stacy and Mary Lou *(was, were)* at the pool.

6. Next time I *(will walk, walked)* another way.

TOPIC 5: ADJECTIVES AND ADVERBS

In this topic area, you'll be asked to decide whether an adjective or an adverb will correctly complete the sentence. Adjectives describe nouns, and adverbs describe verbs.

Directions: Underline the correct word to complete each of the following sentences.

1. The *(intelligent, intelligently)* professor wrote a book.

2. After the game, Howard drove *(quick, quickly)* home.

3. Raoul swam *(graceful, gracefully)*.

TOPIC 6: SENTENCE COMBINING

This topic area asks you to recognize ways to form sentences that make sense and are punctuated correctly. The first one is done for you.

Directions: Draw lines to connect the thoughts that can be combined to make complete, logical sentences.

1. Alex ran for the train,	she missed my party.
2. Rosa lost her wallet;	nevertheless, she forgave us.
3. Tim worked very hard,	but he missed it.
4. Alice was angry;	although he hates music.
5. Because Cathy went to Boston,	so he got the promotion.
6. Mark went to the concert	therefore, she had to borrow money.

TOPIC 7: PUNCTUATION

This topic area will help you learn about your punctuation skills.

Directions: Each of the following sentences needs one punctuation mark. Add the punctuation mark that makes each sentence correct.

1. I ordered pizza salad, and coffee.
2. What happened to the hot water
3. After the soccer team members won the championship they celebrated for two days.
4. Mr. Spagnola your help is needed.
5. I said "I am ready for anything."
6. Tim cant go dancing because he broke his leg.
7. Edwin has three daughters and I have two sons.
8. Celeste Wesson a policewoman, will talk about self-defense.

We ate salad, soup, and saw .

PART II

WRITING SENTENCES

This topic area tests your writing ability.

Directions: Answer the following questions about yourself *in complete sentences*. Write as correctly as you can.

1. Tell three things you do when you have free time.

   I like to clean the house.
   I go shopping whenever I have time.
   We take our kids to Chucky Cheese's on my day off.

2. Write a sentence about what you like to eat for breakfast.

   I like to eat any food, with rice.

3. Tell why a person you love is very important to you.

   Because he cares about me and he loves me.

4. Describe yourself in three or four sentences. You could tell how tall you are, how old you are, what size you are, and what color hair and eyes you have.

   I'm a 5 foot 3 and I am 29 years old

5. If you could have one wish granted, what would that wish be?

Answers start on page 8.

PRE-TEST ANSWER KEY

Part I

Topic 1: Complete Sentences and Subjects

1. b party
2. b computers
3. a Roger
4. a Carla

Topic 2: Nouns

1. school — No specific school is named, so it is not a proper noun and should not be capitalized.
2. women — *Women* is a plural noun, so it is not necessary to add an *s*.
3. bus's — Add *'s* to a singular noun to show possession.
4. boys — Add *s* to make most nouns plural.
5. Aunt — *Aunt* is used as part of Aunt Judy's name in this sentence, so it should be capitalized.
6. doctors' — Several doctors have offices with gray carpeting. Add an apostrophe to a plural noun ending in *s* to show possession.

Topic 3: Pronouns

1. it — The pronoun is the object of the sentence.
2. She — The pronoun is the subject of the sentence.
3. Its — The pronoun must show possession.
4. We — The pronoun is the subject of the sentence.
5. Her — The pronoun must show possession.
6. them — The pronoun is the object of the sentence.

Topic 4: Verbs

1. will receive — The future tense is formed by using *will* with the base verb.
2. laughed — The time clue *Yesterday* tells you to put the verb in the past tense.
3. write — To agree with the pronoun *They*, the verb should not end in *s*.
4. is — Because the two parts of the subject are joined by *or*, the verb agrees with the closest part—*Diane*.
5. were — Because the two parts of the subject are joined by *and*, the verb must agree with a plural subject.
6. will walk — The time clue *Next time* tells you to use the future tense.

Topic 5: Adjectives and Adverbs

1. intelligent — An adjective must be used to describe the noun *professor*.
2. quickly — An adverb must be used to describe the verb *drove*.
3. gracefully — An adverb must be used to describe the verb *swam*.

Topic 6: Sentence Combining

1. Alex ran for the train, but he missed it.
2. Rosa lost her wallet; therefore, she had to borrow money.
3. Tim worked very hard, so he got the promotion.
4. Alice was angry; nevertheless, she forgave us.
5. Because Cathy went to Boston, she missed my party.
6. Mark went to the concert although he hates music.

Topic 7: Punctuation

1. I ordered pizza, salad, and coffee.
2. What happened to the hot water?
3. After the soccer team members won the championship, they celebrated for two days.
4. Mr. Spagnola, your help is needed.
5. I said, "I am ready for anything."
6. Tim can't go dancing because he broke his leg.
7. Edwin has three daughters, and I have two sons.
8. Celeste Wesson, a policewoman, will talk about self-defense.

Part II
Writing Sentences

In this part of the Pre-Test, you had to write on your own. If you had trouble thinking of things to say or writing correctly, don't worry. This section is designed to help you get used to putting your thoughts on paper. It will also help you learn to write correctly.

You may have had a hard time getting ideas on paper. If so, give special effort to journal writing, which is explained on page 57. This kind of writing will help you get going as a writer. Try to write frequently in your journal. Write several times a week—every day if you can. There is a journal writing activity at the beginning of each chapter, but start right away.

You may feel that you need a lot of help in writing correctly. If so, work especially hard on the activities called "Putting Your Skills to Work." These activities are designed to help you practice rules of good English in your writing. Finally, keep in mind that the best way to improve your writing is to write a lot.

Here are some sample answers to the questions that you can compare your answers to. Your answers will be different from these.

1. When I have free time, I jog, watch TV, and read.
2. I like to eat bacon and eggs for breakfast.
3. I love my mother because she brought me into this world.
4. I am nineteen years old. I am a huge person who is over six feet tall. I have dark hair and green eyes.
5. If I could have one wish granted, I would wish for more wishes!

PRE-TEST EVALUATION CHART

Check your answers on pages 8–9. Then come back to this chart. Find the number of each question you missed and circle it in the second column. In addition to reviewing the pages listed below, you may want to work through the first chapter.

	Question Numbers	Study Pages	Number Correct
Topic 1			
Complete sentences	1, 2, 3, 4	70–79	______ /4
Topic 2			
Common and proper nouns	1, 5	87–89	
Singular and plural nouns	2, 4	90–92	______ /6
Possessive nouns	3, 6	92–94	
Topic 3			
Subject pronouns	2, 4	94–96	
Object pronouns	1, 6	96–97	______ /6
Possessive pronouns	3, 5	97–98	
Topic 4			
Verb tenses	1, 2, 6	105–126	
Subject-verb agreement	3, 4, 5	128–137	______ /6
Topic 5			
Adjectives and adverbs	1, 2, 3	145–155	______ /3
Topic 6			
Conjunctions	1, 3		
Connectors	2, 4	162–174	______ /6
Dependent conjunctions	5, 6		
Topic 7			
Comma in a series	1	153–155	
Types of sentences	2	73–75	
Subordinating conjunctions	3	172–174	
Direct address	4	140	
Quotation marks	5	121–122	
Contractions	6	100–102	
Conjunctions	7	165–168	
Phrases that give additional information	8	138	______ /8
		Total Correct	______ /39

PRE-TEST 2: SOCIAL STUDIES

The Social Studies Pre-Test is a guide to using the social studies section. You should take the Pre-Test before you start working on any of the chapters. The questions will test the social studies reading and reasoning skills covered in this section.

Directions: Study each passage or illustration, then answer the questions that follow.

Questions 1 and 2 are based on the following passage.

> The Sultan of Brunei may not control a large nation, but his rule has its rewards. With a fortune worth about $37 billion, Sultan Hassanal Bolkiah is considered the richest man in the world.
>
> His wealth comes from the vast pool of oil lying beneath his small island nation. Thanks to that oil, the sultan is able to give his 369,000 subjects one of the highest standards of living in Asia. No one pays personal income taxes in Brunei, and yet, the government provides a host of social services like free medical care, free primary-school education, and old-age pensions.
>
> The year 1992 was the sultan's 25th year as king, and many people hoped that he would celebrate by restoring democracy to Brunei. Instead, the sultan simply promised to further increase the standard of living. His pampered subjects didn't complain.

1. What is the form of government of Brunei?

    (1) democracy, rule by the people with free elections
    (2) military dictatorship, rule by the head of the armed forces
    (3) monarchy, rule by a single member of a royal family
    (4) theocracy, rule by priests
    (5) oligarchy, rule by a small elite group

2. What is the main idea of this passage?

    (1) The people of Brunei are involved in decision making and planning for the future of the country.
    (2) Brunei is not a very large nation, but the sultan enjoys ruling it.
    (3) The wealthy sultan of Brunei keeps control over his people but provides for them generously.
    (4) The sultan of Brunei is planning to take over neighboring nations in order to enlarge his country.
    (5) The standard of living in Brunei has improved since the sultan celebrated his 25th year on the throne.

Question 3 is based on the following passage.

> As a word-processing teacher, I am often called by companies interested in hiring my students. When they ask for a recommendation, they do not first ask about skills, intelligence, age, or appearance. The first question is almost always about attendance and punctuality.

3. What do companies value most in their word-processing employees?

(1) potential
(2) attractiveness
(3) youth
(4) dependability
(5) knowledge

Questions 4 and 5 are based on the following cartoon.

Background clues: Prison overcrowding in the United States has forced judges to seek alternative ways of punishing people convicted of crimes. Community service, payments to victims, and boot camps are just some of the alternative sentences U.S. judges have used.

"You can take the five years and $60,000 in fines, or you can go for Door Number Two where officer Meryl is standing."

4. When the cartoonist writes, "You can go for Door Number Two where officer Meryl is standing," he is comparing modern trials to

(1) birthday parties
(2) war
(3) classrooms
(4) game shows
(5) horrible ordeals

5. The point of this cartoon is that alternative sentencing

(1) makes punishment a matter of luck
(2) helps trials move more smoothly
(3) is a more humane way of punishing criminals
(4) discourages potential criminals from committing crimes
(5) saves the government a lot of money

Questions 6 and 7 are based on the following passage.

Caroline rushed out to use her brand-new credit card at Sears. She went straight to the home improvement department and bought wallpaper and paint to redecorate the kitchen. She took the supplies to the cashier and handed over her credit card. The cashier made out a sales slip from Caroline's card. After signing the sales slip, Caroline sailed out of the store and immediately started her project.

At the end of the month, Caroline was shocked when she received her statement. She had not realized that the supplies cost so much. The statement listed all her credit purchases and the total amount she owed Sears. She could afford to pay only the minimum payment, not the whole amount she owed. As a result, she had to pay interest to Sears on the unpaid portion.

6. In which of the following situations would you use a credit card in the same way as Caroline did?

(1) buying dinner for your family at McDonald's
(2) renting an apartment from a realtor
(3) buying new shoes at a shoe store
(4) placing a mail order by phone
(5) withdrawing money from an automatic teller machine

7. Caroline had to pay interest to Sears because

(1) she could not afford to make the minimum payment
(2) whenever you buy something with a credit card, you have to pay interest
(3) she could not afford to pay the full amount she owed
(4) she was so shocked when she received her statement
(5) the supplies she bought were on sale

Questions 8 and 9 are based on the following graph.

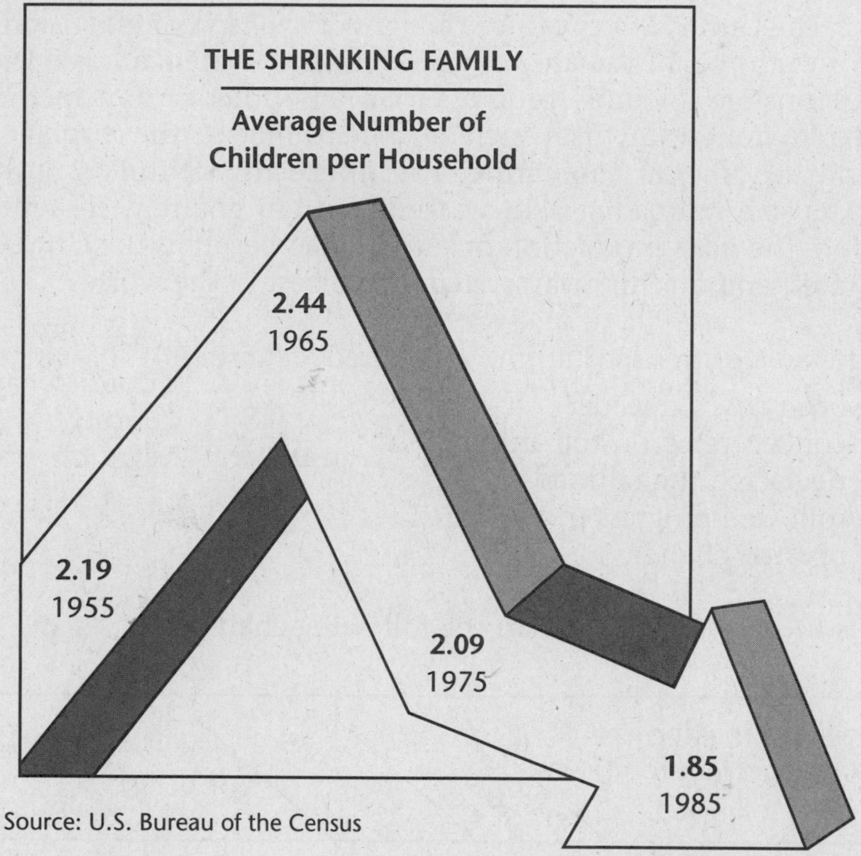

8. In what year did Americans have the greatest number of children per household?
   (1) 1955
   (2) 1965
   (3) 1975
   (4) 1980
   (5) 1985

9. Which of the following is a reasonable conclusion based on this graph?
   (1) American children today generally have fewer brothers and sisters than was the case a generation ago.
   (2) Americans of 1985 were earning more money than thirty years before and could better provide for their children.
   (3) As of 1985, there was a growing need for more elementary schools.
   (4) Most Americans have decided not to have any children because they believe the world is too dangerous.
   (5) An increase in single-parent households has resulted in a decline in the average number of children per household.

Question 10 is based on the following passage.

The United States can be thought of as a land of invention. For example, in the area of transportation, America has been responsible for more progress than any other nation in the world. American firsts include the steamboat, the airplane, and the nuclear submarine. The nineteenth century's most extensive railroad system was built in our country. In addition, the mass production of automobiles began in the United States, and our highway system is the best in the world.

10. In the area of transportation, the United States has

(1) been a world leader
(2) concentrated on the automobile
(3) neglected the railroads
(4) followed progress in Europe
(5) resisted change

Questions 11 and 12 are based on the following chart.

STRATEGIC IMPORTS
(Averages in percent)

	Platinum group metals	Chromium	Vanadium	Manganese	Gold
Share of U.S. imports originating in South Africa (1990–1993)	47%	43%	13%	24%	NA
South Africa's share of world reserves	89%	60%	50%	92%	26%
South Africa's share of world production (1994)	60%	31%	30%	36%	48%

Sources: U.S. Bureau of Mines; United Nations

11. What percentage of the chromium imported into the United States came from South Africa?

(1) 13%
(2) 31%
(3) 43%
(4) 47%
(5) 60%

12. Platinum group metals, chromium, vanadium, and manganese are all important to American industry. What does the chart tell you about the relationship of South Africa to the United States?

(1) The United States has no relationship with South Africa.
(2) South Africa relies on the United States for valuable metals.
(3) The United States could get along easily without imports from South Africa.
(4) South Africa provides the United States with important raw materials.
(5) South Africa lacks natural mineral resources.

Questions 13 and 14 are based on the following passage.

In May 1607, the first permanent English colony in what is now the United States was founded at Jamestown, Virginia. The colonists built their village on a terrible swamp, and then the men spent their time looking for gold. The entire colony would have starved if not for the help of the native chief Powhatan, who gave the settlers food.

The colony struggled along until John Rolfe discovered the American tobacco plant. Virginia began to export tobacco to Europe, where it became very popular. The success of the Virginia colony was assured.

13. After building their village, the first settlers

(1) planted tobacco
(2) attacked the Native Americans
(3) searched for gold
(4) planted food crops
(5) befriended and helped the Native Americans

14. The colonists needed help from the Native Americans

(1) because they did not know how to grow tobacco in Virginia
(2) because they did not produce enough food
(3) to prevent slavery in Virginia
(4) to build the village of Jamestown
(5) to export tobacco to Europe

Questions 15 and 16 are based on the following map.

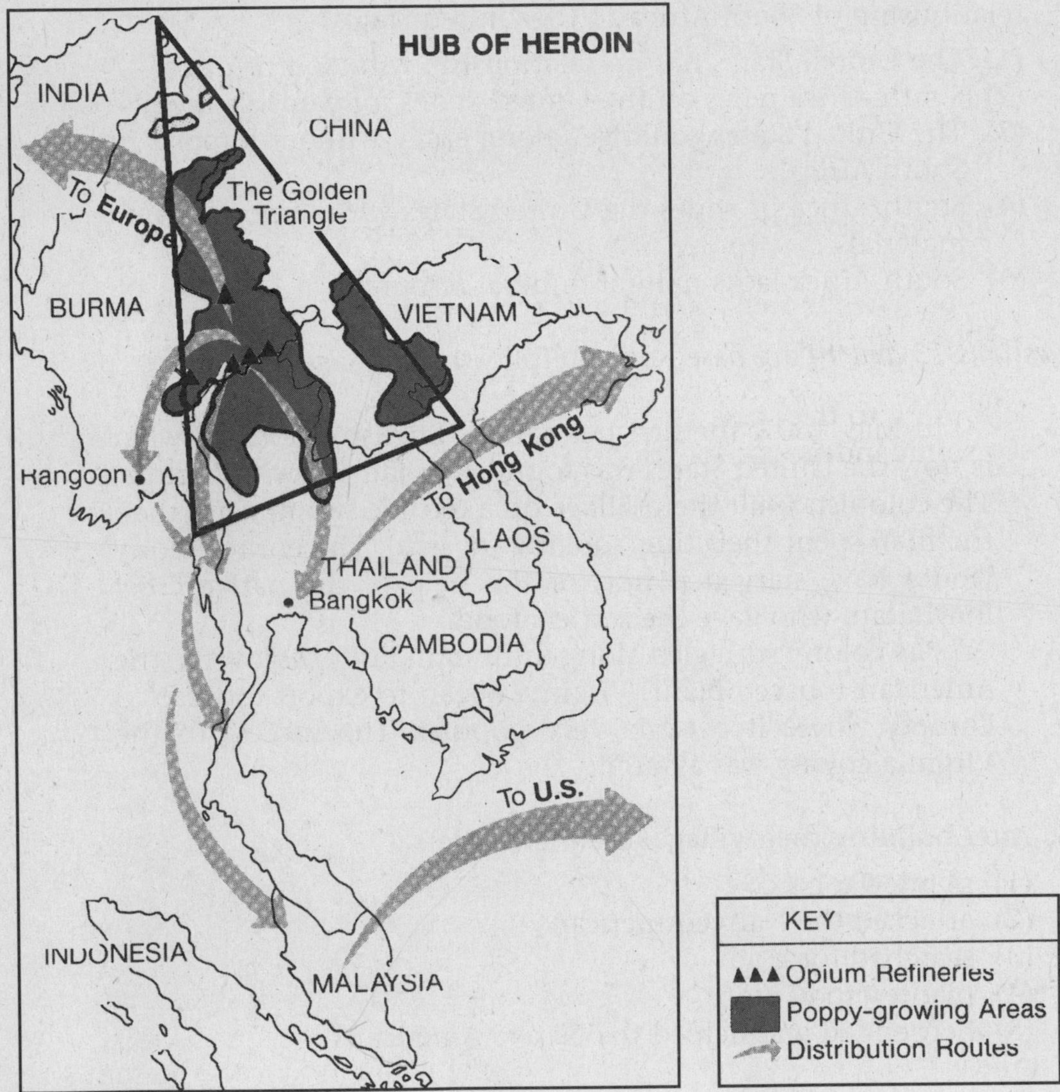

15. The opium refineries in the Golden Triangle are all in
    (1) Bangkok
    (2) Europe
    (3) Rangoon
    (4) India
    (5) poppy-growing areas

16. From Malaysia, heroin is sent to
    (1) Thailand
    (2) Burma
    (3) Hong Kong
    (4) the U.S.
    (5) Europe

Questions 17 and 18 are based on the following passage.

The plow played a vital role for men in search of the American promise of opportunity and independence. The wilderness was the frontier for American men. As long as they could clear new land, plow it, and grow something on it, it was their land. The plow set them free.

However, the city was the frontier for American women. The typewriter gave them a way to earn money and the opportunity to set a course of their own. The business office, not the wilderness, would give women the chance to control their own lives.

17. According to the passage, the machine that most helped women gain economic independence was
    (1) the sewing machine
    (2) the typewriter
    (3) the plow
    (4) the electric mixer
    (5) the automobile

18. The passage describes different opportunities for American women and American men. The key difference the writer describes is that
    (1) women were more dependent than men
    (2) women preferred to live in cities while men preferred to live in log cabins
    (3) women preferred staying at home while men preferred change and adventure
    (4) cities offered women the independence and opportunity that men found in the wilderness
    (5) women planned for the future while men lived for the present

Question 19 is based on the following advertisement.

> **GIVE HER THE FRAGRANCE OF LUXURY**
> Take her away from the ordinary. Give her something she will never forget. A perfume that says "You're special."
> ***Gisell Perfume***
> It costs more, but isn't she worth it?

19. This ad wants you to believe that Gisell perfume
    (1) is used by many famous people
    (2) will make a woman feel special
    (3) is a good buy
    (4) is used by more women than any other perfume
    (5) will drive men wild

Question 20 is based on the following passage.

In the 1840s, many Americans believed in "manifest destiny," the idea that the United States had the right to control all the land from the Atlantic to the Pacific. President Polk used the theory of manifest destiny to justify declaring war on Mexico. As a result of this war, Mexico lost half of its territory and the United States gained most of its southwestern lands, including California.

20. The main idea of this paragraph is that
    (1) the United States used "manifest destiny" to justify taking over half of Mexico
    (2) Mexico lost half its territory in the Mexican War
    (3) the American form of government needs an entire continent to function well
    (4) the United States was right to conquer half of Mexico in order to spread democracy
    (5) Mexico provoked the U.S. into war by opposing "manifest destiny"

Questions 21 and 22 are based on the following passage.

As in many other southern towns, many people in Eastman, Georgia, used to work in a textile mill. After eighty years of operation, the Reeves Brothers mill closed in the mid '80s, laying off 340 people. The economy of this little town was hurt badly by the loss of jobs and wages from the mill.

Bit by bit, however, the town rebounded from the mill closing. When the mill closed, the Standard Candy Company was run by fewer than 100 part-time employees. Now Standard Candy has several hundred full-time workers. Another company, Reynolds Aluminum, added employees to its payroll. A local welding company expanded, and so did another small candy company. In addition, a large discount store opened its doors in Eastman, providing even more jobs.

Perhaps the biggest boost to Eastman's economy was a new Georgia highway that was built right through it. The highway connects Georgia's largest city, Atlanta, with the Georgia seacoast. Because of the highway, products made in Eastman are easier to ship to other places. The highway also allows Eastman to attract tourists driving from Atlanta to the beaches.

21. Over the next five years, it is likely that
    (1) more jobs will be created in Eastman
    (2) the population of Eastman will decline rapidly
    (3) many residents of Eastman will turn to farming to make their living
    (4) most laid-off mill workers will still be out of work
    (5) a major state highway running through Eastman will close

PRE-TEST EVALUATION CHART

Check your answers on page 22; then come back to this chart and find the number of each question you missed and circle it in the second column. Then decide which chapters you should concentrate on. The numbers in **boldface type** are questions based on illustrations.

	Skill	Question Numbers	Number Correct
Chapter 1	• Finding details	17	______ /5
	• Restating information	1	
	• Summarizing information	10	
	• Main idea of a paragraph	20	
	• Main idea of a passage	2	
Chapter 2	• Locating information on a chart	**11**	______ /4
	• Locating information on a graph	**8**	
	• Locating information on a map	**16**	
	• Using a map key	**15**	
Chapter 3	• Sequence	13	______ /3
	• Cause and effect	7	
	• Compare and contrast	18	
Chapter 4	• Inference	14	______ /5
	• Political cartoons	**4, 5**	
	• Hypotheses	23	
	• Predicting outcomes	21	
Chapter 5	• Adequacy of information	24	______ /5
	• Interpreting charts	**12**	
	• Interpreting graphs	**9**	
	• Values	3	
	• Propaganda	19	
Chapter 6	• Application	6, 22	______ /2
		Total Correct	______ /24

PRE-TEST 3: SCIENCE

Because of your life experience, there are many facts about science that you already know. *Science* just means the organized study of the world around you and everything in it. Every time you try to figure out how something works or why something happens, you are thinking scientifically.

Directions: You can use this Pre-Test to test your science reading skills. Read each passage carefully. Look closely at any illustrations that accompany it. Then choose the *one best answer* for each of the questions that follow. Don't worry if you find many of these questions difficult. You will learn how to answer questions like these as you work through this text.

Questions 1 and 2 are based on the following passage.

> Everyone knows what a cold is, and many of us have had one recently. But did you know that a "common cold" can be caused by any one of more than a hundred different viruses? Or that women tend to catch more colds than men, but baby girls actually catch fewer colds than baby boys?
>
> A few people (about 5 percent of the population) seem to be immune to colds. They rarely, if ever, catch one. But that doesn't mean they are the lucky ones. Scientists in West Germany have discovered that people who catch fewer than one cold per year are six times more likely to develop cancer. Maybe having a cold isn't all that bad!

1. What is the best title for this passage?
   (1) Avoid Cancer by Catching a Cold
   (2) Men Catch More Colds
   (3) How to Cure the Common Cold
   (4) Odd Facts About the Common Cold
   (5) The Lucky 5 Percent

2. The "common cold" is probably called "common" because
   (1) many ordinary doctors can cure it
   (2) it is caused by one very common virus
   (3) most people catch one fairly often
   (4) "common" people catch more colds than famous people
   (5) it is unusual in men

Question 3 is based on the following passage and chart.

Hunting laws and regulations have two main purposes: to let game animals reproduce without being disturbed by hunters and to prevent overhunting of the rarer animals. The chart at the right shows some of the rules from the *1987 Wisconsin Hunting Regulations* booklet.

SMALL GAME HUNTING SEASONS*	
Species	**Daily Limit**
Gray & Fox Squirrel	5
Woodcock	5
Jackrabbit	3
Bobwhite Quail	5
Hungarian Partridge	3
Bobcat	1 per season
Snowshoe Hare	Unlimited

** Only selected portions of the chart have been reproduced here. Those seeking complete information should obtain a copy of the original booklet.*

3. From the information in the chart, which of these animals would you infer is the most common?
   (1) gray squirrel
   (2) jackrabbit
   (3) bobwhite quail
   (4) bobcat
   (5) snowshoe hare

Questions 4 and 5 are based on the following passage and diagram.

Keeping the proper amount of air pressure in your automobile tires is important. Incorrect tire pressure can cause extra tire wear. It can also cause accidents. Underinflation can cause a tire to heat up, possibly leading to a blowout on the highway. Overinflation prevents tire tread from fully gripping the road, making the car more likely to skid.

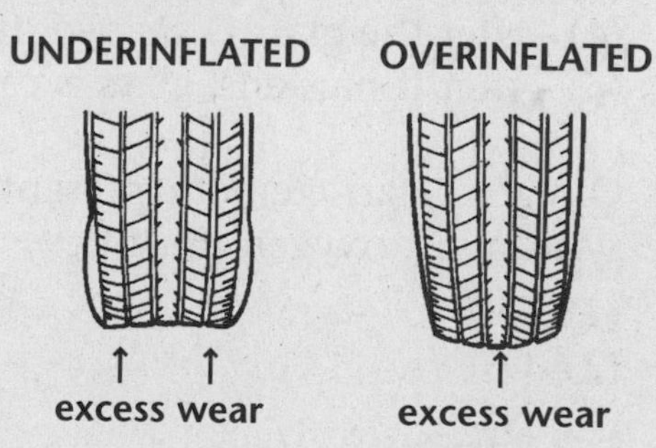

4. An "overinflated" tire means a tire that
   (1) costs too much
   (2) has too little pressure in it
   (3) is badly worn
   (4) has too much air in it
   (5) requires 50 pounds of pressure

5. This passage is most likely to be from which of the following books?
   (1) *Cooking Great Meals on the Road*
   (2) *1,001 Ways to Save Money*
   (3) *Choosing the Right Automobile*
   (4) *Safe Travel in the Air*
   (5) *Tips for New Car Owners*

Questions 6 and 7 are based on the following passage.

People have been making glass for thousands of years, using some of the same methods we use today. Ordinary window glass is made from a mixture of sand (SiO_2), soda (Na_2CO_3), and lime (CaO). This mixture is heated until the different chemicals fuse together into a thick semiliquid. The semiliquid can be blown or pressed or stretched into different shapes before it cools and hardens.

Depending on how it has been mixed and shaped, glass can be used for windows, cups and dishes, lenses in eyeglasses and telescopes, airtight containers for foods and medicines, glass bricks for building, and many other purposes. Glass can even be drawn into a fine thread called fiberglass. Fiberglass can be used for insulation and filters or woven into a handsome fabric for curtains and drapes.

6. Which of the following statements is true, according to the passage?
   (1) Sand, soda, and lime are heated separately and then mixed to make glass.
   (2) Glass must be cool before it can be shaped.
   (3) The basic materials in glass fuse together after they are heated.
   (4) After the glass is shaped, it is heated to make it strong.
   (5) After it hardens, glass is carved into the desired shape.

7. Oxygen is an element present in sand, soda, and lime. The chemical symbol for oxygen must be
   (1) Si
   (2) O
   (3) Na
   (4) C
   (5) Ca

Questions 8 and 9 are based on the following passage and graph.

Weather forecasters use an anemometer to measure the speed of the wind. Below is a graph showing one day's anemometer readings at a certain weather station.

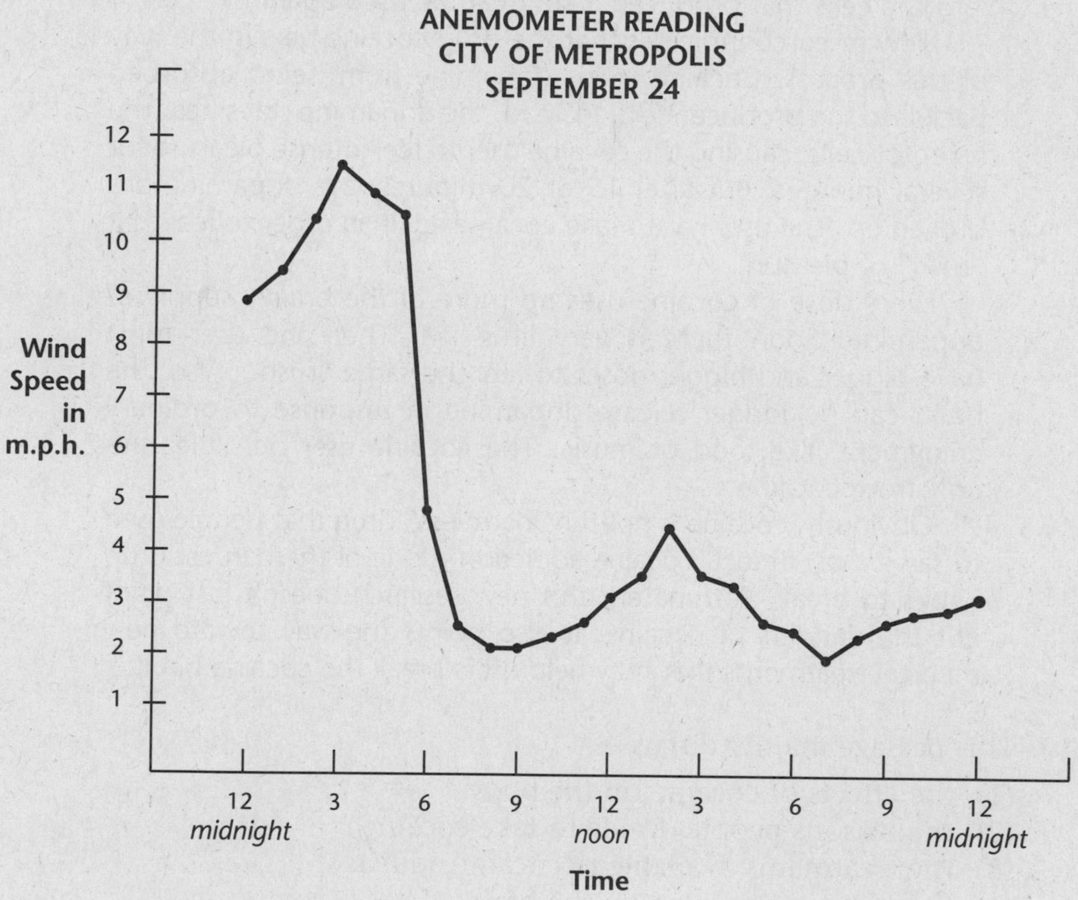

8. Considering that both light and wind are needed to fly a kite successfully, what was the best time to fly a kite in Metropolis on September 24?
   (1) 2 A.M.
   (2) 3 A.M.
   (3) 10 A.M.
   (4) 2 P.M.
   (5) 6 P.M.

9. Since a *thermometer* measures temperature, and an *anemometer* is used to measure wind speed, an *altimeter* is probably used to
   (1) breathe at high altitudes
   (2) hold things attached to tall buildings
   (3) measure altitude in airplanes
   (4) teach women to sing alto music
   (5) plan alternative methods of driving

Questions 10 and 11 are based on the following passage.

When a human being is enjoying something, certain cells in the brain release a chemical called dopamine. When the dopamine travels to other brain cells, called receptors, the person feels pleasure. After a short time, the dopamine is absorbed back into the cells that produced it so it can be used again.

New research indicates that the drug cocaine gets in the way of this process. Cocaine keeps dopamine from being absorbed back into the producer cells. Instead, the dopamine stays near the receptor cells, causing the cocaine user to feel intense pleasure for several minutes. But after 15 or 20 minutes, the dopamine has broken up. The user has to take cocaine again in order to feel that "rush" of pleasure.

Every dose of cocaine uses up more of the brain's supply of dopamine. Soon there is very little left. Then the user must have bigger and bigger doses to feel the same "rush." Also, the brain can no longer release dopamine in response to ordinary enjoyment, like food or music. The cocaine user gets pleasure only from cocaine.

Obviously, cocaine is not the "harmless" drug that people used to say it was. In fact, cocaine addiction is one of the hardest drug habits to break. Fortunately, this new research doesn't just point out the dangers of cocaine. It also points the way toward new medical treatments that may help users break the cocaine habit.

10. This passage mainly discusses

(1) the effects of cocaine on the body
(2) the reasons people decide to take cocaine
(3) the treatments available to cocaine addicts
(4) the effects of cocaine on the brain
(5) the different ways people feel pleasure

11. The author of this passage would be most likely to vote for

(1) more government money to pay for drug-related research
(2) harsher prison sentences for convicted drug users
(3) cuts in funding for drug education programs
(4) government programs to supply addicts with dopamine
(5) shorter prison sentences for drug dealers

Questions 12 and 13 are based on the following passage and diagram.

There are two main scales used to measure temperature today. The **Fahrenheit** scale is used by most people in the United States. The **Celsius,** or centigrade, scale is used by the people of most other countries as well as by scientists all over the world. Use this diagram comparing the two scales to answer the following questions.

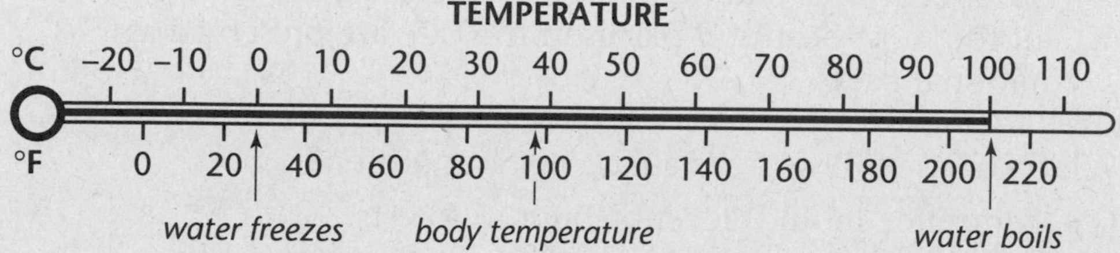

12. What is the boiling point of water on the Celsius scale?

(1) 0°C
(2) 60°C
(3) 98.6°C
(4) 100°C
(5) 212°C

13. Which statement correctly reflects the information in the diagram?

(1) When the temperature outside is 35°C, most people would want to turn on the air conditioner.
(2) The weather is warmer in the United States than in other countries.
(3) The Celsius scale is harder for most people to understand.
(4) Water freezes at a lower temperature in centigrade than it does in Fahrenheit.
(5) 70°F is warmer than 25°C.

Questions 14 and 15 are based on the following passage.

Yellowstone National Park in the western United States was the first national park established in the world. Little was known about this beautiful area, famous for its hot springs, geysers, and spectacular scenery, until after the Civil War, when two different groups of men set out to explore the region.

Judge Cornelius Hedges was a member of one of the expeditions. Around the campfire one night he suggested to his friends that, instead of claiming the land for private profit, they should find a way to preserve the amazing landscape for all the American people to enjoy. Because of their efforts, in 1872 Congress passed the Yellowstone Act, a law that required everything in the park to be preserved in its natural condition.

No one would be allowed to cut down trees or to spoil the park in any way. This law was the foundation for the entire system of national parks in the United States, preserving millions of acres of land.

14. From the passage you can tell that

(1) no one had ever seen the Yellowstone area before 1865
(2) the president did not want to sign the Yellowstone Act
(3) Judge Hedges and his friends acted unselfishly
(4) other countries had national parks before the U.S. had them
(5) all the most beautiful places in the U.S. are preserved in national parks

15. Which of the following is a *fact,* not an opinion?

(1) Campfires should never be built in forests.
(2) Natural beauty is more important than private profit.
(3) The Yellowstone area is famous for its scenery.
(4) Yellowstone National Park is the most beautiful park in the world.
(5) Everyone should spend some time in a national park.

Questions 16 and 18 are based on the following passage and diagram.

When you cut a tree, you can read its life history by counting the number of tree rings in its trunk. Each ring is one year's growth. The inside rings are the earliest, while the outside rings show the tree's most recent growth. Tree rings are easiest to read in deciduous trees, because these trees have a period of almost no growth each winter after their leaves fall.

In a good year, with plenty of water and sunshine, a tree grows a lot, leaving a wide ring as a record of that year. In a bad year, the tree grows only a little, leaving a thin ring. If the tree is attacked by fire or disease, this evidence, too, will show in the tree rings.

16. In the diagram, the tree ring indicated with an arrow is a record of

(1) a good year followed by another good year
(2) a bad year followed by a good year
(3) two bad years in a row
(4) the first year the tree was alive
(5) a good year followed by a bad year

17. From the passage, you can tell that deciduous trees are trees that
    (1) live only in warm climates
    (2) lose their leaves in the fall
    (3) grow very tall
    (4) are very young
    (5) stay green all year

18. Which of the following would be most likely to cause a conflict of values for a tree lover who had a job studying tree rings?
    (1) He would have to cut down trees to study their rings.
    (2) He would feel wrong using trees to study human history.
    (3) He would feel wrong getting paid to study trees.
    (4) He would not really be interested in his work.
    (5) He would not want other people to study tree rings.

Questions 19 and 20 are based on the following passage.

One type of psychotherapy that is becoming more and more popular is family therapy. In family therapy, all the members of a family work together with a counselor. They learn to communicate better and to untangle the relationships among family members. Working with the whole family makes sense when dealing with problems like incest, child abuse, marriage trouble, or teen runaways.

Family therapists believe that many other psychological problems, such as alcoholism, drug abuse, depression, and even school problems, may be caused at least partly by unbalanced family relationships. They believe that one person's problems can affect the whole family. If an individual works with a therapist to "cure" his problem, but then goes back into the same family situation, the problems may start all over again. Family therapy helps build a healthy family, which in turn helps each individual family member.

19. A family therapist would most probably agree with which of the following statements?
    (1) Medical doctors are the best-qualified people to treat psychological problems.
    (2) It is important to be open and honest in your communication.
    (3) Every person is the main cause of his or her own problems.
    (4) It is not necessary to treat an entire family if just one family member has a psychological problem.
    (5) Too much time and money are spent trying to help people with psychological problems.

20. You could infer that one common problem with family therapy is that
    (1) it is not as good as other therapies
    (2) schools won't tell parents about students' problems
    (3) it takes a very long time
    (4) some family members may be unwilling to come to therapy
    (5) it can be done only by a counselor who has a large family

Answers start on page 33.

PRE-TEST ANSWER KEY

1. (4) Choice (4) is the best summary of the ideas in the passage. Choice (1) does not cover the entire passage. Choice (3) is not included in the passage at all. Choices (2) and (5) disagree with the information in the passage.
2. (3) Having a cold is a familiar experience for almost everyone. Choice (2) is untrue, according to the passage. Choices (1) and (4) are not mentioned in the passage.
3. (5) The snowshoe hare is probably the most common animal because the law allows hunters to shoot any number of hares at any time of the year. All the other animals can be shot only at certain times and in certain numbers.
4. (4) This meaning can be figured out from the drawing of an overinflated tire and from the meaning of the prefix *over-*, meaning "too much."
5. (5) The paragraph gives helpful information for car owners. Choice (3) is wrong because the passage does not discuss how to choose an automobile, only how to take care of one. Choice (2) is wrong because the passage talks more about safety than about saving money on tire wear.
6. (3) See the first paragraph for the answer. All the other choices are untrue, according to the passage.
7. (2) O is the only symbol contained in all three chemical formulas.
8. (4) You need daylight and wind to fly a kite successfully. Choices (1) and (2) are wrong because it is dark out at those times. Choices (3)and (5) are not right because the graph shows less wind at those times.
9. (3) The two examples, *thermometer* and *anemometer*, show you that the suffix *meter* indicates something used to measure with.
10. (4) The passage describes how cocaine affects the dopamine supply in the brain. None of the other topics is actually mentioned in the passage.
11. (1) The author would vote for choice (1) because the more we know about drugs, the better prepared we'll be to deal with them.
12. (4) The arrow pointing to "water boils" is at 100°C.
13. (1) According to the diagram, 35°C is equal to about 90°F, a temperature at which most people would want to turn on their air conditioning. Choices (2) and (3) may or may not be true, but they are not shown by the diagram. Choice (4) is impossible. Choice (5) is untrue, according to the diagram.
14. (3) The passage says the team of explorers wanted the land for all the people, instead of just for themselves. Choices (1) and (4) are untrue, according to the passage. Choice (2) is not mentioned at all. Choice (5) is wrong because you could not assume that *all* the beautiful spots are in parks.
15. (3) This fact is mentioned in the first paragraph of the passage. All the other statements are opinions.
16. (5) The indicated ring is wide, showing that it records a good year. The ring next to it toward the outside is narrow, showing a bad year that followed.
17. (2) This is shown by the phrase "each winter after their leaves fall."
18. (1) The values in conflict would be a tree lover's desire to preserve trees and a desire to study their history as required by his or her job.
19. (2) This is mentioned as one of the things that family therapists teach people to do. Choices (3) and (4) are directly opposite the ideas in the passage. Family therapists would not agree with choice (1) because they feel that they are best qualified to help people with psychological problems. They would not agree with choice (5) because this is their life's work.
20. (4) The passage says therapy is best done with all family members.

PRE-TEST EVALUATION CHART

Use the answer key on page 33 to check your answers. Then, on the chart below, circle the number of each question that you missed. If you missed many of the questions that correspond to a certain reading skill, you will want to pay special attention to that skill as you work through this book. The numbers in **boldface type** are questions based on illustrations.

While this test is used to focus on particular reading skills, you will notice that each chapter covers science topics as well as reading skills. Even if you do well on the reading skills in a particular chapter, be sure to go through *all* of the science topics in this section.

	Scientific Method pp. 369–378	**Understanding What You Read** pp. 379–385	**Understanding Illustrations** pp. 401–414	**Analyzing Ideas** pp. 433–442	**Building Vocabulary** pp. 363–369	**Evaluating Ideas** pp. 478–482
Plant and Animal Biology			**16**	**3**	17	18
Human Biology		1, 10		20	2	11, 19
Physics			**12**	**13**	**4**	5
Chemistry				6	7	
Earth Science	15	14	**8**		9	
NUMBER CORRECT:	_____ / 1	_____ / 3	_____ / 3	_____ / 4	_____ / 5	_____ / 4

Total Correct _____ / 20

PRE-TEST 4: READING/LITERATURE AND THE ARTS

The purpose of this Pre-Test is to find your strengths as well as the areas you need to work on. As you take the Pre-Test, don't worry if you have trouble answering a question. Check all your answers and use the evaluation chart on pages 46 to help you and your instructor determine which skills you need to work on most.

Directions: Choose the best answer to each question.

1. Look at the following words: include, chowder, reporter, raven. What is the correct way to divide these words into syllables?
(1) in-clude, chow-der, re-port-er, ra-ven
(2) inc-lude, chow-der, re-port-er, ra-ven
(3) in-clude, chowd-er, re-port-er, ra-ven
(4) in-clude, chow-der, rep-ort-er, ra-ven
(5) in-clude, chow-der, re-port-er, rav-en

2. Use your knowledge of roots, prefixes, and suffixes to match each word with its definition at the right.

(1)	antiaircraft	a.	cover or surround
(2)	enfold	b.	make a copy
(3)	duplicate	c.	cut in order to examine
(4)	interchangeable	d.	against aircraft
(5)	dissect	e.	able to be changed

3. Look at each **boldfaced** word on the left. Find its synonym from the four choices at the right.

(1)	**slumber**	**a.** sleep	**b.** awake	**c.** work	**d.** read
(2)	**gaze**	**a.** gazebo	**b.** glaze	**c.** stare	**d.** haze
(3)	**plain**	**a.** unclear	**b.** vague	**c.** hazy	**d.** clear
(4)	**winner**	**a.** lost	**b.** victor	**c.** failure	**d.** struggle
(5)	**form**	**a.** shape	**b.** from	**c.** produce	**d.** destroy

4. Read the following sentence. Then identify the key words that answer the questions *Who or what?* and *Did what?*

The busy manager became irritable as the piles of work on his desk grew high.

The key words are ______________________ ______________________

5. The earthquake was a **calamity.** People were trapped under buildings, and bridges had collapsed. *Calamity* means
(1) disaster
(2) party
(3) celebration
(4) bridge
(5) surprise

6. Pick the word that best completes the analogy.
red : stop :: green : ____________
(1) yellow
(2) go
(3) slow
(4) yield

Directions: Read each of the following passages. Then answer the questions that come after each passage.

Questions 7–12 are based on the following passage.

Many people prefer to use self-service pumps at gas stations. As a result, routine car checks that gas station attendants used to do are often neglected. However, you can do these simple checks for yourself to help ensure that your car stays in good running order.

First, check the oil level with the dipstick, since running a car without sufficient oil can ruin the engine. You should also check other fluid levels such as the brake fluid, the transmission fluid (if your car is automatic), and the power steering fluid (if your car has power steering). Be sure to follow the precautions that are listed in your driver's manual for the make and model of your car.

To avoid being burned or scalded, make sure the engine is cold before you check to see whether the radiator needs coolant. Tires, too, should be checked for proper air pressure when cool. Too much or too little pressure can cause tires to wear faster.

These regular checks can save excessive wear on your car and may even prevent a frightening experience on the road.

7. The main idea of this selection is that
(1) you should check your oil regularly
(2) you should make routine car checks regularly
(3) you should always check your tire pressure
(4) you should always buy gas at self-service pumps
(5) you should never use self-service pumps

8. According to the author, why have routine car checks often been neglected?
(1) Gas station attendants don't like to do routine car checks.
(2) People are too lazy to bother with routine car checks.
(3) Many people use self-service pumps and don't have attendants check their cars.
(4) Cars are made to function without routine checks.
(5) People aren't as concerned with safety as they once were.

9. The tone of the article is

(1) funny
(2) sad
(3) informational
(4) cheerful
(5) sentimental

10. The statement "Running a car without sufficient oil can ruin the engine" is

(1) a rumor
(2) an opinion
(3) untrue
(4) propaganda
(5) a fact

11. What is the best title for this selection?

(1) Getting Gas at a Self-Service Pump
(2) The Importance of Routine Car Checks
(3) Checking Car Brakes
(4) Checking Fluids in Your Car
(5) Buying a Used Car

12. Fill in the following blanks with details from the selection.

a. Check the ______________ level with the dipstick.

b. Other fluids that need checking are the ________________ fluid, the __________________ fluid for automatics, and the ________________ ____________________ fluid.

c. Be sure to follow precautions listed in your __________________ ___________________.

d. Your engine should be __________________ when you check the radiator.

e. Tires should be checked for pressure when __________________.

Questions 13–16 are based on the following passage.

Meteors are chunks of rock or metal floating out in space. Occasionally, a meteor enters the earth's atmosphere. Caught by the pull of gravity, the meteors plunge toward earth. Most of them burn up in the atmosphere before they hit the ground. Because the glow of their burning makes them visible, people often call them "shooting stars."

Sometimes meteors actually hit the earth. One crashed in the Shandung province of China over 1,300 years ago. It weighed four tons and was shaped like an ox. Because the ancient Chinese regarded the stone as holy and worshiped it, they built a temple nearby. Only recently have researchers determined that the ox-shaped rock was a meteor.

13. People call meteors "shooting stars" because
(1) they float in space like stars
(2) they are the same size as stars
(3) the glow of their burning makes them visible
(4) they light up when they hit the moon
(5) they are ox-shaped

14. Match the facts in the right-hand column with the word that indicates the order in which it is told in the story. Write the number of the fact next to the sequence word that fits it.

Time Order	**Facts**
______ (1) first	**a.** The ancient Chinese regarded the stone as holy.
______ (2) second	**b.** Researchers determined that the ox-shaped rock was really a meteor.
______ (3) third	**c.** They built a temple near it.
______ (4) fourth	**d.** A meteor crashed in Shandung.

15. What causes meteors to plunge toward the earth?
(1) They are caught by the pull of earth's gravity.
(2) They bounce off the moon onto the earth.
(3) They are part of a comet's tail.
(4) They are attracted by the North Pole.
(5) They collide with stars and fall from the sky.

16. Fill in the following blanks with the correct details from the passage.

a. Where did the meteor crash? ______________________________.

b. It weighed ____.

c. It is shaped like an ______________________________.

d. When did it crash? ______________________________.

e. Who determined it was a meteor? ______________________________.

f. When did they determine it was a meteor? ______________________________.

g. The ancient Chinese regarded the stone as ______________________________.

Questions 17–20 are based on the following advertisement.

17. Give one reason the ad gives for buying Kibbles 'n Bits.

____

18. One slogan, "More Bits in Every Bite," is written on the package. What is the other slogan used in the ad?

____

19. The claims in the ad are

(1) opinions
(2) facts

20. The connotations of the words *crunchy*, *chewy*, and *one-of-a-kind* are

(1) positive
(2) negative
(3) neutral

Questions 21–29 are based on the following passage.

Nan's hand shook as she dialed the phone. She listened to it ring, and then Tom's voice came on the phone.

"Hello?"

"Tom, it's me . . . Nan." Her voice quavered.

"What's the matter? Where are you?"

"I'm at the airport. Can you come down and pick me up?"

"I thought you were going to fly down to Miami tonight."

"I was, but I didn't get on the plane."

"Why not? What's the matter? You sound as though you're shook up."

"I am shook up! I can't get myself to *stop* shaking." Nan tried to calm herself. Slowly she said, "The plane crashed just after takeoff. The emergency crews are out there now getting the injured to the hospital. It looks like almost everyone will be OK, but . . ."

"Oh no! Are you all right?"

"I'm fine. I didn't get on the plane. I knew something was wrong because of a dream I had."

"What do you mean, a dream?"

"Last night I dreamed that I was asleep, and I woke up to this funny light coming in my window. I got up and looked out the window and there was this big, black limo . . . the kind they use at funerals to carry the coffin. And then this man looked up and saw me at the window. He waved, and then he said, 'C'mon. There's room for you.' Then I woke up. It scared me because it was such a weird dream."

"Uh, bad dream all right. But what did the dream have to do with you not getting on the plane?"

"Well, I was standing in line waiting to get my boarding pass, when I saw the ticket agent and, Tom, it was the *same* man as the driver in my dream . . . and he said the same thing. He said, 'C'mon, there's room for you!' "

"Then what happened?"

"I ran out of there as fast as I could. I ended up in the observation area where the big windows are. I was shaking so much I just sat down and stared out the windows at the airfield. I thought I was nuts. But a few minutes later I saw it—the plane, I mean. It started to take off, but then it just nosed down and hit the runway. Oh, Tom, it was awful! Please come and get me."

Nan started to cry.

"I'll be right there, Nan. Don't move, I'm coming. Thank goodness you're OK."

Nan heard the phone click. She knew Tom was on his way. She staggered over to a seat and sank down into it, facing away from the huge windows.

21. What is the best title for the story?

(1) Tom's Dream
(2) The Light in the Window
(3) C'mon . . . There's Room for You
(4) The Ticket Agent
(5) Emergency Crew

22. What is the main conflict or problem in the story?

(1) Nan and Tom have an argument about her trip to Miami.
(2) Tom comes to get Nan at the airport.
(3) Tom doesn't believe Nan's story.
(4) Nan's bad dream prevents her from getting on the plane.
(5) Nan's flight to Miami is cancelled.

23. What happens at the climax of the story?

(1) Nan doesn't get on the plane. Then she sees it crash.
(2) Nan calls Tom.
(3) Nan boards the plane.
(4) Tom picks up Nan at the airport in Miami.
(5) Nan realizes she doesn't need to go to Miami.

24. What happens at the conclusion, or end, of the story?

(1) The ticket agent talks to Nan.
(2) Nan has a bad dream.
(3) Nan decides not to board the plane.
(4) Tom agrees to come and help Nan.
(5) Nan starts to shake and cry.

25. What is the tone of the story?
    (1) happy
    (2) peaceful
    (3) sad
    (4) cheerful
    (5) spooky

26. What is the setting of the story?
    (1) a supermarket
    (2) a car
    (3) Tom's apartment
    (4) an airport
    (5) a bus depot

27. How does Nan seem to feel when she calls Tom?
    (1) angry
    (2) frightened
    (3) happy
    (4) hurt
    (5) playful

28. How are the events of Nan's dream similar to the events that really happened?
    (1) Both in her dream and in reality, Nan gets up and looks out her window.
    (2) In Nan's dream, she calls Tom from the airport, just as she did in real life.
    (3) As in her dream, Nan boards the plane before it crashes.
    (4) Both the limo driver and the ticket agent say to her, "C'mon . . . there's room for you."
    (5) Tom forgets to call Nan, as he did in her dream.

29. What does the limo driver in Nan's dream represent?
    (1) a chauffeur
    (2) life
    (3) death
    (4) an airline pilot
    (5) the past

Questions 30–34 are based on the following poem.

A Time to Talk

When a friend calls to me from the road
And slows his horse to a meaning walk,
I don't stand still and look around
On all the hills I haven't hoed,
And shout from where I am, "What is it?"
No, not as there is a time to talk.
I thrust my hoe in the mellow ground,
Blade-end up and five feet tall,
And plod: I go up to the stone wall
For a friendly visit.

—by Robert Frost

30. What does the poet *not do* when a friend calls to him?

(1) decide it's time for a break
(2) join his friend for a chat
(3) put down his hoe
(4) plod over to the stone wall
(5) stand and look at the work he hasn't done

31. When a friend calls to him, the poet

(1) stops working so that he can talk to his friend
(2) keeps hoeing so he can finish his work
(3) waves at his friend and tells him he is too busy to talk
(4) goes to the barn to milk his cows
(5) pretends not to hear his friend

32. From this poem, you can infer that the poet believes

(1) talking to friends is less important than working
(2) talking to friends is more important than working
(3) plowing fields is hard work
(4) his friend shouldn't bother him while he is working
(5) his friend is a lazy worker

33. The hoe is left

(1) lying on the ground
(2) leaning against the stone wall
(3) stuck upright in the dirt
(4) in the barn
(5) resting against a hill

34. You can predict that, after the visit, the poet will probably

(1) return to hoeing
(2) go home
(3) fall asleep
(4) find another friend to talk to
(5) eat dinner

Answers start on page 44.

PRE-TEST ANSWER KEY

1. (1)
2. (1) d (2) a (3) b (4) e (5) c
3. (1) a (2) c (3) d (4) b (5) a
4. *Who or what?* the manager — *Did what?* became irritable
5. (1) Clues are "people were trapped under buildings" and "bridges had collapsed." This could only be a disaster.
6. (2)
7. (2) Choice (2) is the main idea. All other choices are supporting ideas.
8. (3) This idea is stated in the first two sentences of the passage.
9. (3) The facts given in this passage give the passage an informational rather than an emotional tone.
10. (5) The statement can be checked and proven.
11. (2) Choice (5) is not mentioned in the passage. All the other choices refer only to specific details in the passage, not the entire passage.
12. **a.** oil
    b. brake; transmission; power steering
    c. driver's manual
    d. cold
    e. cool
13. (3) The last sentence of the first paragraph states this information.
14. (1) d (2) a (3) c (4) b
15. (1) The third sentence in paragraph 1 gives you this information.
16. **a.** Shandung (China)
    b. four tons
    c. ox
    d. 1,300 years ago
    e. researchers
    f. recently
    g. holy
17. You may have picked either one of the following: " 'cause dogs love crunchy kibbles with chewy bits" OR ". . . one-of-a-kind taste dogs just gotta have"
18. "It better be bits!"
19. (1) Because claims like "dogs love crunchy Kibbles with chewy bits" cannot be proved, the statements in the ad are opinions.
20. (1) The words *crunchy*, *chewy*, and *one-of-a-kind* make the dog food sound appealing for dogs. Therefore, the connotations are positive.
21. (3) Spoken by both the limo driver in her dream and the ticket agent, this phrase upsets Nan so much that she does not board the plane. Therefore, it is central to the story, and a good title for the passage. Choice (1) is inaccurate, since Tom does not have a dream, and choices (2), (4), and (5) all refer to small details within the story.
22. (4) Choice (4) is correct—Nan's bad dream causes the conflict because it prevents her from boarding the plane. Choices (1), (3), and (5) are not supported by the events in the story. Choice (2) is the conclusion, not the conflict, of the story.
23. (1) Choice (1) is the story's climax, and is the correct response. Choice (2) occurs at the beginning of the story, and choices (3), (4), and (5) do not happen.
24. (4) All the other choices occur before the end of the story.
25. (5) The strange supernatural events of the story give a spooky tone to the passage.

26. (4) In line 6, Nan says to Tom, "I'm at the airport." She relates the events of the story in the phone call from the airport, which is the setting.

27. (2) From the following lines, you can tell that Nan is frightened: " 'I am shook up! I can't get myself to *stop* shaking.' Nan tried to calm herself" (lines 11–12), and, " 'Oh, Tom, it was awful! Please come and get me' " (lines 42–43).

28. (4) The limo driver in Nan's dream and the ticket agent at the airport both say, "C'mon . . . there's room for you." Choices (1), (2), (3), and (5) are not supported by the passage.

29. (3) The man in her dream is driving a hearse, "the kind [of limo] they use at funerals to carry the coffin" (lines 22–23). Therefore, the driver represents death.

30. (5) Lines 3–6 support this choice.

31. (1) Lines 9–10 state that the poet goes "up to the stone wall / For a friendly visit."

32. (2) The poet states that there is always time for "a friendly visit," even when he's busy hoeing. Choices (1) and (4) are directly contradicted by the poem. Choices (3) and (5) are not addressed by the poem.

33. (3) In lines 7–8, the poet sticks his hoe "in the mellow ground, / Blade-end up. . . ."

34. (1) The poet does not imply that he thinks hoeing is not important. He says only that he thinks it worth interrupting to talk with a friend who happens to pass by. Therefore, he will probably return to hoeing.

PRE-TEST EVALUATION CHART

Check your answers on pages 44 and 45, and then come back to this chart. Circle the number of each question you missed. This will help you and your instructor decide which chapters you should concentrate on. The numbers in **bold type** are questions based on illustrations.

	Skill	Question Numbers	Number Correct
Chapter 1 **Gaining Meaning from Words**	• Syllables • Word parts • Synonyms and antonyms	1 2 3	_____ /3
Chapter 2 **Understanding What You Read**	• Key words • Words in context • Main ideas • Supporting details, reasons, and examples • Summarizing and paraphrasing	4 5 7, 11, 21 12, 16 30, 31	_____ /9
Chapter 3 **Finding Hidden Meanings**	• Inferences • Predicting outcomes	27, 32 34	_____ /3
Chapter 4 **Organizing Ideas**	• Cause and effect • Comparison and contrast • Sequence • Analogy • Fact and opinion	8, 13, 15 28 14 6 10, **19**	_____ /8
Chapter 5 **Reading Literature**	• Picturing people and setting • Tone and mood • Beginning, conflict, climax, and conclusion • Symbols	26, 33 9, 25 22, 23, 24 29	_____ /8
Chapter 6 **Evaluating What You Read**	• Connotation • Persuasive techniques	**20** **17, 18**	_____ /3
		Total Correct	_____ /34

PRE-TEST 5: MATHEMATICS

On the following pages is an overview of the mathematical skills you will study in Section 5. Part I of this Pre-Test will help you evaluate your strengths and weaknesses in addition, subtraction, multiplication, division, and word problems. Part II of the Pre-Test will help you determine your skills in decimals, fractions, percents, and word problems.

How you do on this Pre-Test may help you decide where to spend most of your study time in this section. However, if you're preparing to take a math test in the future, it is a good idea to read the entire section.

Take your time as you work the problems. When you're finished, check your answers with the answers given on page 52.

PART I

ADDITION SKILLS

1. $\begin{array}{r} 4 \\ 1 \\ +\ 2 \\ \hline \end{array}$

2. $\begin{array}{r} 43 \\ +\ 21 \\ \hline \end{array}$

3. $\begin{array}{r} 23 \\ 12 \\ +\ 4 \\ \hline \end{array}$

4. $\begin{array}{r} 38 \\ +\ 26 \\ \hline \end{array}$

5. $\begin{array}{r} 746 \\ 342 \\ +\ 179 \\ \hline \end{array}$

6. $\begin{array}{r} 3{,}482 \\ 2{,}375 \\ +\ 358 \\ \hline \end{array}$

SUBTRACTION SKILLS

7. $\begin{array}{r} 13 \\ -\ 8 \\ \hline \end{array}$

8. $\begin{array}{r} 53 \\ -\ 21 \\ \hline \end{array}$

9. $\begin{array}{r} 86 \\ -\ 19 \\ \hline \end{array}$

10. $\begin{array}{r} 482 \\ -\ 68 \\ \hline \end{array}$

11. $\begin{array}{r} 480 \\ -\ 29 \\ \hline \end{array}$

12. $\begin{array}{r} 900 \\ -\ 269 \\ \hline \end{array}$

13. $\begin{array}{r} 1{,}060 \\ -\ 473 \\ \hline \end{array}$

MULTIPLICATION SKILLS

14. $\begin{array}{r} 32 \\ \times\ 3 \\ \hline \end{array}$

15. $\begin{array}{r} 43 \\ \times\ 20 \\ \hline \end{array}$

16. $\begin{array}{r} 730 \\ \times\ 302 \\ \hline \end{array}$

17. $\begin{array}{r} 78 \\ \times\ 6 \\ \hline \end{array}$

18. $\begin{array}{r} 76 \\ \times\ 49 \\ \hline \end{array}$

19. $\begin{array}{r} 385 \\ \times\ 193 \\ \hline \end{array}$

DIVISION SKILLS

20. $2\overline{)1{,}462}$

22. $3\overline{)912}$

24. $31\overline{)6{,}479}$

21. $4\overline{)80}$

23. $5\overline{)125}$

25. $345\overline{)7{,}935}$

WORD-PROBLEM SKILLS

26. On her pay stub, Elsie noticed that her gross pay was $1,240. She also read that her deductions were as follows: federal tax, $61.00; state tax, $34.64; social security, $51.24; medical insurance, $10.00; and credit union, $45.50. What is the sum of her federal and state taxes?

27. If Lucinda paid her grocery bill of $13.39 with a twenty-dollar bill, how much change should she receive?

28. At a sale price of $1.03 each, what does a total of twelve cans of orange juice concentrate cost?

29. If he is able to save $24 every month, how many months will it take Loren to save $336?

30. On his diet, Thomas carefully measured all the food he ate. For dinner Tuesday, he cut a steak in two pieces. The uncut steak weighed 1 pound 7 ounces. If the piece he ate weighed 11 ounces, what is the weight of the piece he saved?

31. What is the area of a garage floor that measures 7 yards long by 4 yards wide?

32. The carrying compartment on Peggy's moving van measures 6 feet high by 6 feet wide by 10 feet long. How many boxes, each 1 cubic foot in volume, can be packed into this cargo space?

33. On the three weekends in May that he played golf, Bryce had scores of 98, 111, and 106. What was his average score for these three rounds of golf?

PART II

DECIMAL SKILLS

In each group of decimal fractions below, circle the one with the largest value.

34. .068, .580, .604 .70, .08, .39 .0409, .0410, .049

Round each decimal fraction below to the nearest tenths place.

35. .66 .92 .07 .353 .7089

Add or *subtract* as indicated.

36.

.5	.63	.78	1.35	4.26	12.520
+ .4	+ .34	+ .69	+ .67	+ 1.3	+ 8.25

37.

.9	.89	.385	3.18	5.722	53.006
− .6	−.7	− .286	− .89	− 2.005	− 27.059

Multiply or *divide* as indicated.

38. $\begin{array}{r} .45 \\ \times\ 6 \\ \hline \end{array}$ $\quad$ $\begin{array}{r} .08 \\ \times\ 3 \\ \hline \end{array}$ $\quad$ $\begin{array}{r} 4.7 \\ \times\ .8 \\ \hline \end{array}$ $\quad$ $\begin{array}{r} .74 \\ \times\ .36 \\ \hline \end{array}$ $\quad$ $\begin{array}{r} 4.502 \\ \times\ .26 \\ \hline \end{array}$ $\quad$ $\begin{array}{r} 1{,}000 \\ \times\ 1.39 \\ \hline \end{array}$

39. $6\overline{)2.4}$ $\quad$ $14\overline{)32.76}$ $\quad$ $5\overline{).265}$ $\quad$ $.07\overline{)2.646}$ $\quad$ $12.34 \div 100$

FRACTION SKILLS

Change each improper fraction to a mixed number. Reduce every proper fraction.

40. $\frac{4}{6}$ $\quad$ $\frac{21}{5}$ $\quad$ $\frac{12}{9}$ $\quad$ $\frac{6}{8}$ $\quad$ $\frac{16}{6}$ $\quad$ $\frac{10}{14}$

In each group of numbers below, circle the one with the largest value.

41. $\frac{3}{4}, \frac{7}{8}, \frac{1}{2}$ $\quad$ $2\frac{4}{6}, \frac{15}{6}, 2\frac{15}{18}$ $\quad$ $\frac{7}{5}, \frac{12}{10}, 1\frac{1}{5}$ $\quad$ $\frac{3}{5}, \frac{3}{4}, \frac{3}{6}$

Express each amount below as a fraction of the larger unit indicated.

42. 8 inches = ____ foot $\quad$ 25 minutes = ____ hour $\quad$ 28 weeks = ____ year

Add or *subtract* as indicated.

43. $\begin{array}{r} \frac{5}{7} \\ +\ \frac{1}{7} \\ \hline \end{array}$ $\quad$ $\begin{array}{r} \frac{4}{9} \\ +\ \frac{2}{9} \\ \hline \end{array}$ $\quad$ $\begin{array}{r} 3\frac{1}{4} \\ +\ \frac{2}{4} \\ \hline \end{array}$ $\quad$ $\begin{array}{r} 1\frac{7}{8} \\ +\ \frac{5}{8} \\ \hline \end{array}$ $\quad$ $\begin{array}{r} 3\frac{5}{6} \\ +\ 2\frac{1}{3} \\ \hline \end{array}$ $\quad$ $\begin{array}{r} 13\frac{11}{12} \\ +9\frac{3}{4} \\ \hline \end{array}$

44. $\begin{array}{r} \frac{7}{8} \\ -\ \frac{2}{8} \\ \hline \end{array}$ $\quad$ $\begin{array}{r} \frac{12}{15} \\ -\ \frac{8}{15} \\ \hline \end{array}$ $\quad$ $\begin{array}{r} 6\frac{3}{4} \\ -\ \frac{1}{2} \\ \hline \end{array}$ $\quad$ $\begin{array}{r} 9\frac{3}{8} \\ -\ 5\frac{1}{4} \\ \hline \end{array}$ $\quad$ $\begin{array}{r} 1\frac{1}{3} \\ -\ \frac{2}{3} \\ \hline \end{array}$ $\quad$ $\begin{array}{r} 7\frac{1}{4} \\ -\ 3\frac{5}{8} \\ \hline \end{array}$

45. $\begin{array}{r} \frac{1}{3} \\ +\ \frac{1}{4} \\ \hline \end{array}$ $\quad$ $\begin{array}{r} \frac{3}{5} \\ +\ \frac{3}{4} \\ \hline \end{array}$ $\quad$ $\begin{array}{r} 4\frac{2}{3} \\ +\ 2\frac{3}{4} \\ \hline \end{array}$ $\quad$ $\begin{array}{r} \frac{7}{8} \\ -\ \frac{5}{12} \\ \hline \end{array}$ $\quad$ $\begin{array}{r} 1\frac{2}{3} \\ -\ \frac{3}{4} \\ \hline \end{array}$ $\quad$ $\begin{array}{r} 8\frac{2}{5} \\ -\ 5\frac{2}{3} \\ \hline \end{array}$

Multiply or *divide* as indicated.

46. $\frac{1}{2} \times \frac{3}{4}$ $\frac{6}{8} \times \frac{4}{5}$ $7 \times \frac{3}{4}$ $\frac{1}{3} \times 2\frac{3}{5}$ $3\frac{1}{2} \times 4\frac{3}{8}$

47. $\frac{5}{8} \div \frac{2}{7}$ $\frac{8}{9} \div \frac{3}{4}$ $\frac{4}{5} \div 6$ $2\frac{1}{2} \div \frac{2}{3}$ $1\frac{1}{3} \div 3\frac{5}{6}$

PERCENT SKILLS

Change each percent below to a decimal and a fraction. Write the decimal answer on the first line and the fraction answer on the second line.

48. 25% _____ _____ 37.5% _____ _____ $33\frac{1}{3}$% _____ _____

Change each percent below to a whole number or a mixed decimal.

49. 100% 300% 450% 225%

Determine each number as indicated.

50. 50% of 90 90% of 38 25% of 64 2% of 14

51. .6% of 400 8.8% of 2,000 $\frac{3}{4}$% of 50 $33\frac{1}{3}$% of 57

Determine each percent as asked for below.

52. 12 is what percent of 60? What percent of 64 is 8?

53. 250 is what percent of 50? What percent of 30 is 10?

Determine each number as indicated.

54. 50% of what number is 47? 24 is 40% of what number?

55. .6 is 15% of what number? $33\frac{1}{3}$% of what number is 26?

PRE-TEST ANSWER KEY

Part I
Addition, Subtraction, Multiplication, Division, Word Problems

1. 7	7. 5	13. 587	19. 74,305
2. 64	8. 32	14. 96	20. 731
3. 39	9. 67	15. 860	21. 20
4. 64	10. 414	16. 220,460	22. 304
5. 1,267	11. 451	17. 468	23. 25
6. 6,215	12. 631	18. 3,724	24. 209

25. 23

26.
$$\begin{array}{r} \$61.00 \\ +\ \$34.64 \\ \hline \$95.64 \end{array}$$

27.
$$\begin{array}{r} \$\ 20.00 \\ -\ 13.39 \\ \hline \$\ \ 6.61 \end{array}$$

28.
$$\begin{array}{r} \$1.03 \\ \times\ 12 \\ \hline 206 \\ 103\ \ \\ \hline \$12.36 \end{array}$$

29.
$$\begin{array}{r} \textbf{14 months} \\ \$24\overline{)\$336} \\ -\ 24\ \ \\ \hline 96 \\ -\ 96 \\ \hline 0 \end{array}$$

30.
$$\begin{array}{r} \text{1 lb. 7 oz.} \\ -\ \ \text{11 oz.} \\ \hline \text{12 oz.} \end{array}$$

31.
$$\begin{array}{r} \text{7 yards} \\ \times\ \text{4 yards} \\ \hline \text{28 square yards} \end{array}$$

32. *STEP 1:* 6 × 6 × 10 = 360 cu. feet
STEP 2:
$$\begin{array}{r} \textbf{360 boxes} \\ \text{1 cu. ft.}\overline{)\text{360 cu. ft.}} \end{array}$$

33. *STEP 1:*
$$\begin{array}{r} 98 \\ 111 \\ +106 \\ \hline 315 \end{array}$$
STEP 2:
$$\begin{array}{r} \textbf{105 average score} \\ 3\overline{)315} \\ -3\ \ \\ \hline 015 \\ -\ 15 \\ \hline 0 \end{array}$$

PART II

Decimals, Fractions, Percents

34. .604; .70; .049
35. .7; .9; .1; .4, .7
36. .9; .97; 1.47; 2.02; 5.56; 20.770
37. .3; .19; .099; 2.29; 3.717; 25.947
38. 2.7; .24; 3.76; .2664; 1.17052; 1,390
39. .4; 2.34; .053; 37.8; .1234
40. $\frac{2}{3}$; $4\frac{1}{5}$; $1\frac{1}{3}$; $\frac{3}{4}$; $2\frac{2}{3}$; $\frac{5}{7}$
41. $\frac{7}{8}$; $2\frac{15}{18}$; $\frac{7}{5}$; $\frac{3}{4}$
42. $\frac{2}{3}$; $\frac{5}{12}$; $\frac{7}{13}$
43. $\frac{6}{7}$; $\frac{2}{3}$; $3\frac{3}{4}$; $2\frac{1}{2}$; $6\frac{1}{6}$; $23\frac{2}{3}$
44. $\frac{5}{8}$; $\frac{4}{15}$; $6\frac{1}{4}$; $4\frac{1}{8}$; $\frac{2}{3}$; $3\frac{5}{8}$
45. $\frac{7}{12}$; $1\frac{7}{20}$; $7\frac{5}{12}$; $\frac{11}{24}$; $\frac{11}{12}$; $2\frac{11}{15}$
46. $\frac{3}{8}$; $\frac{3}{5}$; $5\frac{1}{4}$; $\frac{13}{15}$; $15\frac{5}{16}$
47. $2\frac{3}{16}$; $1\frac{5}{27}$; $\frac{2}{15}$; $3\frac{3}{4}$; $\frac{8}{23}$
48. .25, $\frac{1}{4}$; .375, $\frac{3}{8}$; $.33\frac{1}{3}$, $\frac{1}{3}$
49. 1; 3; 4.5; 2.25
50. 45; 34.2; 16; .28
51. 2.4; 176; .375; 18.981
52. 20%; 12.5%
53. 500%; $33\frac{1}{3}$%
54. 94; 60
55. 4; 78

Mathematics Pre-Test Evaluation Chart

On the chart below, circle the number of any problem you missed. The skill and study pages related to each problem are indicated.

Part I

Problem Numbers	*Related Skills*	*Study Pages*
	ADDITION	
1, 2, 3,	Adding small numbers (no carrying)	692–695
4, 5, 6	Adding and carrying	700–702
	SUBTRACTION	
7, 8	Subtracting small numbers (no borrowing)	707–709
9, 10	Subtracting and borrowing	715–717
11, 12, 13	Subtracting from zeros	717–719
	MULTIPLICATION	
14, 15, 16,	Multiplying (no carrying)	725–732
17, 18, 19	Multiplying and carrying	733–737
	DIVISION	
20, 21,	Short division	742–745
22	Using zero as a place holder	746–747
23, 24, 25	Long division	748–758
	WORD PROBLEMS	
26	Addition word problems	697–699
27	Subtraction word problems	712–714
28	Multiplication word problems	732
29	Division word problems	750–752
30	Measurement units word problems	771–786
31	Measurement: area word problems	
32	Measurement: volume word problems	
33	Averages word problems	786–787

Number Correct ______/33 PART I (Questions 1–33)

Part II

Problem Numbers	*Related Skills*	*Study Pages*
	DECIMALS	
34	Recognizing the value of decimal fractions	791–796
35	Rounding decimal fractions	796–798
36	Adding decimal fractions and mixed decimals	798–799
37	Subtracting decimal fractions and mixed decimals	800–801
38	Multiplying decimal fractions and mixed decimals	802–805
39	Dividing decimal fractions and mixed decimals	806–809
	FRACTIONS	
40	Simplifying proper and improper fractions	817–820
41	Recognizing the value of proper and improper fractions	815–816
42	Writing a part as a fraction of a whole	821
43	Adding fractions and mixed numbers	822–824
44	Subtracting fractions and mixed numbers	825–828
45	Finding common denominators for fraction addition and subtraction problems	830–834
46	Multiplying fractions and mixed numbers	838–841
47	Dividing fractions and mixed numbers	841–844
	PERCENTS	
48	Changing percents to decimals and to fractions	857–860
49	Changing percents larger than 100% to whole numbers or to mixed numbers	860
50, 51	Finding part of a whole	867–868
52, 53	Finding what percent a part is of a whole	872
54, 55	Finding the whole when part of it is given	874–875

Number Correct ______/22 PART II (Questions 34–55)

Total Correct _____/55 PARTS I and II (Questions 1–55)

Section 1

LANGUAGE AND WRITING SKILLS

1 Parts of Speech

JOURNAL WRITING: YOUR THOUGHTS ABOUT THE WORLD

A journal is a place to write down your thoughts and feelings about your world. In a journal entry, you begin by writing your first thoughts and end when you don't have anything else to say. A journal entry can be a few sentences, a few paragraphs, or a few pages. Your journal is one place where you don't have to worry about spelling, grammar, or punctuation. Your only concern is your thoughts. Many times, one thought will lead to another, and you may change topics several times in one journal entry.

You can use your journal to sort through thoughts, write letters, argue with your friends, or write about your dreams and goals. Your journal gives you an opportunity to say all the things you've wanted to say.

Your journal is for your eyes only (unless you want to share it with someone). It shows the best of you and sometimes the worst of you! A page from one writer's journal follows. Nothing really special happened to the writer that day, but some things about the day brought special thoughts to her mind.

May 17

Baseball season started today. I never thought I would be spending day after day at Little League games. In grade school, I was always the last person chosen for a team. Being the neighborhood misfit was not the best time of my life. But it helped me learn to not always expect life to be a bed of roses. I really was a lousy ball player. But I had a chance to improve, thank goodness. I never thought I would be an excellent ball player. But my older brother worked with me and helped me. He's a really great guy. . . .

Here are some suggestions for journal writing:

1. Get a special journal notebook.
2. Keep it in a safe place.
3. Keep a pen or pencil with your journal.
4. Set aside a certain time each day for journal writing.
5. Date each entry.

Some people get up fifteen minutes early to write in their journals. Some people write during lunch. Some write before going to bed. It doesn't matter what time you choose. Just pick a time when you can have a few moments of quiet.

Some people write in their journals every day. You don't have to. But if you enjoy journal writing, you will probably find yourself adding to your journal on a regular basis.

While working through this book, you will find suggestions for journal writing at the start of each chapter. These are just suggestions. Feel free to write journal entries on any topic you like.

FREEWRITING

You can use freewriting for this journal entry. *Freewriting* means writing down the thoughts going through your mind. Before you start, decide how long you will be writing. (Ten minutes is a good length of time.) Write down anything that comes into your mind. You don't have to stick with a topic. If you get stuck, write the same word over and over until you think of something else. The important thing is to write without stopping for the full length of time you choose.

JOURNAL ENTRY

Directions: Take some time now to make your first journal entry. If you don't have a special notebook for your journal yet, use a page from any notebook and add it to your journal later.

Choose one of the incomplete sentences below to begin your first journal entry. Finish the sentence and then add other sentences.

My home is. . . .
I wish I were. . . .
My vacation was. . . .
The weekends are. . . .

If you don't like any of these topics, write on anything that interests you. It's *your* journal.

LANGUAGE SKILLS: PARTS OF SPEECH

Let's look quickly at five parts of speech: nouns, pronouns, verbs, adjectives, and adverbs. They are presented here because you often need to be familiar with parts of speech when studying writing skills.

NOUNS

A *noun* names a person, place, thing, or idea.

Here are a few examples of nouns:

Persons	Places	Things	Ideas
uncle	lake	motorcycle	speed
Mr. Archer	stadium	baseball	excitement
Aunt Rose	ocean	shells	health
lawyer	courthouse	bail	crime
president	White House	dog	hate

There are three nouns in the sentence below. Find and circle them.

Aunt Rose wanted to ride her motorcycle to the ocean.

You were right if you circled *Aunt Rose* (a person), *motorcycle* (a thing), and *ocean* (a place). Now try another sentence containing two nouns. One of the nouns is an idea.

The lawyer learned that crime doesn't pay.

The nouns in that sentence are *lawyer* and *crime*.

EXERCISE 1: IDENTIFYING NOUNS

Directions: Circle the nouns in each sentence below.

1. Mr. Archer goes to the stadium because he loves baseball.
2. In Knoxville, Shelley found a new fashion.
3. Aunt Rose finds shells by the ocean.
4. The lawyer paid bail at the courthouse.

Answers start on page 193.

EXERCISE 2: WRITING NOUNS

Directions: Add a noun to each sentence below. Check to see that the nouns you add make sense.

1. Nancy was my best friend in school.
2. My friend thought I was really great.
3. I would like to go on a vacation to Florida.
4. Intelligence is a quality I admire in people.

Answers start on page 193.

PRONOUNS

Pronouns are words that take the place of nouns.

Pronouns are used like nouns. A pronoun stands for the name of a person, place, thing, or idea.

EXAMPLE: **Rosanna** got ice cream on Friday. **She** went to the store.

Both sentences talk about Rosanna. But in the second sentence, the pronoun *she* takes the place of the noun *Rosanna*.

EXAMPLE: Many **cities** get government assistance. **They** use the money for various projects.

Both sentences talk about cities. But in the second sentence, the pronoun *they* takes the place of the noun *cities*.

EXAMPLE: That **dog** looks hungry. **It** probably hasn't eaten for days.

Both sentences talk about a dog. But in the second sentence, the pronoun *it* takes the place of the noun *dog*.

Many useful pronouns are listed in the box below. You'll be studying these pronouns in this book.

Pronouns	
I, me, my, mine	we, us, our, ours
you, your, yours	
he, him, his	
she, her, hers	they, them, their, theirs
it, its	

Find and circle the pronouns in the following sentence.

The landlord wants the rent, and he wants it now.

There are two pronouns in that sentence: *he* and *it*. The pronoun *he* takes the place of *landlord*, and *it* refers to *rent*. Check the box of pronouns on page 60 if you aren't sure which words are pronouns.

They are leaving town, but all of their friends are staying.

You should have circled the pronouns *they* and *their*.

EXERCISE 3: IDENTIFYING PRONOUNS

Directions: In the following sentences, underline the pronouns.

1. He goes to the stadium because he loves baseball.
2. In Knoxville, she found it.
3. She finds them for us by the ocean.
4. He paid bail for me at the courthouse.

Answers start on page 193.

EXERCISE 4: WRITING PRONOUNS

Directions: Replace each noun in parentheses with a pronoun. The first one is done as an example.

1. *(The motorcycle)* ___*It*___ has a top speed of 120 mph.
2. *(Health)* ________ is important whether you are young or old.
3. *(The lawyer)* ________ warned me about getting in trouble again.
4. The president wanted *(his dog)* ________ to behave.

Answers start on page 193.

VERBS

A *verb* is a word that shows action or being.

Some verbs are action words.

EXAMPLES: Gloria **painted** her new apartment.
Jim **fixed** the light in the bathroom.

Other verbs are linking (being) verbs. These verbs link a noun or pronoun to words that rename or describe it.

EXAMPLES: Our street **is** very noisy.
The neighbors **are** Sonia and Larry Petrie.

Following are some samples of both kinds of verbs.

Action	Linking
run, go, ride, love, dance, keep, find, fight, pay, drive, drink, laugh	am, is, are, was, were

Those are only a few examples of verbs. There are thousands of verbs. Any time you talk about what something *is* or *does,* you use one or more verbs. Read the sentence below and underline each verb you find.

Tilly socializes and dances at parties.

Did you underline the words *socializes* and *dances?* Try another sentence—underline the verb.

This party is wonderful.

You were right if you underlined the word *is*.

EXERCISE 5: IDENTIFYING VERBS

Directions: Underline the verb or verbs in the following sentences.

1. Dan rides a motorcycle to the lake.
2. Mr. Archer goes to the stadium because he is a fan.
3. Shelley found a new fashion when she visited Knoxville.

Answers start on page 193.

EXERCISE 6: WRITING VERBS

Directions: Fill in the blanks with action verbs.

1. List five action verbs that tell what people can do with their arms and hands: ________, ________, ________, ________, ________.

2. List five action verbs that tell what people can do with the parts of their faces: ________, ________, ________, ________, ________.

3. List five action verbs that tell what people can do with their minds: ________, ________, ________, ________, ________.

Answers start on page 193.

ADJECTIVES

Adjectives **describe nouns. They tell which one, what kind, or how many.**

You might say to someone, "Meet me by my car." If that person didn't know what your car looked like, he would not be able to meet you. But if you said, "Meet me by the old blue convertible Corvette parked next to the purple shed," he would know exactly which car you meant.

Using adjectives makes a difference. The adjectives *old, blue,* and *convertible* describe the Corvette. The adjective *purple* describes the shed. Your friend would be able to find your car because of the specific information that these adjectives provide.

Here are three lists of common adjectives.

What kind	Which one	How many
big, little, young, old, neat, sloppy, happy, sad, nice, kind, red, blue, white	this, that, these, those	many, few, one, two, some

Find and circle the ten adjectives in the following paragraph.

Many people are happy when they see the red, white, and blue flag of the United States. But some people are sad because they think about friends or family who died in a war. Those persons fought and died in big and little wars.

Check to be sure that all the words you circled are on the list. If you found fewer than ten adjectives, look at the list to find the rest.

EXERCISE 7: IDENTIFYING ADJECTIVES

Directions: These sentences contain adjectives that describe nouns or pronouns. Circle all the adjectives in the sentences.

1. Shelley discovered a new fashion in fuzzy sweaters.
2. Aunt Rose finds big and little shells by the beautiful ocean.
3. The kind lawyer paid the bail at the old courthouse.
4. The president kept a noisy dog in the busy White House.

Answers start on page 193.

EXERCISE 8: WRITING ADJECTIVES

Directions: List adjectives that describe each of the following.

	You	Your home	Your father or mother
1.			
2.			
3.			

Answers start on page 193.

ADVERBS

> *Adverbs* describe verbs. Adverbs can tell how, when, or where.

He writes.

In that sentence, you know that the person writes, but you don't know anything about *how* he writes.

EXAMPLE: He writes **neatly**.

In that sentence, you learn how he writes. The adverb *neatly* describes the verb *writes*.

EXAMPLE: He writes **daily.**

In that sentence, you know *when* he writes. The adverb *daily* describes the verb *writes*. As you can see, an adverb often comes right after the verb it describes.

EXAMPLE: He writes **here.**

In that sentence, you know *where* he writes. The adverb *here* describes the verb *writes*.

In the following sentences, the verbs have been underlined and the adverbs circled. Answer the questions that follow each sentence. The first one has been done as an example.

The judge arrived (late.)

What did he do? ____________

When did he do it? ____________

The victim sobbed (quietly.)

What did she do? ____________

How did she do it? ____________

The judge looked (angrily) at the suspect.

What did he do? ____________

How did he do it? ____________

EXERCISE 9: IDENTIFYING ADVERBS

Directions: Underline the adverbs in the following sentences. Remember, an adverb tells how, when, or where.

1. Uncle Dan rides dangerously. *(How does he ride?)*

2. Mr. Archer arrives early. *(When does he arrive?)*

3. The lawyer paid immediately. *(When did he pay?)*

4. The president's dog barked loudly. *(How did it bark?)*

Answers start on page 193.

EXERCISE 10: WRITING ADVERBS

Directions: Complete the following sentences by writing in adverbs that tell how, when, or where. You can choose adverbs from the following list, or you can think of your own.

sweetly, daily, upstairs, now, there, softly, constantly, proudly, outdoors

1. *(how)* Caroline sings ______________________.
2. *(when)* Caroline sings ______________________.
3. *(where)* The kitten plays ______________________.

Answers start on page 193.

EXERCISE 11: CHAPTER REVIEW

You have had a quick overview of five parts of speech. As you work through this section, you will continue to study nouns, pronouns, verbs, adjectives, and adverbs. The next two exercises are a review of this chapter. Look up any information you need to complete the exercises.

Part 1

Directions: Twenty words are listed below. Decide what part of speech each word is. Write each word in the correct column. The first row has been completed for you.

early	neat	Mr. Archer	listens	he	they	there
slowly	dog	happy	keep	went	you	baseball
now	loves	old	boat	it	nice	

Nouns	Pronouns	Verbs	Adjectives	Adverbs
Mr. Archer	*he*	*listens*	*neat*	*early*

Answers start on page 193.

Part 2

Directions: Add a word to fill in each blank. After the sentence, tell whether you used a noun, pronoun, verb, adjective, or adverb.

	Part of Speech
1. Dan rode his motorcycle to the lake.	noun
2. Mr. Archer went to the stadium.	verb
3. Shelley told me about her new sweater.	adjective
4. Aunt Rose looked everywhere for shells.	adverb
5. The dog ate its ~~his~~ dinner.	Pronoun

Answers start on page 193.

YOUR TURN TO WRITE: AN EVENT IN YOUR LIFE

You have already done some writing—just for yourself. You didn't have to worry about writing neatly and correctly. Now you are going to do a different kind of writing exercise. This exercise asks you to write a paragraph. As you write, keep in mind that others will want to be able to understand your writing. Make your writing as clear and correct as you can.

You will have many writing exercises in this section. Keep all your writing exercises in a notebook or folder. You will be able to reread your exercises and see how your writing is improving.

WRITING PRACTICE

Directions: Put the date at the top of this first exercise and every writing exercise. You will have a record of when you did the writing.

Write a story about an event in your life. Start with the first thing that happened and write down all the information in time order. Write about anything that happened to you, whether it was a very important event in your life or just something that happened the other day. If you can't think of anything to write about, try to start writing by using freewriting. Below are some suggestions for topics:

My first job	My favorite day
The day I almost died	A vacation to . . .
The first time I drove	My best/worst childhood memory

You can choose a different topic to write on. Just be sure to pick a topic that really interests you.

Writing Checklist

- ❑ Have you said all you wanted to say?
- ❑ Are there any changes you want to make?
- ❑ Did you put a date at the top of the writing?

2 Sentences

JOURNAL WRITING: CLUSTERING

Putting your thoughts down can be a little difficult at times. You might feel like writing but find that you don't know where to start. One way to begin writing is to make a word cluster.

Clustering means writing one word in the middle of the page and jotting down around that first word all the thoughts that come to your mind. Don't try to write sentences. Begin by writing words.

An example of clustering follows. The subject is FAMILY. Here are the instructions the writer followed to make the cluster:

1. Write the word FAMILY in the middle of the paper and circle the word.
2. In the space around the word FAMILY, write down any words that pop into your mind on the subject of family and circle those words.
3. Draw arrows connecting the words that seem to go together.
4. Continue doing this until you are ready to write.
5. Write sentences using some or all of the words from the cluster.

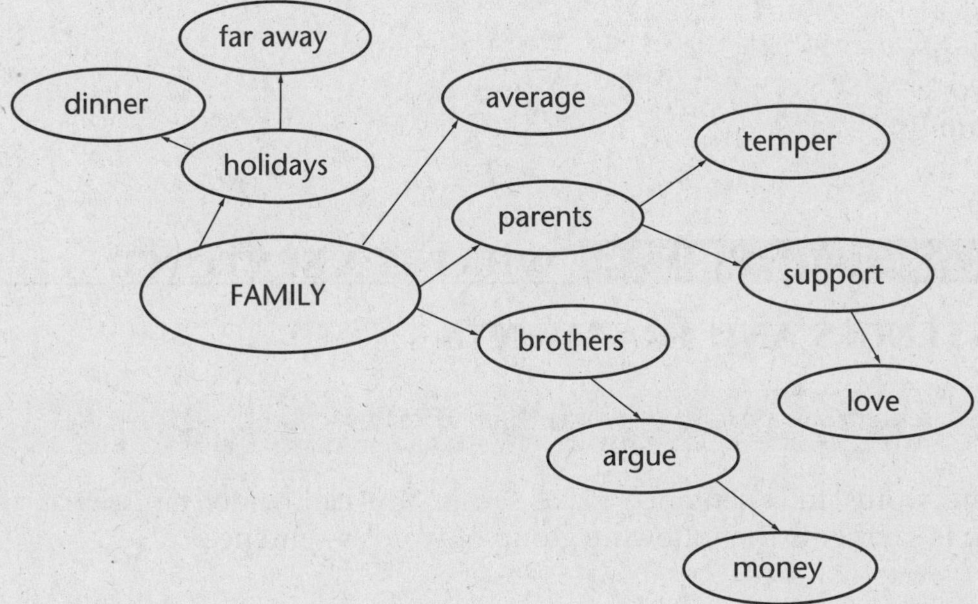

Notice all the circles around the words. Look at the arrows that the writer joined words with. Could some of those words be put together to form ideas and sentences?

You never have to use all the words in a cluster—just the ones that give you something to say. Here are the sentences the writer wrote after making the cluster in the illustration.

> I live with a fairly average family. My parents and I get along, but my dad also has a very bad temper. We may fight sometimes, but they're always there to offer their love and support. My brothers and I don't argue as much anymore because they both live far away now. That makes it hard for the whole family to get together for dinner during the holidays.

JOURNAL ENTRY

Directions: Your entry will be a group of sentences. Write on any topic that interests you. Choose from the topics listed below. Start writing after you've decided on a topic and write until you have nothing else to say. Or begin with a word cluster. Your thoughts will tell you when it is time to begin writing your sentences.

Here is a list of possible topics:

1. Love
2. Money
3. Work
4. Family

LANGUAGE SKILLS: WHAT IS A SENTENCE

SENTENCES AND FRAGMENTS

A *sentence* is a group of words that expresses a complete thought.

The words in a sentence make sense. You can understand what the writer is saying. Is the following group of words a sentence?

EXAMPLE: The man was driving very fast.

That group of words tells a complete thought, so it is a sentence. What about the next group of words?

EXAMPLE: Pulled out behind him.

Those words do not tell a complete thought. Something is missing. The second group of words is a fragment.

A *fragment* does not express a complete thought.

A fragment leaves a question in your mind. In the example you just saw, *who* pulled out behind him? Information can be added to a fragment to make it a complete thought:

EXAMPLE: The police pulled out behind him.

Now you have a complete thought. Now you have a sentence.

COMPLETE SENTENCES:
The police stopped the speeding car.
The driver was drunk.

Each one of those sentences made sense and told a complete thought. You could understand what was being said.

FRAGMENTS:
After the game.
Too many people.
Left early.

You might realize that someone is talking about a game, but a lot of information is left out. What happened *after the game?*

Information can be added to the fragments so that they express complete thoughts. Read the sentences below and compare them with the fragments.

After the game, I wanted to have a good time.
At eight o'clock I was at Ori's party.
Ori's house was so crowded that I left early.

EXERCISE 1: IDENTIFYING SENTENCES AND FRAGMENTS

Directions: Read the following sentences and fragments. In the blank after each group of words, write *S* if it is a sentence or *F* if it is a fragment.

1. April is a mixed-up month. ___S___
2. Income taxes. _______
3. Often celebrate Easter. _______
4. Jewish families often celebrate Passover. _______
5. One day the sun is out. _______

6. Next day snow. ______

7. Do I like April because I'm mixed up too? ______

Answers start on page 194.

EXERCISE 2: TURNING FRAGMENTS INTO SENTENCES

Directions: Each of the following groups of words is a fragment. After each fragment, you will find a question. Answer the question by writing a complete sentence. Use the fragment and add some new information to write your answer. The first one is done as an example.

1. Took the man to jail. *(Who took the man to jail?)*

   The police took the man to jail.

2. Locked him up. *(Who locked him up?)*

   ____

3. His lawyer. *(How did he contact his lawyer?)*

   ____

4. Sleep in jail. *(How did he feel about sleeping in jail?)*

   ____

5. Felt terrible. *(Who or what felt terrible?)*

   ____

Answers start on page 194.

PUNCTUATING PERFECTLY: SENTENCES

A sentence is a group of words that tells a complete thought. It is also a group of words that has a special look. Here is an opportunity for you to do a little detective work about sentences. Look closely at the sentences on this page and then answer the following questions.

What kind of letter does the first word of each sentence begin with?

____

What marks do you find at the ends of the sentences?

____

Did you discover that the first word of each sentence begins with a capital letter? Did you discover that there are punctuation marks at the end of each sentence? You need to remember these two rules when writing a sentence:

1. The first word of each sentence begins with a capital letter.
2. Each sentence ends with a punctuation mark: a period (.), a question mark (?), or an exclamation point (!).

Read on to find out more about when to use these end marks.

EVERY SENTENCE HAS A PURPOSE

There are four different types of sentences. The first type makes a statement (gives information). The second type gives a command (tells someone to do something). The third type asks a question. The fourth type is an exclamation (shows strong feeling). Notice how each example begins with a capital letter and ends with an end mark.

STATEMENT: I want to go bowling.
COMMAND: Take me to the bowling lanes.
QUESTION: Did you get my bowling shoes?
EXCLAMATION: Good grief, I lost again!

Statements

Most of the sentences that you write or read are statements. They give you information about a subject. They end with a period.

STATEMENT: Janet bought four bags of groceries.

Write an example of a statement on the line below.

____

Commands

Commands tell someone to do something. As you have grown up, you have heard a lot of commands from parents, teachers, brothers, or sisters.

COMMANDS:

Clean your room.	Do your homework.
Be home by midnight.	Take your hands off my radio.

Can you think of any other commands? Write them on the next two lines.

____

____

In writing, a command often looks like a statement because a command usually ends with a period. However, a statement just gives information. In a command, the writer is telling the reader to do something. You can mentally fill in the missing word *you* in a command. Here are some examples:

(You) Clean your room.	*(You)* Feed the dog.
(You) Wash the car.	*(You)* Be home by dark.

Questions

A question *asks* something, and it ends with a question mark. Here are some examples of common questions.

What time is it?	How are you?
What's for dinner?	Did the mail come?

On the lines below, write three questions you asked today.

____

____

____

Exclamations

An exclamation shows strong feeling. It ends with an exclamation point. Exclamations are often made at exciting or frightening times. Notice that exclamations all end with exclamation points.

It's a touchdown!	Look out for that car!
That dress is gorgeous!	Let's celebrate!

On the line below, write a sentence that is an exclamation. You might want to think of one you used at a game, at a party, or when you accidentally touched a hot stove.

____

EXERCISE 3: TYPES OF SENTENCES

Directions: Read each of the following sentences. Place the correct end mark (period, question mark, or exclamation point) at the end of each sentence. Then write whether the sentence is a statement, a command, a question, or an exclamation. The first one is done as an example.

1. This is the Rainbow Coffee Shop __.__ __*statement*__
2. Would you like to see a menu ___ __________
3. Get me a glass of water ___ __________
4. This place is on fire ___ __________

Answers start on page 194.

EXERCISE 4: MISTAKES IN SENTENCES

Directions: Each of the following sentences may contain mistakes in punctuation or capitalization. Some may be fragments. Rewrite each sentence correctly. The first one is done as an example.

1. Sky-high rents.
   The rents here are sky-high.
2. Why did they have to tear our building down.
   ____
3. most landlords won't permit pets.
   ____
4. Can't give up my dog!
   ____

Answers start on page 194.

PUTTING YOUR SKILLS TO WORK

Directions: This exercise is for your writing folder or notebook. Write eight sentences. Write two sentences of each kind that you have just studied. After each sentence, indicate whether it is a statement, a command, a question, or an exclamation.

Write your sentences about any topic you wish. When you are finished writing, reread your sentences and use this checklist.

☑ Writing Checklist

- ❑ Does each sentence begin with a capital letter and end with an end mark?
- ❑ Do you have two examples of all four different kinds of sentences? Did you use end marks correctly for each kind?

EVERY SENTENCE HAS A SUBJECT

The ***subject*** of a sentence is the person, place, thing, or idea talked about in the sentence. The sentence will tell what the subject does or is.

To find the simple subject of a sentence, look for the verb in the sentence. If the verb shows action, figure out who or what is performing the action. In the following sentence, what is the action verb? Who performs the action?

EXAMPLE: The dentist pulled all of my wisdom teeth.

In that sentence, the action verb is *pulled*. The person performing the pulling is the dentist, so *dentist* is the subject.

When the verb in a sentence doesn't show action, it is a linking verb. In that case, ask yourself, "Who or what is this sentence about?"

EXAMPLE: My mouth was numb for three hours.

The verb *was* is a linking verb. The sentence is about the writer's mouth, so *My mouth* is the subject.

EXERCISE 5: FINDING THE SUBJECT

Directions: In each of the following sentences, first find the verb and underline it. Then circle the subject. The first one is done as an example.

1. (Chicago) <u>is</u> a big city.
2. People live in interesting neighborhoods.
3. Trains take many workers downtown.

4. The buildings are tall there.

5. People hurry to the train stations.

Answers start on page 194.

TRICKY SUBJECTS

Commands and Questions

The subject of a sentence can come right at the beginning of the sentence. However, the subject can be in many places. Sometimes the way a sentence is written makes finding the subject hard. You learned that you can always add the missing word *you* to a command.

EXAMPLE: Write a letter to your aunt.
(You) Write a letter to your aunt.

The missing *you* is the subject of the sentence.

In a question, part of the verb often comes before the subject. To find the subject, mentally put the sentence back in order as if it were a statement. Here's an example:

Has the president signed the bill?

Here is the question, rearranged as a statement:

The president has signed the bill.

The subject performing the action is the *president*.

Confusing Words and Phrases

Sometimes extra words and phrases in a sentence can confuse you when you are looking for the subject. Remember always to look for the verb. If it is an action verb, who or what is performing the action? If it is a linking verb, who or what is the sentence about?

In the following sentence, words come between the subject and the verb. What is the verb? What is the subject?

The women in the bathroom giggle.

The verb is *giggle*. The performer of the action is the *women*. The words *in the bathroom* come between the subject and the verb. Obviously, a bathroom cannot giggle, so the subject cannot be *the bathroom*!

Now try another example. The following sentence starts out with some words that are not the subject. Find the verb; then find the subject.

In this park, the trees are tall and old.

The verb is *are,* a linking verb. The subject is *the trees*. The verb links the words *tall and old* to *trees*.

EXERCISE 6: FINDING TRICKY SUBJECTS

Directions: Write the subject of each sentence in the blank. Remember that the subject could be the missing *you*. The first one is done as an example.

1. Does Denise come in today? Denise
2. Give Sarah a coffee break at 10:00. ______________
3. Larry, the typist on the left, drinks tea. ______________
4. Is the coffee ready to drink? ______________
5. At 10:00, we go to the lounge. ______________
6. Change the channel, please. ______________
7. Would you like to join us?______________

Answers start on page 194.

EXERCISE 7: WRITING SUBJECTS

Directions: Add subjects to the following sentences.

1. ______________ is my hometown.
2. ______________ is the name of the local paper.
3. In an emergency, ______________ is the best hospital.
4. For bargain prices, ______________ beats all the stores in town.
5. In my opinion, a ______________ looks nicer than any other car.

Answers start on page 194.

EVERY SENTENCE HAS A PREDICATE

The subject is one important part of a sentence. The predicate is the other important part. Everything that isn't part of the subject is part of the predicate.

> The ***predicate*** of a sentence tells what the subject does or is.

The predicate gives information about the subject. There is always a verb in the predicate. This sentence contains an action verb.

EXAMPLE: The mechanic replaced the car's muffler.

There are two parts to that sentence. *The mechanic* is the subject. The predicate is *replaced the car's muffler*. The subject is the person who completed the action. The predicate tells what the subject did. The next sentence contains a linking verb.

EXAMPLE: The muffler is expensive.

There are also two parts to that sentence. *The muffler* is the subject. The predicate is *is expensive*. In that sentence, the predicate tells what the subject is.

EXERCISE 8: WRITING ACTION PREDICATES

Directions: Six one-word subjects are listed below. A predicate has been added to the first one. Add one-word predicates to the last five subjects. Use verbs that tell what the subjects do. (When there is only one word in a predicate, it will always be a verb.)

1. Babies ___cry___.
2. Smoke __________.
3. Flowers __________.
4. Birds __________.
5. Fish __________.
6. Scissors __________.

Answers start on page 194.

EXERCISE 9: WRITING LINKING PREDICATES

Directions: Add two-word predicates to these subjects. One of the words must be a verb. Use linking verbs to tell what the subjects are.

1. Mary ___is___ ___happy___.
2. Our money ___is___ ___gone___.
3. The pool _____ __________.
4. My apartment _____ __________.
5. His motorcycle _____ __________.
6. The tomatoes _____ __________.

Answers start on page 194.

PUTTING YOUR SKILLS TO WORK

Directions: Write a paragraph about someone you know. First, name the person and tell how you know him or her. Second, tell where you spend time together. Third, tell what you do when you spend time together. Finally, tell why you enjoy being with this person. Keep this assignment in your folder or notebook.

☑ Writing Checklist

- ❑ Do you have a subject for each sentence?
- ❑ Do you have a predicate for each sentence?

THE SUBJECTS OF YOUR LIFE

There are a great many important people, places, and things in your life. The most important subjects for you might be your family, your friends, your home, your work, your education, and your activities. You are going to make your own personalized spelling list. Put this exercise in the back of your writing notebook or folder.

Write the heading "The Subjects of My Life" at the top of the page. Complete the lists on the following page with the names of people, places, or things (nouns). The names on the list will be capitalized, since the name of any specific person, place, or thing must begin with a capital letter.

This will be your personalized, capitalized spelling list. If an area does not apply to you, skip it. If you are not sure of the spelling of a name, check with someone. The example below shows part of one person's list.

The Subjects of My Life

People

mother	*Mildred Levy*	boyfriend	*Brian Van Slyke*
father	*Bernard Levy*	best friend	*Clarice Adams*
sister(s)	*Velma Levy*	other friends	*Marva Stein*
	Alice Levy		*Lisa Michaels*

People

mother ____________________ husband or wife

father ____________________ ____________________

sister(s) ____________________ boyfriend or girlfriend

____________________ ____________________

brother(s) ____________________ friend(s), coworkers

____________________ ____________________

teacher(s) ____________________ ____________________

____________________ ____________________

Places

street ____________________ place of work ____________________

school ____________________ restaurant ____________________

city ____________________ park ____________________

county ____________________ shopping center ____________________

state ____________________ theater ____________________

Things

book ____________________ newspaper ____________________

team ____________________ TV show ____________________

☑ Spelling Checklist

- ❑ Is everything spelled correctly?
- ❑ Does every word start with a capital letter? They all should, because they all name specific persons, places, or things.

Complete the following paragraph. Use words from your personalized, capitalized spelling list.

I have lived in ________________ (*state*) for ____________ (*number*) years.

I live on ______________________ (*street*) in ________________ (*town or city*).

______________________ and ______________________ (*names of people in your home*)

live with me. Many of my days are the same. I get up in the

morning and go to ______________________ (*work or school*). When I

get there, ______________________ (*boss or teacher*) tells me what

I have to do for the day. After a hard day, I sometimes stop

to read the ______________________ (*newspaper*) or turn on the TV and

watch the ______________________ (*sports team*). It's a good

way to relax.

EXERCISE 10: CHAPTER REVIEW

Part 1

Directions: Write the simple subject of each of the following sentences in the blank. The first one is done as an example.

1. Juan wants to find a job. ____Juan____
2. A counselor in the unemployment office helps him. ________
3. Each week, Juan goes on at least one job interview. ________
4. The interviewer talked to the manager. ________
5. Give Juan a chance. ________

Part 2

Directions: Read the following five groups of sentences. Four of the five sentences in each group contain one or more mistakes. Circle the letter of the correct sentence in each group.

1. **a.** going back to school is not easy
   b. Students need time to study?
   c. Once the brain is out of gear.
   d. It is difficult to start thinking again.
   e. takes determination.

2. **a.** In high school my grades
   b. Knew I was smart.
   c. I hated to study.
   d. teachers didn't like me?
   e. If I try, I can do it

3. **a.** When I was playing volleyball.
   b. my knee hit the ground hard
   c. Took me to the emergency room.
   d. X rays.
   e. Now I have a plaster cast.

Part 3

Directions: Look at the two pictures on this page. Under each picture, write two things:

- ❑ what is happening in the picture
- ❑ what the characters in the pictures might be saying

Try to write at least one of each of the four types of sentences.

1. ______________________________

____

____

2. ______________________________

____

____

3. ______________________________

____

____

4. ______________________________

____

____

Answers start on page 194.

JOURNAL WRITING: MAKING A WORD PICTURE

When you want to describe something to another person, you need to use a lot of details. For example, if you wrote in a letter to a friend, "The park near our new house is beautiful," your friend would know your opinion, but she would not be able to imagine what the park looked like. You might write something like this:

> The park near our new house is beautiful. It's a block long, and there are trees all around the edges. In the very center of the park is a garden with fragrant flowers. The park is very quiet and peaceful.

When you include details, think about what you can see, hear, smell, feel, and even taste.

WRITING PRACTICE

Directions: This exercise is for your writing folder or notebook. Remember to date the assignment. Use your personalized spelling list from page 81 for this writing. You may even be adding a few new words to the list. Write a paragraph telling about one of three things:

1. Your writing classroom
2. A place you visit often
3. Your choice

Writing Checklist

- ❑ Have you checked your spelling?
- ❑ Have you written complete sentences?
- ❑ Is the first letter of every sentence capitalized?
- ❑ Is there a punctuation mark at the end of every sentence?

3 Nouns and Pronouns

JOURNAL WRITING: WHAT'S ON YOUR MIND?

What's on your mind? What's troubling you? Is something causing you to lose sleep? to lose money? to feel guilty? Are you irritated because you are the only person in your home doing the evening chores while everyone else watches TV? Has a friend jokingly insulted you one time too many?

Write that letter, but don't mail it!

JOURNAL ENTRY

Directions: You now have the opportunity to vent your stored-up anger or frustration without damaging any relationships. Write that person a letter—in your journal. Say anything and everything you've always wanted to say.

Start out with "Dear . . ." and keep writing. Describe what upsets you. Tell the person anything you want. But don't mail the letter. Once you put all your thoughts down and read what you've said, you might find you are capable of taking some action about the situation.

Of course, if you don't feel like writing a letter right now, you're free to write a journal entry on any topic that interests you.

LANGUAGE SKILLS: NOUNS AND PRONOUNS

Nouns and pronouns are both naming words. They tell you whom or what someone else is talking or writing about. You use them to tell whom or what you are talking or writing about. In the following paragraph, the nouns and pronouns are shown in **bold type.**

> Without **nouns it** would be impossible to talk about **people**, **places**, **things**, or **ideas**. How could **you** talk about **your neighbor** if **he** or **she** didn't have a **name**?

Without nouns and pronouns, it is impossible to communicate. As naming words, nouns and pronouns are very similar. They both identify a person, place, thing, or idea.

NOUNS

Nouns identify who or what is being talked about. In this part of the chapter, you will work with several types of nouns.

EXERCISE 1: IDENTIFYING NOUNS

Directions: In the following paragraph, underline all of the nouns. The first two have been underlined as examples.

Nan loves her dog, Fifi. Fifi is a poodle. At the beach, Nan wants to be certain that Fifi does not get too hot. Nan bought a stroller with an awning so Fifi could be in the shade while on the beach. Nan also often buys ice cream for Fifi. Many people on the beach stare at the poodle. The people also stare at Nan!

Answers start on page 195.

COMMON NOUNS AND PROPER NOUNS

Both common and proper nouns name persons, places, things, or ideas. But there is an important difference between them.

A ***common noun*** is the *general* name of a person, place, thing, or idea.
A ***proper noun*** is the *specific* name of a person, place, thing, or idea.

Words like *woman, building, airplane,* and *month* are common nouns. Words like *Lynn, Empire State Building, Concorde,* and *December* are proper nouns.

A common noun never begins with a capital letter (unless it comes at the beginning of a sentence). A proper noun, on the other hand, always begins with a capital letter.

COMMON NOUN: city PROPER NOUN: Detroit

City is a common noun because it names a general type of place. You could be talking about any city in the world. But *Detroit* is a specific place, so it is a proper noun. *Detroit* begins with a capital letter, while *city* does not.

Study the lists below. Notice that, for each common noun on the left, there is a corresponding proper noun on the right.

Common Nouns	Proper Nouns
school	Roosevelt High
car	Chevrolet
store	K-Mart
restaurant	Mama Leone's
day	Friday

Remember that a common noun is a general name, while a proper noun is a specific name. When you are writing proper nouns of more than one word, you usually capitalize all the words. For example, suppose that you are writing the name of a restaurant. You would write *Country Kitchen*, not *Country kitchen*.

EXERCISE 2: COMMON AND PROPER NOUNS

Directions: Below is a list of common nouns. Write the name of a proper noun for each common noun. The first one is done as an example.

1. car: *Honda* ________________
2. senator: ________________
3. company: ________________
4. town: ________________
5. minister: ________________
6. holiday: ________________
7. state: ________________
8. country: ________________
9. organization: ________________
10. doctor: ________________

Answers start on page 195.

Specific Names

Many nouns can be either common or proper. The way they are used will tell you which they are. Words that are used as the specific names of people are proper nouns. However, titles like *senator, doctor, judge, sergeant, vice president, lieutenant, pastor,* and *mayor* are common nouns when they refer to the position. For example, you would write

Kate Jordan is a **senator**.

In that sentence, the word *senator* is used as a job title. It names a position, so it is not capitalized. But you would write

Many people admire **Senator Kate Jordan**.

In that sentence, *Senator* is used as part of a specific name, so the word *Senator* is capitalized. Titles are capitalized when they are used as part of a person's name.

Words that refer to places or things can also be common nouns or proper nouns. Words like *building, school, department,* and *road* are capitalized when they are used as part of a name.

Now look at the following sentences. Capitalize all of the proper nouns.

I went to the doctor.
The nurse said, "doctor rahji will be ten minutes late."
"The doctor had to stop at mercy hospital," the nurse added.
"How far away is the hospital?" I asked.
"It's about two miles down the road," the nurse said.
Just then, a sergeant walked into the office.
"Oh, sergeant jones, you're early," said the nurse.
"There wasn't much traffic on willow road," the sergeant explained.

You should have capitalized *Doctor Rahji, Mercy Hospital, Sergeant Jones,* and *Willow Road.* These are proper nouns because they are used as the names of specific people and places.

EXERCISE 3: CAPITALIZING PROPER NOUNS

Directions: Read the following sentences. If all of the proper nouns in a sentence are capitalized, write *C* for *Correct* in the blank. If you find a proper noun or part of a proper noun that should be capitalized, underline it. Some sentences contain more than one proper noun. The first one is done as an example.

_____ **1.** Mrs. Linkowski first saw the <u>washington monument</u> when she was five.

_____ **2.** New year's eve is aunt Betty's favorite holiday.

_____ **3.** The teachers at brookmont elementary school wrote a letter to mayor carlson.

_____ **4.** My dentist hasn't missed a green bay packers game in seven years.

_____ **5.** Who ran for mayor in the last election?

_____ **6.** Ms. Davis is a member of an organization called mothers against drunk driving.

_____ **7.** The oak valley fire department was too late to save the warehouse.

Answers start on page 195.

SINGULAR NOUNS AND PLURAL NOUNS

Nouns that name one person, place, or thing are called ***singular nouns.*** Nouns that name more than one person, place, or thing are called ***plural nouns.***

Here are some examples:

Singular Nouns	Plural Nouns
bird	birds
husband	husbands
class	classes
child	children

The following sentences show some ways that singular and plural nouns are used.

It is legal to have one **husband**
but illegal to have two **husbands.**

Erma wants to have one **child,**
but Steve wants her to have six **children.**

FORMING PLURALS

There are several rules for making singular nouns plural. Study and practice the following rules. Then complete the second row of each.

1. The usual way to make singular nouns plural is to add an *s*. Here are some examples. Study them carefully and then complete the second and third rows.

planet–planets flower–flowers balloon–balloons

monkey–__________ cake–__________ clown–__________

2. Nouns that end in *s, sh, ch, z,* and *x* have *es* added to the end when they are plural.

bus–buses box–boxes church–churches

dish–__________ waltz–__________ branch–__________

3. Nouns that end in the letter *y* with a consonant before the *y* are made plural by changing the *y* to an *i* and adding *es*.

county–counties salary–salaries city–cities

country–__________ enemy–__________ bully–__________

4. Some nouns do not change form at all when they are plural. If you are ever unsure about whether to change the form of a noun to make it plural, you can check the dictionary.

   sheep deer fish

5. The plurals of some nouns are not formed according to any set of rules. The only way to learn them is to memorize them.

child–children	goose–geese	man–men
woman–________	mouse–________	ox–________

EXERCISE 4: CHANGING SINGULAR NOUNS TO PLURAL

Directions: Read the following sentences. In each sentence, cross out the singular noun that should be plural and write the plural form above it. The first one is done as an example.

women
1. Many ~~woman~~ do not want to work outside the home.
2. Some woman argue that they must work to earn money.
3. Some employer pay women less than men.
4. Salary should be the same for all people who do the same job.
5. Some companies have child care program.
6. Often, several church in a town have day-care centers.
7. City, counties, and towns should do even more to help mothers who must work.

Answers start on page 195.

EXERCISE 5: CORRECTING ERRORS WITH NOUNS

Directions: There is one mistake in each group of sentences below. The mistakes have to do with the use of either singular and plural nouns or common and proper nouns. Read each group of sentences and show which sentence is *not* correct by shading in the box under **a**, **b**, or **c** in the answers.

	a	b	c
1. **a.** Hunger is widespread. **b.** Many people eat only one meals a day. **c.** Some people do not even get one meal.	☐	☐	☐
2. **a.** What can an american do about the problem? **b.** She can support her local food bank. **c.** Food banks are often run by religious groups.	☐	☐	☐

	a	b	c
3. a. They feed any person who is hungry. b. Your religion is not important. c. When parentes say, "My child is hungry!" they are not ignored.	☐	☐	☐

Answers start on page 195.

POSSESSIVE NOUNS

A noun that shows ownership is a ***possessive noun.***

Singular possessive nouns always end in *'s*. Some examples of sentences with singular possessive nouns follow.

To show that Harold owns a jeep, you could write this sentence:

That is **Harold's** jeep.

To show that one boy had a baby hamster, you could write this sentence:

The **boy's** hamster is a baby.

In both of those sentences, *'s* is added to the noun to show possession.

There are times when more than one person owns something. Then you must write ***plural possessive nouns***. When a plural noun ends in *s*, just add an apostrophe (') to make it possessive.

To show that two ladies owned a boat, you could write:

The **ladies'** boat will be launched Tuesday.

An apostrophe (') was added to show possession. As you know, not all plural nouns end in *s*. If a plural noun does not end in *s*, add *'s* to show possession.

To show that several geese laid eggs, you could write this sentence:

The **geese's** eggs will hatch soon.

An *'s* was added to show possession.

Summary of Rules for Possessive Nouns

1. Add *'s* to a singular noun to make it possessive.
   boss*'s* office—one boss has an office
   child*'s* toy—one child has a toy

2. Add *'* to a plural noun ending in *s* to make it possessive.
   bosses*'* offices—several bosses have offices

3. Add *'s* to a plural noun that does not end in *s* to make it possessive.
   children*'s* toys—several children have toys

EXERCISE 6: WRITING POSSESSIVE NOUNS

Directions: Write the possessive form of the following nouns. The first one is done as an example.

1. coach: coach's

2. army: ____________________

3. armies: ____________________

4. woman: ____________________

5. women: ____________________

6. choir: ____________________

7. choirs: ____________________

Answers start on page 195.

EXERCISE 7: MORE PRACTICE WITH POSSESSIVE NOUNS

Directions: Write the possessive form of the first noun in each pair of words. The first one has been done as an example.

1. cat cradle: cat's cradle

2. busboys trays: ____________________

3. Mickey house: ____________________

4. teachers meetings: ____________________

5. coach signals: ____________________

6. neighbors anniversary: ____________________

7. mechanic wrench: ____________________

Answers start on page 195.

PUTTING YOUR SKILLS TO WORK

Directions: This exercise will go in your writing folder or notebook. Practice forming possessive, plural, and proper nouns. According to the following instructions, write five sentences.

- In the first sentence, use the possessive form of *Dracula.*
- In the second sentence, use the possessive form of *sheep.*
- In the third sentence, use the plural form of *city.*
- In the fourth sentence, use the plural form of *woman.*
- In the fifth sentence, use a proper noun with *Detective.*

☑ Writing Checklist

- ❑ Did you use the correct form of each of the five nouns?
- ❑ Are all proper nouns and first words of sentences capitalized?

PRONOUNS

As you learned before, pronouns take the place of nouns. They are used like nouns. They stand for the names of people, places, things, and ideas.

SAMPLE SENTENCES:

Gina is an experienced welder.
She is an experienced welder.

She took the place of *Gina* in the second sentence.

The evening sky was covered with clouds.
The evening sky was covered with them.

Them took the place of *clouds* in the second sentence.

Frank's party lasted only ten minutes.
His party lasted only ten minutes.

His took the place of *Frank's* in the second sentence.

Subject pronouns take the place of the subject of a sentence (like *She* in the sentence *She is an experienced welder.*). ***Object pronouns*** take the place of nouns that are not the subject of a sentence (like *them* in the example above). ***Possessive pronouns*** take the place of possessive nouns (like *his* in the example above). In the chart on the following page are the pronouns you will be studying in this chapter.

Pronouns			
Subject	Object	Possessive Used with a noun	Possessive Used alone
I	me	my	mine
you	you	your	yours
he	him	his	his
she	her	her	hers
it	it	its	its
we	us	our	ours
they	them	their	theirs

SUBJECT PRONOUNS

Subject pronouns are used as the subject of a sentence. You should remember from Chapter 2 that the subject is the person, place, thing, or idea talked about in a sentence. Every sentence tells what the subject is or does. The subject pronouns are *I, you, he, she, it, we,* and *they*.

EXAMPLES:

Adolph said not to listen to the radio.
He said not to listen to the radio.

Adolph is the subject of the sentence, so the pronoun *He* replaces *Adolph*.

The statements are not true.
They are not true.

The statements is the subject. The plural subject pronoun *They* replaces *The statements*.

Wendell and I will be careful.
We will be careful.

Wendell and I is the subject. The subject pronoun *We* replaces *Wendell and I*.

EXERCISE 8: USING SUBJECT PRONOUNS

Directions: On the blanks following these sentences, write the subject pronoun you could use to replace the underlined noun. The subject pronouns are *I, you, he, she, it, we,* and *they*. The first one is done as an example.

1. Linda encouraged her husband Paul to apply for a credit card. _She_

2. Paul seemed qualified for a card. ________

3. Paul and Linda were surprised by the company's response. ________

4. The letter said that Paul's salary was too low. ________

Answers start on page 195.

OBJECT PRONOUNS

Object pronouns are used whenever a pronoun is not the subject and does not show possession. The object pronouns are *me, you, him, her, it, us,* and *them*. Look in the chart on page 95 to see which object pronouns are different from the subject pronouns and which are the same. The object pronoun is in **bold type** in each of the sentences.

EXAMPLES:

Luis gave Ellen a birthday present.
Luis gave **her** a birthday present.

Luis is the subject. Since *Ellen* is not the subject, the object pronoun *her* replaces *Ellen*. Now look at another example.

After school, the bus took Artemas and Titus home.
After school, the bus took **them** home.

In this sentence, *the bus* is the subject. Since *Artemas and Titus* is not the subject, the object pronoun *them* is used.

What pronoun would you use in this sentence? Write it in the blank.

The rosebush gave Arthur great pleasure.
The rosebush gave ________ great pleasure.

You were correct if you wrote *him*. The subject is *The rosebush*, so *Arthur* cannot be the subject. Therefore, *Arthur* must be replaced by the object pronoun *him*.

EXERCISE 9: USING OBJECT PRONOUNS

Directions: In the blank after each sentence, write the object pronoun you could use to replace the underlined noun. The object pronouns are *me, you, him, her, it, us,* and *them*. The first one is done as an example.

1. For the third time, Bob glared at the washing machine. ___*it*___

2. He wrote down the exact dates of each breakdown and handed the list to his landlady. ________

3. Mrs. Perry thanked Bob and promised to speak with the repairman.

____

4. When the machine stayed broken for another week, Bob sent letters to Mrs. Perry and the repair company. ________

5. "I pay my rent on time," wrote Bob. "This situation is unfair to me and the other tenants." ________

6. Bob received a call from Mrs. Perry two days later. ________

Answers start on page 195.

POSSESSIVE PRONOUNS

Possessive pronouns have the same purpose as possessive nouns: they show ownership. Look back at the chart on page 95 and read over the two columns of possessive pronouns. Notice that, unlike possessive nouns, none of the possessive pronouns contain an apostrophe (').

Some possessive pronouns appear with a noun to show who owns the noun. Those possessive pronouns are *my, your, his, her, its, our*, and *their*. The possessive pronouns are shown in **bold type.**

EXAMPLES:

That is Harold's jeep.
That is **his** jeep.

In that sentence, *his* replaces *Harold's* and appears with *jeep* to show who owns the jeep.

The boys' hamster is a baby.
Their hamster is a baby.

In that sentence, *Their* replaces *The boys'* and appears with *hamster* to show who owns the hamster.

The second group of possessive pronouns can stand alone. These pronouns are *mine, yours, his, hers, its, ours*, and *theirs*. Here are some examples of how these pronouns appear in sentences.

The jeep is Harold's.
The jeep is **his**.

The baby hamster is the boys'.
The baby hamster is **theirs**.

In those sentences, the possessive pronouns *his* and *theirs* replace the possessive nouns *Harold's* and *boys'*.

EXERCISE 10: USING POSSESSIVE PRONOUNS

Directions: In the blank following each sentence, write the possessive pronoun that can replace the underlined nouns. The first one is done as an example.

1. Have you seen the Garcias' new day care center? ___their___
2. One reason for the center's popularity is that it's just two blocks from the subway. ________
3. The parents like to help out, so many ideas for games are the parents'. ________
4. Every time Lizzy leaves the center, she tries to take a doll or car that isn't Lizzy's. ________
5. So the Garcias spend time sorting the children's belongings. ________
6. Despite the confusion, Mrs. Garcia often thinks, "This place is really mine and my husband's." ________

Answers start on page 196.

EXERCISE 11: USING PRONOUNS

Directions: Underline the correct pronouns in the following paragraphs. You will be using subject, object, and possessive pronouns. The first one is done as an example.

Karen enjoys *(her, hers)* job at the Adult Learning Center. *(She, Her)* is the staff support specialist. She helps Larry with *(he, his)* teaching. Carol teaches there too and is well liked by *(she's, her)* students. The students look forward to coming to *(their, them)* classes.

The directors of the center are Vicki and George. *(They, Them)* count on government grants to fund the center's programs. *(Their, Theirs)* assistant, Bob, helps *(they, them)* get funding for the programs. *(He, Him)* is a very important member of the staff. All the Adult Learning Center staff members are quick to state, "*(We, Us)* believe in adult education!"

Answers start on page 196.

PRONOUN AGREEMENT

To replace a noun with a pronoun you must figure out whether the noun is a subject, an object, or a possessive. You must know what noun a pronoun is replacing to know what pronoun to use. Is the noun male, female, or neither? Is it singular or plural?

If a female's name is used, you must use *she, her,* or *hers.*

> **Eleanor Roosevelt** never went to grade school. But **she** became a world leader. The world respects **her** contributions to society.

Male names must be replaced with *he, his,* or *him.*

> **Albert Einstein** failed math as a child. However, **his** theory of relativity changed the world of science.

The names of animals, places, things, or ideas must be replaced with *it* or *its*.

> **The United Nations** is in New York City. **It** is a worldwide organization. One of **its** main interests is the children of the world.

Always use a singular pronoun to replace a singular noun and a plural pronoun to replace a plural noun.

> That **book** is interesting. You should read **it**.
> Those **books** are interesting. You should read **them**.

The first example talked about one book, so the pronoun *it* was used to replace the singular noun. The second example talked about more than one book, so the pronoun *them* was used to replace the plural noun.

EXERCISE 12: PRONOUN AGREEMENT

Directions: Fill in each blank with the appropriate pronoun. The word that the pronoun must agree with is in **bold type**. The first one is done as an example.

1. **Will Rogers** hated school and caused extensive damage to school property. In later years, ___he___ became a famous humorist.

2. **Beethoven** was deaf. Although he could not hear ________ music, the world still appreciates it.

3. These **rocks** will make a pretty garden border. I will put ___________ around the edges.

4. The **dogs** may dig up the garden. ___________ run through the yard all the time.

5. These **flowers** were planted last month. I can see __________ leaves coming up now.

6. **Horace and I** have worked hard in the garden. __________ efforts will make this house more beautiful.

Answers start on page 196.

PUNCTUATING PERFECTLY: APOSTROPHES IN CONTRACTIONS

Look at the two sentences below. How are they different?

She is a good person.
She's a good person.

In the second sentence, there is a contraction: *She's*. A contraction is formed when two words are combined into one word. An apostrophe (') shows where one or more letters have been left out when two words are joined. In the example above, the two words *She is* become one word: *She's*. The letter *i* is dropped from the word *is*, and an apostrophe replaces it.

To make a contraction, replace the missing letter or letters with an apostrophe. Study the examples below and then complete the list.

I am *I'm*	she is __________
you are *you're*	they are __________
we will __________	he is __________
(*Hint:* In the item above, remove two letters from *will*.)	it is __________

The correct contractions are *we'll*, *she's*, *they're*, *he's*, and *it's*.

Negatives are formed the same way.

did not *didn't*	is not __________
was not *wasn't*	would not __________
are not __________	had not __________

The correct contractions are *aren't, isn't, wouldn't*, and *hadn't*.

EXERCISE 13: FORMING CONTRACTIONS

Directions: Finish the following list of contractions. The first one has been completed for you.

1. they have ___they've___
2. does not ______
3. he is ______
4. I am ______
5. we are ______
6. is not ______
7. should not ______
8. they will ______

Answers start on page 196.

Contractions and Possessive Pronouns

Apostrophes are used in both contractions and possessive nouns. However, apostrophes are *never* used in possessive pronouns. Be careful not to confuse possessive pronouns with contractions. If you can't tell which to use, substitute the two words the contraction stands for in the sentence to see if they make sense.

Here's an example. Which word correctly completes the sentence?

> *(Its, It's)* cold outside.

As you know, *It's* is a contraction of *It is.* Try substituting *It is* in the sentence. Does the following sentence make sense?

> It is cold outside.

Yes. If you can write *It is*, you can also write the contraction *It's*: It's cold outside.

Now look at another example. Which word is correct?

> That dog is hurt. Something is wrong with *(its, it's)* paw.

Try substituting the words *it is* in the sentence. Does the following sentence make sense?

> Something is wrong with it is paw.

No. That sentence doesn't make sense. So the correct word to complete the sentence must be the possessive pronoun *its*.

> Something is wrong with its paw.

EXERCISE 14: CONTRACTIONS AND POSSESSIVE PRONOUNS

Directions: There are eight errors in the paragraph below. All of the mistakes have to do with contractions and possessives. Find each mistake, cross it out, and write the correct word above it. The first error is corrected for you.

> *It's*
> ~~Its~~ always a good idea to decorate you're home. Even people who don't have much spare time can hang pictures on they're walls and put up curtains. Of course, its harder if your working full-time. Gary, a friend of mine, did a nice job on he's apartment. I hope that he and he's friend Pete will help me out. Their really talented at decorating.

Answers start on page 196.

EXERCISE 15: CHAPTER REVIEW

Part 1

Directions: In this exercise, you will read three ways of writing each sentence. Choose the *correct* sentence by marking choice **a**, **b**, or **c**.

	a	b	c
1. a. Many United states citizens do not want nuclear power. **b.** Many united states citizens do not want nuclear power. **c.** Many United States citizens do not want nuclear power.	☐	☐	☐
2. a. The residents of Harrisburg live close to the power plant. **b.** The Residents of Harrisburg live close to the power plant. **c.** The residents of harrisburg live close to the power plant.	☐	☐	☐
3. a. The residents homes were in danger during the accident. **b.** The resident's home's were in danger during the accident. **c.** The residents' homes were in danger during the accident.	☐	☐	☐

	a	b	c
4. **a.** Some of these citizen's are leading the fight to close all nuclear power plants. **b.** Some of these citizens are leading the fight to close all nuclear power plants. **c.** Some of these Citizens are leading the fight to close all nuclear power plants.	☐	☐	☐

Directions: In each of the following sentences, one or more nouns are incorrect. On the line under the sentence, write the sentence correctly.

5. Years ago, I went to hear senator Stevenson speak.

____

6. The year stevenson ran for president, dad bought a new ford.

____

Directions: Fill each blank in the following sentences with one of the pronouns from the list. You should use each pronoun once.

I they his ours hers us she my

7. After the game, ________ drove my car home.

8. Suzette claimed that the purse was ________.

9. "Throw the Frisbee to ________!" screamed Pablo and Paco.

10. We went to visit the Archers, but ________ weren't home.

11. "Please give me ________ change," requested the diner.

12. "The car that was stolen was ________," cried Betty and Jerry.

Part 2

Use the information you studied in Chapter 2 about complete sentences, punctuation, and subjects of sentences.

Directions: On the line under each exercise, write the sentence correctly. You may have to add words to make a complete sentence.

1. After the party, Dean.

____

2. Look out—it's a raid?

____

3. Will be arrested.

____

Directions: Write the subject of each sentence in the blank. The first one is done as an example.

4. Did you find the album? ___you___

5. Music always cheers me up. ____________

6. Turn on the radio. ____________

7. In a few minutes, the news will come on. ____________

Answers start on page 196.

YOUR TURN TO WRITE: A ONE-SIDED ARGUMENT

In your writing folder or notebook, you are going to share your opinion about something. Below are three possible topics.

1. People over twenty-one should not live with their parents.
2. Parents should not be responsible for their children's illegal actions.
3. Drunk drivers should have to serve time in jail.

WRITING PRACTICE

Directions: Choose one of the topics above (or think of another topic) and state your opinion. There are good points and bad points for everything, but to win this argument present points that support only the side of the issue that you chose.

Writing Checklist

- ❑ Does every sentence you wrote support your opinion?
- ❑ Do all of your pronouns agree with the nouns they replace?
- ❑ Are your nouns used correctly?

4 Verbs

JOURNAL WRITING: AN IMPORTANT PERSON

In this journal entry, try writing an "I just want to tell you how wonderful you are" letter. You now have an opportunity to say how much you appreciate someone. You can probably think of people who have had a positive effect on your life. If you want to, use your journal to write to at least one person who is important to you.

JOURNAL ENTRY

Directions: Has someone helped you to earn extra money? helped you lose weight or become stronger? helped you with your schoolwork? given a sermon that changed your life? had a positive influence on your life?

Have you ever thought, Someday, I'm going to tell that person just how much I appreciate him? Well, this is your chance. Just write "Dear . . ." and continue writing.

LANGUAGE SKILLS: VERBS: FORM AND TENSE

WHAT IS A VERB?

You have already learned some things about verbs in Chapters 1 and 2. You might remember this definition:

> A *verb* is a word that shows action or being.

A verb can be an ***action word*** like *run, jump, skip, drink*, or *dance*. It can also be a ***linking word*** (being word) like *is, am, was*, or *were*.

The following sentences contain verbs. Underline the words that show what a noun is or does.

> The traffic roared through the tunnel.
> Drivers honked horns at each other.
> Many drivers were impatient.
> At the tunnel's exit, a motorcycle cop waited for speeders.

Did you underline *roared, honked, were,* and *waited*? If so, you have a good understanding of verbs.

Below is a list of nouns. In the space next to each noun, write a verb that tells something that the noun does.

husbands ____________________ friends ____________________

wives ____________________ dogs ____________________

cars ____________________

You might have written that dogs bark and friends share. Any word is a correct answer as long as it is a verb.

VERBS TELL TIME

Verbs tell time. When you talk about what you do today, what you did yesterday, and what you will do in the future, you use ***verb tenses***. You change verb tenses to show when events in your life take place.

Think about this very moment as now. A verb that tells what you do now is a ***present-tense*** verb.

> Right now, I **walk** slowly.

Present-tense verbs also tell what you do on a regular basis.

> I always **walk** slowly.

Yesterday took place before now. Anything that happened before now—it doesn't matter how long ago—is part of your past. A verb that tells what you did before is a ***past-tense*** verb.

> Last week, I **walked** slowly.

You also plan to do things tomorrow and weeks, months, and years from now. Anything that happens after now will happen in the future. A verb that tells what you will do at some later time is a ***future-tense*** verb.

Next week, I **will walk** slowly.

Now fill in the blanks below with five verbs showing things you do every day. See if you can put them in the present tense.

Every day I ___sleep___, ___eat___,
___clean___, __________, and __________.

There are things you did yesterday that you did not do today. In the blanks below, list verbs that show things you did yesterday that you did not do today. See if you can put them in the past tense.

Yesterday I ___danced___, __________,
__________, __________, and __________.

Now list verbs that show things that you did not do today but will do tomorrow. See if you can put them in the future tense.

Tomorrow I ___will___ ___shop___, I __________ __________,

I __________ __________, I __________ __________, and I

__________ __________.

RECOGNIZING THE BASE VERB

In the examples on these two pages, you saw the verbs *walk, walked*, and *will walk*. Here they are again:

PRESENT: Right now, I walk slowly.
PAST: Last week, I walked slowly.
FUTURE: Next week, I will walk slowly.

In these examples, the present-tense verb *walk* is the base verb. The past tense is formed by adding an ending, *ed*, to the base verb. The future tense is formed by adding a helping verb, *will*, to the base verb.

The main verb is called the ***base verb.*** Verb tenses are formed by adding endings or helping verbs to the base verb.

As you study verbs in the rest of this chapter, you'll be learning to use base verbs with endings and helping verbs to form different verb tenses correctly.

All verbs change to the future tense according to the same pattern. Some verbs, like *walk,* also change to the present and past tenses according to a regular pattern. These verbs are ***regular verbs***. You'll study how to form regular verbs first. Later in the chapter, you'll study some ***irregular verbs***. Irregular verbs don't follow the regular patterns for changing tenses.

PRESENT TENSE OF REGULAR VERBS

The present tense shows that something is happening right now. It is also used to show that something takes place regularly. To form the present tense, you use the base verb by itself or the base verb plus *s*.

The following box shows how the present tense of the base verb *walk* is formed for different subjects. Notice that *s* is added to the base verb for some of the subjects. An *s* is added to make the verb "agree" with those subjects.

Subject	Present Tense
I, you, we, they, and all plural nouns	walk (base verb alone)
he, she, it, and all singular nouns	walks (base verb + *s*)

In the following sentences, the verbs end in *s* because their subjects are *he, she, it,* or singular nouns:

She **looks** great in her new coat.
Roger **seems** happy enough.
The wind **feels** cool.

In one of the following sentences, the verb should end in *s*. Complete the sentences by writing *dance* or *dances* in each blank.

My grandparents __________ in a contest every year.

My grandmother __________ very gracefully.

For the first sentence, the correct answer is *dance,* since *grandparents* is a plural noun. The correct answer for the second sentence is *dances,* since *grandmother* is a singular noun.

EXERCISE 1: CHOOSING PRESENT-TENSE VERBS

Directions: Circle the subject in each sentence. Then underline the correct verb form. The first one is done as an example.

1. Americans *(enjoy, enjoys)* changes.

2. They *(like, likes)* to see their country grow.

3. I *(love, loves)* being a citizen.

4. I *(find, finds)* that many people are willing to help me.

5. They *(welcome, welcomes)* me with a place to live.

6. My parents still *(live, lives)* in another country.

7. We *(write, writes)* to each other every week.

Answers start on page 196.

PAST TENSE OF REGULAR VERBS

The past tense shows that something took place in the past. Most regular verbs take an *ed* ending to form the past tense. Regular verbs that end in *e* have only the letter *d* added to form the past tense.

Here are some examples of how to form the past tense of regular verbs.

base verb + ending	= past tense
walk + ed	= walked
spell + ed	= spelled
change + d	= changed
love + d	= loved

Now see if you can write some past-tense verbs. The following paragraph has three blanks. Fill in the past tense of the base verb underneath each blank to complete the paragraph.

Two years ago, Al hated (*hate*) exercise. Last year, he walked (*walk*) one mile a day. Now Al walks three miles a day. He looks physically fit. Two years ago, he looked (*look*) terrible. Now he hates to miss his daily exercise.

You should have written *hated, walked,* and *looked*. What letters did you add to the verbs to make them past tense? d & ed

FORMING THE FUTURE TENSE

The future tense shows that something has not happened yet. Here are two sentences using the future tense of the base verbs *fly* and *cry*.

> Maria **will fly** to Puerto Rico.
> She **will cry** when she sees her family.

What helping verb comes before the base verbs *fly* and *cry* to show the future tense? will

The helping verb is *will*. You can form the future tense of any verb by using the helping verb *will* in front of it.

EXERCISE 2: WRITING THE PAST AND FUTURE TENSES

Directions: Write the past and future tenses of the following base verbs. The first one is done for you as an example.

Base Verb	Past	Future
1. look	*looked*	*will look*
2. move	moved	will move
3. live	lived	will live
4. save	saved	will save

Answers start on page 197.

IRREGULAR VERBS

In Exercise 2, you added *d* or *ed* to put each of those verbs in the past tense. Not all verbs change to the past tense according to the regular pattern. There are many irregular verbs, mostly in the past tense. There is only one way to get to know irregular verbs. You must study them until you can remember them.

EXERCISE 3: PAST TENSE OF IRREGULAR VERBS

Directions: Fill in the past tense of as many verbs as you can. When you have filled in as many as you know, turn to the answer key, check your work, and fill in the rest. The first two are done for you as examples.

Base Verb	Past Tense
1. give	I *gave* last month.
2. tell	I *told* him yesterday.

Base Verb	Past Tense
3. see	I __saw__ him the day before he left.
4. come	I __came__ last week.
5. read	I __read__ the paper last Sunday.
6. bring	I __brought__ it some time ago.
7. say	I __said__ so yesterday.
8. make	I __made__ the cake last night.
9. go	I __went__ home yesterday.
10. do	I __did__ it a minute ago.
11. have	I __had__ the book last night.
12. sell	I __sold__ the car four months ago.

Answers start on page 197.

AVOIDING ERRORS WITH IRREGULAR VERBS

In Exercise 3, you filled in the blanks with the past-tense forms of many irregular verbs. None of these forms needed helping verbs. There are some other past tenses that do require helping verbs, but you will not be studying all of those tenses in this chapter. However, some very common mistakes are made when people confuse the different past tenses.

Study the following pair of sentences. The correct sentence uses the form of the past you learned in Exercise 3. It does not require a helping verb. The other sentence contains a mistake because it uses a form that cannot stand alone.

CORRECT: I did my homework already.
INCORRECT: I done my homework already.

The correct past tense of *do* is *did*. The word *done* is used to form a tense that requires a helping verb, so *done* is never correct when it is used alone.

Here are some other similar pairs of sentences. Study each pair to be sure you know which past-tense form can be used without a helping verb.

CORRECT: She went home yesterday.
INCORRECT: She gone home yesterday.

CORRECT: We came home last night.
INCORRECT: We come home last night.

CORRECT: Jesse was helping me.
INCORRECT: Jesse been helping me.

EXERCISE 4: CHOOSING THE CORRECT PAST-TENSE FORM

Directions: Underline the correct verb to complete each of the following sentences. The first one is done as an example.

1. Angie (*seen, saw*) a prowler in the parking lot.
2. Last night the Olshers (*ran, run*) into the Millers.
3. Horace (*was, been*) in that bowling league for years.
4. We (*went, gone*) camping for our vacation.

Answers start on page 197.

IMPORTANT IRREGULAR VERBS

There are three very important irregular verbs. These verbs are used so much that writers must know them in order to write correctly.

The Base Verb *Be*

As you already know, the most common linking verbs are forms of *be*. In fact, forms of *be* are some of the most frequently used verbs.

The verb *be* is very irregular because its forms change for different subjects in both the present tense and the past tense. The forms of the three tenses for *be* are in the following chart. Study and learn them all.

<table>
<tr><th>Subject</th><th>Present</th><th>Past</th><th>Future</th></tr>
<tr><td>I</td><td>am</td><td rowspan="2">was</td><td rowspan="3">will be</td></tr>
<tr><td>he, she, it and all singular nouns</td><td>is</td></tr>
<tr><td>you, we, they, and all plural nouns</td><td>are</td><td>were</td></tr>
</table>

Choose the correct form of *be* to complete the following sentences.

I *(be, am)* furious with those boys.

Tom *(was, were)* about to put his brother in the washing machine.

You *(is, are)* kidding!

In the first sentence, *am* agrees with *I*. In the second sentence, *was* agrees with the singular noun *Tom*. In the third sentence, *are* agrees with *You*.

EXERCISE 5: FORMS OF *BE*

Directions: Underline the correct verb in the following sentences. The first one is done as an example.

1. They *(was, were)* planning to get married.
2. You *(is, are)* going to take bus number five.
3. Erika *(was, were)* angry about the robbery.
4. The station wagon *(is, are)* ready for the junkyard.
5. Ms. Gallagher *(is, are)* concerned about her frequent headaches.
6. My parents (*is, are*) not sure that they want a divorce.
7. Your building (*was, were*) infested with termites.

Answers start on page 197.

The Verbs *Have* and *Do*

There are a few other confusing irregular verbs that we need to use every day. Two of the most common ones are *have* and *do*.

You may already know how to use these verbs correctly most of the time. Try to correct the paragraph below to see how much you already know about those two verbs. Draw a line through each verb you think is incorrect and write the correct form above it. There is one mistake in each sentence.

My brother have to quit his job. His wife don't like it when he leaves home at 5 A.M. to go to work. She have to understand that he will get fired if he comes to work late. My brother's children does not understand him either. They has no time to see him.

The corrected paragraph is on the following page.

My brother **has** to quit his job. His wife **doesn't** like it when he leaves home at 5 A.M. to go to work. She **has** to understand that he will get fired if he comes to work late. My brother's children **do** not understand him either. They **have** no time to see him.

Forms of *Have*

The following chart shows the forms of all three tenses of the irregular verb *have*.

Subject	Present	Past	Future
I, you, we, they, and all plural nouns	have	had	will have
he, she, it and all singular nouns	has		

Remember that the present tense is either *has* or *have* and the past tense is always *had*. The future is always *will have*.

EXERCISE 6: FORMS OF *HAVE*

Directions: Complete the following sentences using the correct form and tense of the verb *have*. The first one is done as an example.

1. Tom __has__ a good job.
   (present)

2. He ________ time to go to the movies each weekend.
   (present)

3. He ________ fun at the movies next weekend.
   (future)

4. After work on Friday, he remembered that he ________ to use an automated teller machine.
   (past)

5. If Tom can't find his personal identification number (PIN), he _______ to contact the bank.
   (future)

Answers start on page 197.

Forms of *Do*

The following chart shows the present-, past-, and future-tense forms of the irregular verb *do*.

Subject	Present	Past	Future
I, you, we, they, and all plural nouns	do	did	will do
he, she, it and all singular nouns	does		

Remember that the present tense is either *do* or *does* and the past tense is always *did*. The future tense is always *will do*.

EXERCISE 7: FORMS OF *DO*

Directions: Complete the following sentences using the correct form of the verb *do*. The first one is done as an example.

1. __Do__ *(present)* you have a monthly household budget?
2. Most people ________ *(present)* not bother to make a budget.
3. If they ________ *(past)*, they might be surprised by where their money goes.
4. My family ________ *(past)* a budget last month, and we were shocked.
5. My brother ________ *(present)* not realize how much money he spends on clothes.
6. In the future we ________ *(future)* a budget each month.

Answers start on page 197.

TIME CLUES TO VERB TENSES

Often you will be able to decide what verb tense (past, present, or future) to use by clue words in a sentence. Words like *now, this minute*, and *today* tell you that the sentence takes place in the present.

Right this minute, I love you.

The clue words are _______________ _______________ _______________.

Words like *yesterday, last year, some time ago*, and *before* tell you that the sentence takes place in the past.

Last year, I loved you.

The clue words are _______________ _______________ .

Words like *tomorrow, in three hours*, and *next year* tell you that the sentence takes place in the future.

Next year, I will love you.

The clue words are _______________ _______________ .

EXERCISE 8: USING TIME CLUES

Directions: Write the correct form of the base verb to complete each sentence. Underline the time clue in each sentence that tells you what tense to choose. The first one is done as an example.

1. *(want)* Today many people ___want___ to lose weight.
2. *(work)* Last year Rob ____________ out to tone up his muscles.
3. *(wake)* Now we ____________ up early every day.
4. *(go)* Tomorrow Anne ____________ to her aerobics class.

Answers start on page 197.

PUTTING YOUR SKILLS TO WORK

Directions: Complete the following exercise. Pay special attention to the verbs. Add this exercise to the others in your writing folder or notebook. Don't forget to date your entry.

Look at the picture. Imagine you are one of the people in the picture. Write a paragraph in your notebook that tells what happened before the scene in the picture (past), what is happening in the picture (present), and what will happen next (future).

Try to use at least two sentences in the past tense, two sentences in the present tense, and two sentences in the future tense. You can use the following sentence as your first sentence.

Matthew's letter said he was coming home on Tuesday.

☑ Writing Checklist

- ❑ Do you have two sentences written in the past tense?
- ❑ Do you have two sentences written in the present tense?
- ❑ Do you have two sentences written in the future tense?
- ❑ Are your verb forms correct?

THE CONTINUING TENSES

Another Way to Form the Present

You have already learned to form the present tense by using the base verb or the base verb plus *s* or *es*. Another present tense, the ***present continuing tense***, shows that an action is continuing in the present. The present continuing tense is formed by using *am, is,* or *are* as a helping verb with the base verb plus *ing*.

EXAMPLE: The clown **is laughing**.

There are two words in the verb of that sentence: *is laughing*. The helping verb is *is*. The base verb is *laugh*. The ending *ing* is added to *laugh*.

Can you pick out the present-continuing-tense verbs in the next two examples? Underline the verbs.

The workers are striking.
I am walking the picket line.

Did you underline *are striking* and *am walking*? They are the verbs in those sentences.

You can add *ing* to any base verb. On the line below, combine the verbs *swear, think,* and *choose* with the *ing* ending. (If a base verb ends in *e*, drop the *e* before adding *ing*.)

____

You should have written *swearing, thinking,* and *choosing*.

Now write the three helping verbs that can be used before the base verb plus *ing* to form the present continuing tense: ____________, ____________, and ____________. The following chart shows all the present continuing forms of the verb *walk*.

Subject	Helping Verb	Base Verb + *ing*
I	am	walking
you, we, they, and all plural nouns	are	
he, she, it and all singular nouns	is	

EXERCISE 9: THE PRESENT CONTINUING TENSE

Directions: Complete each sentence by underlining the correct verb. Make sure that the verb you choose agrees with the subject. The first one is done for you as an example.

1. In my class, everyone *(<u>is studying</u>, are studying)* for an important test.

2. We *(be working, are working)* at different speeds and are good at different things.

3. Anna *(is learning, are learning)* fractions faster than Dave or I.

4. Some students *(is writing, are writing)* sentences with no trouble.

5. I *(is enjoying, am enjoying)* my math class this year because I understand it.

Answers start on page 197.

Another Way to Form the Past

Compare the two sentences below. How are they alike? How are they different?

Rafael is running.
Rafael was running.

The verb in the first sentence is *is running*. That verb is in the present continuing tense. The action is taking place now.

Look at the second sentence. It also uses the word *running*, but the helping verb is *was*. As you know, *was* is a past-tense verb. So that verb is in the ***past continuing tense***, which shows that an action was continuing in the past.

The following chart shows how to form the past continuing tense of the verb *walk* for different subjects.

Subject	Helping Verb	Base Verb + *ing*
you, we, they, and all plural nouns	were	walking
he, she, it and all singular nouns	was	

Complete the following sentences by filling in the correct past continuing form of the base verb.

It *was raining* hard that day.
(rain)

Caren __________________ when she said that.
(joke)

The children __________________ when we got home.
(sleep)

You should have written *was joking* in the second sentence because *Caren* is a singular noun. In the third sentence, *were sleeping* agrees with the plural noun *children*.

EXERCISE 10: THE PAST CONTINUING TENSE

Directions: Complete each sentence below with the correct form of the past continuing tense. Remember, you need to use a helping verb, either *was* or *were*. The base verb must have an *ing* ending. Use the base verb below each blank. The first one is done as an example.

1. It *was raining*, and the streets were slippery as I drove
   (rain)

   to work one morning.

2. I __________________ too fast, and I hit two other cars.
   (drive)
3. The other drivers __________________ when they got out of their cars.
   (smile)
4. "We __________________ in for repairs anyway, so don't worry," they said.
   (go)
5. My boss __________________ for me when I got to work.
   (look)
6. She said that she __________________ me the day off and a big raise.
   (give)
7. Suddenly my alarm clock __________________.
   (ring)
8. I __________________!
   (dream)

Answers start on page 197.

PUNCTUATING PERFECTLY: USING QUOTATION MARKS

Quotation marks ("...") are used for a number of things. You will learn the main use for quotation marks: to show direct quotes.

> ***Quotation marks*** are used to tell the reader that the words between them are exactly what someone said.

EXAMPLE: "Don't do anything I wouldn't do," said Lee.

The words between the quotation marks are a direct quote. You know that Lee said these exact words: *Don't do anything I wouldn't do*. A direct quote repeats the exact words that someone used.

EXAMPLES: "Our team won the championship," said Mike.
Mike said, "Our team won the championship."

Both of those sentences give you the same information. However, in the first example, the direct quote comes first in the sentence. There is a comma (,) after the word *championship* and before the end quotation mark. The period comes after the last word in the sentence, *Mike*.

In the second sentence, the quote is at the end of the sentence. The comma (,) is after the word *said* and in front of the first quotation mark. The period is still at the end of the sentence, but it is inside the end quotation mark.

In the second sentence, the first word of the quote (*Our*) begins with a capital letter even though it is in the middle of the sentence. If a quote is a complete sentence, it always begins with a capital letter.

Practice adding quotation marks to sentences. The sentences below all contain direct quotes. Add quotation marks to show the quotes.

It would take me forever to shine it up, said Pedro.

I really need help with the job, he stated.

Estralita asked, Would you pay me if I helped you?

Then she added, If you drive me to work every day,
I'll help you.

Check the first sentence. Do you have quotation marks before the word *It* and after the comma? In the second sentence, you should have quotation marks before *I* and after the comma. In the third sentence, you should have quotation marks before *Would* and after the question mark. In the final sentence, do you have quotation marks before *If* and after the period?

EXERCISE 11: USING QUOTATION MARKS

Directions: The following sentences form a conversation. Add quotation marks wherever they are needed.

1. I think the best years of a person's life are his teen years, said Raymond.
2. His mother laughed and said, That's because you are a teenager.
3. Actually, you will have more fun once you are an adult, said his twenty-two-year-old brother, John.
4. What will happen to me once I reach thirty? John wondered.
5. You'll be on your way to forty, and believe me, those are really the best years, said Mom.
6. Dad piped in, Oh, I don't know, I think I'm even better-looking at fifty.
7. John asked, How were the sixties, Grandma?

Answers start on page 197.

PUTTING YOUR SKILLS TO WORK

In your writing folder or notebook, write a conversation between a man and a woman. You might want to have them talking about the first time that they met or about their family budget. Or you can think of another topic to have them talk about. The conversation you write should have at least four sentences.

- Sentence 1 should begin with *He said.*
- Sentence 2 should begin with *She replied.*
- Sentence 3 should end with *she added.*
- Sentence 4 should end with *he replied.*

☑ Writing Checklist

- ❑ Do you have quotation marks at the beginning and end of direct quotes in all the sentences?
- ❑ Does the first word inside the quotation marks begin with a capital letter?
- ❑ Is there a comma before the beginning of the quotation in sentences 1 and 2?
- ❑ Is there a comma before the end quotation marks in sentences 3 and 4?

EXERCISE 12: CHAPTER REVIEW

Part 1

To complete this part of the review, you will use the information you have been studying in Chapter 4: verbs and verb tenses.

Directions: Complete the following.

1. Decide whether each verb in the following list is in the past, present, or future tense. Then put each word in the appropriate column of the chart below. Three are done as examples.

will find	**drive**	**will write**	**sang**	**had**	**saw**
claim	**hopes**	**jump**	**is**	**was**	**are**
danced	**will paint**	**will want**	**looked**		

Past	Present	Future
sang	*jump*	*will find*

Directions: Read each sentence carefully. Three ways to write the underlined part of each sentence are given. Choose the way that makes the sentence correct. Choice ***a*** is always the same as the original underlined part.

a b c

2. The community center start a gymnastics program for toddlers. ☐ ☐ ☐

a. start
b. is starting
c. be starting

3. Our neighbors are having a huge argument. ☐ ☐ ☐

a. are having
b. is having
c. having

4. The circus stop here each year. ☐ ☐ ☐

a. stop
b. will stops
c. stops

5. Two years ago, my father decide to go back to school. ☐ ☐ ☐

a. decide
b. decided
c. will decide

6. Todd walk six miles after his car broke down. ☐ ☐ ☐

a. walk
b. walking
c. walked

7. We be ready to leave for school now. ☐ ☐ ☐

a. be
b. is
c. are

8. Velma done the copying three times last week. ☐ ☐ ☐

a. done
b. did
c. will do

9. Theo turn the radio on as soon as he gets home from work. ☐ ☐ ☐

a. turn
b. are turning
c. turns

Part 2

To complete this part of the review, you will have to use the information you studied in Chapters 2 and 3: possessives and contractions, complete sentences, pronouns, and common and proper nouns.

Directions: Each of the following sentences contains one error. Write each sentence correctly on the blank line. The first one is done as an example.

1. Her childrens room is a mess.
   Her children's room is a mess.
2. I cant blame her children for being messy.
   ____
3. Their just like her.
   ____
4. Doesn't like to clean her room either.
   ____

Answers start on page 197.

JOURNAL WRITING: TELLING A STORY

It's time to take out your writing folder or notebook again. You will have two choices.

WRITING PRACTICE

Choice 1

Directions: Think back to high school. Do you remember a typical day in school: classes, your teachers, the kids . . . ? Write at least three paragraphs.

- In the first paragraph, write about a typical day in high school. (Or write about a day on the job or at home.)
- In the second paragraph, write about a typical day in the adult education center.
- In the third paragraph, write about a typical school or work day you would like to have in the future. (Or write about your job or your family in the future.)
- Finally, write a fourth paragraph, sharing some information to tie the first three paragraphs together.

Choice 2

Directions: Try writing a story. Include quotations from the people involved in the story. You might want to tell about meeting someone and falling in love at first sight. Or you might want to tell about a funny experience you had and what people said. Use your imagination! Remember to use quotations from the people involved in the incident.

☑ Writing Checklist

- ❑ If you chose the first exercise, did you use a variety of tenses correctly? Were you able to explain yourself clearly?
- ❑ If you chose the second exercise, do you have quotation marks at the beginning and end of all the direct quotes?

5 Subject-Verb Agreement

JOURNAL WRITING: BRAINSTORMING

Brainstorming means writing all your thoughts about a topic. You write the thoughts down as quickly as possible and in whatever order they pop into your mind. Some of the thoughts may not seem to be a part of the topic. One thought will lead to another. You might even discover that you're thinking faster than you're writing. You don't need to write complete sentences or worry about correct spelling. Just write words and ideas until you don't have anything else to write.

JOURNAL ENTRY

Directions: For this journal entry, brainstorm about one of these three topics or choose your own topic.

- What my perfect job would be like
- Being a teenager (or a mom, or a dad)
- My pet

Brainstorming is part of a writing process. You need to organize your thoughts and then turn them into one or more paragraphs about one topic. One easy way is to number them in the order in which you want to write about them. You might decide not to use all the ideas you brainstormed.

BRAINSTORMING EXAMPLE:

My Pet

1 cat named Misty	*3* doesn't like anyone but me
~~canned cat food stinks~~	*2* gray with white paws
4 sleeps with me at night	~~neighbors have a cat too~~
6 yowls for food	*5* had her kittens under my bed

PARAGRAPH EXAMPLE:

My cat's name is Misty. She is very pretty, with gray fur and white paws. She doesn't like anyone but me, and she sleeps with me every night. When she had kittens, she hid under my bed to give birth. When she is hungry, she sits on the kitchen window sill and yowls noisily for food. She can be a pest, but she is good company for me.

Now it's your turn. Get out your journal, pick your topic, and start brainstorming! Then organize your brainstormed ideas and write at least one paragraph.

LANGUAGE SKILLS: SUBJECT-VERB AGREEMENT

Subject-verb agreement is making the verb in a sentence agree with the subject of that sentence. You practiced subject-verb agreement in Chapter 4, but you'll be studying it more carefully in this chapter.

Except for the irregular verb *be*, which you learned in Chapter 4, verbs change form for different subjects only in the present tense.

PRONOUNS AS SUBJECTS

You will review how to make verbs agree with subject pronouns. Here are the subject pronouns with the correct present tense of the verb *swim*.

I You We They	swim.	He She It	swims.

Which pronouns need a verb that ends in *s*? ______________________

Which pronouns need a verb that does not end in *s?* ______________________

____

Rule for Subject-Verb Agreement with Pronouns

In the present tense, the verb must end in *s* if the subject is *he, she* or *it*. If the subject is *I, you, we,* or *they*, the verb does not end in *s*.

Underline the correct verb to complete each of the following sentences.

They *(<u>swim</u>, swims)* at the beach every Saturday.

He *(laugh, laughs)* at all my jokes.

In the second sentence, *laughs* agrees with *He*.

Usually *s* is added to the end of a base verb for the subjects *he, she,* and *it*. However, when the base verb ends in the letters *s, x, z, sh,* or *ch, es* is added. In the following sentences, the base verbs have *es* added for subject-verb agreement.

She **washes** the car on Sunday mornings.
He **fixes** waffles for breakfast.

EXERCISE 1: SUBJECT-VERB AGREEMENT WITH PRONOUNS

Directions: Underline the correct form of the verb to complete each sentence. Follow the rule for subject-verb agreement with pronouns. The first one is done as an example.

1. He *(own, owns)* a garage on 42nd Street.

2. We *(take, takes)* all our cars and trucks to his shop.

3. They *(come, comes)* back as good as new.

4. She *(thank, thanks)* him for taking good care of her car.

Answers start on page 198.

WHAT ABOUT IRREGULAR VERBS?

Now you'll learn the present tense of one new irregular verb: *go*. Start by looking at another irregular verb. Here are the subject pronouns with the correct present-tense forms of *have:*

I, you, we, they	have
he, she, it	has

Which pronouns need the form of the verb that ends in *s*? ____________

Which pronouns need the form of the verb that does not end in *s*?

____

Did you notice that the rule on page 128 still applies, even though *have* is an irregular verb? Notice that even though spellings are irregular, the forms for *he, she,* and *it* still end in *s*.

Now look at the present-tense forms of *go*.

I, you, we, they	go
he, she, it	goes

As you can see, the forms for *he, she,* and *it* still end in *s,* but an *e* has also been added before the *s*. With the irregular verb *go,* as well as the verb *do,* the *es* ending is used.

Now try applying the subject-verb agreement rule with irregular verbs. Underline the correct form of the verb to complete each of the following.

> He *(do, does)* the dishes this week.
>
> She *(have, has)* the shopping list.
>
> They *(are, is)* in the clothes hamper.

In the first sentence, *does* agrees with *He*. In the second and third sentences, *has* agrees with *She* and *are* agrees with *They*.

Only one verb changes form for different subjects in the past tense. That verb is *be*. Look at the past-tense forms of *be* for different subjects.

Subject	Verb	Subject	Verb
I	was	he, she, it	was
you, we, they	were		

Notice that in the past tense *I was* breaks the subject-verb agreement rule because the verb ends in *s*. This is the only exception to the rule. Underline the correct past-tense form of *be* to complete the following sentences.

> It *(were, was)* done when I left.
>
> They *(were, was)* on the kitchen table.

You should have underlined *was* in the first sentence and *were* in the second sentence.

EXERCISE 2: SUBJECT-VERB AGREEMENT WITH IRREGULAR VERBS

Directions: Underline the correct form of the irregular verb to complete each sentence. Follow the subject-verb agreement rule and refer to the charts of irregular verb forms on pages 112—115 as much as necessary.

1. We *(am, is, are)* happy to see you.
2. They *(have, has)* dinner at 8:00 on most nights.
3. I *(am, are, is)* ready to sing now, Fred.
4. She *(do, does)* whatever her friends tell her.
5. He *(were, was)* on the phone when I arrived.
6. They *(do, does)* the laundry every weekend.
7. You *(were, was)* not invited to this party.
8. He *(go, goes)* to the basketball court every night.

Answers start on page 198.

SINGULAR AND PLURAL NOUNS AS SUBJECTS

The subject of a sentence can be either a subject pronoun, a singular noun, or a plural noun. *Singular* means "one." When a noun is singular, it refers to only one person, place, thing, or idea. *Plural* means "more than one." When a noun is plural, it refers to more than one person, place, thing, or idea. You can easily learn how to make verbs agree with singular subjects and plural subjects.

A singular subject can always be replaced by *he, she,* or *it*. Therefore, a verb must end in *s* to agree with a singular noun. Cross out the subject of the following sentence and replace it with *he, she,* or *it*. Then underline the correct verb.

The alligator (*swim, swims*) slowly through the swamp.

In that sentence, *alligator* is the singular subject. *The alligator* can be replaced by *It*. Therefore, the verb must end in *s*. Here is the correct answer:

It
~~The alligator~~ (*swim, <u>swims</u>*) slowly through the swamp.

A plural subject can always be replaced by *they*, so a verb must not end in *s* to agree with a plural subject. Cross out the plural subject of the following sentence and replace it with *they*. Then underline the correct verb.

The women (*laugh, laughs*) loudly.

In that sentence, *women* is the plural subject. *The women* can be replaced by *They*. The verb must not end in *s* to agree with *They*, so the correct verb is *laugh*.

Here is the subject-verb agreement rule again.

Subject-Verb Agreement Rule

In the present tense, the verb must end in *s* if the subject is *he, she, it,* or a singular noun. If the subject is *I, you, we, they*, or a plural noun, the verb does not end in *s*.

Countable and Uncountable Nouns

It's usually easy to tell whether nouns are singular or plural because they are usually ***countable***. You can have one dog, three cousins, and two radios.

However, you cannot count some things and ideas. Nouns like *knowledge, pain, love, advice,* and *beauty* are ***uncountable***. Uncountable nouns are singular. If you put a pronoun in the place of an uncountable noun, you use the pronoun *it*.

The subject of the following sentence is an uncountable noun. Since *knowledge* can be replaced with *it,* the verb must end in *s.*

It
~~Knowledge~~ *(increase, increases)* your job skills.

EXERCISE 3: SINGULAR AND PLURAL SUBJECTS

Directions: Cross out the subject of each sentence and replace it with *he, she, it,* or *they*. Then underline the correct verb. The first one is done as an example.

It
1. ~~Summer~~ *(are, is)* the best time of the year.

2. Families *(move, moves)* from city to city.

3. The gardens *(look, looks)* gorgeous.

4. Carl *(guide, guides)* tourists through the Everglades.

5. Strength *(give, gives)* a woman confidence.

Answers start on page 198.

TRICKY SUBJECT-VERB AGREEMENT

Sometimes it's a little hard to make a subject and a verb agree. This is especially true when the subject of a sentence has two parts or when a phrase comes between the subject and the verb.

When a sentence has a ***compound subject***, the subject is in two parts, which are always connected by *and, or,* or *nor*. The parts are always nouns or pronouns. This sentence has a compound subject:

> **Ed and Joe** like to eat breakfast at the local diner.

In that sentence, *Ed* and *Joe* are the two parts of the compound subject. The two parts are joined by *and.*

In the next example, the two parts of the compound subject are joined by *or.* See if you can identify and underline the two parts of the compound subject.

> Either Alice or I have to plan the surprise party for our boss.

The two parts of the compound subject in that sentence are *Alice* and *I.* (*Either* is not part of the subject.)

Underline the parts of the compound subjects in the sentences below.

> Mrs. Jones and her daughter love Italian food.
>
> The adults or the teenagers bring the snacks.
>
> Neither she nor her brother is likely to win the contest.

You should have underlined *Mrs. Jones* and *her daughter, The adults* and *the teenagers*, and *she* and *her brother*. (The words *either* and *neither* often appear with compound subjects, but they are never part of the subject.)

Compound Subjects Joined by *And*

Very often, the parts of a compound subject are joined by the word *and.*

> Compound subjects joined by *and* are always plural. They need a verb that agrees with a plural subject.

Underline the parts of the compound subject and circle the verb in each sentence. The first one is done for you.

> Music and art (excite) many people.
>
> Football and baseball thrill millions of sports fans.
>
> Susan and I love movies.

You should have underlined *Football* and *baseball* in the second sentence and *Susan* and *I* in the third sentence. You should have circled *thrill* in the second sentence and *love* in the third sentence. Notice that none of the verbs in the three sentences ends in *s*.

Compound Subjects Joined by *Or* or *Nor*

Deciding which verb to use when the parts of a compound subject are joined by *or* or *nor* takes a little more thought.

> When a compound subject is joined by *or* or *nor*, the verb has to agree with the subject that is closest to the verb.

Underline the two parts of the compound subject in the following sentence. Which part is closest to the verb?

Either Betsy or you **come** home at 3:00 every day.

The two parts of the subject are *Betsy* and *you*. The part of the subject closest to the verb is *you*. According to the subject-verb agreement rule, the pronoun *you* needs a verb that does not end in *s*.

Now look at the sentence again, this time with the parts of the subject switched:

Either you or Betsy **comes** home at 3:00 every day.

Since the part of the subject closest to the verb now is *Betsy*, the form of the verb must agree with a singular subject. According to the subject-verb agreement rule, the singular noun *Betsy* needs a verb ending in *s*.

When the parts of the subject are joined by *nor*, the verb is chosen the same way. The verb agrees with the part of the subject closest to it. Underline the two parts of the compound subject in the following sentence. Then circle the verb that agrees with the closest part of the subject.

Neither Max nor his brothers *(plan, plans)* to visit Mother.

The two parts of the compound subject are *Max* and *his brothers*. The correct verb is *plan*, which agrees with the closest part of the subject, *his brothers*. Remember, a plural subject needs a verb that does not end in *s*.

Now look at the sentence again with the parts of the subject reversed. Circle the verb that agrees with the closest part of the subject in the new sentence.

Neither his brothers nor Max *(plan, plans)* to visit Mother.

The correct verb for that sentence is *plans*, which agrees with the singular subject *Max*.

EXERCISE 4: SUBJECT-VERB AGREEMENT WITH COMPOUND SUBJECTS

Directions: Underline the parts of the compound subject in each sentence. Then circle the correct form of the verb. The first one is done as an example.

1. The local police and the state police (*increase, increases*) their patrols on holiday weekends.
2. You and your parents (*need, needs*) to spend more time together.
3. Neither Nan nor I (*go, goes*) to Canada for Christmas.
4. A local club or businesses (*give, gives*) awards for community service.
5. Newspapers and radio (*help, helps*) people stay informed.

Answers start on page 198.

PUTTING YOUR SKILLS TO WORK

Directions: Take out your writing folder or notebook again. Write ten sentences using compound subjects. Write about anything or anyone you wish. Pay close attention to subject-verb agreement.

In at least two of your sentences, join the parts of the compound subject with the word *and*. In at least two other sentences, use *or* to connect the parts of the subject. In at least two other sentences, use *nor*. Remember to date your writing.

Writing Checklist

- ❑ Do you have at least two sentences using *and,* two sentences using *or,* and two sentences using *nor*?
- ❑ Do the verbs agree with the subjects?

DESCRIBING PHRASES

In many sentences, describing phrases come between the subject and the verb. To make sure the subject and verb agree, you must be able to find the subject and ignore the describing phrase. Here's an example.

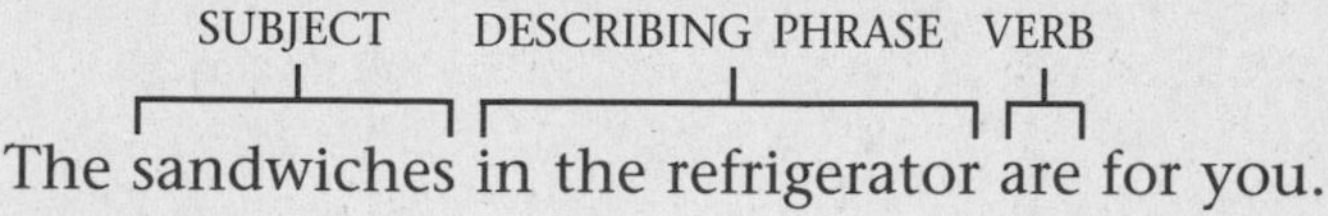

In that sentence, the subject, *sandwiches*, is plural. The verb *are* is correct for a plural subject. Notice that the describing phrase, *in the refrigerator*, does not affect subject-verb agreement.

Now try making the subject and verb agree in a sentence with a describing phrase. Circle the subject of the following sentence and cross out the describing phrase. Then underline the verb that agrees with the subject.

The hinges on the door *(are, is)* rusty.

It makes sense that the hinges would be rusty, so *hinges* has to be the subject of the sentence. The describing phrase is *on the door*. The verb must agree with the plural subject *hinges*, so the correct form is *are*.

Now try one more example. Circle the subject of the following sentence and cross out the describing phrase. Then underline the verb that agrees with the subject.

A car with bucket seats *(hold, holds)* fewer passengers.

The correct verb is *holds*. The subject is *car*, a singular noun. The describing phrase is *with bucket seats*.

EXERCISE 5: SUBJECT-VERB AGREEMENT WITH DESCRIBING PHRASES

Directions: Circle the subject of each sentence. Cross out the describing phrase. Then choose the correct verb to agree with the subject. Remember to follow the subject-verb agreement rule. The first one is done as an example.

1. The (tree) ~~with the red and gold leaves~~ *(change, changes)* color in early October.

2. The children under the tree *(pick, picks)* up the colorful leaves.

3. The father of one of the girls *(arrive, arrives)* early today.

4. Truckers with good sense *(take, takes)* safety precautions.

5. A truck with bad brakes *(have, has)* to be repaired immediately.

6. A driver on a long trip *(go, goes)* to a truck stop to rest.

7. Truckstops on the freeway *(is, are)* busy all night long.

Answers start on page 198.

PUTTING YOUR SKILLS TO WORK

Directions: Write a paragraph about a familiar group or organization. It might be your softball team or a local club. Perhaps you are a great fan of your football team, or a local hockey or track team. If you belong to a church or synagogue or a neighborhood organization, you could write about that.

Before you write your paragraph, try brainstorming about the group you are going to describe. Use ideas from your brainstorming in your paragraph.

☑ Writing Checklist

- ❑ Do all your subjects and verbs agree? Have you used correct verb forms?
- ❑ Have you referred to singular nouns with singular pronouns and plural nouns with plural pronouns?

EXERCISE 6: SUBJECT-VERB AGREEMENT REVIEW

Directions: In this exercise, you will practice all the subject-verb agreement skills you have learned in this chapter. Underline the correct verb to complete each sentence.

1. Nutritious meals and rest *(help, helps)* sick people recover.
2. A grandmother and grandfather *(give, gives)* tender loving care to their grandchildren.
3. Those blankets *(go, goes)* on Maggie's bed.
4. You *(do, does)* not have a chance of getting away with that.
5. Neither the vegetables nor the meat *(look, looks)* good to me.
6. Women in the job training program *(earn, earns)* wages for going to class.
7. Either a colorful poster or flowers *(cheer, cheers)* up a bare office.

Answers start on page 198.

PUNCTUATING PERFECTLY: COMMAS

Commas have many uses. They can be used to interrupt the sentence with additional information, to connect or make transitions between ideas, or to address a person directly.

Commas for Additional Information

When additional information is given about the subject of a sentence, commas are used to set off the information. Notice how a comma comes before and after the additional information in the following example.

Mrs. Stiffler, **my sixth-grade teacher**, really loved teaching.

In the following sentence, the phrase that gives additional information comes at the end of the sentence, so only one comma is needed.

One of my best friends is Harry, **the barber on Ninth Street**.

Now try an example. Add one comma to the following sentence to set off the phrase that gives the additional information.

The best person for that job is Ben an experienced carpenter.

Did you put a comma after *Ben*? The phrase that gives the additional information is *an experienced carpenter*. A phrase that gives additional information always comes directly after the noun it describes.

When you punctuate a phrase that gives additional information, always be careful to put a comma both before *and* after the phrase, unless it comes at the end of the sentence. Here is a common error to avoid:

INCORRECT: Ben, an experienced carpenter can do the job.
CORRECT: Ben, an experienced carpenter, can do the job.

EXERCISE 7: COMMAS WITH PHRASES THAT GIVE ADDITIONAL INFORMATION

Directions: Find the phrase that gives additional information in each of these sentences. Use commas to set off each phrase from the rest of the sentence. The first one is done as an example.

1. The Wizard of Oz, a favorite childhood character, granted wishes.
2. Checkers a game for two is challenging for children and adults.
3. Horror films a frightening form of entertainment attract big audiences.
4. The undercover policeman on the case is Detective Blackwell a member of the vice squad.

Answers start on page 198.

Commas for Connecting Ideas or Making Transitions

Commas are also used to set off short interrupting phrases that connect or make transitions between ideas in a sentence. The following sentences contain examples of these short phrases. Notice that, if you take out the words between the commas, the sentence still tells a complete thought.

I could, **for example**, move to San Francisco.
I might, **on the other hand**, move to Phoenix.

In those sentences, the interrupting phrases come in the middle of the sentence. Two commas are needed—one before and one after the interrupting phrase. However, these phrases could also come at the beginning or the end of the sentence.

I could move to San Francisco, **for example**.
On the other hand, I might move to Phoenix.

Notice that, when the interrupting phrases are moved to the beginning or end of the sentence, only one comma is needed.

Here is a list of common interrupting phrases that connect or make transitions between ideas.

of course	for example
in my opinion	in fact
by the way	on one hand
	on the other hand

EXERCISE 8: PHRASES THAT CONNECT OR MAKE TRANSITIONS BETWEEN IDEAS

Directions: Put commas where they are needed in the following sentences to set off the interrupting phrases. The first one is done as an example.

1. My best friend, of course, would never go out with my boyfriend.

2. I just learned in fact that I'm eating all the wrong foods.

3. Marlene gave up smoking by the way.

4. Andy in my opinion is not mature enough to live on his own.

Answers start on page 198.

Commas for Direct Address

Names used in ***direct address*** are set off by commas. When you use a person's name to speak directly to him or her, the name is set off by commas.

EXAMPLE: Charles, would you please help with this project?

A comma sets off the name *Charles* in that sentence. Only one comma is needed because the name comes first in the sentence.

In the following example, the name used in direct address comes in the middle of the sentence. Two commas are needed to set off *Mr. Littlefield*. Put the commas where they belong.

I hope Mr. Littlefield that you will accept this offer.

You should have put a comma both before and after *Mr. Littlefield*.

The name could also come at the end of the sentence.

EXAMPLE: You had better think twice about that, Fred.

EXERCISE 9: COMMAS IN DIRECT ADDRESS

Directions: Insert commas in these sentences. The first one is done for you.

1. Terry, will you please come for a visit this summer?
2. If I could afford the trip Mary I would surely come.
3. Do you realize how talented you are Paula?
4. In two weeks Mrs. Grant your lease will expire.

Answers start on page 199.

PUTTING YOUR SKILLS TO WORK

Directions: Take out your writing folder or notebook again. This time practice writing a series of sentences.

1. Write two sentences with phrases that give additional information. Make certain you use commas correctly. Here is an example:

   Danielle, an eighth-grader, is taking piano lessons.

2. Write two sentences with phrases that connect or make transitions between ideas. Use commas carefully. You can choose from the list of phrases on page 139. Here is an example:

   Television, in my opinion, is not worth watching.

3. Write two sentences showing direct address. Be careful about comma placement. Here is an example:

   Woody, you are acting like a fool!

☑ Writing Checklist

- ❑ Do you have two sentences showing the use of commas with phrases that give additional information?
- ❑ Do you have two sentences showing phrases that connect ideas? Are the phrases set off by commas?
- ❑ Do you have two sentences showing the use of commas with direct address?
- ❑ Do the subjects of your sentences agree with the verbs?

EXERCISE 10: CHAPTER REVIEW

Part 1

Directions: Find the mistake in each of the following sentences and correct it. If a word needs to be changed, cross out the wrong word and write the correct word above it. If there is a mistake in punctuation, add the correct punctuation or cross out the incorrect punctuation. The first one is done as an example.

1. Lucas and Dena ~~wants~~ *want* to buy a house.

2. A porch or patio give a house an outdoor feeling.

3. Lucas, an excellent cook examines the kitchens carefully.

4. The house with the hardwood floors were too expensive.

5. Neither Lucas nor Dena like the less expensive houses.

6. They are in fact, afraid that they will never find a good house for what they can pay.

Part 2

Directions: Find the mistake in each sentence. On the blank line, rewrite the sentence correctly.

1. Bobs car looks brand-new.

   ____

2. He is very careful to maintain it properly

   ____

3. the required oil change is done every 3,000 miles.

   ____

4. Last month, he change the gas filter, the oil, and the spark plugs.

   ____

5. The best thing to do for a car

   ____

6. It's paint can be preserved with regular waxing.

   ____

Answers start on page 199.

YOUR TURN TO WRITE: AN EVENT IN YOUR LIFE

Take out your writing folder or notebook again. Write three paragraphs about an event in your life. Choose an event as common as a typical work-day or as special as a wedding day.

WRITING ASSIGNMENT

Directions: Pick a topic that can be divided into three parts. In your first paragraph, tell what happened *before* the event. In your second paragraph, tell what happened *during* the event. In the third paragraph, tell what happened *after* the event. Be sure to indent each of your paragraphs. *Indenting* means starting the first word of a paragraph a few extra spaces to the right.

Here is a list of possible events for your paragraphs. Write neatly and correctly. Be especially careful with verbs and commas.

- A holiday celebration
- Interviewing for a job
- The first date with _____
- The first day of school
- Moving to a new home
- Your choice

Writing Checklist

- ❑ Are each of your three paragraphs indented?
- ❑ Do you have commas in the right places?
- ❑ Do your subjects and verbs agree?

6 ADJECTIVES AND ADVERBS

JOURNAL WRITING: STATING YOUR OPINION

Forming an opinion is an art that you can develop by sorting out your thoughts and ideas about a subject. Your opinion is what you think about something. Your opinion on any subject is based on facts, on ideas, and on information you have received from a number of sources. You also form opinions through personal experiences.

Since your journal is private, it is a good place to explore your opinions freely. You can practice sorting out thoughts and using examples and ideas to support your opinions. In this journal entry, you will give your opinion about an issue.

JOURNAL ENTRY

Directions: For this journal entry, choose one of the following opinion statements to write about. Choose one you agree with and have something to say about. You can also make up your own opinion statement. Write the opinion statement you are going to use at the top of a page in your journal.

Income tax should be a flat rate.
Companies should provide free child care.
Teenagers should not be allowed to drop out of high school.
Newspapers should not look into the private lives of public figures.

Next, have a brainstorming session. Write down all the ways you can think of to support your opinion statement. Try to think of lots of arguments and specific details and examples. Then read over your work and mark the ideas you want to include in your writing.

Finally, on a new page, write your opinion sentence again. Follow it with sentences that support your opinion.

LANGUAGE SKILLS: ADJECTIVES AND ADVERBS

WHAT IS AN ADJECTIVE?

Adjectives are words that describe nouns. Adjectives tell what kind, which one, or how many. Adjectives make nouns more specific.

For example, if you say, "James bought a motorcycle," you are not being very specific about the type of motorcycle he bought. Here are two different sentences that use adjectives to explain exactly what kind of motorcycle James bought.

James bought a **big, black, shiny** motorcycle.
James bought a **small, red, inexpensive, used** motorcycle.

In both sentences, you learn that James bought a motorcycle, but there is a big difference between the two motorcycles. The adjectives make each sentence more specific.

Here are three lists of adjectives that are used very often. More examples of adjectives are on page 152.

What Kind	Which One	How Many
tiny, silly, right, sleepy, loud, fast, tight, long	this, that, these, those	none, some, a dozen, much, fourteen (any number)

Using adjectives from the lists above, fill in the blanks in the following sentence.

After driving ___that___ truck for __________ hours, Tim
(which one) (how many)
was __________.
(what kind)

Your sentence should be similar to this:

After driving **that** truck for **fourteen** hours, Tim was **sleepy**.

Adjectives make sentences more specific and more interesting. For example, you can say, "I have a dog," or you can say, "I have a tiny, friendly, curly-haired dog with a ferocious bark." The second sentence is more specific and gives the listener a much better picture of the dog.

The more specific an adjective is, the better it describes what you are talking about. Below are four adjectives. Next to each one, list at least three other adjectives that could describe someone or something more specifically. You can look up the words in a dictionary to get ideas.

Small: *tiny, undersized, trivial*

Nice: ______

Good: ______

Big: ______

EXERCISE 1: CHOOSING ADJECTIVES

Directions: Choose adjectives from the list below to fill in the blanks. Some of the adjectives can be used in more than one of the sentences. The first one is done as an example.

hectic, busy, many, frustrated, small, colorful, expensive, inexpensive, gigantic, numerous

1. *Hectic* shopping takes place during holidays.
2. The ______ stores are overcrowded.
3. In the evening, ______ customers pack the stores.
4. During a sale, bargain hunters fight over ______ purchases.
5. ______ lights decorate the stores.
6. Children sometimes ask for ______ presents.
7. Often parents can afford only ______ presents.

Answers start on page 199.

EXERCISE 2: USING ADJECTIVES

Directions: Fill in each blank in the following sentences with an adjective. The adjective should describe the underlined noun next to the blank. Part of the first one is done as an example.

1. The *middle-aged* (what kind) men play ________ (how many) games of poker once a month.
2. They use ________ (what kind) cards and play on a ________ (what kind) table.
3. The game is played on the ________ (which one) Friday of each month.
4. During the ________ (what kind) game, ________ (how many) pounds of potato chips are eaten.

Answers start on page 199.

PUTTING YOUR SKILLS TO WORK

Directions: Take out your notebook again. Practice using adjectives in this exercise. First, do a quick brainstorming exercise. At the top of a sheet of paper, write your name or the name of a close friend or relative. Then write the first ten adjectives you can think of to describe the person you named. Finally, use at least five of those adjectives and write a paragraph about the person. Be sure to date your entry.

Here is a sample paragraph from a student's list that contained the adjectives *thoughtful, loving, funny, disorganized,* and *oldest.*

> Martha is a very **thoughtful** person who never forgets to send birthday cards. She is a **loving** person and a **funny** lady. However, she is also very **disorganized.** She is the **oldest** employee in her company, yet the boss refuses to let her retire.

☑ Writing Checklist

- ❑ Have you included five adjectives from your list?
- ❑ Do your sentences start with capital letters?
- ❑ Does each sentence have a punctuation mark at the end?

WHERE DO ADJECTIVES BELONG?

An adjective often comes right before the noun it describes.

EXAMPLE: The **happy** child ran through the house.

However, an adjective often can be found in another part of a sentence. You can tell it is an adjective because it describes the noun. It still tells you what kind, which one, or how many. Here is another example:

Tina is happy.

Write the word that describes Tina on this blank. ______________
Even though the word *happy* does not come before *Tina,* it is an adjective because it describes what kind of person she is.

EXERCISE 3: IDENTIFYING ADJECTIVES

Directions: The adjectives in the following sentences may come right before the nouns they describe, but they may not. Circle the adjective in each sentence. The noun that the adjective describes is underlined. The first one is done as an example.

1. Television can be (educational.)
2. The news is informative.
3. Many people watch the news.
4. Sometimes tired viewers go to sleep.
5. Shows about police and detectives are popular.
6. However, they can be violent.

Answers start on page 199.

WHAT IS AN ADVERB?

Adverbs are words that describe verbs. Adverbs can tell how, when, or where.

Here are three lists of adverbs.

How	When	Where
rapidly	today	outside
angrily	later	inside
happily	daily	there
fast	once	here
slowly	again	

Just as adjectives give more information about nouns, adverbs tell you more about verbs. Look at this sentence, which does not contain any adverbs.

Lynn will talk.

That sentence doesn't tell how, when, or where Lynn will talk. By adding an adverb after the verb *talk* you can give more specific information about the verb. The sentence has been rewritten below with a different adverb. Continue rewriting the sentence until you have sentences with adverbs that tell *how*, *when*, and *where*. You may use adverbs from the lists above.

Lynn will talk slowly. *(how)*

Lynn will talk ____________. *(how)*

Lynn will talk ____________. *(when)*

Lynn will talk ____________. *(where)*

Now that you have used three adverbs from the list, see if you can write one of each type using adverbs of your own.

Leon will walk ____________. *(how)*

Leon will walk ____________. *(when)*

Leon will walk ____________. *(where)*

EXERCISE 4: CHOOSING ADVERBS

Directions: Choose an adverb from the list below to describe each verb. Write the adverb in the blank. You will discover that it is possible to use some of the adverbs in more than one place. The first one is done as an example.

hysterically	before	outside	patiently	rapidly
threateningly	nervously	abruptly	strangely	down

1. Andrew laughed *nervously*.
2. He smiled ______________ the show started.
3. He grinned ______________ the theatre.
4. People looked ______________ at him.
5. Tears flowed ______________ from his eyes.
6. He laughed so much, he fell ______________.

Answers start on page 199.

EXERCISE 5: WRITING SENTENCES WITH ADVERBS

Directions: In this exercise you will write three groups of sentences. In each group of sentences, use adverbs that tell *how*, *when*, and *where*. One from each group is done as an example.

1. In this group, use adverbs with the verb *write*.

   a. *(how)* ______________________________

   b. *(when)* *We write daily.*

   c. *(where)* ______________________________

2. In this group, use adverbs with the verb *dance*.

   a. *(how)* *Melinda and Todd dance beautifully.*

   b. *(when)* ______________________________

   c. *where)* ______________________________

3. Finally, in this group, use adverbs with the verb *read*.

   a. *(how)* ______________________________

   b. *(when)* ______________________________

   c. *(where)* Sam will read here.

Answers start on page 199.

WHERE DO ADVERBS APPEAR?

An adverb can come right after the verb it describes. But often an adverb will be found in another part of the sentence. You can tell it is an adverb because it still describes the verb. It tells you how, where, or when. Here are three examples.

> **Angrily**, she turned her back to the group. *(how)*
>
> Eric bought a car **today**. *(when)*
>
> **Yesterday**, the softball team won first place **here**. *(when, where)*

EXERCISE 6: IDENTIFYING ADVERBS

Directions: Circle the adverb in each of the following sentences. There is one adverb in each sentence. The verb that the adverb describes is underlined. The first one is done as an example.

1. Commuters <u>drive</u> (far) to work.
2. Some <u>leave</u> early to miss traffic jams.
3. Many dangerously <u>ignore</u> the speed limit.
4. Mysteriously, police <u>appear</u> to give tickets.
5. A commuter can <u>look</u> everywhere and still not see the police.
6. A safe commuter always <u>travels</u> as if a traffic officer were his passenger.

Answers start on page 200.

ADJECTIVE OR ADVERB?

Adjectives and adverbs are both words that describe. In many cases, they are almost alike. Often a word that is an adjective can be changed to an adverb by adding two letters. These letters are *ly*. Here are two examples:

Adjective	Adverb
sad	sadly
beautiful	beautifully

However, if an adjective ends in *y*, you must change the *y* to *i* and then add the *ly*. Here are two examples:

Adjective	Adverb
angry	angrily
happy	happily

Here are adjectives and adverbs that are very much alike. Circle the adverbs in which *y* is changed to *i*.

Adjective	Adverb
brave	bravely
calm	calmly
hungry	hungrily
general	generally
busy	busily
mysterious	mysteriously
sad	sadly
thoughtful	thoughtfully
usual	usually

The way a word is used in a sentence tells you whether to use the adjective or the adverb form. To describe a noun, use an adjective. To describe a verb, use an adverb.

EXAMPLES:

The **sad** man walked down the street. *(adjective)*
The man walked **sadly** down the street. *(adverb)*

Shelley followed her **usual** route. *(adjective)*
Shelley **usually** followed this route. *(adverb)*

EXERCISE 7: CHOOSING ADJECTIVES OR ADVERBS

Directions: Underline the correct form for each sentence. One of the choices is an adjective, and the other is an adverb. If you are describing a noun, choose the adjective. If you are describing a verb, choose the adverb. The first one is done as an example.

1. Football season is *(fantastic, fantastically)* for the avid sports fan.
2. A fan prepares *(careful, carefully)* for each game.
3. He waits *(calm, calmly)* for the whistle that starts the game.
4. Around him, the *(excited, excitedly)* crowd cheers for their team.
5. He applauds *(loud, loudly)* when his team makes a touchdown.
6. Ten seconds before the end of the game, the quarterback throws a *(magnificent, magnificently)* pass for a touchdown, and the fan goes home grinning.

Answers start on page 200.

PUNCTUATING PERFECTLY: COMMAS IN A SERIES

Sometimes in your writing you may want to use several adjectives or adverbs to describe one noun or verb. How can you punctuate the series of adjectives or adverbs? Use commas to separate three or more items in a series.

EXAMPLE:
The **large, green, spotted, worm-eaten** apple fell from the tree.

Adjectives describing the apple are separated by commas in that sentence.

EXAMPLE:
The chorus began **slowly, carefully, quietly**, and **harmoniously**.

Where would you place commas in the following sentence, which contains three adverbs?

Nina Totenberg speaks calmly clearly and firmly.

You were right if you put commas after *calmly* and *clearly*.

Punctuate a sentence containing four adjectives.

> The long modern sleek curved building won an award for its design.

You should have put commas after *long*, *modern*, and *sleek*.

In addition to adjectives and adverbs, other kinds of words can be used in a series. In the following example, three nouns make up a series. Underline the items in the series. Notice how commas separate the items.

> Please bring coffee, tea, and cream to the meeting.

In that sentence, the items *coffee, tea,* and *cream* are separated by commas. Notice that no comma is placed before the first item *(coffee)* or after the last item (*cream*).

Remember this rule for using commas in a series.

> Commas are used after every item except the last one in a series of three or more items.

It is also very important to remember not to use a comma between only two items.

EXAMPLES:

> Jan and Mark are working today.
> Cincinnati or Austin will host the next cowhands convention.

Read the two sentences that follow. Add commas where necessary. Be sure not to add any extra commas.

> George swims runs and lifts weights to stay in shape.
>
> The Tigers and the Redskins will play a game on Monday.

The first sentence contains a series of three verbs *swims, runs,* and *lifts*. The second sentence needs no commas since only two teams are named.

EXERCISE 8: USING COMMAS IN A SERIES

Directions: Add commas to the following sentences wherever they are needed. Some sentences may not need any commas.

1. The women's club is planning a dinner and a play to celebrate its anniversary.
2. Also included in the program will be speakers awards and music.
3. Sue Almeda Fran Warner Lillian Rutledge and Vanessa Grogan are in charge of inviting guests.
4. Interested enthusiastic dedicated volunteers will be invited.
5. Their husbands or escorts will also be invited.
6. On the menu will be stuffed chicken breasts baked potatoes peas salad rolls ice cream and coffee.
7. The play will require the cooperation of talented interested well-rehearsed participants.

Answers start on page 200.

EXERCISE 9: WRITING SENTENCES WITH SERIES

Directions: Write sentences containing series (or lists) in response to the following. Make certain that you have at least three items separated by commas in each sentence.

1. Write a sentence listing what you will have for dinner one day this week.

   ____

2. Write a sentence using adjectives describing an interesting person you know. ____

Answers start on page 200.

PUNCTUATING PERFECTLY: LETTERS

In your daily life, you may find you want to write two kinds of letters. A *personal letter* is written to stay in touch with someone, to invite someone to an event, or to thank someone for a gift or a kindness. A *business letter* is written to take care of a business matter. You might need to write one to apply for a job, order a gift, or complain about a product or service.

Writing a Personal Letter

In a personal letter, commas are used in a number of places. Use commas correctly in the date, the greeting, and the closing of the letter. Study the sample personal letter. The commas have been circled.

July 14, 1996 — DATE

Dear Georgette, — GREETING

It has been a long time since I wrote to you. Everyone in the neighborhood misses you. We wish you had not moved away. We would like you to visit us this summer. Can you stay with me from August 7 through August 15? I will look forward to your answer. If you can be here, we can go to the local block party. — BODY

Love, — CLOSING

Samantha — SIGNATURE

Commas are used in three places in the sample personal letter:

1. in the date, between the day of the month and the year (July 14, 1996)
2. in the greeting (Dear Georgette,)
3. after the closing (Love,)

The greeting of any letter will usually be Dear ______________. The closing can vary to fit the person receiving the letter. Close a personal letter with any appropriate word. Words like *Love, Sincerely, Affectionately, Fondly, Yours truly*, and other expressions you like to use can end a personal letter. The first word of the closing is always capitalized.

Using the sample letter as a guide, rearrange the parts of the letter on the following page so it is set up and punctuated properly. Rewrite the letter in the blanks.

Affectionately *Susan*

Thank you for the great record album. It completes my collection of oldies but goodies from the sixties. Maybe you will get to listen to all the songs with me before long.

May 10 1997 Dear Tommy

________________ DATE

________________ GREETING

____

____

____

____

____ BODY

____

____

____

______________________ CLOSING

______________________ SIGNATURE

Writing a Business Letter

A business letter is very similar to a personal letter. However, there are a few more parts to a business letter. It should include your address (called the *return address*), the address you are writing to (called the *inside address*), and a typed or printed name under your signature. On the following page is a sample business letter. The punctuation marks have been circled.

15 Tulip Place RETURN
Chicago, IL 60604 ADDRESS
July 14, 1997 DATE

Mr. James West
Western Fields Inc. INSIDE
313 East St. ADDRESS
Chicago, IL 60607

Dear Mr. West: GREETING
Thank you for interviewing me for the hostess position in your company's dining room. After speaking with you, I am sure I would enjoy working at Western Fields Inc. My past food service experience would make me a valuable asset to the company. I look forward to hearing from you in the near future. BODY

Sincerely, CLOSING

Ramona Jones SIGNATURE

Ramona Jones NAME

The business letter format is more detailed than the personal letter format. Here is how punctuation is used:

1. The return address and inside address have a comma between the name of the city and the state (Chicago, IL).
2. The greeting has a colon after the man's name (Dear Mr. West:).
3. A comma follows the closing (Sincerely,). More formal words are used as closings in business letters. *Sincerely* and *Yours truly* are very often used.

Read the short business letter that follows. Then, using the letter to Mr. James West as a sample, put in all the missing punctuation.

227 March Ave.
Rockport MA 08642

December 13 1997

Ms. S. J. Reed
Lightner's Logging Co.
234 Pine Rd.
Rockport MA 08642

Dear Ms. Reed
This is to inform you that the sweater I ordered is too small.
I am returning the sweater to exchange it for a size 44. Please send the larger sweater right away.

Sincerely

Hank Greene

Did you place a comma between the city and state in both the return address and the inside address? Did you place a comma between the day and the year in the date? Is there a colon after the greeting? Do you have a comma after the closing? If so, you have correctly punctuated the letter.

EXERCISE 10: CHAPTER REVIEW

Part 1

Directions: Find the mistake in each sentence. Circle the mistake and rewrite each sentence correctly in the space provided. The first one is done as an example.

1. Ruth is a happily person.
   Ruth is a happy person.
2. The race car moved quick around the track.
   ____
3. Nuts bolts wrenches and tools were thrown around the shop.
   ____
4. The men, and the women agreed that life moves too rapidly.
   ____
5. The business is located in Anchorage Alaska.
   ____
6. The trustworthy young bright babysitter raised her fee.
   ____

7. The soldier looked brave into the eyes of his captors.

____

Part 2

Directions: In this exercise, a part of each sentence is underlined. After the sentence, you will find three possible ways to write the underlined section. The first choice is always the same as the underlined part of the sentence. Choose the best correction and fill in the box under **a**, **b**, or **c** to indicate your answer. The first one is done as an example.

	a	b	c
1. The united states often allows people from other countries to come here to live. **a.** united states **b.** united States **c.** United States	☐	☐	■
2. These People come here looking for opportunities. **a.** People come **b.** People comes **c.** people come	☐	☐	☐
3. They comes from countries like the former U.S.S.R, Poland, China, Mexico, and India. **a.** They comes **b.** They come **c.** Them come	☐	☐	☐
4. One of the first things many immigrants wants to do is learn to speak English. **a.** immigrants wants **b.** Immigrants want **c.** immigrants want	☐	☐	☐
5. Immigrants have difficulty with the language. **a.** Immigrants have **b.** Immigrants has **c.** Immigrant's have	☐	☐	☐
6. An immigrant has to find a new job housing, and friends. **a.** job housing, and **b.** job, housing, and **c.** job housing and	☐	☐	☐

Answers start on page 200.

YOUR TURN TO WRITE: WRITING LETTERS

Take out your writing folder or notebook. Write two short letters for this exercise. One will be a business letter. The other will be a personal letter. They should follow the forms you studied on pages 156–159.

You can use stationery and mail one or both of the letters.

PUTTING YOUR SKILLS TO WORK

Part 1: The Business Letter

Directions: For this part of the exercise, you are to write a short business letter. You may write to a company about a matter of your choosing, or you may use the following suggestion.

Write a letter requesting a copy of the *Consumer Information Catalog.* Write to S. James, Consumer Information Center, P.O. Box 100, Pueblo, CO 81002. If you mail the letter, the Consumer Information Center will send you this catalog of government publications that might be helpful to you.

Part 2: The Personal Letter

Directions: Write a letter to someone you haven't seen in a long time describing your latest vacation, your house or apartment, your car, or a person in your life right now. In this letter use adjectives, adverbs, and items in a series. Be as specific as possible with the descriptions.

Writing Checklist

- ❑ Does your business letter have a return address, a date, an inside address, a greeting, a body, a closing, a signature, and a name?
- ❑ Does your personal letter have a date, a greeting, a body, a closing, and a signature?
- ❑ Is the punctuation correct?
- ❑ Did you use verbs and pronouns correctly?

7 COMBINING SENTENCES

JOURNAL WRITING: USING YOUR IMAGINATION

Most people spend time fantasizing. Does being a champion wrestler, a shift foreman, a glamorous movie star, or a multibillionaire fit your secret fantasy? Does life in the fast lane seem to be calling you, or are you ready to slow down and watch life from an easy chair?

Here is your chance to think through who or what you have always dreamed about being. Use one of the techniques learned earlier in the section to get your thoughts started. Try clustering or brainstorming. Go back to the beginning of Chapter 2 or Chapter 5 if you want to review one of these methods.

JOURNAL ENTRY

Directions: First, put down the name of your desired identity and brainstorm your thoughts about that identity. Then organize your thoughts. After that, write one or more paragraphs on who you would be if you could be anyone in the world. Remember, when you fantasize, you can be anything you want to be.

LANGUAGE SKILLS: COMBINING SENTENCES

COMPOUND SUBJECTS AND PREDICATES

Sentences in which the subjects or predicates have two or more parts will be the topic of this section. Compound subjects and compound predicates will expand your knowledge of sentence structure.

Compound Subjects

A sentence has a compound subject when the subject is in two or more parts. The following sentences have compound subjects. Each part of the subject in each sentence is in **bold type.**

> **Ray** and **Ted** have been going to junior college for one year.
> **Their counselors**, **their teachers**, and **their families** want them to continue their education.

In each of those sentences, the subjects share the same predicate. When you have two sentences with the same or very similar information, often you can combine the subjects.

EXAMPLES:

Ray complained about the cafeteria's food. Ted complained about the cafeteria's food.

Ray and Ted complained about the cafeteria's food.

Read the following pair of sentences. Then, on the blank lines, combine them into one sentence with a compound subject.

The dietitian thought they had valid complaints. The cook thought they had valid complaints.

____

____

You should have written this sentence: *The dietitian and the cook thought they had valid complaints.*

Compound Predicates

Just as you can combine subjects of sentences with similar or related information, you can combine predicates that have the same subject. When you do this, you have a ***compound predicate***.

EXAMPLES:

Ted works in the mornings. Ted studies in the evenings.

Ted works in the mornings and studies in the evenings.

Ray belongs to the Spanish Club. He is its treasurer.

Ray belongs to the Spanish Club and is its treasurer.

Now try combining the following pair of sentences into one sentence with a compound predicate. Write the combined sentence on the blank lines.

The prison library opens early in the morning.
It quickly fills with students.

____

____

You should have written this sentence: *The prison library opens early in the morning and quickly fills with students.*

EXERCISE 1: IDENTIFYING COMPOUND SUBJECTS AND PREDICATES

Directions: Read the following sentences. Decide whether each sentence has a compound subject or compound predicate and underline the compound parts. In the blank, write *CS* if there is a compound subject or *CP* if there is a compound predicate. The first one is done as an example.

__CS__ 1. The immigrants and their host families met at the airport.

_____ 2. They were happy to see each other and were eager to get acquainted.

_____ 3. American food, clothing, and housing seemed strange to the people from other countries.

Answers start on page 200.

EXERCISE 2: COMPOUNDING SUBJECTS AND PREDICATES

Directions: Using a compound subject or compound predicate, combine the following pairs of sentences. The first one is done as an example.

1. Sharon wrote a letter to her parents during lunch.
   She mailed it on her way home.

   Sharon wrote a letter to her parents during lunch and mailed it on her way home.

2. Sharon planned to visit her parents for Thanksgiving.
   Sharon's brother planned to visit them for Thanksgiving, too.

   ____

   ____

3. They were looking forward to seeing their parents.
   They could hardly wait to taste their mother's cooking.

   ____

   ____

Answers start on page 201.

USING CONJUNCTIONS TO COMBINE SENTENCES

Sentences that contain related ideas can be combined to make longer, more interesting sentences. The sentences do not have to have the same subject or the same predicate to be combined.

EXAMPLE:
Rosa lost her sewing job. She has no other skills.
Rosa lost her sewing job, **and** she has no other skills.

In that example, both subjects and both predicates are in the new sentence. You can combine two related sentences by keeping both sentences and putting a joining word between them. These joining words are called ***conjunctions***.

Here are seven common conjunctions and some examples showing how they are used. Notice that a comma comes before the conjunction in each of the example sentences.

Conjunctions

To add information, use *and.*

The night was dark and stormy, **and** the lights went out.

To show a contrast, use *but* or *yet*.

The Laundromat was closed, **but** the manager let me in.
This coat is ten years old, **yet** people still admire it.

To show a cause, and then the effect, use *so*.

The drain was clogged, **so** Margaret called a plumber.

To show the effect, and then the cause, use *for.*

They got a new kitten, **for** their cat had disappeared.

To show two alternatives, use *or.*

Either I'll go to the party, **or** I'll stay home and study.

To show two negatives, use *nor.*

The sun isn't going to come out, **nor** will it rain.

Choosing the Right Conjunction

When you choose a conjunction, be careful to choose one that shows how the two thoughts are related.

EXAMPLE: I ran for the bus, **but** I missed it.

The conjunction *but* shows the contrast between the two thoughts. The person did all he could, but he was not able to reach the bus in time. If he had written, "I ran for the bus, *so* I missed it," the sentence wouldn't make sense. Now look at another example. Notice the conjunction *and.*

Tina joined an aerobics class, and she loves exercising.

You would not say, "Tina joined an aerobics class, *but* she loves exercising." That would make it sound as though aerobics were not exercising.

Read the following sentences. Choose the best conjunction for each (*and, or, for, nor, so, but,* or *yet*). Write it in the blank between the two complete thoughts.

Ed wants to exercise more, ______ he is joining a health club.

Did you choose *so?* If you did, you realized that the first thought is the cause and the second thought is the effect.

Start helping with chores around the house, ______ you will have to move out.

Did you choose *or?* The two thoughts are alternatives—either one or the other will happen.

Don't Overuse Commas

As you have seen, when you join two complete thoughts with a conjunction, a comma comes before the conjunction. You use a comma before a conjunction only when you join two complete thoughts. Remember that a complete thought has *both* a subject and a verb. Here are two sentences that do not contain two complete thoughts. Instead, they have compound predicates.

I ran for the bus **but** missed it.

The second part of the compound predicate, *missed it,* is not a complete thought, so no comma is used before *but.*

Tina joined an aerobics class **and** loves exercising.

The second part of the compound predicate, *loves exercising,* is not a complete thought, so no comma is used before *and.*

Three sentences follow. Only one of them has a conjunction combining two complete thoughts. Find that sentence and put the comma in the correct place.

The car broke down on the highway and Sam had it towed.
The car broke down on the highway but started up again right away.
The car broke down on the highway and was towed.

Did you place your comma in the first sentence after *highway?* The second and third sentences do not have two complete thoughts, so you do not need to add a comma.

EXERCISE 3: PRACTICING WITH CONJUNCTIONS AND COMMAS

Directions: Circle the conjunction in each of these sentences and add commas in the correct places. Each of these sentences contains two complete thoughts. The first one is done as an example.

1. Thrift stores are great places to shop, (and) they have many bargains.
2. Some of the customers who visit them have very little money but others just want to find a good buy.
3. Nice clothes sell quickly so smart customers shop on the day new items are stocked.
4. Men and women go to these stores for clothes but children like to look for toys.
5. Some shops are open at odd hours yet shoppers fill the aisles.

Answers start on page 201.

EXERCISE 4: COMBINING SENTENCES

Directions: Rewrite the following sentences. Add a conjunction and a comma to each set of sentences to form one combined sentence. The first one is done as an example.

and but yet for so or nor

1. Children are fun. Many people enjoy working with them.

   Children are fun, and many people enjoy working with them.

2. Horses are farm animals. People keep them in cities.

   ____

3. Drugs are a serious problem. Many teenagers think they are harmless.

___

___

Answers start on page 201.

PUTTING YOUR SKILLS TO WORK

Directions: Write two short related sentences on each of the following subjects: food, friends, sports. (Or you may pick three topics of your choosing.) First write the short sentences and then rewrite them using a comma and a conjunction to join them. Remember, the conjunctions are *and, but, or, nor, for, so,* and *yet.*

EXAMPLE:

Hot chocolate is a great drink. It has hundreds of calories.
Hot chocolate is a great drink, but it has hundreds of calories.

Write your sentences in your writing folder or notebook and remember to date your work. You will have three sets of sentences that are not combined, and you will have three combined sentences.

☑ Writing Checklist

- ❑ Does each of your combined sentences have a comma before the conjunction?
- ❑ Does each combined sentence have two complete thoughts?
- ❑ Have you chosen a conjunction that shows how your thoughts are related?

USING CONNECTORS

Connectors are another group of joining words you can use to combine sentences. Some common connectors are listed below. Each one has a specific meaning.

Connectors

To show contrast, use *however, nevertheless,* or *instead.*

Brad wants to be a team player; **however**, he loves glory.
Anita was grounded; **nevertheless**, she went out.
Yim wanted to go to school; **instead**, she got a job.

To add more information, use *furthermore* or *moreover.*

You are a good friend; **furthermore**, you are my best friend.
Martin wants to help; **moreover**, he insists on washing the dishes.

To show a cause, and then its effect, use *therefore* or *consequently.*

We love children; **therefore**, we adopted six of them.
Alan enters every contest he can; **consequently**, he often wins.

Punctuating Connectors

Notice that there is a semicolon (;) in front of each connector and a comma after it in each of the sample sentences. Study the following sentences. Circle the connector in each sentence and add semicolons and commas where needed. The first one is done for you.

Todd's chair broke yesterday*;* (therefore*,*) he has to fix it.
Rhonda hurried otherwise she would be late for work.
Amy is 87 today furthermore she intends to live to be 107.

Did you circle *otherwise* and *furthermore?* They are the connectors, and each one should have a semicolon in front of it and a comma following it.

Choosing the Right Connector

Always be careful to choose a connector that shows the relationship between the thoughts in the combined sentence. Look at this example. How does *therefore* show the relationship between the two thoughts?

The women like exercising; **therefore**, they often go to the gym.

In that sentence, *therefore* is used to show that going to the gym is the *effect* of the women's liking exercising.

Now you try. What connector would work well in the following sentence? (See the box above.) Write a logical connector in the blank.

Steve needs a new car; ________________, he has no money.

Did you write *however?* It shows the *contrast* between needing a new car and not having the money to buy one.

EXERCISE 5: CORRECTING SENTENCES WITH CONNECTORS

Directions: In this exercise, a part of each sentence is underlined. After the sentence, you will find three possible ways to write the underlined section. The first option is always the same as the underlined part of the sentence. Choose the option that makes the sentence correct and fill in the box under **a**, **b**, or **c** to indicate your answer. The first one is done as an example.

	a	b	c
1. Kenny has played the banjo since he was <u>three, instead; he</u> is the best banjo picker in town.	☐	■	☐

a. three, instead; he
b. three; consequently, he
c. three, consequently; he

2. The auto industry offers high-paying <u>jobs; therefore, applications</u> have increased. ☐ ☐ ☐

a. jobs; therefore, applications
b. jobs; therefore; applications
c. jobs, therefore, applications

3. I frequently lose my house <u>keys; therefore, I</u> lock my car keys in my car at least once a week. ☐ ☐ ☐

a. keys; therefore, I
b. keys; furthermore, I
c. keys, furthermore; I

4. For some of the armed services, a diploma is <u>required, however; not</u> all branches have this requirement. ☐ ☐ ☐

a. required, however; not
b. required; however, not
c. required; however not

5. Sarah is really <u>bright moreover; she</u> always puts herself down. ☐ ☐ ☐

a. bright moreover; she
b. bright; nevertheless, she
c. bright; moreover, she

Answers start on page 201.

EXERCISE 6: WRITING SENTENCES WITH CONNECTORS

Directions: Join the following sentences using connectors. Remember that the connector that you use has to make sense. Be certain to put the correct punctuation in each sentence.

therefore	**nevertheless**	**furthermore**	**consequently**
moreover	**however**	**instead**	

1. The police searched the neighborhood for drugs. They vowed to jail all dealers.

____

____

2. After the race, the drivers were exhausted. They went to the party.

____

____

3. The Joneses were evicted from their apartment. Mr. Jones lost his job.

____

____

4. Dorothy thought she would get a small raise. She was surprised with a ten percent salary increase.

____

____

5. Electric heat is very expensive. We keep the thermostats turned down to 65 degrees.

____

____

Answers start on page 201.

PUTTING YOUR SKILLS TO WORK

Directions: Take out your writing folder or notebook. Write three sentences using connectors. Use any three of these words: *consequently, furthermore, however, instead, moreover, nevertheless*, and *therefore*. These words must join two related thoughts. You can use your own ideas. Or choose from the following ideas: your family, an accident, your best friend, television, or exercise.

After writing the sentences, circle the connectors and underline the complete thoughts.

☑ Writing Checklist

- ❑ Do you have two complete thoughts in each sentence?
- ❑ Is there a semicolon before each connector?
- ❑ Is there a comma following each connector?
- ❑ Did you use a connector that makes sense in your sentence?

USING SUBORDINATING CONJUNCTIONS

Often you will be able to combine sentences by using another group of conjunctions that show cause, contrast, condition, or time. When these words are used, one part of the sentence becomes dependent on the other part to make sense. Here is a list of some ***subordinating conjunctions*** and examples showing how they are used.

Subordinating Conjunctions

To show cause and effect, use *because* or *since.*

Because she couldn't dance, Sandra stayed home.
Peter took the job **since** the pay was good.

To show contrast, use *though* or *although.*

Though Harry was elected, he doesn't feel victorious.
The Bennets rented the apartment **although** it was too small.

To show condition, use *if.*

If Blair gets home on time, we will go to the game.

To show time, use *when, after,* or *before.*

When the cows come home, Gretna will milk them.
After she milks the cows, Jerry will feed them.
Kenton will sample the milk **before** Kimmy scrubs the milkhouse.

If the subordinating conjunction is the first word in the sentence, place a comma between the two ideas. If the subordinating conjunction is in the middle of the sentence, you should not use a comma.

Now practice using the subordinating conjunctions. The following examples show how to combine two sentences using these conjunctions.

Because and *since* join a cause to an effect.

Sam had no money. He couldn't buy a soda.
Because Sam had no money, he couldn't buy a soda.

I refuse to go to that store. Everything there is overpriced.
I refuse to go to that store **since** everything there is overpriced.

Though and *although* show a contradiction between two ideas.

Running in marathons is exhausting. I enjoy it.
Though running in marathons is exhausting, I enjoy it.

Herman took the job. It meant a huge salary cut.
Herman took the job **although** it meant a huge salary cut.

If shows a condition and a result. If one thing happens, another thing will happen. *If* is attached to the condition.

If the weather is good, we will go swimming tomorrow.
We can go to the park **if** the baby wakes up by 8:30 A.M.

When, after, and *before* are time words. *When* shows that two actions are taking place at the same time. *After* and *before* show the order of two actions. You can tell your reader which action came first.

When you do the dishes, I'll vacuum the floor.
After you do the dishes, I'll vacuum the floor.
I'll vacuum the floor **before** you do the dishes.

EXERCISE 7: COMPLETING SENTENCES WITH SUBORDINATING CONJUNCTIONS

Directions: Fill in the blanks in the following sentences with one of the subordinating conjunctions from the list below. More than one of the conjunctions will work in some sentences. The first one is done as an example.

because	**though**	**if**	**after**
since	**although**	**when**	**before**

1. Bruno will go to work today ____*if*____ he is feeling better.

2. __________ the examination was over, the doctor wrote the report.

3. Fast food restaurants like to hire adults __________ adults are more dependable workers.

4. __________ Bob had retired, his employer asked him to return to work.

Answers start on page 201.

EXERCISE 8: WRITING SENTENCES WITH SUBORDINATING CONJUNCTIONS

Directions: Combine each pair of sentences, using one of the subordinating conjunctions in **bold type**. If the conjunction starts with a capital letter, put it at the beginning of the sentence. Be sure to punctuate your sentences correctly. The first one is done as an example.

if **Though** **Since** **When** **Before** **although**

1. David gets home. We will show him the pictures.
   When David gets home, we will show him the pictures.
2. Chan went to the doctor yesterday. She doesn't feel any better today.
3. The Jellybeans recorded their first big hit in 1964. They were completely unknown.
4. The police will be able to arrest the drug dealer. Maura can identify him in a lineup.
5. Margaret mowed the lawn. Greg agreed to do the raking.
6. Jenka gave me the money. She needed it herself.

Answers start on pages 201.

PUTTING YOUR SKILLS TO WORK

Directions: This exercise is for your writing folder or notebook. Put the date at the top of your paper. Write five sentences using the subordinating conjunctions. Use any five of the following conjunctions:

because if since when though after although before

These words must combine two related ideas in a way that makes sense. You can use your own ideas in the sentences. If you need suggestions, write sentences about these topics: your city, your neighborhood, your vacation, your home.

Writing Checklist

- ❑ Did you combine two ideas in each of your sentences?
- ❑ If a sentence started with a subordinating conjunction, did you separate the two ideas with a comma?
- ❑ If a subordinating conjunction came in the middle of a sentence, did you remember not to separate the ideas with a comma?

PUNCTUATING PERFECTLY: REVIEW OF COMMAS AND SEMICOLONS IN COMBINED SENTENCES

You have been combining related sentences by using three types of joining words. When you used conjunctions like *and, but, or,* and *yet,* you placed a comma in front of the conjunction.

Loretta pushed down the brake pedal, **but** the truck didn't stop.

When you used connectors like *however, nevertheless, consequently,* and *moreover,* you placed a semicolon in front of the connector and a comma after it.

Loretta pushed down the brake pedal; **however**, the truck didn't stop.

Then you used subordinating conjunctions like *because, though, if,* and *after*. You separated the two thoughts with a comma if the sentence began with a subordinating conjunction. If the subordinating conjunction came in the middle of the sentence, you didn't use a comma.

> The truck roared down the hill **because** its brakes failed.
> **Because** its brakes failed, the truck roared down the hill.

EXERCISE 9: PRACTICING PUNCTUATION

Directions: Add the correct punctuation to each of the following sentences. Punctuate all the different kinds of sentences you have studied in this chapter. The first one is done as an example.

1. Being new in town is not easy*;* however*,* there are many support groups.
2. Churches form newcomers groups and community agencies do the same thing.
3. People go to the meetings because they want to make new friends.
4. Some women feel that they will appear to be looking for men consequently they won't attend these meetings.
5. Many men fear that same thing so they stay home, too.
6. Others are more optimistic therefore they go to meet people of both sexes.
7. When people have interests in common they may develop good relationships.

Answers start on page 202.

EXERCISE 10: CHAPTER REVIEW

Part 1

Use the information in this chapter on combining sentences. First answer as many questions as possible without looking back in the chapter. Then go back through the chapter to complete any remaining answers.

Directions: Read the following sentences. Then combine them, as directed, in three different ways.

Getting up for work is not easy. I am usually late.

1. Use *so* with a comma to combine the two sentences.

____

2. Use a semicolon with *therefore* to combine the two sentences.

____

3. Use *Because* and a comma to combine the two sentences.

____

Directions: The underlined parts of the following sentences may contain errors. Select the choice that makes each sentence correct. The first choice will always be the same as the underlined part.

a b c

4. Farsighted adults plan for <u>retirement; and they</u> hope to spend many years enjoying themselves. ☐ ☐ ☐
   a. retirement; and they
   b. retirement, and they
   c. retirement; and, they

5. Workers try to save <u>money, furthermore some</u> businesses offer excellent payroll deduction plans. ☐ ☐ ☐
   a. money, furthermore some
   b. money; furthermore, some
   c. money; furthermore some

6. Businesses offer profit-sharing <u>plans; consequently the</u> employees feel they are a part of the company. ☐ ☐ ☐
   a. plans; consequently the
   b. plans; consequently, the
   c. plans, consequently, the

a b c

7. It is helpful to have savings; instead, you reach retirement age. ☐ ☐ ☐
   a. savings; instead, you
   b. savings; furthermore, you
   c. savings when you

8. Unfortunately, it is not always possible to save earnings because they are needed to pay bills. ☐ ☐ ☐
   a. earnings because
   b. earnings; because
   c. earnings. Because

Part 2

Directions: Find the mistake in each of the following sentences and fill in the box that corresponds to the letter of the mistake. The first one is done for you.

a b c

1. Peanut butter (a), one of America's favorite foods (b), are (c) high in protein. ☐ ☐ ■

2. The nutritionist said (a), "Stress (b) can be relieved with vitamins (c). ☐ ☐ ☐

3. The team members is (a) negotiating their (b) contracts in closed individual sessions (c). ☐ ☐ ☐

4. The students or the teacher (a) are (b) in charge of the report (c). ☐ ☐ ☐

5. Her (a) planned to purchase chips (b), pretzels (c), and dip for the party. ☐ ☐ ☐

6. The womens' (a) support group meets (b) every Wednesday (c). ☐ ☐ ☐

Answers start on page 202.

YOUR TURN TO WRITE: WRITING A PARAGRAPH

Take out your writing notebook or folder again. Remember to date the assignment. Write a paragraph on a consumer issue or a current event. Pick one of the following topics:

- A wise car buyer shops around.
- It's best to buy clothes out of season.
- Vote for ______!
- Join the campaign to stop hunger.
- Drugs are everyone's problem.
- Your choice

PUTTING YOUR SKILLS TO WORK

Directions: Choose a topic that you can relate to and tell why you feel the way you do. Write a paragraph using short sentences. Write at least eight sentences. Then try to combine some of the sentences in your paragraph, using the sentence-combining techniques you have been learning in this chapter. Use the charts on pages 165, 169, and 172 to help you choose good joining words.

Here is a sample from part of a paragraph on voting for a favorite candidate. The first paragraph began as follows:

> Vote for Olga for mayor. She is the best candidate. She has lived here all her life. Olga knows our town very well. She is a Democrat. She gets along with Republicans. . . .

Now look at the same paragraph with combined sentences.

> Vote for Olga for mayor because she is the best candidate. She has lived here all her life and knows our town very well. She is a Democrat; however, she gets along with Republicans. . . .

Spend enough time working on your paragraph to develop it thoroughly. The sentences will relate to each other, and you will be able to combine them easily. Pick your topic and begin writing.

Writing Checklist

- ❑ Do you have at least eight sentences in your paragraph?
- ❑ Have you used sentence-combining methods correctly?
- ❑ Have you combined sentences so that their relationship is clear?

8 Sentences and Paragraphs

JOURNAL WRITING: TODAY'S CONCERNS OR YESTERDAY'S MEMORIES?

Some people spend much of their time thinking about current concerns. Others are caught up in things that happened to them in the past. This journal entry will give you an opportunity to work through one of those two themes. Use any technique you like to start writing.

If you are writing about your current concerns, would you like to see a woman president? Would you like to see the government train people on welfare for new jobs? Perhaps your concerns are more personal. Are you worried about your family? Would you like to tell your neighbors how much you appreciate them? Here's an opportunity to speak your piece.

Maybe you would rather write about the past. Write about your favorite childhood memory or another event from your past. Was there a special birthday celebration? Did someone surprise you with a visit? Were you the class clown in school? Were you good at sports?

JOURNAL ENTRY

Directions: Decide on a topic. Use one of the suggestions above or a topic of your own. Cluster, brainstorm, or just write everything you can about the topic. Enjoy saying what's on your mind or reliving a memory.

LANGUAGE SKILLS: NEW TOPICS IN SENTENCE STRUCTURE

In this chapter, you will be practicing two new ways to put ideas together correctly by using describing phrases and parallel structure. Using these techniques will help to make your sentences more interesting.

USING DESCRIBING PHRASES CORRECTLY

A describing phrase can tell you something about a noun or a pronoun. You have seen examples of describing phrases in Chapter 5. In this chapter, you'll learn more about writing sentences with describing phrases.

Describing phrases must always be placed as close as possible to the word they describe. Here's an example:

> Mona entered the office at midnight. She was carrying the stolen papers.
>
> **Carrying the stolen papers**, Mona entered the office at midnight.

In the combined sentence, the describing phrase *Carrying the stolen papers* tells you something about *Mona*. Therefore, that phrase is placed next to *Mona*.

A describing phrase is ***misplaced*** if it is not placed next to the noun or pronoun it describes. Here is an example of a sentence with a misplaced describing phrase:

> The cowboy entered the saloon wearing matching pistols.

The describing phrase, *wearing matching pistols*, is placed next to *saloon*. The wording of the sentence tells you that the saloon was wearing matching pistols! But your common sense tells you that the cowboy must be wearing them. The sentence could be rewritten clearly in either of the following two ways:

> **Wearing matching pistols**, the cowboy entered the saloon.
>
> The cowboy **wearing matching pistols** entered the saloon.

In both of those examples, the describing phrase *wearing matching pistols* is next to *cowboy*, the word it describes.

On the following page is an example of what happens when describing phrases are misplaced. Look at the picture and read the sentence below it.

We watched the batter hit a home run from box seats.

Your common sense tells you that the batter is not hitting a home run from box seats. The describing phrase, which is in **bold type**, is placed next to the underlined words they describe.

CORRECT: **From box seats,** <u>we</u> watched the batter hit a home run.

Three sentences follow. A describing phrase to insert in each sentence is also given. First underline the word that each phrase describes. Then rewrite the sentences, placing each describing phrase as close as possible to the word it should describe. The first one is done for you.

Please put the <u>presents</u> under the tree. *(that you wrapped)*

Please put the presents that you wrapped under the tree.

Albert saw a dog chasing a cat. *(walking to work)*

____

____

Danny put the ring on Carmen's finger. *(worn by his grandmother)*

____

____

Did you rewrite the sentences like this?

> **Walking to work,** Albert saw a dog chasing a cat.
> Danny put the ring **worn by his grandmother** on Carmen's finger.

EXERCISE 1: IDENTIFYING MISPLACED DESCRIBING PHRASES

Directions: Read the following sentences. Circle the letter of the sentence in each pair that is written correctly. In each correct sentence, underline the describing phrase and circle the word it describes. The first one is done as an example.

1. (a.) The (woman) in purple shoes caught the Frisbee.
   b. The woman caught the Frisbee in purple shoes.

2. a. The desk that is 500 years old was bought in an antique shop near Chicago.
   b. The desk was bought in an antique shop near Chicago that is 500 years old.

3. a. The people yawned through the movie sitting in the front row.
   b. The people sitting in the front row yawned through the movie.

Answers start on page 202.

EXERCISE 2: WRITING SENTENCES WITH DESCRIBING PHRASES

Directions: Insert the describing phrase into each of the following sentences. Be sure to place the phrase next to the word it describes. The first one is done as an example.

1. He let the puppy out. *(wearing only his pajamas and slippers)*
   Wearing only his pajamas and slippers, he let the puppy out.

2. The actors were getting ready to face the audience. *(in their dressing rooms)*
   ____

3. The salesman handed the slacks to Geraldine. *(with the red stripes)*
   ____

4. The team fumbled the ball in the second half. *(in blue uniforms)*
   ____

Answers start on page 202.

PARALLEL STRUCTURE

When writing sentences, you need to use parallel structure to list more than one thing or idea. ***Parallel structure*** means that items are in the same form.

INCORRECT: John likes **to fish** and **boating**.

The forms of the two items are different: *to fish* and *boating*.

CORRECT: John likes **fishing** and **boating**.

The words *fishing* and *boating* both end in *ing*.

CORRECT: John likes **to fish** and **to boat**.

Here's another example.

INCORRECT: The cartoon was funny, short, and was unusual.

The third part of the list now contains a verb *(was)* instead of just an adjective.

CORRECT: The cartoon was **funny, short**, and **unusual**.

The words *funny, short*, and *unusual* are all adjectives that describe *cartoon*.

Here's a sentence that contains longer parallel parts. Underline the two phrases that are in parallel form.

CORRECT: The employer promised to increase salaries and give more coffee breaks.

The two phrases are *increase salaries* and *give more coffee breaks*. Both phrases begin with a verb in the same form.

One of the following sentences has correct parallel structure. The other two do not. On the lines on the next page, rewrite each *incorrect* sentence so that it has parallel structure. Your goal is to choose one form for the parallel parts and follow through with that form.

1. When he was twenty-one, Richard loved dancing, skiing, and to swim.
2. Dorothy is going to school and learning to write.
3. Singing in a rock group and to star in a movie are Claude's goals.

____

____

____

____

SENTENCE 1—CORRECT WAYS:

- When he was twenty-one, Richard loved **dancing, skiing,** and **swimming.**
- When he was twenty-one, Richard loved **to dance, to ski,** and **to swim.**

SENTENCE 3—CORRECT WAYS:

- **Singing** in a rock group and **starring** in a movie are Claude's goals.
- **To sing** in a rock group and **to star** in a movie are Claude's goals.

EXERCISE 3: IDENTIFYING CORRECT PARALLEL STRUCTURE

Directions: Circle the letter of the sentence that has correct parallel structure in each pair below. Underline the parallel parts in the correct sentence. The first one is done as an example.

1. a. Harold loves working, playing, and to watch good movies.
(b.) Harold loves working, playing, and watching good movies.

2. a. Burt can't decide if he wants to be a police officer, a paramedic, or a firefighter.
b. Burt can't decide if he wants to be a police officer, a paramedic, or work for the fire department.

3. a. Mary Jo draws exquisitely and painting superbly.
b. Mary Jo draws exquisitely and paints superbly.

4. a. Alice's car always stalls out and is leaving her stranded.
b. Alice's car always stalls out and leaves her stranded.

Answers start on page 202.

EXERCISE 4: CORRECTING PARALLEL STRUCTURE

Directions: The following sentences contain errors in parallel structure. Rewrite each sentence with correct parallel structure.

1. Homer went to Texas, got a job, built a house, and he got married.

   ____

2. Getting rich and to buy a car are Dorothy's only interests.

   ____

3. Mystery stories have intrigue, excitement, and full of suspense.

   ____

4. Wendy works very hard but is having fun, too.

   ____

Answers start on page 202.

JOURNAL WRITING: PERFECTING PARAGRAPHS

MATCHING VERBS IN A PARAGRAPH

Verb tenses show how things happen in time. In Chapter 4 you studied past, present, and future tenses. When you are writing, the verbs in a paragraph must show the time element of that paragraph.

EXAMPLE—PAST TENSE:

> Mardi **won** first prize in the cooking contest. She **baked** a shoofly pie. It **looked** scrumptious. The Iowa State Fair judges **thought** it **was** delectable.

Notice that every verb in that paragraph is written in the past tense. That tells you that everything happened in the past.

EXAMPLE—PRESENT TENSE:

> The bus **is** very dependable. It **arrives** on time every morning. In bad weather, the driver **drives** cautiously and **gets** all the passengers to work on time.

All the verbs in that paragraph are in the present tense. They show that this information is true in the present.

EXAMPLE—FUTURE TENSE:

> There **will be** a severe blizzard tonight. Cars **will have** trouble staying on the highways. Pipes **will freeze**. Power lines **will break**. Snow emergency plans **will go** into effect. The storm **will cause** many problems.

Since that paragraph was written with future-tense verbs, each verb had the word *will* in front of it.

When you are writing, be careful not to shift tenses unnecessarily. For example, you would not want to write these sentences:

> There will be a blizzard tonight. The storm caused many problems.

The second sentence shifted from the future to the past tense. This shift makes the reader wonder whether the storm has already happened or not. As a result, neither sentence makes any sense.

Write the following paragraph in the past tense. Cross out any verbs that are not written in the past tense and change them to the past tense.

> Albert bought a car phone after he saw mine. He had it put into his car, but he didn't like it. After an hour, he removes it and took it back. The shop owner refuses to refund Albert's money but gave him a store credit.

You should have changed *removes* to *removed* and *refuses* to *refused*.

EXERCISE 5: CHECKING VERB TENSE IN A PARAGRAPH

Directions: Read the following paragraphs. Cross out any verb that is written in an incorrect tense and write the correct verb above it. The new verb should be in the same tense as the other verbs in the paragraph.

Paragraph 1

Glenn loves being outdoors in the Wyoming mountains. He feels close to nature. He was a careful camper. Glenn sets up perfect campsites. A log cabin is his dream.

Paragraph 2

The cabin will have only one big room, and it had a bathroom. It will be furnished very sparsely. Glenn will live in the cabin all year round.

Paragraph 3

A herd of deer lived close to the building spot. They left once the land was cleared. They move to a new home close to a nearby stream.

Answers start on page 203.

PARAGRAPH STRUCTURE

As you continue writing, check each paragraph to make sure that it has a topic sentence and that all the other sentences support that topic.

> The ***topic sentence*** expresses the main idea of the paragraph. It focuses your writing into one specific area. The ***supporting sentences*** give details that explain the topic sentence.

For example, you might decide that you would like to write a paragraph on insurance. However, that is a very broad topic. There are life insurance, health insurance, car insurance, home insurance, and many other kinds of insurance.

So you can narrow your topic by deciding to write on life insurance. That is still a broad topic. It can be narrowed even more. You might decide to write about good reasons to purchase life insurance.

That can be a good topic sentence. It makes the purpose of your paragraph specific. If you wrote the paragraph, you would include only good reasons for buying life insurance. That paragraph might look like this (the topic sentence is in **bold type**):

> **There are three good reasons for buying life insurance.** First, it gives security to your family in case you die. Second, it can give you retirement income. Finally, you can borrow against the policy if you need a loan.

If you have a clear topic sentence, it is much easier to write a well-organized paragraph. The topic sentence in the paragraph above makes it clear that everything in the paragraph is about good reasons for buying life insurance.

Be certain that all the information you include supports the topic sentence. You would not want to include a sentence like *Life insurance is very expensive* in the paragraph above. The cost of life insurance is not related to the topic sentence.

Read the following paragraph. Find the topic sentence and underline it. One sentence in the paragraph does not support the topic sentence. Cross out the sentence that does not belong.

> Riding subways takes a great deal of knowledge. The passengers must know how to read train schedules. They must know where the station platforms are located. Eating candy helps brighten up a long ride. They must know whether to get off at the front or back of the train.

The first sentence is the topic sentence. The sentence about eating candy does not belong in the paragraph.

EXERCISE 6: KNOWING THE TOPIC OF A PARAGRAPH

Directions: Four paragraphs are included in this exercise. Read each paragraph and underline the topic sentence—the sentence that tells the main idea of the paragraph. Then cross out the one sentence in each paragraph that does not support the topic sentence. The first one is done as an example.

Paragraph 1

There are several steps to follow when applying for a job. First, contact the company's personnel office to arrange an interview. Second, arrive for the interview five minutes early. ~~Meeting a friend for lunch makes the day more enjoyable~~. Third, accurately complete the employment application. Fourth, be polite when interviewed and answer all questions completely and honestly. Fifth, when the interview is over, thank the person who conducted the interview. Finally, before the day is over, write a thank-you note to the interviewer and restate a desire to work for that company.

Paragraph 2

Credit cards are convenient, but they can cost large sums of money. Department stores, gasoline stations, banks, and even telephone companies offer credit as a way to encourage spending. Card holders pay interest on the amount they don't pay off each month. Most cards charge interest rates of 17% to 20% or more. Some cards, such as department store cards and gasoline cards, are used to buy items at a specific place.

Paragraph 3

Caring for an infant is very demanding. An infant must be fed many times each day. His or her diapers must be changed several times a day. They are so cute and so much fun to watch. Often the baby needs care in the middle of the night. Once a baby arrives, parents find their time is not their own.

Paragraph 4

Avid television sports fans are called "armchair athletes." These armchair athletes get their exercise walking from the armchair to the refrigerator and back. They build biceps by crushing soda or beer cans and by changing channels. Soda is better for them because it doesn't contain alcohol. These people spend great amounts of energy cheering or booing the teams on the screen.

Answers start on page 203.

PUTTING YOUR SKILLS TO WORK

Directions: Now you have a chance to practice writing a paragraph with a clear topic sentence and good supporting sentences. Take out your writing folder or notebook. Choose *one* of the following topics for your paragraph. Begin by writing a topic sentence. Then write at least four supporting sentences that relate to your topic sentence.

1. Write a paragraph about your best qualities. What are the good things about you?

2. Think of something that is important to you. Write a paragraph explaining why it is so important.

☑ Writing Checklist

- ❑ Does your paragraph have a clear topic sentence?
- ❑ Do all your supporting sentences relate to the topic sentence?
- ❑ Do all your verbs show the right tense?

EXERCISE 7: CHAPTER REVIEW

Directions: Each of the following sentences contains either a misplaced describing phrase or incorrect parallel structure. Rewrite each sentence so it is written correctly and clearly.

1. The cat meowed, whined, and was scratching the door.

   ____

2. Getting a new job and to move to another apartment will improve Flo's life.

   ____

3. The children listened to the story of *The Pokey Little Puppy* eating their cookies.

   ____

4. Grabbing the ball and fighting to the goal line, we watched the quarterback.

   ____

5. The family worked, played, and was living in Missouri for six years.

   ____

6. Everyone should stop, look, and listening before crossing a street.

   ____

7. Joe paid $500 for the used car of his hard-earned money.

   ____

Answers start on page 202.

YOUR TURN TO WRITE: THREE PARAGRAPHS

Put all your writing skills to work. Write three paragraphs. Describe a place or a person in the first paragraph. Tell a story in the second paragraph. State an opinion in the third paragraph.

Make sure each paragraph has a good topic sentence. Write carefully and correctly, using the skills you have learned in this section.

WRITING ASSIGNMENT

Part 1: Descriptive Paragraph

Directions: Describe a place or a person. Use many adjectives to create an interesting word picture. For a place, describe what you see as you look from left to right. Be certain to include any sounds or smells. For a person, tell what he or she looks like—clothes, walk, speech.

Part 2: Story Paragraph

Directions: Tell a story about a very happy or sad event. First, tell what happened that *led up to* the event. Second, tell what happened *during* the event. Finally, tell what happened *after* the event. Remembering these three steps will always help you organize a story.

Part 3: Opinion Paragraph

Directions: Write an opinion. You can begin by using one of these two topic sentences:

> Writing is a very useful skill.
> Writing is not a very useful skill.

Or choose another opinion to write about. Make certain that the supporting sentences tell only why your opinion is a good one. You want to be as convincing as possible.

Writing Checklist

- ❑ Does each paragraph have a topic sentence?
- ❑ Have you used colorful adjectives in the first paragraph?
- ❑ Is there a "before, during, and after" in the second paragraph?
- ❑ Did you support your opinion clearly in the final paragraph?

Language and Writing Skills Answer Key

CHAPTER 1: PARTS OF SPEECH

Exercise 1: Identifying Nouns
page 59

1. Mr. Archer, stadium, baseball
3. Knoxville, Shelley, fashion
3. Aunt Rose, shells, ocean
4. lawyer, bail, courthouse

Exercise 2: Writing Nouns
page 60

Your answers will be different from these. Compare your answers to these sample answers to see if you used similar nouns.

1. Mark
2. mother
3. Alaska
4. Courage

Exercise 3: Identifying Pronouns
page 61

1. He, he
2. she, it
3. She, them, us
4. He, me

Exercise 4: Writing Pronouns
page 61

1. It
2. It
3. He or She
4. it

Exercise 5: Identifying Verbs
page 62

1. rides
2. goes, is
3. found, visited

Exercise 6: Writing Verbs
page 63

Your answers will differ from these. Did you fill in all the blanks with the right kinds of action verbs?

1. sew, draw, paint, write, build
2. breathe, see, talk, hear, smell
3. dream, think, decide, fantasize, invent

Exercise 7: Identifying Adjectives
page 64

1. new, fuzzy
2. big, little, beautiful
3. kind, old,
4. noisy, busy

Exercise 8: Writing Adjectives
page 64

Your answers will be different from these. Make sure that you used adjectives in your answers.

	You	Your home	Your father or mother
1.	smart	new	tough
2.	handsome	tiny	old
3.	likable	two-story	tall

Exercise 9: Identifying Adverbs
page 65

1. dangerously
2. early
3. immediately
4. loudly

Exercise 10: Writing Adverbs
page 66

You may have thought of different adverbs from the ones listed here. Make sure the adverbs you chose tell how, when, and where depending on the instructions.

1. sweetly, softly, proudly
2. daily, now, or constantly
3. upstairs, there, or outdoors

Exercise 11: Chapter Review
pages 66–67

Part 1

Nouns	Pronouns	Verbs
Mr. Archer	he	listens
dog	they	keep
baseball	you	went
boat	it	loves

Adjectives	Adverbs
neat	early
happy	there
old	slowly
nice	now

Part 2

Check to see if you added the correct part of speech to the sentences. You might have a different word, but the part of speech will be the same.

1.	motorcycle	noun
2.	goes	verb
3.	fuzzy	adjective
4.	carefully	adverb
5.	its	pronoun

CHAPTER 2: SENTENCES

Exercise 1: Identifying Sentences and Fragments
pages 71–72

1. S
2. F
3. F
4. S
5. S
6. F
7. S

Exercise 2: Turning Fragments into Sentences
page 72

You won't have written the same sentences as these. Just make sure that each of your sentences tells a complete thought.

1. The police took the man to jail.
2. An officer locked him up.
3. He called his lawyer.
4. He did not want to sleep in jail.
5. He felt terrible.

Exercise 3: Types of Sentences
page 75

1. This is the Rainbow Coffee Shop. *statement*
2. Would you like to see a menu? *question*
3. Get me a glass of water. *command*
4. This place is on fire! *exclamation*

Exercise 4: Mistakes in Sentences
page 75

1. The rents here are sky-high. (The original group of words was a fragment. The answer must be a complete sentence.)
2. Why did they have to tear our building down?
3. Most landlords won't permit pets.
4. I can't give up my dog! (The original group of words was a fragment. Your answer must be a complete sentence.)

Exercise 5: Finding the Subject
pages 76–77

	Subject	Verb
1.	Chicago	is
2.	People	live
3.	Trains	take
4.	buildings	are
5.	People	hurry

Exercise 6: Finding Tricky Subjects
page 78

1. Denise
2. (You)
3. Larry
4. coffee
5. we
6. (You)
7. you

Exercise 7: Writing Subjects
page 78

Only you can be sure if your answers are correct. Look over your answers. Have you answered using the names of persons, places, and things you are familiar with?

Exercise 8: Writing Action Predicates
page 79

Make sure that the predicate you wrote is an action verb.

1. Babies cry.
2. Smoke rises.
3. Flowers grow.
4. Birds sing.
5. Fish swim.
6. Scissors cut.

Exercise 9: Writing Linking Predicates
page 79

Make sure that you used a linking verb in each of your predicates.

1. Mary is happy.
2. Our money is gone.
3. The pool is open.
4. My apartment is neat.
5. His motorcycle was stolen.
6. The tomatoes are red.

Exercise 10: Chapter Review
pages 83–84

Part 1

1. Juan
2. counselor
3. Juan
4. interviewer
5. You (In a command, the subject is always the missing *you*.)

Part 2

1. d
2. c
3. e

Part 3

Here are some sample answers. Your answers will be different.

1–2. A person is at the checkout counter in a store. The clerk might be saying, "Those are on sale today." *(statement)* or "Do you want only one of those?" *(question)*

3–4. A man is talking to his dog in this picture. He might be saying, "Sit up."*(command)* or "Bad dog!" *(exclamation)*

CHAPTER 3: NOUNS AND PRONOUNS

Exercise 1: Identifying Nouns
page 87

Nan loves her **dog**, **Fifi**. **Fifi** is a **poodle**. At the **beach**, **Nan** wants to be certain that **Fifi** does not get too hot. **Nan** bought a **stroller** with an **awning** so **Fifi** could be in the **shade** while on the **beach**. **Nan** also often buys **ice cream** for **Fifi**. Many **people** on the **beach** stare at the **poodle**. The **people** also stare at **Nan**!

Exercise 2: Common and Proper Nouns
page 88

Below are some sample answers. Did you capitalize your proper nouns?

1. Honda
2. Senator Jesse Helms
3. Sears
4. Aliquippa
5. Reverend Zeiders
6. Christmas
7. Vermont
8. China
9. Boy Scouts
10. Dr. Owens

Exercise 3: Capitalizing Proper Nouns
page 89

1. Mrs. Linkowski first saw the **Washington Monument** when she was five.
2. **New Year's Eve** is **Aunt** Betty's favorite holiday.
3. The teachers at **Brookmont Elementary School** wrote a letter to **Mayor Carlson**.
4. My dentist hasn't missed a **Green Bay Packers** game in seven years.
5. C
6. Ms. Davis is a member of an organization called **Mothers Against Drunk Driving**.
7. The **Oak Valley Fire Department** was too late to save the warehouse.

Exercise 4: Changing Singular Nouns to Plural
page 91

1. Many **women** do not want to work outside the home.
2. Some **women** argue that they must work to earn money.
3. Some **employers** pay women less than men.
4. **Salaries** should be the same for all people who do the same job.
5. Some companies have child care **programs**.
6. Often, several **churches** in a town have day-care centers.
7. **Cities**, counties, and towns should do even more to help mothers who must work.

Exercise 5: Correcting Errors with Nouns
pages 91–92

1. b
2. a
3. c

Exercise 6: Writing Possessive Nouns
page 93

1. coach's
2. army's
3. armies'
4. woman's
5. women's
6. choir's
7. choirs'

Exercise 7: More Practice with Possessive Nouns
page 93

1. cat's cradle
2. busboys' trays
3. Mickey's house
4. teachers' meetings
5. coach's signals
6. neighbors' anniversary
7. mechanic's wrench

Exercise 8: Using Subject Pronouns
pages 95–96

1. She
2. He
3. They
4. It

Exercise 9: Using Object Pronouns
pages 96–97

1. it
2. her
3. him
4. them
5. us
6. her

Exercise 10: Using Possessive Pronouns page 98

1. their
2. its
3. theirs
4. hers
5. their
6. ours

Exercise 11: Using Pronouns page 98

Karen enjoys **her** job at the Adult Learning Center. **She** is the staff support specialist. She helps Larry with **his** teaching. Carol teaches there too and is well liked by **her** students. The students look forward to coming to **their** classes.

The directors of the center are Vicki and George. **They** count on government grants to fund the center's programs. **Their** assistant, Bob, helps **them** get funding for the programs. **He** is a very important member of the staff. All the Adult Learning Center staff members are quick to state, "**We** believe in adult education!"

Exercise 12: Pronoun Agreement pages 99–100

1. he
2. his
3. them
4. They
5. their
6. Our

Exercise 13: Forming Contractions page 101

1. they've
2. doesn't
3. he's
4. I'm
5. we're
6. isn't
7. shouldn't
8. they'll (Notice that two letters are removed in this contraction.)

Exercise 14: Contractions and Possessive Pronouns page 102

It's always a good idea to decorate **your** home. Even people who don't have much spare time can hang pictures on **their** walls and put up curtains. Of course, **it's** harder if **you're** working full-time. Gary, a friend of mine, did a nice job on **his** apartment. I hope that he and **his** friend Pete will help me out. **They're** really talented at decorating.

Exercise 15: Chapter Review pages 102–104

Part 1

1. c
2. a
3. c
4. b
5. Years ago, I went to hear **Senator** Stevenson speak.
6. The year **Stevenson** ran for president, **Dad** bought a new **Ford**.
7. I
8. hers
9. us
10. they
11. my
12. ours

Part 2

1. After the party, Dean stayed out very late. (The original group of words was a fragment. Any answer is correct as long as you wrote a complete sentence.)
2. Look out—it's a raid!
3. The gangsters will be arrested. (The original group of words was a fragment. Any answer is correct as long as you wrote a complete sentence.)
4. you
5. Music
6. you (In a command, the subject is always the missing *you*.)
7. news

CHAPTER 4: VERBS

Exercise 1: Choosing Present-Tense Verbs pages 108–109

1. (Americans) <u>enjoy</u>
2. (They) <u>like</u>
3. (I) <u>love</u>
4. (I) <u>find</u>
5. (They) <u>welcome</u>
6. (My parents) <u>live</u>
7. (We) <u>write</u>

Exercise 2: Writing the Past and Future Tenses
page 110

Past	Future
1. looked	will look
2. moved	will move
3. lived	will live
4. saved	will save

Exercise 3: Past Tense of Irregular Verbs
pages 110–111

1. gave
2. told
3. saw
4. came
5. read
6. brought
7. said
8. made
9. went
10. did
11. had
12. sold

Exercise 4: Choosing the Correct Past-Tense Form
page 112

1. saw
2. ran
3. was
4. went

Exercise 5: Forms of *Be*
page 113

1. were
2. are
3. was
4. is
5. is
6. are
7. was

Exercise 6: Forms of *Have*
page 114

1. has
2. has
3. will have
4. had
5. will have

Exercise 7: Forms of *Do*
page 115

1. Do
2. do
3. did
4. did
5. does
6. will do

Exercise 8: Using Time Clues
page 116

Verb	Time Clues
1. want	Today
2. worked	Last year
3. wake	Now
4. will go	Tomorrow

Exercise 9: The Present Continuing Tense
page 119

1. is studying
2. are working
3. is learning
4. are writing
5. am enjoying

Exercise 10: The Past Continuing Tense
page 120

1. was raining
2. was driving
3. were smiling
4. were going
5. was looking
6. was giving
7 was ringing
8. was dreaming

Exercise 11: Using Quotation Marks
page 122

1. "I think the best years of a person's life are his teen years," said Raymond.
2. His mother laughed and said,"That's because you are a teenager."
3. "Actually, you will have more fun once you are an adult," said his twenty-two-year-old brother, John.
4. "What will happen to me once I reach thirty?" John wondered.
5. "You'll be on your way to forty, and believe me, those are really the best years," said Mom.
6. Dad piped in, "Oh, I don't know, I think I'm even better-looking at fifty."
7. John asked, "How were the sixties, Grandma?"

Exercise 12: Chapter Review
pages 123–125
Part 1

1. Past	Present	Future
sang	jump	will find
looked	claim	will write
danced	drive	will want
saw	are	will paint
had		hopes
was		is

2. b
3. a
4. c
5. b
6. c
7. c
8. b
9. c

Part 2

1. Her **children's** room is a mess.
2 I **can't** blame her children for being messy.
3. **They're** just like her.

4. **She** doesn't like to clean her room either. (The original sentence was a fragment. You should have added a subject to make the sentence complete.)

CHAPTER 5: SUBJECT-VERB AGREEMENT

Exercise 1: Subject-Verb Agreement with Pronouns
page 129

1. owns
2. take
3. come
4. thanks

Exercise 2: Subject-Verb Agreement with Irregular Verbs
page 130

1. are	5. was
2. have	6. do
3. am	7. were
4. does	8. goes

Exercise 3: Singular and Plural Subjects
page 132

1. is *Summer* can be replaced by *It*.
2. move *Families* can be replaced by *They*.
3. look *The gardens* can be replaced by *They*.
4. guides *Carl* can be replaced by *He*.
5. gives *Strength* can be replaced by *It*.

Exercise 4: Subject-Verb Agreement with Compound Subjects
page 135

1. increase The parts are *The local police* and *the state police*. A compound subject joined by *and* is always plural.
2. need The parts are *You* and *your parents*. A compound subject joined by *and* is always plural.
3. go The parts are *Nan* and *I*. The verb agrees with *I* because the parts are joined by *nor*, and *I* is the closest part.
4. give The parts are *A local club* and *businesses*. The verb agrees with *businesses* because the parts are joined by *or*, and *businesses* is the closest part.
5. help The parts are *newspapers* and *radio*. A compound subject joined by *and* is always plural.

Exercise 5: Subject-Verb Agreement with Describing Phrases
page 136

	Subject	Verb	Describing Phrase
1.	tree	changes	with the red and gold leaves
2.	children	pick	under the tree
3.	father	arrives	of one of the girls
4.	Truckers	take	with good sense
5.	truck	has	with bad brakes
6.	driver	goes	on a long trip
7.	Truckstops	are	on the freeway

Exercise 6: Subject-Verb Agreement Review
page 137

1. help The compound subject is *Nutritious meals* and *rest*.
2. give The subject is *A grandmother* and *grandfather*.
3. go The subject is *those blankets*.
4. do The subject is *You*.
5. looks The closest part of the compound subject is *meat*.
6. earn The plural subject is *Women*.
7. cheer The closest part of the subject is *flowers*.

Exercise 7: Commas with Phrases That Give Additional Information
page 138

1. The Wizard of Oz, a favorite childhood character, granted wishes.
2. Checkers, a game for two, is challenging for children and adults.
3. Horror films, a frightening form of entertainment, attract big audiences.
4. The undercover policeman on the case is Detective Blackwell, a member of the vice squad.

Exercise 8: Phrases That Connect or Make Transitions Between Ideas
page 139

1. My best friend, of course, would never go out with my boyfriend.
2. I just learned, in fact, that I'm eating all the wrong foods.
3. Marlene gave up smoking, by the way.
4. Andy, in my opinion, is not mature enough to live on his own.

Exercise 9: Commas in Direct Address page 140

1. Terry, will you please come for a visit this summer?
2. If I could afford the trip, Mary, I would surely come.
3. Do you realize how talented you are, Paula?
4. In two weeks, Mrs. Grant, your lease will expire.

Exercise 10: Chapter Review page 142

Part 1

1. Lucas and Dena **want** to buy a house.
2. A porch or patio **gives** a house an outdoor feeling.
3. Lucas, an excellent cook**,** examines the kitchens carefully.
4. The house with the hardwood floors **was** too expensive.
5. Neither Lucas nor Dena **likes** the less expensive houses.
6. They are**,** in fact, afraid that they will never find a good house for what they can pay.

Part 2

1. **Bob's** car looks brand-new.
2. He is very careful to maintain it properly**.**
3. **The** required oil change is done every 3,000 miles.
4. Last month, he **changed** the gas filter, the oil, and the spark plugs.
5. The best thing to do for a car **is to maintain it well**. (The original sentence is a fragment. Any answer that is a complete sentence is correct.)
6. **Its** paint can be preserved with regular waxing.

CHAPTER 6: ADJECTIVES AND ADVERBS

Exercise 1: Choosing Adjectives page 146

You will probably have chosen one of the following adjectives to complete each sentence.

1. Hectic or Busy
2. busy, colorful, many, or numerous
3. many, busy, numerous, or frustrated
4. small, inexpensive, expensive, many, or numerous

5 Colorful, Many, or Numerous

6. expensive, many, gigantic, or numerous
7. inexpensive or small

Exercise 2: Using Adjectives page 147

Your answers should be similar to these. These answers were written by another student.

1. The **middle-aged** men play **forty** games of poker once a month.
2. They use **playing** cards and play on a **card** table.
3. The game is played on the **first** Friday of each month.
4. During the **monthly** game, **two** pounds of potato chips are eaten.

Exercise 3: Identifying Adjectives page 148

The adjectives you should have circled are listed below.

1. educational
2. informative
3. Many
4. tired
5. popular
6. violent

Exercise 4: Choosing Adverbs page 150

As in Exercise 1, many of these sentences have more than one possible answer.

1. *Hysterically*, *strangely*, or *nervously* can tell how he laughed.
2. *Before* tells when he smiled.
3. *Outside* tells where he grinned.
4. *Strangely*, *threateningly*, or *nervously* can tell how people looked.
5. *Rapidly* tells how his tears flowed.
6. *Down* tells where he fell.

Exercise 5: Writing Sentences with Adverbs pages 150–151

Your answers may differ from these. Check to be sure you have used an adverb to modify the verb in each of your sentences.

1. *(how)* The students write carefully.
   (when) We write daily.
   (where) George writes here.
2. *(how)* Melinda and Todd dance beautifully.
   (when) She will dance tomorrow.
   (where) Tim and Lena dance outside.
3. *(how)* I read rapidly.
   (when) Tom read the book yesterday.
   (where) Sam will read here.

Exercise 6: Identifying Adverbs
page 151

Listed below are the adverbs you should have circled.

1. far
2. early
3. dangerously
4. Mysteriously
5. everywhere
6. always

Exercise 7: Choosing Adjectives or Adverbs
page 153

1. *Fantastic* is an adjective describing *what kind* of football season.
2. *Carefully* is an adverb describing *how* a fan gets ready.
3. *Calmly* is an adverb describing *how* he waits.
4. *Excited* is an adjective describing *what kind* of crowd.
5. *Loudly* is an adverb describing *how* the fan applauds.
6. *Magnificent* is an adjective describing *what kind* of pass.

Exercise 8: Using Commas in a Series
page 155

The necessary commas have been added to the following sentences.

1. No commas are needed.
2. Also included in the program will be speakers, awards, and music.
3. Sue Almeda, Fran Warner, Lillian Rutledge, and Vanessa Grogan are in charge of inviting guests.
4. Interested, enthusiastic, dedicated volunteers will be invited.
5. No commas are needed.
6. On the menu will be stuffed chicken breasts, baked potatoes, peas, salad, rolls, ice cream, and coffee.
7. The play will require the cooperation of talented, interested, well-rehearsed participants.

Exercise 9: Writing Sentences with Series
page 155

Your sentences will differ from these. Check your sentences to make sure they are punctuated correctly.

1. On Monday, I will have hot dogs, baked beans, and pickles for dinner.
2. The most interesting person I know is intelligent, handsome, and funny.

Exercise 10: Chapter Review
pages 159–160

Part 1

You should have corrected the sentences as follows.

1. Ruth is a **happy** person. (Use an adjective to tell what kind of person Ruth is.)
2. The race car moved **quickly** around the track. (Use an adverb to tell how the car moved.)
3. Nuts, bolts, wrenches, and tools were thrown around the shop. (Use a comma after every item in a series except the last one.)
4. The men and the women agreed that life moves too rapidly. (No comma is needed with only two items.)
5. The business is located in Anchorage, Alaska. (A comma is needed between the city and state.)
6. The trustworthy, young, bright baby-sitter raised her fee. (Use a comma after every item in a series except the last one.)
7. The soldier looked **bravely** into the eyes of his captors. (Use an adverb to tell how the soldier looked.)

Part 2

1. c *United States* must be capitalized.
2. c *People* should not be capitalized.
3. b The verb should not end in *s* to agree with *They*.
4. c The plural subject *immigrants* needs a verb that does not end in *s*.
5. a Correct as written.
6. b Commas are needed after each item in a series except the last.

CHAPTER 7: COMBINING SENTENCES

Exercise 1: Identifying Compound Subjects and Predicates
page 164

1. CS The immigrants and their host families
2. CP were happy to see each other and were eager to get acquainted
3. CS American food, clothing, and housing

Exercise 2: Compounding Subjects and Predicates
page 164

Your sentences should be very similar to the following.

1. Sharon wrote a letter to her parents during lunch and mailed it on her way home.
2. Sharon and her brother planned to visit their parents for Thanksgiving.
3. They were looking forward to seeing their parents and could hardly wait to taste their mother's cooking.

Exercise 3: Practicing with Conjunctions and Commas
page 167

1. Thrift stores are great places to shop, and they have many bargains.
2. Some of the customers who visit them have very little money, but others just want to find a good buy.
3. Nice clothes sell quickly, so smart customers shop on the day new items are stocked.
4. Men and women go to these stores for clothes, but children like to look for toys.
5. Some shops are open at odd hours, yet shoppers fill the aisles.

Exercise 4: Combining Sentences
pages 167–168

1. Children are fun, and many people enjoy working with them. **OR:** Children are fun, so many people enjoy working with them.
2. Horses are farm animals, yet people keep them in cities. **OR:** Horses are farm animals, but people keep them in cities.
3. Drugs are a serious problem, but many teenagers think they are harmless. **OR:** Drugs are a serious problem, yet many teenagers think they are harmless.

Exercise 5: Correcting Sentences with Connectors
page 170

1. b **2.** a **3.** b **4.** b **5.** b

Exercise 6: Writing Sentences with Connectors
page 171

Pay close attention to the punctuation in the answers. If you did not use the conjunction shown here, make sure your sentence makes sense.

1. The police searched the neighborhood for drugs; moreover, they vowed to jail all dealers.
2. After the race, the drivers were exhausted; nevertheless, they went to the party.
3. The Joneses were evicted from their apartment; furthermore, Mr. Jones lost his job.
4. Dorothy thought she would get a small raise; instead, she was surprised with a ten percent salary increase.
5. Electric heat is very expensive; therefore, we keep the thermostats turned down to 65 degrees.

Exercise 7: Completing Sentences with Subordinating Conjunctions
page 173

1. if, since, when, after, or because
2. After, When, Since, or Because
3. because or since
4. Although, Though, or After

Exercise 8: Writing Sentences with Subordinating Conjunctions
page 174

Your answers may not be exactly like these. Check to make sure your punctuation is correct and your sentences make sense.

1. When David gets home, we will show him the pictures.
2. Though Chan went to the doctor yesterday, she doesn't feel any better today.
3. Before the Jellybeans recorded their first big hit in 1964, they were completely unknown.
4. The police will be able to arrest the drug dealer if Maura can identify him in a lineup.
5. Since Margaret mowed the lawn, Greg agreed to do the raking.
6. Jenka gave me the money although she needed it herself.

Exercise 9: Practicing Punctuation
page 176

1. Being new in town is not easy; however, there are many support groups.
2. Churches form newcomers groups, and community agencies do the same thing.
3. People go to the meetings because they want to make new friends.
4. Some women feel that they will appear to be looking for men; consequently, they won't attend these meetings.
5. Many men fear that same thing, so they stay home, too.
6. Others are more optimistic; therefore, they go to meet people of both sexes.
7. When people have interests in common, they may develop good relationships.

Exercise 10: Chapter Review
pages 177–178
Part 1

1. Getting up for work is not easy, so I am usually late.
2. Getting up for work is not easy; therefore, I am usually late.
3. Because getting up for work is not easy, I am usually late.

4. b	**6** b	**8.** a
5. b	**7.** c	

Part 2

1. c—The verb must agree with the subject. Peanut butter *is*.
2. c—Closing quotation marks are needed.
3. a—The verb must agree with the plural subject *members*, so it must be *are*.
4. b—The verb must agree with the subject closest to it. Teacher *is*.
5. a—The pronoun is the subject of the sentence and should be *She*.
6. a—The apostrophe is in the wrong place; *women's* is correct.

CHAPTER 8: SENTENCES AND PARAGRAPHS

Exercise 1: Identifying Misplaced Describing Phrases
page 183

	Described Word	Describing Phrase
1. a	woman	in purple shoes
2. a	desk	that is 500 years old
3. b	people	sitting in the front row

Exercise 2: Writing Sentences with Describing Phrases
page 183

1. Wearing only his pajamas and slippers, he let the puppy out.
2. The actors in their dressing rooms were getting ready to face the audience. **OR:**
   In their dressing rooms, the actors were getting ready to face the audience.
3. The salesman handed the slacks with the red stripes to Geraldine.
4. The team in blue uniforms fumbled the ball in the second half.

Exercise 3: Identifying Correct Parallel Structure
page 185

1. b. working, playing, watching good movies
2. a. a police officer, a paramedic, a firefighter
3. b. draws exquisitely, paints superbly
4. b. stalls out, leaves her stranded

Exercise 4: Correcting Parallel Structure
page 186

There are several ways to correct some of these sentences. If you did not write the same sentences as those listed below, make sure you have written sentences with correct parallel structure.

1. Homer went to Texas, got a job, built a house, and got married.
2. Getting rich and buying a car are Dorothy's only interests. **OR:**
   To get rich and to buy a car are Dorothy's only interests.
3. Mystery stories have intrigue, excitement, and suspense. **OR:**
   Mystery stories are full of intrigue, excitement, and suspense.
4. Wendy works very hard but has fun, too. **OR:**
   Wendy is working very hard but is having fun, too.

Exercise 5: Checking Verb Tense in a Paragraph page 187

The corrected sentences for each paragraph follow:

Paragraph 1—He is a careful camper.

Paragraph 2—The cabin will have only one big room, and it will have a bathroom.

Paragraph 3—They moved to a new home close to a nearby stream.

Exercise 6: Knowing the Topic of a Paragraph page 189

The topic sentence of each paragraph is the first sentence. The sentences you should have crossed out are listed below.

1. Meeting a friend for lunch makes the day more enjoyable.
2. Some cards, such as department store cards and gasoline cards, are used to buy items at a specific place.
3. They are so cute and so much fun to watch.
4. Soda is better for them because it doesn't contain alcohol.

Exercise 7: Chapter Review page 191

There can be more than one way to correct some of these sentences. If you did not write the same sentences as those listed below, make sure you have avoided using misplaced describing phrases or incorrect parallel structure.

1. The cat meowed, whined, and scratched the door.
2. Getting a new job and moving to another apartment will improve Flo's life.
3. The children eating their cookies listened to the story of *The Pokey Little Puppy.*
4. We watched the quarterback grab the ball and fight to the goal line.
5. The family worked, played, and lived in Missouri for six years.
6. Everyone should stop, look, and listen before crossing a street.
7. Joe paid $500 of his hard-earned money for the used car.

Section 2

SOCIAL STUDIES

1 UNDERSTANDING WHAT YOU READ

In order to understand social studies fully, you will need to master the skills in this section. One of the most basic reading skills is finding details and facts. Another basic reading skill is understanding the meaning of unfamiliar words. You'll start work on these two skills. Later, you'll work on putting ideas in other words by summarizing and restating. Then you'll practice finding the main idea. Studying these skills will lay the groundwork for reading and understanding social studies.

READING SKILL: LOCATING DETAILS AND FACTS

QUESTION WORDS

The first step in understanding what you read is picking out **details**. You look for facts to answer six basic questions: Who? What? Where? When? How? and Why? In the following example, Judge Phillips needs to use all six questions in order to understand the case. She needs the details in order to make a decision.

JUDGE: *Whom* are you here to represent?
LAWYER: My client is Elisa Canter.
JUDGE: *Why* is she here?
LAWYER: To sue the McWatt Shoe Company.
JUDGE: *What* are the grounds for the suit?
LAWYER: Manufacturing a faulty pair of boots that caused an injury.
JUDGE: *When* did this alleged injury take place?
LAWYER: Last Friday night.
JUDGE: *Where* did it happen?
LAWYER: At Ms. Canter's home.
JUDGE: *How* did the boots cause the injury?
LAWYER: The soles stuck to a patch of ice, causing her to fall.

FINDING THE INFORMATION

Now practice finding information for questions asking *who, what, when, where, how,* and *why*. In the following paragraph, the speaker describes his memories of a bread line. See if you can match the correct answer with each question. Write the letter of the answer in the space provided.

> I was walking along the street at that time (1932), and you'd see the bread lines. The biggest one in New York City was owned by William Randolph Hearst. He had a big truck with several people on it, and big cauldrons of hot soup, bread. Fellows with burlap on their feet were lined up all around Columbus Circle, and went for blocks and blocks around the park, waiting.

_____ **1.** Where was this bread line?

_____ **2.** Who was waiting in the bread line?

_____ **3.** When did this scene take place?

_____ **4.** How did William Randolph Hearst give out food to poor people?

(a) He had a big truck with several people on it.

(b) in 1932

(c) in New York City

(d) fellows with burlap on their feet

Make sure you tried each question in the example above on your own before you read the following explanations. Did you match one answer to each question?

1. (c) *Where* question: New York City. (second sentence)

2. (d) *Who* question: "Fellows with burlap on their feet were lined up. . . ." (last sentence)

3. (b) *When* question: 1932 (first sentence)

4. (a) *How* question: "He had a big truck with several people on it. . . ." (third sentence)

EXERCISE 1: FINDING DETAILS

Directions: Following each paragraph are detail questions. Write your answer to each question in the space provided.

> In 1960, television helped elect a new president. Young John Kennedy defeated Richard Nixon in their famous television debates. Many political writers believe that Kennedy's good performance on television led to his narrow victory in the election.

1. Who were involved in the important televised debates of 1960?

____

2. According to many political writers, how did Kennedy win the 1960 presidential election?

____

In 1968, the Public Service Company of New Hampshire began building a nuclear power plant in Seabrook, New Hampshire. It took twenty years to open the plant, and the Public Service Company went bankrupt in the process. There were construction delays and funding problems, but the biggest headache was protesters. They occupied the plant site and the governor's office. They disrupted public hearings and interfered with plant procedures. Eventually, their fight became a symbol of success for anti-nuclear protesters across the nation. Nevertheless, the Seabrook plant opened in 1990.

3. Where is the power plant located?

____

4. When did the plant open?

____

5. How did protesters let the governor of New Hampshire know about their concerns?

____

Answers start on page 351.

EXERCISE 2: MORE PRACTICE IN FINDING DETAILS

Directions: This exercise is in multiple-choice format. Read the paragraphs. Then answer the questions that follow.

When George L. Belair was running for city council in Minneapolis, Minnesota, he gave away some Twinkies to senior citizens. Under Minnesota law, candidates for office are not allowed to give away food or drinks in order to get votes. Because of this law, Mr. Belair was arrested. He had to prove in court that he was not trying to get votes by giving away the cakes.

1. Why was Mr. Belair arrested?
   (1) He tried to bribe a police officer by giving him Twinkies.
   (2) It's illegal to give away a product that people usually have to pay for.
   (3) He had stolen the Twinkies he was giving away.
   (4) He gave free drinks to senior citizens.
   (5) In Minnesota, candidates cannot give away food to get votes.

Since 1945, the human race has had to face the possibility of its own destruction. In August of that year, an American airplane dropped the first atomic bomb on Hiroshima, Japan. That single bomb destroyed the entire city. In the years since that first explosion, the United States has built enough bombs to destroy the entire world. The Soviet Union has also built enough bombs to wipe out the human race. Great Britain, France, India, and China also have nuclear weapons. Humanity's future now depends on countries settling their differences peacefully.

2. The first atomic bomb was dropped by
   (1) the Soviet Union
   (2) the United States
   (3) Germany
   (4) Japan
   (5) China

3. What was the result when the bomb was dropped on Hiroshima?
   (1) The United Nations was formed.
   (2) The Soviet Union built many bombs.
   (3) The entire city of Hiroshima was destroyed.
   (4) The United States destroyed the entire world.
   (5) An American airplane went down.

For many years, large companies have fought with their workers' unions. But greater competition from overseas has forced both sides to look again at the way they work together. One example of a new approach occurred at the Chrysler Corporation. The United Auto Workers worked together with the company and the government to save Chrysler. Workers accepted pay cuts while the company got back on its feet. The president of the auto workers' union became a member of the board of directors. During the crisis, workers and management tried to become partners instead of enemies.

4. Why did the union and Chrysler management decide to work together?
   (1) The government forced them to work together.
   (2) The union president joined the board of directors.
   (3) The company got tired of fighting with the union.
   (4) Greater competition from overseas threatened the company.
   (5) Workers and management wanted to become partners.

Answers start on page 351.

READING SKILL: UNDERSTANDING UNFAMILIAR WORDS

USING THE CONTEXT

When reading social studies, you may find words you don't know. Understanding what you read is harder. Until you figure out the unknown words, what you read might not make sense.

You could look up words in the dictionary. But sometimes you don't have time, or no dictionary is handy. And sometimes the dictionary definitions are hard to understand. However, you can often figure out the meaning of a certain word by reading the words around it. This is called using the ***context*** (words around a word). In this section, you'll practice looking at the context of unfamiliar words to find their meanings.

SYNONYM, DEFINITION, AND COMPARISON CLUES

Often in social studies reading, you will find a ***synonym***—another word with almost the same meaning—near an unfamiliar word. Or you might find an explanation or definition of what the unknown word means. Sometimes in the passage you will find a comparison with something you know or understand. All of these clues can help you figure out what the unknown word means.

EXAMPLE:

> Calvin Coolidge once said, "When more and more people are thrown out of work, **unemployment** results."

In this example, there is a definition clue. The word *unemployment* is explained directly in the sentence. Unemployment happens when people are thrown out of work.

Now try another example. In the following passage, underline the comparison that is a clue to the meaning of the word *homogeneous*.

> The girls at Whitman High School can only be described as **homogeneous.** Like a school of identically shaped and colored fish, they wear the same clothes, eat the same food, and even talk the same.

▶ What does *homogeneous* mean? ______________________

Homogeneous means "alike." The comparison clue is "Like a school of identically shaped and colored fish . . . ." In addition, the passage says that the girls dress, eat, and talk alike.

EXERCISE 3: SYNONYM, DEFINITION, AND COMPARISON CLUES

Directions: In the space provided, write the meaning of the word or phrase in **bold type**. Use the context clues in the sentences—look for a synonym, definition, or comparison.

1. Like the patent medicine sold by phony doctors to cure all kinds of illnesses, industrial growth was supposed to be a **panacea** for the nation's ills.

   panacea ______________________

2. President Andrew Jackson began a dubious American political tradition, the widespread use of **patronage**—giving jobs and favors for political reasons.

   patronage ______________________

3. De Beers Company created a **monopoly** in the diamond industry, controlling production and crushing its competition.

   monopoly ______________________

4. Worker **productivity** has increased as new machines allow one laborer to make much more than before.

   productivity ______________________

Answers start on page 351.

ANTONYM AND CONTRAST CLUES

Sometimes you can figure out the meaning of an unknown word when the nearby words have an *opposite* meaning.

EXAMPLE: As the strike entered its ninth week, the workers had to decide whether to **persist** or to give up.

▶ What does *persist* mean? ______________________________

This example has an antonym clue. An ***antonym*** is a word that is the opposite of a given word. In this example, the workers are choosing between two choices: *to persist* or *to give up*. You can conclude that the opposite of *to persist* is *to give up*. Therefore, *to persist* means "to keep trying."

EXAMPLE: Despite government claims that people were calming down, the violence continued to **escalate**.

▶ What is the meaning of *escalate*? ______________________________

A situation is described that is ***in contrast to***, or the opposite of, another situation. In this sentence, *escalating violence* is the opposite of people becoming calm. You can conclude that ***to escalate*** means "to increase."

Clue words such as *unlike*, *despite*, and *although* may help you identify antonym and contrast clues.

EXAMPLE:

Unlike children in **wealthy** Kenwood, many children in **impoverished** Garfield Park go hungry.

EXERCISE 4: ANTONYM AND CONTRAST CLUES

Directions: The sentences on the left have antonym or contrast clues. Each sentence contains words or phrases with opposite meanings. Choose the letter of the correct answer to each question on the right.

After years without restrictions on the number of immigrants allowed into the country, Congress passed the first **quota** law in 1921.

1. A quota is
   (a) a person from another country
   (b) a numerical limit
   (c) an economic goal

In the late nineteenth century, new cities grew in the Northeast and Midwest. The **squalor** of these new industrial cities contrasted sharply with the beauty of the surrounding countryside.

2. Squalor is
   (a) filth
   (b) large size
   (c) beauty

Despite the desire of Native Americans to live **amicably** with white people, treaties were broken and fighting broke out.

3. To live amicably is to
   (a) control others
   (b) be peaceful
   (c) better oneself

Unlike the Native American tribes, who only wanted to keep their own lands, the United States followed an **expansionist** policy in the nineteenth century.

4. An expansionist policy favors
   (a) improving relations with neighbors
   (b) getting rid of foreign influence
   (c) making the nation larger

Answers start on page 351.

USING THE SENSE OF THE PASSAGE

Sometimes an important word is not defined directly. There may not be any antonyms or contrast clues. In these cases, you must determine the meaning of the word by reading the entire passage. Sometimes you might be able to figure out the meaning of the unknown word by looking at examples given in the rest of the passage. Other times you will have to rely on your overall understanding of the meaning of the passage, as in the following example.

> The great American **megalopolis** stretches over four hundred miles from Boston to Washington, D.C. Including such cities as New York, Newark, Philadelphia, and Baltimore, it is the largest urban area in the United States.

▶ What is a megalopolis?

(1) a large city and its suburbs
(2) a state government
(3) a group of connected cities and suburbs
(4) a large lottery

The phrase *stretches over* gives you the sense of a connected or continuous area (choice 3). Since the megalopolis includes many cities, it would have to include suburban areas.

EXERCISE 5: USING THE SENSE OF THE PASSAGE

Directions: Answer the questions that follows each passage.

> At **the turn of the century,** American life was changing rapidly. The most visible change was in transportation. Cars were beginning to be seen all over the country. And in 1903, the Wright brothers made the first airplane flight. Motorized vehicles were becoming our primary way of getting around.

1. When is meant by *the turn of the century* in this passage?
   (1) around 1700
   (2) around 1800
   (3) around 1900
   (4) in 1903

Congestion in a big city can't be avoided. One experiences it everywhere. Traffic jams are a constant irritation, making one's feet the fastest way to travel most of the time. A crowded elevator and a tightly packed subway train are other reminders of congestion in the city.

2. *Congestion* means
   (1) illness
   (2) confusion
   (3) overcrowding
   (4) poverty

My grandmother was a handsome woman, but she was oversensitive about her hands. They were **gnarled** by years of hard work at a sewing machine and by terrible arthritis.

3. *Gnarled* means
   (1) pretty
   (2) smooth
   (3) twisted
   (4) black

Answers start on page 351.

READING SKILL: RESTATING AND SUMMARIZING

RESTATING DETAILS AND FACTS

"Mom, you're going to love your new home. There will be people there your own age. There will be a nurse on duty at all times. You'll get the medical care you need."

"So you've decided to ship your poor old mother to a nursing home."

Mom has just restated the facts in different words. Being able to ***restate*** details and facts in different words is an important step in understanding what you read. Following is an example of a passage and questions that ask you to identify material that is stated in different words.

(1) The war that had exploded in Europe in 1914 had cut off the flow of immigrants from the old countries. (2) Northern factories, booming on war orders, were short of labor. (3) Manufacturers sent agents south to recruit black workers. (4) They came with free railroad passes in hand or offered cheap tickets to groups of migrants. (5) A "Northern fever" seized the Blacks of the South.

Read the following statements. If the statement is a correct restatement of the sentence or sentences indicated, write *C* in the blank and underline the part of the passage it restates. If not, write *I* for incorrect.

_____ 1. Northern manufacturers preferred southern black workers to European immigrants. (sentences 1–2)

_____ 2. Employers gave southern blacks assistance in moving north to work. (sentence 4)

Read the following explanations to see how you could think through this example correctly:

1. I The passage states that the war in Europe had cut off the flow of immigrants and the factories were short of labor. It doesn't say anything about what kind of workers the manufacturers preferred.

2. C This sentence restates the information in sentence 4. The passage says that the agents of manufacturers encouraged blacks to go north to work by giving them free or cheap railroad tickets.

EXERCISE 6: RECOGNIZING RESTATED INFORMATION

Directions: After reading the passage, read the sentences that follow. If you think that the statement is a correct restatement of part of the passage, write *C* for correct. If not, write *I* for incorrect.

(1) We had good schools in French Corral, better than they had in San Francisco at that time. (2) Most of our teachers were young men who were college graduates out from the East for a chance to make money and go back to take up further studies. (3) . . . The various teachers found a congenial atmosphere in our home and spent many evenings playing cards with my parents.

_____ 1. The young teachers who came to French Corral from the East wanted to start a new life and settle there. (sentence *2*)

_____ 2. Teachers were always welcome in the writer's home. (sentence *4*)

Answers start on page 351.

EXERCISE 7: RESTATING INFORMATION IN YOUR OWN WORDS

Directions: Read each passage. Then, in your own words, answer the questions that follow.

Rockefeller's company, Standard Oil, managed to put a lot of other oil companies out of business. First Rockefeller pressured railroads into lowering their freight charges for Standard Oil shipments. Then he could charge less for his products than other oil companies because his freight costs were lower. If other oil companies managed to stay in business anyway, Rockefeller had another tactic. He would lower his prices in their area until Standard Oil had lured away all the other companies' customers.

1. How did Standard Oil reduce its freight costs?

____

2. How did Standard Oil wipe out its competition?

____

The most successful of the early labor unions was the American Federation of Labor (AFL), founded in 1886 under the leadership of Samuel Gompers. The AFL was a united group of craft unions. Unlike the unsuccessful labor unions, the AFL did not sponsor its own political candidates. It also did not demand radical social change. Instead, the AFL worked toward concrete goals such as higher wages and shorter work hours.

3. What kinds of goals did the American Federation of Labor work toward?

____

4. What did the unsuccessful early labor unions do?

____

Answers start on page 351.

SUMMARIZING DETAILS AND FACTS

When you summarize, you make one statement that gives the main point of a group of details or facts. A summary should contain all of the important ideas. In the following example, practice finding a summary statement that pulls together all the ideas in the original sentences. Read the following three statements:

Henry Ford produced the first low-cost automobile.

Ford was able to save money through mass production of his automobile.

Millions of people were able to own a car for the first time because of the low cost.

Now place a check before the sentence that best summarizes all three of the statements.

______ Mass production has made many products affordable.

______ By creating the mass-produced car, Henry Ford changed America.

______ By using mass production, Ford produced a low-cost car that was bought by millions of people.

The last choice is the correct one: By using mass production (second statement), Ford produced a low-cost car (first statement) that was bought by millions of people (third statement). You can see that all the important ideas are covered.

EXERCISE 8: SUMMARIZING FACTS

Directions: Following each group of statements are three possible summary sentences. Circle the letter of the best summary. Make sure all the important ideas are included in the summary you choose.

1. AT&T's monopoly of long-distance service has ended.
MCI and Sprint now offer long-distance telephone service.
AT&T has had to lay off workers in order to remain competitive.

(a) MCI and Sprint are the telephone companies of the future.
(b) The ending of the AT&T telephone monopoly has led to competition and worker layoffs.
(c) The AT&T telephone monopoly was in violation of anti-trust laws.

2. Hospital costs are higher than most people can afford.
An unexpected illness can be a financial disaster for a family.
Medical insurance pays for hospital costs and doctors' bills.

(a) Medical insurance protects people from large health-care bills.
(b) The United States should adopt a National Health Insurance plan.
(c) Medical costs are too high and should be reduced to help protect families.

Answers start on page 352.

READING SKILL: PUTTING THE DETAILS TOGETHER

TOPIC AND MAIN IDEA

You have practiced finding, understanding, restating, and summarizing details. The next step is to start putting these details together. To get a complete picture of what the writer is talking about, you must determine the topic and the main idea.

The ***topic*** is the subject of a passage. The ***main idea*** is the point the writer wants to make about the topic. The details provide evidence or examples or description to explain the main idea to you.

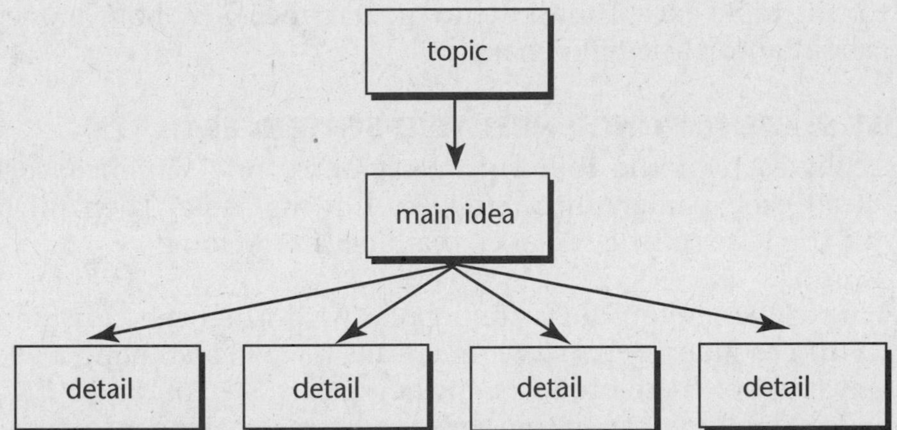

IDENTIFYING THE TOPIC

A ***paragraph*** is a group of sentences that help develop a central point or idea. The topic is what the paragraph is about. One way to determine the topic of a paragraph is to look at the details. Study the details in the paragraph below. Do they suggest a topic, a subject that the whole paragraph relates to?

> The Federal Reserve controls the nation's money supply. Most people need to budget their money very carefully. Many products cater to young consumers. It is very hard to survive on welfare.

You probably are not sure what the topic of this group of sentences is. In fact, there is no single topic. These sentences *look* like a paragraph, but they are not one. For a group of sentences to be a paragraph, they must be about a single topic.

The example that follows is a unified paragraph except for one thing: it contains a sentence that does not belong. Read the paragraph carefully. Decide what the topic of the paragraph is. Then identify the sentence that is *not* about the topic.

(1) Today many people do their banking by automatic teller machine (ATM). (2) ATMs can be found in many places, including department stores and supermarkets. (3) Banks supply their customers with access cards for the machines. (4) You can pay for groceries by check at many supermarkets. (5) Most ATMs can give you money from your account, tell you your account balance, or let you make a deposit.

▶ What is the topic of this paragraph? ______________________

▶ Which sentence does not belong? __________

The topic of this paragraph is *automatic teller machines*. Each sentence is related to this topic except for sentence *4*. Sentence *4* is about money, but it is not about automatic teller machines.

EXERCISE 9: IDENTIFYING UNRELATED SENTENCES

Directions: In each of the following paragraphs, one sentence does not belong. Read each paragraph carefully to find its topic. Then fill in the blank with the letter of the sentence that does not belong.

_____ **1.** **(a)** Japanese products are popular with American consumers. **(b)** For many years now, Americans have been buying a wide variety of these products, including cars, stereos, and VCRs. **(c)** The American automobile industry is making a comeback. **(d)** Japanese restaurants are now becoming very popular in the United States. **(e)** Sushi, a Japanese dish, is almost as well known to Americans as products made by Sony.

_____ **2.** **(a)** The Consumer Price Index (CPI) measures the inflation rate. **(b)** The cost of housing is a major factor in the CPI. **(c)** Food prices often depend on the weather. **(d)** Food and clothing costs are also major factors in the CPI. **(e)** As housing, food, and clothing costs rise, so does the Consumer Price Index.

Answers start on page 352.

FINDING THE MAIN IDEA

Every paragraph has a topic, the subject of the paragraph. And every paragraph has a main idea. The ***main idea*** is the most important thing, or the central point, that the writer wants to say about the topic. Practice finding the topic and the main idea in the following paragraph.

In our free enterprise system, anyone has the right to go into business. If you see a need, you don't need government permission to try to fill it. Whether it is a new computer company or a roadside fruit stand, you have the right to try to sell your products. And if you're successful, the rewards can be great.

▶ What is the topic of this paragraph? ______________________________

▶ What do you think the writer's main point is? ______________________

____

The topic is "starting a business in our free enterprise system." Each sentence is related to this topic. The main idea is more specific than the topic. The main idea is, "In our free enterprise system, anyone has the right to go into business." This main idea tells you the central point of the rest of the sentences.

Now try another example. After the following paragraph are four choices for main idea. Circle the letter of the best choice for the main idea.

> In past decades, most developing countries borrowed billions of dollars from large banks. Today, those loans threaten the world economy. Many developing countries, like Argentina and Brazil, have trouble repaying their loans. Since the world banking system would collapse if the loans went bad, the banks lend these nations more money to pay off their debts. Because of this cycle of borrowing, the world faces a debt crisis.

▶ What is the main idea of this paragraph?

(a) Argentina is having trouble paying back its debts.
(b) The world economy is threatened by a debt crisis.
(c) Today, the world economy has made all countries interdependent.
(d) The United States economy is the largest in the world.

Choice (b) sums up the central point of the paragraph. Choice (a) is too narrow because it is only a specific detail mentioned in the paragraph. Choice (c) is too broad and general. The main idea of this paragraph is more specific—*debt* in the world economy. Choice (d) is not mentioned in the passage at all.

EXERCISE 10: IDENTIFYING THE MAIN IDEA

Directions: Following each paragraph are four choices for main idea. Put *M* by the main idea. Put *N* by the choice that is too narrow. Put *B* by the choice that is too broad. Put *X* by the choice that is not in the passage.

1. In a capitalist economy, most factories and farms are privately owned. In a socialist economy, the society as a whole owns the factories and the farms. Until recently, the Chinese had a socialist economy. But in recent years, the Chinese government has begun to experiment with private ownership. The Chinese are trying to combine the best of socialism and capitalism. In time, perhaps they will develop a com pletely new kind of economy.

_____ (a) Capitalism and socialism are the two main economic systems in the world.
_____ (b China is experimenting by combining capitalism with socialism.
_____ (c) China has successfully controlled the growth of its population.
_____ (d) Most factories and farms are privately owned in a capitalist economy.

2. One measure of a healthy economy is the savings rate. The savings rate measures how much money people deposit in savings accounts. A savings account is a cushion against hard times. It is also a source of money for investment. In the United States, the savings rate is very low. Because of the low savings rate, the United States economy has less money available for investment and less protection against hard times than a country with a higher savings rate has.

_____ (a) The low savings rate in the United States weakens the economy.
_____ (b) A savings account is a cushion against hard times.
_____ (c) The United States faces economic hard times.
_____ (d) Saving rates are important.

Answers start on page 352.

TOPIC SENTENCES

The main idea of a paragraph is sometimes stated directly in one of the sentences of the paragraph. This sentence is called the ***topic sentence***. The topic sentence is often at the beginning of a paragraph. The topic sentence may also occur at the end. Occasionally, it appears in the middle of a paragraph. No matter where the topic sentence appears, all other sentences relate to it. They are ***supporting*** sentences—they support the main idea expressed in the topic sentence.

In the following paragraph, find and underline the topic sentence.

> The Environmental Protection Agency (EPA) is responsible for the quality of our environment. The EPA enforces the Clean Water and Clean Air Acts. It must protect wetlands and other delicate ecosystems. In addition, toxic wastes and their disposal are the EPA's responsibility.

The first sentence introduces the main idea of the paragraph. The EPA is responsible for the quality of the environment. The other three sentences all give examples of the EPA's responsibilities.

In the following example paragraph, the topic sentence has been replaced by two blank lines. Read the paragraph carefully and answer the two questions above the paragraph.

▶ What is the topic? ______________________________

▶ What is the main point being made about the topic? ______________________________

____

Now write a topic sentence for the paragraph that expresses the main idea.

____

____

Only about half of all employees in the United States work a "standard" work week of thirty-five to forty-five hours. Almost a quarter of all employees work fewer than thirty-five hours. The rest work more than forty-five hours each week. However, experts think that these statistics don't tell the whole story. In reality, many of those thirty-five- to forty-five-hour workers may actually work much longer hours.

A good topic sentence for the paragraph might be: *A forty-hour work week is probably not standard for most workers in the United States.*

EXERCISE 11: WRITING TOPIC SENTENCES

Directions: In the following example paragraph, the topic sentence has been replaced by two blank lines. Read the paragraph carefully and answer the questions above the paragraph. Then, on the lines above the paragraph, write a topic sentence that introduces the main idea of the paragraph.

1. What is the topic? ______________________________

   What is the main point being made about the topic?

   ____

   Topic sentence:

   ____

   ____

   The Federal Deposit Insurance Corporation (FDIC) was established in the 1930s after many people lost their life savings when banks failed. Today most bank accounts are insured by the FDIC up to a fixed amount. As a result, if a bank fails, the FDIC will replace money that depositors had in accounts at the failed bank.

2. What is the topic? ______________________________

   What is the main point being made about the topic?

   ____

Topic sentence:

____

____

Housing co-ops are a common kind of consumer co-op. They are owned jointly by the members who live in them. Another common type of consumer co-op is food co-ops. Food co-ops can be large supermarkets or small health-food stores. These co-ops are owned by the members who shop there. Child-care co-ops are preschools and day-care centers owned by members, the parents of the children who attend them.

Answers start on page 352.

FINDING THE MAIN IDEA OF A PASSAGE

The same process is used in finding the main idea of a passage. If you find the main idea of each paragraph in a passage, you will find that they are related. They all point to one main idea for the whole passage. Read the following passage about the 1996 primary elections in New Hampshire. What is the main idea of the first paragraph? the second? the third? What is the one main idea that sums up the whole passage?

Before every presidential election, the Democratic and Republican parties conduct statewide primary elections to measure the popularity of candidates. The nation's first primary election, in New Hampshire, is a presidential candidate's first and probably most powerful opportunity to impress party officials and capture public attention. Successful candidates in the New Hampshire primary often do well nationwide.

Months before the New Hampshire primary, presidential candidates begin making appearances in the state. In the 1996 campaign, the Republican front-runner planned a 10-day campaign tour of New Hampshire. Another candidate hiked border-to-border across the state. Four Republican candidates all campaigned vigorously in the state.

But presidential campaigns involve more than speeches. The Republican candidates tried various strategies in New Hampshire. One candidate began airing campaign commercials months before the primary. Before dropping out of the race, another candidate selected a popular New England politician as his new national finance chairman. A front-runner's staff conducted direct-mail campaigns and telephone surveys. Like other presidential candidates, this candidate also softened his most liberal positions to reassure conservative New Hampshire voters.

main idea of first paragraph: ______________________________

____

main idea of second paragraph: ______________________________

____

main idea of third paragraph: ______________________________

____

The main idea of the first paragraph is that doing well in the New Hampshire primary is very important to presidential candidates. The main idea of the second paragraph is that candidates all make early campaign visits to the state. The main idea of the third paragraph is that the candidates try many strategies in their New Hampshire campaigns.

Now you have looked at the main idea of each paragraph separately. But what about the passage as a whole? Write a main idea for the passage.

____

____

____

You might have written something like this:

> Winning the New Hampshire primary is generally very important to presidential candidates, so they try many strategies to win votes there.

EXERCISE 12: MAIN IDEA OF A PASSAGE

Directions: Read the following passage. Then choose the correct main idea for each of the three paragraphs. Finally, choose the main idea for the passage.

> (1) The Chicago Housing Authority (CHA) has decided to allow renters in one city housing project to manage the project themselves. The tenants of the LeClaire Courts complex have worked toward this decision for three years. They say that tenant management has made living conditions better in housing projects in other large cities.
>
> (2) The new tenant managers will have almost complete control of their housing complex. They will take care of their own maintenance and security and select new tenants. In addition, the CHA has set aside $1 million for repairs in the complex. Residents will decide how the money will be spent. However, the tenant managers will report to the CHA's board of directors.

(3) LeClaire tenants have already formed a management company. A group of about fifteen tenants will be given an intensive three-month training program to learn to manage the housing project. Then they may have as much as two years' follow-up training. When their training period is over, the CHA will allow the tenant company to take over the complex.

1. The main idea of paragraph 1 is:
   (a) The CHA is going to allow tenants of a housing project to manage it themselves.
   (b) Tenant management lowers the quality of life in housing projects.
   (c) Tenant management has succeeded in other major cities.
   (d) LeClaire tenants have worked toward tenant management for three years.

2. The main idea of paragraph 2 is:
   (a) The CHA has set aside $1 million to repair the housing project.
   (b) The CHA will decide how to use the repair money set aside for LeClaire Courts.
   (c) The tenant managers will have almost complete control over LeClaire Courts.
   (d) The tenant managers will have to report to the CHA's board of directors.

3. The main idea of paragraph 3 is:
   (a) The LeClaire tenants have formed a tenant management company.
   (b) About 15 tenants will actually manage the complex.
   (c) After tenant managers are trained, the tenant company will run the complex.
   (d) The tenant managers will not need special training to manage the complex.

4. Choose the sentence below that best summarizes the main idea of the entire passage. Use the main ideas of the individual paragraphs to help you choose the main idea of the passage.
   (a) Tenants lost their battle for control of the LeClaire Courts CHA housing project.
   (b) Following a training period, the CHA board will give a group of tenants almost complete control of their housing project.
   (c) Tenants will be deciding how to spend $1 million in rehab money at the CHA's LeClaire Courts development.
   (d) Tenant management has improved living conditions in public housing in several major cities.

Answers start on page 352.

READING SKILL: READING BETWEEN THE LINES

The information in a passage is not always stated directly. Writers will often provide clues to facts or to their opinions.They will then leave it up to you to figure them out. Figuring out unstated facts and opinions is often called *reading between the lines*. Sometimes it's called ***making an inference.***

INFERRING FACTS

A passage can suggest a fact by giving you clues that you can gather as you read. As you read the following paragraph, watch for clues to Tanya and Mira's ages and their relationship. What is the writer telling you that he is not stating directly?

> Mira and Tanya couldn't decide which television program to watch. There were many different cartoon shows on Saturday morning, and they liked them all. They didn't want to help their father make breakfast. So they decided to ride their bikes.

▶ In what age group are Tanya and Mira?

(1) babies
(2) children
(3) teenagers
(4) young adults
(5) senior citizens

clues: ______________________________

There are several clues that Tanya and Mira are children (choice 2). They were interested in Saturday morning cartoons. They went outside to ride their bikes.

▶ What is the relationship between Tanya and Mira?

(1) sisters
(2) friends
(3) parent-child
(4) co-workers
(5) boyfriend-girlfriend

clue: ______________________________

The third sentence tells you their father is making breakfast (choice 1).

EXERCISE 13: INFERRING FACTS

Part A

Directions: Following this passage are two inferences that can be drawn from the passage. List at least one clue for each inference.

> I had worked hard all day and was very tired. This white man walked back, expecting me to get up and give him my seat. I refused. In most parts of the world, a man would give up his seat to a woman, but I was arrested for refusing to move for the white man. The black community rallied to my support, beginning the famous Montgomery, Alabama, bus boycott.

1. Inference: The incident described in the passage occurred on a bus.

   clues: ____

2. Inference: The speaker in the passage is a black woman.

   clues: ____

Part B

Directions: Read the following passages and answer the questions. The correct answers are not stated directly, but they can be inferred. Find at least one clue that backs up the answer you choose.

> Sam's life was very hard. He was expected to be out working in the cotton fields by sunrise. No matter how hot it was, the foreman kept him working until sunset. His owner had paid $25 for him and expected to get his money's worth.

1. Sam was
   (1) a migrant farm worker
   (2) a slave
   (3) a technician
   (4) the owner of a small farm
   (5) a foreman

> Two hundred of us were working on the floor when the fire broke out. Rolls of fabric were piled everywhere. There was barely enough room to walk between the sewing machines. Some of the other women I work with began to panic when they discovered that the fire escape door was locked. Somehow I managed to get down the stairway and down to the street. I saw women leaping from the windows. It seemed that dead bodies were everywhere.

2. The speaker in the passage was
   (1) an owner of a large mill
   (2) a New England farmer
   (3) an immigrant waiting to enter the United States
   (4) a worker at a factory
   (5) a newspaper reporter writing about a fire

When I took office, the country was in the middle of the worst economic period of its history. Unemployment was very high and many farms and businesses had gone bankrupt. I felt that government should take a more active role in helping people. I proposed programs to Congress to restore people's hope in the future. . . . But, despite all my efforts, hard times continued for some years.

3. The person speaking in this paragraph is
   (1) Douglas MacArthur, a general in the United States Army
   (2) Woody Guthrie, a songwriter who wrote of people's hardships
   (3) Franklin D. Roosevelt, president of the United States from 1933 to 1945
   (4) Samuel Gompers, president of the American Federation of Labor from 1886 to 1924
   (5) Andrew Carnegie, one of the men who built American industry in the 1800s

Answers start on page 352.

INFERRING OPINIONS

You have been learning to infer facts that are not stated directly in a passage. Authors often also imply opinions in their writing. You can infer opinions in the same way as facts—by looking at the evidence. As you read the following passage, ask yourself what the writer might be implying about the effects of watching television. Then answer the question that follows the passage.

I recently discovered that the average school-age child watches an appalling eleven hours of television every week. Imagine everything children could accomplish by spending that time doing something useful! Parents, pitch your television in the garbage tomorrow and get your children involved in something productive like building a tree house together, joining a club, or simply having a private conversation. Teach your children how to use time wisely instead of vegetating on the sofa.

▶ The author believes that watching TV

(1) can be one way of learning
(2) is a horrible waste of time
(3) may be dangerously addictive
(4) makes children violent
(5) reduces the stress in children's lives

You were right if you chose (2), *is a horrible waste of time*. You can figure out what the writer thinks of TV by noticing how she describes activities she *wants* children to pursue.

- First, she contrasts watching TV with "doing something useful."
- She also contrasts it with being "involved in something productive."

These descriptions show you that the writer thinks watching TV is useless and unproductive. In the last sentence she uses the word *vegetating* to describe what it's like to watch TV.

EXERCISE 14: INFERRING OPINIONS

Directions: Read each passage carefully. Answer the questions that follow each passage or cartoon, making sure you have found evidence for the answer you choose.

Franklin D. Roosevelt, president of the U.S. in the 1930s, was crippled by polio. However, most Americans did not realize the extent of his handicap. FDR never discussed his health problems in public, and he was careful to show as few signs of his handicap as possible. The press also helped him by not calling attention to his physical problems. His strategy was so successful that his handicap did not prevent him from being reelected president three times.

1. Why did President Roosevelt want to keep people from being very aware of his handicap?
   (1) He wanted people to believe he was healthy enough to keep up with his responsibilities.
   (2) He didn't want to hurt his social life.
   (3) He didn't want to be reelected because his handicap interfered with his work.
   (4) He enjoyed fooling the American public and controlling the press.
   (5) He wanted to find out how powerful the press could be in shaping public opinion.

Thousands of elderly Japanese men and women are experiencing difficult times. Once, the Japanese were known for their tradition of responsibility and care for their elders. Now most Japanese say that they don't feel they should have to support their aging parents.

2. The passage suggests that, in the past, older Japanese were
   (1) ready to die at sixty-five
   (2) willing to accept their children's lifestyle changes
   (3) living alone on limited incomes
   (4) supported by their children
   (5) saving money so that they could support themselves in retirement

3. When the speaker says "They run in packs and upset the ecosystem," he refers to the actions of
   (1) trees
   (2) wolves
   (3) bad drivers
   (4) people
   (5) park rangers

4. It is the cartoonist's opinion that
   (1) there are too many people moving into Canada
   (2) Canada deserves all the problems it gets
   (3) people are really more dangerous than wolves
   (4) traffic at Yellowstone Park should be better regulated
   (5) wolves are vicious, good-for-nothing animals

Answers start on page 352.

EXPRESSING OPINION IN POLITICAL CARTOONS

A political cartoon expresses the opinion of the artist. Usually political cartoons comment on current events. One key to understanding most political cartoons is *background knowledge* of what was going on in the world when the cartoon was created. In this book, you'll be given background clues to the cartoons.

Another key to understanding political cartoons is *symbols*. A symbol stands for something. For example, a dollar sign ($) stands for money. Political cartoons often use symbols.

A third key to understanding political cartoons is understanding the *titles* and all the *labels*. Always read every word on a cartoon. Notice especially when words label a particular figure or part of the cartoon.

Background clues: In the early 1800s, the Massachusetts legislature, controlled by Governor Gerry, created an oddly shaped voting district. The shape of this new district was designed to help Governor Gerry's political party keep control of the legislature. A cartoonist noted that the district was shaped like a salamander.

The Gerry-mander.

☞ *A new species of Monster*, which appeared in *Essex South District* in January last.

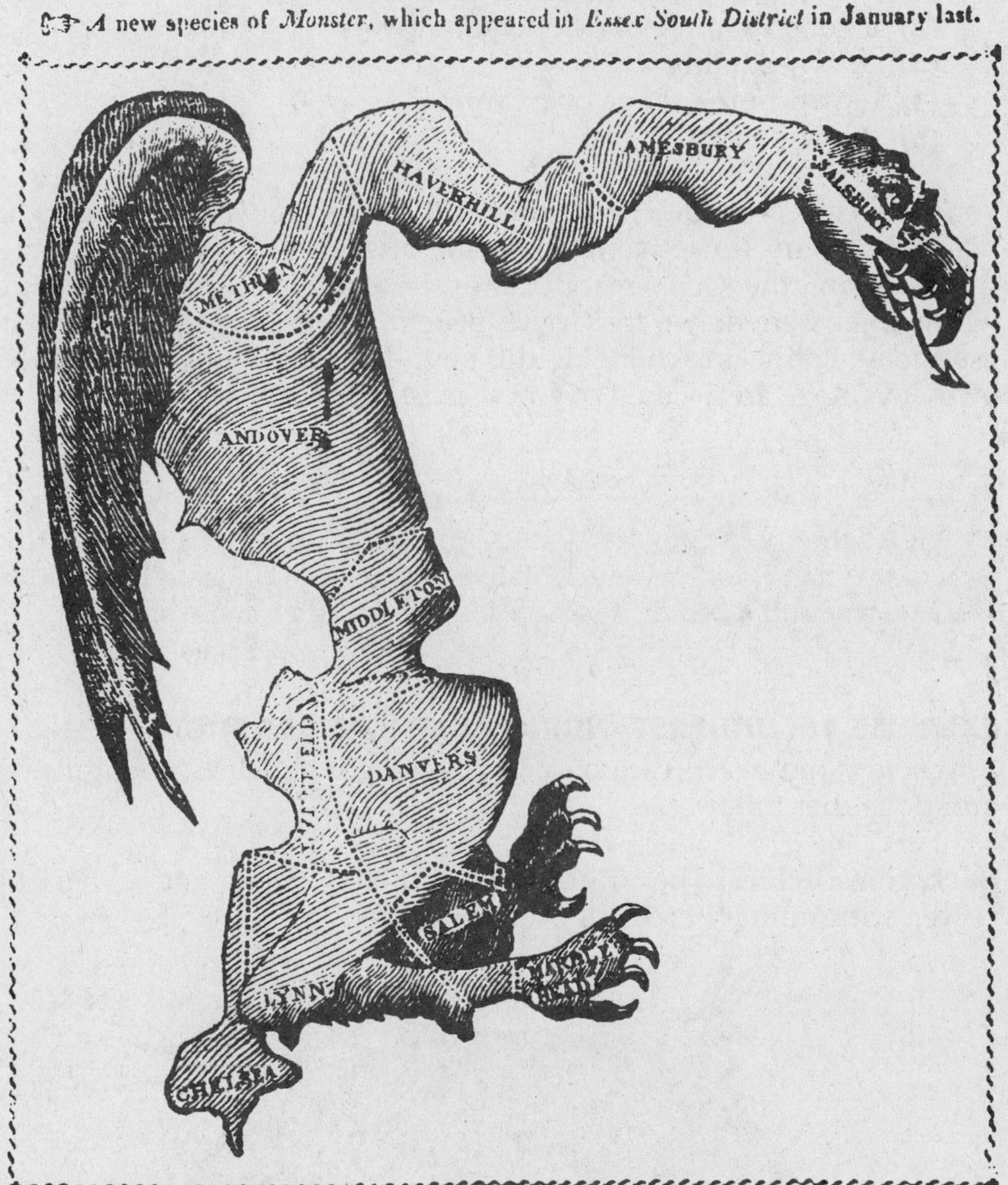

Source: *The Ungentlemanly Art: A History of American Political Cartoons* by Stephen Hess and Milton Kaplan.

▶ What does the cartoonist call the animal in the cartoon? ____________

The animal is called the Gerry-mander.

▶ Whom is the cartoonist criticizing? ________________________________

He is criticizing Governor Gerry. You know this because he called the animal the *Gerry*-mander.

▶ The cartoonist's opinion is that the Essex South District boundaries are

(1) a major creative accomplishment
(2) a good example of democracy at work
(3) drawn unfairly
(4) drawn in the shape of an animal
(5) drawn fairly

You were correct if you chose number (3), *drawn unfairly*. The cartoonist is criticizing Gerry for reshaping a voting district for his own advantage. In this cartoon, the Gerry-mander monster symbolizes the voting district whose lines were drawn for Gerry's benefit. The term *gerrymander* is still in use today. Politicians changing the boundaries of voting districts to their own advantage are accused of *gerrymandering*.

Cartoon Tip

One of the most commonly used symbols in political cartoons is Uncle Sam. He stands for the United States. Uncle Sam is usually a tall man with white hair and a beard. He wears clothes with stars and stripes.

EXERCISE 15: UNDERSTANDING POLITICAL CARTOONS

Directions: Study each cartoon and its background clues; then answer the questions that follow.

Background clues: The United States is a very strong and active military power, with military bases all over the world.

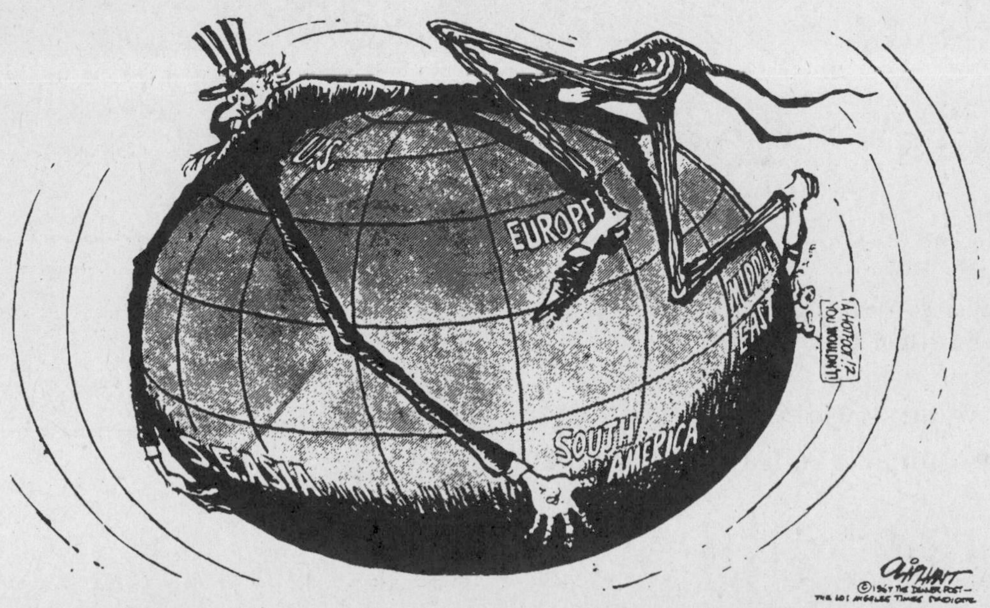

1. What is the cartoon character trying to do?

____

2. The cartoonist's opinion is that the United States
   (1) should act as the policeman of the world
   (2) cannot control the entire world
   (3) should increase its military budget
   (4) should be better respected by foreign governments
   (5) is not doing enough to fight world hunger

Background clues: After the Civil War, New York City politics were controlled by a political organization called Tammany Hall. The boss of Tammany Hall was William Tweed.

3. What is drawn where Tweed's head should be?

____

____

4. The cartoonist's main point is that Boss Tweed
   (1) is an honest man who works for a living
   (2) is a banker
   (3) eats too much
   (4) is corrupt
   (5) is a wealthy man

Source: *The Ungentlemanly Art: A History of American Political Cartoons* by Stephen Hess and Milton Kaplan.

Background clues: This cartoon was drawn at a time when the U.S. economy was starting to recover from a recession.

5. The big fighter sitting in the corner is "Mr. Taxes." What is the name of the skinny fighter knocked out on the floor?

____

6. In the opinion of this cartoonist, taxes
   (1) must increase to save the economy
   (2) are knocking out the economic recovery
   (3) will help the boxing industry
   (4) must be collected for the health of the economy
   (5) are hurting boxers

Answers start on page 353.

EXERCISE 16: CHAPTER REVIEW

Directions: Read the following passages and answer the questions, circling the number of the correct answer.

Questions 1–3 are based on the following passage.

Harriet Hanson was an eleven-year-old girl working in the mill. She later recalled:

I worked in a lower room where I had heard the proposed strike fully, if not vehemently, discussed. I had been an ardent listener to what was said against this attempt at "oppression" on the part of the corporation, and naturally I took sides with the strikers. When the day came on which the girls were to turn out, those in the upper rooms started first, and so many of them left that our mill was at once shut down. Then, when the girls in my room stood irresolute, uncertain what to do . . . I, who began to think they would not go out, after all their talk, became impatient, and started on ahead, saying with childish bravado, "I don't care what you do, I am going to turn out, whether any-one else does or not," and I marched out, and was followed by the others.

As I looked back at the long line that followed me, I was more proud than I have ever been since. . . .

1. The topic of this passage is

(1) a young girl growing up in a mill town
(2) the tragedy of child labor
(3) the rise of the labor movement
(4) life in the early mills
(5) a young girl's role in a mill strike

2. Harriet decided to *turn out*. This meant that

(1) she rearranged her clothes
(2) she went on strike
(3) she told the other workers what to do
(4) she went to the upper rooms
(5) she converted to Catholicism

3. Harriet spoke with childish *bravado*. She showed

(1) great confidence and maturity
(2) a pretense of courage
(3) a lack of responsibility
(4) thoughtfulness
(5) cowardice and fear

Questions 4 and 5 are based on the following passage.

> It has long been true, and prisoners knew this better than anyone, that the poorer you were, the more likely you were to end up in jail. This was not just because the poor committed more crimes. In fact, they did. The rich did not have to commit crimes to get what they wanted; the laws were on their side. But when the rich did commit crimes, they often were not prosecuted, and if they were they could get out on bail, hire clever lawyers, get better treatment from judges. Somehow, the jails ended up full of poor black people.

4. According to the passage, why do the rich commit fewer crimes than the poor?
   (1) They have a better education and stronger reasoning skills than poor people.
   (2) They tend to be more religious than poor people.
   (3) They can get what they want since the law is on their side.
   (4) They can get out on bail, hire clever lawyers, get better treatment from judges.
   (5) They want to set a good example so that others do not resent their good fortune.

5. What is the main idea of this paragraph?
   (1) The poorer you are, the more likely you are to end up in jail.
   (2) Reform is needed to make the criminal justice system work.
   (3) Rich people can afford to hire clever lawyers and pay bail.
   (4) Poor people commit more crimes than rich people.
   (5) The criminal justice system must become tougher on criminals.

Questions 6–8 are based on the following passage.

In the spring of 1903, I went to Kensington, Pennsylvania, where seventy-five thousand textile workers were on strike. Of this number at least ten thousand were little children. The workers were striking for more pay and shorter hours. Every day little children came into Union Headquarters, some with their hands off, some with the thumb missing, some with their fingers off at the knuckle. They were stooped little things, round-shouldered and skinny. . . .

I asked some of the parents if they would let me have their little boys and girls for a week or ten days, promising to bring them back safe and sound. . . . A man named Sweeny was marshall. . . . A few men and women went with me. . . . The children carried knapsacks on their backs in which was a knife and fork, a tin cup and plate. . . . One little fellow had a drum, and another had a fife. . . . We carried banners that said: . . . "We want time to play. . . ."

. . . Our march had done its work. We had drawn the attention of the nation to the crime of child labor.

6. The children carried
   (1) eating utensils and musical instruments
   (2) knives and forks
   (3) the smaller children
   (4) more pay and shorter hours
   (5) a fife and drum

7. What is this passage about?
   (1) a children's march to protest child labor
   (2) an early fund-raising telethon
   (3) the right of children to play
   (4) the textile workers' strike in Kensington
   (5) the abuse and mutilation of children

8. How many textile workers were on strike in Kensington?
   (1) 10
   (2) 1,903
   (3) 7,000
   (4) 10,000
   (5) 75,000

Directions: Read each passage and answer the questions that follow.

Questions 9 and 10 are based on the following passage.

This passage is about Calvin Coolidge, who was president of the United States from 1923 to 1929.

The sudden thrust of the Presidential mantle about his thin shoulders staggered him for a time. He really was a timid person those first few days. He promised to carry on the Harding policies—whatever that might mean—and then lapsed into silence for a month.

During that month he was built into a myth. It was one of the greatest feats of newspaper propaganda that the modern world has seen. It really was a miracle. He said nothing. Newspapers must have copy. So we grasped at little incidents to build up human interest stories and we created a character. He kept his counsel. Therefore he was a strong and silent man. The editorial writers on newspapers which were satisfied with the status quo, the big Eastern journals, created the strong, silent man. Then, in time, as the country found out he was not a superman, neither strong nor silent, they emphasized his little witticisms, his dry wit, and we had a national character—Cal. Everybody spoke of him fondly as "Cal." He was one of us. He was the ordinary man incarnate.

9. Why did the newspapers make up a strong, silent image for President Coolidge?

(1) They admired his strong, silent style of leadership.
(2) They believed silence was a virtue.
(3) The real Coolidge didn't give them anything to write about.
(4) They wanted to make sure the American people understood him.
(5) They wanted to create a miracle.

10. What was the truth about the images of Coolidge?

(1) Calvin Coolidge was a master of public relations when he created his image of "Cal."
(2) The real Calvin Coolidge was different from the public image of him.
(3) Calvin Coolidge was willing to dig for the truth.
(4) Calvin Coolidge was a strong and silent man.
(5) Calvin Coolidge's inspired leadership and great sense of humor have made him one of our most remembered presidents.

Answers start on page 353.

2 Interpreting Graphic Materials

Tables, graphs, and maps are often used in social studies materials. You have seen that it is important to understand written messages. It is just as important for you to understand illustrations. Illustrations can give detailed information without many words, so they are very helpful to both readers and writers. Understanding tables, graphs, and maps will help you in future chapters of this book and in your daily life.

GRAPHIC SKILL: USING TABLES

A table is information organized into columns and rows. The purpose of a table is to allow you to easily locate and compare bits of information. The following example shows the major parts of a table.

EDUCATION COMPLETED, 1940–1990

Since 1940, the following percentage of Americans aged 25 or over had completed high school or college:

	High School Only	Four or More Years of College
1940	24.5%	4.6%
1950	34.3%	6.2%
1960	41.4%	7.7%
1970	55.2%	11.0%
1980	66.3%	16.3%
1990	77.6%	21.3%

Source: U.S. Bureau of the Census

In the table above, the title gives the topic. A sentence below the title gives more information about the topic. The information, or **data**, on a table is organized into rows and columns. A **row** of a table is all the entries on one horizontal line. In the previous table, each row is labeled by a year, such as 1940. The table has two columns. A **column** consists of all the entries on one vertical line. The column headings are "High School Only" and "Four or More Years of College."

UNDERSTANDING A TABLE

Just like a reading passage, every table has a topic. The title usually tells you what a table is about. You can often find more clues to the topic in the headings and sometimes in a subtitle. Look at the table below.

What is this table about? ______________________________

THE NATION'S LARGEST CITIES

1990 Rank	1990 Population	Percentage Change Since 1980
1. New York	7,323,000	+3.5%
2. Los Angeles	3,485,000	+17.4%
3. Chicago	2,784,000	-7.4%
4. Houston	1,631,000	+2.2%
5. Philadelphia	1,586,000	-6.1%
6. San Diego	1,111,000	+26.8%
7. Detroit	1,028,000	-14.6%

Source: *Statistical Abstract of the United States, 1993*

The table is about the percent of population change in the nation's largest cities. You can figure this out by looking at the title and the headings for the columns and rows.

Table-Reading Tip

In order to understand a table, first read the title and all the headings. Don't try to read the data until you understand what the title and headings tell you.

EXERCISE 1: READING THE TITLES AND HEADINGS ON A TABLE

Directions: In your own words, write a sentence telling what the following table is about.

NATIONAL BASKETBALL ASSOCIATION STANDINGS Atlantic Division				
	Wins	Losses	Percentage of Wins	Games Behind
Orlando	18	5	.783	—
New York	16	6	.727	$1\frac{1}{2}$
Miami	12	8	.600	$4\frac{1}{2}$
Boston	11	10	.524	6
Washington	10	10	.500	$6\frac{1}{2}$
New Jersey	9	11	.450	$7\frac{1}{2}$
Philadelphia	3	17	.150	$13\frac{1}{2}$

This table is about ____

____

Possible answers start on page 353.

LOCATING DATA ON A TABLE

In order to find specific data (bits of information) on a table, you must use the column and row headings to locate the information you need. The headings label the vertical and horizontal lines of data. In the following table, the column headings are *1980*, *1990*, and *Percentage Change*. The row headings are the types of foods listed along the left side.

CHANGES IN FOOD CONSUMPTION, 1980–1990 (pounds per person)			
	1980	**1990**	**Percentage Change**
Dairy products	543.2	569.7	+ 4.6%
Red meat	126.4	112.4	–11.1%
Flour and cereal products	144.5	183.5	+26.9%
Fats and oils	57.2	62.2	+ 8.7%

Source: U.S. Department of Agriculture

The data in the table above can be used to help us understand how the American diet changed from 1980 to 1990. Answer the following sample questions based on the table.

▶ What was the number of pounds of red meat consumed (eaten) by the average American in 1990? ________________

First look for the row labeled *Red meat*. Then look for the column labeled *1990*. Draw imaginary lines across from *Red meat* and down from *1990*. The place where the lines cross is the number you are looking for. The average American ate 112.4 pounds of red meat in 1990.

▶ Of the items listed, which food had the greatest percentage change in consumption (use) from 1980 to 1990? ________________

You must look for the largest number in the *Percentage Change* column. That number is 26.9%. Looking across the row, you find that flour and cereal products had the greatest percentage change of the items listed.

▶ By how many pounds did the consumption of flour and cereal products increase from 1980 to 1990? ________________

In order to find the amount of the increase, first find the amount of consumption in 1980 and in 1990. Consumption of flour and cereal products was 144.5 pounds in 1980 and 183.5 pounds in 1990. To find the increase, you need to find the difference between the two numbers, so you subtract: 183.5 – 144.5 = 39.

Table-Reading Tip

If you are asked to find an increase, look for numbers or percentages that become larger over time. When you see a plus (+) sign, such as +18%, the plus sign tells you there was an increase of 18%. If you are asked to find a decrease, look for numbers that become smaller over time. When you see a minus (–) sign, such as –18%, the minus sign tells you there was a decrease of 18%.

EXERCISE 2: FINDING INFORMATION ON A TABLE

Directions: Use the information in the table on the next page to answer the questions that follow the table.

CHANGES IN FOOD CONSUMPTION, 1980–1990 (pounds per capita)			
	1980	1990	Percentage Change
Fresh vegetables	92.5	113.3	+22.5%
Sugar and other sweeteners	123.9	140.7	+13.6%
Fresh fruits	86.9	92.2	+ 6.1%
Poultry	40.6	55.9	+37.7%
Eggs	271.0	233.0	–14.0%
Fish and shellfish	12.4	15.0	+21.0%
Coffee	10.3	10.3	+ 0 %
Source: U.S. Department of Agriculture			

1. In 1990, the average American ate 15 pounds of

   ____

2. Between 1980 and 1990, Americans decreased their consumption of

   ____

3. By what percentage did the consumption of sweeteners increase between 1980 and 1990?

   ____

4. Americans increased their consumption of many foods between 1980 and 1990. What category increased by the greatest percentage?

   ____

Answers start on page 353.

FINDING THE MAIN IDEA OF A TABLE

Like a reading passage, a table may illustrate a main idea. The author may want to make a central point by choosing and displaying data in a certain way. Ask yourself what the table tells you and what its purpose is. Then think of how the data could be summarized in a main idea statement.

Sometimes the main idea of a table will be stated directly in the title or subtitle. Other times you must find the main idea by looking at the headings or by studying the data.

Table-Reading Tip

Because data are easier to read and compare in smaller numbers, tables that compare large numbers often use phrases such as *in thousands* in their subtitle or key. *In thousands* means that each number listed in the table is really 1,000 times that number. So, for example, the number *18* on a table that says *in thousands* actually means *18,000*.

GAINERS AND LOSERS
Union Membership (in thousands)

	1975	**1985**	**1993**
United Steel Workers	1,062	572	421
International Ladies' Garment Workers Union	363	210	133
Communications Workers of America	476	524	472
National Alliance of Letter Carriers	151	186	210
Service Employees International Union	490	688	919

Source: AFL-CIO

Following are four choices for the main idea of "Gainers and Losers." Circle the number of the choice that accurately summarizes the data for the table. What is the main idea of this table?

(1) The largest unions have thousands of members.
(2) In the last eight years, the International Ladies' Garment Workers Union lost almost half its members.
(3) While most unions lost members over the last eighteen years, some have gained members.
(4) In life, there are always gainers and losers.

You were correct if you circled (3). Of the five unions listed, three have lost members over the last eighteen years, while two have gained members. The table makes clear that the "gainers and losers" are the various unions.

EXERCISE 3: MAIN IDEA OF A TABLE

Directions: After each table are five choices for main idea. Choose the one that accurately summarizes the data on the table.

EARNINGS: SEX AND OCCUPATIONS

For every $1,000 made by men in these occupations during 1993, women received the following amounts.

Occupation	Amount	Occupation	Amount
Managers	$667	Security guards	$796
Doctors and lawyers	$765	Farmers/fishers	$883
Technicians	$761	Construction workers	$821
Salespeople	$605	Machine operators/ inspectors	$698
Administrative assistants/ secretaries	$762	Truckers/drivers	$785
Service workers	$893	Laborers	$897

Source: U.S. Bureau of Labor Statistics

What is the main idea of this table?

(1) Traditionally male occupations are now being filled by women.
(2) Women earn less than men in the same occupations.
(3) In most occupations, men are worth more than women.
(4) It costs more to hire a man than it does a woman.
(5) Women's and men's salaries are finally becoming equal.

Answers start on page 353.

GRAPHIC SKILL: READING GRAPHS

A graph allows a reader to spot trends, make comparisons, and draw conclusions from data. Being able to read graphs will help you in many practical situations as well as in social studies. You will look at four types of graphs: pictographs, bar graphs, line graphs, and circle graphs.

FINDING THE TOPIC OF A GRAPH

Like a table, every graph has a topic. The title usually tells you the topic of the graph. Sometimes there is also a subtitle to help you out. Read the titles and then check the other information on the graph, such as the labels and the data, to make sure you have an accurate idea of the topic of the graph.

Look at the sample graph below. What is the topic of this graph?

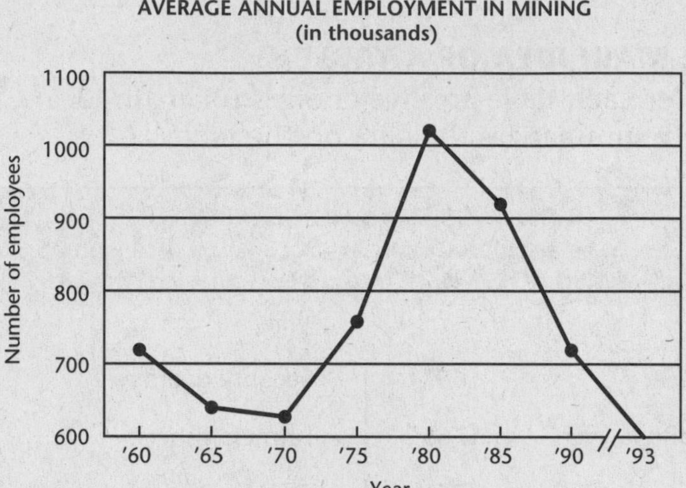

Source: U.S. Bureau of Labor Statistics

This graph shows the average annual employment in mining. The title of this graph tells you what the graph is about.

EXERCISE 4: TOPIC OF A GRAPH

Directions: In the space below each graph, write its topic. Study the titles and other information on each graph carefully before writing.

Graph 1

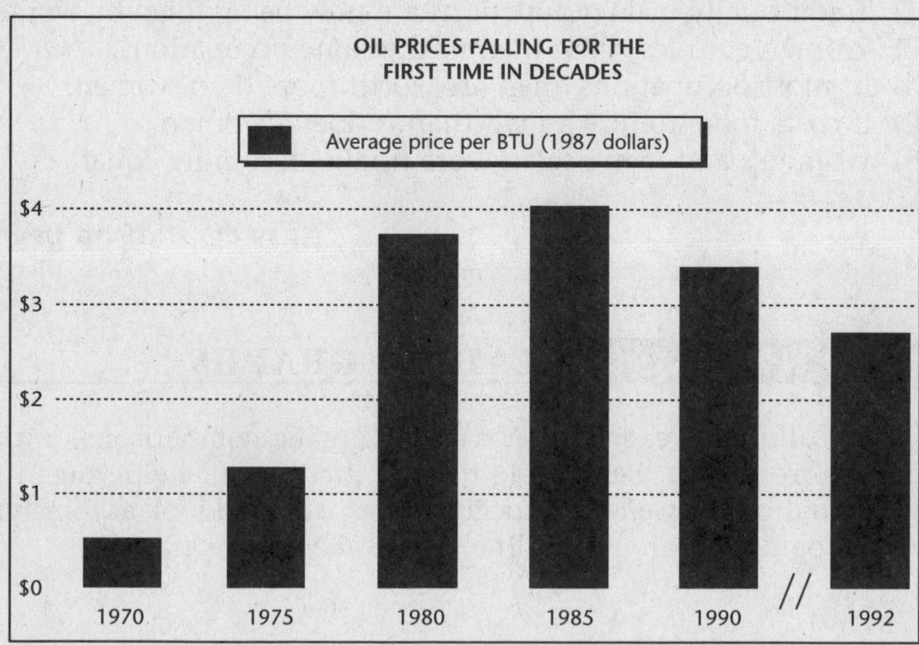

Source: U.S. Energy Information Administration

topic: ______________________________

Graph 2

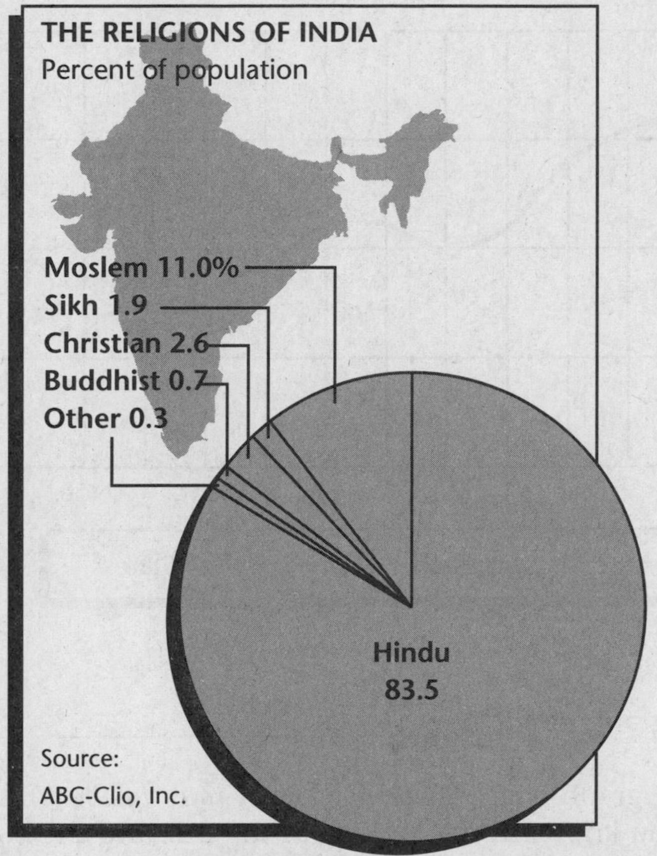

topic: ______________________________

Answers start on page 353.

THE MAIN IDEA OF A GRAPH

Graphs illustrate a point. Usually the main idea will be stated directly in the title or subtitle. To determine the main idea, read the titles and other written information and look at the data. Ask yourself, "What message is the graph giving me?" Then think of a way to summarize the information.

Study the graph on page 250. Read the title, the scale, and the labels and look at the data. Then answer the questions that follow it.

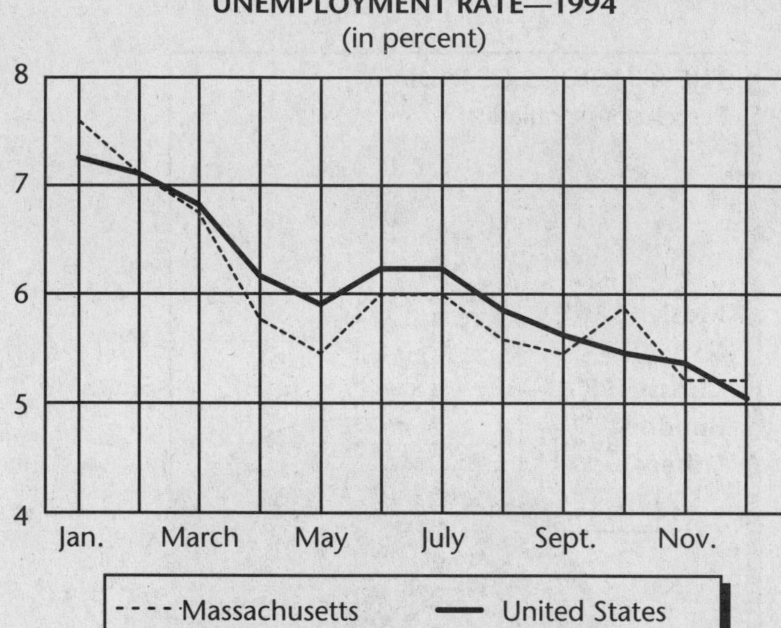

1. What is the graph about? ________________________________

The topic of the graph is *1994 unemployment rates in the United States and Massachusetts*. You know this by looking at the title and the boxed key that contains labels for the two lines.

2. Why are there two lines on the graph? ________________________

There are two lines because two things are being compared. One line stands for the United States as a whole. The other line stands for the state of Massachusetts.

3. The main idea of this graph is that:
(1) The unemployment rates in Massachusetts and the United States generally rose and fell together.
(2) The unemployment rate in the United States peaked at about 7% and then dropped.
(3) The unemployment rate in Massachusetts dipped as low as 5.2% from a high of 7.6%.
(4) The high school dropout rate in Massachusetts is lower than the national average.
(5) Massachusetts had the lowest unemployment rate in the nation.

Choice (1) is correct because it describes the relationship between the two lines. Choices (2) and (3) deal with only one of the two lines. Choice (4) has nothing to do with the graph. Choice (5) is related to the graph, but the graph does not show data for other states.

EXERCISE 5: THE MAIN IDEA OF A GRAPH

Directions: This exercise is based on two graphs. Before you answer any of the questions about a graph, read the title and the other written information and look at the data. Ask yourself about the message of the graph and its purpose. After each graph are one or more "warm-up" questions and then five choices for main idea.

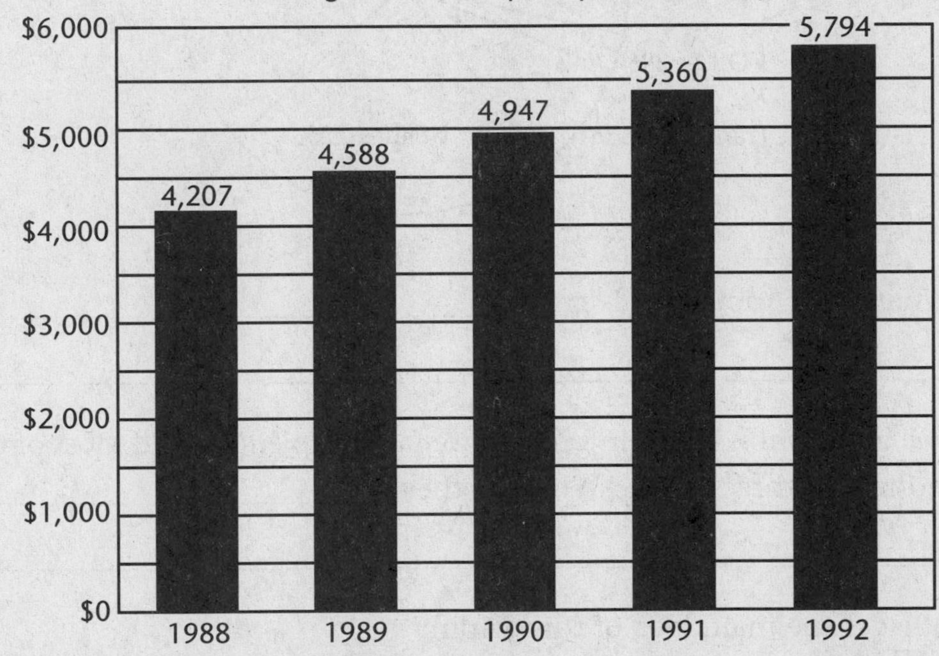

Source: American Hospital Association

1. What trend do you see when you look at the height of the bars changing over time? (A trend is a general direction or pattern of development.)

____

2. What is the main idea of the graph?
   (1) The rate of increase of hospital costs is slowing down.
   (2) Hospital costs increased each year from 1988 to 1992.
   (3) Hospital costs peaked in 1992.
   (4) The high cost of a hospital stay makes health insurance a necessity.
   (5) High hospital costs are a national scandal.

PERSONAL BUDGET OF A
TYPICAL WELFARE RECIPIENT

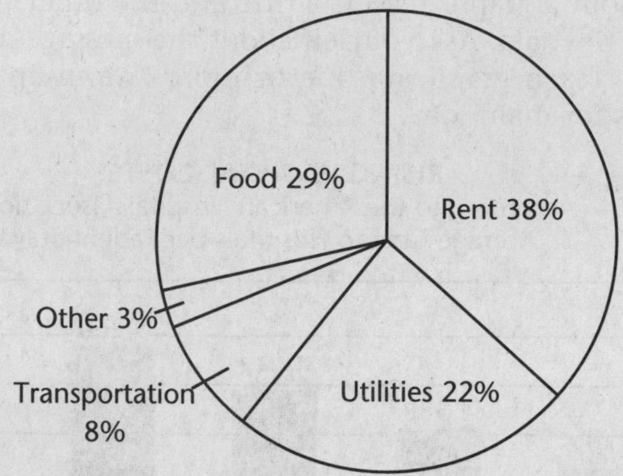

3. What is the topic of this graph? ______________________________

____

4. The graph shows that, in general, welfare recipients spend most of their money on three things. What are they? ______________________

____

5. What is the main idea of this graph?
   (1) Welfare recipients spend a great deal of their income on rent.
   (2) Welfare reform is long overdue.
   (3) Welfare recipients spend most of their money on necessities.
   (4) Welfare recipients do not manage their money wisely.
   (5) When people have to spend most of their income on food, rent, and energy, they go on welfare.

Answers start on page 354.

FINDING INFORMATION ON A PICTOGRAPH

A ***pictograph*** uses symbols to display information. In order to find specific details on a pictograph, you must use the key. The key tells you what the pictures on the graph stand for. For example, look at the following pictograph. Each picture, or symbol, stands for 50 prisoners per 100,000 people. Find the number of prisoners per 100,000 people in Delaware.

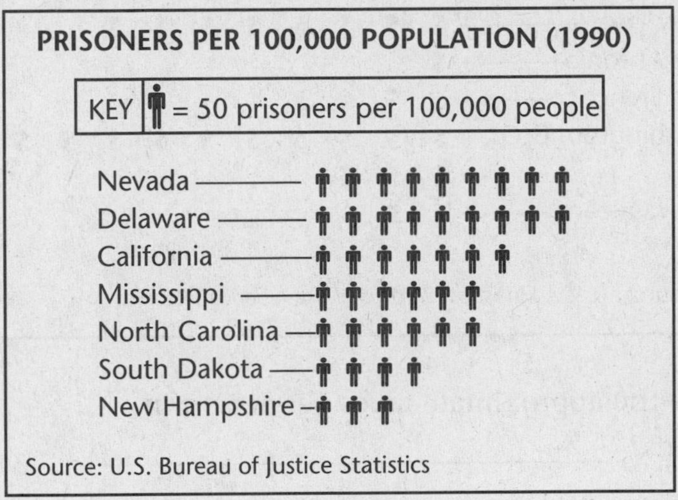

Find the row labeled Delaware. There are nine symbols. The key tells you that each symbol stands for 50 prisoners. Multiply: 9 x 50 = 450. There are about 450 prisoners per 100,000 people in Delaware.

Look again at the pictograph and answer the following questions.

▶ Which states had the highest number of prisoners per 100,000 people?

____

To find the states with the highest number of prisoners per 100,000 people, you must find the longest rows of symbols. Those rows are labeled *Nevada* and *Delaware*.

▶ Which state had the lowest number of prisoners per 100,000 people?

____

To find the state with the lowest number of prisoners per 100,000 people, you must find the shortest row. That row is labeled *New Hampshire*.

Graph-Reading Tip

Pictographs are used to make general comparisons. The information on a pictograph is not exact.

EXERCISE 6: READING PICTOGRAPHS

Directions: Fill in the blanks with the correct information based on the graph.

CITY TAXES PER PERSON

KEY $ = $100

City	
New York	$ $ $ $ $ $ $ $
San Antonio	$
San Francisco	$ $ $ $
Washington, D.C.	$ $ $ $ $ $ $ $ $ $ $ $ $
New Orleans	$ $

Source: *U.S. A Statistical Portrait of the American People*

1. What were the approximate taxes per person in New Orleans? ______________________________

2. Which city's per-person taxes are lower, San Francisco's or New York's? ______________________________

3. What is the main idea of the pictograph "City Taxes per Person"?
   (1) Washington, D.C., is one of the most expensive cities in the country to live in.
   (2) San Antonio and New Orleans have very low city taxes.
   (3) Cities that bring in a lot of tax money are able to provide more services to the public.
   (4) Per-person city taxes in the United States can range widely.
   (5) City taxes in San Francisco are reasonable, so most people could afford to live there.

Answers start on page 354.

READING BAR GRAPHS

A ***bar graph*** uses bars to display information. It gives you a way to compare information quickly and easily. The information is not exact, but you can make good estimates from a bar graph. In order to find specific facts on a bar graph, you must use the scale to read the height of the bars. What is the average life expectancy for women in the United States?

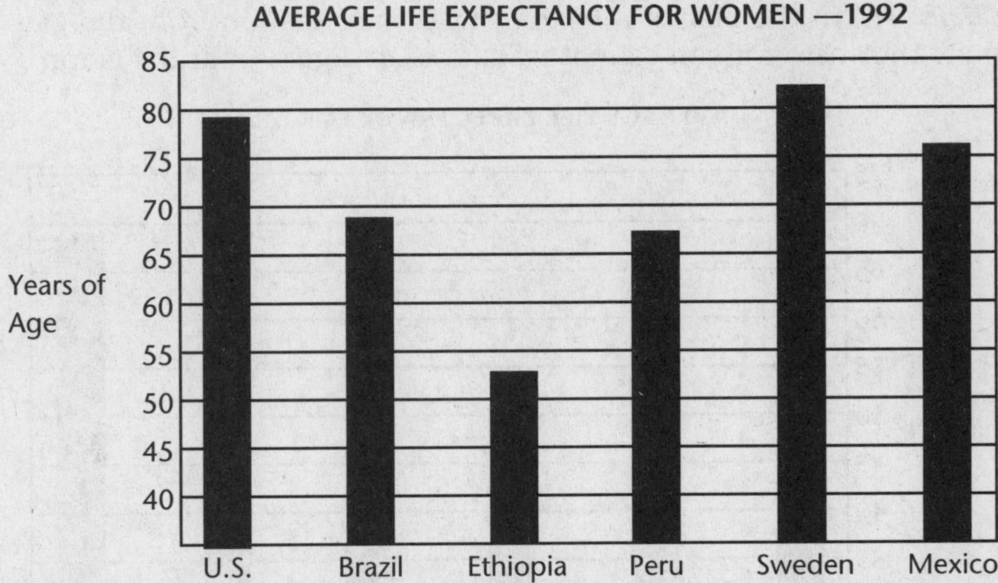

Source: *The World Almanac and Book of Facts*

In order to find the average life expectancy for women in the United States, find the bar labeled *U.S.* Now draw an imaginary horizontal line from the top end of the bar over to the scale. Read the number on the scale. If the line is between two scale entries, estimate the number. In this case, the average life expectancy of women in the U.S. is slightly below 80. A good estimate would be 79 years.

Use the bar graph in the example above to answer the following questions.

▶ What nation had the shortest life expectancy for women? __________

Find the shortest bar. At the bottom of the bar is the name of the country, Ethiopia.

▶ Only one nation on the graph had a life expectancy for women higher than that of the U.S. Which country was that? __________________

Find the U.S. bar. Now draw an imaginary horizontal line across the graph even with the top end of the U.S. bar. Only one bar ends above the line. At the bottom of that bar is the name of the country, Sweden.

Graph-Reading Tip

In multiple-choice questions based on graphs, you can eliminate wrong choices. Since you are usually expected to make estimates based on graphs, there should be one answer choice that is closest to your estimate.

EXERCISE 7: READING BAR GRAPHS

Directions: Fill in the blanks with the correct information from the graph. Estimate the answer if you cannot read an exact figure from the graph.

AVERAGE LIFE EXPECTANCY FOR MEN —1992

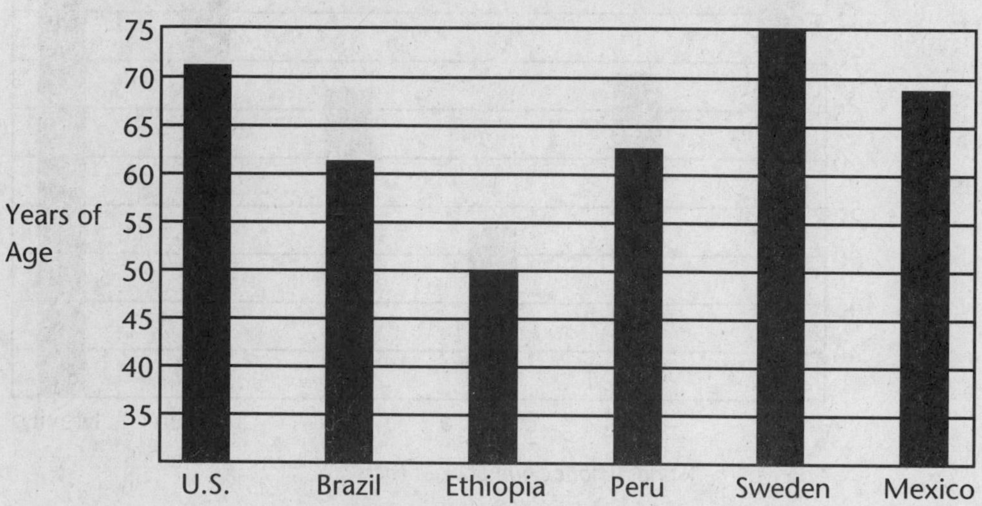

Source: *The World Almanac and Book of Facts*

1. Which nation had an average life expectancy for men of sixty-eight years? ________________

2. Which nation had the longest life expectancy for men? ____________

3. How many nations on the graph had a shorter life expectancy for men than the United States? ________________

4. About how many more years does the average man in Sweden live than the average man in Ethiopia? ________________

Answers start on page 354.

READING LINE GRAPHS

A ***line graph*** is similar to a bar graph in many ways. However, instead of using bars, lines connect different points (called ***data points***). Line graphs are used to show trends or developments. On the side of a line graph is a **vertical scale**. Along the bottom of a line graph is a **horizontal scale**. To read a line graph, you read up from the horizontal scale and across from the vertical scale to a particular point on the line.

Read the titles and other words on the graph before you try reading the data. Study the following line graph and answer the question, "What was the population of London in 1800?"

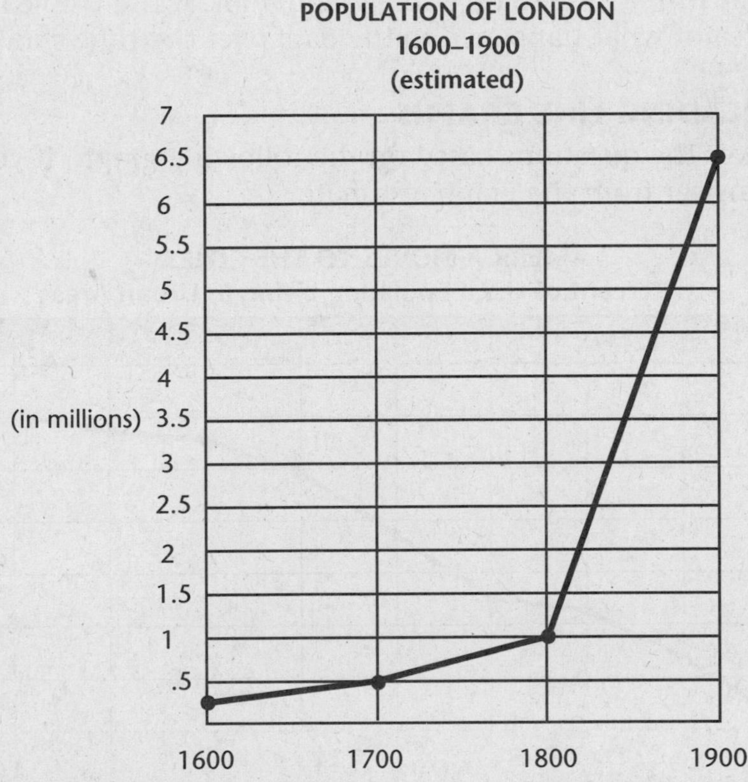

First find *1800* on the horizontal scale (along the bottom of the graph). Now go straight up until you reach the data point for 1800. Now go straight across to the left until you reach the vertical scale. At the height of the data point, the closest number on the vertical scale is 1. That means that the population of London in 1800 was about 1 million.

Use the line graph in the example above to answer the following questions.

▶ In what year shown on the graph did London have its largest population? ________

Look at the line and find the highest point on it. Looking down to the horizontal scale, you find the year 1900. Therefore, London had its largest population in 1900.

▶ Between 1600 and 1900, what happened to the size of London's population? ________

Look at the first point on the line, the shape of the line, and the endpoint of the line. The population of London increased greatly during the period, from less than half a million people to 6.5 million.

To summarize or see a trend on a line graph, look at the whole line and get a general idea of what happened to the data over the time shown.

EXERCISE 8: READING LINE GRAPHS

Directions: Answer the questions based on the following graph. If you can't read an exact answer from the graph, estimate.

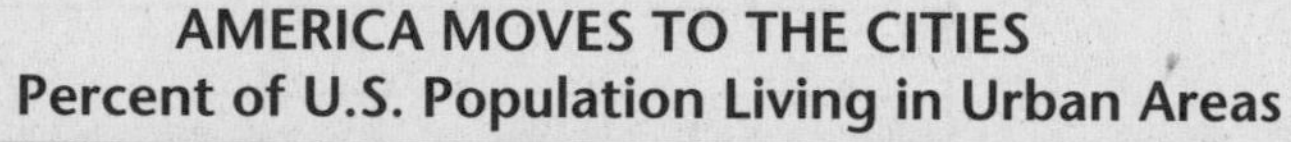

AMERICA MOVES TO THE CITIES
Percent of U.S. Population Living in Urban Areas

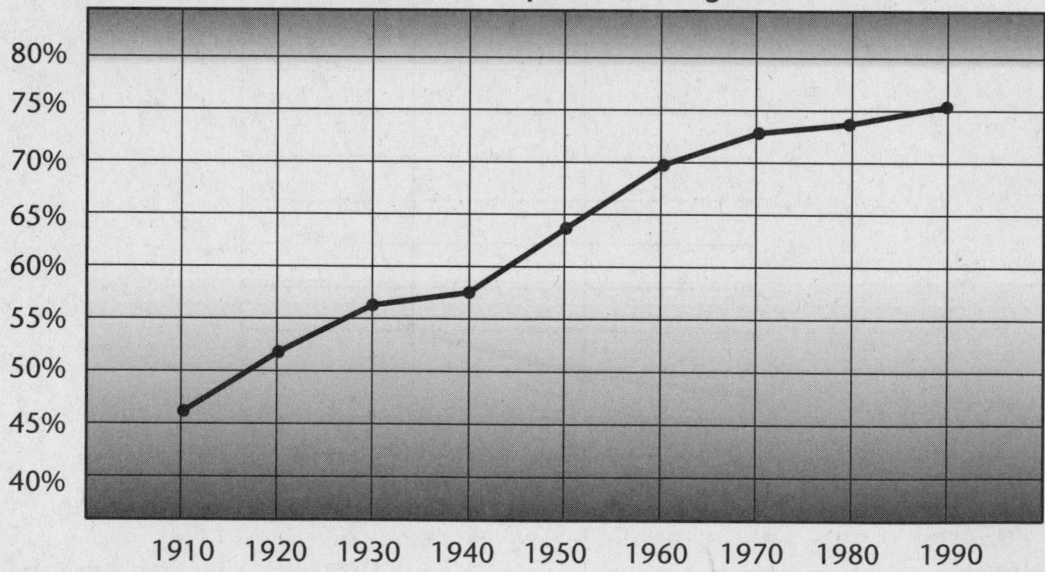

Source: U.S. Bureau of the Census

1. In what year shown on the graph was the percentage of urban population the lowest? ________

2. What percentage of the population of the United States lived in urban areas in 1960? ________

3. Which of the following best describes the trend shown by this line graph?
   (1) The percentage of people living in urban areas of the United States has steadily fallen.
   (2) The percentage of people living in rural areas of the United States has steadily increased.
   (3) The percentage of people living in a few major cities in the United States has risen steadily.
   (4) In 1910, most people lived in the northeastern United States, but by 1980 the population was shifting south and west.
   (5) The percentage of people living in urban areas of the United States rose steadily and then leveled off.

Answers start on page 354.

READING CIRCLE GRAPHS

A circle graph uses parts, or segments, of a circle to display information. Think of the circle graph as a pie. The segments look like slices of the pie. The size of the segment tells how much of the whole it represents.

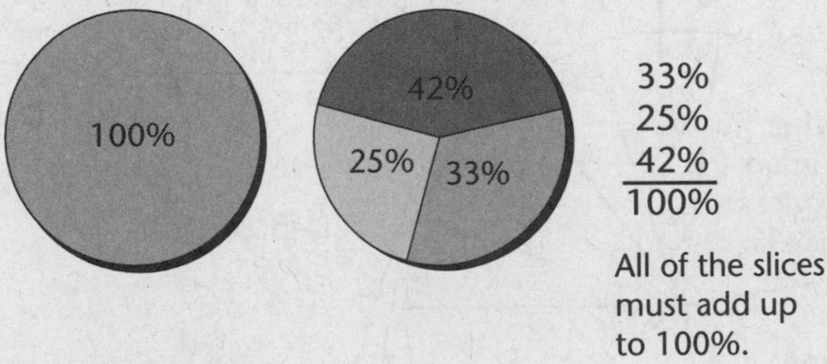

On the following graph, each segment has a label to tell you what it stands for. Find what percent of the U.S. population earned between $10,000 and $14,999.

DISTRIBUTION OF FAMILY INCOME—1990

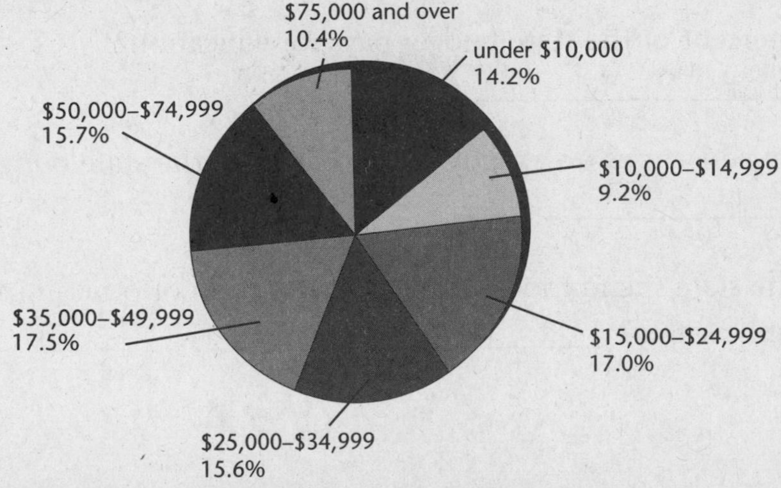

Source: *U.S. A Statistical Portrait of the American People*

First find the segment labeled *$10,000–$14,999*. The percentage *9.2%* is written just below the label of the segment. Sometimes the label and percentage are written in the segment. Other times, especially when the segment is very small, they may be connected to the segment by a line.

Use the circle graph "Distribution of Family Income" to answer the following sample questions.

▶ The largest percentage of families in 1990 were at what income level? ____________________

Find the largest segment—17.5%. It is labeled *$35,000–$49,999*.

▶ In 1990, 10.4% of families were at what income level? ____________

Look for the segment marked *10.4%*. Read the label of that segment: *$75,000 and over.*

EXERCISE 9: READING CIRCLE GRAPHS

Directions: Fill in the blanks with the correct information based on each graph.

THE STATE BUDGET
Where the money goes

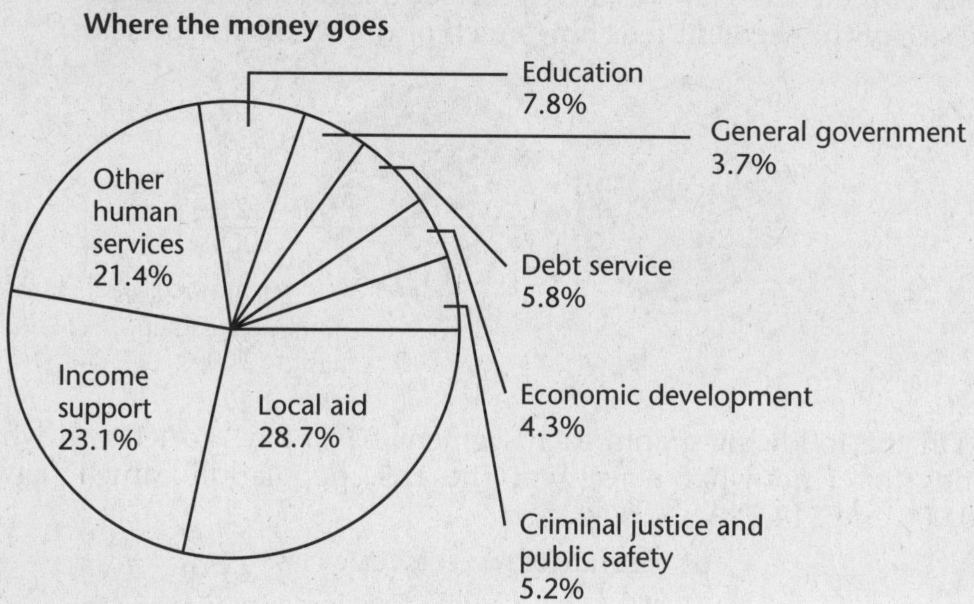
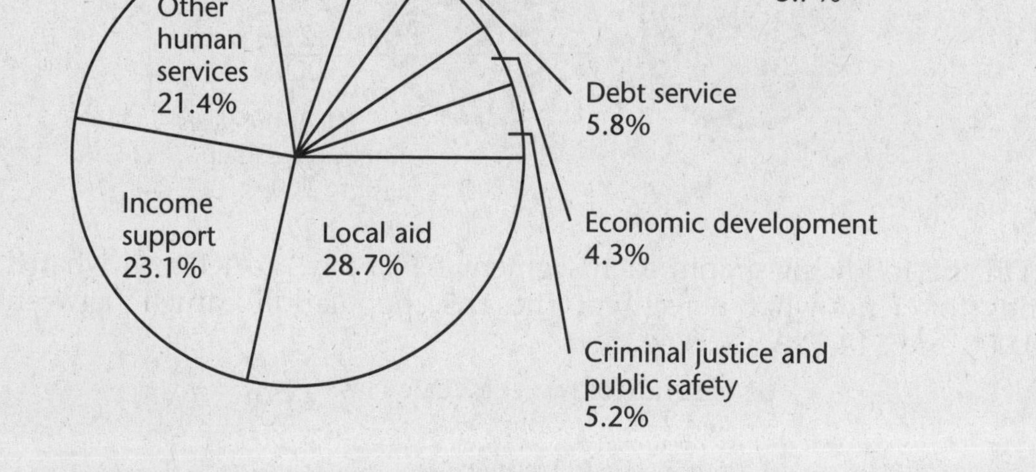

1. What percent of the state budget pays for education?

____

2. What expense uses up exactly 4.3% percent of the state budget?

____

3. Does the state spend more money on education or on criminal justice and public safety? ______________________________________

POPULATION BY AGE GROUP IN THE CITY OF SADDLETOP

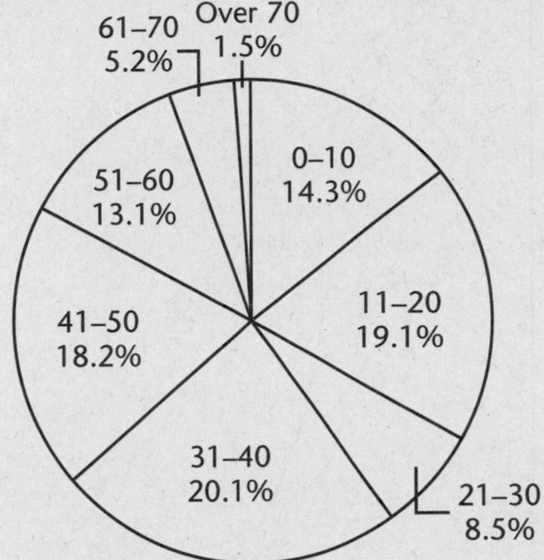

4. What age group makes up the largest percentage of Saddletop's population?____________________

5. What age group below 60 makes up the smallest percentage of the population? ____________________

6. Which age group is larger, the 11–20 group or the 41–50 group?

____

Answers start on page 354.

GRAPHIC SKILL: READING MAPS

A ***map*** is a drawing of the surface of an area. A map could represent your own neighborhood. Or it could represent a city, a state, a country, a continent, or the world.

There are different kinds of maps for different purposes. In this chapter, you will be looking at common parts of maps, including directions, distances, keys, and borders.

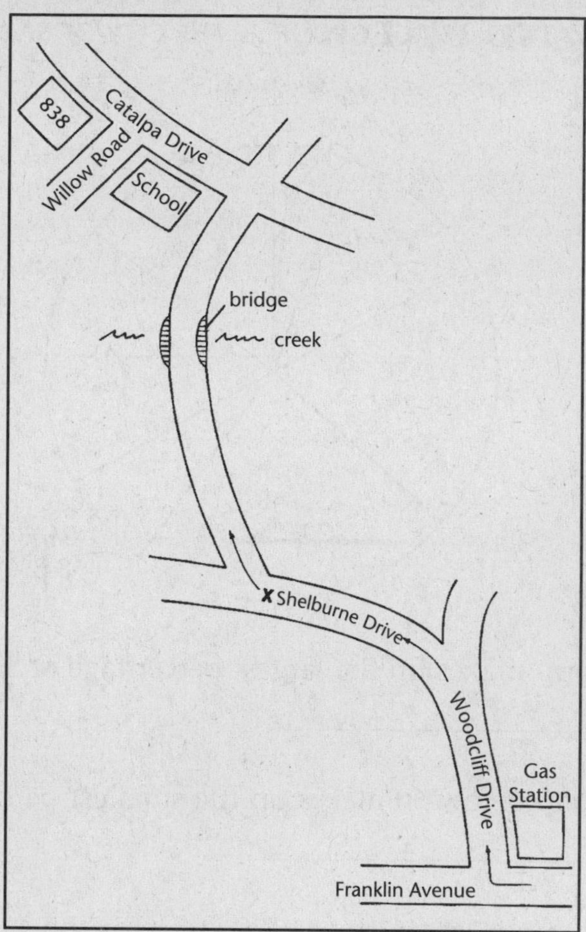

It is easier to follow directions when you use a map. Find the gas station at the corner of Franklin Avenue and Woodcliff Drive. Now follow Woodcliff Drive to where Shelburne Drive forks off from it. Continue along Shelburne Drive to another fork in the road.

Use the map to finish writing directions to 838 Catalpa Drive. Start at the *X* on the map and use landmarks whenever you can.

____

____

SAMPLE DIRECTIONS: Take the right fork. Go straight over a bridge above a small creek. On your left you will see a school. Turn left at the school. You will then be on Catalpa Drive. Continue on Catalpa Drive past Willow Road. On the left you'll find 838 Catalpa Drive.

DIRECTION AND DISTANCE

Different kinds of information are found on a map. There are important symbols on a map that help orient us to it and show how the places fit together. Following is a map of the Baltimore area. The direction symbol in the upper right corner of the map shows that the top of the map is *north.* If north is toward the top of the map, *south* is toward the bottom. *East* is to the right, and *west* is to the left. If you know north you can figure out the other directions.

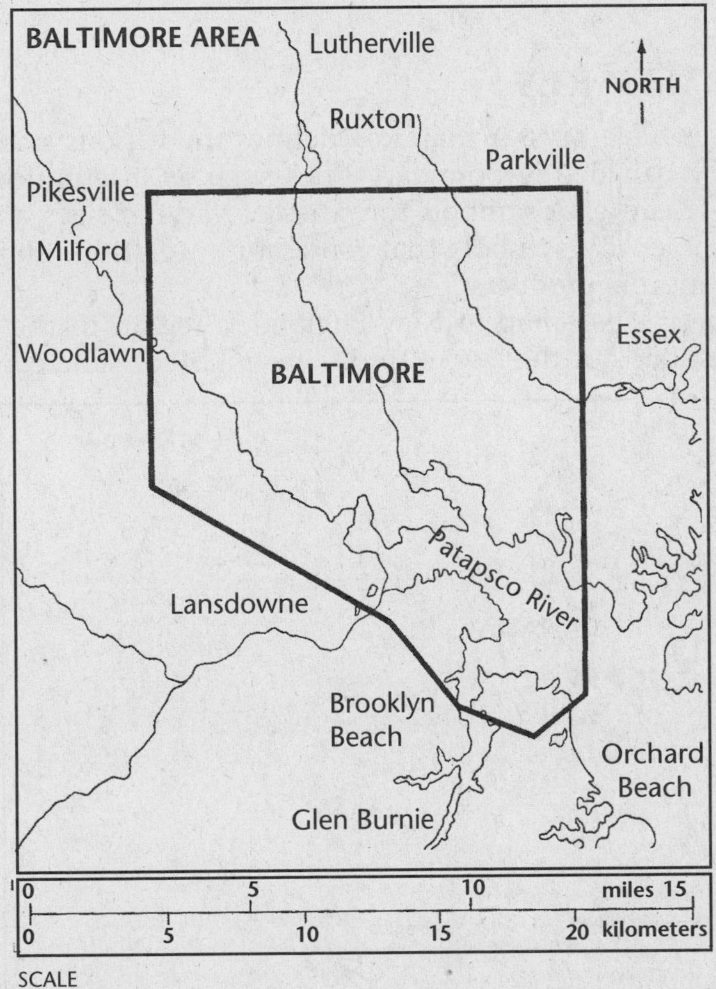

▶ Lutherville is straight north of Baltimore. Name a town that is straight east of Baltimore. ____________________

East is to the right. Therefore, look to the right of Baltimore. The town of Essex is east of Baltimore.

At the bottom of the map is a ***scale*** in miles (and kilometers). You can use the scale to estimate distances. The easiest way to use a scale is to mark off the distance between two places on the edge of a piece of paper. Then put the edge of the paper next to the scale to estimate the distance.

▶ About how many miles is it from Baltimore's west boundary near Woodlawn directly across town to its east boundary?

On the edge of a piece of paper, mark off the distance from the west boundary near Woodlawn straight across to the east boundary. Now line up the left marking for the west boundary with the zero on the scale at the bottom of the map. Your right marking for the east boundary should hit the scale at a little less than 10 miles. Now you know it is a little less than 10 miles from the west boundary to the east boundary of Baltimore.

USING A MAP KEY

Most maps have keys. A **map key** defines the various symbols used on a map. A key can define boundary lines such as international and state boundaries. It can give symbols for cities of varying sizes and for capital cities. It can identify symbols that represent vegetation, climate, population, and economic products.

The following is a map of New England, a region in the northeastern United States. Look at the key to find the symbol for state capitals.

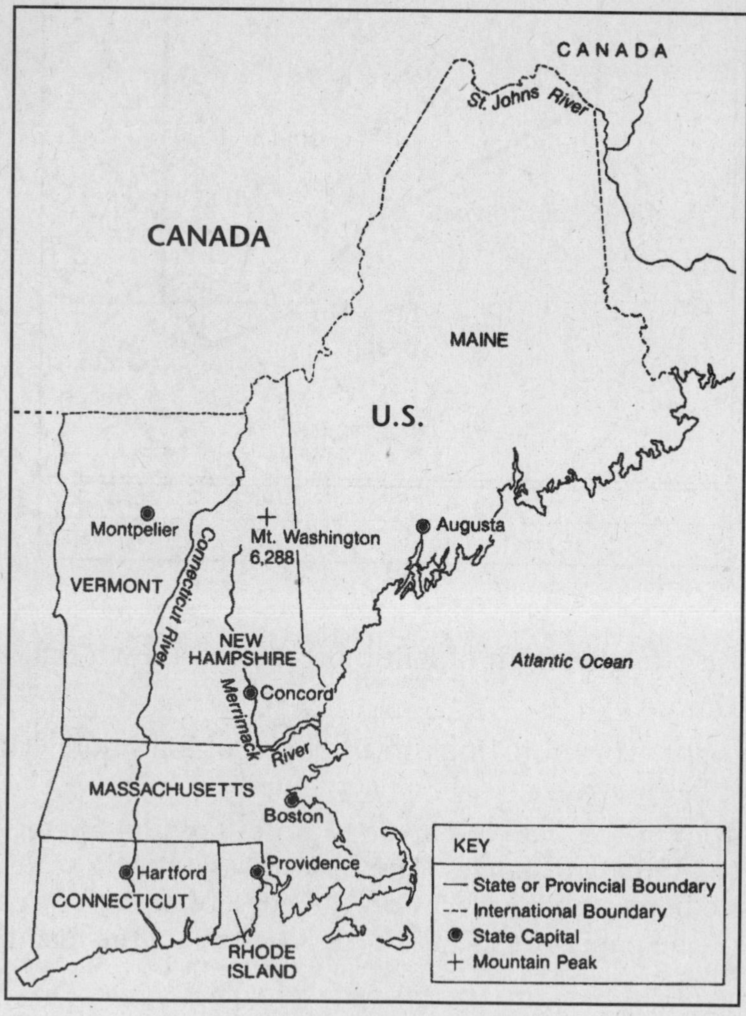

▶ What is the state capital of Connecticut? ____________________

Look at the key to find the symbol for state capitals. Find the state of Connecticut on the map. Now look for the state capital symbol within the state. The symbol is labeled *Hartford*, which is the capital of Connecticut.

Look again at the key to determine what kind of line is used for the international boundary between Canada and the United States.

▶ What river is part of that international boundary? ____________

The key tells you that the international boundary is marked by a dotted line. Following the dotted line, only one river is part of that boundary, the St. Johns River between Maine and Canada.

▶ The only mountain peak marked on this map is Mt. Washington, the highest peak in New England. In what state is Mt. Washington located?

____

The key tells you that the symbol for a mountain is +. Looking for the symbol + on the map, you should be able to locate Mt. Washington, which is in the state of New Hampshire.

EXERCISE 10: USING A MAP KEY

Directions: Brazil is one of the largest countries in the world. It is in South America. Use the map of Brazil to answer the following questions. For some of the questions, you will have to use the key.

1. A major geographical feature of Brazil is a very famous river that runs across the northern part of the country. What is the name of the river?

   ____

2. Part of the southernmost tip of Brazil is a lake. What is the name of the lake? ______________________________

3. The mouth of a river is where it enters the ocean. The mouth of the Amazon River is near what special line that crosses the map?

   ____

4. What is the name of the highest mountain peak in Brazil?

   ____

Answers start on page 354.

HISTORICAL MAPS

Historical maps can help us understand the past. They can show political boundaries of a past time period. They also can be used to illustrate historical trends and events. Sometimes these maps of the past can also help us make sense of the present. Look at the following map of the eastern United States before the American Revolution. What nation controlled the Great Lakes and the region around them?

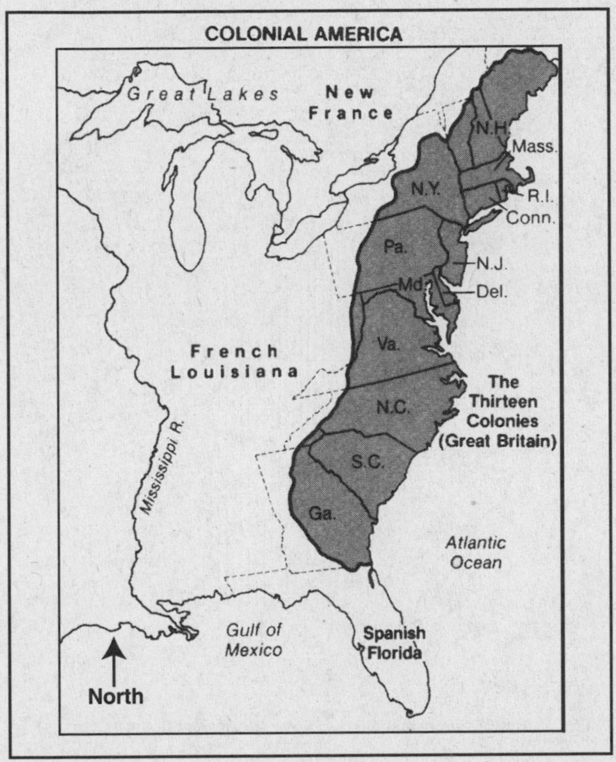

First find the Great Lakes on the map. The area north and east of the Great Lakes is called *New France*. The area south and west of the lakes is called *French Louisiana*. So you know that the whole region was controlled by France.

Use the map of the thirteen colonies to answer the following questions.

▶ What nation controlled Florida? ______________________________

Florida was called *Spanish Florida*, so you know it was controlled by Spain.

▶ What nation controlled a large area to the west of the British colonies?

____

On the map, areas labeled *New France* and *French Louisiana* are west of the thirteen colonies belonging to Great Britain, so the answer is France.

EXERCISE 11: READING HISTORICAL MAPS

Directions: Answer the questions based on the following map.

NATIVE AMERICANS OF NORTH AMERICA

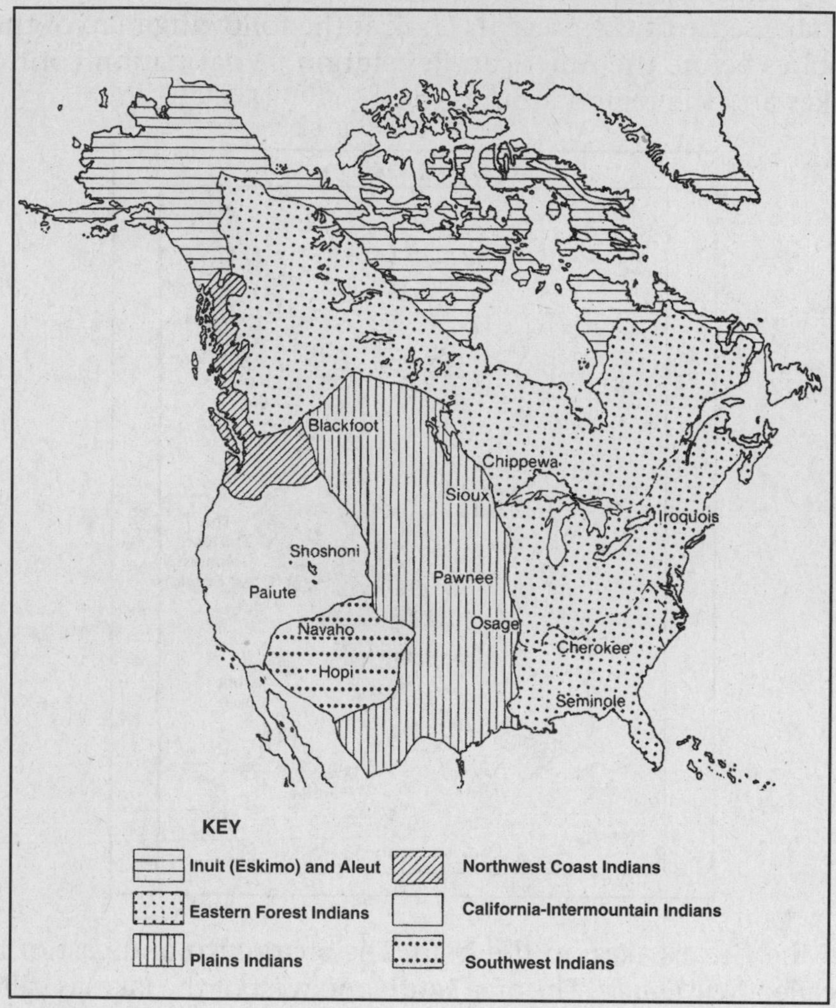

1. The Pawnee were part of which group of Native Americans?
   (1) Eskimo and Aleut
   (2) Eastern Forests Indians
   (3) Plains Indians
   (4) Northwest Coast Indians
   (5) Southwest Indians

2. The far north of the continent was inhabited by which group or groups?
   (1) Inuit (Eskimo) and Aleut
   (2) Eastern Forests Indians
   (3) Plains Indians
   (4) Northwest Coast Indians
   (5) Southwest Indians

Answers start on page 354.

EXERCISE 12: CHAPTER REVIEW

Directions: Study each illustration carefully. Then choose the correct answer.

Questions 1 and 2 are based on the following table.

NUMBER OF ABORTIONS PER 1,000 BIRTHS: 1985
(Entire U.S. = 422 per 1,000)

New York	746	Texas	320
California	640	Ohio	357
Florida	465	Arizona	159
Pennsylvania	348	Mississippi	142
Tennessee	315	Wyoming	125

Source: *Statistical Abstract of the United States 1990,* Bureau of the Census

1. Which of the states listed on the table had the highest number of abortions per 1,000 births in 1985?
   (1) New York
   (2) California
   (3) Tennessee
   (4) Texas
   (5) Wyoming

2. Which of the following states had an abortion rate higher than that of the U.S. overall?
   (1) Ohio
   (2) Arizona
   (3) Florida
   (4) Pennsylvania
   (5) Tennessee

Questions 3 and 4 are based on the following pictograph.

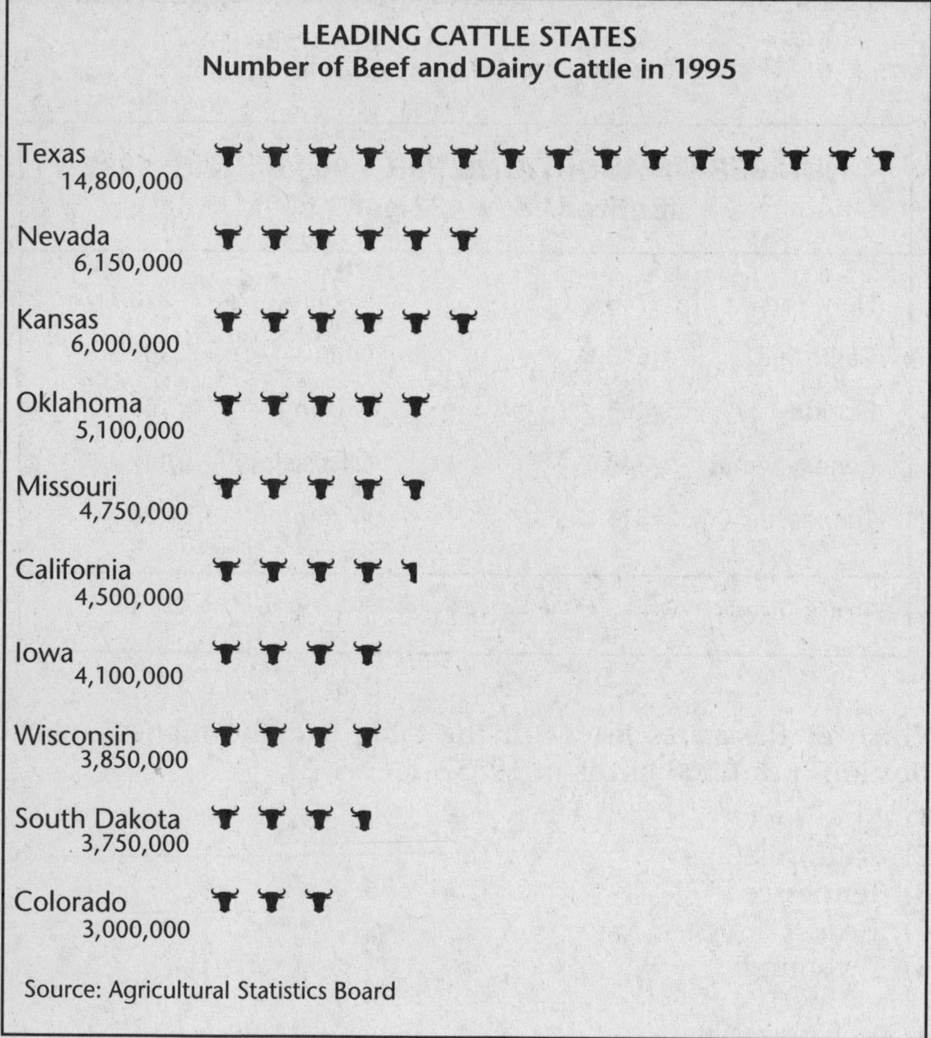

3. Which state had the most beef and dairy cattle in 1995?
   (1) Texas
   (2) California
   (3) Alaska
   (4) Colorado
   (5) Nevada

4. Which state ranked third in total number of beef and dairy cattle in 1995?
   (1) Texas
   (2) California
   (3) Kansas
   (4) Wisconsin
   (5) Colorado

Questions 5 and 6 are based on the following bar graph.

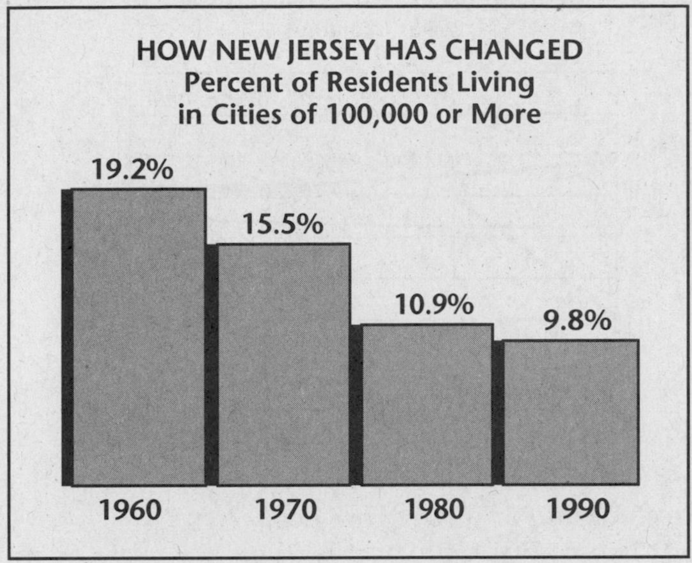

5. What is the main idea of this bar graph?
   (1) New Jersey has changed.
   (2) Over a thirty-year period, a declining number of Americans lived in cities of over 100,000.
   (3) New Jersey's population declined between 1960 and 1990.
   (4) An increasing percentage of New Jersey residents live in cities of 100,000 or more.
   (5) The percentage of New Jersey residents living in cities of 100,000 or more declined between 1960 and 1990.

6. What percent of New Jersey residents lived in cities of 100,000 or more in 1970?
   (1) 19.2%
   (2) 18.3%
   (3) 15.5%
   (4) 10.9%
   (5) 9.8%

Question 7 is based on the following line graph.

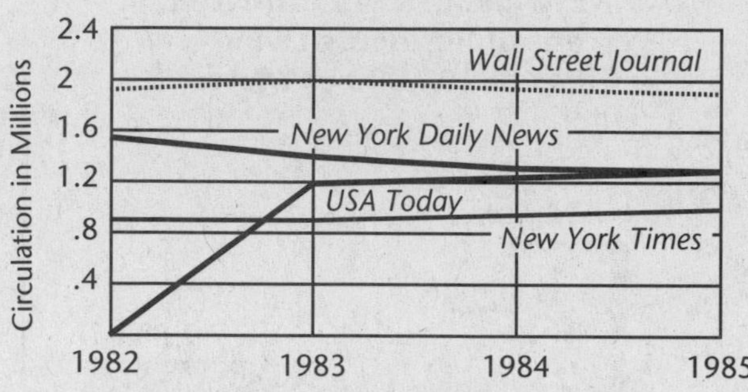

Source: *Boston Globe*/Audit Bureau of Circulations

7. Which two papers had the same circulation in 1985?
   (1) *New York Times* and *USA Today*
   (2) *Wall Street Journal* and *New York Daily News*
   (3) *New York Times* and *Wall Street Journal*
   (4) *USA Today* and *Wall Street Journal*
   (5) *New York Daily News* and *USA Today*

Questions 8 and 9 are based on the following circle graph.

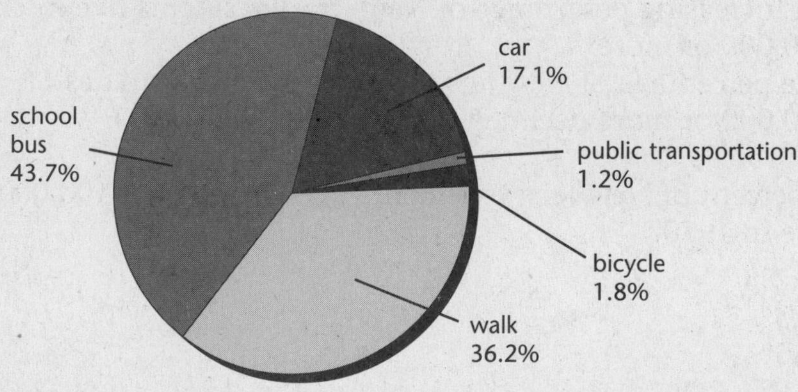

Source: *U.S. A Statistical Portrait of the American People*

8. What percent of children in grades 1–6 travel to school by car?
   (1) 1.2%
   (2) 1.8%
   (3) 17.1%
   (4) 36.2%
   (5) 43.7%

9. 43.7 percent of students in grades 1–6 travel to school by what means?
   (1) walking
   (2) school bus
   (3) car
   (4) bicycle
   (5) public transportation

Questions 10 and 11 are based on the following map.

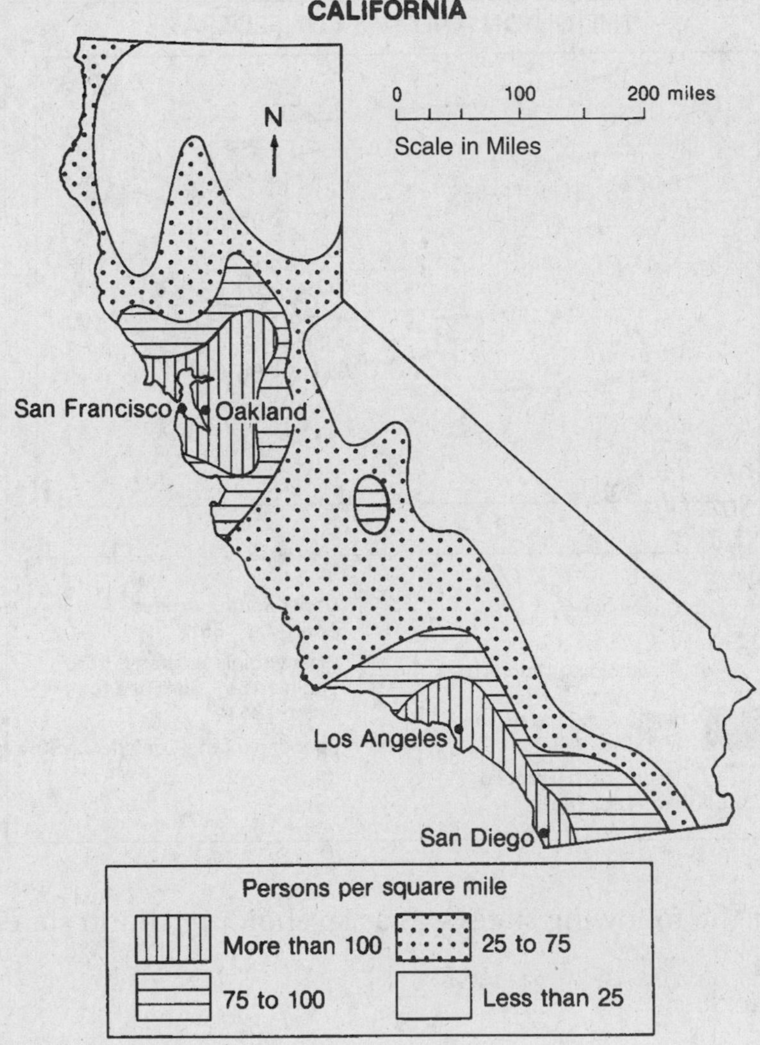

10. What is the population density of the area within 25 miles of San Francisco?
    (1) less than 10
    (2) less than 25
    (3) 25 to 75
    (4) 75 to 100
    (5) more than 100

11. If you drove 200 miles straight north from San Diego and stopped, what would be the population density of the area you stopped in?
    (1) less than 25
    (2) 25 to 75
    (3) 75 to 100
    (4) more than 100
    (5) more than 500

Questions 12 and 13 are based on the following map.

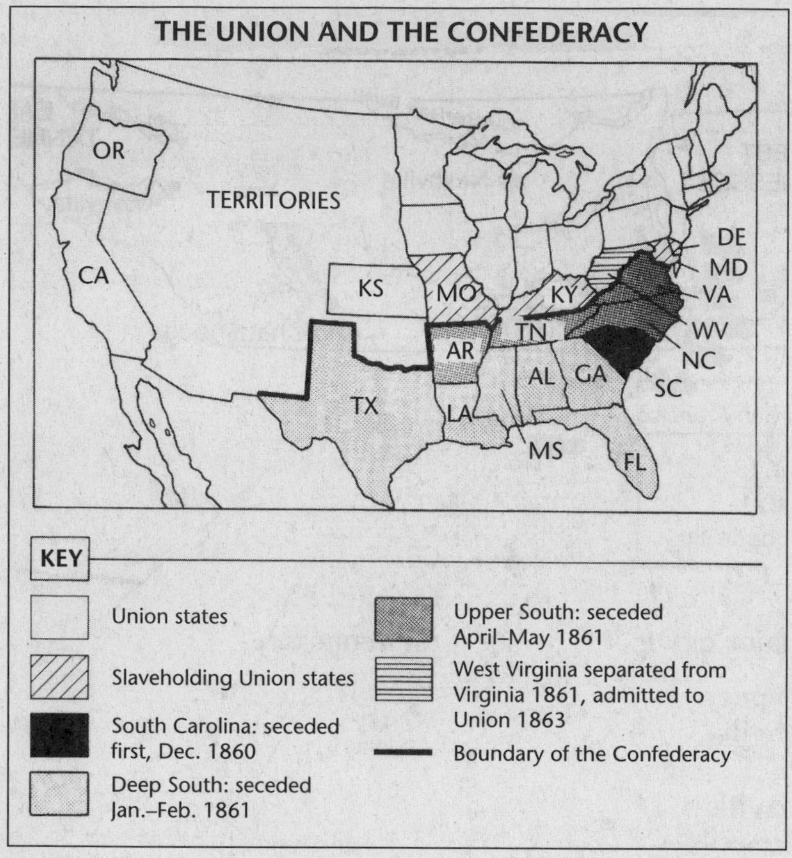

12. Which of the following states was a slaveholding Union state?
    (1) Kansas
    (2) Kentucky
    (3) Texas
    (4) Arkansas
    (5) California

13. What did Texas do during the Civil War?
    (1) It was a Union state that banned slavery.
    (2) It remained a slaveholding Union State.
    (3) It seceded from the Union in December 1860.
    (4) It seceded from the Union in January or February of 1861.
    (5) It seceded from the Union in April or May of 1861.

Questions 14 and 15 are based on the following map.

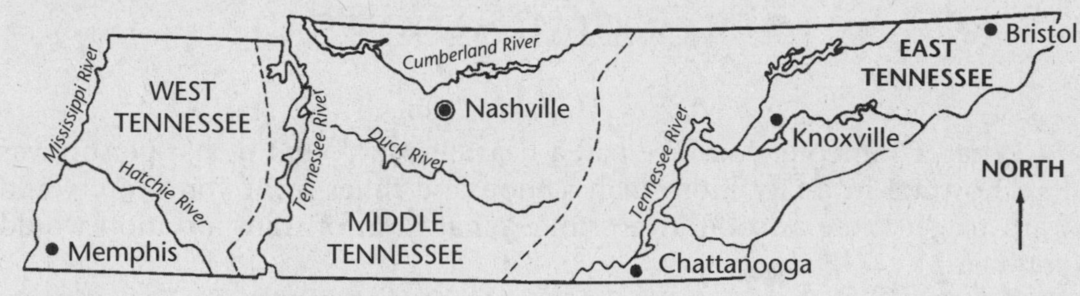

KEY

- ● Major city
- ◉ Capital city
- --- Regional boundary

14. What major city is located in West Tennessee?

(1) Memphis
(2) Nashville
(3) Bristol
(4) Knoxville
(5) Chattanooga

15. What major city is located on the Tennessee River directly east of the state capital?

(1) Memphis
(2) Nashville
(3) Bristol
(4) Knoxville
(5) Chattanooga

Answers start on page 355.

3 Applying Information in Social Studies

What if someone you love had a heart attack? What if that person was in a hospital in a city more than a thousand miles from you? You would want to get there as soon as possible. What form of transportation would you take?

You would probably go by airplane rather than by car, bus, or train. By deciding to take a plane, you would be applying your knowledge of different types of transportation. You would be applying your knowledge to your own needs.

Every day, you put the skills and information you have learned in your life to work for you in different situations. In this chapter, you will be applying information in a passage to new situations. You will also study practical applications of information on maps, charts, and graphs.

APPLICATION: APPLYING INFORMATION IN EVERYDAY LIFE

Often you read or hear information you can apply to your daily needs. You are always picking up information and using it. For example, what do you think you might do to protect yourself or others if you read the following article in your daily newspaper?

> **Tylenol Tragedy**
>
> Police reported that five people in the Chicago area have died from taking Tylenol capsules laced with cyanide. Authorities say that the killer opened the capsules and added the cyanide. The bottles were then resealed and placed on store shelves. At this time the police have no suspects.

▶ What would you do?

____

____

First, you would probably throw away any Tylenol capsules you had. You also wouldn't buy any more until you were sure the capsules were safe. You also might think of warning other people, especially your family, of the danger of taking Tylenol capsules.

By responding to the article, you would have applied the information that Tylenol capsules are dangerous. In the following exercise, you'll practice this skill.

EXERCISE 1: APPLYING INFORMATION IN EVERYDAY LIFE

Directions: Read each passage, then choose the correct answer for each question that follows.

> Regular exercise is more effective than dieting in helping people lose weight. A recent survey found that people who exercised for at least fifteen minutes at least three times per week were able to lose more weight than people using popular weight-loss diets. In a follow-up survey of the same people six months later, most exercisers had maintained their weight loss, while almost half the dieters had already regained what they had lost.

1. Earl wants to lose twenty pounds. Based on the information in the passage, what would be the best way for him to lose the weight and keep it off?
   (1) take diet pills and consume fewer calories
   (2) skip lunch every day
   (3) try a liquid diet
   (4) play tennis or basketball every weekend
   (5) walk briskly three miles at least three times a week

> Automation has transformed the modern office. Computers have replaced the typewriter, and phone systems now allow people to conduct conference calls instead of face-to-face meetings. Many executives use tape recorders instead of dictating to a secretary who takes shorthand. In addition, large amounts of information are stored in databases instead of in file cabinets, and spreadsheet programs have replaced bookkeepers' ledgers. Offices can even send information from their computers to computers in other offices through electronic mail. With all these changes, employers' greatest need now is for people trained to use this new equipment.

2. Karl, who wants to find work in an office, read the previous passage in a brochure on career opportunities. Based on the passage, to help him find and keep a job, he should
   (1) learn to repair electronic equipment
   (2) take a course in shorthand since stenographers are becoming rare
   (3) work hard to increase his typing accuracy
   (4) get training in computer use in business offices
   (5) buy a newspaper and apply for jobs that sound interesting

Answers start on page 355.

APPLICATION: PREDICTING AN OUTCOME

All actions lead to outcomes, some of which you can reasonably predict. Just as you can apply your reading and reasoning skills to recognize a possible cause, you can use these skills to recognize a possible outcome.

The manager of a supermarket advertised a sale on milk, eggs, and orange juice. Check each of the following that are likely outcomes of advertising the sale.

_______ **a.** The store may sell more orange juice than usual.

_______ **b.** The store may order extra milk from its supplier.

_______ **c.** Business at the store may decline overall.

Did you check *a* and *b?* The store would probably sell more orange juice since the price is lower. The store probably would also order extra milk, since larger quantities might be sold at the sale price.

EXERCISE 2: IDENTIFYING PROBABLE OUTCOMES

Directions: Put a check in the blank in front of each likely outcome.

1. A day-care center is starting a program where senior citizens volunteer to help care for the babies at the center.

   _______ **a.** The babies may get less attention.

   _______ **b.** The day-care center may have to charge more for caring for babies.

   _______ **c.** The babies may be touched and held more often.

   _______ **d.** The senior citizens may feel that their help is needed.

2. Sheila just got promoted from a part-time job as a receptionist to a full-time job as a customer service representative.

_______ **a.** Sheila may see her preschool children more than she did before.

_______ **b.** Sheila may learn more about working with people.

_______ **c.** Sheila may be happier about her future.

_______ **d.** Sheila may be able to buy her children new clothes.

_______ **e.** Sheila may have more time to clean her house.

Answers start on page 355.

APPLICATION: IDENTIFYING AUTHORS' PREDICTIONS

We cannot always be certain of the result of something. However, a writer will often try to predict the outcome of an action or a trend. In this part, you'll practice identifying predictions in a passage. In the following example paragraph, look for the prediction the author is making. Answer the question that follows.

> Several states have recently raised the legal drinking age to twenty-one. Lawmakers say that making drinking illegal for eighteen- to twenty-year-olds will help prevent accidents caused by drunken drivers. They argue that younger drinkers are more likely to take chances. However, I feel that making drinking illegal for this age group will increase accidents caused by drunken driving. If eighteen- to twenty-year-olds are kept out of bars, they will drink right in their cars.

▶ What does the writer predict will be the outcome of raising the drinking age to twenty-one?

(1) Accidents caused by drunken drivers will decrease.
(2) Fewer teenagers will drink.
(3) Bars will still allow eighteen- to twenty-year-olds to drink.
(4) Eighteen- to twenty-year-olds will stop drinking.
(5) More accidents will be caused by drunken drivers.

You were right if you chose (5). The author says that raising the drinking age will increase accidents caused by drunken driving.

EXERCISE 3: IDENTIFYING AN AUTHOR'S PREDICTION

Directions: Read each passage and answer the questions that follow.

Colleges and universities have to adjust to changing times. For years, the vast majority of students at these schools were in their late teens and early twenties. Those age groups are now declining in numbers. Many schools are responding to this trend by trying to bring in older students. The colleges' only other choice is to enroll fewer students and become smaller. Few colleges, however, are likely to take that route.

1. The author predicts that colleges and universities will
   (1) become smaller as fewer students enroll
   (2) turn to the federal government for help
   (3) have many more older students
   (4) branch out into other businesses
   (5) encourage students to graduate from high school at an earlier age

Thomas Jefferson thought that small farmers were the most valuable members of society. Jefferson would be disappointed by what's happening in agriculture today. Large farms are the most common type now, and small farms are getting rarer. This trend is likely to continue. In the future, farms will get larger and larger, and small farms will continue to disappear.

2. The author expects that
   (1) there will be larger farms in the future
   (2) a popular movement will lead to more small farms
   (3) the number and size of farms will become stable
   (4) the government will step in to save the family farm
   (5) many large farms will fail to survive

Businesses are feeling pressure from many sides to help fill the needs of working parents. Many companies are allowing either mothers or fathers to go on leave when a new baby is born. Other companies are helping parents make child-care arrangements. A few companies are opening day-care centers in the workplace. These centers are still rare, but they will certainly become more common in the future.

3. The author predicts that
   (1) day-care centers will become less common
   (2) fathers will not be allowed to take leaves when their babies are born
   (3) more mothers will stay home with their children in the future
   (4) businesses will become less concerned with the needs of working parents
   (5) day-care centers in the workplace will become more common

Answers start on page 355.

APPLICATION: PREDICTING BASED ON A PASSAGE

Many times an author gives enough information in a passage so that you can make your own predictions. Be careful to back up your predictions with evidence from the passage. Read the following passage carefully. Choose the answer to the question, basing your choice on the information that is given.

> Computers are everywhere now. Many adults—in the workplace, in school, at home—are struggling to learn the basics of computer operation. In addition, public schools have acquired computers and made them available to children. Soon almost all schoolchildren in the United States will get a lot of experience using computers, both in school and out.

▶ A likely result of children's using computers in school is that
   (1) they will need less computer training when they are adults
   (2) they will become bored by computers and never use them again
   (3) the computer fad will fade as computers are overused
   (4) schools will depend on computers to take over the role of the teacher
   (5) they will learn nothing but how to use computers

The correct answer is choice (1). If all children have a lot of experience using computers, they will not need an introduction to computers when they are adults.

EXERCISE 4: MAKING A PREDICTION BASED ON A PASSAGE

Directions: Read each passage and answer the questions that follow.

> Haiti is, by almost any standard, in a desperate state. Brutal poverty and political terror have crippled Haiti since its independence in 1804. Many Haitians have fled to the United States to escape torture and threats of execution. Those who stay barely make a living. The average Haitian citizen makes $250 a year.

The biggest economic problems facing Haitians are joblessness and inadequate services. An estimated 60 to 90 percent of Haitians are unemployed. That's largely because poor services make it nearly impossible to operate a business. Haitian roads are impassable. Electricity is unavailable outside the capital. And the telephone system only reaches about 5 percent of the population. Any successful program to improve the Haitian economy must address many problems.

1. What problem would a farmer most likely face in Haiti?
   (1) a lack of available farm help
   (2) heavy competition from Haiti's many farmers
   (3) poor quality seeds and grain
   (4) getting farm goods to market
   (5) finding good farm land

2. From the information given in this passage, Haiti could be most helped by
   (1) an improved telephone system
   (2) an open immigration policy
   (3) an increase in utility taxes
   (4) bringing foreign help in to work
   (5) banning the sale of foreign goods

Like many other Native American tribes, the Chukchansi of California use gambling to create jobs on their reservation. According to tribal leaders, over 60 percent of Chukchansi are currently unemployed. So leaders have asked an organization called DreamCatchers to finance and operate a casino on their reservation. Tourists from nearby Yosemite National Park and Sierra National Forest are expected to be the primary customers. The venture will create over 600 well-paying jobs, and Native Americans will be considered first for all positions.

3. DreamCatchers will count on the Chukchansi people to
   (1) gamble in the casino
   (2) plan the casino's future
   (3) serve casino customers
   (4) manage DreamCatcher employees
   (5) invest money

Answers start on page 355.

APPLICATION: APPLYING INFORMATION IN A PASSAGE

In social studies, you are often asked to apply information you read in a passage to answer a question or solve a problem. In the following example, read the passage and make choices. Apply the information in the passage to make the choices.

One hundred fifty years ago, farmers had to make the most of what they had. Typical farm families grew their own food. They also had a variety of farm animals, perhaps including cows, horses, pigs, and sheep. Their everyday clothes might be made from materials grown on the farm, such as wool, leather, cotton, and other fibers. Their homes were made from materials they could gather—wood, stones, even earth.

However, a farm family could not provide for all its needs. Plows, tools, nails, and other metal items were made by a blacksmith. Bowls and plates were made by a potter or imported. Glass windows, storage barrels, and wagon wheels were other items that a farmer had to purchase.

▶ Put a *P* in front of those items that a farm family could *produce* on its farm. Put a *B* in front of those items that a farm family had to *buy*.

______ **1.** wooden spoons

______ **2.** milk

______ **3.** horseshoes

______ **4.** tin lantern

You should have put a *P* in front of 1 and 2. You should have put a *B* in front of 3 and 4.

EXERCISE 5: APPLYING INFORMATION IN A PASSAGE

Directions: Read each passage carefully, then answer the questions that follow.

A variety of government agencies provide services to people who need help. The Department of Health and Human Services provides some benefits, including Aid to Families with Dependent Children. Rehabilitation Services helps people with handicapping conditions get the special programs and services they need. The Federal Council on Aging is an agency that provides the elderly with a variety of resources.

Following are descriptions of some people and the type of assistance they need. In the blank, mark the agency each should go to for help—*H* for Department of Health and Human Services, *R* for Rehabilitation Services, and *A* for the Federal Council on Aging.

______ **1.** A woman with two small children has been abandoned by her husband and has no job.

______ **2.** A seventy-one-year-old woman is lonely and wants to get out and spend time with other people.

______ **3.** A deaf man wants training in order to work with computers.

The development of the American West is limited by a shortage of water. Farmers, businesses and industry, residents, and recreational facilities all compete for water. In the future, communities will have to decide how to use their limited water supply. Will they use their water to grow more crops, to run more factories, to provide for a larger population and more homes, or to expand resorts and recreational facilities?

The city of Kerr has decided that its water will be put to best use for new homes and recreational development. The city is attractive to retired people as well as to tourists. The city council feels that construction of new homes, parks, and resorts will keep Kerr's economy strong.

Under this policy, which of the following requests for water access should the city approve? Write *yes* next to the projects the city *should* approve under the policy. Write *no* next to the projects the city should *not* approve.

______ **4.** St. Mary's Hospital wants to build a new, larger facility to better meet the needs of the growing elderly population.

______ **5.** A chain of amusement parks wants to build a theme park outside Kerr and wants access to the city's water supply.

______ **6.** A farmer wants to buy a large piece of unirrigated land next to his farm. He wants permission to extend his watering system to the unirrigated land.

Answers start on page 356.

APPLICATION: APPLYING MAP INFORMATION

You can apply the information contained on all kinds of maps to real situations and decisions. Maps that you might come across in your everyday life include road maps, subway maps, and weather maps.

One of the most common ways that you might use a map is for deciding how to get from one place to another. For example, when you are trying to figure out a driving route, you look for the most direct route, the one that is closest to a straight line between the two places.

▶ You are a resident of Denver, Colorado. You want to drive to Los Angeles. Based on the interstate map below, describe the shortest route you could take.

____

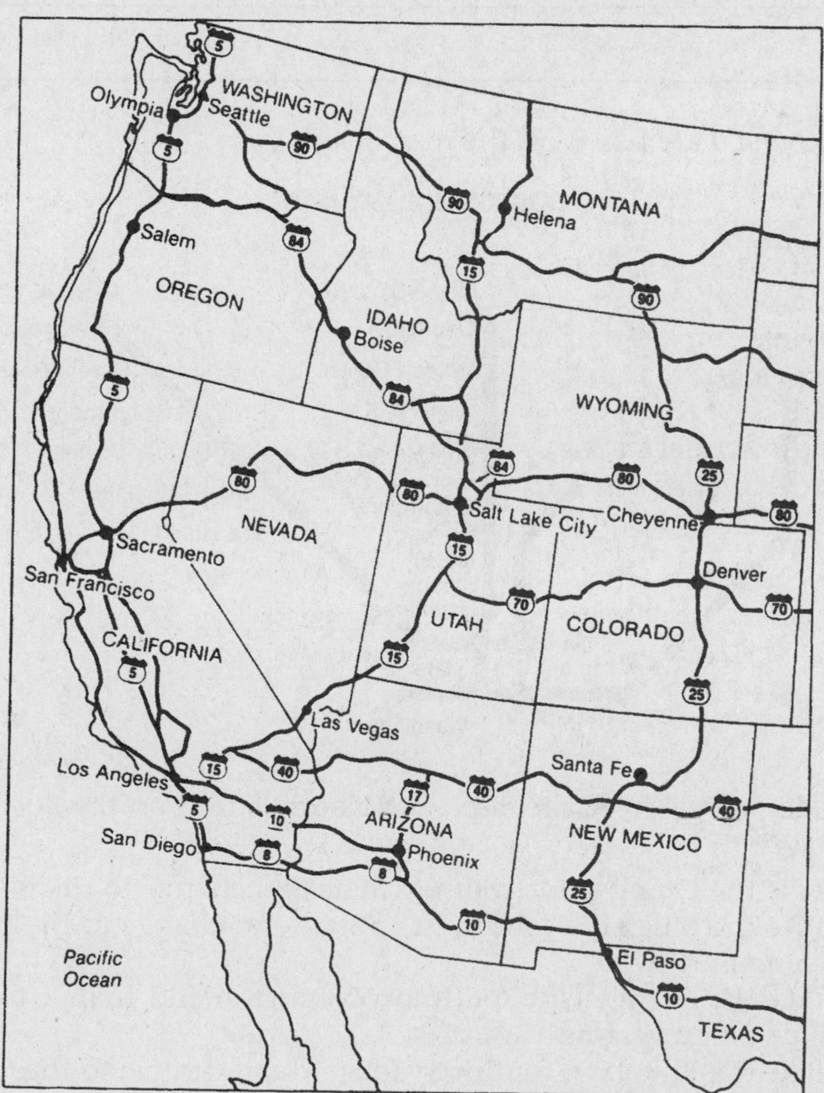

First find Denver and Los Angeles on the map. Then find the route that is closest to a straight line. You should have taken Route 70 west to Route 15, then south on Route 15 to Route 10, and west on Route 10 to Los Angeles.

EXERCISE 6: APPLYING MAP SKILLS

Directions: Use information from the previous map and the one below to answer the following questions. *Questions 1 and 2* are based on the interstate road map on page 285.

1. You live in Olympia, Washington, and want to visit your brother in Cheyenne, Wyoming. What is the most direct route you could take?

___

___

2. You live in San Diego and want to travel to El Paso to see a rodeo. What is the shortest route you could take?

___

___

Questions 3 and 4 are based on the map below.

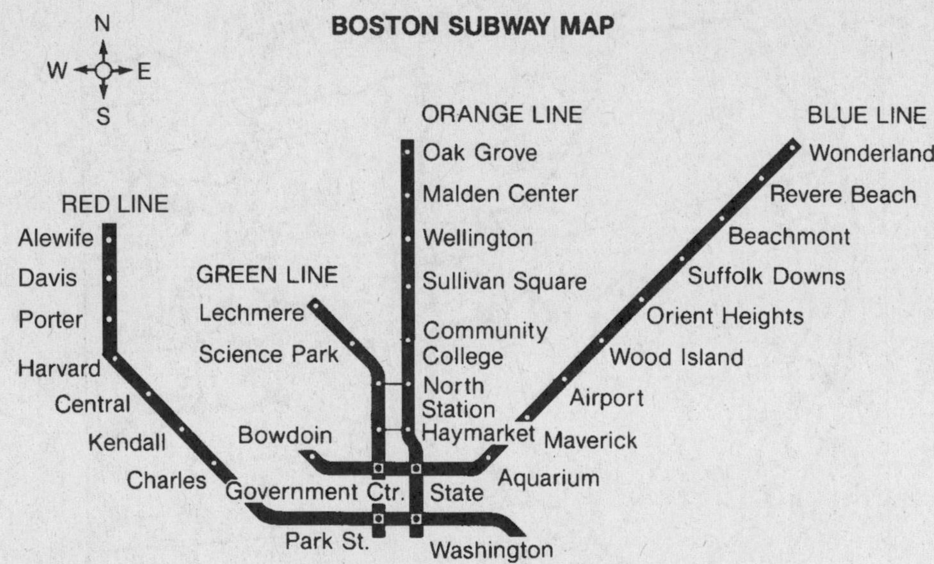

3. How do you get from the airport to North Station on the Boston subway?
   (1) Take the Orange Line south to State and change to the Blue Line.
   (2) Take the Blue Line southwest to State and change to the Red Line going northwest.
   (3) Take the Orange Line south to Washington and change to the Blue Line going northwest.
   (4) Take the Blue Line southwest to State and change to the Orange Line going north.
   (5) Take the Blue Line southwest.

4. A student at Harvard University wants to visit the Science Museum at Science Park. How would she get there by subway?
   (1) Take the Red Line southeast.
   (2) Take the Green Line north.
   (3) Take the Red Line southeast to Park St. and change to the Green Line going north.
   (4) Take the Blue Line southwest to Government Center and change to the Green Line going north.
   (5) Take the Red Line southeast to Park St. and change to the Orange Line going north.

Answers start on page 356.

APPLICATION: APPLYING DATA ON TABLES AND GRAPHS

In social studies, you will often be asked to apply the information on tables and graphs when you need to solve a problem. In the following example, apply the information on the bar graph to figure out what the board of education's long-range plan should be.

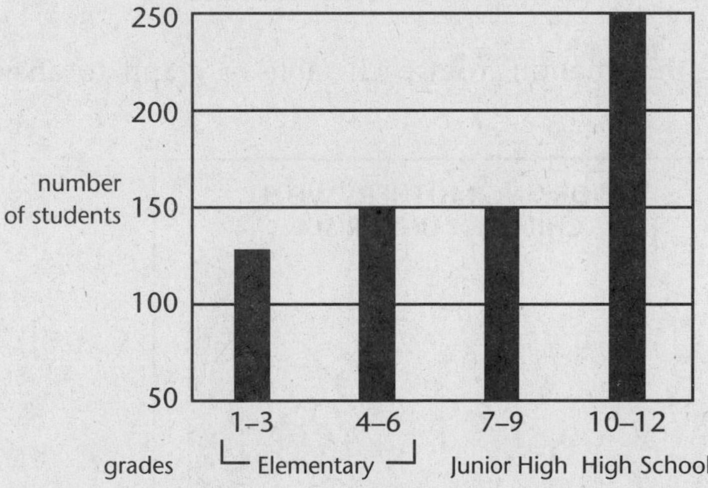

1. How many students are there now in grades 10–12? _______________

There are 250 students. Find grades 10–12 on the horizontal axis. Go to the top of the bar above 10–12 and read the number of students from the vertical axis.

2. In three years, will the student body of the Mozlin High School have increased, decreased, or remained about the same? _______________

The student body in the high school will decrease. Compare the top of the 7–9 bar with the top of the 10–12 bar. In three years the current junior high students (7–9) will be in high school. That means that in three years there will be about 150 students in the high school, many fewer than the 250 there now.

3. Given the information on the bar graph, which of the following should the board of education plan to do within three years?
   (1) hire more high school teachers
   (2) build a second high school
   (3) close the high school, because there won't be any students
   (4) reduce the number of high school teachers
   (5) send overflow students to other schools

The correct answer is choice (4), *reduce the number of high school teachers.* Since there will be fewer students, fewer teachers will be needed. Choices (1), (2), and (5) are incorrect because there will be fewer students. The school should not close, choice (3), since there will still be students.

EXERCISE 7: APPLYING INFORMATION ON TABLES AND GRAPHS

Directions: Use the information from each table or graph to answer the questions.

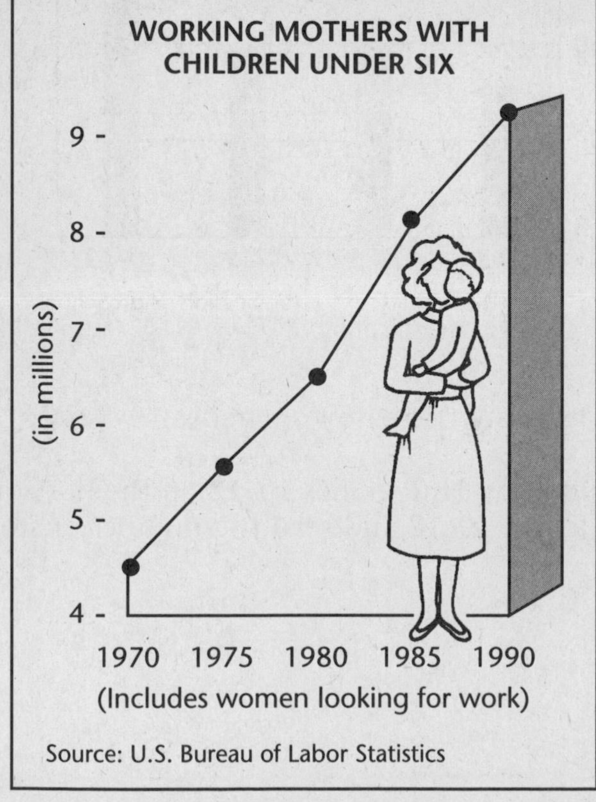

1. The graph shows that the number of working mothers with children under six doubled between 1970 and 1990. Based on this information, a new company that wanted to attract young women into its work force might consider offering
   (1) security guards at night in areas where women work
   (2) Club Med vacations
   (3) on-site day-care facilities
   (4) on-site athletic facilities
   (5) weekly social events in the evenings

CONSUMER REPORTER TELEPHONE COMPARISON

Phone	Price	Durability	Ease of Use
Sunbrand SlimPhone	$55	excellent	poor
Blackdeck Desktop	$75	good	excellent
Radio House Cordless	$85	fair	poor
HomePhone Basic	$25	fair	good

2. Mary is buying a phone for her elderly father, whose hands are stiffened by arthritis. Which phone should she choose?

____

3. Leonard is buying a phone for the kitchen in his home. The phone will be in constant use by his family of six, including his four teenaged children. Which phone should he choose?

____

Answers start on page 356.

EXERCISE 8: CHAPTER REVIEW

Directions: Answer the questions following each passage or illustration.

Question 1 is based on the following paragraph.

In order to ensure a stable food supply for the United States, the U.S. government has an extensive farm support program. This program pays farmers not to plant some of their fields, since we don't need the food right now. These fields are not given up for other uses because they could be needed to produce food in the future. These idle fields could be planted to respond to a national food emergency, such as failure of an important crop because of major drought or disease.

1. Based on the passage, the federal government should *not* pay farmers to preserve unplanted tobacco fields because
   (1) tobacco farmers do not practice sound farm management
   (2) enough tobacco is being produced
   (3) cigarettes have been shown to cause cancer
   (4) tobacco would not be needed in a national food emergency
   (5) the tobacco lobby in Washington has been weakened by antismoking campaigns

Questions 2 and 3 are based on the following passage.

Teenagers today seem angry, and they lack direction. They often express their frustrations through antisocial, even violent, acts such as breaking windows, spray-painting profanity on walls, or stealing cars. Poor children are not the only ones who commit these crimes. These things happen in wealthy suburbs as well.

Because rich teens get in trouble just as deprived teens do, we cannot blame their crimes on their not having money or possessions they want. Instead, we must realize that these young people have almost nothing useful or important to do. They have a lot of energy to use up. If they have no positive outlet for their energy, it will come out in a destructive way.

2. The author of this passage feels that teenagers commit crimes because
   (1) they want money
   (2) they don't have their own cars
   (3) they have nothing useful to do
   (4) they have no outlet for their artistic urges
   (5) they don't know any better

3. Based on the author's theory, which of the following would be a successful way of fighting teen crime?
   (1) raising the drinking age
   (2) giving kids more money to spend
   (3) providing kids with free spray paint
   (4) increasing penalties for juvenile crimes
   (5) having young people do community service work

Question 4 is based on the following passage.

> Since the Charleston became popular in the 1920s, America has been swept by a series of dance fads. Jitterbugging, the twist, and, more recently, disco and break dancing all burst onto the music scene and then faded.

4. A reasonable prediction based on this paragraph would be that
   (1) the Charleston is due for a comeback
   (2) there will be another dance fad in the next few years
   (3) dance crazes will become a thing of the past
   (4) older people will be learning to break-dance
   (5) the next popular dance will start in Japan

Question 5 is based on the following passage.

> Rickerton Park residents are disgusted with mudslinging in Timothy Ayers's aldermanic campaign. Everyone expected a civilized reelection of Democrat Vanessa Alexander; however, Ayers appears determined to humiliate his opponent. He has questioned her sanity, attacked her family, and personally defaced Alexander's campaign posters. These dirty tactics have failed miserably, winning only a 10-point drop for Ayers in the pre-election public opinion polls.

5. Based on the information in the passage, it is reasonable to expect that
   (1) Timothy Ayers will win the election for alderman
   (2) Timothy Ayers will be arrested
   (3) Vanessa Alexander will win the election for alderman
   (4) Vanessa Alexander will withdraw from the race
   (5) Vanessa Alexander will do more mudslinging in her next campaign

Question 6 is based on the following passage.

> Home prices have gone way up in Tristan. The increase isn't because of inflation or a housing shortage. It may be simply because people have expected prices to rise.
>
> In the late 1970s, the same thing happened in California. Eventually people stopped buying homes because the prices got so high, and prices leveled off. The same thing will probably happen soon in Tristan.

6. What does the author believe will happen to the price of Tristan housing soon?
   (1) Prices will level off.
   (2) There will be a crash, with prices declining rapidly.
   (3) Prices will continue to increase rapidly.
   (4) Prices will begin to swing up and down.
   (5) After a brief decline, prices will increase rapidly again.

Questions 7 and 8 are based on the following map.

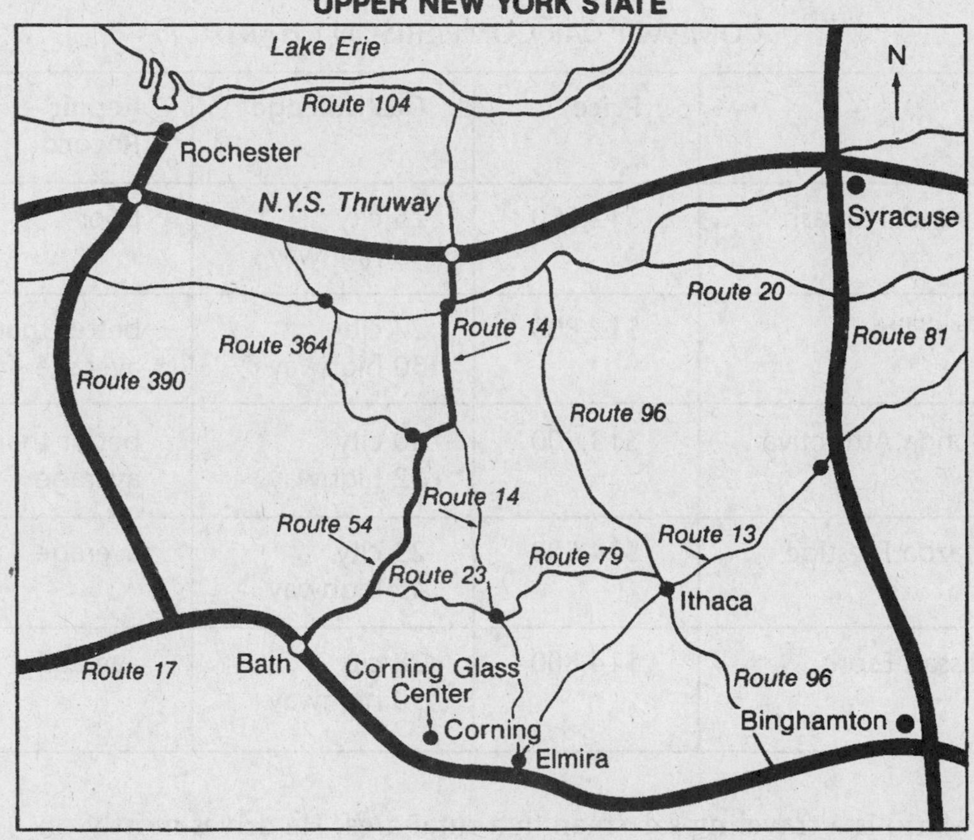

7. You live in Rochester and want to visit the Corning Glass Center in Corning. What is the most direct route you could take?
   (1) Route 390 south to NYS Thruway, east to Route 14, south to Route 17 west
   (2) Route 390 south to NYS Thruway, east to Route 14, south to Route 54, south to Route 17 east
   (3) Route 104 east to Route 14, south to Route 17 west
   (4) Route 390 south to NYS Thruway, east to Route 81, south to Route 17 west
   (5) Route 390 south to Route 17 east

8. The shortest route from the city of Syracuse to the town of Bath is
   (1) NYS Thruway west to Route 14, south to Route 17 west
   (2) NYS Thruway west to Route 14, south to Route 54 south
   (3) NYS Thruway west to Route 390, south to Route 17 east
   (4) Route 81 south to Route 17 west
   (5) Route 81 south to Route 13, south to Route 17 west

Questions 9 and 10 are based on the following chart.

COMPACT CAR COMPARISON CHART			
	Price	**Gas Mileage**	**Repair Record**
Hyundai Splash	$12,500	25 city 45 highway	poor
Geo Elite	$12,800	27 city 50 highway	better than average
Honda Attractiva	$13,900	30 city 52 highway	better than average
Mazda Prestige	$14,500	23 city 45 highway	average
Nissan Esprit	$14,800	28 city 50 highway	average

9. Mario is a traveling salesman in a rural area. He drives mostly on highways and needs a very reliable car. Which car from the chart above should he buy?

(1) Hyundai Splash
(2) Geo Elite
(3) Honda Attractiva
(4) Mazda Prestige
(5) Nissan Esprit

10. Libby cannot afford to pay more than $13,000 for a car. In addition, she wants to buy a car that will have low repair costs. Which car from the chart above should she buy?

(1) Hyundai Splash
(2) Geo Elite
(3) Honda Attractiva
(4) Mazda Prestige
(5) Nissan Esprit

Answers start on page 356.

4 Analyzing Social Studies Materials

Kay asked her friend Peg for a basic cake recipe. First, Peg emphasized the **sequence**, or order, of the steps, in the recipe. Then she explained the **effect** of adding the baking powder to make the cake rise. Finally, she **compared** and **contrasted** a cake made with baking powder with one made without. In the first half of this chapter, we will be looking at these same skills:

Sequence—getting things in the right order

Cause and Effect—understanding what happened and why it happened

Comparison and Contrast—looking at how things and events are the same and how they are different

These three skills will help you to develop a broader skill, that of *recognizing patterns* in social studies materials. This skill will help you to analyze print passages, timelines, graphs, maps, tables, cartoons, and illustrations.

ANALYSIS: RECOGNIZING PATTERNS—SEQUENCE

USING A TIME LINE

Sequence is the organization of events in time order. Most passages present information in time order. In order to make time sequence clear, you can place events on a time line. In this book, you will be using time lines that look like this:

The following example shows how to use this kind of time line.

> The nineteenth century was America's Age of Invention. People like Samuel Morse, Alexander Graham Bell, and Thomas Edison developed devices that changed people's daily lives. "What hath God wrought?" were the immortal words tapped out by Samuel Morse on his telegraph key in 1837.
>
> "Mr. Watson, come here; I want you," was the first sentence ever spoken on a telephone by its inventor, Alexander Graham Bell, in 1876.
>
> "Mary had a little lamb," were the somewhat less than immortal words recorded by Thomas Edison on his gramophone in 1887.

The three events discribed in the passage are the introduction of three inventions: the telegraph in 1837, the telephone in 1876, and the gramophone (phonograph) in 1887. You can use the years to list the three events in order.

1837—telegraph (Morse)
1876—telephone (Bell)
1887—gramophone (Edison)

You could then describe the events on a time line like the following.

earlier

- Samuel Morse introduced the telegraph in 1837.
- Alexander Graham Bell introduced the telephone in 1876.
- Thomas Edison introduced the gramophone in 1887.

later

Here's another passage.

> On October 8, 1871, a cow kicked over a kerosene lamp and started the Great Chicago Fire. In a few hours, the fire spread through the West Side and then jumped the South Branch of the Chicago River. The city was in flames.
>
> Twenty-four hours after it started, the fire was finally put out. Food, clothing, and money began pouring in from all over the world to help the destroyed city.

Make a list of the events in the passage. Then fill in the events on the following time line.

earlier

later

Your completed time line should look like this:

earlier

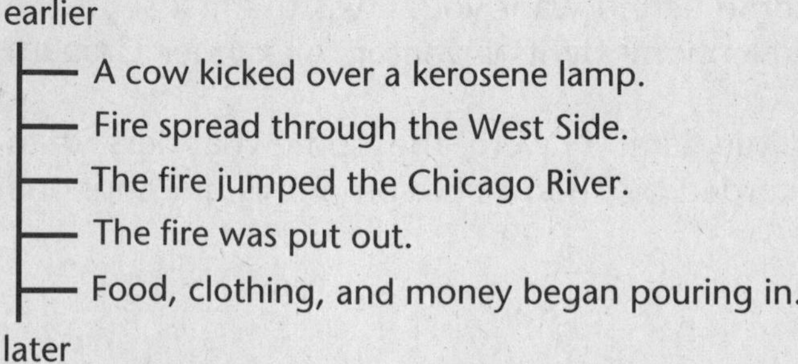
A cow kicked over a kerosene lamp.
Fire spread through the West Side.
The fire jumped the Chicago River.
The fire was put out.
Food, clothing, and money began pouring in.

later

Sequence Tip

Words, as well as dates, can help you identify sequence. When putting events in time order, look for words like *soon, before, after, later, then,* and *while.*

EXERCISE 1: PUTTING EVENTS IN SEQUENCE

Directions: Read the following passage. Number the events listed at the end of the passage in the correct time order and then write them on the time line below.

On January 24, 1848, while building a sawmill for John Sutter, James Marshall found some small stones that he thought might contain gold. About a week later, he went to see Sutter at the local fort to show him the stones. Sutter and Marshall tested the stones and found that they were pure gold. Despite their desire to keep their discovery quiet, word spread fast. Soon groups of men were appearing at the mill, looking for gold. Trying to get rid of them, Marshall then sent them off in all directions. To his surprise, many of them found gold. The California Gold Rush had begun.

______ Marshall sends gold seekers off to look for gold.

______ Marshall and Sutter test the stones to see if they are gold.

______ Groups of men discover gold in the places where Marshall sent them.

______ Marshall discovers gold at Sutter's mill.

earlier

—

—

—

—

later

Answers start on page 356.

SEQUENCE NOT IN TIME ORDER

Passages often present events in an order different from the order in which they occurred. In those cases, you must use clues in the passage to figure out the correct time order. Often you can use dates to help you put events in order, as in the following passage.

> Representing the American colonists, Thomas Jefferson drafted the Declaration of Independence, which was approved in Philadelphia on July 4, 1776. The colonists wanted independence from Great Britain because of many conflicts with England.
>
> For example, in 1763, the British had decided that no colonists would be allowed to settle west of the Allegheny Mountains. This angered many colonists who had hoped to move west. Then the Sugar Act of 1764 and the Stamp Act of 1765 forced the colonists to pay taxes to England. Colonists throughout the thirteen colonies opposed these actions. Ten years later, in 1775, the opposition had grown so strong that fighting broke out between the British and the colonists of Massachusetts. It was only a matter of time before the colonies would become an independent nation.

Number the following events in correct time order, using clues from the passage.

______ The Declaration of Independence is approved.

______ British ban the colonists from moving west of the Allegheny Mountains.

______ Fighting breaks out between the British and the colonists of Massachusetts.

______ The British force the colonists to pay taxes.

Now place the events in order on the time line below.

earlier

later

In this passage, the writer presents events out of time order in order to emphasize the main point. The main idea, that the Declaration of Independence was the result of a long series of conflicts, is made in the second sentence. The description of events in the second paragraph supports that main idea. Even though the approval of the Declaration of Independence happened after the other events, the author mentions it first in order to make his main idea clear. Your completed timeline should look like this:

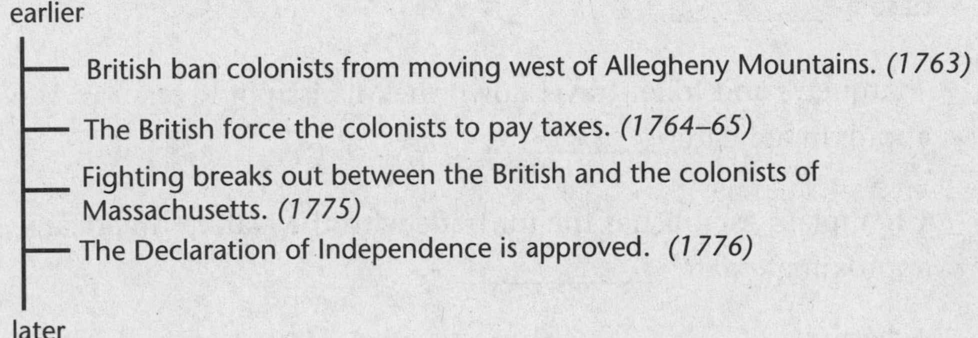
earlier
British ban colonists from moving west of Allegheny Mountains. (1763)
The British force the colonists to pay taxes. (1764–65)
Fighting breaks out between the British and the colonists of Massachusetts. (1775)
The Declaration of Independence is approved. (1776)
later

EXERCISE 2: USING DATES TO IDENTIFY SEQUENCE

Directions: Following this passage is a list of the events described in the passage. Number the events, fill in their dates, and place them in correct order on the time line.

Following the European discovery of America by Christopher Columbus in 1492, other nations sent explorers and settlers to North America. The Spanish were ruthless and bloodthirsty. One Spanish explorer, Hernando De Soto, marched through the southeastern United States from 1539 to 1542. He used torture to force the Native Americans to lead him to gold. Since there was almost no gold to be found, he killed many Native Americans. The worst massacre occurred at their settlement at Mabila on the Alabama River, where De Soto's men murdered several thousand Native Americans.

The French also sent explorers to North America, but they treated the Native Americans well and traded with them. When Jacques Cartier discovered the mouth of the St. Lawrence River in 1534, he opened up Canada to French exploration. From 1603 to 1615, Samuel de Champlain explored parts of southern Canada and northern New York and established the fur trade with the Native Americans. Over fifty years later, Marquette and Joliet traveled down the Mississippi River as far as Arkansas, establishing French claims to the entire Mississippi valley.

______ Columbus discovers America.
date: ____________

______ De Soto murders thousands of Native Americans at Mabila.
approximate date: ____________

______ Cartier discovers the mouth of the St. Lawrence River.
date: ____________

______ Marquette and Joliet travel down the Mississippi River.
approximate date: ____________

______ Champlain establishes the fur trade with the Native Americans.
approximate date: ____________

earlier

later

Answers start on page 356.

SEQUENCE IN GRAPHS

A line graph is well suited to showing a trend over time. By showing how something changes over time, a graph illustrates a sequence very clearly. The following line graph traces the price of chicken at Piggle-Wiggle Supermarkets from 1988 to 1995. Answer the question following the graph by circling the correct choice.

PRICE OF CHICKEN AT PIGGLE-WIGGLE MARKETS

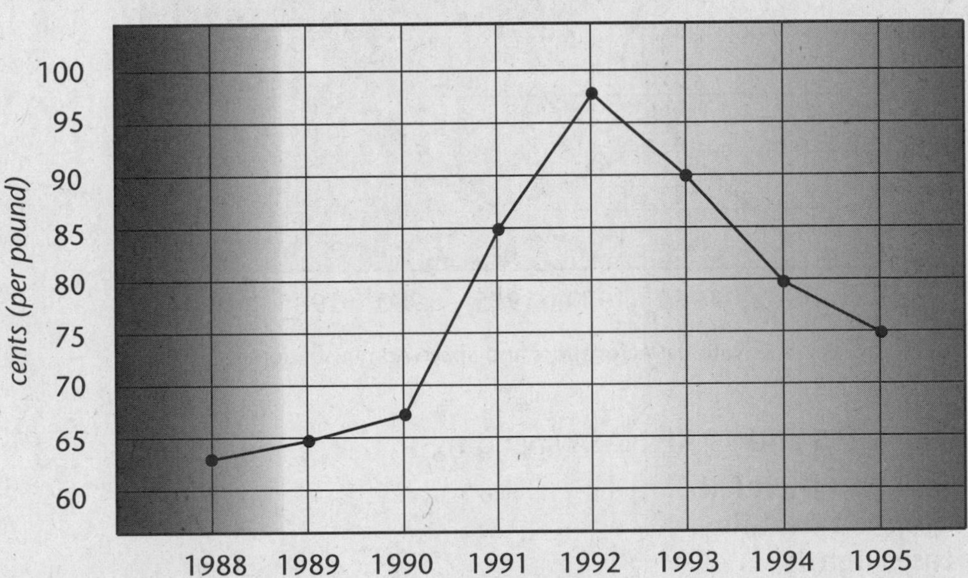

Between 1988 and 1992, the price of chicken at Piggle-Wiggle Markets

(1) went down
(2) went up
(3) went down and then up
(4) went up and then down
(5) remained steady

You were correct if you circled choice (2). Find the data points for 1988 and 1992. Now look at the part of the line between them. The line goes up at each point. This means that the price of chicken went up from 1988 to 1992.

EXERCISE 3: SEQUENCE IN GRAPHS

Directions: Study the following graph, then choose the number of the correct answer to each question.

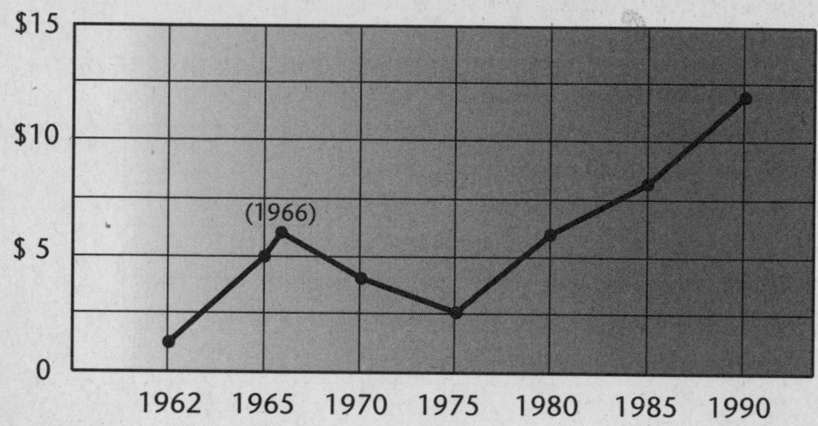

Source: U.S. National Aeronautics and Space Administration

1. Between 1965 and 1970, NASA spending
   (1) rose and then fell
   (2) dropped steadily
   (3) rose slightly
   (4) remained constant
   (5) dropped and then rose

2. Which of the following best describes the pattern of NASA spending between 1962 and 1990?
   (1) It rose steadily.
   (2) It rose, then fell.
   (3) It peaked in 1975.
   (4) It rose until 1966, fell until 1980, then rose again.
   (5) It rose until 1966, fell until 1975, then rose again.

Answers start on page 356.

SEQUENCE ON EXPEDITION MAPS

Maps can depict a chain of events or changes over time. For example, the route of an explorer or an army could be traced on a map. Study the following example to see how looking at the route of the explorers Lewis and Clark can help us understand their journey.

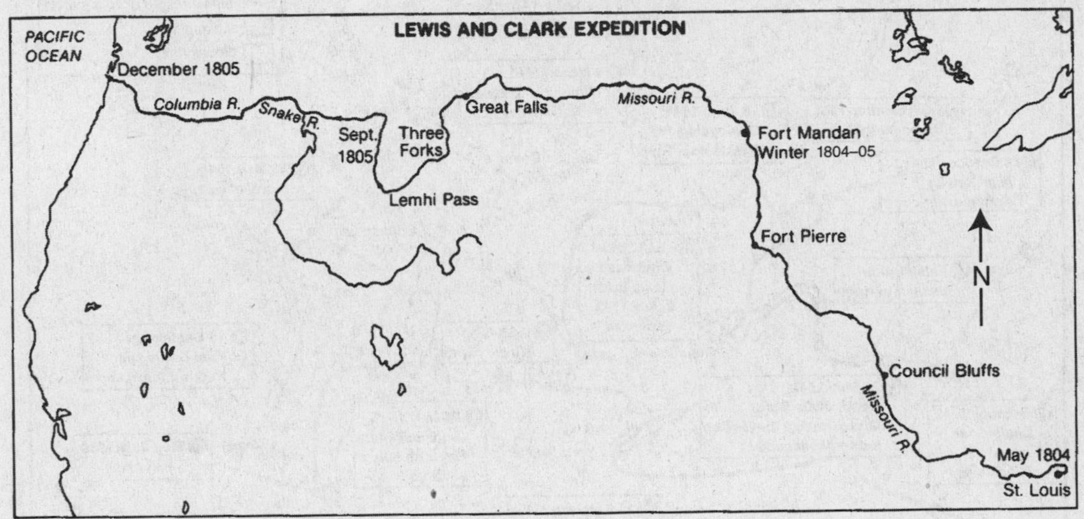

▶ When did Lewis and Clark leave St. Louis? ______________________

Trace along the line that represents the route of Lewis and Clark until you find St. Louis. It is at the eastern end of their route. The date May 1804 is written next to the city. That is the date that Lewis and Clark left St. Louis.

▶ Where did Lewis and Clark spend the winter of 1804–05? ___________

____

Trace the route of the expedition until you find Winter 1804–05. Winter 1804–05 is written below Fort Mandan. Therefore, they spent the winter at Fort Mandan.

▶ When did Lewis and Clark reach the Pacific Ocean? ______________

Trace the route of the expedition until it reaches the Pacific Ocean. Find the date December 1805, which is when the expedition reached the Pacific Ocean.

EXERCISE 4: EXPEDITION MAPS

Directions: Answer each question by circling the number of the correct choice. This map shows the route of a famous explorer through what is now the southeastern United States.

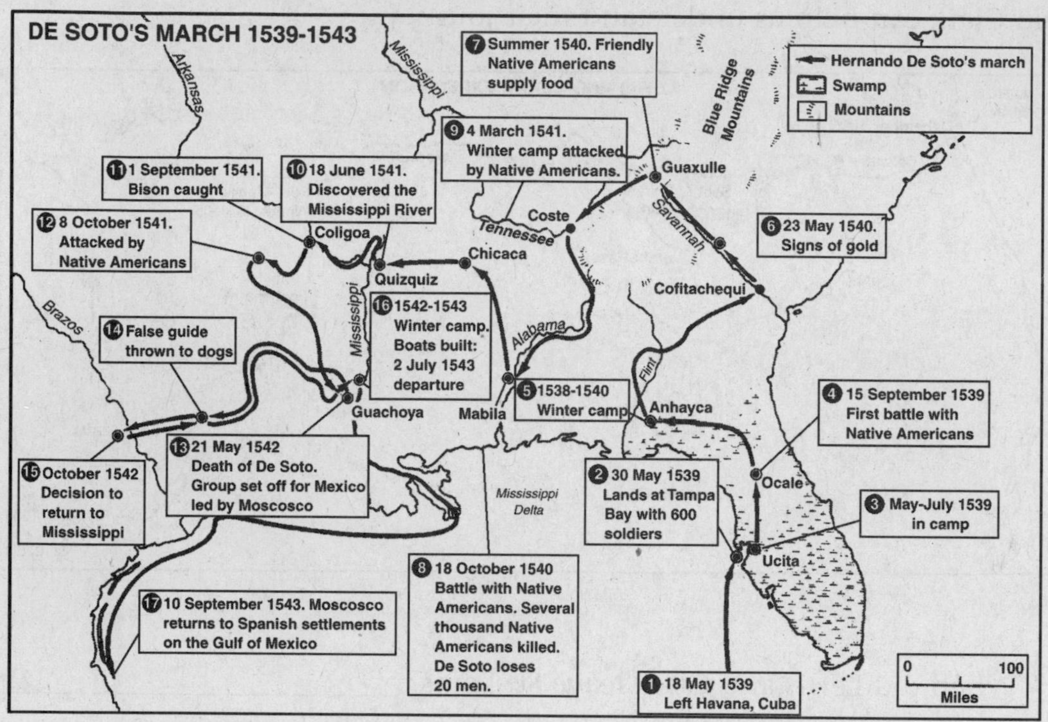

The label in box number 1 tells you when De Soto left Cuba. Box 2 shows you when he landed at Tampa Bay, Florida.

1. Where did friendly Native Americans supply food to De Soto?
   (1) Tampa Bay
   (2) Quizquiz
   (3) Guaxulle
   (4) Mabila
   (5) Ocale

2. When did De Soto die?
   (1) September 1539
   (2) October 1540
   (3) June 1541
   (4) May 1542
   (5) September 1543

3. What important event happened at Quizquiz?
   (1) Several thousand Native Americans were killed.
   (2) De Soto died.
   (3) Friendly Native Americans supplied food.
   (4) A bison was caught.
   (5) The Mississippi River was discovered.

Answers start on page 357.

SEQUENCE ON MAPS OF HISTORICAL CHANGE

Maps can illustrate a trend over time of either growth or decline of an area. The varying boundaries of nations, areas of settlement, or areas of production of a product can all be shown on maps. The map below shows the pattern of settlement of the thirteen original U.S. colonies over time.

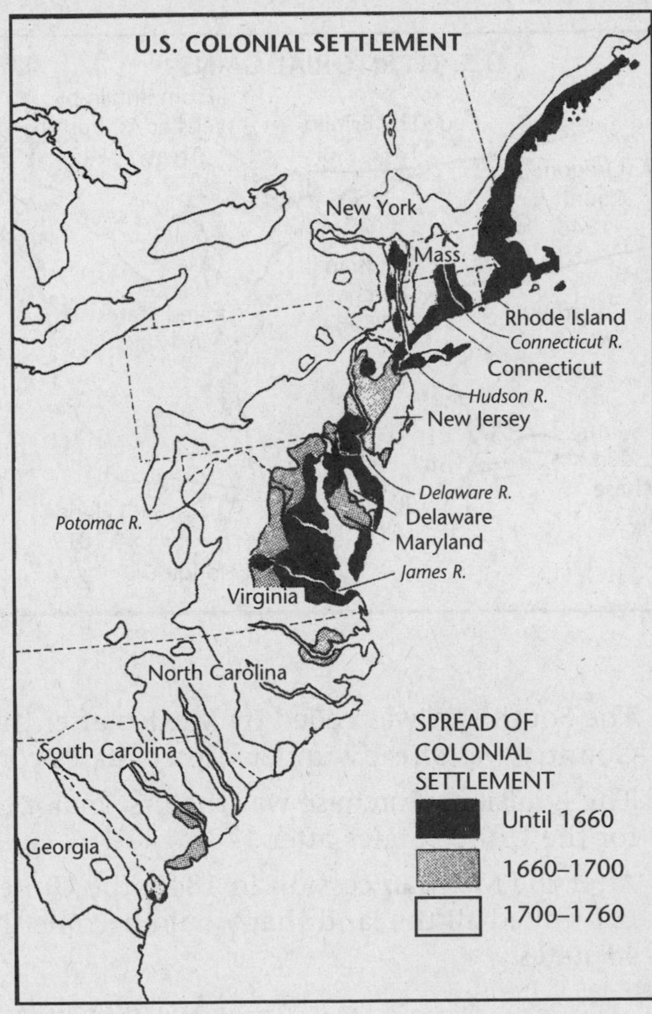

▶ Until 1660, most of the settlement was along the coast of the Atlantic Ocean. True or False? ____________________

You were right if you thought the statement was true. Find the areas that match the key for the areas settled before 1660. These areas are mainly along the coast, as well as along the James, Hudson, and Connecticut rivers.

▶ In general, most of the early colonists settled south of Virginia, with settlement spreading north in later years. True or False? ____________

You were right if you thought the statement was false. Just the opposite is true. The early settlement was in the northern part of the country from Maine to Virginia. Settlement then spread south through the Carolinas and Georgia.

EXERCISE 5: READING MAPS OF HISTORICAL CHANGE

Directions: Mark each statement true (T) or false (F) based on the map. This map shows how the United States expanded into its current 48 connected states.

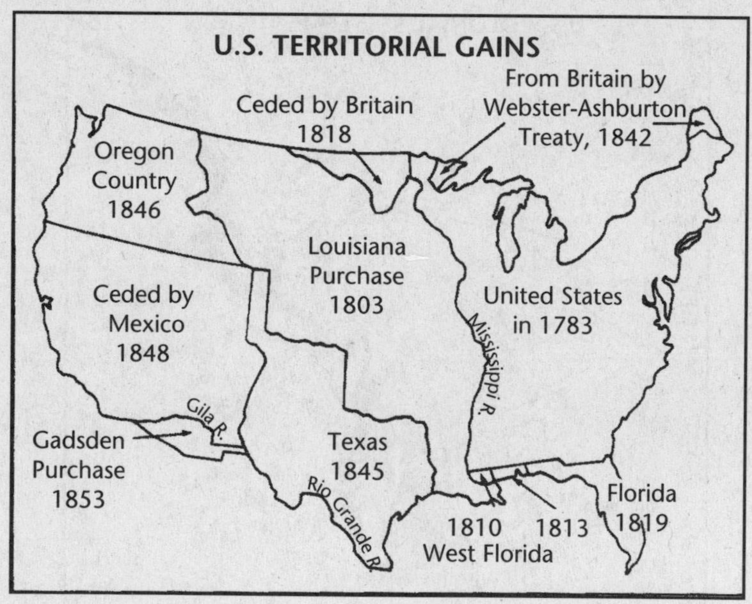

____________ **1.** The Southwest was ceded by Mexico after the Oregon Country was already under United States control.

____________ **2.** The Louisiana Purchase was the first major territorial gain for the United States after 1783.

____________ **3.** After the Mexican cession in 1848, the United States controlled all the land that would become the connected 48 states.

Answers start on page 357.

ANALYSIS: RECOGNIZING PATTERNS—CAUSE AND EFFECT

IDENTIFYING CAUSE AND EFFECT

In order to function in your daily life, you have to understand cause and effect. For example, if your family didn't pay the rent or mortgage every month, you would be evicted from your home. The cause would be not paying the rent or mortgage. The effect would be eviction.

cause:		*effect:*
not paying rent or mortgage	⟶	eviction

Sometimes cause and effect can be very clear. A sixteen-year-old student cuts school sixty-eight days. The effect is that she does not get passing grades. At other times, cause-and-effect relationships are less clear. "I wish I knew what I could have done to help him stop drinking." Much of political debate is about causes and effects. One politician says, "If we raise taxes, the economy will improve." At the same time, another says, "If we lower taxes, the economy will improve."

You should ask yourself, "What happened?" and "Why did it happen?" When you answer the question "What happened?" you understand the ***effect***. When you answer the question "Why did it happen?" you understand the ***cause***. Your reading will often contain clues that can help you decide what is the cause and what is the effect. Read the following sentence. Decide what happened and why it happened, and fill in the blanks.

- ▶ Because it was mismanaged, the company went bankrupt.
- ▶ What happened? ______________________________

  Why did it happen? ______________________________

You should have written "The company went bankrupt" as the answer to the first question and "Because it was mismanaged" as the answer to the second. *Because* is a clue word for the *cause* or the answer to "Why did it happen?"

Cause-and-Effect Tip

In your reading, watch for cause-and-effect clue words and phrases like *because* and *as a result of*. *Before* and *after* sometimes also function as cause-and-effect clue words.

EXERCISE 6: IDENTIFYING CAUSE AND EFFECT

Directions: For each sentence, decide what happened (the effect) and why it happened (the cause) and then fill in the blanks with your choices.

1. Because the wholesale price of coffee had dropped 25%, Colombia found itself in financial trouble.
   What happened? ____________________
   Why did it happen? ____________________

2. The American West developed rapidly after the Civil War because of the railroads.
   What happened? ____________________
   Why did it happen? ____________________

3. Oil prices increased dramatically as a result of the formation of the oil cartel OPEC in 1973.
   What happened? ____________________
   Why did it happen? ____________________

Answers start on page 357.

IDENTIFYING CAUSE AND EFFECT IN A PASSAGE

You cannot depend on a cause and effect always being in the same sentence or being clearly pointed out. In the paragraph below, underline the cause and circle the effect.

> Mothers Against Drunk Driving (MADD), Students Against Drunk Driving (SADD), and Bartenders Against Drunk Driving (BADD) have all campaigned against driving while drinking. The result has been a decrease in traffic accidents.

The key word *result* can help you find what happened (the effect): a decrease in traffic accidents. The first sentence explains why it happened (the cause): MADD, SADD, and BADD all campaigned against drunk driving.

EXERCISE 7: CAUSE AND EFFECT IN A PASSAGE

Directions: Following each passage are questions about cause and effect. Circle the number of the correct choice.

Our continent is named for one of the greatest frauds of all time, Amerigo Vespucci. Vespucci published an account of a voyage he had headed in 1497. This voyage never took place. After reading Vespucci's false account, the king of Portugal asked him to accompany the Portuguese explorer Coelho and write about the voyage. Vespucci went on two voyages commanded by Coelho. In his writings, he took full credit for both voyages and never mentioned Coelho.

Vespucci's accounts were read by many people because he included stories of native sexual customs. In 1507, a young professor of geography in France placed the name *America* on what we now call South America. By the time people agreed that Columbus had really discovered the New World, it was too late. The name *America* had been given to the entire New World.

1. What was the effect of Vespucci's false account of his voyage to the new world in 1497?
   (1) Vespucci became the first explorer to discover America.
   (2) The King of Portugal forced Vespucci to leave Portugal.
   (3) The King of Portugal asked Vespucci to accompany Coelho.
   (4) Coelho gave Vespucci credit for Coelho's expeditions.
   (5) Coelho came to value Vespucci's great knowledge of America.

2. What caused Vespucci's accounts of his voyages with Coelho to be read by so many people?
   (1) He wrote about native sexual customs.
   (2) Vespucci made Coelho famous.
   (3) The whole world focused on the daring Portuguese explorers.
   (4) A French geography professor had all his students study Vespucci's work.
   (5) Vespucci was the famous discoverer of America.

In the 1920s, psychologists Hugh Hartshorne and Mark A. May studied the development of honesty by testing 11,000 children. As a result of the tests, they decided that the children learned honesty mainly through personal relationships and social situations.

Hartshorne and May saw the children imitating adult and peer models a great deal. In other words, they found that the children did what they saw others do, not what they were told to do. If the people they imitated were honest, they tended to be honest.

3. According to Hartshorne and May, children are likely to be honest if
   (1) they are often in social situations
   (2) the people around them are honest
   (3) they are told they should be honest
   (4) their families have plenty of money
   (5) they are punished for dishonesty

Answers start on page 357.

APPLYING CAUSE AND EFFECT

Government has a strong effect on our lives as Americans. American blacks are one group whose lives have been affected, for good or bad, by the actions of the government. In the next exercise, you will be asked to match four actions of government with the effect each action might have had on an individual person.

EXERCISE 8: APPLYING CAUSE AND EFFECT

Directions: Below are listed three documents that greatly influenced conditions for black Americans. Below the documents are quotes that describe the effect of each of these documents. Match each government action with the quote it made possible.

a. Supreme Court separate-but-equal decision—1896
Segregation of public facilities such as schools was declared legal by the Supreme Court.

b. Voting Rights Act—1965
Laws preventing black people from voting were banned by Congress.

c. Civil Rights Act—1964
Discrimination in public places was banned by Congress.

______ 1. "As our first black mayor, I pledge to serve all the people."

______ 2. "I remember when I had to sit in the back of the bus. Now I can sit where I please."

______ 3. "I have to go to a separate school from white people. Some people say it is just as good, but I don't believe them."

Answers start on page 357.

ANALYSIS: RECOGNIZING PATTERNS—COMPARISON AND CONTRAST

LOOKING AT SIMILARITIES

> Despite the great differences among human societies, anthropologists have found an institution they all share. All societies have some form of marriage.

The above paragraph compares the societies of the world. Marriage is the similarity shared by all. A **comparison** can show how two or more things are alike. Read the following paragraph. Then, in the blank provided, write one way that the Coney Island amusement parks were similar.

> New York's Coney Island amusement parks were all designed to send people into a world of pleasure. For instance, Steeplechase Park was nicknamed "The Funny Place." It featured rides such as the human roulette wheel, which sent riders whirling and sprawling. Luna Park was a dream city of bright colors and fanciful decorations. It was exotic, rich, and magical.

▶ How were all the amusement parks similar?

____

The first sentence tells you that all the parks were designed to send people into a world of pleasure. The clue word *all* tells you that a similarity is being described.

EXERCISE 9: IDENTIFYING SIMILARITIES

Directions: In your own words, answer the questions following each passage.

> The populations of three major races, the Caucasians, the Negroes, and the Mongoloids, all developed in a similar way. Large numbers of each race abandoned hunting and gathering and turned to agriculture. The result in each case was population growth among the agricultural groups. Some groups remained hunters and gatherers, such as the Pygmies and Bushmen of Africa and the aborigines of Australia. Those groups now make up only a tiny percentage of the world population.

1. Why did the three major races all experience population growth?

   ____

2. How are the Pygmies and Bushmen of Africa and the aborigines of Australia similar?

   ____

The two nations of Great Britain and Japan have much in common. Both are large island nations separated from the mainland by narrow bodies of water. Both once controlled vast amounts of land and millions of people. Today both Great Britain and Japan are important industrial and trading nations.

3. How is the geography of Great Britain and Japan similar?

____

4. How are the economies of Great Britain and Japan similar today?

____

Answers start on page 357.

LOOKING AT DIFFERENCES

When you **contrast** two things, you concentrate on how they are different. Examining differences as well as similarities helps you get a better picture of what you are studying. Read the following example passage; then use the information in the passage to fill in the chart.

In the past 200 years, technology has changed our lives. For example, while our ancestors depended on horses to travel long distances, today we travel from coast to coast in a few hours on an airplane. When we want to get around town, we may drive a car or take a train or bus.

Another dramatic change we have experienced has been in communication. It once took weeks for the news to travel by boat from England to the United States. Today, through radio and television, we have almost instant access to world events. In addition, world leaders can talk on the telephone even though they may be separated by an ocean.

CONTRAST: 200 YEARS AGO AND TODAY		
	200 Years Ago	**Today**
travel		
overseas communication		

Your chart might look something like this. Did you show how different things are now than they were 200 years ago?

CONTRAST: 200 YEARS AGO AND TODAY		
	200 Years Ago	**Today**
travel	depended on horses, so long-distance travel was very slow	can get around town or even coast to coast very fast
overseas communication	messages had to travel by boat across the ocean	now can talk on the phone overseas; hear radio and TV news the same day something happens

COMPARISON AND CONTRAST IN ILLUSTRATIONS

Maps, charts, and graphs can be used to illustrate comparison and contrast. For example, the map below compares and contrasts black voting rights in Southern states during the early years of the civil rights movement. Answer the questions based on the map.

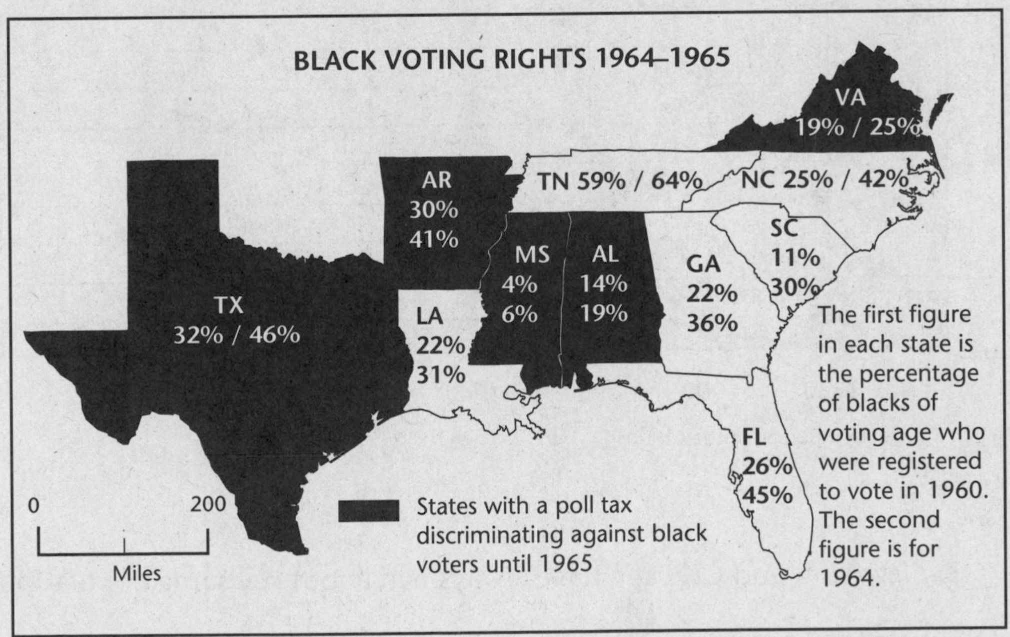

▶ Which five states used a poll tax to discriminate against blacks until 1965? ______________________________

You were right if you listed Texas, Arkansas, Mississippi, Alabama, and Virginia. These states are all shaded black on the map, showing that they used a poll tax.

EXERCISE 10: COMPARISON AND CONTRAST IN ILLUSTRATIONS

Directions: Mark each statement *T* if it is true or *F* if it is false.

Questions 1 and 2 are based on the map "Black Voting Rights" on page 000.

_____ **1.** Of all the states shown, Mississippi showed the smallest increase in black voter registration—only 2% between 1960 and 1964.

_____ **2.** In 1964, Texas had the highest percentage of any southern state of eligible blacks registered, with 46%.

Questions 3–5 are based on the following line graph.

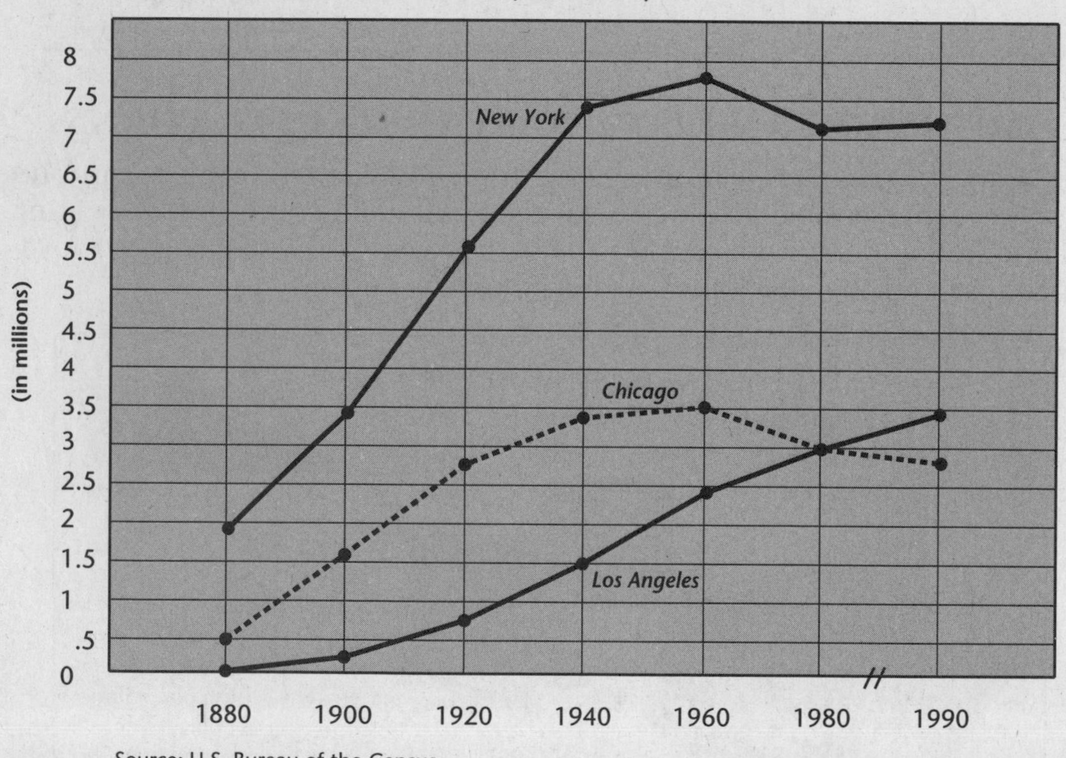

_____ **3.** New York and Chicago have always had about the same population.

_____ **4.** In 1980, Chicago and Los Angeles had about the same population.

_____ **5.** When the population of Chicago was decreasing, the population of Los Angeles was also decreasing.

Answers start on page 357.

The following passage will help introduce you to some additional analytical skills.

> Eileen's eighteen-year-old son Greg just got his driver's license. As she walked into the house with two bags of groceries, Greg rushed to her side, took the bags from her, and put away the groceries. When he finished, Eileen said, "OK, you can have the car tonight."
>
> Eileen was using her analytical skills. She looked at the facts: Greg had never rushed to help her with the groceries before. Greg had just gotten his driver's license.
>
> She realized that he must be rushing to help her in order to get something else. He must want to use the car. Greg also was using his analytical skills. He predicted that if he helped his mother without being asked, she might let him use her car.

In the remainder of this chapter, you will be practicing these analytical skills:

1. Distinguishing fact from opinion

   fact: Greg is helping with the groceries.
   opinion: Greg is a good son.

2. Developing a hypothesis, or educated guess

   Since Greg just got his license, a reasonable explanation of why he is helping is that he wants to use the car.

ANALYSIS: PRACTICING ANALYSIS—FACT AND OPINION

A ***fact*** is a statement that can be proven. An ***opinion*** is a belief that cannot be proven. If you believe that something is true, it still has to be proven to be a fact. Every day, you read and hear both facts and opinions. At times, you may have to give some thought to which is which. When you read social studies material, notice whether a statement you read is fact or opinion. Can a statement be proven? Or is it something the author believes but cannot prove?

Of the following two statements, one is a fact and one is an opinion. Write *F* in the blank before the fact and *O* in the blank before the opinion.

_______ The U.S. Constitution is the greatest political document ever written.

_______ In 1995, there were twenty-six amendments to the U.S. Constitution.

You were right if you thought the first statement was an opinion. The word *greatest* gives the opinion of the writer. The second statement is a fact that can be checked by looking at a copy of the Constitution.

EXERCISE 11: FACT OR OPINION?

Directions: In the blank preceding each sentence, write *F* if the sentence is a fact and *O* if it is an opinion.

1. _______ The United States is a democracy in which people elect their government officials.

2. _______ Democracy is the best form of government.

3. _______ Local governments mismanage their responsibilities of police and fire protection.

4. _______ Local governments have responsibility for the public schools.

5. _______ The vice president has the most unimportant job in the entire federal government.

6. _______ If the president dies in office, the vice president becomes the new president.

Answers start on page 357.

FACTS AND OPINIONS IN A PASSAGE

Writers often tell you facts and express their opinions in the same piece of writing. They use the facts as evidence to back up their opinions. In the following example, see how the author uses facts to support her opinion. Read the paragraph and underline the sentences that contain facts. Circle the sentences that contain opinions.

> The United States is a member of the North Atlantic Treaty Organization (NATO). The members of NATO coordinate their military activity in Europe through the NATO military command. Because we have to work through the NATO chain of command, NATO restricts our ability to act on our own. We should withdraw from NATO because our military needs to be able to work freely in Europe.

The first two sentences are facts. The writer can prove that the United States is a member of NATO. She can also prove that NATO has a military command that coordinates the activity of member nations in Europe. The second two sentences are opinions. It is her opinion that membership in NATO restricts our ability to act on our own. In the last sentence, the word *should* is a clue that the sentence is the opinion of the author.

Fact vs. Opinion Tip

Phrases like *I think, I believe,* and *we should* tell you that the writer is expressing an opinion.

EXERCISE 12: FACTS AND OPINIONS IN A PASSAGE

Directions: For each sentence in each of the following passages, write *F* if the sentence is a fact and *O* if the sentence is an opinion.

Passage 1

> (1) The best political system ever developed is the two-party system of the United States. (2) Since the Civil War, no third party has been able to threaten the political power of either the Democratic Party or the Republican Party. (3) Every president of the last one hundred years has been a member of one of these two parties. (4) No third party has been able to gain control of either house of Congress. (5) The country has been spared the chaos that results when there are more than two parties. (6) And the people have not had to endure the tyranny of one-party rule.

1. ________ 3. ________ 5. ________

2. ________ 4. ________ 6. ________

Passage 2

(1) The book *The Hard Times of Mortimer Mitchell* should not be on the shelves of our high school library. (2) First, the characters take drugs. (3) Second, there are three scenes in the book in which sexual activity between unmarried people is described in detail. (4) Third, the main character murders another character and then goes unpunished. (5) This is not the kind of book that the children in our community should read. (6) A parents' committee should be formed to help the school librarian choose good reading material for our teens.

1. ________ **3.** ________ **5.** ________

2. ________ **4.** ________ **6.** ________

Answers start on page 358.

ANALYSIS: PRACTICING ANALYSIS—DEVELOPING HYPOTHESIS

DISTINGUISHING FACT FROM HYPOTHESIS

Sometimes an author gives the cause of an event or a trend as a statement of fact, as in the following example:

> Ponda did not get to work on time because her car broke down.

Effect: Ponda did not get to work on time.
Cause (fact): because her car broke down

Sometimes, however, a writer is not sure of the cause of an event. He or she makes a good educated guess, a ***hypothesis***. The writer in the following example gives a hypothesis for why something happened.

> Our son Larry called just two days before our fortieth anniversary. We were surprised that he did not mention the anniversary. Then we realized that possibly he was planning a surprise party.

Effect: Larry did not mention the anniversary.
Possible Cause (hypothesis): He was planning a surprise party.

EXERCISE 13: DISTINGUISHING FACT FROM HYPOTHESIS

Directions: Each of the following sentences describes a cause-and-effect relationship. Write *F* in the blank if the cause is stated as a fact. Write *H* in the blank if the cause is stated as a hypothesis.

_______ **1.** The cause of the Air India crash was the explosion of a terrorist bomb.

_______ **2.** As a result of six months of intensive counseling, the Martins decided not to file for divorce.

_______ **3.** Qualified candidates choose not to run for office probably because they don't have enough money.

_______ **4.** Research suggests that brain damage in criminals may be a cause of violent crime.

Answers start on page 358.

IDENTIFYING A HYPOTHESIS

In a social studies passage, an author will often state a cause as a possibility, or hypothesis, rather than as a fact. It is important to recognize when authors are stating facts and when they are suggesting a hypothesis. In the following example, notice that the author does not know for sure why leaders are supporting basic education. But she does give you a possible explanation.

> All over the country, both labor and business leaders are supporting efforts to provide basic education to adults. These leaders may feel that workers will need this basic education in order to get and keep jobs in the future.

▶ According to the passage, what is the most likely cause of the efforts of labor and business leaders to educate adults?

(1) They feel a new spirit of charity.
(2) They want workers to be able to vote in union elections.
(3) In the future, workers will need to have a basic education.
(4) They recognize that labor and business must work together.
(5) They are concerned about a lack of workers for unskilled jobs.

You were right if you chose (3). The author says, "These leaders may feel that workers will need this basic education in order to get and keep jobs in the future."

EXERCISE 14: FINDING THE AUTHOR'S HYPOTHESIS

Directions: Read each passage and answer the questions that follow.

To middle-class Americans, the main purpose of a house is not simply protection from the weather. Instead, a house is an investment. To many, the most important feature of a house is its possible resale value. The focus on resale value has brought about changes in houses. For example, in 1900, only the richest families had two bathrooms in their houses. Now two- and three-bathroom houses are common because the extra bathrooms increase the resale value of a house.

1. Why does the author think that two- and three-bathroom houses are now common in the United States?

(1) Many families have more servants.
(2) Many families are larger and need more than one bathroom.
(3) Extra bathrooms increase the resale value of a home.
(4) Americans have settled down and now have enough time to make additions to their homes.
(5) The homes are designed to house more than one family.

Credit union members are more likely to save money than customers of regular banks. Credit union officials think they know why. Credit union members can have part of their paychecks set aside automatically in a savings account. Credit union officials think that their members are less likely to spend money that they never saw in the first place. In this way, their savings build up.

2. How do credit union officials explain the high rate of savings among their members?

(1) The members bank at regular banks also.
(2) The credit unions encourage them to save through effective advertising.
(3) Credit union officials encourage people who don't want to save money to bank elsewhere.
(4) Credit unions pay a higher rate of interest on savings accounts.
(5) Members won't spend money that they never see in the first place.

Answers start on page 358.

DEVELOPING A HYPOTHESIS

Sometimes a writer leaves it up to you to figure something out. The writer might describe an event or a trend without explaining why it happened. You can often use the evidence in the passage along with your common sense to develop a hypothesis to explain something. Try the following example:

> "We almost had to push the healthier, lighter foods on employees a couple of years ago," recalled Joseph P. Kingrey, president of ARA Services' Business Dining Division. "Lately, it's become a craze."
>
> Indeed, corporate dining facilities are picking up on the same trends that have swept through expensive restaurants. A recent study by the National Restaurant Association indicates that decaffeinated coffee, fresh fruit, and main dish salads are among the fastest-growing items in restaurants.

▶ A possible cause of the increased popularity of main dish salads is

(1) people want to spend less on food
(2) a shortage of high-quality chicken and beef
(3) people are tired of hamburgers and steaks
(4) people have become more concerned about their health
(5) a new, better-tasting lettuce has been developed

You were correct if you chose (4). The passage suggests this explanation in several ways. Healthier, lighter foods have become a craze, and decaffeinated coffee and fresh fruit are becoming more popular. You can put this evidence together and conclude that a likely reason for the growing popularity of salads is that they are healthier. There's no evidence in the passage for the other choices.

EXERCISE 15: MAKING A REASONABLE HYPOTHESIS

Directions: Read each passage and answer the questions that follow.

> Ten years ago tuberculosis, or TB, was disappearing in the United States. However, the number of serious cases is rising again. Most people infected with the tuberculosis bacterium never get sick. Their immune systems keep the disease under control. However, malnutrition, old age, illness, and drug abuse can all weaken the immune system so that tuberculosis has an opportunity to multiply and become dangerous.

1. Which of the following might be one reason why the number of serious TB cases is rising?
   (1) AIDS and homelessness have become more prevalent.
   (2) Smoking is becoming less common in the United States.
   (3) New medicines can help strengthen a patient's immune system.
   (4) People are afraid of tuberculosis, so they avoid contact with people who appear to be sick.
   (5) Most people infected with TB never get sick.

In 1967 the Field Foundation paid a group of doctors to study hunger and malnutrition in certain areas of the United States. These doctors found that many people in the United States were going hungry.

Ten years later, the foundation sent another group of doctors to the same areas. The second group of doctors reported that food aid programs (such as food stamps) had helped people in those regions. In 1967, the doctors had seen many children with swollen stomachs, dull eyes, and open wounds. In 1977, they saw fewer signs of hunger and its related illnesses.

2. In 1967, what was the probable cause of the poor physical condition of many children?
   (1) They were too dependent on handouts from the government.
   (2) They were being neglected by their parents.
   (3) They lived in unsanitary conditions.
   (4) They did not have enough good food.
   (5) There were not enough doctors.

Answers start on page 358.

EXERCISE 16: CHAPTER REVIEW

Directions: Study each passage or illustration carefully. Then choose the correct answer to each question.

Questions 1 and 2 are based on the following map.

SPREAD OF THE COTTON KINGDOM

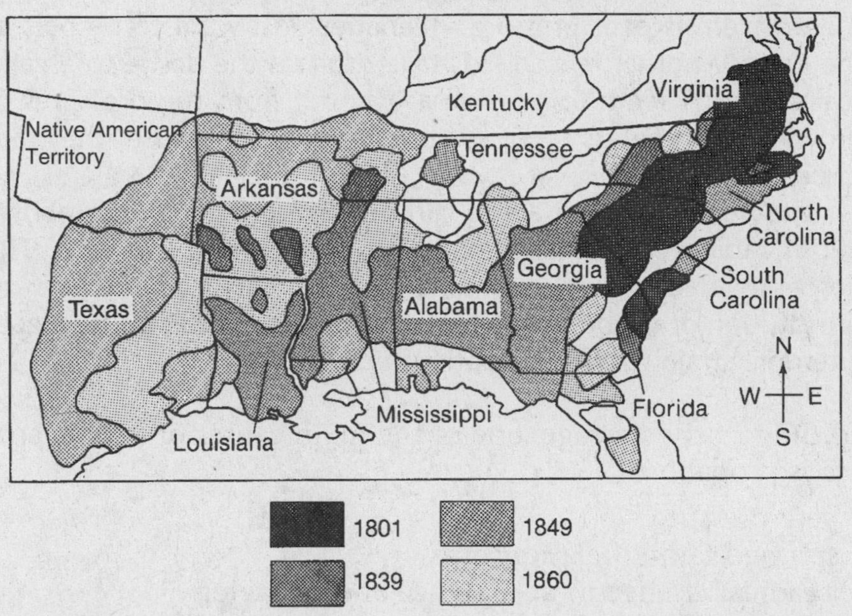

1. In 1801, the Cotton Kingdom was centered in the Carolinas, Georgia, and Virginia. From 1801 to 1860, the spread of the Cotton Kingdom was to
   (1) the north and east
   (2) the south and west
   (3) the east
   (4) Illinois
   (5) the Atlantic coast

2. The areas that had the greatest growth from 1801 to 1839 in land devoted to cotton were
   (1) Texas, Native American Territory, and Arkansas
   (2) the Carolinas, Georgia, and Virginia
   (3) Georgia, Alabama, Mississippi, and Louisiana
   (4) Florida and Texas
   (5) Tennessee, Kentucky, and North Carolina

Questions 3 and 4 are based on the following passage.

The epidemic of adolescent drug abuse continues to rage across the nation. Many reasons are given to explain this problem. Some people say that parents are too easy on their children. Other people say that the problem is caused by people drifting away from religion. Probably one of the main causes of the problem is peer pressure—teenagers just want to be part of the gang. Another reason kids take drugs is the desire to escape reality. Drugs seem to provide a way out from the pressures of growing up. Drugs also seem glamorous because they are forbidden.

The effects of drug abuse can be devastating. A drug abuser might radically change in both appearance and behavior. The desperate need for money to buy drugs can lead the user to prostitution or robbery. In addition, adolescent drug abuse places a terrible strain on family relationships.

3. According to the passage, one of the main causes of adolescent drug abuse is probably

(1) peer pressure
(2) strained family relationships
(3) a radical change in appearance and behavior
(4) a desperate need for money
(5) teen prostitution

4. According to the passage, drug abuse may cause an adolescent to

(1) drift away from religion
(2) commit crimes
(3) want to be part of the gang
(4) become more loving toward his or her family
(5) improve his or her appearance

Questions 5–8 are based on the following passage.

When high-tech industries are struggling, the next high-tech boom may be getting started. When laid-off executives and scientists don't have enough to do, they dream of running their own companies or building new products. So they start new companies offering new products.

Thus, while the giant companies suffer through hard times, dozens of new companies are quietly setting up shop. Often these new firms create the new products of the next boom. When these breakthrough products capture the public's imagination, the new boom explodes. Old and new firms rush to copy the product. The industry shoots into a period of frantic growth that may last two years or more.

Then the public's love affair with the product ends. Or a giant company takes over the whole market. Then the boom is over. The industry slumps back into the next recession. This bust-boom-bust cycle has happened over and over in high technology: in the late 1960s with minicomputers, in the mid-'70s with video games, in the early '80s with personal computers and VCRs, and in the early '90s with video camcorders and cellular phones.

5. How were the high-tech booms of the late 1960s, the mid-'70s, the early '80s, and the early '90s similar?
   (1) They all got started when new firms introduced new products.
   (2) They were all related to the car industry.
   (3) They all ended when one giant company took over the market.
   (4) They all began during times of prosperity.
   (5) They were all dominated by the Japanese.

6. How were the high-tech booms of the late 1960s, the mid-'70s, the early '80s, and the early '90s different?
   (1) Their patterns of boom and decline are different.
   (2) Only in the mid-'70s did firms rush to copy the new product.
   (3) Only in the early '80s was there a major new breakthrough product.
   (4) Different products led each boom.
   (5) Economic conditions were very different while the new products and new companies were getting started.

7. What is the correct sequence of each high-tech boom cycle?
   (1) large companies develop new product, new market booms, industry slumps
   (2) development during previous boom, short recession, new boom
   (3) development of new product by new firm during slow period, boom, industry slumps
   (4) company mergers, development of new product, booming new market, leveling off
   (5) mass advertising campaign, booming sales, new firms created, period of stability

8. According to the passage, which of the following might cause a high-tech boom to end?
   (1) scientists developing a new product
   (2) the public losing interest in the new product
   (3) other firms copying the product
   (4) computers becoming obsolete
   (5) executives getting laid off

Questions 9 and 10 are based on the following bar graph.

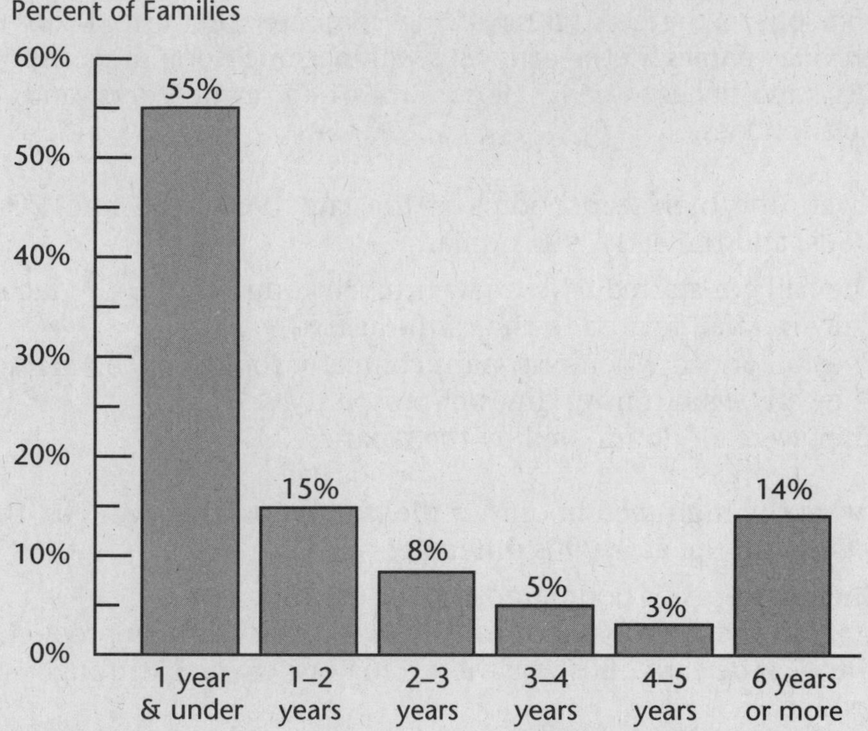

Source: "The Facts About Welfare: Being Poor in Massachusetts." Copyright 1985 by the Office of Research, Planning, and Evaluation, Commonwealth of Massachusetts.

9. According to the graph, how long do more than half of Massachusetts welfare recipients stay on welfare?
   (1) 1 year or less
   (2) 1–2 years
   (3) 3–4 years
   (4) 4–5 years
   (5) 6 years or more

10. Given the information on the chart, it seems that most people go on welfare
   (1) in order to collect benefits for their entire lives
   (2) so that they can afford to have more babies
   (3) to help them get back on their feet at a difficult time
   (4) to avoid their duties as parents
   (5) so that they never have to work again

Questions 11 and 12 are based on the following cartoon.

Background clues: The news media focuses a lot of attention on stories about terrorists, especially when they take hostages.

11. The terrorist in the cartoon says, "Shoot or I'll stop!" To whom is he talking? ______________________________

12. What is the cartoonist's opinion of terrorist actions?
(1) Terrorists are daring and courageous.
(2) Terrorists want their hostages to suffer.
(3) Terrorist actions reduce the number of American tourists traveling abroad.
(4) Terrorists are using the news media to get attention.
(5) News reporting about terrorist actions is biased.

Question 13 is based on the following passage.

> Mel Fisher first heard about two treasure ships that sank in 1622 in a book called *The Treasure Hunter's Guide.* In 1970, Fisher began a sixteen-year search of the ocean floor near Florida, looking for the ships. Fisher had to raise money from 1,200 investors to pay for the costly search. He finally found one of the ships in 1986. It held a treasure of over $400 million worth of jewels and precious metals.

13. Which of the following hypotheses best explains why Mel Fisher was looking for the ships?

(1) He wanted to know how ships were built in the 1600s.
(2) He wanted to publish a book on the dangers of shipping in the 1600s.
(3) He wanted the valuable treasure from the ships.
(4) He was doing research for his book, *The Treasure Hunter's Guide.*
(5) He was working for a group of investors.

Question 14 is based on the following passage.

> In 1940, only 8 percent of black men earned more money than the average white man. By 1980, 29 percent of employed black men earned more money than the average white man.
>
> What brought about this dramatic change? One study examined several major factors: education, the migration of blacks from the South to the North, blacks moving from rural areas into cities, welfare programs, and affirmative action programs. The study concluded that when blacks moved to cities they had better opportunities. However, education enabled blacks to take advantage of these opportunities. Education was the key factor that allowed blacks to succeed.

14. What do the authors of the study believe is the best way to improve the standard of living of black people?

(1) provide educational opportunities
(2) encourage relocation in the South
(3) maintain affirmative action programs
(4) ensure that there is good medical care
(5) encourage migration to urban areas

Answers start on page 358.

5 EVALUATING SOCIAL STUDIES MATERIALS

In this chapter, you will learn to evaluate what you read. When you evaluate, you ask yourself whether something is logical. You will practice judging whether you have enough information to answer a question or solve a problem and whether the information you have is what you need. You will also practice identifying errors in reasoning. And you'll practice recognizing the values that have an effect on beliefs, decision making, and action. Also, you'll learn what propaganda is and how to recognize it.

EVALUATION: HAVING ENOUGH INFORMATION

USING THE INFORMATION IN A PASSAGE

Every day you evaluate whether you have enough information to solve a problem or answer someone's question. Sometimes you evaluate information to make a decision. Read the example paragraph carefully and then decide whether you have enough information to prove the following statements.

> It was 3:00 A.M. Larry was driving at fifty-five miles per hour on the interstate in his 1993 Oldsmobile. An hour before, he had noticed that his gas gauge was on "Empty" as he passed a closed gas station. Suddenly, his engine stopped and his car slowly rolled to a stop.

Put a check in front of each statement that the passage gives you enough information to prove.

______ **1.** Larry's car had engine trouble.

______ **2.** Larry's car had run out of gas.

______ **3.** Larry was coming home from his night job.

1. Not enough information. It is possible that he had engine trouble, since the passage states that the engine stopped, but you can't tell for sure.

2. Enough information. He had driven at fifty-five miles per hour for an hour with the fuel gauge on "Empty."

3. Not enough information. It is possible, but there is not enough information in the passage for proof.

EXERCISE 1: IS THERE ENOUGH INFORMATION?

Directions: Following each passage are four statements. Put a check (✓) in front of each statement that can be proven by using the information in the passage. Put an *X* in front of each statement that cannot be proven based on the passage.

All but one of the sixteen southern states allow the death penalty. In 1992 in those states, there was a total of 1,488 prisoners waiting for execution. Of the thirty-four states outside the South, twenty-one allow the death penalty. In 1992, those states had 1,106 prisoners on death row.

______ **1.** In 1992, there were more prisoners on death row in the sixteen southern states than in all thirty-four other states.

______ **2.** Murder is increasing in the southern United States.

______ **3.** A person convicted of murder in any southern state might not be given the death penalty.

When people talk about the "heartland" of America, they usually mean the Midwest. Some researchers have decided that the "typical American voter" lives in Dayton, a service and manufacturing city on the Miami River in southwestern Ohio. This typical American voter is a housewife whose husband is a machinist—perhaps with General Motors or Delco—and whose brother-in-law is a policeman. She considers herself a Democrat but often votes Republican.

Companies that want to find out what products people will buy also believe that the Midwest is typical. Columbus, Ohio, boasts that companies like to test-market new products there because it offers such a good cross section of the country.

______ **4.** Many companies believe that if a new product is successful in Columbus it will be successful in the nation as a whole.

______ **5.** The "typical American voter" lives in a city.

______ **6.** Ohio will always be the home of the typical American voter.

Answers start on page 359.

USING THE INFORMATION ON A MAP

A map might not always have all the information you need to answer a question. See what information you can get from the following map.

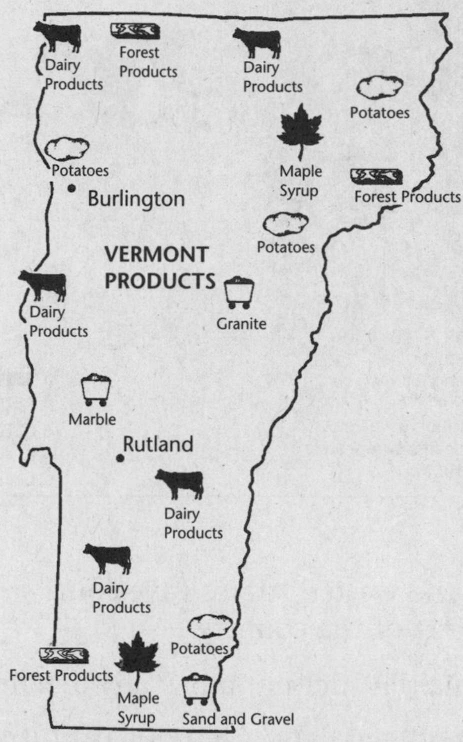

Does the map of Vermont provide enough information to prove the following statements? Put a check (✓) in the blank in front of the statement you can prove. Put an *X* in front of the statement you cannot prove.

______ The capital of Vermont is Montpelier.

______ Potatoes are produced in Vermont.

You were right if you put an *X* in front of the first statement. The map shows a few cities, but not Montpelier. You should have put a check in front of the second statement. Scanning the map, you will see several spots where potatoes are produced.

EXERCISE 2: USING INFORMATION ON A MAP

Directions: Following each map are several statements. In the blank in front of each statement, put a check (✓) if there is enough information on the map to prove the statement true. Put an *X* if there is not enough information.

Questions 1–3 are based on the Vermont products map above.

______ **1.** Vermont's forest products are more important than its potatoes.

______ **2.** Dairy products are Vermont's major source of farm income.

______ **3.** Maple syrup is produced in Vermont.

Questions 4–6 are based on the following map.

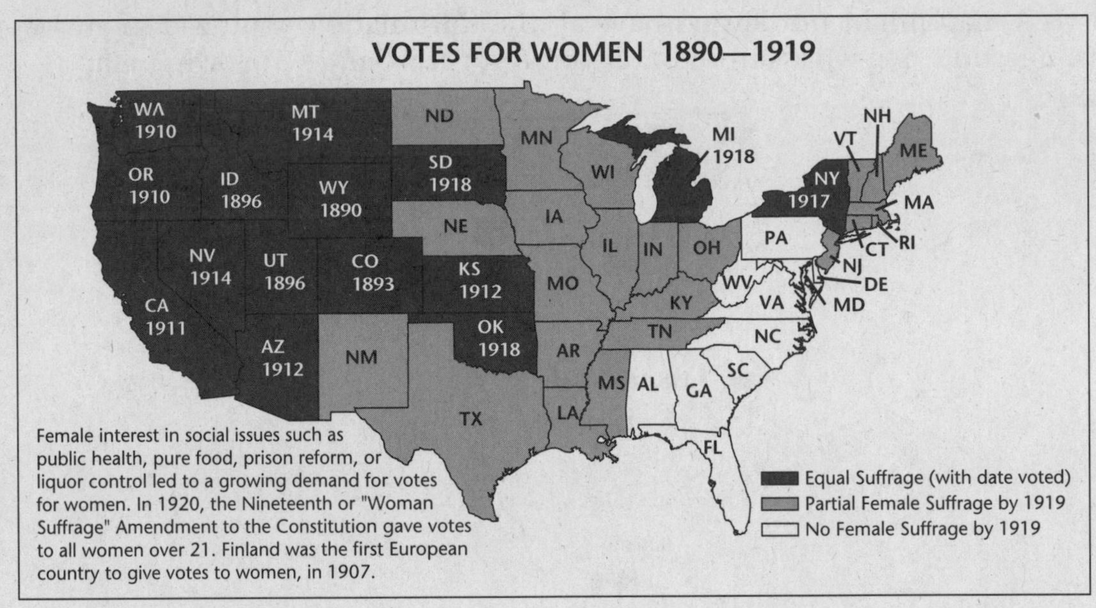

_______ 4. In general, the western states gave equal suffrage to women before the rest of the country.

_______ 5. Pennsylvania (PA) did not allow any female suffrage by 1919.

_______ 6. More women lived in New York in 1917 than in any other state.

Answers start on page 359.

EVALUATION: LOOKING FOR THE RIGHT INFORMATION

Doreen is a feminist—a supporter of women's rights. When she went to vote in the primary for state senator, she found that Marie Home was running against Tom Taylor. Doreen voted for Marie because she was a woman. She later found out that it was Tom, not Marie, who supported the women's issues that were important to her.

Doreen used the wrong information to make an important decision. She wanted a state senator who would support women's issues. She thought that all she needed to know was which candidate was a woman. Unfortunately, her choice went against her desire to have a state senator who would support women's rights.

IRRELEVANT INFORMATION

Irrelevant information isn't really related to the subject being talked about. Sometimes writers try to persuade you to do something by giving you irrelevant but appealing information. Study the following advertisement. Think about what the advertiser wants you to do and what reasons you are given to do it.

WIN THE LARGEST SWEEPSTAKES OF ITS KIND IN AMERICA!

If you are the lucky winner, Ed McMahon, former star of "Star Search" and "The Tonight Show" will hand you your winning check on national TV. We also offer the lowest prices on your favorite magazines!

ORDER THESE GREAT MAGAZINES FROM US TODAY!!!

What does the advertiser want you to do?

____

What irrelevant reasons are given for doing it?

____

The purpose of the ad is to convince you to buy magazines. However, two facts are irrelevant: "the largest sweepstakes of its kind in America" and "Ed McMahon will hand you your winning check." Both are poor reasons to buy the magazines. However, getting your favorite magazine at the lowest price is a good reason to buy the magazines.

EXERCISE 3: IDENTIFYING IRRELEVANT INFORMATION

Directions: Read each passage. First, figure out what the writer wants you to do. Then fill in the reasons that are not relevant to the decision you must make.

Dear Editor,

I want to urge your readers to vote for Gil Cohen for mayor. Everyone agrees that he is more attractive than his opponent. He has years of administrative experience, much more than the other candidate. He has promised to increase the police budget in order to control crime. Finally, people should vote for him because he has spent over $100,000 of his own money to get elected.

Sincerely,
Bernice Cohen

a. What does the writer want her readers to do?

____

b. What irrelevant reasons for doing it does she give?

____

Answers start on page 359.

EXERCISE 4: USING INFORMATION CORRECTLY

Directions: Read each passage; then answer the questions that follow.

Many people outside the United States think of Americans as self-centered and selfish. Yet there is evidence for quite a different view. In 1985, Americans responded to the record "We Are the World" and the Live Aid concert by contributing millions of dollars to famine relief in Africa. A year later, Americans participated in Hands Across America, an event in which millions of people joined hands to raise millions of dollars more to feed hungry Americans.

1. Hands Across America was
   (1) a concert to benefit starving people in Africa
   (2) a record that featured America's most famous singers
   (3) an event that raised millions of dollars to feed hungry Americans
   (4) an event that proved that Americans were self-centered and selfish
   (5) an event that proved that Americans were willing to help needy people from other countries

2. There is enough proof in the passage to show that
   (1) the U.S. government is concerned with world hunger
   (2) Africa is successfully coping with its food problems
   (3) all musicians are concerned with helping others
   (4) Americans are becoming more self-centered
   (5) Americans can show generosity

In recent years, the United States has been divided sharply over the concept of affirmative action. For many years, minorities and women were kept out of jobs and schools because of thei race or sex. Affirmative action programs try to correct past prejudice. Schools and employers using these programs search for qualified women and minorities to fill their openings.

Many Americans believe that hiring should not be influenced by race, sex, or religion. They insist that affirmative action is the wrong way of dealing with prejudice because it is prejudice working in reverse.

3. There is enough information to determine that

(1) affirmative action programs have made up for past prejudice and are no longer needed
(2) affirmative action is not fair to white males
(3) affirmative action will not result in more black people in important jobs
(4) affirmative action is an attempt to make up for past prejudice
(5) affirmative action will be a major issue of the 1990s

The kibbutz is a type of cooperative community found in Israel. In a kibbutz, most things are owned by everyone as a group. The kibbutz owns the land, all farm animals and equipment, and all crops. Sometimes it owns its own factories. In some kibbutzim, even the houses are owned by the community.

4. A kibbutz is a community in which

(1) everybody must learn Hebrew, the language of Israel
(2) new members must be over thirty-five years old
(3) most things are owned in common
(4) children cannot live with their parents
(5) factories are owned by the richest people

Answers start on page 359.

EVALUATION: FINDING ERRORS IN REASONING

In this part of the chapter, you will practice recognizing other errors in reasoning, such as

(a) substituting personal beliefs, desires, or experience for facts:

"I have never gotten a parking ticket on this street; therefore, it must be legal to park here."

(b) making general statements based on one example:

"All those TV offers are rip-offs. My sister sent in $25 for a set of knives, and she never got it."

(c) backward reasoning:

"If all American voters are people over eighteen years old, then all people over eighteen years old are American voters."

Below are two reasons for a certain action. Put a check (✓) in front of the one that shows good reasoning. Put an *X* in front of the one that shows a reasoning error.

Cali, the office manager, is trying to decide whether to purchase new word processing equipment for her office.

______ The staff will get more work done if word processing equipment is purchased and used.

______ Cali thinks the office ought to have the latest and fanciest equipment.

You should have put a check in front of the first reason. A good reason for purchasing new equipment is to improve productivity. You should have put an *X* in front of the second reason. This is an example of substituting a personal desire for good reasons.

EXERCISE 5: RECOGNIZING ERRORS IN REASONING

Directions: Following each statement are two reasons for making a choice or taking an action. Put a check (✓) in the blank before the choice that shows good reasoning. Put an *X* in the blank before the choice that shows an error in reasoning.

1. Mel's Auto Body Shop is in financial trouble.

______ **a.** Since Mel's business has had an excellent financial record for thirty years, Mel is confident his bank will help him.

______ **b.** Since the government bailed out the Chrysler Corporation when it was in financial trouble, it will help out Mel's Auto Body Shop.

2. The Yellowbrick neighborhood decided not to work with the Froston Redevelopment Authority to improve the neighborhood.

_______ **a.** The Froston Redevelopment Authority wiped out the West End neighborhood thirty years ago. Therefore, the same thing will happen to the Yellowbrick neighborhood.

_______ **b.** For over thirty years, the Froston Redevelopment Authority has constantly ignored the wishes of Froston's neighborhoods. Instead, it has listened to wealthy developers. Therefore, it is risky to work with them.

Answers start on page 359.

WHAT IS THE PROBLEM HERE?

It is important for you to be able to explain why reasoning is correct or why it is wrong. In the following exercise, you'll practice identifying and explaining reasoning problems. Try answering the questions based on the following cartoon.

Background clues: Compared to many diseases, AIDS is difficult to catch. Yet, because it is deadly, many people have irrational fears.

▶ Why is the person in this cartoon fired? ______________________________

▶ Why is it ridiculous that this person is getting fired? ________________

The boss is afraid Wilson might have AIDS. It is impossible for the employee to have caught AIDS through this string of people, and it's impossible for AIDS to be passed on through normal office contact.

Now try some sample questions based on the following paragraph.

> A recent research study found that violent behavior might be caused by brain damage and child abuse. All the residents of death row spoken to by the researchers had some brain damage and had been abused in childhood. Because of the results of this study, we should put all brain-damaged people who have been victims of child abuse into mental hospitals.

▶ What does the author suggest should happen to people who have suffered child abuse and brain damage? ____________________

▶ What is the problem with his reasoning? ____________________

The author thinks that these people should be put into mental hospitals. His reasoning is poor because he is reasoning backward. The report stated that the violent people studied were brain-damaged and abused as children. That does not mean that all brain-damaged and abused people will be violent.

EXERCISE 6: ERRORS IN REASONING

Directions: Answer the questions following each passage.

> In 1980, Ronald Reagan was running for president against President Jimmy Carter. He asked the voters if they were better off then than they were four years before. He suggested that, if they were worse off, they should vote for him to replace President Carter. I had had a hard year. My wife died, and my children dropped out of school. I started drinking and got fired from my job. I was doing much worse than four years before. Therefore, I voted for Ronald Reagan for president.

1. The writer of the passage decided to vote for Ronald Reagan because
   (1) he supported Reagan's economic policies
   (2) his life was going badly
   (3) he did not like Jimmy Carter
   (4) he felt that it was time for a change
   (5) he thought Reagan was a great speaker

2. What is the problem with his reasoning? ____________________

____

I read about a study that found that, in general, married men are the happiest group of people. Unmarried women came in second in the happiness study. They were almost as happy with their lives as married men. Unmarried men finished third in the survey. Finally, the unhappiest group in the population was married women.

I am an unmarried woman. My husband left me five years ago, and I am still miserable as a result. Therefore, the study must be wrong. The unhappiest group of people are unmarried women.

3. The study found that the unhappiest group was

(1) married men
(2) married women
(3) unmarried men
(4) unmarried women
(5) children

4. What is the problem with the speaker's reasoning? ________________

____

Answers start on page 359.

EVALUATION: RECOGNIZING VALUES

Everybody has values, those things that they consider important. We often think of the United States as a nation shaped by values. Many of the early settlers from Europe came to America for religious freedom.

It is important to be able to recognize the values of an author or of the people an author writes about. Some people have values that you may think are noble, such as consideration for others or the importance of honesty. Other values can include wanting to make money, getting what you want no matter who gets hurt, concern for world peace, and patriotism. See if you can identify the values being expressed in the cartoon below.

Background clues: The National Rifle Association (NRA) opposes all gun control laws. They believe that all law-abiding Americans have the right to own and use guns.

OF COURSE WE SELL ARMOR-PIERCING BULLETS... WHO KNOWS WHEN YOU'LL SEE A DEER DRIVING A SHERMAN TANK?

▶ What value is being expressed by the shop owner in the cartoon?

(1) patriotism
(2) world peace
(3) human rights
(4) freedom to carry weapons
(5) consideration for others

The correct answer is choice (4), *freedom to carry weapons*. The caption shows that he will sell dangerous ammunition that is clearly not meant to be used against deer. The cartoon does not suggest choice (1), *patriotism*. His willingness to sell something so dangerous eliminates choices (2), (3), and (5).

EXERCISE 7: RECOGNIZING VALUES

Directions: Study each passage or cartoon; then answer the questions that follow.

Conversations about politically correct speech have been taking place at college campuses across the nation. Some school officials, alarmed by incidents of racial and sexual harassment, have adopted speech codes prohibiting hateful language in classrooms and dormitories. They hope to protect minority students from prejudice. Opponents argue that the codes restrict students' and teachers' First Amendment right to free speech. Some students have fought the controversial codes by suing their colleges, generally with success.

1. What value did colleges hope to preserve by adopting speech codes?
   (1) quiet study areas for students
   (2) fair treatment of all people
   (3) access to education for all Americans
   (4) support of the U.S. government
   (5) separation of the sexes in schools

2. What value did opponents of the codes hope to preserve?
   (1) equality among races
   (2) pursuit of money
   (3) freedom to express ideas
   (4) racial hatred
   (5) the right to sue

Background clues: Throughout history each U.S. president has developed a special relationship with the press. The cartoon below comments on the way former President Ronald Reagan seemed to view reporters. It refers to the First Amendment to the U.S. Constitution, which protects the freedom of the press to operate without government interference.

"I propose we reword the First Amendment and make it: FREEDOM FROM THE PRESS."

3. According to the cartoonist, which value was most important to President Reagan?
   (1) freedom of the press
   (2) making money
   (3) power of the president
   (4) solving America's problems
   (5) human rights

4. Based on this cartoon, what value seems to be most important to the cartoonist?
   (1) freedom of the press
   (2) making money
   (3) power of the presidency
   (4) solving America's problems
   (5) human rights

The New England town meeting has been called the purest form of democracy. At the meetings, every voter has the opportunity to "stand up and be counted" on issues that are important to the town. Any group coming to a town meeting has the chance to appeal to the voters by speaking directly to them. One town preservation society thought they had an issue that couldn't lose at the town meeting. They wanted the town to buy an old farm and save the land for recreation and education.

Everybody on the purchase committee wanted a chance to speak to the voters. Despite a poll of voters that showed them strongly in favor of saving open land, the proposed purchase of the farm was badly defeated.

5. What value of the voters did the town preservation society try to appeal to?

(1) the need for efficiency
(2) conservation of open land
(3) the desire for lower taxes
(4) the importance of communication
(5) the spirit of fair play

Answers start on page 359.

EVALUATION: RECOGNIZING PROPAGANDA

Propaganda presents a person, a product, or an idea as good or bad. Its purpose is to convince you. You see examples of propaganda every day. The most common example of propaganda is advertising. Does the following example look familiar?

NEW MEDICAL BREAKTHROUGH!!!

Lose up to 50 Pounds Without Dieting
EAT ALL YOUR FAVORITE FOODS AND STILL LOSE WEIGHT

All of us have seen these kinds of ads before. They pull at our emotions and desires. They tell only the good side of their products and leave out any possible harmful side effects. They are a form of propaganda.

Propaganda uses information to convince a reader. It uses ideas, facts, or accusations to help or hurt a cause. It generally tries to promote a single point of view and is one-sided. Propaganda often distorts facts. Advertisers use a variety of propaganda techniques to convince us to buy their products.

How is this advertiser trying to convince you to buy the product?

TRAIN YOUR VOICE FOR SUCCESS!

Never again will you be overanxious or fearful when meeting new people or speaking in public. You will be absolutely self-confident knowing that your voice can have the resonance of a James Earl Jones, the controlled charm of a Courtney Cox, the poise of a Peter Jennings, or the seductive power of a Julia Roberts!

Order Your Voice-Training Cassette Right Away!

▶ This ad tries to convince you to buy the cassette by claiming that

(1) it can make you speak as well as some famous people
(2) you can become a famous actor if you use it
(3) most people you know have benefited from it already
(4) people who use it get better jobs
(5) you don't need to improve your public speaking skills

The correct answer is choice (1). This is an example of a very common propaganda technique, the "famous or respected person" technique. It uses the names of famous people. The ad tries to get you to think that you'll learn the same techniques that have made these people so successful.

Other common propaganda techniques include:

- **Glittering generalities**—using vague positive words and images

  Our salon's *secret techniques* will bring out the *timeless beauty* in you. Our experts think *age* and *elegance* go hand in hand.

- **Name calling**—connecting a negative image to an idea, a product, a person, or a group

  Stop using *dirty, smelly, smoky* oil. Change to electric heat.

- **Bandwagon**—everybody is doing it

  Join the *Pepsi Generation!* Drink Pepsi Cola.

- **Card stacking**—mentioning only the favorable facts and ignoring the negative facts

  Top Choice Chewing Tobacco gives you that *real tobacco flavor without smoke.* For real tobacco satisfaction, use Top Choice.

  (Not mentioned in the ad are the dangers of smokeless tobacco.)

EXERCISE 8: PROPAGANDA AND ADVERTISING

Directions: Answer the questions following each advertisement.

Eat Chocorich, America's highest-quality candy.
Only the finest chocolate and sugar are used in making Chocorich.

1. According to the ad, you should eat Chocorich because
   (1) everybody eats Chocorich
   (2) famous people eat Chocorich
   (3) eating Chocorich will make you popular
   (4) more people eat Chocorich than any other candy
   (5) other candy makers use lower-quality chocolate and sugar

2. The ad gives only reasons why you *should* eat Chocorich. Can you think of a reason not to eat Chocorich?

____

____

3. This ad appeals to people who believe that
   (1) attractive men have large muscles
   (2) it is a good idea to keep your weight down
   (3) it is important to be healthy
   (4) women like intelligent men
   (5) it is important to be considerate of others

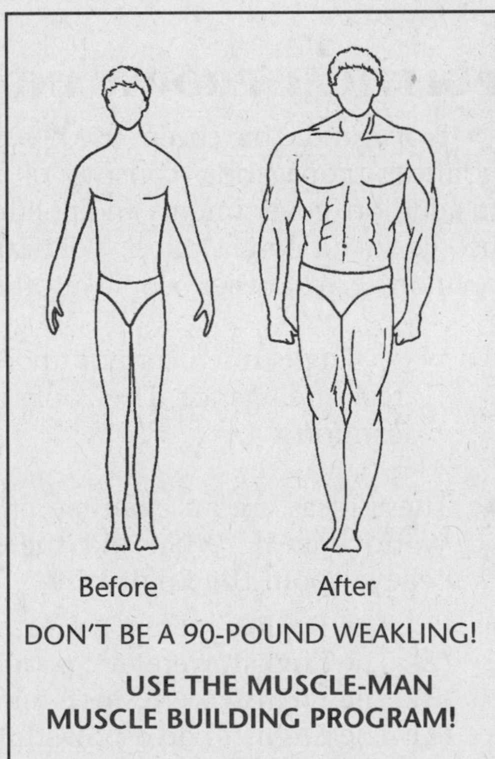

Before
After
DON'T BE A 90-POUND WEAKLING!
USE THE MUSCLE-MAN
MUSCLE BUILDING PROGRAM!

4. Women will be attracted to this ad because
   (1) they look like the woman in the drawing
   (2) they are tired of the summer and want to look ahead to fall
   (3) they are looking for a bargain
   (4) they want to think of themselves as sophisticated
   (5) they do not want to attract attention to themselves

COME TO LESLIE'S!
We have sophisticated styles for fall.

Answers start on page 360.

POLITICAL PROPAGANDA

Propaganda has been used frequently in the political world. A lot of political propaganda consists of advertisements for political candidates. In addition, governments and political candidates use propaganda to convince people to support a cause. Political propaganda is also used to turn public opinion against other people or other countries, as in the following example.

> Englishmen cannot understand great ideas; they lack any real intelligence. They only care about material things and comforts.

▶ These ideas are an example of Italian propaganda at the beginning of World War II. What did the Italian government want its people to believe about the English?

(1) The English were a dangerous enemy who must be feared.
(2) The English were evil people who wanted to destroy the world.
(3) The English were small-minded and could be defeated easily.
(4) The English had a powerful economy that had to be destroyed.
(5) The English were a noble people who should be copied.

The correct answer is choice (3). The writer says that the English lacked real intelligence. The Italian government insulted the English so that the Italian people would be more supportive of the war against the English.

EXERCISE 9: POLITICAL PROPAGANDA

Directions: Answer the questions following each passage or illustration.

Following a disastrous defeat of the Germans by the Soviets at Stalingrad, Goebbels, Hitler's propaganda chief, spoke to the German people. He said that the 300,000 Germans killed in the battle were all heroes. They had slowed down six Soviet armies, which otherwise would be rampaging toward Germany. He claimed that the Germans had been "purified" by the defeat at Stalingrad. It had given them the new strength they required for victory.

1. List two reasons that, according to Goebbels, the defeat at Stalingrad was good for the Germans.

____

____

2. Why would Goebbels have described the terrible outcome of the Battle of Stalingrad as he did?

(1) He believed that military defeats were good for the German spirit.
(2) He thought the Russians might retreat.
(3) He wanted the Americans and British to break their alliance with the USSR.
(4) He didn't want people to realize what a disaster it was.
(5) He wanted Germany to surrender to the Russians.

INTEREST IN HOLISTIC HEALING SKYROCKETS!

Americans nationwide are choosing holistic medicine over traditional treatment.

You, too, can experience the benefits of holistic healing!

3. According to this advertisement, you should try holistic medical treatment because

(1) it works faster than traditional medical treatments
(2) everybody is trying holistic medicine
(3) traditional drugs have unhealthy side effects
(4) a lot of research has gone into the development of holistic medicine
(5) holistic medicines are much cheaper than other treatments

Answers start on page 360.

EXERCISE 10: CHAPTER REVIEW

Directions: Study each passage or picture, then answer the questions that follow.

Questions 1 and 2 are based on the following map.

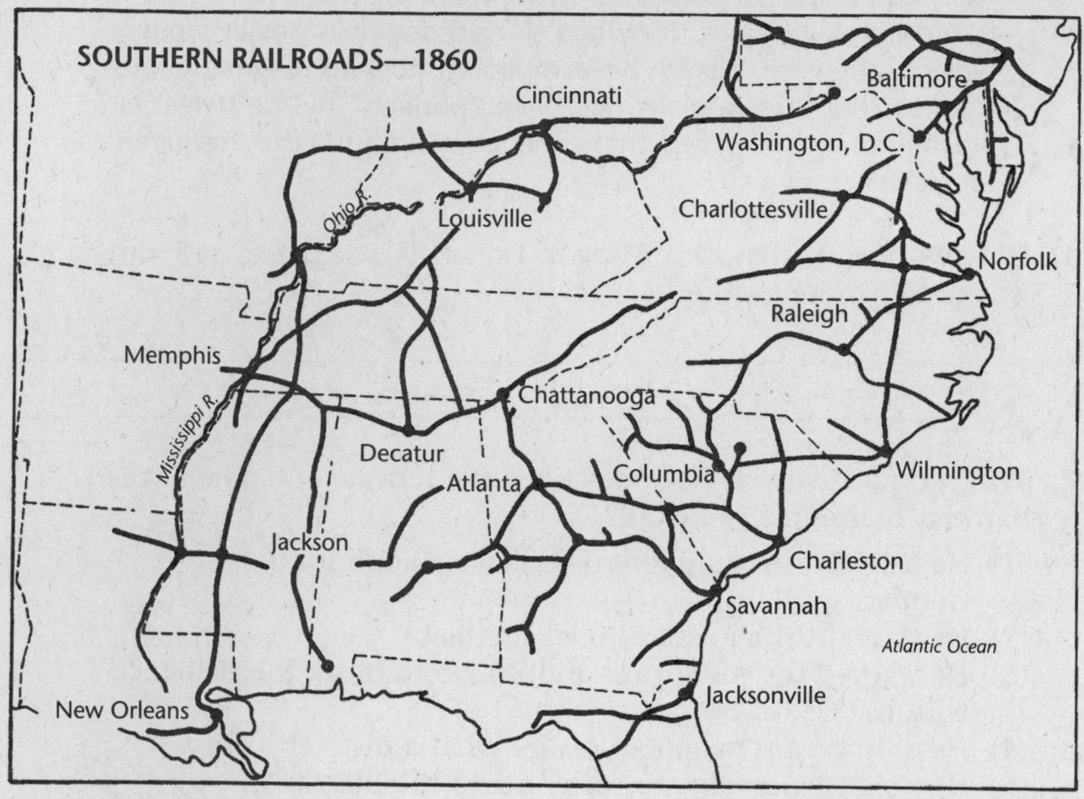

1. According to the map, in 1860 it was impossible to travel by train from
   (1) Jackson to New Orleans
   (2) Atlanta to Columbia
   (3) Atlanta to Chattanooga
   (4) Raleigh to Charlottesville
   (5) Jacksonville to Savannah

2. There is enough information on the map to determine that
   (1) the North would win the Civil War by using the rail system to transport the troops
   (2) Atlanta was the largest city in the South because it was an important railroad junction
   (3) Savannah was the main shipping port for cotton because all cotton grown across the South could be shipped there by train
   (4) the western frontier could not be reached from the South by train
   (5) the South was mostly farmland and, therefore, did not need an extensive rail network

Questions 3 and 4 are based on the following passage.

Amnesty International is a very special organization. It does not support any one form of government or economic system. It does watch out for human rights throughout the world, working on thousands of cases of political imprisonment, torture, and murder. As a result of this work, many people put into prison or tortured for their beliefs have been freed. Governments have been pressured to end their abuse of people who disagree with them. In recognition of its work, Amnesty International was awarded the Nobel Peace Prize.

3. Amnesty International's purpose is

(1) the defeat of conservative politicians
(2) the protection of human rights
(3) the growth of democracy
(4) the winning of major awards
(5) the raising of money through contributions

4. To decide if Amnesty International has been effective, you would want to know

(1) how many awards it has won
(2) whether it has the support of the United States government
(3) if it has helped make governments more respectful of human rights
(4) whether it has fought against imperialism
(5) whether it has been able to raise more money than other human rights groups

Questions 5 and 6 are based on the following passage.

The United Nations was founded after World War II to help nations solve their differences peacefully. While there has not been another world war, the past fifty years have been far from peaceful. For example, in the 1950s, the United Nations sent troops to fight in the Korean War. In addition, there was almost constant war in Southeast Asia and the Middle East for over half a century. And, even though the United Nations sent peace-keeping forces to the Balkans, horrible ethnic wars continued to rage.

Both the Security Council and the General Assembly of the United Nations were supposed to be places where nations could talk about their differences and solve them without violence. Unfortunately, nations have used these forums to attack each other verbally rather than to settle disputes.

5. From the passage, it is clear that
   (1) the United Nations has failed and should be abolished
   (2) the United Nations should be given more money
   (3) the United Nations has promoted war rather than prevented it
   (4) the United Nations still needs to develop ways to solve disputes peacefully
   (5) the United Nations should follow American foreign policy

6. A guiding principle of the United Nations is
   (1) only the strong survive
   (2) the meek shall inherit the earth
   (3) if you have the votes, you have the power
   (4) people should be free to live as they choose
   (5) conflicts should be settled peacefully

Question 7 is based on the following ad.

KEEP AMERICA STRONG!

VOTE FOR VITO AMORELLI FOR U.S. CONGRESS

7. As a voter, what reasonable response might you make to this ad?
   (1) voting for Vito because you want America to be strong
   (2) voting against Vito because you want America to be weak
   (3) not voting at all because it does not matter who is elected
   (4) finding out how Vito proposes to keep America strong
   (5) running for Congress yourself

8. "Equal pay for equal work" has become a rallying cry for women's groups. On the average, women are paid only two-thirds of what a man receives for either the same job or a job of equal difficulty and responsibility. What might be a good reason for a particular man to be paid more than a particular woman for a similar job?
   (1) He needs to be paid more because he must support a family.
   (2) Men are more important than women.
   (3) He has more years of experience than the woman.
   (4) He must save for retirement.
   (5) His pride would be hurt if a woman made as much as he.

Answers start on page 360.

SOCIAL STUDIES ANSWER KEY

CHAPTER 1: UNDERSTANDING WHAT YOU READ

Exercise 1: Finding Details
pages 208–209

Your wording may vary, but your answers should contain the same information as the answers below.

1. John Kennedy and Richard Nixon
2. Kennedy's good performance in the televised debates got him the extra votes he needed.
3. Seabrook, New Hampshire
4. 1990
5. They occupied the governor's office, disrupted public hearings, and interfered with plant procedures.

Exercise 2: More Practice in Finding Details
pages 209–211

1. (5) The second sentence tells you about a law against giving away food or drinks. The third sentence says Mr. Belair was arrested because of this law.
2. (2) The second sentence states that an American plane dropped the first atomic bomb.
3. (3) The third sentence states that the bomb destroyed the entire city.
4. (4) The second sentence states that competition from overseas has forced both sides to look at the way they work together. While the other statements could be true, only (4) is stated directly in the passage as the cause of cooperation.

Exercise 3: Synonym, Definition, and Comparison Clues
page 212

Your wording may vary, but your answers should contain the same information as the answers below.

1. phony cure-all
2. giving jobs and favors for political reasons
3. a company that controls production of a product and has no competition
4. amount of goods produced

Exercise 4: Antonym and Contrast Clues
pages 213–214

1. (b) The contrast clue is "After years without restrictions on the number . . ."
2. (a) The clue is "contrasted sharply with the beauty."
3. (b) The clue is "fighting broke out."
4. (c) The contrast is "unlike the Native American tribes, who only wanted to keep their own lands."

Exercise 5: Using the Sense of the Passage
pages 214–215

1. (3) The Wright brothers' flight in 1903 gives you a clue that it must be around 1900. In addition, the paragraph is talking about changes taking place over time, so the answer shouldn't be a specific year.
2. (3) The paragraph is full of examples of overcrowding—traffic jams, crowded elevators, and crowded subway trains.
3. (3) Age and arthritis would probably make hands twisted.

Exercise 6: Recognizing Restated Information
pages 216

1. I—They wanted "a chance to make money and go back . . ."
2. C—This sentence restates "The various teachers found a congenial atmosphere in our home . . ." *Congenial* means "friendly."

Exercise 7: Restating Information in Your Own Words
pages 217

Your wording may vary, but your answers should contain the same information as the answers below.

1. Rockefeller forced the railroads to charge him low freight costs on his oil shipments.
2. Rockefeller would cut prices for his oil in areas where he had competitors.
3. The AFL promoted clear-cut issues such as rate of pay and the length of the workday.
4. They put up candidates for political office and asked for major changes in American society.

Exercise 8: Summarizing Facts
pages 218

In this exercise, the correct summary is always the choice that contains all the important ideas from the three original statements.

1. (b) 2. (a)

Exercise 9: Identifying Unrelated Sentences
pages 220

1. (c) The other sentences talk about American interest in Japanese products.
2. (c) The topic of the other four sentences is the Consumer Price Index.

Exercise 10: Identifying the Main Idea
pages 221–222

In this exercise, the main idea choice (M) is supported or explained by the details in the rest of the paragraph. The other choices are either too broad (B), too narrow (N), or not mentioned in the passage (X).

1.		2.	
(a)	B	(a)	M
(b)	M	(b)	N
(c)	X	(c)	X
(d)	N	(d)	B

Exercise 11: Writing Topic Sentences
pages 223–224

Although your wording will vary from the answers below, you should have written similar information. Compare your answers to these to be sure you were on the right track.

1. *Topic:* FDIC

   Main Point: FDIC protects people who deposit in a bank.

   Topic Sentence: The purpose of the Federal Deposit Insurance Corporation is to protect people against bank failure.
2. *Topic:* consumer co-ops

   Main Point: There are different kinds, but all are owned by members.

   Topic Sentence: Although there are different kinds of consumer co-ops, they are all owned by their members.

Exercise 12: Main Idea of a Passage
pages 225–226

1. (a) Choice (b) is not true. Choices (c) and (d) are details that tell you more about the main idea.
2. (c) Choices (a) and (d) are details. Choice (b) is not true.
3. (c) Choices (a) and (b) are details that tell you more about the main idea. Choice (d) is not true.
4. (b) Choice (c) is a detail mentioned only in paragraph 2, and choice (d) is a detail mentioned only in paragraph 1. Choice (a) is not true.

Exercise 13: Inferring Facts
pages 228–229

Part A

Check to make sure you have the following information in your answers.

1. The speaker talks about seats, and the last sentence mentions a bus boycott.
2. The speaker says that the black community rallied to her support and points out that in most parts of the world, a man gives up his seat to a woman; so you can infer that she is a black woman.

Part B

1. (2) The clues that Sam had an owner and was bought for $25 tell you that Sam was a slave.
2. (4) The speaker says, "Two hundred of us were working . . ." A factory would have that many workers. By using the pronoun *us*, she tells you she was one of the workers.
3. (3) The speaker says "When I took office . . . ," and he talks about proposing programs to Congress. You also can infer that he was president of the United States by eliminating the other choices.

Exercise 14: Inferring Opinions
pages 230–232

1. (1) The passage tells you how careful Roosevelt was to keep the public eye off his handicap. The last sentence of the passage says that this was a deliberate strategy. You can infer that Roosevelt was making sure that people thought he was healthy and able.
2. (4) The passage says that the Japanese used to be known for taking care of their elders. Now, in contrast, most Japanese don't feel they should have to support their parents.
3. (4) The speaker is a wolf, so "they" must be the people he is watching.
4. (3) The cartoon suggests that people, rather than wolves, should be sent away to protect the ecosystem.

Exercise 15: Understanding Political Cartoons
pages 234–236

You may have worded your answers differently from some of the sample answers below. Check to be sure you have the right information in your answer.

1. He is trying to reach around the whole world.
2. (2) Uncle Sam is clearly not succeeding in his efforts to reach around the world. Notice the desperate look on his face. He is trying to reach and hold on to too many places that are too far away.
3. a bag of money
4. (4) The cartoonist is saying that Boss Tweed controlled New York with money instead of intelligence.
5. Recovery
6. (2) The cartoonist names the two fighters to show you what they stand for. Clearly, Mr. Taxes is beating up Recovery.

Exercise 16: Chapter Review
pages 237–240

1. (5) The passage is a story told by Harriet Hanson. She writes of what she thought and did during the beginning of a mill strike.
2. (2) The word *strike* is used in the third sentence of Harriet's story: "When the day came on which the girls were to turn out, . . . so many of them left that our mill was at once shut down." You can tell from this description that they were going on strike.
3. (2) From what Harriet says, you can imagine that she might be pretending she wasn't afraid to strike. Harriet says she was impatient and childish, eliminating choices (1) and (4). Her following action and her pride in its result shows that she did have a sense of responsibility, eliminating choice (3). Her action was brave, eliminating choice (5).
4. (3) This is stated in the fourth sentence.
5. (1) The main idea is stated in the first sentence. It is supported by two reasons: the poor commit more crimes, and the rich who commit crimes are able to stay out of jail.
6. (1) You must summarize the items listed in the second paragraph: knife, fork, cup, plate, drum, fife. These are all eating utensils and musical instruments.
7. (1) The final paragraph makes the topic clear: ". . . Our march had done its work. We had drawn the attention of the nation to the crime of child labor."
8. (5) This number is given in the first sentence.
9. (3) The passage states, "He said nothing. Newspapers must have copy." You can infer that the newspapers started making things up about Coolidge because he gave them nothing else to write about.
10. (2) The passage implies that the real Calvin Coolidge did not reveal himself to the public. All the country had to go on was "his little witticisms, his dry wit"—not enough to get to know the real Coolidge.

CHAPTER 2: INTERPRETING GRAPHIC MATERIALS

Exercise 1: Reading the Titles and Headings on a Table
pages 242–243

The table is about the ranking of the teams in the Atlantic Division of the NBA.

Exercise 2: Finding Information on a Table
pages 244–245

1. Fish and shellfish
2. Eggs. The word *decreased* tells you that you are looking for a minus sign (–) in the *Percentage Change* column. Eggs is the only category with a minus sign.
3. 13.6%
4. Poultry

Exercise 3: Main Idea of a Table
page 247

(2) In every occupation shown on the table, women earn less than men. None of the other answer choices is based on the table.

Exercise 4: Topic of a Graph
pages 248–249

Graph 1 topic is about the changes in oil prices from 1970 to 1992.

Graph 2 topic is about the percent of Indian people who practice each of India's major religions.

Exercise 5: The Main Idea of a Graph pages 251–252

You wrote some of the answers to this exercise in your own words. The answers you wrote should be similar to the sample answers below.

1. The bars are getting taller, so costs are rising.
2. (2) This choice summarizes the information on the graph. Choices (1) and (3) may be true, but you can't be sure. Choices (4) and (5) are not based on the graph at all.
3. This graph gives a general idea of how people on welfare spend their money.
4. Food, rent, and utilities. These items are the largest parts of the graph.
5. (3) Food, rent, and utilities are necessities. Most of the graph is taken up by these items. Choice (1) is true, but it is only a detail. Choices (2), (4), and (5) are not based on the graph.

Exercise 6: Reading Pictographs page 254

1. $200— Each of the symbols stands for $100.
2. San Francisco's—Comparing the rows for the two cities, you can see that San Francisco has the shorter row.
3. (4) This choice pulls together all the information on the graph. Choice (2) is a detail. Choices (1), (3), and (5) cannot be proven by the graph.

Exercise 7: Reading Bar Graphs page 256

1. Mexico—The bar for Mexico is the only bar that stops between 65 and 70.
2. Sweden—It has the tallest bar.
3. Four—There are four bars shorter than the U.S. bar.
4. 25 years—The bar for Ethiopia reaches 50. The bar for Sweden reaches 75; 75–50 = 25.

Exercise 8: Reading Line Graphs pages 258–259

1. 1910—The lowest point on the graph is at the year 1910.
2. 70%—At 1960 on the horizontal scale, the data point is at 70% on the vertical scale.
3. (5)—The percentage rose every decade until 1970. Since then it hasn't changed much.

Exercise 9: Reading Circle Graphs pages 260–261

1. 7.8%—The label for the Education segment is at the top right corner.
2. Economic development—Scanning the labels and percentages, you should pick out 4.3%.
3. Education—The education segment is 7.8% of the total. The criminal justice and public safety segment is smaller, 5.2%.
4. 31–40—This is the largest segment, 20.1% of the population.
5. 21–30—Among the age groups under 60 years of age, 21–30 is the smallest segment, 8.5%.
6. 11–20—Because these segments are almost the same size, you must read the percentages to answer correctly.

Exercise 10: Using a Map Key page 266

1. The Amazon River—This is the only river shown on the map in the northern part of Brazil.
2. Lake Mirini—It is at the bottom of the map, in the southernmost portion of Brazil.
3. The Equator—The mouth of the Amazon is on the northern coast of Brazil at the Equator.
4. Picó da Neblina—Two high mountains are marked on the map with the + symbol. Picó da Neblina has the higher elevation.

Exercise 11: Reading Historical Maps page 268

1. (3) The Pawnee were in the region cutting through the center of the map. The key shows that the Plains Indians lived in this region.
2. (1) The farthest northern parts of the map match the *Inuit (Eskimo) and Aleut* section of the key.

Exercise 12: Chapter Review
pages 269–275

1. (1) New York had 746 abortions per 1,000 live births. All the other rates listed on the chart are lower.
2. (3) The rate for the entire U.S. is given at the top of the chart as 422. Compare this rate to the rates of the choices (1)–(5). Florida has a rate of 465.
3. (1) The row of symbols for Texas is the longest row.
4. (3) Although Nevada and Kansas have the same number of symbols, the *actual* numbers show Kansas with 6,000,000 and Nevada with 6,150,000.
5. (5) The percentage of New Jersey residents living in cities of 100,000 or more dropped for each decade shown on the graph. The other choices cannot be proven by the graph.
6. (3) The second bar is for 1970. The percent for that bar is 15.5%.
7. (5) 1985 is the last year shown on the graph. At 1985 on the horizontal scale, the lines for *New York Daily News* and *USA Today* merge.
8. (3) This percent is listed with the label for the car riders.
9. (2) If you scan the segments looking for 43.7%, you will find it with the school bus label.
10. (5) The area around San Francisco matches the key for more than 100 persons per square mile.
11. (1) Measure off 200 miles going straight up the map from San Diego. The area there matches the key for less than 25 persons per square mile.
12. (2) Find the part of the key for slave-holding Union states. Then check each of the states that matches that part of the key. Only Kentucky is among the answer choices.
13. (4) Find Texas on the map. Then find the part of the key that matches Texas. That part of the key says "seceded Jan.–Feb. 1861."
14. (1) Find the regional boundary for West Tennessee. The only city shown in West Tennessee is Memphis.
15. (4) Find Nashville and look to the east. Knoxville is directly east of Nashville and is located on the Tennessee River.

CHAPTER 3: APPLYING INFORMATION IN SOCIAL STUDIES

Exercise 1: Applying Information in Everyday Life
pages 277–278

1. (5) The passage states that exercising for at least fifteen minutes at least three times a week is the most effective way to lose weight.
2. (4) The passage says that the greatest office need will be people trained to use modern equipment, such as computers.

Exercise 2: Identifying Probable Outcomes
pages 278–279

You should have checked the following.

1. c, d 2. b, c, d

Exercise 3: Identifying an Author's Prediction
pages 280–281

1. (3) The author says that many schools are appealing to older students in order to keep their enrollments up.
2. (1) The author states that farms will get larger and larger and that small farms will continue to disappear.
3. (5) In the last sentence, the writer states that day-care centers in the workplace will become more common in the future.

Exercise 4: Making a Prediction Based on a Passage
pages 281–282

1. (4) According to the passage, Haiti's roads are impassable, so they couldn't be used to transport farm goods.
2. (1) An improved telephone system would help Haitian businesses grow. Then the businesses could give more people jobs.
3. (3) DreamCatchers will be operating the casino, so DreamCatchers will manage employees, invest profits, and plan the casino's future. That leaves mostly service jobs for the Chukchansi.

Exercise 5: Applying Information in a Passage
pages 283–284

1. H
2. A
3. R
4. yes
5. yes
6. no

Exercise 6: Applying Map Skills
pages 286–287

1. Take Route 5 south to Route 84, Route 84 east to Route 80, and Route 80 east.
2. Take Route 8 east to Route 10 and Route 10 east to El Paso.
3. (4) The airport is on the Blue Line. North Station is on the Orange Line. The two lines intersect at State.
4. (3) Harvard is on the Red Line. Science is on the Green Line. The two lines intersect at Park St.

Exercise 7: Applying Information on Tables and Graphs
pages 288–289

1. (3) The graph shows many women with children under six in the work force. Day care at their workplace is likely to appeal to these women.
2. Blackdeck Desktop—This phone is the easiest to use of all the phones described. A man with arthritis in his hands would need a phone that is easy to use.
3. Sunbrand SlimPhone—This phone is the most durable of all the phones, so it would be most likely to hold up under heavy use.

Exercise 8: Chapter Review
pages 290–294

1. (4) The passage says that the fields are preserved in case they are needed for food production in the future. Tobacco is not a food.
2. (3) In the last paragraph, the author says that teens have nothing useful or important to do. Therefore, their energy comes out in destructive acts.
3. (5) Community service work would give teens a positive outlet for their energy. Therefore, they would not need to commit crimes to use up their energy.
4. (2) The passage tells how different dance fads have come and gone. It is reasonable to expect that there will be another one soon.
5. (3) Vanessa Alexander was popular in Rickerton Park, and her opponent's campaign has only angered voters. It is reasonable to expect that she will win.
6. (1) In the last paragraph, the author describes how prices leveled off in California and says that the same thing will happen in Tristan.
7. (5) First find Rochester and Corning on the map. Then find the route that is closest to a straight line.
8. (2) First find Syracuse and Bath on the map. Then find the route that is closest to a straight line.
9. (3) The Honda Attractiva has the highest highway gas mileage and the best repair record of the choices given.
10. (2) The Geo Elite has a better repair record than the Hyundai Splash, which is the only other car listed that is in Libby's price range.

CHAPTER 4: ANALYZING PATTERNS SOCIAL STUDIES MATERIALS

Exercise 1: Putting Events in Sequence
page 297

- Marshall discovers gold at Sutter's Mill.
- Marshall and Sutter test the stones to see if they are gold.
- Marshall sends gold seekers off to look for gold.
- Groups of men discover gold in the places where Marshall sent them.

Exercise 2: Using Dates to Identify Sequence
pages 299–300

- Columbus discovers America. (1492)
- Cartier discovers the mouth of the St. Lawrence River. (1534)
- De Soto murders thousands of Native Americans at Mabila. (about 1540)
- Champlain establishes the fur trade with the Native Americans. (about 1610)
- Marquette and Joliet travel down the Mississippi River. (about 1660)

Exercise 3: Sequence in Graphs
page 302

1. (1) Looking at the graph between 1965 and 1970 on the horizontal scale, you can see that the line goes up and then goes down.
2. (5) This choice represents the pattern shown on the graph.

Exercise 4: Expedition Maps
pages 304–305

1. (3) Trace De Soto's route and look for a box that tells you that friendly Native Americans supplied food. That box is labeled *7* and it is connected by a line to the dot labeled *Guaxulle*.
2. (4) Continue to trace De Soto's route, looking for his death. Box 13, dated 21 May 1542, tells of De Soto's death.
3. (5) Scan the map to find the circle labeled *Quizquiz*. It is just below box 10, which tells you that De Soto discovered the Mississippi River there.

Exercise 5: Reading Maps of Historical Change
page 306

1. T—The Oregon Country became part of the United States in 1846. Mexico ceded most of the Southwest in 1848.
2. T—The first major purchase shown on the map is the Louisiana Purchase in 1803. All the other new territories were added in later years.
3. F—The Gadsden Purchase (1853) followed the Mexican Cession.

Exercise 6: Identifying Cause and Effect
page 308

1. *What happened?* Colombia found itself in financial trouble.
   Why did it happen? The wholesale price of coffee had dropped 25%.
2. *What happened?* The American West developed rapidly after the Civil War.
   Why did it happen? Because of the railroads
3. *What happened?* Oil prices increased dramatically.
   Why did it happen? The oil cartel OPEC was formed in 1973.

Exercise 7: Cause and Effect in a Passage
pages 309–310

1. (3) The third sentence of the first paragraph says that the king of Portugal asked Vespucci to go after reading Vespucci's false story.
2. (1) The first sentence of the second paragraph tells you this. The clue word *because* makes the cause-and-effect relationship very clear.
3. (2) There is evidence for this answer throughout the passage: The children learned honesty through personal relationships. The children did what they saw others do. If the people the children imitated were honest, the children tended to be honest.

Exercise 8: Applying Cause and Effect
page 310

1. b—Laws banning discrimination against black voters led to a surge in the election of black officials.
2. c—Under the Civil Rights Act, blacks and whites had to be treated the same in such public places as buses.
3. a—Based on this decision, black and white children were segregated into different schools.

Exercise 9: Identifying Similarities
pages 311–312

The words you used in your answers may not be just like the words used in the sample answers below. However, you should have written the same information in your answers.

1. They stopped hunting and gathering food and started farming instead.
2. They are still hunters and gatherers.
3. They are large islands, located not far off the coast of a major continent.
4. They both have a lot of industries and do a lot of trading of goods.

Exercise 10: Comparison and Contrast in Illustrations
page 314

1. T—To make sure this statement is true, you must check all the states to make sure none had an increase of less than 2%.
2. F—Tennessee had a higher percentage, 64%.
3. F—New York has always been much larger than Chicago.
4. T—Both cities had just under 3 million people.
5. F—Chicago's population decreased between 1960 and 1990. Los Angeles gained population between 1960 and 1990.

Exercise 11: Fact or Opinion?
page 316

1. F	3. O	5. O
2. O	4. F	6. F

Exercise 12: Facts and Opinions in a Passage
pages 317–318

Passage 1

1. O 3. F 5. O
2. F 4. F 6. O

Passage 2

1. O 3. F 5. O
2. F 4. F 6. O

Exercise 13: Distinguishing Fact from Hypothesis
page 319

1. F 2. F 3. H 4. H

Exercise 14: Finding the Author's Hypothesis
page 320

1. (3) In the last sentence, the author states that two- and three-bathroom houses are common because the extra bathrooms increase the resale value of a house.
2. (5) The passage states that members can have part of their paychecks deposited directly into their savings accounts and explains that this helps people build their savings.

Exercise 15: Making a Reasonable Hypothesis
pages 321–322

1. (1) Victims of AIDS often get TB because their immune systems have been weakened. Homeless people are also likely to have weakened immune systems due to malnutrition and disease. The other answer choices list trends that would tend to lower the number of TB cases.
2. (4) In 1967, the doctors found that many people were hungry. The symptoms of the children probably occurred because they were not getting enough to eat.

Exercise 16: Chapter Review
pages 323–328

1. (2) As the years passed, more cotton was grown in areas to the south and west (below and to the left) of the 1801 cotton-growing area.
2. (3) The area that matches the key for 1839 shows the growth in cotton land between 1801 and 1839. Large portions of these four states are in this area.
3. (1) The passage states, "Probably one of the main causes of the problem is peer pressure . . ." None of the other choices is given as a possible cause.
4. (2) The passage states, "The desperate need for money to buy drugs can lead the user to prostitution or robbery." These are crimes.
5. (1) The first paragraph tells you that a high-tech boom gets started by new companies offering new products. The last sentence of the passage tells you that the pattern described in the passage applies to all three high-tech booms.
6. (4) The last sentence of the passage lists the different products that created each boom.
7. (3) The three paragraphs describe these steps in order. The first paragraph talks about a new product being created when thinkers don't have enough to do in a slow period. The second paragraph describes the industry boom that follows. The third paragraph describes the industry going into a slump.
8. (2) In the last paragraph, the writer states, "Then the public's love affair with the product ends. . . . Then the boom is over."
9. (1) The tallest bar, 1 year and under, accounts for 55% of the people.
10. (3) Since the majority of people don't stay on welfare for more than a year or two, they must need the welfare payments only to get them through a rough period.
11. The terrorist is talking to the reporters.
12. (4) The cartoonist shows the terrorist taking a hostage in front of a large group of reporters with cameras. The cartoon implies that getting attention from the press is the purpose of taking the hostage.
13. (3) Fisher heard about the ships by reading *The Treasure Hunter's Guide.* He put an extraordinary amount of time and money into his search. The evidence suggests that he was hoping it would pay off in valuable treasure.
14. (1) In the last two sentences, the authors state that education was the key to success.

CHAPTER 5: EVALUATING SOCIAL STUDIES MATERIALS

Exercise 1: Is There Enough Information? page 330

1. ✓ 3. X 5. ✓
2. X 4. ✓ 6. X

Exercise 2: Using Information on a Map pages 331–332

1. X 3. ✓ 5. ✓
2. X 4. ✓ 6. X

Exercise 3: Identifying Irrelevant Information pages 333–334

You may have worded your answer differently from the sample answers below. Check to be sure you included the correct information in your answers.

- **a.** The writer wants people to vote for Gil Cohen for mayor.
- **b.** The irrelevant reasons are (1) he is more attractive than his opponent and (2) he has spent over $100,000 of his own money to get elected.

Exercise 4: Using Information Correctly pages 334–335

1. (3) The last sentence tells you that this event raised millions of dollars to feed hungry Americans.
2. (5) The passage gives examples of Americans raising money for charitable causes.
3. (4) The third sentence of the passage tells you that affirmative action programs try to correct past prejudice. The passage does not contain enough information to prove any of the other choices.
4. (3) The second sentence tells you that in a kibbutz most things are owned by everyone as a group. The other choices are not mentioned in the passage.

Exercise 5: Recognizing Errors in Reasoning pages 336–337

1. a. ✓ 2. a. X
   b. X b. ✓

Exercise 6: Errors in Reasoning pages 338–339

You may have worded your answers differently from the sample answers below. Check your answers to be sure they contain the correct information.

1. (2) The writer says he was doing much worse than he had been four years before, so he voted for Reagan.
2. The problem is that the reasons he was doing badly (his wife dying, his children dropping out of school, his drinking, and losing his job) had nothing to do with the president or the government. These factors should not have influenced his vote.
3. (2) The passage tells you that the unhappiest group was married women.
4. The problem is that she thinks the results of the study are wrong based on the experience of only one person: herself.

Exercise 7: Recognizing Values pages 341–343

1. (2) The passage says the codes were meant to protect students from prejudice, which in this case means unfair treatment on the basis of race or sex.
2. (3) The passage says that opponents think the codes violate the right to free speech, which is the right to express ideas.
3. (3) The caption of the cartoon tells you that Reagan would like to be free from the press, which would mean he would not be criticized by reporters and newswriters. This would add greatly to his power.
4. (1) The cartoonist makes Reagan and his advisors look sinister as they talk about not liking the press. Since the cartoonist is part of the press, it is likely that he would value freedom of the press.
5. (2) The purpose of buying the old farm would be to save the land for education and recreation

Exercise 8: Propaganda and Advertising pages 345–346

1. (5) The ad says that Chocorich is America's highest-quality candy, using only the finest chocolate and sugar. It implies that other candies are made from lower-quality ingredients.
2. Answers will vary.
3. (1) The ad implies that you will look like the muscle-man in the "After" picture if you use this program. Men who want to look like a muscle-man would be attracted to the ad.
4. (4) The ad implies that if you shop at Leslie's, you will look sophisticated.

Exercise 9: Political Propaganda page 347

1. They had slowed down six Soviet armies, and they had been "purified" by the defeat.
2. (4) Goebbels didn't want the Germans to think they were losing the war. If the real extent of the disaster were known, people might become angry with the German government and military leaders.
3. (2) The only thing the ad tells you about holistic medicine is that Americans across the country are trying it, and interest in it is rising. So, the ad is arguing that you should use it simply because it's popular.

Exercise 10: Chapter Review pages 348–350

1. (5) There is no dark line from Jacksonville to Savannah, so there was no railroad.
2. (4) All the train lines end just beyond the Mississippi. Anyone wanting to go farther west would have to travel another way.
3. (2) The passage says that Amnesty International watches out for human rights throughout the world.
4. (3) Since the purpose of the organization is to promote human rights, you would want to know if it was accomplishing that purpose. The other choices would not tell you whether it was.
5. (4) The passage describes all the violent conflicts that rage in the world despite the efforts of the United Nations to keep the peace. The passage does not support the other choices.
6. (5) The first sentence tells you that the United Nations was founded to help nations solve their differences peacefully.
7. (4) The ad does not tell you much about Mr. Amorelli's ideas. You would want to find out more before you decided whom to vote for.
8. (3) Experience usually partly determines what a person's work is worth. The other choices do not relate to what a person's work is worth.

Section 3

SCIENCE

1 SCIENCE KNOWLEDGE AND SKILLS

READING SKILL: LOCATING DETAILS AND FACTS

Scientists use a lot of big words, but most of them are made up of smaller parts. If you understand the parts, you can often figure out the meaning of the word. Sometimes the way a word is used in a sentence is a clue to its meaning.

COMPOUND WORDS

The easiest words to figure out are ***compound*** words. These are words made by putting two other words together. *Mailman*, *lighthouse*, and *bookstore* are all common examples of compound words. A *breakwater* is a line of concrete or rocks that breaks the force of the waves in front of a harbor. *Buttermilk* comes from the milk left after butter is made.

EXERCISE 1: COMPOUND WORDS

Directions: Write each word in the blank after its definition. (You will not use all the words on the list.)

sunspot	horsepower	earthquake	rattlesnake
lifetime	spaceship	catfish	wavelength

1. Power equal to one horse pulling: ____________________
2. A ship that travels in outer space: ____________________
3. A spot on the surface of the sun: ____________________
4. A time when the earth quivers and shakes: ____________________
5. How long a wave of light or sound is: ____________________

Answers start on page 505.

BEFORE AND AFTER: ROOTS, PREFIXES, AND SUFFIXES

Many long words are made up of several word parts put together. The main part of the word is called the ***root*** of the word. For example, the root of *careful* is the word *care.* Beginnings and endings can be added to root words to change the meaning. An addition to the beginning of a word is called a ***prefix***. Something added to the end is called a ***suffix***. Two root words can also be put together to form another word.

Scientific words are often made from roots, prefixes, and suffixes that come from Latin or Greek words or word parts. Following is a chart of some common word parts used in science and everyday English, along with their meanings. Study the chart carefully.

Prefixes	Roots	Suffixes
anti- (against) **di-, bi-** (two, double) **inter-** (among, between) **mal-** (bad, ill) **multi-** (many) **post-** (after) **pre-** (before) **re-** (back, again) **tri-** (three) **un-** (not)	**bio** (life, living) **cardio** (heart) **derm** (skin) **graph, gram** (writing) **hydro** (water) **meter** (measure) **mono** (one, single) **micro** (very tiny) **neur** (nerves) **nuclear** (central, atomic) **therm** (heat)	**-al** (having to do with) **-er, -or, -ist** (person who does something) **-full** (full of) **-itis** (disease or inflammation of) **-less** (without) **-log, -logue** (talk, to speak) **-logy** (the study of)

You can form words by putting these parts together and by using them with other words you know. For example, *biology* is the study of living things. A *biography* is a piece of writing about someone's life, and *biochemistry* is the chemistry of living things. The root *bio* in a word tells you that the word has something to do with life or living things. Likewise, *redo* means to do over again, and an instant *replay* shows a sports play over again. The prefix *re-* always means "back" or "over again."

Knowing the meanings of common word parts can help you figure out many new words. Let's say you read an article about antinuclear protesters. The chart above shows that *anti-* means "against" and *nuclear* can mean "atomic." Antinuclear protesters are probably people protesting against atomic weapons. How would you use the chart to figure out what neuritis is? Since the root *neur* means "nerves," and the suffix *-itis* means "disease," neuritis is a disease of the nerves.

EXERCISE 2: WORD PARTS

Directions: In each group of sentences, choose the correct word for each blank. Do this exercise without a dictionary. Use the chart of prefixes, roots, and suffixes and some words you already know.

-logy (study of)—dermatology, hydrology, neurology

1. The study of the skin is called ____________________.
2. ____________________ is the study of the nervous system.

therm (heat)—thermometer, thermonuclear, biothermal

3. ____________________ energy is heat that comes from living things.
4. A ____________________ is an instrument that measures heat.

tri- (three)—trimonthly, tricycle, trifocals

5. A ____________________ magazine is published quarterly (every three months).
6. Glasses that focus at three different distances are

   ____________________.

cardio (heart)—cardiologist, cardiogram, cardiac

7. A written record of your heartbeat is a ____________________.
8. A doctor specializing in heart disease is a ____________________.

micro (tiny)—micrometer, microbiology, microfilm

9. The study of very tiny living things is called ____________________.
10. A ____________________ is used to measure very small distances.

Answers start on page 505.

CONTEXT CLUES

Often you can figure out a new word by looking at its ***context***, the words around it. Using the context is easiest when the meaning of a new word is given clearly in the sentence. Here are some sentences that give clear definitions of new words:

> Ichthyologists, scientists who study fish, may find the next solution to the world's hunger problem.
>
> One of the worst childhood diseases, scarlet fever, can now be controlled by antibiotics.

From these sentences you can tell that *ichthyologists* are scientists who study fish and that *scarlet fever* is a disease that children used to get. Notice that the explanations of the new words are separated from the rest of the sentence by commas. Sometimes the sentence does not give a complete definition. Even so, there may be ***context clues*** that will tell you at least part of the meaning. Look at this sentence:

> She poured the mixture into the crucible and put it on the burner.

From this sentence you can tell that a crucible must be *some kind of pot that things are heated in.*

EXERCISE 3: USING THE CONTEXT

Directions: Read each sentence. Then write what you think each word in **bold type** means. For this exercise, do not look the words up in the dictionary. Instead, use the context clues in the sentence to help you.

1. The astronomer used her **astrolabe** to measure the distance between the two stars.

   An astrolabe might be ____.

2. Information sent into **cyberspace** can be viewed by computer operators across the nation.

   Cyberspace might be ____.

3. Most plastics are only one color, but this one was **polychromatic**.

   Polychromatic probably means ________________________________.

4. Cats, wolves, and dogs are all **carnivores**, but mice, rabbits, and horses are not.

   Carnivores are probably animals that eat ______________________.

5. **Hydroponic** farming makes it possible to grow vegetables in areas with no fertile soil.

   Hydroponic farming is probably farming without ________________.

Answers start on page 505.

SCIENTIFIC LANGUAGE

Don't be discouraged if a difficult science passage doesn't make sense to you at first. You may have to read it several times. You may need to figure out the meanings of scientific words, go back over tough sentences, and put the whole thing together. Following are the steps to follow when you are reading something difficult.

1. Start to read normally until you run into a sentence that doesn't make sense to you.
2. Go back and read the sentence again more slowly. Sometimes it helps to read it out loud quietly.
3. Look for any words you don't know in the sentence. Try to figure out their meanings, using word parts and context clues. If you have to, look them up in a dictionary.
4. Look at the next few sentences to see if they explain more about the sentence you are working on. Do not read very much further ahead until you understand what is being said.
5. Finally, read the sentence again. Try to put it into simpler words to be sure you have understood it.
6. Read through the passage once this way. Figure out all the hard parts as well as you can. Then read the whole passage once more at a regular speed. This helps you to put all the ideas together.

Restating Ideas

One of the key steps in understanding difficult writing is being able to put complicated sentences into simpler words. Here is an example:

> In considering the experimental results, it would not be wise to take too optimistic a view of the eventual usefulness of the new drug in the treatment of cardiac diseases.

Three words that may be new to you are *optimistic, eventual*, and *cardiac*. Being optimistic means "always expecting the best thing to happen." *Eventual* means "at the end" or "in the long run." Its root, *cardio,* tells you that *cardiac* means "something to do with the heart." Now let's translate the sentence piece by piece.

Original	Simpler Version
In considering the experimental results,	When you look at the results of the experiments,
it would not be wise to	you shouldn't
take too optimistic a view of the eventual usefulness of	expect too much good, in the long run, from using
the new drug in the treatment of cardiac diseases.	the new drug to help people with heart disease.

Putting the simpler version all together, we get

> When you look at the results of the experiments, you shouldn't expect too much good, in the long run, from using the new drug to help people with heart disease.

or even more simply:

> The experiments don't show for sure that the new drug will help people with heart disease.

EXERCISE 4: UNDERSTANDING SCIENTIFIC LANGUAGE

Directions: Rewrite the following sentences in simpler words. Use your knowledge of context clues and word parts and look up words in a dictionary if you need to.

1. The effects of atmospheric pollution are among the most seriously adverse.

   ____

2. The generation of hydroelectric power was the primary development necessary to provide inexpensive residential electricity.

   ____

3. Playthings for young individuals should be constructed to provide intellectual as well as recreational experiences.

   ____

Answers start on page 505.

SCIENCE TOPIC: THE SCIENTIFIC METHOD

Clarence R. Higgenbottom, well-known British millionaire, is found dead on the floor of his library at 7:00 P.M. Saturday. He has been shot through the heart. Inspector Stokes of Scotland Yard is called in to solve the mystery. He discovers facts regarding the weapon, time of death, and known enemies of the victim.

From these facts, Inspector Stokes guesses that businessman John Jones Percy killed Higgenbottom. He gets a search warrant and searches Percy's big house. He finds a Ruger .22 pistol hidden under the front staircase. In a police lab test, the gun fires a bullet marked exactly like the one found in Higgenbottom's body. Percy is arrested for the murder, and another case is solved successfully by the famous Inspector Stokes.

This example shows that detectives and scientists have a lot in common. They both have to figure out mysteries, and they do it mostly in the same way. First a detective or scientist has to decide what problem he is going to work on. Then he collects all the facts he can. Next, he makes a careful guess, based on those facts, about what is really happening. Then he tests his guess by doing an experiment. Finally, he draws a conclusion from his experiment and decides whether his guess was right or not. This way of solving problems is called the ***scientific method***.

Here's a summary of the five steps Stokes followed in solving the crime. You can see how solving a mystery is a lot like using the scientific method.

Solving the Mystery	The Scientific Method
1. Inspector Stokes is assigned to find out "Who killed Higgenbottom?"	**1.** Deciding the question
2. Stokes collects facts to find out what happened.	**2.** Finding the facts
3. Stokes guesses that Percy killed Higgenbottom.	**3.** Forming a hypothesis
4. Stokes searches Percy's house and finds the murder weapon.	**4.** Testing the hypothesis
5. Stokes concludes that his guess is right: Percy is guilty.	**5.** Deciding on a theory

FIRST STEP: DECIDING THE QUESTION

Scientists can often decide what problems they want to work on; there are thousands of questions in our universe waiting for answers. Detectives, on the other hand, are usually assigned a question; they don't have much choice.

It is important to read a question very carefully before you try to answer it. Let's read through a sample question and figure out what kind of answer the writer is looking for.

Question 1. What is the average yearly rainfall in Nebraska?

▶ Will the answer to this question be a word, a number, a place, or somebody's name? ______________________________

(The answer will be a *number*.)

▶ What unit of measure (inches, feet, miles, or whatever) will this answer probably be in? ______________________________

(From listening to the radio weather reports, we know that rainfall is usually measured in *inches*.)

▶ Where do you think you are expected to find the answer to this question?

____

(The information would come from a reading passage, graph, or chart. This is not the kind of information you would be expected to have in your own head.)

Let's look at another question.

Question 2. What would probably happen to people if all the green plants on Earth died?

▶ Will this answer probably be in words or numbers?________________

(The answer will probably be in *words*. The question doesn't ask for a number.)

▶ Where are you expected to find the answer to this question?

____

(If you have studied science, you know how important green plants are, so you should be able to figure out the answer. There might also be something in a reading passage to help you decide the answer to the question.)

SECOND STEP: FINDING THE FACTS

Many things we read and hear every day seem to be facts but may not be. A ***fact*** in science is something that can be proven by ***observation.*** **Measurement** may be used as an aid to observation. With measurement you use a tool such as a ruler or a scale.

Often, we confuse opinions with facts. ***Opinions*** are usually statements that depend upon a person's ***values***. Values are the things someone likes or considers important. Our values matter to us very much, but values cannot be used to prove facts.

Here are some examples of opinions:

- Broccoli tastes horrible.
- Women should work in any field that interests them.
- Blue is the prettiest color.

You may agree or disagree strongly with some of these opinions, but no one can prove them right or wrong.

Fact vs. Opinion Tip

Phrases like *I think, I believe,* and *we should* tell you that an opinion is being expressed.

EXERCISE 5: FACT AND OPINION

Directions: Write *F* before the statements that are facts (that you could prove by observation or measurement) and *O* before the statements that are opinions (that depend on your values).

________ **1.** Denver is a nicer place to live than Chicago.

________ **2.** New York is 92 miles away from Philadelphia.

________ **3.** Everyone should try to earn a high school diploma or GED certificate.

________ **4.** Eighty percent of employers surveyed said they had hired a job applicant with a diploma or GED certificate over an applicant without one.

________ **5.** Listening to music played very loudly can damage a person's ears.

________ **6.** Nuclear power plants ought to be shut down for the next five years.

________ **7.** There have been several accidents at nuclear power plants in the last five years.

Extra Practice: Write three opinions you feel strongly about.

Answers start on page 505.

THIRD STEP: FORMING A HYPOTHESIS

After scientists have collected all the facts they can find out about a particular problem, they use these facts to make a careful guess about the solution. This guess is called a ***hypothesis.*** Two or more guesses are called ***hypotheses.***

Scientists are not the only people who make hypotheses. We all make careful guesses (hypotheses) about things every day. For instance, if your child comes home from school soaking wet, you might ***hypothesize*** (assume) that it is raining outside. Of course, not all hypotheses turn out to be right. It is possible your child walked through a sprinkler or played with water balloons on the way home. But each hypothesis is the best guess made at the time based on all the facts available.

▶ Make a hypothesis for this situation: Your washing machine won't work, and the light over your laundry table won't go on. What do you think has happened? Should you guess that your washing machine is broken?

___

___

(No, because that doesn't explain why the light won't go on either. Your first hypothesis could be that *something is wrong with the electricity*.)

EXERCISE 6: EVERYDAY HYPOTHESES

Directions: Practice making hypotheses with these everyday situations. Write your hypothesis in the space provided.

1. During a big thunderstorm, your lights go off suddenly.

   Your hypothesis: ___

   ___

2. Bill, who works for you, has been asking for time off during hunting season, but you have had to turn him down. On the first day of the season, Bill's wife calls and says that Bill is too sick to come to work.

   Your hypothesis: ___

   ___

3. Your crew leader at work has left his job, and you have a good chance to be promoted to his position. Your boss calls you into her office, saying she has some good news for you.

   Your hypothesis: ___

   ___

Answers start on page 505.

Fitting All the Facts

Of course, most scientific hypotheses are based on more than one or two facts. When you go to the doctor, she bases her ***diagnosis*** (her hypothesis about why you are sick) on many facts. She considers many things, including your temperature, your appearance, any pains or other symptoms, and your ***medical history*** (the sicknesses you and your family have had before).

A good hypothesis must fit all the facts available. A careful scientist never ignores a fact just because it doesn't fit her first ideas. Instead, she changes her ideas to fit all the facts.

EXERCISE 7: CHOOSING HYPOTHESES

Directions: After carefully reading about these situations, choose the number of the hypothesis that best fits each set of facts.

1. A scientist had twelve green plants. All the plants were the same kind and about the same size. He put three plants on a window sill inside a room. He put another three plants in a closet without a light. He put three more plants outside on the ground. He put the last three plants in paper bags with air holes and put them outside.

   All the plants were given good soil and enough water. The plants on the window sill and the plants outside in the open grew well. The plants outside in the bags turned yellow and grew very badly. The plants in the closet died. What was learned from this experiment with green plants?

   (1) Green plants turn yellow due to disease.
   (2) Green plants don't live for very long.
   (3) Green plants need light to grow.
   (4) Green plants cannot grow inside.
   (5) Green plants grow well in closets.

2. Louis Pasteur, a famous scientist who lived over 100 years ago, made an important hypothesis about certain germs called *bacteria*. He noticed that bacteria grew quickly in open jars of liquid, like chicken soup. Bacteria also grew in jars of soup that were sealed tightly so that no air could get in. However, they didn't grow in soup that was sealed tightly in a jar, then boiled and kept sealed after it cooled. What was Pasteur's correct hypothesis?

   (1) Bacteria cannot grow in jars.
   (2) Bacteria must have air to survive.
   (3) Bacteria grow only in chicken soup.
   (4) Bacteria can be killed by boiling.
   (5) Bacteria can live in boiling liquids.

3. Janet kept track of the weather outside and the fuel she burned for the first five months in her new house. She made the following chart showing the facts that she found.

Month	Average Temperature	Weather	Oil Used
September	45	Mostly rainy	60 gal.
October	39	Sunny, some snow	90 gal.
November	23	Rainy and snowy	140 gal.
December	26	Mostly snowy	125 gal.
January	20	Mostly sunny	160 gal.

What did Janet discover about the amount of oil she burned?

(1) More oil was burned when it was not sunny.
(2) More oil was burned when temperatures were lower.
(3) More oil was burned each month as winter went on.
(4) More oil was burned whenever it snowed.
(5) More oil was burned during the holidays.

Answers start on page 505.

EXERCISE 8: FORMING HYPOTHESES

Directions: Write your own scientific hypothesis to fit each of the following situations.

1. A water tester checks the water in a certain river. It is polluted with lead, mercury, and detergent. He walks upstream and passes a small town. He tests the water again and finds lead and mercury, but no detergent. He keeps walking and passes a factory. When he tests the water again, it is clean and not polluted.

   Knowing that water flows downstream, what is the tester's hypothesis about where the detergent is coming from?

2. Carl had a two-inch magnet. He did an experiment to see what it would pick up. The items it would pick up are in List A. The items it would not pick up are in List B.

List A	List B
1-inch steel paper clip	pile of pepper
wet iron nail	1-inch goldfish
tiny iron filings	2-inch copper wire
3-inch steel wire	wet dollar bill

What kind of things can Carl's magnet pick up?

Answers start on page 505.

FOURTH STEP: TESTING THE HYPOTHESIS

Once a scientist has made a hypothesis, he tries to test it—to check it out. This is the fourth step of the scientific method. The most common way for a scientist to check a hypothesis is to do an ***experiment***.

In an experiment, a scientist takes groups of things, called ***subjects***. He puts them in an artificial situation where everything is the same except the variable. A ***variable*** is the one thing he wants to test. He usually leaves at least one subject in its natural state. This natural subject is called his ***control***. Then he records the results of his experiment. He checks to see if the results prove his hypothesis correct or not. It's easier to understand these parts of an experiment when we look at an example from everyday life.

Let's say a house painter has just found out about a new type of paint. He hypothesizes that it will keep its color better than the paint he is regularly using.

He takes ten pieces of wood to test. These are his subjects. He paints five pieces of wood with the new paint and five with the old paint. The new paint is the variable. The pieces of wood with the old paint are the control group.

The painter leaves all of the boards together in his backyard for a month. When he brings the boards back in, he notices that the boards painted with the old paint have faded more than the boards with the new paint. These are the results of the experiment. The painter's hypothesis is correct: the new paint fades less.

In order to really prove his hypothesis, the painter must repeat the experiment with two new sets of boards to see if it comes out the same way again. It would be even better if he had someone else repeat the experiment. Scientists will not accept the results of an experiment unless it is ***reproducible***, that is, unless it can be repeated with the same results. This shows that the first results were not just a coincidence.

The chart below shows the parts of the painter's experiment.

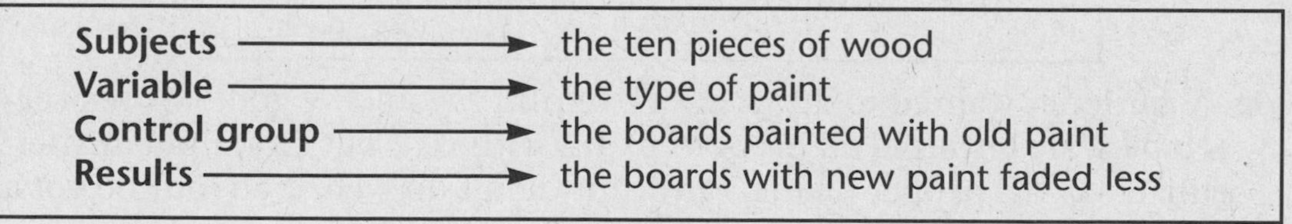

Subjects →	the ten pieces of wood
Variable →	the type of paint
Control group →	the boards painted with old paint
Results →	the boards with new paint faded less

Here is a list of the requirements that we have discussed for a good experiment:

- The subjects need to be similar, and there should be more than one subject in each group.
- All the conditions of the experiment should be the same except for the one variable being tested.
- There should be a control group.
- The results should be reproducible.

If an experiment does not meet these requirements, the results are not ***valid*** and **reliable**. (Valid means getting *true* results. Reliable means getting the *same* results when repeating the experiment.) So the experiment is not very useful. You can see this for yourself by looking at the following experiment. Can you figure out what is wrong with it?

A chef wanted to find out if egg whites could make his pie crust more tender. He made three pies using egg whites in the crusts and three pies without egg whites. As they baked, he noticed that the pies with the egg whites browned more quickly, so he took them out ten minutes early, leaving the other pies in the regular amount of time. When he served the pies, everyone said that the first three were more tender. The chef has decided that using egg whites will make his pie crusts better.

What's wrong? ____

____

▶ The problem with the chef's experiment is that *he didn't keep all the conditions the same*. The variable he wanted to test was the use of egg whites, but he also used different cooking times for the two groups. Maybe it was the egg whites that made the first group of pies more tender; maybe it was the shorter cooking time. He can't be sure, so his experiment is not good.

EXERCISE 9: ERRORS IN EXPERIMENTS

Directions: Tell what is wrong with each of these experiments. Choose from the list below.

- not enough subjects
- subjects were not similar
- conditions of experiment not kept the same
- the experiment was not reproduced

1. A gardener wanted to know if XYZ fertilizer would be good for his vegetables. He fertilized all his bean plants with XYZ but didn't put any fertilizer on his pepper plants. His beans didn't do well at all, but he got a good crop of peppers. He concluded that XYZ fertilizer was no good.

2. A molding machine in a factory was not working very well. About a third of the time, the plastic squirt guns that it was making came out with a flaw in the handle. The repair mechanic adjusted the stamping pressure. Then she ran one gun through. It came out just fine, so the mechanic figured she had solved the problem.

Answers start on page 505.

FIFTH STEP: DECIDING ON A THEORY

Nothing Is Certain!

After a scientist has chosen a problem, collected the facts, formed a hypothesis, and checked it out with several experiments, he is ready to decide if his correct hypothesis is a theory. A ***scientific theory*** is an idea or explanation based on the available facts and experimentation. Scientists are never absolutely sure about any of their theories because new facts can *contradict* the old theories. To contradict something means to imply the opposite of it.

For example, seventy-five years ago scientists had "proven" that the atom was one solid particle that could not be split. Then Einstein and others discovered that atoms could be split, and they discovered atomic energy. Forty years ago, chemical companies had "proven" that DDT was perfectly safe. Now DDT is forbidden for use in this country because it turned out to be deadly to fish, birds, and even people.

Making Decisions

You can use the scientific method to help solve problems in everyday life, too. When you have to make an important decision, you collect all the facts you can about your decision. Then you look at possible solutions. (hypotheses).

You try out these solutions one by one. Sometimes you just try them out in your head, saying to yourself, "What would probably happen if I did this? Or this? Or maybe that?" You might ask some friends for their opinions. If you can, you try out a solution in real life just to see what will happen. Finally, you make your decision, but you can't tell right away whether you have decided correctly. Just as in science, in real life there are very few guarantees.

When you are taking a test, you can use some of this process to help you choose good answers. You are given the question. You read the passage and study any illustrations carefully; this is collecting your facts. Then you look at all the possible answers, checking them out in your head to see which ones make sense. Many people miss questions because they do not read all the answers.

EXERCISE 10: REVIEW OF THE SCIENTIFIC METHOD

Directions: As you read through this real-life example of the scientific method, answer each question as you come to it.

Smallpox is a terrible disease that once killed thousands of people every year. Today doctors think smallpox may be totally gone from the world. This is mostly because of the work of an English doctor named Edward Jenner, who lived from 1749 to 1853.

When Jenner was a young doctor, an epidemic (a sudden spread of a disease) of smallpox broke out. He worked hard to save his patients, but many of them died. He noticed that milkmaids—the women who milked the cows on dairy farms—didn't seem to catch the disease. He decided to find out why.

1. As the first step in his process, what question did Jenner ask himself?

____

He talked to many milkmaids and discovered that the women often caught a disease called cowpox from the cows. This disease caused spots like smallpox, but the spots were only on the women's hands, and the disease wasn't very serious; no one ever died of cowpox. The remarkable thing was that no one who had had cowpox ever seemed to catch smallpox.

2. What hypothesis would you make if you were Jenner?

____

Jenner guessed that having cowpox somehow protected people against smallpox for the rest of their lives.

3. How do you think Jenner decided to test his guess?

____

Jenner decided to check his hypothesis by taking cowpox germs on a needle and deliberately injecting them into people. After these people got over the cowpox, he watched to see if any of them got smallpox. He did this to several people, and none of them got smallpox.

Jenner's idea of deliberately giving someone a mild disease to protect him from a serious disease was the beginning of all our modern vaccinations. At the time, though, many people did not like Jenner's idea. But when it became clear that many lives were being saved, more and more people came to get vaccinated, and Jenner became famous.

Answers start on page 506.

2 Living Things

Many people have trouble understanding technical writing of the kind found in science textbooks. This chapter covers three special reading techniques that can help you understand what you read: restating facts, summarizing, and finding the main idea.

READING SKILL: UNDERSTANDING WHAT YOU READ

RESTATING FACTS

One way to show that you understand something you have read is to ***restate*** it—to say the same thing in different words. You will often be asked to do this on tests. For example, a sentence from a reading passage could say, "Studies show that eating fish oil could help protect you against heart disease." Suppose that a test question asked you to choose a restatement of the information in that sentence. The correct answer to the question might read, "Researchers have found that your chances of getting heart disease may be lower if you consume fish oil."

Notice that the answer means the same thing as the sentence from the passage, but it does not use exactly the same words. When test writers write this type of question, they usually do not use exactly the same words in the answer as they did in the passage. Therefore, you should look for an answer with the same *meaning* as the sentence in the passage.

▶ To see if you've got the idea, try this. Write the numbers from Group One before their restatements in Group Two.

Group One	Group Two
1. Luther Burbank was a very famous plant breeder.	______ His plants helped to improve many people's diets.
2. He was one of the first people to breed hybrid plants.	______ He was one of the most well-known plant breeders around.
3. He developed many of the plants that farmers grow today.	______ Many important food plants were bred by Luther Burbank.
4. Many people eat better today because of Luther Burbank.	______ He was one of the discoverers of hybrid plants.

The correct answers are 4, 1, 3, 2.

EXERCISE 1: RESTATING FACTS

Directions: Restate each of the following facts. Write a new sentence that says the same thing in different words.

1. If you don't smoke, you have less chance of getting lung cancer.

 ____

2. Many GED graduates are successful businessmen and businesswomen.

 ____

3. Nuclear energy is a powerful tool and a dangerous weapon.

 ____

4. Learning is often easier as you get older because you have more experience.

 ____

Answers start on page 506.

SUMMARIZING

Another type of test question might ask you to summarize a passage. To ***summarize*** something is to put all the important points together in one short statement. Look at these facts.

- John decided to start his science experiment.
- He spilled the chemicals he was mixing.
- The Bunsen burner wouldn't light.
- When he finally turned in his results, they were all wrong.

One way to summarize these facts would be to say, "Everything went wrong for John when he tried to do the science experiment."

▶ Now you try it. Choose the statement that best summarizes these facts.

- Most snakes are not poisonous.
- Snakes eat many insects, mice, and rats that otherwise would destroy farmers' crops.
- We need snakes, just as we need most other living things, to keep the natural balance of our world.

▶ What is the best summary of these facts?

(1) Snakes eat insects, mice, and rats.
(2) Most snakes do more good than harm.
(3) Snakes drink milk and strangle babies.
(4) Only farmers need snakes.
(5) Some snakes are poisonous.

Answer (2) is the best summary because it covers all of the facts. Answers (3) and (4) are not true according to the facts listed. Answers (1) and (5) are true, but they each deal with only one fact.

EXERCISE 2: SUMMARIZING

Directions: Read these groups of facts carefully. Circle the number of the correct answer.

- Florence Nightingale was one of the first people to see that nursing had to be a professional job.
- When she went to nurse soldiers wounded in the Crimean War, she was shocked by the poor conditions.
- Most of the "nurses" had no training.
- Florence Nightingale taught them basic ideas of cleanliness and nursing.
- Later she went on to start one of the first real nursing schools.

1. What is the best summary of these facts?

(1) Crimean War nurses had little training.
(2) Soldiers need the best nursing care.
(3) Florence Nightingale was a famous woman.
(4) Crimean War hospitals were very bad.
(5) Florence Nightingale made a big improvement in nursing.

- Aspirin can help stop minor pains like headaches and backaches.
- Aspirin reduces the swelling in joint injuries like sprains and even arthritis.
- Because aspirin makes blood less likely to clot, it can also sometimes be used to prevent heart attacks and strokes.

2. What is the best summary of these facts?

(1) Aspirin has been used for a long time.
(2) Everyone should use more aspirin.
(3) Aspirin has many uses in modern medicine.
(4) Aspirin is good for headaches.
(5) Aspirin can prevent all heart attacks.

Answers start on page 506.

THE MAIN IDEA

You may read something and say to yourself, "What's the point?" You're looking for the author's ***main idea***, the main thought. A ***paragraph*** is a group of related sentences. Every paragraph should have one main idea. The rest of the paragraph is filled with ***details*** that explain or prove the main idea. Here is an example.

MAIN IDEA

> **Albert Einstein was a "slow learner" who turned out to be a real genius.** He didn't learn to talk until he was almost three. Later, he did very poorly in school, especially in mathematics. One teacher even said he was retarded! But when he was grown up, he developed the Theory of Relativity, which is the main scientific theory about nuclear energy. He became known as one of the greatest scientists of our time.

The main idea of this paragraph is in the first sentence: *Albert Einstein was a "slow learner" who turned out to be a real genius.* The rest of the paragraph contains the details that show you how this happened.

Many paragraphs have the main idea in the first sentence, but others do not. Sometimes the author builds up the details and then puts the main idea at the end. Look at this example.

> Nancy kept watching the clock, but it never seemed to move. She hated the sound of the drill and the sight of the other equipment. The numbness in her mouth was beginning to feel uncomfortable. **Nancy could hardly wait for her dentist to finish her root canal.**

MAIN IDEA

This time the main idea was in the last sentence.

At other times, the main idea is somewhere in the middle of the paragraph, as in the example below.

> Women are working as doctors, veterinarians, and laboratory technicians. Some of the most respected science professors at large universities are women. **More and more women are working at scientific jobs that people used to think were only for men.** Several women have even become astronauts and flown in space.

Probably the most difficult type of paragraph is one in which the main idea is never really stated. The author just ***implies*** (hints at) an idea by using details.

> She held her breath as the top of the skull came into sight. Very carefully she brushed away the sand until she could lift it out. It must be over two million years old! Her hands trembled as she realized that she was holding the oldest human bone she had ever seen.

The main idea of this paragraph is that *the woman is very excited about the old skull that she has found.* The author never really says it, but all the details about the way the woman held her breath and how her hands trembled show you how excited she was.

When you are asked to find the main idea, don't choose one of the supporting details. The supporting details are all true, but they are not the main idea. Remember, the main idea is the idea that covers the *whole* paragraph.

EXERCISE 3: FINDING THE MAIN IDEA OF A PARAGRAPH

Directions: In each of the next three paragraphs, underline the sentence that contains the main idea.

1. Cactuses are remarkable plants made to live in one of nature's harshest environments. In place of regular leaves, they have needles that also serve as a good defense against hungry animals. Their stems are full of hollow cells that can store enough water to last for months. They can survive the great heat of the desert sun at noon and the bitter cold of the desert night.

2. Henry Ford's first car had only one cylinder in the engine and ran on bicycle wheels. It was steered with a stick that connected directly to the front wheels. In the 1960s, cars had up to eight cylinders, power steering, power brakes, and even power windows. Cars just seem to get more and more complicated. Present-day cars have electronic ignition, catalytic converters, cruise control devices, and some even have special on-board computers.

3. Allen has red eyes and a runny nose. He is sneezing and coughing, and his skin is all broken out in big, red, itchy patches. Does Allen have some horrible disease? No. In fact, Allen doesn't have a disease at all. He has an allergy. When you have an allergy, your body's defenses react strongly to something normally harmless, like dog hair or ragweed pollen. Allergies can be mild or very serious. Some people have even died of severe allergic reactions. Even though it is only a reaction of your own body, an allergy can really make you miserable!

Answers start on page 506.

THE MAIN IDEA OF A PASSAGE

Test questions often ask you to find the main idea of a passage. Questions that ask you for the "best title" for a passage are also asking for the main idea.

Many passages are longer than one paragraph, but you can use the same skills to find the main idea. In a paragraph, each detail supports the main idea of the paragraph. In a longer passage, each paragraph supports the main idea of the passage. To find the main idea of the passage, first look at the main ideas of the paragraphs. These ideas should all be related and point toward one major main idea for the passage.

Try this method to find the main idea of the following passage. Beneath each paragraph, write the main idea of that paragraph.

> Many animals in Australia belong to a very old group of animals called marsupials. Marsupials raise their young differently than ordinary animals do. Most marsupials give birth when their young are still very undeveloped. These tiny babies are often blind and hairless. They do not have fully developed arms or legs. They must live in their mother's pouch until they are ready to survive in the outside world.
>
> MAIN IDEA: ______________________________
>
> This way of raising young is not as safe as that of other mammals, where the baby is carried inside the mother until it is ready to be born. These old-fashioned animals still survive in Australia only because they didn't have much competition from animals that came into being more recently. Long ago, Australia got cut off from the main part of Asia by a big piece of the ocean. Animals that developed after this couldn't get to Australia since it was too far to swim to.
>
> MAIN IDEA: ______________________________
>
> In recent times, many new animals, like rabbits and sheep, have been brought to Australia. These animals are pushing out the marsupials. If we do not take action to save the marsupials, we may lose some of these interesting animals forever.
>
> MAIN IDEA: ______________________________

The first paragraph explains that *unusual animals called marsupials raise their young from very undeveloped babies.* The second paragraph says that, *because of this, most marsupials survived only in Australia,* where more highly developed animals could not go. The main idea of the last paragraph is that the *marsupials are now threatened by animals brought in by humans.*

▶ Now put all these ideas together. From the following sentences, choose the one that tells the main idea of the whole passage.

(1) All unusual animals need to be protected.
(2) Marsupials are unique because of the way they raise their young.
(3) Many people want to save the marsupials.
(4) The marsupials can survive without any help from us.
(5) The marsupials, a unique group of animals, are now in danger.

If you chose sentence (5), you were correct. This sentence covers all of the ideas in the passage. Sentence (1) is too broad; the passage is not about all unusual animals, just marsupials. Sentence (2) is too narrow; the passage does say that marsupials raise their young in an unusual way, but that is not all it says. Sentence (3) is probably true, but it is not mentioned in the passage. Sentence (4) is false, according to the passage.

EXERCISE 4: FINDING THE MAIN IDEA OF A PASSAGE

Directions: Practice choosing the main idea of this passage. Circle the number of the best answer. Be careful not to choose an answer that is too broad or one that covers only part of the passage.

> One of the most important things that parents buy for a new baby is a crib. Any crib, whether it is bought new or borrowed, should have several safety features. First, the spaces between the bars must not be more than 2 3/8 inches wide. Many old cribs have more widely spaced bars. Today we know that if the spaces are any wider, a young baby might slip through the bars, catch his head, and strangle himself. The same thing can happen if there are fancy designs in the ends of the crib with holes big enough for a baby to catch his head in.
>
> Next, the crib mattress must fit tightly so that the baby can't get caught between the mattress and the sides. The crib must also be built strongly. The bottom springs must not slip out when the child jumps up and down. The side catches must be strong enough to hold the weight of a child without giving way. Finally, the paint or varnish must be lead-free, so the baby can teethe on it without getting lead poisoning.

1. This passage is mainly about
(1) problems babies have during teething
(2) advantages of buying a brand-new crib
(3) fancy designs on cribs
(4) safety features of a crib
(5) safety features of a crib mattress

2. The best title for this passage would be
(1) Keeping Your Baby Safe
(2) Only 2 3/8 Inches Apart
(3) Choosing a Safe Crib
(4) How to Buy Baby Clothes
(5) Choosing an Inexpensive Crib

Answers start on page 506.

SCIENCE TOPIC: PLANTS AND ANIMALS

We share the Earth with millions of other living things, from the smallest bacteria to the huge blue whale. Many of these creatures affect our lives directly. All of them have some of the same needs as human beings: to find food, to escape enemies, and to reproduce. When we learn about other living things, we also learn something about ourselves.

CELLS

Did you know that you are made up of millions of tiny units called ***cells?*** In fact, every living thing is made up of cells. Cells are so small that you can see them only through a microscope; there are thousands of cells in just your little finger. Some cells, like the ones in you, are part of larger, many-celled beings. Other cells live on their own as one-celled creatures.

There are lots of different types of cells. A nerve cell in your brain is very different from a muscle cell in your arm. A human cell is even more different from a cell in the trunk of an oak tree. Still, there are some things that are alike in all cells.

Animal Cells

Look at the diagram of an animal cell to see the major cell parts. Every cell has a ***nucleus***, which is a dark spot, usually near the center of the cell. The nucleus is like the "brain" of the cell. It controls most of what happens inside the cell. The ***chromosomes*** inside the nucleus carry the directions ("blueprints") for making new cells.

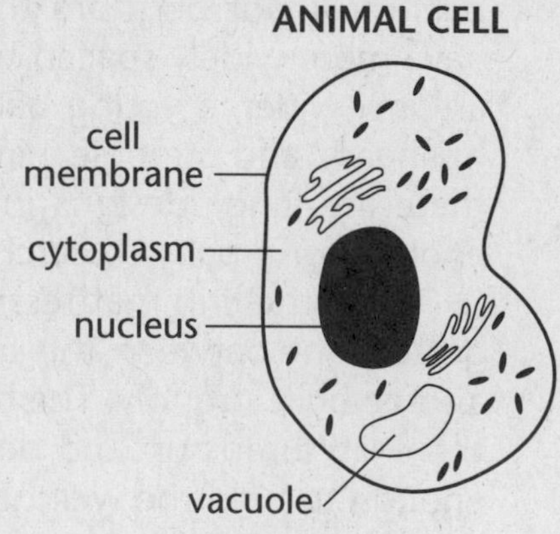

The ***cell membrane*** is a thin wrapping around the outside that holds the cell together. It keeps out many things that could harm the cell, while letting in things the cell needs, like oxygen and food. The inside of the cell is filled with ***cytoplasm***, a clear, jelly-like liquid. The space in the cytoplasm is called a ***vacuole***. Vacuoles store water and food for the cell.

Plant Cells

A plant cell is similar to an animal cell, but there are some differences. In plant cells, a large vacuole often takes up much of the space inside the cell. All plant cells have a ***cell wall*** around the outside of the membrane. This wall is made of a stiff material called ***cellulose***.

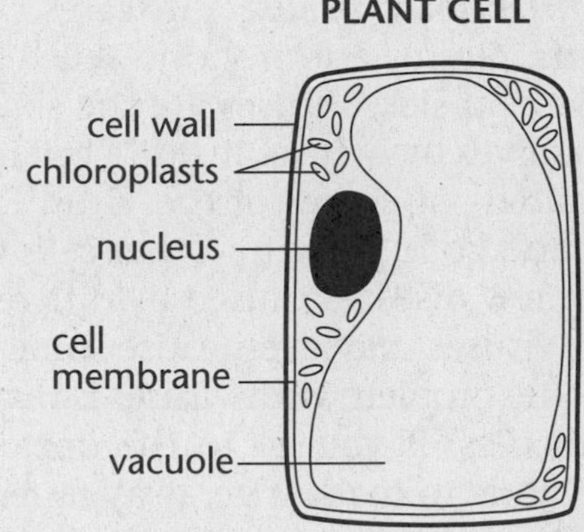

In most plant cells there are also small oval objects called ***chloroplasts***. The chloroplasts contain a green chemical called ***chlorophyll***, which is the chemical that helps green plants make their own food. No animal cells have cell walls or chloroplasts, and no animal can make its own food.

EXERCISE 5: CELLS

Directions: Match the word with its definition.

______ **1.** Cell membrane	**a.** Contain chlorophyll
______ **2.** Cell wall	**b.** Jelly-like liquid inside cells
______ **3.** Cellulose	**c.** Carry "blueprints" for new cells
______ **4.** Chloroplasts	**d.** Directs most cell activities
______ **5.** Chlorophyll	**e.** Stores food and water for the cell
______ **6.** Chromosomes	**f.** Holds animal cells together
______ **7.** Cytoplasm	**g.** Stiff material in cell walls
______ **8.** Nucleus	**h.** Chemical that helps plants make food
______ **9.** Vacuole	**i.** Stiff structure around plant cells

10. One difference between plant and animal cells is that

(1) plant cells have cell walls; animal cells don't
(2) plant cells can't move; animal cells can
(3) plant cells live in water; animal cells don't
(4) plant cells have a nucleus; animal cells don't
(5) plant cells have vacuoles; animal cells don't

Answers start on page 506.

GERMS

Infectious diseases (diseases caught from someone else) are caused by ***germs***. Germs are tiny one-celled living things that invade your body and make you sick. Viruses are the smallest of the three main types of germs. A ***virus*** lives by getting inside a cell in your body and forcing that cell to make hundreds of copies of the virus. Eventually, all the copies burst out of the cell and go looking for other cells to invade. Colds, the flu, and the measles are a few diseases caused by different types of viruses. Some scientists think that viruses may even cause some kinds of cancer.

One problem with viruses is that they are not killed by antibiotics or other medicines. If you go to the doctor with a bad cold, he can't give you an antibiotic to make it go away faster. You usually just have to get through it.

Bacteria are another kind of germ. Different kinds of bacteria cause different diseases, such as strep throat, tetanus, and tuberculosis. Today, many bacteria can be killed by penicillin and other antibiotics. With antibiotics, many diseases that were once very serious can now be cured.

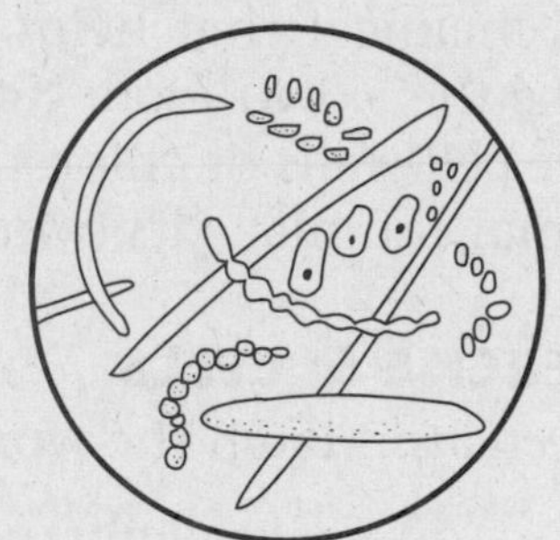

Bacteria under a microscope

Not all bacteria cause diseases, though. Some bacteria are actually helpful. Bacteria are needed to break down dead plants and animals in nature. There is even one kind of bacterium that lives in your intestines and helps your body produce certain vitamins.

Other diseases are caused by protozoans. ***Protozoans*** are larger than bacteria, but they are still single-celled creatures. If you have ever looked at a drop of pond water through a microscope, you have probably seen protozoans swimming around in it. Although most protozoans are harmless, malaria and some forms of diarrhea are caused by types of protozoans. One type of protozoan, the amoeba, is shown at right.

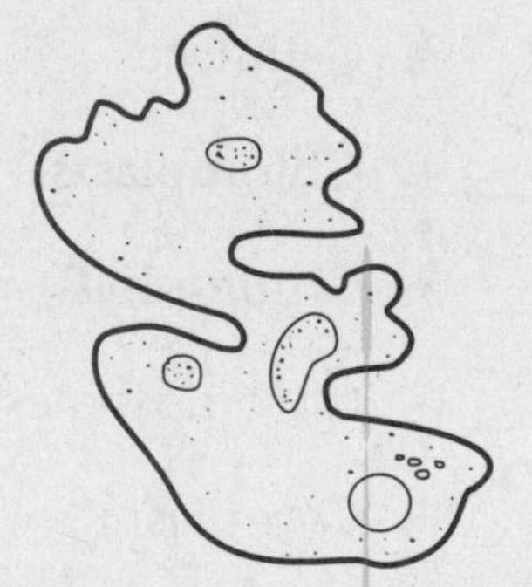

Ameba under a microscope

Viruses, bacteria, and protozoans are all around us, so why aren't we sick all the time? One reason is that a person's body creates defenses against germs it has fought before. We call this building immunity to a disease. One way to build immunity to a disease is to catch it. A better way is to get a shot, called an ***immunization*** or a ***vaccination***, from your doctor. The doctor puts a small number of dead or weakened germs into you. This makes your body create the same defenses it would if you had the real disease, but you don't really get sick.

Immunizations are available for only some diseases. Some immunizations last all through your life, while others have to be repeated every five or ten years. Most immunizations should first be given to people when they are babies.

It is very important to make sure children get all of their immunization shots because those shots protect them from many serious, even deadly, diseases. However, some vaccines can cause some bad side effects. It is wise to ask your doctor about all the risks and benefits of an immunization. Immunizations are available from doctors as well as county public health departments.

EXERCISE 6: GERMS

Directions: Write the best word in each blank to complete the review of this passage.

1. Diseases can be caused by problems inside your body or by ________________ (a) invading from outside of your body. Three types of germs are ________________ (b), ________________ (c), and ________________ (d). Your body builds up some protection, called ________________ (e), to diseases it has fought before. A shot that causes your body to build immunity is called an ________________ (f) or a ________________ (g). Most of these shots should first be given to people when they are ________________ (h). Children should get all their shots to ________________ (i) them against many serious diseases.

Directions: Circle the number of the best answer.

2. What is the main idea of the text about germs?
   (1) Doctors have medicines to cure disease.
   (2) Immunizations can be given by doctors or clinics.
   (3) Most diseases can be prevented.
   (4) People should get immunized to protect themselves.
   (5) Immunizations are given only to babies.

Answers start on page 506.

PLANTS AND PHOTOSYNTHESIS

Unlike animals, plants have the ability to make their own food. Without plants, there would be no food on the Earth. Since animals cannot make their own food, they must eat plants or other animals to survive.

Plants make food using a process called ***photosynthesis***. They use energy from the Sun to combine carbon dioxide, water, and minerals into food. Carbon dioxide is a gas in the air, while water and minerals come from the soil. Plants carrying out photosynthesis also give off oxygen, which all animals, including people, need to breathe.

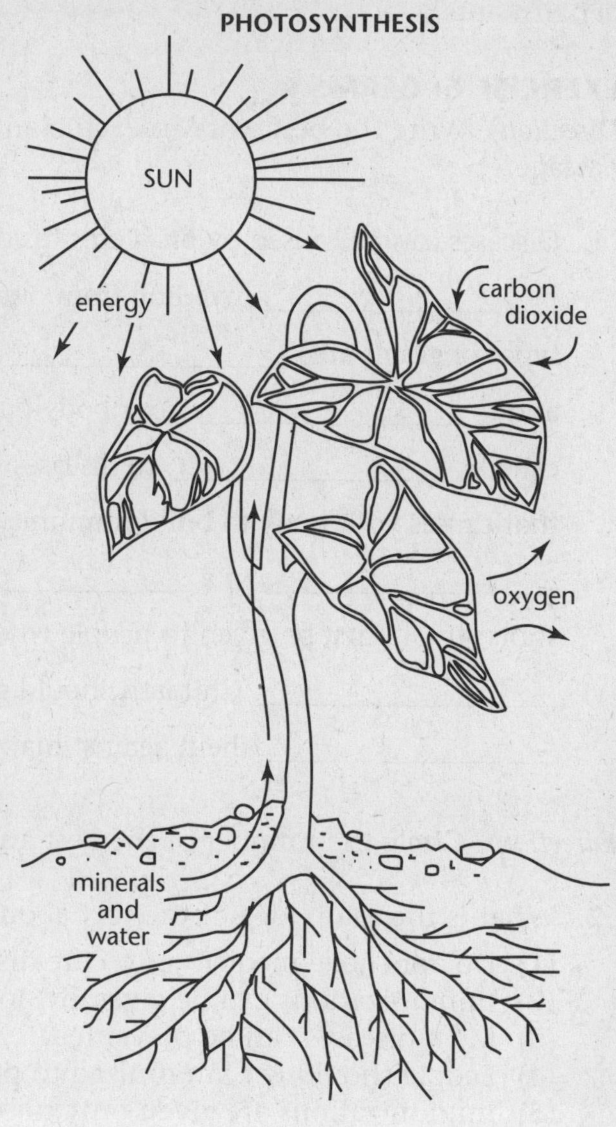

Photosynthesis can take place only in plant cells that have ***chlorophyll***. Scientists have not been able to figure out how to perform photosynthesis in a laboratory. It takes place only in living green plants.

The most advanced plants are members of either the fern family or the seed-bearing plant family. Plants of both of these families use chlorophyll to make their own food.

Less advanced plants called ***fungi*** cannot make their own food because they have no chlorophyll in their cells. They must live off other living things, often things that are dead or decaying. Molds, mildews, and mushrooms are all types of fungi. Some fungi are helpful to people, like the yeast that makes bread rise. Other fungi, like the fungus that causes athlete's foot or the molds that spoil food, are harmful.

The simplest plants have only one cell, like the bacteria we discussed in the last passage and like certain kinds of ***algae*** (green or brown plants that grow in water). Surprisingly, many of these plants do contain chlorophyll.

EXERCISE 7: FOOD FACTORIES

Directions: Read the following statements. Circle *T* if the statement is true or *F* if the statement is false.

T F 1. All fungi are harmful to people.

T F 2. Oxygen is given off during photosynthesis.

Directions: Choose the best answer for each question.

3. What does a plant that contains chlorophyll need to make food?
   (1) energy, water, carbon dioxide, and minerals
   (2) water, carbon dioxide, oxygen, and minerals
   (3) minerals, spores, water, and energy
   (4) carbon dioxide, oxygen, spores, and energy
   (5) oxygen, water, energy, and minerals

4. The main idea of the passage about plants is
   (1) what makes food spoil
   (2) how different plants get or make their food
   (3) different types of one-celled plants
   (4) the way animals get their food
   (5) pollution created by food factories

Answers start on page 506.

EVOLUTION AND CLASSIFICATION

Fossils, the remains of ancient animals and plants, helped scientists discover the story of ***evolution***. Evolution is a theory that explains how life developed on Earth.

Millions of years ago, fossils were made when living things left traces, like footprints or bones, in mud or sand. Over the centuries the mud or sand turned to rock, and the remains were preserved. Other fossils were preserved in tar or in amber, which is ancient tree sap that has hardened to stone. When the Earth was formed, it was a ball of hot, molten (melted) rock and gases. As it began to cool, clouds formed and the first rain fell. The low spots on the cooling Earth filled with water and became oceans. Life began in the oceans, probably about $3^1/_2$ billion years ago.

The first living things were very simple beings like viruses and bacteria. About 3 billion years ago the first true plants developed. These were one-celled algae that could carry out photosynthesis. Much later, about 1 billion years ago, simple one-celled animals developed and fed on the plants. Gradually these single-celled creatures grouped together in colonies. These became the first many-celled plants and animals.

Early Animals

The first many-celled animals lived in the sea. They were all ***invertebrates***—animals without backbones. There are many invertebrates still living today, such as insects, worms, crabs, and jellyfish. The first ***vertebrates*** (animals with backbones) were the fish, which appeared about 550 million years ago. All other vertebrates, including humans, are descended from the fish.

About 400 million years ago, the first descendants of the fish crawled out on land. These were early ***amphibians***. The amphibians had to stay close to the water because they laid their eggs in water. The eggs hatched into tiny creatures that swam with fins and breathed underwater with gills just like fish. When they grew older, these creatures lost their fins and gills, grew legs and lungs, and went out onto the land. You can watch the same thing happening today when tadpoles change into toads or frogs.

The next animals to develop, over 250 million years ago, were the ***reptiles***. Snakes, turtles, and alligators are all reptiles that are alive today. Reptiles look similar to amphibians, but they have scales instead of smooth skin, and they lay their eggs on land rather than in water. A reptile ***embryo*** (the not-yet-born form of an animal) goes through its gill-breathing stage inside the egg. The egg has a tough outer covering to preserve moisture. Some reptiles developed into some of the most amazing animals that ever lived, the giant ***dinosaurs***.

Birds and Mammals

During the last part of the Age of Reptiles, while dinosaurs were still everywhere, two new types of animals began to be seen. ***Birds*** developed from some of the smaller two-legged dinosaurs. ***Mammals*** were small mouselike creatures that came from reptiles that lived before the dinosaurs. Birds and mammals had an advantage over the reptiles; they were ***warm-blooded***. This meant that their bodies stayed at a constant temperature. To help them do this, birds developed feathers, while mammals developed hair. Both of these are much better insulators than scales. This meant that birds and mammals could survive in a colder climate than reptiles.

Birds and mammals also improved on the reptiles' way of having young. Birds lay eggs with shells that are tougher than those of reptile eggs. Mammals developed a whole new way of reproducing. The female mammal carries the embryo inside her body until it is grown enough to survive in the outside world. Then she feeds her young on milk that she makes in her own body. This way of reproducing is safer than egg-laying because the young are better protected.

About 70 million years ago, the dinosaurs and most of their relatives suddenly died out. No one knows why, but some scientists think the cause was a change to cooler, drier weather over most of the Earth. At any rate, only a few families of reptiles survived, and the Age of Mammals began.

The small, furry mammals changed and developed into many of the animals we see today. Dogs, cats, horses, bears, and every animal that bears its young alive and gives milk are members of the class of mammals.

The final part of the story (so far) begins only about 2 million years ago with the coming of the first human. Humans are mammals, since we bear our young alive and feed them with milk. We belong to the primate order in the class of mammals, along with our cousins, the monkeys and apes. To understand better how humans are related to other animals, look at the part of our "family tree" below.

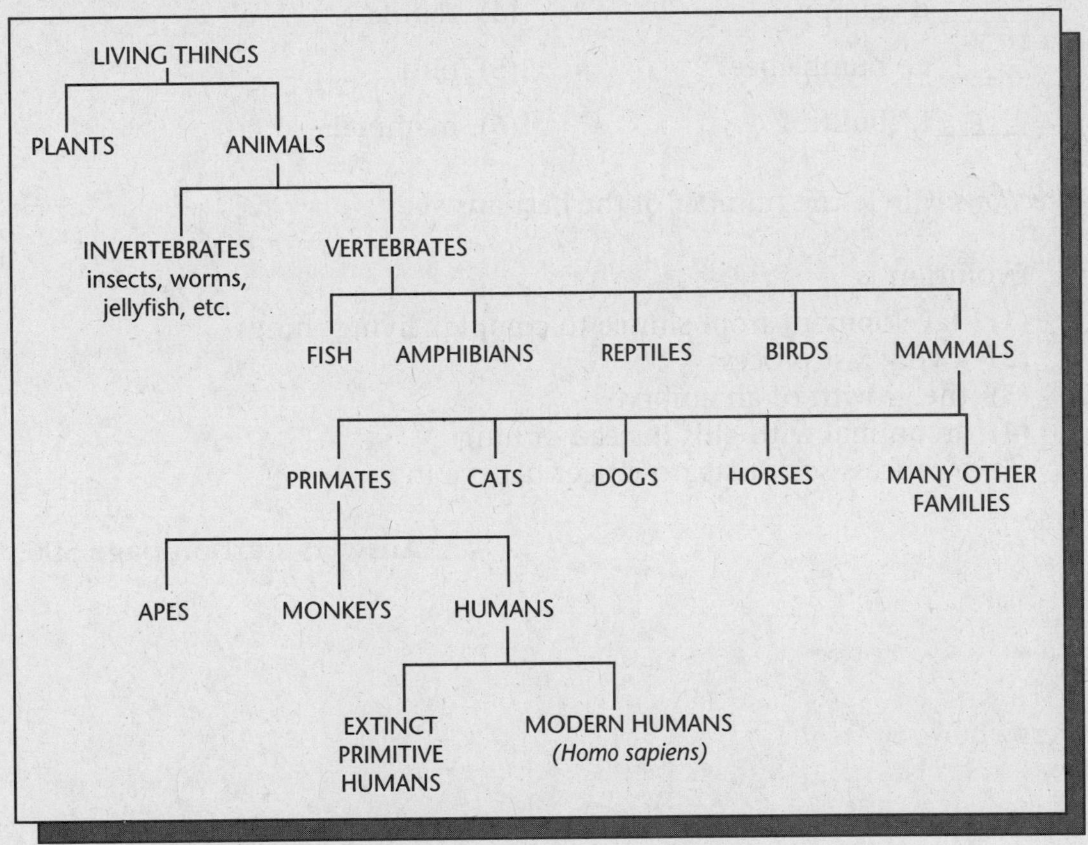

EXERCISE 8: TYPES OF ANIMALS

1. *Directions:* Match each word with its definition.

_____ **a.** invertebrates

_____ **b.** vertebrates

_____ **c.** fish

_____ **d.** amphibians

_____ **e.** reptiles

_____ **f.** birds

_____ **g.** mammals

(1) animals that feed their young with milk

(2) animals that live first in water, then on land

(3) animals without backbones

(4) animals with scales that lay eggs on land

(5) animals that breathe with gills

(6) animals with backbones

(7) animals with feathers

2. *Directions:* Match each animal with the group it belongs to.

_____ a. cow	(1) invertebrate
_____ b. rattlesnake	(2) fish
_____ c. robin	(3) amphibian
_____ d. guppy	(4) reptile
_____ e. bumblebee	(5) bird
_____ f. bullfrog	(6) mammal

Directions: Circle the number of the best answer.

3. Evolution is
   (1) development from simple to complex living things
   (2) a very fast process
   (3) the growth of an embryo
   (4) an animal with gills instead of lungs
   (5) a process scientists no longer believe in

Answers start on page 506.

GENETICS

We all know that children tend to look like their parents, but why? The science that studies this question is called ***genetics***, the study of how things are ***inherited*** (passed along) from parents to children.

Every cell in your body contains a kind of "blueprint" of the plans for your whole body. Inside the nucleus of each cell are tiny threadlike things called ***chromosomes***. The chromosomes are made of ***genes*** strung together like beads. Each pair of genes carries the code for a certain ***trait***: things like the color of your hair or eyes and your size and general shape.

The simplest one-celled plants and animals ***reproduce*** by splitting. For example, each chromosome in a bacterium's nucleus splits into two identical copies. Then the nucleus splits, with one copy of each chromosome going into each new nucleus. Finally, the whole cell splits into two bacteria. Both bacteria start growing again until each of them is the same size as the original cell.

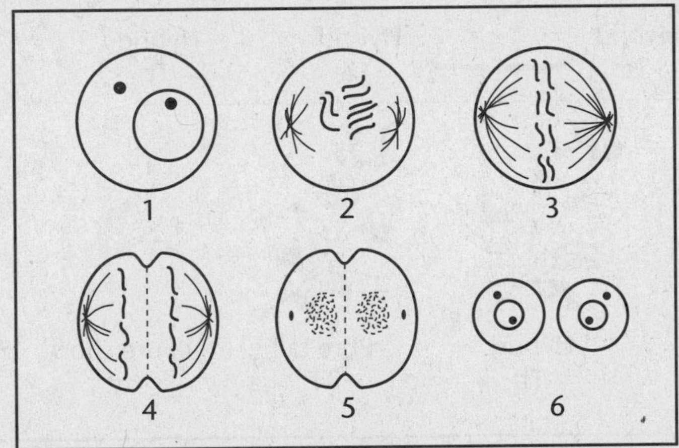

A cell splitting

More advanced plants and animals reproduce sexually. A male cell and a female cell must combine to form the first cell of the new being. This new being gets half its chromosomes from each parent. This way of reproducing allows for more variety. This is because the new being will inherit characteristics from both its father and its mother. It will not be an exact copy of either parent.

Let's look at an example from an experiment done by Gregor Mendel, a monk who first investigated the basic facts of genetics. He crossed a tall pea plant with a dwarf pea plant. Each of the ***offspring*** (the new plants) got a gene for tallness from one parent and a gene for shortness from the other. Plants with mixed parents like this are called ***hybrid*** plants.

The next diagram shows the results of Mendel's experiment.

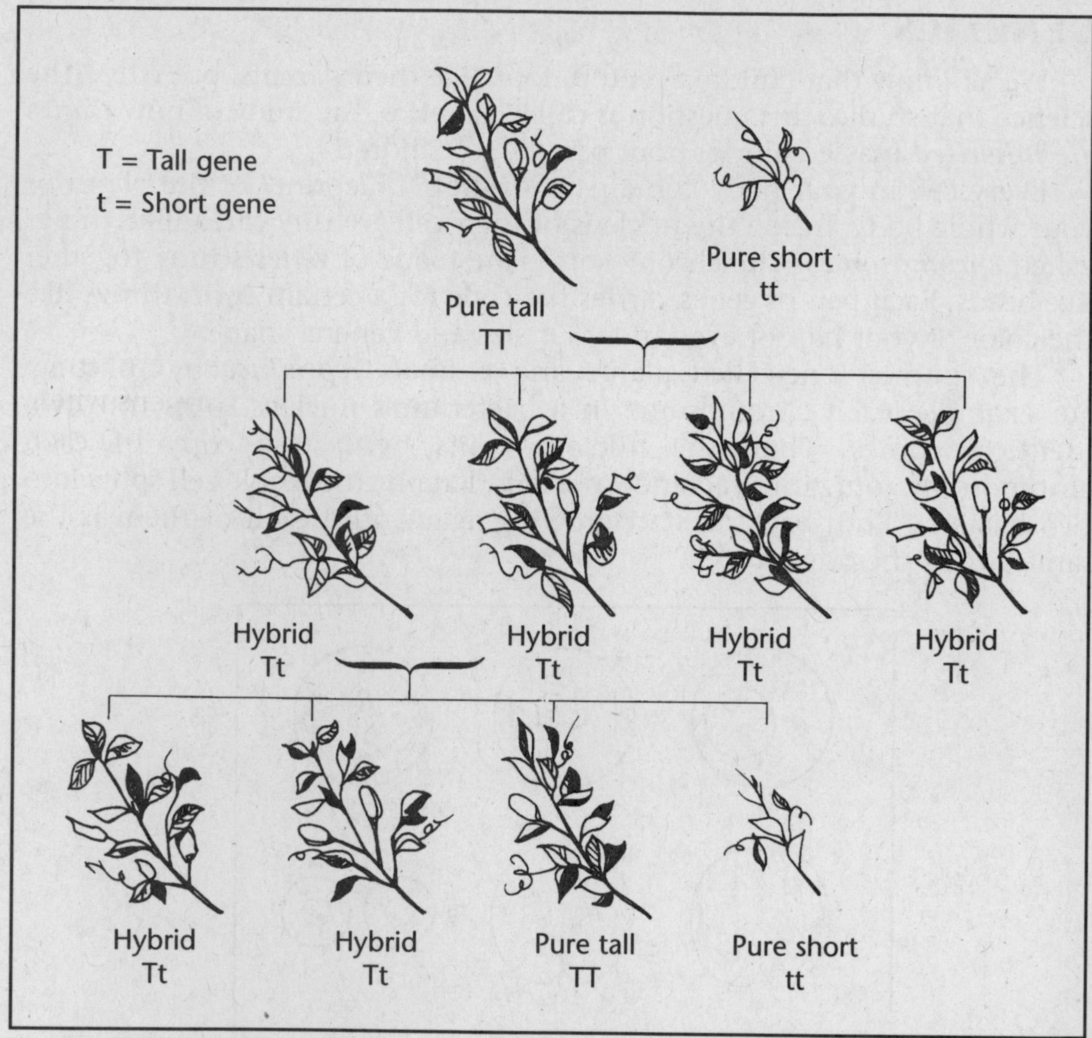

Strangely enough, all the first generation of new plants looked tall, even though they each had one gene for shortness. The gene for tallness is ***dominant.*** This means that the gene for tallness will always override the gene for shortness. The gene that is *not* dominant, in this case the gene for shortness, is called ***recessive.***

As you can see in the diagram above, if two of these hybrid plants are crossed, one-quarter of the offspring will be pure short (tt). This is because they have inherited two genes for shortness, one from each parent. Half of the offspring will be tall but carry a hidden gene for shortness (hybrid Tt). The last quarter will be pure tall plants (TT), plants that carry both genes for tallness.

Inheritance in people works the same way, though it can be more complicated. Sometimes more than one set of genes controls a certain trait, as in skin color.

In humans, many inherited diseases, like juvenile diabetes and Tay-Sachs disease, are the result of recessive genes. This means that a person could be healthy yet be carrying a dangerous gene. If that person marries another person with the same recessive gene, one (or more) of their children could get both recessive genes. Therefore their children could have the disease. People whose families show any of these diseases often have their genes checked before they have children. This is called ***genetic counseling***.

EXERCISE 9: GENETICS

Directions: In hamsters, dark eye color is dominant and light eye color is recessive. First, fill in the following gene chart showing what happens when a dark-eyed hamster with two *DD* genes mates with a light-eyed hamster with two *dd* genes. Then answer the questions that follow.

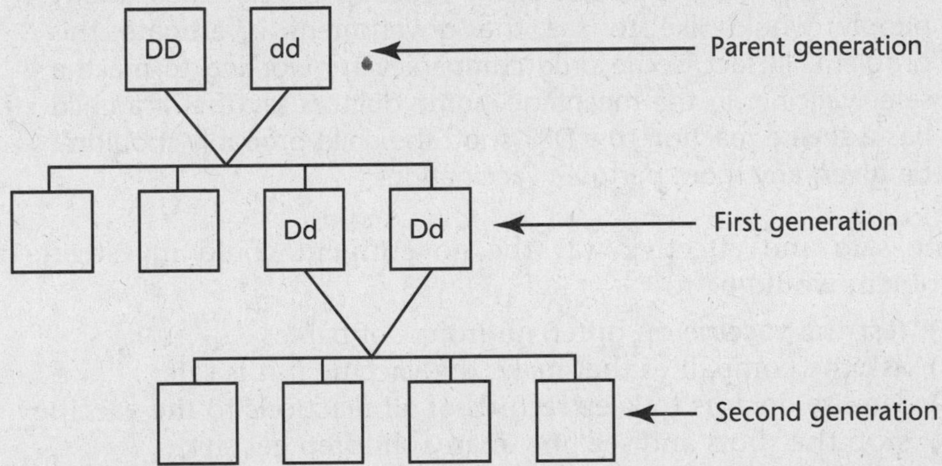

1. In the first generation of hamsters, how many would probably have dark eyes?
2. In the first generation, how many hamsters would carry one recessive gene for light eyes?
3. Two of the first-generation hamsters mate with each other. How many of the offspring out of every four would probably have light eyes and how many would have dark eyes?
4. Three out of four of the second-generation hamsters have dark eyes because they carry the dominant gene (D). How many of these dark-eyed hamsters would probably carry a gene for light eyes?

Answers start on page 507.

EXERCISE 10: CHAPTER REVIEW

Directions: Read each passage carefully. Then circle the number of the one best answer to each question.

Questions 1 and 2 are based on the following passage.

> Vaccines play an important role in keeping children healthy. However, some people are questioning whether the pertussis (whooping cough) vaccine, which is part of the standard DPT shot given to babies, is being used safely. A group called Dissatisfied Parents Together claims that too many children are permanently hurt by reactions to this shot. The American Medical Association admits that pertussis vaccine can cause bad reactions, but it says that the risk of a bad reaction is very small. Many people would like to see the government investigate this problem. In fact, some drug companies are working to make a safer vaccine. In the meantime, some doctors say that if a child has a severe reaction to a DPT shot, the child probably shouldn't be given any more pertussis vaccinations.

1. One safe and effective way the government could investigate this problem would be to
   (1) test the vaccine on different groups of babies
   (2) ask the companies that make the vaccine if it is safe
   (3) require doctors to keep records of all reactions to the vaccine
   (4) stop the shots and see how many children get sick
   (5) take an opinion poll to see how many people think the shots are dangerous

2. If a child has a bad reaction to a DPT shot, some doctors recommend that the child should
   (1) get his next shot later
   (2) not get any more pertussis vaccine
   (3) get his next shot earlier
   (4) stop all shots of any kind
   (5) continue the shots on schedule

Questions 3 and 4 are based on the following passage.

The word *dinosaur* comes from two Greek words, *deinos* ("terrible") and *sauros* ("lizard"). During the long Age of Reptiles, from 225 to 70 million years ago, dinosaurs dominated the Earth. There were dinosaurs that lived in swamps and ate plants. One of these, the huge apatosaurus, was over 90 feet long and weighed 70,000 pounds. There were terrifying meat-eating dinosaurs, such as the allosaurus (50 feet long, 16,000 pounds) and its even larger cousin, the tyrannosaurus rex (50 feet long, 20,000 pounds). There were dinosaurs that glided through the air, like the pterosaurs, and dinosaurs that swam in the ocean. There were even small three-foot-long dinosaurs that ran around on two legs. They probably lived by eating the eggs of their larger relations.

3. The largest dinosaur mentioned in this passage is the

(1) apatosaurus
(2) allosaurus
(3) tyrannosaurus rex
(4) pterosaur
(5) archaeopteryx

4. Which of the following is *not* true according to the passage?

(1) Dinosaurs were reptiles.
(2) Dinosaurs lived 70 million years ago.
(3) Some dinosaurs could swim.
(4) Some dinosaurs were smaller than people.
(5) Dinosaurs ate only meat.

Questions 5 and 6 are based on the following passage.

Some genetic problems are caused by mutations. A mutation happens when radiation, chemicals, or chance causes a sudden change in a gene. The offspring that has that gene will be different from its parents in some way. Some mutations are harmful, like the one that causes some horses to be born with one short leg. When a mutation is life-threatening, the mutated creature will probably not survive to breed, so the damaged gene will not be passed on. Once in a while, a mutation is helpful—for example, a mutation that made one hen lay stronger eggshells than normal. A helpful mutation makes a creature more likely to survive and have offspring who will inherit the new gene. This is called ***natural selection,*** and it is one of the ways evolution happens.

5. A harmful mutation is not usually passed on in animals because the mutated animal
   (1) doesn't want to pass it on
   (2) lays stronger eggs
   (3) has a shorter leg
   (4) is chosen by natural selection
   (5) probably will not survive to breed

6. The idea that successful creatures will have more offspring and pass on their good genes is called
   (1) mutation
   (2) radiation
   (3) survival
   (4) natural selection
   (5) evolution

Questions 7 and 8 are based on the following passage.

> Gardening is a hobby that can be enjoyed by people of all ages. Small children love to plant seeds and will wait impatiently for the first signs of the new plants. Energetic teenagers can get a good tan and a good workout while digging the ground or hoeing the weeds. Parents can share this hobby with their children and stretch the food budget with fresh, home-grown vegetables. Even very elderly people can pick flowers and enjoy the fresh air while sitting out in the garden.

7. The main idea of this passage is that
   (1) gardening is a hobby
   (2) children like gardening
   (3) people of different ages can enjoy gardening
   (4) gardening saves money
   (5) older people can't enjoy gardens

8. What is one opinion stated in this passage?
   (1) Older people can pick flowers.
   (2) Home-grown vegetables help the food budget.
   (3) Gardening is an enjoyable hobby.
   (4) Small children shouldn't work in gardens.
   (5) Digging requires energy.

Answers start on page 507.

3 HUMAN BIOLOGY

READING SKILL: UNDERSTANDING ILLUSTRATIONS

"A picture is worth a thousand words." That old saying can be true even when you're reading a textbook. Sometimes a picture can give you information more quickly and easily than any number of words. Many textbooks and tests use special pictures called diagrams, charts, and graphs. Understanding these special illustrations is a very important reading skill.

DIAGRAMS

The science topics in this chapter are about your body—about some of its many parts and how they work. Many of the articles will have ***diagrams*** to go with them. A diagram is a drawing that shows the parts of something or how a process works.

Look at the diagram below.

AREAS OF THE BRAIN

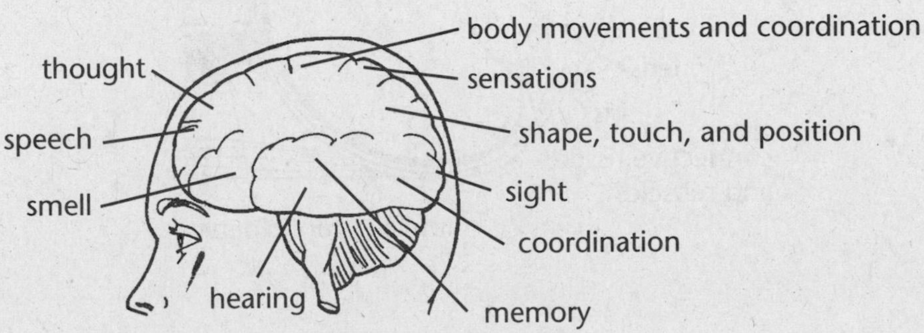

Always look at the ***title*** of a diagram first. The title tells you what the diagram is about. The title of this diagram is "Areas of the Brain." This title tells you that the diagram is showing you different parts of the brain.

Now look at the drawing. It is a drawing of the inside of a person's head. It is not a realistic drawing. Like most diagrams, this drawing has been simplified to get the main point across.

Finally, look at the ***labels***. The labels are words identifying important parts of the drawing. In this diagram, the words are telling which parts of the brain are used to do different things. For example, the part that gets messages from the eyes is at the back of the brain. If a woman were injured at the back of her head, she might lose her sight. The part that directs body movements is at the top of the brain. A person injured here might not be able to move well.

▶ You can use the diagram to figure things out. For instance, what might happen to a man injured at the forehead?

____

If you decided he might have trouble speaking, you were right. You got that information from the diagram.

DIAGRAM-READING TIP

In order to understand a diagram, first read the title. Next, look at the drawing itself. Finally, read all the labels.

EXERCISE 1: DIAGRAMS

Directions: Look at the diagram below and answer the questions.

PARTS OF THE EYE

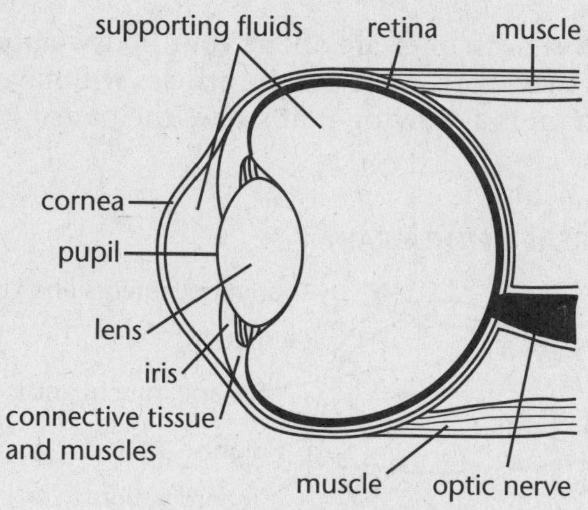

1. What is the opening in front of the lens called? ____________

2. What is the inside of the eye filled with? ____________

3. What is the screen on the back of the eyeball called? ____________

4. What is the name of the nerve that runs out of the back of the eye?

____

5. When a person gets a cataract, the cornea of the eye gets clouded over. Why would this make it hard to see?

____

Answers start on page 507.

COMPARING DIAGRAMS

Sometimes a diagram will have more than one drawing. You should carefully compare the drawings. Look to see how they are alike and how they are different.

Let's look at this diagram with three drawings. Try to answer the questions that follow. Then read on to see if your answers were correct.

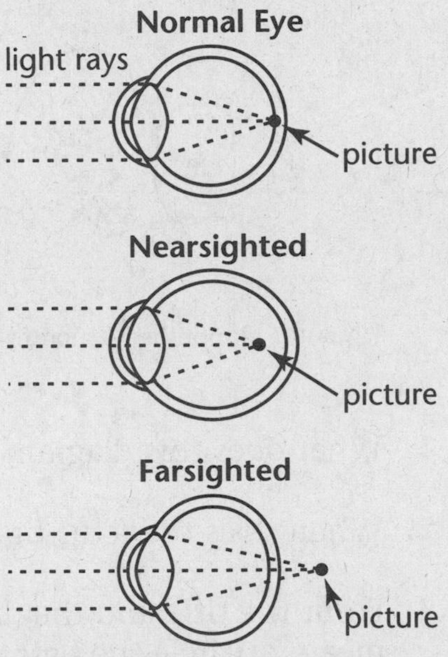

▶ Read the title. What is this diagram about?

____

▶ What is the difference in shape between the normal eye and the nearsighted one?

____

____

▶ What is the difference in shape between the normal eye and the farsighted one?

____

____

VISION AND EYE SHAPE

The title tells us that this diagram is about *the relationship between vision and eye shape*. The *nearsighted* eyeball is *longer* than the normal one; the *far-sighted* eyeball is *shorter*.

When you see something, a picture forms where the light rays focus (come together) in your eye. In a normal eye, the pictures form on the retina.

▶ Where does a picture form in a nearsighted eye? ______________

▶ Where does a picture form in a farsighted eye? ______________

▶ Why do you think that nearsighted and farsighted people have trouble seeing clearly? ______________________________

Because a nearsighted eye is longer, the light rays focus on the picture *ahead of the retina*. In a farsighted eye, they focus *behind the retina*. In both cases, the picture is blurry because *the light rays are not focused exactly on the retina*.

EXERCISE 2: COMPARING DIAGRAMS

Directions: Look at this diagram. Then answer the following questions.

GROWTH OF THE FETUS DURING EARLY PREGNANCY

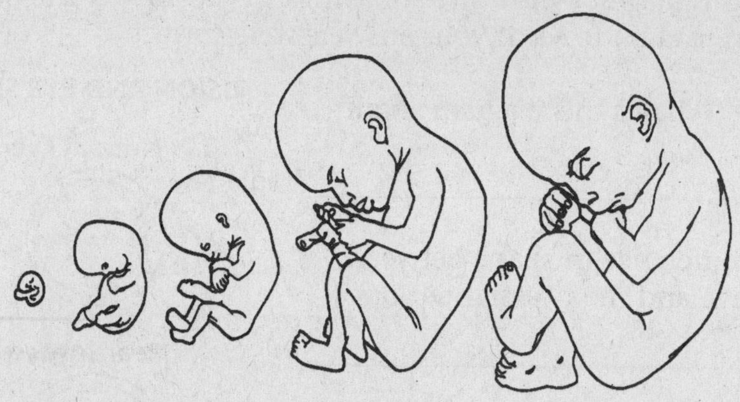

1. What does this diagram show? ______________________________

2. When does the fetus first show toes? ______________________________

3. From the title and the diagram, what do you think the word *fetus* means? (Circle the best answer.)
   (1) a baby
   (2) a deformed head
   (3) a young boy
   (4) an unborn child
   (5) a new drug

Answers start on page 507.

CHARTS

Another way to get information is from charts. Charts are often just tables with lines separating items of information into a series of small boxes. Charts are very useful for organizing information. Here is an example.

Blood Types and Transfusions		
Blood Type	**Can Take Blood from**	**Can Give Blood to**
O	O	O, A, B, AB
A	O, A	A, AB
B	O, B	B, AB
AB	O, A, B, AB	AB

To understand this chart, you have to know that different people have different ***blood types***. There are four main blood types, called *O*, *A*, *B*, and *AB*. If a person gets blood from someone else in a ***transfusion***, it has to be the right blood type. The wrong type of blood could kill someone.

First look at the title of this chart. This chart tells what types of blood are safe to use in transfusions between people with different blood types. Notice that the information in charts is organized in vertical ***columns***. Each column has a ***heading***. The three headings on this chart are "Blood Type," "Can Take Blood from," and "Can Give Blood to." These headings tell you what information each column holds.

Now read the chart across in rows. For example, look at the first blood type, "O." In the second column, the chart lists only "O" again. This means that a person with type O blood can take blood only from another person with type O. Look in the third column. The chart lists types O, A, B, and AB. This means that a person with type O blood can safely give blood to people with any of the four blood types.

Now you try it. Look on the chart for blood type B.

▶ A person with blood type B can take blood from what types? ________

▶ Type B people can give blood to what types? __________________

According to the chart, type B people can take *type O* or *type B* blood. They can give blood to *type B* or *type AB*.

CHART-READING TIP

When reading a chart, first look at the title of the chart. Then read the headings on each of the columns and rows. Do not try to get specific information from the chart until you understand what the chart is about.

EXERCISE 3: CHARTS

Directions: Use this chart to answer the following questions.

Vitamins		
Vitamin	**Source**	**Use in the Body**
A	Fish, butter, eggs, liver, yellow vegetables	Keeps eyes and skin healthy. Helps digestion and breathing.
C	Leafy vegetables, tomatoes, citrus fruits like lemons and oranges	Prevents a disease called *scurvy.*
D	Sunshine, fish oils, liver	Helps to build strong bones and teeth.
E	Vegetable and animal oils	Protects the nervous system and the reproductive system.
B Group		
B_1 (thiamine)	Yeast, liver, nuts, grains, lean pork	Protects the nervous system. Prevents a disease called *beriberi.*
B_2 (riboflavin)	Yeast, wheat germ, liver, meat, eggs	Affects entire body. Prevents skin and mouth diseases.
Niacin	Vegetables, meat, yeast, beer	Prevents skin disorders like pellagra.
B_{12}	Vegetables and liver	Prevents anemia.

1. What eight vitamins does this chart cover? ______________________

2. What disease does vitamin C prevent? ______________________

3. What two vitamins are found in fish? ______________________

4. What three vitamins might a doctor recommend for a skin problem?

____

Answers start on page 507.

LINE GRAPHS

Sometimes a chart is not the best way to show information. For example, Jack wanted to find out how he could make his tomatoes grow bigger, so he experimented. He put a different amount of fertilizer on each row of plants. Then he recorded how many pounds of tomatoes he harvested from each row. He entered his results in a chart.

Fertilizer	Tomatoes	Fertilizer	Tomatoes	Fertilizer	Tomatoes
2 oz.	4 lb.	8 oz.	20 lb.	14 oz.	28 lb.
4 oz.	10 lb.	10 oz.	23 lb.	16 oz.	20 lb.
6 oz.	16 lb.	12 oz.	26 lb.	18 oz.	13 lb.

Jack could take the same information and draw a line graph like the one on the following page. The line graph shows the result of his experiment much better.

A line graph has four parts:

- the title,
- the horizontal axis,
- the vertical axis, and
- the graph line.

First look at the title of a graph to see what the graph will be about. Titles can be important clues to the information you will be expected to find.

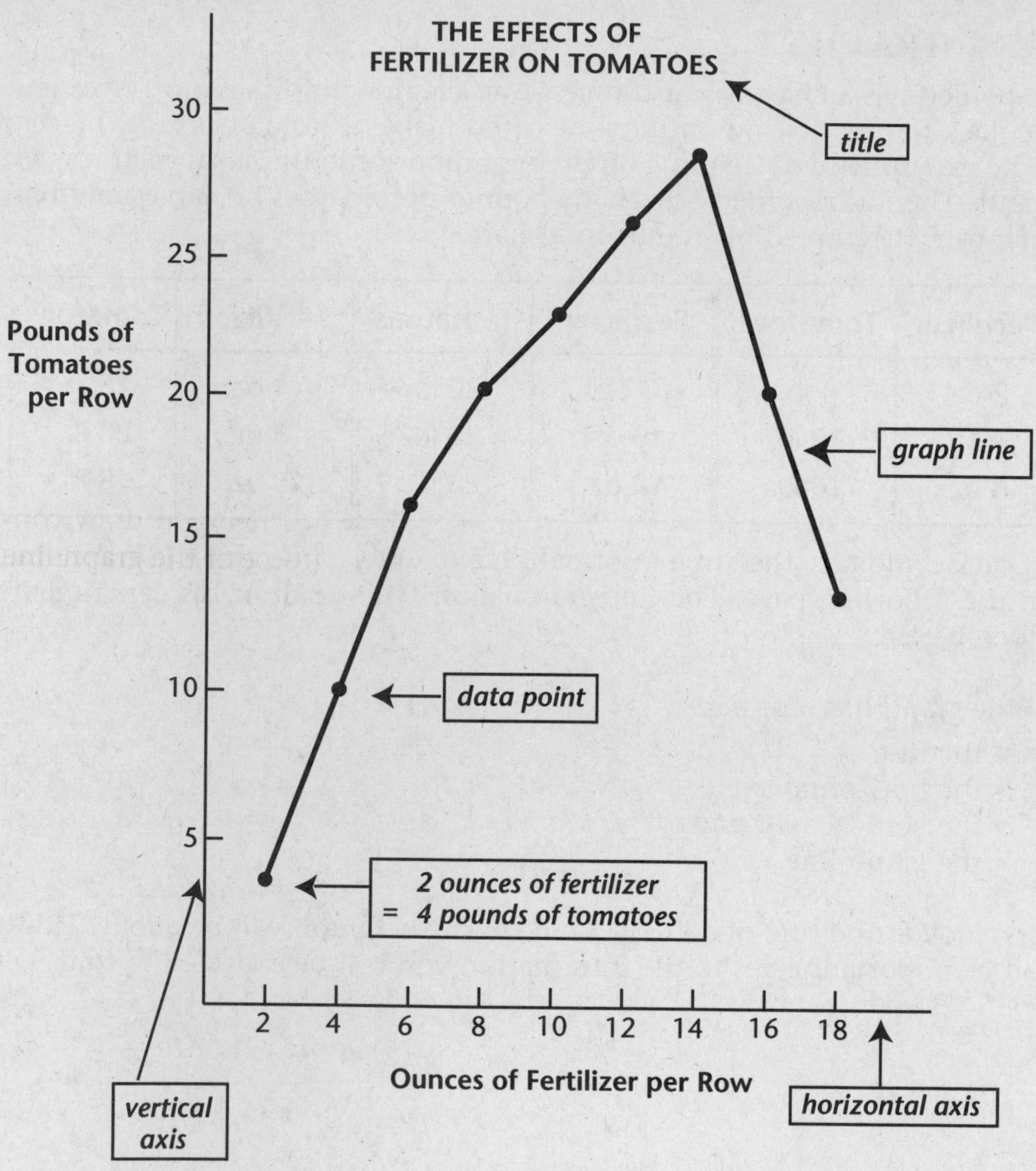

Reading Each Axis

Next look at the two axes. The axis that runs across the paper from left to right is called the ***horizontal axis***. The axis that runs up and down is called the ***vertical axis***. Each axis has a scale of numbers or measurements on it and a label to tell you what the axis is recording. For instance, in this graph the horizontal axis records the ounces of fertilizer Jack used in each row. The vertical axis records the pounds of tomatoes that were picked.

Always read the scales and labels of each axis carefully. Notice that each step on an axis can be more than one unit. In this graph, each step on the vertical axis is equal to five pounds. This is so the graph can fit in the space provided.

The Graph Line

After reading the title and the axis labels, look at the ***graph line*** itself. You can find specific pieces of information using the graph line. For example, you can find the amount of tomatoes that grew with only two ounces of fertilizer (4 pounds). You can also find the maximum amount of tomatoes that grew in one row (28 pounds).

Many graph lines have dots on them, called ***data points***, to help you find particular points on the graph. If a point lies between two steps on the scale, you must ***estimate*** the measurement for that point. If you can't tell just where a certain point on the line falls, use something straight to line up the point with the scale on the axis. (Use a ruler or the edge of a piece of paper.) The graph below shows how to read an *exact* and an *estimated* data point.

The overall shape, or ***trend***, of the graph line can help you draw conclusions about the graph's subject. For example, the shape of the graph line shows that more fertilizer is not always better for tomatoes. Jack could decide to use 14 ounces of fertilizer on each row of his tomatoes next year.

Let's look at another example of a line graph. Examine the graph below, and then try to answer the questions on the following page.

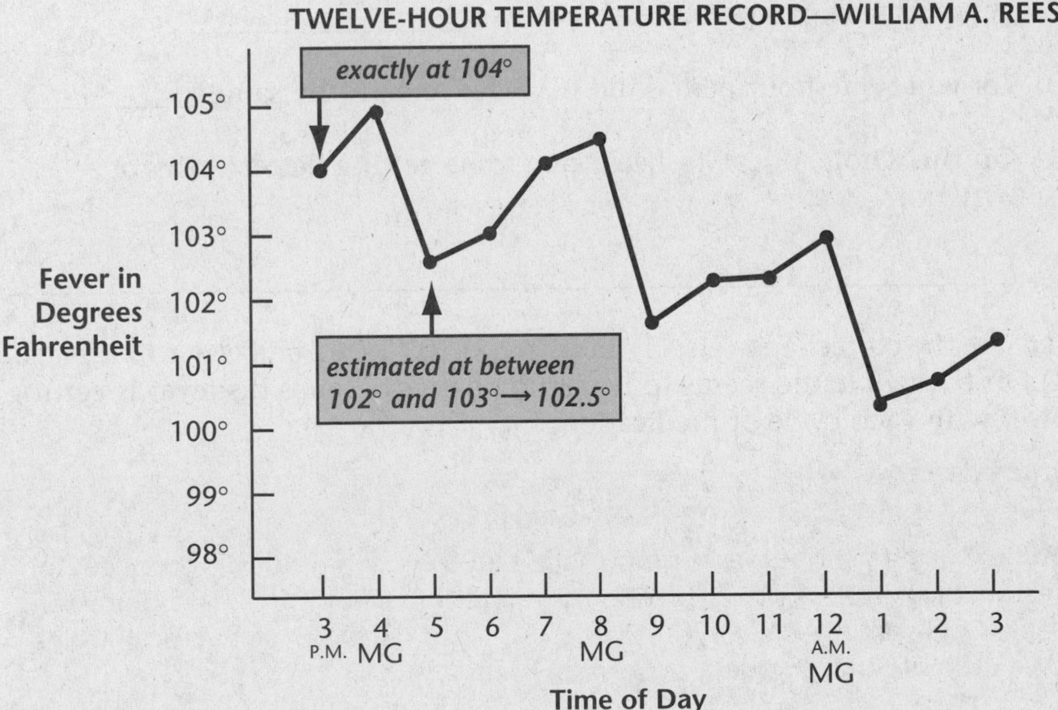

Note: MG = medication given

▶ What is the title of this graph? ________________________________

The title is *Twelve-Hour Temperature Record—William A. Rees*. From this title, we might guess that Mr. Rees is sick, because someone is keeping careful track of his temperature.

▶ What does the horizontal axis measure? ____________________

It measures *time*, in hours.

▶ What does the vertical axis measure? ______________________

It measures *Mr. Rees's fever* on the Fahrenheit scale. The scale (named after Gabriel Fahrenheit) is the same temperature scale we usually use in our daily lives. Scientists and people in other countries often use a different scale, called the Celsius or centigrade scale.

▶ Now look at the graph line and answer these questions.

1. When was Mr. Rees admitted?________________
2. What was his temperature at 6:00 P.M.?________________
3. For what one-hour period did his fever remain the same?__________
4. On the whole, does Mr. Rees seem to be getting better? Why or why not?

   ____

Here are the correct answers: (1) 3:00 P.M. (2) 103°F (3) 10:00 P.M. to 11:00 P.M. (4) On the whole, he seems to be getting better because his fever is getting lower with each cycle of medication.

LINE-GRAPH TIP

When a data point on a graph falls between two values, you need to estimate. For example, in the temperature line graph, the data point for 5 P.M. falls about halfway between 102° and 103° on the vertical scale. We estimate that the data point is at 102.5°.

EXERCISE 4: LINE GRAPHS

Directions: Sarah was prying rocks out of the lawn at her cabin in the mountains. She noticed that she had to use different-sized crowbars to move different rocks. She did some experimenting with this idea, and this graph shows her results.

Look at the graph carefully. Then circle the best answer for each of the following questions.

CROWBARS AND ROCKS

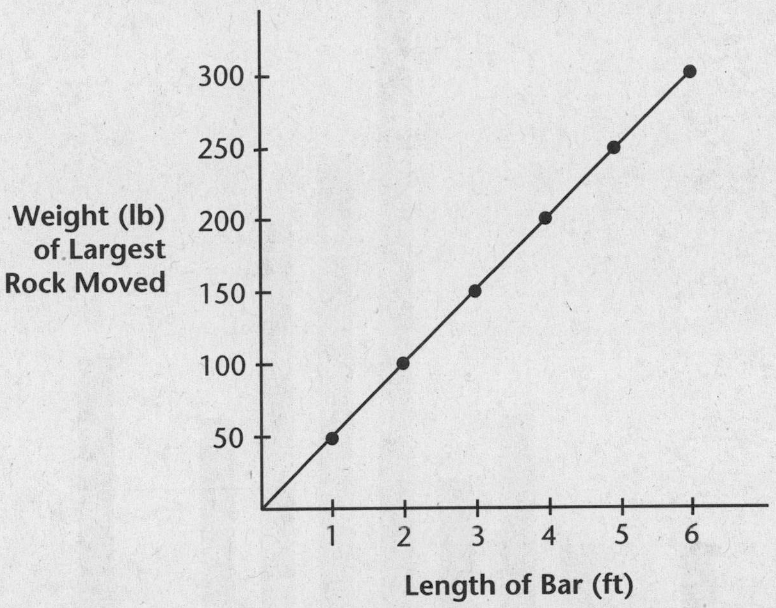

1. What length crowbar helped Sarah move the heaviest rock?
   (1) 2 feet
   (2) 3 feet
   (3) 4 feet
   (4) 5 feet
   (5) 6 feet

2. Which hypothesis could be based on this graph?
   (1) Sarah is an extremely strong person.
   (2) To move a heavy rock, you should use a thick crowbar.
   (3) There were no rocks under 50 pounds on Sarah's lawn.
   (4) The longer the crowbar, the heavier the rock that can be moved.
   (5) Everyone needs a five-foot crowbar to move a 250-pound rock.

3. "Crowbars and Rocks" is not a very accurate title for this graph. Which of the following would be the best title?
   (1) Lengths of Crowbars Needed to Move Different Rocks
   (2) How Sarah Cleared Her Cabin Lawn
   (3) Weights of Rocks That Can Be Moved
   (4) Lengths of Crowbars Commonly Available
   (5) Weights of Rocks on a Mountain Cabin Lawn

Answers start on page 507.

BAR GRAPHS

Another type of graph is a ***bar graph***. A bar graph uses bars instead of lines to show pieces of information. The bars usually come up from the horizontal axis. You read the graph by seeing how high the bars go on the vertical scale. Look at the example that follows.

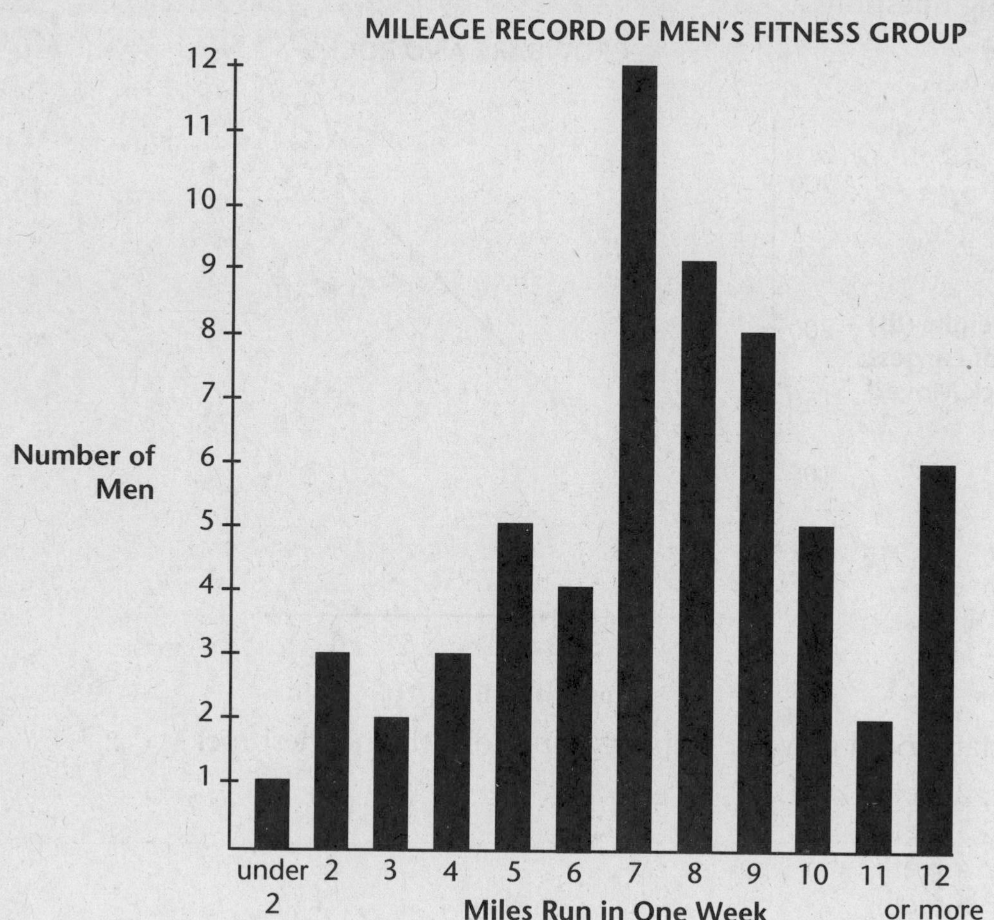

To read this graph, look at the bars coming up from the horizontal axis. Use a straight edge like a piece of paper to line up the top of the bar with the vertical scale.

- ▶ How many men ran just two miles? ____________________
- ▶ What distance was run by exactly eight men? ____________________
- ▶ What exact distance was run by the greatest number of men? ________

Your answers should be as follows: *three men*, *nine miles*, and *seven miles*.

Bar-Graph Tip

On some bar graphs, the bars come out from the vertical axis. To read this type of bar graph, read down from the bar to the value given on the horizontal axis.

EXERCISE 5: BAR GRAPHS

Directions: Look at this bar graph carefully. Then answer each of the following questions.

AVERAGE TEMPERATURES IN VANCOUVER, BRITISH COLUMBIA

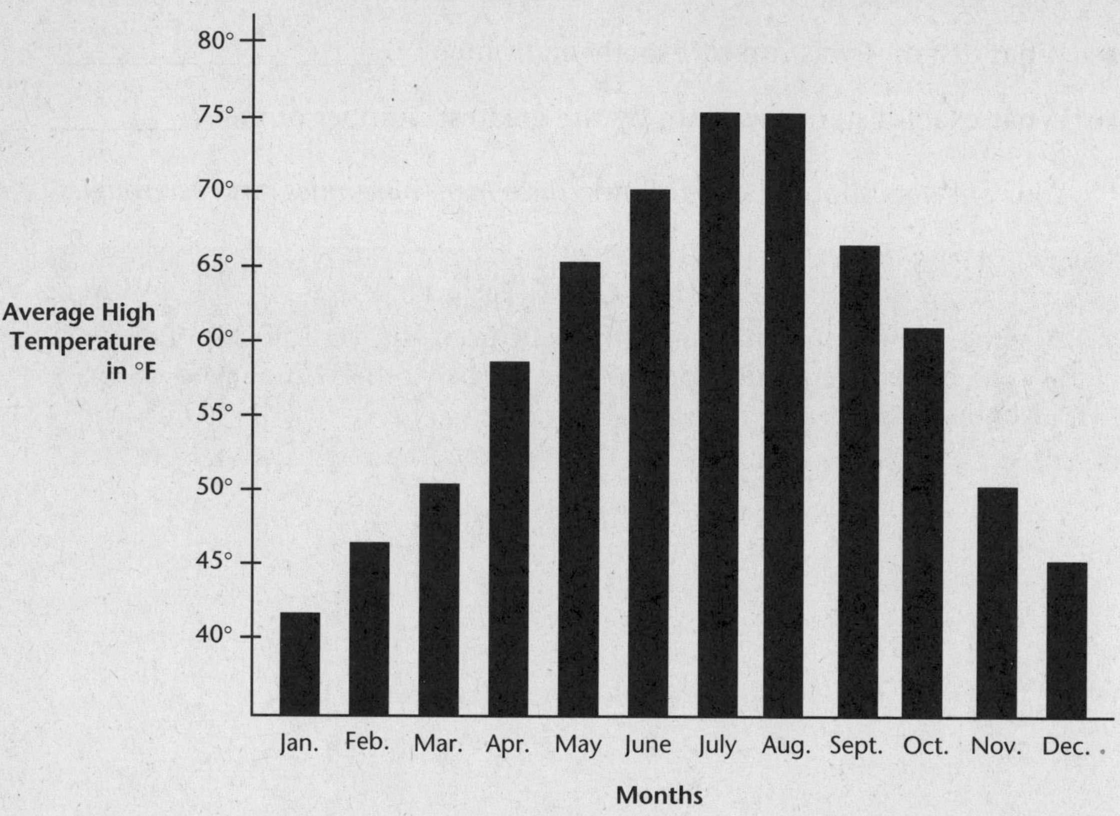

1. Looking at the title, what information do you expect to find on this graph? ____________________

2. What does the horizontal axis show? ____________________

3. What does the vertical axis measure? ____________________

4. How big is each step on the vertical axis? ____________________

5. What is the average high temperature in November? ____________________

6. Which two months are the warmest? ____________________

7. Do you think it often gets below freezing in Vancouver? Why or why not? ____________________

Answers start on page 508.

SCIENCE TOPIC: THE HUMAN BODY

To get the most out of modern medical care, you need to know something about the way your body works. It also helps to know some of the special scientific words used to describe it.

Your body is made up of many different kinds of cells. Similar kinds of cells are grouped together into ***tissues***; for example, we talk of nerve tissue or muscle tissue. Each separate part inside your body is called an ***organ***. Your brain, your stomach, and your liver are all separate organs. Finally, organs and tissues are organized into ***systems***. Each system has a purpose. For example, your ***digestive system*** is the group of organs that help you digest your food. It includes your mouth, your stomach, your intestines, and many other organs. In this chapter we will study several different body systems, how they work, and how to keep them healthy.

BONES AND MUSCLES

All the strength in your body comes from two systems: the ***skeletal system***, containing the bones and their connecting tissues, and the ***muscular system***, which is all the muscles in your body.

The Skeletal System

There are 206 separate bones in your body! Some are large, like the bones in your legs. Others are small, like the delicate bones in your hands. The diagram of a skeleton on page 416 shows some of the most important bones.

Your bones do three important things for you. First, they support your body. Without your skeleton, you would be shapeless, like a jellyfish. You wouldn't be able to move, breathe, or even live. Second, some bones protect different parts of your body. Your hard skull bones protect your brain. Your ribs protect your heart, stomach, and lungs.

Third, inside some of your bones there is a soft substance called ***marrow***. The bone marrow is where most of your blood cells are made.

The skeletal system contains two other kinds of tissue, called cartilage and ligaments. ***Cartilage*** is a stiff kind of tissue, but it is softer than bone. Your nose and the outside of your ears are made of cartilage. Children's bones are said to be "soft." That is because young children's bones have much more cartilage in them. The cartilage hardens up into real bone as they get older.

A ***joint*** is a place where two bones come together. Most joints are padded with cartilage. Bones are held together at the joints by very tough bands of tissue called ***ligaments***. When a doctor says that you have sprained something, like your ankle, she means you have stretched or torn some ligaments. This is usually caused by a sudden bending or twisting of a joint in the wrong direction.

THE HUMAN SKELETON

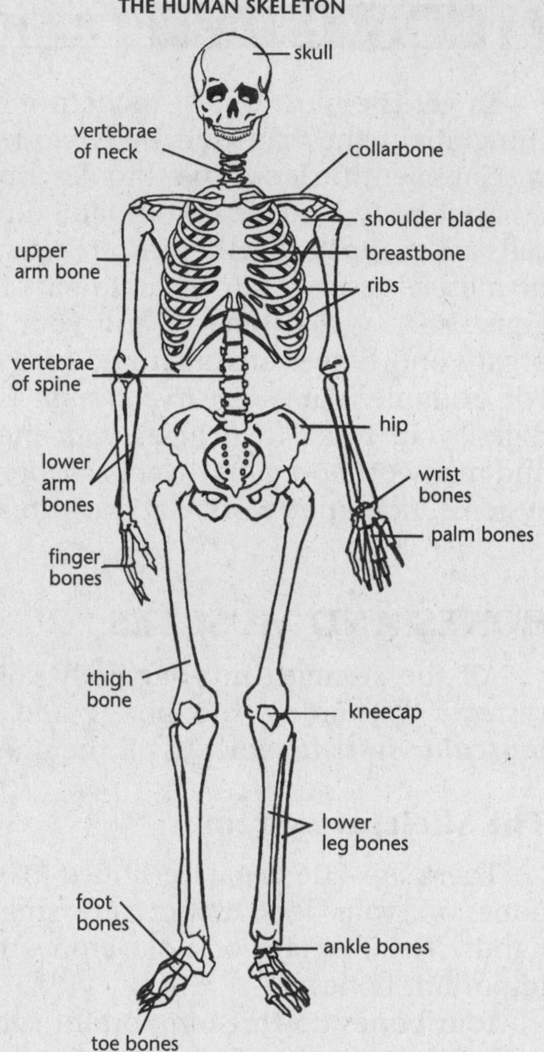

A common problem with the skeleton is ***osteoporosis***, which makes a person's bones become very brittle and breakable. It has many causes. One cause is not having enough calcium in the diet. Osteoporosis is particularly common among older women, which is why women are advised to get lots of calcium all through their lives.

The Muscular System

Muscles are made of special cells that contract to get shorter and relax to get longer. That is how muscles move. Look at this diagram of an arm.

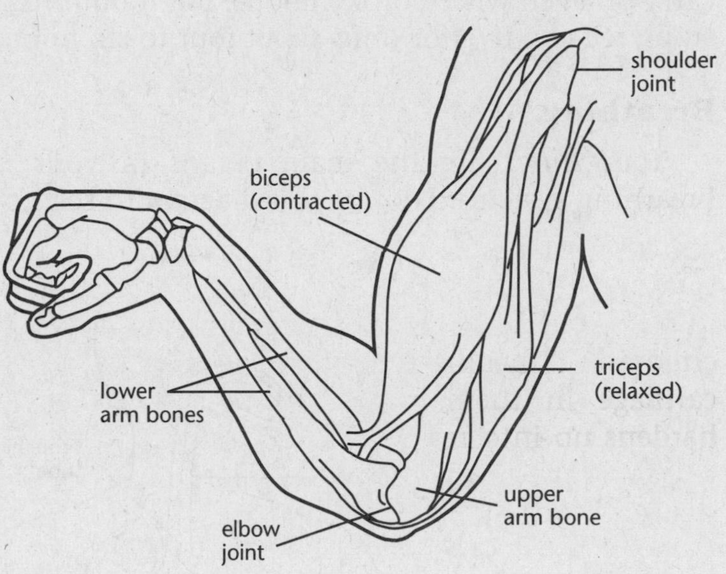

When you tighten your arm muscle, every little cell in that muscle contracts. Your ***skeletal muscles*** are attached to your bones by ***tendons***. When your muscle contracts, it pulls on the tendon, which pulls your arm bone up. Your skeletal muscles are ***voluntary***, which means that you can control their movement.

Two other kinds of muscles are mostly ***involuntary***—not controlled by your conscious mind. ***Smooth muscles*** are the kind in your stomach and intestines. They expand and contract in rhythm to help digest your food and keep it moving through your digestive tract. ***Cardiac muscles*** are especially strong and reliable. They are found only in your heart, which is the most important muscle in your body.

EXERCISE 6: BONES AND MUSCLES

Directions: Circle *T* if the statement is true and *F* if it is false.

T F **1.** There are over 200 bones in your body.

T F **2.** Bones support and protect your body.

T F **3.** Cartilage is harder than bone.

T F **4.** Ligaments attach one bone to another.

T F **5.** Osteoporosis is caused partly by lack of calcium.

T F **6.** Voluntary muscles are not under your control.

T F **7.** Your heart is a muscle.

Directions: Circle the best answer.

8. Look at the diagram of a skeleton in this article. What are the bones in your backbone and neck called?

(1) ribs
(2) palm bones
(3) collarbones
(4) vertebrae
(5) mandibles

Answers start on page 508.

RESPIRATION AND CIRCULATION

Ambulance scenes on TV and in real life tell us just how important our breathing and blood systems are. We can live for days without food and carry on even with a broken bone. But if our breathing or blood circulation stops, we can live for only about four to six minutes.

Breathing

Your ***lungs*** are the main organs in your ***respiratory system*** (your breathing system). Look at this diagram to see how your lungs work.

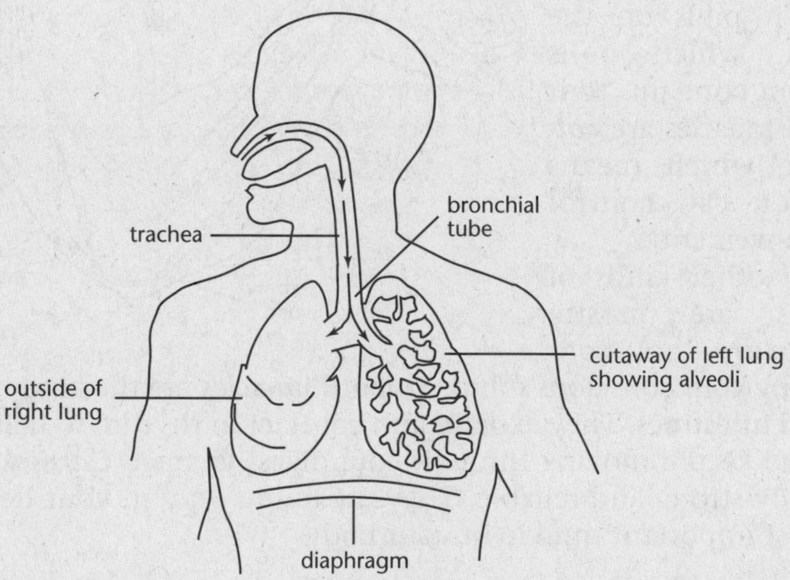

When you breathe in, your ***diaphragm***, a thin, flat muscle that lies under your lungs, pulls down. Your chest muscles pull up and out. This causes suction inside your chest, which makes your lungs expand and pull in air. The air enters through your nose or mouth. It comes down your ***trachea*** (your windpipe). Then it splits and goes down your two ***bronchial tubes*** into your lungs.

Inside your lungs are all kinds of little tubes running to groups of tiny air sacs called ***alveoli***. These sacs get filled with air. Surrounding these sacs are small blood vessels. Some of the oxygen in the air passes into these blood vessels. Carbon dioxide, a waste material in our bodies, moves from the blood vessels into the small air sacs.

Then your diaphragm and your chest muscles relax, putting pressure on your lungs. The air in the alveoli makes the return trip back through the little tubes, into your bronchial tubes, up your trachea, and back out your nose or mouth. Then you are ready to start all over again. You have been doing this twelve to twenty times a minute since the moment you were born, usually without thinking about it.

Smoking can damage your respiratory system. Tars and other chemicals in smoke build up in the alveoli. If you smoke enough, these air sacs may get stiff. Then they can't pull air in or push it out easily anymore. We call this disease ***emphysema***. Persons with emphysema cannot breathe deeply or exercise. Eventually, they cannot breathe at all.

The Circulatory System

The ***circulatory system*** is the body's transport system. It carries food, chemicals, oxygen, and waste materials from place to place in your body.

The center of your circulatory system is your heart. Your heart is an amazing muscle that contracts and relaxes 60 to 80 times every minute of every day of your life. It pumps the blood around and around, through miles of ***blood vessels*** throughout your body.

Blood vessels get rid of carbon dioxide by carrying it to your lungs and picking up oxygen there to take back to your heart. Other blood vessels take oxygen and food out to all the parts of your body. Blood vessels going away from your heart are called ***arteries.*** Blood vessels going toward your heart are called ***veins***. The veins take waste materials away from the cells.

Blood contains three different types of cells. Each kind of cell has a different purpose. The ***red blood cells*** carry oxygen to your body cells. The ***white blood cells*** fight disease by attacking harmful bacteria and viruses in your body. Whenever a blood vessel gets torn, small blood cells called ***platelets*** break along the edge of the wound and release a chemical that causes your blood to clot. Clotting around the wound prevents you from losing too much blood.

You can do a lot to keep your heart and circulatory system healthy. Not smoking, staying reasonably thin, getting regular exercise, and learning to manage tension—all these things will help you avoid high blood pressure and heart attacks, two of the most common killers in America.

EXERCISE 7: HEART, BLOOD, AND LUNGS

Directions: To summarize this article, fill in the blanks in these paragraphs.

Your ____________ (1) are the main organs in your respiratory system. Air comes in your ________________ (2) or ________________ (3), goes down your ______________ (4), into your two ____________________________ (5), and then into small tubes in your lungs that lead to tiny air sacs called ______________ (6). Tiny blood vessels collect ______________ (7) from the air in these sacs and get rid of ______________ ______________ (8).

The ________________ ________________ ________________ (9) in your blood carry oxygen to your body cells. The ________________ ________________ ________________ (10) help your body fight disease. ____________________ (11) carry a chemical that helps your blood clot.

Answers start on page 508.

NUTRITION

Nutrition is the study of the foods, or ***nutrients***, our bodies need. Poor nutrition can be a real problem. It can cause severe depression, high blood pressure, premature births, and many other serious health problems. It can also weaken us so that we are more likely to catch other illnesses.

Our bodies need six types of nutrients: protein, carbohydrates, fats, vitamins, minerals, and water. The following chart shows why we need these nutrients and gives examples of some typical foods containing them.

Nutrients

Nutrient	What It Does	Some Good Food Sources
protein	• provides building material for new cells	meat, fish, eggs, tofu, milk products, beans, soybeans, peanuts
carbohydrates (starches and sugars)	• provides energy	whole-grain bread, tortillas, rice, corn, pasta, desserts
fats	• provides concentrated energy • needed for body chemistry	meat, butter, whole milk, olives, avocado, vegetable oils
vitamins	• needed for enzymes and other body chemistry	fruits, vegetables, liver, whole grains, cod liver oil
minerals	• makes strong bones and teeth • iron needed for blood • needed for body chemistry	milk products, green leafy vegetables, seafood, liver, kelp
water	• needed by *all* parts of the body. Your body is about 70% water.	water, milk, fruit juices

Nutritionists (people who study nutrition) have set up a food guide pyramid that shows what people should eat to get all the nutrients they need. It is important to eat a variety of different foods. Listed below are the average adult's daily requirements. Children, teenagers, pregnant or nursing women, and athletes have slightly different needs.

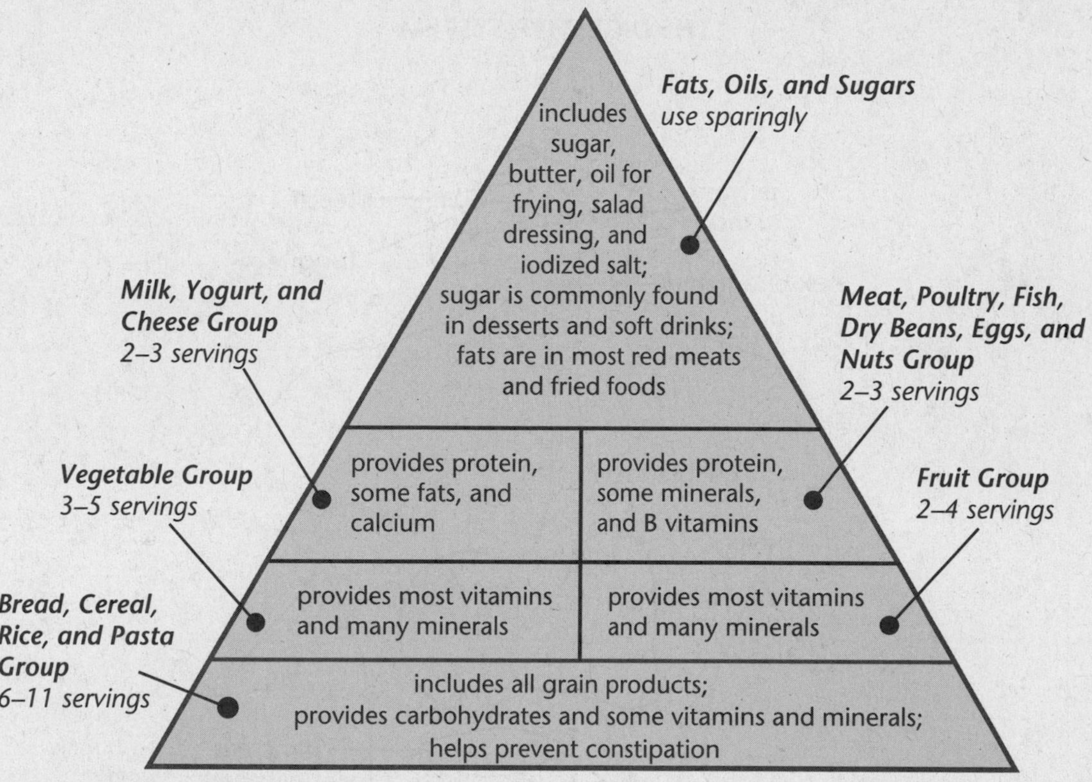

EXERCISE 8: NUTRITION

Directions: Circle the best answer.

1. According to the Nutrients chart on page 420, the main purpose of carbohydrates is to
   (1) build new cells
   (2) provide energy
   (3) make enzymes
   (4) provide liquid
   (5) keep bones healthy

2. Which of the following is an opinion, not a fact?
   (1) It is important to eat a variety of foods.
   (2) Some vitamins are destroyed by cooking.
   (3) Poor nutrition can cause health problems.
   (4) Everyone should take vitamin pills.
   (5) Cheese and meat provide protein.

Answers start on page 508.

THE DIGESTIVE TRACT

The food you eat goes through a long journey and many changes before it is ready to be used by your body. The process of breaking down food into simpler chemicals that the body can use is called ***digestion***. The place where this process happens is the ***digestive tract***.

THE DIGESTIVE SYSTEM

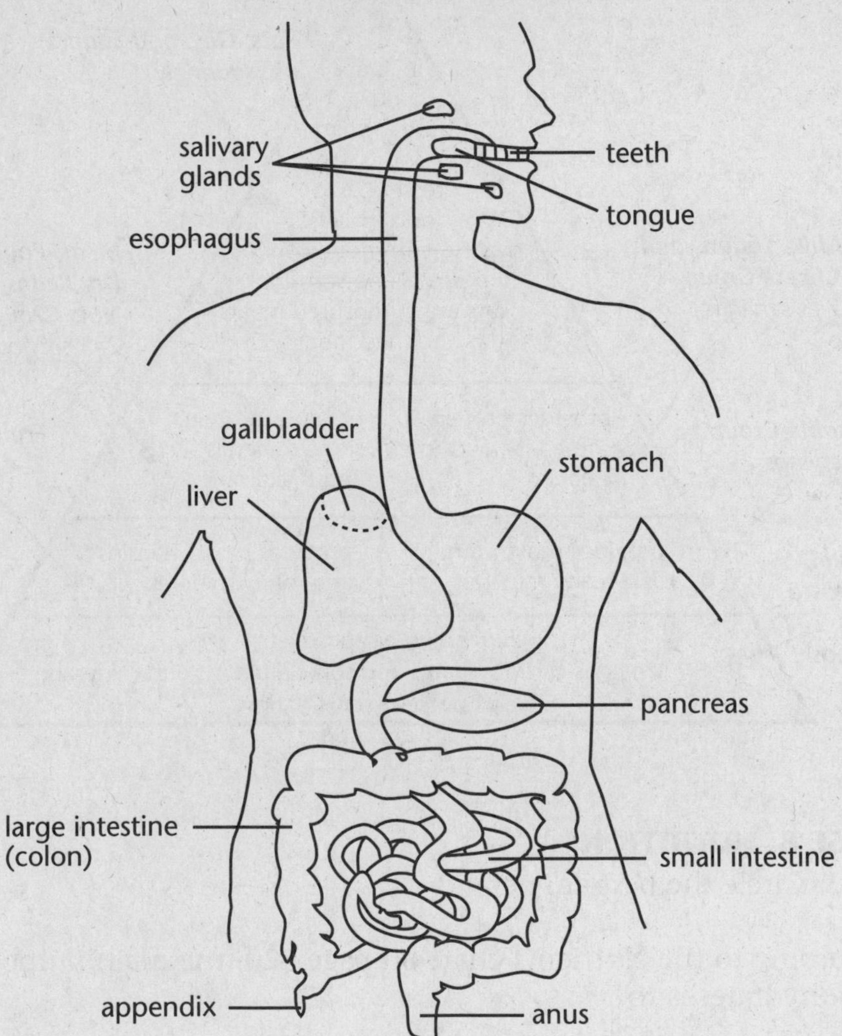

Your digestive tract begins with your mouth. Here food is taken in and ground down into small pieces by your teeth. It is mixed with ***saliva***, which is produced by salivary glands that lie next to your mouth. Saliva moistens the food so that it slides easily down the long tube of your ***esophagus*** into your stomach. The stomach is a muscular sac that turns and squeezes the food, mixing it with a little acid and some enzymes. ***Enzymes*** are special chemicals that help you break down foods. An enzyme in saliva breaks down starches, and two enzymes in your stomach break down proteins.

After the food is mixed and mashed into liquid in your stomach, it goes into your ***small intestine***. The small intestine is over twenty feet long. At its beginning, more enzymes that come from your liver, gallbladder, and pancreas are mixed with the food. These enzymes help you digest fats and complete the digestion of proteins. As the digested food moves along, the nutrients you need are ***absorbed*** (soaked up) through the walls of your small intestine. This leaves only the waste materials and water. These pass into your ***large intestine***, which is wider than your small intestine but only about seven feet long. There most of the water is absorbed back into your body, and what is left passes out of your body through the anus.

EXERCISE 9: DIGESTION

Directions: Match the words to their definitions.

______ **1.** mouth

______ **2.** saliva

______ **3.** salivary glands

______ **4.** esophagus

______ **5.** stomach

______ **6.** small intestine

______ **7.** liver, pancreas, and gallbladder

______ **8.** large intestine

a. organ that absorbs water from waste
b. tube that runs from mouth to stomach
c. organ that absorbs nutrients from food
d. glands that produce saliva
e. organs that dump enzymes into the small intestine
f. liquid that moistens food in the mouth
g. place where food enters the body
h. organ that mixes food with acid

Directions: Circle the best answer.

9. The correct order in which food moves through your digestive system is

(1) stomach, esophagus, small intestine, large intestine
(2) large intestine, small intestine, stomach, esophagus
(3) stomach, large intestine, esophagus, small intestine
(4) esophagus, stomach, small intestine, large intestine
(5) esophagus, small intestine, stomach, large intestine

Answers start on page 508.

THE NERVOUS SYSTEM

Your ***nervous system*** is the communication network of your body. Your ***brain*** is the center of the system. It is like a computer that runs your body, only much more amazing than any computer.

Your ***spinal cord*** is the main link between your brain and the rest of your body. Most of the nerves in your body connect into it. Only some nerves in your head connect directly to your brain. Your spinal cord runs down the middle of the vertebrae in your backbone. Your brain and your spinal cord together are called your ***central nervous system***.

Two kinds of nerves run throughout the rest of your body. ***Motor nerves*** carry messages *from* the brain and spinal cord *to* other parts of your body. These messages tell your body to do things, like move an arm or wink one eye. ***Sensory nerves*** carry messages *to* your brain and spinal cord *from* your body. These nerves tell your brain what is going on around you. They send messages of sights, sounds, tastes, smells, pain, heat, and pressure. There are many sensory nerves in your head, coming from your eyes, nose, mouth, and ears. There are sensory nerves all over your skin, like those in your fingertips, and even some inside your body.

EXERCISE 10: THE NERVOUS SYSTEM

Directions: Trace the path of these messages through your nervous system by filling in the blanks. The first one is done as an example.

You are lying in bed on a cold winter night. The nerve endings in your ____skin____ (1) feel the air getting colder. This message travels up a ________ (2) nerve to your ________ (3) ________ and then up to your ________ (4). Your ________ (5) decides to do something about the cold. It sends a message down a ________ (6) nerve, through your spinal cord, down your arm to your ________ (7), telling it to pull up the blankets. All this happens more quickly than you can realize it, because these messages, called ***nerve impulses***, travel at about one hundred feet per second.

Answers start on page 508.

STRESS AND WELLNESS

Some doctors and ***psychologists***, scientists who study the mind, believe that how you think can affect your health. You know that your brain is connected to every part of your body through your nervous system. Now there is scientific proof that how you think and feel can affect the health of your body.

Stress is caused whenever there is a problem or a change in your life. Of course, everybody has a certain amount of stress; nobody's life is perfect. In fact, stress is necessary. Without stress, we would never learn anything or grow or change. But too much stress can hurt you. It can cause ulcers, heart attacks, and migraine headaches. It can weaken your body's defenses so that you are more likely to catch diseases. It can even make you more likely to have an accident.

When you feel stress, your brain sends a message to your body to release a chemical called ***adrenaline***. Adrenaline speeds up your breathing and your heartbeat. It also makes your muscles tense up. Today you have a different kind of stress. You may have problems like unpaid bills or troubles with kids. If you don't use up all that adrenaline, it stays bottled up inside you and can do some damage.

What can you do about stress? First, you can try to find ways of changing things so that you aren't under so much stress. You can set up a plan to pay those bills or go to a counselor to try to work things out. But sometimes you can't change a stressful situation. Sometimes you don't even want to. A big change might be a good change, but it will still be stressful.

The body-brain link works in two ways. Your body can help your mind deal with stress. If you are under stress, you need to take especially good care of your body. It's important to get enough sleep and eat nutritious meals. Some people take a vitamin-mineral pill every day. Another thing that can help you handle stress is daily exercise. If you go jogging or do aerobic dancing or work out, you give your body a chance to burn up some of that adrenaline. Of course, a person who isn't used to much physical activity should start slowly and check with a doctor first.

EXERCISE 11: STRESS

How do you know when you are under too much stress? Some clues are feeling run-down or getting many headaches or stomachaches. Other clues are the sources of stress in your life. The chart that follows outlines some events that cause stress. The events are listed in order, from the hardest to handle to the easiest.

Directions: Look at this chart and answer the questions that follow.

Events That Often Cause Stress	
1. Death of husband or wife	**11.** Small children in home
2. Divorce	**12.** Tension at work
3. Trouble with the law	**13.** Change in working hours
4. Major personal injury	**14.** Changing to a new school
5. Getting married	**15.** Change in social life
6. Losing a job	**16.** Change in church
7. Retirement	**17.** Taking out a mortgage
8. Pregnancy	**18.** Change in sleeping habits
9. New family member	**19.** Change in eating habits
10. Loss of close friend	**20.** Vacation

1. Some of the events in the list are positive. Why do you think that they cause stress?

____

____

2. What do *all* the events in the list have in common?

____

____

Directions: Circle the one best answer.

3. According to the chart, which of these life events is *least* likely to cause stress?
   (1) having a baby
   (2) getting a ticket for speeding
   (3) getting fired
   (4) going on a diet
   (5) breaking your leg

Answers start on page 508.

PREGNANCY PRECAUTIONS

People used to believe that an unborn baby (called a ***fetus***) was protected from most things that happened to its mother. Now doctors are discovering that the fetus is affected by many things.

If a pregnant woman catches German measles or certain other diseases, her baby might have a ***birth defect.*** The baby might be born with something wrong with his or her mind or body. Some medicines taken by the mother can also cause birth defects. Even some of the most common drugs, like aspirin and sleeping pills, can cause trouble for the fetus. Almost all illegal drugs can cause birth defects. Too much alcohol, even just beer or wine, may hurt a baby and may cause it to be mentally handicapped.

Regular smoking can cause a woman's baby to be born too small or too early. If a mother doesn't get enough of the right kind of foods, especially protein, her baby might also be born weak or underweight. Some problems with fetuses happen for unknown reasons. However, if a pregnant woman follows her doctor's advice and takes good care of herself, she is giving her baby the best possible chance to be born healthy.

EXERCISE 12: PREGNANCY PRECAUTIONS

Directions: List at least four things mentioned in the passage that could hurt a fetus.

1. ______________________________

2. ______________________________

3. ______________________________

4. ______________________________

Answers start on page 508.

EXERCISE 13: CHAPTER REVIEW

Directions: Read each passage carefully. Then circle the number of the best answer to each question.

Questions 1 and 2 are based on the following passage and diagram.

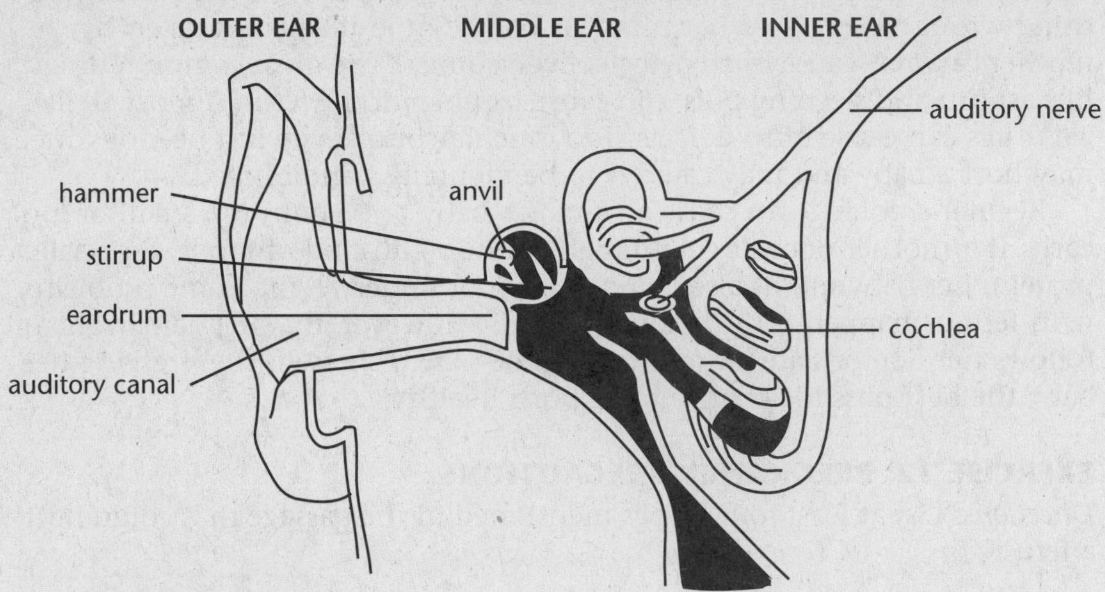

Look at this diagram of the ear. Sound enters the outer ear and travels down the auditory canal to the eardrum. The sound causes the eardrum to vibrate, just as a regular drum vibrates when you hit it. The vibration of the eardrum moves three little bones called the hammer, the anvil, and the stirrup. These three bones transfer the vibration to the inner ear, which contains the cochlea. The cochlea is a coiled tube filled with liquid. The vibrations in this liquid are changed to nerve impulses, or messages, that travel along the auditory nerve to the brain.

1. According to the diagram, the part of the ear that contains the hammer, anvil, and stirrup bones is called the
   (1) outer ear
   (2) auditory canal
   (3) middle ear
   (4) inner ear
   (5) auditory nerve

2. When a person gets an ear infection, the middle ear gets full of fluid. Which hypothesis best explains why someone with an ear infection can't hear as well as usual?
   (1) The fluid prevents the eardrum from vibrating easily.
   (2) The pain makes it hard to hear.
   (3) The fluid makes the inner ear too cold for nerve impulses to travel.
   (4) The fluid helps the sound travel better.
   (5) The pain keeps the person from paying attention.

Questions 3 and 4 are based on the following chart.

Recommended Energy Intake for Average-Sized People		
Category	**Age (years)**	**Energy Needs (calories)**
Children	1–3	(900–1,800)
	4–6	(1,300–2,300)
	7–10	(1,650–3,300)
Males	11–14	(2,000–3,700)
	15–18	(2,100–3,900)
	19–22	(2,500–3,300)
	23–50	(2,300–3,100)
	51–75	(2,000–2,800)
	76+	(1,650–2,450)
Females	11–14	(1,500–3,000)
	15–18	(1,200–3,000)
	19–22	(1,700–2,500)
	23–50	(1,600–2,400)
	51–75	(1,400–2,200)
	76+	(1,200–2,000)

3. According to the chart, about how many calories does a 45-year-old man need?
   (1) 2,000–3,700
   (2) 2,000–2,800
   (3) 1,600–2,400
   (4) 2,300–3,100
   (5) 1,400–2,200

4. Which of these statements is true, according to the information in the chart?
   (1) The older you get, the more calories you need.
   (2) All men need more calories than all women.
   (3) Men need more calories than women of the same age.
   (4) Girls need more calories than boys.
   (5) Children need more calories than teenagers.

Questions 5 and 6 are based on the following passage.

A sexually transmitted disease (STD) is a disease that is passed from one person to another, primarily by sexual contact. Chlamydia, genital herpes, gonorrhea, and syphilis are some of the most common STDs being reported today. Chlamydia, gonorrhea, and syphilis can be cured by antibiotics if treated in the early stages. If left untreated, they can do very serious harm. Chlamydia and gonorrhea, for instance, can cause a severe infection that makes a woman unable to have children.

Because STDs can be so dangerous if not treated, a person who might have an STD should see a doctor. Signs of infection include burning, itching, or sores on the sexual organs. One way to avoid catching an STD is by using latex condoms.

Many people are embarrassed to talk to a doctor about STDs, but doctors are used to talking about private matters. Good doctors treat their patients with respect. Doctors are also required to keep medical information private. Being a little embarrassed is better than having to worry about STDs.

5. The main idea of the passage is that
   (1) people shouldn't get STDs
   (2) doctors are used to talking privately
   (3) people with an STD should see a doctor
   (4) many people are embarrassed by STDs
   (5) STDs cannot be cured

6. Many sexually transmitted diseases can be cured by
   (1) taking vitamins
   (2) waiting for them to go away
   (3) taking over-the-counter drugs
   (4) drinking plenty of fluids
   (5) taking antibiotics

Questions 7 and 8 are based on the following graph.

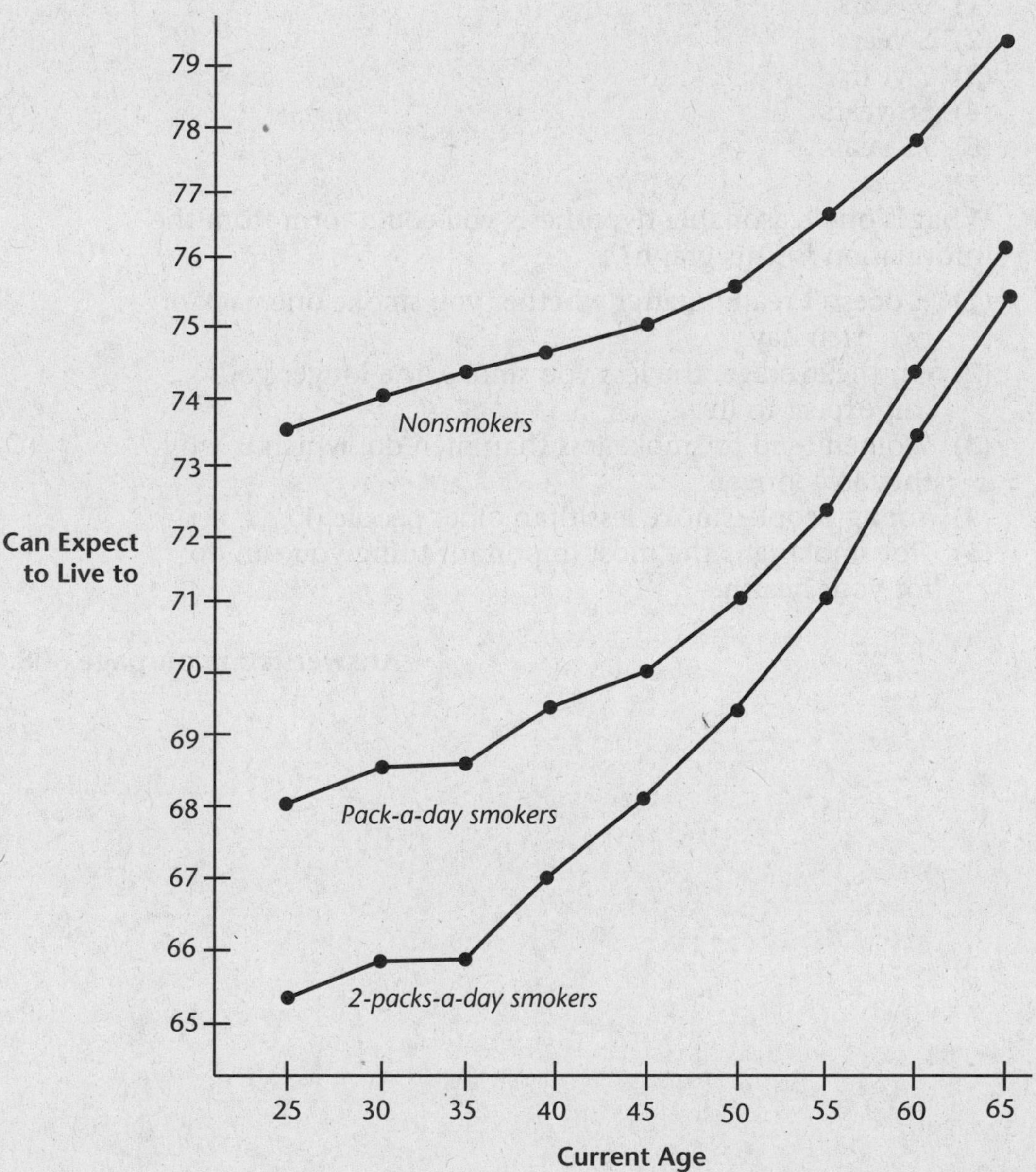

7. An average 45-year-old nonsmoker can expect to live about how many years longer than an average 45-year-old who smokes two packs a day?
   (1) 2 years
   (2) 5 years
   (3) 7 years
   (4) 68 years
   (5) 75 years

8. What is one reasonable hypothesis you could form from the information in this graph?
   (1) It doesn't really matter whether you smoke one pack or two each day.
   (2) On the average, the less you smoke, the longer you can expect to live.
   (3) Women tend to smoke less than men do, which is why they live longer.
   (4) Young people smoke less than older people do.
   (5) Not smoking is the most important thing you can do for your health.

Answers start on page 508.

4 PHYSICS

READING SKILL: ANALYZING IDEAS

One main purpose of education is to make your life easier. The more you know about the world you live in, the better you can handle decisions and problems. The more you know about reading, the easier it will be to do many ordinary things. You will be able to fill out job applications, read instructions, and understand articles in the newspaper. The reading skills covered here will help you pass tests and serve you in other ways.

SEQUENCE

In science it is important to know when something happened. The veterinarian (animal doctor) wants to know when your dog got sick—before or after eating the new food? Many questions on tests ask when something happened. Words like *first, then, next, later, before,* and *after* can give you clues about the ***sequence*** (time order) of events. Groups of words, like *in the meantime* and *during that week,* can also give you clues about time.

Look at these examples:

Before he did the experiment, he got all his equipment together.
Children learn to crawl **first; after that** they learn to talk.
The doctor will see you **next, after** Mrs. Jones.

Notice that the thing that happens first is not always written first in the sentence. You must use the "time" words to determine the sequence.

Sequence Tip

Here is a list of some words that show time order.

first	before	then	afterward
second	after	finally	in the meantime
third	next	later	today

▶ Now read these examples. Underline the time words in the sentences and answer the questions.

1. Louis Pasteur developed a rabies vaccine after he did his famous work on bacteria.

   Which did he work on first, the bacteria or the rabies vaccine?

   ____

In this sentence, *after* is the time-word clue. It tells you that the bacteria work came first, and the vaccine came after that.

2. Before Pasteur's vaccine, a person bitten by a rabid animal was almost sure to die.

   Did more people die of rabies before or after Pasteur's vaccine was developed?

   ____

Before is the time clue here. It tells you that many people died before the vaccine was invented.

Now try your sequence skills on this paragraph. As you read this passage, underline the time words and answer the questions that follow.

> A monarch butterfly, like most insects, goes through four different stages during its life. First, it is only an egg laid on a milkweed plant. Then the egg hatches into a caterpillar, also called a ***larva***. After it grows to its full size, the caterpillar hangs from a twig and splits open its skin. The third stage, called a ***pupa***, emerges. Next, a hard skin forms to cover and protect the pupa. Inside this hard skin, the insect's body parts are slowly changing. Finally, the pupa splits. Out comes an adult butterfly with beautiful orange and black wings. About an hour later, the wings are dry. Then the butterfly flies away.

1. What are the two names for the second stage?

   ________________________ and ________________________

2. What does the caterpillar do before it splits its skin?

   ____

3. What happens to the insect after it forms a pupa? ________________

4. What is the last stage? ________________________________

Now check your answers. You should have underlined these time words in the paragraph: *during, First, Then, After, third, Next, slowly, Finally, About an hour later, Then.* Here are the answers to the four questions above:

1. caterpillar and larva
2. It hangs from a twig.
3. A hard skin develops, and its body parts change.
4. the adult butterfly

EXERCISE 1: SEQUENCING

Directions: Read the following passage. Then order the list of events from earliest to latest by numbering them from 1 to 4. If you want to, underline the time-word clues as you read.

Sir Isaac Newton is known today as the Father of Modern Physics. He is best known for his theory of gravitation. As a boy, he was more interested in building mechanical things than in studying. He was considered a poor student. At fourteen, he had to leave school to help his mother manage the farm. But later, he went back to school. He graduated from Trinity College, Cambridge University in 1665.

The same year, Newton was sitting in his backyard drinking tea. He saw an apple fall from a tree. He said that this gave him the idea of ***gravity***, the idea that all objects in the universe pull toward each other. Objects that are close together pull harder than objects that are far apart. Objects that are heavier pull harder than light objects.

Newton did some of his work on gravitation in 1665 and 1666, but he was not satisfied with it and put it away. Over twenty years later, after he was already a professor and a well-known scientist, a friend persuaded him to publish his theory. After it was published, he received many honors.

_____ **a.** Newton published his theory of gravitation.

_____ **b.** Newton dropped out of school.

_____ **c.** Newton started work on his theory of gravitation.

_____ **d.** Newton became a professor.

Answers start on page 509.

Using Your Head

Sometimes there are no word clues to tell you the sequence of events. But your own common sense can often tell you which event probably came first. Which of these two events happened first?

a. Many children were paralyzed or killed by polio.
b. Jonas Salk discovered a vaccine against polio.

If you said **a** came before **b**, you used good logic. Before the polio vaccine was discovered, many children caught the disease.

▶ Now see if you can put these three statements in logical order.

a. Mr. Jones's flowers are growing well.
b. Mr. Jones sees that his flowers are wilting.
c. Mr. Jones waters his garden.

The logical order is *b, c, a.* First Mr. Jones notices that his flowers are wilting, then he waters them, and then they grow well.

EXERCISE 2: LOGICAL SEQUENCE

Directions: List these groups of events in logical order.

1. **a.** Steam locomotives pulled the first trains.
   b. The steam engine was invented.

   Logical order: ________, ________

2. **a.** Benjamin Franklin discovered that lightning is a form of electricity.
   b. People believed that lightning was a weapon of the gods.
   c. Franklin invented lightning rods to keep buildings safe.

   Logical order: ________, ________, ________

Answers start on page 509.

CAUSE AND EFFECT

What causes heart attacks? Why does gold conduct electricity so well? What happens if a person is exposed to radioactive fallout? Science is concerned with many questions like these, questions about cause and effect.

Why Did It Happen?

A ***cause*** is whatever makes something happen. An ***effect*** is the thing that happens because of the cause. Sometimes there will be words like *because, since,* or *therefore* to give you a clue. Other times you must use your own logic to discover the cause and effect.

▶ Try writing a possible cause for the given effect.

Cause: ______________________________

Effect: Many drivers buy radar detectors.

There can be more than one possible cause for an event. You could have said that *police started to use radar to catch speeders* or that *radar detectors were advertised in many magazines.*

▶ Now try these two:

Cause: Birth control methods were invented.

Effect: ______________________________

Cause: ______________________________

Effect: May Chen's garden grew its best crop of lettuce ever.

Often a single cause will have more than one effect. For instance, say that Lester got up late one morning. Since he got up late, he missed the bus, forgot to pack his lunch, and had a headache all morning. Getting up late caused three separate effects. The invention of birth control methods might have led to lower growth rates, smaller families, and other effects.

A single effect can also have several causes. A great scientific discovery may be the result of one scientist's curiosity, another scientist's lucky accident, and a conference that brought the two scientists together. Good weather, the use of fertilizers, and careful weeding are some of the causes that could have led to May's bumper crop of lettuce.

Cause-and-Effect Tip

As you read, look for cause-and-effect clue words like *because, since, therefore,* and *as a result of.*

EXERCISE 3: CAUSES AND EFFECTS

Directions: Read each paragraph. Identify the causes and effects by filling them in when called for.

Uranium ore must be refined and purified before it can be used in atomic power plants. The pure uranium is shipped to fuel fabrication plants. There it is put into fuel rods that fit into the cores of atomic power reactors. In the power plant, a chain reaction, which is a series of tiny atomic explosions, is kept under careful control. If the chain reaction goes very fast, the whole plant could blow up. If the reaction is slowed down too much, it won't make enough heat.

1. **Cause:** ________________________________

   Effect: The power plant would blow up.

2. **Cause:** The chain reaction goes too slowly.

   Effect: ________________________________

The heat from the chain reaction is used to boil water. The steam that is formed is used to turn giant generators, which make electricity.

3. **Cause:** The chain reaction makes heat.

   Effect: ________________________________

4. **Cause:** ________________________________

   Effect: Electricity is made.

Answers start on page 509.

Science or Superstition?

A time-order relationship is not the same as a cause-effect relationship. Even if one event happens before another, the first event does not necessarily *cause* the second. This kind of confusion is what causes superstitions like these.

I saw a black cat just before I had a bad accident. The black cat must have caused my accident.

I wore my navy suit to the job interview, and I got the job. My navy suit must be lucky.

▶ For practice, read these sentences. Circle those that probably show a true cause-effect relationship.

1. It was minus 25°F last night; now my car won't start.
2. John forgot his vitamins yesterday; now he has a cold.
3. John's sister had a cold last week; now John has a cold.
4. Helen didn't wear her rubber boots; then she slipped and fell on the ice.

Did you circle numbers *1, 3,* and *4?* These are probably true cause-effect relationships. Number *2* is simply in time order: John had to catch his cold from someone else, not just from forgetting his vitamins one day.

EXERCISE 4: FINDING CAUSES AND EFFECTS

Directions: Read the passage and circle the best answer to each question.

Niels Bohr was a Danish scientist who originated the first practical theory about the structure of the atom. His father had been a professor, so when Niels was a child, many people had come to the house to discuss the latest scientific discoveries. When he was older, Bohr went to the University of Copenhagen and earned a doctoral degree in physics.

After he developed his theory of atomic structure, Bohr became very famous. When the Nazis invaded Denmark during World War II, they wanted Bohr to work for them in atomic research. Bohr refused, so they tried to arrest him. He escaped to Sweden and returned to his home only after the war was over.

1. One reason Bohr became interested in science was that
   (1) he was born in Denmark
   (2) he wanted to become famous
   (3) his father was a professor
   (4) he studied physics at a university
   (5) he hated the Germans

2. One effect of his scientific fame was that
   (1) the Nazis invaded Denmark
   (2) the Nazis wanted him to work for them
   (3) he refused to work for the Nazis
   (4) he hated the Nazis
   (5) he went home after the war

Answers start on page 509.

MAKING INFERENCES

Sometimes writers don't directly tell you everything they mean. Instead, they ***imply*** (hint at) some things by the way they write. Here is an example:

> As the sun got higher, Juan wished he had brought a bigger canteen.

Consider all that is implied by this one sentence. Juan is hot and thirsty. He is in a place where water is not easy to get. Also, either he has run out of water or he is worried about running out. None of these things is said directly, but you can tell that they are true.

When a writer implies things without saying them right out, you have to ***infer*** (figure out) what he or she is trying to say. The skill of figuring out what a writer is implying is called ***making inferences***. You could say that you are "reading between the lines." Let's look at another example.

> The study showed that the medicine was perfectly safe. Of course, the study was done by the company that sells the medicine.

▶ What do you think this writer is implying? ______________________

____

The writer is implying that the company *might have rigged the results of the study* so that it could keep selling its medicine.

EXERCISE 5: MAKING INFERENCES

Directions: Read the following statements. Then write your inferences on the lines provided. Notice that some statements imply more than one thing.

1. Cancer of the mouth is increasing among young males, the group most likely to use smokeless tobacco.

   What does the writer imply about smokeless tobacco?

   ____

2. The new easy-care fabrics that followed the invention of polyester fiber have really changed the clothing industry.

   a. What does the writer imply that the new fabrics are made of?

   ____

   b. What does the writer imply about the fabrics before polyester?

   ____

3. The typical American still eats a diet high in fat and sugar, even though heart disease is the number one killer in America.

   a. What does the writer imply about fat and sugar?

   ____

   b. What does the writer imply that a person should do to avoid heart attacks?

   ____

Answers start on page 509.

SCIENCE TOPIC: EVERYDAY PHYSICS

The universe is made up of matter and energy. ***Matter*** is anything that takes up space. A brick, a person, water, the Sun, and even air are all matter. They all take up space.

Energy is anything that can do work. Common forms of energy are electricity, gravity, heat, and light. ***Physics*** is the branch of science that studies matter and energy and the relationship between them.

SIMPLE MACHINES

When you think of machines, you probably think of things like lawn mowers, electric drills, and bulldozers. These machines get power from gasoline and electricity. But some machines, like crowbars and wheelbarrows, use human muscle power. These are called ***simple machines***.

Work

A ***machine*** is anything that helps you do work. Scientists say that ***work*** is using force to move something. (***Force*** is the amount of push needed to move something.) To figure how much work is done, you multiply the force applied by the distance moved. For example, if you lift a 20-pound box 5 feet, you have just done 100 ***foot-pounds*** of work. You multiply the force needed to move the box (20 pounds) by the distance it is moved upward (5 feet).

Now figure the amount of work done in each of these cases. Your answers will be in foot-pounds.

1. A 10-pound fish is lifted 3 feet into a boat. ____________________

The force is 10 pounds; the distance is 3 feet. 10 x 3 = 30 foot-pounds of work done.

2. A 200-pound man climbs an 8-foot ladder. ____________________

The force is 200 pounds; the distance is 8 feet. 200 x 8 = 1,600 foot-pounds of work done.

Often a person wants to do something that requires more force than his or her muscles can give. Simple machines can help. Like most simple machines, the lever trades force for distance. If you use less force, you must move the end of the lever over a longer distance.

Inclined Planes

An ***inclined plane*** (a slope) is another type of simple machine. As with all simple machines, **the work you put into it must equal the work that is done.** Both the work you put in and the work done are figured by multiplying the force times the distance, as shown in this equation:

WORK PUT IN		WORK DONE
F x D	=	F x D

For example, imagine that you want to load your 300-pound motorcycle onto the tailgate of your pickup, which is two feet off the ground. You can't just lift 300 pounds, so you use a ramp, a type of inclined plane.

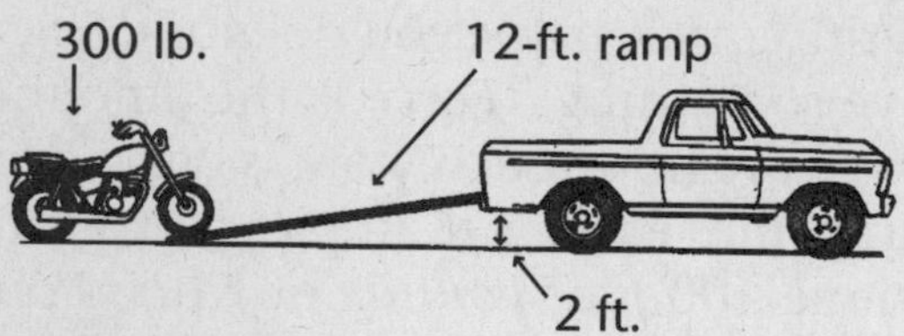

The force is 300 lb., the weight of the motorcycle. The distance is 2 ft., the vertical distance (distance straight upward) that the motorcycle must be moved. Therefore, the ***work that must be done*** is 300 lb. × 2 ft., which equals 600 foot-pounds.

Since the work put in must equal the work done, you know that the ***work put in*** will also equal 600 foot-pounds. You would use an equation like this:

WORK PUT IN		WORK DONE
force x 12 ft.	=	600 foot-pounds

Your ramp is 12 feet long, so 12 feet is the distance. Since you *multiplied*, to find the work done, you *divide* the amount of force needed. You will only need to use a force of 600 ÷ 12, which is 50 pounds, to push the motorcycle up the ramp.

Now suppose that you had a motorcycle that weighed 450 pounds. How much force would you need to push it up the same ramp? The equation would look like this:

WORK PUT IN		WORK DONE
force x 12 ft.	=	450 lb. x 2 ft.

The work to be done is 450 lb. x 2 ft. = 900 foot-pounds. You get this equation:

WORK PUT IN		WORK DONE
force x 12 ft.	=	900 foot-pounds

Dividing 12 into 900, you discover that you will have to use 75 pounds of force.

EXERCISE 6: SIMPLE MACHINES

Directions: Fill in the blanks with the appropriate words.

1. Crowbars, wheelbarrows, and inclined planes are all types of ____________ ____________ (a). With each of these, the work you put in must equal the ____________ ____________ (b). Work is using ____________ (c) to move something. Force is the ____________ ____________ ____________ (d) needed to move something. When you figure how much work is done, your answers are in units of measurement called ____________ (e).

Directions: A hill is also a type of inclined plane. Look at this diagram to answer questions 2 and 3.

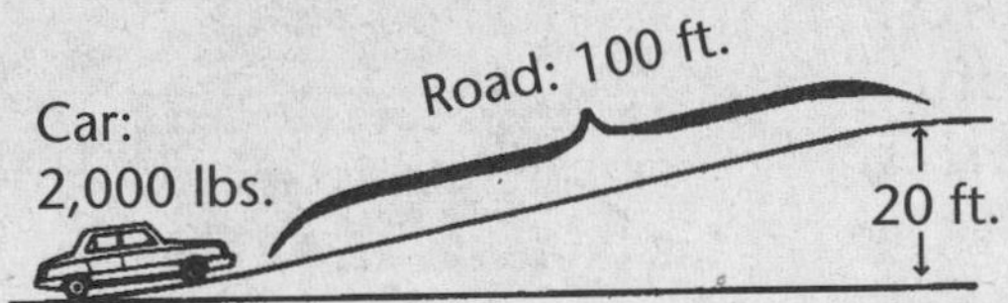

2. You drive your 2,000-pound car up a road to the top of a 20-foot hill. How much work is done?
   (1) 20 foot-pounds
   (2) 2,000 foot-pounds
   (3) 4,000 foot-pounds
   (4) 40,000 foot-pounds
   (5) 200,000 foot-pounds

Answers start on page 509.

WHAT IS A COMPUTER?

Computers are only machines. They can do only what people tell them to do. No computer can do as much as the "computer" you have in your head, your brain. But computers can do arithmetic and other things much faster than people can. They can store a great deal of information and recall it perfectly. Computers have thousands of uses in our society.

Computers control the hookups in the phone system. They do all the accounting for banks and many businesses. Many schools use computers for teaching. Writers and secretaries use word processors. Even the games in video arcades are run by small computers.

Parts of a Computer

A computer must have parts for input, processing, and output. ***Input*** is how information is given to a computer. Many computers have a keyboard, like a typewriter keyboard, for inputting information. Computers also get information from disks and tapes. Some computers read paper cards or tapes with specially coded holes punched in them. Computers in grocery stores use a light device to read a coded group of lines on each can or box of food. Computers that are hooked up to ***modems*** can send and receive information over telephone lines, using a code of very fast beeps.

Output is how the computer gives out information. Many computers have a screen, or ***monitor,*** that shows the output in words or graphics (pictures). Computers are often connected to ***printers***, which print out the information. Computers can also output information onto disks, tapes, and cards and over telephone lines.

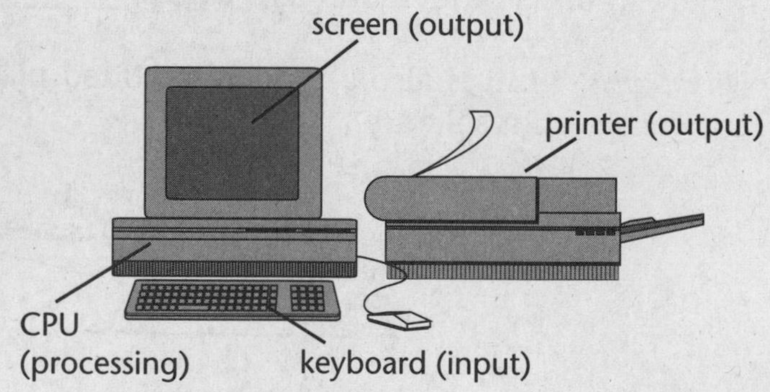

Processing Information

The main work of the computer is done in the ***central processing unit*** (CPU). The CPU is like the computer's brain. It is the part of the computer that makes decisions, does the figuring, and controls the input and output parts. Attached to the CPU are the arithmetic unit, which does the mathematical calculations, and the computer ***memory***. The memory holds the ***program*** (set of instructions) and information needed to do a particular task. You can store information on the computer's hard drive or by outputting it onto floppy disks or other storage media.

Personal computers can help you keep track of your budget, write letters, or run a small business. They can help your kids do their homework, learn new things, or play games. Computers are tools that can make your life easier and fuller.

EXERCISE 7: COMPUTERS

Directions: List the information required.

1. List four ways that computers are used in our society.

____

____

____

____

2. List five input devices for computers.

____

____

3. List five output devices for computers.

____

____

Answers start on page 509.

ELECTRICITY

Imagine a world with no telephones, no refrigerators, no TVs, and no washing machines. A little over a hundred years ago, this was the world that everyone lived in. Then, in 1884, Thomas Edison built the first electric power station in New York City. Now power companies supply electricity to almost every part of the country.

Electricity is the movement of electrons. The atoms of some substances do not hold on to their electrons very tightly. Friction, magnetism, heat, or an outside source can start the electrons flowing from one atom to another. This flow is called an electric ***current***.

Substances that electricity flows through easily are called ***conductors***. Gold, copper, steel, and silver are examples of good conductors. Materials that electricity does not flow through well are called ***insulators***. Rubber, glass, plastic, and most fabrics are insulators. The wires that carry electricity in your home are made of copper or aluminum. They are surrounded by insulation made of plastic, rubber, or fabric.

TYPICAL HOUSEHOLD CIRCUIT

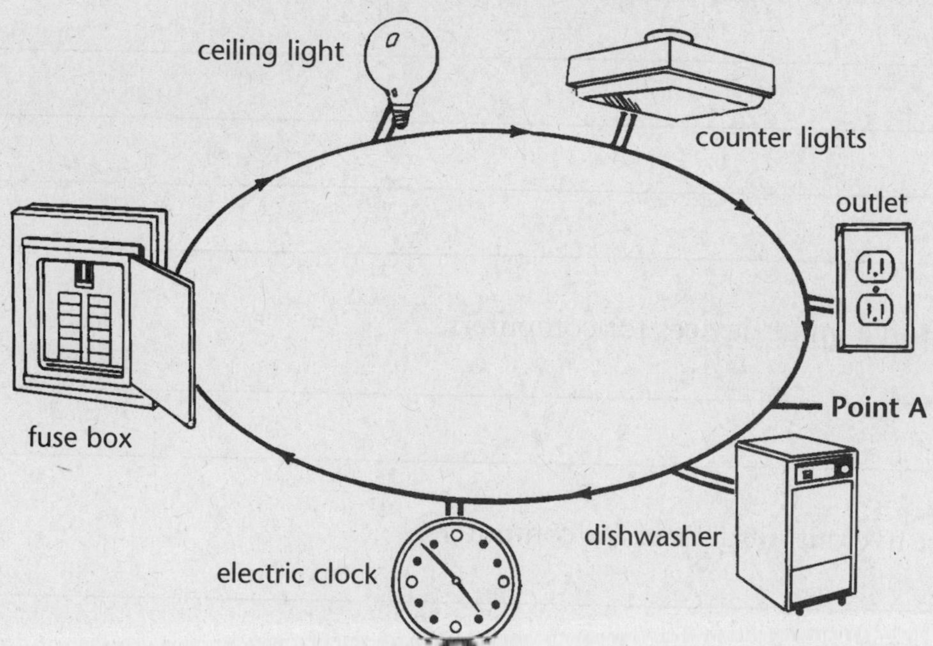

Electricity always flows in a ***circuit***. A circuit must be a complete circle or electricity will not flow. For example, there is electric wiring to each side of the wall sockets in your house. When you plug in and turn on a toaster, the metal prongs of the plug complete the circuit. Electricity flows through the toaster. A light switch works the same way. When you turn it on, you complete the circuit and allow electricity to flow through the light.

A ***short circuit*** happens when the insulation on a wire wears through or when there is a loose connection or break somewhere. The wire touches some other conductor, and the electricity flows along a path different from the one it was supposed to take. An electric current in the wrong place can cause something to get very hot and may even start a fire. An electric current flowing through you can burn you badly or kill you.

Every circuit in a house has a ***fuse***. A fuse is a small strip of metal designed to burn out if too much electricity flows through it. If you have a short circuit, or you try to use too many appliances on one circuit, the fuse will blow. The circuit will be broken. No more electricity will flow in that circuit until you find the problem and replace the fuse. More modern electrical systems have ***circuit breakers*** instead of fuses. A circuit breaker is a switch that turns off whenever too much electricity goes through it.

Electricity is useful, but it can also be dangerous. Electrical cords should be checked regularly for breaks or worn spots. Worn cords or bad plugs on appliances should be replaced. A blown fuse must never be replaced with a penny or another piece of metal. No electrical appliance, even a radio, should be used near water. If it touches the water at the same time you do, you could get a deadly shock, because water is a very good conductor. Children must not be allowed to play with appliances or electric plugs. If there is a young child in the house, all unused outlets should be covered with plastic outlet blanks.

EXERCISE 8: ELECTRICITY

Directions: Look at the sample circuit diagram on page 448. Beginning at the fuse box and following the arrows, number these in order according to the electrical flow. Then, in the spaces below, write down the order in which the electricity flows from object to object. Use the items from the list at right.

1. ______________________
2. ______________________
3. ______________________
4. ______________________
5. ______________________

outlet
counter lights
ceiling light
dishwasher
electric clock

Directions: Circle the number of the best answer.

6. In the diagram on page 448, what would happen if there was a break in the wire at Point A?
   (1) The ceiling light, counter lights, and outlet would still work, but the dishwasher and clock wouldn't.
   (2) The lights would still work because they draw so little electricity.
   (3) The dishwasher and the electric clock would work, but nothing else would.
   (4) Everything would still work.
   (5) Nothing would work.

Answers start on page 509.

NUCLEAR POWER

Like every new discovery, nuclear power has advantages and disadvantages. Here are two selections discussing some of the pros and cons of nuclear power.

Speaker A

America needs nuclear power. Fossil fuels such as coal, natural gas, and oil are becoming more expensive and harder to find. Air pollution laws have also made fossil fuels expensive to burn, due to the multimillion-dollar antipollution devices now required. In addition, depending on fossil fuels means depending on foreign countries for much of our energy needs. This limits our political options and ruins our balance of trade.

Radical environmental groups say that nuclear energy is too dangerous to use. They are ignoring the excellent safety record of nuclear power in the United States. American nuclear power plants are now built with so many safeguards that it is virtually impossible for a serious accident to occur.

In the long run, nuclear power will save the consumer money. The small amount of fuel needed to run a nuclear power plant is much less expensive than the barrels of oil or tons of coal needed to fuel regular power plants. The environment will benefit, too, since nuclear power plants release no acid smoke or filthy discharge.

Speaker B

Nuclear power is just not worth the risks involved. These risks are in three main areas.

First, there is the direct risk of accident. Every year, accidents happen at nuclear power plants, and "small" amounts of radiation leak out. The accident at Chernobyl showed how damaging a major accident can be. Chances are that sooner or later there will be an accident in the United States that cannot be stopped.

Second, there is the constant risk of pollution. Nuclear power plants release large amounts of heated water from their cooling devices. This water increases the growth of algae, killing off some types of fish. This water also carries slight amounts of radiation. The authorities assure us that these amounts are too small to be dangerous, but how can they be sure? The solid nuclear waste produced by nuclear power plants is especially polluting. If just small amounts of it got into our water system, many people would die. No one has yet solved the problem of what to do with these wastes.

Third, there is the danger of terrorist attacks and sabotage. When uranium is being shipped all over the country for power plants, it would be fairly easy for a small group of terrorists to steal enough for a bomb. Nuclear power plants can't have tight enough security to stop a terrorist from getting in and maybe causing a major "accident."

EXERCISE 9: NUCLEAR POWER

Directions: Read the following statements. Put an *A* in front of the ones that you think Speaker A would agree with. Put a *B* in front of the statements that Speaker B would agree with.

______ **1.** Security checks at nuclear power plants should be tougher.

______ **2.** Scientists don't know enough about the effects of small doses of radiation.

______ **3.** Some people exaggerate the dangers of pollution.

Directions: Circle the number of the best answer.

4. Which of these is a fact from selection B?

(1) Other nations are going full speed ahead to develop nuclear power.
(2) It would be fairly easy for a small group of terrorists to steal enough uranium for a bomb.
(3) America needs nuclear power.
(4) The United States would be better off developing solar and wind power and forgetting about nuclear power.
(5) Every year accidents happen at nuclear power plants.

5. Which of these is most likely to be Speaker A?

(1) a doctor studying the effects of radiation
(2) a public relations person for a utility company
(3) a member of an environmental protection group
(4) a scientist doing research on solar energy
(5) a engineer working for an oil company

Answers start on page 509.

LIGHT AND SOUND

Light

Light is the energy that allows us to see. Scientists say that light travels in waves, but they aren't really sure what this means. They do know it travels very fast, about 186,000 miles per second. That means light can travel to the moon and back in less than three seconds. Nothing else in the universe is that fast.

The Sun is our main source of light. Only a little of the Sun's light reaches Earth. The white light we get from the Sun is really a mixture of all different colors of light. Light that goes through a specially shaped piece of glass called a ***prism*** will split into all its different colors. The same thing happens when drops of water in the air split sunlight to make a rainbow.

When light strikes an object, three different things can happen. Light either goes through the object, or it is absorbed or reflected. If the light goes easily through it, we say the object is ***transparent***. Glass, water, and air are mostly transparent. Light rays bend a little when they go through a transparent object. This is how eyeglasses work. The lenses bend the light rays to focus them correctly for your eyes.

Light that doesn't pass through an object is either ***reflected*** (bounced back) or ***absorbed***. Most things reflect some colors of light while absorbing others. The reflected colors are what we see. For example, a blue sofa reflects blue light but absorbs all the other colors. The darker something is, the more light it absorbs. If something absorbs all light, it looks black.

Sound

Sound is caused by the vibration of molecules. For example, someone plucks a guitar string, making it ***vibrate*** (move quickly back and forth). The vibrating string hits the molecules of air around it, making them vibrate. These molecules hit other molecules, until eventually the vibration comes to your ear. The vibrating air moves against your eardrum, making it vibrate too. A nerve carries a message about the vibration from your eardrum to your brain, and you say, "Isn't that great music?"

Sound also moves as a wave, but it moves much more slowly than light. Sound only travels about a fifth of a mile per second in ordinary air. If there is a thunderstorm a distance away from you, you will see the lightning before you hear the thunder. The farther apart the light and sound seem, the farther away the storm is. Sound waves are of different lengths. Shorter sound waves make higher tones, while longer waves make lower tones. Mixed-up combinations of waves just sound like noise. Unlike light, sound can travel best through solid objects. This is because the molecules are closer together in solid things.

EXERCISE 10: LIGHT AND SOUND

Directions: Circle *T* if the sentence is true; *F* if it is false.

T F **1.** Light and sound both travel as waves.

T F **2.** Sound travels faster than light.

T F **3.** White light has no colors in it.

T F **4.** A lens is used to bend light.

T F **5.** You hear sound when your eardrum vibrates.

T F **6.** Sound travels best through air.

Answers start on page 509.

EXERCISE 11: CHAPTER REVIEW

Directions: Read each passage and study each diagram carefully. Then circle the number of the one best answer to each question.

As you know, a lever is one type of simple machine. A basic lever is just a straight object, like a board, balanced on top of a pivot point. Each side of the board can be thought of as an "arm." The pivot point is called the *fulcrum.* A seesaw is a good example of this type of lever.

To check whether or not a lever is balanced, we can use the following equation:

LEFT ARM		RIGHT ARM
Force x Distance	=	Force x Distance

When this equation is used with levers, the *force* is equal to the weight on each arm. We measure the *distance* from each weight to the fulcrum. Look at this example of a level in balance:

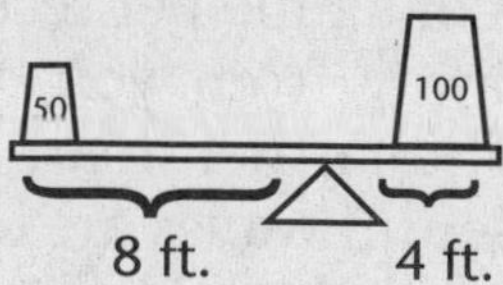

Using the equation above, the numbers for this level look like this:

LEFT ARM		RIGHT ARM
50 lb. x 8 ft.	=	100 lb. x 4 ft.

OR

400 = 400 [balanced]

Question 1 is based on the following diagrams.

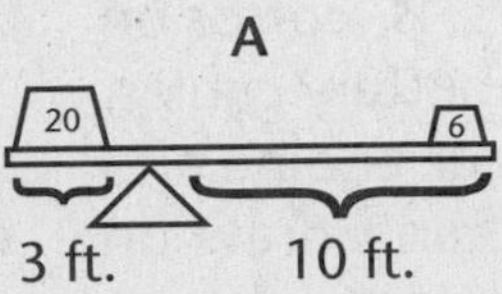

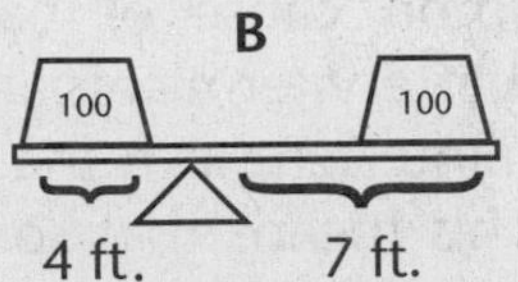

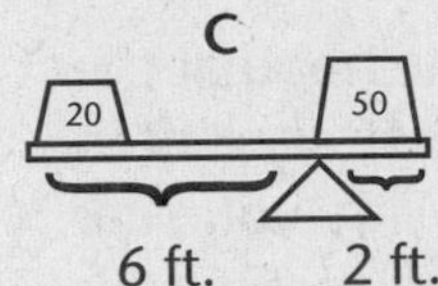

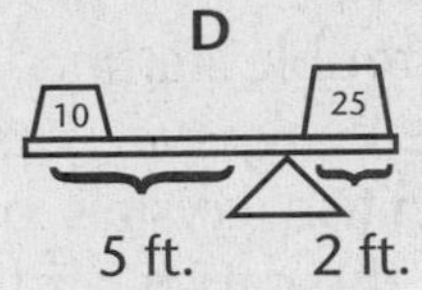

1. Which of the levers above are balanced?
   (1) Lever A only
   (2) Lever B only
   (3) Levers B and C only
   (4) Levers A and D only
   (5) Levers B and D only

2. Look at this drawing of a balanced lever. What will happen if a one-pound weight is added to side A?
   (1) The lever will stay balanced because there are two weights on each side.
   (2) Side B will go down because the weight on top is heavier.
   (3) Side A will go up because it is heavier.
   (4) Neither end will go up or down because one pound isn't enough to make any difference.
   (5) Side A will go down because it is heavier.

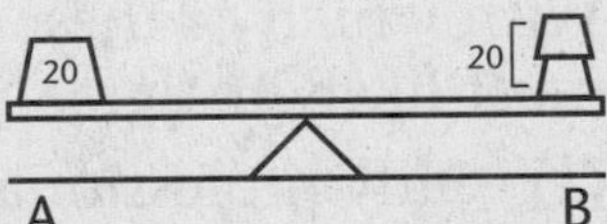

Questions 3 and 4 are based on the following passage.

One common cause of bad starting in cars is corrosion between the battery terminals and the ends of the battery cables. Corrosion can interfere with the circuit between your engine and the battery. This means that sometimes your car can't draw on the battery for starting power, and other times the battery can't recharge correctly.

If you have trouble starting your car, look under the hood at the place where the heavy wire cables connect to your battery. Often you will see whitish crystals on the connections. With your car turned off, take the cables off the terminals. Scrape all the crystals and the dark corrosion off the terminals and the ends of the cables. Make sure there is bright metal on both sides of the connection. This will allow for the best flow of electricity. Replace the cables and try your car again; it may surprise you by starting easily.

3. When should you check your battery terminals for corrosion?

(1) every five years
(2) when your car is using too much gas
(3) whenever you buy a new battery
(4) in the winter
(5) when your car isn't starting well

4. With which of these statements would the author of this passage be most likely to agree?

(1) Only professional mechanics should work on cars.
(2) Most people don't understand written directions.
(3) Most car problems are very difficult to fix.
(4) Most people can learn to do simple car repairs.
(5) Men are better at fixing cars than women.

Questions 5 and 6 are based on the following passage.

Some people get some of their heat directly from the Sun in a process called solar heating. When sunlight hits an object, some of the light rays are absorbed and changed into heat. This is why the Sun feels so good on your back on a chilly day. Some of the Sun's rays are being absorbed by your body and warming you up.

The darker the object, the more light it will absorb and change to heat. The simplest kind of solar heating uses this principle. Large windows are placed on the south side of the house (where the most sunlight comes in). The floors under those windows are covered in dark carpeting, which absorbs the sunlight and releases heat into the room. This type of solar heating, using no special machines or instruments, is called passive solar heating.

Active solar heating systems use special heat collectors lined with black material. Light is often concentrated in these collectors by reflecting metal foil or mirrors. Small electric motors are used to pass air or liquid over the heated metal. This heated air or liquid is then pumped into the heating system of the house.

5. Solar heat collectors use black material because

(1) black is cheaper than colors
(2) black material reflects light best
(3) black material absorbs light best
(4) it is traditional to use black
(5) black cannot be stained by the liquid used

6. What is one big problem with solar heat?

(1) Solar heat collectors are hard to find.
(2) Solar heat can be collected only when the Sun shines.
(3) Most people don't like dark carpeting.
(4) Solar heat is less polluting than other heat sources.
(5) Large windows are expensive to install.

Questions 7 and 8 are based on the following passage and chart.

Sound travels as waves. The stronger the wave, the more pressure it puts on our eardrums and the louder the sound seems to us.

The strength of a sound wave is measured in decibels (dB). On the decibel scale, each increase of 10 units means a sound 10 *times* louder. Therefore, a noise rated at 80 decibels is 10 times louder than one at 70 dB. A noise at 90 dB is 100 times louder than one at 70 dB. Repeated exposure to levels of 90 to 115 dB can cause permanent hearing loss. Lower levels of continuous noise may not damage hearing, but they add to stress and may contribute to stress-related diseases.

Here is a chart showing the decibel ratings for some common noises. Use the chart to answer the following questions.

Sound	Rating
Ordinary conversation	60 dB
Busy street traffic	75 dB
Office adding machines	80 dB
20 feet from a subway train	90 dB
Can manufacturing plant	100 dB
Newspaper printing press	102 to 108 dB
Caterpillar tractor, idling	104 dB
Circular saw	105 to 116 dB
Drills, shovels, trucks operating	108 dB

7. The sound of office adding machines is how many times the sound of ordinary conversation?
   (1) 2
   (2) 10
   (3) 20
   (4) 100
   (5) 200

8. Which of these workers is *most likely* to have job-related hearing loss?
   (1) a heavy-equipment operator
   (2) a worker in a can factory
   (3) a teacher
   (4) a traffic cop
   (5) a secretary

Answers start on page 510.

5 CHEMISTRY

Chemistry is the branch of science that studies matter and how matter changes. ***Matter*** is anything that occupies space and has ***mass*** (bulk). Matter can be a solid, a liquid, a gas, or ***plasma*** (a gas that makes up the Sun and other stars). You'll learn later in this chapter about how matter is made up and how it is arranged. You'll also learn how *elements* (ingredients) combine chemically to form *compounds*.

READING SKILL: UNDERSTANDING SYMBOLS AND FORMULAS

ATOMS AND MOLECULES

All matter is made up of billions of tiny particles called ***atoms***. They are too small to be seen, even with the most powerful microscope. Even so, scientists have learned a lot about atoms by doing experiments.

Each atom is like a tiny sun surrounded by planets. In the center of the atom is the ***nucleus***. The nucleus is made up of ***protons***, which carry a positive electrical charge, and ***neutrons***, which are electrically neutral. ***Electrons*** orbit around the nucleus. They carry a negative electrical charge and move in levels called ***shells***. The drawing of an aluminum atom below shows these parts of an atom.

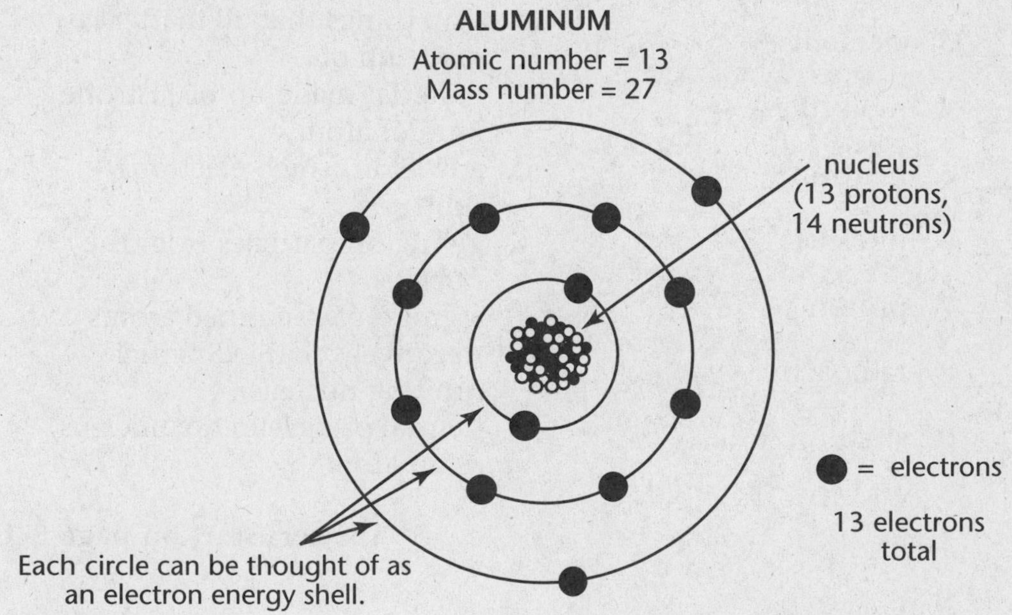

Scientists have found only a little over 100 different kinds of atoms. A material containing only one kind of atom is called an ***element***. Most things are made of more than one kind of atom. When two or more atoms combine, they form a group called a ***molecule***. For example, a molecule of water is made up of two hydrogen atoms and one oxygen atom. There are millions of different ways that the elements can combine, so there are millions of different substances in the universe.

Atomic Energy

The most powerful kind of energy in the universe is the energy that holds the nucleus of every atom together. This energy is called ***atomic energy***. Another name for it is ***nuclear energy***. When the nucleus of an atom is blown apart, an enormous amount of energy is released.

Some elements with many protons in the nucleus, like radium and uranium, lose particles from the nucleus all the time, not just when there is an atomic explosion. We call these elements ***radioactive***. Other elements may become radioactive if they have lots of extra neutrons. Radioactive substances are dangerous to us because the extra neutrons and protons they give off can enter our bodies and cause cancer and other illnesses.

EXERCISE 1: ATOMS AND MOLECULES

Directions: Match the words with their definitions.

_____ 1. atoms
_____ 2. electron
_____ 3. element
_____ 4. molecule
_____ 5. neutron
_____ 6. nucleus
_____ 7. proton
_____ 8. radioactive
_____ 9. shell

a. the center of an atom
b. positively charged particle in the nucleus
c. tiny things that all matter is made up of
d. material made up of just one kind of atom
e. a level in which electrons orbit
f. giving off particles from the nucleus
g. a group of combined atoms
h. negatively charged particle orbiting nucleus
i. neutral particle in the nucleus of an atom

Answers start on page 510.

HOW CHEMICALS COMBINE

Some chemicals combine easily with other chemicals. Other chemicals will combine only with certain special partners. A few chemicals won't combine with anything. Chemicals can combine in simple mixtures, in solutions, and in chemical compounds.

Simple Mixtures

The simplest way in which chemicals get together is in a ***mixture***. A mixture is formed when two or more things are simply mixed together. The materials in a simple mixture are not changed at all. The mixture itself may be uneven, with more of one material at the bottom or at the top.

A good example is a salad, which is a mixture of vegetables. All the vegetables are in the same salad bowl, but the tomatoes are still red, the lettuce is still green, and the peppers still taste sharp. None of the vegetables have changed; they have just been put together.

Solutions

A ***solution*** is a special type of mixture. It has two parts. The material that is dissolved is called a ***solute***. The material it dissolves in is called a ***solvent***. For example, when salt dissolves in water, the salt is the solute and the water is the solvent. The most familiar solutions are formed when solids dissolve in liquids, but you can have a solution using any two types of materials. Examples are a liquid combined with a liquid or a gas combined with a liquid.

A certain amount of solvent can only hold so much of any one solute. For instance, if you try to dissolve more and more salt in a glass of the water, it finally can hold no more. We say that the solution is ***saturated***. Any more salt that is added will just sink to the bottom of the glass; it will not go into solution.

A solution is different from a simple mixture in several ways. For one thing, you can't see any separation between the solute and the solvent. Another difference is that a solution is ***homogenous***, which means it is the same all the way through. Finally, a solution cannot be separated by ***filtration***. This means that both parts of the solution will stay together if you try to separate them by using a screen or pouring them through filter paper.

	SIMPLE MIXTURE Example: sugar & sand	SOLUTION Example: salt & water	COMPOUND Example: water (hydrogen & oxygen)
Can you see the separate parts?	Yes. You can easily see the separate bits of sugar and sand.	No. You can't see the particles of salt at all.	No. Water does not look like hydrogen and oxygen.
Is it homogenous?	No. You can see that in some parts of this mixture there is more sand, and in others there is more sugar.	Yes. The solution is the same all the way through.	Yes. The water is the same all the way through.
Can you separate it by sifting or filtering?	Yes. A fine sifter would let the sugar through while holding the coarser sand particles back.	No. The salt particles in solution would slip through even the finest filter paper along with the water.	No. You cannot separate water into the gases hydrogen and oxygen by sifting or filtering it.
Is the result a totally new substance?	No. The sugar and sand still look, taste, and feel like sugar and sand.	No. The water still looks the same, and even though you can't see the salt, you know it is still there because you can taste it.	Yes. Water is completely different from hydrogen and oxygen. You can see it and drink it, but you can't breathe it.

Compounds

A chemical ***compound*** is very different from a solution or an ordinary mixture. Obviously, the materials in a simple mixture like sugar and sand stay the same. In a saltwater solution, even though you can't see the salt, the taste tells you the salt is still there, basically unchanged. But when two or more materials combine chemically, they form something that can be totally different from the original materials.

For example, hydrogen and oxygen are both invisible gases in the air you breathe. When they combine chemically, they make water, a liquid you can easily see but certainly not breathe. Carbon is a black solid like coal in its pure form. It combines with hydrogen and oxygen to make sugar, something different from coal! Compounds are formed when atoms of two or more elements are bonded together into a single molecule.

EXERCISE 2: MIXTURES, SOLUTIONS, AND COMPOUNDS

Directions: Tell whether each of the following forms a compound, a solution, or a simple mixture by writing *C, S,* or *M* in the blanks.

______ **1.** popcorn and caramel making popcorn balls

______ **2.** carbon and oxygen making carbon dioxide gas

______ **3.** sugar stirred into hot coffee

______ **4.** different types of candies in a dish

______ **5.** oxygen and nitrogen gas making nitrate fertilizer

______ **6.** chocolate powder and hot milk making hot cocoa

Directions: Circle the best answer.

7. Chlorine is a poisonous gas. When chlorine gets together with sodium, it forms a white solid called *salt,* which people eat every day. From this information, you can tell that salt is a
   (1) simple mixture
   (2) poison
   (3) compound
   (4) solution
   (5) solvent

Answers start on page 510.

CHEMICAL FORMULAS

Chemical codes are written in the ordinary abbreviations used by chemists all over the world. Some chemicals have common names that we use every day—for example, water, bleach, alcohol, and cleaning fluid. All chemicals also have a scientific name, using the names of the elements as root words plus some prefixes and suffixes.

The chemical name tells you just what is in a compound. For example, calcium chloride is a compound of calcium and chlorine. Iron oxide is made of iron and oxygen. Sodium hydroxide is a combination of sodium, hydrogen, and oxygen. Notice that the suffix *-ide* is often added to the name of the last element in a compound. This suffix indicates a compound; nothing else has been added to it.

Two other common suffixes do indicate a change, though. The suffixes *-ite* and *-ate* both mean that oxygen has been added to the compound. For instance, hydrogen sulfate is a compound of hydrogen, sulfur, and oxygen. Calcium nitrite contains calcium, nitrogen, and oxygen.

Chemical Symbols and Formulas

To save time and energy, chemists usually use symbols for chemicals. Each of the elements has its own chemical symbol. These symbols are one or two letters taken from the name of the element in either English or some other language. If there are two letters, the first letter is the only one capitalized.

You certainly do not need to memorize the symbols for all of the elements, but there are a few very common ones that you should know. Some of these are listed below.

Name	Symbol
Hydrogen	H
Carbon	C
Nitrogen	N
Oxygen	O
Sodium	Na
Sulfur	S
Chlorine	Cl
Calcium	Ca
Iron	Fe

The chemical formula for every compound is written using the symbols of the elements in it. For instance, hydrogen chloride is written *HCl,* while sodium chloride is *NaCl.*

The chemical symbol for water is H_2O. The *H* and *O* tell you that water is made of hydrogen and oxygen, and the small *2* after the *H* shows that it takes two atoms of hydrogen to combine with one atom of oxygen to make a molecule of water. Whenever there is more than one atom of an element in a molecule, chemists show how many are needed by putting that small number after the symbol for the element. For example, $C_6H_{12}O_6$ is the chemical formula for a simple kind of sugar. This formula shows that it takes 6 carbon atoms, 12 hydrogen atoms, and 6 oxygen atoms to make one molecule of this sugar.

While the number of *atoms* is shown with a small number after the symbol for an element, the number of *molecules* is shown with a large-size number in front of all the elements. For example, two molecules of the simple sugar would be described this way: $2C_6H_{12}O_6$.

EXERCISE 3: CHEMICAL NAMES AND SYMBOLS

Directions: From the list below, write the correct symbol after each chemical name. Look back at the chart on page 464 if you need to.

CaO	$CaCl_2$	CO
HNO_2	H_2S	$NaSO_4$

1. calcium chloride __________
2. calcium oxide __________
3. hydrogen sulfide __________
4. sodium sulfate __________
5. carbon monoxide __________
6. hydrogen nitrite __________

Directions: Circle the best answer for this question.

7. Carbon tetrachloride is the chemical name for a common cleaning fluid. (*Tetra-* is a prefix meaning "four.") Which of these equations correctly describes one molecule of carbon tetrachloride?
   (1) CCl
   (2) $CaCl_2$
   (3) $4CO_2$
   (4) C_4Cl
   (5) CCl_4

Answers start on page 510.

SCIENCE TOPIC: EVERYDAY CHEMISTRY

Many of today's ***chemists*** are more concerned with discovering new combinations of chemicals that do not occur naturally. They use these chemicals to make new types of fabrics, plastics, and many other things. Other chemists are investigating the chemistry that goes on in living things. They are responsible for many new medicines and medical treatments.

ACIDS AND BASES

There are many applications of chemistry in daily life. Some of the most common uses of chemistry are in cooking and cleaning.

One common group of chemicals is called ***acids***. Many foods contain ingredients that are acids. Vinegar, used in pickling, is mainly acetic acid ($HC_2H_3O_2$). Citric acid ($HC_6H_7O_7$) is found in oranges, lemons, and grapefruits and is used as a preservative in many canned foods. Sour milk contains lactic acid ($HC_3H_5O_3$), and baking powder also contains a type of acid.

Acids are also used for cleaning. Vinegar and lemon juice are old standbys for cleaning glass or china. Boric acid (H_3BO_3) is used in eyewash, and sulfuric acid (H_2SO_4) is used to clean corroded metals.

From the examples above, you might guess that most acids have a sour taste. The chemical formula for an acid usually shows an H for hydrogen at the beginning. Chemists test for acids using ***litmus paper***, a special kind of paper that turns red in acid.

Another group of chemicals is known as ***bases***. Many common household chemicals are bases. Most drain cleaners contain sodium hydroxide (NaOH), a very strong base that is commonly known as lye. Washing soda ($NaCO_3$) and baking soda ($NaHCO_3$) are both bases. Ammonia (NH_3) is a base that is used in many kinds of household cleaners. Milk of magnesia ($Mg(OH)_2$) and aluminum hydroxide ($Al(OH)_2$) are both bases used in common antacid medicines.

Most bases are bitter-tasting and have a slippery feel to them. The chemical formulas for many bases show an (OH) group on the end. Litmus paper can be used to test for bases, too, because it turns blue when it touches a base.

Both acids and bases are very ***reactive***; that is, they react easily with other chemicals. This makes them good cleaners; they react with the dirt and grease. But this also makes them very dangerous. A strong acid or base can burn a person very badly because it reacts with the water and other things in the skin. Acids and bases react very easily with each other. If an acid and a base are combined, they will react together to form water and some kind of salt. When this happens, the acid and the base have ***neutralized*** each other.

EXERCISE 4: ACIDS AND BASES

Directions: Complete this review by filling in the blanks.

_____1_____ and _____2_____ are two common groups of chemicals that are very reactive. _____3_____, _____4_____, and _____5_____ are examples of foods containing acids. Three cleaners that are bases include _____6_____, _____7_____, and _____8_____.

There are many ways to tell an acid from a base. Acids taste _____9_____, while bases taste _____10_____. _____11_____ also feel slippery to the touch, but _____12_____ don't. Scientists test acids and bases using _____13_____ paper. This special paper turns _____14_____ when it touches an acid and _____15_____ when it touches a base.

Answers start on page 510.

POISON!

Children under five are the most common victims of poison. Young children do not know what is food and what isn't. They taste everything they find, and many poisons are so strong that even a taste can be very dangerous.

People are often surprised at how many common household items have dangerous chemicals in them. Bleach, drain cleaner, floor polish, and most cleaning supplies can all be deadly. Children have been poisoned by relatively small amounts of ordinary medicines like cough syrups, laxatives, and Tylenol. Cosmetics like eye shadow, face cream, and even lipstick can be ***toxic*** (poisonous) when eaten. Vitamins may seem like candy, but an ***overdose*** can be toxic.

Adults, too, can be poison victims. The most common cause of adult poisoning is drug overdose. Most drug overdoses are accidental. A half-asleep person may accidentally take extra doses of sleeping pills. Someone else may take extra prescription medicine, thinking that if a little is good, a lot will be even better. (Not true!)

Adults can also be poisoned while working around the house. They may breathe toxic fumes (gases) from insecticides, paints, and solvents. Dangerous chlorine gas can be created just by mixing ammonia with bleach or other chlorine-based cleaners. Siphoning gasoline by mouth is not safe; just a few drops of gasoline in the lungs can kill a person.

Safety Precautions

An accident with poison can be a real tragedy. People can help prevent poisonings in their own homes by taking these basic safety precautions.

1. Keep all chemicals, cleaners, cosmetics, and medicines in high cupboards with childproof hooks or locks on them. Return things to these cupboards immediately after use; never leave them out on a countertop or table.
2. Put warning stickers on all poisons. These stickers are available free from your local hospital or poison control center.
3. Don't get children to take medicine by telling them that it is "candy." Never encourage a child to take "just a sip" of an alcoholic drink. Don't leave tobacco, ashes, or alcoholic drinks in rooms where little children may be alone.
4. Read the information on containers of all household products and pay attention to the warnings.
5. Use materials that put out strong fumes only in well-ventilated areas. If you start to feel sick, go out into the fresh air. If you still feel funny, call a doctor or a hospital emergency room.
6. Never put a nonfood substance, like oil or cleaning fluid, in a food container like a Coke bottle or milk carton.
7. Check the label every time you take or give a medicine and use only the amount prescribed.
8. By your telephone, keep a list of the phone numbers of the hospital emergency room and the nearest poison control center.
9. Get a bottle of syrup of ipecac from your drugstore and keep it handy with your other medicines. Syrup of ipecac can be used to make a person vomit (throw up) if he has swallowed poison. Sometimes vomiting will help; sometimes it will just make things worse, so *do not use the ipecac until told to by a health professional.*

CHEMICALS THAT CAUSE DISEASE

Modern chemistry has made our lives longer, fuller, and more comfortable. Without chemistry, there would be no plastic, nylon, rayon, polyester, detergents, photographs, or contact lenses. But chemicals can harm as well as help. Terrible chemical weapons, like nerve gas and napalm, have been used in wars since World War I. Often the damage done by chemicals is not done on purpose. Many times a chemical that people thought was harmless has turned out to have unknown side effects.

For many people, medicines are the most important chemicals. Before 1940, people died from infected wounds and from diseases like strep throat and pneumonia. Now we get a prescription for an antibiotic from the doctor and feel fine in a few days. People with heart disease, high blood pressure, and many other illnesses depend on modern medicines to help them lead normal lives.

But scientists don't know everything about new medicines, and big mistakes have been made. For example, in just the last few years, doctors have discovered that giving children aspirin when they have the flu or certain other viruses may cause a deadly reaction called ***Reye's syndrome***.

Asbestos is one of the most useful chemicals in construction. It is fireproof, makes good insulation, and helps strengthen other materials like concrete and plastic. Millions of tons of asbestos were used in our schools, homes, and stores. Now scientists have discovered that asbestos can cause cancer. There are plans to remove all the open asbestos in public buildings, but for the many people who got cancer the damage is already done.

Chemicals in Food

Another problem involves ***food additives***, chemicals that are added to foods. Preservatives help keep foods from spoiling or going stale. Artificial flavors and flavor enhancers are added to foods to make them taste better. Artificial colors make foods more attractive and appealing. Almost all prepared foods, and many other canned and frozen foods, contain food additives. Food additives have made a great variety of foods available to us in easy-to-fix forms. But scientists are discovering that some additives can be dangerous to our health.

Artificial sweeteners have been a big problem for manufacturers. According to some tests, cyclamates and saccharin, two popular sweeteners, may cause cancer. Another sweetener called *aspartame* (NutraSweet and Equal) was carefully tested before it was used, but some people still say that it gives them headaches and other problems.

Sodium nitrite is a preservative that keeps meat from spoiling. It is used in meats like hot dogs, salami, and bacon. Before sodium nitrite was used, people sometimes got food poisoning from these foods. Now some people say that sodium nitrite should be banned because experiments show that it can cause cancer in animals.

Many people say we must be more careful about the chemicals we use. This can be accomplished through the cooperation of manufacturers, concerned individuals, and government agencies such as the FDA (Food and Drug Administration) and the EPA (Environmental Protection Agency).

EXERCISE 5: DECISIONS ABOUT CHEMICALS

Directions: There are no right or wrong answers to these questions. Write your opinions. Give reasons for your ideas.

1. Do you think people should be allowed to buy artificial sweeteners, even though they may cause cancer?

2. In the mid-1980s, the budgets of agencies like the EPA and FDA were cut. At the same time, more and more money was spent on the military. Do you believe that this was a wise way to spend money?

Directions: Circle the best answer for each question.

3. Which of the following is an opinion, not a fact?
   (1) Some tests show that saccharin may cause cancer.
   (2) Manufacturers should work to make sure that chemicals are safe.
   (3) Artificial colors are intended to make food more appealing.
   (4) Chemistry has been important in the construction business.
   (5) Sodium nitrite can cause cancer in animals.

Answers start on page 510.

DRUG ABUSE

Drugs and medicines can be divided into two groups. Most drugs mainly affect the body. These drugs are rarely ***abused*** because they are not fun to take. But there are many drugs that affect the mind. They can make a person feel very happy or relaxed or full of energy. Because these drugs can make someone feel good in a bad situation, they are often abused.

Drugs may make a person feel good, but they can have some bad effects. Drugs can change a person's picture of reality. Some drugs can cause ***hallucinations***; that is, they can make a person see or hear things that aren't real.

If a person uses a drug regularly, he may come to need that drug. He is ***addicted***. That drug becomes the most important thing in his life. Usually he needs the drug just to handle everyday stress. Without it, he feels as if he might fall apart. This is called a ***psychological dependence***. Some drugs also cause chemical changes in the body. The body comes to need the drug. If a person stops taking the drug, he becomes very sick. This is called a ***physical dependence***.

Commonly Abused Drugs

Marijuana ("grass," "pot") is a dried plant that is usually smoked or eaten. It makes a person feel relaxed, lazy, and a little silly. Once in a while it will make a person feel frightened or depressed. It can cause psychological dependence. Marijuana smoke causes lung damage, just as cigarette smoke does. Heavy use may affect the sex hormones and the ability to have healthy children. THC, the main chemical in marijuana, is used by doctors to treat an eye disease and to help cancer patients tolerate chemotherapy. Hashish is a concentrated form of marijuana.

Hallucinogens are a group of drugs that cause hallucinations. Included in this group are LSD ("acid"), STP, PCP, mescaline, psilocybin, and others. These are very powerful, unpredictable drugs. A person taking these drugs may see beautiful visions or have nightmarish delusions. Some hallucinogens can cause "flashbacks." Hallucinogens may cause brain damage and birth defects.

Amphetamines ("uppers," "speed") are drugs that make a person feel very energetic, awake, and alive. People using speed often don't eat or sleep for days. The use of speed can very easily damage the body, especially the nervous system. Amphetamines are sometimes prescribed by doctors to treat obesity and depression, but they are not used very much anymore because they are so addictive psychologically and physically.

Barbiturates ("downers") are drugs that depress and slow down the whole body. They can make a person feel very relaxed and peaceful. Doctors use them to treat sleeplessness, epilepsy, and many mental illnesses. Barbiturates are physically addictive, and if a person suddenly stops taking them, he or she may die. Taking an overdose of barbiturates, or combining even a small amount with alcohol, can make a person stop breathing.

Cocaine ("coke") is a drug made from the leaves of a South American plant. It is a strong stimulant, and it makes people feel very confident and well. It causes a very strong physical and psychological addiction; once a person starts using cocaine, it is often very hard to stop. One form of cocaine, called "crack," can be deadly even on the first use.

Heroin is the drug many people think of when they think of addicts. Heroin is strongly addictive, both physically and psychologically. Heroin users waste away physically. Because this drug is usually injected, users can get diseases like hepatitis and AIDS from using unclean needles.

Alcohol is not considered a drug by many people, yet it can be a dangerous one. Alcoholics, people addicted to alcohol, number in the millions in this country alone. Researchers say that one in four families is affected by alcoholism. Frequent abuse of alcohol can cause permanent damage to the kidneys, liver, and brain.

Nicotine is the main drug in cigarettes. It is probably the most commonly abused drug in this country. It is a stimulant that speeds up the heartbeat and breathing and raises the blood pressure. Over a period of years, nicotine and other chemicals in tobacco smoke damage the lungs, heart, and blood vessels.

Treatment of Drug Addiction

Drug addiction can affect anyone. People who are psychologically or physically dependent on drugs are caught in a trap. Even if they do not want to use the drugs anymore, often they cannot stop. Sometimes they need medical treatment to be able to stop safely. Help is available from a counselor or special group, like Alcoholics Anonymous or Narcotics Anonymous.

EXERCISE 6: DRUG ABUSE

Directions: Match the drugs in the column on the left with the phrases in the column on the right by writing the correct letters in the blanks.

_____ 1. marijuana

_____ 2. hallucinogens

_____ 3. amphetamines

_____ 4. barbiturates

_____ 5. cocaine

_____ 6. heroin

_____ 7. alcohol

_____ 8. nicotine

a. one deadly kind is called "crack"
b. can damage lungs, heart, and blood vessels
c. usually smoked or eaten
d. can damage kidneys, liver, and brain
e. may cause "flashbacks"
f. should never be combined with alcohol
g. users may not feel the need to eat or sleep
h. usually injected, very addictive

Answers start on page 510.

EXERCISE 7: CHAPTER REVIEW

Directions: Using the information given, circle the best answer for each question.

Questions 1 and 2 refer to the chart below.

Some Elements and Their Chemical Symbols		
Cl—Chlorine Si—Silicon	N—Nitrogen Cu—Copper	O—Oxygen Ag—Silver

1. How many of these compounds contain silver?

   $AgNO_3$ Cu_2O Ag_2O Ag_2S Au_2O

   (1) 1
   (2) 2
   (3) 3
   (4) 4
   (5) 5

2. What is the correct name for CuCl?
   (1) silver calcite
   (2) chlorine sulfate
   (3) copper oxide
   (4) silver chloride
   (5) copper chloride

Questions 3 and 4 are based on the label below.

CAUTION: KEEP OUT OF REACH OF CHILDREN
If bleach is splashed in eyes, flood with water.
Harmful if swallowed. If swallowed, feed milk.
Call a physician or Poison Control Center.
If splashed on skin, flood with water.

3. According to this label, laundry bleach can be harmful to which parts of the body?
   (1) eyes
   (2) stomach
   (3) skin
   (4) all of the above
   (5) none of the above

4. If a person swallows bleach, you should
   (1) flood the person with water
   (2) have the person drink milk
   (3) have the person drink water
   (4) rinse the person's eyes with water
   (5) rinse the person's eyes with milk

Questions 5 and 6 are based on the chart below.

Many people are exposed to dangerous conditions on the job. Following is a chart of some symptoms and possible causes.

Area Affected	Symptoms	Common Causes
Head	headache, dizziness	excessive noise
Nose and Throat	coughing, sneezing, sore throat nasal cancer	ozone, solvents, ammonia, caustic soda, dusts hardwood dusts and resins
Chest and Lungs	dry cough, wheezing, congestion flu-like symptoms shortness of breath after mild exercise	cotton dust, detergent enzymes, beryllium, solvents, TDI metal oxides from welding long-term exposure to asbestos
Ears	ringing, temporary deafness, hearing loss	excessive noise
Eyes	irritation, redness, watering "welder's flash," grainy feeling	gases, fumes, smoke, metal dust, acids ultraviolet radiation
Skin	itching, dryness, redness ulcers, skin cancer	epoxies, solvents, oil, fiberglass, nickel, caustic soda arsenic, pitch, tar, mineral oils, radiation
Nervous System	nervousness, irritability, stress tremors, sleeplessness, speech changes	speed-up, noise, metal poisoning (mercury, lead)
Reproductive System	irregularities in menstruation miscarriage damage to chromosomes or fetus sterilization	polystyrene production, xylene, solvents pesticides, radiation, lead, anesthetic gas lead, mercury, radiation, benzene radiation

5. Betty works in a chemical factory. She has been having problems with her nervous system. According to this chart, what is one possible cause?

   (1) solvents
   (2) metal poisoning
   (3) ozone
   (4) acid fumes
   (5) radiation

6. Workers in another plant are exposed to many different kinds of dust. According to the chart, which of these problems is probably *not* caused by dust?

   (1) irritated eyes
   (2) sore throat
   (3) dry cough
   (4) sneezing
   (5) headache and dizziness

Questions 7 and 8 are based on the following opinions.

Speaker A

There has been a lot of discussion about the "problem" of marijuana. The biggest problems are caused by the laws that make marijuana illegal. If marijuana were legalized, ordinary students would not get a criminal record just for smoking it. People who wanted marijuana would not be forced into contact with criminals who also sell other, more dangerous drugs. If marijuana sellers were licensed, users would not have to worry about poisons or other drugs being mixed with it. Finally, if marijuana were controlled the way alcohol is, people would learn to use it responsibly, just as they do with alcohol.

Speaker B

Some people are calling for the legalization of marijuana. This would be a big mistake. If marijuana were legal, more people would smoke it more often. This would cause an increase in car accidents due to driving under the influence of marijuana. It would slow production and cause more accidents in factories. If marijuana were legal for adults, it would also be easier for underage children to get. Many immature people would try to avoid their problems by getting high instead of learning to deal with their problems. Also, there is new evidence that smoking marijuana may cause sterility, brain damage, and birth defects. Look at all the problems society has with legal alcohol; legalized marijuana would be even worse.

7. Speaker A would probably agree with which of these statements?
   (1) Governments should pass laws to protect people against drugs, even if people don't want to be protected.
   (2) People should be allowed to do what they want, as long as they don't harm others.
   (3) People who smoke marijuana are mostly delinquents and criminals.
   (4) Most people cannot be trusted to take care of themselves.
   (5) Smoking marijuana usually leads to hard drug addiction.

8. Both of these articles are mostly opinion. What is one fact mentioned by Speaker B?
   (1) Some people are now calling for the legalization of marijuana.
   (2) Legalizing marijuana would be a big mistake.
   (3) If marijuana were legal, people would smoke more of it.
   (4) Children should not smoke marijuana.
   (5) Marijuana would be a bigger problem than alcohol if it were legalized.

Answers start on page 510.

6 EARTH SCIENCE

READING SKILL: EVALUATING IDEAS

Should businesses be required to protect the environment, even if that means that jobs will be lost and prices will rise?

Should new medicines that might cure diseases like AIDS be put on the market right away, or should they first go through a five-year testing program to make certain they are useful and safe?

Should the government spend millions to put astronauts in space, or should it spend that money on health care for the elderly?

These are just a few of the questions that our modern society faces because of scientific progress. Scientists are making discoveries every day that will allow us to do things that we have never done before. Every scientific discovery brings problems as well as benefits.

Questions about how science should be used cannot be answered by scientists alone. There is no "scientific" answer that will tell us what we should do. Science can answer only questions about facts. What should be done with those facts is a question of values and beliefs.

VALUES AND BELIEFS

Each person has his or her own ***value system***, a set of beliefs about what is important and what is right and wrong. We develop this value system as we grow, from our life experiences, and from what our family and other people tell us. We use our value system to help us make decisions.

Sometimes our values are in conflict; we cannot do or have everything we want. Often the conflict is between short-term and long-term values. A ***short-term value*** is something that will make us feel good right now. A ***long-term value*** is something that we think is important in the long run.

Sometimes there are conflicts between short-term and long-term values. For example, an inexpensive sewage treatment plant will save the taxpayers money now, but in ten years it may have polluted the local drinking water. Other decisions about science are difficult because of conflicts between important long-term values. For example, everyone agrees that doctors should save lives and that people should die with dignity. But issues like these raise difficult questions: Should patients be allowed to refuse special medical treatment and die in peace? Or should doctors always try to keep patients alive as long as possible?

Some conflicts come about because there is only so much money, time, and effort available to solve problems. Should we spend money on weapons to defend our country or on programs like student grants and food stamps? Should we increase Medicare benefits for older people or provide more nutritious hot lunches in schools? Different groups of people will have different ideas about what is most important.

Suppose your town, like many, uses chemical herbicides (weed killers) along the sides of the roads. Some people want to stop the town from doing this because the chemicals pollute the environment and because a few children get very sick when they are exposed to herbicides. The mayor says that if the town can't use herbicides, it will have to hire extra workers to mow the roadsides. That means higher taxes. The mayor says that the town has been using these chemicals for years, and no one has really been hurt.

▶ If you were voting on this issue, would you vote for or against the use of herbicides? Here are some questions you might consider in making this decision.

1. Which is more important to you, a cleaner environment or lower taxes?
2. Should everyone have to pay more just because a few children are sensitive to these chemicals?
3. Is the mayor probably right that no one has been hurt?

Now write how you would vote and list any other reasons for voting that way.

____

Do you think your answer would be different if you had a brother or sister who was sensitive to herbicides? How about if your family had a low income and you were afraid of losing your home because of higher taxes? To make fair decisions, we have to look at what is best for us personally and what is best for our community.

EXERCISE 1: YOU DECIDE

Directions: Below are several pairs of opposite opinions on current questions about the use of science. Put a check next to the opinion you agree with. Then write three reasons that support your opinion.

1. ________ Scientists should control the genes of unborn children so that the next generation is stronger and smarter.

   ________ Scientists should not try to control the genes of unborn children.

   Reasons that support your opinion:

   a. ____

   b. ____

   c. ____

2. ________ Some areas of government land should be closed to all people so that some wilderness can be preserved.

________ All government lands should be open to tourists and to careful mining, ranching, or lumbering.

Reasons that support your opinion:

a. ____________________

b. ____________________

c. ____________________

3. ________ Employers should have the right to test workers to find out if they are using drugs.

________ Employers should not have the right to do drug testing.

Reasons that support your opinion:

a. ____________________

b. ____________________

c. ____________________

CRITICAL READING

Advertisers want you to buy their products. Politicians want you to vote for them. Even your family and friends will try to persuade you to agree with them and do things their way. To help yourself understand and make clear decisions about important issues, ask yourself these two questions: Am I getting all the facts? If not, where can I go to get more information?

All the Facts, Please

Many times someone will try to persuade you to think or do something without giving you all the facts. For example, an advertiser will say, "Strike detergent is new and improved; buy some today!" However, the ad doesn't say how Strike was improved. Does it clean better, cost less, or just smell nicer? You need this information before you can decide if Strike is the detergent you want to buy.

▶ Look at this statement from a medicine company: "Ninety percent of people surveyed prefer Sager aspirin." List two or more pieces of information you might need before deciding whether to buy Sager aspirin.

1. ____________________

2. ____________________

There are many different facts you might need here. *How many people were surveyed?* If only ten people were surveyed, the results don't mean as much as if thousands were surveyed. *How was the survey done?* Did the questioners choose people at random, or did they question only people who had already bought Sager? *Who did the survey*, an independent company or the Sager company itself? Finally, *why did the people prefer Sager?* Was it cheaper? Did it work best for headaches or perhaps for arthritis?

EXERCISE 2: THE WHOLE STORY

Directions: Read the following persuasive statements. Write at least one question that you would need answered in order to have all the facts.

1. Move to California; we have the best weather in the nation.

   ____

   ____

2. Take vitamins to improve your health.

   ____

   ____

3. Stop your taxes from going up by voting against the new park.

   ____

   ____

4. We must build more roads; we can't stand in the way of progress.

   ____

   ____

5. Chemical X must be banned because it causes cancer in mice.

   ____

   ____

Answers start on page 511.

WHERE TO GO NEXT

It is not always easy to get accurate information on a subject. Your sources of information should have some special knowledge about the subject. It is important to get information from a source that is not ***biased*** (prejudiced toward one side of a question). For example, if you wanted to know which brand of stereo needs the fewest repairs, you wouldn't just ask the salesperson. After all, she wants to sell you her brand. Instead, you could check in a magazine like *Consumer Reports* for the results of independent testing.

One good place to start looking for information is the public library. Libraries have thousands of books and articles on all sorts of subjects. Many people are not sure where to look for things in the library, but librarians are happy to help people find the information they want.

Another good source of information about local questions is your city, town, or county government. If you ask for help with a problem, government workers will often explain exactly what you can do. A letter to your congressperson or senator will often get you information about new laws and government programs to help individuals. Finally, there are citizens' groups organized to deal with many different issues, from wildlife preservation to preventing birth defects. These groups are usually more than happy to provide information on their subjects.

EXERCISE 3: INFORMATION, PLEASE

Directions: Circle the numbers of the *two* best sources of information about each of the following questions.

1. Is the factory in my town polluting our river?
   (1) a publicity release from the factory
   (2) the town health department
   (3) Citizens for a Better Environment
   (4) a friend who fishes on the river all the time

2. If a child has a fever of 101°F, does the child need to see a doctor?
   (1) the doctor's nurse
   (2) the child's grandmother
   (3) a neighbor whose child had a similar fever last week
   (4) the hospital emergency room

3. Are "health foods" really better for you?
   (1) books on nutrition from the library
   (2) the county social services department
   (3) your brother, who is always on a diet
   (4) a clerk at your local health food store

Answers start on page 511.

SCIENCE TOPIC: THE SCIENTIFIC METHOD

People have lived on Earth for hundreds of thousands of years, and they have always been curious. Yet there is always something new to discover about the amazing planet we live on. Even today, we know very little about the deep places in the oceans, and there are probably hundreds of plants and animals that we have not named and classified. Although we still have much to learn about our own planet, we are now taking on an even bigger challenge. We have begun to investigate the other planets and the stars, the universe itself.

THE EARTH'S INTERIOR

Inside the Earth

The Earth is a little like an apple. It has a thin outer layer like a peel, an inner part, and a core. The thin outer part is called the ***crust***. It is very irregular, bumping up into mountains and flattening out in plains. The thickest part of the crust is only about 40 miles thick, but it gives us everything we need for life.

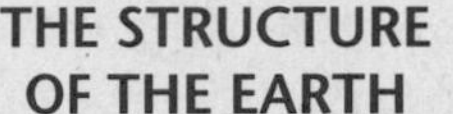

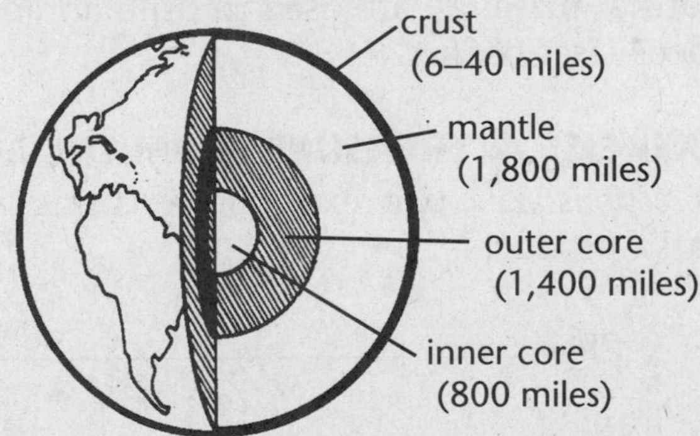

Below the crust is a thick layer called the ***mantle***. No one has ever drilled down into the mantle or the layers beneath it. From studying the way vibrations pass through this layer, scientists believe the mantle is made of solid rock.

Inside the mantle are the ***outer core*** and the ***inner core***. Both cores are probably made of a mixture of iron and nickel. It is very hot inside the Earth, up to 9,000°; the outer core is molten (liquid). The enormous pressures at the center of the Earth have forced the material of the inner core into a solid, very dense state.

Buried Treasure

People dig mines into the Earth's crust to find all kinds of ***minerals*** (natural elements and compounds). Minerals contain materials that we need for many things.

Metals are usually found mixed with other elements in mineral compounds called ***ores***. From different ores, we get iron to make steel for all kinds of building and machinery, copper for electric wires, aluminum for aircraft and kitchen uses, and uranium for use in atomic power plants. Gold and silver ores are used to make coins and in industry.

Oil, coal, and natural gas, called ***fossil fuels***, are minerals that are the remains of plants that lived millions of years ago. These plants died and were buried in layers deep within the Earth, where heat and pressure gradually changed them to coal and oil. During this process, they gave off natural gas, which was trapped under the Earth. Fossil fuels took millions of years to make, but we are using them up very quickly. We burn fossil fuels to get most of the energy for our cars, homes, and industry. We also use them to make many important chemical products, from medicines to plastics. Fossil fuels are so important to us that many people are worried about what will happen if we use them all up.

Throughout history, people have valued jewels such as diamonds, rubies, and emeralds because of their beauty and rarity. Strangely enough, jewels are just ordinary minerals that have been changed into clear and colorful gems by exactly the right amounts of heat and pressure. For instance, rubies are made of aluminum and oxygen, while diamonds are pure carbon, the same material as in black, sooty coal. Besides being used in jewelry, gemstones are used in industry. For example, diamonds, which are the hardest natural material, are used in drills and cutting tools, and rubies are used to focus laser beams.

EXERCISE 4: TREASURE FROM THE EARTH

Directions: List two examples of things you own or use made from these earth products.

1. copper: ______________________________

2. iron: ______________________________

3. aluminum: ______________________________

4. fossil fuels: ______________________________

Directions: Choose the best answer.

5. According to this article, scientists learn about the layers under the Earth's crust by

   (1) drilling down under the crust
   (2) reading science fiction
   (3) going down into the center of the Earth
   (4) measuring vibrations that pass through the Earth
   (5) studying the material that comes out of volcanoes

Answers start on page 511.

SOIL CONSERVATION

When the pioneers first settled our country, a farmer mainly had to have a strong back and lots of energy. Today a successful farmer also needs a lot of scientific knowledge. New machines and chemicals have changed the way people farm. Almost all the good farmland is settled, so farmers can't just move on if they wear out their land. Instead, successful farmers have learned to keep the land from wearing out through soil conservation.

Soil is the loose material found on the top of the Earth's crust. Plants get most of their nutrients (the materials they need to grow) from the soil.

Most of the available nutrients are found in the upper layer of the soil, called the ***topsoil***. Topsoil is a mixture of sand, clay, and humus. ***Humus*** is decaying plant and animal material. It provides many nutrients and keeps the soil spongy so that it can hold air and water. Sand makes the soil loose so that water and air can get in and plant roots can grow easily. Clay helps the soil hold water and provides some necessary minerals. All three materials are needed for good soil.

Beneath the topsoil is the ***subsoil***, which may be sand, clay, gravel, or a mixture of all three. Since subsoil has no humus in it, most plants cannot grow in it directly. Some plants, however, have very deep roots that allow them to get some of their minerals from the subsoil. Both layers of soil rest on the ***bedrock*** that makes up the crust of the Earth.

Soil Damage

If ground is left bare, wind and running water can carry away the topsoil. This process is called ***erosion***. Water erosion is more likely on hilly land, while wind erosion happens most often on flat land with no hedges or windbreaks. Fall plowing adds to the problem of erosion. So do crops like corn and cotton that grow in rows, leaving the soil bare between the plants.

Every year the plants take minerals out of the soil. If these minerals aren't returned to the soil, the soil is soon worn out. Since different crops use different amounts of minerals, soil gets worn out faster when only one type of crop is grown year after year.

Keeping Soil Healthy

Farmers do many things to prevent erosion. They plant lines of trees or bushes, called ***windbreaks***, to slow down the wind as it crosses their fields. They avoid plowing in the fall and plant ***cover crops*** to hold down the soil after they take their main crop off the land. Farmers with hilly land plow sideways around the hills (called ***contour plowing***). Contour plowing leaves the soil in horizontal ridges that catch water, preventing the water from running straight downhill. Some farmers use ***conservation tillage***, which leaves plant material in the top layer of soil to protect it from erosion. All these things help keep valuable topsoil from being blown or washed away.

Farmers add ***fertilizer*** to their soil to keep it from getting worn out. ***Inorganic*** fertilizers are chemicals made in a laboratory that can be added to the soil. Some commonly added chemicals are nitrogen, phosphorus, and potassium. ***Organic*** fertilizer comes from living things, like manure from farm animals, compost, or waste material from crops. Organic fertilizer can be more expensive, and its chemical content is harder to measure exactly. However, only organic fertilizer contains humus, which is necessary for healthy soil.

To preserve the minerals in the soil, farmers sometimes let a field lie ***fallow*** (resting for a year without crops). Farmers also ***rotate*** their crops, growing different crops on the same piece of land each year. A crop like corn, which takes a lot out of the soil, may be followed by clover or alfalfa, crops that help replace some minerals.

EXERCISE 5: SOIL CONSERVATION

Directions: What follows is a list of farming practices. On the line next to each farming practice, write whether the practice *harms* or *helps* the soil. The first one is done for you.

1. Using fertilizer *helps*
2. Planting the same crop every year ________________
3. Letting a field lie fallow ________________
4. Plowing straight up and down hills ________________
5. Planting cover crops ________________
6. Rotating crops ________________
7. Contour plowing ________________

Directions: Circle the number of the best answer.

8. If you had a garden patch with sandy, worn-out soil, what would be the best thing you could do to improve it?
   (1) plant only easy-to-grow things like radishes and beans
   (2) dig in lots of dried manure for fertilizer
   (3) plow it well before planting
   (4) leave it bare all winter to soak up water
   (5) spread pure nitrogen fertilizer on it

Answers start on page 511.

ECOLOGY AND POLLUTION

The study of the balance of nature is called ***ecology***. Ecologists study how living things are related to each other and to the world around them, their ***environment***. All living things depend on their environment and on each other in very complex patterns.

MEADOW FOOD WEB

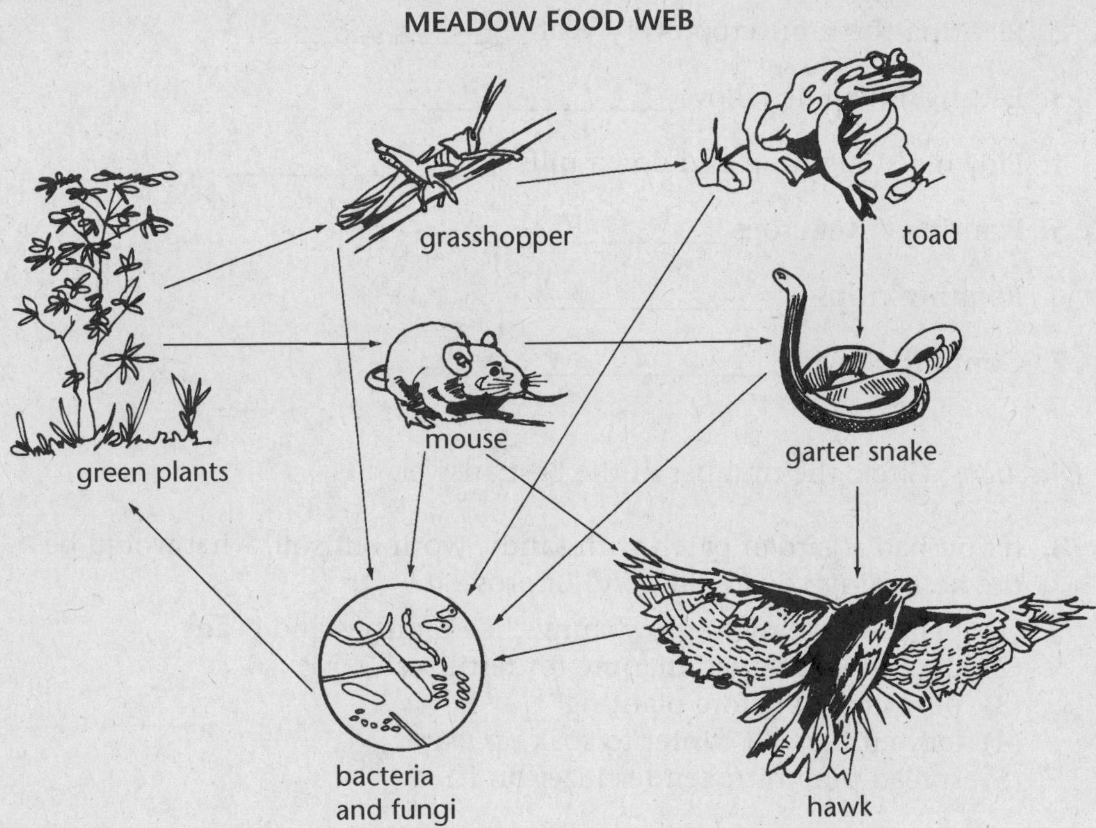

One pattern that ecologists study is called a ***food web***. The basis of any food web is green plants. Green plants are called ***producers*** because they use energy from the Sun to produce food by photosynthesis. Every other living thing depends on the food made by green plants. Animals that eat plants, like grasshoppers and mice, are called ***primary consumers***. Animals that eat other animals, like the toad, the snake, and the hawk in this food web, are all ***secondary consumers***. Finally, ***decomposers*** like bacteria and fungi break down wastes and dead plants and animals. They return their nutrients to the soil for plant food.

If just one link in a food web is disturbed, all the other parts are affected. For an example, look at the food web on page 488.

- If a sudden dry spell prevented the toads from breeding, there would be fewer toads to eat grasshoppers.
- Millions more grasshoppers would survive, so farmers' crops in the area would be under attack from the hungry grasshoppers.
- Snakes would not do well either because there wouldn't be so many toads for them to eat.
- Because there were fewer snakes, there might be fewer hawks, too.

People and the Environment

Humans try to control their environment. Because of this, we often disturb the balance of nature. We cut down forests that provided food and shelter for many kinds of animals and plants. We dam rivers and water our lawns. We burn fossil fuels to heat our homes in winter and cool them in summer. We kill off whole groups of animals for sport or for food.

Our industrial society produces many chemicals that are sometimes released into the environment, causing ***pollution***. Air pollution comes from the chimneys of factories and furnaces and from automobile exhaust. Water pollution can be caused by wastes from homes and factories. Even fertilizers can pollute the water if they wash off farm fields instead of soaking into the ground where they can be used by plants. Pollution is just one of the problems we must address to keep our natural environment safe.

EXERCISE 6: A FOREST ECOSYSTEM

Directions: A group of plants and animals and the local environment they live in are called an ***ecosystem***. Use this diagram of a food web in a forest ecosystem to answer the following questions. Notice that all of the arrows in the food web point to consumers.

FOREST FOOD WEB

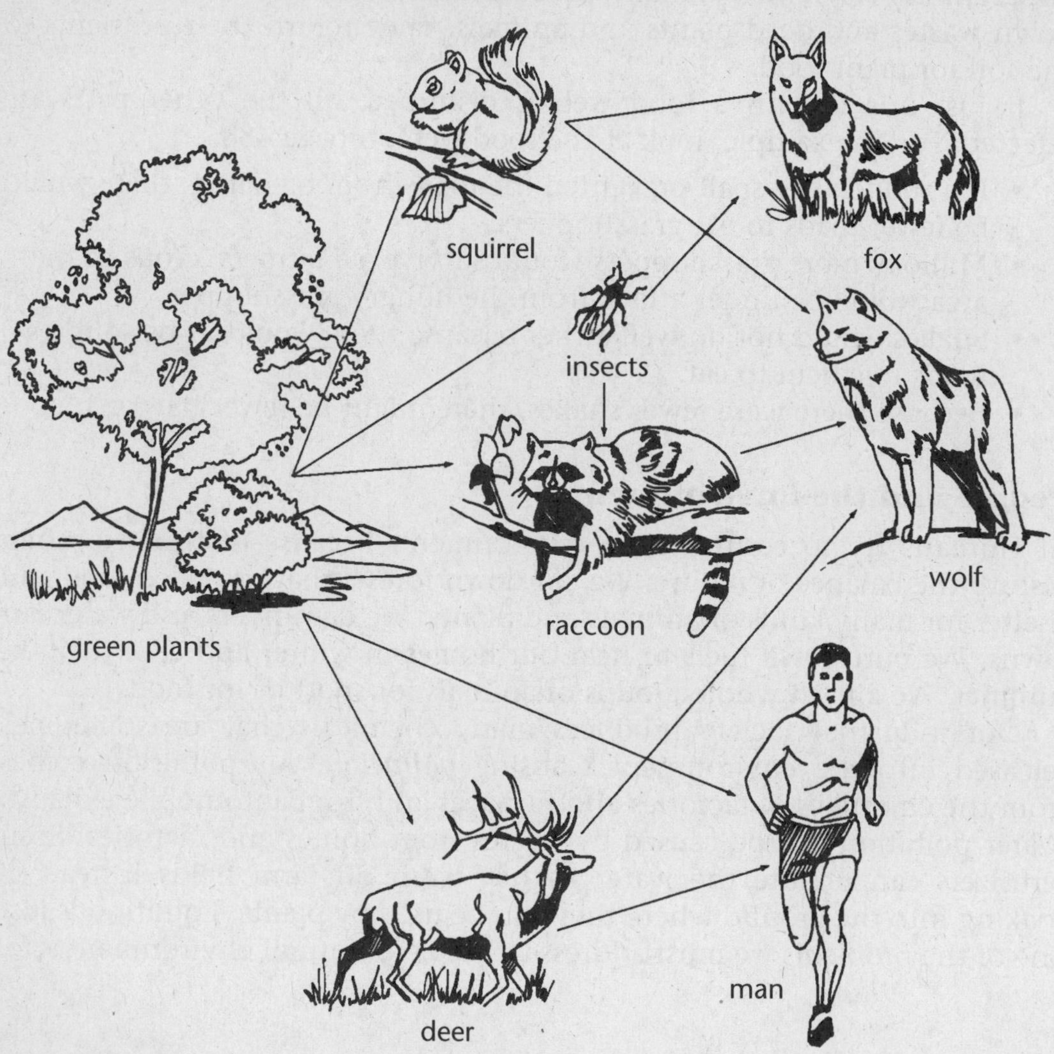

Note: All dead organisms are decomposed by bacteria and fungi, and their nutrients return to the soil to be used by plants.

1. What are the producers in this food web? ______________________

2. What are the primary consumers? ______________________

3. What are the secondary consumers? ______________________

4. What are the decomposers? ______________________

Directions: Circle the number of the best answer.

5. The main point this author is trying to make is that
   (1) people can control their environment
   (2) living things depend on each other and the environment
   (3) some animals eat other animals
   (4) green plants are the most important things on earth
   (5) people often pollute the environment

Answers start on page 511.

WEATHER

One of the first things most people do in the morning is check the weather. Yet the weather is a part of the environment that we really cannot control. We don't even predict it very well. The Earth is surrounded by a blanket of air many miles thick, our ***atmosphere***. Everything that affects the lower part of the atmosphere affects our weather.

Air Pressure

Because air is so light, we don't usually think of it as weighing anything. But each of us has miles of air above our head. Like everything else on Earth, this air is pulled down by gravity. It presses on us with a force of about fourteen pounds per square inch. We don't usually feel this ***air pressure*** unless it suddenly drops. When this happens before a storm, or when we go up in an airplane, it makes our ears pop and can give some people a headache.

Warm air is lighter and cold air is heavier, so weather forecasters can use changes in air pressure as one way to predict the weather. They measure air pressure with an instrument called a ***barometer***, so air pressure is sometimes called ***barometric pressure***.

Wind

Wind is the movement of air. Large masses of air move in predictable patterns around the Earth due to the Earth's rotation (spinning). Weather patterns in the United States mostly move from west to east. Small masses of air move in different directions because of differences in temperature. When air is warm, it becomes lighter and rises. Colder, heavier air moves in close to the ground to take the place of the warm air. This movement of air causes wind. A light wind feels good on a hot day, but strong winds like tornadoes and hurricanes can be very destructive.

Clouds

Clouds are part of the natural water cycle. Water evaporates into warm air. As the air rises, it cools, and tiny droplets of water form. These droplets are so small and light that they just hang in the air, forming a cloud.

Clouds come in many sizes and shapes. ***Cirrus*** clouds are thin, feathery-looking clouds that are usually high up in the atmosphere. ***Cumulus*** clouds are the familiar soft, puffy clouds that look like pieces of cotton wool. Light, white cumulus clouds are usually a sign of good weather. Cumulus clouds with dark, heavy-looking bottoms mean rain or snow is probably on the way. ***Stratus*** clouds are low, flat clouds that often cover the whole sky.

Precipitation

Precipitation is any kind of water that falls from the sky, in the form of rain, snow, sleet, or hail. Each type of precipitation is formed under different conditions. Raindrops are formed when water droplets in a cloud combine into larger and larger drops. When the drops of water get heavy enough, they fall to the ground as rain. If the air cools very quickly, the water droplets freeze before they can combine, and the precipitation falls as snow. If already-formed raindrops go through a very cold air layer on their way to the ground, they freeze into hard little pellets called ***sleet***. ***Hail*** develops when raindrops are blown up and down between layers of warm and cold air, freezing and refreezing. Strong winds can hold hailstones up in the clouds until they are the size of golf balls or even larger.

EXERCISE 7: WEATHER

Directions: Show whether these statements are true or false by putting a *T* or an *F* in front of them. If a statement is false, change the word in *italics* to make it true.

_____ **1.** *Water* pressure is also called barometric pressure.

_____ **2.** Weather in the United States usually moves from *west* to *east.*

_____ **3.** *Cirrus* clouds are soft-looking, puffy clouds.

_____ **4.** Rain, snow, sleet, and hail are all forms of *precipitation.*

_____ **5.** *Snow* is formed when frozen raindrops are blown up and down between layers of warm and cold air.

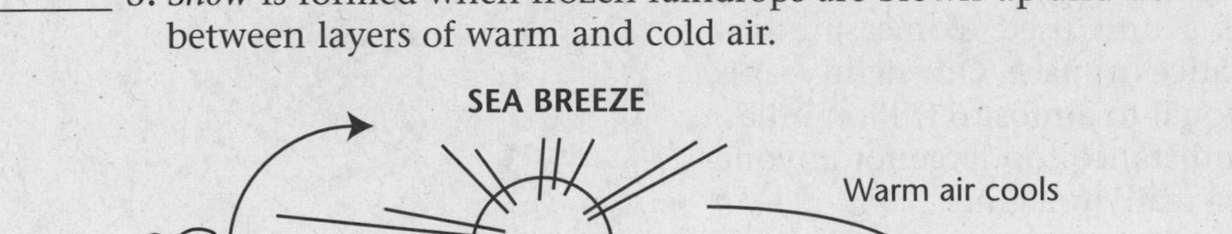

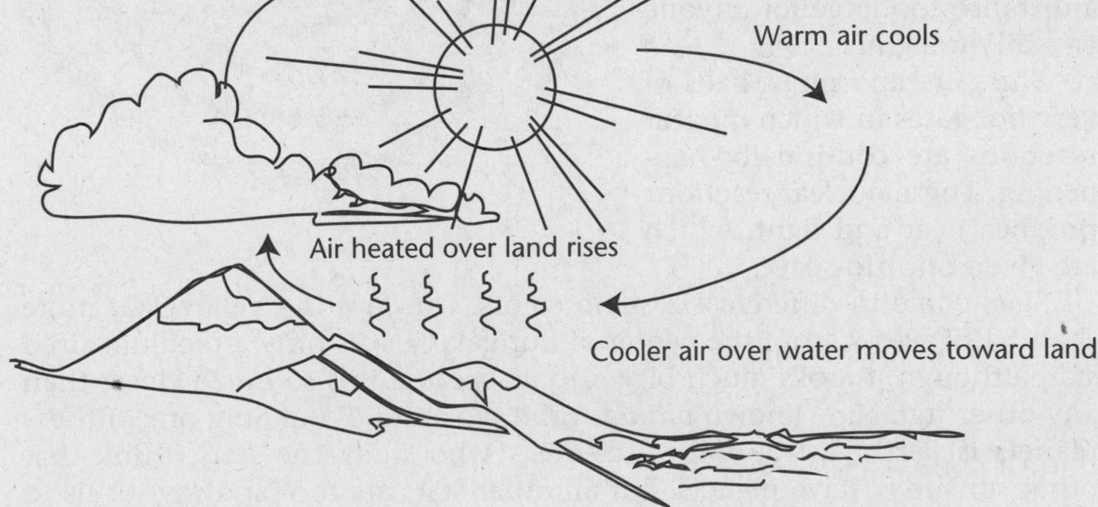

Directions: The diagram above shows why, on a warm day, you can often find a cool breeze blowing from a lake or an ocean. Use this diagram and the information about wind in this article to choose the best answer for this question.

6. Why does the air over the land rise?
   (1) The Sun draws it up by gravity.
   (2) The water is warmer than the land.
   (3) The shade from the cloud makes the air cooler.
   (4) The Sun heats the land and the air over it.
   (5) The strong wind causes friction.

Answers start on page 511.

OUR SOLAR SYSTEM: BEYOND THE EARTH

The ***universe*** is the biggest thing we know. It includes all matter and all space. No one knows where the edge of the universe is; maybe it just goes on forever.

A ***galaxy*** is a group of stars in the universe. Our galaxy is called the Milky Way. It contains about 100 billion stars grouped in a flat spiral pattern that is about 100,000 light-years across. A ***light-year,*** the distance light travels in a year, is a unit used to measure distance in space. One light-year is equal to almost 6 trillion miles, a distance too large for anyone to really imagine.

THE MILKY WAY GALAXY

Stars are enormous balls of very hot gases in which nuclear reactions are continually happening. These nuclear reactions produce heat and light, which are given off into space.

Stars come in different sizes and colors. Our ***Sun*** is a yellow star more than halfway out from the center of our galaxy. It is only a medium-sized star, although it looks much bigger to us because it is so much closer than any other star. Nine known ***planets*** orbit (go around) our Sun; one of these planets is Earth. Astronomers, scientists who study the stars, think that other suns may have planets, but all other stars are too far away for us to see any planets.

The Solar System

The Sun, with all its planets, their moons, and various other things, such as comets and asteroids, is called the ***solar system***.

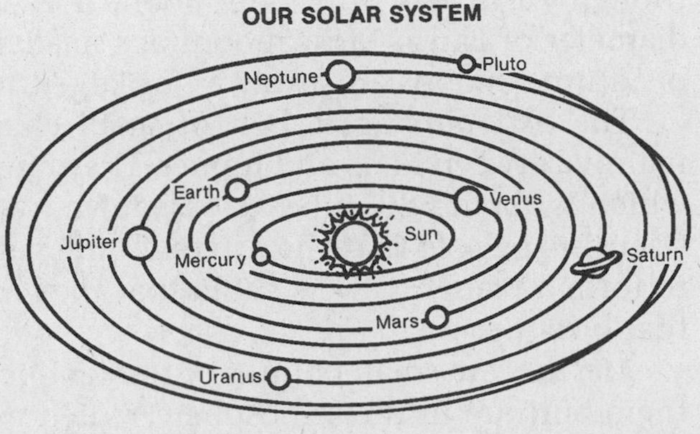

Mercury is the planet closest to the Sun. Mercury rotates very slowly, taking almost 59 Earth days to spin around once. Because of this, one side of Mercury gets very hot while the other side, away from the Sun, gets very cold.

Venus is the second planet from the Sun. It is about the same size as Earth, nearly eight thousand miles in ***diameter*** (distance across, going through the center). Venus is always covered with clouds, so only a few space probes have allowed us to see its surface.

Our Earth is the third planet. It is the only planet known to have life. This may be because it has just the right temperature range. It is neither too hot (like Venus) nor too cold (like Mars) to support life.

Mars, the fourth planet, is about one-half the diameter of Earth. Some scientists think there may once have been life on Mars before the planets cooled off so much. Some even think there might still be life. Others say that life is impossible because the atmosphere is too thin and cold. A space probe sent to Mars did not find any life, but no one can be sure.

Jupiter is the largest planet, more than eleven times the diameter of Earth and over 300 times its mass. The atmosphere of Jupiter is very thick and heavy, made up mostly of hydrogen, methane, and ammonia.

Saturn is the sixth planet from the Sun. It is slightly smaller than Jupiter, and it is known mostly for its beautiful rings. There are three main groups of rings around Saturn, each made up of smaller ringlets. Each ringlet contains many small icy particles that revolve around Saturn and sparkle brightly from reflected sunlight.

Uranus and Neptune are the seventh and eighth planets. They are both very far from the Sun and very cold. They are about the same size, approximately 3 1/2 times the diameter of Earth. The *Voyager* space probes discovered that both planets have small rings and many small moons.

For most of its orbit, Pluto is the farthest planet from the Sun. At times, however, its orbit brings it closer to the Sun than Neptune. Because it is so far away (about 3 1/2 billion miles from the Sun) and so small, Pluto was not discovered until 1930. Little is known about it.

At least seven of the planets have ***moons*** orbiting around them. Jupiter has at least sixteen moons, and more are likely to be discovered. Even though Earth has only one moon, it is a big one, about one-fourth the diameter of Earth. Most moons are smaller. Only four of Jupiter's and one of Saturn's moons are as big as, or larger than, ours.

The ***asteroids*** are a belt of small chunks of rock that orbit the Sun mainly between Mars and Jupiter. They range in size from the largest, Ceres, which is about 580 miles across, down to tiny particles of rock dust. Some scientists believe that the asteroids are matter that never grouped together to form a planet. Others think that they might be the remains of a planet that blew up.

Meteors are small chunks of rock and ice that fall toward Earth. Most of them burn up in the atmosphere. When we see meteors burning up in the atmosphere, we call them "shooting stars." A chunk of meteor that survives its fall and hits the ground is called a *meteorite*.

Comets are good-sized balls of rock and ice. They have very strange orbits. At one end they come very near the sun, while at the other end they swing out far beyond Pluto's orbit. When a comet comes near the Sun, the ice in it begins to melt and then boil away. The gas from the boiling ice reflects the sunlight and looks like a long white "tail."

EXERCISE 8: THE HEAVENLY BODIES

Directions: Write the correct word in front of each definition.

________________ 1. largest planet in the solar system

________________ 2. huge balls of hot gases giving off light and heat

________________ 3. chunks of rock orbiting between Mars and Jupiter

________________ 4. group of stars in the universe

________________ 5. planet with thick layer of clouds

________________ 6. the sun with all its planets, moons, etc.

________________ 7. ball of ice and rock with a long, gaseous "tail"

Directions: Circle the number of the best answer.

8. Considering how the term *solar system* is used in this article, the word *solar* probably means
   (1) very hot
   (2) having to do with the Earth
   (3) far apart
   (4) having to do with the Sun
   (5) related to comets

Answers start on page 512.

A SOLAR ECLIPSE

A solar ***eclipse*** is not magic, although people used to believe it was. A solar eclipse happens when the moon comes between the Earth and the sun. Look at the diagram below.

A SOLAR ECLIPSE

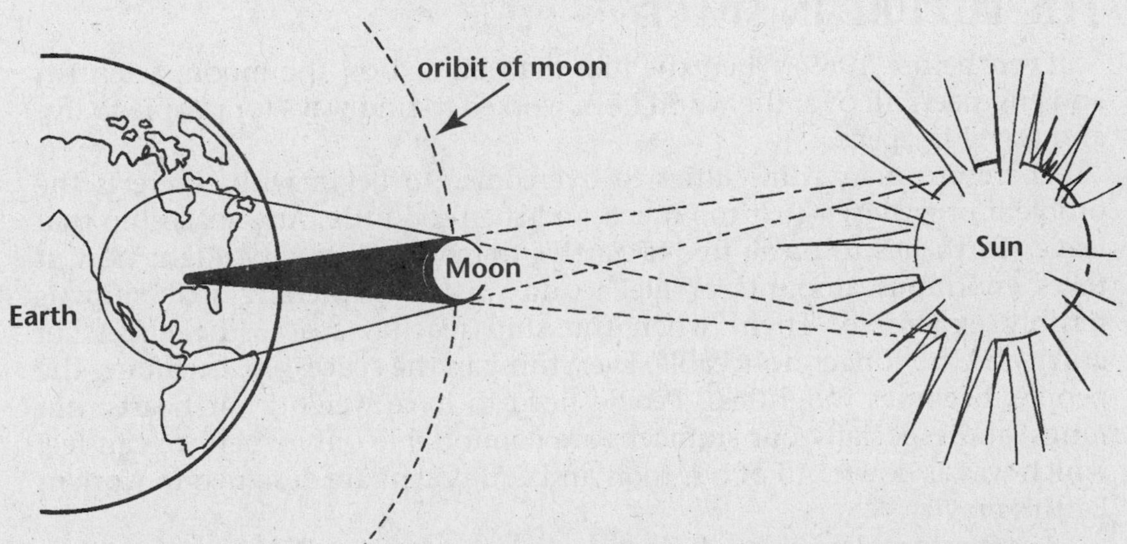

When the moon is directly between the Earth and the Sun, the Sun's rays cannot reach a small part of the Earth (a circular area 169 miles in diameter). If you are standing in this area where the moon's shadow falls, it will seem as if the Sun has disappeared. Actually, the moon is blocking your view of the Sun. It is important, however, to avoid looking at the Sun during an eclipse because doing so may cause permanent damage to your eyes.

If you are near, but not in, the shadow area, only part of the Sun will be blocked. This is called a ***partial eclipse***. Total solar eclipses are rare. When there is one, scientists will travel many miles for the opportunity to study it.

EXERCISE 9: AN ECLIPSE

Directions: Write a few sentences in answer to the following question.

1. What if you had never heard about eclipses and suddenly saw the Sun start to disappear? What might you think, feel, and do?

Directions: Circle the best answer.

2. Which of the following can you infer from the eclipse diagram?
   (1) During a solar eclipse, some people on Earth can't see the Sun or the moon.
   (2) The Earth is almost as big as the Sun.
   (3) Most of the Earth is dark during a solar eclipse.
   (4) Solar eclipses happen mostly at night.
   (5) The moon is closer to the Sun than to the Earth.

Answers start on page 512.

THE FUTURE IN SPACE

Even before 1969, when the first man landed on the moon, scientists and engineers all over the world have worked to find ways for people to live and travel in space.

There are many difficulties to overcome. To begin with, there is the problem of ***gravity***—first too much and then too little. Any spaceship that leaves Earth has to break free of Earth's tremendous gravity. Right now, it takes enormous amounts of fuel to do this, so launching spaceships is terribly expensive. Then, when the ship reaches space, the effects of gravity are no longer noticeable. Everything in the spaceship, including the people, becomes weightless. People need to have weight; our hearts, our lungs, and especially our stomachs are comfortable only when we can feel which way is down. All of our tools and equipment are designed to work in Earth's gravity.

Another problem is air. Space is nearly a ***vacuum***; that is, it is almost totally empty, containing practically no matter, not even air. Any ship that travels in space has to be completely airtight. For long trips, a spaceship would have to carry enough air for all the passengers to breathe, or scientists would need to find a way to break down exhaled carbon dioxide to get pure oxygen again. There would be the same problem on the moon, which has no real atmosphere. Every building would have to be airtight, and some way would be needed to supply oxygen for the people living there.

A third problem is heat. On Earth, our atmosphere controls the Sun's heat for us. In the daytime, it shelters us from the direct rays of the Sun, which would boil us alive. At night, it holds in heat so that we don't freeze solid. In space and on the moon, there is no atmosphere to do this. Special shielding and insulation are needed to protect us.

Space Exploration

With all these difficulties and more, why should we bother with space exploration? This is a question many people are asking now, especially when it seems that the government hasn't enough money to do everything it needs to do right here on Earth.

There are some very practical reasons for investing money and effort in space exploration. Many experiments can best be done in conditions of vacuum or weightlessness, conditions that are easy to find in space. Solving the problems of space travel and communication has already led to many inventions, like new medical monitoring techniques and the microchips used in personal computers. Many raw materials that are becoming scarce on Earth may be found in space, especially in the asteroid belt. Some nations also want to use spaceships or stations for military purposes.

Space exploration also offers tremendous opportunities to learn more about our solar system and our universe. The two *Voyager* space probes taught scientists more about the outer planets than we learned in hundreds of years of telescope observation from Earth. The space-borne Hubble telescope has shown us galaxies more distant than any seen before—and raised new questions about the size of the universe.

However, there is another important, though less obvious, reason for exploring space. Space may well be the next place we will go to learn from nature, to test our abilities and our ideals—our next, and perhaps final, frontier.

EXERCISE 10: THE FUTURE IN SPACE

Directions: Write short answers to the following questions.

1. What are the three main areas of difficulty in space exploration listed in the section of text titled "The Future in Space"?

   ____

2. Do you agree or disagree with the author's idea that our country should spend money on space research? Give at least *three* reasons for your answer and support them.

   a. ____

   b. ____

   c. ____

Directions: Choose the best ending.

3. The author of this part of the text would probably agree that
   (1) people should stick to old, traditional ways
   (2) scientific research is too expensive
   (3) dreaming of new things is useless and impractical
   (4) humanity was never intended to travel in space
   (5) people need a challenge to bring out the best in them

Answers start on page 512.

EXERCISE 11: CHAPTER REVIEW

Directions: Read each passage carefully. Then circle the number of the one best answer to each question.

Questions 1 and 2 are based on the following passage.

There are over 2,000 types of minerals found in the Earth's crust, but they can all be classified in three basic groups. The first type is igneous rock. Igneous rock is formed when hot, liquid rock is pushed up from the center of the Earth and then cools and hardens. Since the whole crust of the Earth was once liquid, most of the crust is made of igneous rock.

Sedimentary rock is often formed under water. For example, some types of sedimentary rock are formed as a layer of sand, mud, small rocks, and shells drifts to the bottom of the ocean each year. As the layers pile up, more and more pressure is put on the bottom layers. As they are pressed together, they gradually turn into rock.

Metamorphic rock is rock that has been changed. If an ordinary igneous or sedimentary rock gets buried deeply under other rocks, sometimes the heat and pressure will cause the rock to change its form. For example, marble is a metamorphic rock made from ordinary limestone.

1. According to the passage, most of the Earth's crust is made of igneous rock because
   (1) there are many volcanoes in the world
   (2) metamorphic rock is changed to igneous rock
   (3) sedimentary rock is found only where oceans have been
   (4) granite is a kind of igneous rock
   (5) the crust was once all hot, liquid rock

2. Limestone contains small shells and bits of fish skeletons. What type of rock must limestone be?
   (1) metamorphic
   (2) sedimentary
   (3) igneous
   (4) useless
   (5) expensive

Questions 3 and 4 are based on the following passage and diagrams.

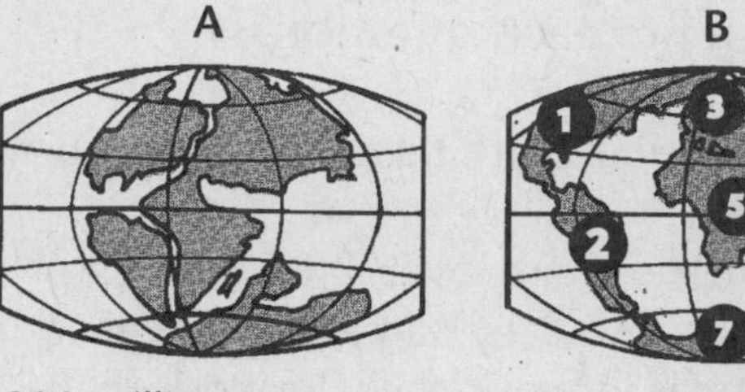

200 million years ago   present

1	North America	5	Africa
2	South America	6	Australia
3	Europe	7	Antarctica
4	Asia		

One of the most interesting ideas in science is the theory of continental drift. Scientists who hold this theory believe that at one time all seven of the continents were in one giant land mass. Gradually, over millions of years, the continents broke apart and shifted to the places where they are today.

There is a good bit of evidence supporting this theory. In the above diagrams, you can see how the western edges of Europe and Africa seem to fit right into the eastern edges of North and South America. Also, similar fossil plants and animals have been found on widely separated continents, like Africa and South America. It is hard to believe that any land-living plant or animal could somehow cross a wide ocean. It is easier to explain if, at one time, Africa and South America lay right next to each other.

Underwater exploration has offered further proof of the drift theory. Scientists have seen rifts in the ocean floor where two plates (continent-sized sections of the Earth's crust) are moving apart and molten rock is flowing out, adding new areas of seafloor.

3. One way to test the idea of continental drift would be to
   (1) watch the continents from a spaceship
   (2) try to push a continent with many large ships
   (3) keep careful records of the positions of the continents over hundreds of years
   (4) measure very carefully to see if the continental edges would still fit together exactly
   (5) see if ancient scientists believed the idea of continental drift

4. Fossils of one certain kind of animal are found in both Africa and South America. If the continental drift theory is true, that animal probably existed
   (1) recently
   (2) about 1,000 years ago
   (3) only after the continents drifted apart
   (4) before the continents drifted apart
   (5) before the Earth's crust began to cool

Questions 5 and 6 are based on the following passage.

Early explorers in Africa and South America wrote about the "endless jungle," the tropical rain forest, dark and tangled and teeming with life. Today, however, the jungle is disappearing; within twenty years there may not be any tropical rain forest left outside of a few parks and reserves.

People are destroying the rain forest. Every year thousands of acres of rain forest are cut down by lumber companies that take the largest trees, destroying the rest in the process. Other people clear many more acres to make farms and ranches. Towns and even cities are springing up in areas that used to be primitive forest.

Why should we care if all the rain forest is eventually gone? One reason is that unusual rain forest plants provide us with many medicines, dyes, and other chemicals. Even more importantly, the rain forest is a major part of the air renewal system of this planet. All the millions of green plants in the rain forest put out enormous amounts of oxygen every day. Without the rain forest, some scientists think there might not be enough green plants on Earth to keep the oxygen level up.

Scientists are concerned about the destruction of the rain forest and what that destruction might do to our planet. We need to listen to their concerns and take steps now to preserve and protect one of our most important natural resources, the tropical rain forest.

5. The main idea of the third paragraph of this passage is that rain forests are
   (1) beautiful
   (2) valuable to us
   (3) being destroyed
   (4) difficult to travel in
   (5) useless and unnecessary

6. Which would probably be the best source of more information about the destruction of the rain forest?
   (1) a pamphlet put out by a lumber company
   (2) your hometown daily newspaper
   (3) a high school chemistry textbook
   (4) articles in an ecology journal
   (5) advertisements for real estate in tropical countries

Questions 7 and 8 are based on the graph below.

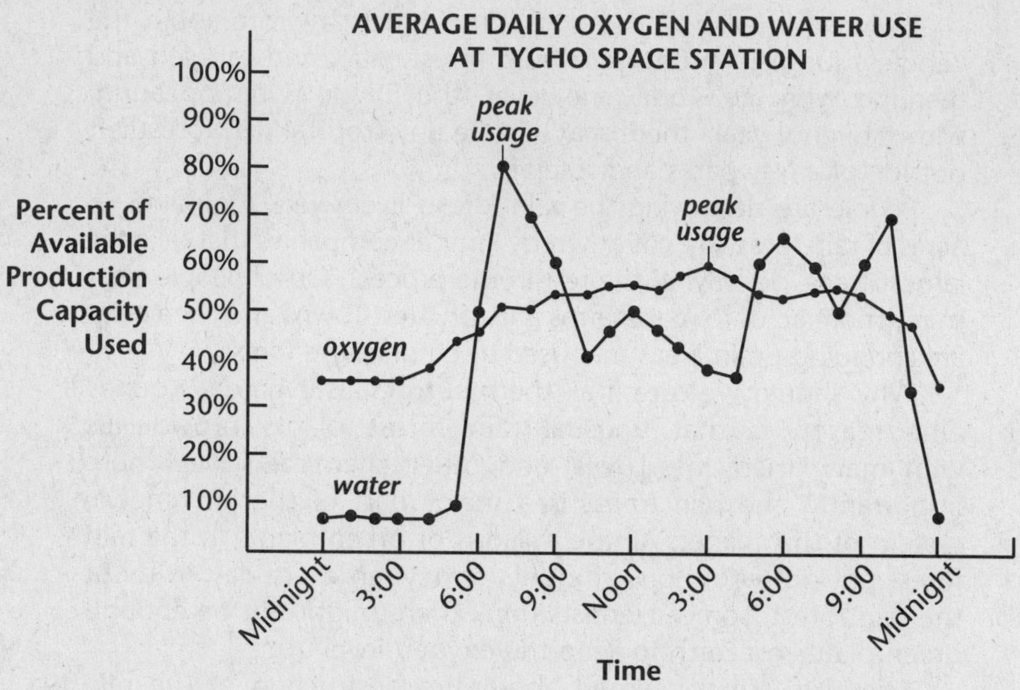

7. Which of the following can you conclude from the graph?
   (1) Water and oxygen show exactly the same pattern of usage.
   (2) Oxygen use changes more during the day than water use.
   (3) Lowest usage of water and oxygen occur at the same time.
   (4) Oxygen is more necessary than water.
   (5) Water and oxygen use both peak at the same time.

8. Which question *cannot* be answered from the information in the graph?
   (1) Are more oxygen-producing plants needed?
   (2) Who uses more water, male or female crew members?
   (3) When is oxygen use highest?
   (4) Do crew members use as much oxygen when asleep?
   (5) Does the crew use all of the water that can be produced?

Answers start on page 512.

SCIENCE ANSWER KEY

CHAPTER 1: SCIENCE KNOWLEDGE AND SKILLS

Exercise 1: Compound Words page 363

1. horsepower
2. spaceship
3. sunspot
4. earthquake
5. wavelength

Exercise 2: Word Parts page 365

1. dermatology
2. Neurology
3. Biothermal
4. thermometer
5. trimonthly
6. trifocals
7. cardiogram
8. cardiologist
9. microbiology
10. micrometer

Exercise 3: Using the Context pages 366–367

Your answers should be similar to these answers, but you may use different words. If you are not sure whether your answer is correct, check with your teacher.

1. An astrolabe might be **an instrument for looking at or measuring stars.**
2. Cyberspace might be **a kind of space that is controlled by computers.**
3. Polychromatic probably means **many-colored**
4. Carnivores are probably **animals that eat meat.**
5. Hydroponic farming is probably **farming without soil.**

Exercise 4: Understanding Scientific Language page 368

There are many ways to simplify these sentences. Here are some sample answers. If you are not sure whether your answer is correct, check with your teacher.

1. Air pollution can have very bad effects.
2. Learning how to use water power to make electricity was necessary in order to make cheap electric power.
3. Children's toys should be educational as well as fun.

Exercise 5: Fact and Opinion page 371

1 O That Denver is nicer is a matter of opinion.

2. F You can measure 92 miles.
3. O Statements about what people should do can never be proven; they are always opinions.
4. F You could prove this by a survey.
5. F You could prove this by measuring the hearing of people who listen to a lot of very loud music.
6. O Statements about what should be done are always opinions.
7. F You could prove this by looking at the records.

Exercise 6: Everyday Hypotheses page 372

Your answers should be similar to these answers, but you may use different words.

1. The storm has caused a power outage.
2. Bill isn't really sick; he's out hunting.
3. You are going to be promoted.

Exercise 7: Choosing Hypotheses pages 373–374

1. (3) The plants without light died, and the plants with little light did not grow well. Therefore, you can hypothesize that green plants need light to grow and live.
2. (4) The bacteria in the jars were killed by the boiling temperatures. Choice (2) is wrong because bacteria grew in a sealed jar with no air.
3. (2) The amount of oil burned is related directly to the average temperature. Choices (1), (4), and (5) are not correct because the most oil was burned in January, when it was sunny, not snowy, and not the holiday season. Less oil was burned in December than in November, so (3) is not right.

Exercise 8: Forming Hypotheses page 374

Your answers should be similar to these answers, but you may use different words. If you are not sure whether your answer is correct, check with your teacher.

1. The detergent is coming from the town. Upstream from the town there was no detergent in the river.
2. Carl's magnet, like all magnets, picks up only things made of iron or steel. It makes no difference how big the object is or whether or not it is wet.

Exercise 9: Errors in Experiments page 376

Your answers should be similar to these answers, but you may use different words.

1. **subjects were not similar** OR **conditions of experiment not kept the same**

   The gardener used pepper plants for one group and beans for the other, so his subjects were not all similar. He couldn't tell if the beans didn't grow because of the fertilizer, because the seeds were bad, because it was a bad year for beans, or for some other reason.

2. **not enough subjects** OR **the experiment was not reproduced**
   The mechanic tried only one squirt gun, so she didn't have enough subjects in her test group. Since the machine was having trouble only a third of the time, maybe the next gun or the one after that would have been flawed. The mechanic needs to reproduce the experiment.

Exercise 10: Review of the Scientific Method
page 378

Your answers should be similar to these answers, but you may use different words.

1. Why didn't milkmaids catch smallpox?
2. Getting cowpox keeps you from catching smallpox.
3. He tested it by giving people cowpox and seeing if it protected them against smallpox.

CHAPTER 2: LIVING THINGS

Exercise 1: Restating Facts
page 380

Your answers should be similar to these answers, but you may use different words.

1. Smoking increases your chances of getting lung cancer.
2. Many people who pass the GED test go on to do well in business.
3. Nuclear energy is very powerful and useful, but it can also do horrible damage.
4. An older person with more experience often learns more easily than a child in school.

Exercise 2: Summarizing
page 381

1. (5) This is the best summary. Choices (1) and (4) are too narrow; each covers only one of the facts given. Choice (3) is too broad, and (2) is not even mentioned.
2. (3) This is the best summary. Choices (1) and (4) are too narrow; each covers only one of the facts. Choice (2) is not mentioned. Choice (5) is not a true statement.

Exercise 3: Finding the Main Idea of a Paragraph
page 383

1. The main idea is "Cactuses are remarkable plants made to live in one of nature's harshest environments." The rest of the paragraph gives you details on how they are able to survive harsh conditions.
2. The main idea is "Cars just seem to get more and more complicated." The rest of the paragraph tells you how simple the first cars were and how they got more and more complicated as time went on.
3. The main idea is "Even though it is only a reaction of your own body, an allergy can really make you miserable." The rest of the paragraph explains how an allergy is a reaction and just how miserable it can be.

Exercise 4: Finding the Main Idea of a Passage
page 385

1. (4) The passage describes safety features a crib should have. Choices (1), (2), (3), and (5) are details.
2. (3) The passage is about a crib's safety features. Choice (1) is too broad, choice (2) is too narrow, and choices (4) and (5) are not mentioned in the passage.

Exercise 5: Cells
page 387

1. f
2. i
3. g
4. a
5. h
6. c
7. b
8. d
9. e
10. (1) The paragraph under the heading "Plant Cells" mentions cell walls. There is no mention of cell walls in animal cells.

Exercise 6: Germs
page 389

1. **a.** germs
   b. viruses
   c. bacteria
   d. protozoans
   e. immunity
   f. immunization
   g. vaccination
   h. babies
   i. protect
2. (4) The paragraph talks about how important it is to get immunized. Choices (1), (2), and (3) are too narrow, covering only one part of the paragraph. Choice (5) is not true according to the passage.

Exercise 7: Food Factories
page 391

1. F Some fungi, like yeast, are helpful.
2. T This is stated in the second paragraph of the text.
3. (1) Check the second paragraph of the text.
4. (2) Choice (2) is the best summary. Choice (1) is only a detail. Choices (4) and (5) are not mentioned.

Exercise 8: Types of Animals
pages 393–394

1. **a.** (3)
   b. (6)
   c. (5)
   d. (2)
   e. (4)
   f. (7)
   g. (1)
2. **a.** (6) A cow gives milk.
   b. (4) A rattlesnake has scales, is cold-blooded, and lays eggs on land.
   c. (5) A robin has feathers.

d. (2) A guppy has a backbone and breathes all its life with gills.
e. (1) A bee has no backbone.
f. (3) A bullfrog first lives in the water as a tadpole, then changes and lives on land.

3. (1) This is the main idea of the first section of this passage.

Exercise 9: Genetics
page 397

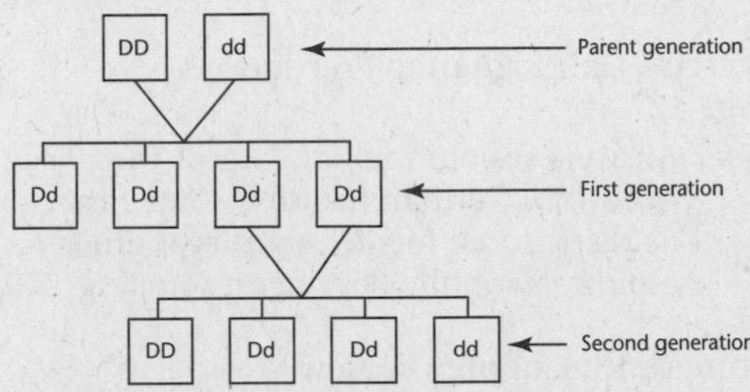

1. All the hamsters would have dark eyes because they all would inherit one dominant gene for dark eyes from one parent.
2. All of them would carry one recessive gene for light eyes from the other parent.
3. One hamster out of four would probably have light eyes; it would probably have gotten one recessive gene from each parent. Three would have dark eyes.
4. Two out of three of the dark-eyed second-generation offspring would carry a light-eye recessive gene.

Exercise 10: Chapter Review
pages 398–400

1. (3) The risk of a bad reaction may be small compared to the risk of disease. Doctors would want to keep giving the vaccine. Choices (1) and (4) are too dangerous. Choices (2) and (5) are just ways of getting opinions, not scientific proof.
2. (2) This is stated in the last sentence of the passage.
3. (1) The size and weight of the apatosaurus are the largest given. The dinosaurs in choices (2) and (3) are both smaller. The pterosaur's size is not given, so (4) is wrong. Choice (5) is not mentioned in the passage.
4. (5) The passage mentions that some dinosaurs ate plants.
5. (5) A mutated animal usually does not survive to breed.
6. (4) See the last sentence of the passage for this definition.
7. (3) Children, teenagers, and adults can all enjoy gardening. Choice (1) is too broad. Choices (2) and (4) are too narrow. Choice (5) is false.
8. (3) Some people enjoy gardening, but others may not. Choices (1), (2), and (5) are facts, not opinions. Choice (4) disagrees with the passage.

CHAPTER 3: HUMAN BIOLOGY

Exercise 1: Diagrams
page 402

1. the pupil
2. supporting fluids
3. the retina
4. the optic nerve
5. If the cornea clouds over, light cannot pass through it to the pupil and into the eye.

Exercise 2: Comparing Diagrams
page 404

1. It shows drawings of a fetus for the first 5 months of pregnancy.
2. at four months
3. (4) Choices (1) and (3) are not right because the title says that this child hasn't been born yet. Choice (2) is wrong; the head looks different because it hasn't grown yet. Choice (5) has nothing to do with the diagram.

Exercise 3: Charts
page 406

1. vitamins A, C, D, E, B_1, B_2, niacin, and B_{12}
2. scurvy
3. vitamins A and D
4. vitamins A, B_2, and niacin

Exercise 4: Line Graphs
page 411

1. (5) The heaviest rock (300 pounds) is the last one on the graph line and corresponds to 6 feet.
2. (4) The direction of the graph shows that longer crowbars move heavier rocks. Choice (2) is wrong because the length of the crowbar is important, not the thickness. Not enough information is given to conclude choice (1) or (3).
3. (1) The main idea of the graph is to show how long a crowbar must be to move rocks of different weights. Choice (3) is not true; some rocks over 300 pounds can be moved by other methods. Choice (4) is not told; other crowbars may be available. Choice (5) is not complete. The graph gives no information for rocks under 50 pounds, but that doesn't mean that there aren't any.

Exercise 5: Bar Graphs
page 414

1. You expect to find information about the average temperatures in Vancouver.
2. It shows the months of the year.
3. It shows the average high temperatures in degrees Fahrenheit.
4. 5°F
5. 50°F
6. July and August
7. No, it probably doesn't get below freezing very often because the lowest average temperature is only 42°F.

Exercise 6: Bones and Muscles
page 417

1. T There are 206 bones.
2. T These are two of the main functions of bones.
3. F Cartilage is softer than bone.
4. T Ligaments are tough bands of tissue that hold bones together at the joints.
5. T One possible cause of osteoporosis is not getting enough calcium.
6. F Voluntary muscles are controlled by you.
7. T Cardiac muscles are found in the heart.
8. (4) See the diagram. Look at the skeleton's spine (backbone) and neck.

Exercise 7: Heart, Blood, and Lungs
page 419

1. lungs	7. oxygen
2–3. nose, mouth	8. carbon dioxide
4. trachea	9. Red blood cells
5. bronchial tubes	10. White blood cells
6. alveoli	11. Platelets

Exercise 8: Nutrition
page 421

1. (2) See the chart. Find carbohydrates in the "Nutrients" column. Then look to the right under "What It Does."
2. (4) A statement about what someone *should* do is usually an opinion. All the other choices are facts.

Exercise 9: Digestion
page 423

1. g	4. b	7. e
2. f	5. h	8. a
3. d	6. c	

9. (4) See the last two paragraphs of the passage for the correct order.

Exercise 10: The Nervous System
page 424

1. skin	4. brain	6. motor
2. sensory	5. brain	7. hand
3. spinal cord		

Exercise 11: Stress
page 426

1. Answers will vary. One possible reason is that these events cause big changes in a person's way of life.
2. Answers will vary. One answer is that they all involve change.
3. (4) "Change in eating habits" is number 19 on the list. The other choices—pregnancy, trouble with the law, losing a job, and personal injury—are all rated as more stressful.

Exercise 12: Pregnancy Precautions
page 427

1–4. Answers should include four of these: bad nutrition, German measles, some other diseases, some medicines, illegal drugs, aspirin, alcoholic beverages, smoking.

Exercise 13: Chapter Review
pages 428–432

1. (3) The diagram shows that these three bones are located in the middle ear.
2. (1) If the eardrum cannot vibrate, the person's hearing is affected. Choices (2) and (5) are wrong because we have no evidence about the effect of pain on hearing. Choice (3) is wrong because the fluid would be at body temperature, not cold. Choice (4) is wrong because, if the sound traveled better, the person would hear better, not worse.
3. (4) See the chart, across from "Males, 23–50."
4. (3) This is true for men and women of all ages. Choice (1) is not true because after 23, people need fewer calories. Choice (2) is wrong because a 19-to-22-year-old woman needs more calories than a 76-year-old man. Choices (4) and (5) are not right according to the chart.
5. (3) The passage talks about why STDs are dangerous and need a doctor's attention. Choices (2) and (4) are in the passage, but they are only details. Choice (1) is not in the passage. Choice (5) is false according to the passage.
6. (5) See the first paragraph. None of the other answers ever cure STDs.
7. (3) The graph shows that a 45-year-old nonsmoker can expect to live until age 75, while a two-packs-a-day smoker of the same age can expect to live only until age 68. The difference is 7 years.
8. (2) The graph shows that people who smoke less tend to live longer. This can be concluded by comparing the lifespans of smokers and nonsmokers.

CHAPTER 4: PHYSICS

Exercise 1: Sequencing
page 436

a. 4 c. 2
b. 1. d. 3

Exercise 2: Logical Sequence
page 437

1. Logical order: b, a. Steam engines must be invented before they can be put into locomotives.
2. Logical order: b, a, c. Before Franklin discovered what lightning really was, people could have believed it was a weapon of the gods. Franklin had to discover what lightning was before he could invent lightning rods.

Exercise 3: Causes and Effects
page 439

Your answers should be similar to these answers, but you may use different words. If you are not sure, check with your teacher.

1. *Cause:* The chain reaction goes very fast.
2. *Effect:* Not enough heat is formed.
3. *Effect:* The water boils.
4. *Cause:* The steam turns giant generators.

Exercise 4: Finding Causes and Effects
pages 440–441

1. (3) Many people came to Bohr's home to talk about science, and that got him interested. Choices (l), (4), and (5) are true, but they did not cause Bohr to become interested in science. Choice (2) is not mentioned in the passage.
2. (2) The Nazis were interested in Bohr because he was well known and respected. All the other events did happen, but they were not caused by his fame.

Exercise 5: Making Inferences
page 442

Your answers should be similar to these answers, but you may use different words. If you are not sure, check with your teacher.

1. Smokeless tobacco can cause mouth cancer.
2. a. They are made of polyester.
   b. They were hard to take care of.
3. a. Too much fat and sugar can help cause heart attacks.
   b. A person should eat less fat and sugar to avoid heart attacks.

Exercise 6: Simple Machines
page 445

1. a. simple machines
   b. work done
   c. force
   d. amount of push
   e. foot-pounds
2. (4) 2,000 pounds x 20 feet = 40,000 foot-pounds.

Exercise 7: Computers
page 447

1. Any four of these are correct: telephones, accounting, banks, businesses, secretaries, writers, teaching, games. Also correct are any other true uses of computers.
2. Any five of these: keyboard, disks, tapes, paper cards, paper tapes, lights, modems, telephone lines.
3. Any five of these: screen, printer, disks, tapes, cards, modems, telephone lines.

Exercise 8: Electricity
page 450

1. ceiling light 4. dishwasher
2. counter lights 5. electric clock
3. outlet

(Check the diagram for the sequence of items 1–5.)

6. (5) Nothing would work because there must be a complete circuit for the electricity to flow at all.

Exercise 9: Nuclear Power
page 452

1. B Speaker B is worried about security not being able to stop terrorists.
2. B Speaker B asks, "How can they be sure?"
3. A Speaker A says the groups worried about nuclear power are "radical."
4. (5) This fact is given in the second paragraph. Choice (1) is a fact from selection A, not B. Choice (3) is an opinion, not a fact, from A. Choice (2) is an opinion from B, not a fact.
5. (2) Obviously Speaker A is in favor of nuclear power. Utility companies are the companies that own and operate nuclear and other types of power plants. Choice (3) would be against nuclear power. Choices (1) and (4) would not necessarily be interested in nuclear power plants at all.

Exercise 10: Light and Sound
page 454

1. T
2. F Light is faster than sound.
3. F White light is a combination of all colors.
4. T
5. T
6. F Sound travels best through solid things.

Exercise 11: Chapter Review
pages 454–458

1. (4) Only levers A and D are balanced. Check this by multiplying the force times the distance on each side.
2. (5) Side A will go down because the heavier side always goes down, even if the difference is only a pound. It does not matter how *many* weights are on each side, but rather how *much* the total weight is on each.
3. (5) The passage tells you to look at the battery if you have trouble starting your car.
4. (4) This answer is implied because the author is clearly directing this at people who do not already know a lot about cars.
5. (3) This is implied in the sentence "The darker the object, the more light it will absorb and change to heat." Choice (2) is incorrect because of the same sentence. Choices (1), (4), and (5) are not mentioned at all in the passage.
6. (2) Solar heat is defined in the passage as heat from sunlight. Choices (1), (3), and (5) are not indicated in any way in the article. Choice (4) is true, but it is not a problem; it is an advantage.
7. (4) As in the example in the passage, a sound twenty decibels higher is actually 100 times louder than the softer sound, because each 10-decibel jump means ten times as much sound. $10 \times 10 = 100$
8. (1) According to the chart, drills, shovels, and trucks put out the most decibels of sound, so a person working with them would have the greatest chance of job-related hearing damage.

CHAPTER 5: CHEMISTRY

Exercise 1: Atoms and Molecules
page 460

1. c	4. g	7. b
2. h	5. i	8. f
3. d	6. a	9. e

Exercise 2: Mixtures, Solutions, and Compounds
pages 462–463

1. M	3. S	5. C
2. C	4. M	6. S

Numbers 2 and 5 are compounds because two chemicals go together to make a completely different substance. Numbers 3 and 6 are solutions because they could not be separated by sorting or filtering. The others are simple mixtures because they would be easy to separate into their original parts.

7. (3) Salt is a compound, rather than a mixture or a solution, because it is an entirely different substance from its original parts. It can't be a poison, since people eat it every day.

Exercise 3: Chemical Names and Symbols
page 465

1. $CaCl_2$	4. $NaSO_4$
2. CaO	5. CO
3. H_2S	6. HNO_2

Check with the chart in this article or your teacher if you missed some of these.

7. (5) It has four chlorine atoms and one carbon atom. Choice (3) has the wrong chemicals. Choices (1), (2), and (4) have the wrong number of chlorine atoms.

Exercise 4: Acids and Bases
page 467

1. Acids
2. bases

3–5. Choose three of these: vinegar, oranges, sour milk, lemons, grapefruit, canned foods

6–8. drain cleaner, washing soda, ammonia

9. sour	13. litmus
10. bitter	14. red
11. Bases	15. blue
12. acids	

Exercise 5: Decisions About Chemicals
page 470

1–2. Answers will vary.

3. (2) A statement that tells you what someone *should* do is an opinion. The other choices are facts from the article.

Exercise 6: Drug Abuse
page 472

1. c	5. a
2. e	6. h
3. g	7. d
4. f	8. b

Exercise 7: Chapter Review
pages 472–477

1. (3) Three of the listed compounds contain Ag, the symbol for silver.
2. (5) CuCl contains copper and chlorine. None of the other chemicals named has these two elements.
3. (4) All three body parts are listed as possible places of damage.
4. (2) See line 3 of the instructions.
5. (2) Metal poisoning is the only choice given that is listed as causing problems with the nervous system.
6. (5) Dust is not listed as one of the causes of headaches and dizziness.
7. (2) Speaker A would disagree with the other choices because he is arguing against the marijuana laws.

8. (1) You could prove how many people want marijuana legalized by taking a poll. Choices (2), (3), and (5) are opinions because no one can prove what could happen in the future. Choice (4) is an opinion because it talks about what people should do.

CHAPTER 6: EARTH SCIENCE

Exercise 1: You Decide
pages 479–480

Answers will vary.

Exercise 2: The Whole Story
page 481

Answers will vary. Here are some possibilities.

1. How hot or cold does it get in California? Is there much rain?
2. Which vitamins should be taken? How much? What specific health problems will each vitamin solve?
3. How much would taxes go up because of the park—closer to $2 or $200?
4. Why are new roads needed? What does the speaker mean by "progress"?
5. Is there evidence that Chemical X causes cancer in humans? How many mice were tested in the study?

Exercise 3: Information, Please
page 482

1. Choices (2) and (3) are good sources. (1) is not a good source because the factory would be biased toward persuading you that it is not polluting the river. (4) is not the best source because the friend is probably not as knowledgeable as the health department or Citizens for a Better Environment.
2. Choices (1) and (4) are the best sources. Neither (2) nor (3) is as knowledgeable, unless one of them happens to be a doctor or nurse.
3. (1) and (2) are the best sources. Your brother [source (3)] is probably not as knowledgeable, and source (4), the health food store clerk, may be biased, since her job depends on people buying health foods.

Exercise 4: Treasure from the Earth
page 484

Answers will vary. Here are some possibilities.

1. copper—electrical wires, kitchen pans, jewelry
2. iron—cars, stainless steel and cast-iron kitchen utensils, wood stoves, steel beams, wrought-iron railings, many tools
3. aluminum—kitchen utensils, foil, electrical wires
4. fossil fuels—gasoline, natural gas, heating oil, polyester clothes, draperies and upholstery
5. (4) This is stated in the third paragraph.

Exercise 5: Soil Conservation
page 487

1. helps
2. harms
3. helps
4. harms
5. helps
6. helps
7. helps
8. (2) The text says that manure is organic fertilizer. Organic fertilizer has humus, which is needed for healthy soil. Choice (5) is incorrect because soil needs more than just nitrogen. Choices (1) and (3) wouldn't help the soil. Choice (4) would cause erosion.

Exercise 6: A Forest Ecosystem
pages 490–491

1. The producers are green plants (the tree, the bush, and the grass). Only green plants can produce food.
2. The primary consumers are the squirrel, the insects, the deer, the raccoon, and the man because they all eat plants.
3. The secondary consumers are the fox, the wolf, the raccoon, and the man because they eat other animals.
4. The bacteria and the fungi are the decomposers.
5. (2) This is the main idea behind ecology. Choice (1) is not correct because people only *partly* control their environment. Choice (4) is wrong because all living things are needed; many plants couldn't survive without animals either. Choices (3) and (5) are in the article but are only details.

Exercise 7: Weather
page 493

1. F **Air** pressure is also called barometric pressure.
2. T
3. F **Cumulus** clouds are soft-looking, puffy clouds.
4. T
5. F **Hail** is formed when frozen raindrops are blown up and down between layers of warm and cold air.
6. (4) Warm air rises. Choice (1) is wrong because the sun's gravity causes an equal (but very small) pull on *all* air on Earth. Choices (2) and (3) are not true according to the diagram. Choice (5) is not mentioned in the diagram.

Exercise 8: The Heavenly Bodies
pages 496–497

1. Jupiter
2. stars
3. asteroids
4. galaxy
5. Venus
6. solar system
7. comet
8. (4) The Sun is the center of the solar system.

Exercise 9: An Eclipse
page 498

1. Answers will vary.
2. (1) Both the sun and the moon are on one side of the Earth, so people on the other side of the Earth can't see them.

Exercise 10: The Future in Space
page 500

1. gravity, air, and heat
2. Answers will vary.
3. (5) The last paragraph shows that the author thinks people need a challenge. Her opinions throughout the article show that she would disagree with the other four statements.

Exercise 11: Chapter Review
pages 501–504

1. (5) See the first paragraph of the passage.
2. (2) Since limestone contains small pieces of sea creatures, it must have formed under the ocean; therefore, it is sedimentary.
3. (3) This method would show whether or not the continents were shifting. Choices (1), (2), and (4) are not practical. Choice (5) is incorrect because ancient scientists weren't always right.
4. (4) The animal must have existed before the continents split in order to be found on both sides of the ocean. That eliminates answers (1), (2), and (3). Choice (5) is impossible; no animals lived on land before the crust cooled.
5. (2) The paragraph lists many examples of how the rain forests are valuable. Choices (1), (3), and (4) are all details. Choice (5) is untrue.
6. (4) The journal would be a good source of information on conservation issues. Sources (1) and (5) would probably be biased. Source (2) might have some information, but it would not be as complete as articles in a specialized journal.
7. (3) Lowest usage of both water and oxygen occur from midnight to 3:00 A.M., presumably because the crew members are all asleep. Choices (1), (2), and (5) are false according to the information on the graph. There is no information on the graph about Choice (4).
8. (2) There is nothing on the graph to show which crew members are using the water.

Section 4

READING/LITERATURE AND THE ARTS

1 GAINING MEANING FROM WORDS

You want to understand whole sentences, paragraphs, and passages. However, do individual *words* ever slow you down? A good vocabulary helps you to understand more of what you read.

There are a number of ways to build your vocabulary. In this chapter we'll look at those ways. First, we'll work on *dictionary skills.* Then we'll study *syllables, word parts,* and *synonyms and antonyms.*

VOCABULARY: DICTIONARY SKILLS

Skillful use of a dictionary is important for adults. It allows you to figure out the meanings of words on your own and to continue to learn in and out of school.

Words represent ideas. If you don't know what a word means, you can't *think* about that idea, much less read with understanding or discuss it. A good vocabulary is important in making progress in school, on the job, and at home. Being able to use a dictionary well is also useful for parents who help their children with homework.

BASIC ALPHABETICAL ORDER

As you know, the dictionary lists words in alphabetical order by the first letter in each word. Look at the three words that follow. In what order would the dictionary list them?

fan corn hit

Look at the first letter of each word. Which letter comes first: *f*, *c*, or *h?* Since *c* comes before *f* or *h, corn* would be first in alphabetical order. Which letter comes next: *f* or *h?* Since *f* comes after *c* but before *h, fan* would be next. Since *h* comes after *f, hit* would be the last word.

corn fan hit

EXERCISE 1: ALPHABETICAL ORDER BY FIRST LETTERS

Directions: The following groups of words are not in alphabetical order. Rearrange them as they would appear in the dictionary.

1. broccoli, lettuce, onion, peas, cauliflower, radish

 ____

2. Ford, Chevrolet, Honda, Toyota, Oldsmobile, Mazda

 ____

3. love, hate, disgust, charm, reject, feel

 ____

Answers start on page 670.

COMPLEX ALPHABETICAL ORDER

You've seen how the dictionary lists words in alphabetical order by the first letter in each word. But many words start with the same letter: *can, cent, chat.*

How does the dictionary sort these out? Read the following rule.

> **Rule:** If the first letters in the words are alike, alphabetize by the second letters. If the first and second letters are the same, alphabetize by the third, and so on.

For example, look at these five words:

can cent chat chart cereal

Since they all begin with *c*, you must look at the *second* letter of each word in order to alphabetize them. Before putting them into a final list, look at the *third* and *fourth* letters.

The correct order is as follows:

can cent cereal chart chat

EXERCISE 2: ALPHABETIZING BEYOND THE FIRST LETTER

Directions: Look at each set of words. Alphabetize them. If they begin with the same first letter, you must alphabetize by the second. If the first two letters are the same, alphabetize by the third, and so on. Write the words in alphabetical order in the blanks provided.

1. needle, nervous, nerd, need, nest

____

2. worry, wrench, wreck, worm, worn

____

3. able, abuse, ache, achieve, about

____

Answers start on page 670.

GUIDE WORDS

Now that you know how to alphabetize words, the *guide words* on a dictionary page will help you locate a word quickly. The guide words are the two words at the top of a dictionary page. The guide word on the left is the first word defined on that page. The guide word on the right is the last word defined on that page. Look at the dictionary page that follows. Note the words *lid* and *lizard* in **boldface type** at the top of the page. By using alphabetical order and guide words, you can quickly decide whether the word you want is on that page, before it, or after it.

lid—lizard

lid *n* a cover for the opening or top of a container
lift *v* to raise from a lower to a higher place
light *adj* easy to carry, having little weight
limerick *n* a humorous verse having a special rhyme scheme
limp *v* to walk unsteadily or with difficulty
linen *n* cloth known for its strength and shine
linger *v* to be slow in leaving
link *n* something that connects one thing to another
lint *n* fuzz from small pieces of yarn and fabric
lion *n* a large, meat-eating cat
lipstick *n* a cosmetic, usually colored, for the lips
liquid *n* a substance that flows like water
list *n* a record or catalog of names or items
listen *v* to pay attention to something you hear
listless *adj* having no energy
liter *n* a metric unit for measuring liquids
literature *n* a body of written work, including prose, poetry, and drama
litter *v* to scatter trash or garbage
lively *adj* energetic, full of spirit
lizard *n* any of a group of long-bodied reptiles

For example, would *lane* be on this page? No, *la* (in *lane*) comes before *li* (in the guide word *lid*), so you would know to turn back a few pages.

Would *loose* be on this page? No, *lo* (in *loose*) comes after *li* (in the guide word *lizard*), so you would know to turn forward a page or so.

Would *list* be on the page? Yes, *lis* (in *list*) comes after *lid* (the guide word) and before *liz* (the guide word *lizard*). Therefore, you know *list* would be on the page.

EXERCISE 3: USING GUIDE WORDS

Directions: Decide whether the following words listed in the left column would be on the page between the guide words, or on a page before or after the guide words. Write *before* if the word on the left comes before the guide words. Write *after* if the word on the left comes after the guide words. Write *same page* if the word would be on the same page as the guide words. The first one is done as an example.

Part 1 GUIDE WORDS: **combat—command**

Words	**Where Words Appear** *(before, after,* or *same page?)*
1. come	same page
2. commit	____________
3. color	____________
4. college	____________
5. compass	____________
6. common	____________
7. comet	____________

Part 2 GUIDE WORDS: **hockey—Holmes**

1. home ____________
2. hike ____________
3. house ____________
4. hospital ____________
5. holiday ____________
6. holdup ____________
7. hoarse ____________

Answers start on page 670.

FINDING RELATED WORDS

Often, dictionaries put the definition of a longer word at the bottom part of the entry for the shorter word from which it's formed. This uses less space than making a separate entry.

What would you look under to find the word *basically?* You were right if you said *basic*. *Basically* is formed from the shorter word *basic*.

EXERCISE 4: FINDING RELATED FORMS OF A WORD

Directions: Look at each word at the left; then write the shorter, related word under which you could find it. The first one is done for you.

To Find	Look Under
1. hollowness	hollow
2. marriageable	__________
3. quickness	__________
4. liquidity	__________
5. guardianship	__________
6. discontentment	__________
7. chargeable	__________

Answers start on page 670.

PRONUNCIATION

Now you'll see how the dictionary can help you pronounce a word that you don't know how to say. For example, look at the word *chic:*

It looks like the word *chick* or *chicken*. But just after the word, the dictionary gives you another spelling between parentheses ( ) or slashes / /, depending on your dictionary: chic (*shēk*)

You already know how to say the *sh* sound at the beginning and the *k* sound at the end of (*shēk*). But you also need to know how to say the *ē*, the vowel sound in the middle.

To know how to say the *ē*, you look at the dictionary's *pronunciation key*. The pronunciation key shows you how to pronounce the vowels in a word by giving you sample words whose vowels sound the same. The pronunciation key may be found on a page at the beginning or at the end of your dictionary. A shortened version of it may appear at the bottom of every other page.

Here is part of the pronunciation key from *Webster's New World Dictionary of the English Language*:

> fat, āpe, cär; ten, ēven; is, bīte; gō, hôrn, to͞ol, look,
> oil, out, up, f~~ur~~ . . .

From this list, find the word with the *e* marked the same as the *e* in (*shēk*): ēven. Now we know that the *e* in *shek* is said the same way as the first *e* in *even*. Therefore, *chic* is pronounced *shēk*.

EXERCISE 5: LOOKING UP PRONUNCIATIONS

Directions: In your dictionary, look up each of the words in the left-hand column. In the middle column, copy from the dictionary the pronunciation given in parentheses ( ). Then compare the pronunciation to the pronunciation key in your dictionary. Find the word in the pronunciation key that has the same vowel sound as the word you looked up, and write it in the third column. The first one is done as an example.

Word	Pronunciation from Dictionary	Word from Pronunciation Key That Matches Vowel
1. chute	(shōōt)	tool
2. reign	______	______
3. aisle	______	______
4. psalm	______	______
5. beau	______	______
6. plague	______	______
7. plaque	______	______

Answers start on page 670.

UNDERSTANDING LABELS

Dictionaries use the following abbreviations for the different kinds of words and their uses. These labels help you know how to use the word.

n = noun	words used to name things
pron = pronoun	words that can be used in place of nouns
*v** = verb	words of action or state of being
adj = adjective	words that describe nouns
adv = adverb	words that describe verbs, adjectives, or other adverbs
prep = preposition	words that give a position in time and space
conj = conjunction	words that connect other words

* You may see *vb*, *vt*, or *vi* in the dictionary. These are all verb forms.

These abbreviations usually appear just after the pronunciation in parentheses. If the word can be used in more than one way (as a noun and a verb, for example), the second label will appear further down in the entry.

EXERCISE 6: UNDERSTANDING DICTIONARY LABELS

Directions: In a dictionary, look up each of the following words. Then write the part(s) of speech given. Some words can be used as more than one part of speech. The first one is done as an example.

Word	Part(s) of Speech
1. bat	noun, verb
2. cross	____________
3. exhibit	____________
4. liquid	____________
5. around	____________
6. rule	____________
7. about	____________
8. but	____________
9. they	____________

Answers start on page 670.

MULTIPLE MEANINGS

Many words have more than one meaning. These different meanings are listed in the dictionary by number, with the most common meaning as number 1, the next most common as number 2, and so forth.

For example, one common meaning of *leave* is "to allow to remain," as in "Leave a sip for me." Another meaning of *leave* is "to abandon," as in "How could Bob leave his wife and children by themselves?"

EXERCISE 7: UNDERSTANDING MULTIPLE MEANINGS

Directions: In each item two sentences contain the same word in **bold type**. However, in each sentence the boldfaced word has a different meaning. Look up the boldfaced word in the dictionary. Pick the meaning that fits the way the word is used in each sentence. Then, write the correct meaning on the blank beneath each sentence. One is done as an example.

1. **a.** I want to **pose** a question.

   Meaning: to propose (a question)

   b. The model held the **pose** for two hours.

   Meaning: a bodily attitude, especially one held for an artist

2. **a.** Newspapers **report** important events.

   Meaning: ______________________________

   b. I have to **report** for work at 8:00 A.M. daily.

   Meaning: ______________________________

3. **a.** We sat in the third **row** of the movie theater.

   Meaning: ______________________________

   b. We had to **row** ashore when it began to rain.

   Meaning: ______________________________

4. **a.** She gave him a sympathetic **pat**.

   Meaning: ______________________________

   b. I used one **pat** of butter on the bread.

   Meaning: ______________________________

5. **a.** Get a new **bar** of soap from under the sink.

   Meaning: ______________________________

   b. He ordered a milkshake at the snack **bar**.

   Meaning: ______________________________

6. **a.** Tom works at a furniture **plant**.

   Meaning: ______________________________

   b. They liked the flowering **plant** but were afraid it wouldn't get enough sunlight in their apartment.

   Meaning: ______________________________

Answers start on page 670.

VOCABULARY: SYLLABLES

Why do you need to know about syllables? Syllables can be combined to make words. Syllables are word parts that form "beats." Breaking words into syllables sometimes provides clues to the meanings of words. Syllables also help you to spell words correctly. Look at these examples:

walk = 1 beat, or 1 syllable
i + deal = 2 beats, or 2 syllables
qui + et + ly = 3 beats, or 3 syllables
in + for + ma + tion = 4 beats, or 4 syllables

There are several rules that can help you decide how to break a word into syllables:

- The Prefix/Suffix Rule
- The VC/CV Rule
- The VCV Rule

You will want to use these rules in the order in which they're given here. First, see if the Prefix/Suffix Rule applies to the word you are dividing (in other words, does the word have a prefix or a suffix?). If it does, use the rule to divide the word. If it doesn't apply, then go on to the next rule listed.

Note: The rules for pronunciation that are given in this vocabulary section may not always agree with the syllable division in the dictionary. The reason is that the dictionary often breaks words by rules other than those relating to pronunciation.

THE PREFIX/SUFFIX RULE

The first rule you need to apply when deciding how to break a word into syllables is the *Prefix/Suffix Rule*. A ***prefix*** is a syllable added to the beginning of a word. A ***suffix*** is a syllable added to the end of a word. Look at the following charts that list common prefixes and suffixes.

Common Prefixes	
pre-	re-
ex-	dis-
in-	un-
pro-	de-
sub-	trans-
non-	mis-

Common Suffixes	
-ing	-ish
-er	-est
-ness	-ment
-ist	-ful
-less	-ship
-tion (say "shun")	-or
	-ly
	-al

The *Prefix/Suffix Rule* tells you to break a word into syllables in the following way:

Prefix	—	Word or Word Part	—	Suffix
1 SYLLABLE		1 OR MORE SYLLABLES		1 SYLLABLE

To use the Prefix/Suffix Rule, you must first decide whether your word contains a prefix or a suffix. The charts you just looked at will help you determine this.

Let's take an example. Look at the following word:

redoing

Does this word have a prefix, a suffix, or both? If you look at the charts on page 524, you can see that it has both; the prefix is *re-* and the suffix is *-ing*. Now let's apply the Prefix/Suffix Rule to the word *redoing*:

re-	+	do	+	-ing
PREFIX		WORD OR WORD PART		SUFFIX

The word *redoing* has now been divided into syllables by using the Prefix/Suffix Rule.

Redoing has both a prefix and a suffix. However, some words may have only a prefix or only a suffix. You can use the Prefix/Suffix Rule for these words as well. For example, the word *export* has only a prefix, so only the prefix part of the Prefix/Suffix Rule is applied, like this:

ex-	+	port
PREFIX		WORD OR WORD PART

Practice applying the Prefix/Suffix Rule to the words in the following exercise.

EXERCISE 8: APPLYING THE PREFIX/SUFFIX RULE

Directions: Break the following words into syllables by breaking the prefix and/or suffix away from the rest of the word. Underline each prefix and/or suffix. Then say each word to yourself. The first one is done as an example.

1. sickness = *sick-ness*
2. subtraction =
3. prevention =
4. misspelling =
5. extended =
6. retirement =
7. swiftly =
8. proposal =

Answers start on page 671.

THE VC/CV RULE

The next rule for breaking words into syllables is the VC/CV Rule. The V stands for *vowel*; the C stands for *consonant*. The VC/CV Rule tells you that if two consonants come together with vowels on either side, you split the word between the two consonants like this:

VC-CV

Let's look at how this rule works with the words *rabbit* and *silver:*

rabbit	silver
↑↑↑↑	↑↑↑↑
VCCV	VCCV

In both words, two consonants come together, with vowels on either side. Therefore, the VC/CV Rule tells you to split the words between the two consonants, like this:

rab-bit	sil-ver
VC-CV	VC-CV

Note: Silent *e*'s at the ends of words and syllables do not count as vowels. Only *sounding* vowels count. For example, look at the silent *e*'s in the syllables in the following words:

re-mote-ly (silent e crossed out)   en-gage-ment (silent e crossed out)

In the words *rabbit* and *silver,* you've seen how the VC/CV Rule works with words that have neither a prefix nor a suffix. Now let's look at how to use the VC/CV Rule with words to which you've already applied the Prefix/Suffix Rule. Look at the following examples:

re-en-ter-ing	un-hap-pi-ness
PREFIX-VC-CV-SUFFIX	PREFIX-VC-CV-SUFFIX

EXERCISE 9: APPLYING THE VC/CV RULE

Part 1

Directions: Use the Prefix/Suffix Rule and the VC/CV Rule to break the following words into syllables. Mark the VC/CV. The first one is done as an example.

1. fragment = *frag-ment* (VC CV)
2. remnant =
3. curtain =
4. appendix =
5. budget =
6. embassy =
7. consistent =
8. filter =

Part 2

Directions: Using the Prefix/Suffix Rule and the VC/CV Rule, break the following words into syllables. Next, underline any prefixes and suffixes. Then say each word to yourself. The first one is done as an example.

1. abnormally = *ab-nor-mal-ly*
2. interception =
3. prospector =
4. interviewer =
5. compartment =
6. correspond =
7. exceptional =
8. organist =

Answers start on page 671.

THE VCV RULE

The third rule to apply when dividing words into syllables concerns *one* consonant falling between two vowels, as in the following examples:

solo = so-lo *or* rapid = rap-id
V-CV VC-V

As you can see, the single consonant can go with either the first vowel or the second vowel, as shown by the VCV Rule that follows:

V-CV *or* VC-V

To judge which way to place the consonant, figure out the vowel sound. A long vowel will end a syllable. With a long vowel, use V + CV, as in the word *solo*:

sō-lō
V-CV

A short vowel will be followed by one or more consonants. With a short vowel, use VC + V, as in the word *rapid*:

răp-ĭd
VC V

EXERCISE 10: APPLYING THE VCV RULE

Directions: Divide the following words into syllables using the VCV rule. Mark long vowels with a (¯), short vowels with a (˘), and silent vowels with a (/). Then say each word to yourself. The first one is done for you.

1. agent = ā gĕnt
2. recent =
3. cabinet =
4. tomato =
5. license =
6. humane =
7. female =
8. limit =

Answers start on page 671.

VOCABULARY: DICTIONARY SKILLS

Now we will be looking at word parts in a different way—as an aid to understanding the *meanings* of words.

PREFIXES

Prefixes (beginning syllables) are sometimes added to whole words we already know in order to change the meaning. For example, the prefix *il-* means "not." When we add *il-* to *legal*, we get *illegal*, which means "not legal."

Prefixes may also be added to word parts called *roots*. **Roots** are the bases on which many words are built. Many roots come from ancient Latin and Greek words.

For example, the prefix *in-* can mean either "in" or "inside." The Latin word *carcer* means "prison." From the prefix *in-* and the Latin root *carcer* we get the English word *incarcerate*. This word means "to put someone in prison." You'll work more on Latin and Greek roots later. Following is a table listing some common prefixes and their meanings.

Prefix	Meaning
re-	again
anti-	against
dis-	not, away, from
un-	not
inter-	between, among

EXERCISE 11: ADDING PREFIXES

Directions: Make a word by adding one of the prefixes in the table to each of the words and roots in the following list. Write the word you formed in the blank provided. With some words and roots, you may be able to use more than one prefix to make a word. Notice how the meaning of the new word you formed differs from the old one. The first one is done as an example.

	Prefix	Word or Root	New Word
1.	*re*	use	*reuse*
2.	________	war	________
3.	________	likely	________
4.	________	ability	________
5.	________	section	________
6.	________	charge	________
7.	________	national	________
8.	________	natural	________

Answers start on page 671.

PREFIXES THAT MAKE OPPOSITES

When added to a word, some prefixes change the meaning of that word to its opposite. Prefixes that often do this are those meaning "not." For example, if you take the prefix *un-* and add it to the word *healthy*, you get the following:

un- + healthy = unhealthy ("not healthy," or the opposite of healthy)

Prefixes that change the meaning of a word to its opposite are listed in the following table.

Prefixes That Change the Meaning to Its Opposite			
Prefix	**Means**	**As in**	**Definition**
un-	not	unable	*not* able
in-	not	incorrect	*not* correct
im-	not	impossible	*not* possible
il-	not	illegal	*not* legal
ir-	not	irresponsible	*not* responsible
non-	not	nonsmoker	*not* a smoker
mis-	wrong	misplace	put in *wrong* place
dis-	not, away from	displease	*not* please
anti-	against	antiwar	*against* war

EXERCISE 12: PREFIXES THAT MAKE OPPOSITES

Directions: Circle the prefix in each of the words that follow. Then write the definition of the word on the blank provided. The first one is done for you.

Word **Meaning**

1. unkind *not kind*
2. irresponsible ______
3. immature ______
4. nonviolent ______
5. disabled ______
6. misspelling ______
7. illegitimate ______
8. inconsiderate ______

Answers start on page 671.

PREFIXES THAT SHOW TIME

Some prefixes have meanings that are related to time. Study the following prefixes and their meanings. Notice that each of these prefixes relates to *when* something is done. Therefore, these prefixes show time.

Prefix	Means	As in	Definition
ante-	before	antedate	to date *before*
pre-	before	prepare	to make ready *before*
post-	after	postpone	to put off until *after*

EXERCISE 13: TIME PREFIXES

Directions: Using the above prefixes and their meanings, match the following definitions on the right with the words or phrases they define on the left. Put the letter of the definition beside the phrase it matches. Use a dictionary if you wish.

Word or Phrase

______ 1. antecedent

______ 2. postpartum examination

______ 3. preholiday sale

______ 4. predetermined amount

______ 5. postoperative examination

______ 6. prehistory

______ 7. postwar

Definition

a. *before* written history

b. examination *after* the birth of a child

c. an examination *after* surgery

d. something that went *before*

e. *after* a war

f. amount determined *before*

g. a sale *before* a holiday

Answers start on page 671.

PREFIXES THAT SHOW PLACE

The following prefixes have meanings related to place or position. They are used to show the relationship between different people or things.

Prefix	Means	As in	Definition
de-	down, away	descend	to go or move *down*
in-, en-	in, inside	enclose	to close something *in*
ex-	out	exit	the way *out*
super-	above, over	supervise	to watch *over* someone's work or progress
pro-	forward	proceed	to move *forward*
sub-	under, below	subzero	to go *under* or *below* zero

EXERCISE 14: PLACE PREFIXES

Directions: Using the above table, match the definition on the right with the correct word or phrase on the left. Write the letter of the definition next to the phrase it matches. You may use a dictionary if you wish.

Word or Phrase

______ 1. degrade someone

______ 2. propel a boat

______ 3. subterranean cave

______ 4. external use only

______ 5. interior use only

______ 6. detract from someone's appearance

______ 7. to make a proposal

Definition

a. use only *outside* the body (as medicine)

b. drive a boat *forward*

c. a cave *under* the earth

d. to put *forward* an idea

e. to disgrace someone or put that person *down*

f. use only *inside* (as paint)

g. take *away* from someone's appearance

Answers start on page 671.

NUMBER PREFIXES

Many prefixes refer to numbers. When they are added to the beginning of words, these number prefixes tell you how many there are of something. Look at the following examples of number prefixes:

uni- = 1, so a uniform is clothing in *one* form
bi- = 2, so a bicycle has *two* wheels

Study the number prefixes and their meanings in the following table.

Number Prefixes			
Prefix	**Means**	**As in**	**Definition**
uni-	one (1)	uniform	*one* form (of clothing)
mono-	one (1)	monotone	*one* tone
bi-	two (2)	bicycle	*two* wheels
du-	two (2)	duplex	a *two*-family house
tri-	three (3)	trio	*three* people
qua-	four (4)	quarter	one of *four* parts

EXERCISE 15: NUMBER PREFIXES

Directions: Using the table of prefix meanings, match the definition on the right with the word or phrase on the left. Write the letter of the definition next to the word or phrase it defines.

Word or Phrase

_______ 1. triplets
_______ 2. bilateral agreement
_______ 3. unit
_______ 4. triangle
_______ 5. quartet
_______ 6. duel
_______ 7. monotheism

Definition

a. agreement between *two* sides
b. having *three* angles
c. *one* thing
d. *three* babies from the same birth
e. musical group having *four* members
f. belief in *one* God
g. fight between *two* people

Answers start on page 671.

MORE PREFIXES

The following table defines some more prefixes. Study them carefully.

Prefix	Means	As in	Definition
co-, col-, com-, con-, cor-	with, together	copilot	person who pilots *with* another
per-	through	permit	to allow to go *through*
auto-	self	automobile	vehicle that moves *itself*
inter-	between, among	international	*between* or *among* nations
intra-	inside	intravenous	*inside* the vein (often called IV in hospitals)
re-	back, again	return, redo	turn *back;* do *again*

EXERCISE 16: MORE PREFIXES

Directions: Match each definition on the right with the correct word or phrase on the left. Write the letter of the definition next to the phrase it matches. Use a dictionary if you wish.

Word or Phrase

______ 1. interstate highway

______ 2. autograph

______ 3. connect two lines

______ 4. interrupt

______ 5. restate a question

______ 6. correlate two ideas

______ 7. to want autonomy

Definition

a. join two lines *with* each other or join them *together*

b. sign your name (write your*self*)

c. cause a break *between* two people talking

d. a highway that goes between states

e. to want to be independent (governing one*self*)

f. relate two ideas *with* each other

g. state a question *again*

Answers start on page 671.

ROOTS AND SUFFIXES

Sometimes prefixes are attached to words that can stand alone. These words are often called *base words* because they form the base on which a new word is built.

Look at the following examples of prefixes added on to base words:

dis- / similar means not / similar
PREFIX / BASE WORD

un- / used means not / used
PREFIX / BASE WORD

LATIN AND GREEK ROOTS

Prefixes are sometimes attached to word parts from Greek or Latin called ***roots***. Many of these word parts cannot stand on their own. Look at the following example.

pre- / dict
PREFIX / ROOT

The root *dict*- comes from the Latin word, *dicere*, meaning "to say or tell." Therefore, *predict* means to say or tell something before, or to tell something that has yet to happen. Weather forecasters *predict* tomorrow's weather. Here's another example:

per- / fect
PREFIX / ROOT

The root *fect* comes from the Latin word, *facere*, meaning "to do." Therefore, *perfect* means to do something through without error. The entire Latin or Greek word is not used. Only a part of the ancient word—the *root*—is used in English. Most of us do not know Latin or Greek, so we need to learn the *root* and its English meaning. Some of the most common roots and their meanings are given in the following table.

Root	Meaning
fect	do
port*	carry
cept, ceive	take
cred	believe, trust
fid	faith
script, scribe*	write

* Note: Some roots, like these, can stand alone as complete words.

Look at the following words. Divide them into prefix, root or base word, and suffix. *Note:* There may not always be a prefix or a suffix.

Word	Prefix	Root or Base Word	Suffix
1. exported	________	________________	________
2. infecting	________	________________	________
3. receiver	________	________________	________
4. except	________	________________	________

Do your answers look like these?

Word	Prefix	Root or Base Word	Suffix
1. exported	ex-	port	ed
2. infecting	in-	fect	ing
3. receiver	re-	ceiv	er
4. except	ex-	cept	—

EXERCISE 17: LOCATING ROOTS AND BASE WORDS

Directions: Study the list of common roots on the preceding page. Then underline the root or base word in each of the words that follow. The first one is done as an example.

1. <u>port</u>able
2. defect
3. transcript
4. inscription
5. transported
6. deceive
7. incredible
8. fidelity

Answers start on page 671.

DEFINING WORDS WITH LATIN OR GREEK ROOTS

By understanding the meaning of Latin and Greek roots, we can understand the meanings of many English words. Take the words *portable* and *telephone*, for example.

Root	Means	As in	Definition
port	carry	portable	able to be carried
tele	distant	telephone	brings sound from a distance

Looking at the meaning of the Greek or Latin root can help you discover the definition of a word. Notice that from time to time you will find minor spelling changes, such as *phone* changing to *phono*, so that the word will be easier to pronounce.

Now you try it. Using the root meanings that are listed below as a guide, match each definition on the right to the word it defines on the left.

Root Meanings	
phone = sound	graph, gram = write
tele = distant	port = carry

Word	Definition
______ **1.** telegraph	**a.** able to be carried
______ **2.** portable	**b.** sound "written down"
______ **3.** phonograph	**c.** written from a distance

(Answers: **1.** c, **2.** a, **3.** b)

EXERCISE 18: LATIN AND GREEK ROOTS

Directions: Study the roots in the table that follows. Then match the definition on the right with the word it defines on the left. (To help you figure out the meaning, the root in each word has been underlined.) Write the letter of the definition next to the word it matches. Use a dictionary if you wish.

Root Meanings	
graph = write	fid = faith
chron = time	sect = cut
bio = life	

Word

_____ 1. synchronize watches

_____ 2. bisect a line

_____ 3. photograph a person

_____ 4. confident he'll succeed

_____ 5. bio graphy of Lincoln

_____ 6. intersection of streets

_____ 7. chronological order

Definition

a. allow light to "write" on film, making a picture

b. where two streets "cut" or cross one another

c. in order by *time*

d. to have *faith* in succeeding

e. *cut* a line in two

f. set to show the same *time*

g. a *written* account of someone's *life*

Answers start on page 672.

SUFFIXES

As you learned earlier, suffixes are syllables added to the ends of words. Most often, they are used to change a word from one part of speech into another part of speech. For example, by adding *-al* to a noun, you can form an adjective. Look at the following example:

Noun	Adjective
person	personal

A few endings or suffixes, like those in the following exercise, have meanings that are useful to know.

EXERCISE 19: FAMILIAR SUFFIXES

Directions: In the following table, study the suffixes and their meanings. Then match the definition on the right with the word it defines on the left. Write the letter of the definition next to the word it matches. Use a dictionary if you wish.

Suffixes

-able, -ible = able to
-ism = belief in, practice of
-ish = like, similar to
-ology = study of
-ful = full of

Word

_______ 1. commercial<u>ism</u>
_______ 2. spite<u>ful</u>
_______ 3. psych<u>ology</u>
_______ 4. child<u>ish</u>
_______ 5. leg<u>ible</u>
_______ 6. ge<u>ology</u>
_______ 7. ideal<u>ism</u>

Definition

a. *study of* the mind and behavior
b. *able to* be read
c. *full of* spite
d. *belief in* ideals
e. *practice of* making money in business or commerce
f. *like* a child
g. *study of* the earth

Answers start on page 672.

VOCABULARY: SYNONYMS AND ANTONYMS

Synonyms are words that have very similar meanings, like the words *thin* and *slender.* ***Antonyms*** are words that have opposite meanings, like the words *hot* and *cold.* You'll be learning how to recognize synonyms and antonyms in the exercises throughout this chapter.

SYNONYMS

As you have just learned, synonyms are words that mean the same or nearly the same thing. The following synonyms are in *italic print.*

couch means about the same thing as *sofa*
rock means about the same thing as *stone*
form means about the same thing as *shape*

EXERCISE 20: FINDING SYNONYMS

Directions: For each word in **bold type** at the left, circle the word that is a synonym from the four choices that follow it. The first one is done as an example.

1. **completed:** began (finished) started delayed
2. **volume:** write author book poem
3. **foundation:** concrete carpenter building base
4. **courageous:** brave foolish afraid cowardly
5. **journey:** airplane passport ticket trip
6. **reasoning:** talking writing thinking pausing
7. **depart:** arrive leave land eat
8. **frequently:** always never often seldom

Answers start on page 672.

EXERCISE 21: FINDING SYNONYMS IN SENTENCES

Directions: As you read each of the following sentences, notice the word in **bold type**. Find another word in each item that is a synonym for the **bold-faced** word and circle it. The first one is done as an example.

1. José was so proud of his **automobile** that he polished (his) car every week.
2. David had **unusual** musical talent. It was rare to see such ability in one so young.
3. People who **perish** in fires often die of inhaling smoke rather than being burned.
4. The **trembling** of the earthquake was so strong that the dishes were shaking in the cupboards.

Answers start on page 671.

ANTONYMS

Words that have opposite meanings are called ***antonyms***. Take a look at the following examples of words and their antonyms:

wet means the opposite of *dry*
tall means the opposite of *short*

EXERCISE 22: FINDING ANTONYMS

Directions: Read each **boldfaced** word at the left and find the antonym for it from the four choices given. Circle the antonym. The first one is done for you.

1. **hot:** warm high (cold) wet
2. **inquire:** answer ask question help
3. **loose:** lose difficult find tight
4. **knowledge:** ignorance learning school book
5. **positive:** decided perfect loud negative

Answers start on page 672.

EXERCISE 23: ANTONYMS IN SENTENCES

Directions: As you read each of the following sentences, find the antonym of the **boldfaced** word and circle it. The first one is done for you.

1. The **dull** finish turned (shiny) as he polished it.
2. The week after the **destruction** of the old office building, construction began on the new park and playground.
3. Although he **approved** of the ideas in the composition, he criticized the grammar and spelling.
4. Her cooking was often **spicy**, for she disliked cooking flavorless meals.

Answers start on page 672.

EXERCISE 24: SYNONYMS AND ANTONYMS IN SENTENCES

Directions: Read the following groups of sentences. Look at the **boldfaced** word in each sentence. Circle a synonym and underline an antonym. The first one is done for you.

1. Heather is **slender**, so she is neither too <u>fat</u> nor too (thin) to be a model.
2. He was **cruel** in his treatment of the children. He never said a kind word but was merciless in his demands.
3. The **freezing** wind cut through his wool uniform. Despite the icy temperatures, he continued walking his beat, but he did wish he had a hot cup of coffee.
4. The **opening** minutes of the movie were boring, but once I got past the beginning, I was fascinated through the ending.
5. The **defective** towels were only slightly damaged but were much cheaper than those that were perfect.
6. The army **proceeded** toward the city, but it advanced only to the river before it retreated under fire.
7. No doubt the carpenter was **skilled**. His expert work only showed how incompetent others were.

Answers start on page 672.

2 Understanding What You Read

How well do you comprehend (understand) what you read? In this chapter we'll look at ways to improve your reading comprehension. We'll study key words in sentences, key words to build main ideas, words in context, main ideas and supporting details, and summarizing and paraphrasing. Let's start with sentences.

STUDY SKILL: KEY WORDS IN SENTENCES

Sometimes long sentences can be confusing, but knowing how to find the *key words* in a sentence can help you understand it better. The key words give you the basic information in a sentence. Any other words used in the sentence simply add details about the information given by the key words. To find the key words in a sentence, ask yourself this question: "*Who* did *what?*"

Let's look at a short example:

Sentence 1: The woman walked.

Key Words: *Who?* The woman *did what?* walked

Now take a look at a longer sentence:

Sentence 2: The beautiful, dark-haired woman in a red dress walked quickly around the corner and out of sight.

Key Words: *Who?* The woman *did what?* walked

As you can see, the key words in Sentences 1 and 2 are the same. The rest of the words in Sentence 2 give you more information about the woman and her walking. However, the basic information is still "The woman walked."

Sentence 3: The plane hit an air pocket.

KEY WORDS: *Who or what?* The plane *did what?* hit an air pocket

Sentence 4: Just as the senior flight attendant began serving lunch to the passenger in seat 3-A, the plane hit an air pocket, splattering the first-class passenger with ham and potato salad.

KEY WORDS: *Who or what?* the plane *did what?* hit an air pocket

Again, the key words in Sentences 3 and 4 are the same.

EXERCISE 1: KEY WORDS IN SENTENCES

1. French painter Paul Gauguin, unhappy in Europe, left his family in Copenhagen to return to the South Seas, where he painted scenes of Tahiti in brilliant color.

   Who or what? ____________________

   Did what? ____________________

2. Harriet Tubman, a famous black woman, rescued thousands from slavery during the American Civil War by personally leading them north through the Underground Railroad.

   Who or what? ____________________

   Did what? ____________________

3. At a news conference today from the Oval Office, the president voiced his disappointment over recent events in the Middle East.

   Who or what? ____________________

   Did what? ____________________

Answers start on page 672.

KEY WORDS TO BUILD MAIN IDEAS

Key words—*who, what, where, when, how* (and sometimes *why*)—help you form knowledge questions. These questions help you build details that relate to the main idea.

When reporters write stories for newspapers, they include the main idea (which is often the headline). They also give information on *who* or *what* the article is about, *what* happened, *where* it happened, *when* it happened, and *how* it happened.

Look at the following diagram to see how these details relate to the main idea.

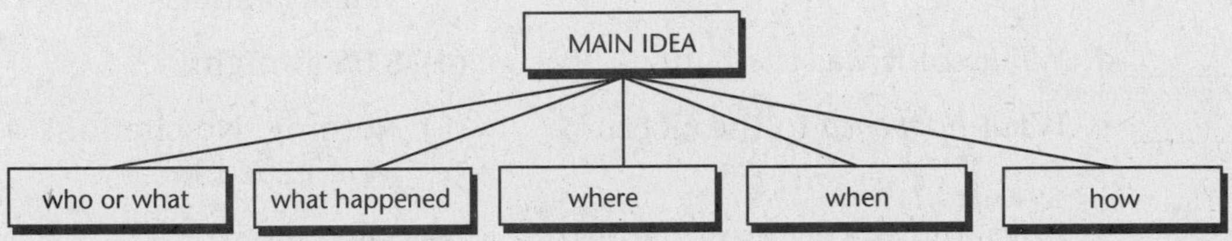

The main idea is in the top box. The boxes connected to the main idea contain the questions that help you identify details in an article. When you read, ask yourself these questions to find the most important details related to the main idea.

EXERCISE 2: MAIN IDEAS IN NEWSPAPER ARTICLES

Directions: Read the following newspaper article. Then answer the questions. Remember that the main idea is often the headline and that details often answer such questions as *who? what? where? when?* and *how?*

Pedestrian Killed

At 8:05 last night, Charles Knight, 62, was hit while attempting to walk across Valencia Street at Compton Avenue against a red light. Witnesses said a light blue pickup truck driven by Sam Glick was moving north on Valencia Street when the accident occurred. Mr. Knight was thrown 20 feet on impact and died instantly. No citations were issued.

1. What is the main idea of the entire article?
   (1) A light blue pickup truck was driven by Sam Glick.
   (2) A pedestrian was hit by a car and killed.
   (3) Sam Glick was driving north on Valencia Street.
   (4) Charles Knight crossed the street against a red light.
   (5) The accident occurred at 8:05 last night.

2. Match the detail questions on the left with the details from the article on the right. Put the number of the correct detail next to the question it answers.

Detail Questions	**Details**
_____ a. *Who* was the victim?	(1) attempting to cross the street
_____ b. *What* was the victim doing?	(2) red
_____ c. *Where* did the accident happen?	(3) moving north on Valencia Street
_____ d. *What* color was the light?	(4) 8:05 at night
_____ e. *What happened* to the victim?	(5) Nothing. No citations were issued.
_____ f. *When* did the accident happen?	(6) Sam Glick
_____ g. *Who* was driving the pickup truck?	(7) Valencia Street at Compton Avenue
_____ h. *Where* was the driver going?	(8) thrown 20 feet and died
_____ i. *What happened* to the driver?	(9) Charles Knight

Answers start on page 672.

VOCABULARY: WORD IN CONTEXT

An important method for defining unfamiliar words is using *context clues*. The ***context*** refers to the words that surround the word you don't know. Often, the context will give you clues that help you figure out what the unfamiliar word means.

CONTEXT CLUES

Let's see how context clues work. As you read the short paragraph that follows, notice how the words in *italic type* give clues to the meaning of the **boldfaced** word.

> Old Mr. Riley was quite **spry** for his age. *Daily he walked several blocks* to buy a newspaper, and I often saw him *working in his garden.*

Since Mr. Riley is described as walking several blocks daily and working in his garden, we can guess that *spry* means active.

> Wilson put on a *heavy coat, a wool scarf, several pairs of socks* inside his boots, and *fur-lined gloves to protect* himself *against* the **frigid** weather.

The clues tell you that Wilson was wearing warm clothes to protect himself. You can infer that if he is wearing warm clothes for protection, the weather must be very cold. Therefore, *frigid* must mean *very cold.*

Now practice this skill by completing the exercises that follow.

EXERCISE 3: WORDS IN CONTEXT

Directions: As you read each sentence that follows, pay special attention to the clues in *italic type* to help you define the **boldfaced** word. Then choose the correct definition of the word from the choices that follow.

1. The police searched his house and found an **arsenal** that included *two rifles, a handgun, several hand grenades,* and *plastic explosives used in making bombs.*

   "Arsenal" means

   (1) a storehouse of weapons
   (2) food
   (3) a house
   (4) used books
   (5) a bomb

2. His **anguish** *over her death* lasted for months. Whenever he spoke of her, *tears welled up in his eyes.*

   "Anguish" means

   (1) happiness
   (2) beauty
   (3) pain
   (4) laughter
   (5) embarrassment

3. The doctor gave her *medicine* to **allay** *the pain,* and she *rested quietly.*

   "To allay" means

   (1) to increase
   (2) to relieve
   (3) to repeat
   (4) to sleep
   (5) to encourage

4. The thief had **eluded** the police *by hiding in the graveyard. The police could not find him.*

   "Eluded" means

   (1) been captured by
   (2) tortured by
   (3) escaped from
   (4) been arrested by
   (5) embraced by

Answers start on page 672.

EXERCISE 4: IDENTIFYING CONTEXT CLUES

Directions: Read each of the following sentences. Underline the words that give clues to the meaning of the **boldfaced** word. Then choose the correct definition of the boldfaced word.

1. The king had **reigned** over his peaceful little kingdom for twenty-five years.

   "Reigned" means

   (1) ruled
   (2) laughed
   (3) fought
   (4) died
   (5) lived

2. The **proprietor** of the floral shop told us he had bought the business twenty years ago.

   "Proprietor" means

   (1) flowers
   (2) store
   (3) worker
   (4) owner
   (5) visitor

3. Since the **polls** will be open until 7:00, I plan to vote on my way home from work.

   "Polls" means

   (1) places to sleep
   (2) places to talk
   (3) places to vote
   (4) places to eat
   (5) places to work

Answers start on page 672.

Examples Given in Context

Sometimes authors give examples that help you understand a word that is new to you. Take a look at the following sentence. Notice the examples that are in *italic type*, and see if they help you understand the **boldfaced** word.

> Any **tragedy**, such as *the death of a loved one* or *loss of a job,* can cause stress.

Although the preceding sentence doesn't actually define the word *tragedy,* the examples of the death of a loved one and loss of a job give us some clues. A tragedy is a sad event.

Notice that the examples were introduced by the phrase *such as*. In other sentences, examples may simply be listed as part of the sentence.

EXERCISE 5: USING EXAMPLES GIVEN IN CONTEXT

Directions: Read each of the following sentences. Look for examples that help explain the **boldfaced** word. Then, circle the best definition from the choices given.

1. While in China, I was unable to read any of the **placards**, such as the railway posters, store signs, and billboards.

   "Placards" means

   (1) speeches
   (2) menus
   (3) newspapers
   (4) written public announcements
   (5) cartoons

2. **Bibliographies** are often placed at the end of a chapter or book to list other books in which you may find more information.

   "Bibliographies" are

   (1) lists of books
   (2) lists of chapters
   (3) lists of words
   (4) lists of authors
   (5) lists of mistakes

3. **Suffixes** such as *-ing, -ed, -s, -ful*, and *-less* may cause spelling changes when added to words.

   "Suffixes" means

   (1) meanings of words
   (2) definitions of words
   (3) endings of words
   (4) beginnings of words
   (5) spelling of words

Answers start on page 673.

Definitions Given in Context

Sometimes authors come right out and give you the definition of a word in a sentence. For example, look at the following sentence.

> **Meteorologists**, *people who study weather and weather patterns*, still have difficulty predicting the weather.

The *italic* words actually define the term *meteorologist.*

In the previous example, the definition was set off from the rest of the sentence by commas. Sometimes the definition of a word will be preceded by the word *or*, as in the following sentence.

> **Acrophobia**, *or fear of heights*, can make life difficult for tightrope walkers who suffer from it.

Review of Context Clues

Context clues can give you more information about a word. They may also give you examples or definitions.

EXERCISE 6: USING DEFINITIONS GIVEN IN CONTEXT

Directions: Read the following sentences to find the definition of each **boldfaced** word given in the sentence. Then circle the best definition from the choices given.

1. **Venison**, or deer meat, must be cooked carefully.

   "Venison" means

   (1) beef
   (2) deer meat
   (3) pork
   (4) lamb
   (5) fish

2. His grandmother preferred **matinees**, or afternoon performances, because she wanted to be home before dark.

   "Matinees" are

   (1) all-night performances
   (2) daily performances
   (3) afternoon performances
   (4) evening performances
   (5) free performances

3. Pioneer women sometimes used a **cistern**, or tank, to catch rain water in order to get soft water for washing.

   "Cistern" means

   (1) basement for storing food
   (2) room for cooking
   (3) tank for storing milk
   (4) tank for catching rain water
   (5) room for doing laundry

Answers start on page 673.

EXERCISE 7: USING CONTEXT CLUES FOR MEANING

Directions: Read each sentence. Look for extra information that will let you guess what the **boldfaced** word means. Then circle the correct definition.

1. Tran Nguyen **emigrated** to the United States with his parents in 1980. It must be difficult to leave the land of your birth and settle in a new country.
   (1) moved to a new country to live
   (2) was a tourist on vacation
   (3) took a business trip
   (4) learned a new language in order to go somewhere
   (5) landed a new job

2. He had thought that brightly colored birds would be **conspicuous**, but try as he might, he could not see even one amid the thick leaves of the jungle.
   (1) in a cage
   (2) eaten
   (3) easy to see
   (4) hard to see
   (5) dangerous

3. The comedy was **hilarious**. The audience laughed loudly all through the show.
   (1) very sad
   (2) very short
   (3) very long
   (4) very funny
   (5) very scary

4. She was so **infuriated** with the salesperson who cheated her that she almost hit him.
   (1) loving
   (2) angry
   (3) selling
   (4) cheating
   (5) sick

5. When the star of the soap opera was killed in a car crash, the show had to be **revised**, or rewritten, to kill the character he had played.
   (1) changed
   (2) killed
   (3) crashed
   (4) left the same
   (5) cancelled

Answers start on page 673.

COMPREHENSION: MAIN IDEA AND DETAILS

If a friend asks about a movie you've seen, you probably respond with a short statement describing what the movie is about. Such a statement gives the ***main idea*** of the movie. For example, let's say you've just watched one of your favorite movies again, *E.T.* When your cousin, who hasn't seen it, asks you what it is about, you say, "It's about a little boy who makes friends with a gentle, funny-looking creature from outer space." When you say this, you state the movie's main idea.

Just as with movies, most of what you read also has a main idea. The main idea is often stated in the title and, sometimes, in the first sentence of a paragraph or a passage. The main idea is supported by specific ideas, or ***details***. These details relate to the main idea in some way.

To see how the main idea and details are related, look at the diagram that follows.

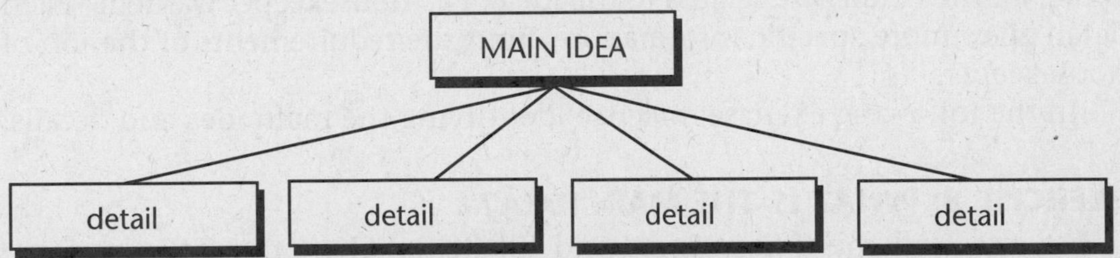

Let's see how this diagram applies to a newspaper want ad. Read the ad that follows to see if you can identify the main idea and details.

Housekeeper Wanted

Must have own transportation. Willing to work 10 hours per week. Salary $15.00 per hour. Be willing to babysit 4-year-old. Call 555-2345.

If we were to make the main idea and related details into a diagram, it would look something like this:

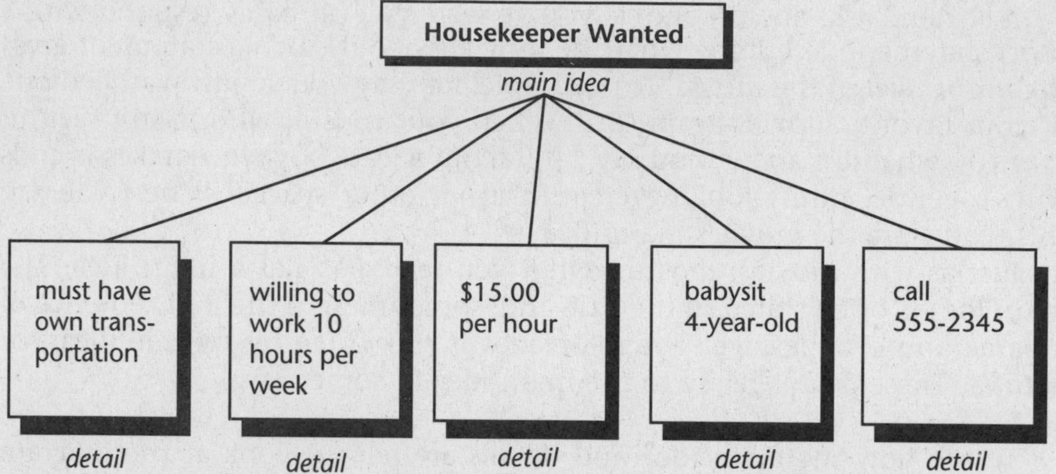

As you can see from the lines connecting the main idea to each detail, all the details are related to the idea of a "housekeeper wanted." Each detail gives more specific information about the requirements of the job of housekeeper.

In the following exercise, practice identifying the main idea and details.

EXERCISE 8: WHAT IS THE MAIN IDEA?

Directions: Read the following ad and fill in the chart that follows. First, write the main idea in the top box. Then write the details in each of the lower boxes.

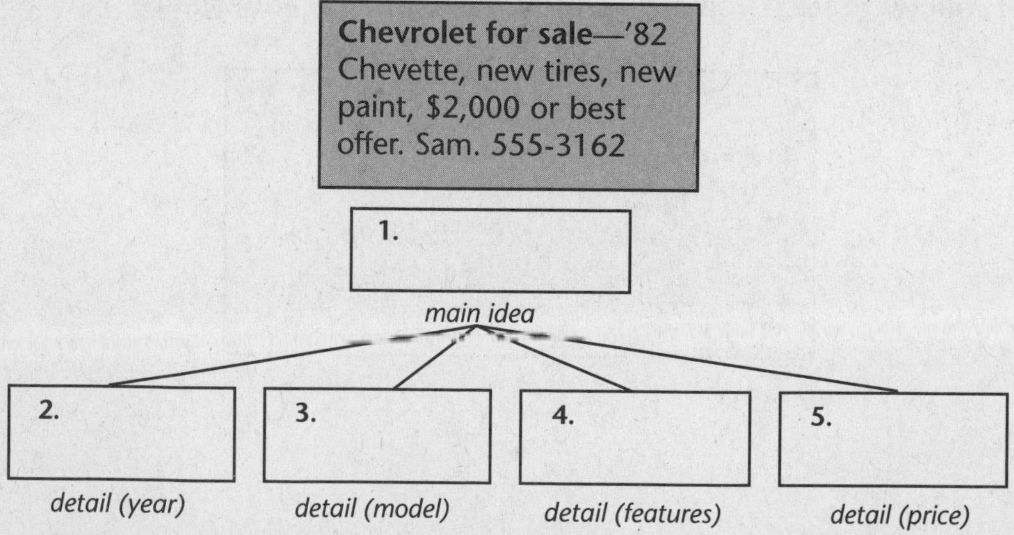

6. Circle the number of the statement below that best explains the term "best offer."

   (1) Sam will only take $2,000 for his car.
   (2) Sam will consider taking less than $2,000.
   (3) Sam wants more than $2,000.
   (4) Sam will give his car away.
   (5) Sam doesn't want to sell his car.

Answers start on page 673.

MAIN IDEAS IN NONFICTION

Nonfiction is the kind of writing that deals with opinions, facts, and reality. Biographies, histories, and essays are examples of nonfiction. The main idea in a paragraph of nonfiction is what the whole paragraph is about. Often, but not always, the first sentence restates the main idea in other words. The sentences that follow the first one give details about the main idea. As you read the paragraph in the next exercise, look for the main idea and details.

EXERCISE 9: MAIN IDEAS AND DETAILS IN NONFICTION

Directions: Read the following paragraph and answer the questions that follow.

The Origin of the Word *Sandwich*

Did you ever wonder where we got the word *sandwich?* It has an interesting origin. Long ago in England, people used a knife to hack a chunk of bread off a loaf and to chop a piece of meat from a roast. Often they ate with their fingers so, of course, their fingers became sticky with food. One nobleman, the Earl of Sandwich, loved to play cards. In fact, he was so fond of playing cards that he hated to leave the table just to eat. Even more, he disliked the cards getting sticky from the greasy meat and bits of food left on his fingers if he ate while playing. One evening he thought of a solution. He ordered his servants to bring him bread and meat. With his knife, he carved off a thin slice of bread. Next, he cut a piece of meat and placed it on the slice of bread. A second slice of bread went on top. Now he could keep his fingers clean by holding the meat between the slices of bread while continuing to play cards. Thus, the Earl invented the first sandwich.

1. What is the main idea of this paragraph?
   (1) The Earl of Sandwich had a passion for playing cards.
   (2) The sandwich was invented by the Earl of Sandwich.
   (3) Long ago, life in England was hard.
   (4) People in medieval England ate with their fingers.
   (5) Most words have interesting origins.

2. Fill in the following chart using the information from the passage.

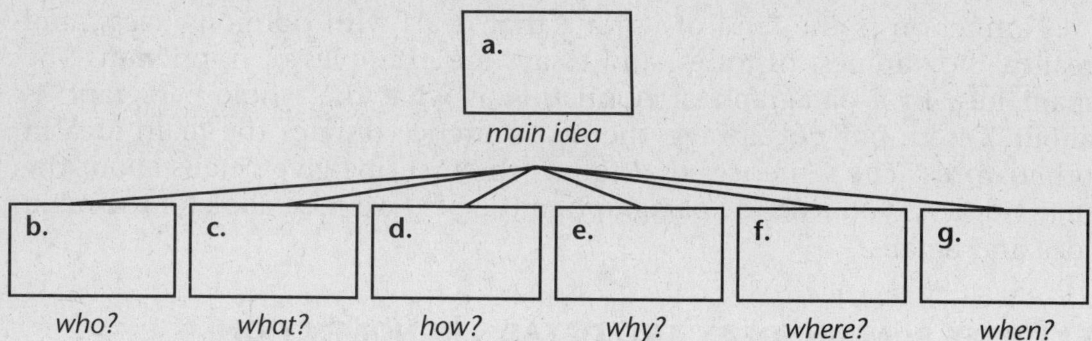

3. If the Earl of Gloucester had invented the sandwich, we would probably call it
   (1) a piece of meat between bread slices
   (2) a sandwich
   (3) a playing card
   (4) a gloucester
   (5) an earl

Answers start on page 673.

AN UNSTATED MAIN IDEA

In what you've read so far, the main idea has been stated directly. Sometimes, however, the main idea is not stated directly. In this case, you need to look at the details to find out what they all relate to. Ask yourself the question, "What is this article mainly about?"

Now let's try finding a main idea that is not directly stated. In the introduction to his book, Garrison Keillor describes an experience he had while on a train trip with his family.

EXERCISE 10: UNSTATED MAIN IDEAS

Directions: Read the following paragraph. Even though the main idea is not stated, see if you can identify it by asking yourself, "What is this article mainly about?" Identify the details by asking *who? what? when? where?* and *how?* Then answer the questions that follow.

I took my son to the men's room and set the briefcase down . . . , and then we went to the cafeteria for breakfast. A few bites into the scrambled eggs I remembered the briefcase, went to get it and it was gone. We had an hour before the southbound arrived. We spent it looking in every trash basket in the station, outside the station, and for several blocks around. I was sure that the thief, finding nothing but manuscripts in the briefcase, would chuck it, and I kept telling him to, but he didn't chuck it where I could see it, and then our time was up and we climbed on the train. I felt so bad I didn't want to look out the window. I looked straight at the wall of our compartment, and as we rode south the two lost stories seemed funnier and funnier to me, the best work I had ever done in my life; I wept for them, and my misery somehow erased them from mind so that when I got out a pad of paper a couple hundred miles later, I couldn't re-create even a faint outline.

—Excerpted from *Lake Wobegon Days*
by Garrison Keillor

1. What would be a good title (statement of main idea) for this paragraph?
   (1) An Author and His Son Travel South
   (2) An Author Cries
   (3) An Author Loses His Manuscripts
   (4) An Author Eats Scrambled Eggs
   (5) An Author Catches a Thief

2. Match the details in the right column with the detail questions in the left column. Write the letter of the detail next to the question it answers.

Detail Questions	**Details**
______ **a.** *Who* lost the stories?	(1) two short stories
______ **b.** *What* happened?	(2) in the men's room of a railroad station
______ **c.** *Where* did he leave it?	(3) before breakfast
______ **d.** *What* was lost?	(4) Keillor lost his briefcase
______ **e.** *When* did he lose them?	(5) the author, Garrison Keillor

Answers start on page 673.

MAIN IDEA IN PASSAGES

Passages are made up of a number of paragraphs. Each paragraph gives you more specific details about the main idea. Just like shorter pieces of writing, passages contain a main idea and details. But because passages are longer than ads and paragraphs, their organization is a little more complicated. The main idea of a passage tells you what the *entire passage*, not just a paragraph, is about.

Details of a passage can be divided into two categories: general and specific. General details are called ***supporting ideas***. These ideas explain the main idea in more depth. Specific details further develop and reinforce the supporting ideas, and consist of examples, reasons, definitions, or characteristics.

The diagram that follows gives you an example of how a passage may be organized. The diagram also shows how the main idea, supporting ideas, and specific details are related to one another.

Notice that in this particular diagram, the main idea has three supporting ideas. One of these supporting ideas uses examples that explain the idea more fully. The second supporting idea uses a reason and a definition. The third supporting idea uses characteristics.

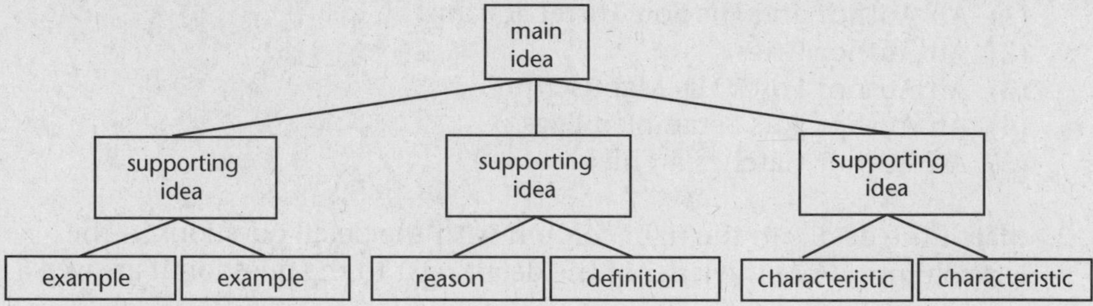

FINDING THE MAIN IDEA AND SUPPORTING IDEAS

As you read the following passage, try to locate the main idea of the entire passage. Then, see if you can identify four supporting ideas in the passage. Finally, notice any *examples, reasons, characteristics,* or *definitions* that help explain the supporting ideas in more depth.

Superstitions

Superstitions, which exist in most societies, are mainly concerned with bad luck. Incidents that are supposed to bring bad luck include walking under a ladder and having a black cat cross your path. Breaking a mirror is supposed to bring seven years of bad luck.

Of course, signs of good luck exist, too. Many people carry good luck charms of all sorts, especially "lucky" coins and rabbits' feet. Placing a horseshoe over a doorway is considered lucky, but only if you place the open end pointing upward so that the good luck can't "run out" of the shoe.

Why do people hold such beliefs? Many psychologists believe that superstitions were created by ancient people to explain events they didn't understand. For example, before it was known that germs and bacteria are the causes of disease, people believed that those who fell ill were victims of "bad luck."

Let's see how a diagram might be used to show how the information is organized in this passage.

SUPERSTITIONS

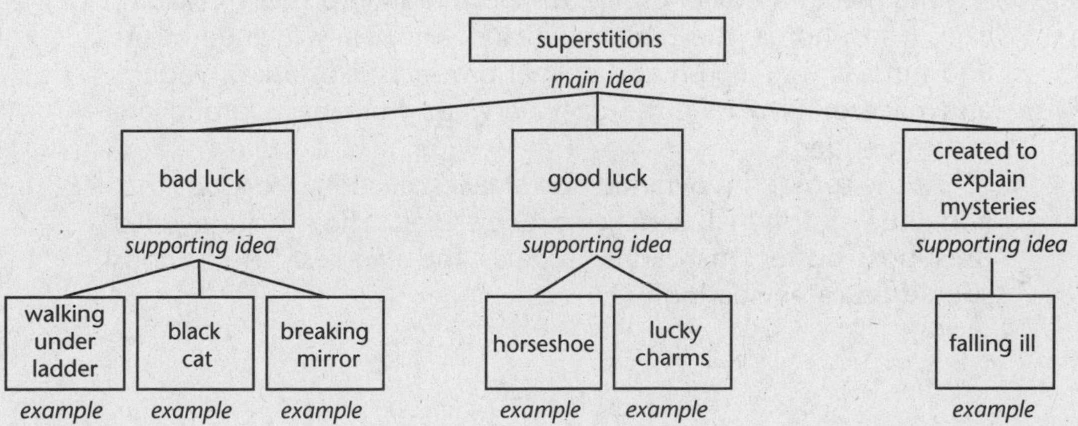

EXERCISE 11: FINDING MAIN AND SUPPORTING IDEAS

Directions: Read the following passage. It contains a main idea, four supporting ideas, and examples of each. Identify these as you read. Then answer the questions that follow. You may find it helpful to draw a diagram.

Basic Food Groups

What is a healthy diet? The answer to that question continues to change. Nutritionists, the people who study food and its effect on health, now believe that there is a better way to describe the nutritional needs of the human body than the basic four food groups we used to learn about in school.

In the early 1990s, nutritionists created a food pyramid to better explain our nutritional needs. At the base of the pyramid is the grain group; on the second level are the fruit and vegetable groups; on the third level are the meat and dairy groups; and at the top is the fats, oils, and sweets group.

Breads, cereals, rice, pasta, and other foods made from grain are the foundation of a healthy diet. Six or more daily servings are recommended because these foods provide B vitamins, iron, carbohydrates, and some protein.

Both the fruit group and the vegetable group provide vitamins, minerals, and fiber. Two to four servings of fruit and three to five servings of vegetables should be eaten every day. Because overcooking reduces the amount of vitamins in fruits and vegetables, it is best to cook these foods only until tender. Many fruits and vegetables can be eaten raw either as a dessert or in a salad. For example, oranges and apples cut into bite-size pieces can be added to a salad for variety.

The meat and dairy groups are both high in protein, calcium, iron, phosphorus, the B vitamins, and zinc. They include beans and nuts as well as fish and animal products like turkey, yogurt, and cheese. Two to three daily servings from each group are recommended.

At the top of the pyramid, the smallest section, are foods that add little nutritional benefit to one's diet. They include salad dressings, butter, margarine, sugars, and candies. These foods should be eaten sparingly.

1. What is the main idea of this passage?
   (1) We should eat meat or fish twice a day.
   (2) Everybody needs milk.
   (3) There are four nutrition levels in the food guide pyramid.
   (4) Nutritionists are people who study food and its effect on health.
   (5) The grain group of food provides the body with energy.

2. The most important supporting ideas in this passage describe the four levels of the food guide pyramid. List each level and then give an example of a food.

   a. ______________________________

   b. ______________________________

   c. ______________________________

   d. ______________________________

Answers start on page 673.

FINDING THE MAIN IDEA AND REASONS

In the next exercise, you'll read a passage that provides reasons to back up its supporting ideas. Reasons explain why something happened.

EXERCISE 12: FINDING REASONS

Directions: As you read the following passage, locate the main idea, the supporting ideas, and the reasons that support them. Then answer the questions that follow.

In 1987, British nobleman Lord Skelmersdale opened the first toad tunnel near Hambledon, England. The toad tunnel, an underground passageway that allows toads to safely cross a road, solved a problem that had been troubling the community for quite a while. Driven by their mating instincts, toads near Hambledon had been migrating from their winter home on one side of the road to the spring ponds where they mate on the other side. As they hopped across the road, many toads were getting run over by passing cars.

The toad tunnel was proposed for two reasons. First, the toads made a slippery, dangerous mess on the road when cars ran over them. Second, people were concerned about the safety of the toads. They had already shown that concern for years by coming at night to scoop the toads into buckets and move them safely across the road. But now the toad tunnel provides a permanent solution to the problem. In fact, it is working so well that other toad tunnels are being planned.

1. What is the main idea of this selection?
   (1) Lord Skelmersdale is a wildlife enthusiast.
   (2) A toad tunnel solved Hambledon's problem with toads.
   (3) Flattened toads are a hazard to drivers.
   (4) The people of Hambledon care about toads.
   (5) Other toad tunnels are being planned.

2. Put a check next to the *two* reasons given in the article for building a toad tunnel.
   ☐ (1) People were concerned about the toads' safety.
   ☐ (2) More toad tunnels will probably be built.
   ☐ (3) Squashed toads made a dangerous mess for cars on the road.
   ☐ (4) Toads cross in pairs to get to the spring ponds.

3. Because the English built the toad tunnel, we can guess that many English people
   (1) hate toads
   (2) dislike Lord Skelmersdale
   (3) are concerned about wildlife
   (4) build tunnels for fun
   (5) like to drive

Answers start on page 673.

DEFINITIONS AND CHARACTERISTICS

In the next exercise, you'll read a passage that uses definitions and characteristics to back them up.

EXERCISE 13: DEFINITIONS AND CHARACTERISTICS

Directions: In the following passage, look for the main idea. Although the passage does not have a title, the main idea is stated in the first paragraph. The article also lists six supporting ideas with definitions and characteristics of each idea. As you read, decide on the main idea of the passage. Find six examples given to explain it. Then answer the questions that follow.

Dr. Hassim Solomon, an expert in criminal behavior, has recently conducted a study of drivers. Dr. Solomon decided that there were six basic types of drivers.

The "Goody Two-Shoes" is a consistently slow driver. This driver believes that she is being extremely careful when really she is dangerous because she interrupts the normal flow of traffic.

The "Conformist," representing eighty percent of all drivers, is the average driver. This driver usually has a good self-concept and likes to obey the law. The Conformist might be tempted to speed if he is late to work or if he has a medical emergency.

The "Underconformist" is always late. This driver speeds to make up for her own poor planning. For example, she oversleeps on the day of a job interview or arrives at an airport just minutes before the plane is due to leave. Her lack of planning causes her to try to "catch up" on the road.

The "Challenger" deliberately exceeds the speed limit. This person loves to argue and is very aggressive in many ways.

The "Situational Deviant" is a person who drives recklessly only in certain situations. He may be a conformist much of the time but drives too fast when drinking alcohol or under the influence of drugs. He often takes his frustrations out on the road.

The "True Deviant" is often different from the rest of society in other aspects of life as well as in driving. This person often gets into trouble with the law and may lose her license. Often she will drive even after her license has been suspended.

1. What is the main idea of the whole passage?
   (1) There are six different types of drivers.
   (2) Dr. Solomon recently conducted a study.
   (3) The "Underconformist" is always late.
   (4) Bad drivers always have excuses.
   (5) Dr. Solomon is an expert in criminal behavior.

2. List the types of drivers described in the passage.

   a. ____________________ d. ____________________

   b. ____________________ e. ____________________

   c. ____________________ f. ____________________

3. In the right-hand column are the characteristics of the first three kinds of drivers. Write the letter of the characteristic next to the type of driver it matches.

______ a. Goody Two-Shoes	(1)	represents eighty percent of all drivers
______ b. Conformist	(2)	disrupts the flow of traffic by driving too slowly
______ c. Underconformist	(3)	is always late because of poor planning and tries to "catch up" on the road

4. In the right-hand column are the characteristics of the last three types of drivers. Write the letter of the characteristic next to the type of driver it matches.

______ a. Challenger	(1)	drives too fast when drinking or using drugs
______ b. Situational Deviant	(2)	is often in trouble with the law and will drive even after his or her license is suspended
______ c. True Deviant	(3)	loves to argue and is aggressive

Answers start on page 673.

COMPREHENSION: SUMMARIZING

You have learned to find the main idea and the details in both short passages and long passages. Now you are ready to learn to summarize. To ***summarize*** means to include only the main idea and the important details.

Here's an example of summarizing in everyday life. Suppose a friend is telling you about a wedding she attended. She might summarize the event this way.

> The bride wore a long white gown with lace, and her bridesmaids were dressed in pale yellow. The groom and ushers wore pale gray suits with yellow ties. The bridesmaids' white and yellow bouquets matched their dresses. Afterward at the reception, there was champagne and cake for everyone. The bride and groom danced the first dance. Then everyone, young and old, danced too. When the bride and groom left, the bride threw her bouquet to a group of us single women. Guess who caught it? I did!

Note that your friend tells you something about the colors worn by the wedding party, but she does not go into detail about who the bridesmaids and ushers were or what the minister said during the ceremony. Next, she briefly describes the reception and tells you that she caught the bouquet. Like all summaries, your friend's description includes only the information she considers to be important, not everything that took place that day.

HOW TO SUMMARIZE

To summarize a passage, you need to find the main idea and the *important* details. Remember, in a summary you don't include *every* bit of information, only what is necessary to understand what's happening. To do this, ask yourself these questions:

Who/What?
Did what?
Where?
When?
How?
Why?

To see how this works, let's look at the following paragraph. As you read the paragraph, ask yourself the questions *who? did what? where? when? how?* and *why?* Match each set of underlined words with the question it answers.

WHO? The *U.S. Treasury Department* has *redesigned paper money for the first time in fifty-seven years*. The new bills now have *a polyester stripe and tiny letters saying "United States of America" around the portrait* on each bill. The reason for the change is that the Treasury Department fears that new, sophisticated color copy machines could produce counterfeit bills that could pass for real bills. Copy machines cannot pick up the polyester stripe because it will not reflect light. The tiny letters around the portrait can't reflect light either, so *these new bills will not be so easy to counterfeit.* **DID WHAT? WHEN? HOW? WHY?**

Now let's look at the answers to the five questions you asked yourself.

Who	the U.S. Treasury Department
Did what?	is redesigning paper money
Where?	we don't know—the paragraph does not say
When?	for the first time in fifty-seven years
Why?	to prevent counterfeiting
How?	with a polyester stripe

You can now put these answers into one sentence and summarize the entire paragraph, like the following:

> The U.S. Treasury Department has redesigned paper money for the first time in fifty-seven years, using a polyester stripe in order to prevent counterfeiting.

Sometimes, as with this paragraph, you will not be able to answer all the questions because some information is not provided. In other cases, the answers to the questions may be given in an order different from the one that appears here.

EXERCISE 14: SUMMARIZING A PARAGRAPH

Directions: As you read the following passage, ask yourself the questions *who/what? did what? where? when? how? why?* Then answer the questions that follow.

> The old lady knelt in the soft, spring earth. She was planting flowers in her garden. Her wrinkled hands dug the hole for each plant. Carefully, she placed a purple petunia in the first hole and then patted the dirt back to fill in the empty space. Then she dug the next hole.
>
> "A red one here, I think," she said to herself.
>
> Soon all the plants were in place. Gently she gave each one water.
>
> "There!" she said, talking to herself again. "Even if the doc says I won't live to see it, there'll be a mass of bright color here in a few months. At least I can leave something pretty behind for other folks to enjoy."

1. On the lines that follow, write the words from the paragraph that answer each question.

   a. Who? ______________________________

   b. Did what? ______________________________

   c. Where? ______________________________

   d. When? ______________________________

   e. How? ______________________________

   f. Why? ______________________________

2. Now write your answers from question 1 as a summary statement by filling in the blanks below.

____

who? *did what?* *where?*

____

when? *how?* *why?*

3. Based on the information in the paragraph, choose the answer that best completes this sentence: The old lady believes that
   (1) bright colors look terrible
   (2) planting flowers isn't worth the trouble
   (3) she should be paid to do gardening
   (4) she is going to die soon
   (5) she will enjoy the flowers next spring

Answers start on page 674.

EXERCISE 15: MORE PRACTICE IN SUMMARIZING

Directions: As you read the following paragraph, ask yourself the questions *who/what? did what? when? where? how?* and *why?* Then complete the exercise.

Manufacturers Try Out Toys On Children

Recently, some toy manufacturers have asked children to try out newly designed toys. One company has a special room in its factory where children may come to play for a six-week period. Toy designers then watch the children as they play. The designers want to know which toys appeal most to children, which toys are played with most often, and which toys hold up the best. They are also concerned about the safety of each toy. By watching children play, toy designers can predict which toys will be good sellers for their company.

1. **a.** Who or what? ______________________
   b. Did what? ______________________
   c. When? ______________________
   d. Where? ______________________
   e. How? ______________________
   f. Why? ______________________

2. Combine the information in question 1 in one or two sentences to summarize the article. Write your summary on the lines provided.

____

____

____

Answers start on page 674.

EXERCISE 16: SUMMARIZING—A REVIEW

Directions: Read the following passage. As you read, look for the main idea, supporting ideas, and details. You will use these to answer questions and write a summary.

No one ever said that being a single parent would be easy. No one ever told me it might get this hard, though, either! Even though Carla is only four years old, I sometimes think that she's more mature than I am.

Working and raising a child at the same time is very stressful. I get up at 5:45 A.M. so that I can get myself ready for work and spend time with Carla while getting her ready for day care. Then I make breakfast and sack lunches for both of us. After that, I'm off to the daycare center to drop Carla off, and then on to work by 7:30. I usually have to work until 6:00, when I pick Carla up. Then comes dinner and a little play time with Carla. Pretty soon it's time for bed. This makes for a long day, especially when a big part of me would rather be spending it at home with Carla than on the job.

I also don't know how I'm supposed to keep up with all of Carla's questions. Even the woman who runs the day-care center comments on her curiosity! Carla will want to know, for instance, why you can't sneeze with your eyes open. If her questions get any harder, I'm going to have to go back to school just to learn how to answer them.

I'm also starting to doubt whether a single parent can have a decent social life. I don't want to sound selfish—having Carla is very important to me—but I would like to go out now and then. I guess that sooner or later, I'll have to sit down and explain the possibility of my dating to her.

Of course, none of these problems is impossible to overcome. I have friends that can help out, and I know that some social workers are trained to give guidance to single parents.

Whenever I feel unprepared or discouraged, I think about the day two years ago that I got custody of Carla. I had been through a bitter divorce, and my ex-wife resented the fact that I would be caring for our daughter. I wasn't even sure that I could handle it. But as soon as I saw Carla after winning custody, I realized that being a good father to her was worth the risk of making mistakes. And I was right.

1. From the information given in the passage, fill in the main idea, supporting ideas, and details in the following chart.

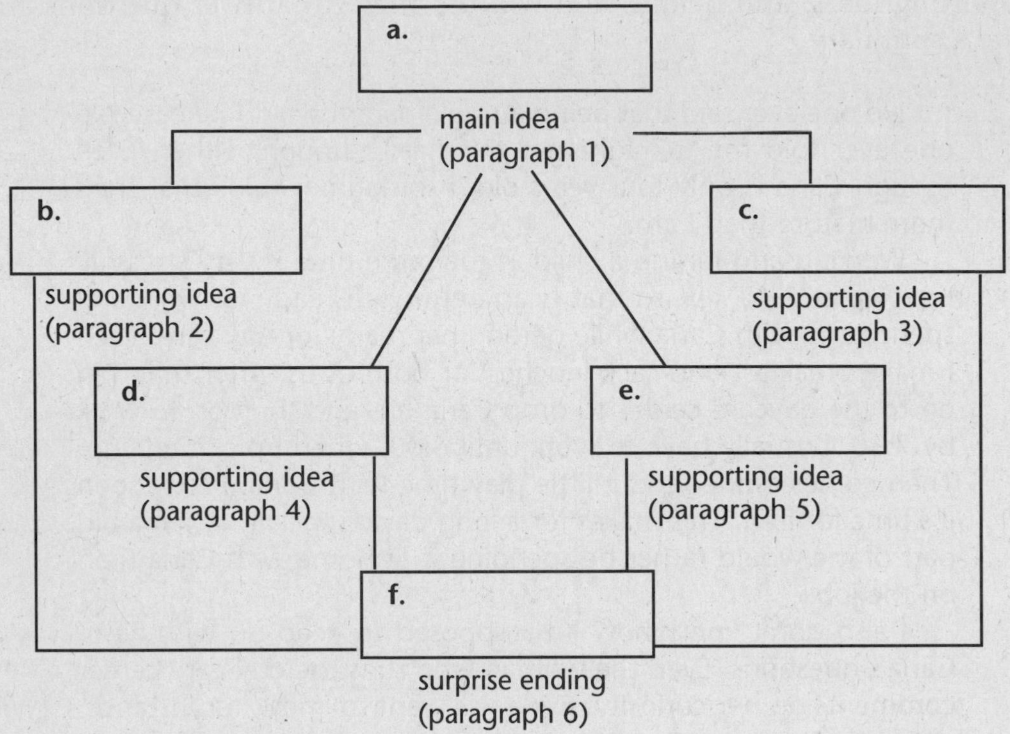

2. In four or five sentences, summarize the selection. Use the information from your chart to help you.

____

____

____

____

____

____

____

3. The fact that a judge awarded custody to the father in this passage suggests that the father is
   (1) wealthy and well traveled
   (2) too old to have another child
   (3) caring and responsible
   (4) frightened of responsibility
   (5) scared that he will never remarry

Answers start on page 674.

3 Finding Hidden Meaning

In Chapter 2 you learned how to identify main ideas. The reading selections directly stated the main idea and backed it up with supporting details. Sometimes, however, the writer only suggests or hints at the main idea, rather than stating it directly. To uncover an idea that is hidden, you must look for details that are stated directly and use them as "clues." A good reader uses details in a passage to figure out the author's suggested message.

In this chapter, we'll look at several skills that can help you uncover those hidden meanings and ideas. We will look at making inferences and predicting. We will also review study skills related to charts and outlines and to following directions.

COMPREHENSION: MAKING INFERENCES

Making an ***inference*** is the process of using information stated directly to figure out an unstated or suggested message. You might think of the process of inference as similar to putting together a jigsaw puzzle. You assemble individual puzzle pieces to form a completed picture. Likewise, when you make an inference, you assemble clues to form an idea that's not directly stated.

You may not realize it, but you use inference in situations every day. For example, suppose you drop by a friend's house. He is usually happy, cheerful, and joking. Today, however, he greets you with a serious face; his voice is grim. You know from previous conversations that he has been worried about his mother's health. You also know the doctor was to call him regarding some medical tests.

What might you infer from your friend's mood? You would probably infer that your friend is upset because the doctor's call brought bad news about his mother's health.

Here are the "clues" (direct information) that would help you make this inference:

- Your friend is usually happy; today he is serious.
- Your friend has been worried about his mother's health.
- The doctor was to call about the results of some tests.

Here's another example of using inference in everyday situations. Suppose you are driving south on a highway when the southbound traffic suddenly stops. Within a few minutes, you hear the wail of a siren, and in your rearview mirror you see a police car, with its lights flashing, coming up behind you on the shoulder. It passes you as you wait in line, followed closely by an ambulance.

What *two* inferences might you draw from these events?

(1) The police are after you.

(2) There has been an accident on the road ahead of you.

(3) The ambulance driver is crazy to follow a police car.

(4) It's all right for the police or an ambulance to use the shoulder of the road in an emergency.

(5) It's fine for anyone to drive on the shoulder when the traffic is stopped.

Did you pick (2) and (4)?
Here are some clues that support inferences (2) and (4):

1. Traffic suddenly stops.
2. The police car has its siren and flashing lights on.
3. The police car is followed by an ambulance.
4. Both the police car and the ambulance are driving on the shoulder of the highway.

From these clues, you can infer that the police car and the ambulance are driving on the shoulder to reach the scene of an accident ahead.

USING INFERENCE IN A CARTOON

You also use inference to understand a cartoon or comic strip. You look at the details of the cartoon—the pictures and the words. Then you use those details as clues to uncover the idea suggested by the cartoonist.

EXERCISE 1: INFERENCE IN A CARTOON

Directions: Look at the following cartoon and the caption beneath it. Notice the details, and think about what you might infer from them. Then answer the questions that follow.

"Mr. Osborne, may I be excused? My brain is full!"

1. Which statements are "clues" *shown directly* by the cartoon? You may choose more than one.
   (1) People are sitting at small tables in rows.
   (2) People are sitting in a living room on couches.
   (3) One young man asks to be excused because his brain is full.
   (4) One young man asks to be excused because he wants to go to the bathroom.
   (5) The book on the front desk is labeled *Algebra*.
   (6) The person at the front has turned his head to look at the young man.

2. Which of the following statements can you *infer* from the cartoon? You may choose more than one.
   (1) The people are in a classroom.
   (2) The teacher's name is Mr. Osborne.
   (3) The people have been watching a movie.
   (4) The class is studying algebra.
   (5) The class is a first grade class.

3. Based on what the young man in the cartoon says, he is probably feeling that
   (1) he wants Mr. Osborne to teach English
   (2) he wants more difficult problems
   (3) he cannot learn any more right now
   (4) he wants to answer the next question
   (5) he wants to become a teacher

Answers start on page 674.

USING DETAILS TO MAKE AN INFERENCE

As you have seen, the clues that you've been using to make inferences are specific details that are stated directly. Read the following paragraph. Notice that the clues, or details, are in **boldfaced type**. See if you can use the clues to make an inference about the paragraph.

> Tuesday morning, Warren turned on the radio, hoping the **weather forecast** would be different from what it had been for the past six days. The announcer said **not to expect** any **cool breezes** or **sunshine,** so Warren grabbed a **raincoat** as he left the house. On the way to work, Warren turned on his **wind-shield wipers** and **headlights,** and got his **umbrella** from the back seat. Everyone at work looked and felt as **damp** and **gloomy** as the weather, so as a surprise Warren arranged to have pizza delivered to the office for lunch.

What kind of day does the paragraph describe?

(1) windy
(2) sunny
(3) rainy
(4) cloudy
(5) dry

Based on the clues, you should have picked (3) rainy.

EXERCISE 2: USING DETAILS TO MAKE AN INFERENCE

Directions: Read the following passage. Then complete the exercises that follow.

"I love the color! It's so neutral it will go with everything!" Lori exclaimed over her birthday present.

"It looks like there's room for all my junk. Let me see. . . ." Lori pulled out her wallet, her makeup bag, her keys, her checkbook, a small package of tissues, and her sunglasses case. She fit each carefully into her gift.

"See, it's perfect! I even have room to spare. And I love the shoulder strap. That will leave my hands free for carrying groceries when I shop and for carrying books when I go to school. Thanks a lot!" Lori grinned as she put the strap on her shoulder and modeled her new present.

1. You can *infer* that Lori's present is a

(1) sweater
(2) purse
(3) coat
(4) pair of earrings
(5) pair of shoes

2. What clues did the author *state directly* that helped you infer what Lori's present might be? You may choose more than one.

(1) wallet, makeup bag, and other items fit into it
(2) groceries
(3) shoulder strap
(4) books

Answers start on page 674.

EXERCISE 3: INFERENCES IN ADVERTISING

In this exercise, you will identify directly stated information and make inferences about a product in an advertisement.

Directions: Read the following ad. Then complete the exercises that follow.

> Lighten up with Lite Brite root beer. Worked hard all day? You deserve it! Drink Lite Brite root beer with your friends, and show them a little class. Bring Lite Brite to your next party for a quick pick-me-up.

1. Which of the following ideas are *directly stated* in the ad? You may choose more than one.
   (1) If you worked hard all day, you deserve to drink root beer.
   (2) Your friends will think you have class if you drink Lite Brite root beer.
   (3) Lite Brite root beer contains vitamins.
   (4) You should take Lite Brite root beer to a party for a quick pick-me-up.

2. Which of the following statements can you *infer* from the ad? You may choose more than one.
   (1) People judge you by the kind of root beer you drink.
   (2) Lite Brite root beer tastes good.
   (3) Lite Brite root beer is cheap.
   (4) People who drink Lite Brite have class.

3. What does this ad want you to believe?
   (1) Drinking root beer makes you a better driver.
   (2) Lite Brite root beer makes you sleepy.
   (3) No one can get fat on Lite Brite root beer.
   (4) Drinking Lite Brite root beer shows class.
   (5) Lite Brite root beer is less expensive than other brands.

Answers start on page 674.

INFERRING IDEAS IN PASSAGES

As you've seen in previous exercises, you can use clues that are stated directly to infer ideas that are only suggested or hinted at. You can also use this process when you read passages like the one that follows.

> In 1972 a Pioneer 10 rocket was fired into space on a scientific mission. Because it will eventually leave the solar system, it carried a plaque with it. The plaque shows pictures of a man and a woman and a picture of the position of Earth within our solar system. The plaque was designed so that any being not of our solar system might understand what humans look like and where they live in the universe.

Did you infer ideas similar to these in the following chart?

Clue or Detail	What You Can Infer From It
1. sending a rocket on a scientific mission	Scientists believe it is important to learn more about the universe.
2. sending a plaque into space	Some scientists may believe there is life somewhere else in the universe.
3. sending a picture of a man and woman into space	Other beings might not resemble humans.
4. sending a picture of the Earth's place in the solar system	Other beings might be able to find the Earth from the picture of the solar system.

EXERCISE 4: INFERRING IDEAS IN PASSAGES

Directions: Read the following passage. Look for clues that will help you make inferences. Then answer the questions that follow.

A War of Symbols

Winston Churchill was Prime Minister of England during World War II when England was attacked by Germany. In the early, terrible days of the war, bombings and lost battles depressed the English people and threatened to destroy their will to fight Hitler's Germany.

Churchill knew he needed a way to cheer up the people. He knew the hated Nazi symbol, the swastika, had originally symbolized good, but the Nazis had changed it into a symbol for power, death, and war. So Churchill invented a symbol, a "V for Victory," that he used whenever he appeared in public. To make the V for Victory sign, he held his hand up, palm out, with the first two fingers raised to form a V.

When English people saw it, they laughed, because if the hand had been reversed, palm in, it would have made a rude gesture. Churchill was telling the people what he really thought of Hitler. The V for Victory gesture soon became known worldwide as a sign of hope.

1. You can infer that Churchill's fellow citizens saw the double meaning in his gesture because the article states that
   (1) English people laughed when they saw the reversed gesture
   (2) English people were becoming depressed with bombings and lost battles
   (3) Churchill was Prime Minister
   (4) the swastika had originally been a symbol for good
   (5) Churchill invented the V for Victory symbol

2. You can infer that without a strong leader like Churchill, England might have lost the war to Germany because the passage states that
   (1) Churchill told the English people what he really thought of Hitler
   (2) the V for Victory sign became known as a symbol of hope
   (3) Churchill invented a symbol
   (4) bombings and lost battles had depressed the people and threatened their will to fight
   (5) Churchill was Prime Minister during World War II

3. The author of this passage would most likely agree that good leaders
   (1) use rude gestures
   (2) leave the country
   (3) never joke
   (4) understand the needs of the people
   (5) don't use symbols

Answers start on page 674.

INFERENCES IN LITERATURE

Inference is most often found in literature, or fictional works. Authors often suggest ideas about the characters and events they create. The reader must infer these suggested ideas because they are not stated directly.

The next exercise provides practice at making inferences about characters and events in fictional works.

EXERCISE 5: INFERENCES IN NARRATIVE

Directions: Read the following story. Then answer the questions that follow.

"Anger is just hurt covered over," Aunt Rosie had said. "If you want to solve the problem, stay in touch with the hurt. Don't let the anger take over, or you'll never get anything worked out. The ego uses anger to build a fence around itself so it won't get hurt again."

I thought about her advice. Les was late again. He'd said he'd be home by six. It was nearly 8:30.

I heard the click of the door. "Stay in touch with the hurt," I told myself.

Les stood hesitantly, as if I were going to throw something.

"Sorry I'm late," he said softly. He had tired lines around his eyes and mouth. His shoulders drooped.

"I felt really hurt that you weren't here when you said you would be. I fixed a really nice dinner, but it's all cold now," I said.

"I'm sorry. I couldn't even call. The boss insisted I go out to that new construction site and settle the change of plans with the foreman. I couldn't even get to a phone to call you ... thanks for not being mad."

Aunt Rosie was right, I thought. If I had hit him full tilt with anger, we'd have just had a big fight. I smiled at him.

"Well, it can't be undone now, I guess," I told him. I wasn't feeling angry anymore.

Les put down his briefcase and drew me into his arms. "Tell you what," he said, "How 'bout Friday night, we'll go out to eat—just to make up for tonight's ruined dinner."

"OK," I agreed. Then to myself I said, "Thanks, Aunt Rosie, you were right. If you want to solve the problem, don't let anger take over. Stay in touch with the hurt."

1. Which of the ideas are *directly stated* in the story? You may choose more than one.
   (1) The woman was angry because her husband did not arrive home on time.
   (2) Aunt Rosie had given the author advice about anger.
   (3) Les was late for dinner.
   (4) Les started a fight.
   (5) If you want to solve a problem, stay in touch with the hurt.

2. Which of the following statements can you *infer* from the story? You may choose more than one.
   (1) Aunt Rosie is a busybody.
   (2) Aunt Rosie is a wise woman.
   (3) The woman loves her husband.
   (4) Les did not intend to make his wife angry.
   (5) The woman did not follow Aunt Rosie's advice because she didn't think it would work.

3. What can you *infer* is the *main idea* of this story?
   (1) Les is late for dinner
   (2) Aunt Rosie gives advice.
   (3) Anger is related to hurt feelings.
   (4) Aunt Rosie gets mad.
   (5) Les is tired when he gets home.

4. With which of the following statements would the author probably agree? You may choose more than one.
   (1) Things are not always what they seem.
   (2) Getting into fights relieves stress.
   (3) If you look behind anger, you will find hurt.
   (4) Married couples who fight should get a divorce.

Answers start on page 675.

COMPREHENSION: PREDICTING

Another skill that will help you improve your reading is **predicting.** Predicting is a skill you already have. When you see someone plant flower seeds in the spring, and then water, weed, and put in fertilizer, you can reasonably predict that soon you'll see beautiful flowers. Predicting is something you do when you watch a movie or a television drama. Predicting what will happen next makes watching more exciting.

PREDICTING WORDS

When reading a passage, good readers can often predict what words will come next. This ability to predict allows them to read smoothly. Readers are able to predict because language often falls into familiar patterns and often repeats ideas.

You already have some skills for predicting words. See how well you can predict the missing words in the next passage. First, read the paragraph. Then go back and fill in the missing words.

> I had lost my wallet. I didn't mind losing ______________
>
> money so much, but __________________ hated the idea of
>
> ______________ my license and credit __________________.

Read the following passage with the missing words filled in, and compare your answers to these:

> I had lost my wallet. I didn't mind losing **the** [or **my**] money so much, but **I** hated the idea of **losing** my license and credit **card** [or **cards**].

Notice that two of the blanks in the paragraph above can have more than one correct answer.

EXERCISE 6: PREDICTING WORDS

Directions: Read the following paragraph. Then reread it, and fill in the numbered blanks with words that fit.

It was Kerry's birthday. We had planned a ______ (1) party for Saturday because ______ (2) in the family had ______ (3) day off. Since the ______ (4) was warm, we decided ______ (5) have a barbecue outside. ______ (6) brought small presents and ______ (7) cards. The party ended ______ (8) a big birthday cake and everyone singing " ______ (9) Birthday to You."

Answers start on page 675.

DIRECTLY STATED PREDICTIONS

Sometimes authors tell you directly what is being predicted, as in the following passage:

> John moved hesitantly through the half open flap of the tent.
>
> "Have a seat!" The fortune-teller sat at a small velvet-covered table. She motioned toward a chair opposite her.
>
> "Cards? Palms? Crystal ball?"
>
> "Uh, palms, I guess." John fumbled in his pocket for the money.
>
> She took the money and bent over his outstretched palm.
>
> "I see long life . . . and many children. Ah . . . but you have been unlucky in love so far. . . . Is that so?"
>
> John nodded.
>
> "Not to worry." The fortune-teller smiled. "All things in their time. You were not ready for such a love as this. But now . . . is almost time." She tossed her head, smiled at him, and looked back at his palm.
>
> "Ah, money, I see much money. One who waits to love you will also bring good luck for money . . . OK! Thank you! Next?"
>
> "Is that all?"
>
> "Isn't it enough?" The fortune-teller led him toward the flap. "Not many have a lucky palm like yours."

What things did the fortune-teller predict for John? You may choose more than one.

(1) a long life
(2) many children
(3) a new car
(4) a new love
(5) a lot of money

[Answers: (1), (2), (4), and (5)]

The next two exercises will give you more practice in identifying directly stated predictions. In the first, you will identify predictions in a cartoon; in the second, in an article.

EXERCISE 7: PREDICTING IDEAS FROM A CARTOON

Directions: Read the following cartoon. Think about what Cathy, the cartoon character, is predicting will happen. Then answer the questions that follow.

cathy® **by Cathy Guisewite**

Cartoon is reprinted with permission.

1. Which of the following statements are *stated directly* in the cartoon? You may choose more than one.
   (1) Cathy always keeps her car clean.
   (2) The inside of Cathy's car is a mess.
   (3) Cathy's car won't start.
   (4) The tow truck operator thinks it is silly for Cathy to clean her car.
   (5) Cathy wants the service department to think she has been taking care of her car.

2. What does Cathy *predict* will happen next?
   (1) She will always clean her car from now on.
   (2) The mechanics won't be able to fix her car.
   (3) Cathy will eat french fries.
   (4) The mechanics will think she hasn't been taking care of her car.
   (5) The mechanics will want to clean her car for her.

3. Based on what the driver of the tow truck says, which one of the following can you reasonably predict about the mechanics who will try to fix Cathy's car?
   (1) They probably won't care whether the inside is clean or dirty.
   (2) They never work on dirty cars.
   (3) They won't be able to fix the car unless it is clean.
   (4) They will all want to date Cathy.
   (5) They will laugh at the inside of Cathy's car.

Answers start on page 675.

EXERCISE 8: DIRECTLY STATED PREDICTIONS

Directions: As you read the following passage, look for predictions that are made. Then answer the questions that follow.

> The term "greenhouse effect" refers to the heating up of Earth's atmosphere. It is caused by the action of the sun on gases that are released when we burn coal, oil, or other fuels. Some scientists predict that if the atmosphere heats up by only two or three degrees, ice at the North and South Poles will melt. The melting ice will be enough to make the oceans rise two to eight feet. All of this may occur in the next 100 years or so.

1. Which of the following are *stated* or *predicted* directly in the paragraph? You may choose more than one.
   (1) The "greenhouse effect" refers to the heating of Earth's atmosphere.
   (2) The heating is caused by the action of the sun on gases released when we burn coal, oil, and other fuels.
   (3) Higher temperatures in the atmosphere will melt part of the ice at the North and South Poles.
   (4) Higher temperatures in the atmosphere will cause more ice to form at the North and South Poles.
   (5) If the polar ice caps melt a little, the oceans may rise two to eight feet.

2. Which *two* of the following statements can be predicted based on the passage? If the oceans rise two to eight feet,
   (1) there will be no change in the land on Earth
   (2) low-lying land will probably be flooded
   (3) salt water may seep into fresh water supplies, making them unusable
   (4) oceans will dry up
   (5) ocean travel will be impossible

Answers start on page 675.

USING INFERENCE TO MAKE PREDICTIONS

Sometimes authors only suggest what is going to happen. In cases like this, you have to *infer* what will happen in the story. To do this, you must use the directly stated information as a clue to help you predict the outcome of a passage.

Listen to a supervisor describe Manuel, one of his workers. See if you can make a prediction about Manuel from the information the supervisor gives you.

> "I'll give this job to Manuel. Manuel may be a little slower than some of the others, but you know he'll do it right. He's dependable. He takes time to figure it out—not just any old way will do for Manuel. When he's finished, there's never a complaint from the customer!"

What does the supervisor say directly about Manuel? He mentions these three characteristics:

- Manuel is slow but dependable.
- Manuel takes time to figure out the problem.
- There are no customer complaints if Manuel does the job.

From this directly stated information, you can predict what will probably happen next. Which one of the following do you predict it will be?

(1) Manuel will do the job, and the customer will be pleased.
(2) There will be complaints if Manuel does the job.
(3) Manuel will be the fastest worker.
(4) The foreman is going to fire Manuel.

Did you pick (1)? Based on the information you were given, you can infer that, if Manuel does the job, the customer will be pleased.

EXERCISE 9: USING INFERENCE TO MAKE PREDICTIONS

Directions: As you read the following passage, think about what predictions you can make about reading to children. Then answer the questions that follow.

Helping Children Become Good Readers

Helping children become good readers begins early. Reading aloud is the first step. Babies as young as six months enjoy hearing Mother Goose rhymes because the little poems have rhythm, and the sounds of the language are fun to hear. Between the age of six and twelve months, babies often point to pictures in books. Parents can help by naming objects in the pictures. It's possible to buy books made of cloth for babies so that they can "pretend read" by turning the pages.

As they grow older, simple story books, such as *The Three Little Pigs* and *Little Red Riding Hood,* can be added. It's important that parents read such stories with some excitement in their voices. Then children learn that reading can be fun. By ages three and four, children enjoy more picture books, ABC books, and somewhat longer stories.

At age four or five, children enjoy visiting a library to pick out books. Many librarians have been specially trained to help find children's books for particular ages and interests. For birthdays and other special days, it is a good idea to give at least one book to a child to be his or her very own.

Long before formal schooling begins, parents can help children prepare to be good readers.

1. Which of the following sentences contain information that is *directly stated* in the passage? You may choose more than one.
   (1) Parents can help children become good readers.
   (2) Parents should read to babies as young as six months.
   (3) Parents should not buy cloth books for babies.
   (4) Simple story books, picture books, ABC books, and somewhat longer story books are recommended for reading to children.
   (5) Parents should buy books as birthday presents.

2. Which one of the following is a logical *prediction?* Children who have been read to as babies will
   (1) be better prepared to learn to read in school
   (2) enjoy television movies more
   (3) hate books
   (4) never learn their ABCs
   (5) be jealous of other children

Answers start on page 675.

STUDY SKILL: CHARTS AND OUTLINES

You have learned how to read a paragraph and fill in a chart that showed the main idea and supporting details in that paragraph. In this study skill, you will be reversing that process. You will first fill in a chart and then use the chart to write your own paragraph. Later, you will also see how outlines can help you write a paragraph with a main idea and supporting details.

CHARTS

Let's take a look at how it's done. First, look at the following partially finished chart below.

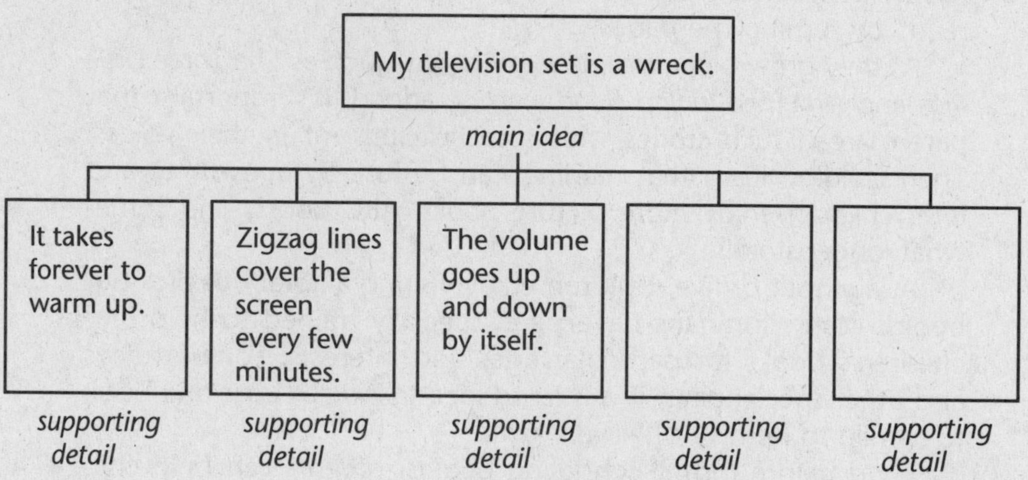

Notice that all the supporting details describe something about the main idea. Use your imagination to think of two more details that support the main idea, *My television set is a wreck*, and then go back and write them in the empty boxes of the preceding chart.

Now read the paragraph that follows. It was written by using the information in the chart you just filled in. Complete the paragraph by writing a sentence or two about the supporting details you added to the chart:

> **My television set is a wreck.** It takes forever to warm up after it's turned on, and the volume goes up and down all by itself. After it's been on for just a little while, zigzag lines cover the screen every couple of minutes. ______________________________
>
> ____
>
> ____

In the preceding paragraph, the main idea is in **bold type**. The supporting ideas that follow the main idea explain it further.

EXERCISE 10: USING CHARTS

Directions: Complete each of the following questions.

1. Describe something or someone you can see from where you are sitting. Do this by filling in the following chart. Put the main idea in the top box, just as shown in the previous example. Then fill in the supporting details with ideas that further describe or explain your main idea. Write as many details as you can think of. (Consider size, weight, shape, texture, color, use, and so on.)

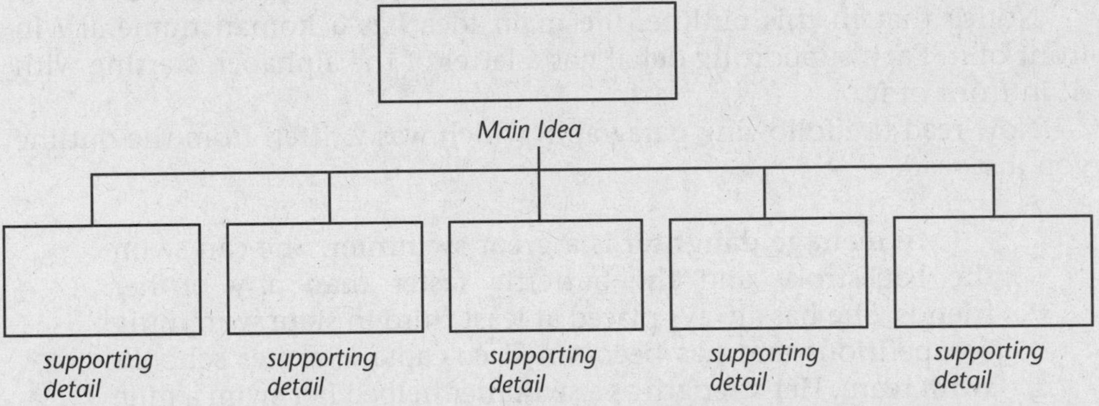

2. Now use the chart you just created to write a paragraph. Begin with your main idea. Then put your supporting details into sentences following the main idea. If you wish, you may combine more than one detail in a sentence. Check what you have written with your teacher or with a friend.

Answers start on page 675.

OUTLINES

An outline can help you organize your ideas and write a paragraph. The difference between a chart and an outline is that a chart may organize ideas *across* the page, while an outline always organizes ideas *down* the page. However, charts and outlines contain the same information: the main idea and supporting details.

Look at this example of an outline:

I. My teenage daughter is a great swimmer. — MAIN IDEA

A. Can swim the backstroke and the butterfly faster than her friends
B. Has always placed at least third in state competitions
C. Has been voted co-captain of her school swim team for her ability
D. Swam a mile to shore after boat overturned

— SUPPORTING DETAILS

Notice that in this outline, the main idea has a Roman numeral *I* in front of it. Each supporting detail has a letter of the alphabet, starting with *A,* in front of it.

Now read the following paragraph, which was written from the outline you just read.

> **My teenage daughter is a great swimmer**. She can swim the backstroke and the butterfly faster than any of her friends. She has always placed at least third in state swimming competitions and has been voted co-captain of her school's swim team. Her strength as a swimmer helped her swim a mile to shore after the boat she was in overturned.

Notice that the main idea in the preceding paragraph is in **bold type**. The supporting details that follow it explain more about the main idea.

EXERCISE 11: USING OUTLINES

Directions: Complete each of the following exercises.

1. Consider what you would do if you won $10,000 in a contest. In the outline that follows, write "I won $10,000" on the main-idea line. Think of at least three things you might do with the money. Write those ideas on the supporting detail lines.

   I. ______________________________

   A. ______________________________

   B. ______________________________

   C. ______________________________

2. Now use the outline you just created to write a paragraph. Put the main idea in the first sentence. You can reword it slightly to make it more interesting. Then add sentences for the supporting details.

Answers start on page 675.

STUDY SKILL: FOLLOWING DIRECTIONS

When we think of following directions, we may first think of finding our way to a certain place. But we follow directions of all kinds. For instance, when a cook follows a new recipe, he is following directions. When a doctor gives you medicine, she tells you when to take it and how much to take. An employer who explains what he or she wants you to do is also giving you directions. As you can see, knowing how to follow directions can be extremely important in your everyday life.

Following directions when doing classwork or while taking a test can be important. Sometimes people do poorly on exercises or tests because they fail to follow the directions. In this study skill, we will look at the parts of directions to make them easier to follow.

DIVIDING DIRECTIONS INTO PARTS

Directions usually come in three parts: What to do? To what? Under what conditions or how? Study these examples:

Part 1	Part 2	Part 3
What to Do?	**To What?**	**Under What Conditions: How? When? or Where?**
Circle	the word	that matches the definition.
Feed	the baby	when he is hungry.
Draw	a line	from the detail to the question it matches.
Donate	blood	at 10:00 tomorrow morning.

Notice that in the preceding table the three parts occur in the same order. This is not always the case. Sometimes the parts of the direction occur in a different order, such as the following:

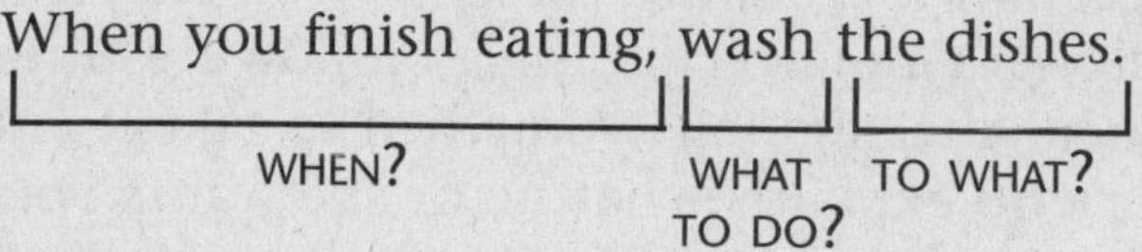

Now let's analyze the following three directions. As you read, notice the order of the three different parts of each direction.

Before opening, read the directions.

PART 1: **What** are you **to do**? *Read*
PART 2: Read **what**? *the directions*
PART 3: **When**? *before opening*

EXERCISE 12: DIVIDING DIRECTIONS INTO PARTS

Directions: Analyze the directions that follow. Then write the three parts of each direction in the correct columns in the table below. The first one is done for you.

1. Analyze the directions that follow.
2. Write the words in the correct columns.
3. Deliver the boxes to the accounting department.
4. Check only the clues that support the reference.
5. Fill in the blank with the correct word.
6. When answering the phone, write down the caller's name.

What to Do?	To What?	Under What Conditions: How? When? or Where?
1. *Analyze*	*the directions*	*that follow.*
2.		
3.		
4.		
5.		
6.		

Answers start on page 675.

FOLLOWING SEVERAL DIRECTIONS

As a student, an employee, and in many other roles, you will often have to follow several directions at once. If you follow the directions in sequence, you will find they are not so confusing. Analyze *each* direction for the three parts you have learned to identify. *Analyze* means to study something complex by reducing it to something simpler.

EXERCISE 13: FOLLOWING SEVERAL DIRECTIONS

1. *Directions:* In the following sentence, underline the context clues that help you figure out the meaning of the word in **bold type**. Then circle the correct definition of the boldfaced word.

   The cup had been **mended** so well that no one could tell that it had ever been broken.

   (1) broken
   (2) repaired
   (3) dropped
   (4) washed
   (5) packed

   Is it right or wrong? If it is wrong, mark the mistake(s).

2. *Directions:* Add lines 3 and 4. Subtract line 5. Write your answer on line 7. If the amount is less than $12, write the total again on line 8. Leave lines 1, 2, and 6 blank.

   1. ________
   2. ________
   3. $10
   4. $ 3
   5. $ 4
   6. ________
   7. $ 9
   8. $12

   Is it right or wrong? If it is wrong, mark the mistake(s).

3. *Directions:* Put the following words in alphabetical order—*can, each, band, dentist, fat, bead.* If the first word starts with B, circle the word. If the first word ends in D, underline the word. If the last word has an A in it, draw a box around the word. If the last word has a T in it, underline the word twice.

   band bead can dentist each fat

   Is it right or wrong? If it is wrong, mark the mistake(s).

Answers start on page 676.

4 Organizing Ideas

In this chapter, you will discover how authors organize their ideas. Authors use a number of different techniques to arrange information in their writing. We will look at four of these techniques:

- Cause and effect
- Comparison and contrast
- Sequence (time order)
- Analogies

You will also learn to read more critically. In particular, you will learn to distinguish fact from fiction.

COMPREHENSION: CAUSE AND EFFECT

In a cause-and-effect relationship, one condition or event makes another one happen. Authors are not the only ones to use cause and effect. In fact, you use this relationship every day. Every time you say the word *because*, you are recognizing why something happened. This is its ***cause***. The ***effect*** is what happened as a result of the cause. For example, look at the following sentence.

José failed the test *because* he did not study.

Effect (*what happened?*):
José failed the test
Cause (*why?*):
because he did not study

The cause-and-effect relationship is the same regardless of the order in which ideas are stated.

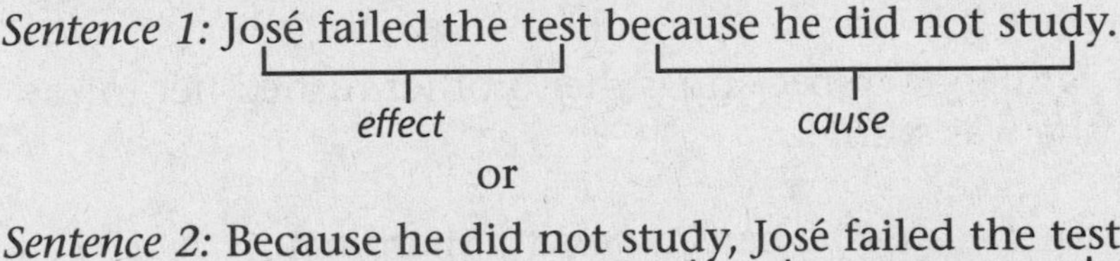

This is so even though sentence 2 states it in the opposite order from sentence 1. We might chart a cause-and-effect relationship in this way:

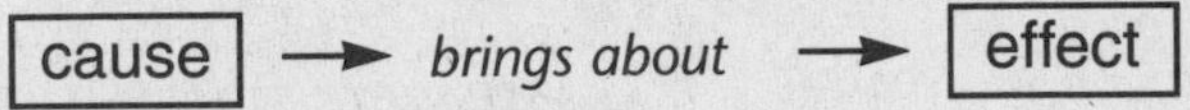

Read the next two pairs of sentences. The sentences in each pair state the same cause-and-effect relationship, but in different orders. See if you can identify the cause and the effect in each sentence. Fill in the appropriate boxes with words from each sentence to show the cause-and-effect relationship.

1. Because Jenny hates liver, she never eats it.

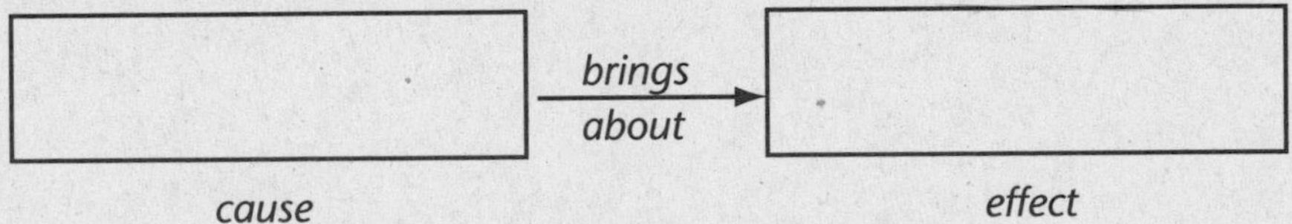

2. Jenny never eats liver because she hates it.

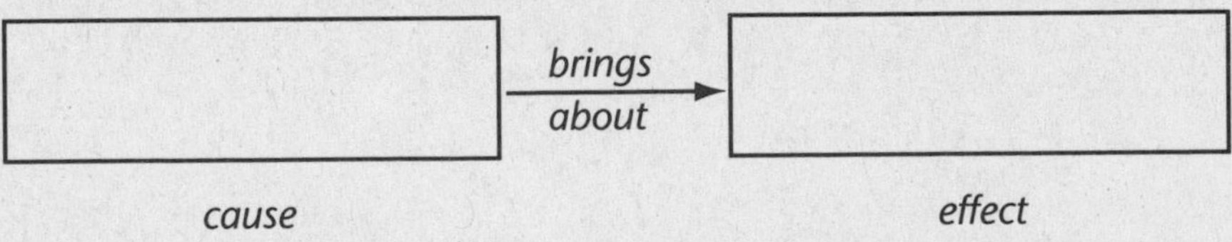

See how your answers compare with these:

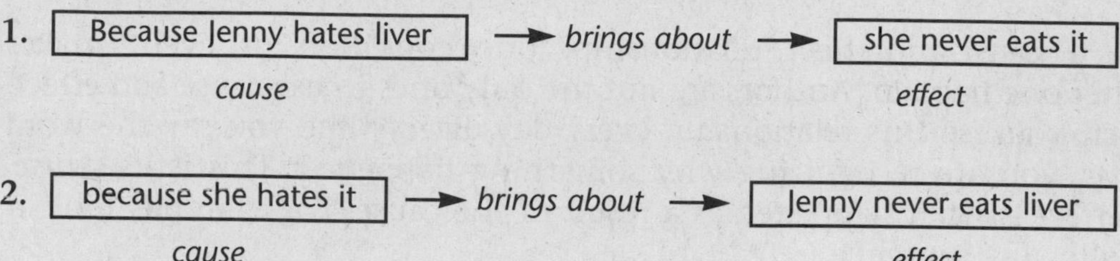
1.
Because Jenny hates liver
brings about
she never eats it
cause
effect
2.
because she hates it
brings about
Jenny never eats liver
cause
effect

EXERCISE 1: IDENTIFYING CAUSE AND EFFECT

Directions: In the following sentences, circle the words that indicate a cause, and underline the words that indicate an effect. The first one has been done for you.

1. Julie fell because she did not see the hole in the sidewalk.
2. Because Carlos added salt instead of sugar, his cake tasted terrible.
3. Because Amy is allergic to bee stings, her brother rushed her to the doctor when she was stung.
4. He had a flat tire because he had run over a sharp nail.
5. Because the radio was so loud, I didn't hear the phone.
6. Pete was exhausted because he had worked overtime.

Answers start on page 676.

UNDERSTANDING SIGNAL WORDS

All of the cause-and-effect sentences thus far have contained the word *because*. The word *because* is called a ***signal word*** because it signals you that a cause is immediately following. *For* and *since* are also signal words that let you know a cause is coming next. Signal words and phrases can also introduce an effect. Some of these include *therefore* and *so*. The following sentences give examples of signal words:

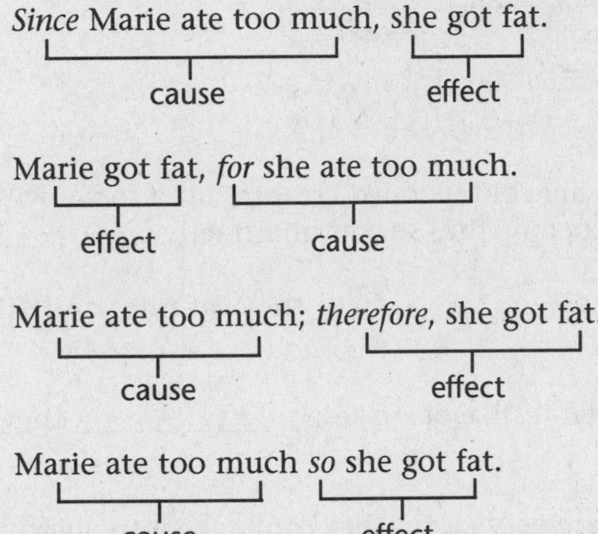

Read the following sentences, and see whether you can identify the cause, the effect, and the signal word. Write *cause* on the line under the part of the sentence that is the cause. Write *effect* on the line under the part of the sentence that is the effect. Then, circle each signal word.

1. The rainfall was heavy; therefore, the river rose four feet.

2. The rainfall was heavy, so the river rose four feet.

Your answers should read:

1. The rainfall was heavy; (therefore,) the river rose four feet.
   cause *effect*
2. The rainfall was heavy, (so) the river rose four feet.
   cause *effect*

EXERCISE 2: IDENTIFYING CAUSE-AND-EFFECT RELATIONSHIPS

Directions: Each of the following sentences contains a cause-and-effect relationship. As you read each sentence, identify the cause and the effect. Then, fill in the blank in each sentence with a signal word that indicates the proper cause-and-effect relationship. Remember to think of the **relationship** of the ideas. The first one is done as an example.

Signal Words	
because	therefore
since	so
for	

1. *Because* snakes are cold-blooded creatures and move with a crawling motion, many people find snakes unattractive.

2. Snakes are useful creatures ______________ they eat mice and other small animals.

3. Some people get over their dislike of snakes; ______________, they may adopt them as pets.

4. ______________ snakes are very clean, they can be kept in apartments.

5. Grant lived next door; ________________, I often saw him with his pet boa constrictor.

6. Boa constrictors do not eat daily, ________________ Grant found that feeding his pet was cheap.

7. ________________ boas need sunshine and fresh air, Grant often took his boa outside.

Answers start on page 676.

CAUSE-AND-EFFECT RELATIONSHIPS IN PARAGRAPHS

You've seen how cause-and-effect relationships occur in sentences. Now we'll take a look at how they occur in paragraphs. Just as you did in sentences, look for signal words in a paragraph. However, even when there are no signal words, a cause-and-effect relationship may still be present.

EXERCISE 3: CAUSE-AND-EFFECT RELATIONSHIPS IN PARAGRAPHS

Directions: Read the following paragraph. Then answer the questions that follow.

> Some scientists are worried about what will happen to people and animals if large forests and jungles in the world are destroyed. The trees and green plants in these forests and jungles produce oxygen, which is released into the atmosphere. Animals and people need this oxygen to breathe. If huge areas of green plants are destroyed, too little oxygen may be produced to keep people and animals alive.

1. What is the *cause* of some scientists' worry?

   ____

2. According to the paragraph, what bad effect would occur if huge forests and jungles are destroyed?
   (1) Shade trees would disappear.
   (2) Oxygen in the atmosphere would be reduced.
   (3) Exotic plants would die out.
   (4) Less farmland would be available.
   (5) Conservationists would protest.

3. A South American country wants to get rid of its forests in order to sell the lumber and to create farmland. Given the information in the paragraph you just read, what do you think scientists might advise the country's leaders to do?
   (1) grow corn and rice only
   (2) burn the forest down
   (3) save part of the forest as it is
   (4) sell the lumber to the United States for building houses
   (5) go ahead and destroy the forests

Answers start on page 676.

EXERCISE 4: MORE PRACTICE IN CAUSE/EFFECT IN PARAGRAPHS

Directions: Read the following paragraph. Remember to pay attention to the relationship of ideas, not just to the signal words. Then answer the questions that follow.

> Whales usually travel down the Pacific coast from Alaska to Mexico in the fall. They make this long trip because they breed and have their young in the warm water near Mexico. In the fall of 1985, one young whale became confused, took a wrong turn, and swam into the San Francisco Bay by mistake. Unable to find the narrow opening back to the sea, the whale began to swim up one of the rivers that flows into the bay. Many people became alarmed because the fresh water in the river can cause severe skin problems for whales. People were afraid the whale might die if he did not return to the salt water of the ocean; therefore, they organized themselves along the river bank and in boats. By using recorded whale noises to attract the lost whale, these people gradually coaxed him back down the river toward the ocean. As a result, the whale swam under the Golden Gate Bridge and was free. Everyone was relieved because the whale was now safe.

1. Whales travel from Alaska to Mexico because they want to

(1) see the scenery
(2) escape whale hunters
(3) breed and have their young
(4) get to San Francisco Bay
(5) die at the end of their journey

2. The whale swam into the bay because he

(1) wanted to explore San Francisco
(2) became confused and took a wrong turn
(3) wanted to hear recorded whale sounds
(4) was tired of swimming
(5) was sick and needed a place to die

3. The people were afraid that

(1) the whale might drown
(2) the fresh water might harm the whale
(3) the whale's huge tail might damage the Golden Gate Bridge
(4) the whale could not swim
(5) he would eat all the fish in the river

4. Why did people use recorded whale noises? ______________________

____

5. What was the effect of the people's efforts? ____________________

____

6. The "whale noises" had been recorded previously in the ocean. When the whale heard them, he followed the boats. It may be that he thought the sounds he heard were of
   (1) boats traveling under the Golden Gate Bridge
   (2) whales feeding
   (3) boats out hunting whales
   (4) airplanes crossing the ocean
   (5) whale hunters

Answers start on page 676.

COMPREHENSION: COMPARISON AND CONTRAST

Besides cause and effect, authors often use the comparison-and-contrast technique to help them organize their ideas. To ***compare*** means to see how things are *alike*. To ***contrast*** means to see how things are *different*. We often use these techniques to describe things in our daily lives.

COMPARING TWO THINGS

Let's try comparing and contrasting the jobs of a *waiter* and a *bridge builder*. Think about how the jobs of a waiter and a bridge builder are *alike*, and list those qualities. Then list the ways in which the jobs of a waiter and a bridge builder are *different*.

Now see how your answers compare with these:

Compare		
Hints	**Waiter**	**Bridge Builder**
Works with other people or alone?	works with others	works with others
Is moving around or seated while working?	moves around while working	moves around while working
Contrast		
Usually works outside or inside?	usually works inside	works outside
Is the job safe or dangerous	safe job	dangerous job

EXERCISE 5: COMPARISON AND CONTRAST

Directions: Read the descriptions with the following pictures. Notice how the cars are compared and contrasted. Then answer the questions that follow.

The 1976 Pontiac Grand Prix weighed 4,048 pounds. This car used more gas than later, lighter models. Because it was made with heavy steel, it was also expensive for auto manufacturers to produce.

The 1994 Pontiac Grand Prix weighed 3,159 pounds, or 889 pounds less than the 1976 model. By redesigning the car and by using aluminum and plastic instead of heavy steel, designers made the car lighter. With the increasingly high price of gas, consumers wanted lighter-weight cars that used less gas than earlier models.

1. Using the information with each picture, fill in the following chart. Then use the chart to help you answer the remaining questions.

	1976 Pontiac Grand Prix	1994 Pontiac Grand Prix
Total weight of each		
Materials used for each		
Cost to produce (cheaper/more expensive)		
Gas use (more/less)		

2. Put a check in the box next to all the statements that show how the two cars are *similar*.
   (1) Both used the same amount of gas.
   (2) Both were made by the same company.
   (3) Both weighed the same amount.
   (4) Both were Grand Prix models.

3. Put a check in the box next to all the statements that show how the two cars were *different*.
   (1) One was built in 1976; one was built in 1994.
   (2) One was built by Ford; the other was built by Pontiac.
   (3) One was heavier than the other.
   (4) One was blue; the other was red.

4. According to the information you just read, what caused auto manufacturers to design lighter-weight cars that used less gas?
   (1) Aluminum and plastic are lighter than steel.
   (2) Lighter, more weatherproof paints were being developed.
   (3) Increased gas prices made consumers want cars that used less gas.
   (4) People could more easily fit the smaller cars into parking places.
   (5) People could change the tires of lighter-weight cars more easily.

Answers start on page 676.

COMPARISON AND CONTRAST IN A PASSAGE

So far, you've learned how to compare and contrast two things. The next exercise will give you practice in recognizing comparison and contrast as they are used in a passage.

EXERCISE 6: COMPARING AND CONTRASTING TWO PEOPLE

Directions: Pretend that you have been introduced to a neighbor of two old school friends of yours. Notice how you learn about the personalities of these two people. You get a description of their similarities and differences. Then answer the questions that follow.

> "Teddy and Will? Sure I know them. Why, I lived in the same apartment house with their momma and daddy for over twenty years. I remember Teddy, the oldest one. He was always so quiet and serious. Why you'd never know a baby lived upstairs—hardly ever cried. But that Will—he was the loud one. He'd shriek and holler when he was hungry. But he could laugh too.
>
> They were as different as day and night as they got older. Teddy was always carryin' books around. I guess he read most of them—got high grades in school. I know 'cause his momma used to tell me. That Will could never have sat long enough to read much—always dashing in and out, up and down the stairs with his friends. He was more sports-minded than his brother. He played on lots of teams at school, and on Sunday you could hear the ball games on his radio way down in my apartment.
>
> "They were both good boys—made their momma proud, they did. Teddy? He went on to school to do something with computers. Will quit school for a while and worked. Later, he went back and got his diploma. He works as a car salesman now—makes good money. Both of them still send their momma money to help out now that their dad is gone. Of course, they visit—especially on holidays. Funny how two brothers can be so different."

1. Who was the older and more serious boy? ______________________

2. Who loved sports? ______________________________________

3. Put a check next to *two* of the ways in which the boys were similar.
   (1) Both had the same parents.
   (2) Both were quiet and serious.
   (3) Both were male.
   (4) Both loved to play sports.

4. Put a check next to *two* of the ways in which the brothers were different.
   (1) One liked to read; the other liked sports.
   (2) One liked his mother; the other didn't.
   (3) One left home; the other still lives with his mother.
   (4) One was quiet; the other was noisy.

5. Based on what you read, you can tell that the neighbor probably
   (1) likes both boys
   (2) likes Teddy better than Will
   (3) likes Will better than Teddy
   (4) dislikes both boys
   (5) wishes she'd had more children

Answers start on page 677.

COMPREHENSION: SEQUENCE (TIME ORDER)

Another technique that authors often use to organize their ideas is ***sequencing***. This means to put things in the order in which they occur. For example, history books often discuss early historical events first. They gradually lead up through history to modern events.

TIME LINE SEQUENCING

One way to diagram a sequence of events is to use a *time line*. A time line is a straight line that marks important events in order of the times when they occurred.

Here's an example of a time line that marks some major wars in U.S. history:

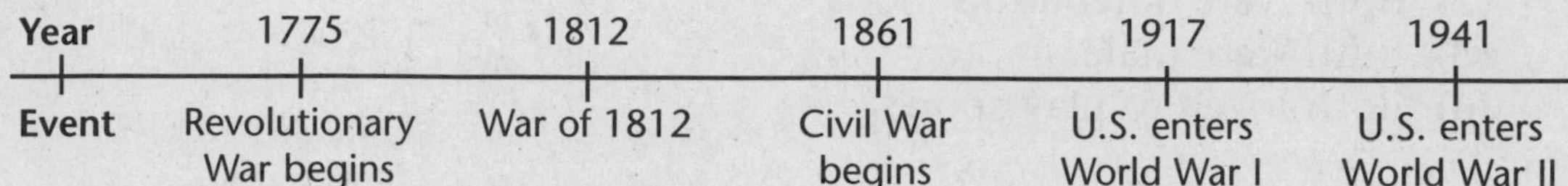

As you can see, the time line records the events from left to right in the order in which they occurred. It's easy to tell from a time line how many years passed between one event and the next. For example, you can tell that 80 years passed between the beginning of the Civil War and the entry of the United States into World War II. You can figure this out by subtracting the year the Civil War began (1861) from the year the United States entered World War II (1941):

1941–1861 = 80 years

EXERCISE 7: UNDERSTANDING A TIME-LINE SEQUENCE

Directions: Read the following timeline of important events in the life of Angela Rodriguez. Starting at the left, read across the time line, noting the events and the dates on which they occurred. Then answer the questions that follow.

1948	1954	1966	1967	1968	1970	1985	1986
born in Memphis, Tennessee	started school	finished high school	married Carlos	daughter Carmen born	son Carlos, Jr. born	divorced Carlos	started college

1. About how old was she when she started school? ______________
2. About how old was she when she finished high school? __________
3. How many years was Angela married to Carlos? ________________
4. Angela returned to school
   (1) before she married Carlos
   (2) before Carlos, Jr. was born
   (3) one year before her divorce
   (4) one year after her divorce
   (5) after Carmen had graduated

Answers start on page 677.

SIGNAL WORDS

Time lines can help chart the sequence of important events in a person's life. Sequencing is also important in the day-to-day events of our lives. For example, most of us follow a sequence of steps when we go about our daily activities of getting up in the morning, going to work or school, cooking, and so on.

Words such as *first*, *next*, and *last* are ***signal words*** that indicate what sequence to follow when doing something. Authors often use words like the following to signal the order of events in a story to the reader.

Signal Words Showing Sequence		
first	later	since
second	then	when
third	after	last
next	before	

EXERCISE 8: SIGNAL WORDS THAT SHOW SEQUENCE

Directions: In the following sentences, underline the signal words that show sequence. If you need to, look at the table above.

1. First, bring the water to a boil. Second, add the eggs. Third, turn down the heat. Then simmer the eggs for fifteen minutes, and last, rinse the eggs with cold water.

2. Before I met her, I was afraid I wouldn't know what to say. After meeting her in person, I found she was friendly, so I relaxed.

3. When I got on the bus, I must have had my wallet because I got my fare out of it. Later, at home, I discovered my wallet was gone.

Directions: Choose the correct answer.

4. You are giving a friend three-step directions to get to a certain restaurant. In your directions, should you use the words *first*, *second*, and *third* for the steps, or should you use *first*, *next*, and *last*?

   (1) first, second, third
   (2) first, next, last
   (3) both (1) and (2) are fine because the sequence is the same

Answers start on page 677.

EXERCISE 9: ARRANGING ITEMS IN CORRECT SEQUENCE

Directions: The following sentences describe how to wash a dog at home. Read all the sentences first and look for signal words that indicate sequence. Then go back and number the sentences in the correct sequence. Write the numbers on the lines provided. (You might try doing the numbers lightly in pencil first until you decide on the exact sequence.)

______ **a.** Then shampoo the dog, starting at the head. Work the shampoo well into its coat, being careful not to get soap in its eyes or nose.

______ **b.** Next, rinse the shampoo off thoroughly.

______ **c.** Finally, dry the dog with the towels.

______ **d.** Before you start, gather together a large sponge, several towels, and some dog shampoo.

Answers start on page 677.

SEQUENCE IN PASSAGES

Sequencing plays an important part in the structure of the passages. Being able to identify the correct sequence will help you understand the ideas the author presents.

EXERCISE 10: UNDERSTANDING SEQUENCE IN A STORY

Directions: As you read the following selection, keep track of the sequence of events. Pay special attention to signal words.

Old Jake Cochran was a gold miner. One night, while searching for gold in the high mountains of Canada, he made his camp by a stream. Near the stream he saw large tracks. He decided they probably belonged to a bear who had come to the stream to fish. Not wanting the animal in the camp, he hung his food from a tree several yards from his tent and his campfire.

Before dawn, Jake was awakened by a crashing sound. He leaped from his sleeping bag to peer out of his tent into the dim light. He saw the back of a huge, fur-covered creature rummaging through his food, which the creature had pulled down from the tree. Jake reached for his gun. First, the creature stood up and growled. Then the creature, looking more like a gigantic man than a bear, turned around to face Jake. It stood upright like a man, but it must have weighed at least a thousand pounds. Its eyes looked human, yet the creature was covered with thick, dark fur. After staring at Jake for what seemed like forever, the creature snatched some food in its front, pawlike hands, then disappeared into the brush with a few long strides.

Jake dropped his gun in relief. He was safe now. But what kind of creature *was* this?

1. Number the events of Jake's adventure in the proper sequence. The first one has been done for you.

   ______ **a.** Jake was awakened by a noise.
   __1__ **b.** Jake camped near a stream.
   ______ **c.** The creature turned around and looked at Jake.
   ______ **d.** Jake saw that a creature had pulled his food down from the tree.
   ______ **e.** The manlike creature disappeared.

2. Given the sequence of events, what do you think Jake might do next?
   (1) move his food into his tent
   (2) move his camp
   (3) call the police
   (4) hide his gun near the stream
   (5) follow the creature

Answers start on page 677.

EXERCISE 11: UNDERSTANDING SEQUENCE IN DIRECTIONS

Directions: As you read the following article, notice the sequence of steps given to solve a problem. Then answer the questions that follow.

Making Decisions

Adults must make many decisions in life. Some of those may include deciding whether or not to move, to marry, to have children, to go back to school, to change jobs, and so forth. Some people make decisions on impulse and regret their decisions later. Others just stew and worry, unable to come to any conclusion. Still others seem able to make good decisions without much hassle. How do these hassle-free decision makers do it?

One helpful way to make a decision is to sit down in a quiet place with a pencil and a sheet of paper. At the top of the paper, write the problem as a question, such as, "Should I move to New Jersey?" or "Should I marry Susan?" or "Should I return to school?" Next, fold the paper in half lengthwise. Then, unfold the paper so that there are two columns. Write "Advantages" at the top of the left-hand column and write "Disadvantages" at the top of the right-hand column.

Now list all the benefits to be gained under "Advantages." Next list all the drawbacks under "Disadvantages." Sometimes a good friend or a relative can help you think of what to put in each column. Last, weigh the advantages and disadvantages in your lists, and then make your decision. If you follow this method, your decisions may be easier to make than you think!

1. What is the main idea of this article?

(1) Adults make decisions on impulse and later regret their decisions.
(2) Adults worry and stew when making decisions.
(3) Listing advantages and disadvantages can make decision making easier.
(4) Friends and relatives can help you make decisions.
(5) Getting married in a hurry is a mistake.

2. Number the following directions in the sequence in which they occurred in the passage. Put a 1 next to the first, a 2 next to the second, and so on.

_____ **a.** List the benefits under "Advantages" and the drawbacks under "Disadvantages."

_____ **b.** Weigh the advantages and disadvantages.

_____ **c.** Write your problem in the form of a question.

_____ **d.** Divide the paper into two columns and label the two columns "Advantages" and "Disadvantages."

_____ **e.** Make your decision.

Answers start on page 677.

STUDY SKILL: ANALOGIES

You have already used the technique of comparison and contrast. Next we will be comparing (finding the similarities of) the relationships between words. In other words, we will be looking first at how one pair of words is related. Then we will see how another pair of words is related in a similar way. These comparisons of similar relationships are called ***analogies***.

FINDING ANALOGIES

An analogy looks like this:

wet : dry :: hot : cold

We translate the dots this way: One set of dots (:) means *is to*. Two sets of dots (::) mean *as*. Therefore, when we substitute words for dots in the preceding analogy, it looks like this:

wet **is to** dry **as** hot **is to** cold

This means that *wet* is related to *dry* in the same way that *hot* is related to *cold*.

Now we need to discover how *wet* and *dry* and *hot* and *cold* are related in the same way.

wet : dry :: hot : cold
Wet is **the opposite** of *dry*, and *hot* is **the opposite** of *cold*.

In both pairs, the relationship of the words is that one is the opposite of the other.

Now that you know how to identify relationships between words, you can fill in a missing word in an analogy. Look at the following example:

fat : thin :: short : ____________

Since this is an analogy, we know that the relationship between *fat* and *thin* is the same as the relationship between *short* and _________. How do we fill in the blank? Follow the steps below, checking your answers as you go.

fat : thin :: short : ___________

Step 1. Translate the dots by filling in the lines below.

fat _____ _____ thin _____ short _____ _____

fat **is to** thin **as** short **is to** ________

Step 2. Now rewrite the analogy by writing the relationship between the first two words in the blank:

fat is the _____________ of thin

fat is the **opposite** of thin

Step 3. Next, write the *same words* that express the relationship between *fat* and *thin* after the third word, *short*:

short is the _______________ of _______________

short is the **opposite** of ______________

Step 4. Complete the analogy.

fat : thin :: short : _________________

fat: thin :: short : **tall**

The word *tall* completes this analogy because it is the opposite of *short.*

The words we've looked at so far have all been opposites of each other. However, this is not always the relationship in an analogy. Next, we will work with analogies that have relationships other than opposites.

Practice completing the next analogy:

finger : hand :: toe : __________

1. finger ______ _____ hand _____ toe _____ _____ _____________
2. finger is a _____ ______ a hand
3. toe is a ______ _____ a ____________
4. finger : hand :: toe : ____________

Compare your answers with these:

1. finger **is to** hand **as** toe **is to** ______________
2. finger is a **part of** a hand
3. toe is a **part of** a ______________
4. finger : hand :: toe : **foot**

Foot completes this analogy because a toe is a *part of* a foot.

EXERCISE 12: WORKING WITH ANALOGIES

Part 1

Directions: Read each analogy. Using the steps you just learned, pick the word that best completes the analogy. Then write the letter of the word you chose in the blank provided.

1. gift : present :: plate : ______
   a. birthday
   b. dish
   c. cup
   d. holiday

2. end : finish :: start : ______
   a. motor
   b. stop
   c. begin
   d. dinner

3. leaf : tree :: petal : ______
   a. grass
   b. vase
   c. flower
   d. forest

4. see : eye :: hear : ______
   a. ear
   b. blink
   c. listen
   d. music

5. pen : write :: car : ______
   a. letter
   b. tire
   c. drive
   d. read

6. ice : cold :: fire ______
   a. hot
   b. chilly
   c. burn
   d. fireplace

Part 2

Directions: Read each of the following analogies. Using the steps you learned earlier, fill in the blank with a word that completes the analogy.

1. music : listen :: book : ________________
2. $: dollar :: % : ________________
3. glass : break :: paper : ________________
4. hour : minute :: pound : ________________
5. spoon : stir :: knife : ________________
6. ring : finger :: belt : ________________

Answers start on page 677.

COMPREHENSION: READING CRITICALLY

Reading critically means analyzing or questioning what you read. You do this to see whether you agree with the author's statements. To analyze an author's writing, you need to determine whether he or she is stating a fact, an opinion, or a generalization.

FACTS

A ***fact*** is a statement that can be proved to be true. For example, the following statement is a fact:

John is six feet tall.

Anybody can measure John and find out whether this is true. Everyone can agree with the statement by checking the evidence—in this case, the measurement. But suppose we said the following:

John is the most handsome man in town.

This statement is *not* a fact because:

- We can't prove that someone is the *most* handsome.
- We can't all agree. (Some people might think Ming or Sam is better looking.)

Read the following statements and decide which of the statements are facts. Remember, facts can be both proved and agreed upon by all.

1. Des Moines, Iowa, is the best place to raise children.
2. Des Moines is a city in Iowa.
3. There are four quarts in a gallon.
4. John's feet are bigger than Ted's.
5. It's a fact that Sally has the greatest parties.

Did you choose statements 2, 3, and 4 as facts? These three sentences can all be proved and agreed upon. On the other hand, sentence 1 is not a fact because we cannot prove which is best, nor would we all agree. For the same reasons, sentence 5 is not a fact, even though it states that it is. What makes a party "great" varies from person to person.

EXERCISE 13: IDENTIFYING FACTS

Directions: Read each statement. Put an *F* for fact next to the statements that are facts. Remember that facts are statements that can be proved and agreed upon by all.

______ **1.** Lincoln was president during the Civil War.

______ **2.** Chocolate ice cream tastes better than vanilla.

______ **3.** Guatemala is in Central America.

______ **4.** Guatemala has an excellent central government.

______ **5.** A solar eclipse occurs when the moon moves between the Sun and the Earth.

______ **6.** It's a fact that the moon causes insanity.

______ **7.** In the United States, citizens may vote at the age of eighteen.

Answers start on page 677.

OPINIONS

An ***opinion*** is what a person *believes* is true. Indeed, it may be "true" for him but not necessarily for others. It is a personal judgment, *not* a fact. Look at the following example of an opinion.

> San Francisco sourdough bread has a better flavor than any other bread on the market.

Some people feel that this bread tastes better than others, but other people may prefer a different kind of bread. Because this statement cannot be proved and all cannot agree, it is an opinion.

Read the following sentences. Then decide which statements are *opinions.*

1. Mary is the kindest person in the world.
2. Mary brought home-cooked food to my family while I was in the hospital.
3. I think Mary needs a pet to care for.

Did you circle sentences 1 and 3 as opinions? They state what someone *believes* is true. Sentence 2, however, is a statement of what happened. We can check with the family to see whether Mary actually brought food daily.

EXERCISE 14: IDENTIFYING FACTS AND OPINIONS

Directions: Read each of the following statements. Write *O* in the blank if it is an opinion (something someone *believes* is true). Write *F* in the blank if it is a fact (something that can be proved).

_______ **1.** Albert has been unemployed for one year.

_______ **2.** Sprucenut baby food is great for babies.

_______ **3.** A fire started in the basement of the house at 1801 Miller Avenue.

_______ **4.** The United States should change its foreign policy regarding South American countries.

_______ **5.** Fall is the most beautiful time of year, with the cold, crisp air and the autumn leaves in colors of gold, yellow, orange, and red.

6. Which of the following statements about opinions is true?
   (1) Opinions are facts.
   (2) Opinions are judgments.
   (3) Opinions are always true.
   (4) Opinions are always false.
   (5) Opinions are never true.

Answers start on page 677.

5 Reading Literature

You've learned some very important reading skills. Now, you will apply them to reading different types of literature passages. ***Fiction*** is a type of literature that describes imaginary people, places, and events. We will look at three different kinds of fictional literature:

- prose fiction
- poetry
- drama

COMPREHENSION: PROSE FICTION

Prose is writing that most closely resembles everyday speech. To really understand what you're reading *and* to make it more interesting, you need to form pictures in your mind.

FORMING PICTURES IN YOUR MIND

How can you picture something in your head? You can take the clues an author gives you and use your imagination to picture them in your mind. When you do this, you enter the world that the author or poet creates. You visit the places he wants to show you and meet the people he introduces you to. You will need to combine ideas directly stated with those ideas that are implied.

Let's look at the picture you can create from the clues given in a single sentence.

> The old gardener leaned heavily on his hoe.

How do you picture the gardener? Ask yourself the following questions to help form a picture in your mind:

1. Is the gardener young or old?
2. Is the gardener standing or sitting?
3. Is the gardener energetic or tired?
4. What has the gardener been doing?
5. How does the gardener's face look? Smooth, or lined with wrinkles?

Compare your answers with these:

1. **old:** The sentence directly states that the gardener is old.
2. **probably standing:** You can infer this since the sentence says the gardener *leaned* on his hoe.
3. **probably tired:** You can infer this because the sentence tells you that the gardener leaned *heavily* on his hoe.
4. **hoeing:** You can conclude from what the sentence says that he has been tilling the ground, or hoeing.
5. **probably wrinkled:** You can infer this since you know the gardener is old, and a person's skin tends to wrinkle as he or she ages.

EXERCISE 1: FORMING PICTURES IN YOUR MIND

Directions: Read the paragraph that follows. See what kind of mental picture the details in the paragraph help you create.

> Great chunks of ice littered the greenish-blue water. Gray mists of fog swirled around the boat, when suddenly through a break in the mist, I could see the glacier. Wedged between two sheer dark gray cliffs, it towered over the boat. It was muddy and rocky toward the top, but the side leaning toward the water contained vertical shafts of white and clear blue. Then suddenly I heard it—a low rumble and then sharp cracking. An immense piece of ice began to topple slowly toward the water.

1. What was floating in the water? ______________________
2. What was at the top of the glacier? ______________________
3. What colors could be seen on the side of the glacier?

   ____
4. What sounds were heard? ______________________
5. What is about to happen? ______________________

   ____

Answers start on page 677.

USING PICTURES TO UNDERSTAND SETTING AND CHARACTERIZATION

Reading becomes much more interesting when you use the details given to create your own mental image about two elements of a story. These elements are **setting** (the time and place of a story) and **characterization** (the traits of the characters in a story).

Setting

Often an author will describe the place and time of a story because the ***setting*** establishes the framework in which the events of a story occur. Think of the importance of the setting to the story in movies and TV shows you have seen. For example, look at the following chart.

Movie/Show	Place	Time
Frankenstein	a gloomy castle on a stormy night	long ago
"Star Trek"	inside a spacecraft and on distant planets	the future

EXERCISE 2: PICTURING A SETTING

Directions: As you read, picture in your mind the setting in the following excerpt. Then answer the questions that follow.

After he had gone eight miles, he came to the graveyard, which lay just at the edge of his own hay-land. There he stopped his horses and sat still on his wagon seat, looking about at the snowfall. Over yonder on the hill he could see his own house, crouching low, with the clump of orchard behind and the windmill before, and all down the gentle hill-slope the rows of pale gold cornstalks stood out against the white field. The snow was falling over the cornfield and the pasture and the hay-land, steadily, with very little wind—a nice dry snow. The graveyard had only a light wire fence about it and was all overgrown with long red grass. The fine snow, settling into this red grass and upon the few little evergreens and the headstones, looked very pretty.

—Excerpted from "Neighbour Rosicky" by Willa Cather

1. The graveyard is located
   (1) in the middle of town
   (2) at the edge of a field
   (3) in a large city
   (4) next to a lake
   (5) near a mountain

2. Which one of the following is *not* in the description?
   (1) a pasture
   (2) a windmill
   (3) a cornfield
   (4) a barn
   (5) a wire fence

3. The main character thinks the scene is
   (1) pretty
   (2) ugly
   (3) funny
   (4) frightening
   (5) upsetting

4. At what time of year does the scene most likely take place?
   (1) winter
   (2) spring
   (3) summer
   (4) fall
   (5) Halloween

Answers start on page 678.

Characterization

In addition to describing the setting, authors help you form a mental picture of a story by showing you what the characters are like. This is called ***characterization***. An author may describe the physical or personality traits of a character. The author may also reveal a character's traits by what the character says and how he or she says it.

Describing a Character

As you read the following paragraph, notice the details the author gives to describe the character. Use the questions that follow to help you form a mental picture of the character.

> The tall, lean runner bent forward to take her position at the starting line. The muscles in her arms and legs grew tight as she prepared to spring at the sound of the starting pistol. Her eyes stared, unblinking, toward the finish line as beads of sweat formed on her forehead and dampened her black hair. One edge of her electric blue shorts fluttered in the hot wind as she waited tensely for the crack of the gun.

1. What sort of position is the runner in? Is she relaxed or tense?

   ____

2. What are her eyes like? ______________________________

3. What is the runner's mood? ___________________________

Compare your answers to these:

1. bent forward, arms and legs tensed
2. unblinking
3. intense and concentrated

EXERCISE 3: PICTURING A CHARACTER FROM A DESCRIPTION

Directions: As you read the following description, try to get a mental picture of how this person looks and acts. Then answer the questions that follow.

> He stood solidly, legs apart, with his hands on his narrow hips. His jaw was set, his face drawn with sharp bones angled beneath the tight skin. His yellowish snake eyes darted everywhere, as though being on guard was a way of life. When he lifted the edges of his mouth as though to smile, there was no laughter or joy in the movement, only cold hardness.

1. The man described is
   (1) happy and smiling
   (2) unfeeling and harsh
   (3) joking and cheerful
   (4) sad and depressed
   (5) friendly and warm

2. His build is
   (1) muscular
   (2) slender
   (3) big-boned
   (4) flabby
   (5) delicate

3. The person describing the man in the passage most likely
   (1) trusts him
   (2) distrusts him
   (3) is pleased with him
   (4) is in love with him
   (5) admires him

Answers start on page 678.

Listening to a Character Talk

Sometimes authors don't give physical descriptions of characters. Instead, they want you to form a picture in your mind about a character from *what* the character says and the *way* he or she says it.

EXERCISE 4: PICTURING A CHARACTER FROM WHAT HE SAYS

Directions: Read the following selection. Form a picture of the speaker in your mind. Then answer the questions that follow.

I ain't been scared o' nothin', but I'll tell ya' I was scared then. See, I'm big, and most guys won't mess with me, but this was different. It wasn't anything you could fight.

I drove my car over to the school . . . s'posed to be a first meetin'. I sat in my car and gripped the steerin' wheel. I thought of all the other things I could be doin' . . . stayin' home to watch TV, or stoppin' at Arnie's . . . the guys are usually hangin' around most nights.

I got out of the car. I walked toward the building. It was all lit up like a shopping center havin' a sale. Other people were walkin' in, too. I looked at them. Some of 'em were dressed pretty good . . . probably smart too . . . smarter than me. I knew they're probably smarter 'n me 'cuz I always felt so dumb in school. That's why I dropped out . . . I got behind 'cuz my folks moved a lot an' I never could catch up, so I quit to get a job so I could get a car. When you're young, you think like that . . . think the only thing in the world is a job and a car so you can impress the girls.

Anyhow, as I say, I stood there watchin' and feelin' stupid. Finally I turned on my heel and went back to the car. I got in and sat there with the keys in the ignition and my right hand about to turn 'em when I thought of Peg and the kids. They were dependin' on me. Now that I got them, I gotta get a better job, and I can't with the education I got. I'm "last hired and first fired" as they say.

So I got back outta the car and fought my gut that was in a knot and found the room and walked in.

That's how I got here, and I'm sure glad I did. I'm gonna get my diploma at night school. I know it. And I also found out we're all in the same boat. I ain't the only one who needs to learn the stuff I missed out on before. We're all the same—ain't nobody here any different.

1. Which of the following phrases best describes the speaker?
   (1) small and shy
   (2) big and strong
   (3) violent and angry
   (4) lonely and single
   (5) quiet and athletic

2. How does the speaker feel at the beginning of the selection?
   (1) pleased because he has a good job
   (2) sad because he is divorced
   (3) happy to be going to work
   (4) afraid others are smarter than he is
   (5) excited because he is going to be a father

3. How does the speaker feel at the end of the selection?
   (1) tricked and cheated
   (2) angry and hurt
   (3) comfortable and confident
   (4) sad and disappointed
   (5) unloved and alone

4. What can you predict will probably happen next?
   (1) The speaker will drop out of school again and never go back.
   (2) The speaker will have ups and downs but will stick with school.
   (3) The speaker will get a divorce and leave his family.
   (4) The speaker will get in a fight with other people in the class.
   (5) The speaker will buy new clothes to wear to class.

Answers start on page 678.

USING LANGUAGE TO CREATE MENTAL PICTURES

Authors use language in special ways to help the reader understand and create a picture of a story. Two of these special ways are the use of **comparisons** and symbols.

Making Comparisons

Sometimes the author wants to make something more exciting or dramatic. Other times the author wants to get the reader to look at something in a different way. To do this the author will often make a comparison of one object or living thing with another, like this:

> When my daughter took her first step, she proudly puffed up her chest like the first robin of spring.

When reading such comparisons, you should ask yourself two questions:

1. What two things is the author comparing? (*daughter and robin*)
2. Why did the author choose that comparison? What is she trying to get you to see? (*that the daughter looked as proud as a spring robin*)

Let's look at two more comparisons. Read the following statements. As you read, ask yourself what comparisons are being made and for what purpose. Then fill in the blanks.

1. The crowd began to depart like so many leaves blowing in an autumn wind.

   The crowd is compared with ______________________________

   What is the author's purpose? ____________________________

2. I watched the light in his eyes flicker and then go out. He was dead.

   Being alive is compared with ______________________________

   Dying is compared with __________________________________

   What is the author's purpose? ____________________________

Are your answers similar to these?

1. *comparison:* The crowd is compared with leaves blowing in an autumn wind.

   purpose: The people are moving off in many directions, not in a straight line.

2. *comparison:* Being alive is compared with a light; dying is compared with a light flickering and then going out.

   purpose: Life is bright but death is dark. Dying can be as quick as turning off a light.

EXERCISE 5: IDENTIFYING COMPARISONS

Directions: Laurence Yep describes the famous San Francisco earthquake by comparing it to objects and animals. As you read the following excerpt, look for comparisons that help you form a mental picture of the events that happen. Then answer the questions that follow.

> It was thirteen days after the Feast of Pure Brightness that the earthquake hit. Just a little after five A.M., . . . I had gotten dressed and gone out to the pump to get some water. The morning was filled with that soft, gentle twilight of spring, when everything is filled with soft, dreamy colors and shapes; so when the earthquake hit, I did not believe it at first. It seemed like a nightmare where everything you take to be the rock-hard, solid basis for reality becomes unreal.
>
> Wood and stone and brick and the very earth became fluidlike. The pail beneath the pump jumped and rattled like a spider dancing on a hot stove. The ground deliberately seemed to slide right out from under me. I landed on my back hard enough to drive the wind from my lungs. The whole world had become unglued. Our stable and Miss Whitlaw's house and the tenements to either side heaved and bobbed up and down, riding the ground like ships on a heavy sea. Down the alley mouth, I could see the cobblestone street . . . twist like a red-backed snake.
>
> —Excerpted from *Dragonwings* by Laurence Yep

1. The author says "It seemed like a nightmare . . ." in line 6–7. What is the author comparing to a nightmare?
   (1) the morning
   (2) the Feast of Pure Brightness
   (3) soft, dreamy colors and shapes
   (4) the earthquake
   (5) Miss Whitlaw's house

2. To what does the author compare the pail beneath the pump in lines 10–11?
   (1) wood and stone and brick and the very earth
   (2) the ground
   (3) a spider dancing on a hot stove
   (4) a bucket
   (5) the soft spring air

3. How does the author describe the movement of Miss Whitlaw's house and the tenements to either side (lines 14–16)? They are
   (1) tumbling down like towers of wooden blocks
   (2) riding the ground like ships on a heavy sea
   (3) twisting like a red-backed snake
   (4) coming unglued, like old wallpaper
   (5) falling like a person who has slipped on ice

4. The author compares the cobblestone street to a red-backed snake (lines 17–18) to show that the street is
   (1) as dangerous as a poisonous red snake
   (2) the same black color as many snakes
   (3) flooded with water because of the earthquake
   (4) red in color and making rippling motions
   (5) shiny like a snake's skin

Answers start on page 678.

Using Symbols

Another method an author can use to help create a "picture" is to use symbols. ***Symbols*** can be either pictures or objects that stand for ideas, people, concepts, or anything else the author decides.

Some symbols are commonly used to represent certain objects or ideas. This practice makes ideas more understandable by connecting them with things you can see. Symbols are a kind of shortcut to communication. The saying "a picture is worth a thousand words" expresses the value of symbols.

Look at the three pictures that follow. Beneath each picture are words identifying what the picture represents, or *symbolizes*

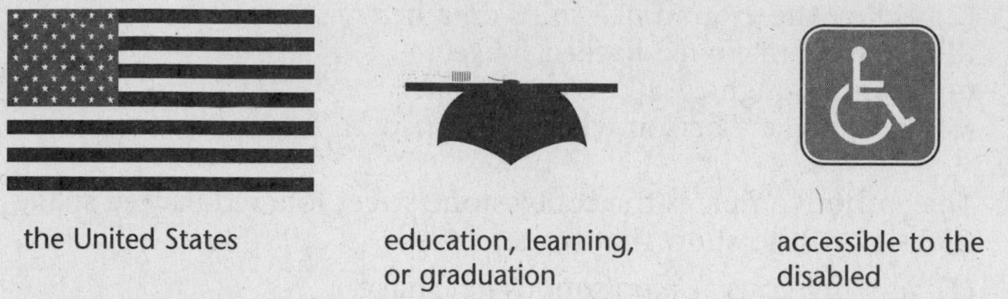

the United States | education, learning, or graduation | accessible to the disabled

Now look at the next set of symbols. On the line beneath each picture, write what the symbol stands for or represents.

1. ____________ 2. ____________ 3. ____________

Compare your answers to the following:

1. no smoking
2. poison
3. liberty

In the next exercise, practice identifying symbols and the things they represent. Remember that a symbol can be a picture, like the ones above, or an object, like a wedding ring.

EXERCISE 6: RECOGNIZING SYMBOLS

Directions: Read the following selections and note the symbol in **bold type** in each. Write what the symbols stand for in the blanks that follow.

1. Finally I spotted the "**golden arches**." I was so hungry, I could hardly wait to order a hamburger.

The symbol stands for ____.

2. We've got big trouble here, Sam, now that the Martin gang rode into town. And I'm going to need your help. Here. Let me pin this **star** on you. Then everybody will know what we stand for.

   The symbol stands for ____.

3. The young woman stepped out of the crowd. She was holding a sign with a **large dove** drawn on it. She walked directly in front of one of the young soldiers standing at attention.

   The symbol stands for ____.

4. I couldn't figure out why Juan was so nervous on our date last Saturday until I saw the jewelry box in his pocket. When I opened it and saw the **diamond ring**, I understood!

   The symbol stands for ____.

Answers start on page 678.

UNDERSTANDING PLOT AND TONE

There are two other elements that you need to know to fully understand a story. They are plot and tone.

Plot

The ***plot*** of a story is a series of events that leads to a believable conclusion. Whether you read a story or watch it being acted out on-screen, a plot contains these four basic elements:

1. the beginning
2. the conflict
3. the climax
4. the conclusion

As the diagram shows, these elements are usually connected in a logical way that draws readers into the story and makes them want to know what will happen next. Being able to predict what happens in a story adds to the suspense. Let's look more closely at each of the four elements of plot:

Beginning	The purpose of the ***beginning*** is to *introduce the characters and setting* of the story. EXAMPLE: a boy, a girl, and the girl's father in a small town
Conflict	Often people think of conflict as meaning a fight or argument. In stories, however, the word ***conflict*** means a *problem to be solved.* EXAMPLE: The boy and girl are in love, but the father hates the boy. CONFLICT (OR PROBLEM): The boy and girl can't get together because of the father.
Climax	The ***climax*** of a story serves two functions: **1.** It is the most exciting part of the story. **2.** It solves the problem. EXAMPLE: The girl falls in the river. } exciting The boy saves the girl. } exciting The father now likes the boy. } problem solved
Conclusion	The ***conclusion*** is simply what happens at the end of the story. EXAMPLE: The girl and boy marry.

Remember that the author or writer may not directly give all the information you need to understand the plot. Therefore, you may need to use the inference and prediction skills you learned earlier to identify the four basic elements of plot.

In the next exercise, you will have a chance to practice identifying the four elements of the plot in a Greek myth. ***Myths*** are stories that try to explain natural occurrences.

The ancient Greeks were great storytellers. They believed in many gods and goddesses, and in nymphs who were the spirits of trees, rivers, rocks, and other elements of nature. This myth tries to explain the reasons for a flower's appearance and the causes of echoes.

EXERCISE 7: READING A GREEK MYTH

Directions: Read the myth that follows. Watch for the beginning, the conflict, the climax, and the conclusion. Then answer the questions that follow.

Echo was a nymph, or spirit of nature. She was beautiful but had one problem. Because she had talked too much, one of the goddesses took away Echo's power of independent speech and allowed her only to repeat what others said.

Echo, like many of the other nymphs, fell madly in love with a handsome young man called Narcissus. Unfortunately Narcissus loved no one but himself. Echo followed him and adored him, but since she could only repeat what others said, she could not begin a conversation with him. She hoped he would notice her and speak first.

One day Narcissus came upon a clear pool. Looking down into the pool's water, he saw the image of a handsome young man.

"I love you," he said to his own reflection.

"I love you," Echo repeated, hoping he would finally look at her.

But Narcissus did not pay any attention to Echo. Instead, still longing for the handsome image in the pool, he leaned too close to the water, fell in, and drowned. After he died, a flower grew where he had sat next to the pool. The flower, called *narcissus,* always hangs its head over water so as to admire its own reflection.

Poor Echo, when she saw that Narcissus was gone, died also, leaving only her voice behind. To this day, Echo can never speak for herself but can only repeat what others say.

1. Who are the main characters?

_______________________________ and _______________________________

2. What is Echo's problem (the conflict) in the story?
   (1) Echo loves Narcissus, but he doesn't love her.
   (2) Narcissus loves Echo, but she doesn't love him.
   (3) Echo and Narcissus love each other.
   (4) Narcissus fell into the pool.
   (5) Echo and Narcissus hate each other.

3. What happens in the climax?
   (1) Echo can finally speak, not just repeat others' words.
   (2) Narcissus falls in love with Echo.
   (3) Both Narcissus and Echo die.
   (4) The other nymphs kill Narcissus.
   (5) Echo and Narcissus are married.

4. What happens at the conclusion (the end) of the story?
   (1) Narcissus and Echo get married and live happily ever after.
   (2) Narcissus drowns in the pool.
   (3) Echo and the other nymphs run away into the forest.
   (4) Narcissus becomes a flower, and Echo leaves only her voice.
   (5) Echo gives birth to her first child.

5. People who suffer from narcissism are those who
   (1) hate themselves
   (2) admire themselves too much
   (3) fall in love too often
   (4) cannot speak
   (5) are overly fond of flowers

Answers start on page 678.

Tone

When an author writes a story, he may express his attitude or feelings about the subject and the characters. This expression of the author's attitude gives a certain ***tone*** to the piece. This tone not only tells you how the *author* feels toward a subject or characters. It also influences how *you,* the reader, feel toward them.

Because the author wants you to feel the same way as he does, he chooses words that he thinks will bring out the same emotions in you. The emotions can be pleasant (such as humor, joy, or peacefulness) or unpleasant (such as fear, horror, or disgust). Nearly any emotion can be the tone of a passage.

Look at the following example. What attitudes or emotions does the author feel? What words does the author use that tell you this?

> The carefree child skipped along under the blossoming trees. A playful puppy trotted after her as fast as he could.

By the use of lighthearted words such as *carefree, skipped, blossoming, playful,* and *trotted,* the author means to paint a pleasant scene that will bring out positive feelings.

In the example that follows, three people have just learned that a friend is pregnant. In the column on the left, read the reaction of each person to this news. Then match the tone from the column on the right with each statement on the left. Write the correct letter in the blank next to each statement.

Reaction	Tone
______ 1. "That's great! Bob is a nice guy. He'll be a wonderful father, I'm sure."	(1) complaining
______ 2. "Now I suppose they'll come crying to me for money to help them. They always want me to bail them out of the scrapes they get into."	(2) eager
______ 3. "Babies are so cute and cuddly. When is she due? Do they want a boy or a girl? Oh, I can't wait to hold it!"	(3) approving

See how your answers compare with these:

1. (3) approving
   This speaker approves of the pregnancy. The father is "a nice guy," and he'll "be a wonderful father."

2. (1) complaining
   You can infer this tone from the speaker's comments, "They'll come crying to me," and, "They always want me to bail them out." This speaker is concerned more about the impact of the pregnancy on his life than on anyone else's.

3. (2) eager
   You can infer this from the words *cute* and *cuddly*, and the phrase "Oh, I can't wait. . . ."

Complete the next exercise for more practice in identifying the tone of a passage.

EXERCISE 8: UNDERSTANDING TONE

Directions: As you read the following passage, picture the person and the scene. Pay particular attention to the words the author uses, and the emotions those words bring out in you. Then answer the questions that follow.

It was an evil night to be driving. The wind drove the rain in great sheets onto the windshield. The wipers could not keep up with the downpour.

Cheri drove slowly. She had left her last client late and probably should have stayed in town, but Sal had demanded that she drive on to Union City. That way, she would be there for the breakfast appointment with a new client.

Suddenly Cheri slammed on her brakes.

"What was that? I thought I saw something in the road. Someone crouching. I must have imagined it. Whoa, I must be tired . . . talking to myself."

Cheri had increased her speed again when she heard a pop. The car swerved savagely to the right.

"Oh no . . . not a flat . . . not tonight—I don't even have a spare." The car rolled to a stop near a ditch. She felt for her flashlight, found it in the glove compartment, and got out of the car. The flashlight beam came to rest on the tire, sagging uselessly against the soggy ground.

"Better try to find help."

Cheri looked through the black trees that lined the road. Somewhere to her left, she heard a dog howl.

Her flashlight stabbed the darkness. She walked back down the road, head down against the driving rain. Then she saw the row of nails on the road. She could see the place where her tires had disturbed them. Someone had deliberately placed a straight line of nails across the right lane.

Her eyes widened in fear. A cold knot gripped her stomach. She began to run, blindly.

1. What was the weather like?

(1) snowing and cold
(2) foggy and damp
(3) raining and windy
(4) sunny and warm
(5) hot and windy

2. Cheri slammed on her brakes because she
   (1) heard a dog howl
   (2) had to get to Union City early in the morning
   (3) suddenly came to a stop sign
   (4) thought she saw someone crouching in the road
   (5) remembered that she should have made a phone call

3. The author uses words like *evil night, black trees, stabbed the darkness, fear,* and *cold knot.* What emotion does the author want you, the reader, to feel?
   (1) happiness
   (2) sadness
   (3) anger
   (4) fear
   (5) embarrassment

4. What conclusion did Cheri draw from what she saw on the road?
   (1) Someone had deliberately placed nails so she would get a flat tire.
   (2) Someone was coming to help her.
   (3) The farmers in the area were friendly.
   (4) The rain would stop soon.
   (5) She would miss her breakfast appointment.

Answers start on page 678.

COMPREHENSION: POETRY

Soon you will be using many of the skills you've already learned in this chapter about reading prose. However, now you will be applying those skills to reading ***poetry***. In addition, you will learn new skills and characteristics that are unique to poetry.

DIFFERENCES BETWEEN POETRY AND PROSE

Some characteristics are unique to poetry. First of all, poetry usually has a different format or structure than does prose. Poetry is traditionally written in short lines, often with a capital letter at the beginning of each line. Some poets use many periods and commas in their work, while others use few. Then how do you read poetry? Read a poem by the sense of the words, *not* line by line. It helps a great deal to read a poem silently first and then aloud. Let the rhythm and sense of the words tell you when to start and stop.

To practice reading poetry by following the sense of the words, read the following poem (first silently, then aloud). Use the letters by the words to help you decide when to begin and when to stop for a breath. (*B* stands for "begin"; *S* stands for "stop.")

Fog

[B] The fog comes
on little cat feet. [S]
[B] It sits looking
over harbor and city
on silent haunches
and then moves on. [S]

—by Carl Sandburg

Did you notice that you only stop in two places—after *feet*, and after the final *on*?

FORMING A PICTURE

To understand prose, it's helpful to use the details the author gives. The same is true of poetry. Look again at Carl Sandburg's poem "Fog." In this poem, Sandburg creates a picture by comparing one thing to another.

Can you tell what two things the poet is comparing in "Fog"? Write them in the blanks that follow:

____________________ is compared to ____________________.

You can tell from the title and the first line that the subject of this poem is fog. What does the poet tell you fog is like? (In other words, to what does the poet compare fog?) In the second line, the words *little cat feet* tell you that the fog is being compared to a cat. The word *haunches* continues this image. The poet is comparing the movement of the fog to that of a cat. By doing so, Sandburg helps you "see" the fog as he does.

EXERCISE 9: FORMING A PICTURE FROM A POEM

Directions: Read the following poem, silently at first, and then aloud. Use the symbols by the words to tell you when to begin and when to stop. (Remember, *B* stands for "begin," and *S* stands for "stop.") As you read, try to picture in your mind what the poet is describing.

.05

[B] If i had a nickel
For all the women who've
Rejected me in my life
I would be the head of the
World Bank with a flunkie
To hold my derby as i
Prepared to fly chartered
Jet to sign a check
Giving India a new lease
On life [S]
[B] If i had a nickel for
All the women who've loved
Me in my life i would be
The World Bank's assistant
Janitor and wouldn't need
To wear a derby [S]
[B] All i'd think about would
Be going home [S]

—by Ishmael Reed

1. The man would be "head of the World Bank" if he had a
   (1) derby
   (2) jet
   (3) nickel for every rejection
   (4) lease
   (5) nickel for every love

2. How do you picture the head of the World Bank?
   (1) rich and famous
   (2) heartbroken and poor
   (3) ugly and unhappy
   (4) sad and lonesome
   (5) angry and scared

3. "Prepared to fly chartered / Jet to sign a check / Giving India a new lease / On life" (lines 7–10) means the man
   (1) can't wait to visit India
   (2) dreams of solving India's poverty
   (3) wants a new lease for his apartment
   (4) needs a job as a travel agent
   (5) doesn't believe anyone can solve India's problems

4. "If i had a nickel for / All the women who've loved / Me in my life i would be / The World Bank's assistant / Janitor . . ." (lines 11–15) means
   (1) women constantly fall in love with the man
   (2) people drop nickels on the street every day
   (3) the man is looking for a job
   (4) the man has not found many women who love him
   (5) the World Bank is looking for an assistant janitor

5. How do you picture the assistant janitor of the World Bank?
   (1) scholarly and wise
   (2) rich and famous
   (3) married and wealthy
   (4) ordinary and poor
   (5) confident and strong

Answers start on page 678.

PARAPHRASING POETRY

Sometimes it's helpful to paraphrase poetic language into everyday language. That means you take the images and symbols that the poet uses and express them in more ordinary words. This technique is especially helpful when a poem is complicated. If you can paraphrase it into everyday language, you can understand its message better.

Take a look at the following poem about children. Read the poem in the left-hand column, first silently, and then aloud. Then, compare the poetry to the everyday language in the right-hand column.

Poem		Paraphrase
Your children are not your children. They are the sons and daughters of Life's longing for itself.	→	Your children don't belong to you. They are part of on-going generations.
They come through you but not from you. And though they are with you yet they belong not to you.	→	They are born to you, and although they live with you, you don't own them.
You may give them your love but not your thoughts, For they have their own thoughts.	→	You can love them, but you can't make them think as you do.
You may house their bodies but not their souls, For their souls dwell in the house of tomorrow, which you cannot visit, not even in your dreams.	→	You can take care of their physical needs, but not their ideas, because they will live in the future, where you cannot go.
You may strive to be like them, but seek not to make them like you. For life goes not backward nor tarries with yesterday.	→	You can try to be like them, but don't ask them to be like you, because they can't go backward.

—Excerpted from *The Prophet* by Kahlil Gibran

As you can see, poetry can be "translated" into everyday language so that it's more easily understood.

Translating a poem into everyday language is also helpful in understanding poems that use symbols. In his poem "Mother to Son," Langston Hughes uses the symbol of stairs to represent life. What can you learn about life from the poet's description of stairs?

EXERCISE 10: PARAPHRASING POETRY

Directions: Read the poem, first silently, and then aloud. Part of the poem has been rephrased as everyday language. Paraphrase the second part into your own words along the side of the poem. Then answer the questions that follow.

Mother to Son

Well, son, I'll tell you: Life for me ain't been no crystal stair.	Life for me hasn't been easy.
It's had tacks in it, And splinters, And boards torn up, And places with no carpet on the floor— Bare.	I've had a lot of tough problems.
But all the time I'se been a-climbin' on, And reachin' landin's, And turnin' corners, And sometimes goin' in the dark Where there ain't been no light. So boy, don't you turn back. Don't you set down on the steps 'Cause you finds it's kinder hard. Don't you fall now— For I'se still goin', honey, I'se still climbin', And life for me ain't been no crystal stair.	

—by Langston Hughes

1. This poem is mainly about a woman who is
   (1) complaining about her life
   (2) giving advice to her son
   (3) punishing her son
   (4) improving her family's situation
   (5) taking a trip with her son

2. What does she mean when she says her stair has "had tacks in it, / And splinters, / And boards torn up, / And places with no carpet on the floor—/ Bare" (lines 3–7)?
   (1) She has had problems in her life.
   (2) The stairs leading to her apartment need fixing.
   (3) She has had an easy life.
   (4) She wants the landlord to make repairs in her building.
   (5) She has been married several times.

3. What does she mean when she says, "And sometimes goin' in the dark / Where there ain't been no light" (lines 12–13)?
   (1) The light needs fixing in her apartment house.
   (2) Sometimes she could not see how to solve her problems.
   (3) She is blind, so she can't see the stairs.
   (4) She turned out the lights so she could save money on electricity.
   (5) She has spent time in the hospital.

4. When she says, "Don't you set down on the steps / Cause you finds it's kinder hard. / Don't you fall now—" (lines 15–17), the speaker is telling her son
   (1) not to give up even when he has problems
   (2) not to go up the steps
   (3) she is tired
   (4) to sit down and rest
   (5) that the steps are too hard to sit on

5. She says her life has *not* been a crystal stair. What would life be like if it *had been* a crystal stair?
   (1) full of splinters and tacks
   (2) full of landings and corners
   (3) hard to climb
   (4) smooth, bright, and easy
   (5) hard to see

Answers start on page 679.

COMPREHENSION: DRAMA

When you go to a play, or ***drama,*** you see actors who take the roles of characters, perform a play's action, and speak the lines. Watching a play is much like seeing a movie or a television show, because you actually see the drama unfold.

Reading a play requires some additional skills. In this section, you will learn how to read and understand a dramatic script.

COMPARING DRAMA AND PROSE

In some ways, reading a play is no different from reading prose or even a poem. What makes reading drama different from reading prose is its format. This is the way words are arranged on the page. As you will see, a dramatic script is easy to recognize because it has a very distinctive format.

One difference in a dramatic script is that the names of the speakers in the play are shown, often in capital letters. Every time a character speaks, his or her name appears beside the lines of dialogue he or she says. In a play, ***dialogue*** is the conversation between characters.

Another format difference is the ***stage directions***, which tell you what the characters are doing as they speak and what their tone of voice is. Stage directions are often printed in *italic type*. You will learn more about stage directions later in this chapter.

Read the following passages carefully. One passage is in prose form, and the other is written in dramatic script form. These two passages are simply different versions of the same scene. John Steinbeck, the author, wrote two versions of *Of Mice and Men* so that the story could be read as a novel or performed onstage. Observe how these passages are similar and how they are different. In the play version, be sure to notice the characters' names in capital letters, the lines of dialogue, and the stage directions.

Novel Version	Play Version
Lennie got up on his knees and looked down at George. "Ain't we gonna have no supper?"	LENNIE: [*Gets up on his knees and looks down at GEORGE, plaintively.*[1]] Ain't we gonna have no supper?
"Sure we are, if you gather up some dead willow sticks. I got three cans of beans in my bindle. You get a fire ready. I'll give you a match when you get the sticks together. Then we'll heat the beans and have supper."	GEORGE: Sure we are. You gather up some dead willow sticks. I got three cans of beans in my bindle.[2] I'll open 'em up while you get a fire ready. We'll eat 'em cold.
Lennie said, "I like beans with ketchup."	LENNIE: [*Companionably*[3]] I like beans with ketchup.
—Excerpted from the novel *Of Mice and Men* by John Steinbeck	—Excerpted from the play version *Of Mice and Men* by John Steinbeck

1 *plaintively* means "sadly"

2 *bindle* is a bedroll, or sack

3 *companionably* means "in a friendly way"

Answer the following questions about the play version of *Of Mice and Men.*

1. What two characters' names are in capital letters?
   ____________________ and ____________________

2. How many stage directions are there? ____________________

Compare your answers with these:

1. Lennie and George
2. two: [*Gets up on his knees and looks down at GEORGE, plaintively.*] and [*Companionably*]

As you probably noticed, the novel version and the play version are similar because they describe the same event: George and Lennie decide what to prepare for supper. The way this event is presented, however, is entirely different.

Novel Version	**Play Version**
• ***A narrator,*** or storyteller, describes the characters' emotions and tells what they are doing. **Example:** Lennie got up on his knees and looked at George.	• ***Stage directions*** describe the characters' emotions and tell the actors what to do. **Example:** LENNIE: [*Gets up on his knees and looks down at GEORGE, plaintively.*]
• ***Dialogue*** is in quotation marks. **Example:** Lennie said, "I like beans with ketchup."	• ***Dialogue*** appears following the name of the character who speaks. **Example:** LENNIE: [*Companionably*] I like beans with ketchup.

THE FORMAT OF DRAMA

Plays are more enjoyable to read when you understand the purpose of (1) acts and scenes, (2) cast lists, and (3) stage directions in scripts.

Acts and Scenes

To make their work easier to follow, playwrights divide their dramas into major sections called ***acts***. If a play is long, a playwright may divide the acts into ***scenes***. A scene always takes place in *one* room or place. When a new scene begins, the location, or setting, changes. The following list of acts and scenes is typical of what you will see when you read a play:

The entire action takes place
in a Manhattan apartment,
on Second Avenue in the upper eighties.

Act One

Scene One: Two-thirty in the morning on a midsummer's day.
Scene Two: Late afternoon, a few days later.

Act Two

Scene One: Mid-September; about one in the afternoon.
Scene Two: Midafternoon, two weeks later.
Scene Three: A late afternoon in mid-December.

—Excerpted from *The Prisoner of Second Avenue* by Neil Simon

On the lines below, write down where the play takes place. Then on the second line, write about how much time passes between the opening of Act One and the close of Act Two.

1. The entire action takes place ________________________________.
2. ________________________ pass between Act One, Scene One and Act Two, Scene Three.

You responded correctly if you said that the action takes place in a *Manhattan apartment*, and that *about five months* pass between Act One, Scene One and Act Two, Scene Three.

Cast Lists

Just after the list of acts and scenes, the playwright introduces the play's characters in a ***cast list***. Often, just the characters' names appear in a cast list. Sometimes, though, the playwright will include each character's age, occupation, physical traits, and personality.

Study the following cast list from the play *The Hot L Baltimore* by Lanford Wilson. As you read, notice what information the playwright provides about each character.

> MR. KATZ: The hotel manager. Thirty-five, balding a little but hiding it. Firm and wary and at times more than a little weary. Dark, in an inexpensive dark suit.
>
> MRS. OXENHAM: The day desk clerk–phone operator. Forty-five and firm; quick-speaking.
>
> BILL LEWIS: The night clerk. Thirty, large-featured, well-built in a beefy way, a handsome but not aggressive face. He covers his difficulty in communicating his feelings for the Girl with a kind of clumsy, friendly bluster.
>
> —Excerpted from *The Hot L Baltimore*
by Lanford Wilson

Now answer the following questions about the characters.

1. How old is Mr. Katz? ____________________

2. What is Bill Lewis's job? ______________________

According to the cast list, Mr. Katz is *thirty-five* and Bill Lewis is a *night clerk*.

Stage Directions

Besides describing how the stage should look, ***stage directions*** also tell the actors how to move around onstage as they perform. Terms like *stage right, stage left,* and *down center* are specific instructions as to where the actors should be when they speak their lines. For example, if a stage direction is *stage right*, the actor should move to the right side of the stage. Read the following stage directions, and see what information they contain.

> VERA: [*Looking fearfully at her husband and moving toward him stage right*] What do you mean, David?

1. How does Vera look at her husband? ____________________

2. Where should she walk as she speaks her line? ____________________

If you answered *fearfully* and *stage right*, you understood this stage direction correctly.

Dialogue

Drama depends mainly on ***dialogue***, or conversation between characters, to gain people's interest and attention. A playwright must write dialogue that is realistic, to the point, and entertaining. In a good play, no line of dialogue is unnecessary. Every word a character says must reveal personality traits and advance the plot or story.

Sometimes a playwright uses punctuation to show an actor exactly how to speak his lines. A dash (—), for example, indicates a pause in a character's speech. Depending on a particular scene, such a pause can indicate hesitation, nervousness, or some sort of interruption. As you read the passages in the following exercises, use these questions to guide you:

1. Where does the scene occur?
   (Remember to picture the characters and setting in your mind.)

2. What information do you get from the stage directions?

3. What is the dialogue about?
   Does it reveal a conflict between characters?

4. How does the playwright's use of punctuation add to the dialogue?

EXERCISE 11: PRACTICE IN READING DIALOGUE

Directions: Using the preceding questions as a guide, read the passage that follows from Agatha Christie's play *Verdict*. Then answer the questions.

KARL: [*Moving to left of the sofa*] I have something to tell you, Inspector. I know who killed my wife. It was not Miss Koletzky.

OGDEN: [*Politely*] Who was it, then?

KARL: It was a girl called Helen Rollander. She is one of my pupils. [*He crosses and sits in the armchair*] She—she formed an unfortunate attachment to me. She was alone with my wife on the day in question, and she gave her an overdose of the heart medicine.

OGDEN: [*Moving down center*] How do you know this, Professor Hendryk?

KARL: She told me herself, this morning.

OGDEN: Indeed? Were there any witnesses?

KARL: No, but I am telling you the truth.

OGDEN: [*Thoughtfully*] Helen—Rollander. You mean the daughter of Sir William Rollander?

KARL: Yes. Her father is William Rollander. He is an important man. Does that make any difference?

OGDEN: [*Moving below the left end of the sofa*] No, it wouldn't make any difference—if your story were true.

—Excerpted from *Verdict* by Agatha Christie

1. Name the occupations of Karl and Ogden.

a. ____________________

b. ____________________

2. What are Karl and Ogden discussing? ____________________________

3. There is a dash between *Helen* and *Rollander* in line 15 to show

(1) the slow, thoughtful way Ogden speaks the name
(2) that someone has interrupted the conversation
(3) that Ogden has trouble speaking
(4) that Karl jumps as Ogden speaks the name *Helen*
(5) that Ogden moves to the left of the sofa

4. What conflict is revealed in this passage?

(1) Karl is jealous of Ogden's feelings for Helen.
(2) Ogden does not believe Karl's explanation of the murder.
(3) Ogden is angry that Miss Koletzky has betrayed him.
(4) Helen and Miss Koletzky are jealous of one another.
(5) Helen and Ogden went to grade school together.

5. After reading the passage, you can infer that this play is probably
   (1) a comedy
   (2) a musical
   (3) a murder mystery
   (4) a tragedy
   (5) a religious drama

Answers start on page 679.

EXERCISE 12: PUTTING IT ALL TOGETHER

This exercise is based on a passage from *The Glass Menagerie*[1] by Tennessee Williams. The main character in this play is Laura Wingfield. Laura is extremely shy and is especially self-conscious about a brace that she wears on one leg. She spends most of her time taking care of her collection of small glass animals.

In this passage, Laura and Jim talk about what Laura is doing with her life. In high school, Laura had a crush on Jim but was too shy to speak to him.

Directions: Read the passage carefully and then answer the questions that follow.

[*Jim lights a cigarette and leans indolently*[2] *back on his elbows smiling at Laura with a warmth and charm which lights her inwardly with altar candles.*[3] *She remains by the table, picks up a piece from the glass menagerie collection, and turns it in her hands to cover her tumult.*[4]]

JIM: [*After several reflective*[5] *puffs on his cigarette*] What have you done since high school?

[*She seems not to hear him.*]
Huh?

[*Laura looks up.*]
I said what have you done since high school, Laura?

LAURA: Nothing much.

JIM: You must have been doing something these six long years.

LAURA: Yes.

JIM: Well, then, such as what?

1 *Menagerie* means a "collection of many different animals."
2 *Indolently* means "lazily."
3 *Lights her inwardly with altar candles* means "she is glowing with pleasure."
4 *Tumult* means "confusion or agitation."
5 *Reflective* means "thoughtful."

LAURA: I took a business course at business college—

JIM: How did that work out?

LAURA: Well, not very—well—I had to drop out, it gave me—indigestion—

[*Jim laughs gently.*]

JIM: What are you doing now?

LAURA: I don't do anything—much. Oh, please don't think I sit around doing nothing! My glass collection takes up a good deal of time. Glass is something you have to take good care of.

JIM: What did you say—about glass?

LAURA: Collection I said—I have one—[*She clears her throat and turns away again, acutely*[1] *shy.*]

JIM: [*Abruptly*][2] You know what I judge to be the trouble with you? Inferiority complex! . . . Yep—that's what I judge to be your principal trouble. A lack of confidence in yourself as a person. You don't have the proper amount of faith in yourself. . . . For instance that clumping you thought was so awful in high school. You say that you even dreaded to walk into class. You see what you did? You dropped out of school, you gave up an education because of a clump, which as far as I know was practically non-existent! A little physical defect is what you have. Hardly noticeable even! Magnified thousands of times by imagination! You know what my strong advice to you is? Think of yourself as *superior* in some way!

—Excerpted from *The Glass Menagerie*
by Tennessee Williams

1 *Acutely* means "very much or extremely."
2 *Abruptly* means "suddenly."

1. What has Laura done since high school?
   (1) dropped out of a business class and cared for her glass collection
   (2) worked at a local store
   (3) married her high school sweetheart and had two children
   (4) graduated from business college
   (5) cared for her sick mother

2. In lines 3–5, Laura picks up a glass animal from her collection to
   (1) prevent Jim from breaking it
   (2) hide her feelings of nervousness and confusion
   (3) show Jim how fragile the piece of glass is
   (4) hide her feelings of anger
   (5) hide it from her brother

3. The dashes in lines 18–19 and 27 reveal that Laura
   (1) stutters
   (2) is hesitant to openly talk to Jim
   (3) has trouble sharing her thoughts with others
   (4) has a severe medical condition
   (5) has indigestion

4. What does Jim mean in lines 36–37 when he says, "you gave up an education because of a clump, which as far as I know was practically non-existent!"
   (1) Jim thinks Laura was right to drop out of high school because of her inferiority complex.
   (2) Jim is sorry that he didn't finish high school.
   (3) Jim thinks Laura dropped out of school because she was self-conscious about a disability that others hardly noticed.
   (4) Jim and the other students used to wonder why she wore the brace.
   (5) Jim knows how popular he was in high school.

Answers start on page 679.

6 Evaluating What You Read

Evaluating what you read means thinking for yourself. Skilled readers locate main ideas and details and understand the organization and hidden meanings of a story. Good readers also question what they read. They know that just because something is in print doesn't necessarily mean that it is true.

This chapter will focus on the words, ideas, and techniques that a writer uses to get you, the reader, to feel or think the same things he or she does. Once you know the author's attitude and purpose, you can decide whether or not you share his or her views. We'll study words and emotions, generalizations, and persuasive techniques.

COMPREHENSION: WORDS AND EMOTION

We understand words on two different levels of meaning. The first level is what the dictionary tells us a word means. We call this meaning the word's ***denotation***. The second level has to do with the positive or negative feelings the word brings out in us. We call this meaning its ***connotation***.

CONNOTATIONS OF WORDS

Compare the two sentences that follow. As you read them, think about what *connotation*, or feeling, each sentence has.

Sentence 1. She was a vision!
Sentence 2. She was a sight!

If *you* were the person being described, which would you prefer to be called: a "vision" or a "sight"? You probably would rather be called "a vision," because the word *vision* brings out positive feelings, while the word *sight* brings out negative feelings.

Read the two pairs of sentences that follow. In each pair, write a plus (+) next to the statement with a positive connotation, and write a minus (–) next to the statement with a negative connotation.

Pair 1

______ 1. Sara has a full figure.

______ 2. Sara is fat.

Pair 2

______ 3. Tom is quite skinny.

______ 4. Tom is quite slender.

The words *full figure* in sentence 1 create a more positive image than *fat* in sentence 2. Likewise, the word *slender* in sentence 4 is more flattering than *skinny* in sentence 3. Of course, some words are neutral; they have neither a positive nor a negative connotation. For example, if someone says, "Please sit on the couch," the word *couch* is neither positive nor negative. It simply means a piece of furniture used for sitting or reclining.

EXERCISE 1: CONNOTATIONS OF WORDS

Directions: Based on their connotations, sort the following pairs of words into the correct diagrams. Put the negative word in each pair into the negative-connotations diagram (–), and put the positive word in each pair into the positive-connotations diagram (+). The first one is done as an example. After you have finished, discuss your answers with others.

Negative Connotations

old

Pairs of Words

1. old, mature
2. jocks, athletes
3. unusual, weird
4. mob, crowd
5. firm, stubborn
6. pushy, assertive

Positive Connotations

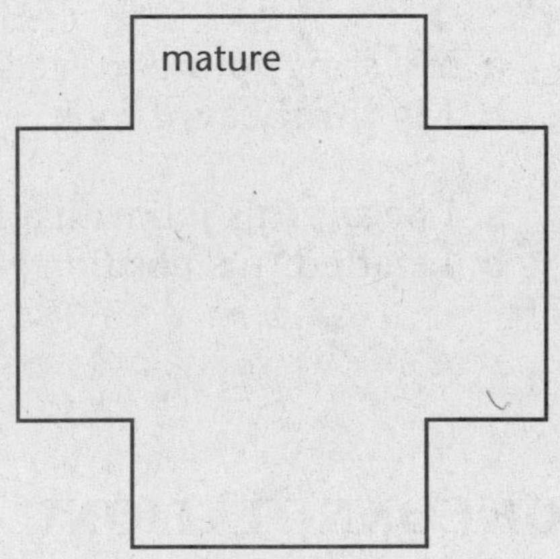

Answers start on page 679.

CONNOTATIONS OF SENTENCES

Words that have the same *denotations* can have very different *connotations*. When these words are used in a sentence, they give the sentence itself a connotation.

For example, look at the next two sentences.

1. Mrs. Benitez was a disciplined and fair supervisor.
2. Mrs. Benitez was a rigid and self-righteous boss.

Although the literal meaning (the denotation) of both sentences is similar, the connotations are quite different. The first sentence has a positive connotation because *disciplined* and *fair* are complimentary. The second sentence has a negative connotation because *rigid* and *self-righteous* are negative.

EXERCISE 2: CONNOTATIONS OF SENTENCES

Directions: Read each of the following pairs of sentences. Based on the connotations of the words in each pair, decide which sentence is positive and which sentence is negative. Mark the positive sentences with a (+) and the negative sentences with a (–).

1. ______ **a.** Mr. Jones, a famous statesman, spoke with strong conviction.
______ **b.** Mr. Jones, a notorious politician, proclaimed his opinions.

2. ______ **a.** My stingy aunt boasted about hoarding money.
______ **b.** My thrifty aunt took pride in saving money.

3. ______ **a.** I began this job with a lousy salary.
______ **b.** I started this position with modest wages.

Answers start on page 679.

USES OF CONNOTATIONS

Connotations of words and sentences can cause you to feel certain emotions. Writers often deliberately use words to bring out these feelings in people. For example, connotations play an important part in euphemisms and advertising.

Euphemisms

Euphemisms are words or phrases that are used to soften a negative event or make something sound better or less objectionable. For example, when someone *dies* (a negative), people often use euphemisms such as "passing away," "going to her reward," or "being with God." These words seem less harsh than the words *dying* and *death*.

EXERCISE 3: TRANSLATING EUPHEMISMS

Directions: Match the euphemism in the left column to its meaning in the right column. Then write the correct letter in the space provided.

Euphemism	Meaning
_____ 1. preowned	a. toilet
_____ 2. powder room	b. grave
_____ 3. garden apartment	c. basement apartment
_____ 4. casualty	d. garbage dump
_____ 5. sanitation engineer	e. garbage collector
_____ 6. final resting place	f. used
_____ 7. landfill	g. dead person

Answers start on page 679.

Product Advertising

So far, you have seen that words have emotional meanings, or connotations. Advertisers know this and use the connotations of words to try to convince you to buy their products. The following ad illustrates this.

> An *exciting* approach to sweater fashion—*high-styled* V-neck with *delicate* rib trimming makes you a *model of fashion!*

The words *exciting, high-styled, delicate,* and *model of fashion* have positive connotations. Advertisers count on your desire to be "high styled" and "exciting" and try to convince you that buying their sweater will make you so.

EXERCISE 4: ANALYZING ADVERTISEMENTS FOR POSITIVE CONNOTATIONS

Directions: Read the following advertisements. Then circle the words in each ad that have positive connotations.

1. A can't-go-wrong classic in silky rayon makes for on-the-go high fashion.

2. Smooth, slinky, sensual. That's what he'll think about you when you wear our newest fragrance.

3. Cozy hideaway with three bedrooms and two baths. Modern kitchen with cupboards galore. A must-see!

4. Let our experienced master mechanics diagnose your car in our modern, computerized auto clinic.

Answers start on page 679.

Political Advertising

Connotations are used not only to sell products, but to "sell" people as well. Political advertising is a good example of this practice. Politicians running for office often describe themselves by using flattering phrases to convince you to vote for them. For example, look at the following political ad.

> Reelect Senator Joan Smith. She understands your needs. She understands your concerns. She works for you!

In the ad, what three reasons are given to convince you to vote for Senator Smith?

The phrases in the ad that have positive connotations are (1) understands your needs; (2) understands your concerns; and (3) works for you.

You can't tell from the commercial how Senator Smith feels about any issue. That's one of the tricky things about political advertising. Often, ads focus on the image or personality of the candidate rather than the issues of the campaign.

Politicians may also use negative connotations to persuade you to vote a certain way. The political cartoon in the following exercise contains words with negative connotations.

EXERCISE 5: ANALYZING POLITICAL LANGUAGE

Directions: Study the following political cartoon. Then answer the questions that follow. (Carefully read the signs in the cartoon as well as the caption to answer the questions.)

"Thank goodness all those negative campaigns are over and done with. Now we can concentrate for the next few years on griping about the winners."

1. Snurt accuses his opponent of being
   (1) mentally ill
   (2) a drug user
   (3) a thespian
   (4) a liar
   (5) unattractive

2. Smith says he will *not* make an issue of his opponent's
   (1) wife
   (2) record
   (3) mental problems
   (4) church
   (5) age

3. Who is accused of having a criminal record?

____

4. Why should you vote for "Rinkledip?"

____

5. What does the woman *predict* they will do for the next few years?

____

6. *Mud slinging* is a term used to describe one candidate making negative statements about another. Given the meaning of *mud slinging*, what does the sign next to the door mean?
   (1) Clean mud off your shoes before you enter.
   (2) The people in charge of the voting booths don't want to mop the floor later.
   (3) Mud puddles are OK as long as they are 50 feet away from the polling place.
   (4) Political campaigning must be 50 feet away from the polling place.
   (5) Dogs are not allowed in the polling place.

Answers start on page 679.

GENERALIZATIONS

Generalizations are similar to opinions in that they are judgments and not factual statements. However, they are somewhat different from opinions because they are statements that offer no exceptions.

Generalizations are so strongly worded that they sound like facts. Compare the two statements that follow. One is an opinion, the other a generalization.

OPINION: I believe students should stay in high school until they graduate.
(*This statement says, "This is what I believe."*)

GENERALIZATION: All students should stay in high school until they graduate.
(*This statement makes no exceptions. It says that all students should stay in school.*)

Notice that the generalization *sounds* like it's a fact because it's so strongly worded. Yet, like the opinion, it can neither be proved nor agreed upon by all.

Because generalizations allow for no exceptions, and the world is *full* of exceptions, you need to recognize generalizations as being different from facts. Generalizations often use words such as *all, none, every, always,* and *never.*

Try identifying some generalizations. Read the two statements that follow. Mark the sentence that expresses an opinion with an *O* and the sentence that expresses a generalization with a *G*.

______ 1. I think Tom lied to you.

______ 2. Telling a lie is always wrong.

Compare your answers with these:

1. *O* At this time and given no more information, we cannot prove 1 is a fact. It is what someone *believes* to be true. Unlike a generalization, this opinion leaves room for exceptions.

2. *G* Most of us have told "white lies" or "fibs" to avoid hurting someone's feelings. We know that the *always* in this statement provides for no exceptions, and there are exceptions to this rule for most people.

EXERCISE 6: IDENTIFYING OPINIONS AND GENERALIZATIONS

Directions: Read the statements that follow. Write an *O* in the blank provided if the statement is an opinion. Write a *G* in the blank if the statement is a generalization. Remember, you are being asked only to analyze what is being said and not to agree or disagree.

______ 1. All Italians are great cooks.

______ 2. I think Thomas was crazy to take that job.

______ 3. All churchgoers are good people.

______ 4. Democrats [Republicans] always know what is best for the country.

______ 5. I believe nuclear energy is the wave of the future.

Answers start on page 680.

PUTTING IT ALL TOGETHER

Now let's put it all together. The following exercise presents opposing views of a single issue—sex education in schools. As you read each paragraph, look for facts, opinions, and generalizations used to support each side's argument.

EXERCISE 7: IDENTIFYING FACTS, OPINIONS, AND GENERALIZATIONS

Directions: Read the following two paragraphs, which contain numbered sentences. Then reread them, identifying each numbered sentence as either a *fact*, an *opinion*, or a *generalization*. Write your answers on the lines provided.

Paragraph 1

Sex Education Should Be Taught at Home

(1) All sex education classes in school are immoral. (2) Only parents should teach the moral judgments that must always accompany information on sex. (3) For more information, you can call Mr. Vincent Bell, leader of Concerned Community Parents.

Sentence 1 ____________________

Sentence 2 ____________________

Sentence 3 ____________________

Paragraph 2

Sex Education Is Needed In Our Schools

(4) Sex education must be taught in our schools if we are going to stop the alarming rise in teenage pregnancy. (5) Trained professionals giving accurate information are always better than well-meaning but uncomfortable or ignorant parents who lack the vocabulary to discuss sex. (6) Mr. Leroy Miller, principal of Taylor Junior High, will speak Sunday at 7:00 P.M. in the school auditorium in support of classroom sex education.

Sentence 4 ____________________

Sentence 5 ____________________

Sentence 6 ____________________

7. Which *two* of the following are facts that could have been used in the preceding arguments?
   (1) a comparison of the pregnancy rate of teens who received sex education and those who did not
   (2) what the mayor said about the issue
   (3) an analysis based on interviews of pregnant teenagers and why they got pregnant
   (4) what the principal of the school thinks

Answers start on page 680.

COMPREHENSION: PERSUASIVE TECHNIQUES

Now you will learn how to identify several techniques that advertisers use to try to persuade you to buy their products. Recognizing these persuasive techniques can help you to make up your own mind about other people's claims.

PLAIN FOLKS AND TESTIMONIAL TECHNIQUES

In the ***plain folks technique***, the appeal is to identify with everyday people. For example, Sam Smith is running for the office of senator. A TV commercial might show him wearing a hard hat and talking to steel workers at a factory. In an agricultural state, he might be shown wearing a work hat and talking to a group of farmers wearing overalls. The idea behind the ad is that because Smith is "plain folks" like you, the viewer, he is *trustworthy*. Therefore, you should vote for him.

The ***testimonial technique*** tries to convince you that the person in the ad can be believed. In this kind of ad, a famous or professional person is shown using the product. By doing so, this person gives a "testimony" (endorsement) for the product. For example, in a TV commercial several years ago, Joe Namath, the former New York Jets football star, wore pantyhose. As the camera zoomed in on his legs, Joe said, "If these pantyhose can make *my* legs look this good, think how good they'll make *your* legs look." The idea behind this kind of ad is that a famous person is trustworthy. Therefore, if he thinks the product is good enough to use, then you should want to use it also.

EXERCISE 8: RECOGNIZING PLAIN FOLKS AND TESTIMONIAL TECHNIQUES

Directions: Read the descriptions of the following ads in Parts 1 and 2. Then answer the questions that follow.

Part 1

A popular TV commercial shows a woman, probably a construction worker, in work clothes and hard hat. A man carrying groceries is wearing jeans and a sport shirt. A young woman is shown playing with a young child. The name of a supermarket is displayed on the screen as voices sing, "You work an honest day, so you want an honest deal."

1. The ad features people dressed in work clothes to appeal to
   (1) wealthy people
   (2) manufacturers of work clothes
   (3) people who work
   (4) supermarket employees
   (5) supermarket owners

2. The ad writers hope that as a result of seeing this ad you will
   (1) get a job
   (2) convince the men in your family to shop for groceries
   (3) shop at the supermarket being advertised
   (4) hire women as construction workers
   (5) get married and start a family

3. The reason a woman is shown wearing a hard hat is to
   (1) appeal to women
   (2) appeal to homemakers
   (3) appeal to male construction workers
   (4) make men angry
   (5) make women angry

4. What *facts* are presented in the ad?
   (1) Anyone who works hard should buy food at that supermarket.
   (2) People who work hard deserve honest deals.
   (3) People who don't work shouldn't eat.
   (4) Construction workers eat more than most people.
   (5) No facts are given.

Part 2

A TV commercial shows an actor dressed in a white jacket. He says, "I'm not a real doctor, but I play one on TV, and I know that Rid Ache works best in relieving headache pain."

5. The actor dresses in a professional-looking white coat rather than in a sport coat and slacks because
   (1) he wants to publicize the TV show he works on
   (2) he looks more attractive in white
   (3) he wants viewers to associate the product with doctors
   (4) he doesn't want to get dirty
   (5) white shows up better on TV

6. Many TV commercials are criticized for not providing more factual information. However, TV commercials can be considered useful because they
   (1) are entertaining
   (2) stop the competition from making money
   (3) are always factual
   (4) let people know what new products are available
   (5) interrupt TV shows

Answers start on page 680.

BANDWAGON AND SNOB APPEAL TECHNIQUES

The ***bandwagon technique*** tries to make you feel left out if you don't join "everybody else" who enjoys a product or believes a certain idea or philosophy. For example, a soft drink company has a TV commercial showing a group of good-looking young people at a beach. Some of them come running into view carrying surfboards. Others arrive on the scene to play a volleyball game on the sand. All are smiling and having a good time. The idea is that if you drink Splash, you will be part of a group having a good time.

The ***snob appeal technique*** implies that wealthy people use a product. If you want to be rich (or appear rich), you should use this product, too. For example, a TV commercial shows a shiny new car called the Diamante. A beautiful woman dressed in an elegant long gown caresses the car as she strolls by it. She is joined by a handsome man in a tuxedo. They get into the car and drive away. The idea behind this ad is that if you want to belong to this privileged group, you should buy a Diamante car.

EXERCISE 9: BANDWAGON AND SNOB APPEAL TECHNIQUES

Part 1

Directions: Study the following ad. Then answer the questions that follow.

IT'S IRRESISTIBLE.

THE ART
OF A
BARGAIN...

I love shopping
at Loehmann's!
Why?
Because, like so
many women
who go there often,
I know that price
is important,
but value is
more important.
May I suggest
that you browse
through Loehmann's
breathtaking array
of designer fashions
soon. I'm sure
you'll find dozens
of great outfits
just as exciting
as the one
I am wearing,
at prices
that have made
Loehmann's famous.

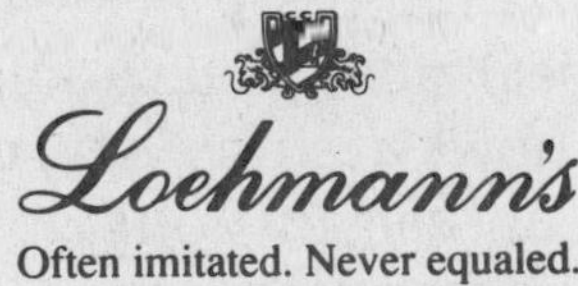

Loehmann's

Often imitated. Never equaled.

1. Which phrase best describes this advertisement?
   (1) trendsetting styles for those on the cutting edge
   (2) homespun fashions for the homemaker
   (3) custom-made finery for elegant living
   (4) tasteful, casual clothing for the older woman
   (5) professional attire for the businesswoman

2. Find three words or phrases that describe the *clothes* available at Loehmann's.

   ____

   ____

   ____

3. By using the phrases, *The art of a bargain, price is important, but . . .*, and *prices that have made Loehmann's famous*, the ad suggests that
   (1) Loehmann's sells cheap clothes
   (2) Loehmann's offers good value for the money
   (3) the clothes at Loehmann's are overpriced
   (4) Loehmann's is having a half-price sale
   (5) Loehmann's is a new store that is not yet well known

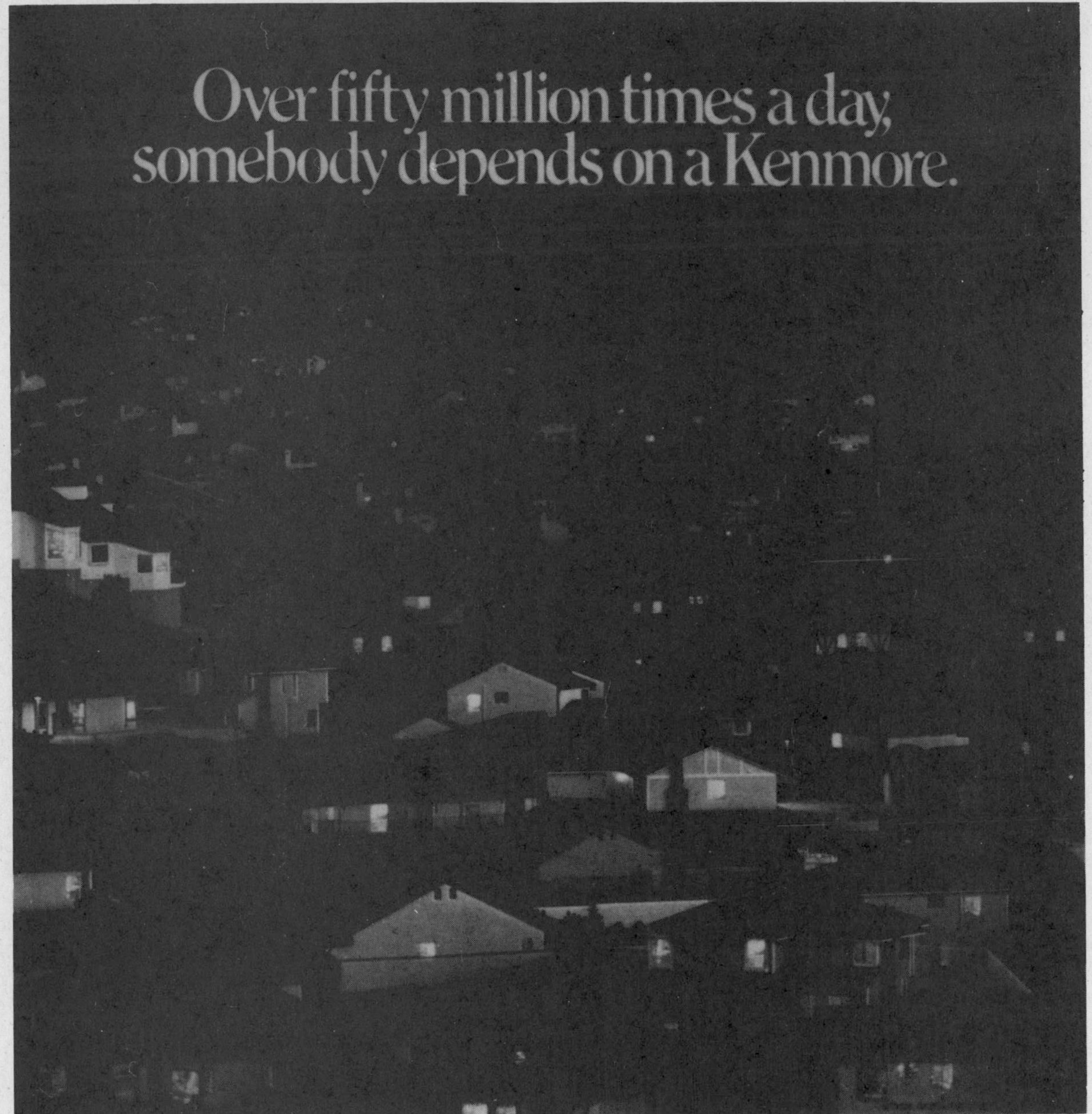

Over the last fifty years, Kenmore appliances have built quite a reputation for reliability.

So much so, in fact, that today more people depend on Kenmore than any other brand in America.

Of course, it's partly because we always insist that our products be as close to immortal as human hands can make them.

But it's also because they're backed by Sears Service—the largest service organization of its kind in the country.

We have more than 15,000 technicians and 12,000 trucks standing by at hundreds of locations across the country, ready to handle any problem—or head off potential ones.

We devote such an extraordinary amount of manpower to service for a very simple reason.

We know that the way we take care of our old ones is the reason so many people buy our new ones.

There's more for your life at
SEARS

Part 2

Directions: Study the ad on page 666 and answer the questions that follow.

4. What kind of technique is used in this ad? ______________________

5. The headline, the second paragraph, and the last paragraph contain phrases that try to get you "on the bandwagon." Write three phrases.

   a. ______________________

   b. ______________________

   c. ______________________

6. Two basic reasons are given for buying Kenmore washers. What are they?

7. Paragraphs 4 and 6 refer to "service" rather than "repair." Why?

8. In Chapter 2 you learned about cause-and-effect relationships. There is a cause-and-effect relationship in the last paragraph of this ad. Fill in the chart with words from the ad.

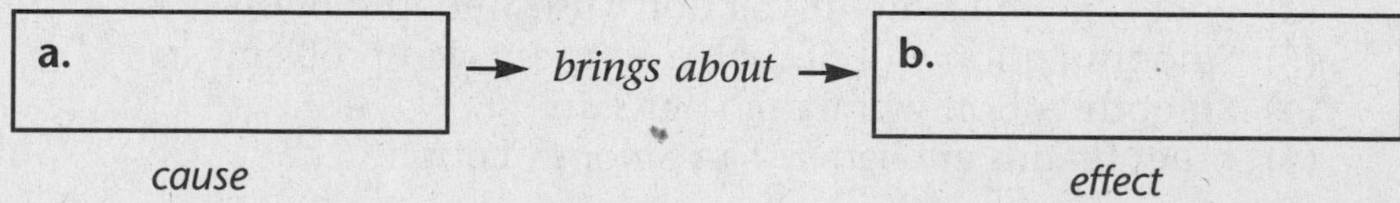

Answers start on page 680.

SLOGANS

Slogans are short phrases or sentences that advertisers hope you will associate with their product. They are designed to give a positive image, not to give facts about the product. For example, when Dwight D. Eisenhower was running for president, people in charge of his campaign used the slogan "I like Ike." The slogan was printed on buttons, posters, bumper stickers, and in much of their radio, TV, and print advertising. "I like Ike" was used because it was positive and it rhymed, making it easy to remember; and it suggested that Eisenhower was "just folks" rather than a former general. Although it gave no facts, the slogan successfully presented a positive image of Eisenhower.

EXERCISE 10: RECOGNIZING SLOGANS

Directions: Read each of the following slogans. Then pick the closest translation of the slogan from the choices that follow.

1. "Better living through chemistry" suggests that
   (1) you should study chemistry
   (2) we all need chemicals in order to live
   (3) advances in chemistry will raise your standard of living
   (4) chemistry is a more useful science than biology
   (5) if chemistry is your hobby, you will live longer

2. The slogan "We know how burgers should be" suggests that
   (1) there are many ways to make good burgers
   (2) you won't like our burgers
   (3) other hamburger chains don't know how to make tasty burgers
   (4) we don't know how to make chicken
   (5) other hamburger chains have less efficient employees

3. "Smooth Lotion—no skin can afford to be without it" suggests that
   (1) Smooth Lotion is too expensive to use on your skin
   (2) your skin will suffer if you don't use Smooth Lotion
   (3) Smooth Lotion will not solve your dry skin problems
   (4) Smooth Lotion will harm your skin
   (5) other brands are better than Smooth Lotion

4. "Come, join us . . . in the safe skies of Eagle" suggests that
   (1) the sky can talk to you
   (2) you should fly on this airline because it is safety-conscious
   (3) you will save money if you fly with this airline
   (4) you should fly on this airline because its staff is friendlier
   (5) you should fly on this airline because it serves better food

5. Which *two* statements best describe slogans?
   (1) Slogans are generalizations.
   (2) Slogans are factual.
   (3) Slogans use words with positive connotations.
   (4) Slogans use words with negative connotations.

Answers start on page 680.

STUDY SKILL: GOOD STUDY HABITS

In the preceding Study Skills, you learned specific skills that help you study better. In this Study Skill, you'll be looking at *how* you study; in other words, you'll examine your *study habits*. Almost everyone can learn to study better by improving study habits.

Read the directions for the survey that follows. Then complete the survey.

EXERCISE 11: GOOD STUDY HABITS

Directions: Read each of the following questions. Then answer *yes* or *no* on the line next to the question. For each question to which you answered *no*, turn to the answer key to find suggestions for improvement.

_____ 1. Do you have a place that is quiet and free of distraction?

_____ 2. Do you surround yourself with the tools of study—sharpened pencils, pens, plenty of paper, textbooks, and a dictionary?

_____ 3. Do you study at regular, planned times?

_____ 4. Do you get right to work without allowing household chores, phone calls, television, and other distractions to keep you from your task?

_____ 5. Do you look over the entire chapter first to see how it's organized and where the main ideas are?

_____ 6. Do you adjust your speed of reading—slow for difficult, complicated tasks and faster for easier reading?

_____ 7. Do you take notes on or underline the main ideas in your text?

_____ 8. Do you review your work? Do you proofread what you've written or review what you've read?

_____ 9. When you hit a difficult section, do you go over it carefully, step by step, to see how to figure it out?

_____ 10. Do you take a short break after an hour or so of studying?

Answers start on page 680.

Reading/Literature and the Arts Answer Key

CHAPTER 1: GAINING MEANING FROM WORDS

Exercise 1: Alphabetical Order— By First Letters
page 516

1. broccoli, cauliflower, lettuce, onion, peas, radish
2. Chevrolet, Ford, Honda, Mazda, Oldsmobile, Toyota
3. charm, disgust, feel, hate, love, reject

Exercise 2: Alphabetizing Beyond the First Letter
page 517

1. need, needle, nerd, nervous, nest
2. worm, worn, worry, wreck, wrench
3. able, about, abuse, ache, achieve

Exercise 3: Using Guide Words
pages 518–519

Part 1

1. same page
2. after
3. before
4. before
5. after
6. after
7. same page

Part 2

1. after
2. before
3. after
4. after
5. same page
6. same page
7. before

Exercise 4: Finding Related Forms of a Word
page 520

To Find	Look Under
1. hollowness	hollow
2. marriageable	marriage
3. quickness	quick
4. liquidity	liquid
5. guardianship	guardian
6. discontentment	discontent
7. chargeable	charge

Exercise 5: Looking Up Pronunciations
page 521

Note: Answers may vary because diction aries use different symbols and key words.

Word	Pronunciation	Key Word
1. chute	sh$\overline{\text{oo}}$t	tool
2. reign	r$\bar{\text{a}}$n	ape
3. aisle	$\bar{\text{i}}$l	bite
4. psalm	säm	far
5. beau	b$\bar{\text{o}}$	go
6. plague	pl$\bar{\text{a}}$g	ape
7. plaque	plak	fat

Exercise 6: Understanding Dictionary Labels
page 522

Word	Parts of Speech
1. bat	*noun, verb*
2. cross	*noun, verb, adjective*
3. exhibit	*verb, noun*
4. liquid	*adjective, noun*
5. around	*adverb, preposition*
6. rule	*noun, verb*
7. about	*adverb, adjective, preposition*
8. but	*preposition, conjunction*
9. they	*pronoun*

Exercise 7: Understanding Multiple Meanings
pages 522–523

Your dictionary's definitions may differ somewhat in wording from these, but the general meanings should be the same.

1. **a.** to propose (a question)
   b. a bodily attitude, especially one held for an artist
2. **a.** to give an account of, as for publication
   b. to present oneself, as for work
3. **a.** any of the lines of seats in a theater
   b. to propel (a boat) with oars
4. **a.** a gentle tap or stroke
   b. a small slice

5. a. a shaped piece of some solid thing
   b. a counter, as for serving snacks or drinks
6. a. the machinery, buildings, etc., of a factory
   b. a small growing thing with leaves, stem, roots, etc.

Exercise 8: Applying the Prefix/Suffix Rule
page 526

1. sick-ness
2. sub-trac-tion
3. pre-ven-tion
4. mis-spell-ing
5. ex-tend-ed
6. re-tire-ment
7. swift-ly
8. pro-pos-al

Exercise 9: Applying the VC/CV Rule
page 527

Part 1

1. frag-ment
   vc cv
2. rem-nant
   vc cv
3. cur-tain
   vc cv
4. ap-pen-dix
   vc cvc cv
5. bud-get
   vc cv
6. em-bas-sy
   vc cvc cv
7. con-sis-tent
   vc cvc cv
8. fil-ter
   vc cv

Part 2

1. ab-nor-mal-ly
2. in-ter-cep-tion
3. pros-pect-or
4. in-ter-view-er
5. com-part-ment
6. cor-res-pond
7. ex-cep-tion-al
8. or-gan-ist

Exercise 10: Applying the VCV Rule
page 528

1. ā-gĕnt
2. rē-cĕnt
3. căb-ĭ-nĕt
4. tō-mā-tō
5. lī-cĕnse
6. hū-māne
7. fē-māle
8. lĭm-ĭt

Exercise 11: Adding Prefixes
page 529

The prefix of each word is underlined.

1. reuse
2. antiwar
3. unlikely
4. disability
5. intersection or dissection
6. discharge or recharge
7. international
8. unnatural

Exercise 12: Prefixes That Make Opposites
page 530

1. unkind, not kind
2. irresponsible, not responsible
3. immature, not mature
4. nonviolent, not violent
5. disabled, not able
6. misspelling, wrong spelling
7. illegitimate, not legitimate
8. inconsiderate, not considerate

Exercise 13: Time Prefixes
page 531

1. d
2. b
3. g
4. f
5. c
6. a
7. e

Exercise 14: Place Prefixes
page 532

1. e
2. b
3. c
4. a
5. f
6. g
7. d

Exercise 15: Number Prefixes
page 533

1. d
2. a
3. c
4. b
5. e
6. g
7. f

Exercise 16: More Prefixes
page 534

1. d
2. b
3. a
4. c
5. g
6. f
7. e

Exercise 17: Locating Roots and Base Words
page 536

1. portable
2. defect
3. transcript
4. inscription
5. transported
6. deceive
7. incredible
8. fidelity

Exercise 18: Latin and Greek Roots
page 538

1. f
2. e
3. a
4. d
5. g
6. b
7. c

Exercise 19: Familiar Suffixes
page 539

1. e
2. c
3. a
4. f
5. b
6. g
7. d

Exercise 20: Finding Synonyms
page 540

You should have circled the following words:

1. finished
2. book
3. base
4. brave
5. trip
6. thinking
7. leave
8. often

Exercise 21: Finding Synonyms in Sentences
page 541

You should have circled the following words:

1. car
2. rare
3. die
4. shaking

Exercise 22: Finding Antonyms
page 541

You should have circled the following words:

1. cold
2. answer
3. tight
4. ignorance
5. negative

Exercise 23: Antonyms in Sentences
page 542

You should have circled the following words:

1. shiny
2. construction
3. criticized
4. flavorless

Exercise 24: Synonyms and Antonyms in Sentences
page 542

1. *circle:* thin
   underline: fat
2. *circle:* merciless
   underline: kind
3. *circle:* icy
   underline: hot
4. *circle:* beginning
   underline: ending
5. *circle:* damaged
   underline: perfect
6. *circle:* advanced
   underline: retreated
7. *circle:* expert
   underline: incompetent

CHAPTER 2: UNDERSTANDING WHAT YOU READ

Exercise 1: Key Words in Sentences
page 544

	Who or what?	*Did what?*
1	Paul Gauguin	left his family
2.	Harriet Tubman	rescued thousands
3.	the president	voiced his disappointment

Exercise 2: Main Ideas in Newspaper Articles
pages 545–546

1. (2) Only choice (2) gives the main idea of the entire article. The other choices all give details from the article.

2. a. (9) **d.** (2) **g.** (6)
b. (1) **e.** (8) **h.** (3)
c. (7) **f.** (4) **i.** (5)

Exercise 3: Words in Context
page 548

1. (1)
2. (3)
3. (2)
4. (3)

Exercise 4: Identifying Context Clues
page 549

1. (1) Underline: king, peaceful little kingdom, twenty-five years
Therefore, *reigned* means ruled.

2. (4) Underline: floral shop, bought the business twenty years ago
Therefore, *proprietor* means owner.

3. (3) Underline: will be open, plan to vote
Therefore, *polls* means places to vote.

Exercise 5: Using Examples Given in Context
page 550

1. (4) 2. (1) 3. (3)

Exercise 6: Using Definitions Given in Context
page 551

1. (2) 2. (3) 3. (4)

Exercise 7: Using Context Clues for Meaning
page 552

1. (1) 4. (2)
2. (3) 5. (1)
3. (4)

Exercise 8: What Is the Main Idea?
page 554

1. Chevrolet for sale
2. 1982 or '82
3. Chevette
4. new tires, new paint
5. $2,000 or best offer
6. (2) No doubt Sam would like $2,000 or even more for the car, but the phrase *or best offer* means he may settle for less.

Exercise 9: Main Ideas and Details in Nonfiction
pages 555–556

1. (2) The entire paragraph is about how and why the Earl of Sandwich invented the sandwich.
2. a. origin of the word *sandwich*
   b. the Earl of Sandwich
   c. invented the sandwich
   d. placed meat between two slices of bread
   e. to keep his playing cards and/or his fingers clean
   f. in England
   g. long ago
3. (4) Since the word *sandwich* comes from its inventor, the Earl of Sandwich, we can assume that if the Earl of Gloucester had been the inventor, it would be called a *gloucester*.

Exercise 10: Unstated Main Ideas
pages 556–557

1. (3) This choice summarizes the whole paragraph.
2. a. (5) c. (2) e. (3)
   b. (4) d. (1)

Exercise 11: Finding Main and Supporting Ideas
pages 560–561

1. (3) This is the only statement that summarizes the whole passage.
2. Examples may vary.
   a. grain; bread/cereal/pasta
   b. fruits and vegetables; oranges/apples
   c. meats and dairy products; turkey/beans/yogurt
   d. fats, oils, and sweets; butter/candy

Exercise 12: Finding Reasons
pages 562–563

1. (2) The entire passage tells how and why a toad tunnel solved Hambledon's problem with toads.
2. (1), (3)
3. (3) In building the tunnel, the English went out of their way to guarantee the safety of the toads. Therefore, you can conclude that many English people are concerned about wildlife.

Exercise 13: Definitions and Characteristics
pages 563–565

1. (1) The entire article is about the six types of drivers.
2. a. Goody Two-Shoes
   b. Conformist
   c. Underconformist
   d. Challenger
   e. Situational Deviant
   f. True Deviant
3. a. (2) 4. a. (3)
   b. (1) b. (1)
   c. (3) c. (2)

Exercise 14: Summarizing a Paragraph pages 567–568

1. **a.** old lady
   b. planted flowers
   c. in her garden
   d. spring
   e. carefully, thoughtfully
   f. to leave something pretty behind for others to enjoy
2. Your summary should be similar to this one:
   An old lady planted flowers in her garden in the spring to leave something pretty behind for others to enjoy.
3. **(4)** According to what the woman says her doctor has told her, you can conclude that the woman thinks that she is going to die soon.

Exercise 15: More Practice in Summarizing page 568

1. **a.** some toy manufacturers
   b. used children to try out toys
   c. recently
   d. special room in their factory
   e. watch children as they play
   f. so that designers can test safety and predict good sellers
2. Your summary statement should be similar to this one: Recently some toy manufacturers have asked children to try out toys in a special room in their factory so that designers can predict which toys will be good sellers and test toy safety.

Exercise 16: Summarizing—a Review pages 569–570

1. **a.** Being a single parent isn't easy.
   b. Working and raising a child is stressful.
   c. I can't keep up with Carla's questions.
   d. It's hard to have a social life.
   e. No problem is impossible to overcome.
   f. Being a good father is worth it.
2. Your summary should be similar to this one:
   No one ever said that being a single parent would be easy. Working and raising a child at the same time is very stressful. I don't know how to keep up with all of Carla's questions, and I'm starting to doubt whether a single parent can have a decent social life. Of course, none of these problems is impossible to overcome, and being a good father to Carla is worth the risk of making mistakes.
3. **(3)** Since the judge awarded custody to the father, the father is probably a caring and responsible person.

CHAPTER 3: FINDING HIDDEN MEANINGS

Exercise 1: Inference in a Cartoon pages 574–575

1. **(1), (3), (5), (6)**
2. **(1), (2), (4)**
3. **(3)** The student's request to leave because his brain is full implies that he cannot take in any more knowledge. Therefore, the other choices do not make sense.

Exercise 2: Using Details to Make an Inference page 576

1. **(2)** Since Lori puts her wallet, makeup bag, keys, checkbook, and tissue in her gift, you can infer that the gift is a purse.
2. **(1), (3)** These two clues clearly describe a purse.

Exercise 3: Inferences in Advertising page 577

1. **(1), (2), (4)** These ideas are all stated directly.
2. **(1), (4)**
3. **(4)** The ad states that you deserve the reward of drinking Lite Brite root beer and that you show class by drinking it.

Exercise 4: Inferring Ideas in Passages pages 579–580

1. **(1)**
2. **(4)**
3. **(4)** Churchill understood that the British people needed a morale boost, and his humorous symbol provided it.

Exercise 5: Inferences in Narrative
pages 580–581

1. (1), (2), (3), and (5) are all stated directly
2. (2), (3), (4)
3. (3)
4. (1), (3) Choices (2) and (4) are not supported by the information given in the passage.

Exercise 6: Predicting Words
page 583

1. birthday
2. everyone/everybody
3. a/the
4. weather/day
5. to
6. Everyone/Everybody
7. birthday/funny
8. with
9. Happy

Exercise 7: Predicting from a Cartoon
pages 584–585

1. (2), (3), (4), and (5) are all shown directly in the cartoon.
2. (4) Cathy says, "I don't want them to think I haven't been taking nice care of it."
3. (1) The tow truck driver's comment indicates that there is so much wrong with the car, the mechanics won't even think about how dirty it is inside.

Exercise 8: Directly Stated Predictions
pages 585–586

1. (1), (2), (3), (5)
2. (2), (3)

Exercise 9: Using Inference to Make Predictions
page 587

1. (1), (2), (4), and (5) are directly stated.
2. (1)

Exercise 10: Using Charts
page 589

The answers in this exercise are given as examples. Yours will be different.

1. MAIN IDEA: our back yard
   SUPPORTING DETAILS: children, swingset, sprinkler, grill, patio
2. Here is a sample paragraph based on the answers given above.

   In the summer, there is a lot of activity in our back yard. Neighborhood children come to play on our swingset and cool off in our sprinkler. For dinner, my wife and I often cook hamburgers on the grill. When we've saved enough money, we're hoping to put in a small patio.

Exercise 11: Using Outlines
page 590

The answers in this exercise are given as examples. Yours will be different.

1. MAIN IDEA I. I won $10,000
   SUPPORTING DETAILS
   A. Buy new clothes
   B. Get gifts for family
   C. Put the rest in the bank
2. Here is a sample paragraph.

   Last month, I won $10,000 in the lottery. It's hard to decide what to do with so much money. First, I'll buy some new clothes so I will feel good about myself at work. Then I'll buy some presents for my family. The rest of the prize money will go into the bank to earn interest!

Exercise 12: Dividing Directions into Parts
page 592

(see chart below)

What to Do?	To What?	Under What Conditions: How? When? or Where?
1. Analyze	the directions	that follow.
2. Write	the words	in the correct columns.
3. Deliver	the boxes	to the accounting department.
4. Check	only the clues	that support the reference.
5. Fill in	the blank	with the correct word.
6. Write down	the caller's name	when answering the phone.

Exercise 13: Following Several Directions
page 593

1. **wrong** You should have marked that *repaired* should be circled; *broken* means the opposite of *mended.*
2. **wrong** You should have marked line 8 as incorrect. It should be $9.
3. **right**

CHAPTER 4: ORGANIZING IDEAS

Exercise 1: Identifying Cause and Effect
page 596

Note: The effects that you should have underlined are here in **bold type**. The causes that you should have circled are in regular type.

1. **Julie fell** because she did not see the hole in the sidewalk.
2. Because Carlos added salt instead of sugar, **his cake tasted terrible.**
3. Because Amy is allergic to bee stings, **her brother rushed her to the doctor when she was stung.**
4. **He had a flat tire** because he had run over a sharp nail.
5. Because the radio was so loud, **I didn't hear the phone.**
6. **Pete was exhausted** because he had worked overtime.

Exercise 2: Identifying Cause-and-Effect Relationships
page 592

1. Because
2. because or since
3. therefore
4. Because or Since
5. therefore
6. so
7. Because or Since

Exercise 3: Cause-and-Effect Relationships in Paragraphs
page 599

1. The cause is about what will happen to people and animals if large forests and jungles in the world are destroyed.
2. (2)
3. (3)The passage states that scientists are worried about the bad effects of destroying forests. Therefore, they would probably advise national leaders to preserve at least part of the forest as it is.

Exercise 4: More Practice in Cause/Effect in Paragraphs
pages 600–601

1. (3)
2. (2)
3. (2)
4. People used recorded whale noises to coax the whale back down the river to the ocean.
5. The whale swam under the Golden Gate Bridge and was free.
6. (2) The sounds described in all the other choices would probably scare the whale away, not coax him toward the sounds.

Exercise 5: Comparison and Contrast
pages 602–603

1.

1976	1994
4,048	3,159
heavy steel	aluminum and plastic
more expensive	cheaper
more	less

2. (2), (4)
3. (1), (3)
4. (3) The passage states that "With the increasingly high price of gas, consumers wanted lighter-weight cars that used less gas." Therefore, you can conclude that this consumer demand caused auto manufacturers to produce lighter-weight cars.

Exercise 6: Comparing and Contrasting Two People
pages 604–605

1. Teddy
2. Will
3. (1), (3)
4. (1), (4)
5. (1) The neighbor's tone is friendly when she mentions both boys, and says "they were both good boys."

Exercise 7: Understanding a Time-Line Sequence
page 606

1. about 6 years old
2. about 18 years old
3. about 18 years
4. (4)

Exercise 8: Signal Words That Show Sequence
page 607

Note: The signal words in each sentence are in **bold type.**

1. First, bring the water to a boil. **Second**, add the eggs. **Third**, turn down the heat. **Then** simmer the eggs for fifteen minutes, and **last**, rinse the eggs with cold water.
2. Before I met her, I was afraid I wouldn't know what to say. **After** meeting her in person, I found she was friendly, so I relaxed.
3. When I got on the bus, I must have had my wallet because I got my fare out of it. **Later**, at home, I discovered my wallet was gone.
4. (3) Choices (1) and (2) are both correct.

Exercise 9: Arranging Items in Correct Sequence
page 608

You should have filled in the blanks in this sequence: 2, 3, 4, 1.

Exercise 10: Understanding Sequence in a Story
pages 608–609

1. You should have filled in the blanks in this sequence: 2, 1, 4, 3, 5.
2. (2) After such a close brush with this scary creature, Jake would probably want to avoid any further contact. Therefore, you can guess that he would probably move his camp.

Exercise 11: Understanding Sequence in Directions
page 610

1. (3)
2. Your directions should be numbered in this sequence: 3, 4, 1, 2, 5

Exercise 12: Working with Analogies
page 613

Part 1

1. b **4.** a
2. c **5.** c
3. c **6.** a

Part 2

1. read **4.** ounce
2. percent **5.** cut
3. tear **6.** waist

Exercise 13: Identifying Facts
page 615

Statements 1, 3, 5, and 7 are facts.

Exercise 14: Identifying Facts and Opinions
page 616

1. F **2.** O **3.** F **4.** O **5.** O
6. (2) Opinions are statements of what someone *believes is true*. Therefore, opinions are judgments and, unlike facts, cannot be proven.

CHAPTER 5: READING LITERATURE

Exercise 1: Forming Pictures in Your Mind
page 619

1. chunks of ice
2. mud and rocks
3. white and clear blue
4. a low rumble and a sharp cracking
5. A huge piece of ice will hit the water and may threaten the safety of the boat and the person.

Exercise 2: Picturing a Setting
page 620

1. (2)
2. (4)
3. (1)
4. (1) The description of the snow tells you that this is a description of a winter scene.

Exercise 3: Picturing a Character from a Description
page 622

1. (2) You know because "His jaw was set" and "there was no laughter or joy in his movement."
2. (2) The words "narrow hips" and "sharp bones" describe a slender build.
3. (2) Lines 4–6 state, "When he lifted the edges of his mouth as though to smile, there was no laughter or joy in the movement, only cold hardness." From this description, you can infer that the person describing this man does not trust him.

Exercise 4: Picturing a Character from What He Says
pages 623–624

1. (2) In the first paragraph, the speaker says "I'm big."
3. (4) The speaker describes these fears in paragraph three.
3. (3) At the end of the selection, the speaker is comfortable with going back to school and feels confident.
4. (2) The student now feels comfortable and confident in his class. Therefore, you can infer that he will probably continue with his classes.

Exercise 5: Identifying Comparisons
pages 626–627

1. (4) The author is comparing the strange effects of an earthquake to a nightmare.
2. (3)
3. (2)
4. (4)

Exercise 6: Recognizing Symbols
pages 628–629

1. McDonald's
2. a sheriff, or law and order
3. peace
4. engagement or marriage

Exercise 7: Reading a Greek Myth
pages 631–632

1. Echo and Narcissus
2. (1)
3. (3)
4. (4)
5. (2) *Narcissism* comes from the name *Narcissus*. Therefore, you can conclude that people who suffer from narcissism think only about themselves.

Exercise 8: Understanding Tone
pages 634–635

1. (3) In paragraph one, the author describes the rainy and windy weather.
2. (4) In paragraphs three and four, Cheri slams on her brakes because she thinks she sees something in the road.
3. (4) Words such as "evil," "black," and "darkness" create fear in the reader.
4. (1) The passage states that "Someone had deliberately placed a straight line of nails across the right lane" (lines 25–26). Cheri then ran away in fear. Therefore, you can infer that Cheri concluded that someone wanted to give her a flat tire.

Exercise 9: Forming a Picture from a Poem
pages 637–638

1. (3) So many women have rejected the man in the poem that if he had a nickel for every rejection, he would be rich—he would be head of the World Bank.
2. (1) rich and famous
3. (2) If the man could give India a "new lease on life," he would solve all of India's problems, including poverty.
4. (4) If he had a nickel for every woman who has loved him, the man says, he'd be poor. So, the man has not found many women who love him.
5. (4) ordinary and poor

Exercise 10: Paraphrasing Poetry
pages 640–642

1. (2) In lines 14, 15, and 17 the speaker tells her boy to keep going.
2. (1) The mother is comparing life to a staircase. When she says her stair has had tacks and splinters, she means she has faced problems.
3. (2) In these lines, the mother describes times in her life that have been dark. In these times, she has not found easy solutions to her problems.
4. (1) The mother is telling her son not to give up.
5. (4) In contrast to a life filled with splinters, corners, and dark places, a crystal stair would be smooth, bright, and easy.

Exercise 11: Practice in Reading Dialogue
pages 647–649

1. a. Karl is a professor.
   b. Ogden is a police inspector.
2. Karl and Ogden are discussing the murder of Karl's wife. The first lines spoken—"I have something to tell you, Inspector. I know who killed my wife."—tell you this.
3. (1) The stage direction on line 15 tells you that Ogden speaks his line "thoughtfully."
4. (2) The last line of the passage reveals this conflict.
5. (3) "*Verdict*" is probably a murder mystery. You can infer this because the two characters in this passage are discussing who murdered Karl's wife.

Exercise 12: Putting It All Together
pages 649–651

1. (1) Laura describes what she has done in the middle of the selection.
2. (2) The stage directions say, "Laura picks up a piece . . . to cover her tumult."
3. (2) The dashes reveal Laura's hesitance to tell Jim what she has been doing. You can tell this because Laura is "acutely shy," and because she says, "Oh, please don't think I sit around doing nothing!"
4. (3) Jim wants Laura to know that her education was more important than a slight disability.

CHAPTER 6: EVALUATING WHAT YOU READ

Exercise 1: Connotations of Words
page 653

1–6.	Negative	Positive
	old	mature
	jocks	athletes
	weird	unusual
	mob	crowd
	stubborn	firm
	pushy	assertive

Exercise 2: Connotations of Sentences
page 654

1. a. +	2. a. –	3 a. –
b. –	b. +	b. +

Exercise 3: Translating Euphemisms
page 655

1. f	3. c	5. e	7. d
2. a	4. g	6. b	

Exercise 4: Analyzing Advertisements for Positive Connotations
page 656

1. can't-go-wrong classic, silky, on-the-go, high fashion
2. Smooth, slinky, sensual
3. Cozy hideaway, modern, galore, must-see
4. experienced, master, modern, computerized, auto clinic

Exercise 5: Analyzing Political Language
pages 657–658

1. (2)
2. (3)
3. Bloomgut
4. "His wife is cuter."
5. She predicts that they will gripe about the winners of the election.
6. (4) Because mud slinging takes place during political campaigns, the sign next to the door means that campaigning must take place at least 50 feet away from the polls.

Exercise 6: Identifying Opinions and Generalizations
page 659

1. G
2. O
3. G
4. G
5. O

Exercise 7: Identifying Facts, Opinions, and Generalizations
pages 660–661

1. generalization
2. generalization
3. fact
4. opinion
5. generalization
6. fact
7. (1), (3) Both of these choices could be backed up by factual data, while choices (2) and (4) are only opinions.

Exercise 8: Recognizing Plain Folks and Testimonial Techniques
pages 662–663

Part 1

1. (3)
2. (3)
3. (1)
4. (5) There are no facts given in this ad. Actors are shown playing roles of everyday people, but no factual information is given about the supermarket being advertised.

Part 2

5. (3)
6. (4) TV commercials can be considered useful in one sense because they show people the new products that are available.

Exercise 9: Bandwagon and Snob Appeal Techniques
pages 664–667

Part 1

1. (4)
2. You should have picked any three of the following: breathtaking array, designer fashions, great outfits, exciting
3. (2)

Part 2

4. Bandwagon
5. a. "fifty million times a day"
   b. "more people depend on"
   c. "so many people buy our new ones"
6. Kenmore washers are reliable and come with good repair service.
7. "Service" has a positive connotation while "repair" has a negative connotation.
8. a. the way we take care of our old ones
   b. the reason so many people buy our new ones

Exercise 10: Recognizing Slogans
page 668

1. (3)
2. (3)
3. (2)
4. (2)
5. (1), (3) Slogans usually are generalizations that contain words with positive connotations.

Exercise 11: Good Study Habits
page 669

1. If you answered "no," you need to find a place that is quiet and free of distraction. Most people study best with absolute quiet. Some people find that *soft* music helps soften distracting noises such as TV in another room. Experiment to see what atmosphere works best for you.
2. Every worker needs his/her tools. A student needs pencils or pens, paper, textbooks and, of course, a dictionary. If you need to buy a new dictionary, try paperback versions that you can carry easily.
3. Experts say that planning study time is important. Put studying into your daily or weekly schedule.
4. Some people spend much time avoiding study. Set a time for study and then discipline yourself to actually do the work. Besides, feeling guilty about *not* studying is unpleasant.

5. It is helpful to look over the material first. Although it may seem like an extra step, it will save you time in your total study period.
6. Don't be afraid to slow down, even to reread any difficult material. But don't forget to speed up when you have easy material. Good readers adjust their speed depending on their purpose for reading and the level of difficulty.
7. Do underline in your text or take notes on separate paper. Some people find that writing information down helps them remember.
8. Be sure to go over or review what you have just read. Telling someone (even a pet) what you just read often helps stick it in *your* memory. Be sure to read over anything you write down. Sometimes a simple word, left out by accident, can change the meaning.
9. Some people just give up when they find something difficult. However, if you reread and try to understand the material step by step, you will find it isn't so difficult after all.
10. Do take short breaks after studying for an hour or so. You'll find you can concentrate better and remember longer. But don't let your break turn into an excuse for not finishing your work. For a break, try getting a cup of coffee or a drink of water. Stand up. Stretch. Walk to a window and look out. Then return to work.

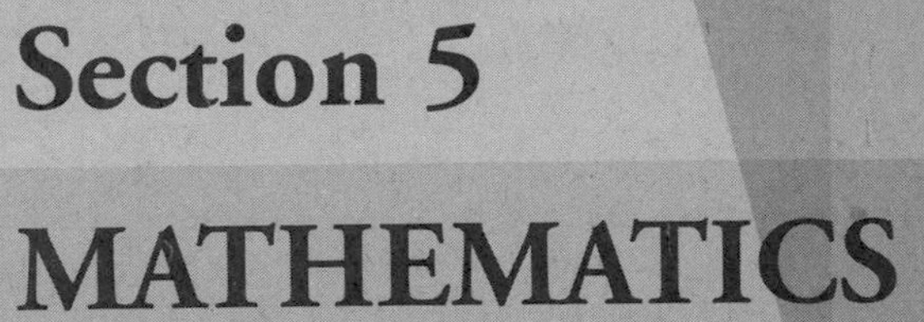

Section 5

MATHEMATICS

1 Whole Numbers

Almost every modern culture has developed a way to count and a way to write counting symbols called ***numbers***. Each number stands for a certain amount, or **value**. Given the choice, you'd probably prefer to earn $21,000 next year rather than $210. The way we use symbols such as 21,000 and 210 to stand for different values is called our ***number system***. You'll be studying our number system in this section. The main focus will be on how numbers are added, subtracted, multiplied, and divided. Also, we'll discuss how numbers are used to solve word problems.

In this first chapter, we'll briefly review the skills of **reading, writing,** and **rounding** whole numbers.

Digits and Place Value

Our number system uses symbols called **digits**. From smallest to largest, the ten digits are **0, 1, 2, 3, 4, 5, 6, 7, 8,** and **9**.

Our counting numbers are called ***whole numbers***. The number 5 is a whole number. So are the numbers 210 and 21,000. 5 is a one-digit whole number, 210 is a three-digit whole number, and 21,000 is a five-digit whole number.

The *value of a digit* in a whole number depends on its place in that number. Because of this, digits are said to have ***place value***. Place value increases as you start at the ones place at the right and move to the left. A 4 in the ones place has a smaller value than a 4 in the thousands place.

The first ten place values of whole numbers are shown below. Starting at the ones place and moving to the left, a comma is used to separate every group of three places.

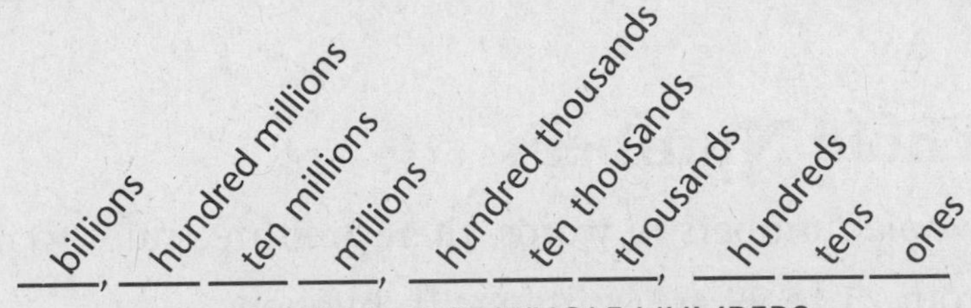

PLACE VALUES OF WHOLE NUMBERS

To find a digit's value, write the digit and follow it with the correct number of zeros to indicate its place value.

EXAMPLE: What is the value of each digit in the number 4,207?

Step 1. 4 is in the thousands place.
4's value is **4 thousand**, which is written 4,000.

Answers to Chapter 1 exercises start on page 909.

Step 2. 2 is in the hundreds place.
2's value is **2 hundred**, which is written 200.

Step 3. 0 is in the tens place.
Thus, there are no tens in the number 4,207.

Step 4. 7 is in the ones place.
7's value is **7 ones**, which is simply written 7.

What is the value of each underlined digit below? The first is done for you.

1. 485 *eighty* **3.** 3,385 ________ **5.** 23,483 ________

2. 685 ________ **4.** 7,890 ________ **6.** 245,000 ________

Reading Whole Numbers

The value of a whole number is made up of the combined values of its digits. The example below shows how to read a whole number in this way.

EXAMPLE: What is the value of 4,032?

Step 1. 4,032 has **4** thousands, **0** hundreds, **3** tens, and **2** ones.

Step 2. 4,032 is read "Four thousand, thirty-two."

Determine the place value of each digit in each number below.

1. 18 has ____ tens and ____ ones.

2. 137 has ____ hundreds, ____ tens, and ____ ones.

3. 4,982 has ____ thousands, ____ hundreds, ____ tens, and ____ ones.

4. 5,420,000 has ____ millions, ____ hundred thousands, and ____ ten thousands.

Writing Whole Numbers

When writing whole numbers in words, there are three rules to remember:

- Numbers from 21 to 99 are written with hyphens.

  EXAMPLE: 45 is forty-five

- The word *and* is not used when writing whole numbers in words.

  EXAMPLE: 126 is one hundred twenty-six not one hundred and twenty-six

- A comma is placed after the word *million*, and after the word *thousand*, but *not* after the word *hundred*.

  EXAMPLE: 3,245,104 three million, two hundred forty-five thousand, one hundred four

Write each of the following numbers in words. The first one is done for you.

1. 47 *forty-seven*
2. 39 __________
3. 238 __________
4. 3,587 __________
5. 38,675 __________

Writing Zero as a Place Holder

Zero is often used as a **place holder**.

When writing a number in symbols, write a zero in each place that is not expressed in words as part of the number. Look at the following examples.

EXAMPLES: seven thousand, sixty-five is 7,065
two million, nineteen thousand, six hundred is 2,019,600
(0 hundred thousands, 0 tens, and 0 ones)

Write each of the following numbers in symbols.

1. three hundred eight __________
2. three thousand, fifteen __________
3. forty-six thousand, eleven __________
4. two hundred nine thousand, four hundred __________
5. six million, three hundred seven thousand __________

Rounding Whole Numbers

- A football sports announcer says that 75,000 people are attending a football game. Actually, 74,839 people are there.

The number 75,000 is called a ***round number***. A round number has zeros to the right of a chosen place value. The number 75,000 has zeros to the right of the thousands place. Thus, 74,839 rounded to the thousands place is 75,000.

One way to round a number is to identify two round numbers that the exact number lies between. Then you simply ask, "Which of these two round numbers is the exact number closer to?"

EXAMPLE 1: Round 74,839 to the nearest 100.

Step 1. To the hundreds place, 74,839 lies between 74,800 and 74,900. 74,800 , 74,839 , 74,900

Step 2. Since 74,839 is closer to 74,800, 74,800 is the rounded answer.

Another way to round a number is to follow the steps given below:

STEPS FOR ROUNDING WHOLE NUMBERS

1. Underline the digit in the place you are rounding to.
2. Look at the digit to the right of the underlined digit.
   a) If the digit to the right is 5 or more, add 1 to the underlined digit.
   b) If the digit to the right is less than 5, leave the underlined digit as is.
3. Put zeros in all places to the right of the underlined digit.

EXAMPLE 2: Round $3,753 to the nearest hundred dollars.

Step 1. Underline the digit in the hundreds place. $3,\underline{7}53$

Step 2. The digit to the right of the 7 is 5. Since 5 is equal to "5 or more," add 1 to the 7. $3,\underline{8}\not{5}\not{3}$

Step 3. Now put zeros in all places to the right of 8. $3,8\underline{00}$

Answer: $3,800

Using either method, round the following numbers.

To the nearest 10

1. 34 ______ 82 ______ 125 ______ $281 ______

To the nearest 100

2. 239 ______ $391 ______ 4,712 ______ $5,351 ______

To the nearest 1,000

3. 4,851 ______ 5,384 ______ $8,901 ______ $12,499 ______

4. Gina earns $1,287 each month. Round Gina's salary to the nearest hundred dollars.

5. The average cost of a three-bedroom house in New Castle is $79,450. Round this cost to the nearest thousand dollars.

Working with Dollars and Cents

The symbols we use when we work with money are the dollar sign $ and the cents symbol ¢.

EXAMPLES: 5 dollars is $5
5 cents is 5¢

We often work with money that combines dollars and cents. To write the total, we use a dollar sign and a ***decimal point***. The decimal point separates the number of dollars from the number of cents. In decimal form, twelve dollars and thirty-five cents is written as

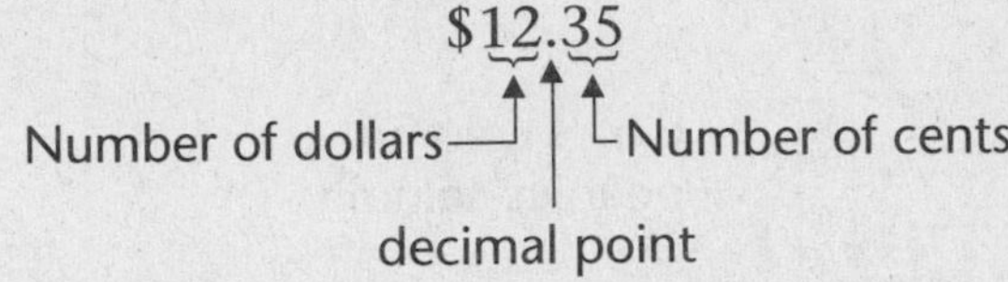

There are five facts to remember about writing dollars and cents in decimal form:

1. Dollars are written to the left of the decimal point.
2. Cents are written in the first two places to the right of the decimal point.
3. When reading (or writing) dollars and cents in decimal form, you read the decimal point as the word *and*.
4. When the amount of cents is between 1¢ and 9¢, write a zero between the decimal point and the cents digit.
   EXAMPLE: Four dollars and six cents is written $4.06.
5. When writing only cents in decimal form, you can write it with or without a zero in the dollar column.
   EXAMPLE: Nineteen cents can be written $0.19 or $.19.

Write each amount below. On the first line, use the cents sign, and on the second line, use the dollar sign and decimal point.The first one is done for you.

1. eight cents ___8¢___ ___$0.08___
2. nine cents ______ ______
3. thirty-five cents ______ ______

Write each of the following amounts using a dollar sign and decimal point. The first amount is completed as an example.

4. Twenty dollars and eight cents ___$20.08___
5. Thirty-two dollars and nine cents ______
6. One hundred fifteen dollars and fifty cents ______

On each line below, fill in the amount shown, using words only. The first one is done for you.

7. $5.07 ___five dollars and seven cents___
8. $23.65 ______
9. $125.50 ______

Rounding Dollars and Cents

You round dollars and cents in the same way you round whole numbers. You can round a monetary amount to the nearest ten cents (dime), nearest dollar, nearest ten dollars, and so on.

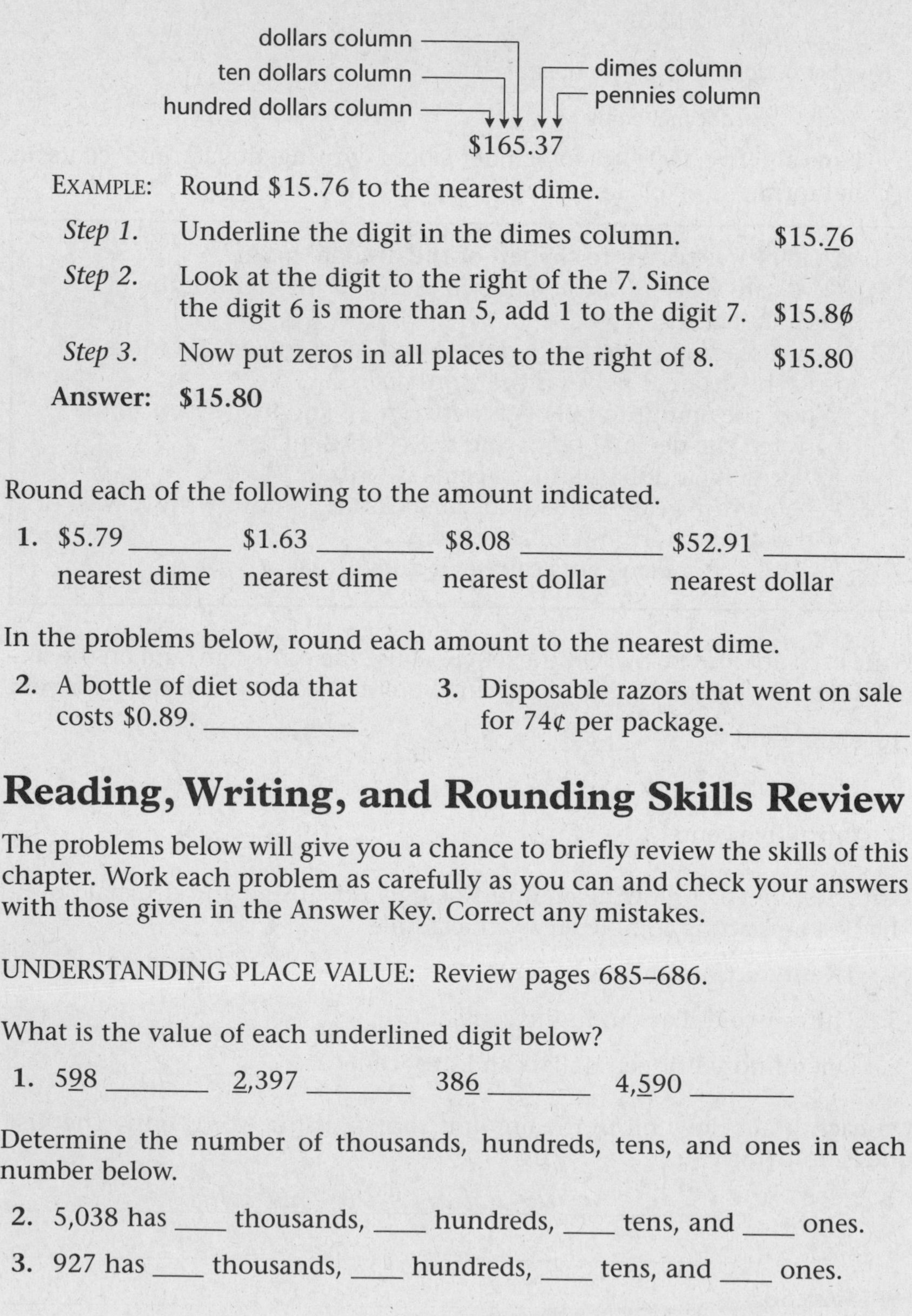

EXAMPLE: Round $15.76 to the nearest dime.

Step 1. Underline the digit in the dimes column. $\$15.\underline{7}6$

Step 2. Look at the digit to the right of the 7. Since the digit 6 is more than 5, add 1 to the digit 7. **$15.8~~6~~**

Step 3. Now put zeros in all places to the right of 8. $15.80

Answer: $15.80

Round each of the following to the amount indicated.

1. $5.79 _______ nearest dime $1.63 _______ nearest dime $8.08 _______ nearest dollar $52.91 _______ nearest dollar

In the problems below, round each amount to the nearest dime.

2. A bottle of diet soda that costs $0.89. __________

3. Disposable razors that went on sale for 74¢ per package. __________

Reading, Writing, and Rounding Skills Review

The problems below will give you a chance to briefly review the skills of this chapter. Work each problem as carefully as you can and check your answers with those given in the Answer Key. Correct any mistakes.

UNDERSTANDING PLACE VALUE: Review pages 685–686.

What is the value of each underlined digit below?

1. $5\underline{9}8$ _______ $\underline{2},397$ _______ $38\underline{6}$ _______ $4,\underline{5}90$ _______

Determine the number of thousands, hundreds, tens, and ones in each number below.

2. 5,038 has ____ thousands, ____ hundreds, ____ tens, and ____ ones.

3. 927 has ____ thousands, ____ hundreds, ____ tens, and ____ ones.

WRITING WHOLE NUMBERS: Review pages 686–687.

Write each of the following numbers in words.

4. 163 ______________________________

5. 4,079 ______________________________

6. 27,000 ______________________________

Write each of the following number phrases as numbers.

7. five hundred seventy-five __________

8. two thousand, forty-six __________

9. four million, six hundred thousand __________

ROUNDING WHOLE NUMBERS AND DOLLARS AND CENTS: Review pages 687–690.

Round each number below as indicated.

10. 76
(tens place)

11. 164
(hundreds place)

12. 2,590
(thousands place)

13. $0.37
(nearest dime)

14. $3.48
(nearest dollar)

15. $67.09
(nearest ten dollars)

2 ADDITION SKILLS

Concepts in Addition

Addition combines two or more numbers.

In symbols we represent addition by the plus sign (+). For example, *five plus three* can be written vertically or horizontally. Numbers being added are called ***addends***. The answer is called the ***sum*** or ***total***.

Written vertically

```
  5 ← addend
+ 3 ← addend
  8 ← sum or total
```

Written horizontally

5 + 3 = 8

addends (5 and 3) ↑ sum or total (8)

Changing the order of addends does *not* change a sum.

5 + 2 = 7 *and* 2 + 5 = 7

Adding zero to a number does *not* change the value of that number.

8 + 0 = 8 *and* 125 + 0 = 125

In daily life, addition problems start out as word questions. To compute an answer, we write mathematical symbols.

a) the **sum** of \$34.82 and \$29.06

```
  $34.82
+  29.06
```

b) seventy cars **plus** thirty cars

```
  70 cars
+ 30 cars
```

Notice that phrases *a* and *b* include **labels**. A *label* is a word or symbol that tells what the numbers refer to. The label in *a* is the dollar sign (\$). The label in *b* is the word *cars*. You can only add amounts with *like* labels.

Solve each problem as indicated.

1.

```
   7      0      9      0     $16    $4.93
 + 0    + 7    + 0    + 9   +   0  + 0.00
```

2. Is the sum of 3 plus 6 equal to the sum of 6 plus 3?

Answers to Chapter 2 exercises start on page 909.

Write each phrase below in numbers. Attach labels where given. Do not do the addition. The first one is done as an example.

3. seven boats plus nine boats

   7 boats + 9 boats

4. The sum of $5.60 and $3.45

5. fifty plus nineteen

6. four dollars and fifty cents plus three dollars and sixteen cents

Adding Single Digits, Columns, and Rows

Practice adding single-digit numbers. **Adding digits two at a time is the way you do all addition.** Practice until you can do each problem quickly with confidence.

1. $\begin{array}{r}7\\+1\\\hline\end{array}$ $\begin{array}{r}5\\+2\\\hline\end{array}$ $\begin{array}{r}0\\+3\\\hline\end{array}$ $\begin{array}{r}1\\+1\\\hline\end{array}$ $\begin{array}{r}1\\+5\\\hline\end{array}$ $\begin{array}{r}6\\+0\\\hline\end{array}$ $\begin{array}{r}2\\+2\\\hline\end{array}$

2. $\begin{array}{r}0\\+1\\\hline\end{array}$ $\begin{array}{r}9\\+0\\\hline\end{array}$ $\begin{array}{r}2\\+5\\\hline\end{array}$ $\begin{array}{r}1\\+6\\\hline\end{array}$ $\begin{array}{r}5\\+3\\\hline\end{array}$ $\begin{array}{r}2\\+7\\\hline\end{array}$ $\begin{array}{r}3\\+1\\\hline\end{array}$

3. $\begin{array}{r}4\\+3\\\hline\end{array}$ $\begin{array}{r}8\\+1\\\hline\end{array}$ $\begin{array}{r}3\\+3\\\hline\end{array}$ $\begin{array}{r}3\\+2\\\hline\end{array}$ $\begin{array}{r}2\\+4\\\hline\end{array}$ $\begin{array}{r}4\\+5\\\hline\end{array}$ $\begin{array}{r}0\\+0\\\hline\end{array}$

4. $\begin{array}{r}7\\+4\\\hline\end{array}$ $\begin{array}{r}8\\+2\\\hline\end{array}$ $\begin{array}{r}6\\+8\\\hline\end{array}$ $\begin{array}{r}8\\+5\\\hline\end{array}$ $\begin{array}{r}7\\+6\\\hline\end{array}$ $\begin{array}{r}2\\+8\\\hline\end{array}$ $\begin{array}{r}9\\+4\\\hline\end{array}$

5. $\begin{array}{r}6\\+9\\\hline\end{array}$ $\begin{array}{r}8\\+3\\\hline\end{array}$ $\begin{array}{r}9\\+6\\\hline\end{array}$ $\begin{array}{r}7\\+8\\\hline\end{array}$ $\begin{array}{r}6\\+5\\\hline\end{array}$ $\begin{array}{r}5\\+8\\\hline\end{array}$ $\begin{array}{r}3\\+7\\\hline\end{array}$

6. $\begin{array}{r}7\\+5\\\hline\end{array}$ $\begin{array}{r}8\\+6\\\hline\end{array}$ $\begin{array}{r}9\\+3\\\hline\end{array}$ $\begin{array}{r}7\\+8\\\hline\end{array}$ $\begin{array}{r}8\\+5\\\hline\end{array}$ $\begin{array}{r}6\\+7\\\hline\end{array}$ $\begin{array}{r}2\\+9\\\hline\end{array}$

7. $\begin{array}{r}6\\+6\\\hline\end{array}$ $\begin{array}{r}8\\+4\\\hline\end{array}$ $\begin{array}{r}9\\+5\\\hline\end{array}$ $\begin{array}{r}5\\+5\\\hline\end{array}$ $\begin{array}{r}9\\+4\\\hline\end{array}$ $\begin{array}{r}7\\+9\\\hline\end{array}$ $\begin{array}{r}3\\+7\\\hline\end{array}$

8. In each matching exercise below, match a sum in the second column with an equal sum in the first column. Write the matching letter on the line before the number. The first one is done for you.

e 1. 8 + 2	a. 8 + 8
___ 2. 6 + 7	b. 4 + 8
___ 3. 7 + 9	c. 6 + 9
___ 4. 9 + 5	d. 6 + 5
___ 5. 8 + 9	e. 7 + 3
___ 6. 7 + 4	f. 6 + 8
___ 7. 5 + 7	g. 9 + 8
___ 8. 8 + 7	h. 9 + 4

Adding a Column of Digits

To add a column of more than two digits, first pick a pair of digits and add them. Then add this sum to the next digit. When possible, first pick a pair of digits whose sum is 10. You may find that this makes adding easier, and you may be less likely to make an error.

EXAMPLE 1: Add: $\left.\begin{array}{r} 5 \\ 2 \end{array}\right\} \; \left.\begin{array}{r} 7 \\ 9 \end{array}\right\} 16$ with $+\,9$

$$\begin{array}{r} 5 \\ 2 \\ \underline{+\,9} \end{array} \qquad \left.\begin{array}{r} 7 \\ 9 \end{array}\right\} 16$$

EXAMPLE 2: Add:

$$\begin{array}{r} 9 \\ 3 \\ \underline{+\,7} \end{array} \qquad \left.\begin{array}{r} 9 \\ \left.\begin{array}{r} 3 \\ +\,7 \end{array}\right\} 10 \end{array}\right\} 19$$

Add the problems below.

1.

9	6	6	2	8	5	7
1	8	5	8	4	5	9
+ 6	+ 2	+ 4	+ 9	+ 6	+ 7	+ 1

2.

7	3	9	1	6	7	2
3	6	3	2	8	5	4
4	2	1	9	4	0	7
+ 2	+ 8	+ 7	+ 4	+ 2	+ 5	+ 3

Adding a Row of Digits

Single-digit addition problems are often written in a row across. Add these the same way you add numbers written in a column. Again, when possible, it may be easier to first add a pair of digits whose sum is 10.

EXAMPLE 1: Add: $\underbrace{\underbrace{6 + 2}_{8} + 5}_{13} =$

$8 + 5$

13

EXAMPLE 2: Add: $4 + 9 + 6 =$

$10 + 9$

19

Add.

1. $4 + 5 + 6 =$
2. $9 + 0 + 3 =$
3. $5 + 7 + 5 =$
4. $8 + 1 + 2 + 6 =$
5. $7 + 2 + 8 =$
6. $7 + 3 + 2 + 4 =$

Find the answers to the word questions below.

7. What do you get when you combine eight gallons, four gallons, and seven gallons of water?
8. What is the total of eight dollars plus nine dollars plus two dollars?

Adding Larger Numbers

Numbers with two or more digits are added one column at a time. First you add the digits in the right-hand column. Then you move to the left and add each column. Continue until you have added each column of digits.

EXAMPLE:

2451 + 1320 1	2451 + 1320 71	2451 + 1320 771	2451 + 1320 3771
Add the ones column	Add the tens column	Add the hundreds column	Add the thousands column

To *check* an addition problem, add the numbers from the bottom to the top. A careful way to check is to switch the numbers and then add again.

EXAMPLE: Add:
```
  2,451
+ 1,320
  3,771
```
Check:
```
  1,320
+ 2,451
  3,771 ✓
```

Add. Check each answer on scratch paper.

1.
```
  50     81     60     24     72     41
+ 15   + 17   + 25   + 15   + 26   + 26
```

2.

528	314	741	327	700	483
+ 261	+ 405	+ 231	+ 112	+ 278	+ 106

3.

42	31	30	18	21	40
21	15	14	11	13	32
+ 22	+ 20	+ 15	+ 10	+ 14	+ 17

Add. Treat each empty digit place as a zero.

EXAMPLE: Add:

$$\begin{array}{r} \boxed{4}\,35 \\ +\quad 60 \\ \hline \boxed{4}\,95 \end{array}$$

4.

734	425	26,300	11,735	14,500
			2,223	12,156
+ 45	+ 61	+ 3,657	+ 1,021	+ 2,031

Adding Dollars and Cents

To add dollars and cents, line up the decimal points and then add the columns as you did when adding whole numbers. Line up the decimal points by placing one directly below the other.

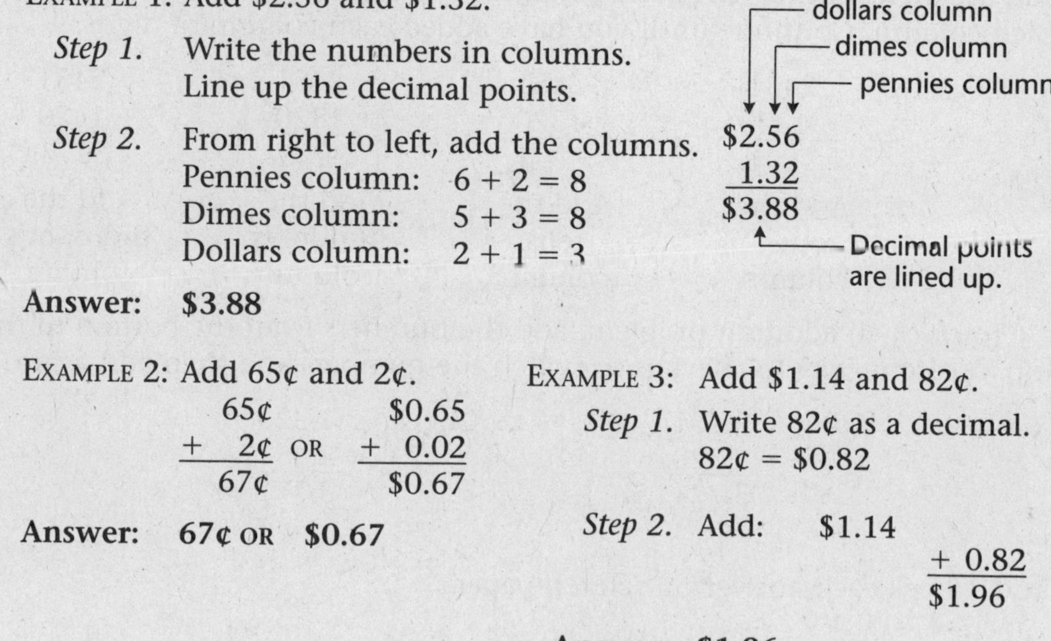

EXAMPLE 1: Add $2.56 and $1.32.

Step 1. Write the numbers in columns.
Line up the decimal points.

Step 2. From right to left, add the columns.
Pennies column: 6 + 2 = 8
Dimes column: 5 + 3 = 8
Dollars column: 2 + 1 = 3

Answer: $3.88

EXAMPLE 2: Add 65¢ and 2¢.

$$\begin{array}{r} 65¢ \\ +\ \ 2¢ \\ \hline 67¢ \end{array} \quad \text{OR} \quad \begin{array}{r} \$0.65 \\ +\ 0.02 \\ \hline \$0.67 \end{array}$$

Answer: 67¢ OR $0.67

EXAMPLE 3: Add $1.14 and 82¢.

Step 1. Write 82¢ as a decimal.
82¢ = $0.82

Step 2. Add:

$$\begin{array}{r} \$1.14 \\ +\ 0.82 \\ \hline \$1.96 \end{array}$$

Answer: $1.96

NOTE: In Example 2, the answer can be expressed either in cents or in decimal form. In Example 3, the 82¢ must first be written in decimal form before the addition can be done.

Add. Remember to include the decimal point and dollar sign in each answer.

1.	\$12.52	\$32.09	\$41.65	\$24.45	\$15.80	\$25.25
	+ 2.31	+ 12.50	+ 14.32	+ 5.13	+ 20.17	+ 10.00

Add. Write each answer two ways. First use the cents symbol. Then use a dollar sign and decimal point.

2. Add 25¢ and 14¢ Add \$0.63 and \$0.16 Add 73¢ and 25¢

Add. As your first step, express each number in decimal form.

3. \$4.52 + 43¢ \$1.25 + 31¢ 75¢ + \$1.10

Introducing Word Problems

A ***word problem*** is a short story that asks a question or tells you to find something. You are given information and are asked to set up and solve a problem.

Understanding the Question

Word problems may be written as a single sentence, or as several sentences. In each type of problem, *the first step is to identify the question and to understand what you are being asked to find.*

EXAMPLE 1: How much does it cost to bowl 3 lines if each line costs \$1.15?

asked to find: cost of bowling 3 lines

EXAMPLE 2: Janice jogs five days a week. On Monday, Wednesday, and Friday, she takes 3-mile runs. On Tuesday and Thursday, she
takes 5-mile runs. *Find how many miles Janice jogs each week.*

asked to find: miles jogged each week

Underline the question in each problem below. Then circle the words within the parentheses that identify what you are asked to find. DO NOT SOLVE THESE PROBLEMS.

1. If Sarah pays $600 per month for rent, how much rent does she pay per year?

   (weekly rent, monthly rent, yearly rent)

2. This year, Manuel paid $2,300 in federal income tax, $426 in state income tax, and $47 in city income tax. Find the amount that Manuel paid in state and federal taxes.

   (federal and state taxes, city tax, total taxes)

3. Road distance between Oak Grove and Rockville is 132 miles. From Rockville to Salem is 91 miles. Driving through Rockville, how many miles is it between Oak Grove and Salem?

   (miles from Rockville to Salem, miles from Oak Grove to Salem, miles from Oak Grove to Rockville)

4. During the week, Jason worked a 35-hour shift, earning $9 per hour. He also worked 3 hours of overtime, earning $13 an hour. Find how much extra money Jason earned this week.

   (total pay, total regular pay, total overtime pay)

Addition Word Problems

Solve the following addition problems. Pay close attention to what the problem asks you to find. Remember to include both a number and a label.

EXAMPLE: A shirt is on sale for $9.75, and a pair of socks is on sale for $1.50. If Bill bought both, how much did he spend?

asked to find: total amount spent

$$\begin{array}{r} \$9.75 \\ +\ 1.50 \\ \hline \$11.25 \end{array} \qquad \text{Check: } \begin{array}{r} \$1.50 \\ +\ 9.75 \\ \hline \$11.25 \end{array} \checkmark$$

Answer: $11.25

Underline the words in each question that identify what you are asked to find. Then solve and check each problem. Problem 1 is completed as an example.

1. If a class contains 23 men and 16 women, how many students are in the class?

23	men	16
+ 16	women	+ 23
39	students	39

2. The distance from Seattle to Portland is 172 miles. If Portland is 114 miles from Eugene, how far is Seattle from Eugene? (Hint: Put the mileage on the diagram below.)

Seattle Portland Eugene

3. David paid $1,245 more for his car than he sold it for. If he sold it for $6,250, what was David's purchase price?

4. If it is now 12 minutes after 8 o'clock, what time will it be in 27 minutes?

5. Ira Thompson makes a monthly rent payment of $415. If his other monthly expenses are $581, what take-home monthly income does he need to pay these expenses?

6. Evening phone rates in Erie are discounted. If the cost of the first minute is 30¢, and the cost of each additional minute is 21¢, what is the cost of a three-minute call?

7. What was the total of John's three bills if his rent was $405; telephone, $21.14; and electricity, $71.25?

8. For their first basketball game of the season, the Bulldogs drew an attendance of 2,324 people. The second game drew 3,042 people, and the third game drew 3,121. Find the combined attendance for these first three games.

Adding and Carrying

Adding two-digit or larger numbers often involves **carrying.** To ***carry*** means to take a digit from the sum of one column and place it at the top of the column to the left.

Carrying to the Tens Column

The example below shows how to carry 10 ones as 1 ten.

EXAMPLE: Add: $\begin{array}{r} 45 \\ +\ 39 \\ \hline \end{array}$ Solution: $\begin{array}{r} \overset{1}{4}5 \\ +\ 39 \\ \hline 84 \end{array}$ Check: $\begin{array}{r} \overset{1}{3}9 \\ +\ 45 \\ \hline 84 \end{array}$ ✓

Step 1. Add the ones column: 5 + 9 = 14
Think of the 14 ones as 1 ten and 4 ones.
Place the 4 under the ones column.

Step 2. Carry the 1 ten to the top of the tens column.

Step 3. Add the tens column: 1 + 4 + 3 = 8

$\begin{array}{r} \overset{1}{4}5 \\ +39 \\ \hline 84 \end{array}$

Carry the 1 ten to the top of the tens column.
Place the 4 under the ones column.
Place the 8 under the tens column.

1. $\begin{array}{r} 48 \\ +\ 7 \\ \hline \end{array}$ $\begin{array}{r} 63 \\ +\ 9 \\ \hline \end{array}$ $\begin{array}{r} 52 \\ +\ 8 \\ \hline \end{array}$ $\begin{array}{r} 69 \\ +\ 36 \\ \hline \end{array}$ $\begin{array}{r} 77 \\ +\ 48 \\ \hline \end{array}$ $\begin{array}{r} 35 \\ +\ 29 \\ \hline \end{array}$

2. $\begin{array}{r} 14 \\ 5 \\ +\ 3 \\ \hline \end{array}$ $\begin{array}{r} 31 \\ 9 \\ +\ 7 \\ \hline \end{array}$ $\begin{array}{r} 27 \\ 16 \\ +\ 6 \\ \hline \end{array}$ $\begin{array}{r} 25 \\ 14 \\ +\ 16 \\ \hline \end{array}$ $\begin{array}{r} 38 \\ 26 \\ +\ 19 \\ \hline \end{array}$ $\begin{array}{r} 56 \\ 47 \\ +\ 29 \\ \hline \end{array}$

Carrying to the Hundreds Column

When the sum of digits in the tens column is 10 or larger, carry to the hundreds column.

EXAMPLE: $\begin{array}{r} \overset{1}{2}95 \\ +\ 73 \\ \hline 368 \end{array}$

3. $\begin{array}{r} 274 \\ +\ 62 \\ \hline \end{array}$ $\begin{array}{r} 883 \\ +\ 95 \\ \hline \end{array}$ $\begin{array}{r} 497 \\ +\ 31 \\ \hline \end{array}$ $\begin{array}{r} 534 \\ 420 \\ +\ 191 \\ \hline \end{array}$ $\begin{array}{r} 556 \\ 482 \\ +\ 181 \\ \hline \end{array}$ $\begin{array}{r} 965 \\ 871 \\ +\ 590 \\ \hline \end{array}$

Carrying to the Thousands Column

When the sum of digits in the hundreds column is 10 or larger, carry to the thousands column.

Example:
```
     1
  6,734
+ 2,841
  9,575
```

4.

			4,435	5,736	8,660
4561	5732	2754	3,520	2,920	7,815
+ 925	+ 656	+ 1825	+ 3,414	+ 1,812	+ 6,903

Carrying to Several Columns

In many addition problems, you may need to carry to several columns in the same problem. The problems below give you practice in developing this skill.

5.

					6,684
674	765	379	8,351	3,573	5,985
+ 87	+ 737	+ 894	+ 769	+ 589	+ 3,481

6.

			56,386	67,389
31,284	54,264	26,473	34,150	52,500
+ 9,785	+ 8,890	+ 7,978	+ 10,854	+ 24,687

Adding Numbers in a Row

When numbers are written in a row, rewrite them in a column before adding. You may want to place the largest number at the top of the column and smaller numbers at the bottom.

EXAMPLE: Add: 452 + 78 + 326

Write the numbers in a column. Line up the hundreds digits (4 and 3), tens digits (5, 2, and 7), and ones digits (2, 6, and 8) directly over one another. Add.

```
  11
  452
  326
+  78
  856
```

Rewrite the following problems in a column and add.

1. 37 + 156 + 40   163 + 57 + 38   75 + 428 + 126

2. 5,354 + 3,365 + 984   23,837 + 7,486 + 5,386

Carrying with Dollars and Cents

Carrying with dollars and cents is done the same way as carrying with whole numbers. You carry a digit across the decimal point as if it weren't there. Remember to place a decimal point and dollar sign in the answer.

EXAMPLE: Add:	Solution:	Check:
$5.75	$\overset{1}{}$\$5.75	$\overset{1}{}$\$2.81
+ 2.81	+ 2.81	+ 5.75
	\$8.56	\$8.56 ✓

Bring the decimal point straight down in the sum and add a dollar sign.

Add as indicated.

1.

\$8.95	\$9.77	\$14.37	\$24.58	\$30.75	\$12.48
+ 1.57	+ .89	+ 3.74	+ 18.63	+ 9.85	+ 9.15

2. \$2.37 + 95¢   \$3.85 + 87¢   \$10.50 + 99¢   \$14.75 + 79¢

Finding Necessary Information

The first step in solving a word problem is understanding what the question asks you to find. *The second step is deciding what information is needed to answer the question.*

What Is Necessary Information?

Given information includes *all* of the numbers and labels that appear in a problem. ***Necessary information*** includes *only* those numbers and labels needed to answer a specific question.

Necessary information may appear anywhere in a problem. Ask yourself, "What information do I need to answer this question?" Then reread the problem carefully and select those numbers that are needed.

EXAMPLE: Lucy planned to spend no more than $20 at the grocery store. She bought a roast for $7.85, vegetables for $5.60, and milk for $1.95. How much did Lucy spend in all?

given information: $20, $7.85, $5.60, $1.95

necessary information: $7.85, $5.60, $1.95

The question asks only about how much Lucy spent. Lucy's spending limit of $20 is not part of the grocery bill. Thus, $20 is **extra information**, information not needed to solve the problem.

In each problem below, underline what you are being asked to find. Then write *only* the information needed to solve the problem on the line below. Be sure to include labels. DO NOT SOLVE THESE PROBLEMS. The first one has been done for you.

1. <u>What is the total price of a quart of milk</u> that costs $0.95 <u>and a loaf of bread</u> that costs $2.09?

   $0.95 $2.09

2. Brenda has lost 13 pounds on her diet. Her weight dropped from 167 pounds to 154 pounds. If she still wants to lose 14 more pounds, how much does Brenda want to lose in all?

   ____

3. How many hours total does Amy work each week if she earns $278 per week working 35 hours as a cook and $4 per hour baby-sitting 8 hours each week?

   ____

4. In Canyonville there are 23,458 registered voters. Of these, 13,228 are men and 10,230 are women. During the November election, 4,572 men voted. If 6,385 women also voted, how many people voted in this election?

   ____

5. What is the total cost of a 7-pound package of chicken when chicken is on sale for $.89 a pound and hamburger is on sale for $1.69?

   ____

Addition Word Problems

In each word problem, watch for words such as *total, altogether,* and *sum* that let you know you should add to find the answer. Solve each addition problem below.

1. In a 50-mile bike race, Sally rode 12 miles the first hour, 9 miles the second hour, and 13 miles the third hour. How many miles altogether did Sally ride during these first 3 hours?

2. There are 14,842 Democrats and 17,463 Republicans registered in Cottage Grove. In the March election, 6,284 Democrats and 5,782 Republicans voted. Only 800 Independents voted. What was the sum of the votes cast in this election?

3. On a trip, Nancy kept a record of her gas use. Her record included: 14 gallons — 209 miles; 17 gallons — 248 miles; and 9 gallons — 173 miles. How many miles total did she drive on her trip?

4. For a barbecue party, Fred bought 3 pounds of chicken, 4 pounds of hamburger, 5 pounds of steak, and 8 pounds of potato salad. How many pounds of meat did Fred buy altogether if he planned to feed between 30 and 40 people?

5. While shopping, Cal bought car oil for $11.95, a shovel for $9.49, dish soap for $1.79, and a rake for $13.50. Find how much Cal paid for the two garden tools.

6. Frank looked at 3 used cars: a Plymouth for $1,695, a Chevrolet for $1,545, and a Ford for $1,275. He chose the Plymouth after the dealer lowered the price to $1,475. He then put on new tires for $276 and put in a radio for $125. What total amount did Frank invest in this car?

Addition Skills Review

Before leaving the chapter on addition, review your addition skills. Work each problem carefully.

1. $\begin{array}{r} 6 \\ +\ 2 \\ \hline \end{array}$ $\quad$ $\begin{array}{r} 8 \\ +\ 7 \\ \hline \end{array}$ $\quad$ $\begin{array}{r} 9 \\ 6 \\ +\ 4 \\ \hline \end{array}$ $\quad$ $5 + 7 =$ $\quad$ $8 + 9 + 2 =$

2. $\begin{array}{r} 23 \\ +\ 16 \\ \hline \end{array}$ $\quad$ $\begin{array}{r} 78 \\ +\ 21 \\ \hline \end{array}$ $\quad$ $\begin{array}{r} 143 \\ +\ 52 \\ \hline \end{array}$ $\quad$ $\begin{array}{r} 634 \\ 121 \\ +\ 23 \\ \hline \end{array}$ $\quad$ $\begin{array}{r} 400 \\ 172 \\ +\ 106 \\ \hline \end{array}$ $\quad$ $\begin{array}{r} 3{,}480 \\ 1{,}002 \\ +\ 315 \\ \hline \end{array}$

3. $\begin{array}{r} 27 \\ +\ 6 \\ \hline \end{array}$ $\quad$ $\begin{array}{r} 43 \\ +\ 9 \\ \hline \end{array}$ $\quad$ $\begin{array}{r} 205 \\ +\ 58 \\ \hline \end{array}$ $\quad$ $\begin{array}{r} 457 \\ +\ 86 \\ \hline \end{array}$ $\quad$ $\begin{array}{r} 687 \\ +\ 159 \\ \hline \end{array}$ $\quad$ $\begin{array}{r} 2{,}380 \\ +\ 638 \\ \hline \end{array}$

4. $\begin{array}{r} 75 \\ 48 \\ +\ 8 \\ \hline \end{array}$ $\quad$ $\begin{array}{r} 87 \\ 36 \\ +\ 21 \\ \hline \end{array}$ $\quad$ $\begin{array}{r} 106 \\ 97 \\ +\ 82 \\ \hline \end{array}$ $\quad$ $\begin{array}{r} 500 \\ 396 \\ +\ 208 \\ \hline \end{array}$ $\quad$ $\begin{array}{r} 1{,}339 \\ 835 \\ +\ 400 \\ \hline \end{array}$ $\quad$ $\begin{array}{r} 13{,}298 \\ 9{,}509 \\ +\ 4{,}582 \\ \hline \end{array}$

5. $\begin{array}{r} \$4.23 \\ +\ 1.10 \\ \hline \end{array}$ $\quad$ $\begin{array}{r} \$6.13 \\ +\ \ .72 \\ \hline \end{array}$ $\quad$ $\begin{array}{r} \$7.46 \\ +\ 2.39 \\ \hline \end{array}$ $\quad$ $\begin{array}{r} \$145.79 \\ +\ 25.89 \\ \hline \end{array}$ $\quad$ $\begin{array}{r} \$2{,}345.65 \\ 1{,}394.05 \\ +\ 375.37 \\ \hline \end{array}$

6. 16 + 8 $\quad$ 47 + 9 $\quad$ 35 + 28 $\quad$ 754 + 395

7. 32 + 18 + 5 $\quad$ 54 + 30 + 17 $\quad$ 343 + 105 + 84

Write each phrase in numbers. Then solve.

8. fourteen plus nine

9. the sum of twenty-five dollars and six dollars

10. thirty-eight pounds added to sixty-seven pounds

Add. Express each number in decimal form.

11. \$0.45 plus 37¢

12. the sum of \$2.34 and 96¢

13. 84¢ plus 59¢

14. What is the sum of 2 quarters, 3 dimes, and 7 pennies?

15. While moving furniture, Ramos moved 9 chairs, 7 tables, and 3 stools. How many pieces of furniture did Ramos move altogether?

16. Walton Stadium holds 46,000 people. At the first game of the season, 32,640 fans showed up. The second game drew only 17,456. The third game brought in only 16,540 fans, although 9,500 tickets were sold before game time. What was the total attendance at these first three games?

3 SUBTRACTION SKILLS

Concepts in Subtraction

Subtraction takes one amount away from another, or finds the difference between two numbers.

In symbols we represent subtraction by the minus sign (−). The words *minus* and *take away* are often used in place of the word *subtract*. You can write a subtraction problem vertically or horizontally. The number being subtracted from is called the ***minuend***. The number being subtracted is called the ***subtrahend***. The answer is called the ***difference***.

Written vertically

```
  9   ← minuend
− 5   ← subtrahend
  4   ← difference
```

Written horizontally

$9 - 5 = 4$ (9 = minuend, 5 = subtrahend, 4 = difference)

You cannot change the order of the minuend and subtrahend in a subtraction problem.

12 − 7 is not the same as 7 − 12.

Subtracting zero from a number does not change the value of that number.

```
  4      26      $9     $15.75
− 0     − 0     − 0    − 0.00
  4      26      $9     $15.75
```

Word phrases that indicate subtraction are most easily solved when written as columns of numbers.

For example, look at how these word phrases are written:

a) the **difference** between $23.45 and $12.00

```
  $23.45
− 12.00
```

b) fifty pounds **minus** thirty-five pounds

```
  50 pounds
− 35 pounds
```

c) nineteen feet **take away** eight feet

```
  19 feet
−  8 feet
```

Solve each problem as indicated.

1.

```
  9      7      13      25      $12     $27.35
− 0    − 0    − 0     − 0     − 0     − 0.00
```

Answers to Chapter 3 exercises start on page 911.

2. Does the difference of twelve subtract seven equal the difference of seven subtract twelve?

Express each phrase below in mathematical symbols. Attach labels where given. You do not need to solve the problems.

3. the difference of nineteen and six

4. one hundred forty-two take away seventy-seven

5. eighty-seven pounds subtract sixty pounds

6. ninety-seven feet minus forty feet

Basic Subtraction Facts

Practice subtracting small numbers. Practice until you can do each problem with confidence.

Minuend (top number) smaller than 10. Subtract.

1.	8	5	9	8	6	4	7	3
	− 6	− 2	− 7	− 4	− 5	− 0	− 3	− 3
2.	7	9	8	7	8	7	9	9
	− 0	− 5	− 5	− 5	− 0	− 6	− 3	− 6
3.	1	5	8	4	9	7	5	2
	− 0	− 5	− 3	− 1	− 8	− 7	− 4	− 0
4.	8	8	7	6	9	6	7	4
	− 2	− 7	− 4	− 6	− 0	− 4	− 2	− 2

Larger minuends. Subtract.

5.	12	14	10	13	11	10	15	11
	− 7	− 7	− 5	− 4	− 7	− 7	− 8	− 5
6.	11	14	13	13	18	10	14	13
	− 9	− 9	− 7	− 6	− 9	− 1	− 5	− 8
7.	11	11	10	12	10	17	10	14
	− 6	− 8	− 4	− 9	− 3	− 9	− 6	− 8

8.	10 − 8	13 − 9	11 − 4	15 − 7	13 − 6	12 − 8	17 − 8	13 − 5
9.	18 − 9	15 − 6	16 − 7	14 − 6	16 − 8	15 − 9	16 − 9	12 − 6

10. Match the problems in both columns that have the same answer. Write the matching letter on the line before the number.

____ **1.** 16 − 8	**a.** 16 − 9
____ **2.** 11 − 9	**b.** 12 − 8
____ **3.** 10 − 9	**c.** 14 − 9
____ **4.** 11 − 7	**d.** 7 − 5
____ **5.** 14 − 8	**e.** 11 − 8
____ **6.** 14 − 7	**f.** 1 − 0
____ **7.** 10 − 5	**g.** 12 − 6
____ **8.** 12 − 9	**h.** 17 − 9

Subtracting Larger Numbers

Larger numbers are subtracted one column at a time. First you subtract the ones column at the right. Then you move to the left and subtract the next column. Continue until you have subtracted each column.

To *check* a subtraction problem, add the difference (answer) to the subtrahend (the bottom number). This sum should equal the minuend (top number).

EXAMPLE:

745 − 321 4	745 − 321 24	745 − 321 424
subtract ones column	subtract tens column	subtract hundreds column

Subtract. Check each answer on scratch paper.

1.	77 − 45	28 − 16	49 − 27	36 − 23	54 − 32	98 − 57	37 − 20

2. 284 − 161   746 − 432   482 − 27   154 − 20   363 − 52   596 − 74   639 − 27

3. 2,476 − 53   7,846 − 31   3,855 − 42   3,495 − 263   2,756 − 505   3,745 − 321   1,485 − 270

Writing Zeros in the Answer

Sometimes when you subtract a column, you get a zero. Except for a zero in the far left column, be sure to write any zero in an answer. Remember, zero holds a place and is part of an answer.

EXAMPLE 1:

$$\begin{array}{r} 567 \\ -\ 465 \\ \hline 102 \end{array}$$

As part of the number, zero gives us an answer of 102, *not* 12.

EXAMPLE 2:

$$\begin{array}{r} 234 \\ -\ 213 \\ \hline 21 \end{array}$$

↑ In this far left column, zero is not written in the answer.

Subtract.

1. 37 − 17   46 − 26   37 − 31   750 − 340   254 − 53   583 − 542   689 − 79

2. 4,628 − 615   1,735 − 535   2,373 − 270   12,474 − 1,471   18,595 − 7,543   23,274 − 13,150   16,648 − 15,433

Find the answer to each word question below.

3. How many miles are left when you subtract 296 miles from 598 miles?

4. What is the difference between two hundred fifty pounds of gravel and two hundred twenty pounds of gravel?

Subtracting Dollars and Cents

To subtract dollars and cents, line up the decimal points and then subtract the columns. Line up the decimal points by placing one directly below the other.

EXAMPLE: Subtract \$2.43 from \$5.89.

Step 1. Write the problem in columns and line up the decimal points. Place \$2.43 directly below \$5.89.

Step 2. From right to left, subtract each column.
Pennies column: 9 − 3 = 6
Dimes column: 8 − 4 = 4
Dollars column: 5 − 2 = 3
Bring down the decimal point.

dollars column
dimes column
pennies column

```
 $5.89
− 2.43
 $3.46
```

Decimal points are lined up.

Answer: **\$3.46**

Subtract. Remember to bring down the decimal points and dollar signs.

1.

\$5.89	\$12.64	\$1.98	\$1.75	\$5.99	\$95.87
− 3.25	− 9.30	− 0.75	− 1.50	− 3.45	− 82.75

Solve each problem as indicated.

2. Subtract \$2.57 from \$14.88.

3. Subtract 75¢ from \$3.99.

4. Subtract \$5.00 from \$9.99.

5. Subtract \$124.50 from \$275.85.

Subtraction Word Problems

Solve each problem. Watch for words that let you know you should subtract to find the answer. Examples are words such as *difference, left,* and *reduction.*

1. Evelyn was born June 3, 1941. How old was she on June 3, 1986?

2. The price of a wool skirt was reduced from $39.99 to $25.50 during the after-Christmas sale. How much is saved with this sale price?

3. George sawed 5 inches off a board that measured 19 inches. How much is left of the longer board?

4. In Prineville, the highest recorded temperature on January 1 is 67°; the lowest recorded temperature is 13°. Find the difference between these two temperatures.

Recognizing Key Words

A word problem may contain clues that tell you whether to add or subtract. Often, key words are the clues found in the question. Look at the use of key words in the following examples:

EXAMPLE 1: Alice earned $47 on Thursday. On Friday, she earned another $36. How much *altogether* did Alice earn on Thursday *and* Friday?

Add: $47 + 36$

Answer: $83

addition key words: *altogether, and*

EXAMPLE 2: Alice earned $47 on Thursday. On Friday, she earned another $36. How much *more* did Alice earn on Thursday *than* on Friday?

Subtract: $47 − 36$

Answer: $11

subtraction key words: *more . . . than*

Addition Key Words
add
and
altogether
both
in all
increased
more
plus
sum
total

Subtraction Key Words
change (money received)
decrease
difference
left
lose (or lost)
more . . . than
reduce (or reduction)
remain (or remaining)
nearer } (and other *-er* comparison words)
farther }

Underline a key word in each problem below. Then, on the line below each problem, write which operation (addition or subtraction) the key words suggest you use to solve the problem. DO NOT SOLVE ANY PROBLEM. The first one is done as an example.

1. How much <u>change</u> did Virginia receive when she paid a $26.45 grocery bill with a check for $30.45?

   subtraction

2. After he received his income tax refund of $235.89, Alan bought a lawnmower for $129 and several garden tools for $30. How much did Alan spend in all?

   ____

3. While driving to San Francisco, Gerry passed a sign that read "San Francisco 187 miles." After she had driven another 60 miles, how much farther did Gerry need to drive?

   ____

4. Peter weighs 184 pounds, much more than his wife, Trixie, who weighs 130 pounds. If they stood on the scale together, what would be their combined weight?

   ____

5. On a local issue during the fall election, 15,657 people voted *yes*. Only 6,542 people voted *no*. How many more *yes* votes were cast than *no* votes?

   ____

6. Frank's shift ended at 8:15. He stayed at work 45 more minutes to finish cleaning the floors. What time did Frank leave work?

   ____

Solving Word Problems

Solve each problem by adding or subtracting. In each problem, pay close attention to what you are asked to find. Be sure to look for key words.

1. The price of a $395 washing machine was reduced to $320 during the Memorial Day sale. How much can Jenny save by buying the machine at this reduced price?

2. At a garage sale, Mrs. Jacobs bought a chair for $17, a table for $47.25, and a lamp for $1.75. What total amount did she pay for these items?

3. When Jill's car engine developed a knocking sound, there was a total of 57,863 miles on the mileage indicator. How many more miles is this than are covered on her 50,000-mile warranty?

4. Robert's bills this month include rent of $535, a car payment of $145, gas and electricity of $167.34, and medical expenses of $97.87. What amount do these bills add up to?

5. During a "price war," Regional Air Lines offered a one-way nonstop flight from New York to Denver for $127.85. Southern Air Lines offered the same flight for $106, but flyers had to change planes in Chicago. Find the difference in price between these two flights.

In each addition or subtraction problem below, underline the necessary information before adding or subtracting. Cross out the unnecessary information. Solve each problem and check your arithmetic.

6. William wants to work a 40-hour week. On Tuesday, his boss increased his 25-hour per week work schedule to include an additional 6 hours on Saturday. How many hours in all does William now work each week?

7. During the "Spring Clearance Sale," Nathan was interested in buying a good used truck. When they reduced the price of a Ford pickup from $3,795 to $2,945, he bought it. If he made a down payment of $825, how much remained for him to pay off?

8. A 3,955-pound full-size car gets 17 miles to the gallon. A 2,630-pound compact car gets more miles to the gallon. How many fewer pounds does the better mileage car weigh?

9. On his dentist bill of $135.80, Dennis made payments of $25, $45.50, and $27.75. During this time, a late charge of $3.75 was added to his bill. So far, what sum has Dennis paid on his total bill?

10. By air, Chicago is 802 miles from New York City and 996 miles from Denver. Also by air, Denver is 1,771 miles from New York City. How much closer is New York City to Chicago than it is to Denver? (Hint: Fill in mileage on the diagram below.)

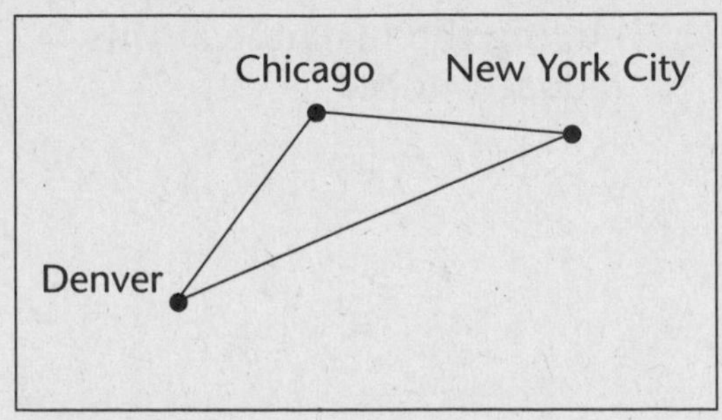

Subtracting by Borrowing

When a digit in the bottom number is larger than the digit above it, you have to **borrow** in order to subtract. The following example shows how to borrow from the tens column in order to subtract the ones column.

EXAMPLE: Subtract: $\begin{array}{r} 53 \\ -\ 27 \\ \hline \end{array}$ Solution: $\begin{array}{r} \overset{4}{\not 5}\ \overset{13}{\not 3} \\ -\ 2\ 7 \\ \hline 2\ 6 \end{array}$ Check: $\begin{array}{r} \overset{1}{2}7 \\ +\ 26 \\ \hline 53 \end{array}$ ✓

Step 1. Since you can't subtract 7 from 3, borrow from the tens column. Take 1 ten from the tens column: cross out the 5 and write a 4 above it. — $\overset{4}{\not 5}3$ — 5 is replaced by 4. (1 ten is borrowed.)

Step 2. Add the borrowed 10 to the 3. Think of this as putting 13 ones in the ones column. (10 + 3 = 13 ones.) — $\overset{4}{\not 5}\ \overset{13}{\not 3}$ — The borrowed 10 is added to the 3 to give 13 ones.

Step 3. Subtract the ones column: 13 − 7 = 6
Subtract the tens column: 4 − 2 = 2 — $\begin{array}{r} \overset{4}{\not 5}\ \overset{13}{\not 3} \\ -\ 2\ 7 \\ \hline \end{array}$ — Each column can now be subtracted.

Answer: 2 6

Borrowing from the Tens Column

Subtract. Check each answer on scratch paper.

1. $\begin{array}{r} 47 \\ -\ 9 \\ \hline \end{array}$ $\begin{array}{r} 20 \\ -\ 6 \\ \hline \end{array}$ $\begin{array}{r} 248 \\ -\ 29 \\ \hline \end{array}$ $\begin{array}{r} 786 \\ -\ 69 \\ \hline \end{array}$ $\begin{array}{r} 472 \\ -\ 107 \\ \hline \end{array}$ $\begin{array}{r} 671 \\ -\ 324 \\ \hline \end{array}$ $\begin{array}{r} 866 \\ -\ 358 \\ \hline \end{array}$

Borrowing from the Hundreds Column

To subtract the tens column, you may need to borrow 10 tens (1 hundred) from the hundreds column.

EXAMPLE: $\begin{array}{r} \overset{3}{\not 4}\ \overset{11}{\not 1}\ 9 \\ -\quad 7\ 3 \\ \hline 3\ 4\ 6 \end{array}$

2. $\begin{array}{r} 148 \\ -\ 92 \\ \hline \end{array}$ $\begin{array}{r} 347 \\ -\ 73 \\ \hline \end{array}$ $\begin{array}{r} 426 \\ -\ 84 \\ \hline \end{array}$ $\begin{array}{r} 744 \\ -\ 463 \\ \hline \end{array}$ $\begin{array}{r} 315 \\ -\ 261 \\ \hline \end{array}$ $\begin{array}{r} 407 \\ -\ 284 \\ \hline \end{array}$ $\begin{array}{r} 566 \\ -\ 391 \\ \hline \end{array}$

Borrowing from the Thousands Column

To subtract in the hundreds column, it may be necessary to borrow 10 hundreds (1 thousand) from the thousands column.

EXAMPLE:

```
   1 13
   2, 3 86
 –    8 74
   1, 5 12
```

3.

5,486	4,583	3,572	4,286	15,297	12,389
– 675	– 720	– 722	– 2,524	– 4,875	– 10,850

Borrowing from Two or More Columns

Sometimes you have to borrow more than once in a single problem. As the example shows, you do this by borrowing from column to column. Be careful to keep track of what number belongs at the top of each column.

EXAMPLE:

```
Subtract:  935        Subtract:  8 12 15
         – 257                   9  3  5
                               – 2  5  7
                                 6  7  8
```

Ones column: You can't subtract 7 from 5. So, borrow 1 ten from the tens column. Change the 3 to 2 and write 15 in place of 5. Subtract 7 from 15.

```
     2 15
   9 3  5
 – 2 5  7
        8
```

Tens column: You can't subtract 5 from 2. Now borrow 1 hundred from the hundreds column. Change the 9 to 8 and write 12 in place of 2. Subtract 5 from 12.

```
   8 12 15
   9  3  5
 – 2  5  7
      7  8
```

Hundreds column: Subtract 2 from 8.

```
   8 12 15
   9  3  5
 – 2  5  7
   6  7  8
```

Answer: 678

Borrowing from the Tens and Hundreds Column

Subtract, and check each problem on scratch paper.

1.

654	845	637	587	320	762	555
– 96	– 79	– 38	– 198	– 267	– 175	– 367

Borrowing from One or More Columns: Mixed Practice

2.

26	31	63	46	237	416	142
– 9	– 8	– 27	– 38	– 65	– 87	– 74

3.	364 − 281	425 − 178	855 − 367	7,354 − 632	2,750 − 820	4,431 − 650
4.	3,475 − 796	5,036 − 847	3,486 − 908	6,475 − 3,887	12,346 − 7,209	34,076 − 19,558

Subtracting from Zeros

Subtraction problems often have zeros in the top number. Since you can't borrow from a zero, you must borrow from the next column. The following example shows how to borrow from the hundreds column when there is a zero in the tens column.

EXAMPLE: Subtract: 503 − 238

Solution:

```
       9
    4 10 13
    5  0  3
  − 2  3  8
    2  6  5
```

Step 1. Since you can't subtract 8 from 3, you must borrow. But you can't borrow from the zero. You borrow from the 5. Cross out the 5 and write a 4 above it. Add the borrowed 1 hundred to the tens column. This puts 10 tens in the tens column.

```
    4 10
    5  0  3
  − 2  3  8
```

Step 2. Now borrow from the 10 tens. Cross out the 10 and write a 9 above it. Add the borrowed 1 ten to the ones column. This puts 13 ones in the ones column.

```
       9
    4 10 13
    5  0  3
  − 2  3  8
```

Step 3. Subtract each column:
Ones column: 13 − 8 = 5
Tens column: 9 − 3 = 6
Hundreds column: 4 − 2 = 2

```
          9
       4 10 13
       5  0  3
     − 2  3  8
Answer: 2  6  5
```

Subtract. Check each problem on scratch paper.

1.	506 − 47	105 − 68	230 − 98	3,501 − 843	5,305 − 1,236	2,502 − 1,825
2.	4,090 − 638	7,050 − 745	3,010 − 193	8,070 − 674	5,040 − 2,733	

Subtracting from a Row of Zeros

In the following example, there is more than one zero in a row in the top number. To subtract, you borrow from the first nonzero digit to the left.

EXAMPLE: Subtract: $\begin{array}{r} 5{,}000 \\ -\,2{,}165 \\ \hline \end{array}$ Solution: $\begin{array}{r} \overset{4}{\not 5},\overset{\overset{9}{\not{10}}}{\not 0}\,\overset{\overset{9}{\not{10}}}{\not 0}\,\overset{10}{\not 0} \\ -\,2,1\,6\,5 \\ \hline 2,8\,3\,5 \end{array}$

Step 1. The first nonzero digit is 5. Cross out the 5 and write 4 above it. Change the first zero to 10. $\overset{4}{\not 5},\overset{10}{\not 0}\,0\,0$

Step 2. Cross out the 10 and write 9 above it. Change the next 0 to 10. $\overset{4}{\not 5},\overset{\overset{9}{\not{10}}}{\not 0}\,\overset{10}{\not 0}\,0$

Step 3. Cross out this 10 and write 9 above it. Change the last 0 to 10. Subtract each column.

$$\begin{array}{r} \overset{4}{\not 5},\overset{\overset{9}{\not{10}}}{\not 0}\,\overset{\overset{9}{\not{10}}}{\not 0}\,\overset{10}{\not 0} \\ -\,2,1\,6\,5 \\ \hline \textbf{Answer: } 2,8\,3\,5 \end{array}$$

NOTE: In this type of problem, all zeros in a row (except the 0 in the ones column) end up as nines.

1. $\begin{array}{r} 200 \\ -\,45 \\ \hline \end{array}$ $\begin{array}{r} 500 \\ -\,73 \\ \hline \end{array}$ $\begin{array}{r} 800 \\ -\,26 \\ \hline \end{array}$ $\begin{array}{r} 6{,}000 \\ -\,3{,}775 \\ \hline \end{array}$ $\begin{array}{r} 32{,}000 \\ -\,16{,}740 \\ \hline \end{array}$ $\begin{array}{r} 15{,}000 \\ -\,8{,}969 \\ \hline \end{array}$

Subtracting Numbers in a Row

When numbers are written in a row, rewrite them in a column before subtracting. The smaller number is placed directly below the larger number. Be sure to place the ones digits in a ones column, tens digits in a tens column, and so on. Remember to borrow when you cannot subtract otherwise.

EXAMPLE: Subtract: 1,507 − 435

Place 435 directly below 1,507 by first lining up the ones digits. Place the 5 below the 7. The tens and hundreds digits will then line up correctly.

Solution: $\begin{array}{r} 1{,}507 \\ -\,435 \\ \hline \mathbf{1{,}072} \end{array}$

Rewrite the following problems in a column and subtract.

1. 98 − 37 483 − 231 2,678 − 1,342

2. 364 − 89 3,486 − 798 506 − 357

3. 800 − 247 1,000 − 429 12,000 − 7,736

Borrowing with Dollars and Cents

Borrowing with dollars and cents is done the same way as borrowing with whole numbers. You borrow from one column to the next as if the decimal point weren't there. When you are done subtracting, be sure to bring down the decimal point.

EXAMPLE:	Subtract:	Solution:	Check:
	$14.00	[3, 10/9, 10] $1~~4~~.~~0~~ ~~0~~	[1 1] 3.27
	− 3.27	− 3.2 7	+ $10.73
		$10.7 3	**$14.00** ✓

Subtract, and check each answer on scratch paper.

1.	$3.45 − 1.28	$6.06 − 2.19	$12.64 − 9.39	$40.82 − 13.95	$153.47 − 74.80	$235.50 − 125.95
2.	$5.00 − 2.37	$8.00 − 4.58	$15.00 − 7.37	$52.00 − 23.83	$300.00 − 142.65	$500.00 − 389.99

3. $5.88 − 89¢ $1.50 − 79¢ $2.00 − 28¢ $5.00 − 63¢

Choosing an Arithmetic Operation

Some addition and subtraction problems contain helpful key words and some don't. Many of the problems contain more information than is needed. Clues are often obtained by drawing a picture or diagram. A drawing is especially helpful in problems where key words are not easy to identify. In the example, there is no single key word that correctly suggests adding.

EXAMPLE: Between noon and 7:00 P.M. on Tuesday, the temperature dropped by 26°. At 7:00 P.M., the temperature was 43° F. What had the temperature been at noon?

26° temperature decrease

← temperature at noon

← 43° F at 7:00

As the picture helps show, the noon temperature is *greater than* either of the two numbers given in the problem. Thus, to find the noon temperature, you add 26° and 43°. You do not subtract.

Add: 43° F
+ 26° F

Answer: 69° F

Drawing a diagram helps because it causes you to think carefully about the numbers in a problem. You must ask yourself, **"Is the number I'm trying to find smaller or larger than the other numbers in the problem?"** Answering this question is the key to solving all addition and subtraction problems.

In problems 1, 2, and 3, use the drawing to help you decide whether to add or to subtract. Then solve each problem and check your answer.

1. Becky Robinson borrowed $1,200 to buy new furniture. So far, she has paid back $850. Not counting any interest charges, how much does Becky still owe?

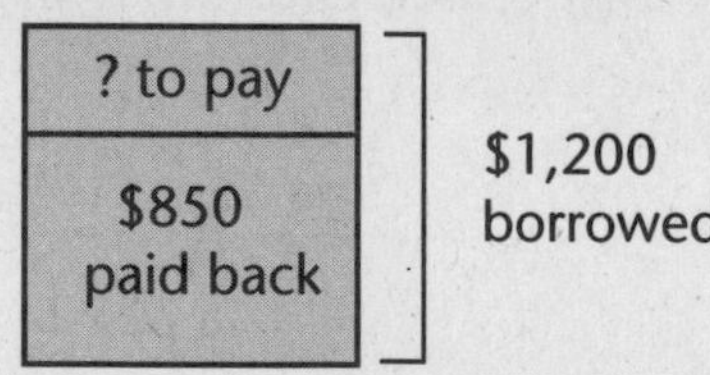

2. Between 8:00 A.M. and 11:00 A.M. on Friday, the temperature rose 28° F. What was the temperature at 11:00 if the temperature at 8:00 was 56° F?

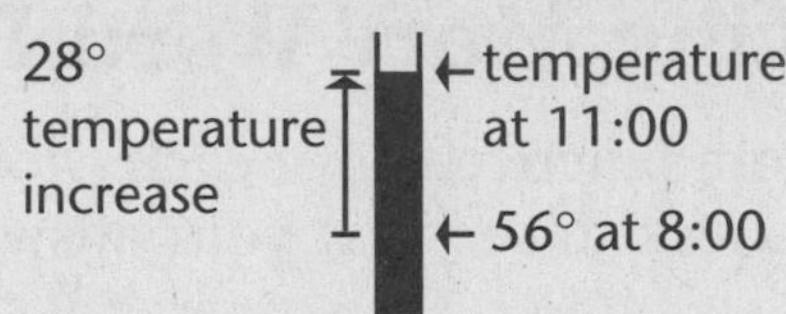

3. The distance between Brady and Dumont is 253 miles. If Yoshi has traveled 128 miles of this distance, what distance does she still have to drive?

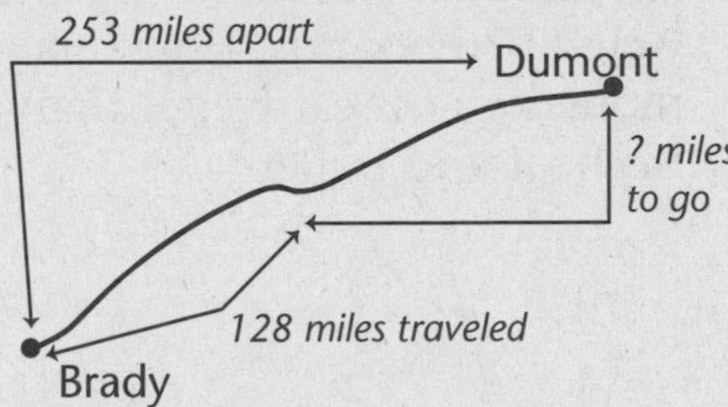

In problems 4, 5, and 6, complete each drawing by filling in the blank lines with numbers from the problems. Then use your completed drawing as a guide and solve each problem.

4. James Olsen paid $236 more in taxes in 1993 than he paid in 1992. If he paid $873 in taxes in 1992, how much did he pay in taxes in 1993?

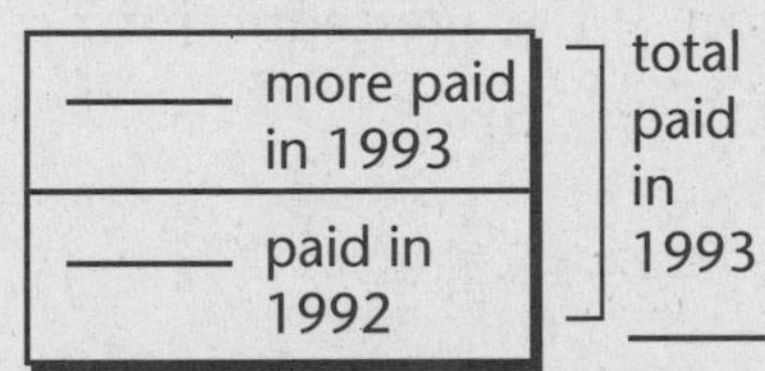

5. Between 7:00 A.M. and noon on Saturday, the temperature rose 34° F. What was the temperature at 7:00 if the noon temperature was 89° F?

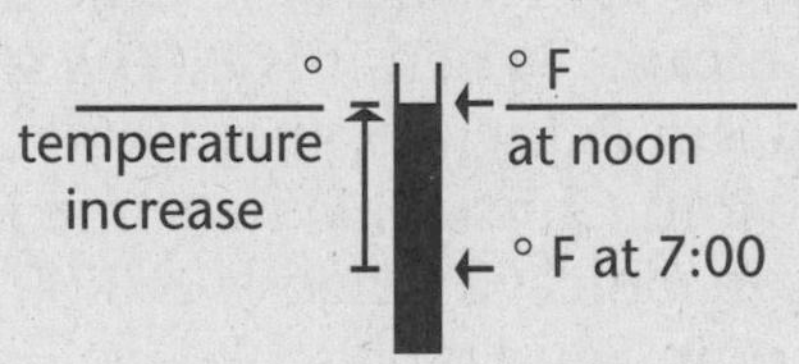

6. The distance between Olene and Glide is 47 miles. From Glide it is only 19 miles to the Double C Ranch. What is the distance between Olene and the ranch if you first go through Glide?

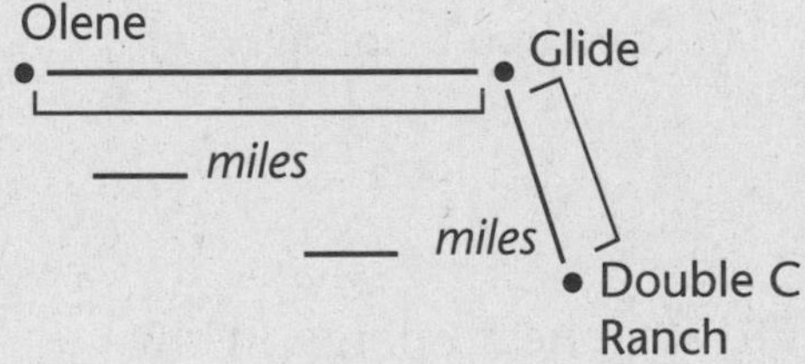

Solving More Word Problems

For more practice, solve each problem carefully and check your arithmetic. Also, check to see that your answer makes sense.

1. Jon's car weighs 3,145 pounds, and his boat and trailer together weigh 876 pounds. How much more does his car weigh than his boat and trailer?

2. After his wages were reduced by $125.75 per month in take-home pay, Robby's monthly check was $1,237.87. What was Robby's monthly check before the wage reduction?

3. The time in San Francisco is 2 hours earlier than the time in Chicago. When it is 8:00 A.M. in San Francisco, it is 10:00 A.M. in Chicago. What time is it in Chicago when it is 3:00 P.M. in San Francisco?

   8:00 A.M. ⟶ 10:00 A.M.
   3:00 P.M. ⟶ ?
   San Francisco   Chicago

4. To save heat energy in the home, it is recommended that thermostats be set no higher than 68 degrees Fahrenheit. How many degrees lower is this than the Jones family thermostat setting of 73 degrees?

5. If Sarah was born on August 6, 1915, in what year did she celebrate her 80th birthday?

6. A mile is the same as 1,760 yards. How many yards farther is a mile than a kilometer, which is about 1,100 yards?

7. Craig drove his car an average of 1,154 miles each month last year. During the first three months this year, he has driven 954 miles, 876 miles, and 1,105 miles. What number of miles has he put on his car so far this year?

8. When Royce and Bev went out to eat, they shared a pizza for $7.95, two salads for $2.98 each, and two soft drinks for $1.20 each. If the tax came to 48¢, what was the total price of their meal?

Word problems are often written as story passages followed by more than one question. Each question requires its own necessary information. Choose this information carefully as you answer each question below.

Questions 9 and 10 refer to the following passage.

> Frank was overweight and decided to go on a diet. Before starting the diet, Frank ate 3,225 calories of food each day. On doctor's orders, Frank reduced his food intake by 750 calories each day. In three months, Frank's weight decreased from 214 pounds to 196 pounds.

9. While on his diet, how many calories of food was Frank allowed each day?

   Information needed:

   Solution:

10. How many pounds did Frank lose during the three-month period?

    Information needed:

    Solution:

Subtraction Skills Review

Review your subtraction skills. Work each problem as carefully as you can and check your answers with the Answer Key. Correct any mistakes.

1.	$9 - 6$	$8 - 8$	$15 - 4$	$14 - 8$	$3 - 0 =$	$12 - 5 =$
2.	$37 - 14$	$46 - 30$	$28 - 7$	$674 - 54$	$483 - 182$	$3{,}448 - 1{,}215$
3.	$35 - 8$	$47 - 19$	$183 - 54$	$325 - 118$	$462 - 278$	$1{,}382 - 718$
4.	$460 - 168$	$705 - 39$	$3{,}047 - 828$	$3{,}050 - 439$	$5{,}030 - 1{,}547$	$9{,}000 - 2{,}583$

5. $5.40 − 1.30 $3.93 − 2.80 $9.46 − 4.39 $8.38 − 2.49 $6.80 − 4.63 $20.00 − 8.49

$5.40	$3.93	$9.46	$8.38	$6.80	$20.00
− 1.30	− 2.80	− 4.39	− 2.49	− 4.63	− 8.49

6. 18 − 9   36 − 8   29 − 14   146 − 27

7. 183 − 97   207 − 183   400 − 137   5,020 − 2,394

8. If Janice paid for an 84¢ hot dog with a five-dollar bill, how much change should she receive?

9. By air, Philadelphia is 738 miles from Chicago. Also by air, Philadelphia is 668 miles from Louisville. How much nearer is Philadelphia to Louisville than it is to Chicago? (Hint: Drawing a diagram might help.)

4 MULTIPLICATION SKILLS

Concepts in Multiplication

Multiplication is a shortcut that takes the place of repeated addition. Instead of adding a number several times, you multiply and get the answer in one step. Here is an example:

- Multiply to find the cost of 4 tires if each tire costs \$62.00.

Solved by multiplication	*Solved by addition*
\$ 62.00	\$ 62.00
× 4	62.00
\$248.00	62.00
	+ 62.00
	\$248.00

Multiplication is represented by the times sign (×). For example, six times four is written in symbols as 6 × 4.

You may see a multiplication problem written vertically or horizontally. The answer is called the ***product.***

Parts of a Multiplication Problem

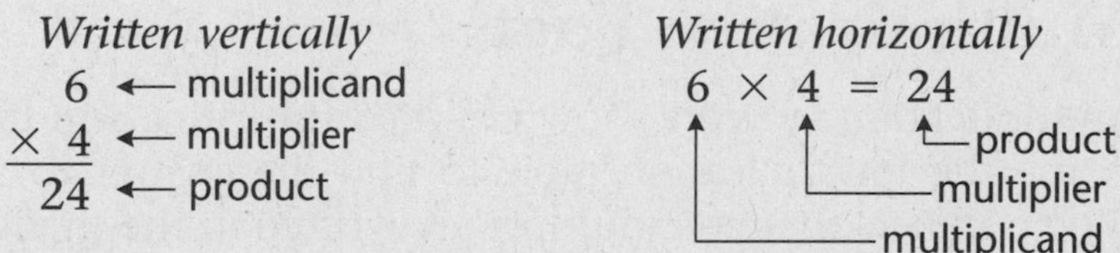

Changing the order of numbers being multiplied does not change the product.

6 × 4 = 24 *and* 4 × 6 = 24

The product of any number times 1 is the same number.

5 × 1 = 5 *and* 28 × 1 = 28

The product of any number times 0 is 0.

8 × 0 = 0 *and* 36 × 0 = 0

Answers to Chapter 4 exercises start on page 912.

Real life multiplication problems can be written with mathematical symbols.

a) thirty-seven **times** nineteen

$$\begin{array}{r}\$37 \\ \underline{\times\ 19}\ \text{people}\end{array}$$

b) one hundred nine **multiplied by** twelve

$$\begin{array}{r}109\ \text{cartons} \\ \underline{\times\ 12}\ \text{eggs}\end{array}$$

Solve each problem below as indicated.

1. $\begin{array}{r}15 \\ \underline{\times\ 1}\end{array}$ $\begin{array}{r}\$.09 \\ \underline{\times\ 1}\end{array}$ $\begin{array}{r}1 \\ \underline{\times\ 7}\end{array}$ $\begin{array}{r}1 \\ \underline{\times\ 8}\end{array}$ $\begin{array}{r}\$1.26 \\ \underline{\times\ \ \ 0}\end{array}$ $\begin{array}{r}0 \\ \underline{\times\ 7}\end{array}$

2. Which two of the following equals the product of 6×3?

$9 + 9 + 9$ $3 + 6$ 3×6 $6 + 6 + 6$

Write the phrases below in mathematical symbols. Attach labels where given. You do not need to do the multiplication.

3. five dollars and eighteen cents times six

4. four hundred miles multiplied by seven

Basic Multiplication Facts

The basic multiplication facts are shown in the **multiplication table** below.

You can use the multiplication table to find the answer to single-digit problems. The numbers that you multiply are written in the shaded row and column. It is a good idea to memorize this table if you don't already know it.

The table does not include 0. For problems involving 0, remember that the product of any number times 0 is 0.

The Multiplication Table

	1	2	3	4	5	6	7	8	9
1	1	2	3	4	5	6	7	8	9
2	2	4	6	8	10	12	14	16	18
3	3	6	9	12	15	18	21	24	27
4	4	8	12	16	20	24	28	32	36
5	5	10	15	20	25	30	35	40	45
6	6	12	18	24	30	36	42	48	54
7	7	14	21	28	35	42	49	56	63
8	8	16	24	32	40	48	56	64	72
9	9	18	27	36	45	54	63	72	81

EXAMPLE: Multiply 6×7:

Step 1. Find 6 in the shaded row across the top.

Step 2. Run your finger down the 6 column until you reach the row starting with a shaded 7.

The square at the intersection contains the answer.

Answer: 42

Multiply. Practice until you can do each problem with confidence.

1.	6×3	8×7	1×9	8×0	6×2	3×9	7×8	5×1
2.	7×0	3×2	7×5	3×8	6×5	0×3	9×8	6×9
3.	4×7	6×8	4×8	7×8	7×3	9×4	8×5	5×2
4.	2×2	4×5	8×4	3×7	7×9	9×8	8×3	3×5
5.	6×2	5×8	2×8	6×3	7×6	8×2	9×5	9×2
6.	5×6	3×9	1×9	2×5	7×2	8×6	4×3	4×4
7.	9×3	2×3	7×7	6×7	5×9	8×8	5×3	5×7
8.	9×2	6×4	3×4	9×7	1×6	7×4	4×9	6×6
9.	8×5	3×3	5×4	8×7	3×2	2×9	3×8	2×1

Multiplying by One Digit

After mastering the basic multiplication facts, you are ready to multiply larger numbers. To multiply by a one-digit number, multiply the top number one digit at a time. Multiply and write the answer from right to left. Make sure you put the product of the ones digit in the the ones column, the product of the tens digit in the tens column, etc.

EXAMPLE:

$$\begin{array}{r} 13\boxed{4} \\ \times \ \boxed{2} \\ \hline \boxed{8} \end{array} \qquad \begin{array}{r} 1\boxed{3}4 \\ \times \ \boxed{2} \\ \hline \boxed{6}8 \end{array} \qquad \begin{array}{r} \boxed{1}34 \\ \times \ \boxed{2} \\ \hline \boxed{2}68 \end{array}$$

multiply the ones digit by 2 | multiply the tens digit by 2 | multiply the hundreds digit by 2

Multiplying Two-Digit Numbers

1. $\begin{array}{r} 21 \\ \times\ 3 \\ \hline \end{array}$ $\begin{array}{r} 32 \\ \times\ 2 \\ \hline \end{array}$ $\begin{array}{r} 11 \\ \times\ 8 \\ \hline \end{array}$ $\begin{array}{r} 71 \\ \times\ 6 \\ \hline \end{array}$ $\begin{array}{r} 80 \\ \times\ 9 \\ \hline \end{array}$ $\begin{array}{r} 83 \\ \times\ 3 \\ \hline \end{array}$ $\begin{array}{r} 81 \\ \times\ 7 \\ \hline \end{array}$

Multiplying Three-Digit Numbers

2. $\begin{array}{r} 312 \\ \times\ 3 \\ \hline \end{array}$ $\begin{array}{r} 141 \\ \times\ 2 \\ \hline \end{array}$ $\begin{array}{r} 232 \\ \times\ 3 \\ \hline \end{array}$ $\begin{array}{r} 721 \\ \times\ 4 \\ \hline \end{array}$ $\begin{array}{r} 432 \\ \times\ 3 \\ \hline \end{array}$ $\begin{array}{r} 911 \\ \times\ 8 \\ \hline \end{array}$ $\begin{array}{r} 630 \\ \times\ 3 \\ \hline \end{array}$

Multiplying by Two Digits

When you multiply by a two-digit number, you multiply the top number by each digit of the bottom number:

- When you multiply by the ones digit, start your answer in the ones column.
- When you multiply by the tens digit, start your answer in the tens column.

The answer of each step of the multiplication process is called a ***partial product.*** The answer of the whole problem is computed by adding the partial products.

EXAMPLE: Multiply: $\begin{array}{r} 42 \\ \times\ 13 \\ \hline \end{array}$ Solution: $\begin{array}{r} 42 \\ \times\ 13 \\ \hline 126 \\ 42 \\ \hline 546 \end{array}$

partial products { 126, 42 ← Treat this blank space as a zero.

Step 1. Multiply 42 by the ones digit: $42 \times 3 = 126$
Write 126.

Step 2. Multiply 42 by the tens digit: $42 \times 1 = 42$
Be sure to write 42, the second partial product, in the tens and hundreds columns. <u>It does not start in the ones column.</u>

Step 3. Add the partial products.

Answer: **546**

Multiply.

32	24	31	40	41	421	512
× 12	× 22	× 11	× 21	× 37	× 43	× 32

Multiplying by Three Digits

When you multiply by a three-digit number, you get three partial products:

- Start the first partial product in the ones column.
- Start the second partial product in the tens column.
- Start the third partial product in the hundreds column.

EXAMPLE: Multiply: 312 × 231

Solution:

```
                         312
                       × 231
            ↗ 1st  →     312
partial products → 2nd →  936
            ↘ 3rd  →    624
                      72,072
```

Step 1. Multiply 312 by the ones digit: $312 \times 1 = 312$

Step 2. Multiply 312 by the tens digit: $312 \times 3 = 936$

Step 3. Multiply 312 by the hundreds digit: $312 \times 2 = 624$

Step 4. Add the partial products. Treat all blank spaces as zeros.

Answer: 72,072

Multiply.

324	211	321	423	3,202	3,112	4,120
× 112	× 121	× 211	× 212	× 212	× 312	× 211

Zeros in Multiplication

When multiplying by zero, you can use a shortcut. Write a 0 directly beneath the 0 in the problem. Then multiply by the next digit and start the new partial product in the next space to the left. Using the shortcut, you do not need to write a partial product that contains only 0s.

EXAMPLE 1: *Shortcut*

```
   21 2
 ×  3 0
 6,36 0
```

Write a 0 beneath the 0 above.

Long Way

```
   212
 ×  30
   000   ←—— This partial product contains only 0s.
  6 36
 6,360
```

The shortcut is to write the second partial product to the left of the zero. This shortcut reduces the number of partial products you write when you multiply by 0. Look at the next two examples carefully.

EXAMPLE 2: *Shortcut* *Long Way*

```
Shortcut        Long Way
    2 4 3          243
 ×    1 1 0     ×  110
    2 4 3 0        000
   24 3           2 43
   26,7 3 0      24 3
                26,730
```

EXAMPLE 3: *Shortcut* *Long Way*

```
Shortcut        Long Way
    3 2 1          321
 ×  1 0 2       ×  102
      6 4 2        642
   32 1 0          000
   32,7 4 2      32 1
                32,742
```

Multiply.

1.

```
   23       43       21       51      321      132      212
 × 20     × 10     × 20     × 40    × 210    × 320    × 210
```

2.

```
  243      421      612      502      212      413      421
× 200    × 400    × 300    × 200    × 103    × 203    × 301
```

Multiplying by 10, 100, and 1,000

The previous shortcut gives us three easy rules to use when either the top number or bottom number is 10, 100, or 1,000.

1. **To multiply a number by 10, attach a 0 to the right of the number.**

EXAMPLES:

```
(1)   35      (2)   278      (3)   10
    × 10          ×  10          × 17
     350          2,780           170
```

2. **To multiply a number by 100, attach two 0s to the right of the number.**

EXAMPLES:

(1)	(2)	(3)
463	3,647	100
× 100	× 100	× 89
46,300	364,700	8,900

3. **To multiply a number by 1,000, attach three 0s to the right of the number.**

EXAMPLES:

(1)	(2)	(3)
457	4,826	1,000
× 1,000	× 1,000	× 27
457,000	4,826,000	27,000

Multiply.

1.	67	634	352	100	10	100
	× 10	× 100	× 100	× 85	× 9	× 76
2.	100	10	1,000	1,000	578	4,586
	× 365	× 14	× 36	× 375	× 1,000	× 1,000

Multiplying Dollars and Cents

When multiplying dollars and cents, multiply as if the decimal point weren't there. Then place the decimal point and dollar sign in the answer to separate dollars from cents.

Remember, cents go in the first two places to the right of the decimal point.

EXAMPLE 1:

Multiply: $4.23 × 3 = $12.69

EXAMPLE 2:

Multiply: $5.31 × 10 = $53.10

Multiply. Remember to write the decimal point and dollar sign in each answer.

1.	$5.30	$4.20	$9.32	$21.11	$6.24	$7.20
	× 3	× 4	× 3	× 8	× 2	× 4
2.	$5.85	$7.36	$7.58	$6.50	$32.69	$7.49
	× 100	× 100	× 10	× 100	× 10	× 1,000

Multiplication Word Problems

A multiplication word problem requires you to multiply to determine an answer. Often, you are given a part of something and are asked to find the total. Or you may be given the price of a single object and then be asked to find the total price of several like objects. Here are two examples:

EXAMPLE 1: Loretta's car gets 21 miles to the gallon. How many miles *total* can she expect to drive on a full tank of 16 gallons?

$$\begin{array}{r} 21 \\ \times\ 16 \\ \hline 126 \\ 21 \\ \hline 336 \end{array}$$

Answer: 336 miles

EXAMPLE 2: If a quart of milk sells for 51¢, what is the price *of* 3 quarts?

$$\begin{array}{r} \$0.51 \\ \times\quad 3 \\ \hline \$1.53 \end{array}$$

Answer: $1.53

Multiplication word problems may also contain key words. In Example 1, the word *total* is a **multiplication key word.** In Example 2, the second word *of* is a multiplication key word.

Because multiplication is a shortcut for addition, it is not surprising that many addition key words are also multiplication key words.

Multiplication Key Words

altogether	times
in all	total
of	twice
multiply	whole
product	

Solve each multiplication problem below. Underline each multiplication key word that you can identify. Not all problems contain key words.

1. John's Men Store sold 21 shirts during a "Saturday Only Sale." If the store made a profit of $4 per shirt, what total profit did John's make on these shirts?

2. Sheila puts $42 a month in a savings account for her infant son. At this rate, how much can she save in all during 1 year's time? (1 year = 12 months)

3. After the weekend sale, a quart of oil will cost twice as much as it does today. What is the regular price if today's sale price is 63¢?

4. June works 40 hours a week as a painter. If she also works an average of 12 overtime hours each week, how many overtime hours does she average each 4-week pay period?

Multiplying and Carrying

When the product of two digits is 10 or more, you must **carry**. As in addition, you place the carried digit at the top of the next column to the left. Then multiply and add the carried digit to the product. The example below shows how to multiply and carry to the tens column.

EXAMPLE: Multiply: $\begin{array}{r} 45 \\ \times\ 7 \\ \hline \end{array}$ Solution: $\begin{array}{r} 45 \\ \times\ 7 \\ \hline 315 \end{array}$

Step 1. Multiply the ones digit: $7 \times 5 = 35$
Think of 35 as 3 tens and 5 ones.
Place the 5 under the ones column.

Step 2. Carry the 3 tens to the top of the tens column.

Step 3. Multiply the tens digit: $7 \times 4 = 28$
Add the carried 3 to 28: $28 + 3 = 31$
Write 31 under the tens and hundreds columns.

$\begin{array}{r} {\scriptstyle 3} \\ 45 \\ \times\ 7 \\ \hline 315 \end{array}$

Carry 3 tens to top of tens column.

Place 5 under ones column.

Remember: Multiply the tens digit before adding the carried digit.

Carrying to the Tens Column

Multiply.

1. $\begin{array}{r} 17 \\ \times\ 2 \\ \hline \end{array}$ $\begin{array}{r} 37 \\ \times\ 6 \\ \hline \end{array}$ $\begin{array}{r} 42 \\ \times\ 5 \\ \hline \end{array}$ $\begin{array}{r} 129 \\ \times\ 3 \\ \hline \end{array}$ $\begin{array}{r} 617 \\ \times\ 4 \\ \hline \end{array}$ $\begin{array}{r} 428 \\ \times\ 3 \\ \hline \end{array}$ $\begin{array}{r} 719 \\ \times\ 2 \\ \hline \end{array}$

Being Careful with Zeros

Multiplying numbers that have one or more zeros can be tricky. But you won't have any trouble if you remember these two rules:

- **The product of any number times 0 is 0.**
- **Multiply the zero first, then add the carried digit.**

EXAMPLE: $\begin{array}{r} \boxed{2}\ \ \\ 507 \\ \times\ \ 3 \\ \hline 1{,}521 \end{array}$

Step 1. $3 \times 7 = 21$ Write the 1, carry the 2.

Step 2. $3 \times 0 = 0$ Add the carried 2 to the 0.
$0 + 2 = 2$
Write the 2 in the tens place.

Step 3. $3 \times 5 = 15$ Write the 15.

2. $\begin{array}{r} 107 \\ \times\ 5 \\ \hline \end{array}$ $\begin{array}{r} 206 \\ \times\ 4 \\ \hline \end{array}$ $\begin{array}{r} 307 \\ \times\ 3 \\ \hline \end{array}$ $\begin{array}{r} 706 \\ \times\ 7 \\ \hline \end{array}$ $\begin{array}{r} 803 \\ \times\ 9 \\ \hline \end{array}$ $\begin{array}{r} 609 \\ \times\ 6 \\ \hline \end{array}$

Carrying to the Hundreds Column

When the product of the tens digit is more than 10, you must carry to the hundreds column.

EXAMPLE:
```
 [1]
 241
× 4
 964
```

3.

482	571	620	461	580	281
× 4	× 2	× 9	× 7	× 6	× 5

Carrying to the Thousands Column

When the product of the hundreds digit is more than 10, you must carry to the thousands column.

EXAMPLE:
```
  [2]
1,[5]1 0
×     [5]
7,[5]5 0
```

4.

5,721	4,632	8,210	7,723	9,610	7,924
× 4	× 3	× 8	× 3	× 7	× 2

Carrying to Two or More Columns

The following example shows how to carry to two or more columns.

EXAMPLE: Multiply: 256 × 7

Solution:
```
  3 4
  256
×   7
1,792
```

Step 1. Multiply the ones digit: $7 \times 6 = 42$
Write the 2 under the ones column.
Carry the 4 to the tens column.

```
   [4]
 2 5[6]
×   [7]
    [2]
```

Step 2. Multiply the tens digit: $7 \times 5 = 35$
Add the carried 4: $35 + 4 = 39$
Write 9 under the tens column.
Carry the 3 to the hundreds column.

```
[3] 4
 2[5]6
×  [7]
 17[9]2
```

Step 3. Multiply the hundreds digit: $7 \times 2 = 14$
Add the carried 3: $14 + 3 = 17$
Write 17 under the hundreds and thousands columns.

5.

167	148	262	376	192	173
× 6	× 5	× 7	× 2	× 5	× 6

6.

1,245	2,327	1,265	2,477	3,586	1,284
× 7	× 4	× 8	× 3	× 2	× 8

Carrying: Mixed Practice

7.	2,476	486	306	57	258	3,587
	× 7	× 9	× 7	× 2	× 8	× 6

Carrying with Larger Numbers

When multiplying larger numbers, carrying may be needed to compute each partial product. The example below shows how to do this.

EXAMPLE: Multiply: 247 × 38

Solution:

```
  247
×  38
 1976
 741
 9,386
```

Step 1. Multiply 247 by 8: (3 and 5 are the carried digits)

```
  3 5
  2 4 7
×   3 8
1 9 7 6
```

NOTE: Each partial product has its own carried digits. It is a good idea to write carried digits lightly in pencil.

Step 2. Multiply 247 by 3: (1 and 2 are the carried digits)

```
   1 2
   2 4 7
 ×   3 8
 1 9 7 6
 7 4 1
```

Step 3. Add the partial products.

Answer: **9,386**

Multiply.

1.	74	58	84	27	96	45
	× 28	× 33	× 67	× 19	× 42	× 36
2.	683	365	565	295	730	625
	× 46	× 27	× 67	× 38	× 29	× 35
3.	407	518	607	730	364	730
	× 285	× 341	× 445	× 378	× 470	× 307

4.

$$\begin{array}{r} 482 \\ \times\ 407 \\ \hline \end{array} \quad \begin{array}{r} 376 \\ \times\ 317 \\ \hline \end{array} \quad \begin{array}{r} 947 \\ \times\ 705 \\ \hline \end{array} \quad \begin{array}{r} 1{,}630 \\ \times\ 706 \\ \hline \end{array} \quad \begin{array}{r} 1{,}846 \\ \times\ 354 \\ \hline \end{array} \quad \begin{array}{r} 3{,}374 \\ \times\ 836 \\ \hline \end{array}$$

Multiplying Numbers in a Row

When numbers are written in a row, rewrite them in columns. To simplify the multiplication, write the larger number as the top number.

EXAMPLE: Multiply: 31×146

With larger number on top

$$\begin{array}{r} 146 \\ \times\ 31 \\ \hline 146 \\ 4\ 38 \\ \hline 4{,}526 \end{array}$$

Write the following problems in columns and multiply. Remember, on some problems you can use a shortcut.

1. 100×766 $\quad$ $1{,}721 \times 240$ $\quad$ 347×583

2. 154×10 $\quad$ 23×589 $\quad$ $400 \times 1{,}663$

Carrying with Dollars and Cents

To carry with dollars and cents, you carry from one column to the next as if the decimal point weren't there.

EXAMPLE 1: Multiply:

$$\begin{array}{r} \scriptstyle 1 \\ \$6.45 \\ \times\ 12 \\ \hline 12\ 90 \\ 64\ 5 \\ \hline \$77.40 \end{array}$$

EXAMPLE 2: Multiply 87¢ by 26.

$$\begin{array}{r} \scriptstyle 1 \\ \scriptstyle 4 \\ \$0.87 \\ \times\ 26 \\ \hline 5\ 22 \\ 17\ 4 \\ \hline \$22.62 \end{array}$$

Multiply.

1. $5.87 × 8 $4.76 × 4 $2.59 × 7 $2.49 × 25 $6.08 × 35 $7.40 × 20

2. $25.50 × 125 $15.30 × 165 $48.35 × 250 $15.69 × 380 $54.80 × 365

3. 73¢ times 12 68¢ times 24 92¢ times 32

Estimating Answers

An estimate is a number that is "about equal" or "close to" the exact answer. Since it is faster to estimate than it is to solve for an exact answer, estimation is a useful tool. It is also a good way to check if an answer is likely to be correct.

To estimate an answer, replace the numbers in the problem with round numbers that are easy to work with. Then solve the problem using the round numbers.

EXAMPLE: Estimate the answer to the addition problem at right.

```
  692
  403
+ 289
```

Round each number to the nearest hundred.
692 rounds to 700
403 rounds to 400
289 rounds to 300

Estimated Answer	Exact Answer
700	692
400	403
+ 300	+ 289
1,400	1,384

Answer: 1,400 is an estimated answer.

Estimate the answer to each problem below. Replace the numbers in the problems with numbers rounded to the hundreds place, except when the numbers can only be rounded to the tens place. Then estimate the answers by using the rounded numbers.

1. 79 + 52 → *80 + 50 = 130*

2. 187 − 98

3. 2,792 + 1,311 + 978

4. 512 × 203

5. $\begin{array}{r} 34{,}893 \\ -\ 12{,}796 \\ \hline \end{array}$

6. $\begin{array}{r} 26{,}923 \\ 17{,}090 \\ +\ 8{,}914 \\ \hline \end{array}$

7. $\begin{array}{r} 516 \\ \times\ 38 \\ \hline \end{array}$

8. $\begin{array}{r} 711 \\ \times\ 89 \\ \hline \end{array}$

9. $\begin{array}{r} 288 \\ 237 \\ +\ 94 \\ \hline \end{array}$

10. $\begin{array}{r} 3{,}248 \\ 2{,}196 \\ +\ 356 \\ \hline \end{array}$

11. $\begin{array}{r} 501 \\ -\ 297 \\ \hline \end{array}$

12. $\begin{array}{r} 179 \\ \times\ 41 \\ \hline \end{array}$

13. $\begin{array}{r} 4{,}597 \\ 2{,}203 \\ +\ 1{,}994 \\ \hline \end{array}$

14. $\begin{array}{r} 89 \\ -\ 42 \\ \hline \end{array}$

15. $\begin{array}{r} 3{,}401 \\ -\ 2{,}599 \\ \hline \end{array}$

16. $\begin{array}{r} 3{,}492 \\ \times\ 103 \\ \hline \end{array}$

Using Estimation in Word Problems

Estimation is a very useful tool for many word problems. Used carefully, estimation enables you to quickly choose an operation and check solutions.

To estimate an answer to a word problem, substitute a round number for one or more numbers that appear in the problem. Then, solve the problem using the round numbers.

EXAMPLE: Helen bought 9 cases of oil on sale for \$11.95 per case. How much did she pay for all 9 cases?

To estimate the answer, substitute \$12 for \$11.95 and multiply:

\$12 × 9 = \$108

Estimated answer: \$108

NOTE: We also could have substituted 10 for 9 and gotten an answer of \$120. However, \$108 is closer to the exact answer, \$107.55.

A good rule to follow when using estimation is this: **Substitute only enough to make an answer easy to compute.** You don't need to substitute a round number for *every* number that appears in a problem.

Following are addition, subtraction, and multiplication problems. In each problem, substitute round numbers as indicated and estimate the answer. Then, using this number as a clue, choose the correct answer from the choices given.

1. Georgia paid for a $13.19 purchase with a twenty-dollar bill. How much change should she get back?

   a) $3.81
   b) $6.81
   c) $13.81

   Substitute $13 for $13.19.

   Estimated answer: *$20 − $13 = $7*

   Exact answer: *b) $6.81*

2. During his regular shift Thursday, Al carried three loads of gravel. The first load weighed 3,119 pounds; the second, 4,089 pounds; and the third, 3,912 pounds. How many total pounds of gravel did Al carry on Thursday?

   a) 11,120
   b) 19,120
   c) 21,120

   Substitute 3,000 for 3,119, 4,000 for 4,089, and 4,000 for 3,912.

   Estimated answer:

   Exact answer:

3. At a price of $14.89 each, what will 21 shirts cost?

   a) $148.29
   b) $249.19
   c) $312.69

   Substitute $15 for $14.89 and 20 for 21.

   Estimated answer:

   Exact answer:

4. Starting with a 71-inch-long board, Bobby cut off a 42-inch piece. What was the length of the piece that remained?

   a) 29 inches
   b) 34 inches
   c) 39 inches

   Substitute 70 for 71 and 40 for 42.

   Estimated answer:

   Exact answer:

Solving Word Problems

Following are addition, subtraction, and multiplication problems for you to solve. In each, estimate the answer and then solve the problem exactly. Write the estimate on the first line and the exact answer on the second line. The first problem is completed as an example.

1. What is the total cost of 19 gallons of gas at a price of $1.29 per gallon?

   Estimate: *$26.00* *Exact:* *$24.51*

estimate	*exact*
$1.30	*$1.29*
× 20	*× 19*
$26.00	*1161*
	129
	$24.51

2. On Monday Alice drove 349 miles. On Tuesday she drove 497 miles. How far did Alice drive on these two days?

   Estimate: ________ *Exact:* ________

3. Norma's car gets 29 miles to the gallon while driving in the city. How many miles of city driving can she expect to do on a full tank of 15 gallons?

Estimate: __________ *Exact:* __________

4. How many calories are in the following meal?

   one hamburger: 403 calories
   one cola drink: 149 calories
   french fries: 296 calories

Estimate: __________ *Exact:* __________

5. At a variety sale, Jack bought a lamp for $12.89, a chair for $3.49, and a box of magazines for $9.95. What total price did he pay for the lamp and chair?

Estimate: __________ *Exact:* __________

6. Mark earns $5.75 per hour as a sales clerk. He is also paid a commission of $6.98 for each suit he sells. How much did Mark earn in June from sales commissions for selling 51 suits?

Estimate: __________ *Exact:* __________

7. At 9:00 A.M. Mary Ann was 197 miles from Chicago. By 11:00 A.M. she had driven 98 miles closer. At that time, how far was she still from Chicago?

Estimate: __________ *Exact:* __________

8. From a 72-inch board, Shelley cut three pieces. These pieces measure 19 inches, 11 inches, and 29 inches. What is the total length of these three smaller boards?

Estimate: __________ *Exact:* __________

Multiplication Skills Review

Review your multiplication skills. Work each problem carefully and check your answers with the Answer Key. Correct any mistakes.

1.	4 × 2	7 × 1	9 × 6	8 × 1	5 × 8	6 × 5 =
2.	32 × 3	60 × 7	143 × 2	34 × 12	231 × 23	423 × 210
3.	15 × 6	46 × 8	423 × 4	309 × 6	381 × 7	384 × 7
4.	47 × 24	86 × 47	50 × 42	482 × 27	705 × 94	375 × 284
5.	$5.60 × 6	$20.14 × 2	$45.49 × 100	$4.58 × 9	$2.48 × 17	$12.40 × 34

6. 163 × 24   54 × 1,000   58 × 137   271 × 152

7. Norma borrowed $5,000 from her credit union to buy a used car. To get the loan, she agreed to pay the credit union $134.14 each month for 48 straight months. What total amount of money will she pay the credit union over the 48-month period?

For problems 8 and 9, write the estimate on the first line and the exact answer on the second line.

8. What is the cost of 19 gallons of gasoline at a price of $1.22 per gallon?

__________ __________

9. If Fran's car gets 41 miles to the gallon, how many miles can she expect to drive on 19 gallons?

__________ __________

5 Division Skills

Concepts in Division

Division splits one amount into equal parts, or finds how many times one number will go into another number. In word problems, you often use division to find a part when you are given a total.

In symbols, division is represented either by the division bracket ($\overline{)\ \ }$) or by the division sign (÷). The number being divided is called the ***dividend***. The number you divide by is called the ***divisor***. The answer is called the ***quotient***.

Parts of a Division Problem

Written with a division bracket	*Written with a division sign*
$4\overline{)36}$ = 9 ← quotient; divisor → 4; dividend → 36	36 ÷ 4 = 9 ← quotient; 36 → dividend; 4 → divisor

Changing the order of divisor and dividend changes the value of the answer.

$2\overline{)8}$ is *not* the same as $8\overline{)2}$

Zero divided by any other number equals zero. $5\overline{)0}$ = 0 $\qquad 0 \div 8 = 0$

***Never* divide by 0. Division by 0 has no meaning.**

Identify the divisor, dividend, and quotient of each solved problem below.

1. $9\overline{)72}$ = 8
   divisor __________
   dividend __________
   quotient __________

2. 14 ÷ 7 = 2
   divisor __________
   dividend __________
   quotient __________

3. 24 divided by 4 is 6.
   divisor __________
   dividend __________
   quotient __________

4. 5 divided into 40 is 8.
   divisor __________
   dividend __________
   quotient __________

Answers to Chapter 5 exercises start on page 914.

Use a division bracket to write each phrase below as a math problem. Remember that the number being divided up goes *inside* the bracket. Attach labels where given. You do not need to solve the problems.

5. How many two-hour segments are there in sixteen hours?

6. What is twenty-four dollars divided into six equal parts?

7. How many times does 7 go into 42?

8. Find the quotient of twenty-five divided by five.

Basic Division Facts

Here are the basic division facts you'll use in division problems. These facts come from the multiplication table. To divide is really to "undo" multiplication. Look at these examples:

To solve:	*You think:*	*In words:*	*Answer:*
$8\overline{)24}$	8 × ___ = 24	8 times <u>what number</u> equals 24?	3
56 ÷ 7	7 × ___ = 56	7 times <u>what number</u> equals 56?	8

Think about multiplication facts as you divide each problem below. Write both the division answer and the multiplication facts below.

1.	$8\overline{)56}$ (8 × ___ = 56)	$2\overline{)4}$ (2 × ___ = 4)	$9\overline{)36}$ (9 × ___ = 36)
2.	$8\overline{)72}$ (8 × ___ = 72)	$4\overline{)12}$ (4 × ___ = 12)	$5\overline{)20}$ (5 × ___ = 20)
3.	54 ÷ 9 = (9 × ___ = 54)	18 ÷ 6 = (6 × ___ = 18)	81 ÷ 9 = (9 × ___ = 81)

Divide as indicated. Write down multiplication facts if you find it helpful.

4.	$2\overline{)10}$	$3\overline{)21}$	$7\overline{)49}$	$8\overline{)24}$	$2\overline{)18}$
5.	$9\overline{)81}$	$4\overline{)16}$	$3\overline{)24}$	$9\overline{)45}$	$5\overline{)10}$

6. $63 \div 7 =$ $48 \div 6 =$ $20 \div 4 =$ $64 \div 8 =$

Write each sentence in symbols and then solve. When given, be sure to include a label as part of the answer.

7. What is forty-five dollars divided by nine? How many times does 8 go into 32? Split 72 coins into 8 equal portions.

8. How many fives are in twenty? What is 56 divided by 8? What is twelve hours divided into four equal parts?

Dividing by One Digit

Now you are ready to divide larger numbers. To divide by a one-digit number, divide the dividend one digit at a time. Write your answer from left to right.

To *check* a division problem, multiply the answer by the divisor. The product should equal the dividend.

EXAMPLE: Divide: $2\overline{)68}$ with 34 above. Check: 34 (answer) × 2 (divisor) = 68 ✓

Divide 2 into 6: $6 \div 2 = 3$ Write 3 above the 6. ($2\overline{)68}$, 3)

Divide 2 into 8: $8 \div 2 = 4$ Write 4 above the 8. ($2\overline{)68}$, 34)

Answer: 34

Divide. Remember to work from left to right. Check each answer on scratch paper.

1. $4\overline{)84}$ $3\overline{)39}$ $2\overline{)48}$ $4\overline{)48}$ $2\overline{)22}$ $3\overline{)63}$ $2\overline{)28}$

2. $2\overline{)224}$ $4\overline{)848}$ $3\overline{)663}$ $3\overline{)969}$ $2\overline{)842}$ $5\overline{)555}$

3. $4\overline{)8,448}$ $2\overline{)4,824}$ $3\overline{)9,639}$ $2\overline{)62,484}$ $3\overline{)96,693}$ $4\overline{)84,488}$

Dividing into Zero

In many division problems the dividend contains one or more zeros. When you divide into zero, you get zero as an answer. Because the zero is part of a number, you must write 0 as part of the answer.

Divide. Check each answer on scratch paper. The first one in each row is given as an example.

Zeros on the End

1. $\begin{array}{r}20\\3\overline{)60}\end{array}$ $2\overline{)40}$ $4\overline{)80}$ $2\overline{)640}$ $3\overline{)960}$ $2\overline{)820}$

Zeros in the Middle

2. $\begin{array}{r}201\\4\overline{)804}\end{array}$ $2\overline{)608}$ $3\overline{)906}$ $5\overline{)5{,}005}$ $3\overline{)9{,}006}$ $4\overline{)4{,}008}$

Dividing into a Smaller Digit

In some problems you can't divide into the first digit of a number. It is smaller than the divisor! In this case, you divide into the first two digits.

EXAMPLE: Divide: $\begin{array}{r}52\\4\overline{)208}\end{array}$ Check: $\begin{array}{r}52\\\underline{\times\ 4}\\208\end{array}$ ✓

You can't divide 4 into 2.
Divide 4 into 20: 20 ÷ 4 = 5
Write 5 above the 0.

$\begin{array}{r}5\\4\overline{)208}\end{array}$

Divide 4 into 8: 8 ÷ 4 = 2
Write 2 above the 8.

$\begin{array}{r}52\\4\overline{)208}\end{array}$

Answer: 52

Divide. Check each answer on scratch paper.

1. $5\overline{)405}$ $6\overline{)306}$ $2\overline{)108}$ $5\overline{)205}$ $4\overline{)2{,}048}$ $5\overline{)1{,}055}$

2. $5\overline{)100}$ $3\overline{)300}$ $4\overline{)804}$ $3\overline{)2{,}706}$ $2\overline{)1{,}060}$ $4\overline{)2{,}008}$

Using Zero as a Place Holder

In many problems, it is the second or third digit that is smaller than the divisor. In these problems, you place a 0 in the answer to hold a place. Then you divide into the next two digits.

EXAMPLE: Divide: $\begin{array}{r}206\\3\overline{)618}\end{array}$ Check: $\begin{array}{r}206\\\times\ 3\\\hline 618\end{array}$ ✓

Step 1. Divide 3 into 6: $6 \div 3 = 2$ $\begin{array}{r}2\\3\overline{)618}\end{array}$
Write 2 above the 6.

Step 2. You can't divide 3 into 1. $\begin{array}{r}20\\3\overline{)618}\end{array}$
Write 0 above the 1.

Step 3. Divide 3 into 18: $\begin{array}{r}206\\3\overline{)618}\end{array}$
$18 \div 3 = 6$
Write 6 above the 8.

Answer: 206

Divide and check your answers.

1. $3\overline{)927}$ $5\overline{)510}$ $6\overline{)636}$ $4\overline{)8,416}$ $2\overline{)2,416}$ $7\overline{)7,728}$

Mixed Practice

2. $6\overline{)240}$ $7\overline{)714}$ $5\overline{)255}$ $8\overline{)640}$ $3\overline{)906}$ $4\overline{)820}$

3. $3\overline{)6,039}$ $4\overline{)8,040}$ $7\overline{)1,407}$ $6\overline{)3,600}$ $2\overline{)1,860}$ $5\overline{)2,505}$

Remainders in Division

A **remainder** is a number that is left over. For example, if you divide 13 compact discs among 4 people, each person gets 3 CDs. Since 4×3 is 12, one CD is left over. Dividing 13 by 4 gives an answer of 3 with a remainder of 1.

Remainders are common in division. You get a remainder each time a number does not divide evenly. The letter *r* is used to stand for *remainder*. In the example above, we would write $13 \div 4 = 3$ r 1.

To check a division problem that has a remainder, *multiply* and then *add* the remainder.

EXAMPLE: Divide:

```
  2 r 3
5)13
 -10
   3
```

Check: Multiply then Add

```
  2        10
× 5      +  3
 10        13 ✓
```

Step 1. 5 does not divide evenly into 13. But 5 does divide evenly into 10. This is as close as we can get to 13.

```
   2
5)13
```

$10 \div 5 = 2$

Write 2 above the 3.

Step 2. Multiply: $2 \times 5 = 10$
Write 10 beneath 13. Subtract: $13 - 10 = 3$

```
   2
5)13
 -10
   3
```

Step 3. Write the remainder 3 as *r 3* next to the 2.

Answer: 2 r 3

Divide. Check each answer.

1. 2)5   4)9   6)8   5)17   8)58   9)62

To solve a division problem correctly, remember these two important rules:

```
  4 r 3
6)27
 -24
   3
```

- The product of the whole number part of the answer *times* the divisor should always be smaller than the dividend.
- The remainder should always be smaller than the divisor.

Cross out each problem below that is solved incorrectly. Then, in the space below, correct each problem that you crossed out.

2.

```
    8        9 r 2      7 r 9      8 r 8       7
10)78      5)47       6)51       8)72       7)49
 - 80       -45        -42        -64        -49
              2          9          8          0
```

Introducing Long Division

Long division is a four-step process that you use for most division problems. Long division is used when you have a remainder before you finish dividing all of the digits.

EXAMPLE: Divide: $4\overline{)92}$

Step 1	*Step 2*	*Step 3*	*Step 4*
$\begin{array}{r} \boxed{2} \\ 4\overline{)\boxed{9}2} \end{array}$	$\begin{array}{r} 2 \\ 4\overline{)92} \\ \boxed{8} \end{array}$	$\begin{array}{r} 2 \\ 4\overline{)92} \\ \boxed{\begin{array}{r} -\underline{8} \\ 1 \end{array}} \end{array}$	$\begin{array}{r} 2 \\ 4\overline{)92} \\ -\underline{8} \\ \boxed{12} \end{array}$

Step 1. Divide 4 into 9. Write 2 over the 9.

Step 2. Multiply: $2 \times 4 = 8$. Write 8 under the 9.

Step 3. Subtract: $9 - 8 = 1$. Write the remainder 1 under the 8.

Step 4. Bring down the 2 and place it next to the remainder 1.

Now repeat the four-step process. Start by dividing 4 into 12.

$$\begin{array}{r} 2\boxed{3} \\ 4\overline{)9\;2} \\ -\underline{8} \\ \boxed{12} \\ -\underline{12} \\ \boxed{0} \end{array}$$

Step 1. Divide 4 into 12. Write the 3 over the 2.

Step 2. Multiply: $3 \times 4 = 12$. Write 12 under the 12.

Step 3. Subtract: $12 - 12 = 0$. Write 0 under the 12.

Step 4. There is no other digit to bring down, and there is no remainder. The problem is done.

Answer: 23

Use long division to divide each problem below. Check each answer on scratch paper.

1. $2\overline{)36}$ $4\overline{)60}$ $6\overline{)78}$ $3\overline{)51}$ $8\overline{)96}$ $5\overline{)75}$

2. $5\overline{)425}$ $7\overline{)105}$ $9\overline{)198}$ $3\overline{)207}$ $4\overline{)300}$ $8\overline{)360}$

Answers with Remainders

As the example at right shows, many problems solved by long division also have a remainder as part of the answer. When you have "brought down" all of the numbers and have finished the division, you may still have a remainder. Solve and check your work.

EXAMPLE:

```
   85 r 3
4)343
 - 32
    23
  - 20
     3
```

3. 5)62 7)89 8)95 6)523 3)137 4)339

Dividing Dollars and Cents

Divide dollars and cents by a whole number as if the decimal point weren't there. Then place the decimal point and dollar sign in the answer. Place the decimal point directly above its place in the dividend.

EXAMPLE 1:

Divide: 6)$4.14

Step 1. Use long division to divide the numbers.

```
     69
6)$4.14
  - 3 6
     54
   - 54
      0
```

Step 2. Place the decimal point and dollar sign in the answer.

```
  $0.69
6)$4.14
```

Answer: $0.69

EXAMPLE 2: What is the quotient of $0.72 divided by 9?

Step 1. Divide:

```
       8
9)$0.72
   - 72
       0
```

Step 2. Place the dollar sign and decimal point in the answer.
Place the decimal point directly above its position in the dividend.
Put a 0 between the decimal point and the 8.

```
  $0.08
9)$0.72
```

Answer: $0.08

Divide.

1. 4)$1.52 7)$2.94 3)$0.24 6)$0.60 8)$0.64 5)$0.45

Use a dollar sign and decimal point to write each answer below.

2. What is the quotient of $7.56 divided by 7? Divide $4.23 by 9. What amount do you get by dividing $0.32 by 8?

Division Word Problems

A division word problem requires you to divide to determine an answer. Often, you are given a quantity and asked to find the size of a part. In other problems, you are given the price of several objects and asked to find the price of a single one. Here are two examples:

EXAMPLE 1: On his trip to Oak Grove, Charlie drove 276 miles in 6 hours. On the *average*, how many miles did he drive *every* hour?

Answer: 46 miles

$$\begin{array}{r} 46 \\ 6\overline{)276} \\ -\underline{24} \\ 36 \\ -\underline{36} \\ 0 \end{array}$$

EXAMPLE 2: If yogurt is on sale at "Four for $1.84," how much does *each* container cost?

Answer: $0.46

$$\begin{array}{r} \$0.46 \\ 4\overline{)\$1.84} \\ -\underline{1\ 6} \\ 24 \\ -\underline{24} \\ 0 \end{array}$$

Division word problems also often contain key words in their questions. In Example 1, the words *average* and *every* are **division key words**. In Example 2, the word *each* is a division key word.

You can usually tell a division key word from a multiplication key word:

- A division key word refers to a single item. In fact, the most common division key words are *each* and *every*. Both of these words mean *one* or *single*.
- Many division key words actually mean "divide." Example words are *split, share,* and *average*.

Following are division key words. Look for examples of the words in the chart as you work the next set of problems.

Division Key Words	
average	every
cut	one
divide(d)	share(d)
each	single
equal pieces	split

Solve each division problem below. Underline each division key word you can find. Each word problem may contain one or more key words.

1. Six people won a lottery that had a value of $4,800,600. If they share the prize equally, what is each person's share?

2. During one 8-hour shift, Amy's Fast Food sold 176 hamburgers. On the average, how many hamburgers did Amy's sell during each hour?

3. If a large pizza is divided into 16 equal slices, how many pieces will each of 4 people get?

4. Louise wants to make 3 shelves out of a board that measures 147 inches long. About how long should she make each piece to get 3 equal pieces?

There are two special types of division word problems that often cause confusion. In the first type, you are asked to find a whole number answer. However, when you divide, your answer contains a remainder. Here is an example:

EXAMPLE 3: John is going to make 3-foot-long shelves out of a 20-foot-long board. How many shelves can he make?

```
   6 r 2
3)20
 -18
   2
```

As shown at right, $20 \div 3 = 6 \text{ r } 2$.

In this example, the question asks "how many shelves?"; this question requires a whole number answer. The answer is *6 shelves*. The leftover piece (2 feet) is less than a shelf and, therefore, is of no use.

In the second type of problem, you *divide* to find a *total*. In fact, the word *total* may be in the question. Yet, this is a division problem.

EXAMPLE 4: If Virginia saves $5 a day in tips, what total number of days will it take her to save $135?

```
     27
$5)$135
  - 10
     35
   - 35
      0
```

Answer: 27 days

NOTE: When both the divisor and the dividend contain a dollar sign, the answer doesn't.

Solve the division problems below.

5. If a dress takes two yards of material to make, how many dresses can be made from nine yards?

6. Amy packs and ships music tapes. She is able to pack 6 tapes in a single mailing box. How many boxes will she need to fill an order for 39 tapes?

More About Long Division

Once you have learned the four steps of long division, you can divide any size number by repeating these steps.

EXAMPLE: Divide: $7\overline{)952}$

1st Division: Divide 7 into 9.

Step 1. Divide: 9 ÷ 7 = 1. Write 1 over the 9.
Step 2. Multiply: 1 × 7 = 7. Write 7 under the 9.
Step 3. Subtract: 9 − 7 = 2. Write 2 under the 7.
Step 4. Bring down the 5 and place it next to the 2.

```
   1
7)9 52
 -7
  2 5
```

2nd Division: Divide 7 into 25.

Step 1. Divide: 25 ÷ 7 = 3. Write 3 over the 5.
Step 2. Multiply: 3 × 7 = 21. Write 21 under the 25.
Step 3. Subtract: 25 − 21 = 4. Write 4 under the 1.
Step 4. Bring down the 2 and place it next to the 4.

```
   1 3
7)9 52
 -7
  2 5
 -2 1
    42
```

3rd Division: Divide 7 into 42.

Step 1. Divide: 42 ÷ 7 = 6. Write 6 over the 2.
Step 2. Multiply: 6 × 7 = 42. Write 42 under the 42.
Step 3. Subtract: 42 − 42 = 0. Write 0 under the 2.
Step 4. There is no other digit to bring down, and there is no remainder. The problem is done.

```
  13 6
7)95 2
 -7
  25
 -21
   4 2
  -4 2
     0
```

Answer: 136

Check your answer by multiplication:

```
  2 4
  136
×   7
  952 ✓
```

Use long division to complete each problem below. Check each answer on scratch paper.

1. $6\overline{)858}$ $3\overline{)822}$ $2\overline{)536}$ $6\overline{)1{,}176}$ $7\overline{)4{,}438}$

Each problem below has a remainder in the answer.

2. $6\overline{)715}$ $3\overline{)827}$ $5\overline{)928}$ $5\overline{)2{,}314}$ $7\overline{)3{,}726}$

Dividing by Two Digits

Dividing by a two-digit number is similar to dividing by a one-digit number. However, there is one difference. The first step is to guess what the answer will be! A good guess can save a lot of time and work.

EXAMPLE: Divide: $13\overline{)39}$

The multiplication facts don't tell you what 39 ÷ 13 is. To find the above quotient, you make a good guess and then multiply to see if you're correct.

For example, try 3:

$$\begin{array}{r} 13 \\ \underline{\times\ 3} \\ 39 \end{array} \checkmark \qquad \begin{array}{r} 3 \\ 13\overline{)39} \\ \underline{-\ 39} \\ 0 \end{array}$$

3 is correct, and there is no remainder.

Answer: 3

NOTE: The number 3 was chosen as a guess because the first number of the divisor (1) divides into the first number of the dividend (3) 3 times. This way of choosing a guess is helpful, but, it doesn't always give the correct answer.

Dividing into a Two-Digit Number

Divide. There are no remainders in row 1. Check each answer on scratch paper.

1. $14\overline{)70}$ $12\overline{)60}$ $16\overline{)64}$ $26\overline{)78}$ $13\overline{)52}$

Row 2 may contain remainders.

2. $15\overline{)60}$ $14\overline{)90}$ $17\overline{)86}$ $25\overline{)75}$ $17\overline{)51}$

Dividing into a Three-Digit Number

When the first two digits of the dividend are smaller than the two digits of the divisor, you must divide into the first three digits. At the right the answer 7 is placed above the 8.

EXAMPLE:

```
     7
24)168
 - 168
     0
```

3. $16\overline{)112}$ $25\overline{)179}$ $32\overline{)160}$ $18\overline{)150}$ $26\overline{)130}$

Dividing Larger Numbers

The four-step process of long division is also used when you divide larger numbers. In the following example, you must divide twice to complete the problem.

EXAMPLE: $23\overline{)828}$

1st Division: Divide 23 into 82.

Step 1. Divide: 82 ÷ 23 = 3. Write 3 over the 2.

Step 2. Multiply: 3 × 23 = 69. Write 69 under the 82.

Step 3. Subtract: 82 − 69 = 13. Write 13 under the 69.

Step 4. Bring down the 8 and place it next to the 13.

```
    3
23)82 8
  -69
   13 8
```

2nd Division: Divide 23 into 138.

Step 1. Divide: 138 ÷ 23 = 6. Write 6 over the 8.

Step 2. Multiply 6 × 23 = 138. Write 138 under the 138.

Step 3. Subtract: 138 − 138 = 0. Write 0 under the 8.

Step 4. There is no other digit to bring down, and there is no remainder. The problem is completed.

```
    3 6
23)82 8
  -69
   13 8
  -13 8
      0
```

Answer: 36

Dividing by Two-Digit Numbers

Complete each problem below. Use multiplication to check each answer on scratch paper.

1. $16\overline{)432}$ $27\overline{)486}$ $15\overline{)855}$ $28\overline{)532}$ $38\overline{)798}$

2. $32\overline{)1{,}312}$ $46\overline{)1{,}426}$ $39\overline{)1{,}092}$ $52\overline{)1{,}144}$ $35\overline{)1{,}750}$

For larger dividends, you may need to divide more than twice to complete the problem. Look carefully at the example at right.

EXAMPLE:

```
     128
 37)4,736
   - 3 7
     1 03
   -   74
      296
   -  296
        0
```

3. $28\overline{)6{,}020}$ $31\overline{)7{,}626}$ $43\overline{)13{,}803}$ $52\overline{)11{,}128}$

Dividing by Three-Digit Numbers

Dividing by three-digit numbers is similar to dividing by two-digit numbers. The first step is to divide into the first 3 (or 4) digits of the dividend.

In the example at right, 237 divides into 2014, the first 4 digits of the dividend. Two divisions are needed to complete this problem.

EXAMPLE:

```
         85
 237)20,145
    - 18 96
       1 185
     - 1 185
           0
```

4. $312\overline{)1{,}560}$ $418\overline{)1{,}672}$ $279\overline{)2{,}232}$ $303\overline{)1{,}212}$

5. $216\overline{)16{,}848}$ $322\overline{)17{,}388}$ $297\overline{)18{,}117}$ $403\overline{)23{,}374}$

Dividing Numbers in a Row

When a division problem is written with a ÷ sign, rewrite the problem with a division bracket ($\overline{)\quad}$). Remember, the number to the right of the ÷ sign is the divisor and goes outside the bracket.

EXAMPLE: Divide: 773 ÷ 24 Rewrite as:

$$\begin{array}{r} 32\text{ r }5 \\ 24\overline{)773} \\ -\underline{72} \\ 53 \\ -\underline{48} \\ 5 \end{array}$$

Answer: 32 r 5

Divide. Check each answer on scratch paper. Some of the problems will have a remainder as part of the answer.

1. 3,240 ÷ 24 5,274 ÷ 41 924 ÷ 231 268 ÷ 12

2. 364 ÷ 16 8,543 ÷ 165 24,566 ÷ 346

Deciding When to Multiply and When to Divide

You need to know when to multiply and when to divide in problem solving. Although key words may be helpful, they are not always present.

In both multiplication and division problems, you are given two numbers and asked to find a third number:

- In multiplication problems, you are given *parts* of a total. You multiply these parts to determine the total.
- In division problems, you are given the *total* and *one part.* You divide the total by the given part to determine the unknown part.

While working on a problem, you may find it helpful to write a **solution sentence.** *A solution sentence uses words to state a problem's solution.* Once you write a solution in words, it is easy to replace words with numbers and then to compute the answer. Solution sentences are especially helpful for difficult problems.

EXAMPLE 1: Stacey bought 4 cartons of pop for the birthday party. If each carton contains 6 bottles, how many bottles did she buy?

The problem is asking for the *total number of bottles* that Stacey bought. You know this even though the word *total* is not mentioned.

Here is a solution sentence for this problem:

total = cartons <u>times</u> bottles in a carton

To find this total, replace words with numbers:

total	=	***4*** (cartons)	×	***6*** (bottles)
total	=	***24 bottles***		

Answer: 24 bottles

EXAMPLE 2: During a weekend clothing sale, Lewis sold $364 worth of A-1 work shirts. If he sold 26 shirts, what was the price of each shirt?

In this problem you are asked to find the price of a single shirt. The price of one shirt is a *part* of $364, the total cost of all 26 shirts.

For a solution sentence we can write:

price = total cost <u>divided by</u> number of shirts

To find this price, replace words with numbers:

price	=	***$364*** (total cost)	÷	***26*** (number of shirts)
price	=	***$14***		

Answer: $14

Each problem below is followed by a *solution sentence*. Complete each sentence by writing either the word *multiplied* or the word *divided* on the blank line. Then, using your solution sentence as a guide, compute the answer to the question.

1. The owner of a grocery store bought 150 loaves of bread for $0.79 per loaf. What price did the owner pay for all the bread?

   total cost of bread = cost per loaf __________ by the number of loaves bought

2. During a weekend trip, Kim drove 161 miles. If she used 7 gallons of gas, how many miles did her car run on each gallon?

   number of miles per gallon = total miles driven __________ by the number of gallons used

3. Farmer Murphy's cows produce 168 gallons of milk each day. Remembering that there are 4 quarts in one gallon, how many quarts of milk is this each day?

   total quarts each day = number of gallons each day __________ by the number of quarts per gallon

To the right of each problem below, circle the correct answer. Answer *a* is computed by multiplication; answer *b* by division. Use only common sense to help you decide which answer to choose. Do not solve any problem.

4. If Gregory plans to drive 2,800 miles in 4 days, how many miles should he plan to drive each day?	a) multiplication: 11,200 b) division: 700
5. A local bakery sells chocolate chip cookies for \$3.40 per dozen. How much will 6 dozen cookies cost?	a) multiplication: \$20.40 b) division: \$0.57
6. Four salesmen sold a total of \$26,968 worth of furniture during April. On the average, how much furniture did each salesman sell that month?	a) multiplication: \$107,872 b) division: \$6,742
7. Jerry's Restaurant sold 352 small colas on Saturday. If each small cup holds 8 ounces of soda, how many ounces of cola did Jerry's sell that day?	a) multiplication: 2,816 b) division: 44

Solving Word Problems

Solve the following multiplication and division problems. As a first step in each problem, you may find it helpful to write a solution sentence. Then choose necessary information and compute an answer.

After solving each problem, check to see that your answer makes sense.

1. At a recent sale, Martha bought a case of oil for $18.96. The case contained 24 one-quart cans of oil. What amount did each quart of oil cost Martha?

2. Out of Stan's monthly check of $1,413, he must pay $485 for rent and an average of $165 for utilities. How much total rent does Stan pay each year?

3. Sonny reads at the rate of 240 words per minute. He once read an entire 88,000-word novel in just over 6 hours! At this rate, how many minutes will it take him to read a short story that contains 8,640 words?

4. Laura looked at a new oak dining set. The table alone cost $449. The set of four chairs costs $356. Laura bought the table and two of the four chairs. What price did Laura pay for each of the chairs?

5. Before José tuned up his car, it would get only 28 miles to the gallon. Now, after being tuned, it gets 37 miles to the gallon. How many miles can José hope to drive now on a full tank of 16 gallons?

6. Jenny is in charge of purchasing picnic supplies for Three Woods Lumber Company's annual picnic. Although 900 people work for the company, she expects that about 2,500 cups will be needed. If a single carton holds 75 cups, how many cartons of cups should she get? (She cannot buy partial cartons, so your answer must not have a remainder.)

7. During a "TV Special" sale, Uptown Music Company shipped 1,238 boxes of compact discs. If each box held 13 compact discs, how many compact discs were shipped in all?

8. A 234-page book contains 72,072 words. On the average, how many words are written on a single page?

Answer the questions that follow each short passage below. The necessary information may be entirely in the passage or it may be partly in the questions themselves.

Questions 9 and 10 refer to the following passage.

> Carol applied for a job as a secretary with a publishing company. As part of the application process, she had to take a 6-minute keyboarding test. During the 6 minutes, she typed 438 words. The manager was impressed, and Carol got the job.
>
> Carol's starting salary was $935 per month. After 6 months she was given a raise. Her new salary was $1,156 per month.

9. How much did Carol earn during the first six months of her employment?

   Information needed:

   Solution:

10. After Carol received a raise, what was her new yearly salary?

    Information needed:

    Solution:

Questions 11 and 12 refer to the passage below.

> Tami borrowed $5,000 from Friendly Finance Company. To repay the loan, Tami must make 24 monthly payments of $237.71 each.
>
> Before deciding on Friendly Finance, Tami also talked with Larry's Loan Company. Larry agreed to a $5,000 loan. But Tami would have to pay back a total of $5,764.80 divided into 24 equal monthly payments. After talking with Larry, Tami decided to get the loan from Friendly.

11. Over the 24-month loan period, what total payments will Tami make to Friendly Finance?

    Information needed:

    Solution:

12. If Tami had gotten the loan from Larry's Loan Company, what would her monthly payments have been?

    Information needed:

    Solution:

Questions 13 and 14 refer to the information below.

> Bill works as a shipping clerk in a food warehouse. His job is to pack cans of food into boxes in preparation for shipment. Last week, Bill was responsible for packing three fish products:
>
> tuna fish—128 cans per box
> salmon—48 cans per box
> sardines—144 cans per box

13. How many boxes does Bill need in order to ship 18,816 cans of tuna fish?

Information needed:

Solution:

14. During this week, he also delivered a special order of 100 boxes of salmon. How many cans of salmon were in this special order?

Information needed:

Solution:

Division Skills Review

Review your division skills. Work each problem as carefully as you can and check your answers with the answers given in the Answer Key. Correct any mistakes.

1. $3\overline{)15}$ $4\overline{)36}$ $5\overline{)40}$ $6\overline{)54}$ $21 \div 7 =$ $28 \div 4 =$

2. $4\overline{)84}$ $3\overline{)936}$ $2\overline{)680}$ $5\overline{)305}$ $4\overline{)4{,}080}$ $3\overline{)600}$

3. $4\overline{)25}$ $6\overline{)40}$ $5\overline{)75}$ $4\overline{)72}$ $7\overline{)377}$ $6\overline{)450}$

4. $6\overline{)275}$ $4\overline{)916}$ $12\overline{)252}$ $16\overline{)384}$ $35\overline{)875}$ $28\overline{)845}$

5. $5\overline{)\$1.50}$ $7\overline{)\$2.31}$ $3\overline{)\$0.96}$ $12\overline{)\$24.84}$ $25\overline{)\$37.50}$

6. $272 \div 4$ $385 \div 24$ $2{,}007 \div 9$ $42{,}845 \div 41$

7. When green onions are selling for "three bunches for $1.38," what price would you pay for a single bunch?

8. If Grace can type 65 words per minute, how many minutes will it take her to type a 2,990-word report?

9. For several months, Betty has had her eye on a microwave oven that she'd like to buy. Its price has been $369.99. Last week when it went on sale for $289.58, Betty bought it. She paid $50.00 down and agreed to pay off the $239.58 balance in 6 equal monthly payments. If no interest is charged, how much will Betty pay each month?

Checking Your Answer

Key words, drawings, and **solution sentences** often provide clues that help you decide how to solve a word problem. You get one more clue when you **check your answer.**

Checking your answer involves two steps:

1. Checking to see that you did the math correctly
2. Checking to see that your answer makes sense

Seeing if your answer makes sense is the most important clue you have for knowing if you worked a problem correctly. You ask yourself, "Is my answer about what I expect it should be?"

To the right of each problem below, circle the answer that makes the most sense. Don't do any computation. Just choose the answer that makes sense to you. Only one answer is correct.

1. Krisa received $31.25 in change after buying a 7-pound roast that cost $13.77. She paid by check. How much did she write the check for?

   a) addition: $45.02
   b) subtraction: $17.48

2. Four friends agreed to evenly share the cost of driving across the country. If each person's share for gas came to $64, what was the total gas bill?

   a) multiplication: $256
   b) division: $16

3. By 6:30 P.M. the temperature had cooled 29° F below its 3:00 P.M. high. If the temperature at 3:00 was 73° F, what was the temperature at 6:30?

   a) addition: 102°
   b) subtraction: 44°

4. A recipe calls for 3 teaspoons of salt to season a meat dish for 6 people. If the cook wanted to prepare the same dish for 18 people, how many teaspoons of salt would be needed?

   a) multiplication: 9
   b) division: 1

5. A youth group divided its membership list into 4 mailing lists. If each mailing list contained 72 names, how many names were on the membership list?

   a) multiplication: 288
   b) division: 18

6. Ernie paid $780 in property taxes last year. Later he got a $75 refund. How much did Ernie end up paying for property taxes after all?

   a) addition: $855
   b) subtraction: $705

Reviewing One-Step Word Problems

A **one-step word problem** is solved by one arithmetic operation. You compute the answer by adding, subtracting, multiplying, or dividing.

While working the following problems, remember to read each problem carefully. Make sure you understand what the question asks you to find. Then choose the **necessary information** and decide which arithmetic operation you wish to use. In some problems **key words** may be helpful. In other problems you may want to make a **drawing** or write a **solution sentence.**

Here are some general guidelines to help you choose the correct operation:

- when combining amounts ⟶ add
- when finding the difference between two amounts ⟶ subtract
- when given one unit of something and asked to find several ⟶ multiply
- when given a part of something and asked to find the total ⟶ multiply
- when given an amount for several and asked to find an amount for one ⟶ divide
- when splitting, cutting, sharing, etc. ⟶ divide

After you've solved each problem, check to make sure your answer makes sense. If it doesn't, redo the problem until you're happy with the answer.

Solve each problem below.

1. Work at the Data Corporation is divided into shifts. Ninety-six people work on day shift, 78 work on swing shift, and 67 work on evening shift. How many people in all does the Data Corporation employ?

2. As a supervisor, Jan earns $8.67 an hour. Ron is a mail clerk and makes $5.49 an hour. What is the difference between what Jan earns each hour and what Ron earns?

3. Jason and three friends agreed to evenly split the cost of renting a camper for the weekend. If the camper rent total was $132.88, what was Jason's share of the cost?

4. A railroad flatcar is carrying 12 new Toyota sport model cars. Each car weighs 2,935 pounds. Compute the total weight carried by this flatcar.

5. After working his regular shift last week, Hank worked 7 overtime hours on Saturday. If overtime pay is $9.25 per hour, how much extra money did Hank earn for this Saturday work?

6. In a game of bridge, 52 cards are dealt out equally to 4 players. As the game begins, how many cards are in each player's hand?

Questions 7 and 8 contain extra information. In each, underline the necessary information and then solve the problem.

7. The Wildcat Football Stadium holds 14,500 people. For the first game of the season, 8,684 fans showed up. The second game drew 9,832, and the third game drew 11,459. What was the combined attendance at the first 3 games?

8. On the hottest day last summer, the temperature soared to its highest point, 104°, at 4:20 P.M. By 8:00 P.M., the temperature was down to 81°. Finally, by 10:30, the temperature had dropped several more degrees. As shown below, how many degrees did the temperature drop between 4:20 and 10:30?

Questions 9 and 10 refer to the following passage.

While shopping at Al's Hardware, Ray bought all 7 items he had written on his shopping list. He was especially pleased to find 3 of those items at sale prices: a new hammer for $7.99, a new hand saw for $13.85, and a 6-pound sack of nails for $5.28.

After paying the clerk $42.00, Ray got back $1.89 in change.

9. How much did Ray spend for the 3 items he bought on sale?

10. What total amount did Ray spend at Al's Hardware?

Questions 11 and 12 refer to the passage below.

Lois borrowed $2,000 from her credit union to buy a used car. To repay the loan, Lois can choose to make payments over either 24 months or 36 months.

If she chooses 24 months, Lois must make 24 equal monthly payments of $102.25 each. If she chooses 36 months, Lois must make 36 equal payments of $74.60.

11. If she chooses the 24-month loan, what total amount will Lois pay to her credit union?

12. If she chooses the 36-month loan, what total amount will Lois pay to her credit union?

6 Special Topics in Math

TOPIC 1: Introduction to Multi-Step Word Problems

The solution of a **multi-step** word problem requires two or more operations. This type of problem is most easily solved by breaking it down into two or more one-step problems. Each step can then be solved by a single operation.

To break down a multi-step problem into simpler one-step problems, it is best to begin by writing a **solution sentence.** To write a solution sentence, use brief phrases and numbers to state a problem's solution as simply as possible.

EXAMPLE: Raphael planned to spend $25.00 at Gene's Men Store. After buying a shirt for $14.45 and a tie for $1.95, how much money did Raphael have left?

To solve this problem, let's first write a solution sentence:

amount left = $25 **minus** $\underbrace{\text{cost of shirt and tie}}_{\text{missing information}}$ together

The total cost of shirt and tie is not given in the problem as a single number. Because it isn't, this amount is called **missing information.** Computing missing information is the first step in finding a problem's solution.

In example 1, the missing information is easily computed:

missing information = cost of shirt and tie together

= $14.45 + $1.95

= **$16.40**

Now the solution sentence can be written with numbers, and the answer can be computed by subtraction:

amount left = $25.00 − $16.40

= **$8.60**

Answer: **$8.60**

Answers to Chapter 6 exercises start on page 917.

Solve each of the following problems. For item 1, we have written a solution sentence and two solution steps as an example. In step 1, you compute the value of the missing information. In step 2, you complete the problem.

1. At HI LIFE GROCERY, Jason bought hamburger for $3.58, a gallon of milk for $1.89, and a box of cereal for $2.79. If he paid the clerk with a twenty-dollar bill, how much change did he receive?

   Solution sentence: change = $20 *minus* total cost of groceries

   STEP 1. *Add* to find the total cost of groceries.

   STEP 2. *Subtract* the total cost of groceries from $20 to determine Jason's change.

2. Each day Monday through Friday, Frieda delivers a newspaper to each of her 121 customers. Last weekend she delivered a total of 257 papers. What total number of papers did Frieda deliver last week?

3. Five friends agreed to split the cost of dinner evenly. Together they had a pizza for $12.75, drinks for $4.30, and salads for $9.45. What was each person's share of the bill?

4. For her church, Shelley made 23 gift packages to give to children following Easter services. Each package contained 79¢ worth of candy, a $1.98 toy, and a 35¢ balloon. How much was the total cost of all 23 packages?

5. Brenda, a plumber, fixed the sink at Mark's house. She charged Mark a total of $75.40. The cost of new parts included $28.50 for a new faucet, $13.65 for tubing, and $0.83 for washers. How much did Brenda charge for her labor?

6. In Dick's pickup he can carry 8 boxes. He can also carry 6 more boxes in a small trailer attached to his pickup. How many boxes can Dick move in 8 trips if he uses both pickup and trailer?

7. Working as a waitress Monday through Thursday, Lita serves about 95 people each day. On Saturday she serves about 165. During the 5 days that Lita works, about how many people does she serve?

8. John and his two brothers split the cost of renting a small trailer tent to take hunting. Daily rental cost is $27.84. If they kept the unit for 5 days, how much would be each brother's share of the rental cost?

Below are more multi-step word problems for you to solve. Each contains extra information. A solution sentence will help you decide what information to use.

9. Angie traded in her old Ford on a newer Toyota. The Ford had 119,724 miles on it. The Toyota showed only 32,696 miles. During the next twelve months, Angie drove the Toyota an average of 1,350 miles each month. At the end of the year, how many miles showed on the Toyota's mileage indicator?

10. In Lewisville there are 26,854 registered voters. During the fall election, 14,725 people voted for Measure #1. Of those who voted, 6,539 were Republicans and 4,891 were Democrats. How many people who voted for Measure #1 were neither Republicans nor Democrats?

Becoming Familiar with Arithmetic Expressions

As you've seen in multi-step word problems, more than one operation may be needed to solve a problem. Here we'll see how arithmetic expressions that contain more than one operation are written and evaluated.

Multiplication and division are always performed before addition and subtraction. Look at these examples:

Arithmetic Expression	*Meaning*	*Computing the Value*
$5 \times 4 + 8$	add 8 to the product of 5×4	Compute the product: $5 \times 4 = 20$ Add 8 to 20: $20 + 8 = $ **28**
$11 - 15 \div 3$	subtract the quotient $15 \div 3$ from 11	Compute the quotient: $15 \div 3 = 5$ Subtract 5 from 11: $11 - 5 = $ **6**

Next, we'll look at the use of parentheses ( ). **Parentheses are used to indicate a single quantity that is to be multiplied or divided.** Using parentheses, no multiplication sign is needed. Here are two examples:

Arithmetic Expression	*Meaning*	*Computing the Value*
$5(9 + 6)$	multiply 5 times the sum of $9 + 6$	Compute the sum: $9 + 6 = 15$ Multiply 15 by 5: $5 \times 15 = $ **75**
$(15 - 6) \div 3$	divide 3 into the difference of $15 - 6$	Compute the difference: $15 - 6 = 9$ Divide 9 by 3: $9 \div 3 = $ **3**

When an expression contains parentheses, follow these steps:

Step 1. Do the arithmetic indicated within parentheses first.

Step 2. Starting at the left, do all multiplication and division.

Step 3. Again starting at the left, do all addition and subtraction, adding or subtracting two numbers at a time.

Study the following examples carefully. A bracket $\underbrace{\hphantom{xxx}}$ indicates the operation performed as you move from one line to the next. Notice that in each step an operation is performed on only two numbers at one time.

EXAMPLES:

1. $57 - \underbrace{8 \times 6} + 5$

$= \underbrace{57 - 48} + 5$

$= 9 + 5$

$= \mathbf{14}$

2. $\underbrace{5 \times 7} + 72 \div 8$

$= 35 + \underbrace{72 \div 8}$

$= 35 + 9$

$= \mathbf{44}$

3. $6\underbrace{(13 - 9)} - 14$

$= \underbrace{6(4)} - 14$

$= 24 - 14$ [since 6(4) means 6×4]

$= \mathbf{10}$

Evaluate each expression below.

1. $5 \times 3 + 9$ $\quad$ $8 \times 5 - 17$ $\quad$ $42 - 8 \times 3 + 4$

2. $36 \div 4 + 8$ $\quad$ $6 \times 5 + 7 \times 8$ $\quad$ $12 \times 3 - 45 \div 5$

3. $8\ (6 + 3)$ $\quad$ $13\ (12 - 5) + 3$ $\quad$ $(28 - 4) \div 6$

4. $9\ (13 - 6) + 5 \times 8$ $\quad$ $36 - (3 + 6 + 4)$ $\quad$ $2\ (8 + 4) - 49 \div 7$

An arithmetic expression is often used to show the computation steps of a multi-step word problem. In many problems, there may be more than one correct solution sentence and arithmetic expression.

Learning to write arithmetic expressions to solve word problems is an important skill. You'll use this skill throughout your study of mathematics.

From the choices at right, circle the one expression that will give the correct answer to each problem.

5. Last week, Greg made 8 deliveries each day Monday through Friday. On Saturday he worked until noon and made 3 more deliveries. How many deliveries total did Greg make during the 6 days?
   a) $8 + 3$
   b) $5\ (8 + 3)$
   c) $5 \times 8 + 3$

6. Shirley planned to divide her penny collection evenly among her 3 children. She had 536 pennies in all. First, she took out 120 pennies she wanted to keep herself. Of the pennies left, how many should she give each child?
   a) $536 \div 3 - 120$
   b) $(536 - 120) \div 3$
   c) $536 - 120 \div 3$

7. Jane gave a clerk a twenty-dollar bill to pay for one gallon of paint and one paintbrush. If the paint cost \$11.95 and the brush cost \$3.45, how much change did she receive?
   a) \$20.00 − (\$11.95 + \$3.45)
   b) (\$11.95 + \$3.45) − \$20.00
   c) \$20.00 − \$11.95 + \$3.45

8. For his cleaning business, Arnie bought 12 gallons of soap at \$9.25 per gallon. He also bought a gallon of deodorizer for \$17.85. What amount did he pay for these supplies?
   a) 12 (\$9.25 + \$17.85)
   b) \$9.25 × 12 + \$17.85
   c) \$9.25 (12 + \$17.85)

9. For Halloween, Betty bought 4 bags of candy. Each bag contained 75 small wrapped candies. If she expected to see about 60 children, about how many candies should Betty give to each child?
   a) $(75 \times 4) \div 60$
   b) $(75 - 60) \div 4$
   c) $4\ (75 \div 60)$

10. George and five friends agreed to evenly split the cost of dinner. They bought a pizza for \$13.50, salads for \$9.00, and drinks for \$3.50. How much did George pay for his share?
   a) (\$13.50 + \$9.00 + \$3.50) ÷ 5
   b) 6 ÷ (\$13.50 + \$9.00 + \$3.50)
   c) (\$13.50 + \$9.00 + \$3.50) ÷ 6

For each problem below, there are two expressions that will give the correct answer. Circle the **two** correct choices to the right of each problem.

11. When fully loaded, Cindy's truck can haul 2,300 pounds of gravel. On Saturday, she hauled 6 full loads. On Sunday, she hauled 5 more full loads. How many pounds of gravel did she haul on these two days?

a) 2,300 (5 + 6)
b) 2,300 × 2
c) 6 + 5(2,300)
d) (2,300 × 5) + (2,300 × 6)
e) 2,300 × 6 + 5

12. Each day he fights fires, Manuel earns $25 more than his regular daily pay of $63. Last week he fought fires on 3 days. How much did he earn during the 5-day week?

a) 5 ($63 + $25)
b) $63 × 5 + $25 × 3
c) $63 × 2 + $25 × 3
d) $63 × 5 + $25 × 2
e) 3 ($63 + $25) + 2 × $63

13. Sam, Frank, and Lois bought a boat. The sale price was $5,600. They also received a $1,200 rebate a month later. If they split all costs evenly, how much did each one end up paying for this boat after they split the rebate? (Remember, a ***rebate*** is money you get returned to you.)

a) ($5,600 + $1,200) ÷ 3
b) ($5,600 ÷ 3) − ($1,200 ÷ 3)
c) ($5,600 ÷ 3) + ($ 1,200 ÷ 3)
d) ($5,600 − $ 1,200) ÷ 3
e) ($1,200 ÷ 3) + $5,600

TOPIC 2: Introduction to Measurement

Measurement is an important part of daily life. Common uses include the measuring of length, weight, liquid measure, and time. A measurement is given as a number and a label. The label is called a ***measurement unit***.

There are two types of measurement units in use in the United States. One is the familiar **standard** or **American system**. The other is the **metric system**. Commonly used units in each system are shown following.

UNITS OF LENGTH

STANDARD SYSTEM		METRIC SYSTEM	
Unit	*Relation to Other Units*	*Unit*	*Relation to Other Units*
inch (in. or ")	Smallest unit	millimeter (mm)	Smallest unit
foot (ft. or ')	1 ft. = 12 in.	centimeter (cm)	1 cm = 10 mm
yard (yd.)	1 yd. = 36 in. 1 yd. = 3 ft.	meter (m)	1 m = 1,000 mm 1 m = 100 cm
mile (mi.)	1 mi. = 5,280 ft. 1 mi. = 1,760 yd.	kilometer (km)	1 km = 1,000 m

1 cm ▬▬

1 inch ▬▬▬▬▬

1 m equals a little more than 39 in.

1 km is about 0.6 mi.

UNITS OF WEIGHT

STANDARD SYSTEM

Unit	*Relation to Other Units*
ounce (oz.)	Smallest unit
pound (lb.)	1 lb. = 16 oz.
ton (T.)	1 T. = 2,000 lb.

METRIC SYSTEM

Unit	*Relation to Other Units*
milligram (mg)	Smallest unit
gram (g)	1 g = 1,000 mg
kilogram (kg)	1 kg = 1,000 g
metric ton (t)	1 t = 1,000 kg

2.2 lb. is approximately 1 kg

UNITS OF LIQUID MEASURE

STANDARD SYSTEM

Unit	*Relation to Other Units*
ounce (oz.)	Smallest unit
pint (pt.)	1 pt. = 16 oz.
quart (qt.)	1 qt. = 2 pt.
gallon (gal.)	1 gal. = 4 qt.

METRIC SYSTEM

Unit	*Relation to Other Units*
milliliter (ml)	Smallest unit
liter (l)	1 l = 1,000 ml
kiloliter (kl)	1 kl = 1,000 l

1 qt. is a little less than 1 liter

UNITS OF TIME

Units of time are identical in both standard (American) and metric systems.

Unit	*Relation to Other Units*	*Unit*	*Relation to Other Units*
second (sec.)	Smallest unit	day (d.)	1 d. = 24 hr.
minute (min.)	1 min. = 60 sec.	week (wk.)	1 wk. = 7 d.
hour (hr.)	1 hr. = 60 min.	year (yr.)	1 yr. = 365 d.

To become more familiar with metric units, do the exercise below.

Fill in each blank with one of the choices within parentheses.

1. A meter is __________ than a yard. (longer, shorter)

2. A kilogram is __________ than a pound. (heavier, lighter)

3. A liter is __________ than a quart. (larger, smaller)

4. A speed of 50 kilometers per hour is __________ a speed of 50 miles per hour. (greater than, less than)

Answer each question below.

5. The smallest metric unit of length is the ___________ .

6. The smallest metric unit of weight is the ___________ .

7. The smallest metric unit of liquid measure is the ___________ .

Circle the larger in each pair of quantities.

8. 10 yards *or* 10 meters.

9. 5 pounds *or* 5 kilograms.

10. 3 quarts *or* 3 liters

Changing from One Unit to Another

A quantity can be written in more than one unit. To **convert** (change) from one unit to another, you use a **conversion factor**.

A conversion factor is a number that relates two different units. The tables of measurements on pages 771–772 list common units and their conversion factors.

Here are a few examples:

Units	*Conversion Factor*	*Units*	*Conversion Factor*
1 foot = 12 inches	12	1 pound = 16 ounces	16
1 yard = 3 feet	3	1 meter = 100 centimeters	100

To change from one unit to another, you use a conversion factor as follows: **To change larger units to smaller units, <u>multiply</u> by the conversion factor.**

EXAMPLE 1: Change 6 yards to feet (feet are smaller than yards).

Step 1. Identify the conversion factor that relates yards and feet.
Since 1 yard = 3 feet, *the conversion factor is 3.*

Step 2. To change yards to feet, multiply by 3.
6 yards $= 6 \times 3 = 18$ feet

Answer: 18 feet

To change smaller units to larger units, <u>divide</u> by the conversion factor.

EXAMPLE 2: Change 64 ounces to pounds (pounds are larger than ounces).

Step 1. Identify the conversion factor that relates ounces and pounds.
Since 1 pound = 16 ounces, *the conversion factor is 16.*

Step 2. To change ounces to pounds, divide by 16.
64 ounces $= 64 \div 16 = 4$ pounds

Answer: 4 pounds

Change each quantity to the unit indicated. As your first step in each problem, identify the correct conversion factor.

Changing Larger Units to Smaller Units: Multiply

1. 7 ft. = _____ in. 8 yd. = _____ ft. 12 cm = _____ mm
2. 3 lb. = _____ oz. 5 km = _____ m 2 kg = _____ g
3. 3 qt. = _____ pt. 2 l = _____ ml 4 min. = _____ sec.

Changing Smaller Units to Larger Units: Divide

4. 36 in. = _____ ft. 300 cm = _____ m 12 pt. = _____ qt.
5. 72 hr. = _____ d. 12 qt. = _____ gal. 120 sec. = _____ min.
6. 24 ft. = _____ yd. 4,000 lb. = _____ T. 80 oz. = _____ lb.

Many times, when smaller units are converted to larger units, there is a remainder.

As the example below shows, this remainder is simply written as the number of smaller units left over.

EXAMPLE: Change 7 feet to yards.

Step 1. Divide 7 feet by the conversion factor 3.

$7 \div 3 = 2 \text{ r } 1$

Step 2. Write the remainder as the number of feet left over.

Answer: 7 feet = 2 yards 1 foot

7. 29 in. = _____ ft. _____ in. 14 ft. = _____ yds. _____ ft.
8. 75 min. = _____ hr. _____ min. 47 oz. = _____ lbs. _____ oz.
9. 240 cm = _____ m _____ cm 26 mm = _____ cm _____ mm
10. 2,500 g = _____ kg _____ g 3,400 ml = _____ l _____ ml

Adding Measurement Units

To add two or more quantities, add each unit of measurement separately and then simplify the sum. An example is shown below for lengths in both the standard and metric systems.

STANDARD SYSTEM

Add:	8 ft. 7 in.
	+ 7 ft. 9 in.
	15 ft. 16 in.
Answer:	**16 ft. 4 in.**

(Since 16 in. = 1 ft. 4 in.)

Addition

Step 1. Add each column separately.

Step 2. Simplify the sum.

METRIC SYSTEM

Add:	6 cm 9 mm
	+ 5 cm 4 mm
	11 cm 13 mm
Answer:	**12 cm 3 mm**

(Since 13 mm = 1 cm 3 mm)

Add the following quantities and simplify each sum.

1.	9 ft. 7 in. + 7 ft. 8 in.	3 mi. 1,500 yd. + 2 mi. 450 yd.
2.	25 m 35 cm + 12 m 86 cm	47 km 750 m + 30 km 500 m
3.	5 lb. 7 oz. + 2 lb. 14 oz.	3 T. 1,300 lb. +1 T. 675 lb.
4.	8 kg 900 g + 5 kg 750 g	12 g 125 mg + 9 g 900 mg
5.	3 pt. 9 oz. + 1 pt. 8 oz.	1 gal. 3 qt. + 1 gal. 2 qt.
6.	2 l 800 ml + 1 l 750 ml	2 kl 900 l + 1 kl 350 l
7.	3 hr. 35 min. + 2 hr. 45 min.	2 d. 18 hr. + 1 d. 7 hr.

Solve each word problem below.

8. Karin made a long garden hose by connecting 3 shorter hoses together. The lengths of the shorter hoses were 5 yd. 2 ft., 4 yd. 1 ft., and 6 yd. 2 ft. What is the combined length of these three hoses?

9. On Saturday Ellen went on a 20 km hike. During the first hour, she walked 4 km 800 m. During the second hour, she walked 5 km 400 m, and during the third, 6 km 100 m. What total distance did she walk in 3 hours?

10. Ervin put a turkey in the oven at 25 minutes after 2:00. If he's supposed to cook it for 3 hours and 45 minutes, at what time should he turn off the oven?

11. At Wong's Market, Yoshi bought 3 bags of rice, each weighing 10 kg 750 g. What is the total weight of rice that Yoshi bought?

Subtracting Measurement Units

To subtract one quantity from another, subtract each unit of measurement separately, starting with the unit in the right-hand column. Borrowing from a larger unit is often necessary and is done in a way similar to borrowing in whole numbers. A borrowed larger unit is changed into smaller units. It is then added to the smaller units already present in the problem. An example of borrowing is shown below for weight measures in both the standard and metric systems.

STANDARD SYSTEM

Subtract: 4 lb. 9 oz.
− 1 lb. 13 oz.

Borrow: 1 lb. = 16 oz.
Add: (16 oz. + 9 oz. = 25 oz.)

Write: ~~4~~ (3) lb. ~~9~~ (25) oz.
− 1 lb. 13 oz.

Answer: **2 lb. 12 oz.**

Subtraction

Step 1. Since it is necessary, borrow 1 whole unit from the left column. Add this borrowed unit to the right column.

Step 2. Subtract each column.

METRIC SYSTEM

Subtract: 3 kg 750 g
− 1 kg 900 g

Borrow: 1 kg = 1,000 g
Add: (1,000 g + 750 g = 1,750 g)

Write: ~~3~~ (2) kg ~~750~~ (1,750) g
− 1 kg 900 g

Answer: **1 kg 850 g**

Use borrowing to subtract the following quantities.

1.
$$\begin{array}{r} \text{5 ft. 3 in.} \\ -\ \text{2 ft. 9 in.} \\ \hline \end{array} \qquad \begin{array}{r} \text{2 mi. 850 yd.} \\ -\ \text{1 mi. 1,500 yd.} \\ \hline \end{array}$$

2.
$$\begin{array}{r} \text{13 m 52 cm} \\ -\ \text{9 m 85 cm} \\ \hline \end{array} \qquad \begin{array}{r} \text{24 km 600 m} \\ -\ \text{21 km 775 m} \\ \hline \end{array}$$

3.
$$\begin{array}{r} \text{4 lb. 5 oz.} \\ -\ \text{2 lb. 8 oz.} \\ \hline \end{array} \qquad \begin{array}{r} \text{2 T. 755 lb.} \\ -\ \text{1 T. 1,550 lb.} \\ \hline \end{array}$$

4.
$$\begin{array}{r} \text{5 kg 150 g} \\ -\ \text{1 kg 875 g} \\ \hline \end{array} \qquad \begin{array}{r} \text{3 t 775 kg} \\ -\ \text{1 t 825 kg} \\ \hline \end{array}$$

5.
$$\begin{array}{r} \text{4 pt. 8 oz.} \\ -\ \text{2 pt. 11 oz.} \\ \hline \end{array} \qquad \begin{array}{r} \text{2 gal. 2 qt.} \\ -\ \text{1 gal. 3 qt.} \\ \hline \end{array}$$

6.
$$\begin{array}{r} \text{1 l 355 ml} \\ -\ \text{850 ml} \\ \hline \end{array} \qquad \begin{array}{r} \text{4 kl 325 l} \\ -\ \text{2 kl 750 l} \\ \hline \end{array}$$

7.
$$\begin{array}{r} \text{2 hr. 45 min.} \\ -\ \text{1 hr. 50 min.} \\ \hline \end{array} \qquad \begin{array}{r} \text{3 d. 15 hr.} \\ -\ \text{1 d. 21 hr.} \\ \hline \end{array}$$

Solve each word problem below.

8. Julia is supposed to bake a beef roast for 3 hours and 15 minutes. If she has already baked it for 1 hour and 45 minutes, how much longer should she leave it in the oven?

9. When Shelley was in the sixth grade, she could throw a baseball 42 yards 2 feet. Now, in the eighth grade, she can throw it 57 yards 1 foot. How much farther can Shelley throw a baseball now than in the sixth grade?

Multiplying Measurement Units

To multiply a quantity by a number, multiply each unit of measurement separately and then simplify the answer. An example is shown below for multiplying length in both the standard and metric systems.

STANDARD SYSTEM

Multiply: 3 yd. 1 ft.
× 4
12 yd. 4 ft.

Answer: 13 yd. 1 ft.
(Since 4 ft. = 1 yd. 1 ft.)

Multiplication
Step 1. Multiply each column.
Step 2. Simplify the product.

METRIC SYSTEM

Multiply: 4 cm 7 mm
× 3
12 cm 21 mm

Answer: 14 cm 1 mm
(Since 21 mm = 2 cm 1 mm)

Multiply the following quantities and simplify each answer.

1. 5 ft. 8 in. × 4 2 mi. 880 yd. × 2

2. 5 cm 6 mm × 2 9 km 550 m × 4

3. 3 lb. 12 oz. × 4 1 T. 825 lb. × 3

4. 5 g 225 mg × 5 2 t 750 kg × 2

5. 1 pt. 7 oz. × 3 2 gal. 3 qt. × 2

6. 2 l 300 ml × 4 3 kl 650 l × 3

7. 3 hr. 25 min. × 4 8 min. 30 sec. × 4

Solve each word problem below.

8. To make a park bench, Brian needed four iron rods, each 6 feet 8 inches long. What total length of rod did Brian need?

9. In Georgia's job, she packages telephones for delivery to electronic supply stores. If each phone weighs 1 kg 250 g, what does a box that contains 12 phones weigh?

10. A recipe for ice cream calls for 1 pint 6 ounces of light cream. What total amount of light cream would be needed to make 5 times as much ice cream?

11. Renée uses pure silver to make jewelry. She uses strands of silver that are 4 cm 3 mm long. What total length of silver does Renée have if she has 6 strands left?

Dividing Measurement Units

To divide a quantity by a number, first divide the number into the largest unit of measurement. Next, change any remainder into the next smallest unit in the problem. Then add the remainder to the smaller units already present. Finally, divide this sum by the number. An example is shown below for weight measures in both the standard and metric systems.

STANDARD SYSTEM

Divide: 1 lb.
3)5 lb. 4 oz.
3
Remainder: → 2

Add: 2 lb. = 32 oz. to second column

Answer: **1 lb. 12 oz.**
3)5 lb. 4 oz
3
2 lb. = 32 oz.
Divide → 36 oz.
36 by 3: 36 oz.

Division
Step 1. Divide the first column.
Step 2. Change the remainder of the first column to the units of the second column. Add this remainder to the second column.
Step 3. Add the numbers in the second column. Divide this sum.

METRIC SYSTEM

Divide: 1 kg
2)3 kg 250 g
2
Remainder: → 1

Add: 1 kg = 1,000 g to second column

Answer: **1 kg 625 g**
2)3 kg 250 g
2
1 kg = 1000 g
Divide→ 1250 g
1250 by 2: 1250 g

Divide the following quantities.

1. 5)7 ft. 6 in. 3)4 mi. 34 yd.

2. 6)16 m 26 cm 2)7 km 488 m

3. 2)3 T. 600 lb. 7)15 kg 470 g

4. 2)5 gal. 2 qt. 3)4 pt. 8 oz.

5. 4)5 l 280 ml 5)7 kl 550 l

6. 2)3 hr. 20 min. 2)3 d. 8 hr.

Solve each word problem below.

7. If Marie wants to cut a 6-foot 8-inch piece of ribbon into five equal pieces, how long should she cut each piece?

8. Arlene is going to cut a large piece of beef into seven rib roasts. If the uncut beef weighs 29 pounds 5 ounces, about how much should each roast weigh?

Learning About Perimeter

The distance around an object is called its ***perimeter***. For example, the distance around a lake is its perimeter. Perimeter is measured in length units. The symbol for perimeter is *P*.

To determine the perimeter of a many-sided figure, just add the lengths of its sides.

EXAMPLE: What is the perimeter of the field at the right? Simplify the answer.

Step 1. Add the lengths of the four sides:

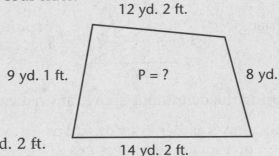

12 yd. 2 ft.
9 yd. 1 ft.
14 yd. 2 ft.
+ 8 yd.
43 yd. 5 ft.

12 yd. 2 ft.
9 yd. 1 ft.
P = ?
8 yd.
14 yd. 2 ft.

Step 2. Simplify the answer:
a) Change 5 ft. to 1 yd. 2 ft.
b) Add 1 yd. 2 ft. to 43 yd.

43 yd.
+ 1 yd. 2 ft.
44 yd. 2 ft.

Answer: The perimeter is 44 yds. 2 ft.

Find the perimeter of each figure below and simplify each answer.

1. P = ________________

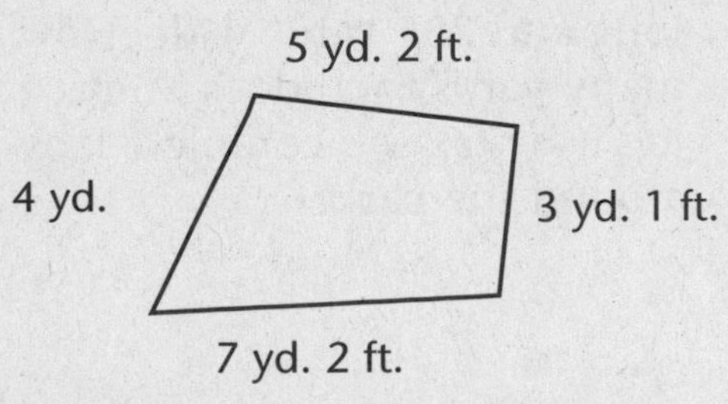

2. P = ________________

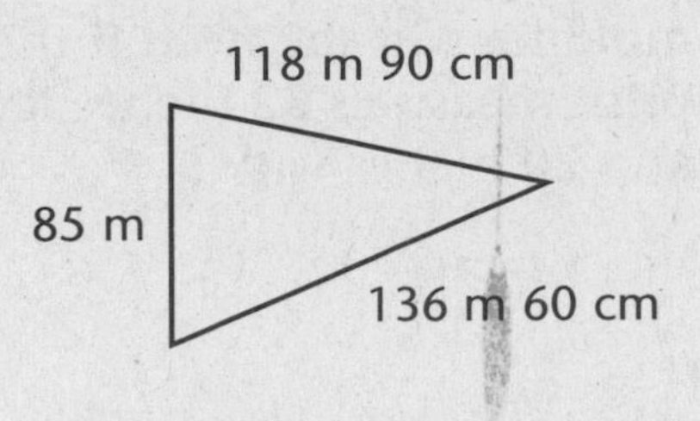

3. P = ____________________

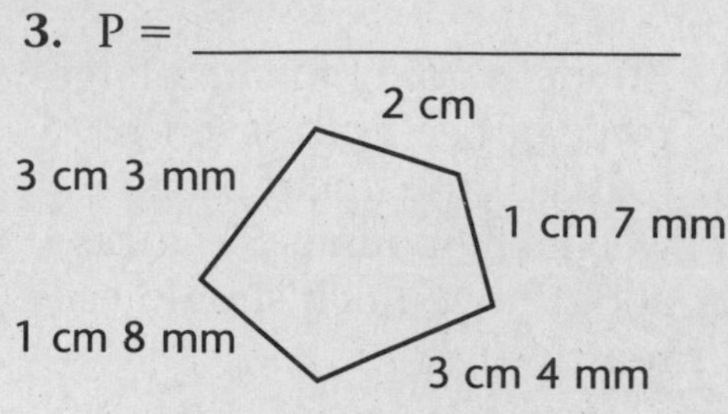

4. P = ____________________

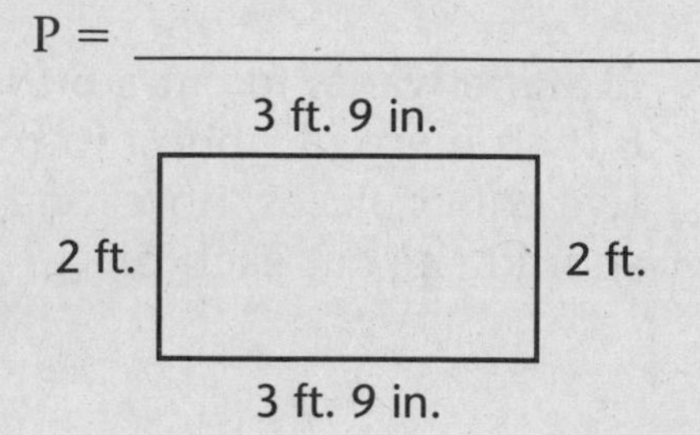

Word problems most often involve finding the perimeter of an object that has a common geometrical shape. The three most common geometrical shapes are the **square**, the **rectangle**, and the **triangle**.

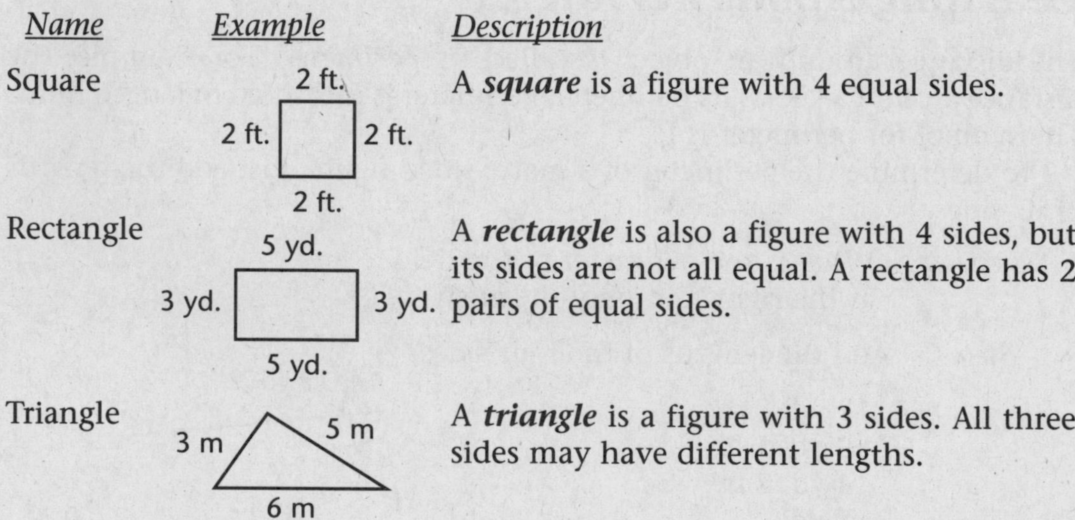

Name	*Example*	*Description*
Square	2 ft. / 2 ft. / 2 ft. / 2 ft.	A ***square*** is a figure with 4 equal sides.
Rectangle	5 yd. / 3 yd. / 3 yd. / 5 yd.	A ***rectangle*** is also a figure with 4 sides, but its sides are not all equal. A rectangle has 2 pairs of equal sides.
Triangle	3 m / 5 m / 6 m	A ***triangle*** is a figure with 3 sides. All three sides may have different lengths.

Using the definitions above, answer the following questions.

5. Amy's garden is in the shape of a square that measures 21 yards on each side. How many yards of fencing must Amy use to enclose the garden?

6. Allison is making a frame for a rectangular print. About how many inches of frame molding will she need if the print measures 32 inches long and 20 inches wide?

7. A piece of cut glass, in the shape of a triangle, is to be enclosed in a solder strip. What length of solder is needed if the glass sides measure 9 cm 4 mm, 12 cm 5 mm, and 14 cm?

8. Mick jogs each afternoon around Oak Park. The rectangular park is 450 yards long and 285 yards wide. How many yards total does Mick jog if he takes 5 complete laps around the park?

Becoming Familiar with Area

Area is a measure of surface. For example, to measure the size of a floor you determine its area. A larger room has more floor space and thus has a larger area than a smaller room. The symbol for area is *A*.

To measure area, you use an **area unit** in the shape of a square. A square has 4 equal sides that meet at right angles.

For example, at right is a scale drawing of a square that measures 1 foot on each side. This area unit is called a ***square foot.***

1 square foot

1 foot

1 foot

Common area units in the standard (or American) system are the **square inch** (sq. in.), **square foot** (sq. ft.), and **square yard** (sq. yd.). Common area units in the metric system are the **square centimeter** (cm^2) and **square meter** (m^2).

The area of a flat figure can be measured by counting the number of square area units that fit inside the figure.

EXAMPLE: What is the area of the rectangle at right?

The rectangle is divided into square area units. As shown, each area unit is 1 square yard.

To find the area of this rectangle, count the number of square yards that fit inside the rectangle.

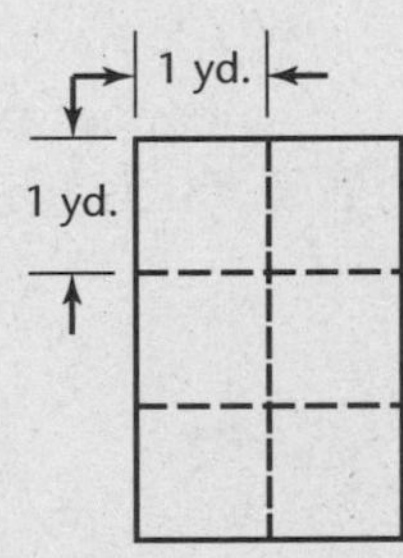

Answer: 6 square yards

Determine the area of each figure below. Be sure to include the correct area unit label as part of each answer.

1. A = ___________

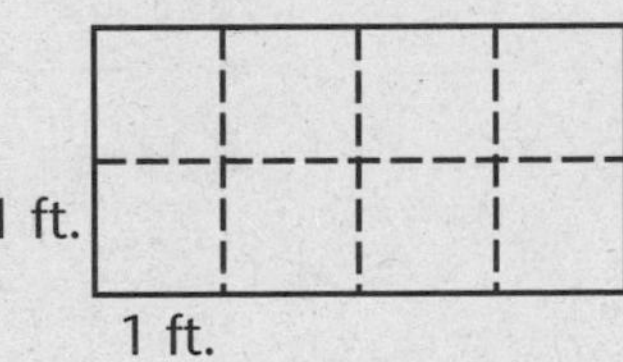

2. A = ___________

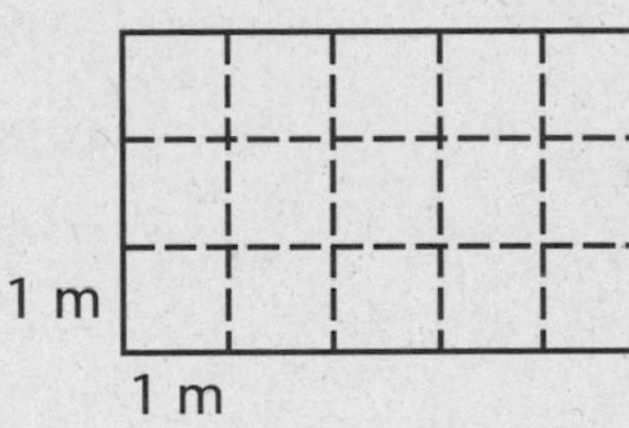

3. A = ___________

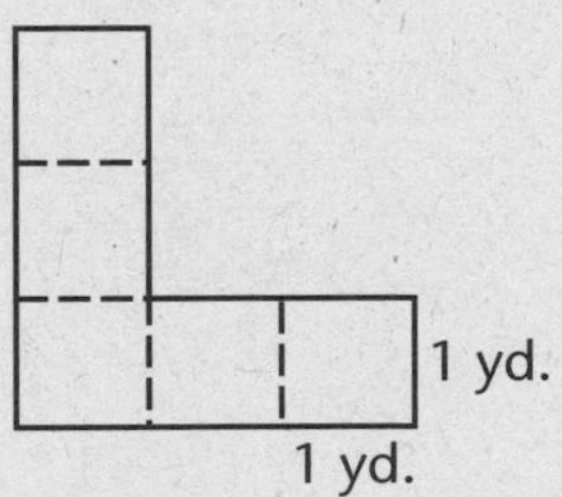

4. A = ___________

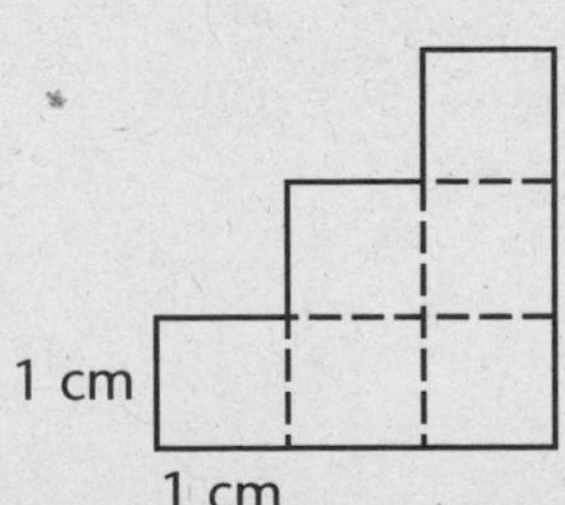

5. A = ___________

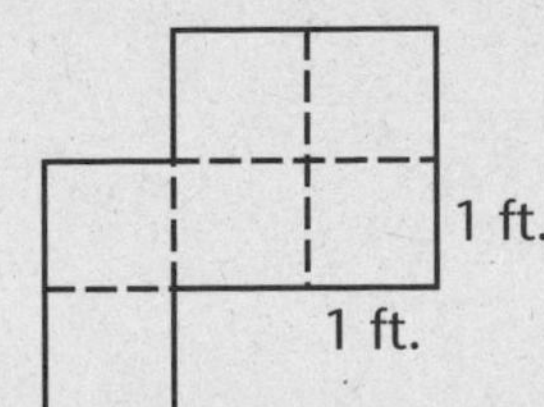

6. A = ___________

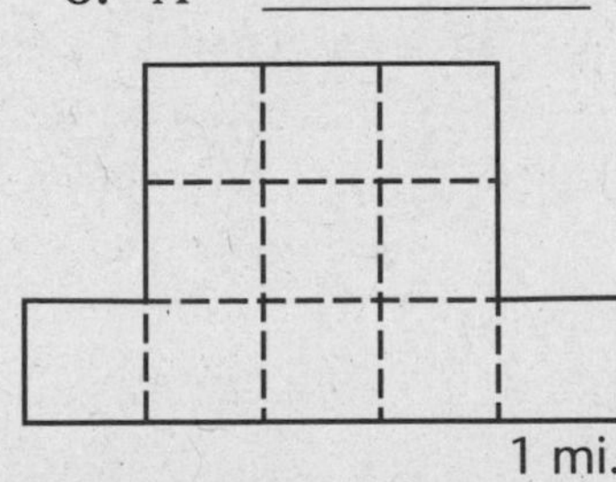

The most common area you'll ever work with is that of a rectangle. Dividing the rectangle below into 1-foot squares, you can see that the rectangle has an area of 24 square feet. Notice that we can get this answer most easily by multiplying the length (6 feet) by the width (4 feet).

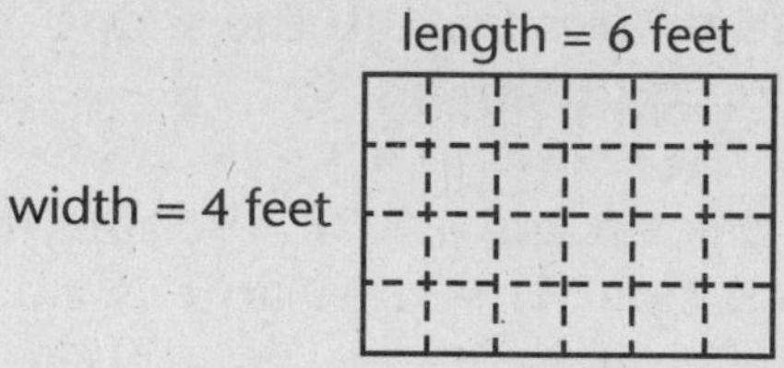

length = 6 feet

width = 4 feet

Area = 6 ft. x 4 ft. = 24 square feet

The drawing gives us a rule to use to find the area of any rectangle:

To find the area of a rectangle, multiply the length by the width.

Use the rule given above to help you answer the following questions.

7. At a cost of $12.50 per square yard, how much would it cost to carpet a room that measures 4 yards long by 3 yards wide?

8. Joan wants to tile her kitchen floor. The floor is in the shape of a rectangle 10 feet long and 7 feet wide. How many tiles will she need if each tile measures 12" by 12" (1 square foot)?

9. How many square yards of Astroturf are needed to cover a football field measuring 120 yards long by 60 yards wide?

10. Guy, a groundskeeper, needs to fertilize a rectangular lawn. The lawn measures 50 meters long and 35 meters wide. If each bag of fertilizer will cover 100 square meters, how many bags will he need to complete the job?

Becoming Familiar with Volume

Volume is a measure of space. For example, volume is the space taken up by a solid object such as a brick. Volume is also the space enclosed by a solid surface. The volume of a box is the space enclosed by its top, its sides, and its bottom. The symbol for volume is *V*.

To measure volume, you use a **volume unit** in the shape of a cube. A cube has 6 surfaces called ***faces***. Each face is a square.

At right is a scale drawing of a cube that measures 1 yard along each edge. (Each square face has 1-yard-long sides.) This volume unit is called a ***cubic yard***.

1 yd.
1 yd.
1 yd.

Common volume units in the standard system are the **cubic inch** (cu. in.), **cubic foot** (cu. ft.), and **cubic yard** (cu. yd.). Common volume units in the metric system are the **cubic centimeter** (cm^3) and **cubic meter** (m^3).

The volume of a figure can be measured by counting the number of cubic volume units that fit inside the figure.

EXAMPLE: What is the volume of the rectangular solid pictured at right?

The rectangular solid is divided into cubic volume units. As shown, each volume unit is 1 cubic foot.

To find the volume of this figure, count the number of cubic feet that fit inside it.

We have numbered the 6 volume units in the front layer, and there are 3 layers.

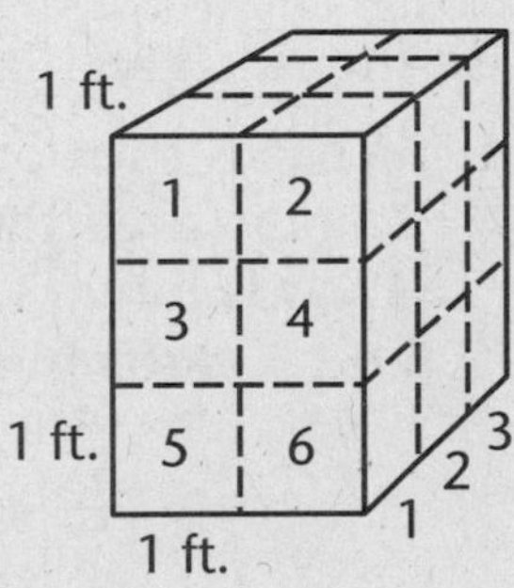

NOTE: There are 6 volume units in each of 3 layers.

Answer: 6 × 3 = 18 cubic feet

Determine the volume of each figure below. Be sure to include the correct volume unit label as part of each answer.

1. V = ___________

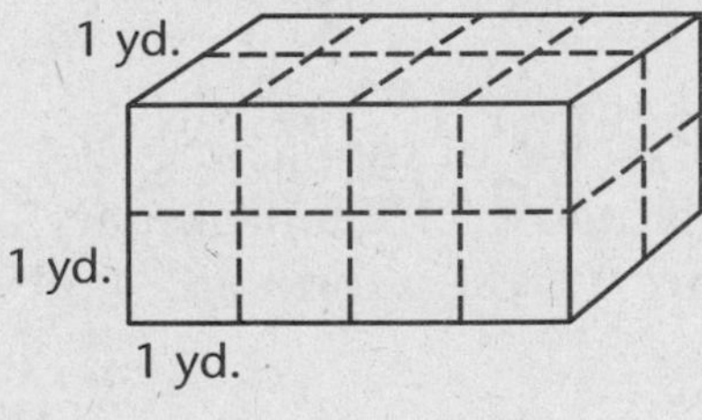

2. V = ___________

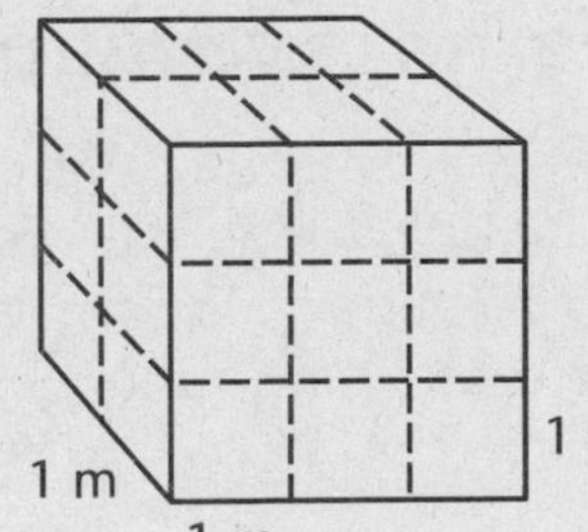

3. V = ___________

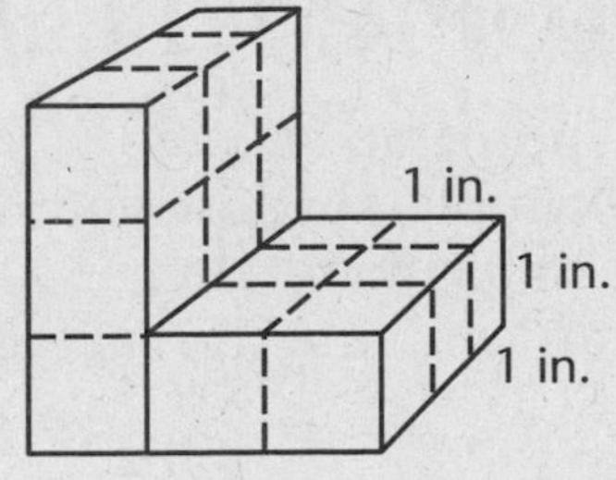

The most common volume you'll ever work with is that of the rectangular solid. Boxes, suitcases, freezers, and rooms all have a rectangular solid shape. Below we have divided a rectangular solid into 24 cubic feet. Notice that we can find this volume most easily by multiplying the length (4 feet) by the width (2 feet) by the height (3 feet).

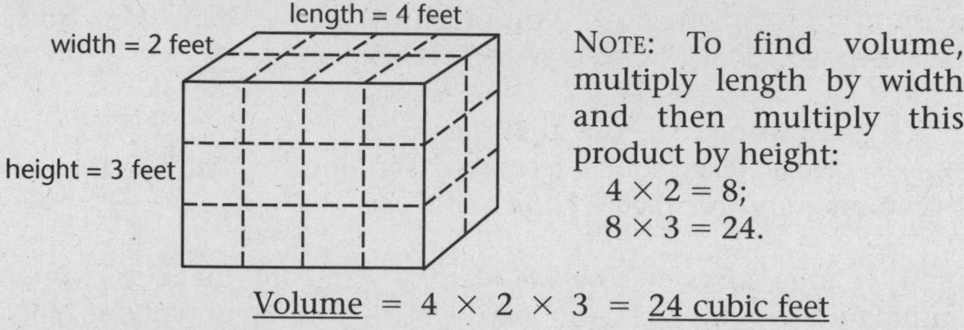

NOTE: To find volume, multiply length by width and then multiply this product by height:
$4 \times 2 = 8;$
$8 \times 3 = 24.$

Volume = $4 \times 2 \times 3$ = 24 cubic feet

This drawing gives us a rule for finding the volume of any rectangular solid:

To find the volume of a rectangular solid, multiply the length by the width by the height.

Use the rule given above to help you answer the following questions.

4. What is the volume of a storage shed that measures 4 yards long, 3 yards wide, and 3 yards high?

5. What is the volume of a small freezer that has inside dimensions of 3 feet, 2 feet, and 2 feet?

6. How many cubic feet of water are in a water bed that is 6 feet long, 5 feet wide, and 1 foot high? If 1 cubic foot of water weighs about 62 pounds, what is the weight of water in this bed when full?

TOPIC 3: Finding an Average

Finding an average is a good way to get a "typical" value of something. For example, suppose your phone bills are as follows: January, \$18.25; February, \$24.05; and March, \$21.60. To get a value for your typical phone bill, you can compute the average of these 3 amounts.

To compute the average of a group of numbers, add the numbers together and then divide by the number of numbers in the group. Your average phone bill is easily computed:

Step 1. Add the 3 bills.

$$\begin{array}{r} \$18.25 \\ 24.05 \\ +\ 21.60 \\ \hline \$63.90 \end{array}$$

Step 2. Divide by 3, the number of numbers added.

$$\begin{array}{r} \$21.30 \\ 3\overline{)\$63.90} \end{array}$$

Answer: $21.30

NOTE: In most problems, as in the example, the average does not turn out to be equal to any of the numbers in the group of numbers you add. However, the average is usually close to the middle value in each group.

Answer each question below.

1. The Jenkins triplets, Bob, Ben, and Bill, weigh 124 pounds, 120 pounds, and 125 pounds, respectively. What is the average weight of these three young men?

2. On a 4-day trip to Canada, Amber drove 480 miles the first day. She then drove 362 miles the second day, 412 miles the third day, and 290 miles on the fourth day. On the average, how many miles did Amber drive each day?

3. Three different models of a 20-inch color TV set sell for $318, $289, and $329. What is the average price of these 3 TV sets?

4. Part of Jed's diet plan is to keep track of the number of calories he eats each day. During the first 2 weeks, he made a list of daily calories as shown below. Using this list, figure out the average number of daily calories Jed ate each week.

   1st week: ____ 2nd week: ____

	1st Week	2nd Week
Monday	1,800	1,925
Tuesday	1,750	2,100
Wednesday	1,770	1,970
Thursday	1,810	1,975
Friday	1,800	1,900
Saturday	1,780	2,080
Sunday	1,820	1,980

5. Over the weekend, the Mueller family rented 3 movies. The first movie was 1 hour 45 minutes long; the second was 2 hours 10 minutes long; and the third was 1 hour 53 minutes. What is the average length of these movies?

TOPIC 4: Squares, Cubes, and Square Roots

Math has many of its own words, symbols, and definitions. These include **squares, cubes,** and **square roots.**

Square of a Number

The ***square*** of a number is that number multiplied by itself.
For example, the square of 6 is $6 \times 6 = 36$.

In symbols, we write the square of a number as a **base** and an **exponent**.

6×6 is written 6^2 ← exponent
↑ base

The exponent (2) tells how many times the base (6) is written in the product when you multiply. The exponent of a square is always 2.
We commonly read 6^2 as "six squared." The **value** of 6^2 is 36.

Cube of a Number

The ***cube*** of a number is that number multiplied by itself twice.
For example, the cube of 6 is $6 \times 6 \times 6 = 36 \times 6 = 216$.

In symbols, we write a cube with an exponent of 3.

$6 \times 6 \times 6$ is written 6^3 ← exponent
↑ base

We commonly read 6^3 as "six cubed." The **value** of 6^3 is 216.

To find the value of the square or cube of a number, you do the multiplication represented by the symbols.

Look at these examples:

Product	*As a base and an exponent*	*Read in words*	*Value*
2×2	2^2	"two squared"	4
5×5	5^2	"five squared"	25
12×12	12^2	"twelve squared"	144
$2 \times 2 \times 2$	2^3	"two cubed"	8
$4 \times 4 \times 4$	4^3	"four cubed"	64
$10 \times 10 \times 10$	10^3	"ten cubed"	1,000

Complete the following chart.

Product	As a base and an exponent	In words
1. 4×4	4^2	*four squared*
2. 5×5		
3. 10×10		
4. 25×25		
5. $3 \times 3 \times 3$	3^3	*three cubed*
6. $8 \times 8 \times 8$		
7. $10 \times 10 \times 10$		
8. $32 \times 32 \times 32$		

Find each value as indicated below.

9. $7^2 =$ ________ 12. $15^2 =$ ________ 15. $7^3 =$ ________

10. $9^2 =$ ________ 13. $20^2 =$ ________ 16. $12^3 =$ ________

11. $12^2 =$ ________ 14. $3^3 =$ ________ 17. $20^3 =$ ________

What Is a Square Root?

The ***square root*** of a number is found by asking, "What number times itself equals this number?" For example, to find the square root of 25 we ask, "What number times itself equals 25?" The answer is 5 because $5 \times 5 = 25$.

The symbol for square root is $\sqrt{}$. Thus, $5 = \sqrt{25}$.

Numbers that have whole number square roots are called ***perfect squares.*** A list of perfect squares is easily made by "squaring" whole numbers. The first 15 perfect squares are shown in the table below.

Table of Perfect Squares

$1^2 = 1$	$6^2 = 36$	$11^2 = 121$
$2^2 = 4$	$7^2 = 49$	$12^2 = 144$
$3^2 = 9$	$8^2 = 64$	$13^2 = 169$
$4^2 = 16$	$9^2 = 81$	$14^2 = 196$
$5^2 = 25$	$10^2 = 100$	$15^2 = 225$

The values in this table can be used to find the square roots of perfect squares.

EXAMPLE: What is the square root of 169?

Find 169 in the column at right.

Since $13^2 = 169$, 13 is the square root of 169.

In symbols, $13 = \sqrt{169}$.

Write each sentence below in symbols. The first one is done as an example.

1. Four is the square root of sixteen. $4 = \sqrt{16}$
2. Ten is the square root of one hundred. ________
3. Nine is the square root of eighty-one. ________
4. Twelve is the square root of one hundred forty-four. ________

Use the Table of Perfect Squares to find each square root below.

5. $\sqrt{64}$ = ______
6. $\sqrt{4}$ = ______
7. $\sqrt{121}$ = ______
8. $\sqrt{25}$ = ______
9. $\sqrt{49}$ = ______
10. $\sqrt{225}$ = ______
11. $\sqrt{1}$ = ______
12. $\sqrt{196}$ = ______
13. $\sqrt{36}$ = ______

7 Decimal Skills

Decimal Fractions

Each of us sees or uses decimal fractions every day. This is because our money system uses them. Decimal fractions are used to represent parts of a dollar called ***cents***. One cent (a penny) is one hundredth of a dollar. As a decimal fraction, hundredths are written as the first two numbers to the right of a decimal point.

Think of a dollar as being divided into 100 parts, each part standing for 1¢. Twenty-seven hundredths of a dollar is 27¢. As a decimal fraction, 27¢ is written as follows:

27¢ = $.27 (Read each as "27 cents" although you can also correctly read $.27 as "27 hundredths of a dollar.")

↑ decimal point

Two of the most common uses of decimal fractions are our money system and the metric measuring system. In the metric system, a meter is divided into 100 equal parts called ***centimeters.*** Because of this, a length such as 35 centimeters is often written as the decimal fraction .35 meter (35 hundredths of a meter).

A mixed decimal is a whole number plus a decimal fraction.

The number 7.29 is an example of a **mixed decimal**. When you read a mixed decimal, you read the decimal point as the word *and*. This is true both for money and for a number standing alone:

$7.29 is read as "Seven dollars *and* twenty-nine cents."

7.29 is read as "Seven *and* twenty-nine hundredths."

Each place in a mixed decimal has a certain **place value**. To the left of the decimal point are the familiar place values of whole numbers.

To the right of the decimal point are the place values of decimal numbers. The first place is the **tenths place**. To the right of the tenths place is the **hundredths place**. Continuing to the right, each new place value decreases by a multiple of ten. Notice that each decimal place value ends in the letters *ths*.

As you study **decimals** (decimal fractions and mixed decimals), you'll want to become familiar with the first six whole number and decimal fraction place value names.

Answers to Chapter 7 exercises start on page 920.

PLACE VALUE NAMES IN MIXED DECIMALS

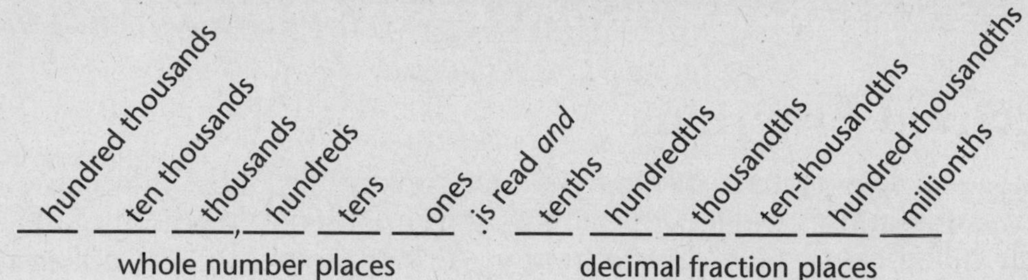

It is helpful to remember that each decimal place stands for part of a whole. Look at the meaning of each of these simple decimal fractions:

Example	*Value*	*Meaning*
.1	one tenth	one part out of 10 parts
.01	one hundredth	one part out of 100 parts
.001	one thousandth	one part out of 1,000 parts
.0001	one ten-thousandth	one part out of 10,000 parts
.00001	one hundred-thousandth	one part out of 100,000 parts
.000001	one millionth	one part out of 1,000,000 parts

The number of digits to the right of the decimal point is called the **number of decimal places.**

Use words to express the value of each **whole number** and **decimal fraction** below.

1. 1,000 ______________________ .001 ______________________
2. 100 ______________________ .01 ______________________
3. 10 ______________________ .1 ______________________
4. 100,000 ______________________ .00001 ______________________
5. 10,000 ______________________ .0001 ______________________

Express the following **mixed decimals** in words.

6. 2.1 ______________________
7. 5.01 ______________________
8. 7.001 ______________________
9. $13.01 ______________________

Reading Decimals

A decimal fraction may have one or more nonzero digits. To read a decimal fraction, first read the number to the right of the decimal point. Read this number just as you'd read a whole number. Then read the place value of the digit farthest to the right. **You can think of a decimal fraction as a number plus a place value.**

Examples	*Number*	*+ Place Value*	*Read as*
.4	4	tenths	4 tenths
.04	4	hundredths	4 hundredths
.35	35	hundredths	35 hundredths
.035	35	thousandths	35 thousandths
.140	140	thousandths	140 thousandths

Although the number 4 in .4 is the same as the number 4 in .04, these decimal fractions have different values. The 4 in .4 is in the tenths place, while the 4 in .04 is in the hundredths place.

Similarly, .35 differs from .035. Each has number 35. But the place value in each is determined by the 5, the farthest digit to the right. In .35 the place value is hundredths. In .035 the place value is thousandths.

When reading a mixed decimal, remember to read the decimal point as the word *and*, connecting the whole number with the decimal fraction.

17.538 is read "17 *and* 538 thousandths."

Show how each of the following decimal fractions is read. Two are done as examples.

1. .5 *5 tenths* .7 ________ .9 ________

2. .12 *12 hundredths* .27 ________ .50 ________

3. .135 ________ .272 ________ .180 ________

4. .2048 ________ .1305 ________ .4000 ________

5. .12348 ________ .83721 ________ .204000 ________

Show how each of the following mixed decimals is read.

6. 5.8 ________ 7.19 ________

7. 6.87 ________ 14.105 ________

8. 29.326 ________ 154.60 ________

9. 3.2442 ________ 18.38724 ________

Writing Zero as a Place Holder

Although the digit 0 has no value, it is used as a **place holder.** Placed between the decimal point and a decimal digit, zero changes the value of a decimal fraction. Placed at the far right of a decimal fraction, zero changes the way the fraction is read but does not change its value.

EXAMPLE 1: The decimal fraction .04 differs from .4 because of the 0 in the tenths place. It is this 0 that *holds* 4 in the hundredths place.

> A zero that comes anywhere between the decimal point and the last nonzero digit is called a ***necessary zero.*** A necessary zero cannot be removed without changing the value of a number.
>
> **Examples of necessary zeros:** $.\underline{0}4$ $.5\underline{0}6$ $3.\underline{0}2\underline{0}5$ $.\underline{00}80$

EXAMPLE 2: The decimal fractions .60 and .6 differ in the way they are read. You read .60 as 60 hundredths, and .6 as 6 tenths. Yet both have the same value. This is similar to the fact that 60 pennies have the same value as 6 dimes.

> Because zeros at the far right do not change the value of a decimal fraction, these zeros are called ***unnecessary zeros.***
>
> **Examples of unnecessary zeros:** .60 .2500 4.7030

Underline each **necessary zero** in each of the decimals below. Circle each **unnecessary zero.**

1.	.05	.106	.007	2.30	4.650
2.	.109	.048	5.070	.2031	5.0040
3.	2.0030	.650	.07700	1.1030	.50050

In each group of three decimal fractions below, circle the two that have the same value.

4.	.03, .003, .030	.405, .450, .45	.61, .061, .610
5.	.015, .0150, .105	.0271, .2710, .271	.0306, .03060, .30600

Writing Decimals

To write a decimal fraction, first decide the **place value** of your number. The place value tells you how far from the decimal point to place the number's last digit.

EXAMPLE: Write **thirty-six thousandths** as a decimal fraction.

Step 1. Identify **thousandths** as the place value. You know this because *thousandths* is the last word of the number. Also, place value is always a word that ends in *th* or *ths*.

Step 2. Write 36. Place the decimal point so that 6 ends up in the thousandths place, the third place to the right. Since 36 is only a two-digit number, use a zero to hold the first place.

0 is written as a place holder

.036

6 ends up in the thousandths place

Answer: **thirty-six thousandths is written as .036**

To write a mixed decimal, remember that the word *and* separates the whole number from the decimal fraction.

Examples	*Written as a decimal*
five hundredths	.05
twenty-one hundredths	.21
sixty-four thousandths	.064
four and three hundred seventeen thousandths	4.317
five and seven tenths	5.7
ninety and sixty-one hundredths	90.61

Write each number below as a decimal fraction or a mixed decimal.

1. nine tenths _____

2. seven hundredths _____

3. thirty-five hundredths _____

4. twenty-seven thousandths _____

5. four and one tenth _____

6. two and nine hundredths _____

7. fifty and twenty hundredths _____

8. six and eighty thousandths _____

9. eight hundred forty-three thousandths _____

10. one hundred seventy-four and sixty-five hundredths _____

11. one thousand four hundred and seventy-five thousandths _____

Comparing Decimal Fractions

Decimal fractions can easily be compared when they have the same number of decimal places. For example, you know that $.40 is larger than $.08. Since each amount is written with two decimal places, you simply compare the number 40 with the number 8.

Rules for Comparing Decimal Fractions

1. Use zeros to give each decimal fraction the same number of places. Remember, placing one or more zeros **to the right** of a decimal fraction does not change its value.

2. Compare the numbers.

EXAMPLE: Which decimal fraction is larger, .07 or .048?

Step 1. Give .07 and .048 the same number of places. To do this, place a zero at the right end of .07: .07 = .070.

Step 2. Compare the numbers 70 and 48. Because 70 is larger than 48, .070 is larger than .048. Therefore, .07 is larger than .048.

Answer: .07 is larger than .048

Place 0 at end

.07 = .070
↑ like this

not at front

.07 = .007
↑ not like this

In each pair below, circle the larger decimal fraction.

1. .32 or .51
2. .137 or .401
3. .29 or .4
4. .3 or .184
5. .66 or .493
6. .76 or .2321
7. .482 or .2673
8. .392 or .6004
9. $.80 or $.56

Arrange each group of numbers below in order. In each group write the smallest number to the left and the largest to the right. The first one is done for you.

10. .43, .8, .134

    .430, .800, .134

    .134, .43, .8

11. .201, .4, .35
12. $.53, $.09, $.28
13. .209, .45, .5
14. .6, .35, .42
15. .611, .64, .174

Rounding Decimal Fractions

To **round a decimal fraction** is to simplify the way it is written. You do this by discarding digits that are not needed.

EXAMPLE 1: Erin earns $7.68 for each hour of overtime she works. How much will she earn in 2.4 hours of overtime work on Saturday?

Step 1. You solve this problem by multiplying $7.68 by 2.4. This multiplication is shown at right.

Notice that the answer contains 3 digits to the right of the decimal point.

```
   $7.68
 ×   2.4
   3 072
  15 36
 $18.432
```

Step 2. To write $18.432 as dollars and cents, we want to keep only two digits to the right of the decimal point. To do this, we **round** $18.432 to $18.43 by discarding the 2.

Answer: **$18.43**

The steps for rounding decimal fractions are almost the same as the steps for rounding whole numbers.

Steps for Rounding Decimal Fractions

1. Underline the digit in the place you are rounding to.
2. Look at the digit to the right of the underlined digit. If the digit to the right is 5 or more, add 1 to the underlined digit. If the digit to the right is less than 5, leave the underlined digit as it is.
3. Discard the digits to the right of the underlined digit.

EXAMPLE 2: Round 2.1749 to the thousandths place.

Step 1. Underline the digit in the thousandths place.
Underline the 4: 2.17$\underline{4}$9.

Step 2. Look at the digit to the right of the 4. The digit is 9. Since 9 is "5 or more," add 1 to the underlined digit 4.
Add 1 to 4: 2.17$\underline{5}$9̸.

Step 3. Discard the digit 9.

Answer: **2.175**

Round each amount below to the nearest cent. For each amount circle one of the two answer choices.

1. $.467: $.46 *or* $.47 $.015: $.01 *or* $.02 $.953: $.95 *or* $.96

2. $6.875: $6.87 *or* $6.88 $83.746: $83.74 *or* $83.75

Round each decimal fraction below as indicated. The first problem in each row is done for you.

To the nearest tenth.

3. .24 *.2* .37 ______ .52 ______ .408 ______ .375 ______

.$\underline{2}$4
↑ less than 5

To the nearest hundredth.

4. .406 *.41* .483 ______ .725 ______ .8715 ______ .3842 ______

.4$\underline{0}$6
↑ 5 or more

To the nearest thousandth.

5. .0273 .027 .8394 _____ .3847 _____ .6283 _____ .93042 _____

.0273
↑ less than 5

6. When regular gas is selling for $1.069 per gallon, what is its price to the nearest cent per gallon?

7. The machinist's blueprint showed that the key should be 2.136 inches long. What length is this to the nearest hundredth inch?

Adding Decimals

To add decimals, line up the decimal points and then add each column just as you do when you add whole numbers. **Place a decimal point in the answer directly below the decimal points in the problem.** Carrying with decimals is done the same way as carrying with whole numbers. **Carry across the decimal point as if it weren't there.**

EXAMPLE 1: Add .23 and .16.

Step 1. Line up the decimal points and add the columns.

$$\begin{array}{r} .23 \\ +\ .16 \\ \hline .39 \end{array}$$

Step 2 Place the decimal point in the answer directly below the decimal points.

Answer: .39

EXAMPLE 2: Add .85 and .63.

Step 1. Line up the decimal points and add the columns. Carry the 1 from the tenths column to the ones column.

$$\begin{array}{r} {}^{1}.85 \\ +\ .63 \\ \hline 1.48 \end{array}$$

Step. 2. Place the decimal point in the answer.

Answer: 1.48

Add.

.3	.42	.624	.9	.645	8.94
+ .2	+ .16	+ .304	+ .7	+ .571	+ 4.46

Zeros as Place Holders

To add numbers that do not have the same number of decimal places, you may find it helpful to use zeros as place holders.

EXAMPLE 5: Add 8, 5.231, and 1.36.

		Line up the decimal points.	*Use zeros as place holders.*
Step 1.	Write a decimal point to the right of the 8, and line up the three decimal points. Use zeros to give each number the same number of decimal places.	8. 5.231 + 1.36	8.000 5.231 + 1.360 14.591
Step 2.	Add the columns.		
Answer:	**14.591**		

Use zeros as place holders to add each problem below.

1.	.56	.6	.232	.743	.864	.92
	+ .2	+ .14	+ .16	+ .2	+ .76	+ .7507

2. .34 + .12 .64 + .5 .345 + .25 .2535 + .12

3. 4 + 3.26 2.175 + .92 5.21 + 3 6.81 + 4.2

4. 7 + 3.61 + 1.3 4.2 + 3 + 2.87 6.81 + 4 + 3.9

Subtracting Decimals

To subtract decimals, place the smaller number directly below the larger number and line up the decimal points. Then subtract, borrowing if necessary, just as you would subtract whole numbers. **Place a decimal point in the answer directly below the decimal points in the problem.**

EXAMPLE 1: Subtract 1.24 from 5.61.

Step 1. Write 1.24 directly below 5.61. Make sure you line up the decimal points. Subtract by borrowing from the tenths column in order to subtract the hundredths column.

Step 2. Place a decimal point in the answer.

Answer: 4.37

Subtract.

1. $\begin{array}{r} .9 \\ -\ .3 \\ \hline \end{array}$ $\begin{array}{r} .8 \\ -\ .1 \\ \hline \end{array}$ $\begin{array}{r} .97 \\ -\ .25 \\ \hline \end{array}$ $\begin{array}{r} 7.4 \\ -\ 3.2 \\ \hline \end{array}$ $\begin{array}{r} 13.9 \\ -\ 5.6 \\ \hline \end{array}$ $\begin{array}{r} 23.67 \\ -\ 7.50 \\ \hline \end{array}$

2. .9 − .7 .8 − .4 1.83 − .92 12.34 − 9.28

3. \$3.75 − \$2.68 \$12.29 − \$7.86 \$7.85 − \$4.59 2.456 − 1.488

To subtract numbers that do not have the same number of decimal places, write in extra zeros as place holders. When necessary, borrow from these zeros in the same way you borrow when subtracting whole numbers. You can borrow across the decimal point as if it weren't there.

EXAMPLE 2: Subtract 3.4 from 5.82.

Line up the decimal points. $\begin{array}{r} 5.82 \\ -\ 3.4 \\ \hline \end{array}$

Use a zero as a place holder. $\begin{array}{r} 5.82 \\ -\ 3.40 \\ \hline 2.42 \end{array}$

Answer: 2.42

EXAMPLE 3: Subtract 2.36 from 9.

Line up the decimal points. $\begin{array}{r} 9. \\ -\ 2.36 \\ \hline \end{array}$

Use two zeros as place holders. $\begin{array}{r} {}^{8}\not{9}.{}^{9}\not{0}{}^{10}\not{0} \\ -\ 2.36 \\ \hline 6.64 \end{array}$

Answer: 6.64

Perform each subtraction below. Place a decimal point to the right of each whole number and write in extra zeros as needed. Be sure to line up the decimal points.

4. .95 − .8   2.56 − 1.8   .3802 − .27   .504 − .3

5. 7 − 5.37   4 − 3.48   3.53 − 2   12 − 4.598

6. .304 − .10   3.46 − 3.1   8 − 4.204

Solving Addition and Subtraction Word Problems

In problems 1 and 2, underline a key word that suggests either addition or subtraction. Then solve each problem.

1. During the first half of baseball season, Hank's batting average was .306. During the second half, his average increased by .048. What was Hank's batting average at the end of the season?

2. The area of the United States is 3.62 million square miles. The area of Canada is 3.85 million square miles. What is the difference in area of these two countries?

Problems 3 and 4 contain extra information. In each problem, circle only the necessary information and then solve the problem.

3. The distance from Joe's house to his workplace is 12.8 miles. His workplace is 5.6 miles north of town. On the way to work he drops his daughter off at school, a distance of 5.9 miles from his house. After he drops her off, how much farther does Joe have to drive to get to his workplace?

4. A machinist cut .025 inch off a shaft that first measured .752 inch across. Since it was still a little too wide, he cut another .003 inch off. Now the shaft fits perfectly. How much did the machinist end up cutting off the shaft?

In problem 5, circle the arithmetic expression that will give the correct answer to each question. You do not need to solve these two problems.

5. Normal human body temperature is 98.6 degrees. When Jill had the flu, her temperature went up to 103.4 degrees. By taking a cool bath, Jill lowered her temperature to 101.7. How much did the bath reduce Jill's temperature?

a) 103.4 − 98.6
b) 103.4 − 101.7
c) 101.7 − 98.6
d) 103.4 + 101.7

In problems 6 and 7, complete the drawings by placing numbers from the problems on the blank lines. Then use the drawings to help you solve each problem.

6. The retail price of a wool sweater at Jessica's Clothes Shop is $59.75. As the owner, Jessica can buy the sweater herself anytime for a price of $39.99. How much markup does Jessica have on this sweater?

Retail price ________

subtract

Owner's price ________

Equals markup ________

7. Sid drew the map at right and measured the following dimensions for his property:

north side:	53.75 meters
east side:	79.69 meters
south side:	51.62 meters
west side:	84.39 meters

Walking clockwise around the eastern edge of the property, how far is it from the northwest corner A to the southwest corner B?

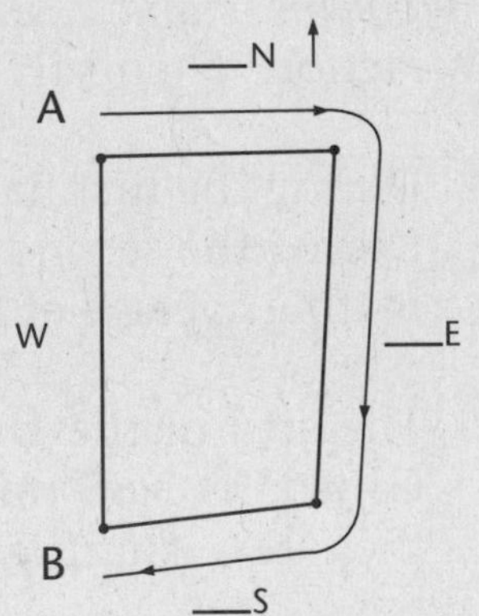

Multiplying Decimal Numbers

When decimal numbers are multiplied, the number of decimal places in the answer must equal the sum of decimal places in the problem.

EXAMPLE: Multiply .385 by .7.

Step 1. Multiply the numbers.

Step 2. Total the number of decimal places in each number being multiplied.

```
  .385     three places
×   .7   + one place
  2695     four places
```

Starting at the right, count over 4 places to the left and place a decimal point in the answer.

.2695 (4 3 2 1)
Start at the right.
← Count to the left.

Answer: .2695

Remember, the number of decimal places in a number is simply the number of digits to the right of the decimal point. A whole number has no decimal places.

Multiplying Decimals by Whole Numbers

Multiply.

1. $\begin{array}{r} {}^{3}8.5 \\ \times\ 6 \\ \hline 51.0 \end{array}$ *one place* / *no place* / *one place* $\quad \begin{array}{r} .74 \\ \times\ 7 \\ \hline \end{array} \quad \begin{array}{r} 126 \\ \times\ .4 \\ \hline \end{array} \quad \begin{array}{r} 23 \\ \times\ .08 \\ \hline \end{array} \quad \begin{array}{r} .89 \\ \times\ 6 \\ \hline \end{array}$

2. $\begin{array}{r} \$.35 \\ \times\ 8 \\ \hline \end{array} \quad \begin{array}{r} 215 \\ \times\ .004 \\ \hline \end{array} \quad \begin{array}{r} \$1.25 \\ \times\ 5 \\ \hline \end{array} \quad \begin{array}{r} 137 \\ \times\ .008 \\ \hline \end{array} \quad \begin{array}{r} \$5.17 \\ \times\ 6 \\ \hline \end{array}$

Multiplying Decimals by Decimals

Multiply.

3. $\begin{array}{r} 6.9 \\ \times\ .3 \\ \hline 2.07 \end{array}$ *one place* / *one place* / *two places* $\quad \begin{array}{r} 8.21 \\ \times\ .07 \\ \hline \end{array} \quad \begin{array}{r} .77 \\ \times\ .8 \\ \hline \end{array} \quad \begin{array}{r} 2.83 \\ \times\ .09 \\ \hline \end{array} \quad \begin{array}{r} .515 \\ \times\ .6 \\ \hline \end{array}$

4. $\begin{array}{r} 1.26 \\ \times\ .32 \\ \hline \end{array} \quad \begin{array}{r} .582 \\ \times\ 6.6 \\ \hline \end{array} \quad \begin{array}{r} .903 \\ \times\ .72 \\ \hline \end{array} \quad \begin{array}{r} 4.74 \\ \times\ 1.6 \\ \hline \end{array} \quad \begin{array}{r} 3.89 \\ \times\ .35 \\ \hline \end{array}$

Rounding Decimal Numbers

Round each answer to the place indicated.

To the nearest tenth.

5. $\begin{array}{r} .24 \\ \times\ 8 \\ \hline 1.92 \end{array} \quad \begin{array}{r} .46 \\ \times\ 4 \\ \hline \end{array} \quad \begin{array}{r} 1.6 \\ \times\ .9 \\ \hline \end{array} \quad \begin{array}{r} .325 \\ \times\ .8 \\ \hline \end{array} \quad \begin{array}{r} 4.61 \\ \times\ 6 \\ \hline \end{array}$

$= 1.\underline{9}2 = 1.9$

To the nearest hundredth.

6. $\begin{array}{r} 4.16 \\ \times\ .8 \\ \hline 3.328 \end{array} \quad \begin{array}{r} 5.28 \\ \times\ .6 \\ \hline \end{array} \quad \begin{array}{r} .35 \\ \times\ .7 \\ \hline \end{array} \quad \begin{array}{r} .52 \\ \times\ .9 \\ \hline \end{array} \quad \begin{array}{r} 7.24 \\ \times\ .06 \\ \hline \end{array}$

$= 3.3\underline{2}8 = 3.33$

In the following example, it is necessary to write a zero as a place holder before the decimal point can be placed in the answer. Can you see why?

EXAMPLE: What is the product of .23 times .14?

```
                     .23   two places
                  × .14    two places
                  { 92
partial products  { 23
                  .0322    four places
```

The answer must have 4 decimal places. This is why we add a zero to the left of the 3 before placing the decimal point in the answer.

7. $.8 \times .2$ $\quad .7 \times .4$ $\quad .9 \times .8$ $\quad .57 \times .8$ $\quad .63 \times .02$

8. $.07 \times .7$ $\quad .05 \times .5$ $\quad .008 \times .07$ $\quad .015 \times .003$ $\quad .106 \times .007$

9. $.0007 \times 6$ $\quad .0006 \times 3$ $\quad 7.2 \times .004$ $\quad .003 \times .08$ $\quad 6.5 \times .009$

Multiplying by 10, 100, or 1,000

Decimal multiplication gives us shortcuts to use when multiplying by 10, 100, or 1,000.

1. **To multiply a decimal by 10, move the decimal point one place to the right.**

EXAMPLE 1: Multiply 2.41 by 10.
$2.41 \times 10 = 2.41$
$= 24.1$

EXAMPLE 2: Multiply .09 by 10.
$.09 \times 10 = .09$
$= .9$

2. **To multiply a decimal by 100, move the decimal point two places to the right.**

EXAMPLE 3: Multiply 5.6 times 100.
5.6 × 100 = 5.60
= **560**

EXAMPLE 4: Multiply:
.3 × 100
.3 × 100 = .30
= **30**

Notice in examples 3 and 4 that zeros have to be added to the right of each number. These zeros hold places so that we can move the decimal point the correct number of places. As you see, these added zeros become part of the whole number answer.

3. **To multiply a decimal by 1,000, move the decimal point three places to the right.**

EXAMPLE 5: Multiply 13.7 by 1,000.
13.7 × 1,000 = 13.700 = **13,700**

Hint: To remember these rules, notice that the decimal point is always moved the same number of places as there are 0s in the multiplying number.

Using the shortcuts, compute each product below. The first one in each row is done as an example.

1. 1.34 × 10 = 13.4   68.3 × 10   2.74 × 10   32.1 × 10   .058 × 10

2. .35 × 10 = 3.5   2.3 × 10 =   .03 × 10 =
.35

3. .253 × 100 = 25.3   .03 × 100 =   21.7 × 100 =
.253

4. 5.14 × 1000 = 5,140   .05 × 1,000 =   74.9 × 1,000 =
5.140

Dividing a Decimal by a Whole Number

To divide a decimal by a whole number, place a decimal point in the answer **directly above its position in the problem.** Then divide the numbers just as you would divide whole numbers.

EXAMPLE: Divide 3.76 by 4.

Step 1. Set up the problem for long division. Place a decimal point in the answer space above the line.

Step 2. Divide as you would divide whole numbers.

Answer: **.94**

$$\begin{array}{r} .94 \\ 4\overline{)3.76} \\ \underline{3\ 6} \\ 16 \\ \underline{16} \\ 0 \end{array}$$

Solve each division problem below.

1. $3\overline{)6.3}$ $7\overline{)4.97}$ $2\overline{).342}$ $5\overline{)3.05}$ $6\overline{).612}$

2. $5\overline{)4.65}$ $9\overline{)20.7}$ $6\overline{)1.452}$ $14\overline{)32.76}$ $20\overline{)132.0}$

When dividing money, be sure to place a dollar sign in the answer.

3. $4\overline{)\$43.36}$ $14\overline{)2.884}$ $16\overline{)\$139.52}$ $6\overline{).936}$ $8\overline{)\$9.44}$

Using Zeros When You Can't Divide

As shown at right, a zero is used to hold a place when you can't divide:

Since you can't divide 4 into 2, put a 0 above the 2. Now divide 4 into 23. Place 5 above the 3 and continue the steps of long division.

EXAMPLE: $4\overline{).236}$

$$\begin{array}{r} \mathbf{.059} \\ 4\overline{).236} \\ \underline{20} \\ 36 \\ \underline{36} \\ 0 \end{array}$$

4. $8\overline{).648}$ $3\overline{).096}$ $7\overline{).0084}$ $12\overline{).108}$ $25\overline{).075}$

5. $9\overline{).297}$ $6\overline{).0774}$ $13\overline{).1053}$ $27\overline{).0567}$ $4\overline{).0504}$

Zeros can also be added to the end of a number to make division possible. At right, a zero is added to 2.4 to give 2.40. Now we can divide by 60.

EXAMPLE:

$$60\overline{)2.4} \rightarrow \begin{array}{r} .04 \\ 60\overline{)2.40} \\ \underline{2\ 40} \end{array}$$

6. $6\overline{).3}$ $8\overline{).4}$ $32\overline{)1.6}$ $40\overline{)2.4}$ $60\overline{)1.2}$

Adding zeros is also useful in many other division problems. As shown in the first example at right, using zeros makes it possible to divide a larger whole number into a smaller whole number. The answer is a decimal fraction.

To divide 5 into 4, add a decimal point and a zero. Then divide.

As shown in the second example, adding several zeros is often a good way to eliminate a remainder in a division problem.

EXAMPLES:

$5\overline{)4}$ $8\overline{)5}$

$$\begin{array}{r} .8 \\ 5\overline{)4.0} \\ \underline{4\ 0} \\ 0 \end{array} \qquad \begin{array}{r} .625 \\ 8\overline{)5.000} \\ \underline{4\ 8} \\ 20 \\ \underline{16} \\ 40 \\ \underline{40} \\ 0 \end{array}$$

Use zeros to divide in each problem below. Add enough zeros in each problem so that division ends with no remainder.

7. $5\overline{)2}$ $4\overline{)1}$ $8\overline{)2}$ $4\overline{)3}$ $5\overline{)6}$

8. $8\overline{)3}$ $4\overline{)7}$ $8\overline{)7}$ $4\overline{)5}$ $16\overline{)5}$

Dividing a Decimal by a Decimal

To divide a decimal by a decimal, the first step is to change the divisor to a whole number. To do this you move the decimal point of the divisor (the number outside the division sign) to the right as far as you can. **Then you move the decimal point in the dividend an equal number of places.**

EXAMPLE: Divide 2.832 by .03.

Step 1. Set up the problem for long division.

Make the divisor (.03) a whole number. Do this by moving the decimal point two places to the right. Then move the decimal point in the dividend (2.832) two places to the right.

$.03\overline{)2.832}$

$$\begin{array}{r} 94.4 \\ 03.\overline{)2\,83.2} \\ \underline{2\,7} \\ 13 \\ \underline{12} \\ 1\,2 \\ \underline{1\,2} \\ 0 \end{array}$$

Step 2. Now divide the whole number (3) into the new decimal number 283.2.

Answer: **94.4**

Moving the decimal point an equal number of places in both divisor and dividend makes sure that the decimal point appears in the correct place in the answer.

Solve each division problem below.

1. $.02\overline{)1.6}$ $.12\overline{).48}$ $3.1\overline{).093}$ $.004\overline{)8.408}$ $.07\overline{)49.14}$

2. $.04\overline{)3.108}$ $.006\overline{)91.44}$ $2.3\overline{).529}$ $.07\overline{)355.6}$ $1.2\overline{)27.84}$

Using Zeros as Place Holders

It is often necessary to add one or more zeros to the dividend before it is possible to move the decimal point to the right.

In example 1 at right, we must move the decimal point two places in order to make the divisor (.04) a whole number. To move the decimal point in the dividend (2.8) two places, we must add one zero.

In example 2, three zeros must be added.

EXAMPLE 1:

$.04\overline{)2.8}$

$$\begin{array}{r} 70. \\ .04\overline{)2.80} \end{array}$$

Answer: 70

EXAMPLE 2:

$.0006\overline{)3.6}$

$$\begin{array}{r} 6000. \\ .0006\overline{)3.6000} \end{array}$$

Answer: 6,000

Divide.

3. $.05\overline{)1.5}$ $.004\overline{)9.36}$ $.017\overline{).306}$ $.024\overline{)19.536}$ $.035\overline{).4970}$

Dividing Whole Numbers by Decimals

To divide a whole number by a decimal, add a decimal point to the whole number. Then add zeros as needed, move the decimal point, and divide.

To divide .08 into 4, the first step is to add a decimal point to 4. Then the decimal points in both .08 and 4. are moved to the right two places, and 8 is divided into 400.

EXAMPLE:

$.08\overline{)4} \longrightarrow \overset{50.}{.08\overline{)4.00}}$

Answer: 50

4. $.06\overline{)12}$ $\quad 1.5\overline{)30}$ $\quad .003\overline{)6}$ $\quad 2.5\overline{)50}$ $\quad .04\overline{)24}$

Dividing by 10, 100, or 1,000

There are shortcuts we can use when dividing decimal numbers by 10, 100, or 1,000.

1. **To divide a decimal by 10, move the decimal point one place to the left.**

   EXAMPLE 1: Divide 3.4 by 10.
   3.4 ÷ 10 = 3.4
   = **.34**

   EXAMPLE 2: Divide 5 by 10.
   5 ÷ 10 = 5.
   = **.5**

2. **To divide a decimal by 100, move the decimal point two places to the left.**

   EXAMPLE 3: Divide 2.5 by 100.
   2.5 ÷ 100
   = 02.5 = **.025**

   EXAMPLE 4: Divide .34 by 100.
   .34 ÷ 100 =
   00.34 = **.0034**

Notice in examples 3 and 4 that zeros have to be added to the left side of each number. These zeros hold places so that we can move the decimal point the correct number of places. These added zeros become part of the answer.

3. **To divide a decimal by 1,000, move the decimal point three places to the left.**

   EXAMPLE 5: Divide 23.56 by 1,000.

   23.56 ÷ 1,000 = 023.56 = **.02356**

   To remember these rules, notice that the decimal point is always moved the same number of places as there are 0s in the dividend.

Using the shortcuts, divide each number below. The first one in each row is done as an example.

1.	5.6 ÷ 10 = .56 5.6	7.5 ÷ 10 =	23.5 ÷ 10 =	525.2 ÷ 10 =
2.	37.2 ÷ 100 = .372 37.2	63.9 ÷ 100 =	3.5 ÷ 100 =	.021 ÷ 100 =
3.	126 ÷ 10 = 12.6 12.6	15 ÷ 100 =	375 ÷ 100 =	12 ÷ 1,000 =

Solving Multiplication and Division Word Problems

In problems 1 and 2, underline a key word that suggests either multiplication or division. Then solve each problem.

1. Sam earns "time and a half" for each hour of overtime he works. His overtime pay rate is found by multiplying his regular pay rate by 1.5. What is Sam's overtime rate when his regular hourly pay is $5.76?

2. While traveling through Vermont, Alice drove 315.9 miles on 13.5 gallons of gas. Knowing this, figure out how many miles Alice can drive on a single gallon of gas.

Problems 3 and 4 contain extra information. In each problem, circle only the necessary information and then solve the problem.

3. A medium-size shipping box is packed with 144 cans of corn and weighs 216 pounds. Each can weighs 1.5 pounds. Packed with the same corn, a large-size box weighs 318 pounds. How many cans does this large-size box contain?

4. Myrna works part-time for Betty's Word Processing Service. Betty charges customers $14.50 per hour for word processing. Of this amount, Myrna is paid $9.28. How much did Myrna make last week if she worked for 21.5 hours?

In problems 5 and 6, look at the list or drawing shown below each problem to find necessary information. Then solve each problem.

5. As shown in her drawing below, a machinist placed 3 nuts of equal width on a bolt to use as a spacer. What length of the 1.5-inch bolt is taken up by the 3 nuts?

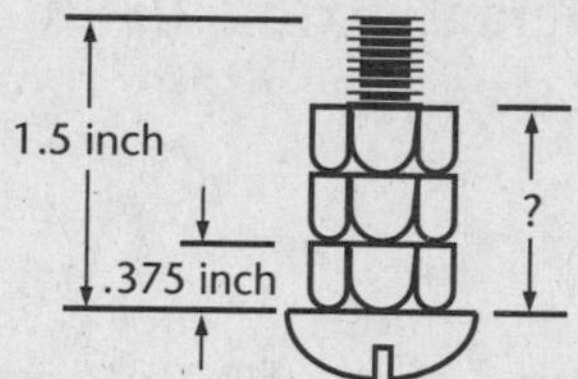

6. For his jewelry-making business, Jason uses small pieces of solid silver wire. As shown below, he wants to divide this long wire into 6 equal lengths. How long should he cut each piece?

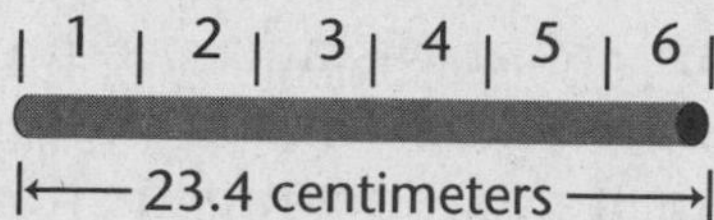

Solving Multi-Step Word Problems

Solve the multi-step problems below.

1. In March Lena bought a new television for $469.88. She made a down payment of $125.00. Because she agreed to pay off the balance in 6 equal monthly payments, she paid no interest charges. Compute the amount of Lena's monthly payment.

2. How much change would you expect to receive if you bought 5.5 pounds of nails on sale for $.97 per pound and you paid with a ten-dollar bill?

3. Last week Ester worked 40 hours at her regular hourly rate of $6.50 per hour. She also worked 6.4 hours of overtime last Saturday. Her overtime rate is $9.75 per hour. How much did Ester earn in all last week?

4. Jannie jogs 1.7 miles each Monday, Wednesday, and Friday. On Tuesday and Thursday she jogs 2.4 miles. How many total miles does Jannie jog each week?

5. As a decimal fraction, one-sixteenth inch is equal to .0625 inch. Russ, a machinist, uses washers that are one-sixteenth inch thick. How much room will be left on a 1-inch-long bolt if he places 5 of these washers on the bolt?

6. At a Thanksgiving Sale, Jerry bought a 3.7-pound package of chicken priced at $.70 per pound, and a 4.6-pound roast priced at $1.75 per pound. What amount did Jerry pay for these two packages of meat?

7. Norm's Road Construction Company is fixing potholes along Airport Drive. The crew can average fixing about .42 miles of road per hour. Working 10 hours each day, how many days will it take them to repair the 21-mile-long road?

8. Mark bought a 23.5-pound sack of potatoes priced at $.24 per pound. If he pays by check, for how much should he write the check if he wants to get $10 back in change?

9. In the metric system, road distance is measured in kilometers. A kilometer is shorter than a mile. In fact, 1 kilometer is equal to .62 mile. Giving your answer in miles, how much shorter is 10 kilometers than 10 miles?

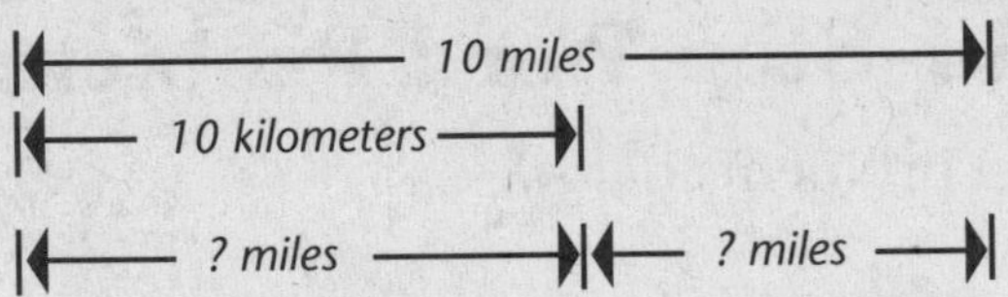

Rounding an answer is useful in a wide variety of decimal word problems. *In problems 10 and 11*, round each answer as indicated.

10. Gasoline prices are always given in dollars, cents, and parts of a cent. For example, a price of $1.299 per gallon means $1.29 and nine-tenths cent per gallon. Rounding to the nearest penny, how much would 18.7 gallons of gas cost at this price?

11. According to the blueprint, Jan is supposed to cut the bushing to a thickness of .2573 inch. The rough-cut bushing starts at .27 inch. How much does Jan need to cut off the bushing to meet the specifications of the blueprint? Express your answer to the nearest thousandth of an inch.

Problems 12 and 13 refer to the following passage.

> Joyce Hernandez manages a service station. Before June 1 she sold unleaded gas at a price of $1.359 per gallon. Then, because of a drop in wholesale prices, she lowered the pump price of unleaded by $.019 per gallon.

12. After June 1, what price did Joyce charge per gallon for unleaded gas?

13. At the lower price, how many gallons of unleaded can you buy for $16.00? Express your answer to the nearest tenth gallon.

Problems 14 and 15 refer to the passage below.

> Jamie wants to decide which of two day-care centers would be the least expensive for her child to attend. Because of her work schedule, Jamie will need to send her child to the center 18 days each month, and the child will need lunch each day.
>
> School for Kids charges by the month. It charges $137.50 for each child enrolled in the program. There is no refund if you don't bring your child every day, and lunch is provided free.
>
> Little Bunnies Center charges by the day. It charges $7.00 per child per day. A $1.00 fee is charged for each lunch for each child.

14. How much would it cost Jamie to send her child to School for Kids each month?

15. What would Jamie have to pay each day if her child went to Little Bunnies Center?

Decimal Skills Review

Review decimal computation skills. Work each problem below as carefully as you can.

In each group of decimal fractions below, circle the two that are equal in value.

1. .004, .040, .04 .390, .039, .39 .100, .010, .10

Round each decimal fraction below to the nearest hundredth.

2. .452 .093 .106 .0075 .4901

Add or subtract as indicated.

3. $.6 + .8$ $.05 + 2.1$ $4.8 - .9$ $6.48 - 4$ $8 - 4.7$

4. $2 + 3.5 + .81$ $5.67 + 2.3 + 3$ $12.4 + 6 + .57$

5. $7.12 − $.89 $25.00 − $15.69 $8.05 − 97¢ $157 − $64.48

Multiply as indicated.

6. $.9 \times 7$ 2.6×5 $12 \times .6$ 7.5×10 26×2.1 100×4.5

7. $.9 \times .5$ $.85 \times .7$ $.054 \times .8$ $5.8 \times .37$ $.56 \times .28$ 12.6×2.8

8. $3.47 \times 1{,}000 =$ $.28 \times 100 =$ $5.9 \times 10 =$

Divide as indicated.

9. $6\overline{)3.06}$ $12\overline{)4.824}$ $8\overline{).096}$ $1.2\overline{)2.472}$ $.7\overline{).385}$

10. $3.5\overline{)1.470}$ $.023\overline{)124.2}$ $.004\overline{)90}$ $4 \div 1{,}000 =$

8 Common Fractions Skills

What is a Common Fraction?

A common fraction stands for one or more parts of a whole. A common fraction is written as a top number above a bottom number. The top number is called the ***numerator***, and the bottom number is called the ***denominator.*** Most often, a common fraction is just called a "fraction."

5 ← numerator	The **numerator** tells how many parts you have.
8 ← denominator	The **denominator** tells how many parts one whole is divided into.

Proper Fractions

The fraction you see most often is a **proper fraction**. In a proper fraction, the top number is always smaller than the bottom number. The value of a proper fraction is always less than 1.

Example 1: $\frac{5}{8}$ A pie is cut into 8 equal pieces. Only 5 pieces remain. $\frac{5}{8}$ of the pie remains. $\frac{3}{8}$ is gone.

Improper Fractions

In an **improper fraction**, the top number is either the same as or larger than the bottom number. The value of an improper fraction is either 1 or larger than 1.

Example 2: $\frac{3}{3}$ The top 3 stands for the number of pieces you have. But 3 is also the number of pieces in 1 whole. Thus, the value of $\frac{3}{3}$ is 1.

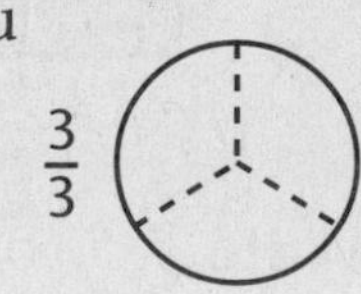

Example 3: $\frac{7}{4}$ One whole is divided into 4 equal pieces. But, you have 7 pieces. This is 3 pieces more than 1 whole. Therefore, the value of $\frac{7}{4}$ is larger than 1.

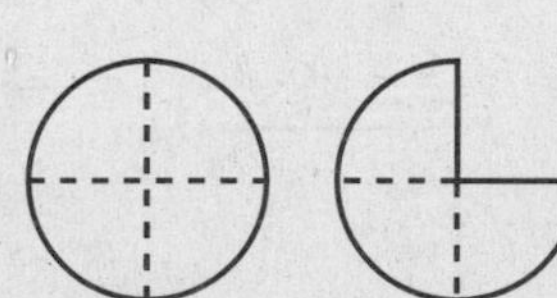

Answers to Chapter 8 exercises start on page 922.

Mixed Numbers

A **mixed number** consists of a fraction written next to a whole number. A mixed number is understood to be the sum of the whole number and the fraction.

EXAMPLE 4: $2\frac{1}{2}$ The whole number 2 stands for 2 whole objects. In addition to the 2 objects, there is $\frac{1}{2}$ object more.

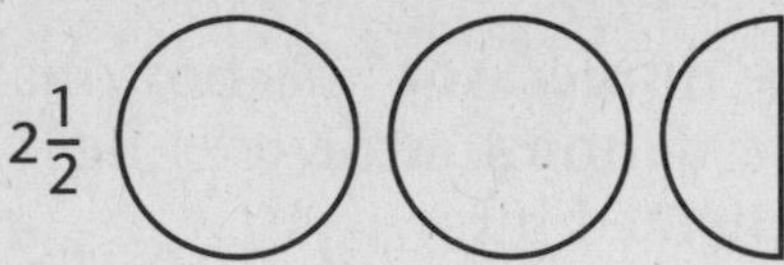

Each whole figure below is divided into equal parts, some shaded and some white. On the first line, write the proper fraction that represents the shaded part. On the second line, write the fraction that represents the unshaded (white) part.

1.

2.

3.

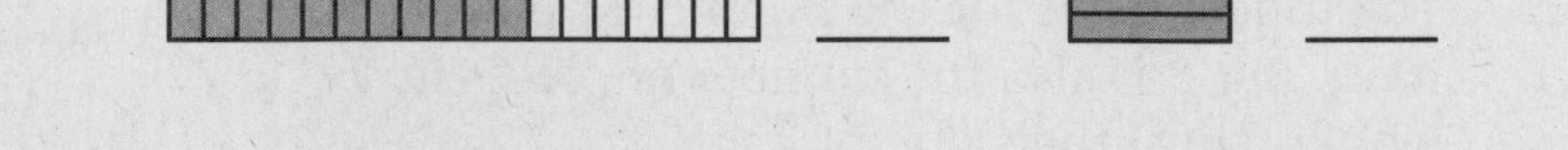

Write *p, i,* or *m,* to indicate whether each of the following numbers is a proper fraction, an improper fraction, or a mixed number.

4. $\frac{4}{5}$ _____ $\frac{9}{8}$ _____ $4\frac{1}{3}$ _____ $\frac{12}{10}$ _____ $2\frac{1}{2}$ _____

On the line following each drawing, write *p, i,* or *m,* to indicate which type of fraction or mixed number each drawing represents. Consider a complete circle as 1 whole.

5.

6.

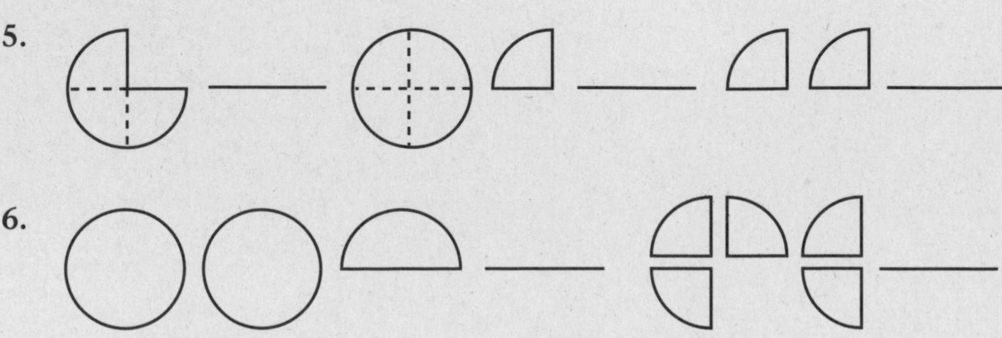

Simplifying Fractions

There are two common ways to simplify the writing of fractions. You'll use both of these throughout your work with fractions.

Reducing Fractions

To reduce a fraction is to rewrite it using smaller numbers. Reducing does not change the value of a fraction. It simply replaces one fraction with another of equal value called an ***equivalent fraction***. Here are three examples of equivalent fractions:

a) $\frac{2}{4} = \frac{1}{2}$ b) $\frac{8}{12} = \frac{2}{3}$ c) $\frac{6}{10} = \frac{3}{5}$

When a fraction is in its simplest form—the smallest numbers possible—it is said to be **reduced to lowest terms.**

Equivalent Fractions

$\frac{2}{4}$ is equal to $\frac{1}{2}$

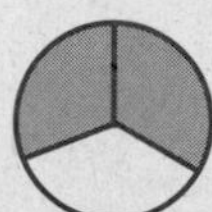

$\frac{8}{12}$ is equal to $\frac{2}{3}$

To reduce a fraction to lowest terms, divide both numerator and denominator by the largest whole number that divides evenly into each.

EXAMPLE 1: Reduce $\frac{3}{9}$ to lowest terms.

Divide both numerator (3) and denominator (9) by 3.

$\frac{3 \div 3}{9 \div 3} = \frac{1}{3}$

Answer: $\frac{1}{3}$

EXAMPLE 2: Reduce $\frac{12}{20}$ to lowest terms.

Divide both 12 and 20 by 2. Divide by 2 again.

$\frac{12 \div 2}{20 \div 2} = \frac{6}{10} = \frac{3}{5}$

Answer: $\frac{3}{5}$

After you reduce a fraction, see if it can be reduced further. Notice that in Example 2, $\frac{12}{20}$ was reduced twice. An alternative would have been to divide both the numerator and denominator by 4. Often it is difficult to see the largest whole number to divide by the first time you reduce, so you have to reduce again.

Reduce each fraction to lowest terms.

1. $\frac{4}{12} =$ $\frac{6}{8} =$ $\frac{4}{6} =$ $\frac{6}{9} =$ $\frac{12}{16} =$

2. $\frac{9}{15} =$ $\frac{15}{25} =$ $\frac{24}{30} =$ $\frac{14}{21} =$ $\frac{10}{20} =$

3. $\frac{3}{9} =$ $\frac{2}{8} =$ $\frac{30}{35} =$ $\frac{14}{28} =$ $\frac{12}{15} =$

Changing Improper Fractions to Mixed Numbers

Many answers to fraction addition and multiplication problems are first written as improper fractions. To write these answers in simplest form, we change them to mixed numbers.

To change an improper fraction to a mixed number, divide the denominator into the numerator.

EXAMPLE 1: Change $\frac{13}{2}$ to a mixed number.

Step 1. Divide 2 into 13:

$$\begin{array}{r} 6 \text{ r1} \\ 2\overline{)13} \\ \underline{12} \\ 1 \end{array}$$

Step 2. Write the remainder (1) over the divisor (2) to form the proper fraction part of the answer.

Answer: $6\frac{1}{2}$

EXAMPLE 2: Change $\frac{12}{8}$ to a mixed number.

Step 1. Divide 8 into 12:

$$\begin{array}{r} 1 \text{ r4} \\ 8\overline{)12} \\ \underline{8} \\ 4 \end{array}$$

$1 \text{ r4} = 1\frac{4}{8}$

Step 2. Reduce the proper fraction.

$\frac{4 \div 4}{8 \div 4} = \frac{1}{2}$

Answer: $1\frac{4}{8} = 1\frac{1}{2}$

On the first line below each picture, write an improper fraction that stands for the amount shown. On the second line, write this same amount as a mixed number.

4. 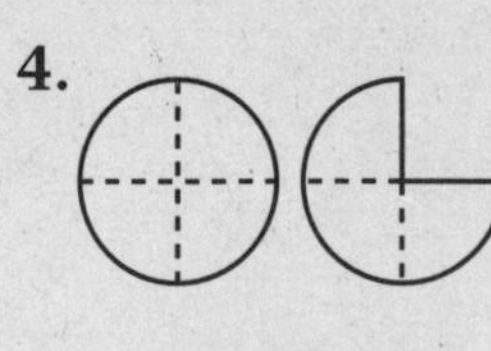

_____ _____

5. 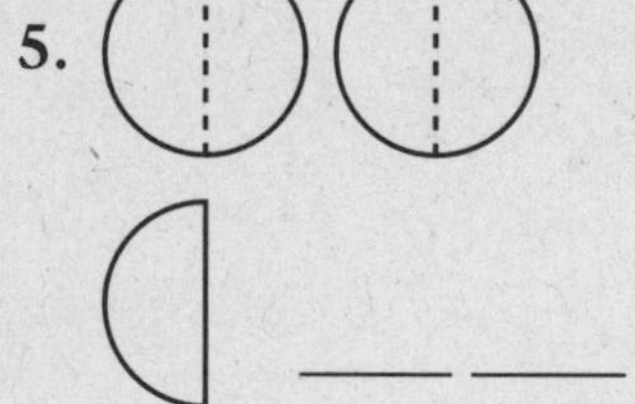

_____ _____

6. 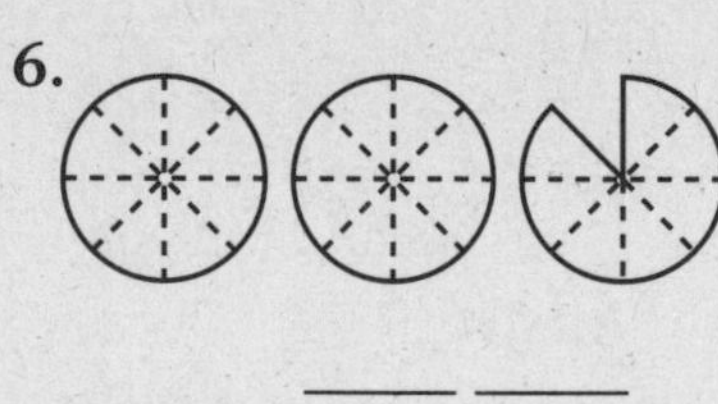

_____ _____

Change each improper fraction below to a mixed number. Reduce proper fractions.

7. $\frac{21}{10} =$ $\frac{5}{2} =$ $\frac{7}{4} =$ $\frac{20}{15} =$ $\frac{22}{4} =$

8. At Leo's Pizza by the Slice, Leo cuts whole pizzas into 8 slices. Monday night there were 21 slices left over. How many pizzas is this? (Hint: $\frac{21}{8}$ pizzas are left over.)

9. Jenny has $\frac{21}{2}$ yards of dress material left on a roll. Does she have enough to sell this as a "half-roll" if a half-roll is supposed to contain at least 10 yards of material?

Raising Fractions to Higher Terms

To raise a fraction to higher terms is to rewrite the fraction using larger numbers. Raising a fraction to higher terms is the opposite of reducing a fraction. In both cases, the fractions remain *equivalent*, or equal in value.

To raise a fraction to higher terms, multiply both numerator and denominator by the same number.

Example 1: Write $\frac{2}{5}$ as a fraction that has 15 as a denominator.

Step 1. Ask yourself, "What number times 5 equals 15?" $\frac{2}{5} = \frac{?}{15}$

You must multiply 2 by the same number to find the missing numerator.

Step 2. To answer the question, divide 5 into 15:

$15 \div 5 = 3$

Step 3. Multiply 2 by 3: $\frac{2 \times 3}{5 \times 3} = \frac{?}{15}$

Divide 5 into 15 and get 3. Multiply 2 by 3 to get the missing numerator, 6.

Answer: $\frac{2}{5} = \frac{6}{15}$

Raise each fraction to higher terms by writing the numerator of each new fraction.

1. $\frac{1}{2} = \frac{}{8}$ $\frac{1}{3} = \frac{}{6}$ $\frac{1}{4} = \frac{}{8}$ $\frac{2}{3} = \frac{}{9}$ $\frac{3}{4} = \frac{}{12}$

2. $\frac{2}{5} = \frac{}{10}$ $\frac{3}{4} = \frac{}{8}$ $\frac{1}{3} = \frac{}{12}$ $\frac{5}{7} = \frac{}{14}$ $\frac{1}{2} = \frac{}{10}$

3. $\frac{1}{3} = \frac{}{15}$ $\frac{2}{5} = \frac{}{30}$ $\frac{5}{14} = \frac{}{42}$ $\frac{11}{12} = \frac{}{24}$ $\frac{4}{7} = \frac{}{42}$

Comparing Common Fractions

Common fractions are easily compared when they have the same denominator. For example, $\frac{3}{4}$ is larger than $\frac{2}{4}$ because 3 is larger than 2. The rules for comparing fractions are easy to follow.

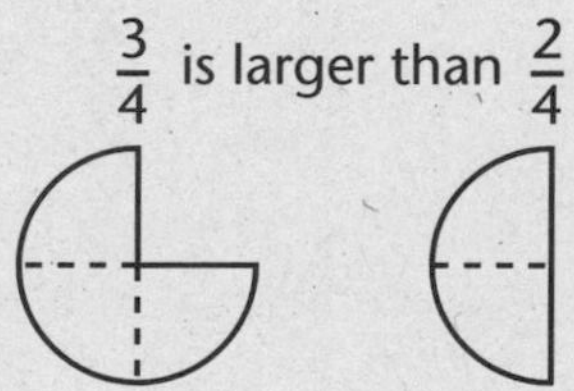

Rules for Comparing Common Fractions

1. Write each fraction so that all fractions have the same (common) denominator. This usually means raising one or more fractions to higher terms.
2. Compare the numerators of the like fractions that result from rule 1.

EXAMPLE: Of the following three fractions, which is the largest and which is the smallest: $\frac{1}{4}$, $\frac{3}{16}$, and $\frac{5}{32}$?

Step 1. To compare, we can choose 32 as a common denominator and rewrite $\frac{1}{4}$ and $\frac{3}{16}$ as fractions with a denominator of 32.

$\frac{1}{4} = \frac{8}{32}$ $\quad \frac{3}{16} = \frac{6}{32}$ $\quad \frac{5}{32}$

Step 2. Compare the numerators of the like fractions: 5, 6, and 8. From smallest to largest, the fractions are:
smallest: $\frac{5}{32}$ middle value: $\frac{6}{32}$ $(\frac{3}{16})$ largest: $\frac{8}{32}$ $(\frac{1}{4})$

Answer: $\frac{5}{32}$ is the smallest. $\frac{1}{4}$ is the largest.

In each pair below, circle the larger fraction. Use the larger denominator in each pair as the common denominator with which to write like fractions.

1. $\frac{2}{3}$ or $\frac{7}{12}$ $\qquad \frac{3}{4}$ or $\frac{10}{12}$ $\qquad \frac{5}{8}$ or $\frac{1}{2}$ $\qquad \frac{7}{8}$ or $\frac{13}{16}$

2. $\frac{1}{4}$ or $\frac{3}{8}$ $\qquad \frac{4}{9}$ or $\frac{1}{3}$ $\qquad \frac{3}{10}$ or $\frac{2}{5}$ $\qquad \frac{6}{7}$ or $\frac{11}{14}$

Arrange each group of three fractions in order. Write the smallest to the left and the largest to the right. Use the largest denominator as the common denominator.

3. $\frac{1}{3}, \frac{5}{12}, \frac{1}{4}$ $\qquad \frac{2}{3}, \frac{7}{9}, \frac{1}{3}$ $\qquad \frac{7}{24}, \frac{3}{8}, \frac{1}{3}$ $\qquad \frac{6}{14}, \frac{4}{7}, \frac{1}{2}$

Finding What Fraction a Part Is of a Whole

Problems of measurement often require you to write one amount as a fraction of a larger unit. We'll discuss this skill on this page.

EXAMPLE: There are 36 inches in a yard. What fraction of a yard is 28 inches?

Step 1. Write a fraction by placing the part (28) over the whole (36). $\frac{28}{36}$

Step 2. Reduce this fraction: $\frac{28}{36} = \frac{28}{36} \div \frac{4}{4} = \frac{7}{9}$

Answer: 28 inches is $\frac{7}{9}$ of a yard.

Express each amount below as a fraction of the larger unit indicated. Write each fraction in its most reduced form.

1. 1 yard = 36 inches

24 inches = _____ yard

30 inches = _____ yard

2. 1 foot = 12 inches

6 inches = _____ foot

10 inches = _____ foot

3. 1 hour = 60 minutes

8 minutes = _____ hour

45 minutes = _____ hour

4. 1 year = 52 weeks

32 weeks = _____ year

48 weeks = _____ year

5. 1 pound = 16 ounces

8 ounces = _____ pound

10 ounces = _____ pound

6. 1 year = 12 months

4 months = _____ year

10 months = _____ year

7. Al makes $1,500 each month on his job as a salesman. If he pays $375 each month for rent, what fraction of his salary is his rent?

8. Lee read 240 pages of a 1,000-page novel. What fraction of the novel has she read?

Adding Like Fractions

Fractions that have the same denominator are called ***like fractions***. For example, $\frac{3}{8}$ and $\frac{5}{8}$ are like fractions, while $\frac{3}{8}$ and $\frac{5}{16}$ are not.

To add like fractions, add the numerators and place the sum over the denominator. Reduce the answer to lowest terms.

EXAMPLE: Add $\frac{7}{16}$ and $\frac{5}{16}$.

Step 1. Add the numerators. $7 + 5 = 12$

Step 2. Place the sum 12 over the denominator 16.

$$\frac{7}{16} + \frac{5}{16} = \frac{12}{16} = \frac{3}{4}$$

Step 3. Reduce $\frac{12}{16}$ to lowest terms. Divide both 12 and 16 by 4.

$$\frac{12 \div 4}{16 \div 4} = \frac{3}{4}$$

Answer: $\frac{3}{4}$

Think of a bar divided into 16 equal parts. Now add as shown.

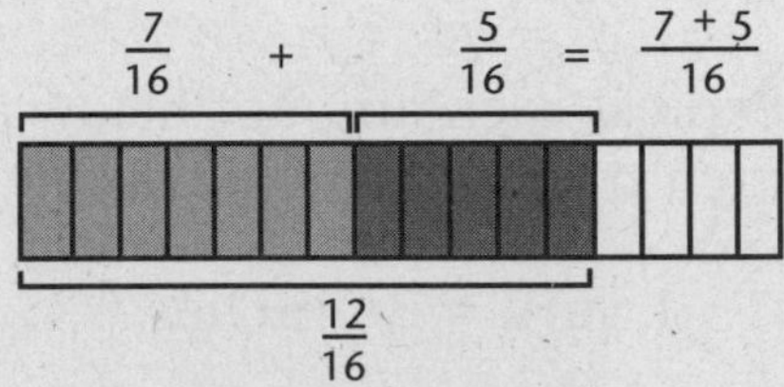

Note: *You do not add denominators.*

Fractions That Add to Less than 1

Add. Write each answer in lowest terms. The first problem in each row is done as an example.

1. $\frac{2}{4} + \frac{1}{4} = \frac{3}{4}$ $\qquad \frac{5}{8} + \frac{2}{8}$ $\qquad \frac{7}{12} + \frac{4}{12}$ $\qquad \frac{5}{9} + \frac{1}{9}$ $\qquad \frac{9}{16} + \frac{5}{16}$

2. $\frac{7}{16} + \frac{4}{16} + \frac{3}{16} = \frac{14 \div 2}{16 \div 2} = \frac{7}{8}$ $\qquad \frac{3}{8} + \frac{2}{8} + \frac{1}{8}$ $\qquad \frac{5}{12} + \frac{3}{12} + \frac{2}{12}$ $\qquad \frac{5}{9} + \frac{1}{9} + \frac{2}{9}$ $\qquad \frac{9}{14} + \frac{3}{14} + \frac{1}{14}$

Fractions That Add to a Whole Number

A fraction that has the same nonzero top and bottom number is always equal to 1.

As shown at right, when fraction addition gives an answer with the same numerator and denominator, write the answer as 1.

EXAMPLE:

$$\begin{array}{r} \frac{7}{10} \\ + \frac{3}{10} \\ \hline \frac{10}{10} = \mathbf{1} \end{array}$$

3. $\begin{array}{r} \frac{6}{9} \\ + \frac{3}{9} \\ \hline \frac{9}{9} = 1 \end{array}$ $\quad \begin{array}{r} \frac{4}{7} \\ + \frac{3}{7} \\ \hline \end{array}$ $\quad \begin{array}{r} \frac{7}{8} \\ + \frac{1}{8} \\ \hline \end{array}$ $\quad \begin{array}{r} \frac{3}{4} \\ + \frac{1}{4} \\ \hline \end{array}$ $\quad \begin{array}{r} \frac{7}{12} \\ + \frac{5}{12} \\ \hline \end{array}$

As the following problems show, fractions may also add up to whole numbers larger than 1.

4. $\frac{3}{4} + \frac{2}{4} + \frac{3}{4}$ $\quad \frac{6}{7} + \frac{6}{7} + \frac{2}{7}$ $\quad \frac{3}{9} + \frac{8}{9} + \frac{8}{9} + \frac{8}{9}$

$= \frac{8}{4} = 2$

Fractions That Add to More than 1

When fraction addition gives an answer that is an **improper fraction**, change the answer to a **mixed number.**

Reduce the proper fraction if possible.

EXAMPLE:

$$\begin{array}{r} \frac{5}{7} \\ + \frac{4}{7} \\ \hline \frac{9}{7} = \mathbf{1\frac{2}{7}} \end{array}$$

5. $\begin{array}{r} \frac{5}{6} \\ + \frac{2}{6} \\ \hline \frac{7}{6} = 1\frac{1}{6} \end{array}$ $\quad \begin{array}{r} \frac{7}{9} \\ + \frac{4}{9} \\ \hline \end{array}$ $\quad \begin{array}{r} \frac{14}{16} \\ + \frac{9}{16} \\ \hline \end{array}$ $\quad \begin{array}{r} \frac{9}{12} \\ + \frac{7}{12} \\ \hline \end{array}$ $\quad \begin{array}{r} \frac{13}{16} \\ + \frac{7}{16} \\ \hline \end{array}$

6. $\begin{array}{r} \frac{4}{5} \\ \frac{3}{5} \\ + \frac{2}{5} \\ \hline \frac{9}{5} = 1\frac{4}{5} \end{array}$ $\quad \begin{array}{r} \frac{2}{3} \\ \frac{2}{3} \\ + \frac{2}{3} \\ \hline \end{array}$ $\quad \begin{array}{r} \frac{7}{8} \\ \frac{5}{8} \\ + \frac{4}{8} \\ \hline \end{array}$ $\quad \begin{array}{r} \frac{7}{9} \\ \frac{5}{9} \\ + \frac{3}{9} \\ \hline \end{array}$ $\quad \begin{array}{r} \frac{11}{12} \\ \frac{9}{12} \\ + \frac{4}{12} \\ \hline \end{array}$

Adding Fractions and Mixed Numbers

To add a fraction and a mixed number, first add the fractions alone. Then bring down the whole number.

If the sum of fractions is an **improper fraction**, change this sum to a **mixed number**. Add the whole number part of the mixed number to the whole number already in the answer.

EXAMPLE:

$$\begin{array}{r} 2\frac{4}{8} \\ +\ \frac{7}{8} \\ \hline 2\frac{11}{8} \end{array} = 2 + 1\frac{3}{8} = 3\frac{3}{8}$$

Add. Reduce the proper fraction if possible.

7. $\begin{array}{r} 4\frac{3}{6} \\ +\frac{1}{6} \\ \hline \end{array}$ $\quad \begin{array}{r} 3\frac{1}{4} \\ +\frac{2}{4} \\ \hline \end{array}$ $\quad \begin{array}{r} 6\frac{5}{8} \\ +\frac{3}{8} \\ \hline \end{array}$ $\quad \begin{array}{r} 4\frac{9}{12} \\ +\frac{2}{12} \\ \hline \end{array}$ $\quad \begin{array}{r} 8\frac{11}{16} \\ +\frac{3}{16} \\ \hline \end{array}$

$4\frac{4}{6} = 4\frac{2}{3}$

8. $\begin{array}{r} 3\frac{5}{8} \\ +\frac{7}{8} \\ \hline \end{array}$ $\quad \begin{array}{r} 5\frac{7}{8} \\ +\frac{5}{8} \\ \hline \end{array}$ $\quad \begin{array}{r} 9\frac{10}{11} \\ +\frac{6}{11} \\ \hline \end{array}$ $\quad \begin{array}{r} 12\frac{2}{3} \\ +\ \frac{2}{3} \\ \hline \end{array}$ $\quad \begin{array}{r} 20\frac{6}{10} \\ +\ \frac{9}{10} \\ \hline \end{array}$

$3\frac{12}{8} = 3 + 1\frac{4}{8}$

$4\frac{4}{8} = 4\frac{1}{2}$

Adding Mixed Numbers

To add mixed numbers, add the fractions and the whole numbers separately.

If the sum of fractions is an **improper fraction**, change this sum to a **mixed number**. Add the whole number part to the sum of whole numbers already in the answer.

EXAMPLE:

$$\begin{array}{r} 3\frac{7}{16} \\ +\ \ 2\frac{11}{16} \\ \hline 5\frac{18}{16} \end{array} = 5 + 1\frac{2}{16} = 6\frac{2}{16} = 6\frac{1}{8}$$

Add. Reduce the proper fraction if possible.

9. $\begin{array}{r} 2\frac{3}{4} \\ +\ 1\frac{1}{4} \\ \hline \end{array}$ $\quad \begin{array}{r} 4\frac{2}{4} \\ +\ 3\frac{1}{4} \\ \hline \end{array}$ $\quad \begin{array}{r} 7\frac{2}{9} \\ +\ 5\frac{4}{9} \\ \hline \end{array}$ $\quad \begin{array}{r} 8\frac{5}{12} \\ +\ 6\frac{3}{12} \\ \hline \end{array}$ $\quad \begin{array}{r} 14\frac{13}{16} \\ +\ 7\frac{1}{16} \\ \hline \end{array}$

$3\frac{4}{4} = 3 + 1 = 4$

10. $4\frac{7}{8} + 2\frac{5}{8}$ $\quad 7\frac{8}{9} + 6\frac{7}{9}$ $\quad 8\frac{7}{8} + 2\frac{5}{8}$ $\quad 15\frac{11}{12} + 13\frac{9}{12}$ $\quad 25\frac{13}{16} + 19\frac{13}{16}$

$= 6\frac{12}{8}$

$= 6 + 1\frac{4}{8}$

$= 7\frac{4}{8} = 7\frac{1}{2}$

Subtracting Like Fractions

To subtract like fractions, subtract the numerators and place the difference over the denominator. Reduce the answer to lowest terms.

EXAMPLE: Subtract $\frac{2}{9}$ from $\frac{8}{9}$.

Step 1. Subtract the numerators. $8 - 2 = 6$

Step 2. Place the difference (6) over the denominator (9).

$$\begin{array}{r} \frac{8}{9} \\ -\frac{2}{9} \\ \hline \frac{6}{9} \end{array}$$

Step 3. Reduce $\frac{6}{9}$ to lowest terms. Divide both 6 and 9 by 3.

$$\frac{6 \div 3}{9 \div 3} = \frac{2}{3}$$

Answer: $\frac{2}{3}$

Think of a circle divided into 9 equal parts.

$\frac{8}{9}$ are there. Subtract $\frac{2}{9}$ and $\frac{8-2}{9} = \frac{6}{9}$ are left.

Note: *You do not subtract denominators.*

Subtracting Two Fractions

Subtract. Write each answer in lowest terms. The first problem in each row is done as an example.

1. $\frac{7}{9} - \frac{3}{9} = \frac{4}{9}$ $\qquad \frac{9}{10} - \frac{2}{10}$ $\qquad \frac{8}{9} - \frac{2}{9}$ $\qquad \frac{7}{8} - \frac{3}{8}$ $\qquad \frac{11}{12} - \frac{8}{12}$

Subtracting Fractions from Mixed Numbers

To subtract a fraction from a mixed number, first subtract the fractions. Then bring down the whole number. Reduce the fraction in the answer if possible.

2. $4\frac{5}{8} - \frac{2}{8} = 4\frac{3}{8}$ $\qquad 5\frac{3}{5} - \frac{2}{5}$ $\qquad 6\frac{4}{6} - \frac{1}{6}$ $\qquad 6\frac{8}{9} - \frac{2}{9}$ $\qquad 9\frac{11}{12} - \frac{10}{12}$

Subtracting Mixed Numbers

To subtract mixed numbers, first subtract the fractions alone. Then subtract the whole numbers. Reduce the proper fraction in the answer if possible.

EXAMPLE:

$$\begin{array}{r} 4\frac{7}{9} \\ -\ 2\frac{1}{9} \\ \hline 2\frac{6}{9} = 2\frac{2}{3} \end{array}$$

3. $\begin{array}{r} 7\frac{2}{3} \\ -\ 3\frac{1}{3} \\ \hline 4\frac{1}{3} \end{array}$ $\quad \begin{array}{r} 2\frac{13}{16} \\ -\ 1\frac{8}{16} \\ \hline \end{array}$ $\quad \begin{array}{r} 9\frac{7}{8} \\ -\ 3\frac{3}{8} \\ \hline \end{array}$ $\quad \begin{array}{r} 4\frac{9}{10} \\ -\ 2\frac{1}{10} \\ \hline \end{array}$ $\quad \begin{array}{r} 14\frac{7}{12} \\ -\ 6\frac{3}{12} \\ \hline \end{array}$

Subtracting Fractions from the Whole Number 1

To subtract a fraction from the whole number 1, change 1 to a fraction. For the numerator and denominator of this new fraction, use the number that is the denominator of the fraction that is being subtracted.

In Example 1, the whole number 1 is changed to $\frac{5}{5}$ since the denominator of the fraction being subtracted is 5.

In Example 2, the whole number 1 is changed to $\frac{8}{8}$. Do you see why?

EXAMPLE 1:

$$\begin{array}{rcr} 1 & = & \frac{5}{5} \\ -\frac{3}{5} & = & \frac{3}{5} \\ \hline & & \frac{2}{5} \end{array}$$

EXAMPLE 2:

$$\begin{array}{rcr} 1 & = & \frac{8}{8} \\ -\frac{3}{8} & = & \frac{3}{8} \\ \hline & & \frac{5}{8} \end{array}$$

4. $\begin{array}{rcr} 1 & = & \frac{3}{3} \\ -\ \frac{2}{3} & = & \frac{2}{3} \\ \hline & & \frac{1}{3} \end{array}$ $\quad \begin{array}{r} 1 \\ -\ \frac{3}{4} \\ \hline \end{array}$ $\quad \begin{array}{r} 1 \\ -\ \frac{1}{5} \\ \hline \end{array}$ $\quad \begin{array}{r} 1 \\ -\ \frac{4}{7} \\ \hline \end{array}$ $\quad \begin{array}{r} 1 \\ -\ \frac{8}{9} \\ \hline \end{array}$

Subtracting Fractions from Whole Numbers

To subtract a fraction from a whole number, you must **borrow** 1 from the whole number. You change the borrowed 1 to a fraction and then subtract.

EXAMPLE:

Problem	*Step 1*	*Step 2*	*Step 3*
$\begin{array}{r} 6 \\ -\ \frac{3}{8} \\ \hline \end{array}$	$\begin{array}{r} 5 + 1 \\ -\ \quad \frac{3}{8} \\ \hline \end{array}$	$\begin{array}{r} 5\frac{8}{8} \\ -\ \frac{3}{8} \\ \hline \end{array}$	$\begin{array}{r} 5\frac{8}{8} \\ -\ \frac{3}{8} \\ \hline 5\frac{5}{8} \end{array}$

Step 1. To subtract $\frac{3}{8}$, you need a fraction to subtract from. As a first step, borrow 1 from the 6.

Step 2. Change the borrowed 1 to the fraction $\frac{8}{8}$. You choose $\frac{8}{8}$ because $\frac{3}{8}$ has 8 as a denominator. Write $5 + \frac{8}{8}$ as $5\frac{8}{8}$.

Step 3. Subtract the fractions: $\frac{8}{8} - \frac{3}{8} = \frac{5}{8}$. Bring down the whole number 5.

Answer: $5\frac{5}{8}$

In row 1, show how each whole number can be rewritten by borrowing a 1 and changing it to a fraction. Write the correct numerator in each blank line. Then subtract.

Skill Builders

1.

$$\begin{array}{rcr} 3 & = & 2\frac{\_}{4} \\ -\ \frac{3}{4} & = & -\frac{3}{4} \\ \hline \end{array} \qquad \begin{array}{rcr} 5 & = & 4\frac{\_}{6} \\ -\ \frac{1}{6} & = & -\frac{1}{6} \\ \hline \end{array} \qquad \begin{array}{rcr} 2 & = & 1\frac{\_}{5} \\ -\ \frac{4}{5} & = & -\frac{4}{5} \\ \hline \end{array} \qquad \begin{array}{rcr} 6 & = & 5\frac{\_}{2} \\ -\ \frac{1}{2} & = & -\frac{1}{2} \\ \hline \end{array}$$

Subtract. Reduce fraction answers when possible.

2.

$$\begin{array}{r} 5 \\ -\ \frac{4}{5} \\ \hline \end{array} \qquad \begin{array}{r} 3 \\ -\ \frac{4}{7} \\ \hline \end{array} \qquad \begin{array}{r} 12 \\ -\ \frac{7}{8} \\ \hline \end{array} \qquad \begin{array}{r} 9 \\ -\ \frac{4}{6} \\ \hline \end{array} \qquad \begin{array}{r} 10 \\ -\ \frac{15}{16} \\ \hline \end{array}$$

Subtracting Mixed Numbers by Borrowing

When the fraction in the bottom number is larger than the fraction above it, you must borrow in order to subtract. The borrowed 1 is changed to a fraction and added to the fraction that is already part of the top number.

EXAMPLE: *Problem* / *Step 1* / *Step 2* / *Step 3*

$$\begin{array}{r} 4\frac{1}{5} \\ -\ 2\frac{4}{5} \\ \hline \end{array} \qquad \begin{array}{r} 3\frac{5}{5}+\frac{1}{5} \\ -\ 2\frac{4}{5} \\ \hline \end{array} \qquad \begin{array}{r} 3\frac{6}{5} \\ -\ 2\frac{4}{5} \\ \hline \end{array} \qquad \begin{array}{r} 3\frac{6}{5} \\ -\ 2\frac{4}{5} \\ \hline 1\frac{2}{5} \end{array}$$

Step 1. You can't subtract $\frac{4}{5}$ from $\frac{1}{5}$, so borrow 1 from the 4. Change the 4 to 3 and write the borrowed 1 as $\frac{5}{5}$. You choose $\frac{5}{5}$ because the fraction $\frac{1}{5}$ has 5 for a denominator.

Step 2. Combine the top fractions: $\frac{5}{5} + \frac{1}{5} = \frac{6}{5}$

Step 3. Subtract the fraction column: $\frac{6}{5} - \frac{4}{5} = \frac{2}{5}$

Subtract the whole numbers: $3 - 2 = 1$

Subtract. Complete the row of partially-worked Skill Builders.

Skill Builders

1.

$$\begin{array}{rcr} 5\frac{3}{8} & = & 4\cancel{5}\overbrace{\frac{8}{8}+\frac{3}{8}}^{\frac{11}{8}} \\ -\ 1\frac{5}{8} & = & -\ 1\frac{5}{8} \\ \hline \end{array} \qquad \begin{array}{rcr} 9\frac{1}{3} & = & 8\cancel{9}\overbrace{\frac{3}{3}+\frac{1}{3}}^{\frac{4}{3}} \\ -\ 4\frac{2}{3} & = & -\ 4\frac{2}{3} \\ \hline \end{array}$$

2. $12\frac{1}{2} - 8\frac{1}{2}$ $\quad$ $21\frac{3}{10} - 15\frac{7}{10}$ $\quad$ $15\frac{9}{12} - 6\frac{11}{12}$ $\quad$ $2\frac{1}{8} - 1\frac{5}{8}$ $\quad$ $3\frac{2}{4} - \frac{3}{4}$

Solving Addition and Subtraction Word Problems

You solve fraction word problems in the same way you solve whole number and decimal word problems. In each problem below, circle the words within the parentheses that best identify what you are asked to find. Then solve the problem.

1. Alice bought $2\frac{2}{3}$ yards of material to make a dress, $2\frac{1}{3}$ yards to make a wrap-around skirt, and $1\frac{2}{3}$ yards to make a blouse. How many total yards of material did Alice buy?

   (amount of material needed, amount of material bought, amount of material left over)

   $$\begin{array}{r} 2\frac{2}{3} \\ 2\frac{1}{3} \\ +\ 1\frac{2}{3} \\ \hline 5\frac{5}{3} = 6\frac{2}{3} \text{ yards} \end{array}$$

2. Nails in bin C are $\frac{3}{8}$ inch longer than nails in bin B. If the nails in bin B are $\frac{5}{8}$ inch long, how long are the nails in bin C?

   (length of nails in bin B, length of nails in bin C, difference in length of the two nail sizes)

3. By comparing the drawings, figure out how much shorter Amy's doll is than Jane's doll.

   (height of Amy's doll, height of Jane's doll, difference in height of the two dolls)

Problems 4 through 7 contain **extra information**. In each problem, write the **necessary information** on the blank line and then solve the problem.

4. When empty, Jean's suitcase weighs $5\frac{1}{8}$ pounds. Packing to go to Chicago, Jean packed $2\frac{3}{8}$ pounds of clothes, a $1\frac{7}{8}$-pound camera, and a pair of shoes that weighed $1\frac{1}{8}$ pounds. What total weight of items did Jean pack inside her suitcase?

____

5. Following the recipe, Saul added $2\frac{1}{3}$ cups milk, $\frac{1}{3}$ cup cream, and $1\frac{2}{3}$ cups sugar in a bowl that holds $7\frac{1}{3}$ cups. How much liquid did he put in that bowl?

____

6. As shown on the map below, Jenny lives farther from the health club than her friend David. Using the distances shown, figure out how far David lives from Jenny.

____

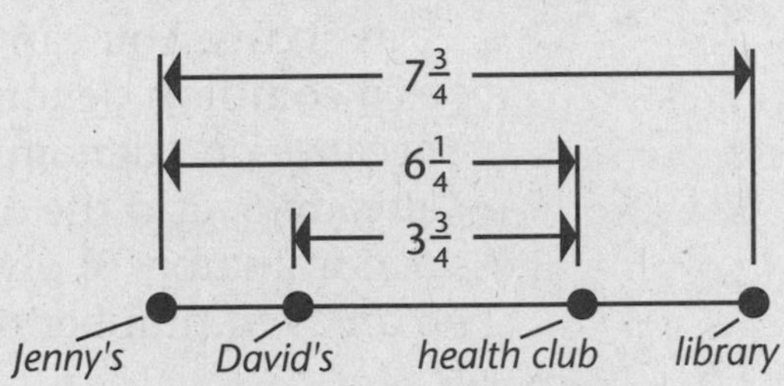

All distances in miles

7. Wally's Seafoods is having a special sale on salmon steaks. His list of prices is shown below. As indicated on the list, how much more salmon do you get for \$8.05 than you get for \$5.85?

Salmon Prices	*Package Size*
\$5.85	$1\frac{3}{4}$ pounds
\$7.05	$2\frac{3}{4}$ pounds
\$8.05	$3\frac{1}{4}$ pounds

____

Adding and Subtracting Unlike Fractions

Unlike fractions—fractions that have different denominators—can be added or subtracted only after they are changed to like fractions.

To change unlike fractions to like fractions, we write them as fractions that have the same number as a denominator. This number is called a ***common denominator***. To do this, we raise at least one fraction to higher terms.

EXAMPLE 1: Add $\frac{2}{3}$ and $\frac{1}{6}$.

Step 1. Choose 6 as a common denominator and rewrite $\frac{2}{3}$ as sixths. You can use 6 as a common denominator because one denominator is already 6, and the other denominator (3) divides into 6 an even number of times.

Step 2. Add the like fractions:

$$\begin{array}{r} \frac{2}{3} = \frac{4}{6} \\ + \frac{1}{6} = \frac{1}{6} \\ \frac{5}{6} \\ \hline \end{array}$$

Answer: $\frac{5}{6}$

EXAMPLE 2: Subtract $\frac{1}{2}$ from $\frac{7}{8}$.

Step 1. Choose 8 as a common denominator and rewrite $\frac{1}{2}$ as eighths.

Step 2. Subtract $\frac{4}{8}$ from $\frac{7}{8}$.

$$\begin{array}{r} \frac{7}{8} = \frac{7}{8} \\ - \frac{1}{2} = \frac{4}{8} \\ \hline \frac{3}{8} \end{array}$$

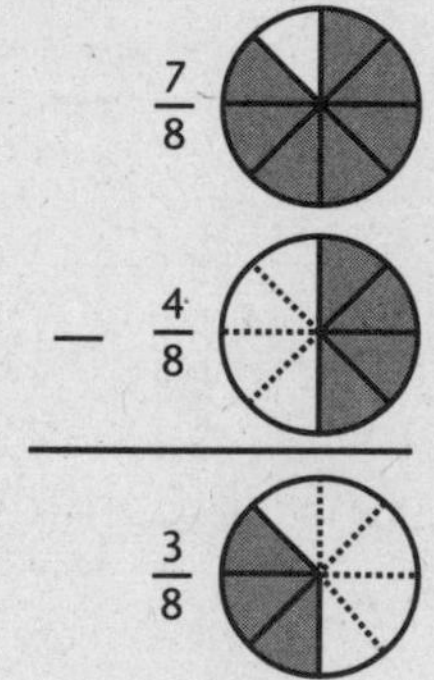

Answer: $\frac{3}{8}$

In rows 1 and 2, raise each fraction to higher terms using the denominator given. Do this by writing the correct numerator on each blank line.

1. $\frac{1}{3} = \frac{\_\_}{6}$ $\qquad \frac{1}{2} = \frac{\_\_}{8}$ $\qquad \frac{2}{3} = \frac{\_\_}{9}$ $\qquad \frac{3}{4} = \frac{\_\_}{8}$ $\qquad \frac{2}{3} = \frac{\_\_}{12}$

2. $\frac{3}{5} = \frac{\_\_}{10}$ $\qquad \frac{3}{4} = \frac{\_\_}{12}$ $\qquad \frac{4}{5} = \frac{\_\_}{15}$ $\qquad \frac{7}{8} = \frac{\_\_}{16}$ $\qquad \frac{3}{7} = \frac{\_\_}{28}$

In rows 3 through 5, add or subtract as indicated. Use the largest denominator in each problem as a common denominator. Reduce answers.

Skill Builders

3. $\frac{1}{3} = \frac{\ }{6}$, $+\frac{3}{6} = \frac{\ }{6}$ $\qquad$ $\frac{3}{5} = \frac{\ }{10}$, $-\frac{3}{10} = \frac{\ }{10}$ $\qquad$ $\frac{7}{8} = \frac{\ }{8}$, $-\frac{3}{4} = \frac{\ }{8}$ $\qquad$ $\frac{1}{2} = \frac{\ }{8}$, $\frac{1}{4} = \frac{\ }{8}$, $+\frac{3}{8} = \frac{\ }{8}$ $\qquad$ $\frac{11}{12} = \frac{\ }{12}$, $\frac{5}{6} = \frac{\ }{12}$, $+\frac{1}{4} = \frac{\ }{12}$

4. $\frac{1}{2} - \frac{1}{6}$ $\qquad$ $\frac{3}{4} + \frac{1}{2}$ $\qquad$ $\frac{4}{7} + \frac{3}{14}$ $\qquad$ $\frac{7}{9} - \frac{2}{3}$ $\qquad$ $\frac{15}{16} - \frac{9}{32}$

5. $\frac{2}{6} + \frac{1}{3} + \frac{1}{6}$ $\qquad$ $\frac{5}{8} + \frac{1}{4} + \frac{1}{8}$ $\qquad$ $\frac{2}{5} + \frac{1}{5} + \frac{3}{10}$ $\qquad$ $\frac{1}{2} + \frac{3}{4} + \frac{1}{8}$ $\qquad$ $\frac{7}{12} + \frac{1}{3} + \frac{3}{4}$

Choosing a Common Denominator

Often, the largest denominator in a problem cannot be a common denominator. **A common denominator must be a number that each denominator divides into evenly.**

Multiplying Denominators Gives a Common Denominator

One way to choose a common denominator is to multiply the denominators in a problem by each other.

For example, at right $4 \times 3 = 12$.

12 can be used as a common denominator because both 4 and 3 divide into 12 evenly.

$$\frac{3}{4} = \frac{9}{12}$$
$$-\frac{1}{3} = \frac{4}{12}$$
$$\frac{5}{12}$$

Multiplying denominators is the best method to use to find a common denominator in most problems. It works well when denominators are small numbers. It also works well when there are more than two denominators in a problem.

In the example, 12 is the smallest whole number that can be used as a common denominator. Because of this, 12 is called the ***lowest common denominator (LCD).***

In each problem below, multiply denominators to find a common denominator, and then add or subtract. The Skill Builders are partially worked for you. Reduce answers.

Skill Builders

1.

$$\begin{array}{r} \frac{1}{2} = \frac{\quad}{6} \\ -\frac{1}{3} = \frac{2}{6} \\ \hline \end{array} \qquad \begin{array}{r} \frac{2}{3} = \frac{\quad}{12} \\ +\frac{1}{4} = \frac{\quad}{12} \\ \hline \end{array} \qquad \begin{array}{r} \frac{4}{5} = \frac{\quad}{20} \\ -\frac{3}{4} = \frac{\quad}{20} \\ \hline \end{array} \qquad \begin{array}{r} \frac{1}{2} = \frac{\quad}{12} \\ \frac{1}{3} = \frac{\quad}{12} \\ +\frac{1}{4} = \frac{\quad}{12} \\ \hline \end{array} \qquad \begin{array}{r} \frac{1}{3} = \frac{\quad}{60} \\ \frac{1}{4} = \frac{\quad}{60} \\ +\frac{1}{5} = \frac{\quad}{60} \\ \hline \end{array}$$

2.

$$\begin{array}{r} \frac{7}{9} \\ -\frac{2}{5} \\ \hline \end{array} \qquad \begin{array}{r} \frac{3}{8} \\ -\frac{1}{3} \\ \hline \end{array} \qquad \begin{array}{r} \frac{3}{4} \\ \frac{1}{2} \\ +\frac{1}{6} \\ \hline \end{array} \qquad \begin{array}{r} \frac{1}{2} \\ \frac{1}{3} \\ +\frac{1}{4} \\ \hline \end{array} \qquad \begin{array}{r} \frac{1}{3} \\ \frac{1}{4} \\ +\frac{1}{5} \\ \hline \end{array}$$

Finding the Lowest Common Denominator

Multiplying denominators always gives a common denominator. However, this method does not always give the **lowest common denominator.**

In the example at right, multiplying 8 times 6 gives 48 as a common denominator.

Notice that 24 will also work as a common denominator. Using 24, you do not need to reduce the answer, and you work with smaller fractions. At right, 24 is the **lowest common denominator.**

Using 48

$$\begin{array}{r} \frac{5}{8} = \frac{30}{48} \\ -\frac{1}{6} = \frac{8}{48} \\ \hline \frac{22}{48} = \frac{11}{24} \end{array}$$

Using 24

$$\begin{array}{r} \frac{5}{8} = \frac{15}{24} \\ -\frac{1}{6} = \frac{4}{24} \\ \hline \frac{11}{24} \end{array}$$

To find the lowest common denominator in any problem, compare the smallest denominator with multiples of the largest denominator. A multiple is found by multiplying a denominator by 1, 2, 3, and so on.

> **The lowest common denominator is the smallest multiple that each denominator divides into evenly.**

Look again at the example:

$\frac{5}{8}$ The multiples of 8 are: 8, 16, 24, 32 . . .

$-\frac{1}{6}$ Find a multiple of 8 that 6 divides evenly into: 6

The smallest multiple of 8 that 6 divides into evenly is 24. Thus, 24 is the lowest common denominator for the example.

Find a common denominator and solve the problem. In the Skill Builders, some multiples of the largest denominator are written for you.

Skill Builders: As your first step, choose the correct multiple to use.

3. $\frac{5}{9} + \frac{1}{6}$ 9, 18, 27 ... 6 ↗ $\frac{5}{6} - \frac{3}{8}$ 6 ↘ 8, 16, 24, 32 ...

4. $\frac{3}{4} + \frac{1}{6}$ $\frac{9}{10} - \frac{3}{4}$ $\frac{11}{12} - \frac{7}{10}$ $\frac{5}{6} - \frac{3}{10}$ $\frac{3}{10} + \frac{5}{14}$

Adding and Subtracting Mixed Numbers

You can add or subtract mixed numbers only if the fractions are **like fractions.** If they are **unlike fractions**, choose a common denominator and rewrite them as like fractions. Use either the method of **multiplying denominators** or the method of **comparing multiples** to choose a common denominator.

- When adding, remember to change any improper fraction answer to a mixed number. Then add the whole numbers together in the answer.
- When subtracting, rewrite unlike fractions as like fractions *before* you do any needed borrowing.
- For all problems, remember to work with fractions first, and then work with whole numbers. Simplify answers when possible.

Adding Mixed Numbers

Write the correct numerator on each blank line. Then complete each problem.

Skill Builders

1. $3\frac{2}{3} = 3\frac{}{6}$, $+\ 1\frac{1}{2} = 1\frac{}{6}$ $5\frac{3}{4} = 5\frac{}{12}$, $+\ 2\frac{1}{3} = 2\frac{}{12}$ $4\frac{3}{5} = 4\frac{}{20}$, $+\ 3\frac{1}{4} = 3\frac{}{20}$ $6\frac{1}{3} = 6\frac{}{12}$, $2\frac{5}{6} = 2\frac{}{12}$, $+\ 1\frac{3}{4} = 1\frac{}{12}$

2. $4\frac{2}{3} + 2\frac{1}{6}$ $\quad$ $5\frac{3}{7} + 4\frac{1}{2}$ $\quad$ $8\frac{3}{8} + 3\frac{2}{5}$ $\quad$ $4\frac{5}{6} + 2\frac{1}{4}$ $\quad$ $12\frac{2}{3} + 9\frac{3}{5}$

3. $4\frac{1}{2} + 2\frac{2}{3} + 1\frac{3}{4}$ $\quad$ $5\frac{3}{8} + 3\frac{1}{4} + 4\frac{1}{2}$ $\quad$ $7\frac{1}{3} + 5\frac{2}{5} + 2\frac{3}{4}$ $\quad$ $12\frac{1}{4} + 11\frac{1}{2} + 9\frac{5}{6}$ $\quad$ $21\frac{2}{3} + 15\frac{3}{5} + 8\frac{1}{2}$

Subtracting Mixed Numbers

Write the correct numerator on each blank line. Then complete each problem.

Skill Builders

4. $7\frac{2}{3} = 7\frac{\_\_}{12}$, $- 5\frac{1}{4} = 5\frac{\_\_}{12}$ $\quad$ $13\frac{5}{6} = 13\frac{\_\_}{12}$, $- 8\frac{3}{4} = 8\frac{\_\_}{12}$ $\quad$ $9\frac{3}{4} = 9\frac{15}{20} = 8\frac{\_\_}{20}$, $- 6\frac{4}{5} = 6\frac{16}{20} = 6\frac{\_\_}{20}$

5. $12\frac{4}{9} - 8\frac{1}{3}$ $\quad$ $17\frac{4}{5} - 10\frac{1}{4}$ $\quad$ $6\frac{3}{8} - 5\frac{7}{16}$ $\quad$ $15\frac{5}{6} - 8\frac{7}{8}$ $\quad$ $29\frac{1}{2} - 17\frac{2}{3}$

Mixed Practice

6. $\frac{2}{3} + \frac{3}{4}$ $\quad$ $3\frac{15}{16} + \frac{7}{8}$ $\quad$ $2\frac{3}{4} - \frac{7}{8}$ $\quad$ $\frac{11}{16} - \frac{1}{4}$ $\quad$ $5\frac{3}{7} - 2\frac{5}{14}$

7. $\frac{9}{10} + \frac{3}{4}$ $\quad$ $4\frac{3}{16} - 2\frac{5}{8}$ $\quad$ $14\frac{5}{9} + 6\frac{2}{3}$ $\quad$ $8\frac{3}{10} - 5\frac{3}{5}$ $\quad$ $13\frac{7}{12} + 7\frac{7}{8}$

Using Substitution to Help Solve Word Problems

One reason fractions are difficult for most people is that they are hard to see in your mind. A technique called ***substitution*** may help you solve fraction word problems. Here's how you use substitution:

- Replace fractions in a problem with small whole numbers.
- Next, read the problem as a whole number problem and decide what problem-solving steps to use—for example, whether to add or to subtract.
- Finally, go back and carry out the same problem-solving steps on the fractions in the original problem.

EXAMPLE:

Original Problem Written with Fractions

A bolt that is $2\frac{5}{16}$ inches long is to be shortened by $\frac{3}{8}$ inch. What length should the bolt be cut?

Substitution Problem Written with Small WholeNumbers

A bolt that is 2 inches long is to be shortened by 1 inch. What length should the bolt be cut?

As written at right, you can see that this is a subtraction problem.You find the answer by subtracting the smaller number 1 from the larger number 2.

Substitution Problem Solution

2 − 1 = 1 inch

Answer: 1 inch

Using the same subtraction step in the original problem, you find the answer by subtracting $\frac{3}{8}$ from $2\frac{5}{16}$.

Answer: $1\frac{15}{16}$ inches

Original Problem Solution

$$\begin{array}{rcrcr} 2\frac{5}{16} & \rightarrow & 2\frac{5}{16} & \rightarrow & 1\frac{21}{16} \\ -\frac{3}{8} & \rightarrow & -\frac{6}{16} & \rightarrow & -\frac{6}{16} \\ \hline & & & & 1\frac{15}{16} \end{array}$$

When you use substitution, it does not matter what small whole numbers you use. Substitute 1 for the smallest fraction or mixed number and 2 or 3 for the largest.

Solve each addition or subtraction problem. Try substituting whole numbers to decide what problem-solving steps to use.

1. Jessica grew $1\frac{1}{4}$ inches last year. This was $\frac{5}{16}$ of an inch more than she grew the previous year. Figure out how much Jessica grew during that previous year.

2. To make a large fruit salad, Janet bought $1\frac{1}{2}$ pounds of grapes, $1\frac{2}{3}$ pounds of strawberries, and $2\frac{1}{4}$ pounds of apples. Mixed together, how many pounds of salad will this fruit make?

When you're not sure which of two fractions is larger, rewrite the fractions to have a common denominator. Then use substitution as before. In problems 3 and 4, substitute 2 for the larger fraction and 1 for the smaller fraction.

3. Connie ordered carpet that was $\frac{11}{16}$ inch thick. The pad underneath it was $\frac{5}{8}$ inch thick. By how much will the carpet and pad raise the level of the floor?

4. On Saturday it rained $\frac{5}{6}$ of an inch. On Sunday it rained another $\frac{7}{8}$ inch. How much more rain fell on one day than on the other?

Solving Addition and Subtraction Word Problems

Following are groups of addition and subtraction word problems. You may find it helpful to use **substitution** to help you visualize what is being described. Remember to change **unlike fractions** to **like fractions** as your first step before either adding or subtracting.

Below are pairs of problems with the same necessary information. Yet each pair contains an addition problem and a subtraction problem. Solve these problems by paying close attention to what each question asks you to find.

1. a) Kate ran $2\frac{3}{4}$ miles on Monday. On Wednesday she ran $3\frac{1}{8}$ miles. How much farther did Kate run on Wednesday than on Monday?

   b) Kate ran $2\frac{3}{4}$ miles on Monday. On Wednesday she ran $3\frac{1}{8}$ miles. How many miles did she run on those two days?

2. a) James has two metal rods. One measures $9\frac{5}{16}$ inches and the other is $5\frac{7}{8}$ inches. What is the length of the two rods placed end to end?

   b) James has two metal rods. One measures $9\frac{5}{16}$ inches and the other is $5\frac{7}{8}$ inches. What is the difference in length between the two rods?

Complete problems 3 and 4 by choosing the word within parentheses that makes each an **addition problem.** Then solve each problem.

3. Georgia went to the store to buy about $6\frac{1}{2}$ pounds of potatoes. Instead, she found a bargain bag of potatoes that weighed $1\frac{2}{3}$ pounds *(less, more)* ________ . How many pounds of potatoes did she end up buying?

4. During May, Friendly Computer stock sold at $34\frac{1}{2}$ per share. By June 15, the price *(rose, fell)* ________ by $1\frac{7}{8}$ points. What price did the stock sell for on June 15?

Complete problems 5 and 6 by choosing the word within parentheses that makes each a **subtraction problem.** Then solve each problem.

5. Norma usually works $4\frac{1}{2}$ hours each Saturday morning. For this Saturday, though, her boss told her that she would go home $\frac{3}{4}$ hour *(earlier, later)* ________ . How many hours can Norma expect to work this Saturday?

6. Last month, Bert lost $3\frac{7}{8}$ pounds on his diet. This month he plans to lose $1\frac{1}{4}$ *(fewer, more)* ________ pounds than he lost last month. How many total pounds is Bert trying to lose this month?

In problems 7 and 8, circle the arithmetic expression that will give the correct answer to each question. You do not need to solve these two problems.

7. Scott has a roll of screen material to make some household repairs. If he cuts off two pieces each $1\frac{1}{2}$ yards wide for windows, and one $3\frac{1}{3}$-yard-wide piece for a door, what total length of screen material will he remove from the roll?

   a) $\frac{5}{2} + \frac{3}{2} - \frac{10}{3}$

   b) $2 + \frac{3}{2} - \frac{10}{3}$

   c) $\frac{3}{2} + \frac{3}{2} + \frac{10}{3}$

   d) $\frac{3}{2} + \frac{3}{2} - \frac{10}{3}$

8. The cookie recipe calls for $1\frac{3}{4}$ cups of flour. If Leonard has only $1\frac{1}{8}$ cups of flour, how much more flour does he need?

   a) $\frac{14}{8} - \frac{9}{8}$

   b) $\frac{13}{8} - \frac{9}{8}$

   c) $\frac{7}{4} - \frac{1}{4}$

   d) $\frac{7}{4} - (\frac{9}{8} + \frac{1}{4})$

Multiplying Fractions

To multiply by a fraction is to take a part of something. For example, to multiply $\frac{1}{4}$ by $\frac{1}{2}$ is to take $\frac{1}{2}$ of $\frac{1}{4}$.

As shown at right, $\frac{1}{2}$ of $\frac{1}{4}$ is $\frac{1}{8}$.

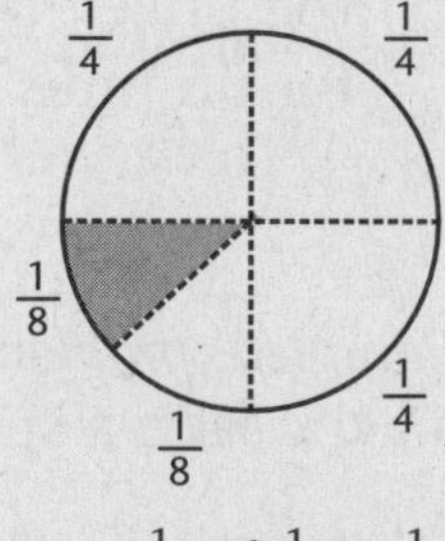

$\frac{1}{2}$ of $\frac{1}{4}$ is $\frac{1}{8}$

or $\frac{1}{2} \times \frac{1}{4} = \frac{1}{8}$

The rule for multiplying fractions is easy to learn.

- Multiply the numerators of the fractions to find the numerator of the answer. In other words, "Top times top equals top."

- Multiply the denominators of the fractions to find the denominator of the answer. You could say, "Bottom times bottom equals bottom."

EXAMPLE 1: Multiply $\frac{1}{2}$ by $\frac{3}{4}$.

Step 1. Multiply the top numbers to find the numerator of the answer. $\frac{1}{2} \times \frac{3}{4} = \frac{3}{}$

Step 2. Multiply the bottom numbers to find the denominator of the answer. $\frac{1}{2} \times \frac{3}{4} = \frac{3}{8}$

Answer: $\frac{3}{8}$

EXAMPLE 2: $\frac{4}{5} \times \frac{3}{8}$

Step 1. Multiply.

$\frac{4}{5} \times \frac{3}{8} = \frac{12}{40}$

Step 2. Reduce the answer.

$\frac{12 \div 4}{40 \div 4} = \frac{3}{10}$

Answer: $\frac{3}{10}$

You use the same rule to multiply both proper and improper fractions. You also use this rule to multiply more than two fractions in the same problem.

Multiply. The first problem in each row is done for you.

1. $\frac{1}{2} \times \frac{1}{3} = \frac{1}{6}$ $\quad \frac{2}{5} \times \frac{2}{9} =$ $\quad \frac{3}{8} \times \frac{1}{2} =$ $\quad \frac{3}{7} \times \frac{3}{10} =$ $\quad \frac{5}{6} \times \frac{3}{4} =$

2. $\frac{1}{3} \times \frac{3}{4} \times \frac{2}{5} = \frac{6}{60} = \frac{1}{10}$ $\quad \frac{2}{3} \times \frac{1}{2} \times \frac{3}{4} =$ $\quad \frac{3}{2} \times \frac{2}{3} \times \frac{4}{5} =$

Using Canceling to Simplify Multiplication

You can use a shortcut called ***canceling*** when you multiply fractions.

To cancel, divide both a top number and a bottom number by the same number. Cancel before you multiply.

Canceling is similar to **reducing** a fraction. However, when you cancel, you simplify fractions **before** you multiply.

EXAMPLE 1: $\frac{2}{9} \times \frac{6}{7}$

With Canceling

Step 1. Divide the right numerator (6) by 3 and divide the left denominator (9) by 3. $\frac{2}{\cancel{9}_3} \times \frac{\cancel{6}^2}{7}$

Step 2. Multiply the rewritten fractions: $\frac{2}{3} \times \frac{2}{7} = \frac{4}{21}$

Answer: $\frac{4}{21}$

Without Canceling

$\frac{2}{9} \times \frac{6}{7} = \frac{12}{63}$

$= \frac{12 \div 3}{63 \div 3}$

$= \frac{4}{21}$

In Example 2, notice how canceling may be used more than once in the same problem.

EXAMPLE 2: $\frac{4}{9} \times \frac{3}{8}$

Step 1. Divide both the 4 and the 8 by 4. $\frac{\overset{1}{\cancel{4}}}{\underset{3}{\cancel{9}}} \times \frac{\overset{1}{\cancel{3}}}{\underset{2}{\cancel{8}}} = \frac{1}{3} \times \frac{1}{2} = \frac{1}{6}$

Step 2. Divide both the 3 and the 9 by 3.

Answer: $\frac{1}{6}$

Skill Builders

3. $\frac{5}{6} \times \frac{3}{4}$ $= \frac{5}{\underset{2}{\cancel{6}}} \times \frac{\overset{1}{\cancel{3}}}{4}$ $\qquad$ $\frac{4}{7} \times \frac{10}{12}$ $= \frac{\overset{1}{\cancel{4}}}{7} \times \frac{10}{\underset{3}{\cancel{12}}}$ $\qquad$ $\frac{12}{9} \times \frac{3}{4}$ $= \frac{\overset{3}{\cancel{12}}}{\underset{3}{\cancel{9}}} \times \frac{\overset{1}{\cancel{3}}}{\underset{1}{\cancel{4}}}$ $\qquad$ $\frac{7}{8} \times \frac{16}{14}$ $= \frac{\overset{1}{\cancel{7}}}{\underset{1}{\cancel{8}}} \times \frac{\overset{2}{16}}{\underset{2}{\cancel{14}}}$

4. $\frac{7}{8} \times \frac{5}{7}$ $\qquad$ $\frac{5}{9} \times \frac{4}{15}$ $\qquad$ $\frac{7}{4} \times \frac{16}{14}$ $\qquad$ $\frac{12}{5} \times \frac{25}{36}$

Multiplying with Fractions and Whole Numbers

To multiply a fraction by a whole number, you must first place the whole number over the number 1. In this way **the whole number is also written as a fraction.** Then you multiply just as you multiply any two fractions. Change any improper fraction answer to a mixed number.

EXAMPLE: $\frac{3}{4} \times 5$

$= \frac{3}{4} \times \frac{5}{1}$

$= \frac{15}{4}$

$= 3\frac{3}{4}$

Multiply. Complete the row of partially-worked Skill Builders.

Skill Builders

5. $\frac{3}{9} \times 6$ $= \frac{3}{9} \times \frac{6}{1}$ $\qquad$ $4 \times \frac{5}{8}$ $= \frac{4}{1} \times \frac{5}{8}$ $\qquad$ $\frac{12}{7} \times 4$ $= \frac{12}{7} \times \frac{4}{1}$ $\qquad$ $8 \times \frac{11}{12}$ $= \frac{8}{1} \times \frac{11}{12}$

6. $\frac{4}{5} \times 6$ $\qquad$ $\frac{7}{8} \times 7$ $\qquad$ $8 \times \frac{11}{12}$ $\qquad$ $5 \times \frac{3}{4}$ $\qquad$ $7 \times \frac{12}{7}$

7. $3 \times \frac{11}{6}$ $\qquad$ $\frac{14}{3} \times 2$ $\qquad$ $8 \times \frac{9}{6}$ $\qquad$ $3 \times \frac{11}{12}$ $\qquad$ $\frac{5}{6} \times \frac{16}{15}$

Multiplying with Mixed Numbers

When a multiplication problem contains one or more mixed numbers, the first step is to change all mixed numbers to improper fractions. Then multiply as before.

Change any improper fraction answer back to a whole number or a mixed number.

EXAMPLE 1:

$\frac{2}{3} \times 3\frac{1}{2}$

$= \frac{{}^{1}\cancel{2}}{3} \times \frac{7}{\cancel{2}_{1}}$

$= \frac{7}{3}$

$= 2\frac{1}{3}$

EXAMPLE 2:

$1\frac{1}{2} \times 2\frac{1}{4}$

$= \frac{3}{2} \times \frac{9}{4}$

$= \frac{27}{8}$

$= 3\frac{3}{8}$

Skill Builders

8. $1\frac{2}{3} \times 3$ $\quad 2 \times 3\frac{3}{4}$ $\quad \frac{5}{6} \times 2\frac{3}{8}$ $\quad 4\frac{1}{2} \times \frac{3}{5}$ $\quad 2\frac{1}{2} \times 3\frac{1}{2}$

$= \frac{5}{3} \times \frac{3}{1}$ $\quad = \frac{2}{1} \times \frac{15}{4}$ $\quad = \frac{5}{6} \times \frac{19}{8}$ $\quad = \frac{9}{2} \times \frac{3}{5}$ $\quad = \frac{5}{2} \times \frac{7}{2}$

= $\quad$ = $\quad$ = $\quad$ = $\quad$ =

9. $\frac{3}{4} \times 1\frac{1}{4}$ $\quad \frac{4}{5} \times 2\frac{5}{6}$ $\quad 3\frac{2}{7} \times 4\frac{1}{3}$ $\quad 6\frac{5}{8} \times 3$ $\quad 2\frac{3}{8} \times 4$

10. $6\frac{7}{10} \times 2$ $\quad 2\frac{3}{4} \times 3\frac{4}{5}$ $\quad 4\frac{1}{3} \times 2\frac{11}{12}$ $\quad 5\frac{2}{7} \times 4\frac{5}{9}$ $\quad 3\frac{3}{10} \times 1\frac{9}{10}$

Dividing Fractions

When you divide, you are finding out how many times one number will go into a second number. This is true for fractions as well as whole numbers.

For example, suppose you want to know how many $\frac{1}{16}$-mile-long sections are in a stretch of road that measures $\frac{3}{8}$ mile long. To find out, you divide $\frac{3}{8}$ by $\frac{1}{16}$.

As shown at right, there are **six** $\frac{1}{16}$ sections in $\frac{3}{8}$.

$\frac{3}{8}$					
$\frac{1}{8}$		$\frac{1}{8}$		$\frac{1}{8}$	
$\frac{1}{16}$	$\frac{1}{16}$	$\frac{1}{16}$	$\frac{1}{16}$	$\frac{1}{16}$	$\frac{1}{16}$

Inverting the Divisor

To divide fractions, invert the divisor (the number you're dividing by) **and change the division sign to a multiplication sign. Then multiply to find the answer.**

To ***invert*** means to "turn a fraction upside down." You do this by interchanging the numerator with the denominator. The top number becomes the bottom number, and the bottom number becomes the top number.

Inverting $\frac{2}{3}$

$\frac{2}{3} \rightarrow \frac{3}{2}$

Before inverting a divisor, you must first change it to a fraction if it's not one already.

- Change a whole number divisor to a whole number over 1.
- Change a mixed number divisor to an improper fraction.

Type of Divisor	*Example*	*Written as a Fraction*	*Inverted*
Proper fraction	$\frac{3}{4}$	$\frac{3}{4}$	$\frac{4}{3}$
Improper fraction	$\frac{12}{7}$	$\frac{12}{7}$	$\frac{7}{12}$
Whole number	5	$\frac{5}{1}$	$\frac{1}{5}$
Mixed number	$2\frac{3}{8}$	$\frac{19}{8}$	$\frac{8}{19}$

Invert each number below. As a first step, change any whole number or mixed number to a fraction.

1. $\frac{8}{3}$ $\quad\frac{11}{2}$ $\quad 9$ $\quad 3\frac{3}{4}$ $\quad 1\frac{7}{8}$

Dividing Fractions by Fractions

To divide one fraction by another, follow these steps:

1. Invert the fraction to the right of the division sign.
2. Change the division sign to a multiplication sign and multiply.

Simplify the answer if possible.

EXAMPLE: $\frac{3}{4} \div \frac{2}{3}$ Invert this fraction. Change this sign.

$= \frac{3}{4} \times \frac{3}{2} = \frac{9}{8}$

Answer: $\frac{9}{8} = 1\frac{1}{8}$

When you divide a fraction by a fraction, the answer may be **less than 1, equal to 1,** or **more than 1.**

Skill Builders

2. $\frac{1}{2} \div \frac{3}{4} \rightarrow \frac{1}{2} \times \frac{4}{3}$ $=$ $\frac{7}{8} \div \frac{7}{8} \rightarrow \frac{7}{8} \times \frac{8}{7}$ $=$ $\frac{4}{5} \div \frac{1}{3} \rightarrow \frac{4}{5} \times \frac{3}{1}$ $=$

3. $\frac{4}{5} \div \frac{4}{5}$ $\frac{5}{6} \div \frac{8}{7}$ $\frac{6}{5} \div \frac{3}{4}$ $\frac{9}{8} \div \frac{4}{3}$ $\frac{1}{2} \div \frac{4}{5}$

4. $\frac{5}{9} \div \frac{5}{9}$ $\frac{12}{3} \div \frac{2}{4}$ $\frac{3}{4} \div \frac{13}{2}$ $\frac{2}{7} \div \frac{14}{5}$ $\frac{15}{4} \div \frac{12}{5}$

Dividing with Fractions and Whole Numbers

Often you may want to divide a fraction by a whole number. To do this, write the whole number as a fraction with a denominator of 1. Then invert the whole number divisor and multiply.

EXAMPLE:

Change
Invert

$$\frac{3}{8} \div 5 = \frac{3}{8} \div \frac{5}{1}$$
$$= \frac{3}{8} \times \frac{1}{5}$$
$$= \frac{3}{40}$$

Dividing a fraction by a whole number gives you an answer that is always smaller than the fraction you started with.

Skill Builders

Change
Invert

5. $\frac{4}{7} \div 2 \rightarrow \frac{4}{7} \div \frac{2}{1}$ $=$ $\frac{8}{5} \div 8 \rightarrow \frac{8}{5} \div \frac{8}{1}$ $=$ $\frac{12}{5} \div 13 \rightarrow \frac{12}{5} \div \frac{13}{1}$ $=$

6. $\frac{3}{4} \div 6$ $\frac{7}{8} \div 4$ $\frac{9}{10} \div 5$ $\frac{8}{2} \div 8$ $\frac{9}{3} \div 5$

You can also divide a whole number by a fraction. Again you write the whole number over the number 1. This time you invert the fraction that is now the divisor.

Note: As the example shows, dividing a whole number or mixed number by a fraction can give a whole number answer.

EXAMPLE:

Change / Invert

$$6 \div \frac{2}{3} = \frac{6}{1} \div \frac{2}{3}$$

$$= \frac{6}{1} \times \frac{3}{2}$$

$$= \frac{18}{2} = 9$$

Skill Builders

7. $5 \div \frac{1}{5} \rightarrow \frac{5}{1} \div \frac{1}{5}$ (Change / Invert) $\qquad 7 \div \frac{3}{4} \rightarrow \frac{7}{1} \div \frac{3}{4} \qquad 12 \div \frac{4}{3} \rightarrow \frac{12}{1} \div \frac{4}{3}$

$= \qquad = \qquad =$

8. $7 \div \frac{2}{3} \qquad 3 \div \frac{1}{4} \qquad 6 \div \frac{3}{8} \qquad 12 \div \frac{6}{2} \qquad 15 \div \frac{3}{2}$

Dividing with Mixed Numbers

Sometimes a division problem contains one or two mixed numbers. The first step is to change the mixed numbers to improper fractions. Then invert the divisor and multiply.

Change any improper fraction answer back to a mixed number.

EXAMPLE 1:	EXAMPLE 2:
$2\frac{1}{3} \div \frac{1}{2}$	$\frac{4}{5} \div 1\frac{2}{3}$
$= \frac{7}{3} \div \frac{1}{2}$	$= \frac{4}{5} \div \frac{5}{3}$
$= \frac{7}{3} \times \frac{2}{1}$	$= \frac{4}{5} \times \frac{3}{5}$
$= \frac{14}{3}$	$= \frac{12}{25}$
$= 4\frac{2}{3}$	

Skill Builders

9.

$1\frac{3}{4} \div \frac{7}{8}$	$2\frac{1}{2} \div 1\frac{2}{3}$	$5 \div 3\frac{1}{2}$	$\frac{3}{5} \div 2\frac{3}{5}$
$= \frac{7}{4} \div \frac{7}{8}$	$= \frac{5}{2} \div \frac{5}{3}$	$= \frac{5}{1} \div \frac{7}{2}$	$= \frac{3}{5} \div \frac{13}{5}$
$= \frac{7}{4} \times \frac{8}{7}$	$= \frac{5}{2} \times \frac{3}{5}$	$=$	$=$
$=$	$=$	$=$	$=$

10. $2\frac{2}{3} \div \frac{2}{3}$ $6\frac{3}{4} \div 2\frac{3}{8}$ $12\frac{1}{2} \div 6$ $\frac{3}{8} \div 4$ $14 \div 3\frac{1}{3}$

Solving Multiplication and Division Word Problems

Fractions are used in a variety of both multiplication and division problems. As you work these problems, remember that your last step is to make sure that your answer makes sense.

Multiplication Word Problems

Most often, fraction multiplication problems are of two types:

- You are asked to find a **part** of a whole. In this type, the word *of* is often used to indicate multiplication.

  EXAMPLE: What is $\frac{3}{4}$ *of* 12 miles? **Answer:** $\frac{3}{4} \times \frac{12}{1} = 9$ miles

- You are given the size of one thing and asked to find the size of many.

  EXAMPLE: If a small package weighs $\frac{1}{3}$ pound, how much do 7 identical packages weigh?

  Answer: $\frac{1}{3} \times \frac{7}{1} = \frac{7}{3}$

  $= 2\frac{1}{3}$ **pounds**

Notice in each example that fraction multiplication is unlike whole number multiplication. **When you multiply a number by a proper fraction, your answer is a smaller number.** This is because you are finding a part of something. Use this fact to help check that each of your answers below makes sense.

Solve the multiplication problems below.

1. If "lean hamburger" is $\frac{1}{5}$ fat, how many ounces of fat are in a 12-ounce hamburger steak? (This is another way of asking, "What is $\frac{1}{5}$ of 12?")

2. Gloria uses $\frac{1}{4}$ of her monthly take-home pay to pay her rent. How much rent does she pay if her monthly take-home pay is $940? (This is another way of asking, "What is $\frac{1}{4}$ of $940?")

Division Word Problems

In a division word problem, you are most often trying to find how many of one object (the **part**) is contained in a second, larger object (the **whole**).

- The whole is the number that is being divided into. The whole must be written to the left of the division sign.
- The part is the number you are dividing by. The part must be written to the right of the division sign.

To divide, you invert the part and then multiply to find an answer. In each problem, be careful to correctly identify which number is the whole and which is the part.

EXAMPLE 1: How many $\frac{1}{2}$-pound steaks can be made out of a package of hamburger that weighs $3\frac{1}{2}$ pounds?

Solution: $3\frac{1}{2} \div \frac{1}{2}$

whole ↑ ↑ part

$= \frac{7}{\cancel{2}_1} \times \frac{\cancel{2}^1}{1}$

$=$ **7 steaks**

EXAMPLE 2: How many books that are $1\frac{1}{4}$ inches thick can be stacked between two shelves that are $13\frac{3}{4}$ inches apart?

Solution: $13\frac{3}{4} \div 1\frac{1}{4}$

$= \frac{55}{4} \div \frac{5}{4}$

$= \frac{\overset{11}{\cancel{55}}}{\cancel{4}_1} \times \frac{\overset{1}{\cancel{4}}}{\cancel{5}_1}$

$=$ **11 books**

Notice, as example 1 shows, fraction division is unlike whole number division:

> **When you divide a number by a fraction smaller than 1, your answer is a larger number than the one you started with.**

Solve the division problems below.

3. The skateboard race covers a total of $1\frac{7}{8}$ miles. How many people will be needed on each team if each person skates for $\frac{3}{16}$ mile?

4. One centimeter is about $\frac{2}{5}$ inch. How many centimeters are in $\frac{7}{8}$ of an inch?

Following are both multiplication and division problems. These problems are designed to increase your problem-solving skills with both fractions and mixed numbers. Notice that the answers to problems 5 and 6 are whole numbers.

5. Not counting any leftover piece, how many $12\frac{3}{4}$-inch pieces of ribbon can be cut from a piece that measures 141 inches in length?

6. Bryan, a jewelry maker, uses $\frac{5}{16}$ ounces of gold for each custom-made ring he designs. How many complete rings can Bryan make when his gold supply is down to $3\frac{5}{8}$ ounces?

Problems 7 and 8 contain extra information. In each problem, circle the necessary information and then solve the problem.

7. The distance around Jake's property is $3\frac{3}{4}$ miles. Across the back boundary it is $\frac{7}{8}$ mile. The local power company has decided to place power line poles along this back boundary. If the poles are to be placed $\frac{3}{64}$ mile apart, about how many will be placed along this boundary?

8. Last year, $\frac{3}{5}$ of the moisture that fell in Klamath was rain, $\frac{3}{10}$ was snow, and $\frac{1}{10}$ was hail or sleet. If Klamath recorded 40 inches of precipitation during the year, how much of it fell as snow?

In problems 9 and 10, necessary information is found to the right of each problem. Use this information to solve the problems.

9. To bake cookies, Mark looked at a cookbook recipe. Part of that recipe is shown at the right. If Mark wanted to make only $\frac{1}{2}$ as many cookies as the recipe provides, how many cups of flour should he use?

Recipe

1 cup shortening

$1\frac{1}{2}$ cups sugar
$1\frac{3}{4}$ cups flour
1 cup raisins

10. Stella has to move the whole pile of sand shown at right. The maximum load she can carry each trip is $1\frac{2}{3}$ tons. Determine how many trips Stella will need to make in order to finish this job. (Hint: the answer is a whole number!)

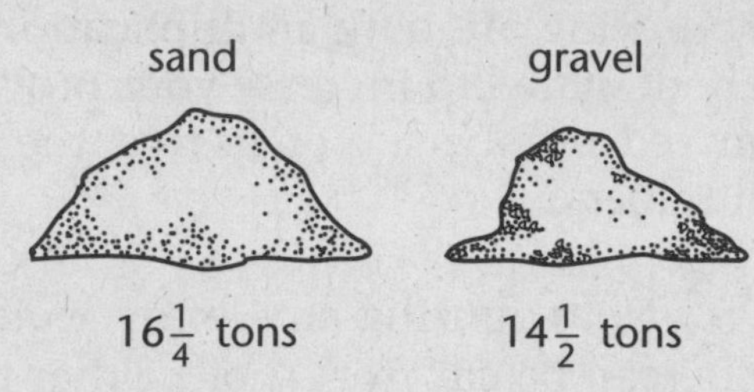

Working with Decimals and Fractions at the Same Time

Decimals and fractions often appear in word problems together. Therefore, you may need to change common fractions to decimal fractions or to change decimal fractions to common fractions.

Changing Common Fractions to Decimal Fractions

To change a common fraction to a decimal fraction, you divide the denominator into the numerator. Follow the rules for dividing decimal numbers.

EXAMPLE: Change $\frac{3}{8}$ to a decimal fraction.

Step 1. Set up the problem for long division. Be sure to place the numerator (3) inside the division bracket.

Step 2. Place a decimal point to the right of the 3, add a zero, and divide.

Step 3. Continue dividing. You will need to add two more zeros before the answer comes out with no remainder.

$$\begin{array}{r} .375 \\ 8\overline{)3.000} \\ \underline{2\,4} \\ 60 \\ \underline{56} \\ 40 \\ \underline{40} \\ 0 \end{array}$$

Answer: $\frac{3}{8} = .375$

Change each fraction to a decimal. **Round** any **repeating decimal** to the hundredths place. Complete the partially-worked Skill Builders first.

Skill Builders

(repeating decimal)

1. $\frac{1}{4} \rightarrow 4\overline{)1.00}$ $\qquad \frac{5}{8} \rightarrow 8\overline{)5.000}$ $\qquad \frac{1}{6} \rightarrow 6\overline{)1.000}$

2. $\frac{2}{4}$ $\qquad \frac{3}{5}$ $\qquad \frac{3}{4}$ $\qquad \frac{7}{10}$ $\qquad \frac{3}{20}$

3. $\frac{1}{8}$ $\frac{1}{3}$ $\frac{6}{15}$ $\frac{2}{3}$ $\frac{5}{11}$

Changing Decimal Fractions to Common Fractions

To change a decimal fraction to a common fraction, write the number in the decimal as the numerator of a fraction. For the denominator of this fraction, write the place value of the final digit in the decimal. Reduce the fraction if you can.

EXAMPLE 1: Write .075 as a fraction.

Step 1. Write 75 as the numerator of a fraction: $\frac{75}{\ }$

Step 2. Since 5 (of the .075) is in the thousandths place, one thousand will be the denominator of the fraction. $\frac{75}{1{,}000}$

Step 3. You can now reduce this fraction by dividing both top and bottom numbers by 25. $\frac{75 \div 25}{1{,}000 \div 25} = \frac{3}{40}$

Answer: $.075 = \frac{3}{40}$

EXAMPLE 2: Write 2.45 as a mixed number.

Step 1. Write .45 as a fraction. $.45 = \frac{45}{100}$

Step 2. Reduce the fraction by dividing both top and bottom numbers by 5. $\frac{45 \div 5}{100 \div 5} = \frac{9}{20}$

Step 3. Replace .45 in the mixed decimal 2.45 by $\frac{9}{20}$ to make a mixed number.

Answer: $2.45 = 2\frac{9}{20}$

Write each of the following numbers as a fraction or mixed number. Reduce each fraction when possible.

4. .2 .5 .25 .75 .95

5. .38 .375 .750 1.7 3.25

6. 9.4 8.125 6.005 3.0375 4.875

Comparing Common Fractions with Decimal Fractions

To compare common fractions with decimal fractions, change the common fractions to decimals. This is by far the easiest way to make a comparison.

With both numbers now expressed as decimals, follow the rules for comparing decimal fractions given on page 000.

EXAMPLE: Which is larger, $\frac{3}{4}$ or .793?

Step 1. Write $\frac{3}{4}$ as a decimal fraction. Dividing 4 into 3, we get $\frac{3}{4} = .75$.

$$\begin{array}{r} .75 = .750 \\ 4\overline{)3.00} \\ \underline{2\,8} \\ 20 \\ \underline{20} \\ 0 \end{array}$$

Step 2. Compare .75 with .793. Give each decimal the same number of places. Do this by adding 0 to the right of .75: .75 = .750.

Since .793 is larger than .750, .793 is larger than .75 ($\frac{3}{4}$).

Answer: .793 is larger than $\frac{3}{4}$.

In each pair, circle the larger value.

1. .249 or $\frac{1}{4}$ $\frac{3}{5}$ or .62 $\frac{7}{8}$ or .859   .128 or $\frac{1}{8}$

To make each comparison below, round each fraction to 3 decimal places. Then circle the larger value in each pair.

2. .334 or $\frac{1}{3}$ $\frac{2}{7}$ or .283 $\frac{7}{9}$ or .804 $\frac{5}{6}$ or .812

3. Which is the smaller area: $\frac{3}{4}$ square yard or .74 square yard?

4. Which represents the larger amount: \$.71 or $\frac{5}{8}$ of a dollar?

5. Which is the heavier amount: 4 ounces or .275 pound?

6. Which is the longer distance: 25 inches or .7 yard?

Comparison Word Problems

A comparison word problem is solved by comparing one value with another. Most often, you are given information in both fraction and decimal form. You may be asked to find the difference in sizes, or you may be asked to write things in the order of their sizes.

To solve a comparison problem, rewrite each fraction as a decimal and then compare decimals as needed.

Solve each comparison problem below.

1. According to the blueprint, Jim should drill a drainage hole "no larger than .24 inch in diameter (distance across)." If he has the three drill bit sizes to choose from as shown at right, which will give him the largest permissible hole?

Bit #	*Diameter*
#1	$\frac{1}{4}$ inch
#2	$\frac{7}{32}$ inch
#3	$\frac{3}{16}$ inch

2. Jill has four items to stack in a display case. She should place the heaviest item on the bottom, then the next heaviest, and so on. The lightest item goes on top. The weight of each item is listed at right.

   Place a letter on each blank line to show the order in which she should stack the items. The letter of the heaviest item goes on the bottom line.

Order	*Item*	*Weight*
____	A	12 ounces
____	B	1.2 pounds
____	C	.78 pounds
____	D	$\frac{4}{5}$ pound

3. Write the times shown at right as mixed decimals (for example, 6.30 hours). Express each answer to two decimal places, and write them in order from the shortest time at the left to the longest at the right.

Joyce:	$6\frac{1}{3}$ hours
Irvin:	6.3 hours
Francis:	6 hours 22 minutes
Ellen:	$6\frac{7}{20}$ hours

__________ __________ __________ __________

Solving Decimal *and* Fraction Word Problems

Many word problems (especially money problems) contain both decimals and fractions. To solve this type of problem, you can change all numbers to the same form. You also can compute with the numbers as they are.

An example can best show each method.

EXAMPLE: Mary Anne bought $5\frac{1}{4}$ yards of dress material for $2.48 per yard. What is the total cost of this material?

Method 1

Step 1. Change $5\frac{1}{4}$ to a decimal.

$5\frac{1}{4} = 5.25$ since $\frac{1}{4} = .25$.

Step 2. Multiply $2.48 times 5.25.

```
   $2.48
 ×  5.25
    1240
    496
  1240
 $130200 = $13.02
```

$13.02

Method 2

Step 1. Change $5\frac{1}{4}$ to an improper fraction.

$5\frac{1}{4} = \frac{21}{4}$

Step 2. Multiply $2.48 times $\frac{21}{4}$.

$\frac{\overset{.62}{\cancel{2.48}}}{1} \times \frac{21}{\cancel{4}_1} = \$.62 \times 21$

$= \mathbf{\$13.02}$

Using either method you prefer, solve the problems below.

1. At Sunday's race, Rhoda ran 3.5 miles in $27\frac{1}{2}$ minutes. On the average, how long did it take Rhoda to run each mile?

2. One-inch-wide wood trim costs $.28 per foot of length. How much does a piece of trim cost that is 6 feet 3 inches long? (Hint: First change 3 inches to a fraction of a foot.)

Solving Multi-Step Word Problems

In each multi-step problem, a solution sentence is written and the missing information is underlined. Solve each problem by first finding the value of the missing information.

1. It takes Steve $\frac{1}{2}$ hour to drive to work each morning and $\frac{3}{4}$ hour to drive home each night. How much total time does Steve spend driving to and from work each 5-day week?

   total time = <u>total driving time each day</u> times 5

   $\underbrace{\frac{1}{2} + \frac{3}{4}}$

   $1\frac{1}{4} \times 5 = 6\frac{1}{4}$ *hours*

2. Jay bought $5\frac{3}{8}$ pounds of chocolate. He gave $3\frac{1}{2}$ pounds of it to his sister. From the chocolate he kept, he made 12 chocolate desserts. How much chocolate did he put in each dessert?

   chocolate in each dessert = <u>total chocolate kept</u> divided by 12

3. To prepare for a picnic, Kimberly bought two packages of hamburger: one marked 2 pounds 5 ounces and one marked 1 pound 7 ounces. Using both packages, how many $\frac{1}{4}$-pound hamburgers can she make? (Hint: First add and then change ounces to a fraction of a pound: 16 ounces = 1 pound.)

   number of hamburgers = <u>total amount of meat</u> divided by $\frac{1}{4}$

4. Monday through Friday, Rita earns her regular salary rate of $8.20 per hour. For each overtime hour she works on Saturday, she makes $1\frac{1}{2}$ times her regular rate. How much does Rita earn during a week in which she works $34\frac{3}{4}$ regular hours and $5\frac{1}{2}$ overtime hours?

   total earned = <u>total regular pay</u> plus <u>total overtime pay</u>

In problems 5 and 6, you may find it helpful to first write a solution sentence to help identify missing information.

5. Rapid Express provides overnight mail delivery service. To mail packages, it charges \$13.40 per pound. Using this service, what is the total cost of mailing three packages with weights of $1\frac{3}{8}$ pounds, $2\frac{1}{4}$ pounds, and $1\frac{1}{2}$ pounds?

6. For the hardware sale, Moses is going to make 15 equal-size bags of mixed screws, bolts, and nuts. First he'll mix $5\frac{3}{8}$ pounds of screws with $4\frac{1}{4}$ pounds of bolts and $3\frac{1}{2}$ pounds of nuts. Then he'll divide this mixture equally into 15 bags. About how much will each bag weigh?

In problems 7 and 8, circle the arithmetic expression that will give the correct answer to each question. You do not need to solve these two problems.

7. For Halloween, Cindy bought a $9\frac{3}{8}$-pound bag of candy chews. She took out $\frac{3}{4}$ pound of the candy to keep for her own family. Then she divided the rest into 50 "treat bags" to give to children. About how much candy was in each treat bag?

   a) $(9\frac{3}{8} \div 50) - \frac{3}{4}$
   b) $(9\frac{3}{8} + \frac{3}{4}) \div 50$
   c) $(50 - 9\frac{3}{8}) \times \frac{3}{4}$
   d) $(9\frac{3}{8} - \frac{3}{4}) \div 50$

8. Martha bought $2\frac{1}{4}$ yards of plain material for \$1.68 per yard, and $3\frac{1}{2}$ yards of print material for \$2.46 per yard. How much did Martha pay for all this material?

   a) $\frac{9}{4} \times 1.68 + \frac{7}{2} \times 2.46$
   b) $(\frac{9}{4} + \frac{7}{2}) \times (1.68 + 2.46)$
   c) $\frac{7}{2} \times 1.68 + \frac{9}{4} \times 2.46$
   d) $(\frac{7}{2} \times \frac{9}{4}) \times (2.46 - 1.68)$

Questions 9 and 10 refer to the following passage.

Stock prices are given in dollars and fractions of dollars. The price quoted is the price of one share. For example, a stock that is quoted at $11\frac{1}{2}$ is selling for $11.50 per share. In May, Sarah bought 15 shares of Best Computer stock, selling at $14\frac{3}{4}$. To buy the stock, Sarah paid the broker a commission of $11.35.

9. Including the commission, how much did Sarah pay for her 15 shares of Best Computer stock?

10. Sarah sold her stock when it was at $17\frac{1}{2}$. If she paid a commission of $13.60, how much money did she receive from the sale?

Questions 11 and 12 refer to the passage below.

To improve his health, Leon went on a special diet and exercise program. While on this program, Leon will lose $1\frac{3}{8}$ pounds each week. The exercise part of the program is as follows:

1st 3 months: Exercise $\frac{1}{2}$ hour per day, 3 days each week.

2nd 3 months: Exercise $\frac{3}{4}$ hour per day, 3 days each week.

After 6 months: Exercise $\frac{3}{4}$ hour per day, 4 days each week.

Leon's plan is to lose 66 pounds and decrease his weight from 256 pounds to 190 pounds.

11. While on this program, how much time will Leon spend exercising each week during the first three months?

12. How many weeks will it take Leon to reach 190 pounds?

Fraction Skills Review

Review fraction computation skills. In each group of common fractions below, circle the two that are equal in value.

1. $\frac{1}{2}, \frac{5}{9}, \frac{4}{8}$ $\quad$ $\frac{3}{9}, \frac{2}{6}, \frac{3}{12}$ $\quad$ $\frac{5}{20}, \frac{3}{15}, \frac{6}{30}$ $\quad$ $\frac{3}{10}, \frac{6}{18}, \frac{9}{30}$

Arrange each group of fractions in order. Write the smallest to the left and the largest to the right. Use the largest denominator as the common denominator.

2. $\frac{5}{12}, \frac{1}{3}, \frac{1}{4}$ $\quad$ $\frac{13}{24}, \frac{5}{12}, \frac{5}{8}$ $\quad$ $\frac{1}{3}, \frac{7}{9}, \frac{2}{3}$ $\quad$ $\frac{9}{20}, \frac{5}{10}, \frac{2}{5}$

Add and subtract as indicated.

3. $\frac{4}{7} + \frac{3}{7}$ $\quad 2\frac{3}{5} + \frac{1}{5}$ $\quad \frac{7}{9} + \frac{2}{3}$ $\quad 4\frac{3}{7} + 2\frac{3}{14}$ $\quad 7\frac{7}{8} + 5\frac{3}{4}$

4. $\frac{7}{9} - \frac{2}{9}$ $\quad \frac{7}{9} - \frac{2}{3}$ $\quad \frac{10}{12} - \frac{1}{6}$ $\quad 5\frac{1}{4} - \frac{5}{8}$ $\quad 9\frac{7}{10} - 2\frac{2}{5}$

Multiply as indicated.

5. $\frac{2}{3} \times \frac{1}{5} =$ $\quad \frac{7}{9} \times \frac{3}{4} =$ $\quad \frac{3}{4} \times 7 =$ $\quad 12 \times \frac{5}{6} =$

6. $2\frac{1}{4} \times \frac{2}{3} =$ $\quad 3\frac{4}{5} \times 5 =$ $\quad 5\frac{3}{8} \times 2\frac{1}{4} =$ $\quad 6\frac{3}{8} \times \frac{9}{2} =$

7. $\frac{1}{2} \times \frac{3}{5} \times \frac{10}{15} =$ $\quad \frac{2}{3} \times \frac{3}{4} \times 5 =$ $\quad 2\frac{1}{2} \times \frac{3}{4} \times \frac{4}{5} =$

Divide as indicated.

8. $\frac{3}{4} \div \frac{1}{2} =$ $\quad \frac{1}{6} \div 3 =$ $\quad 5 \div \frac{3}{10} =$ $\quad \frac{3}{4} \div 3\frac{1}{3} =$

9. $5\frac{3}{5} \div \frac{2}{3} =$ $\quad 1\frac{7}{8} \div 4 =$ $\quad 6\frac{1}{3} \div 7\frac{4}{9} =$ $\quad 5\frac{5}{6} \div 9\frac{1}{2} =$

9 PERCENT SKILLS

Percents

Percent means "hundredth." A percent is most often written as a number followed by the percent symbol %. For example, 5 percent is usually written 5% and means 5 hundredths. Percent is another way to write part of a whole. But, because *percent* means hundredth, **a percent always refers to a whole that is divided into 100 equal parts.**

You write percent as the number of hundredths followed by the percent sign %. For example, 10 percent is written as 10%. **10% means 10 parts out of 100.**

Any percent can easily be written as an equivalent decimal or fraction.

- Percent has the same value as a two-place decimal.
  For example, 35% is equal to .35.
- Percent has the same value as a fraction that has a denominator of 100.
  For example, 35% is equal to $\frac{35}{100}$.

100 equal parts

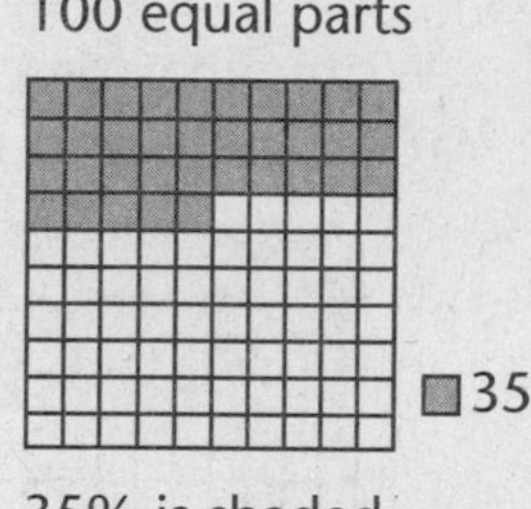

35% is shaded.

Percents, decimals, and fractions are similar, yet we use all three. Each method of writing part of a whole is popular for certain uses. Decimals became the basis of our money system and of the metric measuring system. Fractions became the basis of the English measuring system. Percents became used with such things as store sales, taxes, finance charges, and rates of increase and decrease.

Percents, decimals, and fractions often appear together. **Always change a percent to a decimal or fraction before you do any computations.**

To remember the meaning of percent, look at the % sign.

- When you want to write a percent as a decimal, the two zeros in % remind you of two decimal places. 35% = .35
- When you want to write a percent as a fraction, the two zeros in % remind you of two zeros in the denominator. 27% = $\frac{27}{100}$

Answers to Chapter 9 exercises start on page 926.

In each figure below, show how the shaded part can be written as a **fraction**, as a **decimal**, and as a **percent**.

1. 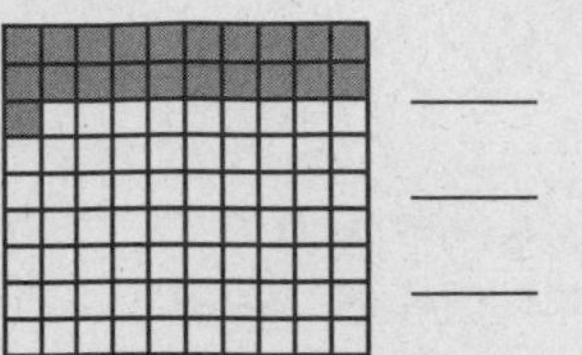 ___ ___ ___

2. 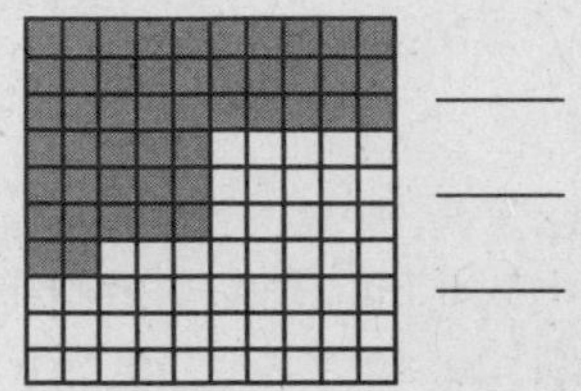 ___ ___ ___

3. 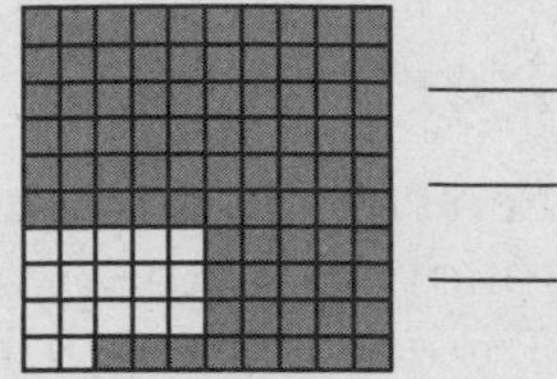 ___ ___ ___

4. 100% always represents a whole amount. At right, 30% of the large square is shaded; 70% is unshaded.

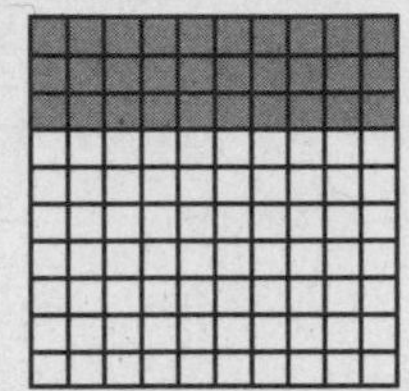

% shaded	30%
% unshaded	70%
total %	100%

Write what percent of each square below is shaded, what percent is unshaded, and what the total of the two percents is equal to.

a) 

% shaded ______
% unshaded______
total % ________

b) 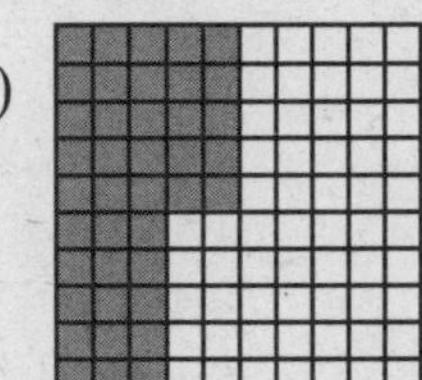

% shaded ________
% unshaded _____
total %_________

5. One hundred students attend classes at Sheldon Community Center. Eighty-nine students showed up for classes on Thursday.

a) What percent of students came to class Thursday?

b) What percent of students did not come to class?

6. There are 100 pennies in 1 dollar. What percent of 1 dollar is each of the following amounts?

a) a penny?

b) a nickel?

c) a dime?

d) a quarter?

Percents, Decimals, and Fractions

It's important to become comfortable with percents, decimals, and fractions. You'll want to learn how you can quickly change from one form to another. We'll start by seeing how to change percents to decimals.

Changing Percents to Decimals

To change a percent to a decimal:

- Move the decimal point two places to the left, adding a zero if necessary.
- Drop the percent sign.
- Drop any unnecessary zeros.

Remember that the decimal point in a whole number percent is understood to be at the right of the whole number even though it is not written.

EXAMPLES:

Percent	Move Decimal Point Two Places Left	Decimal	
35%	35	.35	
80%	80	.80 = .8	← The zero can be dropped.
9%	09 ← Add a zero.	.09	
8.5%	08.5 ← Add a zero.	.085	
62.5%	62.5	.625	

Change each percent below to a decimal. Add zeros where necessary to give *at least* two decimal places. Drop any unnecessary zeros.

1. 55% = 25% = 4% = 8% =

2. 8.8% = 11.5% = 30% = 7.5% =

Changing Fractional Percents to Decimals

A fractional percent is a percent less than 1%. A fractional percent can be written alone such as $\frac{1}{2}$%. It may also be part of a mixed number percent such as $33\frac{1}{3}$%.

To change a fractional percent to a decimal, first use division to change the fraction itself to a decimal. This changes the fractional percent to a decimal percent. Next, move the decimal point two places to the left to change the decimal percent to a decimal fraction.

EXAMPLES:

Fractional Percent		*Decimal Percent*		*Decimal Fraction*
a) $\frac{1}{2}$%	=	.5%	=	.005

Caution: Don't make the mistake of writing $\frac{1}{2}$ % = .5, a commonly-made error!

Graphically

$\frac{1}{2}$% is shaded.

$\frac{1}{2}$% is $\frac{1}{2}$ of 1%.

b) $\frac{1}{4}$%	=	.25%	=	.0025

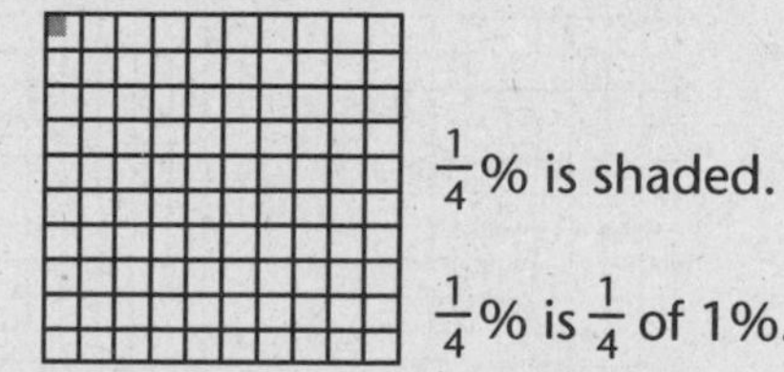

$\frac{1}{4}$% is shaded.

$\frac{1}{4}$% is $\frac{1}{4}$ of 1%.

Note: The graphics at right help you visualize just how small fractional percents really are.

c) $47\frac{4}{5}\% = 47.8\% = .478$

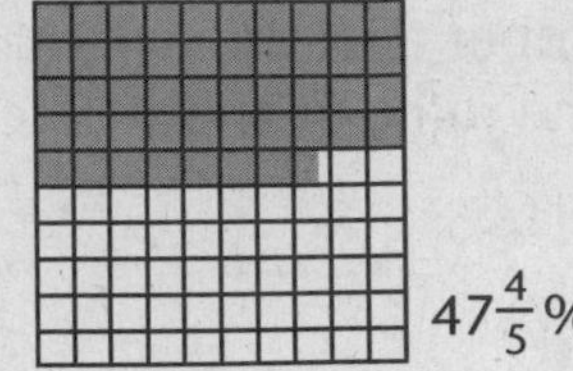

$47\frac{4}{5}\%$ is shaded.

Complete the row of partially-worked Skill Builders. Then change each percent below to a decimal fraction.

Skill Builders

3. $\frac{1}{5}\% = .2\% =$ $\frac{7}{10}\% = .7\% =$ $3\frac{1}{2}\% = 3.5\% =$

4. $\frac{3}{10}\% =$ $\frac{3}{4}\% =$ $7\frac{3}{4}\% =$ $9\frac{3}{8}\% =$

Changing Percents Larger than 100% to Decimals

Once in a while you may see percents that are larger than 100% (larger than a whole unit). When you change such a large percent to a decimal, the answer will be a whole number or a mixed decimal.

EXAMPLES: 1. 300% = 3.00 = **3** 2. 575% = **5.75**

Change each percent below to a whole number or a mixed decimal.

5. 200% = 900% = 485% = 130% =

In each large square below, shade the number of smaller squares that represents each indicated percent. Each large square (1 whole unit) contains 100 equal-size smaller squares.

6. 

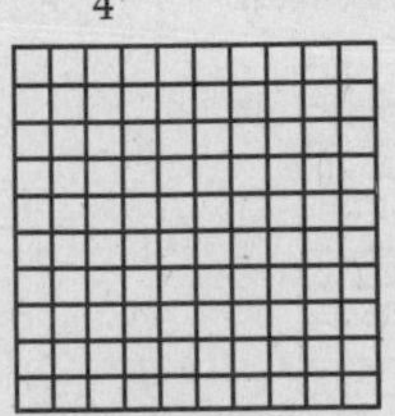

7. $\frac{5}{8}$

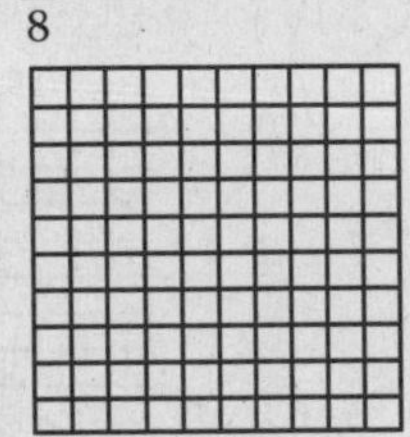

8. $8\frac{8}{10}\%$

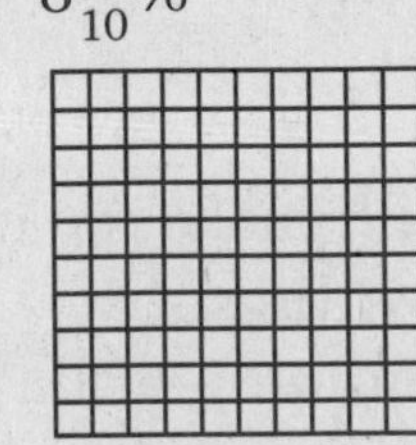

9. $75\frac{2}{3}$

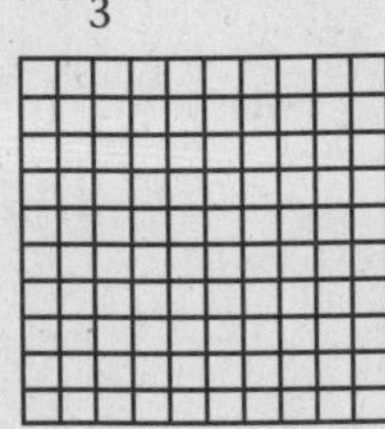

10. 125%

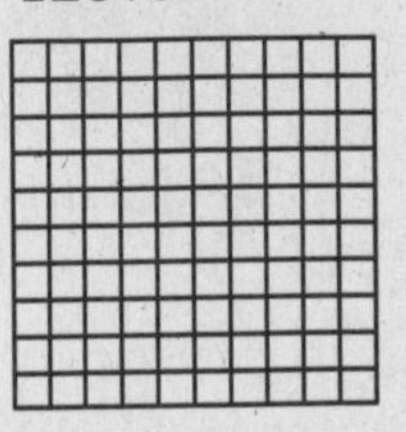

11. 180%

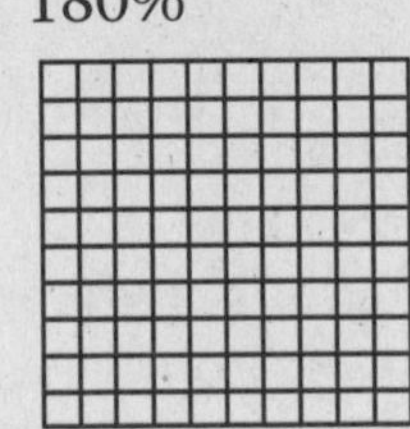

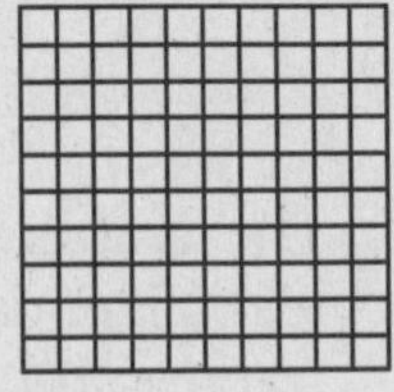

Changing Decimals to Percents

To change a decimal to a percent, simply reverse the rules for changing a percent to a decimal:

- Move the decimal point two places to the right, adding a zero if necessary.
- Write the percent sign after the number.
- Drop any unnecessary zero.
- Drop the decimal point unless the percent contains a decimal fraction.

EXAMPLES:

Decimal	*Move Decimal Point Two Places Right*	*Percent*	
.25	25.	25%	← Drop the point.
.90	90.	90%	
.07	07.	7%	← Drop the unnecessary zero.
.4	40. ← Add a zero.	40%	
.125	12.5	12.5%	
2.5	250. ← Add a zero.	250%	

Change each decimal below to a percent.

12. .75 = .8 = .09 = .375 =

13. .085 = 1.5 = .605 = .7 =

Divide as indicated. Change each decimal answer to a percent.

14. 9 ÷ 10 = 7 ÷ 8 = 4 ÷ 5 = 3 ÷ 8 =

15. 5 ÷ 10 = 8 ÷ 5 = 14 ÷ 4 = 24 ÷ 6 =

Changing Percents to Fractions

To change a percent to a fraction: 1) write the percent as a fraction with 100 as the denominator, 2) reduce the fraction if possible.

EXAMPLE 1: Change 45% to a fraction.

Step 1. Write the percent (45) as a fraction with 100 as the bottom number. $45\% = \frac{45}{100}$

Step 2. Reduce the fraction by dividing top and bottom by 5. $\frac{45 \div 5}{100 \div 5} = \frac{9}{20}$

Answer: $\frac{9}{20}$

Notice that we can also change a percent that's larger than 100% to a mixed number.

EXAMPLE 2: Change 225% to a mixed number.

Step 1. Write the percent (225) as a fraction with 100 as the denominator. $225\% = \frac{225}{100}$

Step 2. Divide 225 by 100. Then reduce the proper fraction remainder.

$$\begin{array}{r} 2\frac{25}{100} = 2\frac{1}{4} \\ 100\overline{)225} \\ \underline{200} \\ 25 \end{array}$$

Answer: $2\frac{1}{4}$

Change each percent below to a fraction.

16. 55% = 40% = 1% = 30% =

17. 50% = 12% = 99% = 20% =

18. 6% = 250% = 475% = 340% =

Changing Fractions to Percents

To change a fraction to a percent: (1) reduce the fraction, (2) change the fraction to a decimal, (3) change the decimal to a percent.

EXAMPLE 1: Change $\frac{3}{4}$ to a percent.

Change $\frac{3}{4}$ to a decimal. Then change the decimal to a percent.

$$4\overline{)3.00} = .75 = \mathbf{75\%}$$
$$\begin{array}{r} 2\,8 \\ \hline 20 \\ 20 \\ \hline \end{array}$$

EXAMPLE 2: Change $\frac{3}{8}$ to a percent.

Change $\frac{3}{8}$ to a decimal and then to a percent.

$$8\overline{)3.000} = .375 = \mathbf{37.5\%}$$
$$\begin{array}{r} 2\,4 \\ \hline 60 \\ 56 \\ \hline 40 \\ 40 \\ \hline \end{array}$$

A **shortcut** that's easy to remember is just to multiply the fraction by 100%. Look how this shortcut simplifies the examples above:

$$\frac{3}{\not{4}_{1}} \times \frac{\overset{25\%}{\not{100}\%}}{1} = \frac{75\%}{1} = 75\% \qquad \frac{3}{8} \times \frac{100\%}{1} = \frac{300\%}{8} = 37.5\%$$

Using either method, change each fraction below to a percent.

19. $\frac{2}{4} =$ $\frac{3}{5} =$ $\frac{1}{4} =$ $\frac{1}{8} =$

20. $\frac{1}{3} =$ $\frac{1}{6} =$ $\frac{7}{25} =$ $\frac{9}{10} =$

21. $\frac{7}{8} =$ $\frac{1}{5} =$ $\frac{2}{3} =$ $\frac{3}{16} =$

Commonly Used Percents, Decimals, and Fractions

Below is a partially-completed chart of the 33 most commonly used percents, decimals, and fractions. The decimals and fractions are written in their most reduced form. Complete this chart by filling in the blank spaces.

Percent	*Decimal*	*Fraction*
10%	.1	$\frac{1}{10}$
	.2	
		$\frac{1}{4}$
30%		
40%		
	.5	
	.6	$\frac{3}{5}$
70%		
	.75	
		$\frac{4}{5}$
	.9	

There are two special fractions that we have not yet mentioned. These are $\frac{1}{3}$ and $\frac{2}{3}$. They are special because their decimal and percent forms include a fraction. This is because $\frac{1}{3}$ and $\frac{2}{3}$ are **repeating decimals.** This simply means that when you write either $\frac{1}{3}$ or $\frac{2}{3}$ as a decimal or percent, you always end up with a remainder.

Because the fractions $\frac{1}{3}$ and $\frac{2}{3}$ often appear in word problems, **you should memorize the three forms of each given below.**

Percent	*Decimal*	*Fraction*
$33\frac{1}{3}\%$	$.33\frac{1}{3}$	$\frac{1}{3}$
$66\frac{2}{3}\%$	$.66\frac{2}{3}$	$\frac{2}{3}$

Word Problems: Percents, Decimals, and Fractions

Answer each question below. Remember to reduce fractions to lowest terms.

1. Bert went to a sale where "all clothes are 25% off."

   a) Express this price reduction as a decimal.

   b) Express this price reduction as a fraction.

2. As of June 15, Mathew had completed $66\frac{2}{3}\%$ of the house he was building.

   a) What fraction of the house had Mathew completed?

   b) What percent of the house remains to be built?

3. A dollar contains 20 nickels.

   a) What fraction of a dollar is 13 nickels?

   b) What percent of a dollar is 13 nickels?

4. A kilometer is a metric distance unit that equals 1,000 meters.

   a) Expressed as a decimal, what part of a kilometer is 350 meters? (Hint: 350 meters is 350 thousandths of a kilometer.)

   b) What percent of a kilometer is 350 meters?

5. A ton is equal to 2,000 pounds.

   a) What fraction of a ton is 1,500 pounds?

   b) What percent of a ton is 1,500 pounds?

Using Percents: The Percent Circle

Percent is used three ways in calculations:

- To find **part** of a whole
  EXAMPLE: What is 10% of 200 pounds?
- To find what **percent** a part is of a whole
  EXAMPLE: What percent of 300 feet is 60 feet?
- To find a **whole** when a part of it is given
  EXAMPLE: If 20% of a bill is $45, how much is the whole bill?

The Percent Circle

To help you learn and remember how to solve each type of problem, we'll use a memory aid called the ***percent circle.*** Notice its uses below and on the pages that follow.

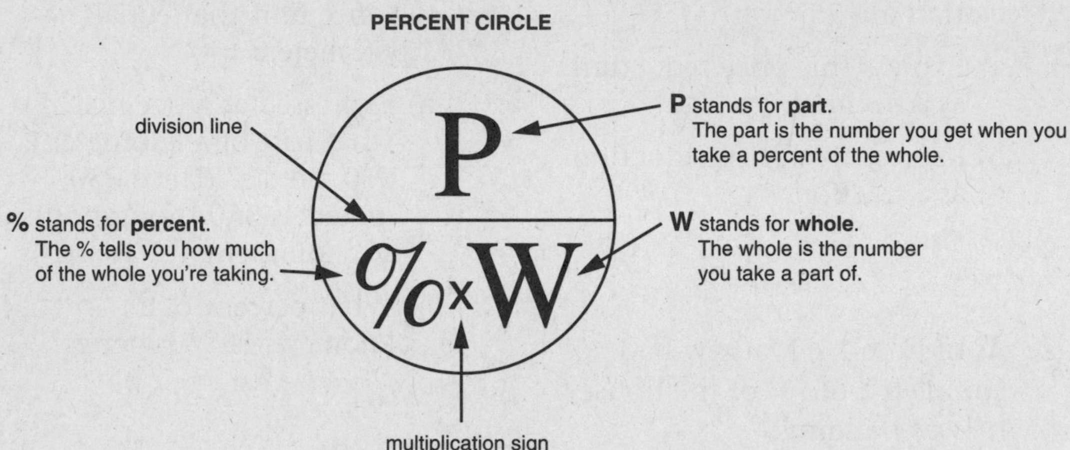
PERCENT CIRCLE
division line
P
P stands for **part**.
The part is the number you get when you take a percent of the whole.
% stands for **percent**.
The % tells you how much of the whole you're taking.
%×W
W stands for **whole**.
The whole is the number you take a part of.
multiplication sign

EXAMPLE 1: Identify the %, W, and P in sentence *a* below:

a) 15% of 300 is 45.

Answer: **% = 15%**

W = 300

P = 45

EXAMPLE 2: Identify the %, W, and P in sentence *b* below:

b) 50 is 25% of 200.

Answer: **% = 25%**

W = 200

P = 50

Using the Percent Circle

You can use the percent circle to remember both multiplication and division problems that involve percents. Simply cover the number you're trying to find. This unknown number is then computed by doing the calculation that the uncovered symbols tell you to do. Since there are three different symbols, we can write three different **percent sentences** as shown below.

I. To find **part** of a whole:

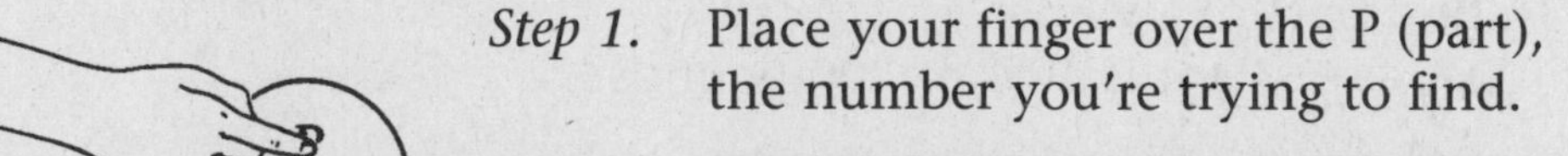
P
% × W

Step 1. Place your finger over the P (part), the number you're trying to find.

Step 2. Read the uncovered symbols: % × W.

Write: P = % × W

Percent Sentence I: **To find the part, you multiply the percent by the whole.**

II. To find what **percent** a part is of a whole:

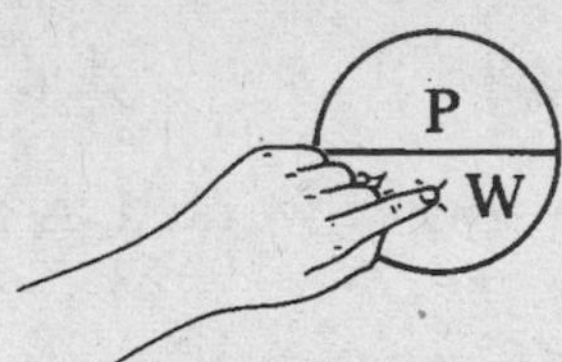

Step 1. Place your finger over the % (percent), the number you're trying to find.

Step 2. Read the uncovered symbols: $\frac{P}{W}$

Write: $\% = \frac{P}{W}$

Percent Sentence II: **To find the percent, you divide the part by the whole.**

Notice that the line that crosses the center of the percent circle is a division line.

III. To find a **whole** when a part of it is given:

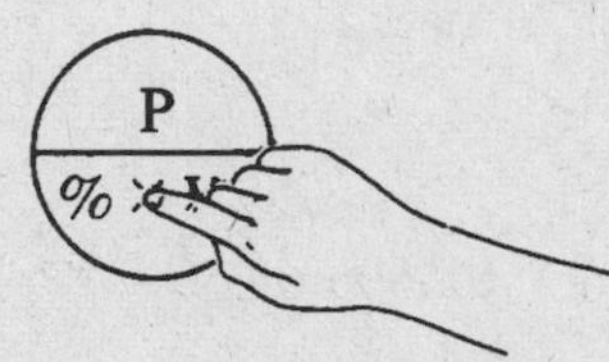

Step 1. Place your finger over the W (whole), the number you're trying to find.

Step 2. Read the uncovered symbols: $\frac{P}{\%}$

Write: $W = \frac{P}{\%}$

Percent Sentence III: **To find the whole, you divide the part by the percent.**

Finding Part of a Whole

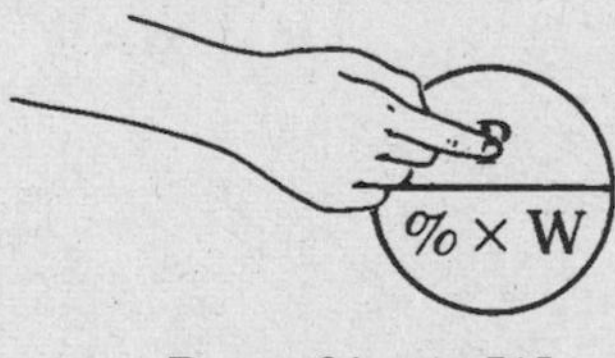

$P = \% \times W$

Percent Sentence: To find part of a whole, multiply the percent by the whole.

How to do it: Change the percent to either a decimal *or* a fraction, and then multiply.

EXAMPLE: Find 25% of 90.

Method 1

Step 1. Change 25% to a decimal.

25% = .25

Step 2. Multiply 90 by .25.

$$\begin{array}{r} 90 \\ \times\ .25 \\ \hline 4\ 50 \\ 18\ 0 \\ \hline 22.50 \end{array} = 22.5$$

Answer: **22.5 (or $22\frac{1}{2}$)**

Method 2

Step 1. Change 25% to a fraction.

$25\% = \frac{25}{100} = \frac{1}{4}$

Step 2. Multiply 90 by $\frac{1}{4}$.

$\frac{1}{4} \times \frac{90}{1} = \frac{90}{4}$

$= 22\frac{2}{4} = 22\frac{1}{2}$

Answer: **$22\frac{1}{2}$ (or 22.5)**

You can use either method, but when the percent is $33\frac{1}{3}\%$ ($= \frac{1}{3}$) or $66\frac{2}{3}\%$ ($= \frac{2}{3}$), always use method 2.

As a review, change each percent in row 1 to either a decimal or a fraction.

1. 50%   34%   125%   75% $6\frac{1}{2}\%$

Solve each problem below. The first problem in each row is worked as an example.

Percents Between 1% and 100%

2. 30% of 50 $33\frac{1}{3}\%$ of 189   50% of 121   7% of 42

30% = .30

$$\begin{array}{r} 50 \\ \times\ .30 \\ \hline 15.00 \end{array}$$

Decimal and Fractional Percents

3. .5% of 12   .25% of 72   .75% of 10   11.5% of 50

.5% = .005

$$\begin{array}{r} 12 \\ \times\ .005 \\ \hline .060 \end{array}$$

4. $\frac{3}{4}\%$ of 40 $\frac{1}{4}\%$ of 100 $8\frac{1}{2}\%$ of 750 $4\frac{3}{4}\%$ of 30

$\frac{3}{4}\% = .75\% = .0075$

$$\begin{array}{r} 40 \\ \times\ .0075 \\ \hline 200 \\ 280 \\ \hline .3000 \end{array} = .3$$

Percents Larger than 100%

5. 200% of 40   500% of 130   150% of 48 $166\frac{2}{3}$ of 12

200% = 2.00 = 2

$(166\frac{2}{3}\% = 1\frac{2}{3})$

$$\begin{array}{r} 40 \\ \times\ 2 \\ \hline 80 \end{array}$$

Word Problems: Finding Part of a Whole

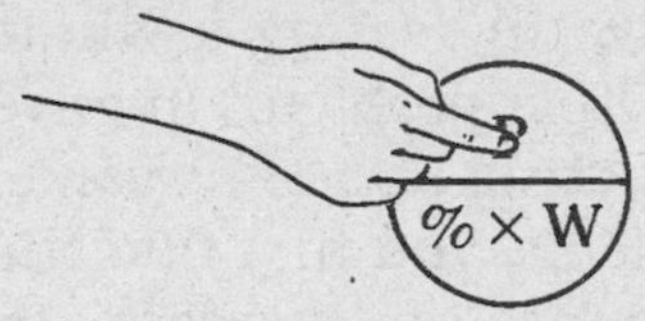

Percent word problems often ask you to find part of a whole amount. This also is a one-step problem in which you change the percent to a decimal or to a fraction. Then you multiply to determine the answer.

$$P = \% \times W$$

EXAMPLE: Lowrey's Real Estate charges a 6% sales commission for each house it sells. When Jan had Lowrey's sell her house, a sales price of $58,400 was agreed upon. How much commission will Lowrey's charge for the sale of Jan's house?

Identify % and W
% = 6%
W = $58,400
P = unknown commission

$58,400	selling price (W)
× .06	× commission rate (%)
$3504.00	commission (P)

To determine the commission, change 6% to .06 and multiply.

Answer: $3,504

Solve each problem below. First identify the percent and the whole.

1. Out of his monthly salary of $1,246, Greig puts 15% in a savings account. At this rate, how much does Greig save each month?

2. During last year, the inflation rate on consumer goods averaged only 4%. How much did the cost of a $285 washing machine increase during this year?

3. Only 23% of the registered voters in Benton County voted in a recent budget election. How many people voted if there are 74,000 registered voters in this county?

4. Because of a company cutback, Randi's salary of $545 a week was cut by 9%. Figure out how much less money Randi will earn each week after the cutback.

Word Problems: Increasing or Decreasing a Whole

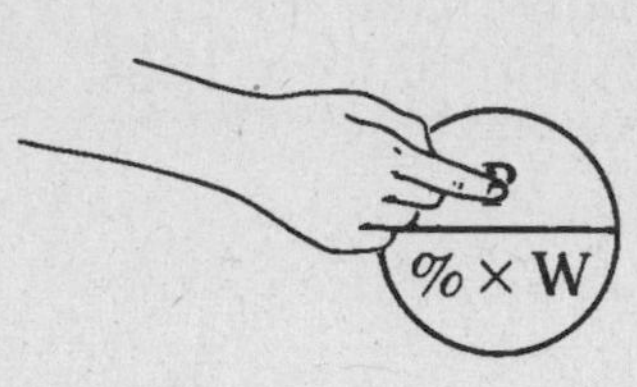

P = % × W

Many word problems involve increasing a whole by **adding** part of its value. Other problems involve decreasing a whole by **subtracting** part of its value. To work these types of problems, you first find the unknown part (the amount of increase or decrease). Then you add or subtract this part from the original whole.

A common example of increasing a whole by adding a part is the sales tax. Other examples are given in the problems below.

SALES TAX: Purchase price = selling price + amount of sales tax

EXAMPLE: A pair of jogging shoes is marked with a selling price of \$46. What is the purchase price if there is a 6% state sales tax?

% = 6%
W = \$46
P = unknown amount of tax
Purchase price = W + P

Step 1. Find the amount of the sales tax. Change 6% to .06 and multiply.

\$46	selling price (W)
× .06	× sales tax rate (%)
\$2.76	amount of tax (P)

Step 2. Add the sales tax to the price of the shoes. This will give the purchase price.

\$46.00	selling price (W)
+ 2.76	+ amount of tax (P)
\$48.76	purchase price

Answer: \$48.76

The following problems involve increasing a whole by adding or subtracting a part of its value.

RATE INCREASE: New amount = original amount + amount of increase

1. Before his raise, José made a monthly salary of \$1,260. What is the amount of José's new salary if he was given a 5% raise?

MARKUP: Selling price = store's cost + markup

2. In Cecil's Men's Store, Cecil pays \$12.00 for the Fashion Plus shirts that he sells. If he adds a 30% markup to his cost, for what price does Cecil sell Fashion Plus shirts?

DISCOUNT: Sale price = original price − amount of discount

3. As a special deal, Beth's friend offered to sell her a new TV at a discount of 40%. How much would Beth have to pay for the set if its regular price was \$640?

RATE DECREASE: New amount = original amount − amount of decrease

4. In order to help the company, employees of Thomas Electronics agreed to a 10% pay cut. What will Shirley's new salary be if before the cut she was earning $746 per month?

DEPRECIATION: New value = original value − amount of depreciation
Note: Depreciation is value lost due to age or wear.

5. A new car depreciates (loses value) 20% during its first year. Much of this loss in value takes place the moment the car is driven off the new car lot because it is no longer a new car! What will be the approximate value of Ellie's new $12,350 car one year after her purchase?

Word Problems: Mixed Practice

Solve each problem below.

1. Bill's Discount Realty charges a real estate commission of only 4%. If Bill sells a house for a sales price of $72,000, how much commission will he earn?

2. Cindy owns and operates "Cindy's Cuts," a hair salon and beauty shop. On each hair product she sells, Cindy makes a profit of 25%. What price does Cindy charge for shampoo that costs her $4.80?

3. Certain machines depreciate at a rate of about 15% each year. At the beginning of his third year of business, Daniel figured that his tractor was worth about $38,000. What value would this tractor have at the end of that third year?

4. While shopping for clothes, Sally saw a sweater marked as "40% off." Determine the amount of the sale price if the original price was listed as $42.50.

In problems 5 and 6, circle the arithmetic expression that will give the correct answer to each question. You do not need to solve these two problems.

5. During the last 3 months, the number of students in Lee's class has increased by 10%. What number of students are in the class now if 3 months ago there were 20?

   a) $(.10 \times 20) + 20$

   b) $20 \div .10 + 20$

   c) $(.10 \times 20) - 20$

   d) $20 - .10 \times 20$

6. The population of Orin has decreased by $33\frac{1}{3}\%$ over the past ten years. Ten years ago 38,700 people lived there. What's the town population now?

   a) $38{,}700 + (\frac{1}{3} \times 38{,}700)$

   b) $(\frac{1}{3} \times 38{,}700) + 10{,}000$

   c) $38{,}700 - (\frac{1}{3} \times 38{,}700)$

   d) $\frac{1}{3} \times 38{,}700$

Finding What Percent a Part Is of a Whole

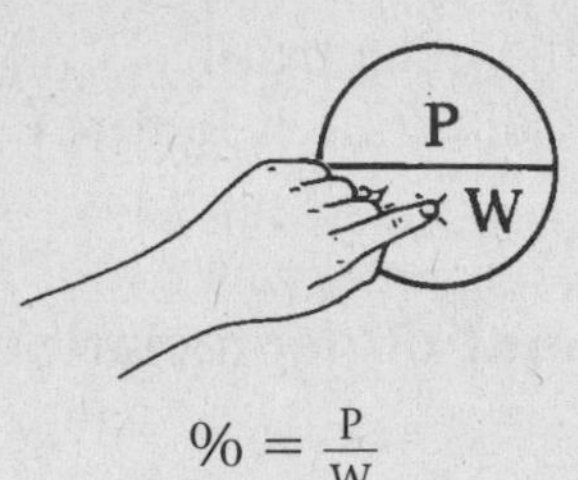

$\% = \frac{P}{W}$

Percent Sentence: To find what percent a part is of a whole, divide the part by the whole.

How to do it: Write a fraction $\frac{P}{W}$. Reduce this fraction, divide, and change the quotient to a percent.

EXAMPLE: 8 is what percent of 32?

Step 1. Write the fraction 8 (P) over 32 (W). Reduce this fraction. $\frac{P}{W} = \frac{8}{32} = \frac{1}{4}$

Step 2. Change $\frac{1}{4}$ to a decimal by dividing 4 into 1:

$\frac{1}{4} = .25$

Step 3. Change the decimal .25 to a percent by moving the decimal point two places to the right and adding a % sign. .25 = 25%

Answer: 8 is **25%** of 32

As you solve each problem below, remember to first write $\frac{P}{W}$ as a fraction. Then reduce this fraction if possible before dividing.

1. 5 is what percent of 25?
2. 8 is what percent of 16?
3. What percent of 60 is 15?
4. What percent of 16 is 2?

The answers to problems 5 and 6 are larger than 100%.

5. 250 is what percent of 125?
6. What percent of 30 is 90?

Word Problems: Finding What Percent a Part Is of a Whole

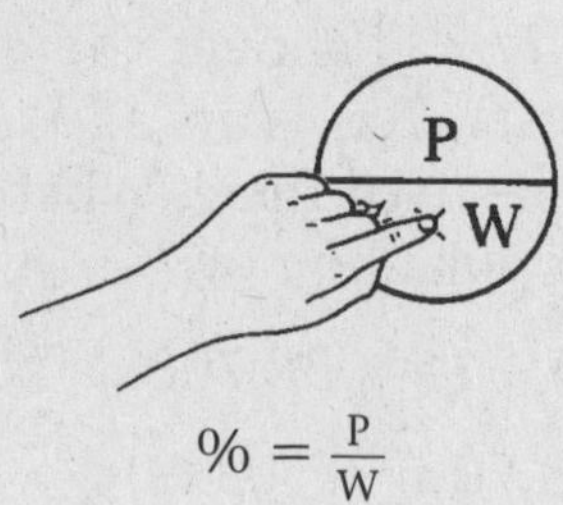

$\% = \frac{P}{W}$

Before writing the fraction $\frac{P}{W}$, You need to identify which number is the part (P) and which is the whole (W).

In almost all word problems you'll work, P is the smaller number and goes on top. Rephrase the question in each problem as follows: "______ is what percent of ______ ?" The number that you choose to follow the word *of* will be W.

Solve each problem below. Remember, always reduce a fraction before dividing.

1. During last year, the price of a \$250 washing machine increased by \$25. What percent of an increase in price is this? (Hint: 25 is what percent of \$250?)

2. Meyer's Department Store pays \$8.00 for each shirt it sells. If each shirt is priced so that the store makes a \$4.00 profit, what percent markup does Meyer's use?

3. Two years after Magda bought a used Chevrolet for \$5,500, its value had decreased by \$1,760. What percent of depreciation is this over the two-year period?

4. Out of Gina's gross monthly pay of \$900, her employer withholds \$171 for federal tax. What percent of Gina's salary is withheld for this tax?

Word Problems: Finding Percent Increase or Decrease

One type of two-step word problem that you'll often see involves finding a percent increase or a percent decrease. In these problems, you divide the **change in an amount** by the **original amount** (the whole). The percent circle is used in the second step of the solution.

EXAMPLE: At a clothing sale, the price of a wool skirt was reduced from \$48 to \$36. What percent price reduction is this?

Step 1. Subtract to find how much the skirt has been reduced in price: \$48 − \$36 = \$12.

\$12 is the **amount of decrease.**

Step 2. Ask yourself, "What percent of \$48 is \$12?"
From the percent circle, write

$\% = \frac{P}{W} = \frac{\$12}{\$48} = \frac{1}{4}$

$$\% = \frac{P}{W} = \frac{\text{amount of decrease}}{\text{original amount}}$$

Step 3. Change $\frac{1}{4}$ to a decimal by dividing 4 into 1. Move the decimal point in the answer two places to the right to find the percent.

$$4\overline{)1.00} = .25 = 25\%$$
$$\begin{array}{r} 8 \\ \hline 20 \\ \underline{20} \end{array}$$

Answer: 25%

Solve each percent increase or percent decrease problem below.

Percent Increase

$$\% \text{ increase} = \frac{\text{P (amount of increase)}}{\text{W (original amount)}}$$

1. During last year, the price of a certain compact car rose from $7,500 to $7,800. What percent increase in price is this?

2. In response to a rise in cheese prices, Tino's Pizza raised the price of its large pizza from $10.00 to $11.50. What percent price increase is this?

Percent Decrease

$$\% \text{ decrease} = \frac{\text{P (amount of decrease)}}{\text{W (original amount)}}$$

3. In order to attract more business, Bob's Hamburgers lowered the price of its cheeseburger from $2.00 to $1.75. What percent price reduction is this?

4. On her diet, Jesse's weight dropped to 135 pounds from 150 pounds. What percent of her original body weight did Jesse lose on this diet?

Mixed Practice

5. Marvin was given a raise last month. His monthly salary went from $1,250 to $1,312.50. What percent of raise is this?

6. Before cooking the ham, Martha measured its weight to be 16 pounds. After cooking, the ham weighed 14 pounds. How much shrinkage (percent decrease) occurred during cooking?

Finding the Whole When a Part Is Given

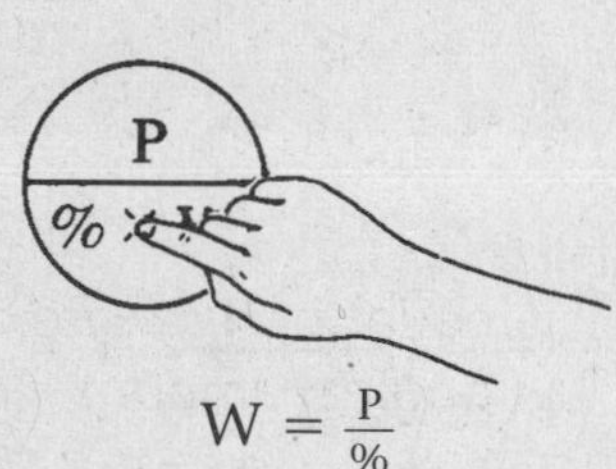

$W = \frac{P}{\%}$

Percent Sentence: To find a whole when part of it is given, divide the part by the percent.

How to do it: Change the percent to either a decimal or fraction and then divide.

EXAMPLE: 40% of what number is 32? (or, "32 is 40% of what whole number?")

Method 1

Step 1. Change 40% to a decimal.

40% = .40

Step 2. Divide .40 into 32. Divide by .4 since .40 = .4.

$$\begin{array}{r} 80. \\ .4\overline{)32.0} \\ \underline{32} \\ 0 \\ \underline{0} \end{array}$$

Answer: 80

Method 2

Step 1. Change 40% to a fraction.

$40\% = \frac{40}{100} = \frac{4}{10} = \frac{2}{5}$

Step 2. Divide 32 by $\frac{2}{5}$.

$\frac{32}{1} \div \frac{2}{5} = \frac{32}{1} \times \frac{5}{2}$

$= \frac{\overset{16}{\cancel{32}}}{1} \times \frac{5}{\cancel{2}_1} = 80$

Answer: 80

Using either method, solve the following problems.

1. 75% of what number is 27?
2. 14 is 7% of what number?
3. $33\frac{1}{3}$% of what number is 123? (Use the fraction form of $33\frac{1}{3}$%.)
4. 56.8 is 8% of what number?

Word Problems: Finding the Whole When a Part Is Given

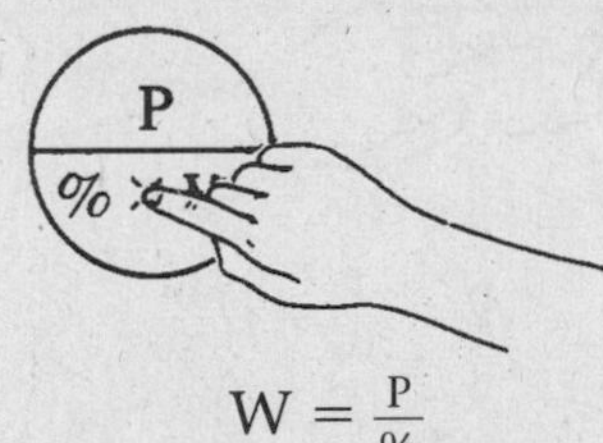

$W = \frac{P}{\%}$

In each problem below, remember to divide the given amount (the part) by the percent. To divide, you can change the percent to either a decimal or a fraction.

When the percent is less than 100%, your answer (the whole) will be larger than the part you start with.

1. Fred pays 25% of his monthly salary for rent. If his monthly rent is $245, what is his monthly salary?

2. When she bought a used Ford, Kelly made a down payment of $480. This amounted to 15% of the purchase price. How much did Kelly pay for the Ford?

3. During May's special election, only 34% of the registered voters went to the ballot box. If 14,280 votes were cast, how many registered voters live in the district?

4. Ahmad was charged $27 during August on the unpaid balance on his Great Western credit card. If Great Western charges a finance charge of 1.5% each month on the unpaid balance, what was Ahmad's unpaid balance at the beginning of August?

5. During the last 3 months, Sal lost 14 pounds while dieting. If this weight is 8% of his original weight, what was Sal's weight before he started the diet?

Finding the Original Price

A common two-step problem involves finding an original price when you know the sale price and you know the discount rate. In this problem, the percent circle is used in the second step of the solution.

EXAMPLE: Jeana bought a dress that was marked "30% off." What was the original price of the dress if Jeana paid only $49?

Step 1. The first step is to determine what percent $49 is of the original price. To do this, subtract 30% from 100%.
100% − 30% = 70% **$49 is 70% of the original price.**

Step 2. Now ask yourself, "70% of what number is $49?"

Solve this problem as you solved the problems on the previous page. Divide $49 by 70% in either decimal or fraction form.
70% = .70 = .7

$$.7\overline{)\$49.0}\quad = 70.$$

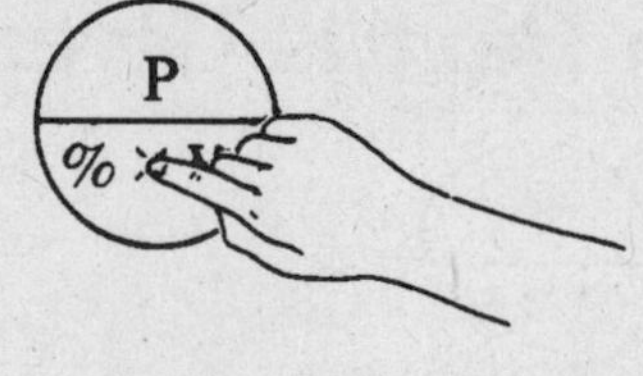

$$W = \frac{P}{\%} = \frac{\$49}{70\%}$$

Answer: **$70**

6. By paying cash, Paul got a 6% discount on a television set. If he paid $451.20 cash for the set, how much would he have paid if he didn't pay cash?

7. Lola went to a special Winter Sale where all furniture was marked 35% off. What was the regular price of a recliner that Lola got on sale for $256?

Percent Word Problems: Mixed Practice

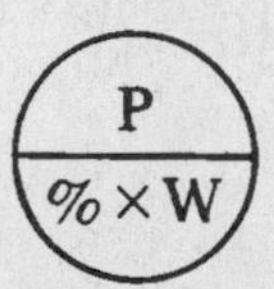

Percent Circle

Use the percent circle to solve each word problem below. As a first step in each problem, decide if you are looking for the part, the percent, or the whole.

Be careful; some problems—such as percent increase and percent decrease—may require two steps to solve.

1. Out of Jeffrey's monthly salary of $1,240, his employer withholds $99.20 for state income tax. What percent of Jeffrey's salary is withheld for this tax?

2. Luis pays $360 each month in rent. However, if he pays on the 1st of each month, he is given a 3% discount. How much should Luis write his rent check for each month he pays on the lst?

3. During a snowstorm, only 36% of the employees of Amer Electronics Company were able to get to work. If only 90 employees reported for work, how many people work for this company?

4. During the month of December, 42% of the babies born at St. Mary's Hospital were girls. If 150 babies were born there during December, how many were girls?

5. Grace bought a sweater at an "After Christmas Sale" that was marked down 30% from its original price. If she paid $21.50 for the sweater on sale, what was its price before the sale?

6. Frieda decided that the May sale was a good time to buy a new television set. At Frank's Discount Center she could get a good deal, but she had to make a down payment of 15%. Frieda chose a new set from the sizes listed at the right. If she made a down payment of $64.50, which model did she buy?

Model	*Original Price*	*Sale Price*
14 in.	$249	$189
17 in.	$399	$329
19 in.	$569	$430
22 in.	$749	$619

Circle the arithmetic expression that will give the correct answer to each question. You do not need to solve these two problems.

7. John LaPlace owns 648 acres of farmland, which he uses for growing crops and raising sheep. Early this spring he plans to plant 360 acres in corn. If this corn takes up 72% of the total acreage he uses for crops, on how many acres does John plant crops?

   a) $648 \div .72$

   b) $(648 - 360) \div .72$

   c) $360 \div .72$

   d) $.72 \times (648 - 360)$

   e) $.28 \times (648 - 360)$

8. After raising the price of the large size cola, Cinema Center has a 25% decrease in the number of large-size colas sold. Before the price increase, they could sell about 340 large-size colas at each movie. About how many can they expect to sell now, after the price increase?

   a) $340 - .25 \times 340$

   b) $340 + .25 \times 340$

   c) $.25 \times 340 - 340$

   d) $.25 \times 340$

   e) $340 - .25 + 340$

Percent Skills Review

Change each percent below to both a decimal and a fraction. Write the decimal answer on the first line and the fraction answer on the second line.

1. 50% ______ ______ 25% ______ ______ 60% ______ ______

2. 75% ______ ______ 12.5% ______ ______ 2.5% ______ ______

Determine each number indicated below.

3. 40% of 60 25% of 200 8% of 12 $33\frac{1}{3}$% of 96

4. .8% of 14 5.5% of 25 $\frac{4}{5}$% of 100 $\frac{3}{4}$% of 50

5. 8.8% of $5,000 300% of 100 125% of 42 250% of 18

6. 8 is what percent of 32?

7. 12 is what percent of 96?

8. What percent of 200 is 31?

9. What percent of 42 is 14?

10. 150 is what percent of 75?

11. What percent of 30 is 66?

12. $33\frac{1}{3}$ is what percent of 100?

13. $\frac{1}{2}$ is what percent of 100?

14. 25% of what number is 19?

15. 50% of what number is 31?

16. 51 is 20% of what number?

17. .3% of what number is 99?

18. $66\frac{2}{3}$% of what number is 32?

19. $33\frac{1}{3}$% of what number is $13\frac{1}{3}$?

20. 12% of what amount is $27.06?

21. $12.76 is 8.8% of what amount?

TOPIC 1: Using Estimation

Estimation can be a tool for other ways to solve problems. **An estimate (or estimated answer) is a number that is "about equal" to an exact answer.** Being able to make an estimate is useful in three ways:

- to check the correctness of your answer to a problem
- to find an approximate answer when an exact answer is not needed
- to quickly pick the most reasonable answer from among choices given on test questions.

Estimation is very useful in understanding and solving mixed decimals, mixed numbers, and percent problems. To make an estimate, replace one or more numbers in a problem with whole numbers. **Choose a whole number that is as close as possible to the mixed decimal or mixed number it replaces.**

Replacing a mixed decimal or mixed number with a whole number is called ***rounding to the nearest whole number***. Rounding can be used to quickly make estimates in multiplication and division problems.

EXAMPLE 1: Estimate $4\frac{7}{8}$ times $7\frac{1}{8}$.

Step 1. Round each mixed number to the nearest whole number.

$4\frac{7}{8} \rightarrow 5 \quad 7\frac{1}{8} \rightarrow 7$

Step 2. Multiply the whole numbers.

Answer: 35

Estimate

$5 \times 7 = 35$

Exact Answer

$$4\tfrac{7}{8} \times 7\tfrac{1}{8} = \frac{39}{8} \times \frac{57}{8} = \frac{2{,}223}{64} = 34\tfrac{47}{64}$$

Note: 35 is close to the exact answer $34\frac{47}{64}$, and it is much easier to compute!

EXAMPLE 2: Estimate the quotient of 322.344 divided by 3.96.

Step 1. Round each mixed decimal to the nearest whole number.

322.344 → 322

3.96 → 4

Step 2. Divide the whole numbers.

Answer: 80.5

Estimate

```
   80.5
4)3220
  32
   2 0
   2 0
     0
```

Exact Answer

```
         81.4
3.96)322 34.4
     316 8
       5 54
       3 96
       1 58 4
       1 58 4
            0
```

Answers to Chapter 10 exercises start on page 929.

Round each number below to the nearest whole number. The first problem in each row is done as an example.

1. $2\frac{1}{6}$ *2* ______ $12\frac{2}{9}$ ______ 14.975 ______ 2.025 ______
2. 8.8% *9%* ______ 4.95% ______ $5\frac{9}{10}$% ______ $13\frac{1}{8}$% ______

Estimate the answer for each problem below by first rounding each number to the nearest whole number. The first problem in each row is done as an example. You need *not* work out the exact answer.

Addition and Subtraction: Estimation is most useful in mixed number problems.

3. $5\frac{7}{8} \rightarrow 6$ / $+ 3\frac{1}{16} \rightarrow + 3$ = *9* $\quad$ $7\frac{15}{16} + 4\frac{1}{6}$ $\quad$ $21.9 - 13.2$ $\quad$ $9.1 - 5.9$

$$\begin{array}{r} 5\frac{7}{8} \rightarrow \quad 6 \\ +\ 3\frac{1}{16} \rightarrow +\ 3 \\ \hline 9 \end{array} \qquad \begin{array}{r} 7\frac{15}{16} \\ +\ 4\frac{1}{6} \\ \hline \end{array} \qquad \begin{array}{r} 21.9 \\ -\ 13.2 \\ \hline \end{array} \qquad \begin{array}{r} 9.1 \\ -\ 5.9 \\ \hline \end{array}$$

Multiplication and Division: Estimation is useful in all problems.

4. $4\frac{1}{8} \times 3\frac{7}{8}$ $\quad$ $5\frac{9}{10} \times 8\frac{1}{5}$ $\quad$ $\begin{array}{r} 8.953 \\ \times\ \ 6.12 \\ \hline \end{array}$ $\quad$ $\begin{array}{r} 17.91 \\ \times\ \ 8.07 \\ \hline \end{array}$

$4 \times 4 = 16$

5. $14\frac{1}{3} \div 2\frac{7}{8}$ $\quad$ $23\frac{1}{5} \div 3\frac{15}{16}$ $\quad$ $4.07\overline{)89.2}$ $\quad$ $2.02\overline{)124.075}$

$14 \div 3 = 4\frac{2}{3}$

6. $8\frac{1}{3}$% of \$93.15 $\quad$ 7.85% of \$125.06 $\quad$ $6\frac{4}{5}$% of 240 $\quad$ 11.9% of 820

8% of \$93

$$\begin{array}{r} \$93 \\ \times\ \ .08 \\ \hline \$7.44 \end{array}$$

Compute an *estimated answer* for each problem below. Then, using this estimate as a clue, circle the *exact answer* from the answer choices given.

7. $5\frac{6}{7} \times 8\frac{1}{9}$
   a) $38\frac{19}{63}$
   b) $47\frac{32}{63}$
   c) $54\frac{57}{63}$

8. $24\frac{7}{8} \div 2\frac{3}{4}$
   a) $4\frac{7}{22}$
   b) $6\frac{3}{22}$
   c) $9\frac{1}{22}$

9. $\begin{array}{r} 5.078 \\ \times\ 2.96 \\ \hline \end{array}$
   a) 12.90538
   b) 15.03088
   c) 19.09828
   d) 23.15948

10. $2.9\overline{)14.674}$
   a) 3.76
   b) 4.06
   c) 4.51
   d) 5.06

11. 24.9% of $145.87
   a) $21.62
   b) $27.83
   c) $36.32
   d) $42.93

12. 5.15% of 19.8
   a) 1.0197
   b) 1.0919
   c) 1.4364
   d) 1.9503

Using Estimation in Word Problems

Estimation is an especially useful tool for solving word problems. In each of the following problems, compute both an estimated answer and an exact answer. Write the estimate on the first line and the exact answer on the second line. The first problem is completed as an example.

1. If chicken is on sale for $1.04 per pound, how much would you pay for a whole chicken that weighs 5.95 pounds?

   $6.00 (estimate) *$6.19* (exact)

estimate

$1.04 → $1.00
5.95 → × 6
$6.00

exact

$$\begin{array}{r} \$1.04 \\ \times\ 5.95 \\ \hline 520 \\ 936 \\ 520 \\ \hline \$6.1880 \end{array}$$

$6.19 (to the nearest penny)

2. How much rock can Ray carry with his truck in 8 loads if he can carry $2\frac{7}{8}$ tons on each load?

_______ _______
estimate exact

3. At birth Sunny was $20\frac{1}{8}$ inches long. By her 1st birthday she had grown $9\frac{1}{16}$ inches. By her 2nd birthday she had grown another $4\frac{3}{4}$ inches. Use this information to determine Sunny's height on her 2nd birthday.

_______ _______
estimate exact

4. What is the difference in width of a shelf that is $19\frac{1}{8}$ inches wide and one that is $11\frac{15}{16}$ inches wide?

_______ _______
estimate exact

5. Jeremy lives in a state that has a 6.9% sales tax. By adding on the sales tax, what would Jeremy pay for a steam iron that has a price tag of $34.19?

_______ _______
estimate exact

6. How many concrete blocks $10\frac{7}{8}$ inches long will it take to cross a patio that measures 33 feet wide? Assume that the blocks are laid end-to-end. (Hint: As a first step, change the patio width to inches only.)

_______ _______
estimate exact

Use estimation to help you quickly choose the correct answer for each problem below. Do not work out the exact answer.

7. If salmon steak is on sale for $3.98 per pound, what is the cost of a package of steaks that weighs 5.037 pounds?

a) $14.95
b) $17.26
c) $20.05
d) $24.76
e) $27.89

8. Three hoses are joined together end-to-end. Determine the length of the combined hoses if the separate hose lengths are as follows: $26\frac{5}{6}$ feet, $31\frac{11}{12}$ feet, and $19\frac{1}{8}$ feet.

a) $71\frac{7}{8}$ feet
b) $73\frac{11}{12}$ feet
c) $75\frac{3}{4}$ feet
d) $77\frac{7}{8}$ feet
e) $98\frac{8}{9}$ feet

9. At a price of $\$1.23\frac{9}{10}$ per gallon, how much would you pay for $14\frac{1}{10}$ gallons of unleaded gasoline?

a) $17.47
b) $18.69
c) $19.82
d) $21.41
e) $23.08

10. Ann's roof measures 60 feet across. If each roof shingle is $5\frac{3}{4}$ inches wide, about how many shingles placed side-by-side would it take to cross this roof?

a) 105
b) 126
c) 150
d) 200
e) 230

11. During the year, the price of a new dishwasher rose by 8.9%. If last year's price was $297.89, what can you expect to pay this year?

a) $324.40
b) $382.60
c) $401.32
d) $417.95
e) $459.00

Estimation Doesn't Always Help

Estimation does not take the place of exact work. As you've seen, **estimation works well when answer choices differ greatly in value from each other.** However, when answer choices are close in value, estimation may lead you to choose a wrong answer. There are two types of problems where you must be careful.

When the numbers are smaller than 1. For example, the answer choices on the right are to a problem where you are to divide $\frac{5}{8}$ by $\frac{15}{16}$. It won't help you to round $\frac{5}{8}$ and $\frac{15}{16}$ to 1; the estimated answer is then also 1. An estimate of 1 won't help you choose from among the answer choices. (Correct answer is c.)

Answer Choices

a) $\frac{9}{16}$ c) $\frac{2}{3}$

b) $\frac{11}{27}$ d) $\frac{7}{9}$

When the answer choices are very close in value. For example, to multiply 3.92 by 2.03, you might write an estimated answer of 8 (found by multiplying 4 by 2).

As you look among the answer choices, you see that each is so close to 8 that you can't be sure which is correct. (Correct answer is b.)

a) 7.8366

b) 7.9576

c) 8.0046

d) 8.1456

e) 8.2046

Use estimation to try to solve each problem below. Then, in your own words, explain why estimation doesn't work in each problem. (The correct answer (*) to each problem is indicated.)

1. Danita bought a 7.08-pound roast that was on sale for $1.93 per pound. How much did this roast cost her?
   a) $13.46
   *b) $13.66
   c) $13.86
   d) $14.16

2. What is $\frac{6}{7}$ of $\frac{15}{16}$ of an inch?
   *a) $\frac{45}{56}$ of an inch
   b) $\frac{99}{112}$ of an inch
   c) $\frac{9}{16}$ of an inch

3. If only 98 out of 202 employees showed up for work during a snowstorm, what percent of employees made it in to work?
   a) 45.3%
   b) 47.2%
   c) 47.9%
   *d) 48.5%

TOPIC 2: Understanding Simple Interest

Interest is money that is earned (or paid) for the use of money.

- If you deposit money in a savings account, a certificate of deposit (CD), or an individual retirement account (IRA), interest is money that the bank pays you for using your money.
- If you borrow money, interest is money that you pay for using the lender's money.

Interest is earned (or paid) on ***principal***—the amount that is deposited or borrowed. ***Simple interest*** can be found if the original principal does not change. We want to study simple interest for several reasons:

1. Interest is part of both the saving and the borrowing of money.
2. Interest problems involve the use of whole numbers, decimals, fractions, and percents. This gives you a chance to practice several math skills at once.
3. To solve an interest problem, we use the ***simple interest formula.*** A formula is a rule that uses letters to stand for words.

The Simple Interest Formula

To determine an amount of interest, you **multiply the principal by the rate by the time.**

In words, Interest = Principal × Rate × Time

As a formula, $\boxed{I = PRT}$

where, I = interest, written in dollars
P = principal: money deposited or borrowed, written in dollars
R = percent rate, written as a fraction or a decimal
T = time, written in years or parts of a year

Written in symbols, I = PRT is called the ***simple interest formula***. This formula is used to compute both the interest earned and the interest paid.

Note: Be sure not to confuse the use of the letter P in the simple interest formula with its use in the percent circle. In I = PRT, P stands for *principal*. In the percent circle, P stands for *part*.

EXAMPLE: What is the interest earned on $400 deposited for 2 years in a savings account that pays 6% simple interest?

Step 1. Identify P, R, and T.

P = principal, the amount deposited = $400

R = percent rate of interest = 6% = $\frac{6}{100}$

T = time, the number of years the money is deposited = 2

In this problem, we write the percent rate as a fraction because we see that canceling can be used to simplify the multiplication. In other problems, multiplication may be easier if you write the percent as a decimal.

Step 2. To compute the interest, first replace the letters in the formula with the values identified in Step 1. Then multiply.

$$I = PRT = 400 \times \frac{6}{100} \times 2$$

$$= \overset{4}{\cancel{400}} \times \frac{6}{\underset{1}{\cancel{100}}} \times 2 = 48$$

Answer: $48

In the problems below, use the simple interest formula I = PRT to find either the interest earned or the interest paid.

Interest Earned

1. What is the interest earned on $500 deposited for 3 years in a savings account that pays 5% simple interest?

2. How much interest would Ms. Phipps earn on a deposit of $1,500 in 1 year if the interest rate was $5\frac{1}{2}$% per year?

Interest Paid

3. At an 11.5% interest rate, how much interest would Sharon have to pay on an $850 loan borrowed for 3 years?

4. How much interest would Andy pay for a loan of $1,200 at 12% if he repaid it at the end of 2 years?

Finding the Total Balance or the Total Owed

Many problems ask you to find the total balance or the total owed at the end of a time period. In these problems, you add the interest to the principal in order to find the total.

EXAMPLE: Mark deposited $250 in a savings account that earns 5.5%. What will be the total in Mark's account after 2 years?

Step 1. Compute the interest earned in 2 years.

I = P R T	250	P	13.75	PR
P = $250	× .055	× R	× 2	× T
R = 5.5% = .055	1 250	PR	27.50	PRT
T = 2	12 50			
I = $27.50	13.750			

Step 2. Add the $27.50 interest to the $250 principal.

$250.00
+ 27.50
$277.50

Answer: **$277.50**

Solve each problem below.

5. Earning simple interest of 5%, what total will be in a money market account of $750 left for a period of 3 years?

6. What will be the total amount owed on a loan if the principal is $2,000, the interest rate is 15%, and the time is 2 years?

Interest for Part of a Year

Although interest is earned (or paid) as a yearly interest rate, not all deposits or loans are made for whole years. To use the simple interest formula for part of a year, write the time either as a decimal or as a fraction.

In Example 1, both the interest rate and the time are written as fractions, and canceling is used to simplify the multiplication.

EXAMPLE 1: What is the interest earned on \$300 deposited for 9 months at an interest rate of 6%?

Step 1. Identify P, R, and T.

$P = 300 \quad R = 6\% = \frac{6}{100} \quad T = 9 \text{ months} = \frac{9}{12} = \frac{3}{4} \text{ year}$

Step 2. Replace the letters in the formula I = PRT with the values identified in Step 1, and then multiply.

$$I = PRT = 300 \times \frac{6}{100} \times \frac{3}{4}$$

$$= {}^{3}\cancel{300} \times \frac{{}^{3}\cancel{6}}{\cancel{100}_{1}} \times \frac{3}{\cancel{4}_{2}} = \frac{27}{2} = 13\frac{1}{2} = 13.50$$

Note: We write $\frac{1}{2}$ as .50 because we want the answer to be

in dollars and cents.

Answer: \$13.50

In Example 2, the time is given as a mixed number. In this problem it looks easier to write time as a mixed decimal and write R as a decimal and then multiply.

EXAMPLE 2: How much interest is paid on a personal loan of \$525 borrowed for $3\frac{1}{2}$ years at a 9% simple interest rate?

$P = 525 \quad R = 9\% = .09 \qquad T = 3\frac{1}{2} = 3.5$

$I = PRT = 525 \times .09 \times 3.5$

$$\begin{array}{r} 525 \\ \times\ .09 \\ \hline 47.25 \end{array} \qquad \begin{array}{r} 47.25 \\ \times\ \ 3.5 \\ \hline 23\,625 \\ 141\,75\ \ \\ \hline 165.375 \end{array}$$

165.375 = 165.38 Rounding to the nearest cent.

Answer: \$165.38

In the following problems, decide whether you are looking for the interest only or the new total balance. Then solve each problem using either decimals or fractions.

1. Olsen Furniture charges 13% simple interest on all purchases. How much interest would Heather pay on a purchase of \$750 if she paid the full amount at the end of 6 months?

2. Brady deposited \$350 in a money market account at his bank. How much interest will his money earn after 15 months if he is paid an interest rate of 6%?

3. Borrowing at a 14% interest rate, how much interest would you pay on an equity loan of \$5,000 held for 5 years?

4. Figure out the interest earned on \$650 deposited for 2 years and 6 months in a certificate of deposit (CD) account that pays 7% interest.

5. How much total money will Jennifer have to repay the bank if she borrows \$900 for 9 months at an interest rate of $11\frac{1}{2}$%?

6. Amber and her husband Don borrowed \$1,400 from their credit union. They signed a note saying that they would pay 8% interest and would pay back the entire amount at the end of 7 months. How much would be due at the end of that time?

Simple Interest Problems: Mixed Practice

On this page you'll have a chance to review several types of simple interest problems.

Questions 1 through 4 refer to the following story.

Mrs. James opened a savings account at her bank. She deposited \$2,800 in an account that paid $6\frac{1}{2}$% simple interest. At the end of 18 months, Mrs. James withdrew all her money. She wanted to use this money as a down payment on a car.

The car she decided to buy was a two-year-old Nissan. The asking price was \$9,000. After Mrs. James got the dealer to reduce the price by 10%, she agreed to buy the car. She gave the dealer all the money she had withdrawn from the bank. She agreed to pay off the balance in one payment at the end of 9 months. For this 9-month loan, the dealer charged her a 6% yearly interest rate.

1. How much money did Mrs. James withdraw from her savings account? (Include both principal and interest.)
2. What price did Mrs. James agree to pay for the car?
3. After giving the dealer her money as a down payment, how much did Mrs. James still owe for the car?
4. At the end of 9 months, how much did Mrs. James have to pay the dealer in order to pay off the loan?

TOPIC 3: Introduction to Data Analysis

Numerical data are a group (often called ***set***) of numbers that are related in some way. An example of numerical data is the set of numbers that stand for the ages of four students in a class.

21 years
20 years
42 years
18 years

Data analysis is the study of numerical data. Data analysis is used in decision making at all levels of society. It is used in schools, businesses, and government agencies.

The Language of Data Analysis

Three words that are often used in data analysis are **mean, median**, and **ratio**. We'll look at the definition and use of each word on the pages ahead.

MEAN

Mean is another word for **average**. You may already know the two steps used to find the average of a set of numbers:

1. First, compute the sum of the set.
2. Second, divide this sum by the number of numbers in the set.

EXAMPLE: Find the mean (average) of the following set of numbers: 38, 52, 25, 19, 67, 63.

Step 1. Compute the sum of the set.

$$\begin{array}{r} 38 \\ 52 \\ 25 \\ 19 \\ 67 \\ +\ 63 \\ \hline 264 \end{array}$$

Step 2. Divide this sum by 6, the number of numbers in the set.

$$\begin{array}{r} 44 \\ 6\overline{)264} \\ \underline{24} \\ 24 \\ \underline{24} \\ 0 \end{array}$$

Answer: Mean = 44

Compute the mean of each set of numbers below.

1. 4, 7, 9, 13, 17
2. \$2.39, \$3.49, \$3.99
3. $1\frac{1}{2}$, $3\frac{3}{4}$, $5\frac{1}{4}$, $6\frac{1}{2}$

MEDIAN

The ***median*** of a set of numbers is the number that is the middle value. To find the median, follow these two steps:

1. Arrange the numbers in order, from smallest to largest.
2. Count the number of numbers in the set:
   a) For an **odd** number of numbers, the median is the middle number.
   b) For an **even** number of numbers, the median is the average of the two middle numbers.

EXAMPLE 1: Find the median in the following set of numbers: 9, 13, 4, 7, 17.

Step 1. Arrange the numbers in order, smallest one first.

4
7
9 ← middle number = median
13
17

Step 2. Since there is an odd number (5) of numbers, the median is the middle value (9).

Answer: Median = 9

EXAMPLE 2: What is the median in the following set of numbers? 38, 52, 25, 19, 67, 63

Step 1. Arrange the numbers in order, smallest one first.

19, 25, 38, 52, 63, 67
↖ ↗
median is average of two middle numbers

Step 2. Since there is an even number (6) of numbers, the median is the average of the two middle numbers, 38 and 52.

$$\begin{array}{r} 38 \\ +\,52 \\ \hline 90 \end{array} \qquad \begin{array}{r} 45 \\ 2\overline{)90} \\ \underline{8} \\ 10 \\ \underline{10} \end{array} \leftarrow \text{median}$$

Answer: Median = 45

Find the median for each set of numerical data below.

4. 6 lbs. 4 oz.
   8 lbs. 3 oz.
   9 lbs. 15 oz.
   6 lbs. 2 oz.
   7 lbs. 5 oz.

5. 87°, 92°, 96°, 95°, 93°, 91°, 90°

6. $1.26, $1.32, $1.18, $1.19, $1.20, $1.31

RATIO

A ***ratio*** is the comparison of two numbers. For example, if there are 8 women in your class and 5 men, the ratio of **women to men is 8 to 5.** The ratio 8 to 5 can be written in symbols in two ways.

- With a colon, the ratio 8 to 5 is written 8:5.
- As a fraction, the ratio 8 to 5 is written $\frac{8}{5}$.

In words, a ratio is always read with the word *to*. Both 8:5 and $\frac{8}{5}$ are read as ratios as "8 to 5." A ratio, like a fraction, is usually reduced to lowest terms. However, an improper fraction ratio such as $\frac{8}{5}$ is not changed to a mixed number.

When you write a ratio, write the numbers in the same order as asked for in the question. Although the ratio of women to men is 8 to 5, the ratio of **men to women is 5 to 8 (or $\frac{5}{8}$).**

Here is another example of a ratio problem.

EXAMPLE: A new car gets 24 miles per gallon during city driving and 38 miles per gallon during highway driving. What is the ratio of highway mileage to city mileage?

Step 1. Write highway mileage as the numerator of the ratio fraction because it is mentioned first in the question.

$$\frac{38}{24} = \frac{\text{highway mileage}}{\text{city mileage}}$$

Step 2. Reduce the ratio fraction $\frac{38}{24}$.

$$\frac{38 \div 2}{24 \div 2} = \frac{19}{12}$$

Answer: 19:12 or $\frac{19}{12}$

In each problem below, remember to express the ratio in lowest terms.

7. On her test, Jan got 26 questions correct out of a total of 32. What is the ratio of her correct answers to the total number of questions?

8. To make the color pink, Andrea mixes 18 ounces of red paint with 12 ounces of white. In this paint mixture, what is the ratio of white paint to red?

9. Dave makes $7.50 per hour while Sam makes only $4.50. What is the ratio of Dave's salary to Sam's?

10. Find the ratio of 1 foot to 1 yard. (Change 1 yard to 3 feet before writing the ratio as a fraction.)

Displaying Numerical Data

Even on tests, numerical data are usually not written just as a group of numbers. Instead, data are presented in the same way you might see them used in magazines and newspapers. As part of this introduction to data analysis, we'll now look at the two most common ways of displaying data: 1) in a **table** and 2) on a **graph**.

Reading a Table

- A ***table*** is simply an orderly arrangement of numbers.

Numerical data appear in a table as rows and columns of numbers. Rows are read from left to right. Columns are read from top to bottom. Word labels (or symbols) tell what information is contained in each row and column.

EXAMPLE: Below is a nutrition chart for several types of grain. This chart contains a table of numerical information. Take note of the title of the chart and all the other information included.

Nutrition Chart

Uncooked grains, 1 cup of each. Protein (*P*), Carbohydrates (*C*), and Fat (*F*), are all given in grams.

	Calories	P	C	F
Barley	936	26	170	5.7
Millet	660	20	150	5.9
Rice, Brown	667	14	140	4.3
Rye Berries	591	21	130	3.9
Wheat Berries	578	24	120	4.7

Questions about a table usually ask you to find a particular value or to compare two or more values.

Example Questions

1. How many grams of carbohydrates are contained in 1 cup of rye berries?

Answers

1. The answer, **130**, is written at the intersection of the "Rye Berries" row and the C (Carbohydrates) column.

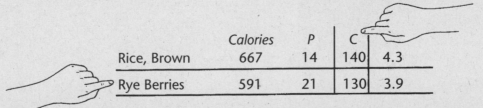

	Calories	*P*	C	
Rice, Brown	667	14	140	4.3
Rye Berries	591	21	130	3.9

2. What is the *average* value of protein in 1 cup of the 5 grains shown?

2. The *average* value is found by adding the 5 protein values together and then dividing by 5.

$$\begin{array}{r} 26 \\ 20 \\ 14 \\ 21 \\ +\ 24 \\ \hline 105 \end{array}$$

Answer: 21 grams

$$5\overline{)105} = 21$$

Answer the questions below about the following nutrition chart. Remember that the title and other parts of the chart can give you important information. Read them carefully.

Nutritional Values of Selected Meats

(Each value is for a six-ounce serving.)

Meat	Calories (nearest 10)	Protein (g*) (nearest 1)	Fat (g*) (nearest 1)	Iron (mg*) (nearest .1)
BEEF				
lean ground	370	47	19	6.0
round steak	440	48	26	5.9
CHICKEN (skinned)				
light meat	280	54	6	2.2
• dark meat	300	48	11	2.9
HAM (lean)	640	40	52	5.2
LAMB (lean)	480	43	32	2.9

* g = grams mg = milligrams

1. How many more grams of fat are contained in six ounces of chicken dark meat than in light meat?

2. Of the meats shown, what is the *median* number of calories for the six-ounce servings of meat shown?

3. What is the *ratio* of the number of calories in lean ham to the number of calories in chicken dark meat?

4. What is the *mean* number of grams of protein for the six-ounce servings of meat shown?

What Is a Graph?

A ***graph*** is a pictorial display of information. As a picture, a graph enables you to get a quick impression of the data being shown. It also enables you to quickly compare one number with another. The four most common types of graphs are the **circle graph**, the **bar graph**, the **pictograph**, and the **line graph**.

Reading a Circle Graph

A circle graph is drawn as a divided circle. Each segment (part) is given a name and value. The whole circle represents all (100%) of the data being displayed.

- In the most common circle graph, each segment is given a percent value. The sum of all segments adds up to 100%. See Graph A below.
- In a second type, each segment is given a number of cents as a value. Here the sum of segments adds up to $1.00. See Graph B below.

EXAMPLES:

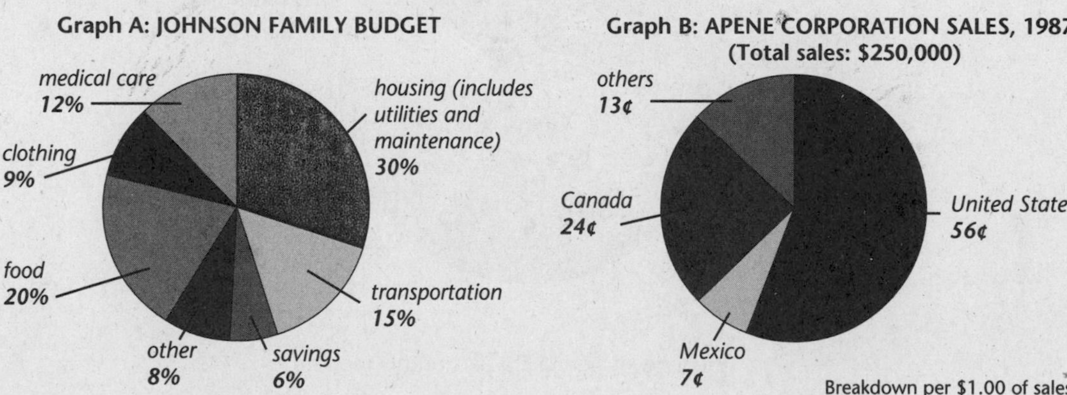

Questions about circle graphs usually ask you to find an amount of money, to find a percent, or to compare two or more values.

Example Questions

GRAPH A

1. How much more of their budget do the Johnsons spend for housing than they spend for food?
2. If the Johnson family monthly income is $3,400, what dollar amount do they pay for housing?

Answers

GRAPH A

1. The answer, **10%**, is computed by subtracting the food percent (20%) from the housing percent (30%).
2. The answer, **$1,020**, is obtained by computing 30% of $3,400.

GRAPH B

1. What percent of Apene sales during 1987 was made in Canada?

2. What dollar amount of sales was made in Canada during 1987?

GRAPH B

1. See the segment labeled "Canada." 24¢ out of each sales dollar means that **24%** of all sales were made in Canada.

2. The dollar amount, **$60,000**, is obtained by computing 24% of $250,000, Apene's total sales during 1987.

Answer each question below about the following circle graph.

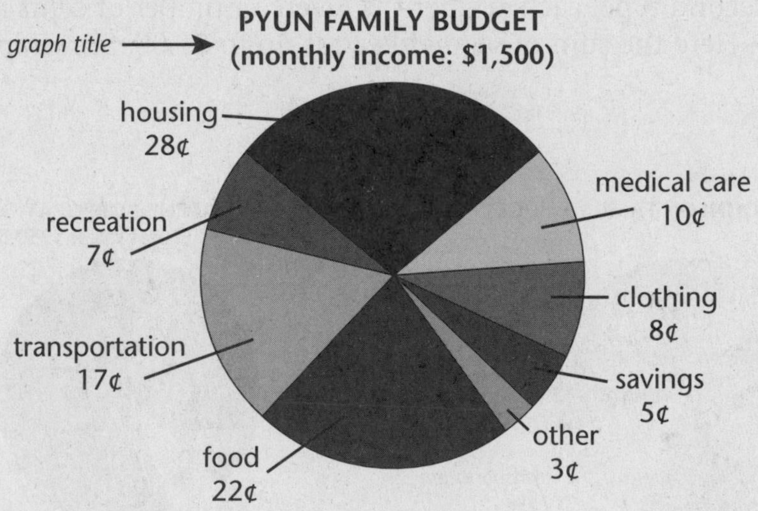

Breakdown per $1.00 of monthly income

5. According to the graph title, what is the Pyun family monthly income?

6. What percent of their monthly income do the Pyuns spend on housing?

7. What is the *ratio* of the amount the Pyuns spend on recreation to the amount spent on medical care?

8. Each month the Pyuns donate $1\frac{1}{2}$% of their monthly income to their church. How many dollars each month is this donation?

Reading a Bar Graph

A bar graph uses thick bars to show data. These bars may be drawn either vertically (up and down) or horizontally (across).

Numerical values are read along numbered scales called ***axes*** that make up the sides of the graph. You read a value for each bar by finding the number on the **axis** that is across from the end of that bar. A long bar will have a greater value than a short bar.

EXAMPLE: Below is a bar graph showing the growth of the population in the United States. Numerical values for the population appear on the left, along the vertical axis. The year the population is measured is written along the bottom, beneath the horizontal axis.

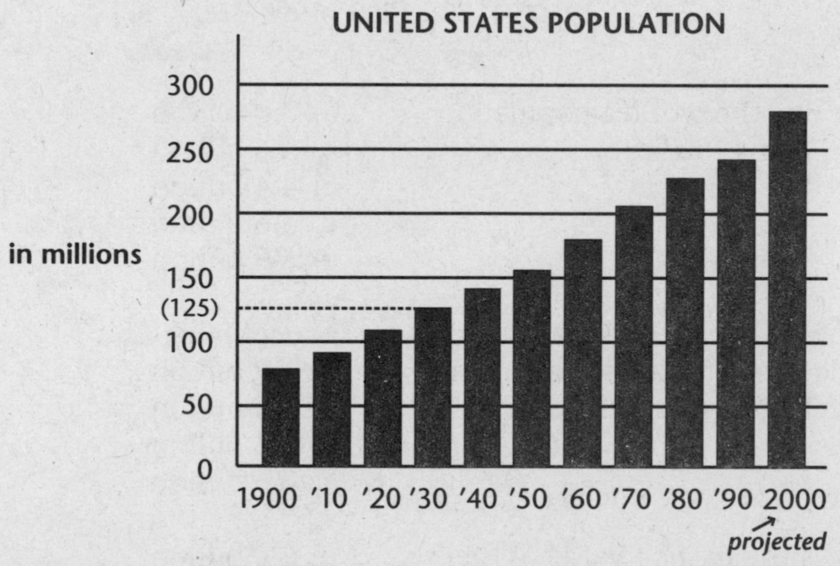

Questions about bar graphs usually ask you to find a specific value or to compare one value with another.

Example Questions

1. What was the United States population in 1930?

2. What is the approximate ratio of the 1960 population to the population in 1900?

Answers

1. First locate the bar that is above the year 1930. Then, scan directly to the left from the top of the bar across to the vertical axis. As read on the axis, the value of the 1930 population is between 100 and 150, or **about 125 million.**

2. To compute the ratio, divide the approximate 1960 population (175) by the approximate 1900 population (75).

   Ratio $= \frac{175}{75} = \frac{7}{3}$

Answer the questions below the following bar graph.

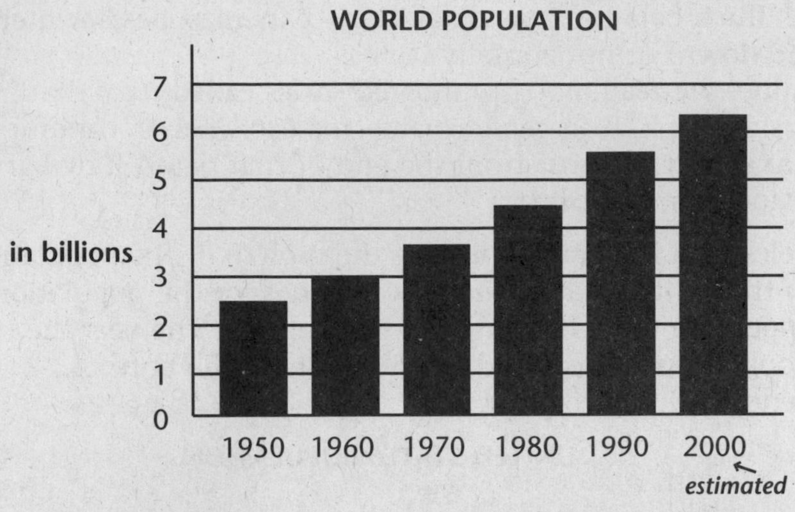

9. What was the world's population in the year 1980?

a) 3.0 billion
b) 3.6 billion
c) 4.4 billion
d) 5.6 billion
e) 5.9 billion

10. By how many people is the world's population estimated to increase between the years 1980 and 2000?

a) 1 billion
b) 1.9 billion
c) 2.5 billion
d) 3.2 billion
e) 3.6 billion

11. What is the *median* value of the population totals for the 6 specific years shown?

a) 2.5 billion
b) 3.0 billion
c) 3.7 billion
d) 4.1 billion
e) 4.8 billion

12. What is the approximate *ratio* of the estimated population in the year 2000 to the actual population in the year 1960?

a) 2 to 1
b) 3 to 1
c) 4 to 1
d) 5 to 4
e) 6 to 5

Reading a Pictograph

A pictograph looks similar to a bar graph. However, a pictograph uses small pictures as symbols. Each symbol has a certain value that is shown in a key written on the graph.

To find the total value of a line of symbols, you multiply the number of symbols by the value of a single symbol. A long line of symbols has a larger value than a short line because it contains more symbols.

EXAMPLE: Below is a pictograph showing the sales of bicycles in the northwest states by the Northwest Bicycle Company. The names of the states are listed along the vertical axis at left. Sales for each state are read as a number of bicycle symbols extending as lines to the right.

Questions about pictographs, like bar graphs, most often ask you to find a specific value or to compare one value with another.

Example Questions

1. For the sales period shown, how many bicycles did Northwest sell in Idaho?

2. What is the ratio of sales in Oregon to the sales in Washington?

Answers

1. The first step is to count the number of bicycle symbols to the right of Idaho. Now multiply these 3 symbols by the value of each symbol, 150.

   Answer = 450 bicycles

2. The easiest way to find this ratio is simply to put the number of Oregon symbols over the number of Washington symbols.

   Ratio $= \frac{4}{8} = \frac{1}{2}$

Answer the questions below about the following pictograph.

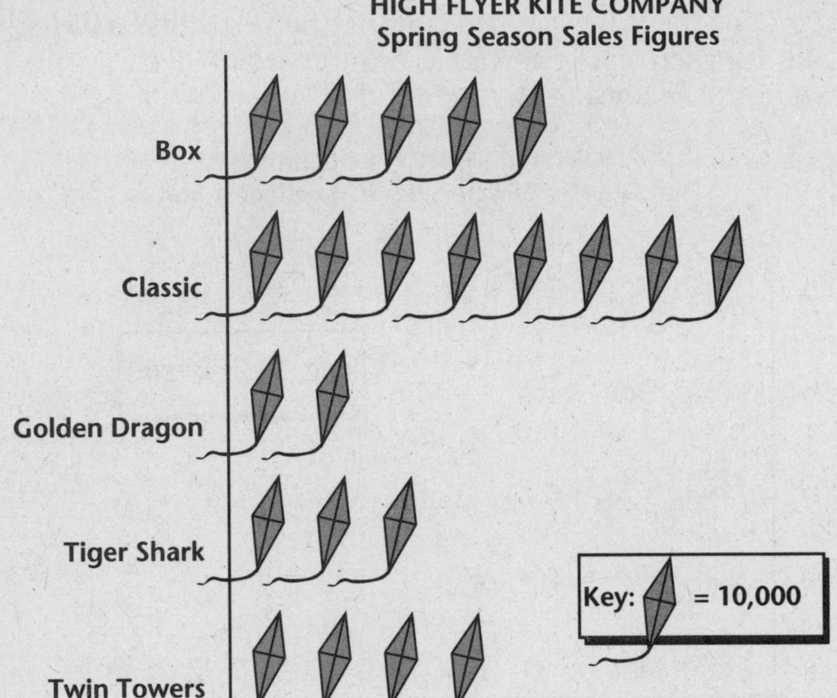

13. What number does the symbol stand for?

14. How many Golden Dragon kites did the High Flyer Company sell during the spring season?

15. What was the total number of kites sold by High Flyer for the time period shown?

16. What is the **ratio** of the number of Box kites sold to the number of Classic kites sold?

17. Out of the 5 styles shown, for which kite did the **median** number of sales occur?

18. What is the **average** number of sales for the various styles of kites sold by High Flyer Company?

Reading a Line Graph

A line graph uses a thin line to show data. Because every point on the line has a value, a line graph shows how data change in a continuous way. You are not limited to just a few points as you are with the other graphs.

Like a bar graph, a line graph has numbered scales called ***axes***. The value of each point on the line is read as two numbers, one taken from each axis.

EXAMPLE: Below is a growth chart that shows how the height of an average-size girl changes between birth and age 10. Height is read along the vertical axis, and the age at which that height occurs is read along the horizontal axis. As an example, dotted lines drawn from a point on the line indicate that an average-size 4-year-old girl has a height of about 40 inches.

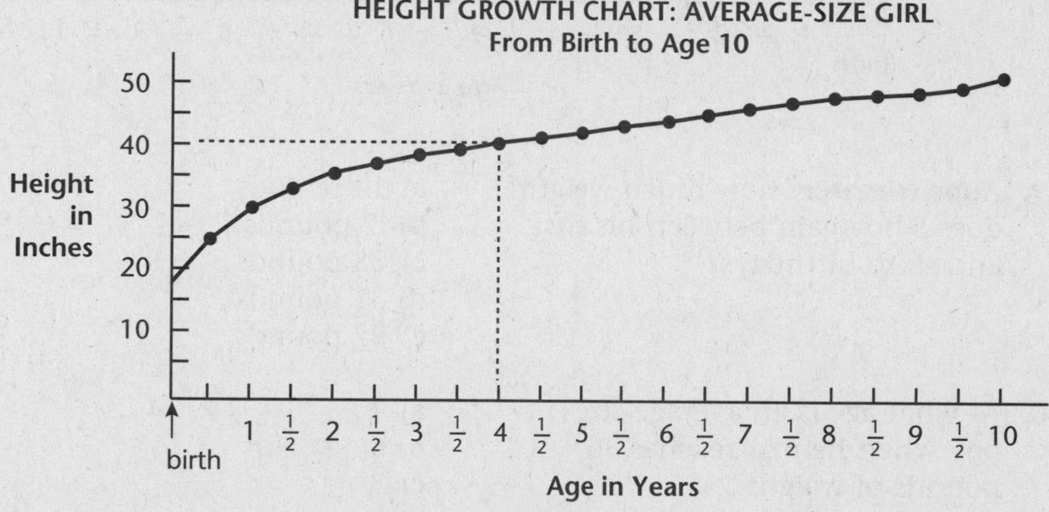

Questions about line graphs usually are concerned with how data are changing as you move from left to right across the graph.

Example Questions

1. During which year is a girl's height increasing most rapidly?

2. What is the approximate ratio of a girl's height at age 8 to her height at age 4?

Answers

1. To answer this question, look for the year at which the graph is rising most rapidly (is the steepest).

   Answer: From birth to age 1

2. To compute this ratio, put the height at age 8 over the height at age 4.

   Answer: $\frac{\text{50 inches}}{\text{40 inches}}$ **or about** $\frac{5}{4}$

Answer the questions below about the following line graph. Choose the best answer from among the answer choices given.

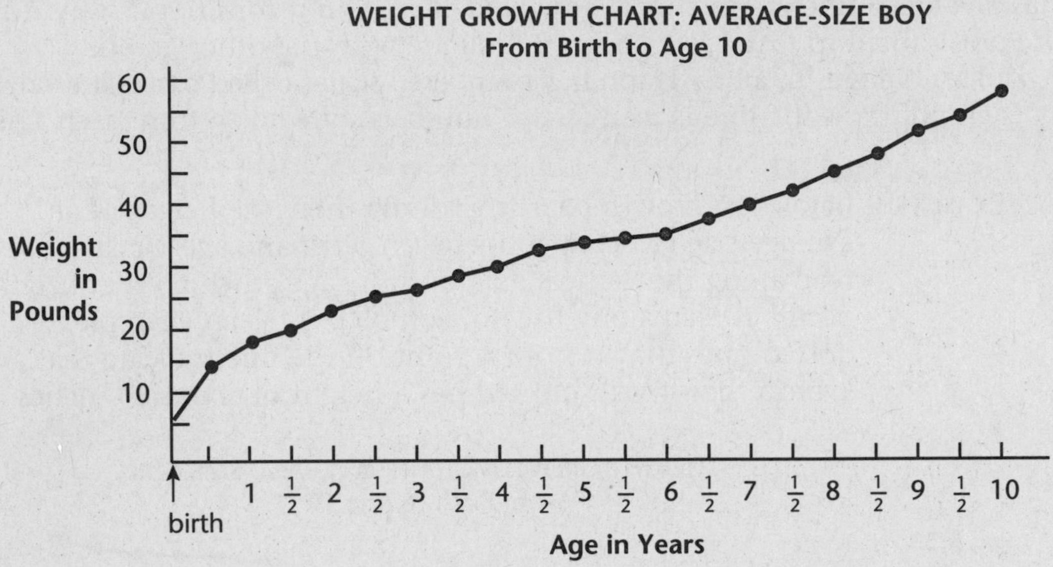

19. Approximately how much weight does a boy gain between his first and sixth birthdays?

a) 14 pounds
b) 17 pounds
c) 25 pounds
d) 31 pounds
e) 37 pounds

20. At what age is an average-size boy when he first reaches 30 pounds of weight?

a) 4
b) 6
c) 8
d) 9
e) 10

21. About how many pounds does a baby boy gain during his first 6 months of life?

a) 3
b) 6
c) 9
d) 12
e) 15

TOPIC 4: Introduction to Probability

Chance and Outcome

Probability is the mathematical study of chance. An example can best show what the word *chance* means.

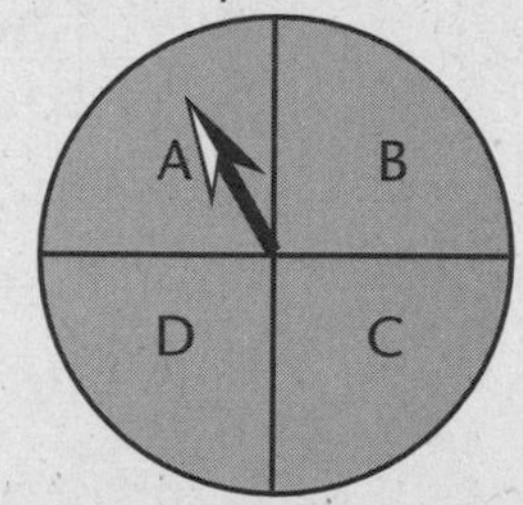

If you spin the spinner at right, you do not know where it will stop. It is equally likely to stop in any of the four sections, A, B, C, or D. We say that "where it stops is left to chance."

We use the word *chance* to indicate our lack of control over how something will turn out. The result is not something that we can predict with certainty.

When we study probability, we call a result an ***outcome***. For each spin of the spinner, there are 4 possible outcomes: A, B, C, and D. Because each section is the same size, each of the 4 outcomes is equally likely to occur.

Expressing Probability as a Number

Probabilities are expressed as numbers ranging from 0 to 1, or as percents ranging from 0% to 100%.

Probabilities of 0 or 1

A probability of 0 (or 0%) means that an outcome cannot possibly occur. For example, the probability that the spinner will stop on E is 0. This is because there is no E on the circle!

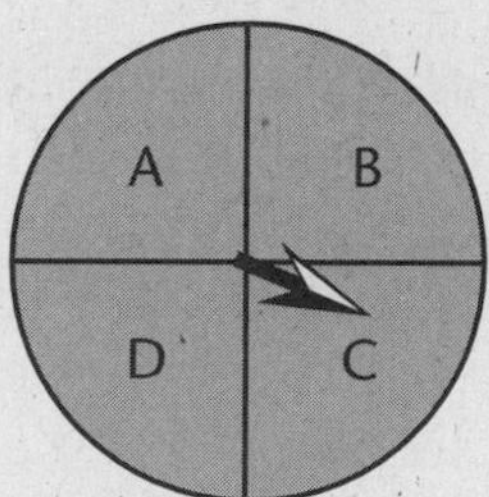

Will it stop at E?
Probability = 0, or 0%

A probability of 1 (or 100%) means that the outcome will occur for sure. In fact, a probability of 1 means that you are sure of an outcome. You can say that the probability that the spinner will stop *somewhere* in the circle is 1. There is no other possibility, assuming that the spinner can't keep spinning forever!

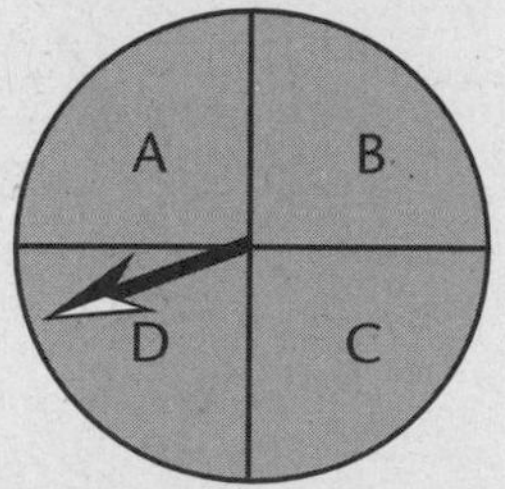

Will it stop on the circle?
(at A, B, C, or D?)
Probability = 1, or 100%

Probabilities Between 0 and 1

Almost all probabilities you'll ever think about will be greater than 0 and less than 1. For example, you might ask, "What is the probability that the spinner will land in section B?"

Answer: Because there are 4 equally likely outcomes, the chance is 1 in 4 that the spinner will land in section B. To express this as a probability, we write a fraction. The denominator of the fraction is equal to 4, the total number of possible outcomes.

The probability that the spinner will stop in section B is $\frac{1}{4}$. Expressed as a percent, the probability is 25%.

Probability of outcome B $= \frac{1}{4}$ **or 25%**

Answer each question below about probability. Express each answer both as a fraction and as a percent.

1. What is the probability that the sun will rise in the east tomorrow?

   fraction: _____ percent: _____

2. What is the probability that you will be younger tomorrow than you are today?

   fraction: _____ percent: _____

3. If you spin the spinner shown below, what is the probability that the spinner will stop in section C?

   fraction: _____ percent: _____

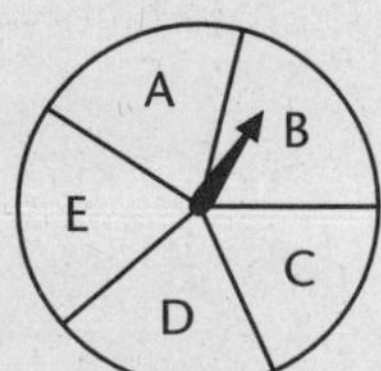

4. Suppose you shut your eyes and choose a penny from the group below. If you don't know where the "head's up" one is, what is the probability that you will choose it on your first try?

   fraction: _____ percent: _____

5. Below is a spinner for a money game. What is the probability that the player will win $50 on one spin?

   fraction: _____ percent: _____

Multiple Chances for the Same Outcome

In some problems an outcome can occur in more than one way. To see how this can happen, look at this next example.

EXAMPLE 1: If you spin the spinner at right, what is the probability that it will stop on an A section?

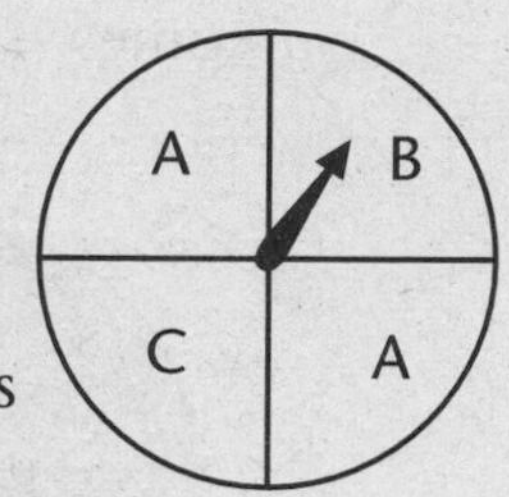

First, notice that the spinner is again equally likely to stop on any one of 4 sections. But, since 2 sections are labeled A, the spinner has 2 chances in 4 of stopping on an A section.

The probability of stopping on an A section is the fraction $\frac{2}{4}$. The numerator 2 is the number of ways outcome A can occur. The denominator 4 is the total number of possible outcomes — the total number of sections in the circle.

Probability of an outcome A = $\frac{2}{4}$ (which can be reduced)

= $\frac{1}{2}$ **or 50%**

Example 1 helps you understand the mathematical definition of probability:

$$\text{Probability of an outcome} = \frac{\text{number of ways an outcome can occur}}{\text{total number of possible outcomes}}$$

EXAMPLE 2: Below are six cards placed on a table. Two are aces and four are kings. If you close your eyes, shuffle the cards around, and then pick a card without looking, what is the probability that you'll pick a king?

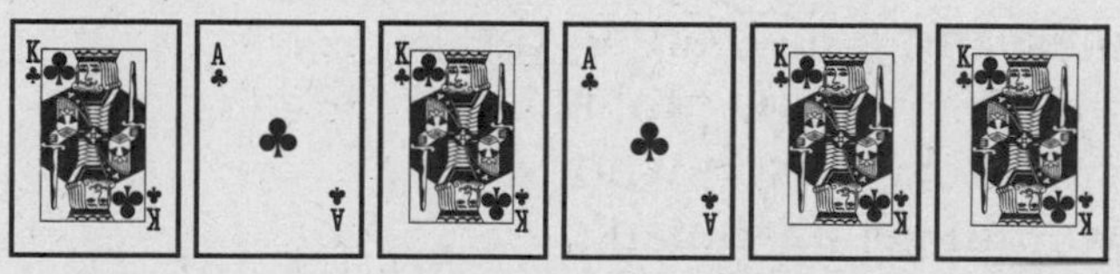

Since there are 6 cards, the total number of possible outcomes is 6. Therefore, 6 is the denominator of the probability fraction.

To determine the numerator, notice that you can choose any one of 4 cards and get a king. This means there are 4 ways that the **king outcome** can occur. Thus, the numerator is 4.

Probability of picking a king = $\frac{4}{6} = \frac{2}{3}$ **or** $\mathbf{66\frac{2}{3}\%}$

Answer each question below. Express each answer as a fraction and as a percent.

6. If you spin the spinner below, what is the probability of an outcome C?

   fraction: _____ percent: _____

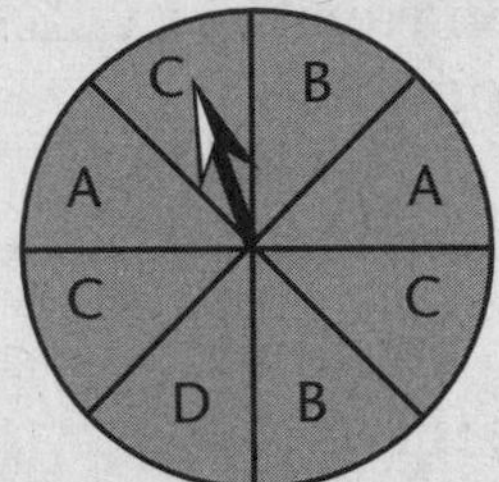

7. If you randomly choose from the cards below, what is the probability that you'll choose a "2" on your first try?

   fraction: _____ percent: _____

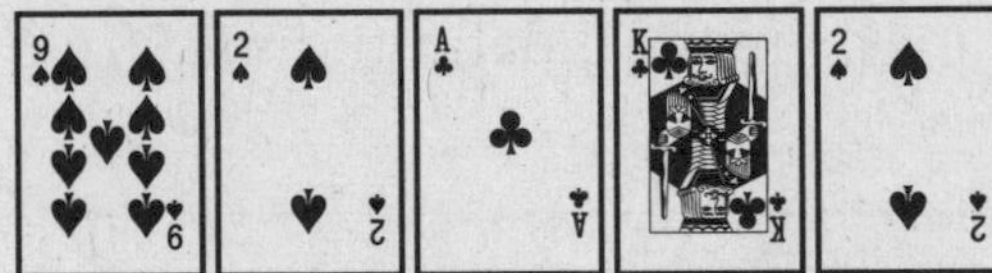

8. For a holiday party, the names of 10 people are "put in a hat." Each person then draws the name of a friend for whom to buy a gift. Four women and 6 men are in the group. What is the probability that the first person who draws will get a woman's name?

   fraction: _____ percent: _____

9. If you randomly pick a number from 1 to 25, what is the probability that the number you pick will be evenly divisible by 3?

   fraction: _____ percent: _____

10. On one roulette wheel, there are 24 numbers colored red, 24 numbers colored black, and 2 numbers colored green. On a single bet, what is the probability of *losing* if you choose both green numbers? (Hint: The probability of losing is the probability that something other than one of the 2 green numbers will be chosen.)

   fraction: _____ percent: _____

Dependent Probabilities

Now we'll look briefly at the topic of **dependent probabilities**. We'll explain with an example.

EXAMPLE: Let's look again at the 6 cards placed on the table. Two are aces and 4 are kings. Again pretend you close your eyes and pick a card. Only this time, pretend you look at it, put it aside, and then pick a second card.

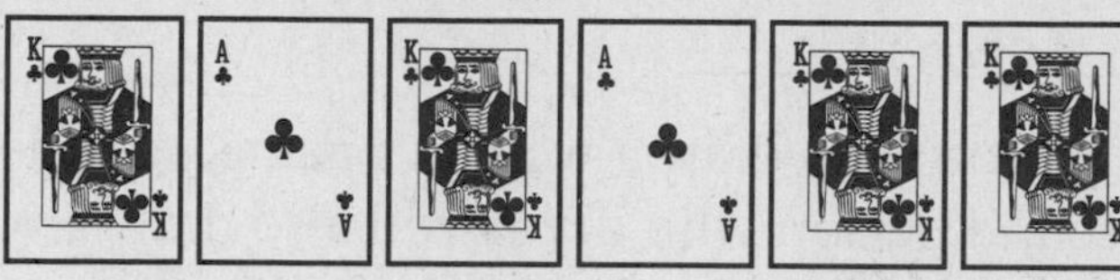

a) What is the probability of picking an ace for your first card? The probability of picking an ace for your first card is $\frac{2}{6} = \frac{1}{3}$. This is because there are 2 aces out of a total of 6 cards.

b) What is the probability of picking a king for your second card?

- The answer to question *b depends on what card you actually get as your first card.* The answer to b is called a ***dependent probability***.

Let's look at the two possible answers to *b*.

Possibility 1: Your first card is a king.

remaining cards:

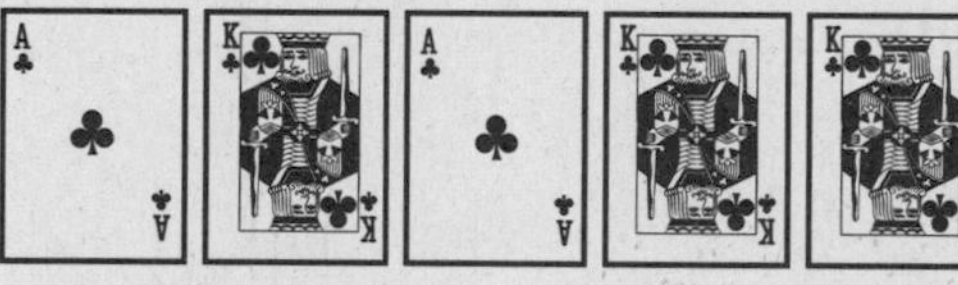

After you pick a card, there are only 5 cards left. If your first card is a king, 3 of the remaining 5 cards are kings and 2 are aces.

In this case, **the probability that you'll choose a king for your second card is $\frac{3}{5}$ or 60%.**

Possibility 2: Your first card is an ace.

remaining cards:

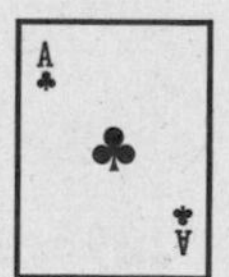

If the first card chosen is an ace, 4 of the remaining 5 cards are kings and 1 is an ace.

In this case, **the probability that you'll choose a king for your second card is $\frac{4}{5}$ or 80%.**

Answer each question below. Express each answer as a fraction and as a percent.

11. During the holidays, 4 friends agreed to exchange gifts. Each person wrote his or her name on a slip of paper. Then each randomly chose the name of a friend. There are 3 women and 1 man in the group.

a) What is the probability that the first person who draws will draw a woman's name?

fraction: _____ percent: _____

b) If the first person does draw a woman's name, what is the probability that the second person who draws will also draw a woman's name?

fraction: _____ percent: _____

12. Lila bought 3 cans of corn and 3 cans of peas. Except for the labels, the cans look identical. As she walked in the door at home, she heard the phone ring. She placed the bag with the cans on the floor and went to the phone. While she talked, Lila's three-year-old son Jeffy peeled the labels off all 6 cans!

a) When she opens a can, what is the probability that Lila will open a can of corn?

fraction: _____ percent: _____

b) If the first can she opens is peas, what is the probability that the second can she opens will also be peas?

fraction: _____ percent: _____

Answer Key

CHAPTER 1: WHOLE NUMBERS

Digits and Place Value
pages 685–686

1. eighty
2. five
3. three thousand
4. eight hundred
5. twenty thousand
6. two hundred thousand

Reading Whole Numbers
page 686

1. 1, 8
2. 1, 3, 7
3. 4, 9, 8, 2
4. 5, 4, 2

Writing Whole Numbers
pages 686–687

1. forty-seven
2. thirty-nine
3. two hundred thirty-eight
4. three thousand, five hundred eighty-seven
5. thirty-eight thousand, six hundred seventy-five

Writing Zero as a Place Holder
page 687

1. 308
2. 3,015
3. 46,011
4. 209,400
5. 6,307,000

Rounding Whole Numbers
pages 687–688

1. 30, 80, 130, $280
2. 200; $400; 4,700; $5,400
3. 5,000; 5,000; $9,000; $12,000
4. $1,300
5. $79,000

Working with Dollars and Cents
pages 688–689

1. 8¢, $0.08
2. 9¢, $0.09
3. 35¢, $0.35
4. $20.08
5. $32.09
6. $115.50
7. five dollars and seven cents
8. twenty-three dollars and sixty-five cents
9. one hundred twenty-five dollars and fifty cents

Rounding Dollars and Cents
page 690

1. $5.80, $1.60, $8.00, $53.00
2. $0.90
3. $0.70

Reading, Writing, and Rounding Skills Review
pages 690–691

1. ninety, two thousand, six, five hundred
2. 5, 0, 3, 8
3. 0, 9, 2, 7
4. one hundred sixty-three
5. four thousand, seventy-nine
6. twenty-seven thousand
7. 575
8. 2,046
9. 4,600,000
10. 80
11. 200
12. 3,000
13. $0.40
14. $3.00
15. $70.00

CHAPTER 2: ADDITION SKILLS

Concepts in Addition
pages 692–693

1. 7, 7, 9, 9, $16, $4.93
2. yes
3. 7 boats + 9 boats
4. $5.60 + $3.45
5. 50 + 19
6. $4.50 + $3.16

Adding Single Digits
pages 693–694

1. 8, 7, 3, 2, 6, 6, 4
2. 1, 9, 7, 7, 8, 9, 4
3. 7, 9, 6, 5, 6, 9, 0
4. 11, 10, 14, 13, 13, 10, 13
5. 15, 11, 15, 15, 11, 13, 10
6. 12, 14, 12, 15, 13, 13, 11
7. 12, 12, 14, 10, 13, 16, 10
8. 1. e
   2. h
   3. a
   4. f
   5. g
   6. d
   7. b
   8. c

Adding a Column of Digits
page 694

1. 16, 16, 15, 19, 18, 17, 17
2. 16, 19, 20, 16, 20, 17, 16

Adding a Row of Digits
page 695

1. 15
2. 12
3. 17
4. 17
5. 17
6. 16
7. 8 gallons + 4 gallons + 7 gallons = 19 gallons
8. $8 + $9 + $2 + = $19

Adding Larger Numbers
pages 695–696

1. 65, 98, 85, 39, 98, 67
2. 789, 719, 972, 439, 978, 589
3. 85, 66, 59, 39, 48, 89
4. 779, 486, 29,957, 14,979; 28,687

Adding Dollars and Cents
pages 696–697

1. $14.83, $44.59, $55.97, $29.58, $35.97, $35.25
2. 39¢ or $0.39, 79¢ or $0.79, 98¢ or $0.98
3. $4.95, $1.56, $1.85

Introducing Word Problems
pages 697–698

1. **Question:** How much rent does she pay per year?
   Find: yearly rent
2. **Question:** What amount did Manuel pay in state and federal taxes?
   Find: federal and state taxes
3. **Question:** Driving through Rockville, how many miles is it between Oak Grove and Salem?
   Find: miles from Oak Grove to Salem
4. **Question:** How much extra money did Jason earn this week?
   Find: total overtime pay

Addition Word Problems
pages 698–699

1. **Find:** How many students are in the class?
   Solution: 23 men
   16 women
   39 students
2. **Find:** How far is Seattle from Eugene?
   Solution: 172 miles
   +114 miles
   286 miles
3. **Find:** the purchase price of car
   Solution: $6,250
   + 1,245
   $7,495
4. **Find:** What time will it be in 27 minutes?
   Solution: 12 minutes
   + 27 minutes
   39 minutes; 8:39
5. **Find:** What take-home monthly income does he need to pay these expenses?
   Solution: $415
   + 581
   $996
6. **Find:** cost of a 3-minute call
   Solution: 30¢
   21¢
   + 21¢
   72¢
7. **Find:** total of John's bills
   Solution: $405.00
   21.14
   + 71.25
   $497.39
8. **Find:** combined attendance for these first 3 games
   Solution: 2,324 people
   3,042 people
   + 3,121 people
   8,487 people

Adding and Carrying
pages 700–701

1. 55, 72, 60, 105, 125, 64
2. 22, 47, 49, 55, 83, 132
3. 336; 978; 528; 1,145; 1,219; 2,426
4. 5,486; 6,388; 4,579; 11,369; 10,468; 23,378
5. 761; 1,502; 1,273; 9,120; 4,162; 16,150
6. 41,069; 63,154; 34,451; 101,390; 144,576

Adding Numbers in a Row
pages 701–702

1. 233, 258, 629
2. 9,703; 36,709

Carrying with Dollars and Cents
page 702

1. $10.52, $10.66, $18.11, $43.21, $40.60, $21.63
2. $3.32, $4.72, $11.49, $15.54

Finding Necessary Information
pages 702–703

1. **Question:** What is the total price of a quart of milk and a loaf of bread?
   Necessary information: $0.95, $2.09
2. **Question:** How much does Brenda want to lose in all?
   Necessary information: 13 pounds, 14 pounds
3. **Question:** How many hours total does Amy work each week?
   Necessary information: 35 hours, 8 hours
4. **Question:** How many people voted in this election?
   Necessary information: 4,572; 6,385
5. **Question:** What is the total cost of a 7-pound package of chicken?
   Necessary information: 7 pounds, $.89 a pound

Addition Word Problems
page 704

1. 12 miles
   9 miles
   +13 miles
   34 miles
2. 6,284 people
   5,782 people
   + 800 people
   12,866 people

3.
```
  209 miles
  248 miles
+ 173 miles
  630 miles
```

5.
```
  $ 9.49
+ 13.50
  $22.99
```

4.
```
  3 pounds
  4 pounds
+ 5 pounds
 12 pounds
```

6.
```
  $ 1,475
      276
+     125
  $1,876
```

Addition Skills Review
pages 705–706

1. 8, 15, 19, 12, 19
2. 39; 99; 195;778; 678; 4,797
3. 33; 52; 263; 543; 846; 3,018
4. 131; 144; 285; 1,104; 2,574; 27,389
5. $5.33; $6.85; $9.85; $171.68; $4,115.07
6. 24; 56; 63; 1,149
7. 55, 101, 532
8. 23
9. $31.00
10. 105 pounds
11. $0.82
12. $3.30
13. $1.43

14.
```
  $.50
   .30
  +.07
  $.87
```

15.
```
  9
  7
 +3
 19
```

16.
```
  32,640
  17,456
 +16,540
  66,636
```

CHAPTER 3: SUBTRACTION SKILLS

Concepts in Subtraction
pages 707–708

1. 9, 7, 13, 25, $12, $27.35
2. no
3. 19 – 6
4. 142 – 77
5. 87 pounds – 60 pounds
6. 97 feet – 40 feet

Basic Subtraction Facts
pages 708–709

1. 2, 3, 2, 4, 1, 4, 4, 0
2. 7, 4, 3, 2, 8, 1, 6, 3
3. 1, 0, 5, 3, 1, 0, 1, 2
4. 6, 1, 3, 0, 9, 2, 5, 2
5. 5, 7, 5, 9, 4, 3, 7, 6
6. 2, 5, 6, 7, 9, 9, 9, 5
7. 5, 3, 6, 3, 7, 8, 4, 6
8. 2, 4, 7, 8, 7, 4, 9, 8
9. 9, 9, 9, 8, 8, 6, 7, 6

10. 1. h
    2. d
    3. f
    4. b
    5. g
    6. a
    7. c
    8. e

Subtracting Larger Numbers
pages 709–710

1. 32, 12, 22, 13, 22, 41, 17
2. 123, 314, 455, 134, 311, 522, 612
3. 2,423; 7,815; 3,813; 3,232; 2,251; 3,424; 1,215

Writing Zeros in the Answer
page 710

1. 20, 20, 6, 410, 201, 41, 610
2. 4,013; 1,200; 2,103; 11,003; 11,052; 10,124; 1,215

3.
```
  598 miles
– 296 miles
  302 miles
```

4.
```
  250 pounds
– 220 pounds
   30 pounds
```

Subtracting Dollars and Cents
page 711

1. $2.64, $3.34, $1.23, $.25, $2.54, $13.12

2.
```
  $14.88
 –  2.57
  $12.31
```

4.
```
  $9.99
– 5.00
  $4.99
```

3.
```
  $3.99
–   .75
  $3.24
```

5.
```
  $275.85
– 124.50
  $151.35
```

Subtraction Word Problems
page 712

1.
```
  1986 years
– 1941 years
    45 years
```

2.
```
  $39.99
– 25.50
  $14.49
```

3.
```
  19 inches
–  5 inches
  14 inches
```

4.
```
  67°
– 13°
  54°
```

Recognizing Key Words
pages 712–713

1. Key word: change; subtraction
2. Key words: in all; addition
3. Key word: farther; subtraction
4. Key words: together, combined; addition
5. Key words: more than; subtraction
6. Key word: more; addition

Solving Word Problems
pages 713–714

1. $395
− 320
$ 75

2. $17.00
47.25
+ 1.75
$66.00

3. 57,863 miles
− 50,000 miles
7,863 miles

4. $535.00
145.00
167.34
+ 97.87
$945.21

5. $127.85
− 106.00
$ 21.85

6. 25 hours
+ 6 hours
31 hours

7. $2,945
− 825
$2,120

8. 3,955 pounds
− 2,630 pounds
1,325 pounds

9. 25.00
45.50
+ 27.75
$98.25

10. 1,771 miles
− 802 miles
969 miles

Subtracting by Borrowing
pages 715–716

1. 38, 14, 219, 717, 365, 347, 508
2. 56, 274, 342, 281, 54, 123, 175
3. 4,811; 3,863; 2,850; 1,762; 10,422; 1,539

Borrowing from Two or More Columns
pages 716–717

1. 558, 766, 599, 389, 53, 587, 188
2. 17, 23, 36, 8, 172, 329, 68
3. 83; 247; 488; 6,722; 1,930; 3,781
4. 2,679; 4,189; 2,578; 2,588; 5,137; 14,518

Subtracting from Zeros
page 717

1. 459, 37, 132, 2,658; 4,069; 677
2. 3,452; 6,305; 2,817; 7,396; 2,307

Subtracting from a Row of Zeros
page 718

1. 155; 427; 774; 2,225; 15,260; 6,031

Subtracting Numbers in a Row
pages 718–719

1. 61; 252; 1,336
2. 275; 2,688; 149
3. 553; 571; 4,264

Borrowing with Dollars and Cents
page 719

1. $2.17, $3.87, $3.25, $26.87, $78.67, $109.55
2. $2.63, $3.42, $7.63, $28.17, $157.35, $110.01
3. $4.99, $.71, $1.72, $4.37

Choosing an Arithmetic Operation
pages 720–721

1. $1,200
− 850
$350

2. 56°
+ 28°
84°

3. 253 miles
− 128 miles
125 miles

4. $873
+ 236
$1,109

5. 89°
− 34°
55°

6. 47 miles
+ 19 miles
66 miles

Solving More Word Problems
pages 722–723

1. 3,145 pounds
− 876 pounds
2,269 pounds

2. $1,237.87
+ 125.75
$1,363.62

3. 3:00 P.M.
+ 2 hours
5:00 P.M.

4. 73 degrees
− 68 degrees
5 degrees

5. 1915
+ 80
1995

6. 1,760 yards
− 1,100 yards
660 yards

7. 954 miles
876 miles
+ 1,105 miles
2,935 miles

8. $7.95
2.98
2.98
1.20
1.20
+ .48
$16.79

9. 3,225 calories
− 750 calories
2,475 calories

10. 214 pounds
− 196 pounds
18 pounds

Subtraction Skills Review
pages 723–724

1. 3, 0, 11, 6, 3, 7
2. 23; 16; 21; 620; 301; 2,233
3. 27, 28, 129, 207, 184, 664
4. 292; 666; 2,219; 2,611; 3,483; 6,417
5. $4.10, $1.13, $5.07, $5.89, $2.17, $11.51
6. 9, 28, 15, 119
7. 86; 24; 263; 2,626
8. $5.00
− .84
$4.16
9. 738 miles
− 668 miles
70 miles

CHAPTER 4: MULTIPLICATION SKILLS

Concepts in Multiplication
pages 725–726

1. 15, $.09, 7, 8, 0, 0
2. 3×6 and $6 + 6 + 6$
3. $5.18 × 6
4. 400 miles × 7

Basic Multiplication Facts
pages 726–727

1. 18, 56, 9, 0, 12, 27, 56, 5
2. 0, 6, 35, 24, 30, 0, 72, 54
3. 28, 48, 32, 56, 21, 36, 40, 10
4. 4, 20, 32, 21, 63, 72, 24, 15
5. 12, 40, 16, 18, 42, 16, 45, 18
6. 30, 27, 9, 10, 14, 48, 12, 16
7. 27, 6, 49, 42, 45, 64, 15, 35
8. 18, 24, 12, 63, 6, 28, 36, 36
9. 40, 9, 20, 56, 6, 18, 24, 2

Multiplying by One Digit
page 728

1. 63, 64, 88, 426, 720, 249, 567
2. 936; 282; 696; 2,884; 1,296; 7,288; 1,890

Multiplying by Two Digits
pages 728–729

384; 528; 341; 840; 1,517; 18,103; 16,384

Multiplying by Three Digits
page 729

36,288; 25,531; 67,731; 89,676; 678,824; 970,944; 869,320

Zeros in Multiplication
page 730

1. 460; 430; 420; 2,040; 67,410; 42,240; 44,520
2. 48,600; 168,400; 183,600; 100,400; 21,836; 83,839; 126,721

Multiplying by 10, 100, and 1,000
pages 730–731

1. 670; 63,400; 35,200; 8,500; 90; 7,600
2. 36,500; 140; 36,000; 375,000; 578,000; 4,586,000

Multiplying Dollars and Cents
page 731

1. $15.90, $16.80, $27.96, $168.88, $12.48, $28.80
2. $585.00; $736.00; $75.80; $650.00; $326.90; $7,490.00

Multiplication Word Problems
page 732

1. **Key word:** total

$$\begin{array}{r} \$4.00 \\ \times \quad 21 \\ \hline 400 \\ 800 \\ \hline \mathbf{\$84.00} \end{array}$$

2. **Key words:** in all

$$\begin{array}{r} \$42 \\ \times 12 \\ \hline 84 \\ 42 \\ \hline \mathbf{\$504} \end{array}$$

3. **Key word:** twice

$$\begin{array}{r} \$.63 \\ \times \quad 2 \\ \hline \mathbf{\$1.26} \end{array}$$

4. $$\begin{array}{r} 12 \\ \times 4 \\ \hline 48 \text{ hours} \end{array}$$

Multiplying and Carrying
pages 733–735

1. 34; 222; 210; 387; 2,468; 1,284; 1,438
2. 535; 824; 921; 4,942; 7,227; 3,654
3. 1,928; 1,142; 5,580; 3,227; 3,480; 1,405
4. 22,884; 13,896; 65,680; 23,169; 67,270; 15,848
5. 1,002; 740; 1,834; 752; 960; 1,038
6. 8,715; 9,308; 10,120; 7,431; 7,172; 10,272
7. 17,332; 4,374; 2,142; 114; 2,064; 21,522

Carrying with Larger Numbers
pages 735–736

1. 2,072; 1,914; 5,628; 513; 4,032; 1,620
2. 31,418; 9,855; 37,855; 11,210; 21,170; 21,875
3. 115,995; 176,638; 270,115; 275,940; 171,080; 224,110
4. 196,174; 119,192; 667,635; 1,150,780; 653,484; 2,820,664

Multiplying Numbers in a Row
page 736

1. 76,600; 413,040; 202,301
2. 1,540; 13,547; 665,200

Carrying with Dollars and Cents
pages 736–737

1. $46.96, $19.04, $18.13, $62.25, $212.80, $148.00
2. $3,187.50; $2,524.50; $12,087.50; $5,962.20; $20,002.00
3. $8.76, $16.32, $29.44

Estimating Answers
pages 737–738

1. 130	**6.** 52,900	**11.** 200
2. 100	**7.** 20,000	**12.** 8,000
3. 5,100	**8.** 63,000	**13.** 8,800
4. 100,000	**9.** 600	**14.** 50
5. 22,000	**10.** 5,800	**15.** 800
		16. 350,000

Using Estimation in Word Problems
pages 738–739

1. b	**3.** c
2. a	**4.** a

Solving Word Problems
pages 739–740

1. **Estimate:**

$$\begin{array}{r} \$1.30 \\ \times \quad 20 \\ \hline \mathbf{\$26.00} \end{array}$$

Exact:

$$\begin{array}{r} \$1.29 \\ \times \quad 19 \\ \hline 11\ 61 \\ 12\ 9 \\ \hline \mathbf{\$24.51} \end{array}$$

2. **Estimate:**

$$\begin{array}{r} 350 \\ +\ 500 \\ \hline \mathbf{850 \text{ miles}} \end{array}$$

Exact:

$$\begin{array}{r} 349 \\ +\ 497 \\ \hline \mathbf{846 \text{ miles}} \end{array}$$

3. Estimate:	Exact:
30	29
× 15	× 15
150	145
30	29
450 miles	**435 miles**

4. Estimate:	Exact:
400	403
150	149
+ 300	+ 296
850 calories	**848 calories**

5. Estimate:	Exact:
$ 13.00	$12.89
+ 3.50	+ 3.49
$ 16.50	**$16.38**

6. Estimate:	Exact:
$ 7.00	$6.98
× 50	× 51
$350.00	698
	3490
	$355.98

7. Estimate:	Exact:
200	197
− 100	− 98
100 miles	**99 miles**

8. Estimate:	Exact:
20	19
10	11
+ 30	+ 29
60 inches	**59 inches**

Multiplication Skills Review
page 741

1. 8, 7, 54, 8, 40, 30
2. 96; 420; 286; 408; 5,313; 88,830
3. 90; 368; 1,692; 1,854; 2,667; 2,688
4. 1,128; 4,042; 2,100; 13,014; 66,270; 106,500
5. $33.60; $40.28; $4,549.00; $41.22; $42.16; $421.60
6. 3,912; 54,000; 7,946; 41,192
7. $134.14
   × 48
   $6,438.72

8. Estimate:	Exact:
$ 1.20	**$23.18**
× 20	
$24.00	

9. Estimate:	Exact:
40	**779 miles**
× 20	
800 miles	

CHAPTER 5: DIVISION SKILLS

Concepts in Division
pages 742–743

1. 9
   72
   8
2. 7
   14
   2
3. 4
   24
   6
4. 5
   40
   8
5. $2\overline{)16}$ hours
6. $6\overline{)\$24}$
7. $7\overline{)42}$
8. $5\overline{)25}$

Basic Division Facts
pages 743–744

1. 7, 2, 4
2. 9, 3, 4
3. 6, 3, 9
4. 5, 7, 7, 3, 9
5. 9, 4, 8, 5, 2
6. 9, 8, 5, 8
7. $5, 4, 9 coins
8. 4, 7, 3 hours

Dividing by One Digit
page 744

1. 21, 13, 24, 12, 11, 21, 14
2. 112, 212, 221, 323, 421, 111
3. 2,112; 2,412; 3,213; 31,242; 32,231; 21,122

Dividing into Zero
page 745

1. 20, 20, 20, 320, 320, 410
2. 201, 304, 302, 1,001; 3,002; 1,002

Dividing into a Smaller Digit
page 745

1. 81, 51, 54, 41, 512, 211
2. 20, 100, 201, 902, 530, 502

Using Zero as a Place Holder
page 746

1. 309, 102, 106; 2,104; 1,208; 1,104
2. 40, 102, 51, 80, 302, 205
3. 2,013; 2,010; 201; 600; 930; 501

Remainders in Division
pages 746–747

1. 2r1, 2r1, 1r2, 3r2, 7r2, 6r8
2.

7 r 8	8 r 3	9
$10\overline{)78}$	$6\overline{)51}$	$8\overline{)72}$
− 70	− 48	− 72
8	3	0

Introducing Long Division
pages 748–749

1. 18, 15, 13, 17, 12, 15
2. 85, 15, 22, 69, 75, 45
3. 12r2, 12r5, 11r7, 87r1, 45r2, 84r3

Dividing Dollars and Cents
page 749

1. $0.38, $0.420, $0.08, $0.10, $0.08
2. $1.08, $0.47, $0.04

Division Word Problems
pages 750–752

1. **Key words:** share, each, equally

   $800,100
   6)$4,800,600
   − 4,800,600
   0

2. **Key words:** average, each

   22 hamburgers
   8)176
   − 16
   16
   − 16
   0

3. **Key words:** divided, each

   4 pieces
   4)16
   − 16
   0

4. **Key words:** cut, each, equal pieces

   49 inches
   3)147
   − 12
   27
   − 27
   0

5. **4 dresses**
   2)9
   − 8
   1

6. **6 r 3**
   6)39
   − 36
   3

   (Amy will need **7** boxes to pack all the tapes.)

More About Long Division
pages 752–753

1. 143, 274, 268, 196, 634
2. 119r1, 275r2, 185r3, 462r4, 532r2

Dividing by Two Digits
pages 753–754

1. 5, 5, 4, 3, 4
2. 4, 6r6, 5r1, 3, 3
3. 7, 7r4, 5, 8r6, 5

Dividing Larger Numbers
pages 754–755

1. 27, 18, 57, 19, 21
2. 41, 31, 28, 22, 50
3. 215, 246, 321, 214
4. 5, 4, 8, 4
5. 78, 54, 61, 58

Dividing Numbers in a Row
page 756

1. 135, 128r26, 4, 22r4
2. 22r12, 51r128, 71

Deciding When to Multiply and When to Divide
pages 756–758

1. **Multiplied:**
   $ 0.79
   × 150
   39.50
   79.
   $118.50

2. **Divided:**
   23 miles
   7)161
   − 14
   21
   − 21
   0

3. **Multiplied:**
   168
   × 4
   672 quarts

4. b
5. a
6. b
7. a

Solving Word Problems
pages 759–761

1. **$0.79**
   24)$18.96
   168
   2 16
   2 16
   0

2. $ 485
   × 12
   970
   4 85
   $5,820

3. **36 minutes**
   240)8640
   − 720
   1440
   − 1440
   0

4. **$89**
   4)$356
   − 32
   36
   − 36
   0

5. 37
   × 16
   222
   37
   592 miles

6. **33 r 25**
   75)2500
   − 225
   250
   − 225
   25

   (Jenny must buy **34** cartons in order to have enough cups.)

7. 1,238
× 13
3 714
12 38
16,094 compact discs

8. **308 words**
234)72072
− 702
1872
− 1872
0

9. $935
× 6
$5,610

10. $1,156
× 12
2 312
11 56
$13,872

11. $237.71
× 24
95084
4 7542
$5,705.04

12. **$ 240.20**
24)$5764.80
− 48
96
− 96
04 8
− 4 8
00

13. **147 boxes**
128)18816
− 128
601
− 512
896
− 896
0

14. 100
× 48
800
4 00
4,800 cans

Division Skills Review
pages 761–762

1. 5, 9, 8, 9, 3, 7
2. 21; 312; 340; 61; 1,020; 200
3. 6r1, 6r4, 15, 18, 53r6, 75
4. 45r5, 229, 21, 24, 25, 30r5
5. $.30, $.33, $.32, $2.07, $1.50
6. 68; 16r1; 223; 1,045

7. **$0.46**
3)$1.38
− 1 2
18
− 18
0

8. **46 minutes**
65)2,990
− 260
390
− 390
0

9. **$39.93**
6)$239.58
− 18
59
− 54
55
− 54
18
− 18
0

Checking Your Answer
pages 762–763

1. a
2. a
3. b
4. a
5. a
6. b

Reviewing One-Step Word Problems
pages 763–765

1. 96
78
+ 67
241 people employed

2. $8.67
− 5.49
$3.18 difference

3. **$33.22 is Jason's share**
4)$132.88
−12
12
−12
08
−8
08
−8
0

4. 2,935
× 12
5870
2935
35,220 pounds

5. $9.25
× 7 hours
$64.75 extra money

6. **13 cards each**
4)52
−4
12
−12
0

7. 8,684
9,832
+11,459
29,975

8. 104°
− 76°
28°

9. $ 7.99
13.85
+ 5.28
$27.12

10. $42.00
− 1.89
$40.11 spent

11. $102.25
× 24
409 00
2 045 0
$2,454.00

12. $74.60
× 36
447 60
2 238 0
$2,685.60

CHAPTER 6: SPECIAL TOPICS IN MATH

TOPIC 1: Introduction to Multi-Step Word Problems pages 766–768

1. *STEP 1:* **Add.**
$ 3.58
1.89
+ 2.79
$ 8.26

STEP 2: **Subtract.**
$20.00
− 8.26
$ 11.74

2. *STEP 1:* **Multiply.**
121
× 5
605 Mon.–Fri. papers

STEP 2: **Add.**
605
+ 257
862 total papers

3. *STEP 1:* **Add.**
$12.75
4.30
+ 9.45
$26.50 total cost

STEP 2: **Divide.**
$ 5.30 per person
5)$26.50
− 25
1 5
− 1 5
00

4. *STEP 1:* **Add.**
$0.79
1.98
+ 0.35
$ 3.12 cost per pkg.

STEP 2: **Multiply.**
$3.12
× 23
936
624
$71.76

5. *STEP 1:* **Add.**
$28.50
13.65
+ 0.83
$42.98 cost of parts

STEP 2: **Subtract.**
$ 75.40
− 42.98
$ 32.42 labor cost

6. *STEP 1:* **Add.**
8
+ 6
14 boxes per trip

STEP 2: **Multiply.**
14
× 8
112 total boxes moved

7. *STEP 1:* **Multiply.**
95
× 4
380 served in 4 days

STEP 2: **Add.**
380
+ 165
545 served in 5 days

8. *STEP 1:* **Multiply.**
$27.84
× 5
$139.20 total rental cost

STEP 2: **Divide.**
$46.40 each brother's share
3)$139.20
− 12
19
− 18
12
− 12
00

9. **Solution sentence:** miles on Toyota's indicator = miles per month times 12 *plus* 32,696

STEP 1:
1,350
× 12
2700
1350
16,200 miles

STEP 2:
16,200
+ 32,696
48,896 miles on indicator

10. **Solution sentence:** number of voters who were neither Republicans nor Democrats = 14,725 *minus* number of Republicans and number of Democrats combined

STEP 1:
6,539
+ 4,891
11,430
Republicans and Democrats

STEP 2:
14,725
− 11,430
3,295
number of voters neither Republican nor Democrat

Becoming Familiar with Arithmetic Expressions pages 768–771

1. 24; 23; 22
2. 17; 86; 27
3. 72; 94; 4
4. 103; 23; 17
5. c
6. b
7. a
8. b
9. a
10. c
11. a, d
12. b, e
13. b, d

TOPIC 2: Introduction to Measurement pages 771–773

1. longer
2. heavier
3. larger
4. less than
5. millimeter
6. milligram
7. milliliter
8. 10 meters
9. 5 kilograms
10. 3 liters

Changing from One Unit to Another pages 773–774

1. 84, 24, 120
2. 48; 5,000; 2,000
3. 6; 2,000; 240
4. 3, 3, 6
5. 3, 3, 2
6. 8, 2, 5
7. 2 ft. 5 in., 4 yds. 2 ft.
8. 1 hr. 15 min., 2 lbs. 15 oz.
9. 2 m 40 cm, 2 cm 6 mm
10. 2 kg 500g, 3 l 400 ml

Adding Measurement Units pages 775–776

1. 17 ft. 3 in., 6 mi. 190 yd.
2. 38 m 21 cm, 78 km 250 m
3. 8 lb. 5 oz., 4 T. 1975 lb.
4. 14 kg 650 g, 22 g 25 mg
5. 5 pt. 1 oz., 3 gal. 1 qt.
6. 4 l 550 ml, 4 kl 250 l
7. 6 hr. 20 min., 4 d. 1 hr.
8. 5 yd. 2 ft.
4 yd. 1 ft.
+ 6 yd. 2 ft.
15 yd. 5 ft. = **16 yd. 2 ft.**
9. 4 km 800 m
5 km 400 m
+ 6 km 100 m
15 km 1300 m = **16 km 300 m**
10. 2:25
+ 3:45
5:70 = **6:10**
11. 10 kg 750 g
10 kg 750 g
+ 10 kg 750 g
30 kg 2250 g = **32 kg 250 g**

Subtracting Measurement Units pages 776–777

1. 2 ft. 6 in., 1,110 yd.
2. 3 m 67 cm, 2 km 825 m
3. 1 lb. 13 oz., 1,205 lb.
4. 3 kg 275 g, 1 t 950 kg
5. 1 pt. 13 oz., 3 qt.
6. 505 ml, 1 kl 575 l
7. 55 min., 1 d. 18 hr.
8. 3 hr. 15 min.
− 1 hr. 45 min.
1 hr. 30 min.
9. 57 yd. 1 ft.
− 42 yd. 2 ft.
14 yd. 2 ft.

Multiplying Measurement Units pages 778–779

1. 22 ft. 8 in., 5 mi.
2. 11 cm 2 mm, 38 km 200 m
3. 15 lb., 4 T. 475 lb.
4. 26 g 125 mg, 5 t 500 kg
5. 4 pt. 5 oz., 5 gal. 2 qt.
6. 9 l 200 ml, 10 kl 950 l
7. 13 hr. 40 min., 34 min.
8. 6 ft. 8 in.
× 4
24 ft. 32 in. = **26 ft. 8 in.**
9. 1 kg 250 g
× 12
12 kg 3000 g = **15 kg**
10. 1 pt. 6 oz.
× 5
5 pt. 30 oz. = **6 pt. 14 oz.**
11. 4 cm 3 mm
× 6
24 cm 18 mm = **25 cm 8 mm**

Dividing Measurement Units pages 779–781

1. 1 ft. 6 in., 1 mi. 598 yd.
2. 2 m 71 cm, 3 km 744 m
3. 1 T. 1,300 lb., 2 kg 210 g
4. 2 gal. 3 qt., 1 pt. 8 oz.
5. 1 l 320 ml, 1 kl 510 l
6. 1 hr. 40 min., 1 d. 16 hr.
7. **1 ft. 4 in.**
5 6 ft. 8 in.
−5
1 ft. = 12 in.
20
− 20
0
8. **4 lb. 3 oz.**
7 29 lb. 5 oz.
−28
1 lb. = 16 oz.
21
− 21
0

Learning About Perimeter pages 781–782

1. 20 yd. 2 ft.
2. 340 m 50 cm
3. 12 cm 2 mm
4. 11 ft. 6 in.
5. 21
× 4
84 yards
6. *STEP 1:*
32 × 2 = 64
20 × 2 = 40
STEP 2:
64
+ 40
104 inches
7. 9 cm 4 mm
12 cm 5 mm
+ 14 cm
35 cm 9 mm
8. *STEP 1:*
450 × 2 = 900 yards
285 × 2 = 570 yards
STEP 2:
900
+ 570
1,470 yards
STEP 3:
1,470 yards
× 5
7,350 total yards

Becoming Familiar with Area pages 783–784

1. 8 sq. feet
2. 15 sq. meters
3. 5 sq. yards
4. 6 sq. centimeters
5. 6 sq. feet
6. 11 sq. miles
7. $12.50
× 12
2500
1250
$150.00
8. *STEP 1:*
A = 10 feet
× 7 feet
70 square feet
STEP 2:
70 tiles
1 sq. foot)70 sq. feet
9. 120 yards
× 60 yards
7,200 sq. yards
10. *STEP 1:*
50 meters
× 35 meters
250
1 50
1,750 sq. meters
STEP 2:
17 r 50
100 sq. meters)1750 sq. meters
− 100
750
− 700
50
(Guy will need **18** bags to do the job.)

Becoming Familiar with Volume pages 785–786

1. 16 cubic yards
2. 18 cubic meters
3. 15 cubic inches
4. *STEP 1:*
4 yards
× 3 yards
12 sq. yards
STEP 2:
12 sq. yards
× 3 yards
36 cubic yards
5. *STEP 1:*
3 feet
× 2 feet
6 sq. feet
STEP 2:
6 sq. feet
× 2 feet
12 cubic feet
6. *STEP 1:*
6 feet
× 5 feet
30 sq. feet
STEP 2:
30 sq. feet
× 1 foot
30 cubic feet
STEP 3:
30 cubic feet
× 62 pounds
60
1 80
1,860 pounds

TOPIC 3: Finding an Average pages 786–787

1. *STEP 1:*
124
120
+ 125
369 pounds
STEP 2:
123 pounds
3)369
− 3
06
− 6
09
− 9
0
2. *STEP 1:*
480
362
412
+290
1,544 miles
STEP 2:
386 miles
4)1544
− 12
34
− 32
24
− 24
0
3. *STEP 1:*
$318
289
+ 329
$936
STEP 2:
$312
3)$936
− 9
03
− 3
06
− 6
0
4. *STEP 1:*

1st week	2nd week
1,800	1,925
1,750	2,100
1,770	1,970
1,810	1,975
1,800	1,900
1,780	2,080
+ 1,820	+ 1,980
12,530	13,930

STEP 2:
1790
7)12530
− 7
55
− 49
63
− 63
00
1990
7)13930
− 7
69
− 63
63
− 63
00
5. *STEP 1:*
1 hr. 45 min.
2 hr. 10 min.
+1 hr. 53 min.
4 hr. 108 min.
STEP 2:
1 hr. 56 min.
3)4 hr. 108 min.
− 3
1 hr. = 60 min.
168 min.
− 15
18
− 18
0

TOPIC 4: Squares, Cubes, and Square Roots
pages 788–789

1. 4^2 four squared
2. 5^2 five squared
3. 10^2 ten squared
4. 25^2 twenty-five squared
5. 3^3 three cubed
6. 8^3 eight cubed
7. 10^3 ten cubed
8. 32^3 thirty-two cubed
9. 49
10. 81
11. 144
12. 225
13. 400
14. 27
15. 343
16. 1,728
17. 8,000

What Is a Square Root?
pages 789–790

1. $4 = \sqrt{16}$
2. $10 = \sqrt{100}$
3. $9 = \sqrt{81}$
4. $12 = \sqrt{144}$
5. 8
6. 2
7. 11
8. 5
9. 7
10. 15
11. 1
12. 14
13. 6

CHAPTER 7: DECIMAL SKILLS

Decimal Fractions
pages 791–792

1. one thousand; one thousandth
2. one hundred; one hundredth
3. ten; one tenth
4. one hundred thousand; one hundred-thousandth
5. ten thousand; one ten-thousandth
6. two and one tenth
7. five and one hundredth
8. seven and one thousandth
9. thirteen dollars and one cent

Reading Decimals
pages 792–793

1. 5 tenths; 7 tenths; 9 tenths
2. 12 hundredths; 27 hundredths; 50 hundredths
3. 135 thousandths; 272 thousandths; 180 thousandths
4. 2,048 ten-thousandths; 1,305 ten-thousandths; 4,000 ten-thousandths
5. 12,348 hundred-thousandths; 83,721 hundred-thousandths; 204,000 millionths
6. 5 and 8 tenths; 7 and 19 hundredths
7. 6 and 87 hundredths; 14 and 105 thousandths
8. 29 and 326 thousandths; 154 and 60 hundredths
9. 3 and 2,442 ten-thousandths; 18 and 38,724 hundred-thousandths

Writing Zero as a Place Holder
pages 793–794

1. .05; .106; .007; 2.30; 4.650
2. .109; .048; 5.070; .2031; 5.0040
3. 2.00300; .650; .07700; 1.1030; .50050
4. .03, .030; .450, .45; .61, .610
5. .015, .0150; .2710, .271; .0306, .03060

Writing Decimals
pages 794–795

1. .9
2. .07
3. .35
4. .027
5. 4.1
6. 2.09
7. 50.20
8. 6.080
9. .843
10. 174.65
11. 1,400.075

Comparing Decimal Fractions
pages 795–796

1. .51
2. .401
3. .4
4. .3
5. .66
6. .76
7. .482
8. .6004
9. $.80
10. .134, .43, .8
11. .201, .35, .4
12. $.09, $.28, $.53
13. .209, .45, .5
14. .35, .42, .6
15. .174, .611, .64

Rounding Decimal Fractions
pages 796–798

1. $.47; $.02; $.95
2. $6.88; $83.75
3. .2; .4; .5; .4; .4
4. .41; .48; .73; .87; .38
5. .027; .839; .385; .628; .930
6. $1.07
7. 2.14 inches

Adding Decimals
pages 798–799

.5; .58; .928; 1.6; 1.216; 13.40

Zeros as Place Holders
page 799

1. .76; .74; .392; .943; 1.624; 1.6707
2. .46; 1.14; .595; .3735
3. 7.26; 3.095; 8.21; 11.01
4. 11.91; 10.07; 14.71

Subtracting Decimals
pages 800–801

1. .6; .7; .72; 4.2; 8.3; 16.17
2. .2; .4; .91; 3.06
3. $1.07; $4.43; $3.26; .968
4. .15; .76; .1102; .204
5. 1.63; .52; 1.53; 7.402
6. .204; .36; 3.796

Solving Addition and Subtraction Word Problems
pages 801–802

1. $\begin{array}{r} .306 \\ +\ .048 \\ \hline .354 \end{array}$

2. $\begin{array}{r} 3.85 \\ -\ 3.62 \\ \hline .23 \end{array}$

3. $\begin{array}{r} 12.8 \\ -5.9 \\ \hline 6.9 \end{array}$

4. $\begin{array}{r} .025 \\ +\ .003 \\ \hline .028 \end{array}$ **inch**

5. b

6. $\begin{array}{r} \$59.75 \\ -\ 39.99 \\ \hline \$19.76 \end{array}$

7. $\begin{array}{r} 53.75 \\ 79.69 \\ +\ 51.62 \\ \hline 185.06 \end{array}$

Multiplying Decimal Numbers
pages 802–804

1. 51; 5.18; 50.4; 1.84; 5.34
2. $2.80; .86; $6.25; 1.096; $31.02
3. 2.07; .5747; .616; .2547; .309
4. .4032; 3.8412; .65016; 7.584; 1.3615
5. 1.9; 1.8; 1.4; .3; 27.7
6. 3.33; 3.17; .25; .47; .43
7. .16; .28; .72; .456; .0126
8. .049; .025; .00056; .000045; .000742
9. .0042; .0018; .0288; .00024; .0585

Multiplying by 10, 100, or 1,000
pages 804–805

1. 13.4; 683; 27.4; 321; .58
2. 3.5; 23; .3
3. 25.3; 3; 2,170
4. 5,140; 50; 74,900

Dividing a Decimal by a Whole Number
pages 806–807

1. 2.1; .71; .171; .61; .102
2. .93; 2.3; .242; 2.34; 6.6
3. $10.84; .206; $8.72; .156; $1.18
4. .081; .032; .0012; .009; .003
5. .033; .0129; .0081; .0021; .0126
6. .05; .05; .05; .06; .02
7. .4; .25; .25; .75; 1.2
8. .375; 1.75; .875; 1.25; .3125

Dividing a Decimal by a Decimal
pages 807–809

1. 80; 4; .03; 2,102; 702
2. 77.7; 15,240; .23; 5,080; 23.2
3. 30; 2,340; 18; 814; 14.2
4. 200; 20; 2,000; 20; 600

Dividing by 10, 100, or 1,000
pages 809–810

1. .56; .75; 2.35; 52.52
2. .372; .639; .035; .00021
3. 12.6; .15; 3.75; .012;

Solving Multiplication and Division Word Problems
pages 810–811

1. $\begin{array}{r} \$5.76 \\ \times\ 1.5 \\ \hline 2880 \\ 576 \\ \hline \end{array}$
   $8.640 = **$8.64**

2. **23.4 miles**
   $13.5\overline{)315.9}$
   $\begin{array}{r} \underline{270} \\ 459 \\ \underline{405} \\ 540 \\ \underline{540} \end{array}$

3. **212 cans**
   $1.5\overline{)318.0}$
   $\begin{array}{r} \underline{30} \\ 18 \\ \underline{15} \\ 30 \\ \underline{30} \end{array}$

4. $\begin{array}{r} \$9.28 \\ \times\ \ 21.5 \\ \hline 4640 \\ 928 \\ 1856 \\ \hline \end{array}$
   $199.52

5. $\begin{array}{l} .375 \text{ inches} \\ \times\ \ 3 \\ \hline \end{array}$
   1.125 inches

6. **3.9 cm**
   $6\overline{)23.4 \text{ cm}}$
   $\begin{array}{r} \underline{18} \\ 54 \\ \underline{-54} \end{array}$

Solving Multi-Step Word Problems
pages 811–813

1. amount of balance =
   $469.88 − 125.00 = $344.88
   monthly payment =
   344.88 ÷ 6 = **$57.48**

2. total cost of nails = 5.5 × .97 =
   5.335 = $5.34
   change = 10.00 − 5.34 = **$4.66**

3. regular earnings = 6.50 × 40 = $260
   overtime earnings = 9.75 × 6.4 =
   $62.40
   total earnings = 260 + 62.40 =
   $322.40

4. M, W, F = 5.1
T + Th = 4.8
total miles = 5.1 + 4.8 = **9.9**

5. thickness of 5 washers = .0625 × 5 = .3125
room left = 1 − .3125 = **.6875**

6. 3.7 × .70 = 2.59
4.6 × 1.75 = 8.05
2.59 + 8.05 = **$10.64**

7. .42 × 10 = 4.2
21 ÷ 4.2 = **5 days**

8. 23.5 × $.24 = $5.64
$5.64 + 10.00 = **$15.64**

9. 10 − 6.2 = **3.8**

10.
```
     $1.299
   ×   18.7
      9093
    10392
    1299
   $24.2913 = $24.29
```
$24.2913 = $24.29

11.
```
    .2700
  − .2573
    .0127 inch = .013 inch
```
.0127 inch = .013 inch

12.
```
  $1.359 old price
  −$.019
  $1.340 = $1.34 per gallon after June 1
```
$1.340 = $1.34 per gallon after June 1

13.
```
             11.9 gallons
  1.34)16.000
      −134
        260
       −134
        1260
       −1206
          54
```
11.9 gallons

14. **$137.50**

15.
```
    $7.00
  + $1.00
    $8.00 per day
```
$8.00 per day

Decimal Skills Review
pages 813–814

1. .040, .04; .390, .39; .100, .10
2. .45; .09; .11; .01; .49
3. 1.4; 2.15; 3.9; 2.48; 3.3
4. 6.31; 10.97; 18.97
5. $6.23; $9.31; $7.08; $92.52
6. 6.3; 13; 7.2; 75; 54.6; 450
7. .45; .595; .0432; 2.146; .1568; 35.28
8. 3,470; 28; 59
9. .51; .402; .012; 2.06; .55
10. .42; 5,400; 22,500; .004

CHAPTER 8: COMMON FRACTIONS SKILLS

What Is a Common Fraction?
pages 815–816

1. $\frac{6}{8}, \frac{2}{8}; \frac{1}{4}, \frac{3}{4}; \frac{3}{6}, \frac{3}{6}$
2. $\frac{2}{5}, \frac{3}{5}; \frac{2}{4}, \frac{2}{4}; \frac{3}{6}, \frac{3}{6}$
3. $\frac{11}{18}, \frac{7}{18}; \frac{2}{6}, \frac{4}{6}$
4. P, I, M, I, M
5. P, M, I
6. M, I

Simplifying Fractions
pages 817–818

1. $\frac{1}{3}; \frac{3}{4}; \frac{2}{3}; \frac{2}{3}; \frac{3}{4}$
2. $\frac{3}{5}; \frac{3}{5}; \frac{4}{5}; \frac{2}{3}; \frac{1}{2}$
3. $\frac{1}{3}; \frac{1}{4}; \frac{6}{7}; \frac{1}{2}; \frac{4}{5}$
4. $\frac{7}{4}; 1\frac{3}{4}$
5. $\frac{5}{2}; 2\frac{1}{2}$
6. $\frac{23}{8}; 2\frac{7}{8}$
7. $2\frac{1}{10}; 2\frac{1}{2}; 1\frac{3}{4}; 1\frac{1}{3}; 5\frac{1}{2}$
8. $2\frac{5}{8}$
9. $\frac{21}{2} = 10\frac{1}{2}$; Yes

Raising Fractions to Higher Terms
page 819

1. 4; 2; 2; 6; 9
2. 4; 6; 4; 10; 5
3. 5; 12; 15; 22; 24

Comparing Common Fractions
pages 815–820

1. $\frac{2}{3}; \frac{10}{12}; \frac{5}{8}; \frac{7}{8}$
2. $\frac{3}{8}; \frac{4}{9}; \frac{2}{5}; \frac{6}{7}$
3. $\frac{1}{4}, \frac{1}{3}; \frac{5}{12}, \frac{1}{3}; \frac{2}{3}, \frac{7}{9}; \frac{7}{24}, \frac{1}{3}; \frac{3}{8}, \frac{6}{14}; \frac{1}{2}, \frac{4}{7}$

Finding What Fraction a Part Is of a Whole
page 821

1. $\frac{2}{3}; \frac{5}{6}$
2. $\frac{1}{2}; \frac{5}{6}$
3. $\frac{2}{15}; \frac{3}{4}$
4. $\frac{8}{13}; \frac{12}{13}$
5. $\frac{1}{2}; \frac{5}{8}$
6. $\frac{1}{3}; \frac{5}{6}$
7. $\frac{375}{1,500} = \frac{1}{4}$
8. $\frac{240}{1,000} = \frac{6}{25}$

Adding Like Fractions
pages 822–824

1. $\frac{3}{4}; \frac{7}{8}; \frac{11}{12}; \frac{2}{3}; \frac{7}{8}$
2. $\frac{7}{8}; \frac{3}{4}; \frac{5}{6}; \frac{8}{9}; \frac{13}{14}$
3. $\frac{9}{9} = 1; \frac{7}{7} = 1; \frac{8}{8} = 1; \frac{4}{4} = 1; \frac{12}{12} = 1$
4. $\frac{8}{4} = 2; \frac{14}{7} = 2; \frac{27}{9} = 3$
5. $\frac{7}{6} = 1\frac{1}{6}; \frac{11}{9} = 1\frac{2}{9}; \frac{23}{16} = 1\frac{7}{16}; \frac{16}{12} = 1\frac{1}{3};$
$\frac{20}{16} = 1\frac{1}{4}$
6. $\frac{9}{5} = 1\frac{4}{5}; \frac{6}{3} = 2; \frac{16}{8} = 2;$
$\frac{15}{9} = 1\frac{2}{3}; \frac{24}{12} = 2$
7. $4\frac{2}{3}; 3\frac{3}{4}; 7; 4\frac{11}{12}; 8\frac{7}{8}$
8. $4\frac{1}{2}; 6\frac{1}{2}; 10\frac{5}{11}; 13\frac{1}{3}; 21\frac{1}{2}$

9. 4; $7\frac{3}{4}$; $12\frac{2}{3}$; $14\frac{2}{3}$; $21\frac{7}{8}$
10. $7\frac{1}{2}$; $14\frac{2}{3}$; $11\frac{1}{2}$; $29\frac{2}{3}$; $45\frac{5}{8}$

Subtracting Like Fractions
pages 825–826

1. $\frac{4}{9}$; $\frac{7}{10}$; $\frac{2}{3}$; $\frac{1}{2}$; $\frac{1}{4}$
2. $4\frac{3}{8}$; $5\frac{1}{5}$; $6\frac{1}{2}$; $6\frac{2}{3}$; $9\frac{1}{12}$
3. $4\frac{1}{3}$; $1\frac{5}{16}$; $6\frac{1}{2}$; $2\frac{4}{5}$; $8\frac{1}{3}$
4. $\frac{1}{3}$; $\frac{1}{4}$; $\frac{4}{5}$; $\frac{3}{7}$; $\frac{1}{9}$

Subtracting Fractions from Whole Numbers
pages 826–827

1. 4, $2\frac{1}{4}$; 6, $4\frac{5}{6}$; 5, $1\frac{1}{5}$; 2, $5\frac{1}{2}$
2. $4\frac{1}{5}$; $2\frac{3}{7}$; $11\frac{1}{8}$; $8\frac{1}{3}$; $9\frac{1}{16}$

Subtracting Mixed Numbers by Borrowing
pages 827–828

1. $3\frac{3}{4}$; $4\frac{2}{3}$
2. 4; $5\frac{3}{5}$; $8\frac{5}{6}$; $\frac{1}{2}$; $2\frac{3}{4}$

Solving Addition and Subtraction Word Problems
pages 828–829

1. amount of material bought

$$\begin{array}{r} 2\frac{2}{3} \\ 2\frac{1}{3} \\ +\ 1\frac{2}{3} \\ \hline 5\frac{5}{3} = 6\frac{2}{3} \text{ yards} \end{array}$$

2. length of nails in bin C

$$\begin{array}{r} \frac{5}{8} \\ +\ \frac{3}{8} \\ \hline \frac{8}{8} = 1 \text{ inch} \end{array}$$

3. difference in height of the two dolls

$$\begin{array}{r} 8\frac{1}{4} \\ -\ 7\frac{3}{4} \\ \hline \frac{2}{4} = \frac{1}{2} \text{ inch} \end{array}$$

4.

$$\begin{array}{r} 2\frac{3}{8} \\ 1\frac{7}{8} \\ +1\frac{1}{8} \\ \hline 4\frac{11}{8} = 5\frac{3}{8} \text{ pounds} \end{array}$$

5.

$$\begin{array}{r} 2\frac{1}{3} \\ +\ \frac{1}{3} \\ \hline 2\frac{2}{3} \text{ cups liquid} \end{array}$$

6.

$$\begin{array}{rcl} 6\frac{1}{4} & = & 5\frac{5}{4} \\ -\ 3\frac{3}{4} & & 3\frac{3}{4} \\ \hline & & 2\frac{2}{4} = 2\frac{1}{2} \text{ miles} \end{array}$$

7.

$$\begin{array}{rcl} 3\frac{1}{4} & = & 2\frac{5}{4} \\ -\ 1\frac{3}{4} & & 1\frac{3}{4} \\ \hline & & 1\frac{2}{4} = 1\frac{1}{2} \text{ pounds} \end{array}$$

Adding and Subtracting Unlike Fractions
pages 830–831

1. 2; 4; 6; 6; 8
2. 6; 9; 12; 14; 12
3. $\frac{5}{6}$; $\frac{3}{10}$; $\frac{1}{8}$; $1\frac{1}{8}$; 2
4. $\frac{1}{3}$; $1\frac{1}{4}$; $\frac{11}{14}$; $\frac{1}{9}$; $\frac{21}{32}$
5. $\frac{5}{6}$; 1; $\frac{9}{10}$; $1\frac{3}{8}$; $1\frac{2}{3}$

Choosing a Common Denominator
pages 831–833

1. $\frac{1}{6}$; $\frac{11}{12}$; $\frac{1}{20}$; $1\frac{1}{30}$; $1\frac{11}{12}$
2. $\frac{17}{45}$; $\frac{1}{24}$; $1\frac{5}{12}$; $1\frac{1}{12}$; $\frac{47}{60}$
3. $\frac{13}{18}$; $\frac{11}{24}$
4. $\frac{11}{12}$; $\frac{3}{20}$; $\frac{13}{60}$; $\frac{8}{15}$; $\frac{23}{35}$

Adding and Subtracting Mixed Numbers
pages 833–834

1. 4, 3, $5\frac{1}{6}$; 9, 4, $8\frac{1}{12}$; 12, 5, $7\frac{17}{20}$; 4, 10, 9, $10\frac{11}{12}$
2. $6\frac{5}{6}$; $9\frac{13}{14}$; $11\frac{31}{40}$; $7\frac{1}{12}$; $22\frac{4}{15}$
3. $8\frac{11}{12}$; $13\frac{1}{8}$; $15\frac{29}{60}$; $33\frac{7}{12}$; $45\frac{23}{30}$
4. 8, 3, $2\frac{5}{12}$; 10, 9, $5\frac{1}{12}$; 35, 16, $2\frac{19}{20}$
5. $4\frac{1}{9}$; $7\frac{11}{20}$; $\frac{15}{16}$; $6\frac{23}{24}$; $11\frac{5}{6}$
6. $1\frac{5}{12}$; $4\frac{13}{16}$; $1\frac{7}{8}$; $\frac{7}{16}$; $3\frac{1}{14}$
7. $1\frac{13}{20}$; $1\frac{9}{16}$; $21\frac{2}{9}$; $2\frac{7}{10}$; $21\frac{11}{24}$

Using Substitution to Help Solve Word Problems
pages 835–836

1. 1 in., $\frac{15}{16}$ in.

$$\begin{array}{rcccl} 1\frac{1}{4} & = & 1\frac{4}{16} & = & \frac{20}{16} \\ -\ \frac{5}{16} & = & \frac{5}{16} & = & \frac{5}{16} \\ & & & & \frac{15}{16} \end{array}$$

2. 6 lb., $5\frac{5}{12}$ lb.

$$\begin{array}{rcl} 1\frac{1}{2} & = & 1\frac{6}{12} \\ 1\frac{2}{3} & = & 1\frac{8}{12} \\ +\ 2\frac{1}{4} & = & 2\frac{3}{12} \\ & & 4\frac{17}{12} = 5\frac{5}{12} \end{array}$$

3. 3 in., $1\frac{5}{16}$ in.

$$\begin{array}{rcl} \frac{11}{16} & = & \frac{11}{16} \\ + \frac{5}{8} & = & \frac{10}{16} \\ \hline \frac{21}{16} & = & 1\frac{5}{6} \end{array}$$

4. 1 in., $\frac{1}{24}$ in.

$$\begin{array}{rcl} \frac{7}{8} & = & \frac{21}{24} \\ -\ \frac{5}{6} & = & -\ \frac{20}{24} \\ \hline & & \frac{1}{24} \end{array}$$

Solving Addition and Subtraction Word Problems pages 836–838

1. a)

$$\begin{array}{rcccl} 3\frac{1}{8} & = & 3\frac{1}{8} & = & 2\frac{9}{8} \\ -\ 2\frac{3}{4} & = & -\ 2\frac{6}{8} & = & -\ 2\frac{6}{8} \\ \hline & & & & \frac{3}{8}\text{ mile} \end{array}$$

b)

$$\begin{array}{rcl} 2\frac{3}{4} & = & 2\frac{6}{8} \\ +\ 3\frac{1}{8} & = & +\ 3\frac{1}{8} \\ \hline & & 5\frac{7}{8}\text{ miles} \end{array}$$

2. a)

$$\begin{array}{rcl} 9\frac{5}{16} & = & 9\frac{5}{16} \\ +\ 5\frac{7}{8} & = & +\ 5\frac{14}{16} \\ \hline & & 14\frac{19}{16} = 15\frac{3}{16}\text{ inches} \end{array}$$

b)

$$\begin{array}{rcccl} 9\frac{5}{16} & = & 9\frac{5}{16} & = & 8\frac{21}{16} \\ -\ 5\frac{7}{8} & = & -\ 5\frac{14}{16} & = & -\ 5\frac{14}{16} \\ \hline & & & & 3\frac{7}{16}\text{ inches} \end{array}$$

3. more.

$$\begin{array}{rcl} 6\frac{1}{2} & = & 6\frac{3}{6} \\ +\ 1\frac{2}{3} & = & +\ 1\frac{4}{6} \\ \hline & & 7\frac{7}{6} = 8\frac{1}{6} \end{array}$$

4. rose.

$$\begin{array}{rcl} 34\frac{1}{2} & = & 34\frac{4}{8} \\ +\ 1\frac{7}{8} & = & +\ 1\frac{7}{8} \\ \hline & & 35\frac{11}{8} = 36\frac{3}{8} \end{array}$$

5. earlier.

$$\begin{array}{rcccl} 4\frac{1}{2} & = & 4\frac{2}{4} & = & 3\frac{6}{4} \\ -\ \frac{3}{4} & = & -\ \frac{3}{4} & = & -\ \frac{3}{4} \\ \hline & & & & 3\frac{3}{4}\text{ hours} \end{array}$$

6. fewer.

$$\begin{array}{rcl} 3\frac{7}{8} & = & 3\frac{7}{8} \\ -\ 1\frac{1}{4} & = & -\ 1\frac{2}{8} \\ \hline & & 2\frac{5}{8}\text{ pounds} \end{array}$$

7. c

8. a

Multiplying Fractions pages 838–841

1. $\frac{1}{6}$; $\frac{4}{45}$; $\frac{3}{16}$; $\frac{9}{70}$; $\frac{5}{8}$
2. $\frac{1}{10}$; $\frac{1}{4}$; $\frac{4}{5}$
3. $\frac{5}{8}$; $\frac{10}{21}$; 1; 1
4. $\frac{5}{8}$; $\frac{4}{27}$; 2; $1\frac{2}{3}$
5. 2; $2\frac{1}{2}$; $6\frac{6}{7}$; $7\frac{1}{3}$
6. $4\frac{4}{5}$; $6\frac{1}{8}$; $7\frac{1}{3}$; $3\frac{3}{4}$; 12
7. $5\frac{1}{2}$; $9\frac{1}{3}$; 12; $2\frac{3}{4}$; $\frac{8}{9}$
8. 5; $7\frac{1}{2}$; $1\frac{47}{48}$; $2\frac{7}{10}$; $8\frac{3}{4}$
9. $\frac{15}{16}$; $2\frac{4}{15}$; $14\frac{5}{21}$; $19\frac{7}{8}$; $9\frac{1}{2}$
10. $13\frac{2}{5}$; $10\frac{9}{20}$; $12\frac{23}{36}$; $24\frac{5}{63}$; $6\frac{27}{100}$

Dividing Fractions pages 841–845

1. $\frac{3}{8}$; $\frac{2}{11}$; $\frac{1}{9}$; $\frac{4}{15}$; $\frac{8}{15}$
2. $\frac{2}{3}$; 1; $2\frac{2}{5}$
3. 1; $\frac{35}{48}$; $1\frac{3}{5}$; $\frac{27}{32}$; $\frac{5}{8}$
4. 1; 8; $\frac{3}{26}$; $\frac{5}{49}$; $1\frac{9}{16}$
5. $\frac{2}{7}$; $\frac{1}{5}$; $\frac{12}{65}$
6. $\frac{1}{8}$; $\frac{7}{32}$; $\frac{9}{50}$; $\frac{1}{2}$; $\frac{3}{5}$
7. 25; $9\frac{1}{3}$; 9
8. $10\frac{1}{2}$; 12; 16; 4; 10
9. 2; $1\frac{1}{2}$; $1\frac{3}{7}$; $\frac{3}{13}$
10. 4; $2\frac{16}{19}$; $2\frac{1}{12}$; $\frac{3}{32}$; $4\frac{1}{5}$

Solving Multiplication and Division Word Problems pages 845–848

1. $\frac{1}{5} \times \frac{12}{1} = \frac{12}{5} = 2\frac{2}{5}$ ounces
2. $\frac{1}{4} \times \frac{940}{1} = \$235$
3. $1\frac{7}{8} \div \frac{3}{16} = \frac{15}{8} \times \frac{16}{3} = 10$
4. $\frac{7}{8} \div \frac{2}{5} = \frac{7}{8} \times \frac{5}{2} = \frac{35}{16} = 2\frac{3}{16}$
5. $141 \div 12\frac{3}{4} = \frac{141}{1} \times \frac{4}{51} = \frac{564}{51} =$
   $11\frac{3}{51}$ or $11\frac{1}{17}$ = 11 pieces
6. $3\frac{5}{8} \div \frac{5}{16} = \frac{29}{8} \times \frac{16}{5} = \frac{58}{5} =$
   $11\frac{3}{5}$ or 11 complete rings
7. $\frac{7}{8} \div \frac{3}{64} = \frac{7}{8} \times \frac{64}{3} = \frac{56}{3} = 18\frac{2}{3}$ poles
8. $\frac{3}{10} \times \frac{40}{1} = 12$ inches
9. $\frac{1}{2} \times 1\frac{3}{4} = \frac{1}{2} \times \frac{7}{4} = \frac{7}{8}$ cup
10. $16\frac{1}{4} \div 1\frac{2}{3} = \frac{65}{4} \times \frac{3}{5} = \frac{39}{4} =$
    $9\frac{3}{4}$ or 10 total trips

Working with Decimals and Fractions at the Same Time
pages 848–849

1. .25; .625; .17
2. .5; .6; .75; .7; .15
3. .125; .33; .4; .67; .45
4. $\frac{1}{5}$; $\frac{1}{2}$; $\frac{1}{4}$; $\frac{3}{4}$; $\frac{19}{20}$
5. $\frac{19}{50}$; $\frac{3}{8}$; $\frac{3}{4}$; $1\frac{7}{10}$; $3\frac{1}{4}$
6. $9\frac{2}{5}$; $8\frac{1}{8}$; $6\frac{1}{200}$; $3\frac{3}{80}$; $4\frac{7}{8}$

Comparing Common Fractions with Decimal Fractions
page 850

1. $\frac{1}{4}$; .62; $\frac{7}{8}$; .128
2. .334; $\frac{2}{7}$; .804; $\frac{5}{6}$
3. .74
4. $.71
5. .275
6. .7 yard

Comparison Word Problems
page 851

1. #2
2. A, C, D, B
3. 6.30; 6.33; 6.35; 6.36
   Joyce: 6.33
   Irvin: 6.30
   Francis: 6.36
   Ellen: 6.35

Solving Decimal *and* Fraction Word Problems
page 852

1. $27\frac{1}{2} \div 3\frac{1}{2} =$
   $\frac{55}{2} \times \frac{2}{7} = \frac{55}{7} = 7\frac{6}{7}$ **minutes**
2. $6\frac{1}{4} \times .28 = \frac{25}{4} \times \frac{7}{25} = \frac{7}{4} =$
   $1\frac{3}{4} =$ **$1.75**

Solving Multi-Step Word Problems
pages 853–855

1. $6\frac{1}{4}$ **hours**
2. $5\frac{3}{8} - 3\frac{1}{2} = \frac{43}{8} - \frac{28}{8} = \frac{15}{8}$
   $\frac{15}{8} \times \frac{1}{12} = \frac{5}{32}$ **lb.**
3. 3 lb. 12 oz. = $3\frac{3}{4}$ lbs.
   $3\frac{3}{4} \div \frac{1}{4} = \frac{15}{4} \times 4 =$
   15 hamburgers
4. 34.75 × 8.20 + 12.30 × 5.5
   $284.95 + $67.65
   $$\begin{array}{r} \$284.95 \\ +\ 67.65 \\ \hline \mathbf{\$352.60} \end{array}$$
5. total weight of 3 pkgs. times $13.40
   $$\begin{array}{r} 1\frac{3}{8} \\ 2\frac{2}{8} \\ +\ 1\frac{4}{8} \\ \hline 5\frac{1}{8} \end{array}$$
   $$\begin{array}{r} 5.125 \\ \times\ 13.40 \\ \hline 2\ 05000 \\ 15\ 375 \\ 51\ 25 \\ \hline 68.67500 \end{array}$$
   68.67500 = **$68.68**
6. total weight divided by 15
   $5\frac{3}{8} + 4\frac{2}{8} + 3\frac{4}{8} = 13\frac{1}{8}$
   $\frac{105}{8} \div 15 = \frac{105}{8} \times \frac{1}{15} = \frac{7}{8}$ **lb.**
7. d
8. a
9. $$\begin{array}{r} 14.75 \\ \times\ 15 \\ \hline 7375 \\ 1475 \\ \hline 221.25 \end{array} \qquad \begin{array}{r} \$221.25 \\ +\ 11.35 \\ \hline \mathbf{\$232.60} \end{array}$$
10. $$\begin{array}{r} 17.50 \\ \times\ 15 \\ \hline 8750 \\ 1750 \\ \hline 262.50 \\ -\ 13.60 \\ \hline \mathbf{\$248.90} \end{array}$$
11. $1\frac{1}{2}$ **hrs.**
12. $66 \div 1\frac{3}{8} = 66 \times \frac{8}{11} =$ **48 weeks**

Fraction Skills Review
pages 855–856

1. $\frac{1}{2}$, $\frac{4}{8}$; $\frac{3}{9}$, $\frac{2}{6}$; $\frac{3}{15}$, $\frac{6}{30}$; $\frac{3}{10}$, $\frac{9}{30}$
2. $\frac{1}{4}$, $\frac{1}{3}$, $\frac{5}{12}$; $\frac{5}{12}$, $\frac{13}{24}$, $\frac{5}{8}$; $\frac{1}{3}$, $\frac{2}{3}$, $\frac{7}{9}$; $\frac{2}{5}$, $\frac{9}{20}$, $\frac{5}{10}$
3. 1; $2\frac{4}{5}$; $1\frac{4}{9}$; $6\frac{9}{14}$; $13\frac{5}{8}$
4. $\frac{5}{9}$; $\frac{1}{9}$; $\frac{2}{3}$; $4\frac{5}{8}$; $7\frac{3}{10}$
5. $\frac{2}{15}$; $\frac{7}{12}$; $5\frac{1}{4}$; 10
6. $1\frac{1}{2}$; 19; $12\frac{3}{32}$; $28\frac{11}{16}$
7. $\frac{1}{5}$; $2\frac{1}{2}$; $1\frac{1}{2}$
8. $1\frac{1}{2}$; $\frac{1}{18}$; $16\frac{2}{3}$; $\frac{9}{40}$
9. $8\frac{2}{5}$; $\frac{15}{32}$; $\frac{57}{67}$; $\frac{35}{57}$

CHAPTER 9: PERCENT SKILLS

Percents
pages 857–858

1. $\frac{21}{100}$; .21, 21%
2. $\frac{47}{100}$; .47; 47%
3. $\frac{83}{100}$; .83; 83%
4. a) % shaded 57%
   % unshaded 43%
   total % 100%
   b) % shaded 40%
   % unshaded 60%
   total % 100%
5. a) 89%
   b) 11%
6. a) 1%; b) 5%; c) 10%; d) 25%

Percents, Decimals, and Fractions
pages 858–863

1. .55; .25; .04; .08
2. .088; .115; .30; .075
3. .002; .007; .035
4. .003; .0075; .0775; .09375
5. 2; 9; 4.85; 1.3
6. $20\frac{1}{4}$%

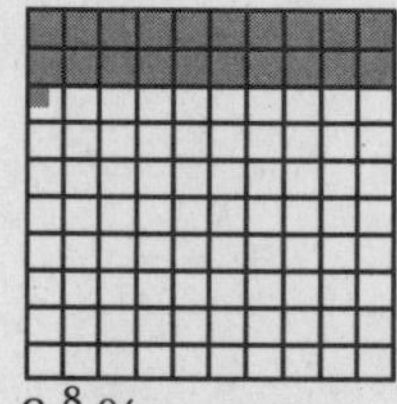

7. $\frac{5}{8}$%

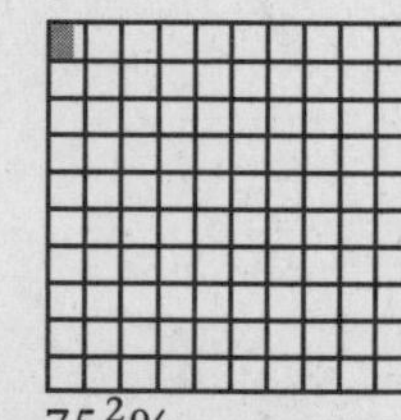

8. $8\frac{8}{10}$%

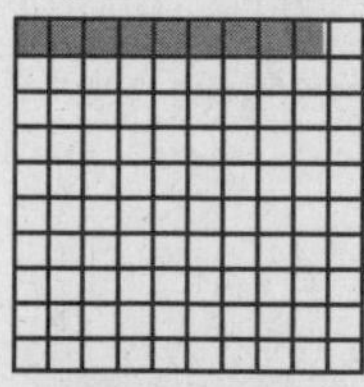

9. $75\frac{2}{3}$%

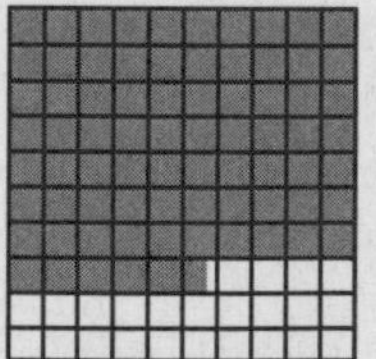

10. 125%

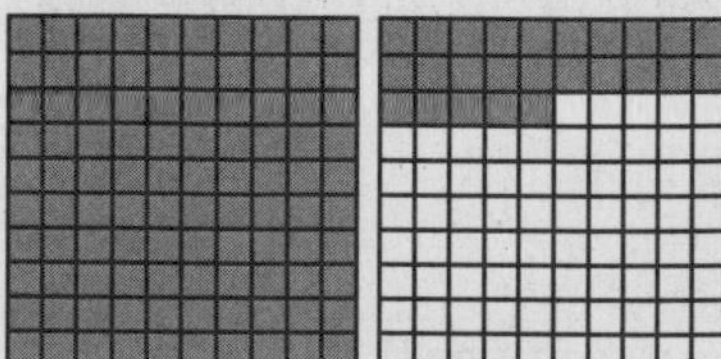

11. 180%

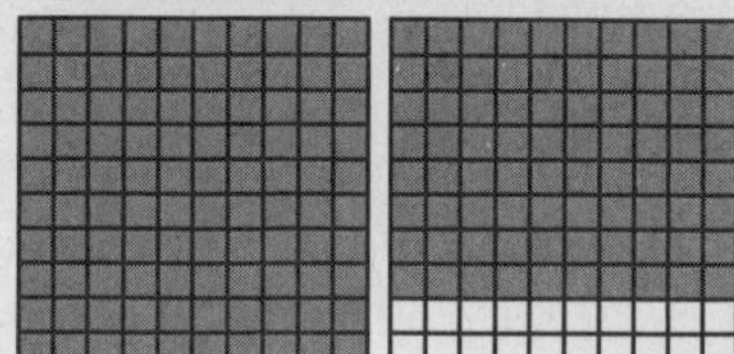

12. 75%; 80%; 9%; 37.5%
13. 8.5%; 150%; 60.5%; 70%
14. 90%; 87.5%; 80%; 37.5%
15. 50%; 160%; 350%; 400%
16. $\frac{11}{20}$; $\frac{2}{5}$; $\frac{1}{100}$; $\frac{3}{10}$;
17. $\frac{1}{2}$; $\frac{3}{25}$; $\frac{99}{100}$; $\frac{1}{5}$
18. $\frac{3}{50}$; $2\frac{1}{2}$; $4\frac{3}{4}$; $3\frac{2}{5}$
19. 50%; 60%; 25%; 12.5%;
20. $33\frac{1}{3}$%; $16\frac{2}{3}$%; 28%; 90%
21. 87.5%; 20%; $66\frac{2}{3}$%; 18.75%

Commonly Used Percents, Decimals, and Fractions
page 864

10%	.1	$\frac{1}{10}$
20%	.2	$\frac{1}{5}$
25%	.25	$\frac{1}{4}$
30%	.3	$\frac{3}{10}$
40%	.4	$\frac{2}{5}$
50%	.5	$\frac{1}{2}$
60%	.6	$\frac{3}{5}$
70%	.7	$\frac{7}{10}$
75%	.75	$\frac{3}{4}$
80%	.8	$\frac{4}{5}$
90%	.9	$\frac{9}{10}$

Word Problems: Percents, Decimals, and Fractions
page 865

1. a) .25
   b) $\frac{25}{100} = \frac{1}{4}$
2. a) $66\frac{2}{3}\% = \frac{2}{3}$
   b) $\frac{3}{3} - \frac{2}{3} = \frac{1}{3} = 33\frac{1}{3}\%$
3. a) $\frac{13}{20}$
   b) $\frac{13}{20} = .65 = 65\%$
4. a) $\frac{350}{1000} = .35$
   b) .35 = 35%
5. a) $\frac{1500}{2000} = \frac{3}{4}$
   b) $\frac{3}{4} = .75 = 75\%$

Finding Part of a Whole
pages 867–868

1. .5 or $\frac{1}{2}$; .34 or $\frac{17}{50}$; 1.25 or $1\frac{1}{4}$; .75 or $\frac{3}{4}$; .065 or $\frac{13}{200}$
2. 15; 63; 60.5; 2.94
3. .06; .18; .075; 5.75
4. .3; .25; 63.75; 1.425
5. 80; 650; 72; 20

Word Problems: Finding Part of a Whole
page 869

1. % = 15%
   W = $1,246
   P = unknown
   $1,246 × .15 = 62 30 + 124 6 = **$186.90**
2. % = 4%
   W = $285
   P = unknown
   $285 × .04 = **$11.40**
3. % = 23%
   W = 74,000
   P = unknown
   74,000 × .23 = 2,220 00 + 14,800 0 = **17,020.00**
4. % = 9%
   W = $545
   P = unknown
   $545 × .09 = **$49.05**

Word Problems: Increasing or Decreasing a Whole
pages 870–871

1. $1,260 × .05 = $63.00; $1,260 + 63 = **$1,323**
2. $12.00 × .30 = 0000 + 3 600 = $3.6000; $12.00 + 3.60 = **$15.60**
3. $640 × .40 = $256.00; $640.00 − 256.00 = **$384.00**
4. $746 × .10 = 0 00 + 74 6 = $74.60; $746.00 − 74.60 = **$671.40**
5. $12,350 × .20 = 00 00 + 2 470 0 = $2,470.00; $12,350 + 2,470 = **$14,820**

Word Problems: Mixed Practice
page 871

1. $72,000 × .04 = **$2,880.00**
2. $4.80 × .25 = 24 00 + 96 0 = $1.20 00; $4.80 + 1.20 = **$6.00**
3. $38,000 × .15 = 1 900 00 + 3 800 0 = $5,700.00; $38,000 − 5,700 = **$32,300**
4. $42.50 × .40 = $17.0000; $42.50 − 17.00 = **$25.50**
5. a
6. c

Finding What Percent a Part Is of a Whole
page 872

1. 20%
2. 50%
3. 25%
4. 12.5%
5. 200%
6. 300%

Word Problems: Finding What Percent a Part Is of a Whole
pages 872–873

1. 25; 250
   $\frac{25}{250} = \frac{1}{10}$
   $1.00 \div 10$: 10)1.00; 1 0; 00; 00; 0 — **.10 = 10%**
2. $\frac{4}{8} = \frac{1}{2}$
   8)4.0; 4.0; 0 — **.5 = 50%**
3. $\frac{1760}{5500} = \frac{8}{25}$
   25)8.00; 7 5; 50; 50; 0 — **.32 = 32%**
4. $\frac{171}{900} = \frac{19}{100}$ = **19%**

Word Problems: Finding Percent Increase or Decrease
pages 873–874

1. $7,800 − 7,500 = $ 300
   $\frac{300}{7500} = \frac{1}{25}$
   25)1.00; 1 00; 0 — **.04 = 4%**

2. $11.50 − 10.00 = $ 1.50

$\frac{1.50}{10.00} = \frac{3}{20}$

20)3.00 = .15 = 15%
20
1 00
1 00
0

3. $2.00 − 1.75 = $ .25

$\frac{.25}{2.00} = \frac{1}{8}$

8)1.0000 = .125 = $12\frac{1}{2}$%
8
20
16
40
40
0

4. 150 − 135 = 15

$\frac{15}{150} = \frac{1}{10}$

10)1.00 = .10 = 10%
1 0
00
00
0

5. $1,312.50 − 1,250.00 = $ 62.50

$\frac{62.50}{1250} = \frac{1}{20}$

20)1.00 = .05 = 5%
1 00
0

6. 16 − 14 = 2

$\frac{2}{16} = \frac{1}{8}$

8)1.000 = .125 = $12\frac{1}{2}$%
8
20
16
40
40
0

Finding the Whole When a Part Is Given
pages 874–875

1. 36
2. 200
3. 369
4. 710

Word Problems: Finding the Whole When a Part Is Given
pages 875–877

1. .25)245.00 = $980.
225
20 0
20 0
00
00
0

2. .15)480.00 = $3,200
45
30
30
0 00
0 00
0

3. .34)14280.00 = 42,000
136
68
68
00 00
00 00
0

4. .015)27.000 = $1,800.
15
12 0
12 0
000
000
0

5. .08)14.00 = 1 75.
8 0
6 0
5 6
40
40
0

6. 100% − 6% = 94%

.94)451.20 = $4 80.
376
75 2
75 2
0

7. 100% − 35% = 65%

.65)256.0000 = 3 93.846 = **$393.85**
195
61 0
58 5
2 50
1 95
550
520
300
260
400
390

Percent Word Problems: Mixed Practice
pages 877–878

1. P = $99.20
% = unknown
W = $1,240

1,240)99.20 = .08 = **8%**
99.20
0

2. P = unknown
% = 3%
W = $360

$360 × .03 = $10.80

$360.00 − 10.80 = **$349.20**

3. P = 90
% = 36%
W = unknown

.36)90.00 = **250.**
72
18 0
18 0
00

4. P = unknown
% = 42%
W = 150

150 × .42
3 00
60 0
63.00

5. P = $21.50
% = 70%
W = unknown

100% − 30% = 70%

.70)21.50000 = 30.714 = **$30.71**
21 0
500
490
100
70
300
280

6. P = unknown
% = 15%
W = $64.50

$$\begin{array}{r} 4\,30.\ \mathbf{19\ in.} \\ .15\overline{)64.50} \\ \underline{60\ \ \ } \\ 4\,5\ \\ \underline{4\,5\ } \\ 00 \\ \underline{00} \end{array}$$

7. c
8. a

Percent Skills Review
pages 878–879

1. .5, $\frac{1}{2}$; .25, $\frac{1}{4}$; .6, $\frac{3}{5}$
2. .75, $\frac{3}{4}$; .125, $\frac{1}{8}$; .025, $\frac{1}{40}$
3. 24; 50; .96; 32
4. .112; 1.375; .8; .375
5. $440; 300; 52.5; 45
6. 25%
7. 12.5%
8. 15.5%
9. $33\frac{1}{3}$%
10. 200%
11. 220%
12. $33\frac{1}{3}$%
13. .5%
14. 76
15. 62
16. 255
17. 33,000
18. 48
19. 40
20. $225.50
21. $145

CHAPTER 10: MORE SPECIAL TOPICS IN MATH

TOPIC 1: Using Estimation
pages 880–882

1. 2; 12; 15; 2
2. 9%; 5%; 6%; 13%
3. 9; 12; 9; 3
4. 16; 48; 54; 144
5. $4\frac{2}{3}$; $5\frac{3}{4}$; 22.5; 62
6. $7.44; $10; $16\frac{4}{5}$; $98\frac{2}{5}$
7. b
8. c
9. b
10. d
11. c
12. a

Using Estimation in Word Problems
pages 882–884

1. **$6.00, $6.19**
2. **24, 23**

estimate
$8 \times 3 = \mathbf{24}$

exact
$8 \times 2\frac{7}{8} = \frac{8}{1} \times \frac{23}{8} = \mathbf{23}$

3. **34, $33\frac{15}{16}$**

estimate

$$\begin{array}{lcr} 20\frac{1}{8} & \rightarrow & 20 \\ 9\frac{1}{8} & \rightarrow & 9 \\ 4\frac{3}{4} & \rightarrow & \underline{+\ 5} \\ & & \mathbf{34} \end{array}$$

exact

$$\begin{array}{rcl} 20\frac{1}{8} & = & 20\frac{2}{16} \\ 9\frac{1}{16} & = & 9\frac{1}{16} \\ +\ 4\frac{3}{4} & = & 4\frac{12}{16} \\ \hline & & \mathbf{33\frac{15}{16}} \end{array}$$

4. **7, $7\frac{3}{16}$**

estimate

$$\begin{array}{lcr} 19\frac{1}{8} & \rightarrow & 19 \\ 11\frac{15}{16} & \rightarrow & \underline{-\ 12} \\ & & \mathbf{7} \end{array}$$

exact

$$\begin{array}{rcl} 19\frac{1}{8} & - & 11\frac{15}{16} = \\ 19\frac{2}{16} & = & 18\frac{18}{16} \\ -\ 11\frac{15}{16} & - & 11\frac{15}{16} \\ \hline & & \mathbf{7\frac{3}{16}} \end{array}$$

5. **$36, $36.55**

estimate
6.9% → 7%
$34.19 → $34

$$\begin{array}{r} \$34 \\ \underline{\times\ .07} \\ \$2.38 \end{array} \rightarrow \$2$$

$$\begin{array}{r} \$34 \\ \underline{+\ \ \ 2} \\ \mathbf{\$36} \end{array}$$

exact

$$\begin{array}{r} \$34.19 \\ \underline{\times\ \ .069} \\ 30771 \\ \underline{2\,0514\ } \\ 2.35911 \end{array} \rightarrow 2.36$$

$$\begin{array}{r} \$34.19 \\ \underline{+\ \ 2.36} \\ \mathbf{\$36.55} \end{array}$$

6. 36, $36\frac{12}{29}$

estimate

$10\frac{7}{8}" \rightarrow 11"$

$33' \rightarrow 396"$

$$\begin{array}{r} 36 \\ 11\overline{)396} \\ \underline{33} \\ 66 \end{array}$$

exact

$$396 \div 10\frac{7}{8}$$
$$= 396 \div \frac{87}{8}$$
$$= \frac{396}{1} \times \frac{8}{87}$$
$$= \frac{3168}{87} = \frac{1056}{29}$$
$$= 36\frac{12}{29}$$

7. c $4 × 5 = **$20**

8. d

$$\begin{array}{r} 27 \\ 32 \\ +\ 19 \\ \hline \mathbf{78} \end{array}$$

9. a

$$\begin{array}{r} 1.24 \\ \times\ 14 \\ \hline 4\ 96 \\ 12\ 4 \\ \hline \mathbf{17.36} \end{array}$$

10. b

$$\begin{array}{r} 60 \\ \times\ 12 \\ \hline 120 \\ 60 \\ \hline 720 \text{ inches} \end{array} \qquad \begin{array}{r} \mathbf{120 \text{ shingles}} \\ 6\overline{)720} \\ \underline{6} \\ 12 \\ \underline{12} \end{array}$$

11. a

$$\begin{array}{r} \$300 \\ \times\ .09 \\ \hline \$27.00 \end{array} \qquad \begin{array}{r} \$300 \\ +\ 27 \\ \hline \mathbf{\$327} \end{array}$$

Estimation Doesn't Always Help
pages 884–885

1. 7 × 2 = 14
   The answer choices are too close in value.
2. 1 ÷ 1 = 1
   The numbers are smaller than 1.
3.
$$\begin{array}{r} .50 \\ 200\overline{)100.00} \\ \underline{100\ 00} \\ 00 \\ \underline{00} \end{array}$$
   The answer choices are too close in value.

TOPIC 2: Understanding Simple Interest
pages 885–887

1. P = $500
   R = 5% = .05
   T = 3

$$\begin{array}{r} \$500 \\ \times\ .05 \\ \hline \$25.00 \end{array} \qquad \begin{array}{r} \$25 \\ \times\ 3 \\ \hline \mathbf{\$75} \end{array}$$

2. P = $1,500
   R = $5\frac{1}{2}$% = .055
   T = 1

$$\begin{array}{r} \$1{,}500 \\ \times\ .055 \\ \hline 7\ 500 \\ 75\ 00 \\ \hline \$82.500 \end{array} = \mathbf{\$82.50}$$

3. P = $850
   R = 11.5% = .115
   T = 3

$$\begin{array}{r} \$850 \\ \times\ .115 \\ \hline 4\ 250 \\ 8\ 50 \\ 85\ 0 \\ \hline \$97.750 \end{array} \qquad \begin{array}{r} \$97.75 \\ \times\ 3 \\ \hline \mathbf{\$293.25} \end{array}$$

4. P = $1,200
   R = 12% = .12
   T = 2

$$\begin{array}{r} \$1{,}200 \\ \times\ .12 \\ \hline 24\ 00 \\ 120\ 0 \\ \hline \$144.00 \end{array} \qquad \begin{array}{r} \$144 \\ \times\ 2 \\ \hline \mathbf{\$288} \end{array}$$

5. P = $750
   R = 5% = .05
   T = 3

Step 1:

$$\begin{array}{r} \$750 \\ \times\ .05 \\ \hline \$37.50 \end{array} \qquad \begin{array}{r} \$37.50 \\ \times\ 3 \\ \hline \$112.50 \end{array}$$

Step 2:

$$\begin{array}{r} \$750.00 \\ +\ 112.50 \\ \hline \mathbf{\$862.50} \end{array}$$

6. P = $2,000
   R = 15% = .15
   T = 2

Step 1:

$$\begin{array}{r} \$2{,}000 \\ \times\ .15 \\ \hline 100\ 00 \\ 200\ 0 \\ \hline \$300.00 \end{array} \qquad \begin{array}{r} \$300.00 \\ \times\ 2 \\ \hline \$600.00 \end{array}$$

Step 2:

$$\begin{array}{r} \$2{,}000 \\ +\ 600 \\ \hline \mathbf{\$2{,}600} \end{array}$$

Interest for Part of a Year
pages 888–889

1. P = $750
   R = .13
   T = 6 mos. = .5 year

$$\begin{array}{r} \$750 \\ \times\ .13 \\ \hline 22\ 50 \\ 75\ 0 \\ \hline \$97.50 \end{array} \qquad \begin{array}{r} \$97.50 \\ \times\ .5 \\ \hline \$48.750 \\ \mathbf{\$48.75} \end{array}$$

2. P = $350
R = .06
T = 15 mos.
$= 1\frac{3}{12}$ years
$= 1\frac{1}{4}$ years
= 1.25 years

$$\begin{array}{r} \$350 \\ \times \quad .06 \\ \hline \$21.00 \end{array}$$

$$\begin{array}{r} 1.25 \\ \times \quad 21 \\ \hline 125 \\ 250 \\ \hline \mathbf{\$26.25} \end{array}$$

3. P = $5,000
R = .14
T = 5

$$\begin{array}{r} \$5,000 \\ \times \quad .14 \\ \hline 200\ 00 \\ 500\ 0 \\ \hline \$700.00 \end{array} \qquad \begin{array}{r} \$700 \\ \times \quad 5 \\ \hline \mathbf{\$3,500} \end{array}$$

4. P = $650
R = .07
T = 2 years 6 months
= 2.5 years

$$\begin{array}{r} \$650 \\ \times \quad .07 \\ \hline \$45.50 \end{array}$$

$$\begin{array}{r} \$45.50 \\ \times \quad 2.5 \\ \hline 22\ 750 \\ 91\ 00 \\ \hline \$113.750 \\ \mathbf{\$113.75} \end{array}$$

5. P = $900
R = .115
T = 9 mos.
$= \frac{9}{12} = \frac{3}{4} = .75$

$$\begin{array}{r} \$900 \\ \times \quad .115 \\ \hline 4\ 500 \\ 9\ 00 \\ 90\ 0 \\ \hline \$103.500 \end{array}$$

$$\begin{array}{r} \$103.50 \\ \times \quad .75 \\ \hline 5\ 1750 \\ 72\ 450 \\ \hline \$77.6250 \end{array}$$

$$\begin{array}{r} \$900.00 \\ + \quad 77.63 \\ \hline \mathbf{\$977.63} \end{array}$$

6. P = $1,400
R = .08

$$\begin{array}{r} \$1,400 \\ \times \quad .08 \\ \hline \$112.00 \end{array}$$

$$\frac{112}{1} \times \frac{7}{12} = \frac{196}{3}$$

$$\begin{array}{r} 65.33 \\ 3\overline{)196.00} \\ 18 \\ \hline 16 \\ 15 \\ \hline 1\ 0 \\ 9 \\ \hline 10 \\ 9 \\ \hline 1 \end{array} \qquad \begin{array}{r} \$1,400.00 \\ + \quad 65.33 \\ \hline \mathbf{\$1,465.33} \end{array}$$

Simple Interest Problems: Mixed Practice pages 889–890

1. P = $2,800
R = .065
T = 18 months = 1.5 years

$$\begin{array}{r} 2,800 \\ \times \quad .065 \\ \hline 14\ 000 \\ 168\ 00 \\ \hline \$182.000 \end{array} \qquad \begin{array}{r} \$182 \\ \times \quad 1.5 \\ \hline 91\ 0 \\ 182 \\ \hline \$273.0 \end{array} \qquad \begin{array}{r} \$2,800 \\ + \quad 273 \\ \hline \mathbf{\$3,073} \end{array}$$

2. $$\begin{array}{r} \$9,000 \\ \times \quad .10 \\ \hline \$900.00 \end{array} \qquad \begin{array}{r} \$9,000 \\ - \quad 900 \\ \hline \mathbf{\$8,100} \end{array}$$

3. $$\begin{array}{r} \$8,100 \\ - \ 3,073 \\ \hline \mathbf{\$5,027} \end{array}$$

4. P = $5,027
R = .06
$T = \frac{9}{12} = \frac{3}{4} = .75$

$$\begin{array}{r} \$5,027 \\ + \quad 273 \\ \hline \$301.62 \end{array}$$

$$\begin{array}{r} \$301.62 \\ \times \quad .75 \\ \hline 150810 \\ 211134 \\ \hline \$226.2150 \end{array}$$

$$\begin{array}{r} 5,027.00 \\ + \quad 226.22 \\ \hline \mathbf{\$5,253.22} \end{array}$$

TOPIC 3: Introduction to Data Analysis pages 890–892

1. 10
2. $3.29
3. $4\frac{1}{4}$
4. 7 lbs. 5 oz.
5. 92°
6. $1.23
7. $\frac{26}{32} \div \frac{2}{2} = \frac{13}{16}$
8. $\frac{12}{18} \div \frac{6}{6} = \frac{2}{3}$
9. $\frac{\$750}{\$450} \div \frac{\$150}{\$450} = \frac{5}{3}$
10. $\frac{1}{3}$

Displaying Numerical Data pages 893–902

1. 5 g
2. 405 calories
3. $\frac{640}{300} = \frac{32}{15}$
4. $46\frac{2}{3}$g
5. $1,500
6. 28%
7. $\frac{7}{10}$
8. $$\begin{array}{r} \$1,500 \\ \times \quad .015 \\ \hline 7\ 500 \\ 15\ 00 \\ \hline 22.500 \\ \mathbf{\$22.50} \end{array}$$
9. c
10. b
11. d
12. a
13. 10,000 kites
14. 20,000
15. $$\begin{array}{r} 50,000 \\ 80,000 \\ 20,000 \\ 30,000 \\ + \ 40,000 \\ \hline \mathbf{220,000} \end{array}$$
16. $\frac{5}{8}$
17. Twin Towers
18. $$\begin{array}{r} \mathbf{44,000} \\ 5\overline{)220,000} \\ 20 \\ \hline 20 \\ 20 \\ \hline 0000 \\ 0000 \\ \hline \end{array}$$

19. b
20. a
21. c

TOPIC 4: Introduction to Probability
pages 903–908

1. 1; 100%
2. 0; 0%
3. $\frac{1}{5}$; 20%
4. $\frac{1}{3}$; $33\frac{1}{3}$%
5. $\frac{1}{8}$; $12\frac{1}{2}$%
6. $\frac{3}{8}$; $37\frac{1}{2}$%
7. $\frac{2}{5}$; 40%
8. $\frac{2}{5}$; 40%
9. $\frac{8}{25}$; 32% (3, 6, 9, 12, 15, 18, 21, 24)
10. $\frac{48}{50} = \frac{24}{25}$; 96%
11. a) $\frac{3}{4}$; 75%
    b) $\frac{2}{3}$; $66\frac{2}{3}$%
12. a) $\frac{1}{2}$; 50%
    b) $\frac{2}{5}$; 40%

POST-TESTS

POST-TEST 1: LANGUAGE AND WRITING SKILLS

The Language and Writing Skills Post-Test will show you how much you remember about the information you studied in this section. Take the test without looking back for help or answers.

The Post-Test has been divided into two sections. The first part is a test of your overall knowledge of language skills. The second part is a test of your writing ability and asks you to write a paragraph.

Once you complete the test, check your answers with the Answer Key starting on page 942. Then fill out the evaluation chart. This chart will tell you which sections of the book you might want to review.

PART I

TOPIC 1: NOUNS AND PRONOUNS

This section tests your knowledge of nouns: common and proper nouns, singular and plural nouns, and possessive nouns. It also tests your knowledge of subject, object, and possessive pronouns.

Directions: Each of the following sentences has an underlined part. Below each sentence are three options for writing the underlined part. Choose the option that makes the sentence correct. The first option is always the same as the underlined part of the original sentence.

1. Both Tom and Jeff wanted to be elected Captain of the community softball team.
   (1) Both Tom and Jeff wanted to be elected Captain
   (2) Both Tom and Jeff wanted to be elected captain
   (3) both Tom and Jeff wanted to be elected captain

2. They have played on the team for five years.
   (1) They
   (2) Them
   (3) Their

3. Their both excellent softball players.
   (1) Their
   (2) Theirs
   (3) They're

4. On Saturday, the players votes were counted.
   (1) players
   (2) players'
   (3) player's

5. The men with the most votes was Jeff.
   (1) men
   (2) mans
   (3) man

6. Jeff will assign they to their positions.
   (1) they
   (2) them
   (3) him

7. The games will be played at Hope Valley park
   (1) Hope Valley park
   (2) Hope valley park
   (3) Hope Valley Park

TOPIC 2: VERBS

This section tests your knowledge of verbs: forming verb tenses, using time clues to verb tense, irregular verb forms, and subject-verb agreement.

Directions: Underline the correct form of the verb to complete each sentence.

8. The students in the class *(are, is)* happy with their grades.

9. Your advice *(were, was)* what saved our garden.

10. Next week, Jim *(will race, raced)* in the track meet.

11. The manager *(plan, plans)* to quit her job after payday.

12. The strength of these workers *(make, makes)* any job easy.

13. Last night, Sheila *(announces, announced)* her engagement.

14. Bill or I *(drive, drives)* the car pool every Wednesday.

15. Right now Uncle Ray *(is standing, was standing)* on his head.

16. You *(have, has)* got to tell Bruce the truth.

17. My uncles *(tell, tells)* terrible jokes.

18. They *(do, does)* their taxes on April 15 every year.

TOPIC 3: SENTENCE STRUCTURE

This section tests your knowledge of different methods for combining ideas in sentences: using joining words, describing phrases, and parallel structure.

Directions: Each of the following sentences has an underlined part. Below each sentence are three options for writing the underlined part. Choose the option that makes the sentence correct. The first option is always the same as the underlined part of the original sentence.

19. The rain lasted for three days, but the rivers were flooded.

(1) days, but
(2) days; so
(3) days, so

20. The fish are frying in the pan that we caught at the lake.

(1) are frying in the pan that we caught at the lake
(2) that we caught at the lake are frying in the pan
(3) are frying in the lake that we caught in the pan

21. The nurse smelled smoke, however, she called for help.

(1) smoke, however, she
(2) smoke; however, she
(3) smoke; consequently, she

22. The president talked, laughed, and he was joking.

(1) he was joking
(2) he joked
(3) joked

23. Sally bumped into the table walking across the room.

(1) Sally bumped into the table walking across the room.
(2) Walking across the room, Sally bumped into the table.
(3) Walking across the room, the table bumped into Sally.

24. When the curtain fell the audience cheered.

(1) fell the
(2) fell; the
(3) fell, the

25. Farhad wants his family to come to the United States; therefore, he is saving money for their tickets.

(1) States; therefore, he
(2) States; instead, he
(3) States; nevertheless, he

26. Jennifer can take the job if, she buys a car.

(1) job if, she
(2) job, if she
(3) job if she

27. Norma is tired, but she is still working.

(1) tired, but
(2) tired, so
(3) tired, before

TOPIC 4: PUNCTUATION

This section tests your knowledge of many punctuation marks you have studied in this text.

Directions: Only one of the sentences in each of the following groups is punctuated correctly. Circle the number of the correct sentence.

28. (1) Terry screamed, "Shut the door."
(2) Terry screamed, "Shut the door!"
(3) Terry screamed, Shut the door!

29. (1) Sandy, will you please give me a call?
(2) Sandy will you please give me a call?
(3) Sandy, will you please give me a call.

30. (1) Mrs. Popovich a true friend, cooked dinner for me.
(2) Mrs. Popovich a true friend cooked dinner for me.
(3) Mrs. Popovich, a true friend, cooked dinner for me.

31. (1) The movers can't get the piano up the stairs.
(2) The movers cant' get the piano up the stairs.
(3) The movers cant get the piano up the stairs.

32. (1) Science, English math, and literature are important subjects to study.
(2) Science English math and literature are important subjects to study.
(3) Science, English, math, and literature are important subjects to study.

PART II

WRITING A PARAGRAPH

Directions: This part of the Post-Test will give you a chance to demonstrate how well you write. Pick just one of the three suggested topics. Read the choices carefully. You should brainstorm or cluster ideas before you begin writing. When you finish writing, go back and reread what you have written. Check to be certain that you have used the information you learned about writing paragraphs. Also check spelling, capitalization, punctuation, and sentence structure. Then make any needed changes.

Topic 1

Think of a person that you admire—a close friend, a coworker, a parent, or any person you think highly of. In a paragraph, explain why you admire that person. What things about the person do you respect most?

Topic 2

Imagine what your perfect job would be like. Where would you work? What would you do? Describe your perfect job in a paragraph with lots of details.

Topic 3

Almost all of us have a good love story to tell, whether it is about ourselves or someone else. Think of a love story you could tell. It could be sweet or sad, silly or serious, or some of each. Write a paragraph telling your love story.

Answers start on page 942.

POST-TEST ANSWER KEY

Part I

Topic 1: Nouns and Pronouns

1. (2) The noun *captain* should not be capitalized because it is not used as a person's title.
2. (1) No correction is necessary.
3. (3) If you substitute *They are* in the sentence, it makes sense.
4. (2) The plural noun must be made possessive.
5. (3) Only one man could have gotten the most votes.
6. (2) The object pronoun must be used because it is not the subject of the sentence. The pronoun must be plural to agree with *their*.
7. (3) All three words should be capitalized to show that this is the specific name of the park.

Topic 2: Verbs

8.	are	The verb must agree with the plural subject *students*.
9.	was	The subject, *advice*, is singular.
10.	will race	The time clue *Next week* tells you to use the future tense.
11.	plans	The subject, *manager*, is singular.
12.	makes	The subject is *strength*, a singular noun.
13.	announced	The time clue *Last night* tells you to use the past tense.
14.	drive	The two parts of the subject are joined by *or*. The verb must agree with the closest part of the subject, *I*.
15.	is standing	The time clue *Right now* tells you to use the present continuing tense.
16.	have	Use *have* to agree with *You*.
17.	tell	The subject, *uncles*, is plural.
18.	do	This verb form agrees with *They*.

Topic 3: Sentence Structure

19. (3) The conjunction *so* shows that the first part of the sentence caused the second part.
20. (2) The original sentence says that we caught the pan at the lake. The describing phrase *that we caught at the lake* should be placed next to *fish*.
21. (3) The connector *consequently* shows that the first part of the sentence caused the second part. Note also the correct punctuation for this connector.
22. (3) For parallel structure, the items *talked*, *laughed*, and *joked* must be in the same form.
23. (2) The original sentence says that the table was walking across the room. The describing phrase *walking across the room* must be placed next to *Sally*.
24. (3) When a subordinating conjunction comes first in a sentence, the two ideas in the sentence are separated by a comma.
25. (1) No correction is necessary.
26. (3) No comma is needed when the subordinating conjunction comes in the middle of the sentence.
27. (1) No correction is necessary.

Topic 4: Punctuation

28. (2) This sentence contains a direct quote that shows strong emotion.
29. (1) This sentence is a question. The name *Sandy* is used in direct address and must be set off with comma.
30. (3) The renaming phrase *a true friend* must be set off by commas.
31. (1) The apostrophe takes the place of the missing letters when the word *cannot* is made into a contraction.
32. (3) Commas must be placed after every item in a series except the last one.

Part II
Writing a Paragraph

In this part of the Post-Test, you had to write a paragraph on your own. If possible, have an instructor work with you to evaluate your paragraph. If you are evaluating your paragraph on your own, be sure to put it aside for a day or two first. Then use the following questions to help you.

1. Does your paragraph have a clear topic sentence? Topic sentences are explained on pages 188–190.
2. Do the other sentences in the paragraph support the topic sentence? Supporting sentences are discussed on pages 188–190.
3. Did you have trouble coming up with ideas to put in your paragraph? If so, review clustering on pages 69–70 and brainstorming on pages 127–128.
4. Did you have trouble with punctuation, verbs, pronouns, or other areas of grammar? If so, you can find pages to review in the Table of Contents.

If you want to try writing another paragraph, go back to Section II of the Post-Test. Choose another of the topics to write about and evaluate it in the same way. Remember, the best way to improve your writing is to write!

POST-TEST EVALUATION CHART

Check your answers on pages 942–943. Then find the number of each question you missed on the chart and circle it in the second column. Then you will know which pages you might need to review.

	Item Number	Review Pages	Number Correct
Topic 1: Nouns and Pronouns			
Nouns	1, 4, 5, 7	87–93	
Pronouns	2, 3, 6	94–99	______ /7
Topic 2: Verbs			
Verb tense	10, 13, 15	105–120	
Subject-verb agreement	8, 9, 11, 12, 14, 16, 17, 18	128–137	______ /11
Topic 3: Sentence Structure			
Conjunctions	19, 27	165–168	
Connectors	21, 25	169–171	
Describing phrases	20, 23	181–183	
Parallel structure	22	184–186	
Subordinating conjunctions	24, 26	172–174	______ /9
Topic 4: Punctuation			
Quotation marks	28	121–122	
Types of sentences	29	73–76	
Contractions	31	100–102	
Commas	30, 32	138–141	______ /5
	Total Correct		______ /32

POST-TEST 2: SOCIAL STUDIES

The Social Studies Post-Test should give you a good idea of how well you have learned the skills you have studied in this section. You should take the Post-Test after you have completed all the chapters.

Directions: Study each passage or illustration, then answer the questions that follow.

Questions 1 and 2 are based on the following passage.

> That man over there says that a woman needs to be helped into carriages and lifted over ditches. . . . Nobody ever helps me into carriages, or over mud-puddles, or gives me any best place. And a'nt I a woman?
>
> Look at my arm! I have ploughed, and planted, and gathered into barns, and no man could head me! And a'nt I a woman?
>
> I would work as much and eat as much as a man, when I could get it, and bear the lash as well. And a'nt I a woman?
>
> I have borne thirteen children and seen 'em most all sold off to slavery, and when I cried out with my mother's grief, none but Jesus heard me! And a'nt I a woman?

1. Who is the speaker in this passage?

(1) a modern politician running for office
(2) a black woman who was a slave
(3) a wealthy, nineteenth-century Southern woman
(4) an early settler in New England
(5) a twentieth-century feminist

2. When the speaker in this passage says, "Look at my arm! I have ploughed, and planted, and gathered into barns, and no man could head me!," she means that

(1) she could work as hard as any man
(2) she was forced to do work that women shouldn't have to do
(3) she loved planting and harvest time
(4) she appreciates the help that men have given her
(5) a real woman must do hard physical labor

Questions 3 and 4 are based on the following passage.

How many languages do you speak? Only one? Actually, whenever you speak you use a particular form of language called a dialect, and your dialect probably changes to suit your listeners. A dialect consists of a special vocabulary, unique pronunciations, and certain habitual ways of organizing words in sentences.

No two people speak in exactly the same way, but any group of individuals that spends time together or shares interests will develop unique speech patterns that eventually become a dialect. For instance, residents of the same geographic area will share an accent and vocabulary. Similarly, people with the same occupation, like astronauts and doctors, usually develop their own special jargon.

3. What do people who speak the same dialect have in common?

(1) Their voices are almost identical.
(2) They were born in the same generation.
(3) They put sentences together in similar patterns.
(4) They share the same opinions and beliefs.
(5) It is difficult for outsiders to understand them.

4. Which of the following groups of people would most likely speak the same dialect?

(1) people with red hair
(2) people who surf at Huntington Beach
(3) people who write a lot of letters
(4) people who hate their jobs
(5) people who eat Primo brand spaghetti sauce

Questions 5 and 6 are based on the following illustration.

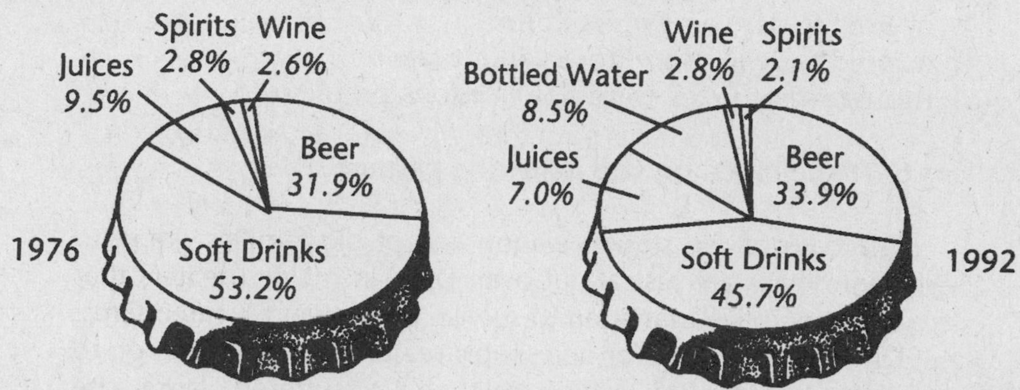

5. Which of the following was a new factor in the drink market in 1992?
   (1) juices
   (2) soft drinks
   (3) beer
   (4) bottled water
   (5) wine

6. From 1976 to 1992, which type of beverage suffered the greatest loss of market share?
   (1) beer
   (2) bottled water
   (3) wine
   (4) juices
   (5) soft drinks

Question 7 is based on the following passage.

> "I can't make a . . . thing out of this tax problem," complained President Warren G. Harding to a friend. "I listen to one side and they seem right and then—God!—I talk to the other side and they seem to be right. . . . I know that somewhere there is a book that will give me the truth, but I couldn't read the book. I know somewhere there is an economist who knows the truth, but I don't know where to find him and haven't the sense to know him and trust him when I find him. God! What a job."

7. The main idea of this paragraph is that Warren G. Harding
   (1) provided leadership on the tax issue
   (2) did not know what to do about the tax problem
   (3) needed to hire a new economist
   (4) wanted to read more books about taxes
   (5) thought that taxes were not a serious problem

Questions 8–10 are based on the following passage.

The days of the station wagon and of big families going to drive-in movies are just about over. Drive-in movie theaters that are still open have managed to survive by showing X-rated films.

Drive-ins are dying for one simple reason—people don't go to them anymore. Box office sales have suffered from the popularity of VCRs and theatres in shopping malls.

Drive-in owners are also tempted to sell to land-hungry developers, who are willing to pay big bucks for property near major highways. One by one, the drive-ins are being replaced by shopping centers and industrial parks.

8. Drive-ins are losing customers because
   (1) land has become more expensive
   (2) people have smaller families than they used to
   (3) VCRs and mall theaters are taking away business
   (4) there are fewer X-rated films
   (5) industrial parks are being built on their former sites

9. The main idea of this passage is that
   (1) the days of the drive-in are just about over
   (2) drive-ins will survive by showing X-rated movies
   (3) drive-ins cannot compete with VCRs and mall theatres
   (4) drive-ins are being bought up by land-hungry developers
   (5) drive-ins are an important part of American life

10. Given the information in this passage, you might predict that in ten years
   (1) drive-ins will make a strong comeback
   (2) land prices will go down
   (3) automakers will stop making station wagons
   (4) many existing drive-ins will be closed
   (5) there will be more X-rated films

Questions 11 and 12 are based on the following chart.

U.S. PETROLEUM IMPORTS BY SOURCE (thousands of barrels per day)					
Source	1978	1979	1980	1981	1982
Arab OPEC	2,963	3,056	2,551	1,848	840
Other OPEC	2,788	2,581	1,749	1,475	1,273
Non-OPEC	2,613	2,819	2,609	2,672	2,928
Total	8,364	8,456	6,909	5,995	5,041

11. American oil imports peaked in the year

(1) 1978
(2) 1979
(3) 1980
(4) 1981
(5) 1982

12. Based on this chart, you could conclude that between 1979 and 1982

(1) imported oil from Arab OPEC members dropped dramatically
(2) Americans increased their dependence on foreign oil
(3) OPEC expanded its influence in the United States
(4) United States demand for oil remained steady
(5) Americans ended their dependence on foreign oil

Question 13 is based on the following illustration.

Background Clues: In 1995, Congress considered several welfare reform bills. Members of Congress wanted the states, instead of the federal government, to control major welfare programs. This would mean that each state would decide which welfare programs to fund and in what amounts.

13. The cartoonist thinks that welfare programs are
    (1) full of problems
    (2) best run by state governments
    (3) very helpful
    (4) a good way to retrain workers
    (5) encouraging people to have children

Questions 14–16 are based on the following passage.

Sociologist David Riesman, in his book *The Lonely Crowd,* describes two types of Americans. First is the inner-directed person whose life is controlled by his or her own strongly held inner values. An example of an inner-directed man is the rugged frontiersman, who has to rely on himself while he works on his homestead.

The second type of American is other-directed. Other-directed people are more interested in the approval of other people than in personal values. A member of a teenage gang and a successful mid-level manager in a large company are examples of other-directed people.

14. Which ad might appeal to an inner-directed man?

(1) A lone, good-looking cowboy on a horse is lighting a cigarette. The ad reads, "This is Marlboro country."
(2) "Subaru is the largest-selling car in New England."
(3) "Come join millions! Celebrate the 100th anniversary of the Statue of Liberty in New York."
(4) "Come to Disney World, the dream vacation for every child!"
(5) "Buy Crest, America's best-selling toothpaste."

15. An other-directed person generally

(1) is a gang member
(2) needs the approval of others
(3) likes to be in the wilderness
(4) is an independent thinker
(5) works as a manager

16. An example of an other-directed person is

(1) an independent, millionaire oilman
(2) a bad-tempered, foul-mouthed tennis star
(3) a nun who can no longer follow church teachings
(4) a practicing member of a religious sect
(5) a hermit who lives in a cave

Question 17 is based on the following ad.

WOMEN!

Fight the Equal Rights Amendment!
It will not help you—It will hurt you.

The Equal Rights Amendment is a threat to all women. If it passes, it will rob you of

- your right to be a homemaker
- your protection from being drafted and serving in combat
- your right to alimony

17. The writers of the above ad wanted women to believe that passage of the Equal Rights Amendment would have
    (1) taken privileges away from women
    (2) promoted male control of society
    (3) required that men and women use the same bathrooms
    (4) ensured that women dominated society
    (5) been fair to both men and women

Questions 18 and 19 are based on the following passage.

Over one hundred years ago, Henry David Thoreau went to jail to protest the Mexican War. In recent times, many people have followed Thoreau's example and openly broken a law in order to bring public attention to injustice.

The great Indian leader Gandhi took Thoreau's ideas further. When convicted of breaking a law, Gandhi would serve a prison sentence rather than pay the smallest fine. In prison, he went on hunger strikes to draw even more attention to himself and his cause, the independence of India from Great Britain.

When good and caring people are thrown in jail for their beliefs, it often makes others think about the laws and conditions that they are trying to change. Peaceful but determined protesters in the United States, such as Martin Luther King, Jr., were inspired by Gandhi and adapted his ideas to the struggle for racial equality. When King and others were jailed for their beliefs, they helped many Americans realize that segregation was wrong. Their example helped strike down the laws that kept segregation alive.

18. After Martin Luther King, Jr., went to jail,
   (1) Thoreau was jailed for his beliefs
   (2) segregation laws in the United States started changing
   (3) India won its independence from Great Britain
   (4) Gandhi went on a hunger strike
   (5) the United States fought the Mexican War

19. It is the author's opinion that
   (1) Thoreau opposed the Mexican War
   (2) Gandhi went to jail rather than pay fines
   (3) Martin Luther King, Jr., used the nonviolent tactics of Gandhi
   (4) Gandhi was a great leader
   (5) segregation laws are no longer legal in the United States

Questions 20 and 21 are based on the following map.

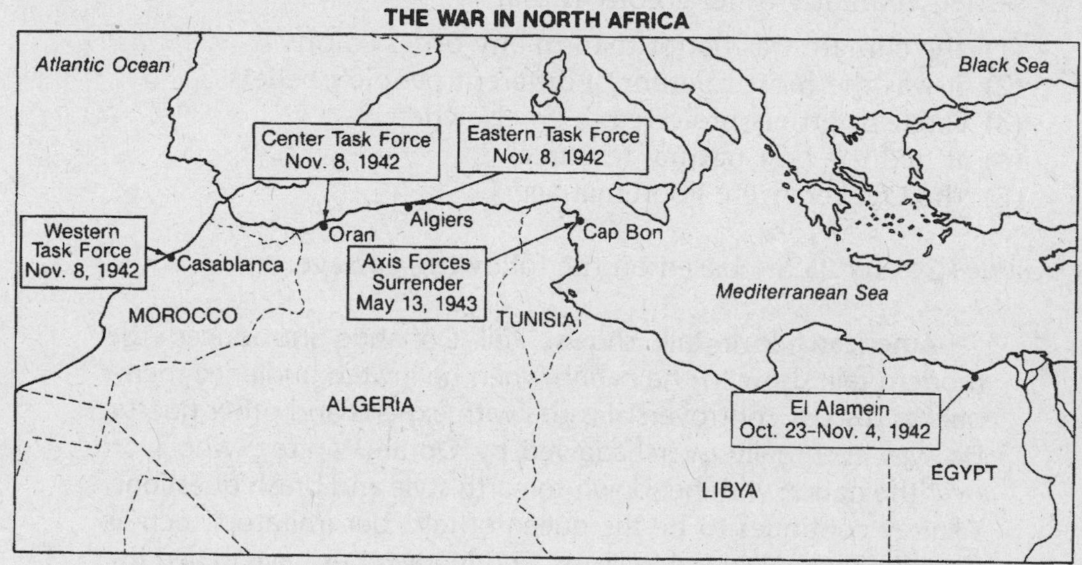

20. In what country did the Axis forces in North Africa surrender?
   (1) Egypt
   (2) Libya
   (3) Tunisia
   (4) Algeria
   (5) Morocco

21. How much time elapsed from the first Allied victory in North Africa at El Alamein on November 4, 1942, to the landing of the Western, Center, and Eastern Task Forces at Casablanca, Oran, and Algiers?
   (1) 6 months
   (2) 3 months
   (3) 23 days
   (4) 1 week
   (5) 4 days

Questions 22 and 23 are based on the following passage.

Of all the original thirteen colonies, Pennsylvania attracted the most non-English settlers. It was also the colony that had the greatest tolerance of religious and cultural differences. It had been founded by Quakers, led by William Penn, who wanted to create a colony based on religious freedom and fairness to all people.

22. An important value of the founders of Pennsylvania was
(1) economic freedom
(2) separation of nationalities
(3) conversion of the Indians to Christianity
(4) religious freedom
(5) return to nature

23. A likely reason that Pennsylvania attracted more non-English settlers than any other colony is that
(1) the climate was better than in any other colony
(2) it was the most tolerant of different people's beliefs
(3) English settlers preferred to go elsewhere
(4) it had the best natural resources
(5) the Quakers were good managers

Questions 24 and 25 are based on the following passage.

Americans love talk shows. Phil Donahue introduced the modern talk show to the nation when he invited audience members to discuss controversial issues with experts and other guests. He was eventually overshadowed by Oprah Winfrey, who won over the nation with her down-to-earth style and brash questions. Winfrey continues to be the queen of talk, but imitators such as Geraldo Rivera, Montel Williams, and Jenny Jones have joined the fight for a piece of the huge talk show audience. Talk shows have been criticized for stirring up conflict and focusing on overly sensational topics. Nevertheless, they get consistently high ratings.

24. According to the passage, the host of the most popular talk show is
(1) Phil Donahue
(2) Oprah Winfrey
(3) Geraldo Rivera
(4) Montel Williams
(5) Jenny Jones

25. There is enough information in the passage to determine that
    (1) Americans will watch shows about controversial issues
    (2) Americans prefer newer shows to older shows
    (3) the popularity of Geraldo Rivera will be short-lived
    (4) "The Oprah Winfrey Show" is better than "Donahue"
    (5) talk shows are valuable educational experiences

Question 26 is based on the following passage.

Canada is the second largest nation in the world, but it is defended by a tiny military less than half the size of the United States Marine Corps.

The Canadian army has fewer than 300 troops protecting 3.5 million square miles of northern territory. An amusement park in Edmonton has more submarines than the Canadian navy. In fact, Canada's territories are so sparsely monitored that a Nazi weather station, built secretly on the Canadian coast in 1943, went undiscovered until 1981.

Nevertheless, Canada's military has earned an international reputation for protecting the peace in other nations. Canadian troops are currently deployed on 14 different United Nations peacekeeping operations.

26. According to the passage, the Canadian armed forces are unable to
    (1) defend themselves
    (2) purchase submarines
    (3) monitor Canadian territory
    (4) recruit enough soldiers
    (5) stay out of United Nations operations

Answers start on page 956.

POST-TEST ANSWER KEY

1. (2) The speaker says she could "bear the lash," and the last paragraph states that she had borne thirteen children and seen most of them sold as slaves.
2. (1) She describes heavy farm work that she did. When she says that no man could "head" her, she means that no man could do any more work than she.
3. (3) The first paragraph tells you that a dialect includes certain ways of organizing sentences.
4. (2) The second paragraph tells you that people develop a dialect when they spend time together or share an interest. The surfers at Huntington Beach do both.
5. (4) All of the choices except bottled water appear on the graph for 1976 as well as on the graph for 1992.
6. (5) Among the choices, both juices and soft drinks lost market share. However, soft drinks lost a larger percentage of market share than juices did.
7. (2) The first sentence states the main idea: "I can't make a . . . thing out of this tax problem." In the rest of the paragraph, Harding describes his confusion and need for guidance.
8. (3) In the second paragraph, you are told that box office sales have suffered from the popularity of VCRs and theatres in shopping malls.
9. (1) The first sentence states that the days of the station wagon and big families going to the drive-in are just about over. The rest of the passage paints a bleak future for the remaining drive-ins.
10. (4) The last sentence states that the drive-ins are being replaced by shopping centers and industrial parks. There is no indication that the trend will reverse.
11. (2) The highest number in the "Total" row is 8,456, which is in the 1979 column.
12. (1) Imports from Arab OPEC countries dropped from 3,056,000 barrels a day in 1979 to 840,000 barrels a day in 1982. If you test the other choices against the data on the chart, you can see that none is true.
13. (1) The symbol labeled *welfare* is a can of worms. When we call something "a can of worms," we mean that it is full of problems.
14. (1) The lone cowboy looks like a tough, independent individual, an inner-directed person.
15. (2) *Other-directed* is defined in the second paragraph as a person who is more interested in the approval of other people than in values.
16. (4) A devout member of a religious sect would look for approval from others in the sect.
17. (1) The writers of the ad listed some privileges that women might want. The ad says that if the Equal Rights Amendment passes, women will not be able to have these privileges.
18. (2) The last sentence states that, after King and others were jailed, the laws began changing.
19. (4) Gandhi did many important things, and many people consider him a great leader. This is a personal belief. The other choices are facts that can be proven.
20. (3) According to the map, the Axis forces surrendered on May 13, 1943, at Cap Bon in Tunisia.
21. (5) According to the map, the Western Task Force at Casablanca, the Center Task Force at Oran, and the Eastern Task Force at Algiers, all landed on November 8, 1942, just four days after the end of the battle of El Alamein.

22. (4) The passage states that the colony had the greatest tolerance of religious differences and that the Quakers wanted to create a colony based on religious freedom.

23. (2) Since the colony was the most tolerant of other people's beliefs, it makes sense that it would attract people who were different from the English.

24. (2) The passage states that Oprah Winfrey is the queen of talk.

25. (1) The fact that talk shows get consistently high ratings is evidence that Americans will watch shows about controversial issues.

26. (3) The passage tells you that Canadian territory is sparsely monitored. It also tells you that the tiny Canadian military must protect a lot of territory. There is no evidence for the other choices.

POST-TEST EVALUATION CHART

Use the answer key on pages 956–957 to check your answers. Then, find the number of each question you missed on this chart and circle it in the second column. Then you will know which chapters you might need to review.

	Skill	Item Numbers	Number Correct
Chapter 1	• Finding details • Words in context • Restating information • Summarizing information • Main idea of a paragraph • Main idea of a passage	24 15 2 26 7 9	______/6
Chapter 2	• Locating information on a chart • Locating information on a graph • Interpreting graphs • Locating information on a map	11 5 6 20	______/4
Chapter 3	• Application	14, 16	______/2
Chapter 4	• Fact and opinion • Inference • Political cartoons • Hypotheses • Predicting outcomes	19 1 13 23 10	______/5
Chapter 5	• Sequence • Sequence on maps • Cause and effect • Compare and contrast	18 21 8 3	______/4
Chapter 6	• Adequacy of information • Interpreting charts • Logical reasoning • Values • Propaganda	25 12 4 22 17	______/5
		Total Correct	______/26

POST-TEST 3: SCIENCE

This two-part Science Post-Test will help you find out what you have learned from this section. Part I will test how well you remember some of the science words and ideas you have learned in this book. Part II will test your ability to understand science passages in multiple-choice format.

This test is not timed. Do the best you can without looking at the rest of the section. Then see pages 970–971 to find out how to evaluate your answers.

PART I: SCIENCE KNOWLEDGE

SECTION A: SCIENCE TERMS

Directions: These are some of the scientific words you need to know. In each group, write the letter of the correct definition in front of each word.

Group 1

1. ________ atmosphere
2. ________ chromosomes
3. ________ chlorophyll
4. ________ erosion
5. ________ fossil fuels
6. ________ nucleus
7. ________ litmus paper
8. ________ work

a. the center of a cell
b. oil, coal, and natural gas
c. using force to move something
d. green chemical that plants use to make food
e. threadlike groups of genes in cell nucleus
f. the layer of air around the Earth
g. the wearing away of earth by water or wind
h. turns red in acids, blue in bases

Group 2

9. ________ conductor
10. ________ ecology
11. ________ enzymes
12. ________ nerves
13. ________ invertebrate
14. ________ matter
15. ________ solution
16. ________ toxic

a. carry messages to and from brain
b. chemicals that help digest food
c. anything that takes up space
d. poisonous
e. the study of the balance of nature
f. any animal without a backbone
g. anything electricity flows through easily
h. substance that cannot be separated by filtering

SECTION B: TRUE/FALSE

Directions: Write *T* (true) or *F* (false) in the blank before each statement. Then make all false statements into true statements by changing one or more of the words in **bold type** (see the example).

carbohydrates
Example: __F__ **Proteins**, ~~**monohydrates**~~, **fats**, **vitamins**, **minerals**, and **water** are the six main nutrients your body needs.

______ 17. The **vibration** of molecules in matter is what causes **sound**.

______ 18. Photosynthesis is how **fungus** plants use sunlight to make food from carbon dioxide, water, and minerals.

______ 19. **Reptiles** lay their eggs in water and change as they grow up from gill-breathing tadpoles to lung-breathing land animals.

______ 20. A **recessive** gene will always override a **dominant** gene.

______ 21. Your lungs are the main organs in your **digestive** system.

______ 22. White light is really made up of **many different colors**.

______ 23. An **atom** of a chemical compound is made up of two or more **molecules**.

______ 24. A person who needs a drug regularly to handle everyday stress is **psychologically dependent** on the drug.

______ 25. Cover crops, windbreaks, crop rotation, conservation tillage, and contour plowing are all ways to prevent **soil erosion**.

PART II: READING SKILLS

Directions: Read each passage or study the illustration carefully. Then circle the one best answer for each of the questions following. Feel free to look back in the passage to help yourself answer the questions.

Questions 26 and 27 are based on the following passage and graph.

John Washington is a wildlife manager in a national forest. His job is to make sure that all the animals in the forest are doing well and that there are not too many or too few of any one species of animal.

In the forest live a few wood ducks. For the past five years, John has been trying to increase the number of wood ducks by setting out artificial nesting boxes near streams and ponds. Every year he kept records of the number of wood ducks seen in the forest, to see if his experiment is working. Here is a graph of his results.

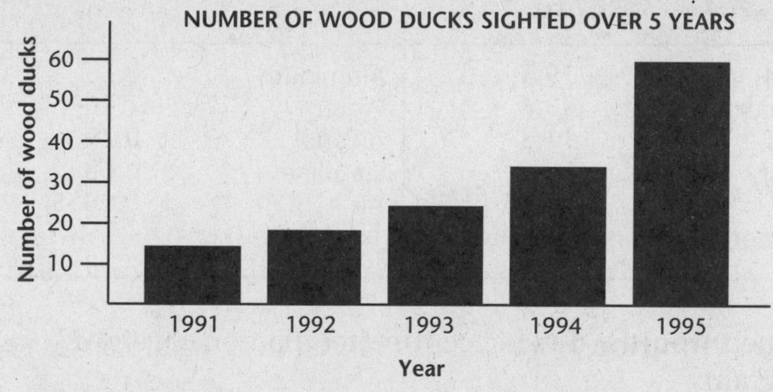

26. About how many wood ducks were sighted in the year John started his experiment?
    (1) 5
    (2) 15
    (3) 25
    (4) 40
    (5) 60

27. What is the hypothesis John is testing with his experiment?
    (1) Wildlife managers should take care of animals.
    (2) There aren't enough wood ducks in the forest.
    (3) The wood ducks need more nesting places in the forest.
    (4) People can count wood ducks accurately.
    (5) Wood ducks breed every five years.

Questions 28 and 29 are based on the following passage and chart.

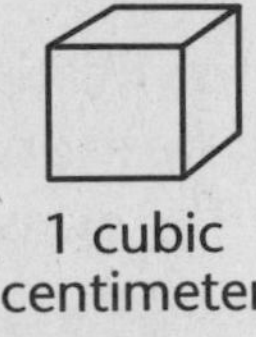

Physicists use the idea of density to describe different materials. Very dense materials are very heavy. Iron and lead are dense materials. In contrast, Styrofoam is not dense at all and is quite light.

The density of something is expressed in the number of grams that a cubic centimeter of that substance weighs (in the metric system of measurement). For example, one cubic centimeter of pure iron weighs 7.86 grams; we say that iron has a density of 7.86 grams per cubic centimeter. The density of a pure substance is always the same. If you had two cubic centimeters of iron, they would weigh exactly twice as much, or 15.72 grams.

The chart below shows the densities of some common substances.

Material	Density (in g/cm^3)	Material	Density (in g/cm^3)
Gold	19.3	Aluminum	2.7
Mercury	13.6	Water	1.00
Lead	11.3	Alcohol	0.79
Silver	10.5	Gasoline	0.68
Iron	7.86	Air	0.0013
Diamonds	3.5		

28. How much would a 6-cubic centimeter diamond weigh?
(1) 3.5 grams
(2) 6 grams
(3) 9.5 grams
(4) 21 grams
(5) 35 grams

29. An archeologist dug up an old crown. There were 30 cubic centimeters of metal in the crown, and it weighed 315 grams. What was the crown made of?
(1) gold
(2) lead
(3) silver
(4) iron
(5) aluminum

Questions 30 and 31 are based on the following passage.

Spaceships of the future will probably be very different from our present-day rockets and shuttles. First, they will be designed to remain in space all the time, using small shuttles to carry passengers and freight up and down to planets. Because of this, they won't have any wings or the traditional pointed nose necessary to move through air.

These spaceships will also probably be much bigger. The spaceships we have today must be fairly small because it takes a great deal of fuel for even a small ship to escape the Earth's gravity. In the future, spaceships traveling between the stars may be large enough to carry thousands of people, plus enough plants for oxygen and fresh food and perhaps even some animals for meat. A really large ship could be a complete, well-balanced ecosystem, able to survive on its own for years.

30. Why are present-day rockets pointed at the nose?

(1) They look more military that way.
(2) They aren't big enough to be round.
(3) They have to move through air.
(4) The instruments have to point forward.
(5) They have no wings.

31. Why would you infer that a spaceship traveling to other stars might need to be a complete ecosystem?

(1) It costs less that way.
(2) It will take a long time to travel between stars.
(3) It takes less fuel to travel in a large ship.
(4) People like to have plants and animals around.
(5) Fresh food is better than canned or frozen food.

Questions 32–34 are based on the following passage.

About one out of every twenty young children has a common behavioral problem called attention deficit disorder (ADD). Children with this problem are also called hyperactive children. A child with ADD is almost always moving, even when sleeping or watching TV. He usually has trouble paying attention to anything for more than a minute or two, so he often doesn't get very much done. He often gets distracted or frustrated very easily and may have trouble waiting for anything.

Parents who suspect their child may have ADD should have the child examined by a team including a child psychologist, a neurologist, and a developmental pediatrician. Children with ADD can often be helped by special behavior management techniques, special diets, or medicines, but each child is different. Treatment may have to change as the child grows and changes. No treatment should be started or medicines given on the advice of an ordinary family doctor or pediatrician alone. With the right help, children with ADD can grow up to be happy, healthy, and capable people.

32. The first paragraph mainly tells

(1) how children usually behave
(2) how to help a child with ADD
(3) how active children of different ages should be
(4) how an ADD child acts differently from other children
(5) how to keep a child from being distracted or frustrated

33. From the passage you can infer that

(1) some foods may make ADD worse in some children
(2) only boys get ADD
(3) children with ADD will probably not get better
(4) all children with ADD must take special medication
(5) children with ADD like to watch TV

34. According to the passage, who would be able to tell whether a child is hyperactive?

(1) the family's doctor
(2) a group of medical specialists
(3) the child's teacher
(4) another parent with a hyperactive child
(5) the child's grandparents, who have experience with how children act

Questions 35 and 36 are based on the following passage and graph.

Below is a solubility graph showing how a new vitamin powder called Vitamix dissolves in milk at different temperatures. Use this graph to answer the next three questions. (Note: Liters and milligrams are measurements from the metric system. You can still read the graph without knowing exactly how much a milligram or a liter is.)

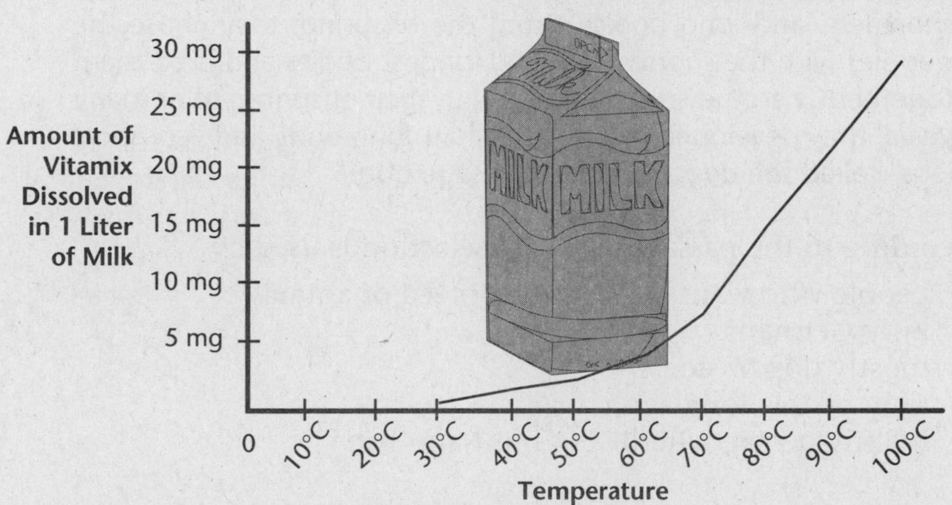

35. The general trend of the graph line shows that

(1) hot liquids dissolve powders better than cool liquids
(2) the higher the temperature, the less Vitamix will dissolve
(3) the more liquid used, the more Vitamix will dissolve
(4) the more Vitamix is dissolved, the lower the temperature will get
(5) the higher the temperature, the more Vitamix will dissolve

36. How was the information for this graph probably obtained?

(1) Many people happened to notice how much Vitamix would dissolve in milk at different temperatures.
(2) Someone did an experiment on dissolving Vitamix in water.
(3) A survey was taken.
(4) Several people did experiments on dissolving Vitamix in milk.
(5) A famous scientist predicted how Vitamix would dissolve in milk.

Questions 37 and 38 are based on the following passage.

Artificial selection has been used for centuries by people who wanted to develop new, more useful types of animals. In artificial selection, a breeder chooses animals closest to the type he or she wants and then breeds them together. Then the most desirable of the offspring are bred together again.

This process of breeding can continue for many generations. For example, to develop a type of dog to go down holes after badgers, some German dog owners bred together dogs with short legs and long bodies. From the offspring, they chose the puppies with the shortest legs and longest bodies and bred them together. Then they did the same with their offspring. After many years, they developed a dog with a low, long body and very short legs, called the *dachshund*, or "sausage dog."

37. According to the passage, artificial selection is used by

    (1) people who want an improved breed of animal
    (2) only Germans
    (3) mostly dog breeders
    (4) only people long ago
    (5) mainly people who like to hunt and fish

38. From the information in the passage, you could infer that dachshunds are nicknamed "sausage dogs" because they

    (1) eat a lot of sausage
    (2) used to cost the same as a sausage
    (3) are the same color as sausage
    (4) are shaped somewhat like a sausage
    (5) were perfected by a person named Sausage

Questions 39 and 40 are based on the following passage.

The first "record player" was a very strange machine. It was patented by Thomas A. Edison in 1877. It didn't play records as we know them but instead played cylinders covered with tinfoil or wax. A recording could be made on the cylinder by speaking or singing at a large diaphragm, a flexible disk sort of like the top of a drum. This diaphragm was connected to a needle. Sound waves from the voice caused the diaphragm to vibrate, which made the needle move up and down, pressing grooves into the wax or foil.

To play the "record," the process was simply reversed. The cylinder was turned, making the needle move up and down in the groove. The needle, in turn, made a small diaphragm vibrate, causing it to reproduce the original sounds. These sounds came out through a big horn, like a megaphone, which amplified them (made them louder). As you may imagine, the sounds were not very clear. Also, the foil or wax "records" wore out very quickly. Record players have come a long way since 1877.

39. According to the passage, which of the following is *not* true?

(1) There were recording machines before 1900.
(2) Thomas Edison invented an early type of "record player."
(3) Early "record players" had a needle.
(4) Early amplifiers were not electronic.
(5) Wax or foil records could be played over a period of many years.

40. From the information in the passage, you can tell that sound waves can cause solid objects to

(1) wear out
(2) vibrate
(3) disappear
(4) get old
(5) break

Questions 41 and 42 are based on the following diagram.

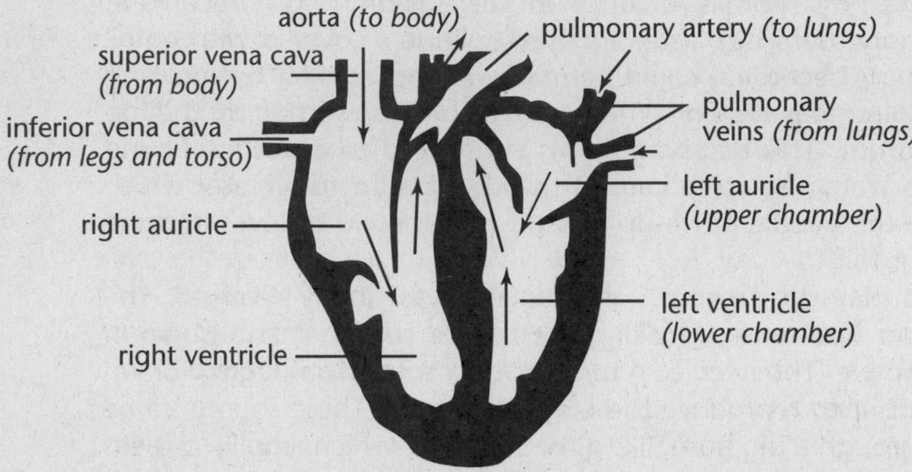

41. According to the diagram, which of these statements is true?

(1) There are three main chambers (sections) in the heart.
(2) Some veins lead directly into the ventricles.
(3) Blood flows from the auricles into the ventricles.
(4) No arteries or veins lead directly to the body.
(5) Blood flows from one ventricle directly into the other.

42. From the diagram you can tell that the word *pulmonary* means something to do with the

(1) heart
(2) brain
(3) lungs
(4) body
(5) blood

Questions 43 and 44 are based on the following passage.

Many ecologists today are concerned about the problem of acid rain. Acid rain is rain that picks up sulfuric acid pollution in the air and then falls into lakes and streams. After a while the water becomes too acidified for many fish and plants to live in.

No one has proven what causes acid rain. Some scientists believe that burning coal in power plants puts too much sulfur in the air, which forms sulfuric acid when it rains. Other scientists think that most of the sulfur in the air comes from car exhaust fumes. Still others say that the lakes are getting acid from the soil around them or the plants in them and not from the rain at all. Right now, different groups of scientists are testing their own hypotheses. They need to find out what causes acid rain and how it affects lakes and streams.

43. Something is *acidified* when it

(1) dies
(2) falls like rain
(3) becomes less acidic
(4) is beautiful
(5) becomes more acidic

44. The author of this passage would probably agree that

(1) the problem of acid rain will be easy to solve
(2) acid rain is not really very important
(3) there should be more research on the acid rain problem
(4) most people know the cause of acid rain
(5) acid rain is a problem only for fishermen and boaters

Answers start on page 970.

POST-TEST ANSWER KEY

Part I: Science Knowledge
Section A: Science Terms

Group 1

1. f	**5.** b
2. e	**6.** a
3. d	**7.** h
4. g	**8.** c

Group 2

9. g	**13.** f
10. e	**14.** c
11. b	**15.** h
12. a	**16.** d

Section B: True/False

17. T

18. F Photosynthesis is how **green** plants use sunlight to make food from carbon dioxide, water, and minerals.

19. F **Amphibians** lay their eggs in water and change as they grow up from gill-breathing tadpoles to lung-breathing land animals.

20. F A **dominant** gene will always override a **recessive** gene.

21. F Your lungs are the main organs in your **respiratory** system.

22. T

23. F A **molecule** of a chemical compound is made up of two or more **atoms**.

24. T

25. T

Part II: Reading Skills

26. (2) The bar for 1991 is halfway between 10 and 20. This can be estimated at 15.

27. (3) John is hoping that providing more nesting places will increase the number of ducks.

28. (4) According to the chart, 1 cm^3 (cubic centimeter) of diamonds weighs 3.5 grams, so 6 cm^3 would weigh 6 times 3.5 g, which equals 21 grams.

29. (3) If you divide 315 g by 30, you get 10.5 g per cubic centimeter, which is the density given in the chart for silver.

30. (3) The passage talks about "the traditional pointed nose necessary to move through air."

31. (2) This answer is implied by the final sentence in the passage and by your knowledge of the enormous distances between stars.

32. (4) The first paragraph describes an ADD child's behavior. Choice (1) does not cover all that is in the first paragraph. Choices (2), (3), and (5) are not covered in the first paragraph at all.

33. (1) You can tell that some foods may make ADD worse because the passage says that some children can be helped by a special diet.

34. (2) The passage says a team of doctors is needed. It specifically says that a regular family doctor or pediatrician should not handle this problem alone. A teacher, family member, or other parent would be even less expert.

35. (5) The graph line shows that more Vitamix dissolved as the temperature of the mixture got higher, so choices (2) and (4) cannot be correct. Choice (3) is not right because nothing was on the graph about using different amounts of liquid. Choice (1) is not correct because this graph gives information only about Vitamix dissolving in milk, not about all powders in all liquids.

36. (4) The graph shows data from experiments. Choices (3) and (5) are incorrect because this graph is based on observed facts, not just opinions. Choice (1) is wrong because it is unlikely that people would just "happen" to notice exact temperatures and amounts of Vitamix dissolved. Choice (2) is wrong because the experiment is about Vitamix and milk, not water.

37. (1) See the first sentence.

38. (4) The passage describes dachshunds as being long and low, with very short legs; thus, somewhat sausage-shaped. Choices (1), (2), (3), and (5) are not mentioned in the passage at all.

39. (5) The passage says that the "foil or wax 'records' wore out very quickly."

40. (2) The passage says that "sound waves from the voice caused the diaphragm to vibrate," and the diaphragm is a solid object.

41. (3) On each side, the arrows come down from the auricles into the ventricles.

42. (3) The pulmonary artery leads to the lungs, and the pulmonary veins come back from the lungs.

43. (5) The passage says that water becomes *acidified* when acid falls into it.

44. (3) In the last sentence, the author says that scientists need to find out what causes acid rain. Choices (2) and (5) are not correct because the author says that this is a problem that many people are worried about.

POST-TEST EVALUATION CHARTS

Since the Science Post-Test is divided into two parts, you should use the following two-step method to evaluate your answers.

First, use the answer key on pages 970–971 to check your answers to Part I: Science Knowledge. Then look at the chart below. Find the number of each question you missed on this chart and circle it in the second column. Then you will know which science topics you might need to review.

Next, use the answer key to check your answers to Part II: Reading Skills. Then go to the chart on page 973. Circle the number of each question that you missed. By looking at the row labeled "Number Correct," you will be able to decide which reading skills you need to review.

PART I: SCIENCE KNOWLEDGE

Science Topic	Item Number	Number Correct
Plant and Animal Biology pages 386–397	2, 3, 6, 13, 18, 19, 20	_____ /7
Human Biology pages 415–427	11, 12, 21	_____ /3
Physics pages 443–454	8, 9, 14, 17, 22	_____ /5
Chemistry pages 459–472	7, 15, 16, 23, 24	_____ /5
Earth Science pages 483–500	1, 4, 5, 10, 25	_____ /5

_____ /25 TOTAL

PART II: READING SKILLS

	Plant and Animal Biology	Human Biology	Physics	Chemistry	Earth Science	NUMBER CORRECT
The Scientific Method pages 369–378	27			36		_____ /2
Understanding What You Read pages 379–385	37	32	39		30	_____ /4
Understanding Illustrations pages 401–414	**26**	**41**	**28**	**35**		_____ /4
Analyzing Ideas pages 433–442	38	33	**29**, 40		31	_____ /5
Building Vocabulary pages 363–368		**42**			43	_____ /2
Evaluating Ideas pages 478–482		34			44	_____ /2

The numbers in **bold type** are questions based on illustrations.

Part I: _____ /25 TOTAL

Part II: _____ /19 TOTAL

Combined: _____ /44 TOTAL

POST-TEST 4: READING/LITERATURE AND THE ARTS

The purpose of this Post-Test is to see how much you have improved your reading skills. Take the test to see which skills you have mastered and which skills you still need to work on. Check all of your answers and use the evaluation chart on page 983.

1. Look at the following words: remark, boulder, prospector, cement. What is the correct way to divide these words into syllables?

   (1) rem-ark, boul-der, pros-pec-tor, ce-ment
   (2) re-mark, bould-er, pros-pec-tor, ce-ment
   (3) re-mark, boul-der, prosp-ect-or, ce-ment
   (4) re-mark, boul-der, pros-pec-tor, cem-ent
   (5) re-mark, boul-der, pros-pec-tor, ce-ment

2. Use your knowledge of roots, prefixes, and suffixes to match each word with its definition at the right.

(1)	anteroom	**a.**	ship under water
(2)	submarine	**b.**	ruled by a king or queen
(3)	monarchy	**c.**	not being faithful
(4)	intrastate	**d.**	outer or waiting room
(5)	infidelity	**e.**	within a state

3. Look at each **boldfaced** word on the left. Find its antonym from the four choices at the right.

(1)	**superior**	**a.** inferior	**b.** important	**c.** superb	**d.** higher
(2)	**friend**	**a.** companion	**b.** party	**c.** stranger	**d.** relative
(3)	**failure**	**a.** frustration	**b.** unhappiness	**c.** sadness	**d.** success
(4)	**stench**	**a.** stink	**b.** fragrance	**c.** smell	**d.** decay
(5)	**survive**	**a.** die	**b.** exist	**c.** live	**d.** continue

4. Read the following sentence. Then identify the key words that answer the questions *Who or what?* and *Did what?*

The bomb squad, acting on a phone tip, disarmed the bomb before it blew up and injured anyone.

The key words are ______________________ ______________________

5. Pam baked her **quota** of three dozen cookies for the holiday party. *Quota* means

   (1) special recipe
   (2) party members
   (3) share or amount required
   (4) contest or bake-off
   (5) club membership

6. Pick the word that best completes the analogy.
end : begin :: stop : ________

(1) eat
(2) move
(3) finish
(4) start

Directions: Read each of the following selections. Then answer the questions that follow.

Questions 7–10 are based on the following passage.

Buying a used car can be a tricky business, but you have a better chance of finding a good buy if you follow expert consumer advice.

First, go to the library and look up the models that most interest you. Consumer guides can give you valuable repair and recall information. Second, take someone with you who knows cars, or ask permission to take the car to a reputable mechanic to look over. The fee you pay the mechanic may save you money in the long run.

Also, check the car yourself. Look for evidence of damage in the body work or windshield. Keep in mind that a new paint job may hide evidence of an accident. Check the interior for signs of heavy wear—a sure sign that the car has many miles on it. Check the tires for uneven tread wear, a sign of possible problems with steering, brakes, or suspension. Check under the hood for oil stains, rust stains, frayed wiring, loose or cracked hoses, worn fan belts, and loose battery terminals. Any one of these could cause you problems later.

Finally, take the car for a test drive. Check the acceleration, braking, and handling. Be sure the lights, horn, and turn indicators work. If everything seems in order, you probably have found a used car worth buying.

7. What is a good title for this passage?

(1) How to Check Tire Treads
(2) How to Find a Mechanic
(3) How to Buy a Used Car
(4) How to Follow Expert Consumer Advice
(5) How to Repair a Faulty Engine

8. If you follow the advice in the article, what does the author predict will happen?

(1) The car will break down within a week.
(2) You will save more money by buying a new car.
(3) You will have found a good mechanic.
(4) The car will never break down.
(5) You will have found a car worth buying.

9. The main purpose of this article is to
   (1) give factual information on buying a used car
   (2) tell you which model of car to buy
   (3) get you to look under the hood carefully
   (4) get you to hire a mechanic
   (5) warn you about used car salesmen

10. Fill in the blanks with details from the selection.

    a. When buying a used car, you can get help from ______________,

    someone who ______________ ______________, or a ____________.

    b. You can check the car yourself for evidence of damage to the

    ________________ ________________ or ______________.

    c. You should check the ________________ for signs of heavy wear.

    d. The tires should be checked for ________________

    ________________ ________________.

    e. When you test drive a car you should check the ______________,

    ________________, and ______________.

    f. Also, you should make sure the ______________, ______________,

    and ________________ ________________ are working.

Questions 11–15 are based on the following passage.

Louis Pasteur was a French chemist who lived in the nineteenth century. Pasteur believed that scientists should tackle practical problems in their research. Therefore, he looked at the problem of food spoilage. Most scientists in Pasteur's time believed food spoiled because of natural chemical changes that took place within the food. However, Pasteur believed that tiny organisms in the air fell on the food, therefore causing it to spoil. He proved his theory was correct when he first heated broth to kill any organisms in it, and then sealed the broth. The broth did not spoil as long as it was sealed. But when the broth was later opened and exposed to air, it spoiled.

Pasteur applied the same principles to preventing wine and vinegar from spoiling. Then he turned his attention to preserving beer. His methods were so effective that England was able to ship beer to its colonies in Africa and India. Later, the same technique was also used to preserve milk. Even today, most of the milk we buy is labeled "pasteurized" after the man who devised ways to prevent food from spoiling.

11. Contrast what Pasteur believed with what most scientists of his day believed.

Most nineteenth-century scientists believed that food spoiled because

of ____________________ ____________________, while Pasteur believed

______________________________ caused food to spoil.

12. Pasteur heated the broth because he

(1) wanted to make it taste better
(2) thought it would kill the organisms in it
(3) wanted to add organisms
(4) thought he would change its chemistry
(5) wanted to imitate other scientists

13. Pasteur used his preserving technique on several foods. Number them in the order in which Pasteur successfully preserved them.

____ **a.** milk

____ **b.** beer

____ **c.** wine and vinegar

14. How did Pasteur's preserving technique affect England's colonies?

____

15. Where did we get the term *pasteurized*?

____

Questions 16–22 are based on the following passage.

Juan stomped into my office. "I'm gonna kill him!"

"Um . . . You sound angry. Who are you going to kill?"

"Ko! I thought we were friends. But he just insulted me!"

"I thought you were friends, too. You've been good about helping him learn English and explaining football to him. He seemed to like you. What happened?"

"He . . . well, he tried to hold my hand as we walked down the hall to go to lunch. I nearly smacked him."

"Oh, I see."

"Yeah? Well, I don't!"

"He didn't mean what you thought. You see, in his country, men show their friendship for one another by walking arm in arm or hand in hand. To hold hands with a woman in public is considered very improper. He really was trying to be your friend. He just didn't know that American culture is different from his, not just in spoken language, but in what body language means. It works both ways. Our gesture for 'come here,' " I wiggled my fingers toward myself with my palm up, "is an insult in his country. It's used to call animals. They use this gesture."

I demonstrated a "come here," but with my palm down.

"You mean every country has its own gestures with different meanings?"

"Well, not quite. But there are differences in gestures among different peoples of the world. What means one thing in one place can mean something quite different in another. So, I really think Ko just wants to be friends."

"Really? He doesn't think . . . Well, I guess I've got a lot more to explain to him than just football . . . See ya."

16. What characters are named in the story?

____________________ and____________________

17. Who is telling the story?
   (1) Juan's father
   (2) Ko
   (3) Ko's father
   (4) A soccer coach
   (5) An unnamed person

18. What is the conflict or problem to be solved?
   (1) The author is angry with Juan.
   (2) The author doesn't understand Ko.
   (3) Ko is angry because Juan tried to hold his hand.
   (4) Juan is angry because Ko tried to hold his hand.
   (5) Juan is angry with the author.

19. What happens at the climax?
   (1) Ko tries to hold Juan's hand.
   (2) The author throws Juan out of the office for being such a nuisance.
   (3) Juan asks for a change in lunch schedule.
   (4) Juan understands that gestures mean different things in other cultures.
   (5) The author agrees that Ko insulted Juan.

20. What happens at the conclusion, or end, of the story?
   (1) Ko punches Juan in the nose.
   (2) Juan punches the author.
   (3) Juan decides to explain things to Ko.
   (4) Juan gets into a fight with Ko.
   (5) Juan asks the author to talk with Ko.

21. What can you predict will happen next?
    (1) Juan and Ko will work out their misunderstanding.
    (2) Ko will ask a female coworker to lunch.
    (3) The author will be angry with Ko.
    (4) Juan will go back to school evenings.
    (5) Juan and Ko will *not* work out their misunderstanding.

22. What can you infer about Ko?
    (1) Ko wants to be a doctor.
    (2) Ko wants to insult Juan.
    (3) Ko was born in the United States.
    (4) Ko works hard at his studies.
    (5) Ko is new to the United States.

Questions 23–27 are based on the following passage.

Good afternoon, ladies and gentlemen. My name is Maria Godellas and I am a candidate in the race for mayor of Ridgemont.

As many of you know, I have lived in Ridgemont all my life. My father still works in the steel mill, and my mother is a part-time nurse at Ridgemont General Hospital. My work experience includes five years as assistant to Police Chief Stewart and two years as a paralegal. More recently, after taking a two-year leave to care for my infant daughter, I was elected head of the City Planning Commission.

These jobs have given me a special understanding of Ridgemont as well as a deep affection for its people. At the police station, I observed how and why crime rates rise and fall, fought discrimination, and worked with teen offenders. As head of the Planning Commission, I've expanded local business, and brought in money and jobs through the Annual Ridgemont Fair. I've also been able to meet most of you and see how hard you work to provide for your families.

Like most of you, I know what it is to work an eight—or ten—hour day and then go home to a family. Every day, I see the increasing need for more dependable day care, better schools, and improved health care.

Support Maria Godellas and you support the values that Ridgemont was built on—family, equality, stability. Join me and together we will watch Ridgemont prosper.

23. What is the purpose of this speech?

____

24. Paragraph two contains mainly
    (1) facts
    (2) opinions

25. Words such as "understanding," "compassion," and "justice" are
    (1) positive
    (2) negative
    (3) neutral

26. "Like most of you, I know what it is to work an eight—or ten—hour day . . ." suggests which persuasive technique?
    (1) testimonial
    (2) plain folks
    (3) bandwagon
    (4) snob appeal

27. "Join me and together we will watch Ridgemont prosper" is
    (1) a fact
    (2) a statement of proof
    (3) a true statement
    (4) a rumor
    (5) a slogan

Questions 28–33 are based on the following passage.

Friendship

OH, THE COMFORT—the inexpressive comfort of feeling
safe with a person,
Having neither to weigh thoughts,
Nor measure words—but pouring them
All right out—just as they are—
Chaff* and grain together—
Certain that a faithful hand will
Take and sift them—
Keep what is worth keeping—
And with the breath of kindness
Blow the rest away.

—by Dinah Maria Mulock Craik

* *Chaff* refers to unnecessary seed coverings that are thrown away. Therefore, the word *chaff* means something worthless or unnecessary.

28. What activity does the poet describe doing with her friend?
(1) meditating
(2) celebrating
(3) talking
(4) laughing
(5) arguing

29. What do the "chaff and grain" in line 6 symbolize?
(1) friends and enemies
(2) the outer covering of wheat seeds
(3) brothers and sisters
(4) useless and useful ideas
(5) the ups and downs of friendship

30. How does the poet feel about her friend?
(1) uneasy because her friend won't understand her
(2) suspicious that her friend will gossip about her to others
(3) sad because their friendship is over
(4) fearful that her friend will criticize her
(5) comfortable talking about anything with her

31. When the poet says, "Certain that a faithful hand will / Take and sift them—" (lines 7–8), she means that her friend
(1) throws away any unused grain
(2) helps her get her work done
(3) cannot listen because she is too busy working
(4) ignores any unwise or silly comments the poet makes
(5) enjoys working with her hands

32. What is the main idea of this poem?
(1) A good friendship lasts a long time.
(2) To keep a good friend, you must think before you speak.
(3) Chaff and grain are necessary to have a good friendship.
(4) A good friend focuses mainly on your positive qualities.
(5) A good friend focuses mainly on your bad qualities.

33. What is the tone of this poem?
(1) funny
(2) informational
(3) thinking seriously
(4) sad
(5) resentful

34. Think about this expression: "Democrats are always for change." Which of the following is the expression?
(1) a testimonial
(2) the bandwagon technique
(3) a slogan
(4) a generalization
(5) a fact

Answers start on page 982.

POST-TEST ANSWER KEY

1. (5)
2. (1) d (2) a (3) b (4) e (5) c
3. (1) a (2) c (3) d (4) b (5) a
4. *Who or what?* the bomb squad — *Did what?* disarmed the bomb
5. (3) The clue is the phrase "of three dozen cookies," which tells how many she needed to bring.
6. (4)
7. (3) The entire passage gives you advice or things to look for when buying a used car.
8. (5) The last sentence of the passage supports this choice.
9. (1) As you saw in question 1, the best title for this passage is "How to Buy a Used Car." Therefore, the purpose of the article is to give factual information on buying a used car.
10. a. consumer guides, knows cars, mechanic
    b. body work, windshield
    c. interior
    d. uneven tread wear
    e. acceleration, braking, handling
    f. lights, horn, turn indicators
11. chemical changes; organisms
12. (2) Lines 8–12 support this statement.
13. a. 3
    b. 2
    c. 1
14. England was able to ship beer to its colonies in Africa and India.
15. From the name of the scientist, Louis Pasteur
16. Juan, Ko
17. (5) The first-person pronoun *my* (line 1) tells you right away that an unnamed person is telling the story of Juan and Ko.
18. (4) The entire passage centers around the conflict caused by Ko's attempt to hold Juan's hand.
19. (4) Once Juan understands the reasons for Ko's behavior, he is no longer angry.
20. (3) The last paragraph supports this response.
21. (1) From the last paragraph, you can conclude that Juan will explain to Ko why he was angry, and they will again be friends.
22. (5) Since Juan has helped Ko learn about English and football, you can conclude that Ko is a newcomer to the United States.
23. The candidate's purpose is to convince people to vote for her.
24. (1) Paragraph two contains facts, or statements that can be proved.
25. (1) The words *understanding, compassion*, and *justice* imply that Maria Godellas cares about Ridgemont and its citizens in a positive way.
26. (2) Maria Godellas uses the phrase "Like most of you" to identify herself with the everyday people she is addressing.
27. (5) This phrase is a slogan because it presents a brief, positive image of the candidate.
28. (3) The poet's reference to pouring out words and thoughts (lines 4–5) indicates that she is describing talking with a friend.
29. (4) In lines 3–4, the poet talks about words and thoughts. When she refers to *chaff* (something worthless) and *grain* (something valuable), she is referring to useless and useful ideas or thoughts.
30. (5) The words *comfort, safe, faithful*, and *kindness* imply that the poet trusts and feels comfortable with her friend.
31. (4) The poet is sure that her friend will pay attention to the ideas that are valuable and ignore the other ideas.
32. (4) The entire poem focuses on friends who support your positive qualities and ignore the negative ones.
33. (3) The poet is thinking about how much she enjoys talking to her friend.
34. (4) Many Democrats may favor change, but not necesarily all of them as this generalization states.

POST-TEST EVALUATION CHART

Use the answer key on page 982 to check your answers. Then, find the number of each question you missed on this chart and circle it in the second column. Then you will know which chapters you might need to review.

	Skill	Item Numbers	Number Correct
Chapter 1 Gaining Meaning from Words	• Syllables • Word parts • Synonyms and antonyms	1 2 3	_____ /3
Chapter 2 Understanding What You Read	• Key words • Main ideas • Words in context • Supporting details, reasons, and examples • Summarizing and paraphrasing	4 7, 32 5 10, 15 9, 23	_____ /8
Chapter 3 Finding Hidden Meanings	• Inference • Predicting outcomes	22, 30 8, 21	_____ /4
Chapter 4 Organizing Ideas	• Cause and effect • Comparison and contrast • Sequence • Analogy • Fact and opinion	12, 14 11 13 6 24	_____ /6
Chapter 5 Reading Literature	• Picturing people and setting • Tone and mood • Beginning, conflict, climax, and conclusion • Symbols • Poetry	16, 17 33 18, 19, 20 29 28, 31	_____ /9
Chapter 6 Evaluating What You Read	• Connotation • Generalizations • Persuasive techniques	25 34 26, 27	_____ /4
		Total Correct	_____ /34

POST-TEST 5: MATHEMATICS

The following questions will give you a chance to review briefly many of the skills you've learned in Section 5. In Part I questions are divided into the four computation skills and word-problem skills. In Part II the questions deal with decimals, fractions, percents, word problems, and special topics.

Work carefully and answer every question. When you finish, check your answers with the answers given on pages 993–994.

PART I

ADDITION

1. $6 + 2 + 0 =$

2. $26 + 13$

3. $31 + 23 + 12$

4. $58 + 29$

5. $\$6.37 + 2.74$

6. $675 + 359 + 63$

7. $4{,}274 + 3{,}138 =$

SUBTRACTION

8. $17 - 9$

9. $68 - 35$

10. $875 - 89$

11. $\$23.48 - 10.09$

12. $408 - 256$

13. $800 - 378 =$

14. $\$500.00 - \$453.63 =$

MULTIPLICATION

15. 53×2

16. 52×30

17. 530×201

18. 98×73

19. $\begin{array}{r} 678 \\ \times\ 607 \\ \hline \end{array}$

20. 236 × 19 =

21. 4,508 × 1,000 =

DIVISION

22. $9\overline{)45}$

23. $3\overline{)6{,}369}$

24. $3\overline{)627}$

25. $5\overline{)4{,}515}$

26. $7\overline{)94}$

27. $4\overline{)\$1.32}$

28. $12\overline{)360}$

29. $279\overline{)2{,}232}$

30. 240 ÷ 16 =

31. 7,973 ÷ 12 =

WORD-PROBLEMS

Solve each of the following word problems. For each problem, circle the letter of the correct answer from the answer choices given.

32. On Monday's shopping trip, Marilyn bought a lamp for \$23.49, a table for \$49.50, 2 vases for \$19.95 apiece, and a serving plate for \$12.79. What total amount did Marilyn pay for the lamp and the 2 vases?
    a) \$ 43.44
    b) \$ 63.39
    c) \$ 66.93
    d) \$105.73
    e) \$125.68

33. At a cost of \$1.49 per bottle, how much do 21 bottles of cola cost?
    a) \$14.90
    b) \$21.29
    c) \$30.00
    d) \$31.29
    e) \$41.29

34. While dieting, Ruth lost 4 pounds during May and 5 pounds during June. How many pounds did she lose altogether if her weight dropped from 145 pounds on May 1 to 131 pounds on August 1?
    a) 5
    b) 9
    c) 14
    d) 18
    e) 23

35. Allison applied for a word processing job that required a typing speed of at least 65 words per minute. She was given a 6-minute timed typing test. On this test, she typed 348 words. How many words per minute did Allison average on this test?
    a) 58
    b) 59
    c) 65
    d) 390
    e) 2,088

36. At a hardware sale, Roy bought a drill on sale for $39.95 and six screwdrivers on sale for 99¢ each. How much change should Roy receive if he pays for these items with two twenty-dollar bills and a ten-dollar bill?

a) $ 1.04
b) $ 4.11
c) $ 5.94
d) $ 9.06
e) $14.11

37. A recipe for tangy punch calls for 2 qt. 1 pt. of lime soda. This will be enough punch for 8 large servings. If Jill wants to make 6 times this much punch, how much lime soda should she use? Express your answer in the largest units possible.

a) 3 gal. 6 pt.
b) 3 gal. 3 qt.
c) 4 gal. 1 qt.
d) 6 gal. 2 qt.
e) 12 qt. 6 pt.

38. A roll of R-30 insulation covers 64 square feet of surface. If each roll costs $25.50, how much will it cost to insulate a ceiling that is in the shape of a rectangle measuring 40 feet long by 32 feet wide?

a) $ 51.00
b) $125.00
c) $255.00
d) $375.00
e) $510.00

39. During league play on Saturday night, Ellen bowled 4 games, all above her year-long average of 142. The scores of her 4 games were 144, 151, 167, and 146. What was Ellen's average score for just these 4 games?

a) 142
b) 144
c) 145
d) 148
e) 152

40. Wilma has a large storage freezer in the shape of a rectangular solid. The inside dimensions of this freezer are as follows: length = 4 feet; width = 2 feet; and height = 3 feet. How many cubic feet of storage space does this freezer contain?

a) 9
b) 24
c) 81
d) 124
e) 234

PART II

DECIMALS

41. When gas is selling for $1.368 per gallon, how much would you actually have to pay for a total purchase of 1 gallon?

    a) $1.30 d) $1.38
    b) $1.36 e) $1.39
    c) $1.37

42. The distance between Tami's office and the library is about .8 miles. From the library to the post office is 1.4 miles. Passing the library on the way, how many miles is Tami's office from the post office?

    a) .6 d) 2.2
    b) 1.2 e) 2.8
    c) 1.8

43. Bernie purchased an electric drill on sale for $39.99. He also bought a set of drill bits for $16.49. How much change will Bernie receive if he pays for these items with three $20 bills?

    a) $1.32 d) $3.52
    b) $1.98 e) $4.02
    c) $2.92

44. Brandi paid $5.23 for 3.6 pounds of chicken. At this rate, how much is she paying for each pound? Express your answer to the nearest penny.

    a) $1.41 d) $17.69
    b) $1.45 e) $18.79
    c) $1.53

45. For exercise, Roger walks around Fenton Park on each of three days during the week. On each of the other four days he walks 1.5 miles around the neighborhood school. If the distance around Fenton Park is 3.2 miles, how many miles total does Roger walk for exercise each week?

    a) 4.7 d) 15.6
    b) 9.6 e) 25.2
    c) 11.4

46. Opal and 3 friends agreed to split the cost of lunch. Each agreed to pay an equal amount. The bill included the items listed below. From this bill, determine Opal's share of the bill.

    Sandwiches: $13.78,
    Salads: $6.04,
    Drinks: $3.74, Desserts: $7.08

    a) $7.66 d) $8.36
    b) $7.96 e) $8.76
    c) $8.16

47. At a January sale, Gordon bought a microwave oven for $379. He made a down payment of $59. He then agreed to pay off the balance in 3 equal monthly payments. If he was charged no interest, which arithmetic expression correctly shows the amount of each of Gordon's monthly payments?

    a) $379 – $59
    b) ($379 + $59) ÷ 3
    c) $379 – ($59 ÷ 3)
    d) ($379 – $59) ÷ 3
    e) $379 ÷ 3 – $59

FRACTIONS

48. There are 52 weeks in a year. What fraction of a year is 36 weeks?

a) $\frac{9}{52}$ b) $\frac{3}{5}$ c) $\frac{9}{13}$ d) $\frac{13}{9}$ e) $\frac{26}{9}$

49. Leon invited several friends over for dinner on Tuesday evening. For that dinner he prepared 3 steaks. One weighed $\frac{5}{8}$ pound, the second weighed $1\frac{1}{2}$ pounds, and the third weighed $\frac{3}{4}$ pound. How many pounds of steak did Leon prepare?

a) $1\frac{5}{8}$ b) $1\frac{9}{14}$ c) $1\frac{7}{8}$ d) $2\frac{7}{8}$ e) $3\frac{7}{8}$

50. During the first week of his diet, Ernie lost a total of $1\frac{5}{8}$ pounds. During the second week, he lost only $\frac{9}{16}$ pounds. How much more did Ernie lose the first week than

the second week? Express your answer in pounds.

a) $\frac{1}{16}$ b) $\frac{9}{16}$ c) $1\frac{1}{16}$ d) $2\frac{1}{16}$ e) $2\frac{3}{16}$

51. Marian spends $\frac{1}{4}$ of her monthly income of $1,224 for rent. She also spends $\frac{1}{8}$ of her income on food. Knowing this, determine

what amount Marian pays for rent each month.

a) $203
b) $306
c) $350
d) $424
e) $618

52. Gail is lining up packages according to weight. She places the heaviest package at the left and the lightest package at the right. Which listing below shows the correct order in which Gail should line up the 4 packages labeled below?

Package	Weight
A	$\frac{7}{8}$ pound
B	.8 pound
C	$\frac{5}{7}$ pound
D	.79 pound

a) B, C, A, D
b) A, C, B, D
c) C, D, B, A
d) A, C, D, B
e) A, B, D, C

53. Norm cut a 17-foot-long "two-by-four" into 9 pieces as follows: First, he cut off a piece that measured $5\frac{5}{6}$ feet long. Next, he cut off a piece that measured $6\frac{1}{2}$ feet long. Last, he cut the remaining piece into 7 equal pieces. Assuming no waste as he cut, how many inches long are each of these 7 short pieces?

a) 7 b) 8 c) 9 d) 10 e) 11

54. For use in his auto shop, Curt bought $\frac{3}{4}$ pound of lock washers and $\frac{5}{8}$ pound of assorted washers. Each type of washer costs $1.29 per pound. He paid for his purchase with a $20 bill. Which arithmetic expression below correctly shows the amount of change he should receive?

a) $\$20 + \$1.29\,(\frac{3}{4} + \frac{5}{8})$

b) $\$20 - \$1.29 \div (\frac{3}{4} + \frac{5}{8})$

c) $\$20 - \$1.29\,(\frac{3}{4} + \frac{5}{8})$

d) $\$20 - \frac{3}{4} + \frac{5}{8}$

e) $\$1.29\,(\frac{3}{4} + \frac{5}{8}) - \$20$

PERCENTS

55. By the time he went to bed Saturday night, Alan had completed 30% of the work he hoped to get done that weekend. What fraction of the work had he completed by that evening?

    a) $\frac{3}{100}$ b) $\frac{3}{10}$ c) $\frac{1}{3}$ d) $\frac{3}{7}$ e) $\frac{3}{4}$

56. At the end of each month Vera is given a 4% bonus based on the dollar value of sales she makes. If she sold $2,658 worth of clothes during July, how much would Vera's bonus be for that month?

    a) $47.82 d) $106.32
    b) $66.45 e) $2,764.32
    c) $98.72

57. One mile is equal to 5,280 feet. What percent of a mile is 440 yards?

    a) 12.5% d) 37.5%
    b) 25% e) 66%
    c) $33\frac{1}{3}$%

58. Before Leslie was laid off from her job at the auto factory, she earned $11.25 per hour. On her new job as a paint salesperson, she earns $7.50 per hour. What percent salary decrease has Leslie taken in accepting this new job?

    a) $16\frac{2}{3}$% d) $33\frac{1}{3}$%
    b) 25% e) $37\frac{1}{2}$%
    c) 30%

59. During a time of high inflation, the cost of food products rose 8% between January and September. At this rate, what would you expect the price of a loaf of bread to be in September if it sold for $1.25 in January?

    a) $.10 d) $1.33
    b) $1.15 e) $1.35
    c) $1.29

60. On the local news it was reported that 17% of the citizens of Portland who were of voting age favored lowering the speed limit within the city limits. The newscaster said that 35,190 people would favor this change. From this information, figure out how many people of voting age live in Portland.

    a) 207,000 d) 307,000
    b) 227,000 e) 351,900
    c) 267,000

61. Chun paid a sale price of $31.85 for a bedspread that was marked "35% off original price" and $63.70 for a quilt. What would she have paid for the bedspread if it hadn't been on sale?

    a) $20.70 d) $66.85
    b) $42.00 e) $147.00
    c) $49.00

62. As an appliance salesperson, Will is paid a monthly salary of $620. He also receives a 2% commission on the dollar value of sales that he makes during the month. Which arithmetic expression correctly shows the amount of Will's monthly pay during a month in which he makes $3,980 in sales?

a) .02 × $3,980
b) .02 ($620 + $3,980)
c) (.02 × $3,980) − $620
d) (.02 × $3,980) + 620
e) (.02 × $620) + $3,980

SPECIAL TOPICS

63. Using the drawing, determine the difference in length between the two sizes of screws shown. Express your answer to the nearest sixteenth of an inch.

a) $\frac{5}{16}$ b) $\frac{7}{16}$ c) $\frac{9}{16}$ d) $\frac{11}{16}$ e) $\frac{13}{16}$

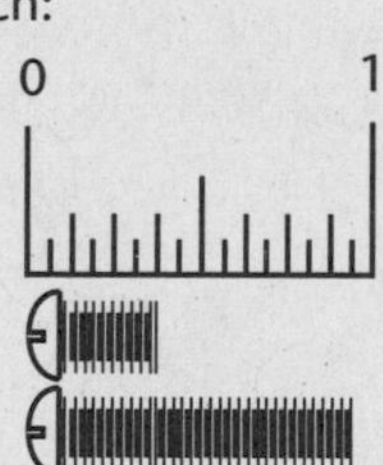

64. When he put a new starter on his Japanese sports car, Adam noticed that the new starter was 6 millimeters longer than the old starter. If the old starter is 19.2 centimeters long, how many centimeters long is the new starter?

a) 19.26 d) 19.8
b) 19.6 e) 25.2
c) 19.62

65. Using the simple interest formula I = PRT, determine the amount of interest you'd pay on a loan of $3,000 borrowed for 2 years 8 months at an interest rate of 12%.

a) $90.80 d) $908.00
b) $96.00 e) $960.00
c) $800.00

66. In Beth's Monday night class there are five women students and six men. Looking at the list of their ages shown below, figure out the *mean* (average) age of these women students.

Mary	18
Joyce	35
Amy	37
Helen	52
Sarah	68

a) 37 b) 42 c) 52 d) 56 e) 59

67. To make a fruit salad for the school picnic, Wanda mixed 6 cups of chopped apples, 4 cups of sliced bananas, $1\frac{1}{2}$ cups of blueberries, $2\frac{1}{2}$ cups of strawberries, and 4 cups of oranges. In this salad, what is the *ratio* of oranges to apples?

a) $\frac{2}{3}$ b) $\frac{6}{5}$ c) $\frac{3}{2}$ d) $\frac{1}{2}$ e) $\frac{1}{4}$

68. Suppose you randomly choose two cards from those shown at right. If your first card turns out to be a face card, what is the probability that your second card will be a 4?

a) 5%
b) 13%
c) 20%
d) 25%
e) 75%

Questions 69 and 70 refer to the circle graph at the right.

69. How many registered voters are there in Linn County?

a) 26,500
b) 29,150
c) 55,650
d) 66,250
e) 100,000

70. What percent of the registered voters in Linn County are not registered as either Democrats or Republicans?

a) 4%
b) 7%
c) 9%
d) 12%
e) 16%

REGISTERED VOTERS OF LINN COUNTY

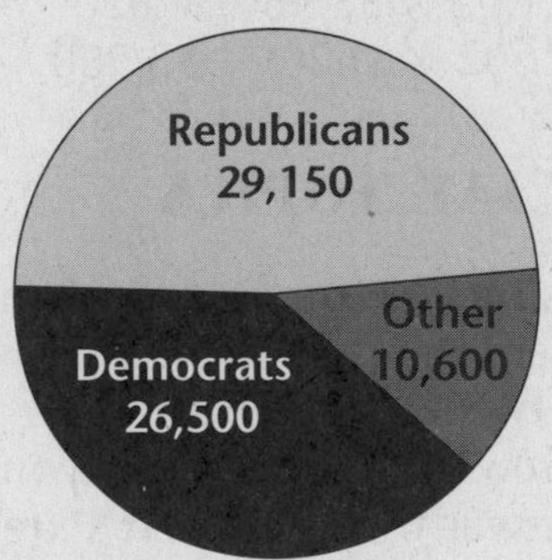

POST-TEST ANSWER KEY

PART I
Addition, Subtraction, Multiplication, Division, Word Problems
pages 985–987

1. 8	15. 106	28. 30
2. 39	16. 1,560	29. 8
3. 66	17. 106,530	30. 15
4. 87	18. 7,154	31. 664 r 5
5. $9.11	19. 411,546	32. b
6. 1,097	20. 4,484	33. d
7. 7,412	21. 4,508,000	34. c
8. 8	22. 5	35. a
9. 33	23. 2,123	36. b
10. 786	24. 209	37. b
11. $13.39	25. 903	38. e
12. 152	26. 13 r 3	39. e
13. 422	27. $.33	40. b
14. $46.37		

PART II
Decimals, Fractions, Percents, Special Topics
pages 988–992

41. c

42. d $1.4 + .8 = 2.2$

43. d $\$39.99 + 16.49 = \$56.48$ $\quad \$20 \times 3 = \$60$ $\quad \$60.00 - 56.48 = \$3.52$

44. b $\$1.45\frac{10}{36}$

3.6)5.230
36
1 63
1 44
190
180
10

45. d $3.2 \times 3 = 9.6$ miles $\quad 1.5 \times 4 = 6.0$ miles

$9.6 + 6.0 = 15.6$ miles

46. a $\$13.78 + 6.04 + 3.74 + 7.08 = \$30.64$

$\$7.66$
4)30.64
28
2 6
2 4
24
24
0

47. d

48. c $\frac{36}{52} = \frac{9}{13}$

49. d

$\frac{5}{8} = \frac{5}{8}$
$1\frac{1}{2} = 1\frac{4}{8}$
$+ \frac{3}{4} = \frac{6}{8}$
$1\frac{15}{8} = 2\frac{7}{8}$

50. c

$1\frac{5}{8} = 1\frac{10}{16}$
$- \frac{9}{16} = -\frac{9}{16}$
$1\frac{1}{16}$

51. b

$306
4)1,224
− 12
24
24
0

or $1,224 \times .25$ = 6120 + 1448 = $306.00

52. e

A. .875
8)7.000
6 4
60
56
40
40

C. $.71\frac{3}{7}$
7)5.00
4 9
10
7
3

B. .8 D. .79

53. b

$17 = 16\frac{6}{6}$
$- 5\frac{5}{6} = 5\frac{5}{6}$
$11\frac{1}{6}$

$11\frac{1}{6} = 10\frac{7}{6}$
$- 6\frac{1}{2} = 6\frac{3}{6}$

$4\frac{4}{6} = 4\frac{2}{3}$ feet = 56 inches

$56 \div 7 = 8$

54. c

55. b $30\% = \frac{30}{100} = \frac{3}{10}$

56. d $\$2,658 \times .04 = \$106.32$

57. b

1760 yards
3)5280
3
22
21
18
18
0
0

$\frac{440}{1760} = \frac{44}{176}$
$\frac{1}{4} = 25\%$

58. d $\$11.25 - 7.50 = \$3.75$

$.33\frac{1}{2} = 33\%$
11.25)3.7500
3 375
3750
3375
375

59. e
$$\begin{array}{r} \$1.25 \\ \times\ \ .08 \\ \hline .1000 \end{array} \qquad \begin{array}{r} \$1.25 \\ +\ .10 \\ \hline \mathbf{\$1.35} \end{array}$$

60. a
$$\begin{array}{r} \mathbf{207{,}000.} \\ .17\overline{)35190.00} \\ \underline{34} \\ 119 \\ \underline{119} \\ 00\ 00 \\ \underline{00\ 00} \\ 0 \end{array}$$

61. c
$$\begin{array}{r} 100\% \\ -\ \ 35\% \\ \hline 65\% \end{array} \qquad \begin{array}{r} \mathbf{49} \\ .65\overline{)31.85} \\ \underline{26\ 0} \\ 5\ 85 \\ \underline{5\ 85} \\ 0 \end{array}$$

62. d

63. c
$$\begin{array}{rcr} \frac{15}{16} & = & \frac{15}{16} \\ -\frac{3}{8} & = & -\frac{6}{16} \\ & & \frac{9}{16} \end{array}$$

64. d
$$\begin{array}{r} 19.2 \\ +\ \ .6 \\ \hline \mathbf{19.8} \end{array}$$

65. e P = \$3,000
R = .12
T = $2\frac{8}{12}$ years = $2\frac{2}{3}$ years
$$\begin{array}{r} \$3{,}000 \\ \times\ \ \ .12 \\ \hline 60\ 00 \\ \underline{300\ 0} \\ \$360.00 \end{array} \qquad \frac{360}{1} \times \frac{8}{3} = \mathbf{\$960}$$

66. b
$$\begin{array}{r} 18 \\ 35 \\ 37 \\ 52 \\ +\ \ 68 \\ \hline 210 \end{array} \qquad \begin{array}{r} \mathbf{42} \\ 5\overline{)210} \\ \underline{20} \\ 10 \\ \underline{10} \\ 0 \end{array}$$

67. a $\frac{4}{6} = \frac{2}{3}$

68. d $\frac{1}{4}$
$$\begin{array}{r} .25 = \mathbf{25\%} \\ 4\overline{)1.00} \\ \underline{8} \\ 20 \\ \underline{20} \end{array}$$

69. d
$$\begin{array}{r} 26{,}500 \\ 29{,}150 \\ +\ 10{,}600 \\ \hline \mathbf{66{,}250} \end{array}$$

70. e
$$\begin{array}{r} .16 = \mathbf{16\%} \\ 66{,}250\overline{)10{,}600.00} \\ \underline{6\ 625\ 0} \\ 3\ 975\ 00 \\ \underline{3\ 975\ 00} \\ 0 \end{array}$$

Mathematics Post-Test Evaluation Chart

On the chart below, circle the number of any problem you missed. The skill and study pages related to each problem are indicated.

Part I

Problem Numbers	*Related Skills*	*Study Pages*
	ADDITION	
1, 2, 3	Adding small numbers (no carrying)	692–699
4, 5, 6, 7	Adding and carrying	700–704
	SUBTRACTION	
8, 9	Subtracting small numbers (no borrowing)	707–714
10, 11	Subtracting and borrowing	715–717
12, 13, 14	Subtracting from zeros	717–718
	MULTIPLICATION	
15, 16, 17	Multiplying (no carrying)	725–732
18, 19, 20, 21	Multiplying and carrying	733–737
	DIVISION	
22, 23	Short division	742–745
24, 25	Using zero as a place holder	746
26, 27, 28	Long division	748–758
29, 30, 31		
	WORD PROBLEMS	
32	Addition word problems	697–699
34	Subtraction word problems	712–713
33	Multiplication word problems	738–740
35	Division word problems	750–752
36, 37	Multi-Step word problems	766–771
38	Measurement: area word problems	783–784
40	Measurement: volume word problems	785–786
39	Averages word problems	786–787

Number Correct _______/40 Part I (Questions 1–40)

Mathematics Post-Test Evaluation Chart

Part II

Problem Numbers	*Related Skills*	*Study Pages*
	DECIMALS	
41	Rounding Off	796–798
42, 64	Adding Decimals	798–799
43	Subtracting Decimals	800–801
45	Multiplying Decimals	802–805
44, 46	Dividing Decimals	806–810
47	Multi-Step Word Problems	811–813
	FRACTIONS	
48	Reducing Fractions	817
49	Adding Fractions	822–824
50, 63	Subtracting Fractions	825–827
51	Multiplying Fractions	838–841
53	Dividing Fractions	841–844
54	Multi-Step Word Problems	845–848
52	Changing Fractions to Decimals	848–849
	PERCENTS	
55	Changing Percents to Fractions	862
57	Finding Percent of Whole	866–867
56	Finding Part of Whole	867–868
59	Finding Part + Original	870–871
58	Percent Decrease	873–874
60, 61	Finding the Whole	874–876
62	Percent Word Problem	877–878
	SPECIAL TOPICS	
65	Interest	885–890
66	Mean and Median	890–891
67	Ratio	892
68	Probability	903–908
69, 70	Graphs	895–902

Number Correct _______/30 Part II (Questions 41–70)

Total Correct _______/70 Parts I and II (Questions 1–70)

INDEX

D

E

F

Q

R

W

Z